THE GREENHILL
DICTIONARY
OF
MILITARY
QUOTATIONS

THE GREENHILL
DICTIONARY
OF
MILITARY
QUOTATIONS

EDITED BY
LIEUTENANT-COLONEL PETER G. TSOURAS, USAR (RET)

GREENHILL BOOKS, LONDON
STACKPOLE BOOKS, PENNSYLVANIA

Greenhill Books

The Greenhill Dictionary of Military Quotations first published 2000
by Greenhill Books, Lionel Leventhal Limited, Park House,
1 Russell Gardens, London NW11 9NN
and
Stackpole Books, 5067 Ritter Road, Mechanicsburg, PA 17055, USA

British Cataloguing in Publication Data
The Greenhill dictionary of military quotations
1.War - Quotations, maxims, etc.
I.Tsouras, Peter II. Dictionary of military quotations
355′.02

ISBN 1-85367-390-0

Library of Congress Cataloging-in-Publication Data
The Greenhill dictionary of military quotations / edited by Peter G. Tsouras
p.   cm.
Includes bibliographical references and index.
ISBN 1-85367-390-0
1. War–Quotations, maxims, etc. 2. Military art and science–Quotations, maxims, etc.
I. Tsouras, Peter
PN6084.W35 G74 2000
355.02–dc21   00-038076

Edited and designed by Ian Penberthy   Typeset by The Shadetree Press, East Sussex

Printed and bound in Great Britain by The Bath Press, Bath

DEDICATION

I dedicate this book to America's touchstone of valour

The United States Marine Corps

Honour bright and razor sharp –
velociraptors in an age of sheep

and to

A scholar of war and a friend

David Chandler

Hark Now Hear the Drum

Verse 1

Hark now the drums beat up again
For all good soldiers, gentlemen.
Let us list and march I say
Over the hills and far away!

Chorus

Over the hills and o'er the Main,
To Flanders, Portugal and Spain
Queen Anne commands and we obey.
Over the hills and far away!

Verse 2

Here's forty shillings on the drum,
For them that volunteer to come.
With shirts and coats and present pay,
Over the hills and far away!

Chorus

Verse 3

While old friends our absence mourn,
We with honours shall return.
Then we'll sing both night and day.
Over the hills and far away.

Chorus

Early 18th-century English army song

Contents

8   **Contents**

Contents

Contents

Acknowledgements

THE GREENHILL DICTIONARY OF MILITARY QUO-
TATIONS is based on my book *Warriors' Words*.
Since its publication nearly a decade ago, I have
expanded, revised and reorganised the work, reviewing every quotation and adding 2,400 more, with three
new indexes for well-known quotations, battles and
campaigns, and generals, soldiers and war leaders.
My appreciation for the help I received in creating the
original edition still stands, perhaps even more so
now that the better part of a decade has passed. A
repetition of my thanks, with a few changes for the
sake of the passing years, is entirely in order.

Without the cheerful and efficient help of six librarians, whose profession is the unsung guardian of our
heritage, this work could not have been prepared. My
special thanks to Debbie Brannan, Meg Nicholas
(now Keish), Carol Norton, Anita Parrin, Holly Wilson
and Carol Wong for their diligence, good will and
friendship. However, their invaluable assistance
would have been for nought if my wife, Patricia, had
not had the patience to help me with the mysteries of
word processing, much of which still bewilders this
computer coward who is more at home with reed
pens and papyrus. Not the least proof of her forbear-
ance and affection was that she willingly shared the
family computer when she had equally pressing dead-
lines. My thanks also to Dr. John Turner for suggesting sources for the ancient Middle East, and to the
late Bruce Watson, my friend and mentor. Bruce, you
are still sorely missed.

To my colleagues and friends during Operations
Desert Storm and Desert Shield, I offer my salute, and
I treasure the memories, particularly of James Tate III
for his wisdom, friendship and integrity; of Elmo C.
'Mo' Wright, Jr., comrade and companion who
trudged the endless corridors of the Pentagon with
me to deliver countless special briefings; of Colonel
James Solomon (Commander, US Army Intelligence
and Threat Analysis Center), Colonel James Pardew
(Chief, Foreign Intelligence, the Army Staff) and
Brigadier-General (later Major-General) John F.
Stewart (Commander, US Army Intelligence Agency
and later G2, Third US Army in Desert Storm and
Desert Shield) – the right men at the right time in the
right place – whose revolution in intelligence support
for the US Army prepared the way for victory. Colonel
Pardew's good-natured appreciation for the right quotation inspired me to finish this book. I still cherish his
award for the gallant defence of a quotation in a draft
briefing for the Chief of Staff.

For this current edition, I wish to thank a couple of
old Army buddies for their help in getting this project
going – Colonels Leonard Hawley and James
Etchechury, who have informed me that the first edition was of daily use in the Pentagon and the White
House. I also extend my thanks for the gracious assistance of Colonel Michael F. Monagan, Chief, History
and Museums Division, U.S. Marine Corps, and to the
librarians of the Navy Library, Washington Navy Yard,
particularly Glen Helm and Barbara Auman. To my
friends, those Marines now in civilian life who made
work so interesting, Robert Fontaine and William F.
Johnson, and Terrence Gardner, an old army hand, I
offer my heartfelt thanks for advice and suggestions;
also to Major Chris Tomlinson for his embodiment of
the best in the living tradition of the British Army –
Chris, I can still hear you humming 'Over the hills and
far away'! To fellow writers of military history, your
advice has been invaluable. Philip Haythornthwaite's
recommendations, in particular, were a guided tour
through the history of British arms. Thanks also to
other keen pairs of eyes – Greg Oviatt, Alfred Price,
Kenneth Macksey, Mike Spick, Paul Britten Austin,
Andrew Uffindell and Ian V. Hogg.

I am also grateful for the permissions granted to
use quotations from the following sources:

The Art of War by Sun Tzu, translated by Lionel
Giles, part of a collection within *Roots of Strategy*,
edited by Thomas R. Phillips; used with
permission of Stackpole Books.
The Art of War by Sun Tzu, translated by Samuel
Griffith, translation copyright © 1963 by Oxford
University Press; used by permission of Oxford
University Press.
Battle Studies by Charles Ardant du Picq, translated
by John L. Greely and Robert C. Cotton; used with
permission of Stackpole Books.
Bringing up the Rear by S.L.A. Marshall, 1979, with
permission of the S.L.A. Marshall Collection,
University of Texas in El Paso.
The Broken Spears by Miguel Leon-Portilla, © 1962,
1990 by Miguel Leon-Portilla; expanded and
updated edition © 1992 by Miguel Leon-Portilla;
reprinted by permission of Beacon Press, Boston.
The Campaigns of Alexander by Arrian, translated by
Aubrey de Sélincourt (published as *Arrian: The
Life of Alexander the Great*, 1958, by Penguin
Classics; revised edition, 1971); copyright © the
Estate of Aubrey de Sélincourt, 1958.
The Edge of the Sword by Charles de Gaulle;
copyright © 1960 by Criterion Books, Inc., and
Faber and Faber Ltd; reprinted by permission of
HarperCollins Publishers, Inc.

Fighting for the Future by Ralph Peters; copyright © 1999 by Ralph Peters; used with permission of Stackpole Books.

First to Fight by Victor Krulak; copyright © 1984, 1991 by the United States Naval Institute; used with permission of the Naval Institute Press.

The History of the Indies of New Spain by Fray Diego Duran, translated by Doris Heyden; copyright © 1994 by the University of Oklahoma Press; reprinted by permission of the publisher.

The Iliad by Homer, translated by Robert Fagles; translation copyright © 1990 by Robert Fagles; Introduction and Notes copyright © 1990 by Bernard Knox; used by permission of Viking Penguin, a division of Penguin Putnam, Inc.

Ideals of the Samurai by William Scott Wilson; copyright © 1982 by William Scott Wilson; reprinted by permission of the publisher, Ohara Publications, Inc.

Instructions of Frederick the Great to His Generals, Frederick the Great, 1747, translated by Thomas R. Phillips; part of a collection within *Roots of Strategy*, edited by Thomas R. Phillips; used with permission of Stackpole Books.

It Doesn't Take a Hero by General H. Norman Schwarzkopf and Peter Petre; copyright © 1992 by H. Norman Schwarzkopf; used by permission of Bantam Books, a division of Random House, Inc.

Jomini's Art of War by Antoine Henri Jomini, edited by J.D. Hittle; used with permission of Stackpole Books.

Leading the Way, edited by Al Santoli; copyright © 1993 by Al Santoli; reprinted by permission of Ballantine Books, a division of Random House, Inc.

Marine! The Life of Lt. Gen. Lewis B. (Chesty) Puller, USMC by Burke Davis; copyright © 1990 by Burke Davis; used with permission of Little, Brown and Company, Inc.

Mastering the Art of War (the works of Zhuge Liang and Liu Ju), translated by Thomas Cleary, © 1989; reprinted by arrangement with Shambhala Publications, Inc., Boston.

Maurice's Strategikon: Handbook of Byzantine Military Strategy, translated by George T. Dennis; copyright © 1984 University of Pennsylvania Press; reprinted by permission of the publisher.

Memoirs of Field Marshal Montgomery by Bernard Law Montgomery, reprinted with permission of A.P. Watt Ltd, on behalf of Viscount Montgomery of Alamein, CBE.

Men Against Fire by S.L.A. Marshall, 1947, with permission of the S.L.A. Marshall Collection, University of Texas in El Paso.

The Military Institutions of the Romans by Vegetius, translated by John Clarke, part of a collection within *Roots of Strategy*, edited by Thomas R. Phillips; used with permission of Stackpole Books.

The Mind of Napoleon: A Selection of His Written and Spoken Words, translated by J. Christopher Herold; copyright © 1995 Columbia University Press; reprinted with permission of the publisher.

My Reveries Upon the Art of War, Maurice de Saxe, 1832, translated by Thomas R. Phillips; part of a collection within *Roots of Strategy*, edited by Thomas R. Phillips; used with permission of Stackpole Books.

The Military Maxims of Napoleon by Napoleon, translated by General Burnod, 1827; part of a collection within *Roots of Strategy*, edited by Thomas R. Phillips; used with permission of Stackpole Books.

On War by Carl von Clausewitz, translated by Michael Howard and Peter Paret; copyright © 1976 by Princeton University Press; reprinted by permission of Princeton University Press.

The Patton Papers (two volumes), edited by Martin Blumenson, published by Houghton Mifflin Co., 1972–1974; reprinted with permission of Blanche C. Gregory, Inc., on behalf of the author.

Pre-Columbian Literatures of Mexico, by Miguel Leon-Portilla, translated by Grace Lobanov and the author, University of Oklahoma Press, 1969.

Plutarch on Sparta, translated by Richard J.A. Talbert, Penguin Classics, 1988; translation copyright © J.A. Talbert, 1988.

The Rise of the Roman Empire by Polybius, translated by Ian Scott-Kilvert, Penguin Classics, 1979; copyright © Ian Scott-Kilvert, 1979.

The Rommel Papers by Field Marshal Erwin Rommel, 1953; used with permission of HarperCollins Publishers Ltd.

Strategy by B.H. Liddell Hart; published by Faber and Faber Ltd, 1954; reprinted with permission of David Higham Associates, on behalf of B.H. Liddell Hart.

Thoughts on War by B.H. Liddell Hart; published by Faber and Faber Ltd, 1944; reprinted with permission of David Higham Associates, on behalf of B.H. Liddell Hart.

War As I Knew It by George S. Patton; copyright © 1947 by Beatrice Patton Walter, Ruth Patton Totten and George Smith Totten; copyright © renewed 1975 by Major General George Patton, Ruth Patton Totten, John K. Waters, Jr. and George P. Waters; reprinted by permission of Houghton Mifflin Co.; all rights reserved.

Peter G. Tsouras
2000

Preface

'I HAD IT FROM XENOPHON . . .'

IN JUNE 1758, the British Army was laying siege for the second time in that century to the great French fortress of Louisburg, the iron gate of Canada. Then Brigadier General James Wolfe hurried the French defenders back into their works with his skilled use of light infantry to turn one flank and then another. The rest of the British force was no less impressed with the manoeuvre than the dazed French now shut up in Louisburg. A brother officer, more perceptive than the rest, remarked that Wolfe's tactics reminded him of an account by Xenophon in the *Anabasis*, the March of the Ten Thousand Greeks. It is not recorded if Wolfe smiled. If he did, it was probably out of exasperation, as he replied, 'I had it from Xenophon, but our friends here are astonished at what I have done because they have read nothing.'

A century and a half later, another British soldier exemplified not the art of war, as Wolfe had at Louisburg, but the art of leadership and the nature of man in war. Private Richard Chuck was serving in Mesopotamia in 1916, in the company of the future Field Marshal Viscount Slim of Burma, then a young officer in one of the war-raised reserve battalions of his regiment. The soldier was a former Royal Naval seaman who had been discharged as an 'Incorrigible Rogue' just before the war and then had been conscripted into the Army; he was the bane of every NCO in the company, an affront to the neat and orderly side of Army life and seemingly indifferent to the reputation of his regiment, the Warwicks. In this he appeared little different from most of the soldiers in Slim's company, middle-aged family men who had not volunteered, but who had been conscripted and had not been well thought of for it. The company was assaulting Turkish positions along a dike when machine-gun fire scythed through the ranks and mortars rained down on them. Half of the men went down, while the rest tried hopelessly to worm their way into the salt-pan desert. Slim saw doom stretching out its hand to his shrinking company. Then, despite the machine-gun fire and mortars, up stood the 'Rogue'. He bellowed, 'Heads up the Warwicks! Show the _____ yer cap-badges.' Slim then recounted:

> Even in that pandemonium a few men heard him as his great form came bullocking through them. They had no cap-badges for we wore Wolseley helmets, but they heard the only appeal that could have reached them – to the Regiment, the last hold of the British soldier when all else has gone. The half dozen around Chuck heard, their heads came up too; in a moment the whole line was running forward. We cursed the wire as it tore at us, but we were through, looking down on brown faces, grey uniforms, and raised hands and dirty white rags held aloft.[1]

It is my hope that this book will help the aspiring soldier as well as the military professional and enthusiast, also to learn 'from Xenophon', the 'Incorrigible Rogue' and the almost 800 other individuals quoted. Theirs is much of the distilled wisdom of 4,000 years of the profession of arms and experience of war, from the sack of Summerian Ur c. 2000 BC to the present day. As conflicts from the end of the second millennium continue to smoulder, we dare not forget the eternal seriousness of war. This lament of Ur is not so different from more recent scenes.

> Dead men, not potsherds
> Covered the approaches,
> The walls were gaping,
> the high gates, the roads,
> were piled with dead.
> In the side streets, where feasting crows would
>   gather,
> Scattered they lay.
> In all the streets and roadways bodies lay.
> In open fields that used to fill with dancers,
> they lay in heaps.
> The country's blood now filled its holes,
> like metal in a mould;
> Bodies dissolved – like fat left in the sun.[2]

[1] Field Marshal Viscount William Slim, *Unofficial History* (Cassell, London, 1959), p. 50.

[2] Joan Oates, *Babylon* (Thames and Hudson, London, 1979), p. 52.

There is a numbing sameness to such wails of horror throughout the history of war, but if war holds such constants in its left hand, it holds the new in its right. For war is ever the realm of the new and change; not to change passes you to the blood-soaked left hand of war, a grim reality check. The right hand holds in its open palm glittering new ideas, such as those of Ralph Peters, the modern von Clausewitz:

> The only thing of which I am certain is that the next century's revolution in weaponry will involve forms of behavior control and mental intrusion. Attacking the human body has been a sloppy and inefficient means of making war. Attacking the mind may prove the culmination of military history.[3]

To the traditional means of making war, Peters addresses the all-too-often forgotten moral questions of war, particularly important at this time:

> We rule the skies and seas, and possess the power to rule the land when we are sufficiently aroused. But we have not learned to understand, much less to rule, minds and hearts and souls. The only moral we need to cull from the *Iliad* is that it is foolish to underestimate the complexity and determination of the killers from the other shore.[4]

This book of over 6,000 quotations, however, despite its reach across four millennia, is not the easy one-stop answer to the art of war. It is a place to start.

I have chosen nearly 500 subject areas for quotation. Basic terms, such as helmet and rifle, I have left to elementary experience and a general dictionary. The subject headings address concepts that are the essence of the profession of arms, the realm of ideas rather than objects, for example 'Change', 'The Indirect Approach' and 'War' itself, divided into 20 sub-categories. The human side of war is equally represented under headings such as 'The Regiment', 'Morale', 'Fear' and, let us never forget, 'Killing', 'Mothers', 'Those Left Behind', 'Wives' and more add the forgotten dimension of those who have suffered so much without even the warrior's passions as slight reward. Lieutenant General Harold G. Moore touches the pain:

> They are the gold star children, war's innocent victims, and their pain shimmers across the years pure and undimmed. They pass through life with an empty room in their hearts where a father was supposed to live and laugh and love.
> All their lives they listen for the footstep that

will never fall, and long to know what might have been.[5]

As a senior analyst working on the Korean War for the US-Russian Joint Presidential Commission on POW/MIAs (1992–93), I have seen exactly the searching souls he has described. It is the daughters, mostly – middle-aged women, mothers and grandmothers even – successful and mature, but still they search.

Included also are the matters of the soldier's heart, the living, spiritual dimensions of human beings in war – 'Cohesion', 'Comradeship', 'Fallen Comrades' and 'Religion'. King David's grief over fallen Jonathan lives on:

> How are the mighty fallen in the midst of the battle! O Jonathan, thou wast slain in thine high places.
>
> I am distressed for thee, my brother Jonathan: very pleasant has thou been unto me: thy love to me was wonderful, passing the love of women.
>
> How are the mighty fallen, and the weapons of war perished.[6]

As does the desperate plea of Agamemnon rallying the Greeks, as Man-Killing Hector stormed their camp.

> Now be men, my friends! Courage, come, take heart!
> Dread what comrades say of you here in bloody combat!
> When men dread that, more men come through alive –
> when soldiers break and run, good-bye glory, good-bye all defenses.[7]

And Shakespeare's rendition of Henry V's speech to his army before the Battle of Agincourt in 1415:

> We few, we happy few, we band of brothers;
> For he to-day that sheds his blood with me
> Shall be my brother.[8]

Still bright also is the clear beauty of simple and utter faith, an inextricable part of 'The Nelson Touch':

> When I lay me down to sleep, I recommend myself to the care of Almighty God; when I awake I give myself up to his direction. Amidst all the evils that threaten me, I will look up to Him for help, and question not but that He will either avert

[3] Ralph Peters, *Fighting for the Future* (Stackpole Books, Mechanicsburg, PA.,1999), p. 209.
[4] Ibid., 'New Old Enemies', *Parameters*, Summer 1999.
[5] Harold G. Moore, *We Were Soldiers Once . . . And Young: Ia Drang – The Battle That Changed the War in*
Vietnam (Random House, New York, 1992), p. 337.
[6] II Samuel 1.25–27.
[7] Homer, *The Iliad*, 5.610–14, tr. Robert Fagles (Penguin Books, New York, 1990), p. 181.
[8] William Shakespeare, *Henry V*, 1599, Act IV, 3.59.

them or turn them to my advantage. Though I know neither the time nor the place of my death, I am not at all solicitous about it, because I am sure that He knows them both, and that He will not fail to support and comfort me.[9]

Here is a fraternity of soldiers, first and foremost. Most of them have long since turned to dust, but their deeds and experiences remain as vital and as insightful as when they trod the earth with thunder and acclaim. Follow them to their original sources – the histories, memoirs, textbooks and works of theory. Open an old book that smells, feels and looks of another time. Be your own Odysseus when he summoned the ghosts of Achilles and Agamemnon from Hades to speak to him. If you let them, they will speak across time to you of problems of leadership and command, of logistics, of tactics and strategy, the sinews of their art. They will speak to you of the human heart, comradeship, example, sacrifice, glory and death. They are not dead as long as they are remembered. And they are exhilarating company. If you are a serving soldier, the reward is not merely the satisfaction of a good read. It can also be, as Wolfe so aptly stated, the road to success, and at the price of a small butcher's bill.

Wherever possible, I have included the full quotation to provide the greatest understanding of the source's intent. All too often, the most glib part of a quotation has been lifted out of its context and turned around in its meaning. A good example is Admiral Farragut's admonition to one of his captains in battle, which is often cited as being a demand for the strict obedience to orders: 'I want none of this Nelson business in my squadron.' Here the reference is to Nelson at the Battle of Copenhagen, where he put his spyglass over the eyepatch covering his blind eye when looking at the signal to withdraw from action, saying, 'I have a right to be blind.' However, a more complete citation reveals Farragut to be very much in the Nelson tradition:

On Farragut's quarterdeck: 'Captain, you begin early in your life to disobey orders. Did you not see the signal flying for near an hour to withdraw from action? . . . I want none of this Nelson business in my squadron.'

Later In Farragut's cabin: 'I have censured you, sir, on my quarterdeck, for what appeared to be a disregard of my orders. I desire now to commend you and your officers and men for doing what you believe right under the circumstances. Do it again whenever in your

judgment it is necessary to carry out your conception of duty.'[10]

The exercise of the profession of arms is the basic requirement for inclusion in this book. Into this fraternity, however, enter some of Athena's daughters – Joan of Arc with banner of Fleurs-de-lis before the English forts surrounding Orleans:

I used to say to them, 'go boldly in among the English,' and then I used to go boldly in myself.[11]

Others of them have seen the grimmest side of war – Florence Nightingale, Clara Barton, Mary Livermore and Mary Bickerdyke.

Mary 'Mother' Bickerdyke, as described by her contemporary, Mary Livermore, during the American Civil War saw duty as clearly as any man who rushed to the colours:

'Where did you get these articles?' he [an officious officer] inquired; 'and under whose authority are you at work?'

She paid no heed to his interrogatories, and, indeed, did not hear them, so completely absorbed was she in her work of compassion. Watching her with admiration for her skill, administrative ability, and intelligence, – for she not only fed the wounded men, but temporarily dressed their wounds in some cases, – he approached her again: –

'Madam, you seem to combine in yourself a sick-diet kitchen and a medical staff. May I inquire under whose authority you are working?'

Without pausing in her work, she answered him, 'I have received my authority from the Lord God Almighty; have you anything that ranks higher than that?'[12]

Of necessity, only those who had the talent, time and inclination to write are represented here. Fate also plays a part: the fact that no first-hand account of Alexander survives is simply a great misfortune. While Alexander is quoted as far as the sources allow, it is nothing to what could have been included if his Royal Journal and Ptolemy's history or any other first-hand source had survived. Only the glittering fragments remain, such as when he faced down the mutiny of the Macedonians at Ophis in 323 BC:

But does any man among you honestly feel that he has suffered more for me than I have

---

[9] David Howarth and Stephen Howarth, *Nelson: The Immortal Memory* (Dent, London, 1986).
[10] Admiral David Glasgow Farragut to Lieutenant Winfield Scott Schley, executive officer of the USS *Richmond*, during the action at Port Hudson, March 1863, quoted in Christopher Martin, *Damn the Torpedos!* (Abelard, Schuman, New York, 1970).

[11] Joan of Arc to her inquisitors who intimated that her success was due to luck, 3 March 1430, quoted in Edward Creasy, *Decisive Battles of the World* (The Colonial Press, New York, 1899), p. 215.
[12] Mary A. Livermore, *My Story of the War* (Hartford, CT, 1887).

suffered for him? Come now – if you are wounded, strip and show your wounds, and I will show mine. There is no part of my body but my back which has not a scar; not a weapon a man may grasp or fling the mark of which I do not carry upon me. I have sword-cuts from close fight; arrows have pierced me, missiles from catapults bruised my flesh; again and again I have been struck by stones or clubs – and all for your sakes: for your glory and gain.[13]

We are left only with the consolation of Arrian's devoted and first-class history, written almost 500 years after the death of Alexander.

Unfortunately, accident and scholars more interested in literary merit and moral lessons, and not students of war, preserved what little survived the destruction of the classical world, the destruction of the Library of Alexandria and the later burning of the libraries of Constantinople by French barbarians in 1204. We can only shudder when we realise how close Homer and Thucydides came to extinction, yet somehow these giants survived to enrich our study of the art of war.

Some of the history of the ancient Middle East has come to life through archaeology. The deeds of Thutmose III, Rameses II and Sargon II are known again, but of their thoughts there is very little. Still, the deeds evoke powerful images, such as Rameses II's valour at Kadesh (1284 BC), where the Hittites surprised his camp and cut him off from even his escort; he rallied his men by charging single-handed among the mass of Hittite chariots and cut a way through:

I charged all countries, while I was alone, my infantry and my chariotry having forsaken me. Not one among them stood to turn about. I swear, as Re loves me, as my father, Atum, favors me, that as for every matter which his majesty has stated, I did it in truth, in the presence of my infantry and my chariotry.[14]

The great warlords of pre-literate societies, unfortunately, are remembered only in surviving oral traditions; they have no tongues to tell us what they learned. So Shaka Zulu is almost completely denied the place his military genius deserves, as are Pachacutec and Ahuitzotl, both of whom have been called the Alexanders of their worlds.

Strangely, there is one notable exception – Tlacaelel, the great Aztec priest-warrior and generalissimo. Tlacaelel ordered a history of the Aztecs to be recorded in the pictorial writing of Mesoamerica, supplemented by the oral histories of professional mnemonic historians. He took a great interest in this document, in its unique form on fig tree bark paper and in human memory. It is from these surviving sources that the great Fray Diego Durán wrote his *History of the Indies of New Spain*; and through the gentle Franciscan friar, the blood-soaked Tlacaelel speaks once again in his promulgation of the Aztec warrior code:

. . . we order that glory and honor and greatness not be inherited simply because one is born of nobles but must be acquired in war, by brave deeds . . . And those courageous warriors will be awarded insignia of valor not once but many times and will be given gold and silver, precious stones, jewels, fine feathers. All of these can used by them always, and by no others. These things will remind them of us after we are dead; we will be remembered by our sons and grandsons and all our descendants.[15]

Through him you can hear the thunder rumble from the huge snake-skin drum atop the Great Temple of Tenochtitlan, summoning the Aztecs to battle, 'Courage, Mexica!'

Recent modern scholarship has brought to English significant works by Byzantine soldiers, chief among whom is the Emperor Maurice. His military classic, *The Strategikon*, together with his *Three Byzantine Military Treatises* were translated by George Dennis in 1984 and 1985. The Byzantine blend of the utterly practical and the religious comes through clearly:

Before getting into danger, the general should worship God. When he does get into danger, then, he can with confidence pray to God as friend.[16]

Similarly, Thomas Cleary has brought to English-speaking readers the works of the great Chinese captains, Zhuge Liang and Liu Ji in *Mastering the Art of War* (1989). The world of ancient China, where the scholar and general were often the same, was where the most subtle thoughts on war were set down and eagerly read and copied in a strong and unbroken tradition from the T'ai Kung (c. 1000 BC) to Mao Tse-tung; for example, the great Zhuge Liang (AD 180–234) wrote:

To overcome the intelligent by folly is contrary to the natural order of things; to overcome the foolish by intelligence is in accord with the natural order. To overcome the intelligent by intelligence, however, is a matter of opportunity.

There are three avenues of opportunity: events, trends, and conditions. When

---

[13] Arrian, *The Campaigns of Alexander*, 7.10, tr. Aubrey de Sélincourt (Penguin Books, London, 1971), p. 363.
[14] James Breasted, *Ancient Records of Egypt*, (University of Chicago Press, Chicago, 1906), p. 147, Vol. II.
[15] Diego Durán, *History of the Indies of New Spain*, 1581,

tr. Doris Heyden (University of Oklahoma Press, Norman and London, 1994).
[16] Maurice, *The Strategikon: Handbook of Byzantine Military Strategy*, tr. George Dennis (University of Pennsylvania Press, Philadelphia, 1984) p. 83.

opportunities occur through events but you are unable to respond, you are not smart. When opportunities become active through a trend and yet you cannot make plans, you are not wise. When opportunities emerge through conditions but you cannot act on them, you are not bold.

Those skilled in generalship always achieve their victories by taking advantage of opportunities.[17]

William Scott Wilson has done the same for the art of war in medieval Japan in *Ideals of the Samurai* (1982).

Caesar was the first great captain to immortalise the work of his sword with his pen. His fashion was not repeated on any scale in the West until the modern era, which has been increasingly rich in its memoirs, beginning in the 18th century with De Saxe's *Mes Reveries* and Suvorov's *The Science of Victory*, and accelerating so much that Churchill was heard to remark after World War II that his generals were selling themselves dearly.

Since the American Civil War, it has almost become *de rigueur* for senior officers to write their war memoirs. So we have almost all of them, from Alexander of Tunis to Zhukov. Others were lucky enough to have a friend or military secretary who was inspired to record events and words – Scipio Africanus had Polybius, and Belisarius had Procopius. To our great loss, the words of other great captains, such as Marlborough, were never written down or have been lost. Lee the Incomparable and Nelson of Immortal Memory, on the other hand, were so beloved that every word they uttered was seized upon and preserved like gold nuggets. Wellington and Napoleon were survived by their stupendous collections of official business and correspondence, and by the numerous memoirs of their colleagues.

Of course, the soldier-scholar, by his very nature, is well-represented – Sun Tzu, Xenophon, Machiavelli, Clausewitz, Liddell Hart and Fuller. For Sun Tzu, the first of the great soldier scholars to leave a legacy, which in many ways has never been surpassed, I have relied on one of the first translations, that by Lionel Giles in 1911. This continues to hold its own, despite a deluge of more recent efforts. We know more of the Prussian Carl von Clausewitz. No library soldier he – his writings were based on the many opportunities provided by Napoleon to amass a great deal of military experience in the field – his students laughed at the broken veins in his nose and cheeks,

making sly asides about his affection for the bottle. Silly boys, those rosy marks were caused by frostbite during Napoleon's invasion of Russia in 1812. Despite the intellectual and prose structure of German philosophy, one can still hear the whistle of the wind off the Russian snows. For this, we appreciate the splendid modern translation, which has become the indisputable standard, the Princeton University's edition of his *On War*, translated by Michael Howard and Peter Paret.

While frequently of value, the words of priest, scholar and diplomat are no more appropriate here than a lawyer's comments in a textbook on surgery. There is no substitute for wielding either scalpel or sword in medicine and war. I also include in this company the great national war leaders, such as Lincoln, Clemenceau, Franklin Roosevelt and Thatcher. There is also something to be gained here from the occasional incompetent; as Wellington observed, 'I learnt what one ought not to do, and that is always something.'[18]

Of course, I have exercised an editor's prerogative of being inconsistent here and there to please myself and, it is hoped, the reader. Some opportunities are too good to miss. For example, Ralph Waldo Emerson: 'I hate quotations; tell me what you know.' Two pillars of the Western canon that I have included, simply because of their manifest majesty and authority, are the Bible and Homer. What greater reason could there be for the Bible's inclusion than Exodus 15.3: 'The LORD is a man of war: The LORD is his name.'

Homer finds an especially honoured place. In *The Iliad*, I am convinced you can read many of the lines composed by the Achaean bards who accompanied their royal masters to Troy to record their glories, much as the Norse bards followed their Viking kings on campaign. The purpose was both informative and entertaining no matter how much they composed to royal taste.[19] In the hands of Homer, the story displays a profound and unsurpassed understanding of men in war:

War – I know it well, and the butchery of men.
Well I know, shift to the left, shift to the right my
tough tanned shield. That's what the real drill,
defensive fighting means to me. I know it all,
how to charge in the rush of plunging horses – I
know how to stand and fight to the finish, twist
and lunge in the War-god's deadly dance.
On guard![20]

[17] Thomas Cleary, tr. and ed., *Mastering the Art of War* (Shambhala Press, Boston, 1989), p. 45.
[18] Wellington's observation after the disastrous British campaign in Holland, 1794–95, in which he served as the colonel of the 33rd Foot. Earl Stanhope, *Conversations with the Duke of Wellington*, 1888, p. 182.
[19] Michael Wood, *In Search of the Trojan War* (Facts on File Publications, New York and Oxford, 1985), pp. 10–11, 20–21, 91. *The Iliad* contains many references to specific

features of the city and the local geography that only an eye-witness at the time could have made, for example, a trained observer – a bard – gathering details for his royal compositions. Some of these, I believe, have survived the endless retellings of the poems that eventually were compiled into *The Iliad*.
[20] Hector to Telamonian Ajax as they began their duel, quoted in Homer, *The Iliad*, 7.271–281, tr. Robert Fagles (Viking, New York, 1990).

And women too:

'That cry – that was Hector's honored mother I heard! My heart's pounding, leaping up in my throat, the knees beneath me paralyzed – Oh I know it . . . something terrible's coming down on Priam's children. Pray god the news will never reach my ears! Yes but I dread it so – what if great Achilles has cut my Hector off from the city, daring Hector, and driven him out across the plain, and all alone? – He may have put an end to that fatal headstrong pride that always seized my Hector – never hanging back with the main force of men, always charging ahead, giving ground to no man in his fury!'

So she cried, dashing out of the royal halls like a madwoman, her heart racing hard, her women close behind her. But once she reached the tower where soldiers massed she stopped on the rampart, looked down and saw it all – saw him dragged before the city, stallions galloping, dragging Hector back to Achaea's beaked warships – ruthless work. The world went black as night before her eyes, she fainted, falling backward, gasping away her life breath . . . she flung to the winds her glittering headdress, the cap and the coronet, braided band and veil, all the regalia golden Aphrodite gave her once, the day that Hector, helmet aflash in sunlight, led her home to Troy from her father's house with countless wedding gifts to win her heart.[21]

The very best of the war correspondents, though engaged in what most soldiers consider an odious profession, somewhere between pest and spy, sometimes come close to Homer's standard. These exceptions are, like Homer – who put an unerring finger on the pulse of man in war – Kipling, the young Churchill, Constantin Simonov and Ernie Pyle who were ever welcome in the mess.

Most soldiers quoted herein wrote at the end of their careers. Others were more prolific throughout their military service, and attempting to determine rank at the moment of literary conceptions presents an endless number of 'Gordian Knots'. Therefore, I have resorted to the highest rank held. A few wore uniform only briefly, and at relatively junior rank, among them Justice Oliver Wendell Holmes Jr. and President Theodore Roosevelt. Soldiers in antiquity are not referred to by rank, which would be difficult, if not impossible, to determine. Some great commanders are referred to by their titles alone, such as the great English dukes, Marlborough and Wellington, whose reputations outshone any insignia of military rank. Of course, Napoleon,

although officially Napoleon I, Emperor of the French, is simply Napoleon. The name alone kept the whole of Europe in terror for almost 20 years. In the end, he was stripped of everything but that enduring reputation:

Many faults, no doubt, will be found in my career; but Arcole, Rivoli, the Pyramids, Marengo, Austerlitz, Jena, Friedland – these are granite: the tooth of envy is powerless here.[22]

Titles of nobility are also included. Sometimes they were a delight – in those cases where they were earned – such as Marshal of France Michel Ney, Duc d'Elchingen and Prince de la Moskova! If anything, Ney was under-titled. Field Marshal Viscount Allenby of Meggido falls into that category as well. The British field marshal viscounts embody in their titles the far-flung campaigns of the British Army – Khartoum, Meggido, Alamein, Burma.

When possible, I have given the source and date of the quotation. Unfortunately, this has not always been viable; in such cases, I have cited the birth and death dates of the source.

Where there are several translations, mostly those from antiquity, I have selected those that best express the particular theme. The range of translation will come as a great surprise to the reader used to a single standard in more modern works. The following two translations of the same passage in Pericles' funeral oration for the Athenian dead (431/430 BC) in Thucydides' *Peloponnesian War*, 2.42, by the scholar translators Benjamin Jowett and Richard Crawley, show the range of style and interpretation possible:

They resigned to hope their unknown chance of happiness; but in the face of death they resolved to rely upon themselves alone. And when the moment came they were minded to resist and suffer, rather than to fly and save their lives; they ran away from the word of dishonor, but on the battlefield their feet stood fast, and in an instant, at the height of their fortune, they passed away from the scene, not of their fear, but of their glory.[23]

Thus choosing to die resisting, rather than to live submitting, they fled only from dishonour, but met danger face to face, and after one brief moment, while at the summit of their fortune, left behind them not their fear, but their glory.[24]

The translations of Sun Tzu's *The Art of War* and Homer's *The Iliad* are infinitely more varied, something readily apparent to anyone who has

---

[21] Ibid. Andromache, wife of Hector, on the news of his death at the hands of brilliant Achilles, 22.530–555.
[22] Conversation on St Helena, quoted in Christopher Herold, ed., *The Mind of Napoleon* (Columbia University Press, New York, 1955).

[23] Thucydides, *The Peloponnesian War*, tr. Benjamin Jowett (Bantam, New York, 1960), p. 119.
[24] Thucydides, *History of the Peloponnesian War*, tr. Richard Crawley (James Dent & Sons, London, 1910), p. 125.

noticed whole shelves now devoted to different translations of both masterpieces.

Although I have chosen freely from among the rich range of translations, I have preferred to stick to the clarity of Lionel Giles' *The Art of War*. Homer yields endless insight, enriched by the nuances of his many translators. So rich, indeed, is this resource that the choice is daunting, but I have found the first and the last to be the best translations of *The Iliad*. They are John Dryden's great effort[25] of almost 300 years ago and Robert Fagles' breathtaking translation of 1990.

The delight of Fagles' translation is its fidelity to Homer's medium – the spoken not the written word, although that, too, is unsurpassed. Listening to Derek Jacobi's narration of this translation brings one closer to the golden time when the blind bard himself sang of the Anger of Achilles. I cannot recommend the book and the tape too highly.[26]

Rage – Goddess, sing the rage of Peleus' son Achilles murderous, doomed, that cost the Achaeans countless losses, hurling down to the House of Death so many sturdy souls, great fighters' souls, but made their bodies carrion, feasts for the dogs and birds.

Begin, muse, when the two first broke and clashed, Agamemnon lord of men and brilliant Achilles.[27]

One imagines them all listening to the Bard still. At one table brilliant fire-eaters like Suvorov and Patton. At another are the scholar-soldiers – Sun Tzu, von Clausewitz, Fuller and Liddell Hart. By themselves, stiff and dour, are Heaven's captains – Tlacaelel and Cromwell. Over there are the mighty men of war, flinty commanders of great hosts – Scipio, Marlborough, Montgomery and Zhukov. By them, the knightly warriors *'sans peur et sans reproche'* – Belisarius, Saladin, Bayard and Lee. In the corner huddled together are the artists of the subtle strategem, the clever ones – Philip of Macedon, Wu Ch'i, Hannibal. And there, where the light pools around them from great windows, are those in love with adventure and glory – Rameses II, young again and boasting of his courage at Kadesh to a smiling Alexander, shining in the midst of everlasting renown.

Peter G. Tsouras
Lieutenant Colonel, USAR (Ret)
Alexandria, Virginia
2000

---

[25] When reading Dryden, the modern reader is struck by the odd sound of the gods' names in their Latin form. Until the middle of the last century, the Greek names were so unfamiliar that this Latinate convention was followed. Today the opposite applies.

[26] I strongly recommend the audio tape of Robert Fagles' translation of *The Iliad*, read by Derek Jacobi, who was certainly possessed by the Muse: Homer, *The Iliad, Classics on Cassette*, HBP 19495 (Penguin-HighBridge Audio, 1992).

[27] Homer, *The Iliad*, tr. Robert Fagles (Viking Penguin, New York, 1990), p. 77.

THE GREENHILL
DICTIONARY
OF
MILITARY
QUOTATIONS

A

ABILITY

THE WINDS AND WAVES are always on the side of the ablest navigators.
> Edward Gibbon, *Decline and Fall of the Roman Empire*, 1776.

WIN with ability, not with numbers.
> Field Marshal Prince Aleksandr V. Suvorov, quoted in Danchenko and Vydrin, *Military Pedagogy*, 1973.

GREAT EVENTS hang by a thread. The able man turns everything to profit, neglects nothing that may give him one chance more; the man of less ability, by overlooking just one thing, spoils the whole.
> Napoleon, 25 September 1797, quoted in R.M. Johnston, ed., *The Corsican*, 1910.

I CONSIDER that in the army there are no princes. There are men, officers, colonels, generals; and there is the commander-in-chief who must be more capable than all the others, and who must stand far above them.
> Napoleon, 1805, letter to Soult, quoted in S.J. Watson, *By Command of the Emperor*, 1957.

UNQUESTIONABLY, victory or defeat in war is determined mainly by the military, political, economic and natural conditions on both sides. But not by these alone. It is also determined by each side's subjective ability in directing the war. In his endeavour to win a war, a military strategist cannot overstep the limitations imposed by the material conditions; within these limitations, however, he can and must strive for victory. The state of action for a military strategist is built upon objective material conditions, but on that stage he can direct the performance of many a drama, full of sound and colour, power and grandeur.
> Mao Tse-tung, 'Problems of Directing China's Revolutionary War', December 1936, *Selected Military Writings*, 1967.

THIS is a long tough road we have to travel. The men that can do things are going to be sought out just as surely as the sun rises in the morning. Fake reputations, habits of glib and clever speech, and glittering surface performance are going to be discovered . . .
> General of the Army Dwight D. Eisenhower, *At Ease: Stories I Tell My Friends*, 1967.

ACTION

NOT A THOUGHT in your heads for works of battle.
What becomes of them now, the pacts and oaths we swore?
Into the flames with councils, all the plans of men,
the vows sealed with the strong, unmixed wine,
the firm clasp of the right hand we trusted!
We battle on in words, always, mere words,
and what's the cure? We cannot find a thing.
No matter how many years we wrangle here.

Agamemnon – never swerve, hold to your first plan of action,
lead your armies headlong into war!
> Homer, *The Iliad*, 2.401–410, c. 800 BC, tr. Robert Fagles, 1990; Nestor attempting to infuse purpose into the Acheaen leadership, which was fragmenting over the quarrel between Agamemnon and Achilles.

THE PROOF of battle is action, proof of words, debate.
No time for speeches now, it's time to fight.
> Homer, *The Iliad*, 16.730–732, c. 800 BC, tr. Robert Fagles, 1990; Patrocles chiding Meriones for engaging in taunts with Aeneas rather than in combat.

IT IS a common mistake in going to war to begin at the wrong end, to act first, and wait for disaster to discuss the matter.
> Thucydides, *History of the Peloponnesian War*, 1.78, c. 404 BC, tr. Richard Crawley, 1910; the Athenian delegation's argument to the Spartans to avoid war, 432 BC.

MY BUSINESS is to succeed, and I'm good at it. I create my Iliad by my actions, create it day by day.
> Napoleon, 1804, conversation with Pope Pius VII at Fountainbleu, quoted in Alfred Comte de Vigny, *Servitude and Grandeur of Arms*, 1857.

IT IS even better to act quickly and err than to hesitate until the time of action is past.
> Major General Carl von Clausewitz, *On War*, 1832, tr. Michael Howard and Peter Paret, 1976.

ACTION IN WAR is like movement in a resistant element. Just as the simplest and most natural of movements, walking, cannot easily be performed in water, so in war it is difficult for normal efforts to achieve even moderate results.
> Major-General Carl von Clausewitz, *On War*, 1.7, 1832, tr. Michael Howard and Peter Paret, 1976.

ACTION IN WAR is not continuous but spasmodic. Violent clashes are interrupted by periods of observation, during which both sides are on the defensive. But usually one side is more strongly motivated, which tends to affect its behavior: the offensive element will dominate, and usually maintain its continuity of action.
> Major-General Carl von Clausewitz, *On War*, 3.16, 1832, tr. Michael Howard and Peter Paret, 1976.

YOU ASK ME why I do not write something. . . . [I] think one's feelings waste themselves in words. They ought to be distilled into actions and into actions which bring results.
> Florence Nightingale (1820–1910), quoted in Cecil Woodham-Smith, *Florence Nightingale*, 1951.

HE who does something at the head of one Regiment, will eclipse him who does nothing at the head of a hundred.
> Abraham Lincoln, 31 December 1861, letter to Major General David Hunter.

NOTHING is so ruinous to an army as doing nothing – it is as demoralizing as a defeat. My men have been looking at the enemy and living in the mud for three months. I cannot endure it much longer.
> Major-General Daniel E. Sickles, 30 January 1862, letter to a friend, Sickles Papers, Library of Congress.

NOW, GENTLEMEN, let us at once to bed, and rise with the dawn, and see if to-morrow we cannot *do something!*
> Lieutenant-General Thomas J. Jackson, during the Seven Days' Battles, 30 June 1862, quoted in Mary Anne Jackson, *Life and Letters of General Thomas J. Jackson*, 1892.

WE cannot afford to be idle, and though weaker than our opponents in men and military equipments, must endeavor to harass if we cannot destroy them.
> General Robert E. Lee, 30 September 1862, letter to President Jefferson Davis.

IF YOU REMAIN one more week at Nashville, I cannot prevent your removal. As I wrote you when you took command, the Government demands action, and if you cannot respond to that demand someone else will.
> Major-General Henry W. Halleck, to Major-General Rosecrans, December 1862, *The War of the Rebellion: A Compilation of the Official Records of the Union and Confederate Armies*, Vol. XX, Part 2, p. 117, U.S. Government Printing Office, 1880–1901.

THERE IS always hazard in military movements, but we must decide between the possible loss of inaction and the risk of action.
> General Robert E. Lee, letter to James A. Seddon, 8 June 1863, *The War of the Rebellion: A Compilation of the Official Records of the Union and Confederate Armies*, Vol. XLV, p. 868, U.S. Government Printing Office, 1880–1901.

AND PERHAPS the most influential reflection of all: "In war it is often less important what one does than how one does it. Strong determination and perseverance in carrying through a simple idea are the surest routes to one's objective."
> Field Marshal Helmuth Graf von Moltke (1800–1891), quoted in Kessel, *Moltke*, 1957.

WE ARE face to face with our destiny and we must meet it with a high and resolute courage. For us is the life of action, of strenuous performance of duty; let us live in the harness, striving mightily; let us rather run the risk of wearing out than rusting out.
> President Theodore Roosevelt, address at the opening of the gubernatorial campaign, New York City, 5 October 1898; 'The Duties of a Great Nation', *Campaigns and Controversies, XIV, The Collected Works of Theodore Roosevelt*, 1926.

A MAN who waits to believe in action before acting is anything you like, but he's not a man of action. It is as if a tennis player before returning a ball stopped to think about his views of the physical and mental advantages of tennis. You must act as you breathe.
> Georges Clemenceau, conversation with Jean Martet, 18 December 1927, quoted in *Clemenceau, the Events of His Life as Told by Himself to His Former Secretary, Jean Martet*, 1930.

WHEN A MAN asks himself what is meant by action he proves that he isn't a man of action. Action is a lack of balance. In order to act you must be somewhat insane. A reasonably sensible man is satisfied with thinking.
> Georges Clemenceau, conversation with Jean Martet, 1 January 1928, quoted in *Clemenceau, the Events of His Life as Told by Himself to His Former Secretary, Jean Martet*, 1930.

IN TACTICS, action is the governing rule of war.
> Marshal of France Ferdinand Foch, *Precepts and Judgments*, 1919.

THE ESSENTIAL THING is action. Action has three stages: the decision born of thought, the order or preparation for execution, and the execution itself. All three stages are governed by the will. The will is rooted in character, and for the man of action character is of more critical importance than intellect. Intellect without will is worthless, will without intellect is dangerous.
> Colonel-General Hans von Seekt, *Thoughts of a Soldier*, 1930.

WHEN FACED with the challenge of events, the man of character has recourse to himself. His instinctive response is to leave his mark on action, to take responsibility for it, to make it his own business. . . . he embraces action with the pride of a master; for if he takes a hand in it, it will become his, and he is ready to enjoy success on condition that it is really his own, and that he derives no profit from it. He is equally prepared to bear the weight of failure, though not without a bitter sense of satisfaction. In short, a fighter who finds within himself all the zest and support he needs, a gambler more intent on success than profits, a man who pays his debts with his own money lends nobility to action. Without him there is but the dreary task of the slave; thanks to him, it becomes the divine sport of the hero.

General Charles de Gaulle, *The Edge of the Sword*, 1932.

THE RELIEF which normally follows upon action after a long period of tension – that vast human sigh of relief – is one of the most recurrent phenomena of history, marking the onset of every great conflict. The urge to gain release from tension by action is a precipitating cause of war. (February 1929.)

Captain Sir Basil Liddell Hart, *Thoughts on War*, 1944.

IN CRITICAL and baffling situations, it is always best to return to first principle and simple action.

Sir Winston S. Churchill (1874–1965).

ACTION IS NECESSARY to maintain the morale of a military force and no commander can afford to miss an opportunity for his troops to win glory by successful action. The effect is two-headed, it invigorates his forces and discourages the enemy. Final victory cannot be won by hit-and-run tactics. Real victories must be won in main engagements, and he who recognizes an opportunity for such an action should proceed, if necessary, without orders from above or even in the face of contrary orders from a higher command out of touch with the situation.

Lin Piao, 1946, quoted in Ebon, *Lin Piao*, 1970.

ACTIVITY

IF THE ENEMY is taking his ease, he can harass him; if well supplied he can starve him; if quietly encamped, he can force him to move.

Appear at points which the enemy must hasten to defend; march swiftly to places where you are not expected.

Sun Tzu, *The Art of War*, 6, c. 500 BC, tr. Giles, 1910.

WHAT DO WE DO with a man who refuses to accept either good fortune or bad? This is the only general who gives his enemy no rest when he is victorious, nor takes any himself when he is defeated. We shall never have done with fighting him, it seems, because he attacks out of

confidence when he is winning, and out of shame when he is beaten.

Hannibal, 210 BC, of the Roman Consul Marcellus upon whom he had just inflicted a reverse at Numistro, but who immediately offered battle again, quoted in Plutarch, *The Lives*, c. AD 100, (*Makers of Rome*, tr. Ian Scott-Kilvert, 1965).

ONCE you engage in battle it is inexcusable to display any sloth or hesitation; you must breakfast on the enemy before he dines on you.

Kai Ka'us Ibn Iskander, Prince of Gurgan, *A Mirror for Princes*, 1082.

WHEN YOU SET OUT to war, be not inactive, depend not upon your captains, nor waste time in drinking, eating, or sleeping. Set the sentries yourselves, and take your rest only after you have posted them at night at every important point about your troops; then take your rest, but arise early. Do not put off your accoutrements without a quick glance about you, for a man may thus perish suddenly through his own carelessness.

Grand Prince Vladimir II Monomakh of Kiev (1053–1125), *The Testament of Vladimir Monomakh*, in Basil Dmytryshyn, *Medieval Russia: A Source Book*, 1967.

I AM UP AND ABOUT when I am ill, and in the most appalling weather. I am on horseback when other men would be flat out on their beds, complaining. We are made for action, and activity is the sovereign remedy for all physical ills.

Frederick the Great (1712–1786), quoted in Christopher Duffy, *Military Life of Frederick the Great*, 1986.

WHAT WOULD I DO if I were the enemy? What project could I form? Make as many as possible of these projects, examine them all, and above all reflect on the means to avert them. If you find yourself unable put it right at once! Often, through an hour's neglect, an unfortunate delay loses a reputation that has been acquired with a great deal of labor. Always presume that the enemy has dangerous designs and always be forehanded with the remedy.

Frederick the Great, *Instructions to His Generals*, 1747, tr. Phillips, 1940.

YOU will not be in a Worse Situation, nor your arms in less Credit if you should meet with Misfortune than if you were to Remain Inactive.

Major-General 'Mad' Anthony Wayne, November 1777, letter to George Washington.

ACCUSTOM YOURSELF to tireless activity . . .

Field Marshal Prince Aleksandr V. Suvorov (1729–1800), quoted in W. Lyon Blease, *Suvorof*, 1920.

ACTIVENESS is the most important of all
attributes of the military. . . . Hurry, your
excellency! Money is dear; human life still dearer,
but time is dearest of all.

> Field Marshal Prince Aleksandr V. Suvorov, 1799,
> during the Italian Campaign, quoted in Savkin, *Basic
> Principles of Operational Art and Tactics*, 1972.

ACTIVITY, Activity, Speed!

> Napoleon, 17 April 1809, order to Marshal of France
> Massena before Eckmühl during the Austrian
> Campaign, quoted in R.M. Johnston, ed., *The
> Corsican*, 1910.

THE HISTORY of warfare so often shows us the
very opposite of unceasing progress toward the
goal, that it becomes apparent that immobility and
inactivity are the normal state of armies in war, and
action is the exception.

> Major-General Carl von Clausewitz, *On War*, 3.16,
> 1832, tr. Michael Howard and Peter Paret, 1976.

A FUNDAMENTAL PRINCIPLE is never to remain
completely passive, but to attack the enemy frontally
and from the flanks, even when he is attacking us.

> Major-General Carl von Clausewitz, *Principles of
> War*, 1812.

MY OWN FEEBLE VOICE if called on will be to
pursue and fight, march rapidly, whip the enemy,
then turn back and give battle to the foe which may
be in front. In war much is gained by activity.

> Lieutenant-General William J. Hardee, to Mrs. Shover,
> 9 November 1861, quoted in Hughes, *General William
> J. Hardee*, 1965.

WE MUST make this campaign an exceedingly
active one. Only thus can a weaker country cope
with a stronger; it must make up in activity what it
lacks in strength. A defensive campaign can only be
made successful by taking the aggressive at the
proper time. Napoleon never waited for his
adversary to become fully prepared, but struck him
the first blow.

> Lieutenant-General Thomas J. 'Stonewall' Jackson,
> letter before the Battle of Chancellorsville, April 1863,
> quoted in Mary Anne Jackson, *Life and Letters of
> General Thomas J. Jackson*, 1892.

THE MOST advantageous thing of all is an
offensive operation against an opponent who stays
where he is. However, an active enemy will not sit
with his arms folded but will himself try to mount
an attack.

> Marshal of the Soviet Union Mikhail N. Tukhachevskiy,
> 1924, quoted in Simpkin, *Deep Battle*, 1987.

THERE IS one great maxim which throughout the
history of war has more often than not proved
successful, and this maxim is: "When in doubt, hit
out." When the soldier, whether private or general,

does not know what to do, he must strike; he must
not stand still, for normally it is better to strike and
fail than it is to sit still and be thrashed.

> Major-General J. F. C. Fuller, *Foundations of the
> Science of War*, 1926.

IN WAR, the policy of least exertion always risks
being paid for dearly.

> General Charles de Gaulle, *Salvation
> 1944–1946*, 1960.

WAS IT PERMISSIBLE to show the enemy that we
were capable only of defense and twisted about on
the same spot, like bound rabbits before the hunter
charging his rifle?

> Marshal of the Soviet Union Vassili I. Chuikov, 1962,
> of the decision on 31 October 1942 to counter-attack
> at Stalingrad, quoted in Nathan Leites, *The Soviet
> Style in War*, 1982.

ADAPTABILITY/ADAPTATION

DO NOT REPEAT the tactics which have gained you
one victory, but let your methods be regulated by the
infinite variety of circumstances.

> Sun Tzu, *The Art of War*, 6, c. 500 BC,
> tr. Giles, 1910.

AS SOON as they made these discoveries the
Romans began to copy Greek arms, for this is one
of their strong points: no people are more willing to
adopt new customs and to emulate what they see is
better done by others.

> Polybius, *Histories*, 6.25, c. 125 BC (*The Rise of the
> Roman Empire*, tr. Ian Scott-Kilvert, 1987).

THE "MOUNTAIN-SEA" SPIRIT means that it is bad
to repeat the same thing several times when fighting
the enemy. There may be no help but to do
something twice, but do not try it a third time. If you
once make an attack and fail, there is little chance of
success if you use the same approach again. If you
attempt a technique which you have previously tried
unsuccessfully and fail yet again, then you must
change your attacking method.

If the enemy thinks of the mountains, attack like
the sea; and if he thinks of the sea, attack like the
mountains. You must research this deeply.

> Miyamoto Musashi, *A Book of Five Rings*, 1645, tr.
> Victor Harris, 1984.

AFTER THE WAR, when I presented my order of
recall, I met General Fuji, the Chief of the General
Staff of the 1st Army, and told him I was anxious to
know what changes in the Japanese Regulations
would be introduced owing to their experiences in
the war; he answered: "So am I. We will wait to
see what new Regulations for the Service
Germany will issue on the basis of the reports that
the officers who have been sent here will make,

and we will translate these Regulations as we did the former ones."
General Max Hoffman, *War Diaries and Other Papers*, II, 1929; observation while attached as an observer to the Japanese Army during the Russo-Japanese War, 1904–1905.

VICTORY SMILES upon those who anticipate the changes in the character of war, not upon those who wait to adapt themselves after they occur.
General Giulio Douhet, *Command of the Air*, 1921.

I HAVE only one merit: I have forgotten what I taught and what I learned.
Marshal of France Ferdinand Foch, quoted in Monteilhet, *Les Institutions Militaires de la France*, 1932.

IT IS also greatly in the commander's own interest to have a personal picture of the front and a clear idea of the problems his subordinates are having to face. It is the only way in which he can keep his ideas permanently up to date and adapted to changing conditions. If he fights his battles as a game of chess, he will become rigidly fixed in academic theory and admiration of his own ideas. Success comes most readily to the commander whose ideas have not been canalised into any one fixed channel, but can develop freely from the conditions around him.
Field Marshal Erwin Rommel, *The Rommel Papers*, 1953.

IN ANY PROBLEM where an opposing force exists, and cannot be regulated, one must foresee and provide for alternative courses. Adaptability is the law which governs survival in war as in life – war being but a concentrated form of the human struggle against environment.
Captain Sir Basil Liddell Hart, *Strategy*, 1954.

SENIOR LEADERSHIP still sometimes has the desire to take the chaos out, to make the world orderly. Some people stay in the military because they want to live in an orderly world. They like to live on bases with traffic moving slowly and all the grass cut. So there is a desire to reject all chaos and try to make war orderly. What we realistically need is a unique organization that can thrive and do its best job in a chaotic situation.
Colonel Michael Wyly, 'Chaos', Al Santoli, ed., *Leading the Way: How Vietnam Veterans Rebuilt the U.S. Military*, 1993.

IN BATTLE, versatility allows a commander to act with certainty and decisiveness amid the fog and friction of mortal combat. In training, it spurs us to press the edge of the envelope, to try new ideas, to dare great things and to grow as individuals and as an army. It is a characteristic that springs from a certain knowledge of the basics of our craft. And that certain knowledge gives great leaders the confidence to improvise solutions – to move well beyond the situations we may forsee today.
General Gordan R. Sullivan, 'Leadership and All That Jazz', *Military Review*, 8/1994.

ADMINISTRATION

THE GOOD CONDITION of my armies comes from the fact that I devote an hour or two every day to them, and when I am sent the returns of my troops and my ships each month, which fills twenty large volumes, I set every other occupation aside to read them in detail in order to discern the difference that exists from one month to another. I take greater pleasure in this reading than a young lady would get from reading a novel.
Napoleon to Joseph Bonaparte, 20 August 1806, *Correspondance de Napoléon Ier, publié par ordre de l'Empereur Napoléon III*, No. 10672, Vol. XIII, 1858–1870.

MY LORD,
If I attempted to answer the mass of futile correspondence that surrounds me, I should be debarred from all serious business of campaigning. I must remind your Lordship – for the last time – that so long as I retain an independent position, I shall see that no officer under my Command is debarred, by attending to the futile drivelling of mere quill-driving in your Lordship's office, from attending to his first duty – which is, and always has been, so to train the private men under his command that they may, without question, beat any force opposed to them in the field.
Duke of Wellington, 1810, letter (attributed) to the Secretary of State for War.

MY RULE was to do the business of the day in that day.
The Duke of Wellington, quoted in Stanhope, *Conversations with the Duke of Wellington*, 1888.

I NEVER KNEW what to do with a paper except to put it in a side pocket or pass it to a clerk who understood it better than I did.
General of the Army Ulysses S. Grant, quoted in S.L.A. Marshall, *The Armed Forces Officer*, 1951.

ALTHOUGH revolutionary government, none was ever so much under the domination of red tape as the one at Richmond. The martinets who controlled it were a good deal like the hero of Molière's comedy, who complained that his antagonist had wounded him by thrusting in carte, when according to the rule, it should have been in tierce. I cared nothing for the form of a thrust if it brought blood. I did not play with foils.
Colonel John S. Mosby, *Mosby's War Reminiscences*, 1887.

NEARLY ALL of my clerical force is broken down . . . The fact is, I never saw so much writing; and yet Drayton, who does as much as any of them, says it is all necessary. So I tell them to go on. I do not mind signing my name. Although I write all my own letters, some one has to copy them. My fleet is so large now that it keeps us all at work the whole time.

> Admiral David G. Farragut, quoted in Alfred Thayer Mahan, *Admiral Farragut*, 1892.

THERE HAS BEEN a constant struggle on the part of the military element to keep the end – fighting, or readiness to fight – superior to mere administrative considerations. . . . The military man, having to do the fighting, considers that the chief necessity; the administrator equally naturally tends to think the smooth running of the machine the most admirable quality.

> Rear Admiral Alfred Thayer Mahan, *Naval Administration and Warfare*, 1908.

THE MORE I SEE of war, the more I realize how it all depends on administration and transportation. . . . It takes little skill or imagination to see where you would like your forces to be and when; it takes much knowledge and hard work to know where you can place your forces and whether you can maintain them there.

> Field Marshal Viscount Wavell of Cyrenaica (1883–1950).

. . . THERE MUST be a clear-cut, long-term relationship established between operational intentions and administrative resources. Successful administrative planning is dependent on anticipation of requirements.

> Field Marshal Viscount Montgomery of Alamein, *Memoirs of Field Marshal Montgomery*, 1958.

SUCCESS cannot be administered.

> Admiral Arleigh Burke, speech, 1962.

PAPER-WORK will ruin any military force.

> Lieutenant-General Lewis B. 'Chesty' Puller, quoted in Burke Davis, *Marine!*, 1962.

ADMIRALS

THERE IS in the naval profession a specialized technical mentality which blocked all my plans. No sooner had I proposed a new idea than I had [Admiral] Ganteaume and the whole navy on my neck: "Sire, this is impossible." – "Why?" – "Sire, the winds don't allow it, and then the doldrums, the currents" – and with that they stopped me short. How can a man argue with people who speak a different language?

> Napoleon, 1816, quoted in Christopher Herold, *The Mind of Napoleon*, 1955.

IT IS DANGEROUS to meddle with admirals when

they say they can't do things. They have always got the weather or fuel or something to argue about.

> Sir Winston Churchill, December 1941, to Secretary of War Frank Knox.

THE ADMIRALS are really something to cope with – and I should know. To change something in the na-a-vy is like punching a feather bed, you punch it with your right and you punch it with your left until you are finally exhausted and then you find the damn bed just as it was before you started punching.

> President Franklin D. Roosevelt (1882–1945), quoted in the *San Diego Union*, 20 November 1987.

WE HAD GENERALS who were Admirals and Admirals who wanted to be Generals. Generals acting as Admirals are bad enough but it was the Admirals who wanted to be Generals who imperilled victory among the coral islands.

> General Holland M. 'Howlin Mad' Smith, *Coral and Brass*, 1949.

[ADMIRAL HALSEY] was of the same aggressive type as John Paul Jones, David Farragut, and George Dewey. His one thought was to close with the enemy and fight him to the death. The bugaboo of many sailors, the fear of losing ships, was completely alien to his conception of fighting.

> General of the Army Douglas MacArthur, *Reminiscences*, 1964.

THE TOTAL VESSELS lost by both navies had been about the same, but we could replace ours, even increase their numbers; the Japanese could not. Our other losses were of a different character; leaders like Admirals Scott and Callaghan are not easy to replace. Their deaths remind us that admirals still die on the bridges of their flagships while generals die in bed.

> General Merrill B. Twining, *No Bended Knee*, 1994. Scott and Callaghan were lost in the naval battles in the Solomon Islands.

ADVERSITY

THE NOBLE and courageous man is known by his patience in adversity.

> The Inca Emperor Pachacutec (d. 1470), quoted in Garcilaso de la Vega, *Royal Commentaries of the Incas*, 1989.

THE OFFICERS should feel the conviction that resignation, bravery, and faithful attention to duty are virtues without which no glory is possible and no army is respectable, and that firmness amid reverses is more honorable than enthusiasm in success – since courage alone is necessary to storm a position whereas it requires heroism to make a difficult retreat before a victorious and enterprising enemy, always opposing to him a firm and unbroken front.

> Lieutenant-General Antoine-Henri Baron de Jomini, *Summary of the Art of War*, 1838, tr. Mendell and Craighill, 1862.

CAMPAIGNS AND BATTLES are nothing but a long series of difficulties to be overcome. The lack of equipment, the lack of food, the lack of this or that are only excuses; the real leader displays his quality in his triumphs over adversity, however great it may be.

> General of the Army George C. Marshall, 18 September 1941, address to the first Officer Candidate Class, Fort Benning, Georgia.

YOU'RE ALL RIGHT as long as you're winners; I'm a hell of a general when I'm winning, anybody is, but it's when you're not winning – and I have not always been winning, if you had been a British general at the start of a war you'd know that – it is then that the real test of leadership is made.

> Field Marshal Viscount Slim of Burma, 8 April 1952, speech to the U.S. Army Command and General Staff College.

ADVICE

WHEN MEN counsel reasonably, reasonable success ensues; but when in their counsels they reject reason, God does not choose to follow the wanderings of human fancies.

> Themistocles, 480 BC, urging the Peloponnesians not to abandon the defence of Salamis during the Persian invasion of Greece, quoted in Herodotus, *The Persian Wars*, 8, tr. George Rawlinson.

I BELIEVE that a general who receives good advice from a subordinate officer should profit by it. Any patriotic servant of the state should forget himself when in that service, and look only to the interests of the state. In particular, he must not let the source of an idea influence him. Ideas of others can be as valuable as his own and should be judged only by the results they are likely to produce.

> Frederick the Great, *General Principles of War*, 1748.

THERE ARE GENERALS who need no advice; who judge and decide for themselves, and their staffs merely execute orders. Such generals are stars of the first magnitude, appearing only once in a century.

> Field Marshal Helmuth Graf von Moltke, *Italian Campaigns of 1859*, 1904.

AGGRESSION

WHEN ASSUR, the great lord, in order to show to the peoples the immensity of my mighty deeds, extended my kingship over the kings of the four regions, and

made great my name; [when] he caused my hands to bear a stern scepter, for the annihilation of my foes, the land sinned against Assur, they treated [him] with scorn, they rebelled. To rob, to plunder, to extend the border of Assyria, they [the gods] empowered me. After Assur and the great gods, my lords, commanded me to march over distant roads, wearying mountains and mighty sands, thirsty regions, – with trusting heart, I marched in safety.

> Esarhaddon (680–669 BC), King of Assyria, quoted in Luckenbill, *Ancient Records of Assyria and Babylonia*, II, 1926.

LET US engage in anger, convinced that nothing is more legitimate between adversaries than to claim to satisfy the whole wrath of one's soul in punishing the aggressor, and nothing more sweet, as the proverb has it, than the vengeance upon an enemy which it will now be ours to take. That enemies they are and mortal enemies you all know, since they came here to enslave our country, and if successful had in reserve for our men all that is most dreadful, and for our children and wives all that is most dishonorable, and for the whole city the name which conveys the greatest reproach.

> Gylippus, Summer 413 BC, to the Syracusans before the last great naval battle with the Athenians in the harbour of Syracuse, quoted in Thucydides, *History of the Peloponnesian War*, 7.68, c. 404 BC, tr. Richard Crawley, 1910.

MEN RISE from one ambition to another: First, they seek to secure themselves against attack, and then they attack others.

> Niccolo Machiavelli, *Discourses*, 1517.

IF AGGRESSORS are wrong above, they are right below.

> Napoleon, *Maxims*, 1804–1815.

THERE IS never a convenient place to fight a war when the other man starts it.

> Admiral Arleigh A. '31-Knot' Burke (1901–1996)

WE RULE the skies and seas, and possess the power to rule the land when we are sufficiently aroused. But we have not learned to understand, much less to rule, minds and hearts and souls. The only moral we need to cull from the *Iliad* is that it is foolish to underestimate the complexity and determination of the killers from the other shore.

> Lieutenant-Colonel Ralph Peters, 'New Old Enemies', *Parameters*, Summer 1999.

AGGRESSIVENESS

TURKISH RAIDS are to be beaten off in the usual way: aggressively, the details depending on circumstances and on the common sense, skill, courage and determination of Messieurs the officers.

Field Marshal Prince Aleksandr V. Suvorov, 1773, on the Danube, quoted in K. Ossipov, *Suvorov*, 1945.

OUR COUNTRY will, I believe, sooner forgive an officer for attacking an enemy than for letting it [*sic*] alone.

Admiral Viscount Nelson, 3 May 1794, letter during the attack on Bastin.

I DO NOT ADVISE rashness, but I do desire resolute and actual fighting, with necessary casualties.

General of the Army Phillip H. Sheridan, 23 September 1864, message to Major-General Averell.

MY RULE IS: if you meet the weakest vessel, attack; if it is a vessel equal to yours, attack; and if it is stronger than yours, also attack . . .

Admiral Stepan O. Makarov (1849–1904).

HOW IS IT POSSIBLE to vanquish the enemy except by a blow over the head? And for this it is necessary to attack him, to spring upon him. This was known to army leaders in biblical times.

Leon Trotsky, 1922, *Military Writings*, 1969.

HOLD what you've got and hit them where you can.

Admiral of the Fleet Ernest J. King, December 1941, admonishment to the hard-pressed commanders in the Pacific in the face of the Japanese onslaught after Pearl Harbor.

WHAT COUNTS is not necessarily the size of the dog in the fight – it's the size of the fight in the dog.

General of the Armies Dwight D. Eisenhower, 31 January 1958, Republican National Convention.

AN ARMY which thinks only in defensive terms is doomed. It yields initiative and advantage in time and space to the enemy – even an enemy inferior in numbers. It loses the sense of the hunter, the opportunist.

General Sir David Fraser, *And We Shall Shock Them*, 1983.

AIRBORNE

THE FÜHRER was very upset by the heavy losses suffered by the parachute units [on Crete in 1941], and came to the conclusion that their surprise value had passed. After that, he often said to me: 'The day of parachute troops is over.'

General Kurt Student, 1945, quoted in B.H. Liddell Hart, *The German Generals Talk*, 1948.

A STANDARD QUESTION for a new man was why he had volunteered for parachuting and whether he enjoyed it. On one occasion, a bright-eyed recruit startled me by replying to the latter question with a resounding, "No, sir." "Why then, if you don't like jumping did you volunteer to be a parachutist?" I asked. "Sir, I like to be with people who do like to jump," was the reply. I shook his hand vigorously and assured him that there were at least two of us of the same mind in the Division.

General Maxwell D. Taylor, *Swords and Ploughshares*, 1972.

I WAS CONFIDENT that we were reasonably well prepared. There is enormous residual self-confidence in a parachute battalion. People don't wonder whether they can do things.

Lieutenant-Colonel Hugh Pike, 1982, commanding 3 Para during the Falklands War.

MY FIRST 11 years in the military were in the old Horse Cavalry. Although the Army's Airborne Forces undeniably originated in the Infantry, and though their outstanding World War II leaders were mostly ex-Infantrymen, they nevertheless seem to me to have inherited the tradition and esprit of the Cavalry. I think this is because military esprit is part derived from mobility: forces inherently able to move faster have options and capabilities slower forces don't have and therefore feel better about themselves.

Airborne esprit is further enhanced by the soldier's knowledge that he repeatedly does something many men cannot force themselves to do; jump out of airplanes. . . .

General Hamilton H. Howze, *A Cavalryman's Story*, 1996.

AIR POWER

FIND THE ENEMY and shoot him down, anything else is nonsense.

Captain Manfred Baron von Richthofen, 1917, opinion of air combat, quoted in Toliver and Constable, *Fighter Aces of the Luftwaffe*, 1977.

THE MILITARY MIND always imagines that the next war will be on the same lines as the last. That has never been the case and never will be. One of the great factors in the next war will be aircraft obviously. The potentialities of aircraft attack on a large scale are almost incalculable.

Marshal of France Ferdinand Foch (1851–1929).

I HAVE a mathematical certainty that the future will confirm my assertion that aerial warfare will be the most important element in future wars, and that in consequence not only will the importance of the Independent Air Force rapidly increase, but the importance of the army and navy will decrease in proportion.

General Giulio Douhet, *Command of the Air*, 1921.

IT IS PROBABLE that future war will be conducted

by a special class, the air force, as it was by the armored knights of the Middle Ages.
Brigadier-General William 'Billy' Mitchell, *Winged Defense*, 1924.

THE ADVENT of air power, which can go straight to the vital centers and either neutralize or destroy them, has put a completely new complexion on the old system of making war. It is now realized that the hostile main army in the field is a false objective, and the real objectives are the vital centers.
Brigadier-General William 'Billy' Mitchell, *Skyways: A Book on Modern Aeronautics*, 1930.

TOM, you've never believed in air. Never get out from under the air umbrella; if you do, you'll be for it. And as you flutter up to heaven all you'll say is – "My gosh, some sailor laid a hell of a mine for me!"
Marshal of the Royal Air Force Sir Arthur Harris, to Admiral Tom Phillips, commanding the squadron that included HMS *Prince of Wales* and *Repulse*, which were later sunk by Japanese carrier aircraft in the Far East in 1942, an action in which Phillips also perished, *Bomber Offensive*, 1947.

VICTORY, speedy and complete, awaits the side that employs air power as it should be employed.
Marshal of the Royal Air Force Sir Arthur Harris (1892–1984).

IF WE LOSE the war in the air, we lose the war, and we lose it quickly.
Field Marshal Viscount Montgomery of Alamein (1887–1976).

WHEREAS to shift the weight of effort on the ground from one point to another takes time, the flexibility inherent in Air Forces permits them without change of base to be switched from one objective to another in the theatre of operations.
Field Marshal Viscount Montgomery of Alamein (1887–1976).

IN OUR VICTORY over Japan, airpower was unquestionably decisive. That the planned invasion of the Japanese Home islands was unnecessary is clear evidence that airpower has evolved into a force in war co-equal with land and sea power, decisive in its own right and worthy of the faith of its prophets.
General Carl A. Spaatz, 'Evolution of Air Power', *Military Review*, 6/1947.

ONE of the outstanding characteristics of air-power proved to be its flexibility and the terrific concentration made possible by a unified air command – a unity only achieved by a faith born of mutual understanding between all branches and ranks of the air forces.
Air Chief Marshal Lord Tedder, *With Prejudice*, 1948.

AIR WARFARE cannot be separated into little packets; it knows no boundaries on land and sea other than those imposed by the radius of action of the aircraft; it is a unity and demands unity of command.
Air Chief Marshal Lord Tedder, *With Prejudice*, 1948.

ANYONE who has to fight, even with the most modern weapons, against an enemy in complete command of the air, fights like a savage against modern European troops, under the same handicaps and with the same chances of success.
Field Marshal Erwin Rommel, *Rommel Papers*, 1953.

THE IDEA that superior air power can in some way be a substitute for hard slogging and professional skill on the ground in this sort of war is beguiling but illusory. Air support can be of immense value to an army; it may sometimes be its salvation. But we must have a care not to misread the lessons of . . . the closing years of World War II. The truth that we should take to heart is that armies can fight – and not only defensively – in the face of almost total air superiority. . . . All this is cold comfort for anyone who hopes that air power will provide some cheap short cut to victory.
Air Marshal Sir John Slessor, 'Air Power and World Strategy', *Foreign Affairs*, October 1954.

AIR STRIKES are so tempting, so swift, so seemingly surgical. We might be able to win a war by air, though, so far, no one had. "The trouble with airpower," I had warned the President, "is that you leave the initiative in the hands of your enemy. He gets to decide when he's had enough." We were planning a full campaign – air, land, sea, and space – to remove the decision from Saddam's hands.
General Colin Powell, of the planning for Desert Storm, *My American Journey*, 1995.

THAT'S THE NATURE of an air campaign. The initiative is in the hands of your opponent because you are not going in to take the initiative away by putting ground troops in.
General Colin Powell, interview in *USA Today*, 17 May 1999.

ALLIANCES/ALLIES/COALITION WARFARE

IF PEOPLE want to be in the front ranks of a flight, I prefer to see them in our enemies' ranks rather than our own.
Xenophon, *Anabasis*, 3.2, c. 360 BC (*The March Up Country*, tr. W.H.D. Rouse, 1959); 401 BC, commenting on former allies of the Greeks who fled to the enemy at the Battle of Cunaxa.

ALLIANCES, to be sure, are good, but forces of one's own are still better.
Frederick William of Brandenburg (the Great Elector), *Political Testament*, 1667.

'TIS OUR TRUE POLICY to steer clear of permanent alliances with any portion of the foreign world.
> President George Washington, 17 September 1796, farewell address.

IT IS BETTER to have a known enemy than a forced ally.
> Napoleon, *Political Aphorisms*, 1848.

THE ALLIES we gain by victory will turn against us upon the bare whisper of our defeat.
> Napoleon, *Political Aphorisms*, 1848.

THE PROVERBIAL WEAKNESS of alliances is due to inferior power of concentration.
> Rear Admiral Alfred Thayer Mahan, *Naval Strategy*, 1911.

GRANTING the same aggregate of force, it is never as great in two hands as in one, because it is not perfectly concentrated.
> Rear Admiral Alfred Thayer Mahan, *Naval Strategy*, 1911.

I CANNOT BELIEVE that the British Army will refuse to do its share in this supreme crisis . . . history would severely judge your absence. . . Monsieur le Maréchal, the honor of England is at stake!
> Marshal of France Joseph Joffre, 5 September 1914; appeal to Field Marshal French, commanding the British Expeditionary Force (BEF), to participate in the counter-attack that would be the First Battle of the Marne, quoted in Barbara Tuchman, *The Guns of August*, 1962.

IN MILITARY OPERATIONS against the Imperial German Government you are directed to cooperate with the forces of the other countries employed against the enemy; but in so doing the underlying idea must be kept in view that the forces of the United States are a separate and distinct component of the combined forces, the identity of which must be preserved. This fundamental rule is subject to such minor exceptions in particular circumstances as your judgment may appprove. The decision as to when your command or any of its parts is ready for action is confided to you, and you will exercise full discretion in determining the manner of cooperation.
> Secretary of War John Baker, 1917, instructions to General John J. Pershing upon assumption of command of the American Expeditionary Force (AEF).

AMERICA has joined forces with the Allied Powers, and what we have of blood and treasure are yours. Therefore, it is that with loving pride we drape the colors in tribute of respect to this citizen of your great republic. And here and now, in the presence of the illustrious dead, we pledge our hearts and our

honor in carrying this war to successful issue. Lafayette, we are here.
> Colonel Charles E. Stanton, 4 July 1917, Paris, as General John J. Pershing placed a wreath at the tomb of the Marquis de Lafayette, quoted in Henry F. Woods, *American Sayings*, 1945.

I WAS NO MORE than conductor of an orchestra. . . . A vast orchestra, of course. . . . Say, if you like, that I beat time well! Has the music stopped? Are we tired of the tune? We must start a new one. Never stop. . . . The true meaning of the unified command is not to give orders, but to make suggestions. . . . One talks, one discusses, one persuades. . . . One says, "That is what should be done; it is simple; it is only necessary to will it."
> Marshal of France Ferdinand Foch, commander of allied forces during World War I, quoted in Liddell Hart, *Foch: The Man of Orleans*, 1931.

ANY ALLIANCE whose purpose is not the intention to wage war is senseless and useless.
> Adolf Hitler, *Mein Kampf*, 1925.

NEGATIVE GOALS frequently are more widespread when waging a coalition war because the egotistic interests of each ally thrust him toward offering the others the honor of striking the enemy while he himself vigilantly guards and protects his own forces for the final hour to force consideration of his interests when concluding the peace. Therefore, coalition wars rather assume a positional nature than the single combat of two states. . . .
> General A.A. Svechin, *Strategy*, 1927.

IN WAR I would deal with the Devil and his grandmother.
> Joseph Stalin (1879–1953).

IF HITLER invaded hell, I would make at least a favourable reference to the devil in the House of Commons.
> Sir Winston S. Churchill, 1941, upon supporting the Soviet Union after the German invasion of 22 June.

THERE IS only one thing worse than fighting with allies – and that is fighting without them.
> Sir Winston S. Churchill (1874–1965).

EXTREMISTS on both sides of the water can indulge in all the backbiting and name-calling that they please – they can never get away from the historical truth that the United States and the British Empire, working together, did a job that looked almost impossible at the time it was undertaken.
> General of the Armies Dwight D. Eisenhower, 13 July 1946, letter to Lord Ismay, quoted in Stephen Ambrose, *Eisenhower*, I, 1983.

HISTORY testifies to the ineptitude of coalitions in waging war. Allied failures have been so numerous and their inexcusable blunders so common that professional soldiers had long discounted the possibility of effective allied action unless available resources were so great as to assure victory by inundation. Even Napoleon's reputation as a brilliant military leader suffered when students in staff colleges came to realize that he always fought against coalitions – and therefore against divided counsels and diverse political, economic, and military interests.

> General of the Army Dwight D. Eisenhower, *Crusade in Europe*, 1948.

ALLIED EFFECTIVENESS in World War II established for all time the feasibility of developing and employing joint control machinery that can meet the sternest tests of war. The key to the matter is a readiness, on highest levels, to adjust all nationalistic differences that affect the strategic employment of combined resources, and, in the war theater, to designate a single commander who is supported to the limit. With these two things done, success rests in the vision, the leadership, the skill, and the judgment of the professionals making up command and staff groups; if these two things are not done, only failure can result.

> General of the Army Dwight D. Eisenhower, *Crusade in Europe*, 1948.

IN WAR it is not always possible to have everything go exactly as one likes. In working with Allies it sometimes happens that they develop opinions of their own.

> Sir Winston Churchill, *The Hinge of Fate*, 1950.

A TOO COMPLETE victory inevitably complicates the problem of making a just and wise peace settlement. Where there is no longer the counter-balance of an opposing force to control the appetites of the victors, there is no check on the conflict of views and interests between the parties to the alliance. The divergence is then apt to become so acute as to turn the comradeship of common danger into the hostility of mutual dissatisfaction – so that the ally of one war becomes the enemy in the next.

> Captain Sir Basil Liddell Hart, *Strategy*, 1954.

WAR without allies is bad enough – with allies it is hell!

> Air Marshal Sir John Slessor, *Strategy for the West*, 1954.

A CLUE to why coalition warfare failed in Vietnam was given by a North Vietnamese Army (NVA) major in Hanoi a week before Saigon's fall. "You should not feel badly," he said. "You have done more than enough . . . more than enough." Even worse than the mortification of being in the enemy's capital while he is celebrating your defeat is the humiliation of his trying to lessen your discomfort with reassuring

words. Yet the NVA major was more correct than he knew. We failed in Vietnam because we attempted to do too much.

> Colonel Harry G. Summers, Jr., *On Strategy: The Vietnam War in Context*, 1981.

I WAS OPERATING with the starting assumption that there was no single target that was more important, if struck, than the principle of Alliance consensus and cohesion.

> General Wesley Clark, on holding the NATO alliance together during the bombing campaign against Serbia, quoted in 'The Commander's War', *Washington Post*, 21 September 1999, p. A16.

AMATEURS

THERE ARE three ways in which a ruler can bring misfortune upon his army:
(1) By commanding the army to advance or to retreat, being ignorant of the fact that it cannot obey. This is called hobbling the army.
(2) By attempting to govern the army in the same way as he administers his kingdom, being ignorant of the conditions which obtain in an army. This causes restlessness in the soldier's [sic] minds.
(3) By employing the officers of his army without discrimination, through ignorance of the military principle of adaptation to the circumstances. This shakes the confidence of the soldiers.

> Sun Tzu, *The Art of War*, 3, c. 500 BC, tr. Giles, 1910.

GENERALS ought to be given advice, in the first place from men of foresight, the experts who have specialized in military affairs, and who have learned from experience; secondly, from those who are on the spot, who see the terrain, who know the enemy, who can judge the right moment for action, who are, as it were, shipmates sharing the same danger. Therefore, if there is anyone who is confident that he can advise me about the best interest of the nation in the campaign which I am now about to conduct, let him not deny the state his services – let him come with me to Macedonia. I will assist him by providing his passage, his horse, his tent, yes, and his travelling money. If anyone finds this prospect too irksome, and prefers the ease of the city to the hardships of campaign, let him not steer the ship from his place on shore.

> Lucius Aemilius Paulus, 168 BC, upon his departure for the campaign in which he would defeat Perseus, King of Macedonia, at the Battle of Pydna, quoted in Livy, *The History of Rome*, 44.22, c. AD 17 (*Rome and the Mediterranean*, tr. Henry Bettenson, 1976).

I WELL KNOW the character of that senseless monster the people, unable either to support the present or to foresee the future, always desirous of attempting the impossible, and of rushing headlong to its ruin. Yet your unthinking folly shall not induce me to permit your own destruction, nor to betray the trust committed to me by my sovereign and yours. Success in war depends less on intrepidity than on prudence to await, to distinguish, and to seize the decisive moment of fortune. You appear to regard the present contest as a game of hazard, which you might determine by a single throw of the dice; but I, at least, have learnt from experience to prefer security to speed. But it seems that you offer to reinforce my troops, and to march with them against the enemy. Where then have you acquired your knowledge of war? And what true soldier is not aware that the result of a battle must chiefly rest on the skill and discipline of the combatants? Ours is a real enemy in the field; we march to a battle, and not to a review.

> Count Belisarius, AD 538, when the population of Rome, in desperation, urged a battle during the siege by the Goths, in Mahon, *Life of Belisarius*, 1829.

THE COMMANDERS of armies are more to be pitied than one would think. Without listening to them, all the world denounces them, the newspapers ridicule them, and yet, of the thousands who condemn them, there is not one that could command even the smallest unit.

> Frederick the Great (1712–1786).

THE KIND of person who could not lead a patrol of nine men is happy to arrange armies in his imagination, criticise the conduct of a general, and say to his misguided self: "My God, I know I could do better if I was in his place!"

> Frederick the Great, 14 July 1745.

LET NO MAN be so rash as to suppose that, in donning a general's uniform, he is forthwith competent to perform a general's functions; as reasonably might he assume that in putting on the robes of a judge he was ready to decide any point of law.

> Dennis Hart Mahan, *Advance-Guard, Out-Post, and Detachment Service of Troops, with the Essential Principles of Strategy and Grand Tactics*, 1863.

I AM SORRY, as you say, that the movements of the armies cannot keep pace with the expectations of the editors of papers. I know they can regulate matters satisfactorily to themselves on paper. I wish they could do so in the field. No one wishes them more success than I do & would be happy to see them have full swing. Genl Floyd has the benefit of three editors on his staff. I hope something will be done to please them.

> General Robert E. Lee, letter to his wife, 7 October 1861, quoted in Clifford Dowdey and Louis Manarin, ed., *The Wartime Papers of Robert E. Lee*, 1961.

[MAJ. GEN. Benjamin] Butler's whole course down there seems marked by the two faults which seem inseparable from civilian generals (excepting those who have a natural aptitude for military affairs, which B. has not): too great rashness & too great timidity in constant alternation. His ignorance of war leads him constantly to require impossibilities from his subordinates and to fear impossibilities from the enemy.

> John Hay, diary entry for June 21, 1864, *Lincoln and the Civil War in the Letters of John Hay*, 1939, p. 195.

THIS IS a very suggestive age. Some people seem to think that an army can be whipped by waiting for rivers to freeze over, exploding powder at a distance, drowning out troops, or setting them to sneezing; but it will always be found in the end that the only way to whip an army is to go out and fight it.

> General of the Army Ulysses S. Grant, January 1865, quoted in Horace Porter, *Campaigning with Grant*, 1906.

ALTHOUGH since the days of Nimrod war has been the constant occupation of men, the fingers of one hand suffice to number the great commanders. The "unlearned" hardly think of usurping Tyndalls' place in the lecture room, or of taking his cuneiform bricks from Rawlinson; yet the world has been much more prolific of learned scientists and philologers than of able generals. Notwithstanding, the average American (and, judging from the dictatorship of Maitre Gambetta, the Frenchman) would not have hesitated to supersede Napoleon at Austerlitz or Nelson at Trafalgar. True, Cleon captured the Spartan garrison, and Narses gained victories, and Bunyan wrote the "Pilgrim's Progress;" but pestilent demagogues and mutilated guardians of Eastern zenanas have not always been successful in war, nor the great and useful profession of thinkers written allegory. As men without knowledge have at all times usurped the right to criticise campaigns and commanders, they will doubtless continue to do so despite the protests of professional soldiers, who discharge this duty in a reverent spirit, knowing that the greatest is he who commits the fewest blunders.

> Lieutenant-General Richard Taylor, *Destruction and Reconstruction*, 1879.

WHEN, in complete security, after dinner in full physical and moral contentment, men consider war and battle, they are animated by a noble ardor which has nothing in common with reality. How many of them, however, at that moment would be ready to risk their lives? But oblige them to march for days and weeks to arrive at the battle front, and on the day of battle oblige them to wait a few minutes or hours to deliver it. If they were honest, they would testify how much the physical fatigue and the mental anguish that preceded action have lowered their morale, how much less eager to fight they are than a month before, when they arose from the table in a generous mood.

> Colonel Charles Ardant du Picq, *Battle Studies*, 1880, tr. Greely, 1957.

ALL THOSE who criticize the dispositions of a general ought first to study military history, unless they have themselves taken part in a war in a position of command. I should like to see such people compelled to conduct a battle themselves. They would be overwhelmed by the greatness of their task, and when they realized the obscurity of the position, the exacting nature of enormous demands made on them, they would doubtless be more modest.

General Erich Ludendorff, *My War Memories, 1914–1918*, 1919.

ALL THE MORE HONOUR to those gifted professional soldiers who have shown creative brains, but also all the more reason why we should preserve an open and receptive mind to the far larger stream of ideas which have come from "amateurs," from Roger Bacon and Leonardo da Vinci down to the Volunteers who simplified our cumbrous drill and developed our musketry and tactical instructions. Nor can we forget that the decisive new weapon of the World War, the tank, owed its introduction principally to "amateurs" in the face of stubborn opposition from the supreme professional opinion. It may also be significant that the one soldier who contributed notably to its causation was an engineer and an imaginative writer. (March 1923.)

Captain Sir Basil Liddell Hart, *Thoughts on War*, 1944.

THE ATMOSPHERE in Washington in that period [1964] is difficult, indeed impossible, to re-create. There were conferences almost weekly, at government expense, to gather in judgments from all possible quarters on what was to be done to carry the war to a successful conclusion. These huddles would bring together professors and self-appointed experts on guerrilla warfare from all parts of the country. The collective contribution to the national cause may have been two degrees above zero. Government was proceeding according to the notion that, if enough persons are collected, some inspired thoughts of value will inevitably flow outward. It reminds me of the Army thesis that if two half-wits are assigned to a task, you get a whole wit, whereas the mathematical prospect is, more accurately, that what comes out will be a quarter-wit.

Brigadier-General S.L.A. Marshall, 'Thoughts on Vietnam', in Thompson, *Lessons of Vietnam*, 1977.

CIVILIAN LEADERS in the Pentagon and State Department . . . obliged MACV [Military Assistance Command Vietnam] to quantify the success of American combat operations. . . . They scoffed at the principles of war. They were convinced the ground war could be confined within the borders of South Vietnam, neatly wrapped in their computer spreadsheets. They were also convinced that if Westmoreland followed their directives faithfully, all the little boxes could be checked, the graph lines would run true, and victory would be inevitable.

Major-General John K. Singlaub, *Hazardous Duty*, 1991.

HE IS neither a strategist nor is he schooled in the operational art, nor is he a tactician, nor is he a general, nor is he a soldier. Other than that he's a great military man, I want you to know.

General H. Norman Schwarzkopf, 28 March 1991, in response to a journalist's question concerning Saddam Hussein's ability as a military strategist.

OUT THERE among you are the cynics, the people who scoff at what you're learning here. The people that scoff at character, the people that scoff at hard work. But they don't know what they're talking about, let me tell you. I can assure you that when the going gets tough and your country needs them, they're not going to be there. They will not be there, but you will. . . . After Vietnam, we had a whole cottage industry develop basically in Washington, D.C., that consisted of a bunch of military fairies that had never been shot at in anger, who felt fully qualified to comment on the leadership ability of all the leaders of the United States Army. They were not Monday morning quarterbacks, they were the worst of all possible kind, they were Friday afternoon quarterbacks. They felt qualified to criticize us even before the game was played. . . . And they are the same people who are saying, my goodness, we have terrible problems in the armed forces because there are no more leaders out there, there are no more combat leaders. Where are the Eisenhowers? Where are the Bradleys? Where are the MacArthurs? Where are the Audie Murphys? . . . Coming from a guy who's never been shot at in his entire life, that's a pretty bold statement.

General H. Norman Schwarzkopf, 15 May 1991, address to the Corps of Cadets at West Point.

AMBITION

I WAS at the head of our troops, and his majesty beheld my bravery. I brought off a chariot, its horses, and him who was upon it as a living prisoner, and took them to his majesty. One [the King] presented me with gold in double measure.

Ahmose Son of Ebana (Egyptian naval officer, 18th Dynasty), in James H. Breasted, *Ancient Records of Egypt*, 1906.

DON'T YOU THINK that I have something worth being sorry about, when I reflect that at my age Alexander was already king over so many peoples, while I have never yet achieved anything really remarkable?

Julius Caesar (100–44 BC), after reading an account of Alexander's triumphs, quoted in Plutarch, *The Lives*, c. AD 100 (*The Fall of the Roman Republic*, tr. Rex Warner, 1972).

IN PRIVATE ENTERPRISES men may advance or recede, whereas they who aim at empire have no alternative between the highest success and utter downfall.

Cornelius Tacitus, *Histories*, 104–109 A.D., 2.74, tr. Alfred J. Church and William J. Brodribb.

A MAN'S WORTH is no greater than the worth of his ambitions.

Marcus Aurelius, *Meditations*, 7.3, c. 170, tr. Maxwell Staniforth.

I CANNOT, if I am in the field of glory, be kept out of sight: wherever there is anything to be done, there Providence is sure to direct my steps.

Admiral Viscount Nelson, early 1797, letter to his wife, while stationed in Genoa, quoted in Robert Southey, *Life of Nelson*, 1813.

AMBITION is the main driving power of men. A man expends his abilities as long as he hopes to rise; but when he has reached the highest round, he only asks for rest. I have created senatorial appointments and princely titles, in order to promote ambition, and, in this way, to make the senators and marshals dependent on me.

Napoleon, quoted in F.M. Kircheisen, *Memoirs of Napoleon I*, 1929.

BESIDES, as far as I am concerned, I have no ambition – or, if I have any, it is so natural to me, so innate, so intimately linked with my existence that it is like the blood that circulates in my veins, like the air I breathe. It causes me to act neither more precipitately, nor in any way differently, than do the natural motives that move me. I never am obliged to fight either for or against ambition. Ambition never is in a greater hurry than I am; it merely keeps pace with circumstances and with my general way of thinking.

Napoleon, conversation, 1804, quoted in Christopher Herold, ed., *The Mind of Napoleon*, 1955.

BUT ALL THAT . . . he will learn will be of little use to him if he does not have the sacred fire in the depths of his heart, this driving ambition which alone can enable one to perform great deeds.

Napoleon, *Correspondance de Napoléon Ier, publié par ordre de l'Empereur Napoléon III*, XXXII, p. 379.

A DIFFERENT HABIT, with worse effect, was the way that ambitious officers, when they came in sight of promotion to the general's list, would decide that they would bottle up their thoughts and ideas, as a safety precaution, until they reached the top and could put these ideas into practice. Unfortunately, the usual result, after years of such self-repression for the sake of ambition, was that when the bottle was eventually uncorked the contents had evaporated.

Captain Sir Basil Liddell Hart, quoted by Josiah Bunting, 'The Conscience of a Soldier', *Worldview*, 10/1973.

AMBITION, not so much for vulgar ends, but for fame, glints in every mind.

Sir Winston S. Churchill (1874–1965).

ANALYSIS

NAPOLEON once said: "I have always liked analysis, if I were to be seriously in love, I should analyse my love bit by bit. Why? and How? are questions so useful that they cannot be too often asked. I conquered rather than studied history; that is to say, I did not care to retain and did not retain anything that could not give me a new idea; I disdained all that was useless, but took possession of certain results which pleased me." In other words, he taught himself "How to think" which is the harvest of all true education, civil or military.

Major-General J.F.C. Fuller, *Lectures on F. S. R. II*, 1931, quoting Napoleon, 25 January 1803.

THE ANALYSTS write about war as if it's a ballet . . . like it's choreographed ahead of time, and when the orchestra strikes up and starts playing, everyone goes out and plays a set piece.

What I always say to those folks is, "Yes, it's choreographed, and what happens is the orchestra starts playing and some son of a bitch climbs out of the orchestra pit with a bayonet and starts chasing you around the stage." And the choreography goes right out the window.

General H. Norman Schwarzkopf, interview in *The Washington Post*, 5 February 1991.

ANALYSIS is a skill that requires native talent as well as lengthy apprenticeship. It requires great specialization and does not fit into the standard Army officer or NCO moulds or career patterns. . . . Military intelligence can tell you how many tanks are out there – but it is a rare MI soldier who can tell you what the enemy is likely to do with those tanks, let alone look deep into the mind of the enemy commander. After brief training courses (and sometimes even without even that), we declare soldiers "analysts." We might as well declare them open-heart surgeons.

Lieutenant-Colonel Ralph Peters, 'Military Intelligence: The Broken Branch', *Army Times*, 13 April 1998.

APPEASEMENT

AND THAT is called paying the Dane-geld;
But we've proved it again and again,
That if once you have paid him the Dane-geld
You never get rid of the Dane.

Rudyard Kipling, *Dane-Geld*.

THIS IS the second time there has come back from Germany to Downing Street peace with honour. I believe it is peace in our time.

Prime Minister Neville Chamberlain, 30 September

1938, from 10 Downing Street upon his return from meeting Hitler at Munich, where Britain and France abandoned Czechoslovakia to its fate.

ENGLAND has been offered a choice between war and shame. She has chosen shame and will get war.
 Sir Winston S. Churchill, September 1938, speech in the House of Commons on Munich Agreement.

REALIZING that common sense and common decency alike dictate the futility of appeasement, we shall never try to placate an aggressor by the false and wicked bargain of trading honor for security. Americans, indeed all free men, remember that in the final choice a soldier's pack is not so heavy a burden as a prisoner's chains.
 President Dwight D. Eisenhower, 20 January 1953, First Inaugural Address.

AN APPEASER is one who feeds the crocodile – hoping it will eat him last.
 Sir Winston S. Churchill, *Reader's Digest*, December 1954.

ARMY
The Nature of Armies

THERE IS no need for me to enlarge upon the battles which the Romans fought and lost against Hannibal, for the defeats they suffered had nothing to do with weapons or formations, but were brought about by Hannibal's cleverness and military genius. This point I made sufficiently clear in my descriptions of the battles in question, and there are two pieces of evidence which support my conclusion. The first is the manner in which the war ended, for as soon as a general of ability comparable to Hannibal's appeared on the Roman side it was only a short while before victory was theirs. The second is provided by Hannibal himself, who as soon as he had won his first battle discarded the equipment with which he had started out, armed his troops with Roman weapons, and continued to use these till the end of the war.
 Polybius, Histories, 18.28, c. 125 BC (*The Rise of the Roman Empire*, tr. Ian Scott-Kilvert, 1987).

TO AID in understanding our treatise on tactical matters, let it be noted that the entire force on campaign is comprised of the following. First are the combat troops, the force armed for offensive action, which is called an armed force or an army. Then come the technical groups such as stonecutters, metalworkers, carpenters, and the like, who need to be on hand for siege operations and for other special work. Third, there are the supply services which provide bread, wine, meat, and other necessities.
 Anonymous Byzantine general, *Strategy*, c. AD 534, in George Dennis, *Three Byzantine Military Treatises*, 1985.

THE IDEAL ARMY would be the one in which every officer would know what he ought to do in every contingency; the best possible army is the one that comes closest to this. I give myself only half the credit for the battles I have won, and a general gets enough credit when he is named at all, for the fact is that a battle is won by the army.
 Napoleon, 1817, conversation. Gaspard Gourgaud, *Sainte Hélène: Journal inédit de 1815 à 1818*, II, quoted in Christopher Herold, ed., *The Mind of Napoleon*, 1955.

WAR is a special activity, different and separate from any other pursued by man. This would still be true no matter how wide its scope, and though every able-bodied man in the nation were under arms. An army's military qualities are based on the individual who is steeped in the spirit and essence of this activity; who trains the capacities it demands, rouses them, and makes them his own; who applies his intelligence to every detail; who gains ease and confidence through practice, and who completely immerses his personality in the appointed task.
 Major-General Carl von Clausewitz, *On War*, 3.5, 1832, tr. Michael Howard and Peter Paret, 1976.

I HAVE NEVER seen so teachable and helpful a class as the Army generally. Give them opportunity promptly and securely to send money home and they will use it. Give them schools and lectures and they will come to them. Give them books and games and amusements and they will leave off drinking. Give them suffering and they will bear it. Give them work and they will do it. I would rather have to do with the Army generally than with any other class I have attempted to serve.
 Florence Nightingale, letter to her sister from the Crimea, March 1856, quoted in Cecil Woodham-Smith, *Florence Nightingale, 1820–1910*, 1951.

WHEN AN ARMY starts upon a campaign, it resolves itself speedily into two parts, one that means to keep out of harm's way if possible, and the other that always keeps with the colors.
 Major-General George B. McClellan (1826–1885), quoted in *Tenting Tonight*, 1984.

THE ARMY is the most outstanding institution in every country, for it alone makes possible the existence of all civic institutions.
 Field Marshal Helmuth Graf von Moltke (1800–1891).

THE ARMY has its common law as well as its statute law; each officer is weighed in the balance by his fellows, and these rarely err. In the barrack, in the mess, on the scout, and especially in battle, a man cannot – successfully – enact the part of a hypocrite or flatterer, and his fellows will measure him pretty fairly for what he is.
 General of the Army William T. Sherman (1820–1891).

THE REAL OBJECT of having an army is to provide for war.

> Elihu Root, *Annual Report of the Secretary of War*, 1899.

AN ARMY is still a crowd, though a highly organized one. It is governed by the same laws. . . and under the stress of war is ever tending to revert to its crowd form. Our object in peace is so to train it that the reversion will become extremely slow.

> Major-General J.F.C. Fuller, *Training Soldiers for War*, 1914.

AN ARMY is to a commander what a sword is to a soldier, it is only worth anything in so far as it receives from him a certain imulsion.

> Marshal of France Ferdinand Foch, *Precepts and Judgments*, 1919.

ALL THROUGH HISTORY there have been recurring cycles of two schools of war; the one tending towards the adoption of small professional forces relatively well trained. The other towards the utilization of masses and mob psychology. Both schools have usually foundered on the rock of compromise, when the first sought to increase its numbers and the second its discipline . . .

> General George S. Patton, Jr., January 1928, *The Patton Papers*, I, 1972.

AN ARMY is an institution not merely conservative but retrogressive by nature. It has such natural resistance to progress that it is always insured against the danger of being pushed ahead too fast. Far worse and more certain, as history abundantly testifies, is the danger of it slipping backward. Like a man pushing a barrow up a hill, if the soldier ceases to push, the military machine will run back and crush him. To be deemed a revolutionary in the army is merely an indication of vitality, the pulse-beat which shows that the mind is still alive. When a soldier ceases to be a revolutionary it is a sure sign that he has become a mummy. (Jan. 1931.)

> Captain Sir Basil Liddell Hart, *Thoughts on War*, 1944.

AN ARMED FORCE differs from an armed mob, or crowd of men, not so much in its armament but in that it is disciplined, is organised, and is under control. A crowd may at times be courageous beyond belief, but it possesses little staying power, and is as quickly depressed as elated by outward circumstances. Courage in itself is insufficient, and to it must be added what is called morale, a complex quality depending upon honour to the cause, loyalty to the leader, confidence in one's skill and the skill of one's comrades, and in an innate feeling that everyone is doing his utmost to win and that no one will leave a comrade in the lurch. Morale endows a force of men with a feeling of superiority and invincibility, it is cultivated by common-sense, sound organisation, efficient arms and equipment, and the realisation that those in command are skilful, brave and just.

> Major-General J.F.C. Fuller, *Lectures on F. S. R. II*, 1931.

THEIR TASK is to destroy. The balance sheet of their activities shows a hideous total of broken lives, of wealth destroyed, of nations ground to powder, of work brought to nothing, of efforts frustrated, and happiness maimed and killed. The wreckage of war is beyond counting. Land left fallow, fire, and famine, such are its material consequences. But, in brooding on the evil, do we not tend to forget the children born into safety, the lives lived out in security as the result of the toil and sacrifice of our soldiers? But for the strength of armies what tribe, what city, and what states could ever have been established? Protected by that human shield, fields have been sown and reaped and men have been able to work on undisturbed. The clash of arms has made possible all material progress. History cannot measure the debt owed by the wealth of nations, their network of communications, their ships upon the seas, to the lust for conquest.

> General Charles de Gaulle, *The Edge of the Sword*, 1932.

THE NATURE of armies is determined by the nature of the civilization in which they exist.

> Captain Sir Basil Liddell Hart, *The Ghost of Napoleon*, 1933.

ARMIES are created to serve the policy of states. And no one knows better than you yourself that strategy should include not only the given circumstances of military technique, but also the moral elements.

> General Charles de Gaulle, 5 January 1945, letter to Dwight D. Eisenhower, *Salvation: 1944–1946*, 1959.

AN ARMY is an organized mob and the cement which bonds it together is discipline and mutual confidence. More therefore than all plans and schemes based on material factors, the art of battle consists in maintaining and strengthening the psychological cohesion of one's own troops while at the same time disrupting that of the enemy's.

> General Andre Beaufre, *Introduction to Strategy*, 1965.

A MAN can be selfish, cowardly, disloyal, false, fleeting, perjured, and morally corrupt in a wide variety of other ways and still be outstandingly good in pursuits in which other imperatives bear than those upon the fighting man. He can be a superb creative artist, for example, or a scientist in the very top flight, and still be a very bad man. What the bad man cannot be is a good sailor, or soldier, or airman. Military institutions thus form a repository of moral resource that should always be a source of strength within the state.

> General Sir John Hackett, 'The Military in the Service of the State', *War, Morality, and the Military Profession*, 1986.

THE ARMY, despite its long-standing reputation for enforced homogeneity, is not an ant colony. Within the Army's vast hierarchy – which determines everything from career patterns to day-to-day chains of command – there is great diversity of experience. Orders are issued and obeyed, and yet highly individualistic people grow and flourish.

It took me many years to appreciate the subtle benefits that grow out of these paradoxical, sometimes contradictory elements. When the Army is functioning at its best, it can be stable without being stultifying. It can take risks without posing undue risks to people's lives. It can create individual "laboratories," within which offices and noncommissioned officers can experiment with the tools and techniques of leadership.

> Lieutenant-General William G. Pagonis, *Moving Mountains*, 1992.

A STRONG ARMY is not one that fights, but one that by the very fact of its existence destroys ideas of aggression. Let's have troops whose existence means that nobody will want to tangle with us.

> General-Lieutenant Aleksandr Lebed, *Trud* (Moscow), 11 October 1995.

Peacetime Army

OUR LONG garrison life spoiled us, and effeminacy and desire for and love of pleasure, have weakened our military virtues. The entire nation must pass through the School of Misfortune, and we shall either die in the crisis, or a better condition will be created, after we have suffered bitter misery, and after our bones have decayed.

> Field Marshal August Graf von Gneisenau (1760–1831), quoted in Balck, *Development of Tactics*, 1922.

IN TIMES of peace we have neglected much, occupied ourselves with frivolities, flattered the people's love of shows and neglected war.

> Field Marshal August Graf von Gneisenau, 1806, on the mobilisation of Prussia leading to the disasters at the Battles of Auerstadt and Jena, quoted in Seeley, *Life and Times of Stein*, 1878.

ONE SHOULD BE CAREFUL not to compare this expanded and refined solidarity of a brotherhood of tempered, battle-scarred veterans with the self-esteem and vanity of regular armies which are patched together only by service-regulations and drill. Grim severity and iron discipline may be able to preserve the military virtues of a unit, but it cannot create them. These factors are valuable, but they should not be overrated. Discipline, skill, good will, a certain pride, and high morale, are the attributes of an army trained in times of peace. They command respect, but they have no strength of their own. They stand or fall together. One

crack, and the whole thing goes, like a glass too quickly cooled.

> Major-General Carl von Clausewitz, *On War*, 3.5, 1832, tr. Michael Howard and Peter Paret, 1976.

IT IS particularly necessary to watch over the preservation of armies in the interval of a long peace, when they are most likely to degenerate. It is important to foster the military spirit in the armies and to exercise them in great maneuvers which, though but faintly resembling those of actual war, still are of decided advantage in preparing them for war.

> Lieutenant-General Antoine-Henri Baron de Jomini, *Summary of the Art of War*, 1838, tr. Mendell and Craighill, 1862.

IT MUST BE OBVIOUS, therefore, that periods of tranquility are rich in sources of friction between soldiers and statesmen, since the latter are for ever trying to find ways of saving money, while the former are constantly urging increased expenditure. It does, of course, occasionally happen that a lesson recently learned, or an immediate threat, compels them to agree.

> General Charles de Gaulle, *The Edge of the Sword*, 1932.

IT IS IN PEACE that regulations and routine become important and that qualities of boldness and originality are cramped. It is interesting to note how little of normal peace soldiering many of our best generals had – Cromwell, Marlborough, Wellington, and his lieutenants, Graham, Hill, Craufurd.

> Field Marshal Viscount Wavell of Cyrenaica, *Soldiers and Soldiering*, 1953.

OUR TRADITIONAL FAULT – the one against which I coped hopelessly in earlier days of the Eighth Air Force – went all the way back to Langley Field. There they had the usual Base commander and Group commander. The Base commander wanted to mow the grass; the Group commander wanted to fly his airplanes. . . . Answer? They mowed the grass.

Because why? Because the Base commander made out the efficiency report on the Group commander. He got rated whether his grass was cut or not, or whether his buildings were painted. By gad, that's what he was going to do: mow grass.

> General Curtis LeMay, *Mission With LeMay*, 1965.

. . . TIMID BEHAVIOR is an outgrowth of peace, where promotion may be sought through a low profile and low risk, in contrast to war, where the rewards come to the leader whose visibility and accompanying risks are high. Another stimulus to prudent silence in today's peacetime environment is the pernicious tendency for any fitness report marking short of perfect to be interpreted as a signal that the officer suffers some grave professional or personality defect.

All of this reality may be discouraging to the military man blessed with a creative mind. Realistically, however, he has no cause to expect his life to be tranquil, nor does he have reason to expect always to be understood. Marine Maj. Earl Ellis was a classic creative mind of the first quarter of this century. Most of his Marine Corps peers saw him as an ill-tempered rum pot, but history now regards him as a misunderstood visionary who saw accurately the nature of the 1941–1945 Pacific War long before it happened.

> Lieutenant-General Victor H. 'The Brute' Krulak, 'A Soldier's Dilemma', *Marine Corps Gazette*, 11/1986.

Standing Army

FRITZ, pay close attention to what I am going to say to you. Always keep up a good and strong army – you won't have a better friend and you can't survive without it. Our Neighbors want nothing more than to bring about our ruin – I am aware of their intentions, and you will come to know them as well. Believe me, don't let wishful thinking run away with you – stick to what is real. Always put your trust in a good army and in hard cash – they are the things which keep rulers in peace and security.

> Frederick William I, 1731, advice to his son, the future Frederick the Great.

I AM PERSUADED and as fully convinced, as I am of any one fact that has happened that our Liberties must of necessity be greatly hazarded, if not entirely lost, if their defence is left to any but a permanent standing Army, I mean one to exist during the War.

> General George Washington, 2 September 1776, letter to the President of Congress, *The Writings of George Washington*, VI, 1932, p. 5.

HAD WE KEPT a permanent Army on foot, the enemy would have had nothing to hope for, and would, in all probability, have listened to terms long since.

> General George Washington, 10 August 1780, letter to the President of Congress, *The Writings of George Washington*, XIX, 1937, p. 410.

THE JEALOUSIES of a standing Army, and the Evils to be apprehended from one, are remote; and in my judgment, situated and circumstanced as we are, not at all to be dreaded; but the consequence of wanting one, according to my Ideas, . . . is certain, and inevitable Ruin.

> General George Washington, *The Writings of George Washington*, VI, 1932, p. 112.

THE COUNTRY must have a large and efficient army, one capable of meeting the enemy abroad, or they must expect to meet him at home.

> The Duke of Wellington, letter, 28 January 1811.

THE TERRIBLE POWER of a standing army may usually be exercised by whomever can control its leaders, as a mighty engine is set in motion by the cranking of a handle.

> Winston S. Churchill, *The River War*, 1899.

ONE of the main arguments against armies is their futility; but, if this be true, this argument can with equal force be directed against peaceful organizations; for surely it is just as futile to keep vast numbers of a nation on the brink of starvation and prostitution, as happens in nearly all civilized countries to-day, as it is to keep an insignificant minority of this same nation on the brink of war.

> Major-General J.F.C. Fuller, *The Reformation of War*, 1923.

ARTILLERY

BLESSED be those happy ages that were strangers to the dreadful fury of these devilish instruments of artillery, whose inventor I am satisfied is now in hell, receiving the reward of his cursed invention, which is the cause that very often a cowardly base hand takes away the life of the bravest gentleman.

> Miguel de Cervantes, *Don Quixote*, 1615.

ULTIMO ratio regum (The final argument of kings).

> Motto, c. 1660, inscribed on French artillery by order of Louis XIV.

THE OBJECT of artillery should not consist of killing men on the whole of the enemy's front, but to overthrow it, to destroy parts of this front, . . . then they obtain decisive effects; they make a gap.

> Field Marshal Francois Comte de Guibert, *Essai général de tactique*, 1773.

IT USED to be our custom to form regiments from the largest men possible. This was done for a reason, for in the early wars it was men and not cannon that decided victory, and battalions of tall men advancing with the bayonet scattered the poorly assembled enemy troops – with the first attack. Now artillery has changed everything. A cannon ball knocks down a man six feet tall just as easily as one who is only five feet seven. Artillery decides everything, and infantry no longer do battle with naked steel.

> Frederick the Great, *A History of My Own Times*, 1789, tr. Holcroft.

THE ARTILLERY, like the other arms, must be collected in mass if one wishes to obtain decisive results.

> Napoleon, *Correspondance de Napoléon Ier, publié par ordre de l'Empereur Napoléon III*, XIX, No. 15338, p. 116.

GREAT BATTLES are won with artillery.

> Napoleon, letter to Prince Eugène, *Correspondance*

de Napoléon Ier, publié par ordre de l'Empereur Napoléon III, XXVI, No. 20929, p. 458.

IN SIEGE WARFARE, as in the open field, it is the gun which plays the chief part; it has effected a complete revolution . . . It is with artillery that war is made.
> Napoleon, 1809, after the Battle of Loebau, *Correspondance de Napoléon Ier, publié par ordre de l'Empereur Napoléon III*, XXX, p. 447.

THE BETTER the infantry, the more one must husband and support it with good batteries. . . .
> Napoleon, *Correspondance de Napoléon Ier, publié par ordre de l'Empereur Napoléon III*, XXXI, pp. 328–329.

LEAVE the artillerymen alone. They are an obstinate lot.
> Napoleon, quoted in Bellemy, *Red God of War*, 1987.

IT IS NECESSARY to be familiar with artillery . . . [and] I believe every officer ought to serve in the artillery, which is the arm that can produce most of the good generals. . . . To be a good general you must know mathematics; it serves to direct your thinking in a thousand circumstances.
> Napoleon, conversation on St. Helena, quoted in Gaspard Gourgaud, *Sainte Hélène*, II, 1899, in Jay Luvaas, *Napoleon on the Art of War*, 1999.

TAYLOR: "What are you using, Captain, grape or canister?"
Bragg: "Canister, General."
Taylor: "Single or double?"
Bragg: "Single."
Taylor: "Well, double-shot your guns and give 'em hell."
> General Zachary Taylor to Captain Braxton Bragg, 23 February 1847, at the Battle of Buena Vista, in K. Jack Bauer, *The Mexican War*, 1974.

YOU CAN'T describe the moral lift,
When in the fight your spirit weary
Hears above the hostile fire
Your own artillery.
Shells score the air like wavy hair
From a forward battery,
As regimental cannon crack
While, from positions further back,
In bitter sweet song overhead
Crashing discordantly
Division's pounding joins the attack;
Mother like she belches shell;
Gloriously it flies, and well,
As, with a hissing, screaming squall,
A roaring furnace, giving all,
she sears a path for the infantry . . .
> Aleksandr Tvardovskiy, 1943, from the narrative poem, *Vasily Tyorkin*, tr. Chris Bellemy, *Red God of War*, 1987.

I DO NOT have to tell you who won the war. You know our artillery did.
> General George S. Patton, Jr., quoted in R.E. Dupuy, *The Military Heritage of America*, 1956.

IF there is one thing a dogface loves, it is artillery – his own.
> Audie Murphy, *To Hell and Back*, 1949.

DURING the 1972 offensive, we had to fight against tanks. What I learned from those battles I carried into the Gulf: "An infantryman can deal with tanks." What you can't deal with is if you are outgunned by enemy artillery.
As a result of that experience, in our planning process for Desert Storm we concentrated on taking out enemy artillery. We knew that could be the biggest casualty producer . . .
> General Walter Boomer, 'Up Front', Al Santoli, ed., *Leading the Way: How Vietnam Veterans Rebuilt the U.S. Military*, 1993.

THE ART OF WAR

IN MILITARY AFFAIRS nothing is more important than certain victory. In employing the army nothing is more important than obscurity and silence. In movement nothing is more important than the unexpected. In planning nothing is more important than not being knowable.
> The T'ai Kung, c. 1100 BC (*The Seven Military Classics of Ancient China*, tr. Ralph Sawyer, 1993).

THE ART of war is, in the last result, the art of keeping one's freedom of action.
> Xenophon (430–c. 355 BC).

IT IS BIAS to think that the art of war is just for killing people. It is not to kill people, it is to kill evil. It is a strategem to give life to many people by killing the evil of one person.
> Yagyu Munenori, late 16th century, quoted in Thomas Cleary, *The Japanese Art of War*, 1991.

THE ART of war is divided between art and strategem. What cannot be done by force, must be done by strategem.
> Frederick the Great, *Instructions to His Generals*, 1747, tr. Phillips, 1940.

THE THREE military arts. First – Apprehension, how to arrange things in camp, how to march, how to attack, pursue, and strike; for taking up position, final judgement of the enemy's strength, for estimating his intentions.
Second – Quickness . . .
This quickness doesn't weary the men. The enemy doesn't expect us, reckons us 100 versts away, and if a long way off to begin with – 200, 300 or more – suddenly we're on him, like snow on the

head; his head spins. Attack with what comes up, with what God sends; the cavalry to begin, smash, strike, cut off, don't let slip, hurra!

Brothers do miracles!

Third – Attack. Leg supports leg, arm strengthens arm; many men will die in the volley; the enemy has the same weapons, but he doesn't know the Russian bayonet. Extend the line – attack at once with cold steel; extend the line without stopping. . . . the Cossacks to get through everywhere. . . . In two lines is strength; in three, half as much again; the first breaks, the second drives into heaps, the third overthrows.

> Field Marshal Prince Aleksandr V. Suvorov, *The Science of Victory*, 1796.

ONE MAY TEACH tactics, military engineering, artillery work about as one teaches geometry. But knowledge of the higher branches of war is only acquired by experience and by a study of the history of the wars of great generals. It is not in a grammar that one learns to compose a great poem, to write a tragedy.

> Napoleon, quoted in Foch, *Principles of War*, 1913.

THE ART of war consists, with a numerically inferior army, in always having larger forces than the enemy at the point which is to be attacked or defended. But this art can be learned neither from books nor from practice: it is an intuitive way of acting which properly constitutes the genius of war.

> Napoleon, 1797, dictation, *Correspondance de Napoléon Ier, publié par ordre de l'Empereur Napoléon III*, Vol. III, p. 163, quoted in Christopher Herold, ed., *The Mind of Napoleon*, 1955.

CONCENTRATION of forces, activity, activity with the firm resolve to die gloriously: these are the three great principles of the military art that have always made fortune favourable in all of my operations. Death is nothing; but to live defeated and ingloriously is to die every day.

> Napoleon, 30 July 1800, quoted in R.M. Johnston, ed., *The Corsican*, 1910.

THE WHOLE ART of war consists in a well-reasoned and extremely circumspect defensive, followed by rapid and audacious attack.

> Napoleon, during the Prussian campaign of 1806, *Correspondance de Napoléon Ier, publié par ordre de l'Empereur Napoléon III*, Vol. XIII, No. 10558, p. 10.

THE ART of war is a simple art; everything is in the performance. There is nothing vague about it; everything in it is common sense; ideology does not enter into it.

> Napoleon, 1818, conversation, quoted in Gaspar Gougraud, *Sainte Hélène: Journal inédit de 1815 à 1818*, II, quoted in Christopher Herold, ed., *The Mind of Napoleon*, 1955.

THE ART of war is like everything that is beautiful

and simple. The simplest moves are the best. If Macdonald, instead of doing whatever he did, had asked a peasant for the way to Genoa, the peasant would have answered, "Through Bobbio" – and that would have been a superb move.

> Napoleon, 1818, conversation, quoted in Gaspar Gourgaud, *Sainte Hélène: Journal inédit de 1815 à 1818*, II, quoted in Christopher Herold, ed., *The Mind of Napoleon*, 1955.

THE ART of war is an immense study, which comprises all others.

> Napoleon, quoted in Christopher Herold, ed., *The Mind of Napoleon*, 1955.

THE ART of war is no more than the art of augmenting the chances which are in our favor.

> Napoleon (1769–1821).

THE WHOLE ART of war consists in getting at what lies on the other side of the hill, or, in other words, what we do not know from what we do know.

> The Duke of Wellington (1769–1852), quoted in *The Croker Papers*, III, 1885, and David Chandler, *The Campaigns of Napoleon*, 1966.

THE ART of war deals with living and with moral forces. Consequently, it cannot attain the absolute, or certainty; it must always leave a margin for uncertainty, in the greatest things as much as in the smallest. With uncertainty in one scale, courage and self-confidence must be thrown into the other to correct the balance. The greater they are, the greater the margin that can be left for accidents.

> Major-General Carl von Clausewitz, *On War*, 1.1, 1832, tr. Michael Howard and Peter Paret, 1976.

ESSENTIALLY, then, the art of war is the art of using the given means in combat; there is no better term for it than the conduct of war. To be sure in its widest sense the art of war includes all activities that exist for the sake of war, such as the creation of the fighting forces, their raising, armament, equipment, and training.

> Major-General Carl von Clausewitz, *On War*, 2.1, 1832, tr. Michael Howard and Peter Paret, 1976.

IT MUST NOT be concluded that the art of war has arrived at that point that it cannot make another step towards perfection. There is nothing perfect under the sun! And if a committee were assembled under the presidency of the Archduke Charles or Wellington, composed of all the strategic and tactical notabilities of the age, together with the most skillful generals of engineers and artillery, this committee could not yet succeed in making a perfect, absolute and immutable theory on all branches of war, especially on tactics!

> Lieutenant-General Antoine-Henri Baron de Jomini, *Summary of the Art of War*, 1838, tr. Mendell and Craighill, 1862.

OF ALL THEORIES on the art of war, the only

reasonable one is that which, founded upon the study of military history, admits a certain number of regulating principles, but leaves to natural genius the greatest part in the general conduct of a war without trammeling it with exclusive rules.

On the contrary, nothing is better calculated to kill natural genius and to cause error to triumph, than those pedantic theories, based upon the false idea that war is a positive science, all the operations of which can be reduced to infallible calculations.

> Lieutenant-General Antoine-Henri Baron de Jomini, *Summary of the Art of War*, 1838, tr. Mendell and Craighill, 1862.

JACKSON: The business of a soldier is to fight. Armies are not called out to dig trenches, or throw up breastworks, and live in camps, but to find the enemy, and strike him; to invade his country, and do him all possible damage in the shortest possible time.
Graham: This would involve great destruction of both life and property.
Jackson: Yes, while it lasted; but such a war would of necessity be of brief continuance, and so would be an economy of prosperity and life in the end. To move swiftly, strike vigorously, and secure all the fruits of the victory is the secret of successful war.

> Lieutenant-General Thomas J. 'Stonewall' Jackson, 1861, conversation with the Rev. James Graham at Lexington, quoted in Graham, 'Some Reminiscences of Stonewall Jackson', *Things and Thoughts*, I, 1901.

ALWAYS MYSTIFY, mislead and surprise the enemy if possible; and when you strike and overcome him, never let up in pursuit so long as your men have strength to follow, for an army routed, if hotly pursued, becomes panic-stricken, and can then be destroyed by half their number. The other rule is, never fight against heavy odds, if by any possible maneuvering you can hurl your own force on only a part, and that the weakest part, of your enemy and crush it. Such tactics will win every time, and a small army may thus destroy a large one in detail, and repeated victory will make it invincible.

> Lieutenant-General Thomas J. 'Stonewall' Jackson, 1862, quoted by John D. Imboden in Underwood and Buel, ed., *Battles and Leaders of the Civil War*, II, 1887–1888.

THE ART of war is simple enough. Find out where your enemy is. Get at him as soon as you can. Strike at him as hard as you can and as often as you can, and keep moving on.

> General of the Army Ulysses S. Grant (1822–1885) – attributed.

ONE DOES simply what one *can* in order to apply what one *knows*.

> Marshal of France Ferdinand Foch, *The Principles of War*, 1913.

THEY FORGET that the whole art of war is to gain your objective with as little loss as possible.

> Field Marshal Viscount Montgomery of Alamein, 8 November 1917, letter to his mother, quoted in Nigel Hamilton, *Monty*, 1981.

WAR RESTS on many sciences, but war itself is not a science – it is a practical art, a skill. The Prussian stategist, King Frederick II was fond of saying that war is a trade for an ignoramus, an art for a man of talent and a science for a genius. But he told a lie. This is false. For an ignoramus war is not a trade because ignorant soldiers are the cannon fodder of war and not at all its "tradesmen." As is well known, each trade requires a certain schooling; and for those who are correctly schooled in military affairs war is therefore a "trade." It is a cruel, sanguinary trade, but a trade nonetheless, that is, a skill with certain habits which are elaborated by experience and correctly assimilated. For gifted people and those of genius, this skill becomes transformed into a high art.

> Leon Trotksy, 1 April 1922, remarks at the 11th Congress of the Communist Party, *Military Writings*, 1969.

WAR is an art and as such is not susceptible of explanation by fixed formula.

> General George S. Patton, Jr., 'Success in War', *The Infantry Journal Reader*, 1931.

WAR is a science which depends on art for its application.

> Captain Sir Basil Liddell Hart, 'Strategy', *Encyclopaedia Britannica*, 1929.

WHEREAS the other arts are, at their height, individual, the art of war is essentially orchestrated.

> Captain Sir Basil Liddell Hart, *Thoughts on War*, 1944.

I'VE BEEN STUDYING the art of war for forty-odd years. When a surgeon decides in the course of an operation to change its objective . . . he is not making a snap decision but one based on knowledge, experience and training. So am I.

> General George S. Patton, Jr., on being accused of making snap decisions.

THE CONDUCT of war, like the practice of medicine, is an art, and because the aim of the physician and surgeon is to prevent, cure, or alleviate the diseases of the human body, so should the aim of the statesman and soldier be to prevent, cure, or alleviate the wars which inflict the international body.

> Major-General J.F.C. Fuller, *The Conduct of War*, 1961.

THE SCIENCE of war stops short of the need for military judgment, the impact of moral forces, the influence of chance, and other similar factors. We thus conclude that the conduct of war is ultimately an art, an activity of human creativity and intuition powered by the strength of the human will. The art of war requires the intuitive ability to grasp the essence of a unique battlefield situation, the creative ability to devise a practical solution, and the strength of purpose to execute the act.

> General Alfred M. Gray and Major John Schmitt, *Warfighting*, United States Marine Corps, 1989.

ATTACK

THE KING also boasts of his wisdom in military matters. He knows when to strike and when to avoid combat . . . "attacking him who attacks . . . since, if one is silent after attack, it strengthens the heart of the enemy. Valiance is eagerness, cowardice is to slink back," he tells us, adding "he is truly a coward who is repelled upon his border."

> Sesostris III (1887–1849 BC), Pharaoh of Egypt, quoted in James Breasted, *Ancient Records of Egypt*, I, 1906.

FORWARD, even with only a spear.

> Samurai proverb, quoted in Inoguchi and Nakajima, *The Divine Wind*, 1958.

DECLINE the attack unless you can make it with advantage.

> Field Marshal Maurice Comte de Saxe, *My Reveries*, 1732, tr. Phillips, 1940.

GENTLEMEN, the enemy stands behind his entrenchments, armed to the teeth. We must attack him and win, or else perish. Nobody must think of getting through any other way. If you don't like this, you may resign and go home.

> Frederick the Great, 5 December 1757, to his officers before the Battle of Leuthen.

FOR IT IS a general rule in war that he who begins the attack has already half the victory, and fortune generally favours the resolute and the brave, and very often, indeed, the rash.

> Lieutenant-General Johann von Ewald, *Treatise on the Duties of Light Troops*, 1790.

THE DITCH isn't deep, the wall isn't high; fling yourself into the ditch; leap over the wall, charge with the bayonet, strike, chase, take prisoner.
  Storm.
  The enemy runs into the town, turn his guns against him, fire hard down the streets, keep up a lively bombardment; go after him at once . . . the enemy surrenders, spare him; the walls occupied, after the plunder.

> Field Marshal Prince Aleksandr V. Suvorov, *The Science of Victory*, 1796.

THE IMPACT of an army, like the total mechanical coefficients, is equal to the mass multiplied by the velocity.

> Napoleon, 30 July 1800, quoted in R.M. Johnston, *The Corsican*, 1910.

ATTACK inspires a soldier, it adds to his power, rouses his self-reliance, and confuses the enemy. The side attacked always overestimates the strength of the attacker.

> Field Marshal August Graf von Gneisenau (1760–1831), quoted in R.E. Dupuy, *The Military Heritage of America*, 1956.

A FEARFUL discharge of grape from all their artillery whistled through the British ranks. Myers was killed; Cole and the three colonels, Ellis, Blakney, and Hawkshawe, fell wounded, and the fuzileer battalions, struck by the iron tempest, reeled, and staggered like sinking ships. Suddenly and sternly recovering, they closed on their terrible enemies, and then was seen with what strength and majesty the British soldier fights. In vain did Soult, by voice and gesture, animate his Frenchmen; in vain did the hardiest veterans, extricating themselves from the crowded columns, sacrifice their lives to gain time for the mass to open out on such a fair field; in vain did the mass itself bear up, and fiercely striving, fire indiscriminately upon friends and foes, while the horsemen hovering on the flank threatened to charge the advancing line. Nothing could stop that astonishing infantry. No sudden burst of undisciplined valour, no nervous enthusiasm, weakened the stability of their order; their flashing eyes were bent on the dark columns in their front; their measured tread shook the ground; their dreadful volleys swept away the head of every formation; their deafening shouts overpowered the dissonant cries that broke from all parts of the tumultuous crowd, as foot by foot and with a horrid carnage it was driven by the incessant vigour of the attack to the farthest edge of the hill. In vain did the French reserves, joining with the struggling multitude, endeavour to sustain the fight; their efforts only increased the irremediable confusion, and the mighty mass giving way like a loosened cliff, went headlong down the ascent. The rain flowed after in streams discoloured with blood, and fifteen hundred unwounded men, the remnant of six thousand unconquerable British soldiers, stood triumphant on that fatal hill!

> Lieutenant-General William F.P. Napier, *History of the War in the Peninsula*, III, 1831, of the attack of the fusilier brigade at the Battle of Albuera, 16 May 1811.

THE ATTACK should be like a soap bubble, which distends itself until it bursts.

> Major-General Carl von Clausewitz, *On War*, 1832, tr. Michael Howard and Peter Paret, 1976.

INASMUCH as the nature of our soldiers lends itself better to offense than to defense, the chiefs shall not forget that in case of emergency they should take the offensive.

> General Jose de San Martin, April 1818, instructions before the Battle of Maipú, in Ricardo Rojas, *San Martin*, 1957.

I WAS TOO WEAK to defend, so I attacked.

> General Robert E. Lee (1807–70) – attributed.

WHEN we are fighting there is no need to think of defense. A positive attack is the best form of defense . . . the vital point in actual warfare is to apply to the enemy what we do not wish to be applied to ourselves and at the same time not to let the enemy apply it to us . . . we must always forestall them.

> Admiral Marquis Heihachiro Togo, 15 May 1905, quoted in Dennis and Peggy Warner, *The Tide at Sunrise*, 1974.

MY CENTER is giving way, my right is pushed back, situation excellent, I am attacking.

> Marshal of France Ferdinand Foch, 8 September 1914, message to Marshal Joffre at the First Battle of the Marne, quoted in Liddell Hart, *Reputations: Ten Years After*, 1928.

OUGHT I in these circumstances to assume the offensive myself or stand on the defensive? According to the invariable rule which I followed throughout the War, whenever there was the slightest possibility, I determined to attack vigorously.

> General Aleksei A. Brusilov, September 1914, *A Soldier's Notebook*, 1930.

EVERY ATTACK, once undertaken, must be fought to the finish; every defense, once begun, must be carried on with the utmost energy.

> Marshal of France Ferdinand Foch, *Precepts and Judgments*, 1919.

ONE MUST create an irresistible battering ram.

> Marshal of the Soviet Union Mikhail N. Tukhachevskiy, 1924, in Richard Simpkin, *Deep Battle*, 1987.

THE NORMAL PURPOSE of an attack is the infliction of death wounds and destruction on the enemy troops with a view to establish both physical and moral ascendancy over them. The gaining of ground in such a combat is simply an incident; not an object.

> General George S. Patton, Jr., 1 November 1926, letter to his wife, *The Patton Papers*, I, 1972.

NAPOLEON once said, "I attack to be attacked." What he meant was that he threw forward a small fraction of his forces for the enemy to bite on, and when his adversary's jaws were fixed he moved up his large reserves – the capital of his tactical bank – and struck his real blow. . . .

> Major-General J.F.C. Fuller, 'Co-ordination of the Attack', *The Infantry Journal*, 1/1931.

ATTACK is the chief means of destroying the enemy, but defence cannot be dispensed with. In attack the immediate object is to destroy the enemy, but at the same time it is self-preservation, because if the enemy is not destroyed, you will be destroyed. In defence the immediate object is to preserve yourself, but at the same time defence is a means of supplementing attack or preparing to go over to the attack. Retreat is in the category of defence and is a continuation of defence, while pursuit is a continuation of attack. It should be pointed out that destruction of the enemy is the primary object of war and self-preservation the secondary, because only by destroying the enemy in large numbers can one effectively preserve oneself. Therefore attack, the chief means of destroying the enemy, is primary, while defence, a supplementary means of destroying the enemy and a means of self-preservation, is secondary. In actual warfare the chief role is played by defence much of the time and by attack for the rest of the time, but if war is taken as a whole, attack remains primary.

> Mao Tse-tung, *On Protracted War*, May 1938.

WE ARE so outnumbered there's only one thing to do. We must attack.

> Admiral Andrew Cunningham, 11 November 1940, before attacking the Italian fleet at Taranto.

WHEN the situation is obscure, attack.

> Colonel-General Heinz Guderian (1888–1954) – attributed.

MANTON EDDY who took over Doc's corps asked me when I told him his job: "How much shall I have to worry about my flank?"

I told him that depended on how nervous he was. He has been thinking a mile a day good going. I told him to go fifty and he turned pale . . .

> General George S. Patton, Jr., August 1944, *The Patton Papers*, II, 1974.

AFTER a question-and-answer session I tried to set a tone for the coming months. "Let me leave you with one thought, guys. In order for this to succeed – because the enemy is still going to outnumber us – it is going to take, for lack of a better word, killer instinct on the part of all of our leaders out there." I pointed again at the map. "What I'm saying is when the Marines hit the wire right here and when the Army forces hit the wire over here, there's going to be none of this bullshit, 'Well, I think we're going to go in and probe a little bit and see if we can get through.' We need commanders in the lead who absolutely, clearly understand that they *will get through*. And that once they're through they're not going to stop and discuss it. They are going to go up there and destroy the Republican Guard. I cannot afford to have commanders who do not understand that it is attack, attack, attack, attack, and destroy every step of the way. If you have somebody who doesn't understand it, I would strongly recommend that you consider removing him from command and putting in somebody that can do the job."

General H. Norman Schwarzkopf, address to his senior commanders on 14 November 1990, as he outlined his battle plan for Desert Storm, *It Doesn't Take a Hero*, 1992.

ATTRITION

THE ENEMY must fight his battles far from his home base for a long time. . . . We must further weaken him by drawing him into protracted campaigns. Once his initial dash is broken, it will be easier to destroy him.

Marshal Trang Hung Dao (Vietnam), c. 1284.

PRINCE MAURICE would lie in a camp till he had starved half his men, if by lying there he could but starve two-thirds of his enemies; so that, indeed, the war in Holland had more of fatigue and hardships in it, and ours had more of fighting and blows. Hasty marches, long and unwholesome encampments, winter parties, counter-marching, dodging, and intrenching, were the exercises of his men, and often time killed more men with hunger, cold and diseases than he could do with fighting; not that it required less courage, but rather more, for a soldier had at any time rather die in the field a la coup de mousquet, than be starved with hunger, or frozen to death in the trenches.

Nor do I think to lessen the reputation of that great general, for it is most certain he ruined the Spaniards more by spinning the war thus out in length, than he could possibly have done by swift conquest; for had he, Gustavus like, with a torrent of victory, dislodged the Spaniard from all the twelve provinces in five years (whereas he was forty years in beating them out of seven) he had left them rich and strong at home, and able to keep the Dutch in constant apprehension of the return of his power; whereas, by the long continuance of the war, he so broke the very heart of the Spanish monarchy, so absolutely and irrecoverably impoverished them that they have ever since languished of the disease, till they are fallen from the most powerful to be the most despicable nation in the world.

Daniel Defoe (1659–1731), *Memoirs of a Cavalier*, 1889.

WE LOST fifty per cent more men than did the enemy, and yet there is sense in the awful arithmetic propounded by Mr. Lincoln. He says that if the same battle were to be fought over again, every day, through a week of days, with the same relative results, the army under Lee would be wiped out to its last man, the Army of the Potomac would still be a mighty host, the war would be over, the Confederacy gone, and peace would be won at a smaller cost of life than it will be if the week of lost battles must be dragged out through yet another year of camps and marches, and deaths in hospitals rather than upon the field. No general yet found can face the arithmetic, but the end of the war will be at hand when he shall be discovered.

A summary of President Abraham Lincoln's comments to one of his secretaries after the Battle of Fredericksburg in late December 1862.

MY OBJECT in war was to exhaust Lee's army. I was obliged to sacrifice men to do it. I have been called a butcher. Well, I never spared lives to gain an object; but then I gained it, and I knew it was the only way.

General of the Army Ulysses S. Grant, quoted in Chancellor, *An Englishman in the American Civil War*, 1971.

THE OLD WARS were decided by their episodes rather than by their tendencies. In this (modern) war the tendencies are far more important than the episodes. Without winning any sensational victories, we may win. . . . Germany may be defeated more fatally in the second or third year of the war than if the Allied armies had entered Berlin in the first.

Sir Winston S. Churchill, November 1915, speech in the House of Commons.

IN THE STAGE of the wearing out struggle losses will necessarily be heavy on both sides, for in it the price of victory is paid.

Field Marshal Earl Douglas Haig, *Dispatches*, 1919.

AN ENEMY may be worn out by physical and moral action; this, though the usual method of defeating him, is also, frequently, the most uneconomical method, for the process of disintegration is mutually destructive.

Major-General J.F.C. Fuller, *The Reformation of War*, 1923.

OF WHAT USE is decisive victory in battle if we bleed to death as a result of it?

Sir Winston S. Churchill (1874–1965).

BUT ATTRITION is a two-edged weapon and, even when skilfully wielded, puts a strain on the users. It is especially trying to the mass of the people, eager to see a quick finish – and always inclined to assume that this can only mean the enemy's finish.

Captain Sir Basil Liddell Hart, *Strategy*, 1954.

ATTRITION is not a strategy. It is, in fact, irrefutable proof of the absence of any strategy. Any commander who resorts to attrition admits his failure to conceive of an alternative. He rejects warfare as an art. . . . He uses blood in lieu of brains.

General Dave R. Palmer, *Summons of the Trumpet*, 1978.

GENERAL WESTMORELAND thought he had found the answer to the question of how to win this war: He would trade one American life for ten or eleven or twelve North Vietnamese lives, day after day, until Ho Chi Minh cried uncle. Westmoreland would learn, too late, that he was wrong; that the American people didn't see a kill ratio of 10–1 or even 20–1 as any kind of bargain.
> Lieutenant-General Harold G. Moore, *We Were Soldiers Once . . . And Young*, 1992.

AUDACITY

IMPETUOSITY and audacity often achieve what ordinary means fail to achieve.
> Niccolo Machiavelli, *Discourses*, 1517.

IN AUDACITY and obstinacy will be found safety.
> Napoleon, *Maxims of War*, 1831.

WITH AUDACITY one can undertake anything, but not do everything.
> Napoleon, *Maxims of War*, 1831.

IF THE THEORY of war does advise anything, it is the nature of war to advise the most decisive, that is the most audacious.
> Major-General Carl von Clausewitz, *Principles of War*, 1812.

NEVER FORGET that no military leader has ever become great without audacity.
> Major-General Carl von Clausewitz, *Principles of War*, 1812.

FOR GREAT AIMS we must dare great things.
> Major-General Carl von Clausewitz, *Principles of War*, 1812.

THEY WANT WAR too methodical, too measured; I would make it brisk, bold, impetuous, perhaps sometimes even audacious.
> Lieutenant-General Antoine-Henri Baron de Jomini, *Summary of the Art of War*, 1838, tr. Mendell and Craighill, 1862.

IN WAR nothing is impossible, provided you use audacity.
> General George S. Patton, Jr., *War As I Knew It*, 1947.

IF YOU TAKE A CHANCE, it usually succeeds, presupposing good judgement.
> Lieutenant-General Sir Gifford Martel, quoted in S.L.A. Marshall, *The Armed Forces Officer*, 1951.

AUDACITY is nearly always right, gambling nearly always wrong.
> Captain Sir Basil Liddell Hart, quoted in Richard Simpkin, *Race to the Swift*, 1985.

AUDACE, audace, toujours audace. [Audacity, audacity, always audacity.]
> Motto on plaque outside U.S. Army Command and General Staff College, Fort Leavenworth, Kansas.

AUFTRAGSTAKTIK

OBEDIENCE is the principle, but man stands above the principle. . . . who is right in battle is decided in most cases by success . . .
> Field Marshal Helmuth Graf von Moltke (1800–1891).

WHEN a detachment is made, the commander thereof should be informed of the object to be accomplished, and left as free as possible to execute it in his own way . . .
> General of the Army William T. Sherman, *Memoirs of General W.T. Sherman*, 1875.

I DO NOT propose to lay down for you a plan of campaign . . . but simply lay down the work it is desirable to have done and leave you free to execute it in your own way. Submit to me, however, as early as you can, your plan of operations.
> General of the Army Ulysses S. Grant, 4 April 1864, instructions to General William Sherman, *Personal Memoirs of U.S. Grant*, 1885.

AUFTRAGSTAKTIK is what I would like to call the leadership action which we saw for the first time in full action in our Exercise Rule 88 and also emphasized for lower leadership in Exercise Rule 06 in the same sense, by which the higher leader does not give his subordinate a binding order, but more an excerpt from his own thought process, through which he demands from [the subordinate] the intellectual cooperation for the accomplishment of the mission.
> General Otto von Moser, 1912, quoted in *Infantry*, January–February 1991.

COMMAND and control of armed forces is an art, a creative activity based on character, ability, and mental power. . . . Mission-oriented command and control is the first and foremost command and control principle in the army, of relevance in war even more than in peace. It affords the subordinate leader freedom of action in the execution of his mission, the extent depending on the type of mission to be accomplished.
> HDv 100/100, Leadership Manual of the Bundeswehr.

I OBJECTED as forcefully as I knew how. I argued and railed. I told them in the bluntest terms that they should not interfere. They did not know the target or the terrain as I did. They did not know our units and commanders as I did. They did not know the enemy and what could be expected of him as I did. It was their business to tell me *what* to do. The goal, the target – their job was to define that as carefully as they were able. If they did not want this particular target, fine. They should choose another, or none. But they should not take it on themselves to tell me *how* to do it. When it came to how, there should be as little interference as possible with the commander in the field. My position was then (as it is now) that the upper echelon should intervene only if they are actually on the battlefield, if they know everything intimately, if they are forward where they can see and understand all the elements that affect the conduct of the battle.

General Ariel Sharon, discussing the raid on the Jordanian headquarters at Kalkilya in 1956, *Warrior*, 1989.

AUTHORITY

MILITARY AUTHORITY, directing the armed forces, is a matter of the authoritative power of the leading general.

If the general can hold the authority of the military and operate its power, he oversees his subordinates like a fierce tiger with wings, flying over the four seas, going into action whenever there is an encounter.

If the general loses his authority and cannot control the power, he is like a dragon cast into a lake; he may seek the freedom of the high seas, but how can he get there?

Zhuge Liang (AD 180–234), *The Way of the General* (*Mastering the Art of War*, tr. Thomas Cleary, 1989).

WHEN SOLDIERS forge ahead and do not dare to fall back, this means they fear their own leaders more than they fear the enemy. If they dare to fall back and dare not forge ahead, this means they fear the enemy more than they fear their own leaders. When a leader can get his troops to plunge right into the thick of raging combat, it is his authority and sternness that brings this about.

The rule is "To be awesome and yet caring makes a good balance."

Liu Ji (1310–1375), *Lessons of War* (*Mastering the Art of War*, tr. Thomas Cleary, 1989).

. . . THE ONLY WAY an officer could acquire influence over the Confederate soldier was by his personal conduct under fire . . . every atom of authority has to be purchased with a drop of blood.

Colonel George Grenfell, statement to a foreign observer during the American Civil War, quoted in Richard Holmes, *Acts of War*, 1985.

DISCIPLINE and morale influence the inarticulate vote that is constantly taken by masses of men when the order comes to move forward – a variant of the crowd psychology that inclines it to follow a leader. But the Army does not move forward until the motion has carried. "Unanimous consent" only follows cooperation between the individual men in the ranks.

Lieutenant-General James G. Harbord, *The American Army in France*, 1936.

BUT WE CAN GO one step beyond General Harbord's suggestion that the multiplied individual acceptance of a command alone gives that command authority. It is not less true that the multiplied rejection of a command nullifies it. In other words authority is the creature rather than the creator of discipline and obedience. In the more recent experiences of our arms, under the stresses of battle, there are many instances of troops being given orders, and refusing to obey. In every case, the root cause was lack of confidence in the wisdom and ability of those who led. When a determining number of men in ranks have lost the will to obey, their erstwhile leader has *ipso facto* lost the capacity to command. *In the final analysis, authority is contingent upon respect far more truly than respect is founded upon authority*.

Brigadier-General S.L.A. Marshall, *The Armed Forces Officer*, 1951.

THE COMMANDER must establish personal and comradely contact with his men but without giving away an inch of his authority.

Field Marshal Erwin Rommel, *The Rommel Papers*, 1953.

B

BATTLE
The Cost of Battle

I HOPE TO GOD that I have fought my last battle. It is a bad thing to be always fighting. While in the thick of it I am too much occupied to feel anything; but it is wretched just after. It is quite impossible to think of glory. Both mind and feelings are exhausted. I am wretched even at the moment of victory, and I always say that, next to a battle lost, the greatest misery is a battle gained. Not only do you lose those dear friends with whom you have been living, but you are forced to leave the wounded behind you. To be sure, one tries to do the best for them, but how little that is! At such moments every feeling in your breast is deadened. I am now just beginning to regain my natural spirits, but I never wish for any more fighting.
> The Duke of Wellington, July 1815, to Lady Shelley after Waterloo.

BRAVE MEN die in battle.
> Major-General William S. Rosecrans, 31 December 1862.

MOUNTAINS, rivers, grass and trees: utter desolation
For ten miles the wind smells of blood from this new battlefield.
The steed advances not, men speak not.
> General Maruseki Nogi, after the Battle of Nanshan, 1904, quoted in Dennis and Peggy Warner, *The Tide at Sunrise*, 1974.

The Dynamics of Battle

ARES drove them [Trojans], fiery-eyed Athena drove the Argives,
and Terror and Rout and relentless Strife stormed too,
sister of manslaughterer Ares, Ares' comrade-in-arms –
Strife, only a slight thing when she first first rears her head
but her head soon hits the sky as she strides across the earth.
Now Strife hurled down the leveler Hate amidst both sides,
wading into the onslaught, flooding men with pain.
> Homer, *The Iliad*, 4.510–16, c. 800 BC, tr. Robert Fagles, 1990.

THE RESULT of a battle depends on the instantaneous flash of an idea. When you are about to give battle concentrate all your strength, neglect nothing; a battalion often decides the day.
> Napoleon, 30 July 1800, quoted in R.M. Johnston, ed., *The Corsican*, 1910.

THE BATTLE is completely lost; but it is only two o'clock, we have time to gain another to-day.
> General Louis Desaix, 14 June 1800, to Napoleon during the Battle of Marengo; quoted in Louis de Bourrienne, *The Memoirs of Napoleon Bonaparte*, II, 1855.

THERE IS a moment in engagements when the least manoeuvre is decisive and gives the victory; it is the one drop of water which makes the vessel run over.
> Napoleon (1769–1821), 'Precis des guerres de J. Cesar', *Correspondance de Napoléon Ier, publié par ordre de l'Empereur Napoléon III*, Vol. XXXII, 1858–1870.

THE BUSINESS of the English Commander-in-Chief being first to bring an Enemy's fleet to Battle on the most advantageous terms to himself, (I mean that of laying his Ships close on board the Enemy, as expeditiously as possible); and secondly to continue them there until the Business is decided.
> Admiral Viscount Nelson, 1805, from the Order to the Fleet before the Battle of Trafalgar.

BETWEEN a battle lost and a battle won, the distance is immense and there stand empires.
> Napoleon, 15 October 1813, on the eve of the Battle of Leipzig.

THE ISSUE of a battle is the result of a single instant, a single thought. The adversaries come into each other's presence with various combinations; they mingle; they fight for a length of time; the decisive moment appears; a psychological spark makes the decision; and a few reserved troops are enough to carry it out.
> Napoleon, 4–5 December, 1815, conversation on Saint Helena, quoted in Las Casas, cited in Christopher Herold, ed., *The Mind of Napoleon*, 1955.

A BATTLE sometimes decides everything; and sometimes the most trifling thing decides the fate of a battle.
> Napoleon, 9 November 1816, letter on Saint Helena.

IN A BATTLE like in a siege, skill consists in
converging a mass of fire on a single point: once the
combat is opened, the commander who is adroit will
suddenly and unexpectedly open fire with a
surprising mass of artillery on one of these points,
and is sure to seize it.
    Napoleon, *The Military Maxims of Napoleon*,
    tr. Burnod, 1827.

A BATTLE is a dramatic action which has its
beginning, its middle, and its end. The battle order of
the opposing armies and their preliminary
maneuvers until they come to grips form the
exposition. The countermaneuvers of the army which
has been attacked constitute the dramatic
complication. They lead in turn to new measures and
bring about the crisis, and from this results the
outcome or denouement.
    Napoleon, dictation on Saint Helena, quoted in
    Christopher Herold, ed., *The Mind of Napoleon*, 1955.

WHAT IS the battle? It is a struggle by the main
force – but not just an insignificant action fought for
secondary objectives, not simply an attempt to be
abandoned if one realizes early enough that its
object is difficult to attain: it is a struggle for real
victory, waged with all available strength.
    Secondary objectives may combine with the
principal one even in a battle, and the battle itself will
be colored by the circumstances that gave rise to it.
Even battle is connected with a still larger entity of
which it is only a part. But since the essence of war
is fighting, and since the battle is the fight of the main
force, the battle must always be considered as the
true center of gravity of the war. All in all, therefore,
its distinguishing feature is that, more than any other
type of action, battle exists for its own sake alone.
    Major-General Carl von Clausewitz, *On War*, 4.9,
    1832, tr Michael Howard and Peter Paret, 1976.

BATTLE is the bloodiest solution. While it should
not simply be considered as mutual murder – its
effect . . . is rather a killing of the enemy's spirit
than of his men – it is always true that the
character of a battle, like its name, is slaughter
(*Schlacht*), and its price is blood.
    Major-General Carl von Clausewitz, *On War*, 4.11,
    1832, tr Michael Howard and Peter Paret, 1976.

THE MAJOR BATTLE is therefore to be regarded as
concentrated war, as the center of gravity of the entire
conflict or campaign. Just as the focal point of a
concave mirror causes the sun's rays to converge into
a perfect image and heats them to maximum intensity,
so all forces and circumstances of war are united and
compressed to maximum effectiveness in battle.
    Major-General Carl von Clausewitz, *On War*, 4.11,
    1832, tr. Michael Howard and Peter Paret, 1976.

COMBATS may be quite independent of scientific
combinations; they may become essentially

dramatic; personal qualities and inspirations and
a thousand other things frequently are the
controlling elements.
    Lieutenant-General Antoine-Henri Baron de Jomini,
    Summary of the Art of War, 1838, tr. Mendell and
    Craighill, 1862.

BATTLES have been stated by some writers to be
the chief and deciding features of war. This assertion
is not strictly true, as armies have been destroyed by
strategic operations without the occurrence of
pitched battles, merely by a succession of
inconsiderable affairs. It is also true that a complete
and decided victory may bring similar results even
though there may have been no grand strategic
combinations. But it is the morale of armies, as well
as of nations, more than anything else, which makes
victories and their results decisive.
    Lieutenant-General Antoine-Henri Baron de Jomini,
    Summary of the Art of War, 1838, tr. Mendell and
    Craighill, 1862.

BATTLES are won by slaughter and manoeuvre.
The greater the general, the more he contributes to
the manoeuvre, the less he demands in slaughter.
    Sir Winston S. Churchill, *The World Crisis*, II, 1923.

BATTLE is an orgy of disorder. No level lawns or
marker flags exist to aid us strut ourselves in vain
display, but rather groups of weary wandering men
seek gropingly for means to kill their foe. The
sudden change from accustomed order to utter
disorder – to chaos, but emphasize the folly of
schooling to precision and obedience where only
fierceness and habituated disorder are useful.
    General George S. Patton, Jr., 27 October 1927,
    lecture 'Why Men Fight', *The Patton Papers*, I, 1972.

IRRESPECTIVE OF PLANS and organization, all
battles quickly resolve themselves into a series of
more or less isolated head-on conflicts between
small groups of combatants.
    General George S. Patton, Jr., 30 January 1928, letter,
    The Patton Papers, I, 1972

BUT BATTLE must not be seen as some kind of
smooth-running conveyor belt on which the various
technical combat resources are merged. Battle is a
complex and fickle thing. So command and control
must be ready to deal with abrupt changes in the
situation, and sometimes to reshape an earlier
plan radically.
    Marshal of the Soviet Union Mikhail N. Tukhachevskiy,
    1931–32, quoted in Richard Simpkin, *Deep Battle*, 1987.

BATTLE should no longer resemble a bludgeon
fight, but should be a test of skill, a manoeuvre
combat, in which is fulfilled the great principle of
surprise by striking "from an unexpected direction
against an unguarded spot."
    Captain Sir Basil Liddell Hart, *Thoughts on War*, 1944.

BATTLES are won by fire and by movement. The purpose of the movement is to get the fire in a more advantageous place to play on the enemy flank. This is from the rear or flank.

General George S. Patton, Jr., *War As I Knew It*, 1947.

WHILE the battles the British fight may differ in the widest possible ways, they have invariably two common characteristics – they are always fought uphill and always at the junction of two or more map sheets.

Field Marshal Viscount Slim of Burma, *Unofficial History*, 1959

The Human Factor

BATTLE is the ultimate to which the whole life's labor of an officer should be directed. He may live to the age of retirement without seeing a battle; still, he must always be getting ready for it as if he knew the hour and the day it is to break upon him. And then, whether it come late or early, he must be willing to fight – he must fight.

Brigadier-General C.F. Smith to Colonel Lew Wallace, September 1861.

IT WOULD BE a service to humanity and to one's people to dispel this illusion and show what battles are. They are buffooneries, and none the less buffooneries because they are made terrible by the spilling of blood. The actors, heroes in the eyes of the crowd, are only poor folk torn between fear, discipline and pride. They play some hours at a game of advance and retreat, without ever meeting, closing with, even seeing closely, the other poor folk, the enemy, who are as fearful as they but who are caught in the same web of circumstance.

Colonel Charles Ardant du Picq, *Battle Studies*, 1880, tr. Greely, 1957.

IT IS always necessary in battle to do something which would be impossible for men in cold blood.

Colonel Louis Louzeau de Grandmaison, February 1911, lecture at the *École de Guerre*.

BATTLES are decided in favor of the troops whose bravery, fortitude, and especially, whose endurance, surpasses that of the enemy's; the army with the higher breaking point wins the decision.

General of the Army George C. Marshall, *Memoirs of My Service in the World War* (written 1919–1923), published 1976.

BATTLE is the most magnificent competition in which a human being can indulge. It brings out all that is best; it removes all that is base. All men are afraid in battle. The coward is the one who lets his fear overcome his sense of duty. Duty is the essence of manhood.

General George S. Patton, Jr., 27 June 1943, to the

officers of the 45th Infantry Division before the invasion of Sicily.

BATTLE is not a terrifying ordeal to be endured. It is a magnificent experience wherein all the elements that have made man superior to the beasts are present: courage, self-sacrifice, loyalty, help to others, devotion to duty. As you go in, you will perhaps be a little short of breath, and your knees may tremble. . . . This breathlessness, this tremor, are not fear. It is simply the excitement every athlete feels just before the whistle blows – no, you will not fear for you will be borne up and exhalted by the proud instinct of our conquering race. You will be inspired by a magnificent hate.

General George S. Patton, Jr., 20 December 1941, address to the Second Armored Division, *The Patton Papers*, II, 1974.

WHEN THINGS are going badly in battle the best tonic is to take one's mind off one's own troubles by considering what a rotten time one's opponent must be having.

Field Marshal Viscount Wavell of Cyrenaica, *Other Men's Flowers*, 1944.

THE ACID TEST of battle brings out the pure metal.

General George S. Patton, Jr., *War As I Knew It*, 1947.

BATTLE is more than a combination of fire and movement. It is the integration of fire, movement, and consciousness. The commander, therefore, cannot rest content with guiding the fire and directing the movement; he must guide the soldier's mental reactions to battle. Hence the commander is responsible for the mental preparation of his men no less than for their physical and technical training and their being brought to battle. Paternal concern for the soldier and his welfare does not mean pampering him; far from it. Soldiers wrapped in cotton-wool will fall helpless victims to the terrors of war, being unprepared to meet the most terrible of all dangers. Sincere concern, on the other hand, will win the soldier's confidence and will prepare him to face the most trying circumstances.

General Yigal Allon, *The Making of Israel's Army*, 1970.

THE ART of battle consists in maintaining and strengthening the psychological cohesion of one's own troops while at the same time disrupting that of the enemy.

General André Beaufre, *An Introduction to Strategy*, 1965.

Love of Battle

AND NOW, what's more, the courage inside
  my chest
is racing faster for action, full frontal assault –
feet quiver beneath me, hands high for the onset!

And Telamonian Ajax joined him, calling out,
"I can feel it too, now, the hands on my spear,
invincible hands quivering tense for battle, look –
the power rising within me, feet beneath me rushing
    me on!
I even long to meet this Hector in single combat,
blaze as he does nonstop for bloody war!"

> Homer, *The Iliad*, 13.89, c. 800 BC, tr. Robert Fagles,
> 1990; Little Ajax to Great Ajax as they rallied to stop
> the Trojan assault on the Greek camp.

IT IS WARM WORK; and this day may be the last to
any of us at a moment. But mark you! I would not be
elsewhere for thousands.

> Admiral Viscount Nelson, at the Battle of
> Copenhagen, quoted in Robert Southey, *Life of
> Nelson*, 1813.

MY OFFICIAL REPORT is a lifeless affair, an exact
statement of facts which have a certain value, but
that which makes the thrilling interest of a battle is
the personal incident, and of that I could, if I had
leisure, tell a good deal . . . A battle so lifts a man
out of himself that he scarcely recognizes his identity
when peace returns and with it quiet occupations.

> Major-General Andrew A. Humphreys, letter to a
> friend, 11 July 1863, of the Battle of Gettysburg,
> quoted in Henry H. Humphreys, *Andrew Atkinson
> Humphreys: A Biography*, 1924.

IN THOSE PERIODS of engagement, when he's
shooting at you and you're shooting at him, or
when you can see them or when they're coming
at you . . . it is the most exhilarating moment in
your life.

It's a symphony: You can hear sporadic small-
arms fire. That grows. When you know you're
engaged is when you hear your machine guns start.
And his machine guns pick up and by that time you
realize, "Okay, give me artillery."

And then you gotta see what's going on, and you
go up on the ridge . . . and here they come . . . You
almost think, "Boy, I wish I had a camera." It's
beautiful.

> General Carl E. Mundy, *The Washington Post*, 5 June
> 1999, p. C2.

The Purpose of Battle

IT IS a paradox to hope for victory without fighting.
The goal of the man who makes war is to fight in the
open field to win a victory.

> Field Marshal Prince Raimond Montecuccoli, *Memorie
> della guerra*, 1703.

BATTLES concerning which one cannot say why
and to what purpose they have been delivered are
commonly the resource of ignorant men.

> Field Marshal Maurice Comte de Saxe, *My
> Reveries*, 1732, tr. Phillips, 1940.

THE MAN who does things without motive or in spite
of himself is either insane or a fool. War is decided
by battles, and it is not finished except by them.
They have to be fought, but it should be done
opportunely and with all the advantages on your
side. . . . Advantages are procured in battles every
time that you determine to fight, or when a battle that
you have meditated upon for a long time is a
consequence of the maneuvers that you have made
to bring it on.

> Frederick the Great, *Instructions to his Generals*, 1747,
> tr. Phillips, 1940.

BATTLES decide the fate of a nation. In war it is
absolutely necessary to come to decisive actions
either to get out of the distress of war or to place
the enemy in that position, or even to settle a
quarrel which otherwise perhaps would never be
finished. A wise man will make no movement
without good reason, and a general of an army will
never give battle if it does not serve some
important purpose. When he is forced by his enemy
into battle it is surely because he will have
committed mistakes which force him to dance to
the tune of his enemy.

> Frederick the Great, *Instruction militaire*, 1761.

MAXIM 15. The first consideration of a general who
offers battle should be the glory and honour of his
arms; the safety and preservation of his men is only
the second; but it is in the enterprise and courage
resulting from the former that the latter will most
assuredly be found. . . .

> Napoleon, *The Military Maxims of Napoleon*,
> tr. George D'Aguilar, 1831 (David Chandler,
> ed., 1987).

WAR as we study it, positive in its nature, permits
only of positive answers: there is no result without
cause; if you seek the result, develop the cause,
employ force.

If you wish your opponent to withdraw, beat him;
otherwise nothing is accomplished, and there is only
one means to that end: the battle.

> Marshal of France Ferdinand Foch, *Principles of
> War*, 1913.

BATTLES are the principal milestones in secular
history. Modern opinion resents this uninspiring truth,
and historians often treat the decisions of the field as
incidents in the dramas of politics and diplomacy.
But great battles, won or lost, change the entire
course of events, create new standards of values,
new moods, new atmospheres, in armies and
nations, to which all must conform.

> Sir Winston S. Churchill, *Marlborough*, 1933.

BATTLES in which no one believes should not
be fought.

> Field Marshal Viscount Wavell of Cyrenaica,
> 'Recollections' (unpublished), 1946.

BATTLEFIELD

. . . A DANCING floor of Ares.

> Epaminondas (c. 418–362 BC) describing the Boetian Plain, quoted in Plutarch, *The Lives*, c. AD 100 (*The Age of Alexander*, tr. Ian Scott-Kilvert, 1965).

THE BATTLEFIELD is the place:
Where one toasts the divine liquor in war,
Where are stained red the divine eagles,
Where the jaguars howl,
Where all kinds of precious stones rain from ornaments
Where wave headdresses rich with fine plumes,
Where princes are smashed to bits.

> Aztec poem, quoted in Michael D. Coe, *Mexico: From the Olmec to the Aztecs*, 1994.

BOYS, remember that it is my custom to sleep on the battlefield!

> Napoleon, 14 June 1800, at the Battle of Marengo as he rallied his men, quoted in F.M. Kircheisen, *Memoirs of Napoleon I*, 1929.

AFTER THE BATTLE of Eylau, the Emperor spent several hours daily on the battlefield. . . . To visualize the scene one must imagine, within the space of one square league, nine or ten thousand corpses; four or five thousand dead horses; rows upon rows of Russian field packs; the remnants of guns and swords; the ground covered with cannon balls, shells,and other ammunition; and twenty-four artillery pieces, near which could be seen the corpses of the drivers who were killed while trying to move them – all this sharply outlined on a background of snow. A sight such as this should inspire rulers with the love of peace and the hatred of war.

> Napoleon, 2 March 1807, 64th Bulletin (Napoleon composed most of the Bulletins personally), quoted in Christopher Herold, ed., *The Mind of Napoleon*, 1955.

THE COUNTRYSIDE is covered with dead and wounded. This is not the pleasant part of war. One suffers, and the soul is oppressed to see so many sufferers.

> Napoleon, March 1807, to Josephine after the Battle of Eylau, *Correspondance de Napoléon Ier, publié par ordre de l'Empereur Napoléon III*, XIV, No. 11813, p. 304.

THE VILLAGE of Fuentes de Oñoro, having been the field of battle, has not been much improved by the circumstance.

> The Duke of Wellington, 3–5 May 1811, *The Dispatches of Field Marshal the Duke of Wellington, During His Various Campaigns in India, Denmark, Portugal, Spain, the Low Countries and France*, VII, 1834–1838.

FROM EARLY MORNING the Emperor was out in all parts of the battlefield, supervising with utmost care the collection and removal of the wounded, Russian as well as French. Never was a battlefield so thickly strewn with dead. In the village round which the attack had centred, the Russian dead lay in heaps. On the plateau behind it the ground was covered with the corpses of Litowski's and Ismaelowski's Guards, slaughtered by our guns. The Emperor carefully examined every portion of this battlefield, the positions of each corps, the movements they had made, the difficulties they had had to overcome. At each point he demanded minute details of everything that had happened, dealt out praise and encouragement, and was greeted by his troops with all their wonted enthusiasm.

> General Armand de Caulaincourt, on the aftermath of Borodino on 8 September 1812, *With Napoleon in Russia*, 1935.

IT WAS a beautiful, calm, moonlight night. Suddenly a dog, which had been hiding under the clothes of a dead man, came up to us with a mournful howl, and then disappeared again immediately into his hiding place. He would lick his master's face, then run up to us again, only to return once more to his master. It seemed as if he were asking both for help and revenge. Whether it was the mood of the moment, whether it was the place, the time, the weather, or the action itself, or whatever it was, it is certainly true that nothing on any battlefield ever made such an impression on me. I involuntarily remained still, to observe the spectacle. This dead man, I said to myself, has perhaps friends, and he is lying here abandoned by all but his dog! What a lesson nature teaches us by means of an animal.

> Napoleon, 1–3 December 1815, conversation on St. Helena about one of the battles of the Italian campaign of 1796–1797, reported by Las Casas, quoted in Kircheisen, ed., *The Memoirs of Napoleon I*, 1929.

THERE IS in every battlefield a decisive point, the possession of which, more than of any other, helps secure the victory, by enabling its holder to make proper application of the principles of war. . . .

The decisive point of a battlefield is determined . . . by the character of the position, the bearing of different localities upon the strategic object in view, and finally, by the arrangement of the contending forces.

> Lieutenant-General Antoine-Henri Baron de Jomini, *Summary of the Art of War*, 1838, tr. Mendell and Craighill, 1862.

THE DOMINANT feeling of the battlefield is loneliness.

> Field Marshal Viscount Slim of Burma, June 1941, to the officers of the Tenth Indian Infantry Division.

THE BATTLEFIELD is the epitome of war. All else in war, when war is perfectly conducted, exists but to serve the forces of the battlefield and to assure success on the field.

> Brigadier-General S.L.A. Marshall, *Men Against Fire*, 1947.

THE BATTLEFIELD is cold. It is the loneliest place which men may share together.

To the infantry soldier new to combat, its most unnerving characteristic is not that it invites him to a death he does not seek. To the extent necessary, a normal man may steel himself against the chance of death.

The harshest thing about the field is that it is empty. No people stir about. There is little or no sign of action. Overall there is a great quiet which seems more ominous than the occasional tempest of fire.

It is the emptiness which chills a man's blood and makes the apple harden in his throat. It is the emptiness which grips him with paralysis. The small dangers which he had faced in his earlier life had always paid their dividend of excitement. Now there is great danger, but there is not excitement about it.
> Brigadier-General S.L.A. Marshall, *Men Against Fire*, 1947.

I HAVE always regarded the forward edge of the battlefield as the most exclusive club in the world.
> General Sir Brian Horrocks, *A Full Life*, 1960.

THE BAYONET

THE ONSET of Bayonets in the hands of the Valiant is irresistible.
> Major-General John Burgoyne, extract from his orderly book, 1777.

THE BULLET is a mad thing; only the bayonet knows what it is about.
> Field Marshal Prince Aleksandr V. Suvorov, *The Science of Victory*, 1796.

FIRE SELDOM but accurately. Thrust the bayonet with force. The bullet misses, the bayonet doesn't. The bullet's an idiot, the bayonet's a fine chap. Stab once and throw the Turk off the bayonet. Bayonet another, bayonet a third; a real warrior will bayonet half a dozen and more. Keep a bullet in the barrel. If three should run at you, bayonet the first, shoot the second and lay out the third with your bayonet. This isn't common but you haven't time to reload. . . .
> Field Marshal Prince Aleksandr V. Suvorov, *The Science of Victory*, 1796.

THE BAYONET has always been the weapon of the brave and the chief tool of victory.
> Napoleon (1769–1821).

21ST, (1796) Verona: The general-in-chief has reviewed Masséna's and Augereau's divisions. He has seen with pleasure the good condition of the troops, but with regret the scarcity of bayonets.

I had sooner see a soldier without his breeches than without his bayonet.
> Napoleon, quoted in R.M. Johnston, ed., *The Corsican*, 1910.

WHEN bayonets deliberate, power escapes from the hands of the government.
> Napoleon, *Political Aphorisms*, 1848.

THE PEOPLE never chafe themselves against naked bayonets.
> Napoleon, *Political Aphorisms*, 1848.

RANGERS of Connaught! It is not my intention to expend any powder this evening. We'll do this business with cold steel.
> General Sir Thomas Picton, 6 April 1812, to the 88th Foot before the assault on Badajoz.

HAVE YOU not got your bayonets?
> Sir George Cathcart: At Inkerman on 5 November 1854, when word came that his division was low on ammunition.

COL B.E. BEE: General, they are beating us back! Stonewall Jackson: Then, sir, we will give them the bayonet!
> At the First Battle of Bull Run, 21 July 1861, *Charleston Mercury*, 25 July 1861.

UNDER divine blessing, we must rely on the bayonet when firearms cannot be furnished.
> Lieutenant-General Thomas J. 'Stonewall' Jackson, letter accompanying his requisition for 1,000 pikes, 9 April 1861.

NOT A MOMENT was about to be lost! Five minutes more of such a defensive, and the last roll-call would sound for us! Desperate as the chances were, there was nothing for it, but to take the offensive. I stepped to the colors. The men turned towards me. One word was enough, – "BAYONET!" – It caught like fire, and swept along the ranks. The men took it up with a shout, one could not say, whether from the pit, or the song of the morning star! It was vain to order "Forward." No mortal could have heard it in the mighty hosanna that was winging the sky. Nor would he wait to hear. There are things still as the first creation, "whose seed is in itself." The grating clash of steel in fixing bayonets told its own story; the color rose in front; the whole line quivered for the start; the edge of the left-wing rippled, swung, tossed among the rocks, straightened, changed curve from scimitar to sickle-shaped; and the bristling archers swooped down upon the serried host – down into the face of half a thousand! Two hundred men!
> Major-General Joshua L. Chamberlain, of the bayonet charge of his 20th Maine at Little Round, Gettysburg on 2 July 1863, 'Through Blood and Fire at Gettysburg', *Hearst's Magazine*, 1913.

THE BRISTLING POINTS and the glitter of the bayonets were fearful to look upon as they were levelled in front of a charging line; but they were

rarely reddened with blood. The day of the bayonet is passed.
> General John B. Gordon, *Reminiscences of the Civil War*, 1903.

ALL TOO MANY of our men lost their lives in trying to "close with the bayonet" and "kill with cold steel" as prescribed, so that they were shot down at close range by cooler-headed opponents who realized that the bullet outreaches the bayonet until the range is closed to less than two yards. More wisely, most of the German troops did not even fix their bayonets, lest the drag should disturb their aim in firing.
> Captain Sir Basil Liddell Hart, *The Memoirs of Captain Liddell Hart*, I, 1965.

THE LAURELS of victory are at the point of the enemy bayonets. They must be plucked there; they must be carried by a hand-to-hand fight if one really means to conquer.
> Marshal of France Ferdinand Foch, *Precepts and Judgments*, 1919.

I BEG LEAVE to remind the [Cavalry] Board that very few people have ever been killed with the bayonet or the saber, but the fear of having their guts explored with cold steel in the hands of battle maddened men has won many a fight.
> General George S. Patton, Jr., January 1941, reply to the Cavalry Board's solicitation of his views, *The Patton Papers*, II, 1974.

THE ATTACK will be pressed with the ruthless vigor that has routed every enemy formation opposing the 3rd Div. All men will be brought to the highest possible state of offensive spirit prior to the jump-off. *Bayonets will be sharpened.*
> General John W. O'Daniel, March 1945, order to the Third Infantry 'Rock of the Marne' Divison, as it attacked into Germany, quoted in Weigley, *Eisenhower's Lieutenants*, 1981. (The Third Infantry Division was the only Allied infantry division mentioned by name in the German Army war diary and was described as the best among the Allies.)

IF you're close enough to stick 'em, you're close enough to shoot 'em.
> Bill Mauldin's 'Willie and Joe' to a recruit in the movie *Willie and Joe*.

FEW MEN are killed by the bayonet; many are scared by it. Bayonets should be fixed when the fire fight starts.
> General George S. Patton, Jr., *War As I Knew It*, 1947.

"HOW do you get a bayonet out of a Jap, once you've got it in!" I asked. . . .
"Shoot it out," he told me. And that's what the Marines did at Saipan and Guadalcanal on the rare occasions that they used bayonets.
> General Holland M. 'Howlin' Mad' Smith and Percy Finch, *Coral and Brass*, 1948.

THAT WEAPON ceased to have any major tactical value at about the time the inaccurate and short-range musket was displaced by the rifle. But we have stubbornly clung to it – partly because of tradition which makes it inevitable that all military habits die a slow death, but chiefly because of the superstition that the bayonet makes troops fierce and audacious, and therefore likely to close with the enemy.
> Brigadier-General S.L.A. Marshall, *The Soldier's Load and the Mobility of a Nation*, 1980.

WITH THEIR BAYONETS on their rifles, these young soldiers, looking grim and determined, moving forward through the thick mist of dawn – it is a sight I shall never forget. A lot of the enemy were killed with those bayonets.
> Lieutenant-Colonel Hugh Pike, 1982, of the attack of his battalion, 3 Para, at the Battle of Mount Longdon on 12 June 1982 during the Falklands War.

THE BEST YOU CAN

I DO the very best I know how – the very best I can; and I mean to keep doing so until the end. If the end brings me out all right, what is said against me won't amount to anything. If the end brings me out wrong, ten angels swearing I was right would make no difference.
> President Abraham Lincoln, quoted in Francis Carpenter, *Six Months at the White House*, 1867.

I HAVE been placed on duty here to conduct operations under the direction of the President. It will give me great pleasure to do everything I can to relieve him & serve the country, but I do not see either advantage or pleasure in my duties. But I will not complain, but do my best. I do not see at present either that it will enable me to see much more of you. In the present condition of affairs no one can foresee what may happen, nor in my judgment is it advisable for any one to make any arrangements with a view to permanency or pleasure. We must all do what promises the most usefulness.
> General Robert E. Lee, letter to his wife upon his assignment as chief military advisor to Jefferson Davis, 14 March 1862, quoted in Dowdey and Manarin, ed., *The Wartime Papers of Robert E. Lee*, 1961.

NOW, as I said before this, perhaps I erred in judgment, for I take this occasion to say to you, and through you to the President, that I have no pretensions to any superior capacity for the post he has assigned me to; that all I can do is to exert my utmost efforts and do the best I can; but that the moment those who have a right to judge my actions think, or feel satisfied, either that I am wanting or that another would do better, that moment I earnestly desire to be relieved, not on my own account, but on account of the country and the cause.

Major-General George Gordon Meade, unofficial telegram to Major-General Halleck in response to his expression of Lincoln's disappointment that Lee was not destroyed when backed up to the rain-swollen Potomac after the Battle of Gettysburg, 31 July 1863, *The War of the Rebellion: A Compilation of the Official Records of the Union and Confederate Armies*, Series I, Vol. XXVII, Part I, pp. 104 and 108, U.S. Government Printing Office, 1880–1901.

I HOPE for the best results as I am always hopeful; put my shoulder to the wheel with my best judgment, and trust to God for the rest.

Admiral David Glasgow Farragut, a week before forcing the passage into Mobile Bay, July 1864, quoted in Mahan, *Admiral Farragut*, 1892.

YOU MUST DO your damnedest and win. Remember that is what you live for. Oh you must! You have got to do some thing! Never stop until you have gained the top or a grave.

General George S. Patton, Jr., while a cadet at West Point, quoted in Carlo D'Este, *Patton: A Genius For War*, 1995.

BLITZKRIEG

MILITARY TACTICS are like unto water; for water in its natural course runs away from high places and hastens downwards. So in war, the way to avoid what is strong is to strike what is weak.

Water shapes its course according to the ground over which it flows; the soldier works out his victory in relation to the foe whom he is facing.

Therefore, just as water retains no constant shape, so in warfare there are no constant conditions.

He who can modify his tactics in relation to his opponent and thereby succeed in winning, may be called a heaven-born captain.

Sun Tzu, *The Art of War*, 6, c. 500 BC, tr. Giles, 1910.

THE RULE of offensive warfare is that those who go the easy way prevail over their opponents. If your enemies are garrisoned in several places, there will inevitably be some places stronger and better manned than others. In that case, you should keep your distance from their strong points and attack their weak points; avoid places where they have many troops and strike where they have few – then you will not fail to win.

Liu Ji (1310–1375), Lessons of War, quoted in Cleary, *Mastering the Art of War*, 1989.

IN SEEKING a better solution I carried out a series of improvised tactical "war games", and by a combination of thought with test evolved a method of attack in which exploitation would become a semi-

automatic process – "each grade of commander", from the platoon upwards, "moving his reserves in the wake of whichever of his forward sub-units is making the best progress", instead of risking the loss of time, surprise, and opportunity by waiting until reports filtered back. Based on a recognition of the practical condition that "success is usually uneven and progress unequal", it was designed "to turn opportunism into a system", so that a progressive infusion of resources should go on as quickly and continuously as possible along the line of least resistance. At first I thought of calling it the "expanding spearhead", but then happened to watch a stream in flood and saw how aptly the water's natural process of penetrating and circumventing obstacles corresponded to my tactical concept, so decided to use the descriptive term "expanding torrent". Some years later, when I read Sun Tzu's two-thousand-year-old book on *The Art of War*, I found that he had used a close simile.

Captain Sir Basil Liddell Hart, 1920, *The Memoirs of Captain Liddell Hart*, I, 1965.

MOBILITY, Velocity, Indirect Approach. . .

Colonel-General Heinz Guderian (1888–1954).

WE HAD SEEN a perfect specimen of the modern Blitzkrieg; the close interaction on the battlefield of army and air force; the violent bombardment of all communications and of any town that seemed an attractive target; the arming of an active Fifth Column; the free use of spies and parachutists; and above all, the irresistable forward thrust of great masses of armour.

Sir Winston S. Churchill, *The Gathering Storm*, 1948.

IN THE SERIES of swift German conquests, the air force combined with the mechanized elements of the land forces in producing the paralysis and moral disintegration of the opposing forces and of the nations behind. Its effect was terrific, and must be reckoned fully as important as that of the panzer forces. The two are inseparable in any valuation of the elements that created the new style of lightning war – the blitzkrieg.

Captain Sir Basil Liddell Hart, *Strategy*, 1954.

BLOODSHED

I DO NOT WANT them to get used to shedding blood so young; at their age they do not know what it means to be a Moslem or an infidel, and they will grow accustomed to trifling with the lives of others.

Saladin to Beha-ed-Din, when Saladin's children asked if they might kill a prisoner, 1191.

IF YOU WISH to be loved by your soldiers, husband their blood and do not lead them to slaughter.

Frederick the Great, *Instructions to His Generals*, 1747, tr. Phillips, 1940.

NOTHING honors a general more than keeping his serenity in danger and facing it when there are chances of winning; but nothing so much eclipses his name as the useless shedding of the blood of his men.
> General Jose de San Martin, 1818, quoted in Rojas, *San Martin*, 1957.

KINDHEARTED people might . . . think there was some ingenious way to disarm or defeat an enemy without too much bloodshed, but pleasant as it sounds, it is a fallacy that must be exposed . . . It would be futile – even wrong – to try and shut one's eyes to what war really is from sheer distress at its brutality.
> Major-General Carl von Clausewitz, *On War*, 1.1, 1832, tr. Michael Howard and Peter Paret, 1976.

WE ARE NOT INTERESTED in generals who win victories without bloodshed. The fact that slaughter is a horrifying spectacle must make us take war more seriously, but not provide an excuse for gradually blunting our swords in the name of humanity. Sooner or later someone will come along with a sharp sword and hack off our arms.
> Major-General Carl von Clausewitz, *On War*, 4.11, 1832, tr. Michael Howard and Peter Paret, 1976.

IN SUCH dangerous things as war, the errors which proceed from a spirit of benevolence are the worst. . . . He who uses force unsparingly, without reference to the bloodshed involved, must obtain a superiority if his adversary uses less vigor in its application. The former then dictates the law to the latter, and both proceed to extremities, to which the only limitations are imposed by the amount of counteracting force on each side.
> Major-General Carl von Clausewitz, *On War*, 1832, tr. Graham, 1918.

WOUNDS which in 1861, would have sent a man to the hospital for months, in 1865 were regarded as mere scratches, rather the subject of a joke than of sorrow. To new soldiers the sight of blood and death always has a sickening effect, but soon men become accustomed to it, and I have heard them exclaim on seeing a dead comrade borne to the rear, "Well, Bill has turned up his toes to the daisies."
> General of the Army William T. Sherman, *Memoirs of General W.T. Sherman*, 1875.

WAR is only a means to results. . . . These being achieved, no man has the right to cause another drop of blood to be shed.
> Marshal of France Ferdinand Foch, quoted in Liddell Hart, *Through the Fog of War*, 1938.

WHAT the American people want to do is fight a war without getting hurt. You cannot do that any more than you can go into a barroom brawl without getting hurt.
> Lieutenant-General Lewis B. 'Chesty' Puller, 1951, quoted in Davis, *Marine!*, 1962.

BOLDNESS

THRUST IN fearlessly: however foreign a man may be, in every crisis it is the high face which will carry him through.
> Homer, *The Odyssey*, Bk 7, c. 800 BC, tr. T.E. Lawrence, 1932, Athena's admonition to Odysseus to boldly enter the feasthall of the Phaeacians.

MY CONCLUSION is, then, that as fortune is variable and men fixed in their ways, men will prosper as long as they are in tune with the times and will fail when they are not. However, I will say that in my opinion it is better to be bold than cautious, for fortune is a woman and whoever wishes to win her must importune and beat her, and we may observe that she is more frequently won by this sort than by those who proceed more deliberately.
> Niccolo Machiavelli, *The Prince*, 1513.

I WISH to have no connection with any ship that does not sail fast; for I intend to go *in harm's way*.
> Admiral John Paul Jones (1747–1792).

DESPERATE AFFAIRS require desperate measures.
> Admiral Viscount Nelson (1758–1805).

THE MEASURE may be thought bold, but I am of the opinion the boldest are the safest.
> Admiral Viscount Nelson, 24 March 1801, to Sir Hyde Parker urging vigorous action against the Russians and Danes.

PERHAPS I should not insist on this bold maneuver, but it is my style, my way of doing things.
> Napoleon, 1813, letter to Prince Eugene.

MAXIM 25. When two armies are in order of battle, and one has to retire over a bridge, while the other has the circumference of the circle open, all the advantages are in favour of the latter. It is then a general should show boldness, and strike a decided blow, and manoeuvre upon the flank of his enemy. The victory is in his hands.
> Napoleon, *The Military Maxims of Napoleon*, tr. George D'Aguilar, 1831 (David Chandler, ed., 1987).

BUT THIS noble capacity to rise above the most menacing dangers should also be considered as a principle in itself, separate and active. Indeed, in what field of human activity is boldness more at home than in war?
  A soldier, whether drummer boy or general, possesses no nobler quality; it is the very metal that gives edge and luster to the sword.
> Major-General Carl von Clausewitz, *On War*, 3.10, 1832, tr. Michael Howard and Peter Paret, 1976.

A DISTINGUISHED commander without boldness is unthinkable. No man who is not born bold can play such a role, and therefore we consider this quality the first prerequisite of the great military leader.

> Major-General Carl von Clausewitz, *On War*, 3.10, 1832, tr. Michael Howard and Peter Paret, 1976.

THE POWER of the various emotions is sharply reduced by the intervention of lucid thought and more, by self-control. Consequently, boldness grows less common in the higher ranks. Even if the growth of an officer's perception and intelligence does not keep pace with his rise in rank, the realities of war will impose their conditions and concerns on him. Indeed their influence on him will be greater the less he really understands them. In war, this is the main basis for the experience expressed in the French proverb, "The same man who shines at the second level is eclipsed at the top." Nearly every general known to us from history as mediocre, even vacillating, was noted for dash and determination as a junior officer.

> Major-General Carl von Clausewitz, *On War*, 3.10, 1832, tr. Michael Howard and Peter Paret, 1976.

BOLDNESS governed by superior intellect is the mark of a hero. This kind of boldness does not consist in defying the natural order of things and in crudely offending the laws of probability; it is rather a matter of energetically supporting that higher form of analysis by which genius arrives at a decision: rapid, only partly conscious weighing of the possibilities. Boldness can lend wings to intellect and insight; the stronger the wings then, the greater the heights, the wider the view, and the better results; though a greater prize, of course, involves greater risks.

> Major-General Carl von Clausewitz, *On War*, 3.10, 1832, tr. Michael Howard and Peter Paret, 1976.

WHILE RASHNESS is a crime, boldness is not incompatable with caution, nay, is often the quintessence of prudence.

> Major-General J.E.B. Stuart, General Order No. 26, Cavalry Tactics, July 30, 1863, *Letters of Major General James E.B. Stuart*, 1990.

"SAFETY FIRST" is the road to ruin in war.

> Sir Winston S. Churchill, 3 November 1940, telegram to Anthony Eden.

A BOLD GENERAL may be lucky, but no general can be lucky unless he is bold. The general who allows himself to be bound and hampered by regulations is unlikely to win a battle.

> Field Marshal Earl Wavell, *Generals and Generalship*, 1941.

THE FIGHT was carried to the enemy at all times and in all places and he was driven from every place he held by the resolute attack of men who were not afraid to die. God favors the bold and the strong of heart . . .

> General Alexander A. Vandegrift, message to the Marine First Division on Guadalcanal indicating that elements of the division had taken nearby Tulagi island, Navy Department Press Release, 29 August 1942.

I CAN always pick a fighting man and God knows there are few of them. I am happy they are sending you to the front at once. I like generals so bold that they are dangerous. I hope they give you a free hand.

> General John J. Pershing, 21 October 1942, to General George Patton before his departure for the invasion of North Africa, quoted in *The Patton Papers*, II, 1974.

IT IS my experience that bold decisions give the best promise of success. But one must differentiate between strategical or tactical boldness and military gamble. A bold operation is one in which success is not a certainty but which in case of failure leaves one with sufficient forces in hand to cope with whatever situation may arise. A gamble, on the other hand, is an operation which can lead either to victory or to the complete destruction of one's forces. Situations arise where even a gamble may be justified – as, for instance, when in the normal course of events defeat is merely a matter of time, when the gaining of time is therefore pointless and the only chance lies in an operation of great risk.

> Field Marshal Erwin Rommel, *The Rommel Papers*, 1953.

THERE ARE occasions when daring and risky operations, boldly executed, can pay great dividends.

> General Matthew B. Ridgway, *Soldier: The Memoirs of Matthew B. Ridgway*, 1956.

BOLDNESS is superior to timidity in every instance and is at a disadvantage only in the face of nervy, calculating patience which allows the enemy to commit himself irrevocably before striking – a form of boldness in its own right.

> General Alfred M. Gray and Major John Schmitt, *Warfighting*, United States Marine Corps, 1989.

BOLDNESS is an essential moral trait in a leader, for it generates combat power beyond the physical means at hand.

> General Alfred M. Gray and Major John Schmitt, *Warfighting*, United States Marine Corps, 1989.

BRAVERY

WITHOUT a sign his sword the brave man, draws,
And asks no omen but his country's cause.

> Homer, *The Iliad*, 12.283, c. 800 BC, tr. Alexander Pope, 1743.

THEY ARE surely to be esteemed the bravest

spirits who, having the clearest sense of both the pains and pleasures of life, do not on that account shrink from danger.

Thucydides, *The History of the Peloponnesian War*, 2.40, 404 BC, tr. Benjamin Jowett, 1881.

WHOEVER wants to see his own people again must remember to be a brave soldier: that is the only way of doing it. Whoever wants to keep alive must aim at victory. It is the winners who do the killing and the losers who get killed.

Xenophon, *Anabasis*, 3.2, c. 360 BC (*The Persian Expedition*, tr. Rex Warner, 1965).

FEW MEN are born brave; many become so through training and force of discipline.

Flavius Vegetius Renatus, *Military Institutions of the Romans*, AD 378, tr. Clark, 1776.

THE BRAVE MAN [is] tall, very tall, small, fat, thin, very fat, very thin, somewhat like a stone pillar, moderately capable, good of appearance. The brave man [is] an eagle [or] an ocelot warrior, scarred, painted, courageous, brave, resolute.

The good, the true brave man [is] one who stands as a man, who is firm of heart, who charges, who strikes out at [the foe]. He stands as a man, he rallies, he takes courage; he charges, he strikes out at the foe. He fears no one, none can meet his gaze.

The bad brave man [is] one who leads others to destruction by his deception, who secretly puts one in difficulty; who visits others' houses; who yells; who slays others viciously, who treacherously forsakes one, who swoons with terror. He becomes frightened, he swoons with terror, he secretly puts one in difficulty.

An Aztec account of the brave man, quoted in Fray Bernardino de Sahagún, *General History of the Things of New Spain, Book 10 – The People*, 1961.

HE SUPPOSES all men to be brave at all times and does not realize that the courage of the troops must be reborn daily, that nothing is so variable, and that the true skill of a general consists in knowing how to guarantee it by his dispositions, his positions, and those traits of genius that characterize great captains.

. . . it is of all the elements of war the one that is most necessary to learn.

Field Marshal Maurice Comte de Saxe, *My Reveries*, 1732, tr. Phillips, 1940.

I HAVE a Constitution hardy enough to encounter and undergo the most severe tryals, and, I flatter myself, resolution to Face what any Man durst, as shall be prov'd when it comes to the Test.

General George Washington, 29 May 1754, to Robert Dinwiddie, *The Writings of George Washington*, I, 1931, p. 60.

ONE cannot think that blind bravery gives victory over the enemy.

Field Marshal Prince Aleksandr V. Suvorov (1729–1800).

WHEN soldiers brave death, they drive him into the enemy's ranks.

Napoleon, 14 November 1806, to a regiment of chasseurs before the Battle of Jena.

NO, shoot them all, I do not wish them to be brave.

Lieutenant-General Thomas J. 'Stonewall' Jackson, 2 June 1862, to Colonel John Patton who deplored the necessity of killing three especially brave Union cavalrymen, quoted in Patton, 'Reminiscences of Jackson', Virginia Historical Society.

I COULD NOT HELP admiring in their misfortunes those brave men who were about to sign a capitulation which would deprive them of the forts they had so confidently and gallantly defended, and who, when all was over and no more could be done, gave up without brag or bluster, and made no excuses for their failure.

I cannot help admiring bravery even in a bad cause, and when I went over the works and saw to what a dreadful hammering the Confederates had been subjected, I thought it not without honor for any one to have fought on the other side.

Admiral David Dixon Porter, describing the bearing of the officers of Fort Jackson upon its surrender on 27 April 1862, *Incidents and Anecdotes*, 1885.

EACH MAN must think not only of himself, but think of his buddy fighting beside him. We don't want yellow cowards in this army, to send back to the States after the war and breed more like them. The brave men will breed brave men. One of the bravest men I saw in the African campaign was one of the fellows I saw on top of a telegraph pole in the midst of furious fire while we were plowing towards Tunis. I stopped and asked him what in the hell he was doing there at a time like that. He answered, "Fixing the wire, sir." Isn't it a little unhealthy right now, I asked. "Yes sir, but this God damn wire has got to be fixed."

General George S. Patton, Jr., 1944, speech.

IF WE TAKE the generally accepted definition of bravery as a quality which knows not fear, I have never seen a brave man. All men are frightened. The more intelligent they are, the more they are frightened. The courageous man is the man who forces himself, in spite of his fear, to carry on. Discipline, pride, self-respect, self-confidence, and the love of glory are attributes which will make a man courageous even when he is afraid.

General George S. Patton, Jr., *War As I Knew It*, 1947.

I DO NOT BELIEVE that there is any man who

would not rather be called brave than have any other virtue attributed to him.

　Field Marshal Viscount Slim of Burma, *Courage and Other Broadcasts*, 1957.

MY DEFINITION of bravery is when a person does what he honestly believes is the best thing for him to do at any particular time. So the majority of my life can be linked up with show-off, or daredevil. The bravest man in the world would be the man who acts as he honestly thinks best more particular times than anyone else. Little wonder, then, that so many of the true acts of bravery go unheralded, while the spectacular or daredevil antics are played up.

　Colonel Gregory 'Pappy' Boyington, *Baa Baa Black Sheep*, 1958.

WHEN I was in the navy I served in an office staffed by over a hundred temporary officers of the Royal Navy Voluntary Reserve. As civilians in uniform we found in many instances that the only way to get things done quickly was to short-circuit the system by getting verbal decisions and letting the paper work tag along later. This required senior officers of the regular navy to give verbal decisions involving the expenditure of thousands of pounds without any paper cover. These officers were as brave as lions and would have risked their lives in a destroyer torpedo attack without a second thought, but they balked at risking their jobs on a verbal decision. Now and again we would find some cheerful young commander or captain who did not hesitate, who was as brave in the office as he was at sea. Commenting on such a regular officer and on his way of doing business we would say, "He's a good one. I bet he's got private means." Invariably investigation proved we were right. The officers who were brave in the Admiralty were the officers who had an independent income, who could afford to resign from the navy if necessary without bringing financial disaster to their wives and children. It started as a joke with us to say that brave officers in the office probably had private means, and then it got beyond a joke and turned into an axiom.

　Nevil Shute, *Slide Rule and Other Proceedings*, 1954.

BROTHERHOOD

TEARS welled up as they looked at him, and they appeared not as an army visiting its king but one attending a funeral. The grief was especially intense among those at his bedside. Alexander looked at them and said: "After my death will you find a king who deserves such men?"

　Curtius, of Alexander the Great's farewell to the Macedonians on his deathbed, 323 BC, *The History of Alexander*, 10.5.1, c. AD 45, tr. John Yardley, 1984.

ADAPT YOURSELF to the environment in which your lot has been cast, and show true love to the fellow-mortals with whom destiny has surrounded you.

　Emperor Marcus Aurelius, *Meditations*, 6.39, c. AD 161–180, tr. Staniforth.

IN THE MARINES, recruit training is the genesis of the enduring sense of brotherhood that characterizes the Corps. In that twelve-week period, an almost mystical alchemy occurs. Young adults from diverse areas of the country and backgrounds are immersed in an environment wherein they are able to perceive, understand, and finally accept as dogma the essential Marine Corps virtues.

　New recruits are told, the day they enter recruit training, that "A Marine Believes – in his God, in his Country, in his Corps, in his buddies and in himself." When I commanded the San Diego Recruit Depot in 1960, I had the words painted on a sign at the entrance to the receiving area where the recruits, awaiting processing, had an opportunity to contemplate their meaning. To read those words is easy, but to believe and to follow them is quite a different matter. Nevertheless, the instinct to practice them in fair times and foul is the bedrock of the Marines' brotherhood, and the way that instinct is created in a few short weeks is a wondrous thing.

　Lieutenant-General Victor H. 'The Brute' Krulak, *First to Fight*, 1984.

BUREAUCRACY

THE ANCIENTS had a great advantage over us in that their armies were not trailed by a second army of pen-pushers.

　Napoleon (1769–1852) quoted in Christopher Herold, ed., *The Mind of Napoleon*, 1955.

GENTLEMEN:

　Whilst marching to Portugal to a position which commands the approach to Madrid and the French forces, my officers have been diligently complying with your request which has been sent to H.M. ship from London to Lisbon and then by dispatch rider to our headquarters.

　We have ennumerated our saddles, bridles, tents and tent poles, and all manner of sundry items for which His Majesty's Government holds me accountable. I have dispatched reports on the character, wit, spleen of every officer. Each item and every farthing has been accounted for, with two regrettable exceptions for which I beg you your indulgence.

　Unfortunately, the sum of one shilling and ninepence remains unaccounted for in one infantry battalion's petty cash and there has been a hideous confusion as to the number of jars of raspberry jam issued to one cavalry regiment during a sandstorm in western Spain. This reprehensive carelessness may be related to the pressure of circumstances since we are at war with France, a fact which may come as a bit of surprise to you gentlemen in Whitehall.

This brings me to my present purpose, which is to request elucidation of my instructions from His Majesty's Government, so that I may better understand why I am dragging an army over these barren plains. I construe that perforce it must be one of two alternative duties, as given below. I shall pursue one with the best of my ability but I cannot do both.

1. To train an army of uniformed British clerks in Spain for the benefit of the accountants and copy-boys in London, or perchance,

2. To see to it that the forces of Napoleon are driven out of Spain.

The Duke of Wellington (1769–1852), to the War Office during the Peninsular War (1808–1814) – attributed.

ALTHOUGH a revolutionary government, none was ever so much under the domination of red tape as the one at Richmond. The martinets who controlled it were a good deal like the hero of Moliere's comedy, who complained that his antagonist had wounded him by thrusting in carte, when according to the rule, it should have been in tierce. I cared nothing for the form of a thrust if it brought blood. I did not play with foils.

Colonel John S. Mosby, *Mosby's War Reminiscences*, 1887.

THE BUSINESS of even the most military department . . . is in itself more akin to civil than to military life: but it by no means follows that those departments would be better administered under men of civil habits of thought than by those of military training. The method exists for the result, and an efficient fighting body is not to be attained by weakening the appreciation of military necessities at the very fountainhead.

Rear Admiral Alfred Thayer Mahan, *Naval Administration and Warfare*, 1908.

IT [the bureaucracy] . . . tends to overvalue the orderly routine and observance of the system by which it receives information, transmits orders, checks expenditures, files returns, and in general, keeps with the Service the touch of paper; in short, the organization which has been created for facilitating its own labors.

Rear Admiral Alfred Thayer Mahan, *Naval Administration and Warfare*, 1908.

THIS MAN, with all his charm, sincerity and self-sacrificing hard work, was one of the type who, through a profound sense of duty, coupled with a microscopic vision of the reality of things, spent hours every day blowing blue pencil dust into the military machine, and in consequence nearly brought our part of it to a standstill. To get a new establishment through his office was like playing golf on a course with a hundred bunkers between each green. Every item was scrutinised, criticised and discussed, and then re-scrutinised, re-criticised and re-discussed *ad infinitum*, with the result that delays were never ending. It was bureaucracy in a nightmare.

Major-General J.F.C. Fuller, *Memoirs of an Unconventional Soldier*, 1936.

WHILE giving lip service to the humanitarian values and while making occasional spectacular and extravagant gestures of sentimentality, those whose task it was to shape personnel policy have tended to deal with man power as if it were motor lubricants or sacks of potatoes. They have destroyed the name and tradition of old and honored regiments with the stroke of a pen, for convenience's sake. They have uprooted names and numbers which had identity with a certain soil and moved them willy-nilly to another soil. They have moved men around as if they were pegs and nothing counted but a specialist classification number. They have become fillers-of-holes rather than architects of the human spirit.

Brigadier-General S.L.A. Marshall, *Men Against Fire*, 1947.

WELL, you're apt to get so tied up in administrative processes, in peacetime that you forget exactly what you're in business for. The emphasis is on something else – not on a ruckus which doesn't exist. But when you get out there and start fighting, it is the people who are actually *fighting* who see these things and realize that they are necessary. Then they've still got to prod and slug and struggle, all the way up through the normal bureaucracy which every military organization owns.

General Curtis LeMay, *Mission With LeMay*, 1965.

SEVERAL YEARS in this field have led me to think that the mentality of our military leaders, indeed the mentality of the bulk of both military and civilian mid-level executives in the Pentagon, has become largely that of efficiency-worshiping functionaries. That in itself is a harmless enough state of affairs as long as business-as-usual and riding the bicycle of bureaucratic procedure continues to be the order of the day. But my experience – as a fighter pilot operating from aircraft carriers at sea, observing from first hand the unprecedented battle and intelligence scenes of the Vietnam War, and eight years of prison-camp revelations – impressed me how such mindsets breed disaster when the unexpected occurs, and then it becomes necessary to steer an institution into uncharted waters.

Admiral James Stockdale, 'Educating Leaders', *Washington Quarterly*, Winter 1983.

BUZZWORDS

THERE ARE three things against which the human mind struggles in vain: stupidity, bureaucracy, and catchwords. All three are perhaps alike in as much as they are necessary. I prefer to leave the hopeless fight against stupidity to my more sagacious contemporaries; admit unqualified defeat in my struggle with military bureaucracy; and propose . . . to join battle with a few catchwords in the military sphere at home.

If I admit the necessity for catchwords I mean that they are necessary for all those who are unable to think for themselves. This necessity or utility of catchwords is thus unimpugnably demonstrated, and the following observations have no other object than to stimulate some one or other of my aforesaid contemporaries to think for himself and, whenever a catchword is uttered, to confront him with the question, Is it true?

In my own professional military sphere I make war on catchwords and slogans for the very definite reason that here their effect can and indeed must be deadly, in the literal sense of the word, because human lives are sacrificed to military catchwords – assuredly not from any evil intention, but simply from lack of independent thought.

Colonel-General Hans von Seekt, *Thoughts of a Soldier*, 1930.

C

CALCULATION

NOW the general who wins a battle makes many calculations in his temple ere the battle is fought. The general who loses a battle makes but few calculations beforehand. Thus do many calculations lead to victory, and few calculations to defeat: How much more no calculation at all! It is by attention to this point that I can see who is likely to win.
  Sun Tzu, *The Art of War*, 1, c. 500 BC, tr. Giles, 1910.

THE REASONABLE course of action in any use of arms starts with calculation. Before fighting, first assess the relative sagacity of the military leadership, the relative strength of the enemy, the size of the armies, the lay of the land, and the adequacy of provisions. If you send troops out only after making these calculations, you will never fail to win.
  Liu Ji (1310–1375) *Lessons of War*, quoted in Thomas Cleary, *Mastering the Art of War*, 1989.

WAR is essentially a calculation of probabilities.
  Napoleon (1761–1821).

NOTHING is attained in war except by calculation. During a campaign whatever is not profoundly considered in all its details is without result. Every enterprise should be conducted according to a system; chance alone can never bring success.
  Napoleon, 6 June 1806, letter to his brother Joseph, quoted in, *Correspondance de Napoléon Ier, publiée par ordre de l'Empereur Napoléon III*, III, 1858–1870, p. 163.

MILITARY SCIENCE consists in calculating all the chances accurately in the first place, and then in giving accident exactly, almost mathematically, its place in one's calculations. It is upon this point that one must not deceive oneself, and yet a decimal more or less may change all. Now this apportioning of accident and science cannot get into any head except that of a genius. . . . Accident, hazard, chance, call it what you may, a mystery to ordinary minds, becomes a reality to superior men.
  Napoleon (1769–1821), quoted in Mme. de Rémusat, *Memoirs 1802–08*, 1895, cited in Chandler, *The Campaigns of Napoleon*, 1966.

IN SHORT, absolute, so-called mathematical factors never find a firm basis in military calculations. From the very start there is an interplay of possibilities, probabilities, good luck and bad that weaves its way throughout the length and breadth of the tapestry. In the whole range of human activities, war most closely resembles a game of cards.
  Major-General Carl von Clausewitz, *On War*, 1.1, 1832, tr. Michael Howard and Peter Paret, 1976.

IN SEEKING to upset the enemy's balance, a commander must not lose his own balance. He needs to have the quality which Voltaire described as the keystone of Marlborough's success – "that calm courage in the midst of tumult, that serenity of soul in danger, which the English call a cool head." But to it he must add the quality for which the French have found the most aptly descriptive phrase – "le sens du practicable". The sense of what is possible, and what is not possible – tactically and administratively. The combination of both these two "guarding" qualities might be epitomised as the power of cool calculation. The sands of history are littered with the wrecks of finely conceived plans that capsized for want of ballast.
  Captain Sir Basil Liddell Hart, introduction to Erwin Rommel, *The Rommel Papers*, 1953.

CAMP FOLLOWERS

THE DEMI-BRIGADES, are expressly forbidden to carry with them more women than the laundresses the law provides for. Every woman found with the army and not duly authorized shall be publicly whipped.
  Napoleon, 28 March 1797, at Goritz, quoted in R.M. Johnston, ed., *The Corsican*, 1910.

THE FIELD MARSHAL desires that when the commanding officers . . . send non-commissioned officers or soldiers to England, from the corps under their command respectively, on any account whatever, they will take care that such men do not take with them from this country any woman who is not married to the person with whom she may cohabit. . . . any individual taking a woman over to England, is to have a certificate from his commanding officer that she is his wife.
  The Duke of Wellington, 6 January 1818, at Cambrai, *Selections from the General Orders of Field Marshal the Duke of Wellington During His Various Commands 1799–1818*, Gurwood, ed., 1847.

ONCE BEFORE I had passed an evening in the ADSEC billet at the Hotel Harscamp in Namur while motoring back to Luxembourg from First Army. I recall the name of that hotel clearly. It was dusk and we had stopped in town to inquire of a GI the way to the Harscamp.

"Whores' camp?" At first he looked puzzled but then he brightened with the thought, "say – d'ya mean they really got one here?"

General of the Army Omar N. Bradley, *A Soldier's Story*, 1951.

CANNAE

A COMPLETE battle of Cannae is rarely met in history. For its achievement, a Hannibal is needed on the one side and a Terrentius Varro on the other, both cooperating for the attainment of the great objective.

A Hannibal must possess, if not a superiority in numbers, the knowledge of how to create one. It is desirable for this purpose that the general combine in himself something of a Scharnhorst . . . to weld together a strong army; something of a Moltke to assemble it solely against the principal enemy; of a Frederick the Great or a Napoleon to direct the principal attack against the flank or rear. . . . Lastly there are needed subordinate commanders well trained in their profession and able to comprehend the scheme of maneuver of higher headquarters.

All the desirable qualifications will not be met with or combined in a single person on either side. A few of Hannibal's qualities and some of the means at his disposal have been possessed by other generals in history. Terrentius Varro, on the other hand, has existed during all periods of history.

Field Marshal Alfred Graf von Schlieffen, *Cannae*, 1931.

THE BASIC LAWS of battle remained unchanged since Hannibal's victory over the Consul Terentius Varro at Cannae. A battle of annihilation can still be fought according to the same plan which Hannibal devised many centuries ago. The enemy front should not be the objective of the main attack. Neither the main concentration of force nor the reserve should be used against the enemy front. Only the smashing of the enemy's flanks is essential. Annihilation is complete if the enemy is also attacked from the rear.

Field Marshal Alfred Graf von Schlieffen, *Cannae*, 1931.

ACCORDING to the principle of Cannae a broad battle line goes forth against a narrower, but generally deeper one. The overlapping wings turn against the flanks, the cavalry preceding them, against the rear. Should the flanks be separated from the center, for some reason or other, it is not necessary to assemble them against the latter in order to continue jointly the march for a surrounding attack, as they can immediately advance, by the shorter road, against flank or rear. This was what Moltke called "the junction of separated units on the field of battle" and declares it the hightest achievement of a general. It is also the most effective and, of course, the most risky.

Field Marshal Alfred Graf von Schlieffen, *Cannae*, 1931.

THE BATTLE of Cannae clearly shows that the decisive victory is not the result of a brilliant strategic idea, nor of its effective and skillful execution alone. Victory is also dependent upon the attitude of the enemy commander, who must be caught unawares and ignorant of the true intentions of his opponent until it is no longer possible for him to act on his own initiative. The blow must fall swiftly and unexpectedly; strength must be met by weakness if a battle of annihilation shall materialize. . . . One belligerent must surprise, the other must be surprised. Only when the two commanders play these respective roles will a battle lead to the annihilation of one army.

General Waldemar Erfurth, *Surprise*, tr. Possony, 1943.

THE CAPTAIN

THE REST are nothing once the captain's down!

Homer, *The Odyssey*, 22.266, c. 800 BC, tr. Robert Fagles, 1990.

A BRAVE CAPTAIN is a root, out which as branches the courage of his soldiers doth spring.

Sir Philip Sidney (1554–1586).

A CAPTAIN cannot be too careful of the company the state has committed to his charge. He must pay the greatest attention to the health of his men, their discipline, arms, accoutrements, ammunition, clothes and necessaries.

His first object should be, to gain the love his men, by treating them with every possible kindness and humanity, enquiring into their complaints, and when well founded, feeling them redressed. He should know every man of his company by name and character. He should often visit those who are sick, speak tenderly to them, see that the public provision, whether of medicine or diet, is duly administered, and procure them besides such comforts and conveniences as are in his power. The attachment that arises from this kind of attention to the sick and wounded, is almost inconceivable; it will moreover be the means of preserving the lives of many valuable men.

Major-General Friedrich Baron von Steuben, *Revolutionary War Drill Manual*, 1794.

THE COMPANY is the true unit of discipline, and the captain is the company. A good captain makes a good company, and he should have the power to reward as well as punish. The fact that soldiers would naturally like to have a good fellow for their captain is the best reason why he should be appointed by the colonel, or by some superior authority, instead of being elected by the men.

General of the Army William T. Sherman, *Memoirs of General W.T. Sherman*, II, 1875.

A LOUD-MOUTHED, profane captain who is careless of his personal appearance will have a loud-mouthed, profane, dirty company. Remember what I tell you. Your company will be the reflection of yourself. If you have a rotten company it will be because you are a rotten captain.

Major C.A. Bach, U.S. Army, 1917, farewell instructions to the graduating student officers, Fort Sheridan, Wyoming.

THERE IS no freer man alive than a captain of cavalry in command of his own troop.

General Jonathan M. Wainwright, quoted in Duane Schultz, *Hero of Bataan*, 1981.

THE COMPANY COMMANDER is a living example to every man in his organization. To be an officer means to set an example for the men. The officer must be his soldier's incarnation of soldiery, his model. If the German officer is inspired by this mission, the best and deepest qualities of his soul will be awakened; his life's aim will be fulfilled if he succeeds, through knowledge, demeanor, and conviction, in forcing his troops to follow him. This is the manly purpose for which it is worthwhile to stake life in order to win life.

German Army, Company Commander, quoted in U.S. War Department, *German Military Training*, 17 September 1942.

CAREERISM

A CAREERIST keeps his mouth shut and his shoes shined.

Major Edward R. Neary, 1966, University of Utah ROTC.

A WORD about the virus of hypocrisy. Battles have been lost, opportunities missed, and reputations ruined where subordinates busied themselves telling the commander what they believed he wanted to hear rather than what they knew to be true. The sycophant is one of the great devils of the military world. He has an extraordinary capacity to survive, indeed to prosper – a melancholy condition that is less a product of his own ability to ingratiate himself with his superior than it is a measure of the weakness of the superior himself.

It becomes quickly apparent when a commander would rather hear his own views played back than risk hearing ideas that may in some way be repugnant to him. This egotistic behavior will cause the opportunists immediately to set about making themselves agreeable rather than useful.

Unless they are very lucky, both the flawed commander and the patronizing subordinate are headed for trouble – the former led into poor decisions and the latter put to the guillotine by the first no-nonsense commander he encounters.

Lieutenant-General Victor H. 'The Brute' Krulak, 'A Soldier's Dilemma', *Marine Corps Gazette*, 11/1986.

AN IMPORTANT lesson of the Vietnam War was the lack of continuity of leadership. Most officers served three to six months with a unit and then transferred. Ever since, I have repeatedly stated, "We killed Marines as a result of changing leaders every six months." Because just as a commander got his feet on the ground and began to understand a little bit about the terrain and the enemy, the System moved him. For a very selfish reason: To give more officers exposure to command. That was an absolutely bullshit and immoral reason.

General Walter Boomer, 'Up Front', Al Santoli, ed., *Leading the Way: How Vietnam Veterans Rebuilt the U.S. Military*, 1993.

INHERENT in all this [military service] is the individual's willingness to subordinate personal interests for the good of one's unit, one's service, and one's country. We can ill afford individuals who become "sunshine soldiers" or get focused on careerism. Instead, we need professionals who strive to be the best at their current job and who realize they attain individual advancement through the success of their unit or work center.

Careerism can be most damaging in the case of leaders. If subordinates perceive leaders as self-consumed with career concerns, then they will be unwilling to forgo personal goals for the good of the unit and the Air Force.

General Ronald R. Fogelman, *Airpower Journal*, Fall 1995.

CASUALTIES

MOURN NOT for houses and lands, but for men; men may gain these, but these will not gain men.

Pericles, 432 BC, urging war against Sparta, Thucydides, *The Peloponnesian War*, 1.143, c. 404 BC, tr. Benjamin Jowett, 1881.

QUINTUS FABIUS, upon being urged by his son to seize an advantageous position at the expense of a few men, asked: "Do you want to be one of those few?"

Fabius Maximus (d. 203 BC), quoted in Frontinus, *Stratagems*, 4.6, c. AD 84–96, tr. Charles E. Bennett, 1925.

QUINTILLIUS VARUS, Give me back my legions (*Quintili Vare, legiones redde*).

> Augustus Caesar, AD 9, in despair after the loss of three irreplaceable legions in the Battle of the Teutoberger Wald, quoted in Suetonius, *On the Life of the Caesars*, 23, AD 121.

O MY LORD, I do not marvel at such deaths, nor do they fill me with fear. This is how wars are fought! Remember Huitzilihuitl the Elder, our forebear and king, who died in Colhuacan before we were born; behold how he left behind him eternal glory as a valiant man. The Aztec nation needs bold men such as those who lie before you. This is Mexico-Tenochtitlan, and men who are even more courageous than these will rise here. How long and how deeply must we mourn the deceased? If we stay here weeping we shall not be able to accomplish more important matters.

> Tlacaelel, c. 1450, to his brother, Motecuhzoma I, on the death of two of their brothers in the last campaign of the war to subjugate the Chalcas, quoted in Diego Durán, *The History of the Indies of New Spain*, 1581, tr. Doris Heyden, 1994.

ALL GREAT captains, chieftains, and men of charge have holden for a maxim to preserve by all means possible the lives of their soldiers, and not to employ and hazard them upon every light occasion, and therewithal to esteem the preservation of the lives of a very few of their soldiers before the killing of great numbers of the enemy.

> John Smythe (c. 1580–1631), *Certain Discourses Military*, 1966.

IT IS very difficult to do one's duty. I was considered a barbarian because at the storming of the Praga 7,000 people were killed. Europe says that I am a monster. I myself have read this in the papers, but I would have liked to talk to people about this and ask them: is it not better to finish a war with the death of 7,000 people rather than to drag it on and kill 100,000.

> Field Marshal Prince Aleksandr V. Suvorov (1729–1800), on the Polish deaths in the storming of the fortified Praga suburb in Warsaw, 15 October 1794, during the Polish revolt, quoted in Philip Longworth, *The Art of Victory*, 1966.

WE HAD a great battle yesterday; victory is mine, but my losses are very heavy; the enemy's losses, which were heavier, do not console me. The great distance at which I find myself makes my losses even more accutely felt.

> Napoleon, 9 February 1807, after the Battle of Eylau, quoted in R.M. Johnston, ed., *The Corsican*, 1910.

I COULD LICK those fellows any day, but it would cost me 10,000 men, and, as this is the last army England has got, we must take care of it.

> The Duke of Wellington, October 1810, of the French army led by Marshal Masséna, held at bay in Portugal,

quoted in John Fortescue, *History of the British Army*, VII, 1899–1930.

I ARRIVED here about two this day, and received your letter of the 17th . . . Your loss, by all accounts, has been very large; but I hope that it will not prove so large as was first supposed. You could not be successful in such an action without a large loss, and we must make up our minds to affairs of this kind sometimes, or give up the game.

> The Duke of Wellington, in reply to General Beresford's report on the great losses he had suffered at the Battle of Albuera on 16 May 1811, *The Dispatches of Field Marshal the Duke of Wellington, During His Various Campaigns in India, Denmark, Portugal, Spain, the Low Countries, and France*, VII, 1834–1838, p. 558.

IT IS a familiar experience that the winner's casualties in the course of an engagement show little difference from the loser's. Frequently there is no difference at all, and sometimes even an inverse one. The really crippling losses, those the vanquished does not share with the victor, only start with his retreat. The feeble remnants of badly shaken battalions are cut down by cavalry; exhausted men fall by the wayside; damaged guns and caissons are abandoned, while others are unable to get away quickly enough on poor roads and taken by the enemy's cavalry; small detachments get lost in the night and fall defenseless into the enemy's hands. Thus a victory usually only starts to gather weight after the issue has already been decided. . . .

> Major-General Carl von Clausewitz, *On War*, 4.4, 1832, tr. Michael Howard and Peter Paret, 1976.

THE CONCERNED officer taking advantage of the situation will always seek a means of economizing manpower and thus reducing the number of people exposed to danger.

> Admiral P.S. Nakhimov, during the siege of Sevastopol, 1855, *Dolumenti i Materialy*, 1954.

. . . IT MAY BE SAID that the effort should have been made to test the value of my judgment, or, in other words, that I should encounter what I believed to be certain defeat, so as to prove conclusively that victory was impossible. Considering how sacred is the trust of the lives of the brave men under my command, but willing as I am to shed their blood and my own where duty requires and my judgment dictates that sacrifice will not be in vain, I cannot be a party to a wanton slaughter of my troops for any mere personal gain.

> Major-General George G. Meade, after his decision not to assault the Confederate entrenchments at Mine Run, November 1863, *The War of the Rebellion: A Compilation of the Official Records of the Union and Confederate Armies*, Series I, Vol. XXIX, Part I, p. 18, U.S. Government Printing Office, 1880–1901.

MEN who march, scout, and fight, and suffer all the hardships that fall to the lot of soldiers in the field, in order to do vigorous work must have the best bodily sustenance, and every comfort that can be provided. I knew from practical experience on the frontier that my efforts in this direction would not only be appreciated, but required by personal affection and gratidute; and, further, that such exertions would bring the best results to me. Whenever my authority would permit I saved my command from needless sacrifices and unnecessary toil; therefore, when hard or daring work was to be done I expected the heartiest response, and always got it. Soldiers are averse to seeing their comrades killed without compensating results, and none realize more quickly than they the blundering that often takes place on the field of battle. They want some tangible indemnity for the loss of life, and as victory is an offset the value of which is manifest, it not only makes them content to shed their blood, but also furnishes evidence of capacity in those who commanded them. My regiment had lost very few men since coming under my command, but it seemed, in my eyes of all who belonged to it, that casualties to the enemy and some slight successes for us had repaid every sacrifice, and in consequence I had gained not only their confidence as soldiers but also their esteem and love as men, and to a degree far beyond what I then realized.
> General of the Army Philip H. Sheridan, *Personal Memoirs*, I, 1888.

HIS MAJESTY'S millions conquer the strong foe.
Field battles and siege result in mountains of corpses.

How can I, in shame, face their fathers?
Songs of triumph today, but how many have returned?
> General Maresuki Nogi, 1905, at the surrender of Port Arthur, quoted in Dennis and Peggy Warner, *The Tide at Sunrise*, 1974.

LET THERE BE dismissed at once, as preposterous, the hope that war can be carried on without some one or something being hurt.
> Rear Admiral Alfred Thayer Mahan, *Some Neglected Aspects of War*, 1907.

WAR consumes men; that is its nature. . . . That the large masses which were led into battle would suffer heavy casualties, in spite of all tactical counter-measures, was unfortunately a matter of course.
> General Erich von Ludendorff, *My War Memories, 1914–1918*, 1919.

AFTER ALL, the most distressing and the most expensive thing in war is – to get men killed.
> Major-General J.F.C. Fuller, *Memoirs of an Unconventional Soldier*, 1936.

A BIG butcher's bill is not necessarily evidence of good tactics.
> Field Marshal Viscount Wavell of Cyrenaica, 1940, reply to Churchill when reproached for evacuating British Somaliland with ony 260 casualties.

THERE'S NO more effective way of creating bitter enemies of the Army than by failing to do everything we can possibly do in a time of bereavement, nor is there a more effective way of making friends for the Army than by showing *WE ARE PERSONALLY INTERESTED IN EVERY CASUALTY WHICH OCCURS*.
> General of the Army George C. Marshall, Army Chief of Staff, 1944.

I WAS very careful to send to Mr. Roosevelt every few days a statement of our casualties. I tried to keep before him all the time the casualty results because you get hardened to these things and you have to be very careful to keep them always in the forefront of your mind.
> General of the Army George C. Marshall (1880–1959).

THE SUCCESSFUL soldier wins his battles cheaply so far as his own casualties are concerned, but he must remember that violent attacks, although costly at the time, save lives in the end.
> General George S. Patton, Jr., *War As I Knew It*, 1947.

IN BATTLE, casualties vary directly with the time you are exposed to effective fire. Your own fire reduces the effectiveness and volume of the enemy's fire, while rapidity of attack shortens the time of exposure. A pint of sweat will save a gallon of blood.
> General George S. Patton, Jr., *War As I Knew It*, 1947.

WELL if there was economy of life, it is something for which I will be grateful to the end of my days. When I thought about the number who were killed, nothing could console me except the thought maybe by God's grace and hard effort we had saved some that might otherwise have been slain.
> General of the Army Douglas MacArthur, 11 May 1949, quoted by Douglas Southall Freeman at the US Naval War College.

FAR FROM BEING a handicap to command, compassion is the measure of it. For unless one values the lives of his soldiers and is tormented by their ordeals, he is unfit to command. He is unfit to appraise the cost of an objective in terms of human lives.
To spend lives, knowingly, deliberately – even cruelly – he must steel his mind with the knowledge that to do less would cost only more in the end. For if he becomes tormented by the casualties he must endure, he is in danger of losing sight of his strategic objectives. Where the objective is lost, the war is prolonged and the cost becomes infinitely worse.
> General of the Army Omar Bradley, *A Soldier's Story*, 1951.

I PERSONALLY have experienced the job of writing letters of condolence by the hundreds, by the thousands, to bereaved mothers and wives. That is a very sobering experience.

General of the Army Dwight D. Eisenhower (1890–1969).

AS IN ALL BATTLES the dead and wounded came chiefly from the best and the bravest.

Field Marshal Lord Carver, *El Alamein*, 1962.

YOU FIND YOURSELF encountering considerable tragedy . . . in overcoming a natural grief concerning casualties among the people whom you've led. You possess a natural inborn repugnance against killing people; yet you know you're going to have to do it. It's rough. It used to be particularly vile when I realized that I'd lost someone, and felt that I shouldn't have lost him. That's when it really comes home to you. I lost them because I made a mistake or somebody else made a mistake.

You must wring the greatest possible benefit out of every lesson.

And you must train yourself grimly to adopt a philosophical attitude with regard to those losses. If you're going to fight you're going to have some people killed. But if you have done everything humanly possible to prepare for that mission and plan it properly, and you have observed that it was properly executed, and you have attained the results which you wished to attain – Then you can think, and feel in your heart, "The losses were paid for."

I think every man who has had to nerve himself into the grim responsibility of leading other men in combat will agree to this:

You have to pay a price in warfare,and part of the price is human life.

So, while you don't like to see people killed, if you're going to fight you're going to have those losses. And, if you keep flying under simulated combat conditions and in every sort of weather, you're going to have losses. But if you've done the best you can in the way of preparation, planning, and execution, then you feel that if those people who were sacrificed came up in front of your desk and looked you in the eye, you could look them in the eye and say, "I think it was a good operation."

If you can't imagine yourself doing that, then you ought to start worrying.

While it tortured me to lose people in the ETO and in the Pacific, I think that in most cases I would be willing to meet them, and I would say, "Well, you were properly expended, Gus. It was part of the price."

Can't tell. I might meet them eventually.

General Curtis LeMay, *Mission With LeMay*, 1965.

IT HAS long seemed to me that the hard decisions are not the ones you make in the heat of battle. Far harder to make are those involved in speaking your

mind about some harebrained scheme which proposes to commit troops to action under conditions where failure seems almost certain, and the only results will be the needless sacrifice of priceless lives. When all is said and done, the most precious asset any nation has is its youth, and for a a battle commander ever to condone the unnecessary sacrifice of his men is inexcusable. In any action you must balance the inevitable cost in lives against the objectives you seek to attain. Unless the results to be expected can reasonably justify the estimated loss of life the action involves, then for my part I want none of it.

General Matthew Ridgway, 'Leadership', *Military Review*, 10/1966.

EVERY WAKING and sleeping moment, my nightmare is the fact that I will give an order that will cause countless numbers of human beings to lose their lives. I don't want my troops to die. I don't want my troops to be maimed.

It is an intensely personal, emotional thing for me. . . . Any decision you have to make that involves the loss of human life is nothing you do lightly. I agonize over it.

It's not purely a question of accomplishing the mission. . . . But it's a question of accomplishing the mission with a minimum loss of human life and within an effective time period.

General H. Norman Schwarzkopf, interview in *The Washington Post*, 5 February 1991.

. . . THE QUESTION of casualties. Norman Schwarzkopf and I were very close on this point. He, still haunted by hideous memories of Vietnam, was anxious to keep American casualties to a minimum. I felt the same. Strongly as I supported the international crusade against Saddam Hussein, I did not see that this war was worth a lot of British dead. . . .

General Sir Peter de la Billière, *Storm Command*, 1992.

DESERT STORM left one awful legacy: It imposed the idea that you must be able to fight the wars of the future without suffering losses. The idea of zero-kill as an outcome has been imposed on American generals. But there is no such thing as a clean or risk-free war. You condemn yourself to inactivity if you set that standard.

General Phillippe Morillon, French Commander in Bosnia 1993, in Jim Hoagland, 'Even America Gets the Blues', *The Washington Post*, 14 December 1993.

A SERIOUS ATTACK would have involved risk to pilots and aircraft, and Washington wants to conduct military operations on the cheap, at least politically. During a past interview, [Osma] bin Laden pointed to our precipitate withdrawal from Somalia after we won a street battle and suffered a handful of casualties. He claimed Americans are cowards who retreat as soon as they are bloodied.

He is wrong about our troops, but right about our government.

Lieutenant-Colonel Ralph Peters, 'We Don't Have the Stomach For This Kind of Fight', referring to the cruise missile attacks on terrorists in Afghanistan and Sudan in response to attacks on U.S. embassies, *The Washington Post*, 30 August 1998.

CAVALRY

NOBODY ever lost his life in battle from the bite or kick of a horse; it is the men who do whatever is done in battle. And then we are on a much more solid foundation than cavalrymen, who are up in the air on horseback, and afraid not only of us but of falling off their horses: we, on the other hand, with feet planted on the earth can give much harder blows to those who attack us, and are much more likely to hit what we aim at. There is only one way in which cavalry have an advantage over us, and that is that it is safer for them to run away than it is for us.

Xenophon, *Anabasis*, 3.2, c. 360 BC (*The Persian Expedition*, tr. Rex Warner, 1965); of course, the cavalryman had a much less stable seat before the development of the saddle in the Dark Ages.

I AM also sure that there are young men who can be filled with enthusiasm for serving in the cavalry if one describes the splendour of a cavalryman's life. . . .

Xenophon, *How To Be A Good Cavalry Commander*, c. 360 BC (*Hiero the Tyrant and Other Treatises*, tr. Robin Waterfield, 1997).

. . . PLEASURE is what nearly all cavalry training involves. It is the closest a man can get, as far as I know, to flying, and that is something people long to be able to do.

Xenophon, *How To Be A Good Cavalry Commander*, c. 360 BC (*Hiero the Tyrant and Other Treatises*, tr. Robin Waterfield, 1997).

THOSE WHO FACE the dizzying heights and cross the dangerous defiles, who can shoot at a gallop as if in flight, who are in the vanguard when advancing and in the rearguard when withdrawing, are called cavalry generals.

Zhuge Liang (AD 180–234), *The Way of the General* (*Mastering the Art of War*, tr. Thomas Cleary, 1989).

WHY THEN should it seem wonderful that a firm and compact body of infantry should be able to sustain a cavalry attack, especially since horses are prudent animals and when they are apprehensive of danger cannot easily be brought to rush into it? You should also compare the force that impels them to advance with that which makes them retreat; you will then find that the latter is much more powerful than the former. In the one case, they feel nothing but the prick of a spur, but in the other they see a rank of pikes and other sharp weapons presented to them.

So, you can see from both ancient and modern examples that good infantry will always be able not only to make headway against cavalry but generally to get the better of them. But if you argue that the fury with which the horses are driven to charge an enemy makes them consider a pike no more than a spur, I answer that even though a horse has begun to charge, he will slow down when he draws near the pikes and, when he begins to feel their points, will either stand stock still or wheel off to the right or left. To convince yourself of this, see if you can can ride a horse against a wall; I fancy you will find very few, if any – however spirited they may be – that can be made to do that.

Niccolo Machiavelli, *The Art of War*, 1521.

AS FOR the cavalry attack, I have considered it necessary to make it so fast and in such close formation for more than one reason: (1) so that this large movement will carry the coward along with the brave man; (2) so that the cavalryman will not have time to reflect; (3) so that the power of our big horses and their speed will certainly overthrow whatever tries to resist them; and (4) to deprive the simple cavalryman of any influence in the decision of such a big affair.

Frederick the Great, *Instructions to His Generals*, 1747, tr. Phillips, 1940.

CAVALRY is useful before, during, and after the battle.

Napoleon, *Correspondance de Napoléon Ier, publiée par ordre de l'Empereur Napoléon III*, Vol. XXXI, 1858–1870, p. 426, note 4.

GENERAL LLOYD asks what is the use of large amounts of cavalry. I say that it is impossible to fight anything but a defensive war, based on field fortification and natural obstacles, unless one has practically achieved parity with the enemy cavalry; for if you lose a battle, your army will be lost.

Napoleon, *Correspondance de Napoléon Ier, publiée par ordre de l'Empereur Napoléon III*, XXXI, 1858–1870, p. 428, note 5.

CAVALRY needs audacity and practice; above all it must not be dominated by the spirit of conservatism or avarice.

Napoleon, *Correspondance de Napoléon Ier, publiée par ordre de l'Empereur Napoléon III*, XXXI, 1858–1870, p. 428.

WITHOUT CAVALRY, battles are without result.

Napoleon, *Correspondance de Napoléon Ier, publiée par ordre de l'Empereur Napoléon III*, XXXI, 1858–1870, p. 427.

MAXIM 51. VICTOR or vanquished, it is of the greatest importance to have a body of cavalry in reserve, either to take advantage of victory or to secure a retreat. The most decisive battles lose half their value to the conqueror when the want of cavalry prevents him from following up his success and depriving the enemy of the power of rallying.

> Napoleon, *The Military Maxims of Napoleon*, tr. George D'Aguilar, 1831 (David Chandler, ed., 1987).

MAXIM 86. A cavalry general should be a master of practical science, know the value of seconds, despise life and not trust to chance.

> Napoleon, *The Military Maxims of Napoleon*, tr. Burnod, 1827.

OUR CAVALRY is the most delicate instrument in our whole machine. Well managed, it can perform wonders, and will always be of use, but it is easily put out of order in the field . . . if any serious accident were to happen to a large body . . . while we should be forward in the plains, we are gone, and with us our political system, our allies, &c . . . The General Officer of a brigade or division of cavalry must have eyes and ears about him . . .

> The Duke of Wellington, 16 March 1813, to E. Cooke, quoted in Julian Rathbone, ed., *Wellington's War: His Peninsular Dispatches*, 1984.

USEFUL as cavalry may be against simple bodies of broken, demoralized troops, still opposed to the whole, it becomes again only the auxiliary arm, because the troops in retreat can reemploy fresh reserves to cover their movement, and therefore, at the next trifling obstacle of ground, by combining all arms they can make a stand with success.

> Major-General Carl von Clausewitz, *On War*, 4.12, 1832, tr. Michael Howard and Peter Paret, 1976.

THE PRINCIPAL VALUE of cavalry is derived from its rapidity and mobility. To these characteristics may be added its impetuosity, but we must be careful lest a false application be made of the last.

> Lieutenant-General Antoine Henri Baron de Jomini, *Summary of the Art of War*, 1838, tr. Mendell and Craighill, 1862.

AN ATTACK of cavalry should be sudden, bold, and vigorous. The cavalry which arrives noiselessly but steadily near the enemy, and then, with one loud yell leaps upon him without a note of warning, and giving no time to form or consider anything but the immediate means of flight, pushing him vigorously every step with all the confidence of victory achieved, is the true cavalry; while a body of men equally brave and patriotic, who halt at every picket and reconnoiter until the precious surprise is over, is not cavalry.

> Major-General J.E.B. Stuart, General Order No. 26, Cavalry Tactics, July 30, 1863, *Letters of Major General James E.B. Stuart*, 1990.

TO RENDER cavalry efficient it is necessary that the officers and men should be of a superior order of intelligence, and that they should fully understand the care of their horses, which should be active and enduring. Officers and men should be excellent horsemen, skilful in the use of their weapons, and thoroughly instructed in the work of reconnaissance. It is really much more difficult to form reliable cavalry at short notice than to instruct artillery or infantry.

> Major-General George B. McClellan, *McClellan's Own Story*, 1887.

FROM the very beginning of the war the enemy had shown more wisdom respecting his cavalry than we. Instead of wasting its strength by a policy of disintegration he, at an early day, had organized his mounted force into compact masses, and plainly made it a favorite; and, as usual, he was now husbanding the strength of his horses by keeping them to the rear, so that in the spring he could bring them out in good condition for the impending campaign.

> General of the Army Philip H. Sheridan, upon his taking command of the cavalry corps of the Army of the Potomac at Brandy Station, early April 1864, *Personal Memoirs*, 1888.

I BELIEVE I was the first cavalry commander who discarded the sabre as useless and consigned it to museums for the preservation of antiquities. My men were as little impressed by a body of cavalry charging them with sabres as though they had been armed with cornstalks. . . . I think my command reached the highest point of efficiency as cavalry because they were well armed with two six-shooters and their charges combined the effect of fire and shock.

> Colonel John S. Mosby, *Memoirs*, 1917.

THE CAVALRY is always the aristocratic arm which loses very lightly, even if it risks at all. At least it has the air of risking all, which is something at any rate. It has to have daring and daring is not so common. But the merest infantry engagement in equal numbers costs more than the most brilliant cavalry raid.

> Colonel Charles Ardant du Picq, *Battle Studies*, 1880, tr. Greely, 1957.

THE POSSESSION of a horse furnishes a man in the hour of his greatest danger with the means of saving himself and it cannot be expected of him that he should not avail of it.

> Field Marshal Colmar Baron von der Goltz, *The Nation in Arms*, 1887.

IN ONE RESPECT a cavalry charge is very like ordinary life. So long as you are all right, firmly in your saddle, your horse in hand, and well armed, lots of enemies will give you a wide berth. But as soon as you have lost a stirrup, have a rein cut, have dropped your weapon, are wounded, or your horse is wounded, then is the moment when from all quarters enemies rush upon you.

> Sir Winston S. Churchill, *The River War*, 1899.

STUBBORN and unshaken infantry hardly ever meet stubborn and unshaken cavalry. Either the infantry run away and are cut down in flight, or they keep their heads and destroy nearly all the horsemen by their musketry.

Sir Winston S. Churchill, *The River War*, 1899.

FOR MY PART I maintain it would be as resonable to introduce the elephants of Porus on to a modern battle-field as regiments of lancers and dragoons who are too much imbued with the true cavalry spirit to use fire-arms and too sensible, when it comes to the pinch, to employ their boasted *armes blanche*.

General Sir Ian Hamilton, military attaché's report on the Russo-Japanese War, *Soul of an Army*, 1921.

"NO LONGER like Frederick at the end of the day do we hurl our jingling squadrons upon the tottering foe." No indeed; better not: they might still have one of those machine guns with them which refuses to totter.

General Sir Ian Hamilton, comment in his introduction to General Hans von Seekt, *Thoughts of a Soldier*, 1930.

BUT NOW from the direction of the enemy there came a succession of grisly apparitions; horses spouting blood, struggling on three legs, men staggering on foot, men bleeding from terrible wounds, fish-hook spears stuck right through them, arms and faces cut to pieces, bowels protruding, men gasping, crying, collapsing, expiring. . . . The blood of our leaders cooled. . . . They remembered for the first time that we had carbines.

Sir Winston S. Churchill, of the British cavalry charge with lance and sabre at Omdurman, 1898, *My Early Life*, 1930.

IN WAR only what is simple can succeed. I visited the staff of the Cavalry Corps. What I saw there was not simple.

Field Marshal Paul von Hindenburg, at the 1932 German Army manoeuvres, quoted in Guderian, *Panzer Leader*, 1953.

AS TO the Army, heaven knows that we have suffered enough from what is known in the services and outside as the "cavalry mind." For the past century and more, even to the outbreak of war in 1939, nobody had much chance of promotion to high command in the army unless he was a cavalry soldier, and it is perfectly well known that in order to get cavalry soldiers as far as high command, it was often necessary to excuse them from the more difficult qualifications in the intervening stages of their career. Unfortunately, they were too apt to develop the mentality of the animals they were so enthusiastic about. If some such provision had not been made, the working infantry, sappers, and gunners would generally have reached the higher posts first, but, as it is,

how many of the high commanders of the last 150 years, up to 1939, were cavalry officers? Because of the cavalry influence, and consequently, of this system of making appointments, the idea of using cavalry inevitably persisted for a quarter of a century after the presence of a horse on a battlefield could only be considered a symptom of certifiable lunacy.

Air Marshal Sir Arthur 'Bomber' Harris, *Bomber Offensive*, 1947.

CELERITY

IF YOU have resolved to attack an entrenched enemy, do it at once and do not allow him time to perfect his works.

Frederick the Great, *Instructions to His Generals*, 1747, tr. Phillips, 1940.

PROMPTNESS is the greatest of military virtues, evincing, as it does, zeal, energy and discipline. The success of arms depends more upon celerity than any one thing else.

Lieutenant-General D.H. Hill, 7 September 1863, circular to his troops at Chattanooga.

THE FLAG OFFICER, having heard all the opinions expressed by the different commanders, is of the opinion that whatever is to be done will have to be done quickly, or we shall be again reduced to a blockading squadron, without the means of carrying on the bombardment, as we have nearly expended all the shells and fuses and material for making cartridges.

Admiral David G. Farragut, general order issued before running past the forts guarding the city of New Orleans, April 20, 1862, quoted in Loyall Farragut, *The Life of David Glasgow Farragut*, 1879.

I BELIEVE in celerity. Five minutes may make the difference between victory and defeat.

Admiral David G. Farragut, quoted in Christopher Martin, *Damn the Torpedos!*, 1970.

CENSORSHIP

THE PUBLISHERS have to understand that we're never more than a miscalculation away from war and that there are things we're doing that we just can't talk about.

President John F. Kennedy (1917–1963).

VIETNAM was the first war fought without censorship. Without censorship, things can get terribly confused in the public mind.

General William C. Westmoreland, *A Soldier Reports*, 1976.

I'M NOT ALLOWED to say how many planes joined

the raid but I counted them all out, and I counted them all back.

Brian Hanrahan, 1 May 1982, reporting on BBC TV the British attack on Port Stanley airport during the Falklands War.

CENTRE OF GRAVITY

ONE MUST KEEP the dominant characteristics of both belligerents in mind. Out of these characteristics a certain center of gravity develops, the hub of all power and movement, on which everything depends. That is the point against which all our energies should be directed.

Major-General Carl von Clausewitz, *On War*, 8.4, 1832, tr Michael Howard and Peter Paret, 1976.

FOR ALEXANDER, Gustavus Adolphus, Charles XII, and Frederick the Great, the center of gravity was their army. If the army had been destroyed, they would all have gone down in history as failures. In countries subject to domestic strife, the center of gravity is generally the capital. In small countries that rely on large ones, it is usually the army of their protector. Among alliances, it lies in the community of interest, and in popular uprisings it is the personalities of the leaders and public opinion. It is against these that our energies should be directed. If the enemy is thrown off balance, he must not be given time to recover. Blow after blow must be aimed in the same direction: the victor, in other words, must strike with all his strength and not just against a fraction of the enemy's. Not by taking things the easy way – using superior strength to filch some province, preferring the security of this minor conquest to great success – but by constantly seeking out the center of his power, by daring to win all, will one really defeat the enemy.

Major-General Carl von Clausewitz, *On War*, 8.4, 1832, tr Michael Howard and Peter Paret, 1976.

THEY (the North Vietnamese Politburo) were . . . correct in the selection of a strategic center of gravity. They knew, especially after their battlefield defeat in the Ia Drang, that it could not be the US Army. Neither could it be the Army of the Republic of Vietnam (ARVN) as long as the United States was acting as its protector. They knew they did not have the military means to threaten our homeland or even to seize Saigon, the capital of South Vietnam. Based on their successful experiences against the French the center of gravity that they identified was the alliance between the United States and South Vietnam, and particularly the "community of interest . . . personalities of the leaders and public opinion."

Colonel Harry G. Summers, Jr., *On Strategy: The Vietnam War in Context*, 1981.

HERE'S HOW an offense might look. But there's

one more important thing: the Republican Guard is another center of gravity of Iraq's army. While you're running your phase-one campaign over Iraq . . . I want the Republican Guard bombed the very first day, and I want them bombed every day after that. They're the heart and soul of his army and therefore they will pay the price.

General H. Norman Schwarzkopf, on the planning for the air portion of Desert Storm, *It Doesn't Take a Hero*, 1992.

CHANCE

SO NOW, each of you, turn straight for the enemy, live or die – that is the lovely give and take of war.

Homer, *The Iliad*, 17.261–262, c. 800 BC, tr. Robert Fagles, 1990; Hector, rallying the Trojan allies to help carry off the body of Patrocles, whom he had just slain.

IF IT really was Achilles who reared besides the ships, all the worse for him – if he wants his fill of war. I for one, I'll never run from his grim assault. I'll stand up to the man – see if he drags off glory or I drag it off myself! The god of war is impartial: he hands out death to the man who hands out death.

Homer, *The Iliad*, 18.359–362, c. 800 BC, tr. Robert Fagles, 1990; Hector, rallying the Trojan host after they had been driven back from their attempt at burning the Greek ships by Achilles.

CONSIDER the vast influence of accident in war, before you are engaged in it. As it continues, it generally becomes an affair of chances, chances from which neither of us is exempt, and whose event we must risk in the dark.

Thucydides, *History of the Peloponnesian War*, 1.78, c. 404 BC, tr. Richard Crawley, 1910; speech of the Athenian delegation to the Spartans arguing against war, 432 BC.

THEY DID NOT REFLECT on the common chances of war where such trifling causes as groundless suspicion or sudden panic or superstitious scruples frequently produce great disasters, or when a general's mismanagement or a tribune's mistake is a stumbling block to an army.

Julius Caesar, *The Civil War*, c. 45 BC, (*The Gallic War and Other Writings of Julius Caesar*, tr. Moses Hadas, 1957).

THE FRENCH are what they were in Caesar's time, and as he described them, brave to excess but unstable. . . . As it is impossible for me to make them what they ought to be, I get what I can out of them and try to leave nothing of importance to chance.

Field Marshal Maurice Comte de Saxe, September 1746, letter to Frederick the Great.

IN WAR something must be allowed to chance and

fortune seeing it is, in its nature, hazardous and an option of difficulties.
  Major-General Sir James Wolfe, 5 November 1757, letter to Major Rickson.

THE ART of war lies in calculating odds very closely to begin with, and then in adding exactly, almost mathematically, the factor of chance. Chance will always remain a sealed mystery for average minds.
  Napoleon, 28 December 1796, in Milan, quoted in R.M. Johnston, ed., *The Corsican*, 1910.

THE OUTCOME of the greatest events is always determined by a trifle.
  Napoleon, 7 October 1797, letter to the Minister for Foreign Affairs.

SOMETHING must be left to chance; nothing is sure in a sea fight above all.
  Admiral Viscount Nelson, 9 October 1805, in a memorandum to the fleet off Cadiz before the Battle of Trafalgar.

IT IS now quite clear how greatly the objective nature of war makes it a matter of assessing probabilities. Only one more element is needed to make war a gamble – chance: the very 1st thing that war lacks. No other human activity is so continuously or universally bound up with chance. And through the element of chance, guesswork and luck come to play a great part in war.
  Major-General Carl von Clausewitz, *On War*, 1.1, 1832, tr. Michael Howard and Peter Paret, 1976.

WAR is the realm of chance. No other human activity gives it greater scope: no other has such incessant and varied dealings with this intruder. Chance makes everything more uncertain and interferes with the whole course of events.
  Major-General Carl von Clausewitz, *On War*, 3.3, 1832, tr. Michael Howard and Peter Paret, 1976.

ONE MUST CONSIDER two factors, the first of which is known: one's own will, the other unknown: the will of the opponent. To these must be added factors of another kind, impossible to foresee, such as the weather, sickness, railroad accidents, misunderstandings, mistakes, in short all factors of which man is neither the creator nor master, let them be called luck, fate or providence. War must not, however, be waged arbitrarily or blindly. The laws of chance show that these factors are bound to be as often favorable as unfavorable to one or the other opponent.
  Field Marshal Helmuth Graf von Moltke, cited in Foch, *Principles of War*, 1913.

ALWAYS REMEMBER, however sure you are that you can easily win, there would not be a war if the other man did not think he also had a chance.
  Sir Winston S. Churchill, *My Early Life*, 1930.

PART OF RISK is the ungovernable element of chance. The element of chance is a universal characteristic of war and a continuous source of friction. Chance consists of turns of events that cannot reasonably be foreseen and over which we and our enemy have no control. The uncontrollable potential for chance alone creates psychological friction. We should remember that chance favors neither belligerent exclusively. Consequently, we must view chance not only as a threat but also as an opportunity, which we must be ever ready to exploit.
  General Alfred M. Gray and Major John Schmitt, *Warfighting*, United States Marine Corps, 1989.

CHANGE

THE ESSENCE of the principles of warriors is responding to changes; expertise is a matter of knowing the military. In any action it is imperative to assess the enemy first. If opponents show no change or movement, then wait for them. Take advantage of change to respond accordingly, and you will benefit.
  The rule is "The ability to gain victory by changing and adapting according to opponents is called genius."
  Liu Ji (1311–1375), *Lessons of War*, quoted in Thomas Cleary, *Mastering the Art of War*, 1989.

THERE IS NOTHING more difficult to take in hand, more perilous to conduct, or more uncertain in its success, than to take the lead in the introduction of a new order of things.
  Niccolo Machiavelli, *The Prince*, 1513.

GENTLEMEN: I hear many say, "What need so much ado and great charge in caliver, musket, pike, and corselet? Our ancestors won many battles with bows, black bills, and jacks." But what think you of that? Captain: Sir, then was then, and now is now. The wars are much altered since the fiery weapons first came up.
  Robert Barret, *The Theory and Practice of Modern Wars*, 1598.

TO SAY that the enemy will adopt the same measures is to admit the goodness of them; nevertheless they will probably persist in their errors for some time, and submit to be repeatedly defeated, before they will be reconciled to such a change – so reluctant are all nations to relinquish old customs.
  Field Marshal Maurice Comte de Saxe, *My Reveries*, 1732, tr. Phillips, 1940.

THE STUDENT will observe that changes in tactics have not only taken place after changes in weapons, which reasonably is the case, but that interval between such changes has been unduly long. An improvement of weapons is due to the energy of one or two men, while changes in tactics have to overcome the inertia of a conservative class.
  Rear Admiral Alfred Thayer Mahan (1840–1914).

WE MUST TRY, by correctly foreseeing what is coming, to anticipate developments, and thereby to gain an advantage which our opponents cannot overcome on the field of battle. That is what the future expects us to do.

> General Friedrich von Bernhardi, quoted in Hermann Foertsch, *The Art of Modern Warfare*, 1940.

VICTORY always smiled on one who was able to renew traditional forms of warfare, and not on the one who hopelessly tied himself to those forms.

> General Giulio Douhet (1869–1930).

THUS for a hundred years we find the French knights charging English archers; for another hundred years or so, cavalry charging musketeers and riflemen; and I suppose we shall see for yet another hundred years infantry charging tanks. What for, indeed what for? Not to win a battle, for the impossibility of this is obvious to a rhinoceros. No; but to maintain the luxury of mental indolence in the head of some military alchemist. Thinking to some people is like washing to others. A tramp cannot tolerate a hot bath, and the average general cannot tolerate any change in preconceived ideas; prejudice sticks to his brain like tar to a blanket.

> Major-General J.F.C. Fuller, *The Foundations of the Science of War*, 1926.

PHILOSOPHERS and scientists have shown that adaptation is the secret of existence. History, however, is a catalogue of failures to change in time with the need. And armies, which because of their role should be the most adaptable of institutions, have been the most rigid – to the cost of the causes they upheld. Almost every great soldier of the past has borne witness to this truth. But it needs no such personal testimony, for the facts of history, unhappily, prove it in overwhelming array. No one can in honesty ignore them if he has once examined them. And to refrain from emphasizing them would be a crime against the country. For it amounts to complicity after the event, which is even more culpable when the life of a people, not merely of one person, is concerned. In the latter case there may be some excuse for discreet silence, as your testimony cannot restore the dead person to life. But in the former case there is no such excuse – because the life of a people will again be at stake in the future. (Dec. 1932.)

> Captain Sir Basil Liddell Hart, *Thoughts on War*, 1944.

THE ONLY THING harder than getting a new idea into the military mind is to get an old one out.

> Captain Sir Basil Liddell Hart, *Thoughts on War*, 1944.

IN MILITARY AFFAIRS, especially in contemporary war, one cannot stand in one place; to remain, in military affairs, means to fall behind; and those who fall behind, as is well known, are killed.

> Joseph Stalin (1879–1930), quoted in Garthoff, *Soviet Military Doctrine*, 1953.

THROUGH ALL THIS welter of change, your mission remains fixed, determined, inviolable – it is to win our wars.

> General of the Army Douglas MacArthur, Thayer Award Speech, U.S. Military Academy at West Point, 12 May 1962.

THE HISTORY of wars convincingly testifies . . . to the constant contradiction between the means of attack and defense. The appearance of new means of attack has always inevitably led to the creation of corresponding means of counteraction, and this in the final analysis has led to the development of new methods for conducting engagements, battles, and operations and the war in general.

> Marshal of the Soviet Union Nikolai V. Ogarkov, quoted in *Kommunist* (Moscow), 1978.

CHANGE typifies the modern world. You can either deal with change or it will deal with you.

> General Gordon R. Sullivan, 1 July 1993, speech to the Reserve Officers Association, Nashville, Tennessee.

PERHAPS the most enduring impact that flowed from the battle for Belleau Wood was an attitudinal one – our institutional commitment to change. Belleau Wood, in many ways, constituted a strategic inflection point for the Marine Corps. In the business world, a strategic inflection point occurs when your competition develops a new product or your market changes so that what you produced in the past is no longer desired. At Belleau Wood, the Marine Corps discovered that warfare had changed, and we had failed to adapt to those changes. The 4th Brigade paid the price in blood. Those who survived never forgot that lesson, and they vowed that the Corps would never again be caught unprepared. They became the innovators, risk takers, and visionaries who championed amphibious assault in the 1920s, close air support in the 1930s, and vertical envelopment in the 1950s. They were the architects that built the force-in-readiness that we are the proud stewards of today.

As I walked through the Belleau Wood and the wheatfields that surround it, I tried to distill what lessons the current generation of Marines could glean from the veterans of Belleau Wood. In my mind the most important one is that we can never rest upon our laurels. Yes, we are the world's finest naval air-ground, combined arms fighting force. Without doubt, the Marine Corps performed brilliantly in DESERT STORM. In many ways we are still basking in the warm glow of that victory, much like the Marine veterans of the First World War were tempted to do in the 1920s. But, those veterans knew they must change. They knew that they needed to accept the risks associated with developing new concepts for the ever-changing battlefield. They weathered the failures and the setbacks. They sparred with the naysayers. But, they never rested upon their laurels. As a result, instead of being the victim of a strategic inflection point as they were at Belleau Wood, they caused one in the Second World War.

General Charles C. Krulak, 'The Legacy of Belleau Wood', *Marine Corps Gazette*, 7/1998.

MANKIND is a constant in a changing world. We love the familiar, and find change hard. The conflicts in which our military will engage in the coming years will have many topical causes; at bottom, however, there will be only two: Man's nature, and the effects of change upon him.

Lieutenant-Colonel Ralph Peters, 'Our New Old Enemies', *Parameters*, Summer 1999.

CHAPLAINS

A REGIMENTAL CHAPLAIN came to Puller's tent one night in December.

"Colonel, I want you to get out an order for me."

". . . What's on your mind? Maybe I can give a hand."

"Well, I want you to prohibit all these good Protestant boys from joining the Catholic Church."

"Holy smoke, man, we can't do that. If you fellows would get down to work like the Catholic chaplains, you'd have no trouble."

Lieutenant-General Lewis B. 'Chesty' Puller, December 1943, on New Guinea, commenting on how he could always find Catholic chaplains forward with the fighting men, quoted in Burke Davis, *Marine!*, 1962.

[GENERAL MONTGOMERY insisted that] everyone must be imbued with the burning desire to "kill Germans". "Even the padres – one per weekday and two on Sundays!"

Major-General Sir Francis de Guingand, *Operation Victory*, 1947.

A CHAPLAIN visits our company. In a tired voice, he prays for the strength of our arms and for the souls of the men who are to die. We do not consider his denomination. Helmets come off. Catholics, Jews, and Protestants bow their heads and finger their weapons. It is front-line religion: God and the Garand.

First Lieutenant Audie Murphy, *To Hell and Back*, 1949.

OUR CHAPLAINS were crucial for morale. I used them with our front line troops. Because of this, a senior chaplain criticized me for exposing our chaplain too often to combat. My answer was: He is where the men need him, where there are wounded and dying. When he's back in the chapel, in the rear, none of the soldiers who really need him can get to him. I went so far as to close the chapel to encourage the chaplain to spend most of his time with troops in difficult areas. One of our chaplains in the Brigade was awarded the Medal of Honor, the highest valor award in the military.

Major-General Bernard Loeffke, *From Warrior to Healer*, 1998.

CHARACTER

A MAN should be upright, not kept upright.

Emperor Marcus Aurelius Antoninus, *Meditations*, c. AD 161–180, tr. George Long.

ONE should not associate with people whose conduct is poor. In the *Shih Chi* it says, "If you don't know a man's character, investigate who his friends are."

Takeda Nobushige, *Opinions in 99 Articles*, 1588 (*Ideals of the Samurai*, tr. William Wilson, 1982).

THE SUCCESS of my whole project is founded on the firmness of the conduct of the officer who will command it.

Frederick the Great, *Instructions to His Generals*, 1747, tr. Phillips, 1940.

WAR must be carried on systematically, and to do it you must have men of character activated by principles of honor.

General George Washington (1732–1799).

MY CHARACTER and good name are in my own keeping, Life with disgrace is dreadful. A glorious death is to be envied.

Admiral Viscount Nelson, 10 March 1795, journal entry.

TRUE CHARACTER always pierces through in moments of crisis . . . There are sleepers whose awakening is terrifying.

Napoleon, 8 November 1816, St. Helen, quoted in Emmanuel Las Casas, *Mémorial de St. Hélène*, 1840.

A MILITARY LEADER must possess as much character as intellect. Men who have a great deal of intellect and little character are the least suited; they are like a ship whose masts are out of proportion to the ballast; it is preferable to have much character and little intellect. Those men whose intellect is mediocre and whose character is in proportion are likely to succeed in their profession. The base must equal the height.

Napoleon, dictation at Saint Helena, in Christopher Herold, ed., *The Mind of Napoleon*, 1955.

WE REPEAT again: strength of character does not consist solely in having powerful feelings, but in maintaining one's balance in spite of them. Even with the violence of emotion, judgment and principle must still function like a ship's compass, which records the slightest variations however rough the sea.

Major-General Carl von Clausewitz, *On War*, 1.3, 1832, tr. Michael Howard and Peter Paret, 1976.

A STRONG FAITH in the overriding truth of tested principles is needed; the *vividness* of transient impressions must not make us forget that such truth as they contain is of a lesser stamp. By giving precedence, in case of doubt, to our earlier convictions, by holding to them stubbornly, our actions acquire that quality of steadiness and consistency which is termed strength of character.

Major-General Carl von Clausewitz, *On War*, 1.3, 1832, tr. Michael Howard and Peter Paret, 1976.

YOU MAY BE whatever you resolve to be.

A maxim of Lieutenant-General Thomas J. 'Stonewall' Jackson, originally from Joel Hawes, *Letters to Young Men, on the Formation of Character &c*, 1851.

PRIVATE and public life are subject to the same rules; and truth and manliness are two qualities that will carry you through this world much better than policy, or tact, or expediency, or any other word that was ever devised to conceal or mystify a deviation from a straight line.

General Robert E. Lee, from his post-war writings, quoted in William Jones, *Life and Letters of Robert Edward Lee*, 1906.

HONESTY in its widest sense is always admirable. The trite saying that "Honesty is the best policy" has met with the just criticism that honesty is not policy. This seems to be true. The real honest man is honest from conviction of what is right, not from policy.

General Robert E. Lee, a note found in his desk at Washington College after his death, quoted in A.L. Long, *Memoirs of Robert E. Lee*, 1886.

AN INSURANCE COMPANY offered him a salary of $10,000 to become their president, and sent a distinguished Confederate soldier to secure his acceptance. To his reply that he could not discharge its duties without giving up the presidency of the College, and that he could not do that, the reply was made, "We do not wish you to give up your present position, General, or to discharge any duties in connection with our company. The truth is that we only want your name connected with the company. That would amply compensate us for the salary we offer you." General Lee's face flushed, and his whole manner indicated his displeasure as he replied, "I am sorry, sir, that you are so little acquainted with my character as to suppose that my name is for sale at any price."

General Robert E. Lee, quoted in William Jones, *Life and Letters of Robert Edward Lee*, 1906.

THE LESSON impressed on me as I stand here and my heart and mind traverse your faces, and the years that are gone, is that in a great, momentous struggle like this commemorated here, it is character that tells. I do not mean simply nor chiefly bravery. Many a man has that, who may become surprised or disconcerted at a sudden change in the posture of affairs. What I mean by character is a firm seasoned substance of soul. I mean such qualities or acquirements as intelligence, thoughtfulness, conscientiousness, rightmindedness, patience, fortitude, long-suffering and unconquerable resolve.

Major-General Joshua L. Chamberlain, 'Dedication of the 20th Maine Monument at Gettsyburg, Oct. 3, 1898', Waldoboro, 1891.

WE KNOW NOT of the future, and cannot plan for it much. But we can hold our spirits and our bodies so pure and high, we may cherish such thoughts and such ideals, and dream such dreams of lofty purpose, that we can determine and know what manner of men we will be whenever and wherever the hour strikes, that calls to noble action. . . no man becomes suddenly different from his habit and cherished thought.

Major-General Joshua L. Chamberlain, address at Gettysburg, 3 October 1893, *Dedication to the Twentieth Maine Monuments on the Battlefield of Gettysburg*, 1895.

IT IS NOT the critic who counts, not the man who points out how the strong man stumbled, or where the doer or deeds could have done them better, the credit belongs to the man who is actually in the arena, whose face is marred by dust and sweat and blood; who strives valiantly; who errs and comes short again and again; who knows the great enthusiasms, the great devotions, and spends himself in a worthy cause; who, at the best, knows in the end the triumph of high achievement; and who, at the worst, if he fails, at least fails while daring greatly, so that his place shall never be with those cold and timid souls who know neither victory nor defeat.

President Theodore Roosevelt (1858–1919).

A SOUND BODY is good; a sound mind is better; but a strong and clean character is better than either.

President Theodore Roosevelt, 24 May 1904, address at Groveton College.

BY GREATNESS of character a general gains command over himself, and by goodness of character he gains command over his men, and those two moods of command express the moral side of generalship.

Major-General J.F.C.Fuller, *The Foundations of the Science of War*, 1926

SOME VIRTUE is required which will provide the army with a new ideal, which, through the military elite, will unite the army's divergent tendencies and fructify its talent. This virtue is called character which will constitute the new ferment – character the virtue of hard times.

General Charles de Gaulle, *The Edge of the Sword*, 1932.

WAR is the severest test of spiritual and physical strength. In war, character outweighs intellect. Many stand forth on the field of battle, who in peace would remain unnoticed.

Generals Werner von Fritsch and Ludwig Beck, *Troop Leadership*, 1933, quoted in U.S. War Department, 'What is the test of human character?'

HAPPILY no democracy can be prepared in the German sense for war – we are of course paying in full for this freedom of the mind – but it should and can be prepared to fight evil; a free people is only ready to resist aggression when the Christian virtues flourish, for a man of character in peace is a man of courage in war.

Lord Moran, 12 May 1943, preface to *The Anatomy of Courage*, 1945.

IT IS probably this: that man will know how to be patient in the midst of hard circumstance, and can continue to be personally effective while living through whatever discouragements beset him and his companions.

Brigadier-General S.L.A. Marshall, *The Armed Forces Officer*, 1950.

OF THE MANY personal decisions that life puts upon the military officer, the main one is whether he chooses to swim upstream. If he says yes to that, and means it, all things then begin to fit into place. Then will develop gradually but surely that well-placed inner confidence that is the foundation of military character. From knowing of what to do comes the knowing of how to do, which is likewise important. The preeminent quality that all great commanders have owned in common is a positiveness of manner and of viewpoint, the power to concentrate on means to a given end, to the exclusion of exaggerated fears of the obstacles that lie athwart the course.

Brigadier-General S.L.A. Marshall, *The Armed Forces Officer*, 1950.

HE MUST HAVE 'character', which simply means that he knows what he wants and has the courage and determination to get it. He should have a genuine interest in, and a real knowledge of, humanity, the raw material of his trade; and, most of all, he must have what we call the fighting spirit, the will to win. You all know and recognize it in sport, the man who plays his best when things are going badly, who has the power to come back at you when apparently beaten, and who refuses to acknowledge defeat. There is one other moral quality I would stress the mark of the really great commander as distinguished from the ordinary general. He must have a spirit of adventure, a touch of the gambler in him.

Field Marshal Viscount Wavell of Cyrenaica, *Soldiers and Soldiering*, 1953.

THE AVERAGE general envies the buck private; when things go wrong, the private can blame the general, but the general can blame only himself. The private carries the woes of one man; the general carries the woes of all. He is conscious always of the responsibility on his shoulders, of the relatives of the men entrusted to him, and of their feelings. He must act so that he can face those fathers and mothers without shame or remorse. How can he do this? By constant care, by meticulous thought and preparation, by worry, by insistence on high standards in everything, by reward and punishment, by impartiality, by an example of calm and confidence. It all adds up to character.

Q: If a man has enough character to be a good commander, does he ever doubt himself? He should not. In my case, I doubt myself. Therefore, I am probably not a good commander.

General Joseph Stilwell, quoted in preface to Anton Myrer, *Once an Eagle*, 1968.

INTELLIGENCE, knowledge, and experience are telling prerequisites [for a commander]. Lack of these may, if necessary, be compensated for by good general staff officers. Strength of character and inner fortitude, however, are decisive factors. The confidence of the men in the ranks rests upon a man's strength of character.

Field Marshal Erich von Manstein, *Lost Victories*, 1958.

CHARACTER is the bedrock on which the whole edifice of leadership rests. It is the prime element for which every profession, every corporation, every industry searches in evaluating a member of its organization. With it, the full worth of an individual can be developed. Without it – particularly in the military profession – failure in peace, disaster in war, or, at best, mediocrity in both will result.

General Matthew B. Ridgway, 'Leadership', *Military Review*, 10/1966.

IT HAS BEEN SAID that man's character is the reality of himself. I don't think a man's strength of character ever changes. I remember a long time ago when someone told me that a mountain might be reported to have moved, I could believe or disbelieve it, as I wished, but if anyone told me that a man had changed his character, I should not believe it.

General of the Army Omar N. Bradley, 'Leadership', *Parameters*, Winter 1972.

A MAN of character in peace is a man of courage in war. Character is a habit. The daily choice of right and wrong. It is a moral quality which grows to maturity in peace and is not suddenly developed in war. The conflict between morality and necessity is eternal. But at the end of the day the soldier's moral dilemma is only resolved if he remains true to himself.

General Sir James Glover, 'A Soldier and His Conscience', *Parameters*, 9/1983.

GLIB, cerebral, detached people can get by in positions of authority until the pressure is on. But when the crunch comes, people cling to those they know they can trust – those who are not detached, but involved – those who have consciences, those who can repent, those who do not dodge unpleasantness. Such people can mete out punishment and look their charges in the eye as they do it. In different situations, the leader with the heart, not the bleeding heart, not the soft heart, but the Old Testament heart, the hard heart, comes into his own.

Admiral James Stockdale, 'Educating Leaders', *Washington Quarterly*, Winter 1983.

OF GREAT IMPORTANCE in shaping the character of a young man is both the school, the public organizations, the traditions of the heroic feat and labor which is cultivated in the nation, but still an inestimable role here is played by the family. I am speaking of myself. In the circle of parents and sisters the emotional principles and the core were formed and to which I have kept all of my life.

Admiral of the Fleet of the Soviet Union Sergei S. Gorshkov, quoted in Ablamanov, *Admiral*, 1986.

CHIEF OF STAFF

WHAT ought to be done, I know only too well; what is going to be done, only the gods know.

General Gerhard von Scharnhorst, while Chief of Staff (completely ignored) to the Duke of Brunswick, commander of the Prussian armies destroyed at the Battles of Jean and Auerstadt, 14 October 1806.

THESE REPORTS, as you know, Monsieur le Marechal, are not for my personal benefit; for I am nothing in the army. I receive in the Emperor's name the reports of the marshals and I sign on his behalf, so personally I have no ax to grind. But His Majesty stipulates that detailed reports on everything which occurs are to be sent to me: for better or worse, nothing should be concealed from the Emperor. I require you therefore to be so kind as to keep me advised of all that occurs in your corps, in the same way as the other marshals.

Marshal of France Louis Berthier, Prince de Neuchatel, Prince de Wagram (Napoleon's Chief of Staff), March 1807, to Marshal Soult, quoted in S.J. Watson, *By Command of the Emperor: A Life of Marshal Berthier*, 1957.

IN MY CAMPAIGNS Berthier was always to be found in my carriage. During the journey I used to study the plans of the situation and the reports sent in, sketch out my plans for battle from them, and arrange the necessary moves. Berthier would watch me at work, and at the first stopping-place or rest, whether it was day or night, he made out the orders and arrangements with a method and an exactness that was truly admirable. For this work he was always ready and untiring. That was Berthier's special merit. It was very great and valuable, and no one else could have replaced Berthier.

Napoleon (1769–1821), on his chief of staff, Marshal of France Louis Berthier, quoted in Christopher Herold, ed., *Memoirs of Napoleon*, 1955.

MAXIM 74. To know the country thoroughly; to be able to conduct a reconnaissance with skill; to superintend the transmission of orders promptly; to lay down the most complicated movements intelligibly, but in a few words and with simplicity; these are the leading qualifications which should distinguish an officer selected for the head of the staff.

Napoleon, *The Military Maxims of Napoleon*, tr. George D'Aguilar, 1831 (David Chandler, ed., 1987).

WELL! If I am to become a doctor, you must at least make Gneisenau an apothecary, for we two belong together always. . . . Gneisenau makes the pills which I administer.

Field Marshal Prince Gebhard von Blücher (1742–1819), describing his chief of staff, August von Gneisenau, upon receiving an honorary degree at Oxford after the Napoleonic Wars.

THE BEST MEANS of organizing the command of an army, in default of a general approved by experience, is to: (1) Give the command to a man of tried bravery, bold in the fight and of unshaken firmness in danger. (2) Assign as his chief of staff a man of high ability, of open and faithful character, between whom and the commander there may be perfect harmony. The victor will gain so much glory that he can spare some to the friend who has contributed to his success.

Lieutenant-General Antoine-Henri Baron de Jomini, *Summary of the Art of War*, 1838, tr. Mendell and Craighill, 1862.

I DON'T BELIEVE in a chief of staff at all, and any general commanding an army, corps, or division, that has a staff-officer who professes to know more than his chief, is to be pitied.

General of the Army William T. Sherman, *Memoirs of General W.T. Sherman*, 1875.

IT HAS sometimes been thought that the defects of an army commander, such as inexperience, inadequate training, weakness of character, may be made good by assigning an exceptionally qualified man as chief of staff. Experience, however, has shown that these attempts invariably fail. Why the experiment has been tried so often through history calls for study.

All men have some weak points and the more vigorous and brilliant a person may be, the more strongly these weak points stand out. It is highly desirable, even essential, therefore, for the more influential members of a general's staff not to be too much like the general, or the shadows will be even more distinct. Ideally, the general and his principal assistants should in a sense supplement one another. Such a mutually supplementary relationship, however, produces desirable results only when the general himself is fully qualified for his office in all professional respects. Mutual supplementation is often misinterpreted, however, to mean that a lack of some indispensable quality in the general may be compensated for by some special talents in the chief of staff. This is a dangerous error.

> Archduke Albert of Austria (1817–1895), quoted in Hugo von Freytag-Loringhoven, *The Power of Personality in War*, 1911, tr. Spaulding, 1938.

AS I KNEW from my own experience, the relations between the Chief of Staff and his General, who has the responsibility, are not theoretically laid down in the German Army. The way in which they work together and the degree to which their powers are complementary are much more a matter of personality. The boundaries of their respective powers are therefore not clearly demarcated. If the relations between the General and his Chief of Staff are what they ought to be, these boundaries are easily adjusted by soldierly and personal tact and the qualities of mind on both sides.

I myself have often characterized my relations with General Ludendorff as those of a happy marriage. In such a relationship how can a third party clearly distinguish the merits of the individuals? They are one in thought and action, and often what the one says is only the expression of the wishes and feelings of the other.

> Field Marshal Paul von Hindenburg, *Out of My Life*, 1920.

THE COMMANDER himself takes the responsibility for giving orders and must listen to the advice of one man alone: the Chief of Staff assigned to him. The decision is taken by these two together and when they emerge from their privacy there is one decision and one only. They have reached it together; they two are one. If there was any difference of opinion, then by evening the two parties to this happy matrimonial council no longer know which gave way. The outside world and the history of war learn nothing of any tiff. In this unification of two personalities lies the security of command. It is all the same whether the order is signed by the General Officer Commanding or, according to our old custom, by the Chief of Staff on his behalf. . . . Thus the relation between the two is

built up entirely on confidence; if there is no confidence they should part without delay. A relation of this kind cannot be reduced to rule; it will and must always vary according to situation and personality. Thus it is obvious that the correct combination of personalities is of decisive importance for success.

> Colonel General Hans von Seekt, *Thoughts of a Soldier*, 1930.

IT IS only by the appointment of the right Chief of Staff that a Commander's brilliant talents for leadership can be fully displayed, or that compensation can be found for his weaknesses.

> Colonel-General Hans von Seekt, *Thoughts of a Soldier*, 1930.

THE CHIEF OF STAFF of 48th Panzer Corps was Colonel von Mellenthin, whom I had known from the Chir River days. An extraordinarily happy partnership began with this outstanding staff officer. On the Chir we had already got to understand one another quickly and with few words. Now a brief discussion every morning – often simply a short indication of something on the map – was enough to put the two of us in tune for the whole day.

During years of working together not the slightest ill-feeling ever arose between us, and we also agreed that one should get things down with as little staff work as possible. We never loaded units with unnecessary bits of paper. Whatever could be disposed of verbally – and that meant most things, including operations orders – was done verbally.

We often changed places on visits to the front line, as a staff officer can also only work properly when he maintains the closest contact with the men on the spot and knows the terrain himself.

> General Hermann Balck, November 1943, quoted in F.W. von Mellenthin, *German Generals of World War II*, 1977.

HAVE a good chief of staff.

> Field Marshal Viscount Montgomery of Alamein (1887–1976), advice on the requirements for a general.

BETWEEN the commander and his chief of staff in a division or larger unit there should be thorough mutual respect, understanding, and confidence with no offical secrets between them. Together they form a single dual personality, and the instructions issuing from the chief of staff must have the same weight and authority as those of the commander himself.

But this does not mean that a commander who delegates such authority to his chief of staff can allow his chief to isolate him from the rest of the staff. If that happens, the commander will soon find himself out of touch, and the chief of staff will be running the unit.

> General Matthew B. Ridgway, 'Leadership', *Military Review*, 10/1966

A GOOD Chief of Staff becomes the voice of his commander: he reflects his commander's views, carries out his orders and interprets them in detail. If I had suddenly said to Ian, 'We're going to move the Division to a new location next week,' it would have been his responsibility to interpret that decision in the form of specific orders and to set the whole move in motion. A Chief of Staff has a responsible and demanding job, but also one of considerable influence: he needs to be a man with experience and judgment.

General Sir Peter de la Billière, *Storm Command*, 1992.

CHIVALRY

HIS HELMET flashed as Hector nodded: "Yes, Ajax, Since god has given you power, build and sense and you are the strongest spearman of Achaea, let us break off this dueling to the death, at least for today. We'll fight again tomorrow, until some fatal power decides between our armies, handing victory down to one side or another. . . .

Come, let us give each other gifts, unforgetable gifts, so any man may say, Trojan soldier or Argive, 'First they fought with heart-devouring hatred, then they parted, bound by pacts of friendship.'"
With that he gave him his silver-studded sword, slung in its sheath on a supple, well-cut sword-strap, and Ajax gave his war-belt, glistening purple. So both men parted, Ajax back to Achaea's armies, Hector back to his thronging Trojans – overjoyed to see him still alive, unharmed, striding back, free of the rage and hands of Ajax still unconquered. They escorted him home to Troy – saved, past all
their hopes –
While far across the field the Achaean men-at-arms escorted Ajax, thrilled with victory, back to
Agamemnon.

Homer, *The Iliad*, 7.300, c. 800 BC, tr. Robert Fagles, 1990.

ALEXANDER on the following day entered the tent accompanied by Hephaestion, and that Darius's mother, in doubt, owing to the similarity of their dress, which of the two was the King, prostrated herself before Hephaestion, because he was taller than his companion. Hephaestion stepped back, and one of the Queen's attendants rectified her mistake by pointing to Alexander; the Queen withdrew in profound embarrassment, but Alexander merely remarked that her error was of no account, for Hephaestion, too, was an Alexander – a 'protector of men'.

Arrian, the meeting of Alexander and the mother of Darius whom the Persian had abandoned in his flight after the Battle of Issus, 1 October 333 BC, *The Campaigns of Alexander*, 2.13, c. AD 150, tr. Aubrey de Sélincourt, 1987; in Greek, the name Alexander means 'Protector of Men'.

WHEN HE FIGHTS with his foes in battle, let him not strike with weapons concealed, nor with such as are barbed, poisoned, or the points of which are blazing with fire.

Let him not strike one who in flight has climbed on an eminence, nor a eunuch, nor one who joins the palms in supplication, nor one who flees with flying hair, nor one who sits down, nor one who says 'I am thine;'

Nor one who sleeps, nor one who has lost his coat of mail, nor one who is naked, nor one who is disarmed, nor one who looks on without taking part in the fight, nor one who is fighting with another foe.

Nor one whose weapons are broken, nor one who has been grievously wounded, nor one who is in fear, nor one who has turned to flight; but in all cases let him remember the duty of honourable warriors.

The Laws of Manu, India, c. AD 200.

THE TREATMENT, in general, that we have received from the enemy since our surrender, has been perfectly good and proper. But the kindness and attention that have been shown to us, by the French officers in particular – their delicate sensibility of our situation, their generous and pressing offer of money, both public and private, to any amount – have really gone beyond what I can possibly describe; and will, I hope, make an impression on the breast of every officer, whenever the fortune of war should put any [of] them into our power.

General Marquis Cornwallis, 20 October 1781, letter to Sir Henry Clinton, announcing his surrender at Yorktown, quoted in Henry Lee, *Memoirs of the War in the Southern Department*, 1869.

STRIKE at the enemy with humane treatment as effectively as with weapons.

Field Marshal Prince Aleksandr V. Suvorov (1729–1800), quoted in *Soviet Military Review*, 11/1979.

AS A SOLDIER, preferring loyal and chivalrous warfare to organized assassination if it be necessary to make a choice, I acknowledge that my prejudices are in favour of the good old times when the French and English Guards courteously invited each other to fire first – as at Fontenoy – preferring them to the frightful epoch when priests, women and children throughout Spain plotted the murder of isolated soldiers.

Lieutenant-General Antoine Henri Baron de Jomini, *Summary of the Art of War*, 1838, tr. Mendell and Craighill, 1862.

YOU COULD have seen the strawberries, bouquets, and other nice things the ladies sent me, you would think me pretty well off. The young men of the regiment wonder why it was that I would be the recipient of some much favor – they forgot that rank will tell. These ladies regarded us as knights, their champions. The cavalry had some spirited engagements with the enemy, with glorious results. The ladies of Maryland made a great fuss, begging autographs, etc. We protected and honored these ladies and they showered us with attention and gratitude. I found the most demonstrative joy on the part of most of the ladies. Chivalry has its rewards.

Major-General J.E.B. Stuart, September 1862, during the Antietam campaign, quoted in Mitchell, ed., *The Letters of Major General James E. B. Stuart*, 1990.

OUR SOUTHERN IDEALS of patriotism provided us with the concepts of chivalry. I tried to excell in these virtues, but others provided a truer interpretation of gallant conduct. A devoted champion of the South was one who possessed a heart intrepid, a spirit invincible, a patriotism too lofty to admit a selfish thought and a conscience that scorned to do a mean act. His legacy would be to leave a shining example of heroism and patriotism to those who survive.

Major-General James E.B. Stuart, 3 December 1862, letter to R.H. Chilton, Virginia Historical Society.

THERE WAS more than a little expression of chivalrous feeling. Union troops shared the contents of canteens and haversacks with the prisoners. One Confederate remembered, "Many of them taking off their hats as we went to the rear, and remarking that we had 'done well,' 'No troops could have done more,' and then offering us a part of their rations."

Anonymous Confederate soldier on the treatment of prisoners taken in Pickett's Charge, 3 July 1863, quoted in George R. Stewart, *Pickett's Charge*, 1991.

WE WANT to make our nation entirely one of gentlemen, men who have a strong sense of honour, of chivalry towards others, of playing the game bravely and unselfishly for their side, and to play it with a sense of fair play and happiness for all.

Lieutenant-General Sir Robert Baden-Powell, *Headquarters Gazette*, 1914.

CHIVALRY governed by reason is an asset both in war and in view of its sequel – peace. Sensible chivalry should not be confounded with the quixotism of declining to use a strategical or tactical advantage, of discarding the supreme moral weapon of surprise, of treating war as if it were a match on the tennis court – such quixotism as is typified by the burlesque of Fontenoy, "Gentlemen for France, fire first." This is merely stupid. So also is the traditional tendency to regard the use of a new weapon as "hitting below the belt," regardless of whether it is inhuman or not in comparison with existing weapons. . . .

But chivalry . . . is both rational and far-sighted, for it endows the side which shows it with a sense of superiority, and the side which falls short with a sense of inferiority. The advantage in the moral sphere reacts on the physical.

Captain Sir Basil Liddell Hart, *A Greater Than Napoleon: Scipio Africanus*, 1926.

THE MILITARY CODE which he [the soldier] perpetuates has come down to us from even before the age of knighthood and chivalry. It embraces the highest moral laws and will stand the test of any ethics or philosophies ever promulgated for the uplift of mankind. Its requirements are for the things that are right, and its restraints are from the things that are wrong. Its observance will uplift everyone who comes under its influence.

General of the Army Douglas MacArthur, 11 July 1935, address to veterans of the Rainbow Division (42nd Infantry) quoted in Douglas MacArthur, *A Soldier Speaks*, 1965.

GENERALS think war should be waged like the tourneys of the Middle Ages. I have no use for knights. I need revolutionaries.

Adolf Hitler, to Herman Rauschning, 1940.

LET IT NOT be thought that the age of chivalry belongs to the past.

Sir Winston S. Churchill (1874–1965).

ROMMEL gave me and those who served under my command in the Desert many anxious moments. There could never be any question of relaxing our efforts to destroy him, for if ever there was a general whose sole preoccupation was the destruction of the enemy, it was he. He showed no mercy and expected none. Yet I could never translate my deep detestation of the regime for which he fought into personal hatred of him as an opponent. If I say, now that he is gone, that I salute him as a soldier and a man and deplore the shameful manner of his death, I may be accused of belonging to what Mr. Bevin has called the "trade union of generals." So far as I know, should such a fellowship exist, membership in it implies no more than recognition in an enemy of the qualities one would wish to possess oneself, respect for a brave, able and scrupulous opponent and a desire to see him treated, when beaten, in the way one would have wished to be treated had he been the winner and oneself the loser. This used to be called chivalry: many will now call it nonsense and say that the days when such sentiments could survive a war are past. If they are, then I, for one, am sorry.

Field Marshal Sir Claude Auchinleck, the foreword to Desmond Young, *The Desert Fox*, 1950.

CIRCUMSTANCES

IN CONCLUSION, then, we have done our part by writing down these things just as our predecessors handed them to us, as well as from our own experience, which goes back a long time. It is up to you, now to apply it to the circumstances that are likely to arise. The outcome of war is not brought about according to the will of men but, just as the affairs of each are weighed, by the providence of God on high.

The Emperor Nikephoros II Phokas, *Skirmishing*, c. AD 969, quoted in Dennis, *Three Byzantine Military Treatises*, 1985.

THE CIRCUMSTANCES of war are sensed rather than explained.
Field Marshal Maurice Comte de Saxe (1696–1750).

MAXIM 105. Conditions on the ground should not alone decide the organization for combat, which should be determined from consideration of all attending circumstances.
Napoleon, *The Military Maxims of Napoleon*, 1827, tr. Burnod, 1827.

THIS PLASTICITY of mind cannot be cultivated during war, except by an occasional genius; the generality of soldiers simply cannot change if they are dogma-ridden. The only way to prevent this ossification of mind is to accept nothing as fixed, to realize that the circumstances of war are ever-changing, and that, consequently, organization, administration, strategy and tactics must change also; and if during peace time we cannot change them in fact, we can nevertheless change them in theory, and so be mentally prepared when circumstances require that changes should be made.
Major-General J.F.C. Fuller, *Lectures on F.S.R. III*, 1932.

THE ART of war has no traffic with rules, for the infinitely varied circumstances and conditions of combat never produce exactly the same situation twice. . . .

It follows, then, that the leader who would become a competent tactician must first close his mind to the alluring formulae that well-meaning people offer in the name of victory. To master his difficult art he must learn to cut to the heart of a situation, recognize its decisive elements and base his course of action on these. The ability to do this is not God-given, nor can it be acquired overnight; it is a process of years. He must realize that training in solving problems of all types, long practice in making clear, unequivocal decisions, the habit of concentrating on the question at hand, and an elasticity of mind, are indispensible requisites for the successful practice of the art of war.

The leader who frantically strives to remember what someone else did in some slightly similar situation has already set his feet on a well-traveled road to ruin.

. . . . Every situation encountered in war is likely to be exceptional. The schematic solution will seldom fit. Leaders who think that familiarity with blind rules of thumb will win battles are doomed to disappointment. Those who seek to fight by rote, who memorize an assortment of standard solutions with the idea of applying the most appropriate when confronted by actual combat, walk with disaster. Rather, it is essential that all leaders – from subaltern to commanding general – familiarize themselves with the art of clear, logical thinking. It is more valuable to be able to analyse one battle situation correctly, recognize its decisive elements and devise a simple, workable solution for it, than to memorize all erudition ever written of war.
General of the Army George C. Marshall, ed., *Infantry in Battle*, 1939.

IN ECONOMY as in politics or strategy, there exists, I believe, no absolute truth. There are only circumstances.
General Charles de Gaulle, *Salvation 1944–1946*, 1960.

ONE MUST NOT THINK in absolutes either in military theory or in practical military affairs.
Marshal of the Soviet Union Nikolai V. Ogarkov, *History Teaches Vigilance*, 1985.

CITIZEN SOLDIERS

CEASE to hire your armies. Go yourselves, every man of you, and stand in the ranks and either a victory beyond all victories in its glory awaits you, or falling you shall fall greatly, and worthy of your past.
Demosthenes, *Third Phillipic*, 341 BC; calling upon the Athenians to form citizen armies again rather than rely upon mercenaries to face the great danger posed by Philip of Macedon.

AFTER they have elected the consuls, they proceed to appoint military tribunes; fourteen are drawn from those who have seen five years' service and ten from those who have seen ten. As for the rest, a cavalryman is required to complete ten years' service and an infantryman sixteen before he reaches the age of forty-six, except for those rated at less than 400 drachmae worth of property who are assigned to naval service. In periods of national emergency the infantry are called upon to serve for twenty years and no one is permitted to hold any political office until he has completed ten years' service.
Polybius, *Histories*, 6.19, c. 125 BC (*The Rise of the Roman Empire*, tr. Ian Scott-Kilvert, 1987).

WHEN we assumed the Soldier, we did not lay aside the citizen; and we shall most sincerely rejoice with you in that happy hour when the establishment of American liberty, upon the most firm and solid foundations, shall enable us to return to our Private Stations in the bosom of a free, peaceful and happy Country.
General George Washington, 26 June 1775, address to the New York legislature, *Writings*, III, 1931, p. 305.

WHEN MEN are irritated and their passions inflamed, they fly hastily and cheerfully to arms: but, after the first emotions are over . . . a soldier reasoned with upon the goodeness of the cause he is engaged in and the inestimable rights he is contending for, hears you with patience and acknowledges the truth of our observations, but adds that it is of no more importance to him than others. The officer makes you the same reply, with this further remark, that his pay will not support him, and he cannot ruin himself and his family to serve his country, when every member of the community is equally interested and benefited by his labors.
General George Washington, *Writings*, VI, 1932.

REMEMBER, soldiers, that first and foremost you are citizens. Let us not become a greater scourge to our country than the enemy themselves.

   General Lazare Carnot, 1792, address to the *Armée du Nord*.

THE INDIVIDUAL who refuses to defend his rights when called by his government, deserves to be a slave, and must be punished as an enemy of his country and friend to his foe.

   Major-General Andrew Jackson, proclamation to the people of Louisiana upon the British invasion, 21 September 1814.

THESE MEN are not an army; they are citizens defending their country.

   General Robert E. Lee, 15 May 1864, to Lieutenant-General A.P. Hill, referring to the Army of Northern Virginia.

CIRCUMSTANCES would, of course vary the character of these lines, and in special cases the engineer would plan particular works. . . . the intelligence of the soldiers was such that their eye for a position was often as quick and keen as that of any of their officers. Foreign officers, visiting the army, often expressed their amazement at seeing the troops of the line doing instantly and without engineering assistance what was elsewhere done by a corps of sappers under direction of the scientific staff.

   Major-General Jacob D. Cox, of the natural talent and initiative found among the Union's citizen soldiers, *Atlanta*, 1882.

THE ARMIES of Europe are machines: the men are brave and the officers capable; but the majority of the soldiers in most of the nations of Europe are taken from a class of people who are not very intelligent and who have very little interest in the contest in which they are called upon to take part. Our armies were composed of men who were able to read, men who knew what they were fighting for, and could not be induced to serve as soldiers, except in an emergency when the safety of the nation was involved, and so necessarily must have been more than equal to men who fought merely because they were brave and because they were thoroughly drilled and inured to hardships.

   General Ulysses S. Grant, *Personal Memoirs*, I, 1885.

SHERMAN'S ARMY, after all the deletions, numbered about sixty thousand effective men. All weak men had been left to hold the rear, and those remaining were not only well men, but strong and hardy, so that he had sixty thousand as good soldiers as ever trod the earth; better than any European soldiers, because they not only worked like a machine but the machine thought. European armies know very little what they are fighting for, and care less.

   General Ulysses S. Grant, of Sherman's army as it

prepared to march north from Savannah, early October 1864, *Personal Memoirs*, II, 1885.

MONTGOMERY understood this "civilian army" as few before him. The rigid old type discipline was not enforced. Human weaknesses were fully appreciated, and the man's lot made as easy for him as possible. This is why he was so lenient as regards dress, and why a certain amount of "personal commandeering" – technically I suppose it might be called "looting" – was winked at. Even when on occasions a unit did not behave in battle as well as it might have done, Montgomery gave them a chance to put things right. All in all he realized that the Prussian type of discipline was not suited to the "civilian" soldier of the Empire.

   Major-General Sir Francis de Guingand, *Operation Victory*, 1947.

PEOPLE KNOW what they should do and they have the courage and confidence in each other to do it. . . . They will do anything even though they feel that life and society have dumped all over them; they can still drive on and fight like demons, march like Jackson, and soldier like the very dickens when they have to. . . it fills me with inspiration. They are truly the great people of this war. . . the forgotten civilians who will probably never receive their due for their valor on the fields of battle.

   Major Alexander Hottell, 1969 journal entry during the Vietnam War, quoted in John F. Murray, *Fallen Warriors*, 1996.

CIVIL AFFAIRS

WHEN ENTERING the territory of an offender do no violence to the shrines of the deities. Do not hunt over the rice fields or damage the earth-works. Do not burn houses or cut down trees. Do not seize domestic animals or grain or agricultural implements. Where you find old people or children allow them to go home unharmed, and do not antagonize even able-bodied men if they do not challenge you. And see that the enemy wounded have medical treatment.

   Ssu Ma Jang Chu, *The Precepts of Ssu Ma Jang Chu*, c. 500 BC, quoted in A.L. Sadler, *Three Military Classics of China*, 1944.

BUT OF ALL the methods that can be taken to gain the hearts of a people, none contribute so much as remarkable examples of continence and justice; such was the example of Scipio in Spain when he returned a most beautiful young lady, safe and untouched, to her father and husband; this was a circumstance which was more conducive to the reduction of Spain than any force of arms could have ever been. Caesar acquired such reputation for his justice in paying for the wood which he cut down to make palisades for his camps in Gaul, that it greatly facilitated the conquest of that province.

Niccolo Machiavelli, *The Art of War*, 1521.

SET OFF with all diligence. Give orders for this affair. You shall be answerable to me for it. What! If they ruin my people, who will feed me? Who will support the expenses of the state? Who will pay you your pensions, gentlemen? As God's alive, to take from my people is taking from myself.

Henry IV (Henry of Navarre) (1553–1610), King of France, upon ordering the investigation of pillage by his troops.

IT IS EVIDENT that a taste for plunder has up until now been one of the principal attractions that has caused many to choose the soldier's trade and that in the present time debauchery and plunder have on occasion taken the place of pay for very many of the troops. A wise prince may tolerate it, although for the apparent good that it seems to accomplish, it causes an infinite number of great evils. All writers on political subjects are agreed that if there is one area where severity is absolutely necessary for a sovereign, it is with regard to his soldiers. The oppression that people suffer from them is so evident that there is no need to embark on a long discourse to convince you of it, or to show how the sovereign suffers indirect losses from it through a reduction in his revenues. . . . Being by honor bound to secure their states from the violence of foreigners, they should be even more eager to protect them from pillage by their own troops. And you must not delude yourself, in weighing the interests of the peasant and the soldier, as many others do, that those men who have enlisted in your troops should mean that much more to you than the rest of the subjects, or that it is to your interests to favor them more than the others.

Louis XIV, *Mémoires de Louis XIV*, 1860, quoted in David Ralston, *Soldiers and States*, 1966.

IF YOU CAN WIN over the whole country so much the better. At least organize your partisans. The friendship of the neutral country is gained by requiring the soldiers to observe good discipline and by picturing your enemies as barbarous and badly intentioned; if they are Catholic, do not speak about religion; if they are Protestant, make the people believe that a false ardor for religion attaches you to them. . . .

Frederick the Great, *Instructions to His Generals*, 1747, tr. Phillips, 1940.

FRIENDS, I promise you this conquest; but there is one condition you must swear to fulfill – to respect the people whom you liberate, to repress the horrible pillaging committed by scoundrels incited by our enemies. Otherwise you would not be the liberators of the people; you would be their scourge; . . . Plunderers will be shot without mercy; already, several have been . . .

Napoleon, 27 March 1796, at Nice.

WE COME to give you liberty and equality, but don't lose your heads about it – the first person who stirs without permission will be shot.

Marshal Pierre-Francois Lefebvre, upon occupying a Franconian town earlier in his career, quoted in David Chandler, *The Campaigns of Napoleon*, 1966.

PLEASE GIVE positive orders that all the Arabic type we have be packed immediately, and that citoyen Langlès take charge of it. I also beg you to give orders that the Greek type be packed: I know we have some, as Xenophon is being printed; and it won't matter so very much if Xenophon is held up for three months.

Napoleon, 26 March 1798, to the Minister of the Interior, quoted in R.M. Johnston, ed., *The Corsican*, 1910.

IT DEPENDS on justice, freedom from corruption, and unswerving truth to one's word and to every obligation one has undertaken.

The Duke of Wellington, 1798, defining the bases on which British rule in India would be maintained, cited in Arthur Bryant, *The Great Duke*, 1972.

THE ROMAN LEGIONS protected all religions. You will find here customs different from those in Europe. You must accommodate yourselves to them. The people amongst whom we are to mix differ from us in the treatment of women; but in all countries he who violates is a monster. Pillage enriches only a small number of men; it dishonours us; it destroys our resources; it converts into enemies the people whom it is our interest to have for friends.

Napoleon, 22 June 1798, proclamation to the troops, aboard the *Orient* on the voyage to Egypt, quoted in Louis de Bourrienne, *Memoirs of Napoleon Bonaparte*, I, 1855.

I WOULD SACRIFICE Gwalior, or every frontier of India, ten times over, in order to preserve our credit for scrupulous good faith, and the advantages and honor we gained by the late war and the peace; and we must not fritter them away in arguments, drawn from over-strained principles of the laws of nations, which are not understood in this country. What brought me through many difficulties in the war, and the negotiations for peace? The British good faith, and nothing else.

The Duke of Wellington, 1804, *The Dispatches of Field Marshal the Duke of Wellington, During His Various Campaigns in India, Denmark, Portugal, Spain, the Low Countries, and France*, III, 1834–1838.

THE PEOPLE of Portugal deserve well of the army; they have in every instance treated the soldiers well; and there never was an army so well supplied, or which had so little excuse for plunder, if any excuse can in any case exist. But if the Commander of the Forces should not by these and other measures be enabled to get the better of these practices, he is determined to report to His Majesty, and send into garrison those corps who shall continue them; as he prefers a small but disciplined and well ordered body of troops to a rabble, however numerous; and he is resolved not to be the instrument of inflicting upon the people of this country the miseries which result from the operations of such a body.

The Duke of Wellington, 26 May 1809, at Ovea in Portugal, *Selections from the General Orders of Field Marshal the Duke of Wellington During His Various Commands 1799–1818*, Gurwood, ed., 1847.

OUR SUCCESS and everything depends upon our moderation and justice and upon the good discipline of the troops. I despair of the Spaniards. They are in so miserable a state that it is really hardly fair to expect that they will refrain from plundering a beautiful country into which they enter as conquerors, particularly adverting to the miseries which their own country has suffered from its invaders. Without any pay and food, they must plunder, and if they plunder, they will ruin us.

The Duke of Wellington, early 1814 during the invasion of southern France when he was trying to win the good will of the French population, quoted in Arthur Bryant, *The Great Duke*, 1972.

MAXIM 70. The conduct of a general in a conquered country is full of difficulties. If severe, he irritates and increases the number of his enemies. If lenient, he gives birth to expectations which only render the abuses and vexations inseparable from war the more intolerable. A victorious general must know how to employ severity, justice, and mildness by turns, if he would allay sedition, or prevent it.

Napoleon, *Military Maxims of Napoleon*, tr. George D'Aguilar, 1831 (David Chandler, ed., 1987).

WE HAVE already arrived at the place of our destiny, and now courage must finish the labor of constancy. Remember that your great duty is to console America and that you are not here to make conquests but to liberate peoples. The Peruvians are your brothers. Embrace them and respect their rights, as you respected those of the Chileans after Chacabuco.

General Jose de San Martin, 1820, address to his army, quoted in Ricardo Rojas, *San Martin*, 1957.

ALTHOUGH I have served in my profession in several countries, and among foreigners, some of whom professed various forms of the Christian religion, while others did not profess it at all; I never was in one in which it was not the bounden duty of the soldier to pay proper deference and respect to whatever happened to be the religious institutions or ceremonies of the place.

The Duke of Wellington, 8 April 1829, speech to the House of Lords.

IMPRESS upon the men the importance of going through the State in an orderly manner, abstaining from taking anything not absolutely necessary for their subsistence whilst traveling. They should try to create as favorable an impression as possible upon the people and advise them if it will do any good, to make efforts to have law and order established within the Union.

General Ulysses S. Grant, letter to Major-General Sherman, Vicksburg, 6 August 1863, *Papers of USG*, IX, 1982.

THE VIETNAMESE fighter has always taken care to observe point 9 of its Oath of Honour:
"In contacts with the people, to follow these three recommendations:
– To respect the people
– To help the people
– To defend the people . . . in order to win their confidence and affection and achieve a perfect understanding between the people and the army."

General Vo Nguyen Giap, *People's War – People's Army*, 1961.

CIVILIAN CONTROL OF THE MILITARY

PRESBYTERIAN cleric: "'Tis against the will of the nation: there will be nine in ten against you."
Cromwell: "But what if I should disarm the nine, and put a sword in the tenth man's hand?"

Oliver Cromwell, shortly after dissolving Parliament in 1649.

IT MAY BE PROPER constantly and strongly to impress upon the Army that they are mere agents of Civil power: that out of Camp, they have no other authority than other citizens, that offences against the laws are to be examined, not by a military officer, but by a Magistrate; that they are not exempt from arrests and indictments for violations of the law.

General George Washington, 27 March 1795, letter to Daniel Morgan, *Writings*, XXXIV, 1940, p. 160.

IT IS MELANCHOLY to be obliged to act against one's countrymen. I hope sincerely it will never be our case; but, as soldiers, we engaged not only to fight the foreigner; but also to support the Government and laws, which have long been in use and framed by wiser men than we.

General Sir John Moore, 1798, address to his Irish troops in Cork.

SO LONG as I hold a commission in the Army I have no views of my own to carry out. Whatever may be the orders of my superiors, and law, I will execute. No man can be efficient as a commander who sets his own notions above the law and those whom he is sworn to obey. When Congress enacts anything too odious for me to execute I will resign.

General Ulysses S. Grant, 22 March 1862, letter to Congressman Elihu B. Washburne, *Personal Memoirs and Selected Letters*, 1990.

NOTHING – but it made me think of the man whose horse kicked up and stuck his foot through the stirrup. He said to the horse, "If you are going to get on I will get off."

> Abraham Lincoln, reply to Governor Andrew when asked what he would say to General McClellan's advice on how to carry on the affairs of the nation, quoted in Carl Sandburg, *Abraham Lincoln*, 1925.

I HAVE HEARD in such a way as to believe it, of your recently saying that both the army and the government needed a dictator. . . . Only those generals who gain successes can set up dictators. What I ask you now is military success, and I will risk the dictatorship.

> President Abraham Lincoln, 26 January 1863, letter to Major-General Joseph Hooker.

I CANNOT SAY to the public I approve this and I disapprove that. I have no right to say this, as it might embarrass the execution of measure fully decided on. It is my duty to strengthen the hands of the President as Commander-in-Chief, not to weaken them by factious opposition.

> Major-General Henry W. Halleck (1815–1872), to General Sherman, *The War of the Rebellion: A Compilation of the Official Records of the Union and Confederate Armies*, Vol. XXIV, Part 3, p. 498, U.S. Government Printing Office, 1880–1901.

THERE IS one thing more I will say in favor of these two officers [Sherman and McPherson]. They may be relied upon for an honest and faithful performance of their duties regardless of what may be their private views of the policy pursued. Neither will they ever discourage, by word or deed, others from a faithful performance of their duties. In a word they are not men to discuss policy whilst their country requires their services.

> General Ulysses S. Grant, 18 January 1864, letter to Senator H. Wilson, Chairman of the Military Committee of the U.S. Senate, encouraging him to support the confirmation of Sherman and McPherson as brigadier-generals in the Regular Army, quoted in *Papers of USG*, X, 1982.

IT IS ALWAYS dangerous for soldiers, sailors or armies to play at politics.

> Sir Winston S. Churchill (1874–1965).

IF THERE IS one basic element in our Constitution, it is civilian control of the military.

> President Harry S. Truman, *Memoirs*, 1955.

ONCE WAR had come, however, the die was cast, I was quite clear in my own mind that for me, as a member of the Armed Forces, there was only one possible course – to fight against our external enemies. The stronger the moral determination of the forces under my command, the greater would be their fighting value. It is the moral obligation of every fighting man unreservedly to support the government of his country when it goes to war. To expect a commander to accept the heavy responsibilities which devolve upon him in war and at the same time to bother his head about internal conditions, let alone to enter upon a struggle against the political leadership of his own country, is asking altogether too much of him.

> Admiral Karl Dönitz, *Memoirs, Ten Years and Twenty Days*, 1959.

MILITARY SUBSERVIENCE to political control applies to existing policy, not to policy debates. The political process requires the unfettered opinions of military leaders, and military leaders who lack the courage to offer such opinions are just as accountable to their people as the politicians who have secured their silence.

> James H. Webb, Jr., 'The Silence of the Admirals', *Proceedings*, 1/1999.

CIVIL–MILITARY RELATIONS

"SO NOW they are openly recalling me," he said, "for years they have tried covertly to force my return by refusing me any money and reinforcements. The Roman people did not conquer Hannibal; many times their armies were decimated and put to rout. It is the senate of Carthage which has defeated me, through hatred and jealousy."

> Hannibal, 203 BC, upon his recall from Italy to defend Carthage from a Roman landing in Africa, quoted in Livy, *Annals of the Roman People*, c. 25 BC–AD 17 (Livy: *A History of Rome*, 30, tr. Moses Hadas and Joe Poe, 1962).

THE ADVANCE and retirement of the army can be controlled by the general in accordance with prevailing circumstances. No evil is greater than commands of the sovereign from the court.

> Chia Lin, Tang Dynasty, AD 618–905.

. . . . THAT A GENERAL during the campaign need not follow court orders is sound military law.

> Emperor Kublai Khan (1215–1294).

A GENERAL to whom the sovereign has entrusted his troops should act on his own initiative. The confidence which the sovereign reposes in the general's ability is authorization enough to conduct affairs in his own way.

> Frederick the Great, *General Principles of War*, 1748.

WHERE the state is weak, the army rules.

> Napoleon, 9 January 1808, remark.

MAJOR BRISCOE, I am but the nominal commander. The President and Secretary of State have interfered with my intended operations, and I fear for the success of the day.

> General William H. Winder, 24 August 1814,

Commander of the American forces at the Battle of Bladensburg, quoted in *Military Review*, 4/1981.

TO LEAVE a great military enterprise or the plan for one to purely military judgment and decision is a distinction which cannot be allowed, and is even prejudicial; indeed, it is an irrational proceeding to consult professional soldiers on the plan of a war, that they may give a purely military opinion upon what the cabinet ought to do . . .
Major-General Carl von Clausewitz, *On War*, 1832, tr. Graham, 1918.

IF IN ordinary times, under the restrictions of constitutional forms, governments subjected to all the changes of an elective legislature are less suitable than others for the creation or preparation of a formidable military power, nevertheless in great crises these deliberative bodies have sometimes attained very different results and have concurred in developing the national strength to the fullest.
Lieutenant-General Antoine-Henri Baron de Jomini, *Summary of the Art of War*, 1838, tr. Mendell and Craighill, 1862.

THE ACTION of a cabinet in reference to the control of armies influences the boldness of their operations. A general whose genius and hands are tied by an Aulic council five hundred miles distant cannot be a match for one who has liberty of action, other things being equal.
Lieutenant-General Antoine-Henri Baron de Jomini, *Summary of the Art of War*, 1838, tr. Mendell and Craighill, 1862.

NO MAN is warranted in feeling pride in the deeds of the Army and Navy of the past if he does not back up the Army and Navy of the present.
President Theodore Roosevelt, 15 October 1903, speech at the dedication of the monument to General William Tecumseh Sherman in Washington.

IN SEEKING to trace all the great mistakes and blunders committed during the Civil War to defects in our military system, it is important to bear in mind the respective duties and responsibilities of soldiers and statesmen. The latter are responsible for the creation and organization of our resources, and, as in the case of the President, may further be responsible for their management or mismanagement. Soldiers, while they should suggest and be consulted on all details of organization under our system, can alone be held responsible for the control and direction of our armies in the field.
So long as historians insist upon making our commanders alone responsible for disasters in time of war, so long will the people and their representatives fail to recognize the importance of improving our system.
Colonel Emory Upton, *The Military Policy of the United States Since 1775*, 1904.

A POPULAR OUTCRY will drown the voice of military experience.
Rear Admiral Alfred Thayer Mahan, *Naval Strategy*, 1911.

THESE MEN are at this moment fighting in the hardest battle of the war, fighting it with heroism which I can find no phrase worthy to express. And it is we who for a mistake made in such and such a place, or which may not even have been made, demand explanations, on the field of battle of a man worn with fatigue. It is of this man that we demand to know whether on such and such a day he did such and such a thing! Drive me from this place if that is what you ask, for I will not do it.
Georges Clemenceau, speech in the Chamber of Deputies, Paris, 4 June 1918, at the height of the last great German offensive of WWI, quoted in Lewis Copeland, ed., *The World's Great Speeches*, 1952.

THERE IS a certain book, "Vom Kriege," which never grows old. Its author is Clausewitz. He knew war, and he knew men. We had to listen to him, and whenever we followed him it was to victory. To do otherwise meant disaster. He gave a warning about the encroachment of politics on the conduct of military operations. In saying this, I am far from passing a judgment upon the orders we now received. I may have criticized in thought and word in 1914, but to-day I have completed my education in the rough school of reality, the conduct of operations in a coalition war. Experience tempers criticism, indeed frequently reveals how unfounded it has been. During the war we have times without number attempted to think: "He is a lucky man who has an easier soldier's conscience than ours, and who has won the battle between his military convictions and the demands of politics as easily as we have." The political tune is a ghastly tune! I myself during the war seldom heard in that tune those harmonies which would have struck an echo in a soldier's heart. Let us hope that if ever our Fatherland's dire necessity involves a summons to arms again, others will be more fortunate in this respect than we were!
Field Marshal Paul von Hindenburg, *Out of My Life*, 1920.

A MATTER of more immediate importance is that the nation should realize the necessity for having educated leaders – trained statesmen – to conduct its war business, if and when war should again come along. This is a direction in which much-needed preparation can be made without the expenditure of cash, and it may be the means of saving tens of thousands of lives and hundreds of millions of money. In all trades and professions the man who aims at taking the lead knows that he must first learn the business he proposes to follow: that he must be systematically trained in it. Only in the business of war – the most difficult of

all – is no special training or study demanded from those charged with, and paid for, its management.
Field Marshal Sir William Robertson, *From Private to Field-Marshal*, 1921.

THE REAL headquarters of Armies in these days are not to be found in the field abroad, but at the seat of government at home; and plans of campaigns are, and must be, now analyzed and criticised by civilian Ministers in a way quite unknown a few decades ago. The military chief must be prepared to expound and justify, lucidly and patiently, the plans for which he seeks ministerial sanction, and he must also be prepared to explain and substantiate his objections to such alternative plans as Ministers themselves may suggest.
Field Marshal Sir William Robertson, *From Private to Field-Marshal*, 1921.

ALL THE reproaches that have been levelled against the leaders of the armed forces by their countrymen and by the international courts have failed to take into consideration one very simple fact: that policy is not laid down by soldiers, but by politicians. This has always been the case and is so today. When war starts, the soldiers can only act according to the political and military situation as it then exists. Unfortunately it is not the habit of politicians to appear in conspicuous places when the bullets begin to fly. They prefer to remain in some safe retreat and to let the soldiers carry out "the continuation of policy by other means."
Colonel-General Heinz Guderian, *Panzer Leader*, 1953.

WHILE political goals shape war and influence it from one moment to the next, it is the soldier's duty to insure that he will not be confronted with insoluble tasks by his political leaders (as happened in June 1941).
General Reinhard Gehlen, *The Service*, 1972.

THIS IS not to say that the civilian strategists were wrong. The political scientists provided a valuable service in tying war to its political ends. They provided answers to "why" the United States ought to wage war. In like manner the systems analysts provided answers on "what" means we would use. What was missing was the link that should have been provided by the military strategists – "how" to take the systems analyst's means and use them to achieve the political scientist's ends.
Colonel Harry G. Summers, Jr., *On Strategy: The Vietnam War in Context*, 1981.

COHESION

EVERY MAN reported and one [the King] mustered an army of Pharaoh which was under command of this king's son. He made troops, commanded by commanders, each man with his village . . .
Pharaoh Ammenhotep III (1411–1375 BC), quoted in James Breasted, *Ancient Records of Egypt*, II, 1906.

THE WORST cowards, banded together, have their power.
Homer, *The Iliad*, 13.281, c. 800 BC, tr. Robert Fagles, 1990.

IT IS THE PART of a wise general to station brothers in rank besides brothers, friends besides friends, and lovers besides their favorites. For whenever that which is in danger near by is more than ordinarily dear the lover necessarily fights more recklessly for the man beside him. And of course one is ashamed not to return a favour that he has received, and is dishonoured if he abandons a benefactor and is the first to flee.
Onasander, *The General*, AD 58, (Aeneas Tacticus, Aclepiodotus, Onasander, tr. The Illinois Greek Club, 1923).

HAVING FORMED his company . . . he (the captain) will then arrange comrades. Every Corporal, Private and Bugler will select a comrade of the rank differing from his own, i.e. front and rear rank, and is never to change him without permission of his captain. Comrades are always to have the same berth in quarters; and that they may be as little separated as possible, in either barracks or the field, will join the same file on parade and go on the same duties with arms when it is with baggage also.
British Army *Regulations of the Rifle Corps*, 1800, prepared under the aegis of Sir John Moore.

VICTORY and disaster establish indestructable bonds between armies and their commanders.
Napoleon, *Political Aphorisms*, 1848.

SOLIDARITY and confidence cannot be improvised. . . . It is time we should understand the lack of power in mob armies.
Colonel Charles Ardant du Picq, *Battle Studies*, 1880, tr. Greely, 1957.

TODAY the soldier is often unknown to his comrades. He is lost in the smoke, the dispersion, the confusion of battle. He seems to fight alone. Unity is no longer insured by mutual surveillance. A man falls, and disappears. Who knows whether it was a bullet or the fear of advancing farther that struck him down?
Colonel Charles Ardant du Picq, *Battle Studies*, 1880, tr. Greely, 1957.

A WISE ORGANIZATION ensures that the personnel of combat groups changes as little as possible, so that comrades in peacetime shall be comrades in war.
Colonel Charles Ardant du Picq, *Battle Studies*, 1880, tr. Greely, 1957.

THE THING in any organization is the creation of a soul.

> General George S. Patton, July 1941, *The Patton Papers*, II, 1974.

IT IS therefore noted as a principle that, all other things being equal, the tactical unity of men working together in combat will be in the ratio of their knowledge and sympathetic understanding of each other. Lacking these things, though they be well-trained soldiers, they are not likely to adhere unless danger has so surrounded them that they must do so in order to survive,and even then, quick surrender is the more probable result.

> Brigadier-General S.L.A. Marshall, *Men Against Fire*, 1947.

. . . . THE INHERENT unwillingness of the soldier to risk danger on behalf of men with whom he has no social identity. When a soldier is unknown to the men who are around him he has relatively little reason to fear losing the one thing that he is likely to value more highly than life – his reputation as a man among other men.

However much we may honor the "Unknown Soldier" as the symbol of sacrifice in war, let us not mistake the fact that it is the "Known Soldier" who wins battles. Sentiment aside, it is the man whose identity is well known to his fellows who has the main chance as a battle effective.

> Brigadier-General S.L.A. Marshall, *Men Against Fire*, 1947

THE BEST tactical results obtain from those dispositions and methods which link the power of one man to that of another. Men who feel strange with their unit, having been carelessly received by it, and indifferently handled, will rarely, if ever, fight strongly and courageously. But if treated with common decency and respect, they will perform like men.

> Brigadier S.L.A. Marshall, *The Armed Forces Officer*, 1950.

DURING the period of four to six weeks we had been enabled to complete the training and equipment of the troops, to make them familiar with the country, to continue to build field fortifications, to prepare work of destruction, and to lay mines and minefields. The homogeneity of the units thus became very different from what is usually the case with hastily mobilized troops immediately thrown into battle. These circumstances were calculated to produce calm and confidence before the trials in front of us.

> Field Marshal Carl Gustav Baron von Mannerheim, citing the preparation of the Finnish Army before the Soviet attack in 1939, *The Memoirs of Marshal Mannerheim*, 1953.

COMMITMENT is the thing. Soldiers in the ranks have rarely, over the ages, fought for king, country, freedom, or moral principle. More than anything else, men have fought and winners have won because of a commitment – to a leader and to a small brotherhood where the ties that bind are mutual respect and confidence, shared privation, shared hazard, shared triumph, a willingness to obey, and determination to follow. . . . bravery, as we recognize it and reward it, is far more than anything else a matter of commitment to the hero's leader or peers.

> Lieutenant-General Victor H. 'The Brute' Krulak, *First to Fight*, 1984.

THE COLOURS

LANDING was difficult . . . while our soldiers were hesitating, chiefly because of the depth of the water, the standard-bearer of the Tenth, with a prayer that his act might rebound to the success of the legion, cried, "Leap down, men, unless you want to betray your eagle to the enemy; I, at least shall have done my duty to my country and my general." As he said this, in a loud voice, he threw himself overboard and began to advance against the enemy with the eagle. Then our men called upon one another not to suffer such a disgrace, and with one accord leaped down from the ships. Seeing this their comrades from the nearest ships followed them and advanced close to the enemy.

> Julius Caesar, of the first Roman landing in Britain, *The Gallic War*, c. 51 BC, tr. Moses Hadas, 1957.

INQUISITOR: Did you ask your saints if, by virtue of your banner, you would win every battle you entered, and be victorious?
Joan: They told me to take it up bravely and God would help me.
Inquisitor: Which helped you more – you your banner, or your banner you?
Joan: As to whether victory was my banner's or mine, it was all our Lords's.

> Joan of Arc, 17 March 1431, *Joan of Arc In Her Own Words*, 1996.

THE SOLDIERS should make it an article of faith never to abandon their standard. It should be sacred to them; it should be respected; and every type of ceremony should be used to make it respected and precious.

> Field Marshal Maurice Comte de Saxe, *My Reveries*, 1732, tr. Phillips, 1940.

WHEN THE PROUD and sensitive sons of Dixie came to a full realization of the truth that the Confederacy was overthrown and their leader had been compelled to surrender his once invincible army, they could no longer control their emotions, and tears ran like water down their shrunken faces. The flags which they still carried were objects of undisguised affection. These Southern banners had gone down before overwhelming numbers; and torn by shells, riddled by bullets, and laden with the powder and smoke of battle, they aroused intense emotion in the men who had so often followed them to victory. Yielding to overpowering sentiment, these high-mettled men began to tear the flags from the staffs and hide them in their bosoms, as they wet them with burning tears.

The Confederate officers faithfully endeavored to check this exhibition of loyalty and love for the old flags. A great majority of them were duly surrendered; but many were secretly carried by devoted veterans to their homes, and will be cherished forever as honored heirlooms.

There was nothing unnatural or censurable in all this. The Confederates who clung to these pieces of battered bunting knew they would never again wave as martial ensigns above embattled hosts; but they wanted to keep them, just as they wanted to keep the old canteen with a bullet-hole through it, or the rusty gray jacket that had been torn by canister. They loved those flags, and will love them forever, as mementoes of the unparalleled struggle. They cherish them because they represent the consecration and courage not only of Lee's army but of all the Southern armies, because they symbolize the bloodshed and the glory of nearly a thousand battles.

> General John B. Gordon, describing the surrender at Appomattox, *Reminiscences of the Civil War*, 1903.

THE COLORS

You cannot choose your battlefield,
God does that for you;
But you can plant a standard
Where a standard never flew.

> Stephen Crane (1871–1900).

AND HENCE it was that when one man in every two, or even two in every three, had fallen in Hoghton's Brigade the survivors were still in line by their colours, closing in towards the tattered silk which represented the ark of their covenant – the one thing supremely important in the World.

> Sir John Fortescue, of the Battle of Albuera, 1811, quoted in Richardson, *Fighting Spirit*, 1978.

A MAN is not a soldier until he is no longer homesick, until he considers his regiment's colours as he would his village steeple; until he loves his colours, and is ready to put hand to sword every time the honour of the regiment is attacked.

> Marshal of France Thomas R. Bugeaud (1778–1846), quoted in Thomas, *Les Transformations de l'Armée Française*, 1887.

I STILL SEE that the old flagpole still stands. Have your troops hoist the colors to its peak, and let no enemy ever haul them down.

> General of the Army Douglas MacArthur, 2 March 1945, to Colonel George M. Jones whose 503rd Regimental Combat Team had just recaptured Corregidor from the Japanese.

IN THE SMALL closed world of the military, great victories, great defeats, and great sacrifices are never forgotten. They are remembered with battle streamers attached to unit flags. Among the scores of streamers that billow and whirl around the flags of all the battalions of the 1st Cavalry Division there is one deep-blue Presidential Unit Citation streamer that says simply: PLEIKU PROVINCE.

School children no longer memorize the names and dates of great battles, and perhaps that is good; perhaps that is the first step on the road to a world where wars are no longer necessary. Perhaps. But we remember those days and our comrades, and long after we're gone that long blue streamer will still caress proud flags.

> Lieutenant-General Harold G. Moore, of the Battle of the Ia Drang Valley, 14–17 November 1967, *We Were Soldiers Once . . . And Young*, 1992.

COMBAT

MEN who fought at a distance worked with
  frequent breaks,
dodging painful arrows that showered side-to-side.
But men who held the center suffered agonies,
thanks to the haze and carnage –
ruthless bronze hacking their lines to pieces,
there where the bravest fought.

> Homer, *The Iliad*, 17.431–436, c. 800 BC, tr. Robert Fagles, 1990.

COMBAT is the only effective force in the world; its aim is to destroy the enemy's forces as a means to a further end. That holds good even if no actual fighting ocurs, because the outcome rests on the assumption that if it came to fighting, the enemy would be destroyed.

> Major-General Carl von Clausewitz, *On War*, 1832, tr. Michael Howard and Peter Paret, 1976.

COMBATS may be quite independent of scientific combinations; they may become essentially dramatic; personal qualities and inspirations and a thousand other things frequently are the controlling elements.

> Lieutenant-General Antoine-Henri Baron de Jomini, *Summary of the Art of War*, 1838, tr. Mendell and Craighill, 1862.

A FORCE engaged is out of the hand of its commander.

> Colonel Charles Ardant du Picq, *Battle Studies*, 1880, tr. Greely, 1957.

IF YOUR BAYONET breaks, strike with the stock; if the stock gives way, hit with your fists; if your fists are hurt, bite with your teeth.

> General Mikhail I. Dragomirov, *Notes for Soldiers*, 1890.

NOTHING is more exhilarating than to be shot at without result.
Sir Winston S. Churchill, *The Malakand Field Force*, 1898.

COMBAT is organized armed conflict between the subunits, units, and formations of belligerents and is the main form of tactical actions on land, in the air, and at sea; it manifests itself in strikes coordinated in terms of objective, place, and time, fire, and maneuver aimed at routing (destroying) the enemy or taking him prisoner and of taking or holding important areas (lines, objectives). Combat is the only means of achieving victory.
Colonel-General V.G. Reznichenko, *Taktika*, 1984.

I DEFINE combat as a violent, planned form of physical interaction (fighting) between two hostile opponents, where at least one party is an organized force, recognized by governmental or *de facto* authority, and one or both opposing parties hold one or more of the following objectives: to seize control of territory or people; to prevent the opponent from seizing and controlling territory or people; to protect one's own territory or people; to dominate, destroy, or incapacitate an opponent. . . .
There are two key points in this definition that I wish to emphasize. Though there may be much in common between military combat and a brawl in a barroom, there are important differences. The opponents in military combat are to some degree organized, and both represent a governmental or quasi-governmental authority. There is one other essential difference: the all-pervasive influence of fear in a lethal environment. People have been killed in barroom brawls, but that is exceptional. In military combat there is the constant danger of death from lethal weapons employed by opponents with deadly intent. Fear is without question the most important characteristic of combat.
Colonel T.N. Dupuy, *Understanding War*, 1987.

IT IS only in the movies that assault rifles fire endlessly, all bullets hit the target with tremendous accuracy, and even if they die, the main characters do this handsomely and with reading-book correctness, accompanying their death or victory with shouts and exclamations appropriate to the place and moment. This is not so in practice. War is difficult, dirty, bloody work. Specifically work! The combat episodes themselves, that which, strictly speaking, customarily is considered war, are rather swift. All the rest of the time you are moving forward, crawling, digging in, maintaining and repairing equipment, and arranging for delivery of ammunitions and provisions. This is unskilled work; there is little here that is heroic. And this work is accompanied by lots of unexpected things of an objective and subjective nature.
Colonel-General Aleksandr I. Lebed, *I Cry For This Great Country*, 1995.

COMBINED ARMS

YOU HEAR that Phillip goes where he pleases not by marching his phalanx of infantry, but by bringing in his train light infantry, cavalry, archers, mercenaries, and other such troops.
Demosthenes, quoted in Duncan Head, *Armies of the Macedonian and Punic Wars*, 1982.

MAXIM 47. Infantry, cavalry, and artillery are nothing without each other. They should always be so disposed in cantonments as to assist each other in case of surprise.
Napoleon, *The Military Maxims of Napoleon*, tr. George D'Aguilar, 1831 (David Chandler, ed., 1987).

WE KNOW WELL what happens when a single arm is opposed to two others.
Major-General Carl von Clausewitz (1780–1831).

IT IS NOT so much the mode of formation as the proper combined use of the different arms which will ensure victory.
Lieutenant-General Antoine-Henri Baron de Jomini, *Summary of the Art of War*, 1838, tr. Mendell and Craighill, 1862.

THERE IS still a tendency in each separate unit . . . to be a one-handed puncher. By that I mean that the rifleman wants to shoot, the tanker to charge, the artilleryman to fire. . . . That is not the way to win battles. If the band played a piece first with the piccolo, then with the brass horn, then with the clarinet, and then with the trumpet, there would be a hell of a lot of noise but no music. To get the harmony in music each instrument must support the others. To get harmony in battle, each weapon must support the other. Team play wins. You musicians of Mars must not wait for the band leader to signal you. . . . You must each of your own volition see to it that you come into this concert at the proper place and at the proper time.
General George S. Patton, Jr., 8 July 1941, address to the men of the Second Armored Division, *The Patton Papers*, II, 1974.

TO ACHIEVE VICTORY on any scale it is important to secure the cooperation between all arms of the service both in operational elements and tactical formations on the terrain (or at least on the sand table). . . .
Marshal of the Soviet Union Georgi K. Zhukov, 1941, *Reminiscences and Reflections*, 1985.

IN ORDER to maximize combat power, we must use all the available resources to best advantage. To do so, we must follow a doctrine of combined arms. Combined arms is the full integration of arms in such a way that in order to counteract one, the enemy must make himself more vulnerable to another. We pose the enemy not just with a problem, but with a dilemma – a no-win situation.

General Alfred M. Gray and Major John Schmitt, *Warfighting*, United States Marine Corps, 1989.

COMMAND

AS FAR as I am concerned, I would rather be the first man here than the second in Rome.

Julius Caesar (100–44 BC), while 'crossing the Alps he came to a small native village with hardly any inhabitants and altogether a miserable-looking place,' quoted in Plutarch, *The Lives*, c. AD 125 (*The Fall of the Roman Republic*, tr. Rex Warner, 1972).

A PRINCE should therefore have no other aim or thought, nor take up any other thing for his study, but war and its organization and discipline, for that is the only art that is necessary to one who commands, and it is of such virtue that it not only maintains those who are born princes, but often enables men of private fortune to attain to that rank.

Niccolo Machiavelli, *The Prince*, 1513.

HE WHO WISHES to be obeyed must know how to command.

Niccolo Machiavelli, *Discourses*, 1517.

IN ALL well-ordered militias the commendation and sufficiency of all generals, colonels, captains, and other officers hath consisted in knowing how to command, govern, and order their armies, regiments, bands, and companies, and to win the love of their soldiers by taking great care of their healths and safeties, as also by all examples of virtue and worthiness not only by instruction but also by action in their own persons, venturing their lives in all actions against the enemy amongst them, and therewithal accounting of them in sickness and health or wounds received as of their own children; and whereas, again, all colonels and captains of horsemen according to all discipline have used to serve amongst their horsemen on horseback, and all colonels and captains of footmen, yea, even the very lieutenants general and kings themselves, if their armies and forces of the field have consisted more of footmen than of horsemen, have always used by all discipline military upon the occasion of any battle to put their horses from them and to serve on foot, and to venture their lives in the former ranks.

John Smythe (c. 1580–1631), *Certain Discourses Military*, 1966.

THERE ARE no bad regiments; there are only bad colonels.

Napoleon (1769–1821).

I CANNOT OBEY any longer. I have tasted the pleasure of command, and I cannot renounce it. My decision is taken. If I cannot be master, I shall quit France.

Napoleon, 1798, before the Egyptian expedition, to Miot de Melito, quoted in Louis de Bourrienne, *The Memoirs of Napoleon Bonaparte*, I, 1855.

I LIKE to walk alone . . .

The Duke of Wellington, 7 July 1801, to his brother, Henry Wellesley, after the news that he had been superseded in command after his brilliant victories in India by a senior officer, Wellington MSS, quoted in Elizabeth Longford, *Wellington: Years of the Sword*, 1970.

IF OFFICERS desire to have control over their commands, they must remain habitually with them, industriously attend to their instruction and comfort, and in battle lead them well.

Lieutenant General Thomas J. 'Stonewall' Jackson, *Letter of Instruction to Commanding Officers*, November 1861.

HOW can I trust a man to command others who cannot command himself?

General Robert E. Lee (1807–1870), quoted in Douglas Southall Freeman, *Douglas Southall Freeman on Leadership*, 1993.

NO MAN can tell how he will act in a responsible position, till he finds himself in it.

Admiral David G. Farragut, quoted in Loyall Farragut, *The Life of David Glasgow Farragut*, 1879.

THE ONLY PRIZE much cared for by the powerful is power. The prize of the general is not a bigger tent, but command.

Justice Oliver Wendell Holmes, February 15, 1913, speech at Harvard Law School, *The Occasional Speeches of Oliver Wendell Holmes*, 1962.

THE ART of command is not that of thinking and deciding for one's subordinates as though one stood in their shoes.

Marshal of France Ferdinand Foch, *Precepts and Judgments*, 1919.

THE POWER to command has never meant the power to remain mysterious.

Marshal of France Ferdinand Foch, *Precepts and Judgments*, 1919.

IT IS often argued that the possession of original ideas is different from, or even incompatible with, the power of executive command. The gulf between these two faculties is narrower than is commonly supposed. The conception of ideas implies mental initiative, while the moral courage required to express them publically and with vigour in the face of tradition-bound seniors indicates a strong personality, for the role of pioneer or reformer is

rarely a popular one. These two qualities of mental initiative and strong personality, or determination, go a long way towards the power of command in war – they are, indeed, the hallmark of the Great Captains. (March 1923.)
Captain Sir Basil Liddell Hart, *Thoughts on War*, 1944.

YOUR GREATNESS does not depend upon the size of your command, but on the manner in which you exercise it.
Marshal of France Ferdinand Foch, quoted in Aston, *Biography of Foch*, 1929.

WHENEVER a General was offered an inferior command and refused it, he did very wrong. You should always accept the command offered to you when it is an active one. I would have taken over any command, however small, without hesitation. And I would have commanded it in such a way that I should soon have been given a more important one.
Marshal of France Ferdinand Foch (1851–1929), quoted in Recouly, *Marshal Foch*, 1929.

TO COMMAND troops is certainly the greatest pleasure of military life, but above all is this the case when one is a captain or a colonel. For the captain, by reason of his immediate contact with the rank and file, which in the French Army is intelligent, active and devoted; for the colonel, because of the influence he exerts on a body of officers imbued with the noblest sentiments, competent in their trade and of proved devotion. It is through his officers that a colonel moulds his regiment so that it becomes in time the very image of the commander.
Marshal of France Ferdinand Foch, *Memoirs of Marshal Foch*, 1931.

THE REGULAR ARMY to-day has a high proportion of competent staff officers, but a much lower proportion of senior officers with the gift for training or the personality for command. And it may be remarked that the value of 'tact' can be over-emphasized in selecting officers for command: positive personality will evoke a greater response than negative pleasantness. (May 1939.)
Captain Sir Basil Liddell Hart, *Thoughts on War*, 1944.

YOU ARE probably busier than I am. As a matter of fact, commanding an army is not such a very absorbing task except that one has to be ready at all hours of the day and night . . . to make some rather momentous decision, which frequently consists of telling somebody who thinks he is beaten that he is not beaten.
General George S. Patton, Jr., letter, 11 October 1944, *The Patton Papers*, II, 1974.

THE LEADER who depends for success on the strength of his personality soon learns that in combat the discount rate is very high indeed. Manners and appearance continue to command respect for the individual only when he is capable of carrying his proportionate part of the burden. The criterion of command is the ability to think clearly and work hard rather than to strike attitudes or accept disproportionate risks.
Brigadier-General S.L.A. Marshall, *Men Against Fire*, 1947.

AT THE TOP there are great simplifications. An accepted leader has only to be sure of what it is best to do, or at least have his mind made up about it. The loyalties which center upon number one are enormous. If he trips, he must be sustained. If he makes mistakes, they must be covered. If he sleeps, he must not be wantonly disturbed. If he is no good, he must be pole-axed.
Sir Winston S. Churchill, *Their Finest Hour*, 1949.

COMMAND is not a prerogative, but rather a responsibility to be shared with all who are capable of filling up the spaces in orders and of carrying out that which is not openly expressed though it may be understood. Admittedly, it is not easy for a young officer, who by reason of his youth is not infrequently lacking in self-assurance and in the confidence that he can command respect, to understand that as a commander he can grow in strength in the measure that he succeeds in developing the latent strength of his subordinates. But if he stubbornly resists this premise as he goes along in the service, his personal resources will never become equal to the strain which will be imposed upon him, come a war emergency. The power to command resides largely in the ability to see when a proper initiative is being exercised and in giving it moral encouragement. When an officer feels that way about his job and his men, he will not be ready to question any action by a junior which might be narrowly construed as an encroachment upon his own authority. Of this last evil come the restraints which reduce men to automatons, giving only that which is asked, or less, according to the pressing of a button.
Brigadier-General S.L.A. Marshall, *The Armed Forces Officer*, 1950.

FROM GENERAL MARSHALL I learned the rudiments of effective command. Throughout the war I deliberately avoided intervening in a subordinate's duties. When an officer performed as I expected him to, I gave him a free hand. When he hesitated, I tried to help him. And when he failed, I relieved him.
General of the Army Omar Bradley, *A Soldier's Story*, 1951.

I BELIEVE in "personal" command, i.e. that a commander should never attempt to control an operation or a battle by remaining at his H.Q. or be content to keep touch with his subordinates by cable, W/T or other means of communication. He must as far as possible see the ground for himself to confirm or correct his impressions of the map;

his subordinate commanders to discuss their plans and ideas with them; and the troops to judge of their needs and their morale. All these as often as possible. The same of course applies to periods of preparation and periods between operations. In fact, generally the less time a commander spends in his office and the more he is with the troops the better.

Field Marshal Viscount Wavell of Cyrenaica, *Soldiers and Soldiering*, 1953.

AS TO the moral factors in command, it is always worth while to bear in mind the following:
(a) Two-thirds of the reports which are received in war are inaccurate; never accept a single report of success or disaster as necessarily true without confirmation.
(b) Always try to devise means to deceive and outwit the enemy and throw him off balance; the British in war are usually very lacking in this low cunning.
(c) Attack is not only the most effective but easiest form of warfare and the moral difference between advance and retreat is incalculable. Even when inferior in numbers, it pays to be as aggressive as possible.
(d) *Finally, when things look bad and one's difficulties appear great, the best tonic is to consider those of the enemy*.

Field Marshal Viscount Wavell of Cyrenaica, *Soldiers and Soldiering*, 1953

IT WAS GOOD FUN commanding a division in the Iraq desert. It is good fun commanding a division anywhere. It is one of the four best commands in the service – platoon, battalion, a division, and an army. A platoon, because it is your first command, because you are young, and because, if you are any good, you know the men in it better than their mothers do and love them as much. A battalion, because it is a unit with a life of its own; whether it is good or bad depends on you alone; you have at last a real command. A division, because it is the smallest formation that is a complete orchestra of war and the largest in which every man can know you. An army, because the creation of its spirit and its leadership in battle give you the greatest unit of emotional and intellectual experience that can befall a man.

Field Marshal Viscount Slim of Burma, *Defeat Into Victory*, 1956.

COMMAND must be direct and personal.

Field Marshal Viscount Montgomery of Alamein, *The Memoirs of Field Marshal Montgomery*, 1958.

THE COMMAND of troops in war is an art, a free creative activity based on character, ability and powers of intellect.

HDV 100/1, *Truppenfuehrung*, 1962 (troop leadership in the Bundeswehr).

IT WAS my first command. It was the small unit, the group unit. I knew the four squadrons. I could never know any other four squadrons as well as I knew those four, because, when I had more rank and more command and more responsibility, I would be bound to lose out on the proportionate intimacies. I went on to command air wings and air divisions, and then to command even larger assemblages in the field. And finally to command all of SAC; and eventually to my job as Chief of Staff of the United States Air Force.

But the 305th – It was my 305th, our 305th.

General Curtis LeMay, *Mission With LeMay*, 1965.

BATTLE COMMAND is not complicated. To me it has three parts. The first is character; values, such as physical courage, mental courage (the courage to be who you really are), integrity, loyalty and selfless commitment to your mission and your troops. These all make a difference. The second is the competence to know what to do. Soldiers have every right to expect their commanders to know the nuts and bolts of the profession, to know how to make decisions, to outthink the enemy, and to put their units in a position to outfight him. The third is leadership – the skills to motivate and otherwise lead an organization of people to accomplish its mission at least cost to them, and sometimes in directions and in situations where they would rather not go.

General Fred Franks, Jr., quoted in Tom Clancy with General Fred Franks, Jr. (ret), *Into the Storm*, 1998.

COMMAND is tough, risky, lonely – the most challenging job an officer can have. But it also is the very emblem of traditional military service. It is what dedicated officers always have lived for and aspired to. The greatest experience of my life has been the privilege of commanding Marines at the platoon and company levels. And what is a military service whose leaders do not aspire to command? It becomes a gutless bureaucracy, pushing papers and taking a paycheck.

James H. Webb, Jr., 'The Silence of the Admirals', *Proceedings*, 1/1999.

THE COMMANDER

MASTER SUN said: "The traits of the true commander are: wisdom, humanity, respect, integrity, courage, and dignity. With his wisdom he humbles the enemy, with his humanity he draws the people near to him, with his respect he recruits men of talent and character, with his integrity he makes good on his rewards, with his courage he raises the morale of the men, and with his dignity he unifies his command. Thus, if he humbles his enemy, he is able to take advantage of changing circumstances; if the people are close to him, they will be of a mind to go to battle in earnest; if he employs men of talent and wisdom, his secret plans will work; if his rewards and punishments are invariably honored, his men will give their all; if the morale and courage of his troops is heightened, they will of themselves be increasingly martial and intimidating; if his command is unified, the men will serve their commander alone.

Sun Tzu, c. 500 B.C., a passage recovered from Wang Fu's (AD 76–157) *Advice to the Commander* and not found in *The Art of War*, quoted in *Sun Tzu: The Art of Warfare*, tr. and ed. Roger Ames, 1993.

. . . . THE DETAILS depend on the circumstances, the judgment, the skill and on the bravery of the man in command.

Field Marshal Prince Aleksandr V. Suvorov (1729–1800).

AN ARMY of lions commanded by a deer will never be an army of lions.

Napoleon, '*Précis des guerres de Frederic II*', *Correspondance de Napoléon Ier, publiée par ordre de l'Empereur Napoléon III*, Vol. XXX, 1858–1870.

THE FOREMOST quality of a commander is to have a cool head, receiving accurate impressions of what is happening without ever getting excited, or dazzled, or intoxicated by good or bad news. The successive or simultaneous sensations that the commander received during the course of a day are classified in the mind and occupy only as much attention as they deserve, for good sense and judgment flow from the comparison of several sensations taken into equal consideration. There are men who, by the moral and physical composition, distort a picture of everything. No matter how much knowledge, intellect, courage and other good qualities they might have, nature has not called them to command armies or to direct the great operations of war.

Napoleon, '*Précis des guerres de Frederic II*', *Correspondance de Napoléon Ier, publiée par ordre de l'Empereur Napoléon III*, Vol. XXXII, 1858–1870, pp. 182–183.

NO VICTORY is possible unless the commander be energetic, eager for responsibilities and bold undertakings; unless he possess and can impart to all the resolute will of seeing the thing through; unless he be capable of exerting a personal action composed of will, judgment, and freedom of mind in the midst of danger.

Marshal of France Ferdinand Foch, *Precepts and Judgments*, 1919.

THERE IS required for the composition of a great commander not only massive common sense and reasoning power, not only imagination, but also an element of legerdemain, an original and sinister touch, which leaves the enemy puzzled as well as beaten.

Sir Winston S. Churchill, *The World Crisis*, 1923.

TO BE a successful commander, one must combine qualities of leadership with a knowledge of his profession. Either without the other is of much avail.

Admiral Raymond A. Spruance, 'Thesis on Command', U.S. Naval War College, 11 September 1926.

INITIATIVE and the desire to crawl into any crack in the enemy combat formations must be the main qualities of every commander.

Marshal of the Soviet Union Mikhail N. Tukhachevskiy (1893–1937), quoted in Savkin, *The Basic Principles of Operational Art and Tactics*, 1972.

SORTING OUT muddles is really the chief job of a commander.

Field Marshal Viscount Wavell of Cyrenaica, 'Training of the Army for War', *Journal, Royal United Services Institution*, 2/1933.

IN THE profoundest sense, battles are lost and won in the mind of the commander, and the results are merely registered in his men.

Captain Sir Basil Liddell Hart, *Colonel Lawrence: The Man Behind the Legend*, 1934.

IN SEEKING VICTORY, those who direct a war cannot overstep the limitations imposed by the objective's conditions; within these limitations, however, they can and must play a dynamic role in striving for victory. The state of action for commanders in a war must be built upon objective possibilities, but on the state they can direct the performance of many a drama, full of sound and colour, power and grandeur.

Mao Tse-tung, *On Protracted War*, 1938.

A COMMANDER should have a profound understanding of human nature, the knack of smoothing out troubles, the power of winning affection while communicating energy, and the capacity for ruthless determination where required by circumstances. He needs to generate an electrifying current, and to keep a cool head in applying it.

Captain Sir Basil Liddell Hart, *Thoughts on War*, 1944.

IN MY EXPERIENCE, all very successful commanders are prima donnas, and must be so treated. Some officers require urging, others require suggestions, very few have to be restrained.

General George S. Patton, Jr., *War As I Knew It*, 1947.

AMONG the ever-pressing problems of the commander is the seeking of means to break down the natural timidity of the great majority of his men. This he can never do unless he is sufficient master of himself that he can come out of his own shell and give his men a chance to understand him as a human being rather than as an autocrat giving orders. Nothing more unfortunate can happen to the commander than to come to be regarded by his

subordinates as unapproachable, for such a reputation isolates him from the main problems of command as well as its chief rewards.
  Brigadier-General S.L.A. Marshall, *Men Against Fire*, 1947.

THERE ARE . . . personal traits which *greatly aid* the commander in reaching a decision. Spiritual power, strength of character, maturity of mind, and personal experience are particularly valuable assets in this respect. Self-appraisal and unceasing efforts at self-improvement are imperative for a commander. An important aspect of any personal experience is the fact that, during its course, the commander has had an opportunity for self-analysis. Out of the great variety of different temperaments and characters, the man with a *cool head and an aggressive spirit* has the best prerequisites for success. The other way around, things would work out badly.
  Colonel-General Dr. Lothar Rendulic, *The Command Decision*, MS No. D 080 A, Office of the Chief of Military History, 15 March 1947.

THE COMMANDER is the backbone of the military unit. The command personnel constitute the skeleton which holds the separate limbs of an army together and supports them as a single, closely-knit military organization. The capability, devotion and courage of the combatants – in other words the practical ability of the army – are related directly to the ability of their commanders, of each of their commanders individually within the limits of his particular responsibilities, of all their commanders together in so far as they are collectively responsible for the army as a whole and all its undertakings.
  General Yigal Allon, *The Making of Israel's Army*, 1970.

I HAVE DEVELOPED almost an obsession as to the certainty with which you can judge a division, or any other large unit, merely by knowing its commander intimately. Of course, we have had pounded into us all through our school courses that the exact level of a commander's personality and ability is always reflected in his unit – but I did not realize, until opportunity came for comparisons on a rather large scale, how infallibly the commander and unit are almost one and the same thing.
  General of the Army Dwight D. Eisenhower, *At Ease: Stories I Tell My Friends*, 1967.

MEN are of no importance. What counts is who commands.
  General Charles de Gaulle, *New York Times Magazine*, 12 May 1968.

FOR CONFIDENCE, spirit, purposefulness, aggressiveness flow down from the top and permeate a whole command. And in the same way do anxiety and lack of resolution on the part of a commander put their indelible stamp upon his men.
  General Matthew B. Ridgeway, quoted in *Military Review*, 6/1987.

COMMANDING GENERAL/ COMMANDER-IN-CHIEF

THE RESPONSIBILITY for a martial host of a million lies in one man. His is the trigger of its spirit.
  Wu Ch'i (430–381 BC).

HAVING by this service won a universally acknowledged reputation for bravery, he in subsequent times refrained from exposing his person without sufficient reason when his country reposed her hopes of success on him – conduct characteristic not of a commander who relies on luck, but on one gifted with intelligence.
  Polybius, referring to Scipio Africanus, *Histories*, c. 125 BC, quoted in Liddell Hart, *A Greater Than Napoleon: Scipio Africanus*, 1926.

A COMMANDER-IN-CHIEF therefore, whose power and dignity are so great and to whose fidelity and bravery the fortunes of his countrymen, the defense of their cities, the lives of the soldiers, and the glory of the state, are entrusted, should not only consult the good of the army in general, but extend his care to every private soldier in it. For when any misfortunes happen to those under his command, they are considered as public losses and imputed entirely to his misconduct.
  Flavius Vegetius Renatus, *Military Institutions of the Romans*, c. AD 378, tr. Clark, 1776.

I HAVE FORMED a picture of a general commanding which is not chimerical – I have seen such men.
  The first of all qualities is COURAGE. Without this the others are of little value, since they cannot be used. The second is INTELLIGENCE, which must be strong and fertile in expedients. The third is HEALTH.
  He should possess a talent for sudden and appropriate improvisation. He should be able to penetrate the minds of other men, while remaining impenetrable himself. He should be endowed with the capacity of being prepared for everything, with activity accompanied by judgment, with skill to make a proper decision on all occasions, and with exactness of discernment.
  Field Marshal Maurice Comte de Saxe, *My Reveries*, 1732, tr. Phillips, 1940.

THE FIRST QUALITY of a general in chief is a great knowledge of the art of war. This is not intuitive, but the result of experience. A man is not born a commander. He must become one. Not to be anxious; to be always cool; to avoid confusion in his commands; never to change countenance; to give his orders in the midst of battle with as much composure as if here perfectly at ease. These are proofs of valor in a general.

Field Marshal Prince Raimondo Montecuccoli (1609–1680), *Commentarii Bellici*, 1740, quoted in Barker, *The Military Intellectual and Battle*, 1975.

LET what will arrive, it is the part of the general-in-chief to remain firm and constant in his purposes: he must be equally superior to elation in prosperity and depression in adversity, for in war good and bad fortune succeed each other by turns, and form the ebb and flow of military operations.

Field Marshal Prince Raimondo Montecuccoli (1609–1680), *Commentarii Bellici*, 1740, quoted in Barker, *The Military Intellectual and Battle*, 1975.

REMEMBER that you are a commander-in-chief and must not be beaten; therefore do not undertake anything with your troops unless you have some strong hope of success.

The Duke of Wellington, 11 May 1809, to General Beresford, *The Dispatches of Field Marshal the Duke of Wellington, During His Various Campaigns in India, Denmark, Portugal, Spain, the Low Countries, and France*, IV, 1834–1838, p. 296.

MAXIM 73. The first qualification in a general-in-chief is a cool head – that is, a head which receives just impressions, and estimates things and objects at their real value. He must not allow himself to be elated by good news, or depressed by bad.

The impressions he receives, either successively or simultaneously in the course of the day, should be so classed as to take up only the exact place in his mind which they deserve to occupy; since it is upon a just comparison and consideration of the weight due to different impressions that the power of reasoning and of right judgment depends.

Some men are so physically and morally constituted as to see everything through a highly coloured medium. They raise up a picture in the mind on every slight occasion and give to every trivial occurrence a dramatic interest. But whatever knowledge, or talent, or courage, or other good qualities such men may possess, nature has not formed them for the command of armies, or the direction of great military operations.

Napoleon, *The Military Maxims of Napoleon*, tr. George D'Aguilar, 1831 (David Chandler, ed., 1987).

MAXIM 77. Generals-in-chief must be guided by their own experience or their genius. Tactics, evolutions, the duties and knowledge of an engineer or an artillery officer may be learned in treatises, but the science of strategy is only to be acquired by experience, and by studying the campaigns of all the great captains.

Gustavus Adolphus, Turenne, and Frederick the Great, as well as Alexander, Hannibal, and Caesar,

have all acted upon the same principles. These have been: to keep their forces united; to leave no weak part unguarded; to seize with rapidity on important points.

Such are the principles which lead to victory, and which, by inspiring terror at the reputation of your arms, will at once maintain fidelity and secure subjection.

Napoleon, *The Military Maxims of Napoleon*, tr. George D'Aguilar, 1831 (David Chandler, ed., 1987).

THE CHARACTER of the man is above all other requisites in a commander-in-chief.

Lieutenant-General Antoine-Henri Baron de Jomini, *Summary of the Art of War*, 1838, tr. Mendell and Craighill, 1862.

ONLY the Head of the Government, the Statesman who has decided for war, and that with a clear conscience, shoulders the same or a bigger burden of responsibility than that of the Commander-in-Chief. In his case it is a question of one great decision only, but the Commander of an army is faced with decisions daily and hourly. He is continuously responsible for the welfare of many hundred-thousands of persons, even of nations. For a soldier there is nothing greater, but at the same time more overwhelming, than to find himself at the head of an army or the entire field army of his country.

General Erich Ludendorff, *My War Memories, 1914–1918*, 1919.

IN MY youthful days I used to read about commanders of armies and envied them what I supposed to be a great freedom in action and decision. What a notion! The demands upon me that must be met make me a slave rather than a master. Even my daily life is circumscribed with guards, aides, etc., etc., until sometimes I want nothing so much as complete seclusion.

General of the Army Dwight D. Eisenhower, 27 May 1943, letter to his wife, Mamie, quoted in *Letters to Mamie*, 1978.

IN MY OPINION, generals – or at least the Commanding General – should answer their own telephones in the daytime. This is not particularly wearisome because few people call a general, except in emergencies, and then they like to get him at once.

General George S. Patton, *War As I Knew It*, 1947.

THERE ARE three types of commanders in the higher grades:
1. Those who have faith and inspiration, but lack the infinite capacity for taking pains and preparing for every foreseeable contingency – which is the foundation of all success in war. These fail.
2. Those who possess the last-named quality to a degree amounting to genius. Of this type I would cite Wellington as the perfect example.

3. Those who, possessing this quality, are inspired by a faith and conviction which enables them, when they have done everything possible in the way of preparation and when the situation favours boldness, to throw their bonnet over the moon. There are moments in war when, to win all, one has to do this. I believe such a moment occurred in August 1944 after the Battle of Normandy had been won, and it was missed. Nelson was the perfect example of this – when he broke the line at St. Vincent, when he went straight in to attack at the Nile under the fire of the shore batteries and with night falling, and at the crucial moment at Trafalgar.

> Field Marshal Viscount Montgomery of Alamein, *The Memoirs of Field Marshal Montgomery*, 1958.

COMMAND SELECTION

IN CHOOSING their centurions the Romans look not so much for the daring or fire-eating type, but rather for men who are natural leaders and possess a stable and imperturbable temperament, not men who will open the battle and launch attacks, but those who will stand their ground even when worsted or hard-pressed, and will die in defence of their posts.

> Polybius, *Histories*, 6.24, c. 125 BC (*The Rise of the Roman Empire*, tr. Ian Scott-Kilvert, 1987).

THE GENERAL should be manly in his attitudes, naturally suited for command, profound in his thinking, sound in his judgment, in good physical condition, hardworking, emotionally stable. He should instill fear in the disobedient, while he should be gracious and kind to others. His concern for the common good should be such that he will neglect nothing at all that may be to its advantage. The general must be judged by his actions, and it is preferable that he be chosen for command on the basis of his record.

> Anonymous Byzantine general, c. AD 527–565, *On Strategy* (*Peri Strategias*), quoted in George Dennis, *Three Byzantine Military Treatises*, 1985.

MINDS which have been trained mechanically triumph in peacetime over those possessing true insight and genius.

> General Gehard von Scharnhorst (1755–1831), quoted in de Gaulle, *The Edge of the Sword*, 1932.

DAILY in the Muese-Argonne, officers were assigned to command of regiments, brigades, divisions, or other important positions to replace casualties, some of which were not due to the enemy. Frequently they took over their duties in a situation which might be characterized as a bad mess; their officers and troops were scattered about on the terrain, under the fire of the enemy; deficiencies and special difficulties had to be ascertained. Yet there was rarely time for a pause in which to size up the officers and the troops, check over the supplies and material, and make a calm survey of the situation. Action was demanded and often within the first hour. A renewed attack was usually required the following morning. It should be obvious that the successful handling of such situations required a very special type of man, a type that frequently is in difficulties in a peace regime.

> General of the Army George C. Marshall, *Memoirs of My Service in the World War* (written between 1923 and 1926), finally published 1976.

POWERFUL PERSONALITIES equipped with the qualities needed in the fighting soldier, and capable of standing up to the tests of great events, frequently lack that surface charm which wins popularity in ordinary life. Strong characters are, as a rule, rough, disagreeable, and aggressive. The man in the street may, somewhat shyly, admit their superiority and pay them lip service, but they are not often liked and, therefore, seldom favored. When it comes to choosing men for high positions, the lot usually falls on the pleasing and docile rather than on the meritorious.

> General Charles de Gaulle, *The Edge of the Sword*, 1932.

THE VALUE of "tact" can be over-emphasized in selecting officers for command: positive personality will evoke a greater response than negative pleasantness.

> Captain Sir Basil Liddell Hart, *Thoughts on War*, 1944.

THE NEXT POINT, still a human one, is the selection of commanders. Probably a third of my working hours were spent in the consideration of personalities. In dealing with subordinates, justice and a keen sense of fairness are essential – as also is a full measure of human consideration. I kept command appointments in my own hand, right down to and including battalion or regimental level. Merit, leadership, and ability to do the job, were the sole criteria; I made it my business to know all commanders, and to insist on a high standard.

> Field Marshal Viscount Montgomery of Alamein, *The Memoirs of Field Marshal Montgomery*, 1958.

A LOT of what makes a leader is personality-driven. In our military there will always be people who have the courage to stand up for their convictions. The question is will they be retired as colonels. Or whether they will be allowed to make their way to the top.

> James Webb, 'Policy Decisions', Al Santoli, ed., *Leading the Way: How Vietnam Veterans Rebuilt the U.S. Military*, 1993.

COMMON SENSE

WHEN ONE is intent on an object, common sense will usually direct one to the right means.

> The Duke of Wellington (1769–1852), quoted in Philip Henry Stanhope, *Notes of Conversations with the Duke of Wellington, 1831-1851*, 1888.

I ATTRIBUTE it entirely to the application of good sense to the circumstances of the moment.

> The Duke of Wellington (1769–1852), when asked to what characteristic of mind he attributed his invariable success, quoted in William Fraser, *Words of Wellington*, 1889.

THE ART of war does not require complicated maneuvers; the simplest are the best, and common sense is fundamental. From which one might wonder how it is generals make blunders; it is because they try to be clever. The most difficult thing is to guess the enemy's plan, to sift the truth from all the reports that come in. The rest merely requires common sense; it is like a boxing match, the more you punch the better it is. It is also necessary to read the map well.

> Napoleon, 29 January 1818, St. Helena, quoted in R.M. Johnston, ed., *The Corsican*, 1910.

I THOUGHT I detected in the management what I had never discovered before on the battlefield – a little common sense. Dash is handsome, genius glorious; but modest, old-fashioned, practical everyday sense is the trump after all.

> A staff officer's observation of Ulysses S. Grant, quoted in Williams, *McClellan, Sherman, and Grant*, 1962.

WHILE exceptional ability is desirable in a general, common sense is essential. Yet there is a peculiar danger in the latter quality unless it is accompanied by the former faculty. For many men of strong common sense but limited education are apt to feel uneasy in dealing with those who are intellectually better equipped. And the too common result is that they become more than normally sensitive to the arguments, especially the negative arguments, of intellectual second-raters, clever but uncreative – the class which produces most of the mouthpieces of orthodoxy. And the purely practical man is too often led to yield, against his better judgment, because he feels incapable of combating their objections. (April 1929.)

> Captain Sir Basil Liddell Hart, *Thoughts On War*, 1944.

COMMUNICATION

IF INTERCOMMUNICATION between events in front and ideas behind are not maintained, then two battles will be fought – a mythical headquarters battle and an actual front-line one, in which case the real enemy is to be found in our own headquarters. Whatever doubt exists as regards the lessons of the 1st war, this is one which cannot be controverted.

> Major-General J.F.C. Fuller, quoted in George Marshall, ed., *Infantry in Battle*, 1939.

Lines of Communication

THE SECRET of war lies in the secret of the lines of communication. . . . Strategy does not consist of making half-hearted dashes at the enemy's rear areas; it consists in really mastering his communications, and then proceeding to give battle.

> Napoleon, 1806, comment to Jomini, quoted in David Chandler, *The Campaigns of Napoleon*, 1966.

LET ME HEAR from you more frequently; in a combined manoeuvre like this it is only by very frequent communication that we can achieve the best results. We are at the crisis of the campaign; they did not anticipate what we are attempting to do; woe betide them if they hesitate and if they lose a single day.

> Napoleon, to Marshal Soult, 6 October 1806, quoted in R.M. Johnston, ed., *The Corsican*, 1910.

MAXIM 12. An army ought only to have one line of operation. This should be preserved with care, and never abandoned but in the last extremity.

> Napoleon, *The Military Maxims of Napoleon*, tr. George D'Aguilar, 1831 (David Chandler, ed., 1987).

THE LINE that connects an army with its base of supplies is the heel of Achilles – its most vital and vulnerable point.

> Colonel John S. Mosby, *Mosby's War Reminiscences*, 1887.

COMMUNICATIONS dominate war; broadly considered, they are the most important single element in strategy, political or military.

> Rear Admiral Alfred Thayer Mahan, *The Problem of Asia and its Effects on International Relations Naval and Civil*, 1900.

FREE SUPPLIES and open retreat are two essentials to the safety of an army or a fleet.

> Rear Admiral Alfred Thayer Mahan, *Naval Strategy*, 1911.

ALL MILITARY organizations, land or sea, are ultimately dependent upon open communications with the basis of national power.

> Rear Admiral Alfred Thayer Mahan, *Naval Strategy*, 1911.

NINE TIMES out of ten an army has been destroyed because its supply lines have been severed.

> General of the Army Douglas MacArthur, 23 August 1950, to the Joint Chiefs of Staff.

TO EXPLOIT the principles of war for our purpose and base ourselves upon strategic indirect approach, so as to determine the issue of the fighting even before fighting has begun, it is necessary to achieve the three following things:
(a) to cut the enemy's lines of communication, thus paralyzing his physical build-up;
(b) to seal him off from his lines of retreat, thus undermining the enemy's will and destroying his morale;

(c) to hit his centres of administration and disrupt his communications, thus severing the link between his brain and his limbs.

Reflection on these three aims proves the truth of Napoleon's saying: "The whole secret of the art of war lies in the ability to become master of the lines of communications."

General Yigael Yadin, *Bamachaneh* (The Israel Forces' Journal), 9/1949, condensed in Liddell Hart, *Strategy*, 1954.

IN PLANNING any stroke against the enemy's communications, either by manoeuvre round his flank or by rapid penetration of a breach in his front, the question will arise as to the most effective point of aim – whether it should be directed against an immediate rear of the opposing force, or further back.

In general, the nearer to the force that the cut is made, the more immediate the effect; the nearer to the base, the greater the effect. . . .

A further consideration is that while a stroke close in rear of the enemy force may have more effect on the minds of the enemy troops, a stroke far back tends to have more effect on the mind of the enemy commander.

Captain Sir Basil Liddell Hart, *Strategy*, 1954.

COMPETENCE

A SCORPION will sting because it has poison; a soldier can be brave when he can rely on his equipment. Therefore when their weapons are sharp and their armor is strong, people will readily do battle. If the armor is not strong, it is the same as baring one's shoulders. If a bow cannot shoot far, it is the same as a close-range weapon. If a shot cannot hit the mark, it is the same as having no weapon. If a scout is not careful, it is the same as having no eyes. If a general is not brave in battle, it is the same as having no military leadership.

Zhuge Liang (AD 180–234), *The Way of the General*, quoted in Thomas Cleary, *Mastering the Art of War*, 1989.

THE GENERAL should be ignorant of none of the situations likely to occur in war. Who can attempt to accomplish what he does not understand? Who is able to furnish assistance in situations whose dangers he does not understand?

The Emperor Maurice, *The Strategikon*, c. AD 600 (*Maurice's Strategikon*, tr. George Dennis, 1984).

OFFICERS can never act with confidence until they are masters of their profession.

Major-General Henry Knox (1750–1806).

THE OFFICERS know that I myself am not ashamed to work at this. . . . Suvorov was Major, and Adjutant, and everything down to Corporal; I myself looked into everything and could teach everybody.

Field Marshal Prince Aleksandr V. Suvorov (1729–1800), quoted in W. Lyon Blease, *Suvorof*, 1926.

OUR OBJECT ought to able to have a good army rather than a large one.

General George Washington, 15 September 1780.

ONE MUST UNDERSTAND the mechanism and power of the individual soldier, then that of a company, a battalion, a brigade and so on, before one can venture to group divisions and move an army. I believe I owe most of my success to the attention I always paid to the inferior part of tactics as a regimental officer. There are few men in the Army who knew these details better than I did; it is the foundation of all military knowledge.

The Duke of Wellington (1769–1852), quoted in John Croker, *The Croker Papers*, I, 1884.

THE TRUE WAY to be popular with the troops is not to be free and familiar with them, but to make them believe you know more than they do.

General of the Army William T. Sherman, 11 November 1864, letter to Rev. Henry Lay.

A COMPETENT LEADER can get efficient service from poor troops, while on the contrary an incapable leader can demoralize the best of troops.

General of the Armies John J. Pershing, *My Experiences in the World War*, 1931.

COMRADESHIP AND
THE BAND OF BROTHERS

AND IT came to pass, when he made an end of speaking unto Saul, that the soul of Jonathan was knit with the soul of David, and Jonathan loved him as his own soul.

And Saul took him that day, and would let him go no more home to his father's house.

Then Jonathan and David made a covenant, because he loved him as his own soul.

And Jonathan stripped himself of the robe that was upon him, and gave it to David, and his garments, even to his sword, and to his bow, and to his girdle.

I Samuel 18:1–4, after David slew Goliath.

NOW BE MEN, my friends! Courage, come, take heart!
Dread what comrades say of you here in bloody combat!
When men dread that, more men come through alive – when soldiers break and run, good-bye glory, good-bye all defenses.

Homer, *The Iliad*, 5.610–14, c. 800 BC, tr. Robert Fagles, 1990; Agamemnon rallying the Achaeans.

IT IS FURTHER recorded in these documents that the soldiers were passionately eager to seem him; some hoped for a sight of him while he was still alive; others wished to see his body, for a report had gone round that he was already dead, and they suspected, I fancy, that his death was being concealed by his guards. But nothing could keep them from a sight of him, and the motive in almost every heart was grief and a sort of helpless bewilderment at the thought of losing their king. Lying speechless as the men filed by, he yet struggled to raise his head, and in his eyes there was a look of recognition for each individual as he passed. . . .
  Arrian, of Alexander the Great's farewell to the Macedonians on his deathbed, 323 BC, *The Campaigns of Alexander*, 7.26 c. AD 150, tr. Aubrey de Sélincourt, 1987.

MY FIRST WISH would be that my military family, and the whole Army, should consider themselves as a band of brothers, willing and ready to die for each other.
  General George Washington, 21 October 1798, letter to Henry Knox, *Writings*, XXXVI, 1941, p. 508.

A NEVER-TO-BE-FORGOTTEN evening was the one spent at our home by the officers who were to start upon their overland trip to the South at 12 o'clock that night. General and Mrs. Johnston were of the party. Before leaving, the General said to his wife, "Come, sing me one or two of the old songs you used to sing, 'Mary of Argyle,' and 'Kathleen Mavourneen.'" She complied reluctantly in the presence of such an audience, saying, with deep emotion, that she felt as though her music days were over. Those songs will ever be remembered by the survivors of that mournful gathering. All were endeavoring to conceal, under smiling exteriors, hearts that were filled with sadness over the sundering of life-long ties, and doubts as to the result of their sacrifice. The most crushed of the party was Major Armistead, who, with tears, which were contagious, streaming down his face, and hands upon Mr. Hancock's shoulders, while looking him steadily in the eye, said, "Hancock, good-by; you can never know what this has cost me, and I hope God will strike me dead if I am ever induced to leave my native soil, should worse come to worst." . . . I, as well as my husband, believed he courted the death that finally came to him at Gettysburg, for I have often heard it related how bravely he came to the front of his brigade, waving his sword, and how he was shot through the body, and fell within our lines, asking to be taken to Hancock's tent. At the same moment my husband had fallen with what was supposed, at the time to be a mortal wound. Three of the six from whom we parted that evening in Los Angeles were killed in front of General Hancock's troops, and others wounded.
  Almira Hancock, *Reminiscences of General Hancock*, 1887.

CONSIDER your corps as your family; your commander as your father; your comrade as your brother; your inferior as a young relative. Then all will be happy and friendly and easy. Don't think of yourself, think of your comrades; they will think of you. Perish yourself, but save your comrades.
  General Mikhail I. Dragomirov, *Notes for Soldiers*, 1890. Note: The last sentence is a quote from Suvorov.

A MYSTERIOUS fraternity born out of smoke and danger of death.
  Stephen Crane, *The Red Badge of Courage*, 1893.

THESE VOICES, these quiet words, these footsteps in the trench behind me recall me at a bound from the terrible loneliness and fear of death by which I had been almost destroyed. They are more to me than life, those voices, they are more than motherliness and more than fear, they are the strongest, most comforting thing there is anywhere, they are the voices of my comrades.
  Erich Maria Remarque, *All Quiet On the Western Front*, 1929.

THE SOLDIER'S FIELD of activity is man, who controls science, technics and material. The army is a combination of many men with the same serious aim. This gives the soldier's profession a quite peculiar bond of unity, a corporate sense which we call comradeship. The term is extremely comprehensive. If we start out from the notion of responsibility we find that "comradeship" means "one for all," for each man bears, in his own way and in his own place, a share of the responsibility for the welfare, the ability, the achievements, and the life of others. For the senior, the leader, the superior, this means the duty of correcting, of training, of supervising others; for the junior, the novice, the subordinate, it means the duty of conscious, voluntary subordination. Love and confidence are the two great components of comradeship.
  Colonel-General Hans von Seekt, *Thoughts of a Soldier*, 1930.

GREAT ACHIEVEMENTS in war and peace can only result if officers and men form an indissoluble band of brothers.
  Field Marshal Paul von Hindenburg, 1934, proclamation to the German Army.

I HAVE always tried to crack a joke or two before, and you have been friendly and laughed at them. But today I am afraid I have run out of jokes, and I don't suppose any of us feel much like laughing. The Kelly has been in one scrap after another, but even after we have had men killed the majority survived and brought the old ship back. Now she lies in fifteen hundred fathoms and with her more than half our shipmates. If they had to die, what a grand way to go, for now they all lie together in the ship we loved. . . .

We have lost her, but they are still with her. There may be less than half the Kelly left, but I feel that each of us will take up the battle with even stronger heart. . . . You will all be sent to replace men who have been killed in other ships, and the next time you are in action remember the Kelly. As you ram each shell home into the gun, shout 'Kelly!' and so her spirit will go on inspiring us until victory is won. I should like to add that there isn't one of you I wouldn't be proud and honoured to serve with again. Goodbye, good luck, and thank you all from the bottom of my heart.

> Admiral Lord Louis Mountbatten of Burma (when he was a lowly destroyer captain), his farewell to the survivors of the crew of the *Kelly* in Alexandria after the loss of the gallant ship in the battle of Crete, 1941.

. . . NOT BECAUSE their presence was going to make a lot of difference to the big scheme of the war, and not to uphold the traditions of the umpteenth regiment. A lot of guys don't know the name of their regimental commanders. They went back because they knew their companies were shorthanded, and they were sure that if someone else in their squad or section were in their shoes, and the situation was reversed, those friends would come back to make the load lighter on them.

> Bill Mauldin, commenting on 'how men sneaked back to their units rather than spend time convalescing after discharge from hospital', *Up Front*, 1945.

I HOLD IT to be one of the simplest truths of war that the thing which enables an infantry soldier to keep going with his weapons is the near presence or the presumed presence of a comrade.

> Brigadier-General S.L.A. Marshall, *Men Against Fire*, 1947.

MEN who have been in battle know from first-hand experience that when the chips are down, a man fights to help the man next to him, just as a company fights to keep pace with its flanks. Things have to be that simple. An ideal does not become tangible at the moment of firing a volley or charging a hill. When the hard and momentary choice is death, the words once heard at an orientation lecture are clean forgot, but the presence of a well-loved comrade is unforgettable. In battle the most valued thing at hand is that which becomes most stoutly defended. All values are interpreted in terms of the battlefield itself. Yet above and beyond any symbol – whether it be the individual life or a pillbox commanding a wadi in Sahara – are all of the ideals which press upon men, causing them to accept a discipline and to hold to the line even though death may be at hand.

> Brigadier-General S.L.A. Marshall, *Men Against Fire*, 1947.

WHY DOES the soldier leave the protection of his trench or hole in the ground and go forward in the face of shot and shell? It is because of the leader who is in front of him and his comrades who are around him. Comradeship makes a man feel warm and courageous when all his instincts tend to make him cold and afraid.

> Field Marshal Viscount Montgomery of Alamein, *A History of Warfare*, 1968.

IN SUCH A UNIT as the 101st, it was a constant task to impress on the officers the folly, indeed the unfairness, of unnecessarily exposing themselves to enemy fire. The strength of a fighting outfit is the mutual respect of all its members of whatever rank. Shared danger breeds admiration for the hard, utter intolerance for the weak, and a fierce loyalty to comrades. Students of military history have often tried to determine why some men fight well and others run away. It never seemed to me that ideological motives or political or moral concepts had much to do with it. If I could get any of my men to discuss a matter so personal as their honest reaction to combat, they would tell me that they fought, though admittedly scared, because "I couldn't let the other boys down" or "I couldn't look chicken before 'Dog Company'." These are simple reasons for simple virtues in simple men whom it is an ennobling privilege to command. For their officers, that privilege carries with it the responsibility to stay alive and look after them. This was a sound precept but one hard to impress on the officers of the 101st who, like their men, didn't want to "look chicken."

> General Maxwell Taylor, *Swords and Ploughshares*, 1972.

THE BALD, red hills with their sandbag bunkers, the banter and frolic of dirt-covered grunts, the fearful intensity of contact. . . . Down south his men were on patrol, or digging new perimeters, or dying, and he was nothing if he did not share that misery.

> James Webb, *Fields of Fire*, 1978.

THIS DAY I am proud to be a Canadian, and I am prouder still to belong to the "band of brothers" who volunteered for overseas service. Today I don't despise the [Canadians] who refuse overseas duty – I pity them, for they will never know what it is to be a man among men. Men! Not supermen, just men, who have learned to act together from no selfish motives but as comrades willing to risk death for one another. After the busting of the Hitler Line, the squirmings of the politicians and the war profiteers and the other gutless wonders at home won't bother us as much. By God, we *know* who *we* are, and what we amount to.

> Captain Farley Mowat, Hastings and Prince Edward Regiment, *My Father's Son: Memories of War and Peace*, 1992.

ANOTHER and far more transcendent love came to us unbidden on the battlefields, as it does on every battlefield in every war man has ever fought. We discovered in that depressing, hellish place, where death was our constant companion, that we loved

each other. We killed for each other, we died for each other, and we wept for each other. And in time we came to love each other as brothers. In battle our world shrank to the man on our left and the man on our right and the enemy all around. We held each other's lives in our hands and we learned to share our fears, our hopes, our dreams as readily as we shared what little else good came our way.
Lieutenant-General Harold G. Moore, *We Were Soldiers Once . . . And Young*, 1992.

ONE of the lasting truths about being a soldier is that friendships formed with comrades in arms are the deepest and most enduring.
General Fred Franks, Jr., quoted in Tom Clancy with General Fred Franks, Jr. (ret), *Into the Storm*, 1998.

MY FIRST CONCERN was not that I might fail God and country, although I certainly hoped that I would not. I was afraid to fail my friends. I was afraid to come back from an interrogation and tell them I couldn't hold up as well as they had. However I measured my character before Vietnam no longer mattered. What mattered now was how they measured my character. My self-regard became indivisible from their regard for me. And it will remain so for the rest of my life.
Captain John McCain, Jr., of his imperishable bond with his fellow POWs, *Faith of My Fathers*, 1999.

CONCENTRATION

THE FEW [are the ones] who prepare against others; the many [are the ones] who make others prepare against them.
Sun Tzu, *The Art of War*, 6, c. 500 BC, tr. Ralph Sawyer, 1985.

ONE should never risk one's whole fortune unless supported by one's entire forces.
Niccolo Machiavelli, *Discourses*, 1517.

THERE IS an ancient rule of war that cannot be repeated often enough: hold your forces together, make no detachments, and, when you are ready to fight the enemy, assemble all your forces and seize every advantage to make sure of success. This rule is so certain that most of the generals who have neglected it have been punished promptly.
Frederick the Great, *Instructions to His Generals*, 1747, tr. Phillips, 1940.

PETTY GENIUSES attempt to hold everything; wise men hold fast to the most important points. They parry great blows and scorn little accidents. There is an ancient apothegm: he who would preserve everything, preserves nothing. Therefore, always sacrifice the bagatelle and pursue the essential! The essential is to be found where big bodies of the enemy are. Stick to

defeating them decisively, and the detachments will flee by themselves or you can hunt them down without difficulty.
Frederick the Great, *Instructions to His Generals*, 1747, tr. Phillips, 1940.

IT IS an ancient rule of war, and I am just repeating it – if you separate your forces you will be beaten in detail. When you give battle you must concentrate all the troops you can – you cannot find a better use for them.
Frederick the Great, *Principes Généraux de la Guerre*, 1748, quoted in Christopher Duffy, *The Military Life of Frederick the Great*, 1985.

I AM DEBOUCHING in Saxony with my whole army in three columns. You lead the right; half a day's march behind you is the corps of Marshal Ney, and one day's march behind you are 10,000 Bavarians; all of which totals more than 50,000 men. Marshal Bernadotte leads the centre; behind him Marshal Davout's corps is marching, with the greater part of the Reserve Cavalry and my Guard; which totals over 70,000 men. (Bernadotte) will debouch through Kronach. The 5th corps leads my left, and I am followed by the corps of Marshal Augereau. They will come through Coburg and Saalfeld, and will make upwards of 40,000 men. The day you reach Hof, the rest of the army will be in line with you. I shall hold myself in general at the centre. With so great a preponderance in numbers, and so closely concentrated, you will realize, that my purpose is not to jump at chances but to attack the enemy, wherever they choose to make a stand, with double their numbers.
Napoleon, 5 October 1806, to Marshal Soult at the beginning of the campaign against Prussia, quoted in R.M. Johnston, ed., *The Corsican*, 1910.

TRUE MILITARY ART consists of the ability to be stronger than the enemy at the given moment.
Military art is the art of separating for life and uniting for battle.
On the battlefield there is no such thing as a surplus battalion or squadron.
Commanders who save fresh forces for operations after the battle will almost always be defeated.
Napoleon's sayings on concentration, quoted in V.Ye. Savkin, *Basic Principles of Operational Art and Tactics*, 1972.

MAXIM 28. No force should be detached on the eve of a battle, because affairs may change during the night, either by the retreat of the enemy, or by the arrival of large reinforcements to enable him to resume the offensive, and counteract your previous dispositions.
Napoleon, *The Military Maxims of Napoleon*, tr. George D'Aguilar, 1831 (David Chandler, ed., 1987).

MAXIM 29. When you have resolved to fight a battle,

collect your whole force. Dispense with nothing. A single battalion sometimes decides the day.
> Napoleon, *The Military Maxims of Napoleon*, tr. George D'Aguilar, 1831 (David Chandler, ed., 1987).

NEVER DIVIDE your forces where the outcome is to be decided. . . . Major goals may be achieved only by decisive attacks. Therefore the most important art of a general consists of the following: *correctly determine the moment and points when and where such decisive attacks can be delivered* with the greatest probability of favorable results. Such a decisive attack is possible only with a superiority in forces at the point at which it is delivered. . . . These principles, lying in the nature of war and being the sole ones leading to decisive results, permit a definition of military art as follows: *it consists of the art of concentrating and using numerically superior forces at the decisive point*.
> Archduke Charles of Austria (1771–1847), quoted in V.Ye. Savkin, *Basic Principles of Operational Art and Tactics*, 1972.

THE BEST STRATEGY is always *to be very strong*; first in general, and then at the decisive point. Apart from the effort needed to create military strength, which does not always emanate from the general, there is no higher and simpler law of strategy than of *keeping one's forces concentrated*.
> Major-General Carl von Clausewitz, *On War*, 3.11, 1832, tr. Michael Howard and Peter Paret, 1976.

WAR is the impact of opposing forces. It follows that the stronger force not only destroys the weaker, but that its impetus carries the weaker force along with it. This would seem not to allow a protracted, consecutive employment of force: instead, the simultaneous use of all means intended for a given action appears as an elementary law of war.
> Major-General Carl von Clausewitz, *On War*, 3.12, 1832, tr. Michael Howard and Peter Paret, 1976.

CONCENTRATION sums up in itself all the other factors, the entire alphabet of military efficiency in war.
> Lieutenant-General Antoine-Henri Baron de Jomini, quoted in Richard Simpkin, *Race to the Swift*, 1985.

ONE great principle underlies all the operations of war – a principle which must be followed in all good combinations. It is embraced in the following maxims:
1. To throw by strategic movements the mass of an army, successively, upon the decisive points of a theater of war, and also upon the communications of the enemy as much as possible without compromising one's own.
2. To maneuver to engage fractions of the hostile army with the bulk of one's own forces.
3. On the battlefield, to throw the mass of the forces upon the decisive point, or upon that portion of the hostile line which it is of the first importance to overthrow.

4. To so arrange that these masses shall not only be thrown upon the decisive point, but that they shall engage at the proper times and with ample energy.
   This principle has too much simplicity to escape criticism . . . .
> Lieutenant-General Antoine-Henri Baron de Jomini, *Summary of the Art of War*, 1838, tr. Mendell and Craighill, 1862.

ANOTHER RULE – never fight against heavy odds, if by any possible maneuvering you can hurl your own forces on only a part, and then the weakest part, of your enemy and crush it. Such tactics will win every time, and a small army may thus destroy a large one in detail, and repeated victory will make it invincible.
> Lieutenant-General Thomas J. 'Stonewall' Jackson, 1862, quoted in G.F.R. Henderson, *Stonewall Jackson*, 1898.

I ALWAYS make it a rule to get there first with the most men.
> Lieutenant-General Nathan Bedford Forrest (1821–1877). Note: This statement has often been rendered popularly as 'Git thar furst with the mostest.'

TO REMAIN separated as long as possible while operating and to be concentrated in good time for the decisive battle, that is the task of the leader of large masses of troops.
> Field Marshal Helmuth Graf von Moltke, *Instructions for Superior Commanders of Troops*, 1869.

IN ANY military scheme that comes before you, let your first question be, Is this consistent with the requirement of concentration?
> Rear Admiral Alfred Thayer Mahan, *Naval Strategy*, 1911.

THE FUNDAMENTAL OBJECT in all military combinations is to gain local superiority by concentration.
> Rear Admiral Alfred Thayer Mahan, *Naval Strategy*, 1911.

IT IS NO USE to get there first unless, when the enemy arrives, you have also the greater men – the greater force.
> Rear Admiral Alfred Thayer Mahan (1840–1914).

ONE MUST NOT rely on the heroism of the troops. Strategy must furnish tactics with tasks easy to accomplish. This is obtained in the first place by the concentration in the place of the main blow of forces many times superior to those of the enemy.
> Marshal of the Soviet Union Mikhail N. Tukhachevskiy, 1920, quoted in Leites, *The Soviet Style in War*, 1982.

THE PRINCIPLE OF CONCENTRATION.
Concentration, or the bringing of things or ideas to a point of union, presupposes movement; movement of

ideas, especially in an army, is a far more difficult operation than the movement of men. Nevertheless, unless ideas, strategical, tactical and administrative, be concentrated, cohesion of effort will not result; and in proportion as annuity of action is lacking, so will an army's strength, moral and physical, be squandered in detail until a period be arrived at in which the smallest result will be obtained from every effort.

Major-General J.F.C. Fuller, *The Reformation of War*, 1923.

TO HAVE at the decisive moment, at the decisive point, an overwhelming superiority of force – this law of military success is also the law of political success, especially in that seething and bitter war of classes which is called revolution.

V.I. Lenin, quoted in Leon Trotsky, *The History of the Russian Revolution*, 1932.

ALL THROUGH HISTORY, from the days of the great phalanx of the Roman Legion, the master law of tactics remains unchanged; this law is that to achieve success you must be superior at the point where you intend to strike the decisive blow.

Field Marshal Viscount Montgomery of Alamein, 'The Growth of Modern Infantry Tactics', *Antelope*, 1/1925.

MY STRATEGY is one against ten, my tactic ten against one.

Mao Tse-tung, quoted in Dennis and Ching Ping Bloodworth, *The Chinese Machiavelli*, 1976.

I DON'T CARE how many tanks you British have so long as you keep splitting them up the way you do. I shall just continue to destroy them piecemeal.

Field Marshal Erwin Rommel, 1941, to a captured British brigadier, quoted in Alan Moorehead, *The March to Tunis*, 1943.

CONCENTRATION is supposed to be exceptional only because people do not try and, in this, as in so many things, starve within an inch of plenty.

S.L.A. Marshall, *The Armed Forces Officer*, 1950.

THE PRINCIPLES of war, not merely one principle, can be condensed into a single word – "concentration." But for truth this needs to be amplified as the "concentration of strength against weakness." And for any real value it needs to be explained that the concentration of strength against weakness depends on the dispersion of your opponent's strength, which in turn is produced by a distribution of your own that gives the appearance, and partial effect of dispersion. Your dispersion, his dispersion, your concentration – such is the sequence, and each is a sequel. True concentration is the fruit of calculated dispersion.

Captain Sir Basil Liddell Hart, *Strategy*, 1954.

THE ENEMY found himself face to face with a contradiction: without scattering his forces it was impossible for him to occupy the invaded territory; in scattering his forces, he put himself in difficulties. His scattered units would fall easy prey to our troops, his mobile forces would be more and more reduced and the shortage of troops would be all the more acute. On the other hand if he concentrated his forces to move from the defensive position to cope with us with more initiative, the occupation forces would be weakened and it would be difficult for him to hold the invaded territory. Now, if the enemy gives up occupied territory, the very aim of the war of re-conquest is defeated.

General Vo Nguyen Giap, referring to General Navarre's dilemma in the First Indochina War, *People's War – People's Army*, 1961.

OPPOSE the strategy of striking with two "fists" in two directions at the same time, and uphold the strategy of striking with one "fist" in one direction at a time.

Mao Tse-tung, *Selected Military Writings*, 1967.

CONFIDENCE

THE TROOPS must have confidence in the orders of their seniors. The orders of their superiors is the source whence discipline is born.

Wu Ch'i (430–381 BC), *Art of War*, quoted in Sun Tzu, *The Art of War*, c. 500 BC, tr. Samuel Griffith, 1969.

REMEMBER, that already danger has often threatened you and you have looked it triumphantly in the face; this time the struggle will be between a victorious army and an enemy already once vanquished.

Alexander the Great, October 333 BC, address to his army before the Battle of Issus, quoted in Arrian, *The Campaigns of Alexander*, 2.7, c. AD 150, tr. Aubrey de Sélincourt, 1987.

WHENEVER despondency or fear has fallen on an army because the enemy has received reinforcements or gained an advantage, then especially the general should show himself to his soldiers gay, cheerful and undaunted. For the appearance of the leaders brings about a corresponding change in the minds of the subordinates, and if the general is cheerful and has a joyful look, the army also takes heart, believing that there is no danger . . .

Onasander, *The General*, AD 58, (*Aeneas Tacticus, Aclepiodotus, Onasander*, tr. The Illinois Greek Club, 1923).

THE CONSUL Valerius Laevinus, having caught a spy within his camp, and having entire confidence in his own forces, ordered the man to be led around, and observing that, for the sake of terrifying the enemy, his army was open to inspection by the spies of the enemy, as often as they wished.

Frontinus, *Stratagems*, 4.7, c. AD 84–96, tr. Charles E. Bennett, 1925.

TROOPS are not to be led into battle unless confident of success.

Flavius Vegetius Renatus, *Military Institutions of the Romans*, c. AD 378, tr. Clark, 1776.

WHEN the general leads his men out to battle, he should present a cheerful appearance, avoiding any gloomy look. Soldiers usually estimate their prospects by the appearance of the general.

The Emperor Maurice, *The Strategikon*, c. AD 600 (*Maurice's Strategikon*, tr. George Dennis, 1984).

IN CONNECTION with military matters, one must never say that something can absolutely not be done. By this, the limitations of one's heart will be exposed.

Asakura Norikage (1477–1555) *Soteki Waki*, c. 1550 (*Ideals of the Samurai*, tr. William Wilson, 1982).

ONE SHOULD NEVER display a weak attitude, even though he may be with sympathetic relatives or retainers. In the *San Lueh* it says, "If a man loses his courage, his servants and soldiers will lose their respect for him."

Takeda Nobushige (1525–1561), *Opinions in 99 Articles*, (*Ideals of the Samurai*, tr. William Wilson, 1982).

THERE IS plenty of time to win this game, and to thrash the Spaniards too.

Sir Francis Drake, 20 July 1588, while playing bowls when the Spanish Armada was sighted.

THIS IS a maxim that the most experienced captains of this era hold to be true: that many more battles are won by well ordered ranks and by a fine appearance than by gun shot or blows from a sword. Such well ordered ranks make one appear confident, and it seems that it is sufficient merely to give the appearance of being brave, since most often our enemies will not await us long enough to let us show if we are in actual fact . . .

Louis XIV, *Mémoires de Louis XIV*, 1860, quoted in David Ralston, *Soldiers and States*, 1966.

EVERY MAN passed through my hands, and he was told that nothing more remained for him to know, if only he did not forget what he had learned. Thus he was given confidence in himself, the foundation of bravery.

Field Marshal Prince Aleksandr V. Suvorov (1729–1800), quoted in W. Lyon Blease, *Suvorof*, 1920.

A GREAT AND GOOD general is . . . in himself an host; for his influence, insinuating itself into every member of the military body, connects and binds the whole together imperceptibly, but firmly and securely. Such confidence in a leader is the charm against a panic.

Robert Jackson, *A Systematic View of the Formation, Discipline, and Economy of Armies*, 1804.

I AM THINKING of the French I am going to fight. I have not seen them since the campaigns in Flanders [1793–1794] when they were capital soldiers, and a dozen years of victory under Bonaparte must have made them better still. 'Tis enough to make one thoughtful. But though they may overwhelm me, I don't think they will outmanoeuvre me. First, because I am not afraid of them, as every one else seems to be, and secondly, because (if all I hear about their system is true) I think it a false one against steady troops. I suspect all the continental armies are half-beaten before the battle begins. I at least will not be frightened beforehand.

The Duke of Wellington, early July 1808, conversation with John Croker on the eve of the Peninsular War, cited in Charles Oman, *Wellington's Army*, 1913.

THE SPANIARDS make excellent soldiers. What spoils them is that they have no confidence in their officers – this would ruin any soldiers – and how should the Spaniards have confidence in such officers as theirs?

The Duke of Wellington, during the Peninsular War (1808–1813), quoted in John Croker, *The Croker Papers*, III, 1884

DEPEND upon it. It requires time for a general to inspire confidence or to feel it; for you will never have confidence in yourself until others have confidence in you.

The Duke of Wellington to Earl Stanhope, *Notes on the Conversations with the Duke of Wellington*, 1888.

CONFIDENCE, the dawn of victory, inspired the whole line.

Major-General Winfield Scott, May 1814, letter, quoted in Eisenhower, *Agent of Destiny*, 1997.

I THINK, in summing up my reflections, that it would be useless to advise colonels of infantry regiments to avoid, with the greatest care, a reverse at the opening of the campaign. The least check has more influence than is generally supposed upon remaining operations of the campaign: it diminishes confidence in the men, by raising mistrust of the commander's talents. The least success, on the contrary, impresses upon the troops, from the very beginning, that just military pride which doubles their strength, and serves as a presage of a series of brilliant feats.

Marshal of France Michel Ney, Duc d'Elchingen, Prince de la Moskova, *Memoirs of Marshal Ney*, 1834.

THE GENERAL commanding would warmly express to the officers and men under his command his joy in their achievements, and his thanks for their brilliant gallantry in action, and their patient obedience under the hardships of forced marches, often more painful to the brave soldier than the dangers of battle. The explanation of the severe exertions to which the Commanding General called the army, which were endured by them with such cheerful confidence in him, is now given in the victory of yesterday. He receives this proof of their confidence in the past with pride and gratitude, and asks only a similar confidence in the future.

> Lieutenant-General Thomas J. 'Stonewall' Jackson, thanks to his army after the Battle of Winchester, 26 May 1862, quoted in R.I. Dabney, *Life of Jackson*, 1866.

NO MATTER what may be the ability of the officer, if he loses the confidence of his troops, disaster must sooner or later ensue.

> General Robert E. Lee, 8 August 1863, letter to Jefferson Davis.

AS I TOLD YOU on the 5th, it pleased God to grant me one of the hardest earned victories of my life, and one momentous to the country, over the rebel ram Tennessee. I always said I was the proper man to fight her because I was one of those who believed I could do it successfully. I was certainly honest in my convictions and determined in my will, but I did not know how formidable the Tennessee was.

> Admiral David G. Farragut, 8 August 1864, quoted in Loyall Farragut, *The Life of Admiral David Glasgow Farragut*, 1879.

YOU WERE the only commander of that army whom men and officers were disposed to trust and confide in without reserve. While at Dalton, I frequently heard this subject, of the unbounded confidence of the men in 'Old Joe,' discussed among the officers, who seemed but little, if any, exceeded by the rank and file in this respect. The officers seemed to regard this feeling as a great element of strength (as it certainly was), and looked upon it as a part of their duty to cherish and promote it. The army had confidence *in itself*, and had long been wanting a commander in whom they could place reliance. The consequence was that it *surrendered to you*; they gave you their *love* and *unlimited confidence*, were willing to follow you, advancing or retreating, and you could have led them wherever you chose. At the time of the retreat from Resaca, and perhaps for a few days following, this feeling of *entire trust* in you abated; but it speedily revived, and was as perfect as ever when you retired. I cannot imagine it possible for an army to entertain more personal affection for a commander, or to place more implicit reliance on one, than that army did for you. I believe the last man of them would have willingly died at your bidding.

 . . . Another officer advanced the opinion that it was because they believed General Johnston would take care of them and not expose them to danger. I interrupted, and asserted emphatically that such ideas did great injustice to an army; that the true reason of their confidence in General Johnston was, they trusted his skill and judgement, and believed that, whenever he issued an order for battle, they would fight to some

purpose. They *would* have engaged the enemy under your command, on the day you left it, with as much cheerfulness and confidence, as on the day the campaign opened. . . . The Army of Tennessee *loved* you and *confided in you implicitly*, as an army of brave men will love and confide in *skill*, *pluck*, and *honor*. . . .

> Lieutenant-General Alexander P. Stewart, 11 February 1868, appraisal of General Joseph E. Johnston's relationship with his Army of Tennessee, quoted in Joseph Johnston, *Narrative*, 1874.

CONFIDENT language by a military commander is not usually regarded as evidence of competence.

> General Joseph E. Johnston, 18 July 1864; his tart rejoinder to President Davis' relief of him, citing in part his lack of confidence that he could defeat Sherman who was at the gates of Atlanta, *Narrative*, 1874.

MY ARMY is now in the very condition to be supplied with recruits. We have good corporals and sergeants, and some good lieutenants and captains, and those are more important than generals. They all seem to have implicit confidence in me. They observe success at points remote, as in this case of Atlanta, and they naturally say that the old man knows what he is about. They think I know where every road and by-path is in Georgia, and one soldier swore that I was born on Kenesaw Mountain.

> General William T. Sherman, letter to General Halleck after taking Atlanta, 3 September 1864, *The War of the Rebellion: A Compilation of the Official Records of the Union and Confederate Armies*, Series I, Volume XXXVIII, Part 5, pp. 793–794, U.S. Government Printing Office, 1880–1901.

I NEVER SAW a more confident army. The soldiers think I know everything and that they can do anything.

> General William T. Sherman, letter to his wife after taking Savanna, 16 December 1864, *Home Letters*, 1909.

MY SUCCESS had been so uninterrupted that the men thought that victory was chained to my standard. Men who go into a fight under the influence of such feelings are next to invincible, and generally are the victors before it begins.

> Colonel John S. Mosby, *Mosby's War Reminiscences*, 1887.

PERSONAL BRAVERY of a single individual alone is not decisive on the day of battle, but rather bravery of the corps, and the latter rests on the good opinion and the confidence that each individual soldier places in the corps to which he belongs.

> Field Marshal Colmar von der Goltz (1843–1916), *Rossbach und Jena*.

IN EACH BATTLE there is a moment when even the bravest soldiers feel like fleeing. This panic is caused by the lack of confidence in their own courage. However, any event, any pretext can return confidence to them. The highest military art is to create these events or pretexts.

> Mikhail V. Frunze (1885–1925), quoted in Gareyev, *M.V. Frunze, Military Theorist*, 1985.

IF CONFIDENCE be indeed "half the battle", then to undermine the enemy's confidence is more than the other half – because it gains the fruits without an all-out fight. (April 1929.)

> Captain Sir Basil Liddell Hart, *Thoughts on War*, 1944.

LATE ONE NIGHT during the war, after a certain serious decision had been taken, my chief coadjutor came to me full of doubts as to whether our decision had been right. "Let it be," I answered. "Only military academies fifty years hence will know for certain whether we did right or wrong."

> Colonel General Hans von Seekt, *Thoughts of a Soldier*, 1930.

FOR TWO WEEKS Puller had commanded the rear of the First Marine Division, cut off in the Chosin Reservoir region by hundreds of thousands of Chinese Communist troops. The colonel was visiting a hospital tent where a priest administered last rites to Marine wounded when a messenger came:

"Sir, do you know they've cut us off? We're entirely surrounded."

"Those poor bastards," Puller said, "They've got us right where we want 'em. We can shoot in every direction now."

> Lieutenant-General Lewis B. 'Chesty' Puller, 1950, as narrated in Burke Davis, *Marine!*, 1962.

FINALLY, that confidence is the *sine qua non* of all useful military power. The moral strength of an organic unit comes from the faith in the ranks that they are being wisely directed and from faith up top that orders will be obeyed. When forces are tempered by this spirit, there is no limit to their enterprise. They become invincible. Lacking it, however, any military body, even though it has been compelled to toe the mark in training, will deteriorate into a rabble under conditions of extraordinary stress in the field, as McDowell's Army did at Bull Run in the American Civil War, and as Hitler's Armies did in 1945 after the Rhine had been crossed at Remagen.

> Brigadier-General S.L.A. Marshall, *The Armed Forces Officer*, 1950.

HOWEVER DESPERATE the situation, a senior commander must always exude confidence in the presence of his subordinates. For anxiety, topside, can spread like cancer down through the command.

> General of the Army Omar Bradley, *A Soldier's Story*, 1951.

THE GENERAL who sees that the soldier is well fed and looked after, and who puts him into a good

show and wins battles, will naturally have his confidence. Whether he will also have his affection is another story. . . . But does it matter to a general whether he has his men's affection so long as he has their confidence? He must certainly never court popularity. If he has their appreciation and respect it is sufficient. Efficiency in a general his soldiers have a right to expect; geniality they are usually right to suspect. Marlborough was perhaps the only great general to whom geniality was always natural.

> Field Marshal Viscount Wavell of Cyrenaica, *Soldiers and Soldiering*, 1953.

PROBABLY one of the greatest assets a commander can have is the ability to radiate confidence in the plan and operations even (perhaps especially) when inwardly he is not too sure about the outcome.

> Field Marshal Viscount Montgomery of Alamein, *The Memoirs of Field Marshal Montgomery*, 1958.

SENIOR OFFICERS decrying the low morale of their forces evidently do not realize that the esprit of the men is but a mirror of their confidence in their leadership. Confidence in leaders is an accepted ingredient of organizational spirit. However, dissentions among the top command, like a single drop of poison in wine, can destroy all partakers.

> General of the Army Omar Bradley, *A General's Life*, 1983.

ALLIED COMMANDS depend on mutual confidence. How is mutual confidence developed? You don't command it. . . . By development of common understanding of the problems, by approaching these things on the widest possible basis with respect to each other's opinions, and above all, through the development of friendships, this confidence is gained in families and in Allied Staffs.

> General of the Army Dwight D. Eisenhower, quoted in Joint Pub 1, *Joint Warfare of the US Armed Forces*, 1991.

NO MATTER the pressure, I kept in mind that people were always looking to me as a commander. So I was very careful not to convey my internal stress or fatigue to the people around me. I always made it a point of trying to look rested, no matter how tired. I always tried to smile. Not frivolous laughter, but keeping in good humor. I walked around with a smile, saying, "How you doing today? How's it going?" If I had doubts, I kept them to myself. I had a deputy, Colonel Tom Olson, who was my confidant. In private I had frank discussion with him.

> General Charles Horner, of the pressure during the initial build-up in Desert Shield, 'Trip Wire', Al Santoli, ed., *Leading the Way: How Vietnam Veterans Rebuilt the U.S. Military*, 1993.

THE INTANGIBLE INGREDIENTS of competent force are spirit, morale, and leadership by example. When discipline and self-respect breaks down, that usually starts at the top. If the senior leadership becomes a hierarchy of compromise, when it comes time to make life or death decisions, troops won't believe that their superiors are looking out for their best interest. And as a result, they won't perform very well.

James Webb, 'Policy Decisions', Al Santoli, ed., *Leading the Way: How Vietnam Veterans Rebuilt the U.S. Military*, 1993.

CONSCIENCE

LABOR to keep alive in your breast that little spark of celestial fire called conscience.

General George Washington (1732–1799).

I KNOW I shall be relieved, but I could not order an assault against my conscience. I would rather a thousand times to be relieved, charged with tardiness or incompetency, than have my conscience burdened with a wanton slaughter uselessly of brave men, or having jeopardized the great cause by doing what I thought was wrong.

Major-General George G. Meade, to Colonel Biddle of his staff after his decision not to assault the Confederate entrenchments at Mine Run, November, 1863, quoted in Pennypacker, *General Meade*, 1901.

IN THIS SOLEMN HOUR it is a consolation to recall and to dwell upon our repeated efforts for peace. All have been ill-starred, but all have been faithful and sincere. This is of the highest moral value – and not only moral value, but practical value – at the present time, because of the wholehearted concurrence of scores of millions of men and women, whose cooperation is indispensable and whose comradeship and brotherhood are indispensable, is the only foundation upon which the trial and tribulation of modern war can be endured and surmounted. This moral conviction alone affords that ever-fresh resilience which renews the strength and energy of people in long, doubtful and dark days. Outside, the storms of war may blow and the lands may be lashed with the fury of its gales, but in our own hearts this Sunday morning there is peace. Our hands may be active, but our consciences are at rest.

Sir Winston S. Churchill, 3 September 1939, upon the declaration of war against Germany, *Blood, Sweat, and Tears*, 1941.

THE ONLY GUIDE to a man is his conscience; the only shield to his memory is the rectitude and sincerity of his actions. It is very imprudent to walk through life without this shield, because we are so often mocked by the failure of our hopes and the upsetting of our calculations; but with this shield, however the fates may play, we march always in the ranks of honour.

Sir Winston S. Churchill, 12 November 1940, tribute in the House of Commons to the late Neville Chamberlain.

DESPITE HIS DOUBTS about the universal validity of the deliverances of conscience, our model officer recognizes that there is in himself an instinctive resistance to actions inconsistent with principles of behavior he learned to follow early in his career. Perhaps this is the voice of his professional conscience; if so, he is happy to have one to keep him straight and will give it due heed. However, he is most unsympathetic with officers who use conscience as an excuse for dereliction of duty or the avoidance of dangerous or unpleasant tasks. In his view, such conduct is worthy of the disdain accorded the soldier who does not discover until the eve of battle that he is a conscientious objector.

General Maxwell D. Taylor, 'A Do-It-Yourself Professional Code for the Military', *Parameters*, 12/1980.

ONCE a soldier's conscience is aroused, it defines a line he dare not cross and deeds he dare not commit, regardless of orders, because those very deeds would destroy something in him which he values more than life itself. If the path of military operations and this line of a soldier's conscience collide, disobedience and mutiny erupt.

Lieutenant-General Sir James Glover, 'A Soldier and His Conscience', *Parameters*, 9/1983.

A MAN OF WAR fights better if his mind is at peace. And a quiet yet active conscience is where a sustained effort is made to enlighten and educate the soldier, and where leadership by persuasion rules. If the soldier is to retain an open conscience, he rejects at his peril the society of which he is part. This is not to say that he should necessarily mirror that society's standards, but rather that he must steadfastly preserve his own discipline, professionalism, and self-respect.

Lieutenant-General Sir James Glover, 'A Soldier and His Conscience', *Parameters*, 9/1983.

CONSCIENTIOUS OBJECTOR

NO MAN who is not willing to bear arms and to fight for his rights can give a good reason why he should be entitled to the privilege of living in a free community.

President Theodore Roosevelt, *Thomas Hart Benton*, 1897.

THERE ARE only two classes who, as categories, show courage in war – the front-line soldier and the conscientious objector.

Captain Sir Basil Liddell Hart, *Thoughts on War*, 1944.

WHEN I was in Washington to receive the Congressional Medal of Honor, in this line-up to receive the same honor was a young fellow who bore the Red Cross. He was a hospital corpsman, and as he stepped by I really got a big lump in my throat. This man had one eye shot out as well as many other injuries. He had been a conscientious objector (before the war), but he had earned his medal by proving what he thought was right. He had received his injuries while picking up Marines on the fire-swept hills on Iwo Jima. He had then, in his own way, really fought for what he believed.

Colonel Gregory 'Pappy' Boyington, *Baa Baa Black Sheep*, 1958.

CONSCRIPTION

I HAVE, it is true, many conscripts in my army, but they are Frenchmen. Four years ago did I not with a feeble army drive before me hordes of Sardinians and Austrians, and scour the face of Italy? We shall do so again. The sun which now shines on us is the same that shone at Arcola and Lodi.

Napoleon, May 1800, at the beginning of the Marengo campaign, quoted in Louis de Bourrienne, *Memoirs of Napoleon Bonaparte*, II, 1855.

YOU HAVE the impudence to talk of the conscription in France; it wounds your pride because it fell upon all ranks. Oh, how shocking, that a gentleman's son should be obliged to defend his country, just as if he were one of the mob!

The conscription did not crush a particular class like your press-gang, nor the rabble, because they were poor. My rabble would have become the best educated in the world. All my exertions were directed to illuminate the mass of the nation instead of brutalizing them by ignorance and superstition.

Napoleon, 18 February 1818, on St. Helena, quoted in R.M. Johnston, ed., *The Corsican*, 1910.

CONSCRIPTION forms citizen armies. Voluntary enlistment forms armies of vagrants and good-for-nothings. The former are guided by honor; mere discipline controls the latter.

Napoleon (1769–1821), quoted in Christopher Herold, ed., *The Mind of Napoleon*, 1955.

CONSCRIPTION is the vitality of a nation, the purification of its morality, and the real foundations of all its habits.

Napoleon, *Political Aphorisms*, 1848.

THE SOUTH, as we all knew, were conscripting every able-bodied man between the ages of eighteen and forty-five; and now they had passed a law for the further conscription of boys from fourteen to eighteen, calling them the junior reserves, and men from forty-five to sixty to be called the senior reserves. The latter were to hold the necessary points not in immediate danger, and especially those in the rear. General Butler, in alluding to this conscription, remarked that they were thus "robbing both the cradle and the grave," an expression which I afterwards used in writing a letter to Mr. Washburn.

General Ulysses S. Grant, of the last months of the American Civil War, *Personal Memoirs*, II, 1885.

GRANT SAYS the Confederates, in their endeavors to get men, have robbed the cradle and the grave; if that is the case, I must say their ghosts and babies fight well!

Major-General George G. Meade, comment to his staff, 12 December 1864.

AS I HAVE SAID, the whole South was a military camp. . . . The cause was popular, and was enthusiastically supported by the young men. The conscription took all of them. Before the war was over, further conscription took those between fourteen and eighteen years of age as junior reserves, and those between forty-five and sixty as senior reserves. It would have been an offense, directly after the war and perhaps it would be now, to ask any able-bodied man in the South, who was between the ages of fourteen and sixty at any time during the war, whether he had been in the Confederate army. He would assert that he had, or account for his absence from the ranks. Under such circumstances it is hard to conceive how the North showed such superiority of force in every battle fought. I know they did not.

General Ulysses S. Grant, *Personal Memoirs*, II, 1885.

THE SYSTEM of conscription has always tended to foster quantity at the expense of quality.

Captain Sir Basil Liddell Hart, *The Untimeliness of a Conscript Army*, 1950.

ANY RECRUITER will tell you that the incentive for enlistment is it [being drafted] is inevitable if you don't.

Lieutenant-General Lewis B. Hershey, director of the Selective Service System, address at the American University, Washington, D.C., 11 December 1966, quoted in *The New York Times*, 12 December 1966.

CONTACT

AT LAST the armies clashed at one strategic point, they slammed their shields together, pike-scraped pike with the grappling strength of fighters armed in bronze and their round shields pounded, boss on welded boss, and the sound of struggle roared and rocked the earth. Screams of men and cries of triumph breaking in one breath, fighters killing, fighters killed, and the ground streamed blood. Wildly as two winter torrents raging down from the mountains, swirling into a valley, hurl their great waters together, flash floods from the wellsprings plunging down in a gorge and miles away in the hills a shepherd hears the thunder – so from the grinding armies broke the cries and crash of war.

Homer, *The Iliad*, 4.517–528, c. 800 BC, tr. Robert Fagles, 1990.

ANOTHER WOMAN, in reply to her son who

declared that the sword he had was a small one, said: 'Then extend it by a stride.'

> An anonymous Spartan mother, quoted in Plutarch, *The Lives*, c. AD 100 (*Plutarch on Sparta*, tr. Richard Talbert, 1988).

AT THE LUXEMBOURG, during the provisional consulate, he [Abbé Siéyès] often awakened his colleague Napoleon, and harassed him about the new plots which he heard of every moment from his private police. "But have they corrupted our guard?" Napoleon used to say. "No." "Then go to bed. – In war, as in love, my dear Sir, we must come to close quarters to conclude matters. It will be time enough to be alarmed when our 600 men are attacked.

> Napoleon, November 1799, quoted in Emmanuel Las Casas, *The Life, Exile, and Conversations of the Emperor Napoleon*, II, 1890.

WHEREVER the enemy goes, let our troops go also.

> General of the Army Ulysses S. Grant, 1 August 1864, dispatch to General Halleck about Sheridan's operations in the Shenandoah Valley.

BEAR IN MIND, the object is to drive the enemy south; and to do this you want to keep him always in sight. Be guided in your course by the course he takes.

> General of the Army Ulysses S. Grant, 5 August 1864, orders to General Sheridan about the upcoming operations in the Shenandoah Valley, quoted in Sheridan, *Personal Memoirs of P.H. Sheridan*, 1888.

IN MODERN BATTLE, which is delivered with combatants so far apart, man has come to have a horror of man. He comes to hand-to-hand fighting only to defend his body, or if forced to it by some fortuitous encounter. . . . It may be said that he seeks to catch the fugitive only for fear that he will turn and fight.

> Colonel Charles Ardant du Picq, *Battle Studies*, 1880, tr. Greely, 1957.

CONTACT (a word which perhaps better than any other indicates the dividing line between tactics and strategy).

> Rear Admiral Alfred Thayer Mahan, *The Influence of Sea Power Upon History*, 1890.

IF YOUR SWORD is too short, take one step forward.

> Admiral Marquis Heihachiro Togo, 15 May 1905.

CONTACT is information of the most tangible kind, an enemy met with is an enemy at grips, and, as in a wrestling match, contact is likely to be followed by much foot-play. Time still remains the decisive factor, time wherein to modify a plan according to the information contact gains.

> Major-General J.F.C. Fuller, *Armoured Warfare*, 1943.

INFANTRY must move forward to close with the enemy. It must shoot in order to move. . . . To halt under fire is folly. To halt under fire and not fire back is suicide. Officers must set the example.

> General George S. Patton, Jr., *War As I Knew It*, 1947.

BOYS, we've been seeking the enemy and now we have found them. They are in front of us, behind us, and on both our flanks.

> Lieutenant-General Lewis B. 'Chesty' Puller, December 1950, at the Chosin Reservoir when the Chinese entered the Korean War, Puller Collection, Marine Corps Historical Division.

CONTINGENCY

THE SHARP general takes into account not only probable dangers, but also those which may be totally unexpected.

> The Emperor Maurice, *The Strategikon*, c. AD 600 (*Maurice's Strategikon*, tr. George Dennis, 1984).

IN BATTLES and in every action against the enemy the wise general, even the most courageous, will keep in mind the possibility of failure and defeat and will plan for them as actually occurring.

> The Emperor Maurice, *The Strategikon*, c. AD 600 (*Maurice's Strategikon*, tr. George Dennis, 1984).

MAXIM 2. In forming the plan of a campaign, it is requisite to foresee everything the enemy may do, and to be prepared with the necessary means to counteract it.

Plans of campaign may be modified ad infinitum according to circumstances, the genius of the general, the character of the troops, and the features of the country.

> Napoleon, *The Military Maxims of Napoleon*, tr. George D'Aguilar, 1831 (David Chandler, ed., 1987).

MAXIM 8. A general-in-chief should ask himself frequently in the day, What should I do if the enemy's army appeared now in my front, or on my right, or on my left? If he have any difficulty in answering these questions he is ill posted, and seek to remedy it.

> Napoleon, *The Military Maxims of Napoleon*, tr. George D'Aguilar, 1831 (David Chandler, ed., 1987).

CONTRACTORS

THERE IS NOTHING performed by contractors which may not be much better executed by intelligent officers. They make immense fortunes at the expense of the state which ought to be saved. They destroy the army, horse and foot and even hospitals, by furnishing the worst of everything.

> Major-General Henry Lloyd (1720–1783), *History of the Late War in Germany*, 1766–1782, quoted in Liddell Hart, *The Sword and the Pen*, 1976.

[CIVILIAN-CONTROLLED] BUREAUX, not to speak of the contractors, are the born enemies of all that tends to put the details of military administration into military hands.

Field Marshal Francois Comte de Guibert (1744–1790), quoted in Alfred Vagts, *A History of Militarism*, 1937.

IN THE COUNCILS of government we must guard against the acquisition of unwarranted influence, whether sought or unsought, by the military-industrial complex. The potential for the disastrous rise of misplaced power exists and will persist.

President Dwight D. Eisenhower, 17 January 1961, farewell address as President.

INCREASINGLY, our national defense is a business, and its business is not defense. . . . the reason is greed. Anyone who has served in the Pentagon has slipped on the slime trails that retired generals and admirals leave in their wake as they navigate the hallways bearing a defense contractor's business card with their name on it. . . . When, in the mid-1980s, a few voices on Capitol Hill called for closing this particular revolving door, representatives from the defense industry and the threatened officers themselves put on their red-white-and-blue war paint and chanted that the defense industry needed the expertise of senior officers. But colonels and captains, warrant officers and sergeants are the ones who have current expertise. Generals and admirals have connections.

Lieutenant-Colonel Ralph Peters, 'Hucksters in Uniform', *The Washington Monthly*, 5/1999.

CONTROL

THE CONTROL of a large force is the same in principle as the control of a few men: it is merely a question of dividing up their numbers.

Fighting with a large army under your command is nowise different from fighting with a small one: it is merely a question of instituting signs and signals.

Sun Tzu, *The Art of War*, 5, c. 500 BC, tr. Giles, 1910.

AND THEREFORE those skilled in war avoid the enemy when his spirit is keen and attack him when it is sluggish and his soldiers homesick. This is control of the moral factor.

In good order they await a disorderly enemy; in serenity, a clamorous one. This is control of the mental factor.

Close to the field of battle, they await an enemy coming from afar; at rest, an exhausted enemy; with well-fed troops, hungry ones. This is control of the physical factor.

Sun Tzu, *The Art of War*, c. 500 BC, tr. Samuel Griffith, 1963.

AFTER GAINING a victory the general who pursues

the enemy with a scattered and disorganized army gives away his victory to the foe.

The Emperor Maurice, *The Strategikon*, c. AD 600 (*Maurice's Strategikon*, tr. George Dennis, 1984).

"FIRM" command of "one's" troops by no means always signifies real control in battle. Frequently "firm" command may even run counter to development of the tactical process. Commanders who seek to control their entire order of battle "firmly", "on a tight rein", are apt to hold back the offensive during a penetration or pursuit and thus damage their chances of success.

Marshal of the Soviet Union Mikhail N. Tukhachevskiy, 1931–1932, quoted in Richard Simpkin, *Deep Battle*, 1987.

I HAVE KNOWN commanders who considered that once their plan was made and orders issued, they need take no further part in the proceedings, except to influence the battle by means of their reserves. Never was there a greater mistake. The modern battle can very quickly go off the rails. To succeed, a C.-in-C. must ensure from the beginning a very firm grip on his military machine; only in this way will his force maintain balance and cohesion and thus develop its full fighting potential. This firm grip does not mean interference, or cramping the initiative of subordinates; indeed, it is by the initiative of subordinates that the battle is won. The firm grip is essential in order that the master plan will not be undermined by the independent ideas of individual subordinate leaders at particular moments in the battle. Operations must develop within a predetermined pattern of action. If this is not done the result will be a compromise between the individual conceptions of subordinates about how operations should develop; alternatively, operations will develop as a result of situations created by subordinate action and in a way which does not suit the master plan. A third alternative is that the initiative might pass to the enemy. The master plan must never be so rigid that the C.-in-C. cannot vary it to suit the changing tactical situation; but nobody else may be allowed to change it at will – and, especially, not the enemy.

Field Marshal Viscount Montgomery of Alamein, *The Memoirs of Field Marshal Montgomery*, 1958.

HALF OF CONTROL during battle comes from the commander's avoiding useless expenditure of the physical resources of his men while taking action to break the hold of fear.

Brigadier-General S.L.A. Marshall, *The Soldier's Load and the Mobility of the Nation*, 1980.

CO-OPERATION

BUT LET SOME other chosen warriour join,
To raise my hopes, and second my design.
By mutual confidence, and mutual aid,

Great deeds are done, and great discov'ries made;
The wise new prudence from the wise acquire,
And one brave hero fans another's fire.

> Homer, *The Iliad*, 10.263–268, c. 800 BC, tr. Alexander
> Pope, 1743; Diomedes asking for a companion to
> accompany him in his reconnaissance of the Trojan
> camp.

TRUE COOPERATION requires that a subordinate should not carry out his superior's ideas in a merely wooden manner, but should do everything in his power to contribute to the full execution of his superior's intentions, using his intelligence to foresee any obstacles which may arise to prevent him carrying out the orders he receives, and taking measures accordingly. On the other hand, it is for the superior to furnish his subordinate with full indication of his intentions, so that the latter may bring his intelligence, instead of mere mechanical obedience, to bear upon the problems which will confront him. (Dec. 1919.)

> Captain Sir Basil Liddell Hart, *Thoughts on War*, 1944.

THE PRINCIPLE OF CO-OPERATION. Co-operation is a cementing principle; it is closely related to economy of force, and therefore to concentration, but it differs from both of these principles, for while mass is the concentrated strength of the organism and economy of force the dispersed strength which renders the former stable, co-operation may be likened to the muscular tension which knits all the parts to the whole. Without co-operation an army falls to pieces. In national wars, the value of co-operation is enormously enhanced, fusing, as it does, the body and soul of a nation into one intricate self-supporting organism. All must pull together, for such wars are the wars of entire nations, and, whatever may be the size of the armies operating, these should be looked upon as national weapons, and not as fractions of nations whose duty is to fight while the civil population turns thumbs up or thumbs down. Gladiatorial wars are dead and gone.

> Major-General J.F.C. Fuller, *The Reformation of
> War*, 1923.

REMEMBER also that in battle, and battles are tests of military structure, the object of each side is not to kill for the sake of killing, but for the sake of disorganizing, for military strength does not reside in individuals, but in the co-operation of individuals and masses. Co-operation depends on control; and the endurance of force depends on maintenance. Every plan must have a threefold base; it must permit of the existing structure of an army remaining unaltered, or as unaltered as possible; it must permit of the existing system of control working without friction; and it must permit of the administrative units carrying out their duties without let or hinderance.

> Major-General J.F.C. Fuller, *The Foundations of the
> Science of War*, 1926.

MY PERSONAL PHILOSOPHY is that the best outfits are those wherein a procedure is developed whereby every man who has an idea on a particular subject may bring it forward at the time of the discussion, without the slightest criticism or hesitation. He argues for his point of view when you're discussing exactly how you're going to proceed. He shouldn't hang back because his idea may appear radical, or because the bulk of the crowd may not agree with it.

Everyone steps forward and expresses an idea. Once the decision is made, however –
"This is the way we're going to do it."

Bang. Everybody complies. If a man doesn't comply, his official head should roll. He may have thought originally that we should all zig instead of zag. After hearing every argument, after listening carefully to all testimony relating to the subject, the commander has decided to zag. Everybody had better zag.

> General Curtis LeMay, *Mission With LeMay*, 1965.

MUCH WILL BE SAID about the success of joint operations during DESERT SHIELD and DESERT STORM. . . . what carried the day was that we, the component commanders, shook hands and said, "We're not going to screw this up, we're going to make it work." And it did.

> Vice Admiral Stanley R. Arthur, Commander
> NAVCENT, quoted in Joint Pub 1, *Joint Warfare of the
> US Armed Forces*, 1991.

CORRUPTION

FOR HE [Aristides], when Themistocles once was saying that he thought the highest virtue of a general was to understand and foreknow the measures the enemy would take, replied, "This, indeed, Themistocles, is simply a necessity, but the excellent thing in a general is to keep his hands from taking money."

> Aristides (c. 530–c. 468 BC), to Themistocles, quoted
> in Plutarch, *The Lives*, c. AD 100, tr. John Dryden.

SOPHOCLES, a general ought not only to have clean hands but also clean eyes.

> Pericles, c. 431 BC, to his fellow general who admired
> a beautiful youth, quoted in Plutarch, *The Lives*,
> c. AD 100, tr. John Dryden.

AN AVARICIOUS GENERAL can be the ruin of his own people and an object of contempt to the enemy.

A general who loves luxury can destroy the whole army.

> The Emperor Maurice, *The Strategikon*, c. AD 600
> (*Maurice's Strategikon*, tr. George Dennis, 1984).

. . . SUCH OF OUR MEN of war as, neglecting and condemning all true honor and discipline military, have brought in amongst us a most shameful and detestable art and discipline of carousing and drunkenness, turning all matters military to their own profit and gain, neglecting to love and to win the love of their soldiers under their governments and charges, making in a manner no account of them nor of their lives. In such sort as by their evil conduction, starving and consuming of great numbers and many thousands of our most brave English people, as also by their infinite other disorders, they have made a far greater war upon the crown and realm of England and English nation than anyways upon the enemies of our country.

> John Smythe (c. 1580–1631), *Certain Discourses Military*, 1966.

BY GOD, Mr. Chairman, at this moment I stand astonished at my own moderation!

> Robert Lord Clive, 1773, in reply to a Parliamentary inquiry into charges of corruption during his conquests in India.

SUCH DEARTH of public spirit, and such want of virtue, such stock-jobbing, and fertility in all the low arts to take advantage of one kind or another. . . . I never saw before and I pray God's mercy that I may never be witness to again!

> General George Washington (1732–1799), quoted in Lynn Montross, *War Through the Ages*, 1944.

THERE IS something in corruption which, like a jaundiced eye, transfers the color of itself to the object it looks upon, and sees everything stained and impure.

> Thomas Paine, *The American Crisis*, 1776–1783.

MEN WELL DESERVE the contempt I feel for them. I have only to put some gold lace on the coats of my virtuous republicans and they immediately become just what I wish them.

> Napoleon, 1802, conversation with his private secretary, Louis de Bourrienne, *Memoirs of Napoleon Bonaparte*, II, 1855, Vol. II.

COUNCIL OF WAR

COME WITH ME instantly, sword in hand, if you wish to save our country. The enemy's camp is nowhere more truly than in the place where such thoughts can rise!

> Scipio Africanus, on bursting into a council of panic-stricken Patricians who were planning to abandon Rome after the disaster of Cannae in 216 BC, quoted in Livy, *The History of Rome*, c. AD 17 (*The War With Hannibal*, tr. Aubrey de Sélincourt, 1972).

FOR THE ISOLATED DECISION of one man, unsupported by others, can see no farther than his own ingenuity, but that which has the additional testimony of councillors guarantees against mistake. However, the general must neither be so undecided that he entirely distrusts himself, nor so obstinate as not to think that anyone can have a better idea than his own; for such a man, either because he listens to every one else and never to himself, is sure to meet with frequent misfortune, or else, through never listening to others but always to himself, is bound to make many costly mistakes.

> Onasander, *The General*, AD 58, quoted in *Aeneas Tacticus, Aclepiodotus, Onasander*, 1923.

IT DOES NOT HELP to assemble the whole army in council, or to keep sending for men when they are off duty. These things only cause discord in the army.

> The Emperor Maurice, *The Strategikon*, c. AD 600 (*Maurice's Strategikon*, tr. George Dennis, 1984).

MY SADDLE is my council chamber.

> Saladin, c. 1180, quoted by Ibn al-Athir in *Recueil des Historiens des Croisades*, 1872–1906.

YOU HAVE BEEN with your council and I have been with mine. Believe me that the counsel of my Lord will be accomplished and will stand, and the counsel of yours will perish.

> Joan of Arc, 6 May 1429, after the capture of the English fortress of the Augustines, *Joan of Arc In Her Own Words*, 1996.

OTHERWISE we should have wasted all our time in discussions, diplomatical, tactical, enigmatical; they would have smothered me, and the enemy would have settled our arguments by smashing up our tactics.

> Field Marshal Prince Aleksandr V. Suvorov (1729–1800).

IF A MAN consults whether he is to fight, when he has the power in his own hands, it is certain that his opinion is against fighting.

> Admiral Viscount Nelson, August 1801, letter.

HOLD NO COUNCIL of war, but accept the views of each, one by one. . . . the secret is to make each alike . . . believe he has your confidence.

> Napoleon, 12 January 1806, letter to Joseph Bonaparte.

WHENEVER I hear of Councils of War being called, I always called them as "cloaks for cowardice" – so said the brave Boscawen, and from him I imbibed this sentiment.

> Admiral Lord St. Vincent, 1809, speech at the opening of Parliament.

MAXIM 65. The same consequences which have uniformly attended long discussions and councils of war will follow at all times. They will terminate in the adoption of the worst course, which in war is always the most timid, or, if you will, the most prudent. The only true wisdom in a general is determined courage.

> Napoleon, *The Military Maxims of Napoleon*, tr. George D'Aguilar, 1831 (David Chandler, ed., 1987).

COUNCILS OF WAR are a deplorable resource and can be useful only when concurring in opinion with the commander, in which case they may give him more confidence in his own judgment, and, in addition, may assure him that his lieutenants, being of his opinion will use every means to insure the success of the movement.
    Lieutenant-General Antoine-Henri Baron de Jomini, *Summary of the Art of War*, 1838, tr. Mendell and Craighill, 1862.

I NEVER HELD a council of war in my life.
    General of the Army Ulysses S. Grant (1822–1885) – attributed.

IF THE COMMANDER . . . feels the need of asking others what he ought to do, the command is in weak hands.
    Field Marshal Helmuth Graf von Moltke, 20 January 1890, letter.

A COUNCIL OF WAR never fights, and in a crisis the duty of the leader is to lead and not to take refuge behind the generally timid wisdom of a multitude of councilors.
    President Theodore Roosevelt, *Autobiography*, 1913.

NOT EVERY ACT is favoured with such happy conception or such easy birth. Meetings, discussion, committees, councils of war, etc., are the enemies of vigorous and prompt decision and their danger increases with their size. They are mostly burdened with doubts and petty responsibilities, and the man who pleads for action ill endures the endless hours of discussion.
    Colonel-General Hans von Seekt, *Thoughts of a Soldier*, 1930.

ON PRINCIPLE, I am opposed to all councils of war, so I did not send for the Army commanders to ask their advice as to the possibilities of success or the general plan; but, since momentus events were impending, I thought it very important to convene my immediate collaborators so as to explain to them my decisions, and, in case of any misunderstandings, clear up any points they might find obscure or hard to grasp. If this is done, those leaders who are neighbors in the field can talk things over together and thus avoid friction and bickerings which otherwise would be inevitable.
    General Aleksei A. Brusilov, *A Soldier's Notebook*, 1930.

WHY, you may take the most gallant sailor, the most intrepid airman, or the most audacious soldier, put them at a table together – what do you get? The sum total of their fears.
    Sir Winston S. Churchill (1874–1965).

TO HEAR some people talk, however, one would think that the way to win the war is to make sure that every Power contributing armed forces and branches of these armed forces is represented on all councils and organizations which have to be set up, and that everybody is fully consulted before anything is done. That is, in fact, the most sure way to lose a war.
    Sir Winston S. Churchill, 27 January 1942, speech in the House, *Maxims and Reflections*, 1949.

YOU'VE TOLD ME all the reasons why the project is not feasible. This meeting is now adjourned and will reconvene in fifteen minutes. When you return I want to hear from you the action you propose to take in order to get the job done.
    Admiral William F. 'Bull' Halsey, to his staff, 1943, quoted in Potter, *Bull Halsey*, 1985.

IT IS ESSENTIAL to understand the place of the "conference" when engaged on active operations in the field. By previous thought, by discussion with his staff, and by keeping in close touch with his subordinates by means of visits, a commander should know what he wants to do and whether it is possible to do it. If a conference of his subordinates is then necessary, it will be for the purpose of giving orders. He should never bring them back to him for such a conference; he must go forward to them. Then nobody looks over his shoulder. A conference of subordinates to collect ideas is the resort of a weak commander.
    Field Marshal Viscount Montgomery of Alamein, *The Memoirs of Field Marshal Montgomery*, 1958.

I COULD almost hear my father's voice telling me as he had so many years before, "Doug, councils of war ever breed timidity and defeatism."
    General of the Army Douglas MacArthur, *Reminiscences*, 1964.

COUNTER-ATTACK/SPOILING ATTACK

LO, while his majesty sat talking with the princes, the vanquished chief of Kheta came, and the numerous countries, which were with him. They crossed over the channel on the south of Kadesh, and charged into the army of his majesty while they were marching, and not expecting it. Then the infantry and chariotry of his majesty retreated before them, northward to the place where his majesty was. Lo, the foes of the vanquished chief of Kheta surrounded the bodyguard of his majesty, who were by his side.
    When his majesty saw them, he was enraged against them, like his father, Montu, lord of Thebes. He seized the adornments of battle, and arrayed himself in his coat of mail. He was like Baal in his hour. Then he betook himself to his horses, and led quickly on, being alone by himself. He charged into the foes of the vanquished chief of Kheta, and the numerous countries that were with him. His majesty was like Sutekh, the great in strength, smiting and slaying among them; his

118   C

majesty hurled them headlong, one upon another into the water of the Orontes.

"I charged all countries, while I was alone, my infantry and my chariotry having forsaken me. Not one among them stood to turn about. I swear, as Re loves me, as my father, Atum, favors me, that, as for every matter which his majesty has stated, I did it in truth, in the presence of my infantry and my chariotry."

Rameses II, 1284 BC, his personal counter-attack at the Battle of Kadesh, the first detailed account of such a manoeuvre, quoted in James Breasted, *Ancient Records of Egypt*, 1906.

AFTER A VICTORY the general should not allow the men to break ranks right away. For it has happened often enough that the enemy, on noticing that our men have let down their guard in their rejoicing and have broken ranks, have regained their courage, come back to fight and turned victory into defeat.

The Emperor Maurice, *The Strategikon*, c. AD 600 (*Maurice's Strategikon*, tr. George Dennis, 1984).

MAXIM 23. When you are occupying a position which the enemy threatens to surround, collect all your force immediately, and menace him with an offensive movement. By this manoeuvre you will prevent him from detaching and annoying your flanks, in case you should judge it necessary to retire.

Napoleon, *The Military Maxims of Napoleon*, tr. George D'Aguilar, 1831 (David Chandler, ed.,1987).

COUNTERATTACK is the soul of defense. Defense is in a passive attitude, for that is the negation of war. Rightly conceived it is an attitude of alert expectation. We wait for the moment when the enemy shall expose himself to a counterstroke, the success of which will so far cripple him as to render us relatively strong enough to pass to the offensive ourselves.

Julian Corbett, *Some Principles of Maritime Strategy*, 1911.

YESTERDAY we were on the defense, we retreated, but today we went over to the offensive.

. . . We all . . . had thought thus: first we would stop the enemy, then we would bring up forces, prepare, and, finally . . . throw ourselves on the enemy. Reality turned out to be different, harsher, and more exacting: . . . we did not find the time to . . . prepare. . . . It became necessary, figuratively speaking, just to turn around one's left shoulder to strike the enemy under whose pressure we had still been retreating yesterday.

Marshal of the Soviet Union Kirill S. Moskalenko, early December 1941, on the approaches to Moscow, quoted in Nathan Leites, *The Soviet Style in War*, 1982.

I CALCULATED that it is only by a counterstrike that one can disrupt the enemy's . . . preparation for a

new offensive. To force the enemy to take the offensive earlier than at the time which he had set is more advantageous for us than to sit and wait until he is fully prepared.

Marshal of the Soviet Union Vassili I. Chuikov, the Soviet offensive in Stalingrad, 12 October 1942, quoted in Nathan Leites, *The Soviet Style in War*, 1982.

COUP D'OEIL

THE *COUP D'OEIL* is a gift of God and cannot be acquired; but if professional knowledge does not perfect it, one only sees things imperfectly and in a fog, which is not enough in these matters where it is so important to have a clear eye. . . . To look over a battlefield, to take in at the first instance the advantages and disadvantages is the great quality of a general.

Chevalier Jean-Charles de Folard (1669–1752), *Nouvelles Découvertes sur la Guerre*, 1724.

THE ABILITY of a commander to comprehend a situation and act promptly is the talent which great men have of conceiving in a moment all the advantages of the terrain and the use that they can make of it with their army. When you are accustomed to the size of your army you soon form your *coup d'oeil* with reference to it, and habit teaches you the ground that you can occupy with a certain number of troops.

Use of this talent is of great importance on two occasions. First, when you encounter the enemy on your march and are obliged instantly to choose ground on which to fight. As I have remarked, within a single square mile a hundred different orders of battle can be formed. The clever general perceives the advantages of the terrain instantly; he gains advantage from the slightest hillock, from a tiny marsh; he advances or withdraws a wing to gain superiority; he strengthens either his right or his left, moves ahead or to the rear, and profits from the merest bagatelles.

Frederick the Great, *Instructions to His Generals*, 1747, tr. Phillips, 1940.

. . . THE ABILITY to assess a situation at a glance, to know how to select the sight for a camp, when and how to march, and where to attack.

Field Marshal Prince Aleksandr V. Suvorov, *The Science of Victory*, 1796.

SPEED, Quick Grasp, Shock.

Field Marshal Prince Aleksandr. V. Suvorov (1729–1800).

IN WAR everything is perception – perception about the enemy, perception about one's own soldiers. After a battle is lost, the difference between victor and vanquished is very little; it is, however, incommensurable with perception, for two or three cavalry squadrons are enough to produce a great effect.

> Napoleon, 22 September 1808, letter to his brother Joseph, *Correspondance de Napoléon Ier, publiée par ordre de l'Empereur Napoléon III*, No. 14343, Vol. XVII, 1858–1870, p. 526.

MY GREAT TALENT, the one that distinguished me the most, is to see the entire picture distinctly.

> Napoleon, quoted in Gaspard Gourgaud, *Journal inédit de 1815 à 1818*, n.d.

THERE IS A GIFT of being able to see at a glance the possibilities offered by the terrain. . . . One can call it the *coup d'oeil* and it is inborn in great generals.

> Napoleon (1769–1821).

ON THE FIELD of battle the happiest inspiration (*coup d'oeil*) is often only a recollection.

> Napoleon, cited in Richard Simpkin, *Race to the Swift*, 1985.

IF THE MIND is to emerge unscathed from this relentless struggle with the unforeseen, two qualities are indispensible: *first, an intellect that, even in the darkest hour, retains some glimmerings of the inner light which leads to truth; and second, the courage to follow this faint light wherever it may lead*. The first of these qualities is described by the French term *coup d'oeil*; the second is determination.

> Major-General Carl von Clausewitz, *On War*, 1.3, 1832, tr. Michael Howard and Peter Paret, 1976.

COUP D'OEIL therefore refers not alone to the physical but, more commonly, to the inward eye. The expression, like the quality itself, has certainly always been more applicable to tactics, but it must also have its place in strategy, since here as well quick decisions are often needed. Stripped of metaphor and of the restrictions imposed by the phrase, the concept merely refers to the quick recognition of a truth that the mind would ordinarily miss or would perceive only after long study and reflection.

> Major-General Carl von Clausewitz, *On War*, 1.3, 1832, tr. Michael Howard and Peter Paret, 1976.

A GENERAL thoroughly instructed in the theory of war but not possessed of military *coup d'oeil*, coolness, and skill, may make an excellent strategic plan and be entirely unable to apply the rules of tactics in presence of an enemy. His projects will not be successfully carried out, his defeat will be probable. If he is a man of character he will be able to diminish the evil results of his failure, but if he loses his wits he will lose his army.

> Lieutenant-General Antoine-Henri Baron de Jomini, *Summary of the Art of War*, 1838, tr. Mendell and Craighill, 1862.

THE PROBLEM is to grasp, in innumerable special cases, the actual situation which is covered by the mist of uncertainty, to appraise the facts correctly and to guess the unknown elements, to reach a decision quickly and then to carry it out forcefully and relentlessly.

> Field Marshal Helmuth Graf von Moltke (1800–1891).

NINE-TENTHS of tactics are certain, and taught in books: but the irrational tenth is like the kingfisher flashing across the pool and that is the test of generals. It can only be ensured by instinct, sharpened by thought practicing the strokes so often that at the crisis it is as natural as a reflex.

> Colonel T.E. Lawrence, 'The Science of Guerrilla Warfare', *Encyclopaedia Britannica*, 1929.

A VITAL FACULTY of generalship is the power of grasping instantly the picture of the ground and the situation, of relating the one to the other, and the local to the general. It is that flair which makes the great executant. (Oct. 1933.)

> Captain Sir Basil Liddell Hart, *Thoughts on War*, 1944.

THE ACID TEST of an officer who aspires to high command is his ability to be able to grasp quickly the essentials of a military problem, to decide rapidly what he will do, to make it quite clear to all concerned what he intends to achieve and how he will do it, and then to see that his subordinate commanders get on with the job. Above all, he has got to rid himself of all irrelevant detail; he must concentrate on the essentials, and on those details and only those details which are necessary to the proper carrying out of his plan – trusting his staff to effect all necessary co-ordination.

> Field Marshal Viscount Montgomery of Alamein, *The Memoirs of Field Marshal Montgomery*, 1958.

COURAGE
General

THE PRINCIPLE on which to manage an army is to set up one standard of courage which all must reach.

> Sun Tzu, *The Art of War*, 11, c. 500 BC, tr. Giles, 1910.

I AM WELL AWARE, soldiers, that words cannot inspire courage, and that a spiritless army cannot be rendered active, or a timid army valiant, by the speech of the commander. Whatever courage is in the heart of a man, whether from nature or from habit, so much will be shown by him in the field; and on him whom neither glory nor danger can move, exhortation is bestowed in vain; for the terror in his breast stops his ears.

> Catiline, 62 BC, speech delivered to his soldiers before the battle in which he suffered defeat and death in rebellion against Rome.

THE COURAGE of the soldier is heightened by the knowledge of his profession.

> Flavius Vegetius Renatus, *Military Institutions of the Romans*, c. AD 378, tr. Clark, 1776.

THE COURAGE of the troops must be reborn daily. . . . nothing is so variable . . . the true skill of the general consists in knowing how to guarantee it.
Field Marshal Maurice Comte de Saxe, *My Reveries*, 1732, tr. Phillips, 1940.

THE MORE COMFORT the less courage there is.
Field Marshal Prince Aleksandr V. Suvorov, quoted in *Soviet Military Review*, 11/1979.

PAY NOT attention to those who would keep you far from fire: you want to prove yourself a man of courage. If there are opportunities, expose yourself conspicuously. As for real danger, it is everywhere in war.
Napoleon, 2 February 1806, to Joseph, *Correspondance de Napoléon Ier, publiée par ordre de l'Empereur Napoléon III*, No. 9738, Vol. XI, 1858–1870, p. 573.

SOLDIERS, you have done all that I expected! You have balanced numbers by courage. You have gloriously marked the difference that lies between the soldiers of Caesar and the armed hordes of Xerxes.
Napoleon, 24 April 1809, to the army, during the Austrian campaign, quoted in R.M. Johnston, ed., *The Corsican*, 1910, p. 164.

COURAGE is like love; it must have hope for nourishment.
Napoleon, *Maxims*, 1804–1815.

WAR is the realm of danger; therefore *courage* is the soldier's first requirement.
  Courage is of two kinds: courage in the face of personal danger, and courage to accept responsibility, either before the tribunal of some outside power or before the court of one's own conscience.
Major-General Carl von Clausewitz, *On War*, 1.3, 1832, tr. Michael Howard and Peter Paret, 1976.

THE MOST essential qualities for a general will always be: *first*, a high moral courage, capable of great resolution; *second*, a physical courage which takes no account of danger. His scientific or military acquirements are secondary to these.
Lieutenant-General Antoine-Henri Baron de Jomini, *Summary of the Art of War*, 1938, tr. Mendell and Craighill, 1862.

THE WELL-KNOWN Spanish proverb, "He was a brave man on such a day," may be applied to nations as to individuals. The French at Rossbach were not the same people as at Jena, nor the Prussians at Prenzlau as at Dennewitz.
Lieutenant-General Antoine-Henri Baron de Jomini, *Summary of the Art of War*, 1838, tr. Mendell and Craighill, 1862.

ONE MAN with courage makes a majority.
American saying attributed to Andrew Jackson (1767–1845).

THERE IS, of course, such a thing as individual courage, which has a value in war, but familiarity with danger, experience in war and its common attendants, and personal habit, are equally valuable traits, and these are the qualities with which we usually have to deal in war. All men naturally shrink from pain and danger, and only incur their risk from some higher motive, or from habit; so that I would define true courage to be a perfect sensibility of the measure of danger, and a mental willingness to incur it, rather than that insensibility to danger of which I have heard far more than I have seen. The most courageous men are generally unconscious of possessing the quality; therefore, when one professes it too openly, by words or bearing, there is reason to mistrust it. I would further illustrate my meaning by describing a man of true courage to be one who possesses all his faculties and senses perfectly when serious danger is actually present.
General of the Army William T. Sherman, *Memoirs of General W.T. Sherman*, 1875.

A GREAT MANY MEN, when they smell battle afar off, chafe to get into the fray. When they say so themselves they generally fail to convince their hearers that they are as anxious as they would like to make believe, and as they approach danger they become more subdued. This rule is not universal, for I have known a few men who were always aching for a fight when there was no enemy near, who were as good as their word when the battle did come. But the number of such men is small.
General of the Army Ulysses S. Grant, *Personal Memoirs of U.S. Grant*, 1885.

AT THE GRAVE of the hero we end, not with sorrow at the inevitable loss, but with the contagion of courage; and with a kind of desperate joy we go back to the fight.
Justice Oliver Wendell Holmes (1841–1935).

IN SPORT, in courage, and in the sight of Heaven, all men meet on equal terms.
Sir Winston S. Churchill, *The Malakand Field Force*, 1898.

IT IS NOT SO MUCH a question of destroying the enemy troops as of destroying their courage. Victory is yours as soon as you convince your opponent his cause is lost. . . . One defeats the enemy not by individual and complete annihilation, but by destroying his hopes of victory.
Field Marshal Colmar Baron von der Goltz, quoted in Foch, *Principles of War*, 1913.

COURAGE . . . is that firmness of spirit, that moral

backbone, which, while fully appreciating the danger involved, nevertheless goes on with the undertaking. Bravery is physical; courage is mental and moral. You may be cold all over; your hands may tremble; your legs may quake; your knees may be ready to give way – that is fear. If nevertheless, you go forward; if in spite of this physical defection you continue to lead your men against the enemy, you have courage. The physical manifestations of fear will pass away. You may never experience them but once.

Major C.A. Bach, 1917, address to graduating new officers, Fort Sheridan, Wyoming.

I THINK the death penalty will cease pretty soon. The debates on it in the House make my blood boil. I wish I could talk to some of the old stagers for a few minutes, about funk & courage. They are the same quality, you know. A man who can run away is a potential V.C.

Colonel T.E. Lawrence, letter to Ernest Thurtle, 1 April 1924, quoted in *The Letters of T.E. Lawrence*, 1988.

COURAGE is rightly esteemed the first of human qualities, because . . . it is the quality that guarantees all others.

Sir Winston S. Churchill, *Great Contemporaries*, 1937.

. . . BUT COURAGE which goes against military expediency is stupidity, or, if insisted upon by a commander, irresponsibility.

Field Marshal Erwin Rommel (1881–1944).

COURAGE is fear holding on a minute longer.

General George S. Patton, Jr., quoted in James Carlton, ed., *The Military Quotation Book*, 1990.

AFTER a quarter of a century I am driven to ask again "Is courage common?" I find it difficult now, living in soft security, to speak from the bench. Twice in my lifetime I have seen boys grow to men, only to be consumed by war, and I have come to think of this almost every day. War is only tolerable when one can take part in it, when one is a bit of the target and not a pensioned spectator. Yet when the death of husband or son or brother has grown distant and the world is free to think again without impiety that courage is not common, men will remember that all the fine things in war as in peace are the work of a few men; that the honour of the race is in the keeping of but a fraction of her people.

Baron Charles MacMoran Wilson Moran, 12 May 1943, preface to *The Anatomy of Courage*, 1945.

NO SANE MAN is unafraid in battle, but discipline produces in him a form of vicarious courage.

General George S. Patton, Jr., *War As I Knew It*, 1947.

THERE IS NO better ramrod for the back of a senior who is beginning to buckle than the sight of a junior who has kept his nerve. Land battles, as to the fighting part, are won by the intrepidity of men in grade from private to captain mainly. Fear is contagious, but courage is not less so. The courage of any one man reflects in some degree the courage of all those who are within his vision. To the man who is in terror and bordering on panic, no influence can be more steadying than that of seeing some other man near him who is retaining self-control and doing his duty.

Brigadier-General S.L.A. Marshall, *The Armed Forces Officer*, 1950.

I DON'T BELIEVE there is any man, who in his heart of hearts, wouldn't rather be called brave than have any other virtue attributed to him. And this elemental, if you like unreasoning, male attitude is a sound one, because courage is not merely a virtue; it is *the* virtue. Without it there are no other virtues. Faith, hope, charity, all the rest don't become virtues until it takes courage to exercise them. Courage is not only the basis of all virtue; it is its expression. True, you may be bad and brave, but you can't be good without being brave.

Field Marshal Viscount Slim of Burma, *Courage and Other Broadcasts*, 1957.

COURAGE is the greatest of all virtues, for without it there are no other virtues. . . . As officers you will, of course, accept greater hazards than your men. You will be first in danger, but an officer must have more than the ordinary physical courage. Anyone can be brave for five minutes. You will not only be braver than the men you lead; you will be brave *for longer*. You will go on being brave when others falter; brave not only in danger, but brave in hardship, in loneliness and, perhaps most difficult of all, in those long periods of inactivity, of boredom that come at times to all soldiers. In failure, too, you will show your courage. We can all be brave when we are winning. I'm a hell of General when everybody is whooping along and the enemy's on the run. But you won't always be winning. If you had ever been a British General at the start of a war you would know what I mean. You'll find some day when things are bad, whether you're the Commanding General or the Platoon Commander, there will come a sudden pause when your men stop and look at you. No one will speak; they will just look at you – look at you and ask, dumbly, for leadership. Their courage is ebbing; you must make it flow back – and it is not easy. You will never have felt more alone in your life.

Field Marshal Viscount Slim of Burma, *Courage and Other Broadcasts*, 1957.

THERE IS NOTHING like seeing the other fellow run to bring back your courage.

Field Marshal Viscount Slim of Burma, *Unofficial History*, 1959.

COURAGE in the commander is a prior condition for courage in his men and for their ability to carry out orders promptly and well. It takes courage and daring to overcome the fears of battle and the trials of armed combat. The commander must also have the courage of his convictions, defying when necessary entrenched, conventional ideas. He must dare to make his views heard in front of his superiors and among his colleagues when permitted to do so, notwithstanding the contrary opinions of those he is addressing.

General Yigal Allon, *The Making of Israel's Army*, 1970.

GENERALLY SPEAKING, there is no more sincere or inspiring form of courage than that which shuns display and seeks the modest unostentatious way. Under certain conditions, however, the most modest of commanders will be compelled to make a show of courage either by paying an unexpected visit under fire to the front line or by taking the lead when advancing upon the enemy's positions. Yet one point must constantly be borne in mind: courage comes of cool thought and knowledge, never of hot-headedness or lack of knowledge. The kind of courage needed by a commander is serious and purposeful, not rash or adventurous.

General Yigal Allon, *The Making of Israel's Army*, 1970.

THERE ARE two kinds of courage, physical and moral, and he who would be a true leader must have both. Both are the products of the character-forming process, of the development of self-control, self-discipline, physical endurance, of knowledge of one's job and, therefore, of confidence. These qualities minimize fear and maximize sound judgment under pressure – with some of that indispensable stuff called luck – often bring success from seemingly hopeless situations.

Putting aside impulsive acts of reckless bravery, both kinds of courage bespeak an untroubled conscience, a man at peace with God. An example is Colonel John H. Glenn who was asked after his first rocket flight if he had been worried, and who replied: "I am trying to live the best I can. My peace had been made with my Maker for a number of years, so I had no particular worries."

General Matthew B. Ridgway, 'Leadership', *Military Review*, 10/1966.

LEADERS must study fear, understand it, and be prepared to cope with it. Like fear, courage takes many forms, from a stoic courage born of reasoned calculation to a fierce courage born of heightened emotion. Experience under fire generally increases courage, as can realistic training by lessening the mystique of combat. Strong leadership which earns the respect and trust of subordinates can limit the effects of fear. Leaders should develop unit cohesion and esprit and the self-confidence of individuals within the unit. In this environment a Marine's unwillingness to violate the respect and trust of his peers will overcome personal fear.

General Alfred M. Gray and Major John Schmitt, *Warfighting*, United States Marine Corps, 1989.

Moral Courage

AS TO moral courage, I have rarely met with two-o'clock-in-the-morning courage; I mean instantaneous courage.

Napoleon, 4–5 December 1815, quoted in Emmanuel Las Casas, *Mémorial de Sainte Hélène*, 1840.

WORDS FAIL to describe the demands that are made of a soldier in battle. To go "over the top" under enemy fire is, indeed, an heroic act, but it is by no means the most difficult. How much resolution and readiness to shoulder responsibility is required of a man who either has to lead or send others to certain death. Those are acts the appalling nature of which no one can imagine who has not himself had to perform them.

General Erich Ludendorff, *My War Memories 1914–1918*, 1919.

I FELT MY DUTY to take up the cudgels. The country's safety was at stake, and I said so bluntly. The President turned the full vials of his sarcasm upon me. He was a scorcher when aroused. The tension began to boil over. For the third and last time in my life that paralyzing nausea began to creep over me. In my emotional exhaustion I spoke recklessly and said something to the general effect that when we lost the next war, and an American boy, lying in the mud with an enemy bayonet through his belly and an enemy foot on his dying throat, spat out his last curse, I wanted the name not to be MacArthur, but Roosevelt. The President grew livid. "You must not talk that way to the President!" he roared. He was right, of course, right, and I knew it almost before the words had left my mouth. I said that I was sorry and apologized. But I felt my Army career was at an end. I told him he had my resignation as Chief of Staff. As I reached the door his voice came with that cool detachment which so reflected his extraordinary self-control, "Don't be foolish, Douglas; you and the budget must get together on this."

Dern had shortly reached my side and I could hear his gleeful tones, "You've saved the Army." But I just vomited on the steps of the White House.

General of the Army Douglas MacArthur, 1933, MacArthur's stand to save the National Guard from a mortal budget slash by Roosevelt, *Reminiscences*, 1964.

DETERMINED leadership is vital, and nowhere is this more important than in the higher ranks. Other things being equal the battle will be a contest between opposing wills.

Generals who become depressed when things are

not going well, and who lack the drive to get things done, and the moral courage and resolution to see their plan through to the end, are useless in battle. They are, in fact, worse than useless – they are a menace – since any lack of moral courage, or any sign of wavering or hesitation, has very quick repercussion down below.

Field Marshal Viscount Montgomery of Alamein, 10 November 1942.

NOW these two types of courage, physical and moral, are very distinct. I have known many men who had marked physical courage, but lacked moral courage. Some of them were in high places, but they failed to be great in themselves because they lacked it. On the other hand, I have seen men who undoubtedly possessed moral courage very cautious about taking physical risks. But I have never met a man with moral courage who would not, when it was really necessary, face bodily danger. Moral courage is a higher and a rarer virtue than physical courage.

Field Marshal Viscount Slim of Burma, *Courage and Other Broadcasts*, 1957.

TO TEACH moral courage is another matter – and it has to be taught because so few, if any, have it naturally. The young can learn it from their parents, in their homes, from school and university, from religion, from other early influences, but to inculcate it in a grown-up who lacks it requires not so much teaching as some striking emotional experience – something that suddenly bursts upon him, something in the nature of a vision. That happens rarely, and that is why you will find that most men with moral courage learnt it by precept and example in their youth.

Field Marshal Viscount Slim of Burma, *Courage and Other Broadcasts*, 1957.

IT TAKES COURAGE, especially for a young officer, to check a man met on the road for not saluting properly or for slovenly appearance, but, every time he does, it adds to his stock of moral courage, and whatever the soldier may say he has a respect for the officer who does put him up.

Field Marshal Viscount Slim of Burma, *Defeat Into Victory*, 1956.

IT HAS long seemed to me that the hard decisions are not the ones you make in the heat of battle. Far harder to make are those involved in speaking your mind about some harebrained scheme which proposes to commit troops to action under conditions where failure seems almost certain, and the only results will be the needless sacrifice of priceless lives. When all is said and done, the most precious asset any nation has is its youth, and for a battle commander ever to condone the unnecessary sacrifice of his men is inexcusable. In any action you must balance the inevitable cost in lives against the objectives you seek to attain. Unless the results to

be expected can reasonably justify the estimated loss of life the action involves, then for my part I want none of it.

General Matthew B. Ridgway, 'Leadership', *Military Review*, 9/1966.

I REMEMBER the day I was ready to go over to the Oval Office and give my four stars to the President and tell him, "You have refused to tell the country they cannot fight a war without mobilization; you have required me to send men into battle with little hope of their ultimate victory; and you have forced us in the military to violate almost every one of the principles of war in Vietnam. Therefore, I resign and will hold a press conference after I walk out of your door."

I made the typical mistake of believing I could do more for the country and the Army if I stayed in than if I got out. I am now going to my grave with that lapse in moral courage on my back.

General Harold K. Johnson, quoted in Lewis Sorely, 'To Change a War', *Parameters*, Spring 1998.

BRAVERY is the quintessence of the soldier . . . But moral courage – the strength of character to do what one knows is right regardless of the personal consequences – is the true face of conscience. Sacking your best friend, facing up rather than turning the blind eye, accepting that the principle at stake is more important than your job . . . Such actions demand moral courage of a high order.

Lieutenant-General Sir James Glover, 'A Soldier and His Conscience', *Parameters*, 9/1983.

DURING MEETINGS, so-called leaders often sit on their hands when it is time to raise a hand and speak up. Leadership requires courage – courage to make waves, courage to take on your bosses when they are wrong, and the courage of convictions. Every Robert E. Lee needs a James Longstreet to tell him exactly the way it is.

Major-General Perry M. Smith, 'Learning to Lead', *Marine Corps Gazette*, 1/1997.

CANDOR and moral courage go together. An officer's responsibility in the policy-making process – whether in the warroom or advising the President – entails total candor. Once a final policy decision is made, he has an obligation to support that decision as if it were his own – with a huge exception. On matters of deep principle – duty, honor, country - there can be no compromise. Duty demands that a naval officer speak out. General George C. Marshall explained that "It is hard to get men to do this, for this is when you lay your career, perhaps your commission, on the line." But any officer truly willing to give his life for his country must also be willing to give up his job.

Lieutenant David A. Adams, 'Chance Second Chances', winner, Vincent Astor Memorial Leadership Essay, *Proceedings*, 6/1998.

Physical Courage

COURAGE in face of personal danger is also of two kinds. It may be indifference to danger, which could be due to the individual's constitution, or to his holding life cheap, or to habit. In any case, it must be regarded as a permanent *condition*. Alternatively, courage may result from such positive motives as ambition, patriotism, or enthusiasm of any kind. In that case courage is feeling, an emotion, not a permanent state.

These two kinds of courage act in different ways. The first is the more dependable; having become second nature, it will never fail. The other will often achieve more. There is more reliability in the first kind, more boldness in the second. The first leaves the mind calmer; the second tends to stimulate, but it can also be blind. *The highest form of courage is a compound of both.*

Major-General Carl von Clausewitz, *On War*, 1.3, 1832, tr. Michael Howard and Peter Paret, 1976.

AS TO physical courage, although sheer cowardice (i.e., a man thinking of his own miserable carcass when he ought to be thinking of his men) is fatal, yet, on the other hand, a reputation for not knowing fear does not help an officer in his war discipline: in getting his company to follow him as the Artillery of the Guard followed Drouot at Wagram. I noticed this first in Afghanistan in 1879 and have often since made the same observation. If a British officer wishes to make his men shy of taking a lead from him let him stand up under fire whilst they lie in their trenches as did the Russians on the 17th of July at the battle of Motienling. Our fellows are not in the least impressed by such bravado. All they say is, "This fellow is a fool. If he cares so little for his own life, how much less will he care for ours."

General Sir Ian Hamilton, *The Soul and Body of an Army*, 1921.

WHEN it comes to combat, something new is added. Even if they have previously looked on him as a father and believed absolutely that being with him is their best assurance of successful survival, should he then show himself to be timid and too cautious about his own safety, he will lose hold of them no less absolutely. His lieutenant, who up till then under training conditions has been regarded as a mean creature or a sniveler, but on the field suddenly reveals himself as a man of high courage, can take moral leadership of the company away from him, and do it in one day.

On the field there is no substitute for courage, no other binding influence toward unity of action. Troops will excuse almost any stupidity; excessive timidity is simply unforgivable . . .

Brigadier-General S.L.A. Marshall, *The Armed Forces Officer*, 1950.

COMPLETE COWARDS are almost non-existent.

Another matter for astonishment is the large number of men and women in any group who will behave in an emergency with extreme gallantry. Who they will be you cannot tell until they are tested. I long ago gave up trying to spot potential VCs by their looks, but, from experience, I should say that those who perform individual acts of the highest physical courage are usually drawn from two categories. Either those with quick intelligence and vivid imagination or those without imagination and with minds fixed on the practical business of living. You might almost say, I suppose, those who live on their nerves and those who have not got any nerves. The one suddenly sees the crisis, his imagination flashes the opportunity and he acts. The other meets the situation without finding it so very unusual and deals with it in a matter of fact way.

Field Marshal Viscount Slim of Burma, *Courage and Other Broadcasts*, 1957.

COURT MARTIAL

. . . IT IS RECOLLECTED, to be a fundamental maxim, in our military trials, that the Judge advocate prosecutes in the name of and in behalf of the United States.

General George Washington, *Writings*, XIV, 1936, p. 449.

COURT! I have no time to order courts! I can't blame an officer who seeks to put his ship close to the enemy. Is there any other vessel you would like to have? Breese, make out Selfridge's orders to the Conestoga.

Admiral David D. Porter, upon being asked when he would initiate a court of inquiry to try the commander of a gunboat who had just lost his vessel to a mine in the Yazoo river while manoeuvring to fire on the Rebel positions in December 1862, quoted in *Memoirs of Thomas O. Selfridge, Jr.*, 1928.

THE PRESENCE of one of our regular civilian judge-advocates in an army in the field would be a first-class nuisance. Too many courts-martial in any command are evidence of poor discipline and inefficient officers.

General William T. Sherman, *Memoirs*, 1875.

THE POPULAR conception of a court-martial is half a dozen blood-thirsty old Colonel Blimps, who take it for granted that anyone brought before them is guilty – damme, sir, would he be here if he hadn't done something? – and who at intervals chant in unison, "Maximum penalty – death!" In reality courts-martial are almost invariably composed of nervous officers, feverishly consulting their manuals; so anxious to avoid a miscarriage of justice that they are, at times, ready to allow the accused any loophole of escape. Even if they do steel themselves to passing a sentence, they are quite prepared to find it quashed because they have forgotten to mark something 'A' and attach it to the proceedings.

Field Marshal Viscount Slim of Burma, *Unofficial History*, 1959.

I WISH to record the opinion that trial under the old Manual of Court Martial came closer to providing real justice than any other American system of jurisprudence: the accused was brought promptly to trial, while the memory of witnesses were fresh; court routines were simple and quickly accomplished, which resulted in trials themselves being short and to the point; the rules of evidence, while eminently fair to the accused, served to allow the truth to become known; and the court itself was composed of officers with a good understanding of the law. I agree with the statement, I believe by the eminent Elihu Root, that if I as the accused were innocent of a crime I would rather be tried by a military court than any other tribunal; but if guilty I would wish to be tried by any tribunal other than a military one.

General Hamilton H. Howze, *A Cavalryman's Story*, 1996.

COWARDICE/COWARDS

WHY have you not launched the attack? Are you standing in chariots of water? Did you also turn to water? . . . If you were to fall down before him, you . . . would either kill him, or at least, frighten him! But instead you acted like a "fairy"!

Hattusili I, 1650–1620 BC, letter to the commander of his army besieging the city of Ursa.

AND TALL HECTOR nodded, his helmet flashing: "All this weighs on my mind too, dear woman. But I would die of shame to face the men of Troy and the Trojan women in their long robes if I would shrink from battle now, a coward."

Homer, *The Iliad*, 6.5–522–525, c. 800 BC, tr. Robert Fagles, 1990; Hector telling his wife, Andromache, that he feared for what would become of her if he died in battle, but that he feared shame more.

IN OTHER CITIES whenever a man shows himself to be a coward his only punishment is that he is called a coward. . . . But in Sparta anyone would be ashamed to dine or to wrestle with a coward. . . . In the streets he must get out of the way . . . he must support his unmarried sisters at home and explain to them why they are still spinsters, he must live without a wife at his fireside . . . he may not wander about comfortably acting like someone with a clean reputation or else he is beaten by his betters. I don't wonder that where such a load of dishonor burdens the coward death seems preferable instead of a dishonored and shameful life.

Xenophon, *Constitution of the Spartans*, 9.4–6, c. 360 BC.

ANOTHER WOMAN, when her sons fled from a battle and reached her, said: "In making your escape, vile slaves, where is it you've come to? Or do you plan to creep back in here where you emerged from?" At this she pulled up her clothes and exposed her belly to them.

Plutarch, quoting an anonymous Spartan woman, *The Lives*, c. AD 100, (*Plutarch on Sparta*, tr. Richard Talbert, 1988).

THE MOST SEDITIOUS is the most cowardly.

Cornelius Tacitus, *Annals*, 4, c. AD 116.

BE REMISS in nothing whilst you are in the battle, for if any mark of fear or cowardice is revealed in you, even if you had a thousand lives you would be unable to save a single one, and the humblest person could overwhelm you. Cowardice results either in your being slain or in the besmirching of your name. Once you become notorious among men for poltroonery and for a display of sloth and feebleness in such circumstances as these, and for failing your comrades, you will be disgraced amongst your friends and associates. Neither repute nor comfort will be left to you; amongst your contemporaries you will be stricken with shame. Death is preferable to such a life, and it is far better to die in good odour than to spend one's life in disrepute.

Kai Ka'us Ibn Iskander, *A Mirror For Princes*, 1082, tr. Levy, 1951.

HE WHO does not go to war, even though he be the king's son, from now on will be deprived of all these things. He will have to wear the clothing of the common man, of the man who has no [fighting] spirit.

And in this cowardice, his weak heart, will be known by all.

He will not wear cotton garments.

He will not wear feathers, he will not receive flowers like the great lords.

He will not receive tobacco,

he will not drink chocolate, he will not eat fine foods.

He will be held in contempt as man of low rank.

He will be made to do manual labor even though he be of royal blood, even though he be one of us or a close kinsman.

And let this be the inviolable law;

That he who does not got to war will be scorned, he will not be respected, nor will he consort with, nor converse with, nor eat with the brave warriors. But he will be treated as an outcast, as something putrid, vile.

He will be made to wait until the brave warriors have eaten, have drunk, and then he will receive what is left over.

Tlacaelel, c. 1450, the promulgation of the Aztec code of the warrior, quoted in Durán, *The History of the Indies of New Spain*, 1581, tr. Doris Heyden, 1994.

A COWARD, when taught to believe, that if he

breaks his Ranks, and abandons his Colours, will be punished with Death by his own party, will take his chance against the Enemy, but the man who thinks little of the one, and is fearful of the other, Acts from present feelings regardless of consequences.

General George Washington, 9 February 1776, to the President of Congress.

WHEN I ASK can war make any man a coward it is no answer to point to men who were cowards before they were soldiers. Such men went about wearing labels for all to read. From the first they were plainly unable to stand this test of men. They had about them the marks known to our calling of the incomplete man, the stamp of degeneracy. The whole miserable issue could have been foretold, the man was certain to crack when the strain came.

Lord Moran, *The Anatomy of Courage*, 1945.

ALL MEN are timid on entering any fight. Whether it is the first fight or the last fight, all of us are timid. Cowards are those who let their timidity get the better of their manhood.

General George S. Patton, Jr., *War As I Knew It*, 1947.

CRITICISM

I SHOULD BE more faint-hearted than they make me, if, through fear of idle reproaches, I should abandon my own convictions. It is no inglorious thing to have fear for the safety of our country, but to be turned from one's course by men's opinions, by blame, and by misrepresentations, shows a man unfit to hold an office such as this, which, by such conduct, he makes the slaves of those whose errors it is his business to control.

Quintus Fabius Maximus, 'The Delayer', 218 BC, to those who criticised him for delaying, hence 'Fabian' tactics of harassment rather than open battle with Hannibal in the Second Punic War, quoted in Plutarch, *The Lives*, c. AD 100, tr. John Dryden.

. . . ROOM for a military criticism as well as a place for a little ridicule upon some famous transactions of that memorable day. . . . But why this censure when the affair is so happily decided? To exercise one's ill-nature? No, to exercise the faculty of judging. . . . The more a soldier thinks of the false steps of those that are gone before, the more likely he is to avoid them.

Major-General Sir James Wolfe (1727–1759), reflections on the Battle of Culloden, quoted in Liddell Hart, *Great Captains Unveiled*, 1927.

YOU SEE the dash which the Common Council of the city of London have made at me! I act with a sword hanging over me, which will fall upon me whatever may be the result; but they may do what they please. I shall not give up the game here as long as it can be played.

The Duke of Wellington, on criticism of his 1809

campaign in Spain and retreat to Portugal, *The Dispatches of Field Marshal the Duke of Wellington, During His Various Campaigns in India, Denmark, Portugal, Spain, the Low Countries, and France*, V, p. 403, 1834–1838.

THERE'S A MAN for you! He is forced to flee from an army that he dares not fight, but he puts eighty leagues of devastation between himself and his pursuers. He slows down the march of the pursuing army, he weakens it by all kinds of privation – he knows how to ruin it without fighting it. In all of Europe, only Wellington and I are capable of carrying out such measures. But there is a difference between him and myself: In France . . . I would be criticized, whereas England will praise him.

Napoleon, c. 1810, conversation on Wellington's retreat to Portugal, quoted in Jean Antoine Chaptal, *Mes Souvenirs sur Napoléon*, 1893.

I BELIEVE there was a good deal of this sort of spirit at one time, before I had laid hold of the public opinion, both in the army and the country, but I kept never-minding it, quite sure that all would come right in good season.

The Duke of Wellington, *The Croker Papers*, Vol. I, p. 347, Notes 1826, cited in Elizabeth Longford, *Wellington: The Years of the Sword*, 1970.

IF I TRIED to read, much less answer all the criticisms made of me and all the attacks leveled against me, this office would have to be closed for all other business – I do the best I know how, the very best I can – I mean to keep on doing this, down to the very end.

President Abraham Lincoln, quoted in Russell B. Reynolds, *The Officer's Guide, 1970–1971 Edition*, 1970.

THE GREAT NUMBER of attacks made upon me by the press of the Country is my apology for not writing to you oftener, not desiring to give any contradiction to them myself. – You have interested yourself so much as my friend that should I say anything it would probably be made use of in my behalf. I would scorn being my own defender against such attacks except through the record which has been kept of all my official acts and which can be examined at Washington at any time.

To say that I have not been distressed at these attacks upon me would be false, for I have a father, mother, wife & children who read them and are distressed by them and I necessarily share with them in it. Then too all subject to my orders read these charges and it is calculated to weaken their confidence in me and weaken my ability to render efficient service in our present cause. One thing I will assure you of however: I can not be driven from rendering the best service within my ability to suppress the present rebellion, and when it is over retiring to the same quiet it, the rebellion, found me enjoying.

> General Ulysses S. Grant, letter to Congressman Elihu B. Washburne, 14 May 1862, after the Battle of Shiloh, quoted in Bruce Catton, *Grant Moves South*, 1960.

I HAVE NO objection to the President using any thing I have ever written to him as he sees fit – I think however for him to attempt to answer all the charges the opposition will bring against him will be like setting a maiden to work to prove her chastity . . .

> General Ulysses S. Grant, letter to Congressman Elihu B. Washburne, 21 September 1864, *Personal Memoirs and Selected Letters*, 1990.

I ALWAYS REMEMBER the Japanese soldier who outraged the senses of patriotism and duty in his superior officer by saying, "In Osaka I would get five yen for digging this gun pit; here I only get criticism."

> General Sir Ian Hamilton, *The Soul and Body of an Army*, 1921.

WE MUST REMEMBER that man remains man and that his heart does not change. Secondly, we must remember that the means of war do not change and that the intelligence of man must keep pace with these changes. We must keep minds subtle and active, and never let ourselves be hypnotized by traditions; we must criticize ourselves, and criticize our criticisms; we must experiment and explore.

> Major-General J.F.C. Fuller, *Sir John Moore's System of Training*, 1925.

THERE IS NO progress without criticism. . . . Curiosity leads to an investigation – which opens discussion – which gives rise to opinion – which breeds criticism – which results in improvement.

> Colonel James C. Breckinridge, *Marine Corps Gazette*, 12/1929.

IN AN INSTITUTION such as the Army the hierarchical system and the habit of subordination, most necessary in its right place, preclude criticism to a degree unknown in other professions, and that would be hardly comprehensible to a scientific mind. This reflection reminds me of the humorous, yet serious, warning of my beloved old chief: "You'll learn that generals are as sensitive as prima-

donnas." I have long learned to appreciate his wisdom. (Feb. 1933.)

> Captain Sir Basil Liddell Hart, *Thoughts on War*, 1944.

MUCH MILITARY CRITICISM is no better than "wisdom after the event" – although not in the usual sense of this facile retort so popular with the friends of the commander whose conduct is called into question. Soldiers who ought to know better, are as addicted as laymen to the habit of judging by results, and of concentrating their attention on the way a plan works out. Even at the best, criticism of performance is difficult – the properties of the general's instrument and the conditions in which it operates are so variable. Moreover, accident plays such an immense part in any result. The truest basis of criticism lies in the general's appreciation and plan – in his conception rather than in its execution. For if we know the orbit of his thought we have a reasonable guide as to how far he was fitted, mentally, for his task. Here we have a real standard for military criticism, a standard created by many centuries of recorded experience. (Aug. 1934.)

> Captain Sir Basil Liddell Hart, *Thoughts on War*, 1944.

I DO NOT resent criticism, even when, for the sake of emphasis, it parts for the time with reality.

> Sir Winston S. Churchill, speech to the House of Commons, 22 January 1941.

I HAVE benefited enormously from criticism and at no point did I suffer from any perceptible lack thereof.

> Sir Winston S. Churchill, quoted in Omar Bradley, 'On Leadership', *Parameters*, 9/1981.

I LIKE commanders on land and sea and in air to feel that between them and all forms of public criticism the Government stands like a strong bulkhead. They ought to have a fair chance, and more than one chance.

> Sir Winston S. Churchill (1874–1965).

I FEEL that retired general officers should never miss an opportunity to remain silent concerning matters for which they are no longer responsible. Having said that, I believe a few general (no pun intended) comments are in order.

> General H. Norman Schwarzkopf, *It Doesn't Take a Hero*, 1992, his memoirs after retirement.

D

DANGER

THE ROMANS also have an excellent method of encouraging young soldiers to face danger. Whenever any have especially distinguished themselves in a battle, the general assembles the troops and calls forward those he considers to have shown exceptional courage. He praises them first for their gallantry in action and for anything in their previous conduct which is particularly worthy of mention, and then he distributes gifts. . . . These presentations are not made to men who have wounded or stripped an enemy in the course of a pitched battle, or at the storming of a city, but to those who during a skirmish or some similar situation in which there is no necessity to engage in single combat, have voluntarily and deliberately exposed themselves to danger.
> Polybius, *Histories*, 6.39, c. 125 BC (*The Rise of the Roman Empire*, tr. Ian Scott-Kilvert, 1987).

REMEMBER also that God does not afford the same protection in unprovoked as in necessary dangers.
> Count Belisarius, April, AD 531.

IF I HAD BEEN censured every time I have run my ship, or fleets under my command, into great danger, I should long ago have been *out* of the Service, and never *in* the House of Peers.
> Admiral Viscount Nelson, March 1805, letter to the Admiralty.

TO SOMEONE who has never experienced danger, the idea is attractive rather than alarming. You charge the enemy, ignoring bullets and casualties, in a surge of excitement. Blindly you hurl yourself toward icey death, not knowing whether you or anyone else will escape him. Before you lies that golden prize, victory, the fruit that quenches the thirst of ambition. Can that be so difficult? No, and it will seem even less difficult than it is. But such moments are rare; and even they are not, as is commonly thought, brief like a heartbeat, but come rather like a medicine, in recurring doses, the taste diluted by time.
> Major-General Carl von Clausewitz, *On War*, 1.4, 1832, tr. Michael Howard and Peter Paret, 1976.

DANGER is part of the friction of war. Without an accurate conception of danger we cannot understand war.
> Major-General Carl von Clausewitz, *On War*, 1.4, 1832, tr. Michael Howard and Peter Paret, 1976.

NOT TILL I SEE day light ahead do I want to lead, but when danger threatens and others slink away I am and will be at my post.
> General of the Army William T. Sherman, August 1861, unaddressed letter.

SHOULD THE GENERAL consistently live outside the realm of danger, then, though he may show high moral courage in making decisions, by his never being called upon to breathe the atmosphere of danger his men are breathing, this lens will become blurred, and he will seldom experience the moral influences his men are experiencing.
> Major-General J.F.C. Fuller, *Generalship: Its Diseases and Their Cure*, 1933.

THE MAJOR BATTLE is only a skirmish multiplied by one hundred. The frictions, confusions, and disappointments are the same. But there is this absolute difference – that the supreme trial of the commander in war lies in his ability to overcome the weaknesses of human nature in the danger, and those are matters which he cannot know in full unless he has served with men where danger lies.
> Brigadier-General S.L.A. Marshall, *Men Against Fire*, 1947.

SINCE WAR is a violent enterprise, danger is a fundamental characteristic of war. And since war is a human phenomenon, fear – the human reaction to danger – has a significant impact on the conduct of war. All men feel fear. Leadership must foster the courage to overcome fear both individually and within the unit. Courage is not the absence of fear; rather, it is the strength to overcome fear.
> General Alfred M. Gray and Major John Schmitt, *Warfighting*, United States Marine Corps, 1989.

DARING

FOR GREAT AIMS we must dare great things.
> Major-General Carl von Clausewitz, *Principles of War*, 1812, tr. Gatzke, 1942.

IN WAR . . . all action is aimed at probable rather than certain success. The degree of certainty that is lacking must in every cause be left to fate, chance, or whatever you like to call it. . . . But we should not habitually prefer the course that involves the least uncertainty. That would be an enormous mistake. . . .

There are times when the utmost daring is the height of wisdom.

> Major-General Carl von Clausewitz, *On War*, 2.5, 1832, tr. Michael Howard and Peter Paret, 1976.

WHO dares wins.

> Motto of the Special Air Service (SAS).

DEATH

DEATH cut him short. The end closed in around him.
Flying free of his limbs
his soul went winging down to the House of Death
wailing his fate, leaving his manhood far behind,
his young and supple strength.

> Homer, *The Iliad*, 16.1001–1005, c. 800 BC,
> tr. Robert Fagles, 1990; the death of Patrocles at the
> hands of Hector.

BOTH ARMIES battled it out along the river banks –
they raked each other with hurtling bronze-tipped
   spears.
And Strife and Havoc plunged in the fight, and
   violent Death –
now seizing a man alive with fresh wounds, now one
   unhurt, now hauling a dead man through the
   slaughter by the heels,
the cloak on her back stained red with human blood.
So they clashed and fought like living, breathing men
grappling each other's corpses, dragging off the dead.

> Homer, *The Iliad*, 18.621–628, c. 800 BC, tr. Robert
> Fagles, 1990; one of the scenes on the shield fashioned
> by the smith god, Hephaestus, for brilliant Achilles.

IN A COURT OF LAW, just as in warfare, neither I nor any other ought to use his wits to escape death by any means. In battle it is often obvious that you could escape being killed by giving up your arms and throwing yourself upon the mercy of your pursuers, and in every kind of danger there are plenty of devices for avoiding death if you are unscrupulous enough to stick at nothing. But I suggest, gentlemen, that the difficulty is not so much to escape death; the real difficulty is to escape from doing wrong. In this present instance I, the slow old man, have been overtaken by the slower of the two, but my accusers, who are clever and quick, have been overtaken by the faster – by iniquity.

> Socrates, 399 BC, parting words to his friends after
> having been condemned to death by the Athenian
> assembly for impiety, quoted in Plato, *Socrates' Defense
> (Apology)*, c. 380 BC (*Plato: The Collected Dialogues*,
> Edith Hamilton, ed., tr. Hugh Tredennick, 1938).

I COMPREHEND the secret, the hidden:
O my lords!
Thus we are,
We are mortal,
men through and through
we all will have to go away,

we all will have to die on earth.
Like a painting,
we will be erased.
Like a flower,
we will dry up
here on earth . . .
Think on this my lords,
eagles and ocelots,
though you be of jade,
though you be of gold
you also will go there
to the place of the fleshless.

> Nezahualcoyotl (1402–1472), King of Texcoco, quoted
> in Miguel Leon-Portilla, *Native Mesoamerican
> Spirituality*, 1980.

COURAGEOUS Aztecs, Tezcocans, Tepances, and all the men from the provinces: there is nothing we can do here but conquer or die. For this we have come. Our enemy shows valor and a brave heart and has decided to defend the city. I beg of you to demonstrate bravery in this endeavor, for to die is to live forever in perpetual honor and glory.

> Motecuhzoma II Xocoyotl, 1506, at the siege of
> Quetzaltepec in Oaxaca, quoted in Durán, *History of
> the Indies of New Spain*, tr. Doris Heyden, 1994.

ONE WHO IS a samurai must before all things keep constantly in mind, by day and by night, from the morning when he takes up his chopsticks to eat his New Year's breakfast to Old Year's night when he pays his yearly bills, the fact that he has to die. That is his chief business.

> Daidoji Yuznan (early 17th century), quoted in
> A.L. Sadler, *The Code of the Samurai*, 1988.

IT IS the cause, and not the death, that makes the martyr,

> Napoleon (1769–1821), quoted in Sarah A. Tooley,
> *The Life of Florence Nightingale*, 1905.

THESE three things you must always keep in mind: concentration of strength, activity, and a firm resolve to perish gloriously. These are the three principles of the military art which have disposed luck in all my military operations. Death is nothing, but to live defeated and without glory is to die everyday.

> Napoleon, 12 December 1804, letter to General
> Lauriston, *Correspondance de Napoléon Ier, publié
> par ordre de l'Empereur Napoléon III*, 1858–1870.

IN THIS *Templars*, there is only one well-drawn character: that of a man who wants to die! That is not true to life, that is useless. Gentlemen, one must wish to live and know how to die.

> Napoleon, 1 December 1805, philosophising to his
> staff on the play by Raynouard on the eve of the Battle
> of Austerlitz, quoted in Philippe Paul, *Un Aide de
> camp de Napoléon: Mémoires du comte de Ségur*, I,
> 1894–1895.

IT IS PART of a sailor's life to die well.
  Commodore Stephen Decatur, on the death of Captain James Lawrence of the USS *Chesapeake* after the engagement of 1 June 1813.

MY FATHER, we must all die sooner or later, and if my time has come nothing will hold it back. It is far, far, better to die with the joy of battle in the heart than to pine away with age, or like a sick ox in a kraal. I have lived by the spear and I shall die by it. That is a man's death. You would not deprive me of that, who are my friend as well as my father?
  Mgobozi, October 1826, to his king, Shaka Zulu, who urged him not to throw away his life in battle the next day, quoted in E.A. Ritter, *Shaka Zulu*, 1955.

I WOULD THAT all could look on death as a cheerful friend, who takes us from a world of trial to our true home. All our sorrows come from a forgetfulness of this great truth. I desire to look on the departure of my friends as a promotion to another and a higher sphere, as I do believe that to be the case with all.
  General Charles 'Chinese' Gordon (1833–1885), quoted in Paul Charrier, *Gordon of Khartoum*, 1965.

I SEE the scene as clearly as on that December day of 1862. That noble, Christian soul passing away; the timid, stricken brother by his side, all of us repeating together the scriptures and his saying to me, pitifully, before consciousness left him, "Please stay with me to the end, for Charlie never saw any one die." When I rose from the side of the couch where I had knelt for hours, until the last breath had faded, I wrung the blood from the bottom of my clothing before I could step, for the weight about my feet. Dreadful days, dear dear sister. . . .
  Clara Barton, quoted in Percy Epler, *The Life of Clara Barton*, 1915.

FEW are wholly dead:
Blow on a dead man's embers
And a live flame will start.
  Robert Graves, 'To Bring the Dead to Life', *Collected Poems*, 1961.

AND when he gets to Heaven,
To Saint Peter he will tell:
"One more Marine reporting, Sir –
I've served my time in Hell."
  Marine Grave inscription on Guadalcanal, 1942

IN BLOSSOM today, then scattered:
Life is so like a delicate flower.
How can one expect the fragrance
To last for ever?
  Vice Admiral Takijiro Ohnishi, Commander of the Kamikaze Special Attack Force – a special calligraphic presentation to his staff after the organisation of the Kamikaze (1944), quoted in Inoguchi and Nakajimi, *The Divine Wind*, 1958.

DEATH stands at attention, obedient, expectant, ready to serve, ready to shear away the peoples en masse; ready, if called on, to pulverize, without hope of repair, what is left of civilization. He awaits only the word of command. He awaits it from a frail, bewildered being, long his victim, now – for one occasion – his Master.
  Sir Winston S. Churchill, *The Gathering Storm*, 1948.

DEATH in combat is not the end of the fight but its peak, and since combat is a part, and at times the sum total of life, death which is the peak of combat, is not the destruction of life, but its fullest, most powerful expression.
  General Moshe Dayan, address in honour of Natan Altermann, 1971.

ONE THING he [General Patton] said always stuck with me, for it was contrary to what I had believed up to that moment, but when I had been in combat only a short while, I knew he was right. Speaking to all of us late one afternoon as we assembled in the North African sunset, he said, "Now I want you to remember that no sonuvabitch ever won a war by dying for his country. He won it making the other poor dumb bastard die for his country."
  General James M. Gavin, *On to Berlin*, 1978.

DECEPTION

ALL WARFARE is based on deception. Hence, when able to attack, we must seem unable; when using our forces we must seem inactive; when we are near, we must make the enemy believe that we are away; when far away, we must make him believe we are near. Hold out baits to entice the enemy. Feign disorder, and crush him.
  Sun Tzu, *The Art of War*, 1, c. 500 BC, tr. Giles, 1910.

A CAVALRY COMMANDER should also devise tricks of his own, suitable for his situation. The basic point is that deceit is your most valuable asset in war. . . . If you think about it, you will find that the majority of important military successes have come about as a result of trickery. It follows, then, that if you are to take on the office of commander, you should ask the gods to allow you to count the ability to deceive among your qualifications, and should also work on it yourself.
  Xenophon, *How To Be A Good Cavalry Commander*, c. 360 BC (*Hiero the Tyrant and Other Treatises*, tr. Robin Waterfield, 1997).

WHEN he was censured for operating mostly by trickery and fraud in a way unworthy of Heracles, and for achieving no honest success, he used to laugh and say that fox-skin had to be stitched on wherever lion-skin would not stretch.
  Plutarch, paraphrasing Lysander, (k. 395 BC), *The*

Lives, c. AD 100, (*Plutarch on Sparta*, tr. Richard Talbert, 1988).

IT IS very important to spread rumors among the enemy that you are planning one thing; then go and do something else. Your plans about major operations should not be made known to many, but to just a few and those very close to you.

The Emperor Maurice, *The Strategikon*, c. AD 600 (*Maurice's Strategikon*, tr. George Dennis, 1984).

WHEN a delegation comes from the enemy, inquire about the leaders of the group, and on their arrival treat them very friendly, so their own people will come to suspect them.

The Emperor Maurice, *The Strategikon*, c. AD 600 (*Maurice's Strategikon*, tr. George Dennis, 1984).

IN HIS MOVEMENTS the general should act like a good wrestler; he should feint in one direction to try to deceive his adversary and then make good use of the opportunities he finds, and in this way he will overpower the enemy.

The Emperor Maurice, *The Strategikon*, c. AD 600 (*Maurice's Strategikon*, tr. George Dennis, 1984).

THOUGH FRAUD in other activities be detestable, in the management of war it is laudable and glorious, and he who overcomes an enemy by fraud is as much to be praised as he who does so by force.

Niccolo Machiavelli, *Discourses*, III, 1517.

IN A BATTLE even the most skilful soldiers find it difficult to estimate the enemy's numbers, and as a rule, one is apt instinctively to exaggerate the number. But if one is foolish enough to accept an inflated estimate of the enemy's forces, then every cavalry colonel on reconnaissance espies an army, and every captain of light infantry battalions. Again I repeat that in war morale and opinion are half the battle. The art of the great captain has always been to make his troops appear very numerous to the enemy, and the enemy's very few to his own. So that to-day, in spite of the long time we have spent in Germany, the enemy did not know my real strength. We are constantly striving to magnify our numbers. Far from confessing that I had only 100,000 men at Wagram, I am constantly suggesting that I had 220,000. In my Italian campaigns, in which I had only a handful of troops, I always exaggerated my numbers. It served my purpose, and has not lessened my glory. My generals and practised soldiers could always perceive, after the event, all the skilfulness of my operations, even that of having exaggerated the numbers of my troops.

Napoleon, 10 October 1809, quoted in R.M. Johnston, ed., *The Corsican*, 1910.

ALWAYS MYSTIFY, mislead, and surprise the enemy, if possible; and when you strike and overcome him, never give up the pursuit as long as your men have strength to follow; for an army routed, if hotly pursued, becomes panic-stricken, and can then be destroyed by half their number.

Lieutenant-General Thomas J. 'Stonewall' Jackson, quoted in G.F.R. Henderson, *Stonewall Jackson*, 1898.

IF I CAN deceive my own friends, I can make certain of deceiving the enemy.

Lieutenant-General Thomas J. 'Stonewall' Jackson, 1862.

TO ACHIEVE victory we must as far as possible make the enemy blind and deaf by sealing his eyes and ears, and drive his commanders to distraction by creating confusion in their minds.

Mao Tse-tung, *On Protracted War*, 1938.

"IN WARTIME" I said, "truth is so precious that she should always be attended by a bodyguard of lies." Stalin and his comrades greatly appreciated this remark when it was translated, and upon this note our formal conference ended gaily.

Sir Winston S. Churchill, *The Second World War: Closing the Ring*, 1951.

I THOUGHT I knew something about war, until I went to China and saw their deception techniques. I had already been in combat for four years, during three tours in Vietnam. And I had been Army Attaché in the Soviet Union. But when a Chinese general walks into a base, the first thing he looks for is the ways that his troops might deceive the enemy. Second, he looks at the camouflage.

Major-General Bernard Loeffke, 'Who Goes There?', Al Santoli, ed., *Leading the Way: How Vietnam Veterans Rebuilt the U.S. Military*, 1993.

DECISION/DECISIVENESS

IACTA alea est. (The die is cast.)

Julius Caesar, upon crossing the Rubicon, the act which precipitated the Roman Civil War, 49 BC.

IT IS ESSENTIAL to be cautious and take your time in making plans, and once you come to a decision to carry it out right away without any hesitation or timidity. Timidity after all is not caution, but the invention of wickedness.

The Emperor Maurice, *The Strategikon*, c. AD 600 (*Maurice's Strategikon*, tr. George Dennis, 1984).

ON THE OTHER HAND, experience shows me that, in an affair depending on vigour and dispatch, the generals should settle their plan of operations so that no time may be lost in idle debate and consultations when the sword is drawn; that pushing on smartly is the road to success, and more particularly so in an affair of this sort; that nothing is to be reckoned an obstacle to your undertaking which is not found really so on trial; that in war something must be allowed to chance and fortune, seeing that it is in its nature hazardous, and an option of difficulties; that the greatness of an object should come under consideration, opposed to the impediments that lie in the way; that the honour of one's country is to have some weight; and that, in particular circumstances and times, the loss of a thousand men is rather an advantage to a nation than otherwise, seeing that gallant attempts raise its reputation. . . . whereas the contrary appearances sink the credit of a country, ruin the troops, and create infinite uneasiness and discontent at home.

> Major-General Sir James Wolfe, quoted in Liddell Hart, *Great Captains Unveiled*, 1927.

ONCE you have made up your mind, stick to it; there is no longer any *if* or *but*. . . .

> Napoleon, 18 February 1812, to Marshal Marmont, *Correspondance de Napoléon Ier, publié par ordre de l'Empereur Napoléon III*, No. 18503, Vol. XXIII, 1858–1870, p. 229.

WAR is waged only with vigor, decision, and unshaken will; one must not grope or hesitate.

> Napoleon, 6 June 1813, to General Bertrand, *Correspondance de Napoléon Ier, publié par ordre de l'Empereur Napoléon III*, No. 20090, Vol. XXV, 1858–1870, p. 363.

THE COMMANDER is compelled during the whole campaign to reach decisions on the basis of situations which cannot be predicted. All consecutive acts of war are, therefore, not executions of a premeditated plan, but spontaneous actions, directed by military tact. The problem is to grasp in innumerable special cases, the actual situation which is covered by the mist of uncertainty, to appraise the facts correctly and to guess the unknown elements, to reach a decision quickly and then to carry it out forcefully and relentlessly. . . . It is obvious that theoretical knowledge will not suffice, but that here the qualities of mind and character come to a free, practical and artistic expression, although schooled by military training and led by experiences from military history or from life itself.

> Field Marshal Helmuth Graf von Moltke, quoted in Earle, ed., *The Makers of Modern Strategy*, 1943.

VARIOUS INCIDENTS may happen which may necessitate a certain deviation from the original plan here and there. It will not be possible to ask the commander for orders in this case, since telegraph and other communications may not work. The corps commander will be faced with the necessity of arriving at a decision of his own. In order that this decision should meet the ideas of the commander-in-chief he must keep the corps commanders sufficiently informed, while, on the other hand, the latter must continuously strive to keep in mind the basic ideas of all the operations and to enter into the mind of the commander-in-chief.

> Field Marshal Alfred Graf von Schlieffen, *Dienstschriften*, II, 1938.

ONCE you have taken a decision, never look back on it.

> Field Marshal Viscount Allenby of Meggido, quoted in Archibald Wavell, *Allenby, Soldier and Statesman*, 1943.

SOMETIMES a commander who cannot make decisions will, by fussing and fuming, try to persuade himself and others that he is taking an active part in the operation. He will give his personal attention to details of secondary importance, and satisfy his desire to leave his impress on the action by interfering in an aimless sort of way.

> General Charles de Gaulle, *The Edge of the Sword*, 1932.

THE FIRST DEMAND of war is decisive action. Everyone, the highest commander and the most junior soldier, must be aware that omissions and neglect incriminate him more severely than mistake in the choice of means.

> Generals Werner von Fritsch and Ludwig Beck, *Troop Leadership*, 1933, quoted in U.S. War Department, *German Military Training*, 17 September 1942.

IN FORTY HOURS I shall be in battle, with little information, and on the spur of the moment will have to make the most momentous decisions. But I believe that one's spirit enlarges with responsibility and that, with God's help, I shall make them and make them right.

> General George S. Patton, Jr. (1885–1945).

A DECISION . . . is not a *problem in simple arithmetic*, but a *creative act*. Even in instances in which a decision is not the outcome of lengthy deliberations, the way leading up to a decision involves a complicated mental process in which, among other factors, also the *temperament* of the individual finds expression. Intuition and *keen sense of perception* play a considerable role. Even if the commander has a large quantity of reference material at his disposal, and even if he has sufficient time for careful evaluation of all known factors, it still remains true that *the process by which a decision is reached is, in the final analysis, nearly always a secret which, in most instances, remains insoluable even to the person who has arrived at the decision*.

> Colonel-General Dr. Lothar Rendulic, *The Command Decision* (MS No. D 080 A), Department of the Army, Office of the Chief of Military History, 15 March 1947.

AFTER A BATTLE is over people talk a lot about how decisions were methodically reached, but actually there's always a hell of a lot of groping around.

> Admiral Frank J. Fletcher (1885–1973).

THE MOMENT of decision-making was a difficult one for the commanding general. You must decide on a great cause and give yourself entirely only to one often very risky but very necessary decision. In these cases thought works intensely and is full of contradictions. One is that the desired decision encounters all kinds of objections in terms of calculations; another is that enormous difficulties are encountered in implementing it; a third is that what is tempting, simple, and safe frees one of all concerns and legal liability. That is how doubts, difficulties, and strivings intertwine. But a decision definitely has to be made. This demands great courage and enormous willpower.
> Marshal of the Soviet Union R.Ya. Malinovsky, quoted in V.S. Golubovich, *Marshal R.Ya. Malinovsky*, 1974.

IN MAKING an attack, there can be no vacillation or indecision, even though a bayonet charge be involved. Any vacillation will result in greater casualties, loss of victory, and general discouragement of the whole force.
> General Lin Piao, 1946, quoted in Ebon, *Lin Piao*, 1970.

IT IS CUSTOMARY to treat "estimate of the situation" as if it were pure mathematical process, pointing almost infallibly to a definite result. But this is contrary to nature. The mind of man does not work that way, nor is it consistent with operational realities. Senior commanders are as prone as even the newest junior lieutenant to labor in perplexity between two opposing courses of action during times of crisis, and then make their decisions almost with the abruptness of an explosion. *It is post-decision steadiness more than pre-decision certitude which carries the day*. A large part of decision is intuitive; it is the byproduct of the subconscious. In war, much of what is most pertinent lies behind a drawn curtain. The officer is therefore badly advised who would believe that a hunch is without value, or that there is something unmilitary about the simple decision to take some positive action, even though he is working in the dark.
> Brigadier-General S.L.A. Marshall, *The Armed Forces Officer*, 1951.

THE POWER of decision develops only out of practice. There is nothing mystic about it. It comes of a clear-eyed willingness to accept life's risks, recognizing that only the enfeebled are comforted by thoughts of an existence devoid of struggle.
> Brigadier-General S.L.A. Marshall, *The Armed Forces Officer*, 1951.

ANY MAN facing a major decision acts, consciously or otherwise, upon the training and beliefs of a lifetime. This is no less true of a military commander than of a surgeon who, while operating, suddenly encounters an unsuspected complication. In both instances, the men must act immediately, with little time for reflection, and if they are successful in dealing with the unexpected it is upon the basis of past experience and training.
> Admiral of the Fleet Ernest J. King, *Fleet Admiral King, Naval Record*, 1952.

THE MATTER of "decision" is vital. The modern tendency is to avoid taking decisions, and to procrastinate in the hope that things will come out all right in the wash. The only policy for the military leader is decision in action and calmness in crisis: no bad doctrine for the political leader as well.
> Field Marshal Viscount Montgomery of Alamein, *The Memoirs of Field Marshal Montgomery*, 1958.

WHEN ALL is said and done the greatest quality required in a commander is "decision"; he must be able to issue clear orders and have the drive to get things done. Indecision and hesitation are fatal in any officer; in a C-in-C they are criminal.
> Field Marshal Viscount Montgomery of Alamein, *The Memoirs of Field Marshal Montgomery*, 1958.

WHEN A DECISION is taken belatedly, its execution inevitably leads to haste.
> Marshal of the Soviet Union Vasili I. Chuikov, 1962, quoted in Leites, *The Soviet Style in War*, 1982.

IT WAS an example of inflexibility in the pursuit of previously conceived ideas that is, unfortunately, too frequent in modern warfare. Final decisions are made not at the front by those who are there, but many miles away by those who can but guess at the possibilities and potentialities.
> General of the Army Douglas MacArthur, *Reminiscences*, 1964.

COMMAND is a pretty lonesome job. There are multiple decisions which you have to make entirely by yourself. You can't lean on anybody else. And a good commander, once he issues an order, must receive complete compliance. An indecisive commander cannot achieve instant compliance. Or one who is unable to make up his own mind and tries to lean on his subordinates will never achieve instant compliance either.
> General Curtis LeMay, *Mission With LeMay*, 1965.

HE (the leader) cannot afford to be ambiguous.
Ever since I was a boy and read about Gettysburg, I've thought that ambiguity was the reason for Lee's losing the battle. Lee said, "General Ewell was instructed to carry the hill occupied by the enemy, if he found it practicable. . . ." I call that leaning on a subordinate, most definitely. Ewell didn't find the attack practicable; so he didn't attack that late afternoon or early evening. During the night the Federals heavily reinforced, and were never driven from their ridges, but instead repelled every Confederate attack poised against them.
Lee left it up to Ewell to make a decision which I

feel that great general should have made himself. And Lee was a great general. Figure it out if you can.
General Curtis LeMay, *Mission With LeMay*, 1965.

THE FLOW of battle may sometimes change conditions or create new tasks no amount of advance planning could have allowed for. Then the success or failure of the entire mission may well depend on the resourcefulness, the training, the alertness, the decisiveness of the leaders of even the smallest units. The ability to make prompt decisions and to execute them vigorously is best bred in men who, through confidence in their troops and in their superiors, have persuaded themselves that they are unbeatable. Unrelenting attention to detail, concern for the well-being of every member of every unit, painstaking checking out of each assignment with the men charged with performing it – all these help instill that self-confidence, that sense of belonging to a tightly organized and well-fed organization, the feeling that can give momentum to a whole force and make it truly unconquerable.
General Matthew B. Ridgway, *The Korean War*, 1967.

WHEN ONE STARTS a war, one has to understand that this is a serious thing, that blood is not water. If, having measured seven times, you did decide to cut, then cut quickly and firmly, to the end. Hesitating and thinking are for the time before you start the war. By the way, thinking is useful at any time. But once you start fighting for real, you have to understand: You fight until you win, not "until elections."
General Aleksandr I. Lebed, *Nezavisimya Gazeta* (Moscow), 3 April 1996.

TOP LEADERS usually must make prudent decisions when they only have about 60 percent of the information they need. Leaders who demand nearly all the information are usually months or years late making decisions.
Major-General Perry M. Smith, 'Learning to Lead', *Marine Corps Gazette*, January 1997.

IN THE FUTURE, formations will operate far more swiftly and in smaller increments than in even the most successful divisional attacks during Desert Storm, but this is the reborn paradigm: go fast, hit the enemy's weakness, keep on hitting him, and don't stop moving. This is very old military wisdom. Somehow, somewhere between the National Training Center and Carlisle, many of us forgot it. Too often, we elevate safety of decision over decisiveness. We may admire Jackson, but we imitate McClellan.
Lieutenant-Colonel Ralph Peters, *Fighting for the Future*, 1999.

DECLARATION OF WAR

THE ROMAN ambassadors had been received at Carthage. After they had heard the Carthaginians'

statement of their case, they spoke no word in reply, but the senior member of the delegation pointed to the bosom of his toga and declared to the Senate that in its folds he carried both peace and war, and that he would let fall from it whichever they instructed him to leave. The Carthagian Suffete answered that he should bring out whichever he thought best, and when the envoy replied that it would be war, many of the senators shouted at once, "We accept it!" It was on these terms that the Senate and the Roman ambassadors parted.
Polybius, on the Roman declaration of war against Carthage beginning the Second Punic War, 219 BC, *Histories* (*Rise of the Roman Empire*, tr. Ian Scott-Kilvert, 1987).

TO SUCH A TASK we can dedicate our lives and our fortunes, everything that we are and everything that we have, with the pride of those who know that the day has come when America is privileged to spend her blood and her might for the principles that gave her birth and happiness and the peace which she has treasured. God helping her, she can do no other.
President Woodrow Wilson, 2 April 1917, asking Congress to declare war against Germany.

I AM SPEAKING to you from the cabinet room at 10 Downing Street. This morning the British Ambassador in Berlin handed the German Government a final note stating that, unless we heard from them by eleven o'clock that they were prepared at once to withdraw their troops from Poland, a state of war would exist between us. I have to tell you now that no such undertaking has been received, and that consequently this country is at war with Germany.
Prime Minister Neville Chamberlain, 3 September 1940, announcing Great Britain's declaration of war against Germany.

YESTERDAY, December 7, 1941 – a date which will live in infamy – the United States was suddenly and deliberately attacked by the naval and air forces of the empire of Japan. . . .

The facts of yesterday and today speak for themselves. The people of the United States have already formed their opinions and well understand the implications to the very life and safety of our nation.

As Commander-in-Chief of our armed forces, I have directed that all measures be taken for our defense.

Always remember the character of the onslaught against us.

No matter how long it may take us to overcome this premeditated invasion, the American people, in their righteous might, will win through to absolute victory. . . .

With confidence in our armed forces, with the unbounding determination of our people, we will gain the inevitable triumph. So help us God.

I ask that the Congress declare that since the unprovoked and dastardly attack by Japan, on December 7, 1941, a state of war has existed between the United States and the Japanese Empire.

President Franklin D. Roosevelt, 8 December 1941, asking Congress to declare war on Japan after the attack on Pearl Harbor.

DEFEAT

DEAD MEN, not potsherds
Covered the approaches,
The walls were gaping,
the high gates, the roads,
were piled with dead.
In the side streets, where feasting crows would
  gather,
Scattered they lay.
In all the streets and roadways bodies lay.
In open fields that used to fill with dancers,
they lay in heaps.
The country's blood now filled its holes,
like metal in a mould;
Bodies dissolved – like fat left in the sun.

A Summerian account of the fall of Third Dynasty Ur (c. 2000 BC), quoted in John Oates, *Babylon*, 1979.

THOSE who reached my boundary, their seed is not; their heart and their soul are finished forever and ever. As for those who had assembled before them on the sea, the full flame was in their front, before the harbor-mouths, and a wall of metal upon the shore surrounded them. They were dragged, overturned, and laid low upon the beach; slain and made heaps from stern to bow of their galleys. While all their things were cast upon the water. Thus I turned back the waters to remember Egypt; when they mention my name in their land, may it consume them, while I sit upon the throne of Harakhte, and the serpent-diadem is fixed upon my head, like Re.

Rameses III, c. 1190 BC, record of the Northern War, quoted in James Breasted, *Ancient Records of Egypt*, 1906.

ONCE MORE may I remind you that you have beaten most of the enemy's fleet already; and, once defeated, men do not meet the same dangers with their old spirit.

Phormio, address to the Athenian Navy, 429 BC, quoted in Thucydides, *The Peloponnesian War*, c. 404 BC, tr. Benjamin Jowett, 1881.

TROOPS defeated in open battle should not be pampered or, even if it seems like a good idea, take refuge in a fortified camp or some other strong place, but while their fear is still fresh, they should attack again. By not indulging them they may with greater assurance renew the fighting.

The Emperor Maurice, *The Strategikon*, c. AD 600 (*Maurice's Strategikon*, tr. George Dennis, 1984).

BROKEN SPEARS lie in the road;
we have torn our hair in our grief.
The houses are roofless
and their walls are red with blood.

Worms are swarming
in the streets and plazas,
and walls are spattered with gore.
The water has turned red, as if it were dyed,
and when we drink it,
it has the taste of brine.

We have pounded our hands in despair
against the adobe walls,
for our inheritance, our city,
is lost and dead.
The shields of our warriors were its defense
but they could not save it.

We have chewed dry twigs and salt grasses;
We have filled our mouths with dust and bits of adobe;
We have eaten lizards, rats, and worms. . . .

An Aztec account of the fall of Tenochtitlan in 1521, about 1528, quoted in Miguel Leon-Portilla, *The Broken Spears*, 1962.

A GENERAL of great merit should be said to be a man who has met with at least one great defeat. A man like myself who has gone his whole life with victories alone and suffered no defeats cannot be called a man of merit, even though he gains in years.

Asakura Norikage (1474–1555) *Soteki Waki*, c. 1550 (*Ideals of the Samurai*, tr. William Wilson, 1982).

CALM YOURSELF, young man. One may be beaten by my army without dishonour!

Napoleon, 2 December 1805, at Austerlitz to a captured young Russian officer who was demanding to be shot for having lost his artillery, quoted in Claude Manceron, *Austerlitz*, 1966.

TROPHIES APART, there is no accurate measure of loss of morale; hence in many cases the abandonment of the fight remains the only authentic proof of victory. In lowering one's colors one acknowledges that one has been at fault and concedes in this instance that both might and right lie with the opponent. This shame and humiliation, which must be distinguished from all other psychological consequences of the transformation of the balance, is an essential part of victory.

Major-General Carl von Clausewitz, *On War*, 4.4, 1832, tr. Michael Howard and Peter Paret, 1976.

WHEN THIS ARMY is defeated and when I am driven from this line, it will be when I have so few men left they will not want for any trains.

General of the Army Ulysses S. Grant, May 6, 1864, comment to a staff officer at the Battle of the Wilderness who said that the trains would be vulnerable if the army was defeated.

NO ONE who is not a seaman can realize the blow which falls upon the human heart of a commander, upon the sinking of his ship. It is not merely the loss of a battle – it is the overwhelming of his household, as it were, in a great catastrophe. The Alabama had not only been my battle-field, but my home, in which I had lived two long years, and in which I had experienced many vicissitudes of pain and pleasure, sickness and health. My officers and crew formed a great military family, every face of which was familiar to me; and when I looked upon my gory deck, toward the close of the action, and saw so many manly forms stretched upon it, with the glazed eye of death, or agonizing with terrible wounds, I felt as a father feels who has lost his children – his children who had followed him to the uttermost ends of the earth, in sunshine and storm, and been always true to him.

> Rear Admiral Raphael Semmes, *Memoir of Service Afloat*, 1868.

MEN ARE easily elated or depressed by victory. As to being prepared for defeat, I certainly am not. Any man who is prepared for defeat would be half-defeated before he commenced. I hope for success; shall do all in my power to secure it and trust to God for the rest.

> Admiral David G. Farragut, letter to his wife, 11 April 1862, quoted in Loyall Farragut, *The Life of David Glasgow Farragut*, 1879.

HE WOULD SIT and talk in the twilight . . .

Once, I remember he sat still for sometime by the window and his face looked so sad. He spoke of the Southern people, of their losses, privations, and sufferings, and also of our vain struggle. "I cannot sleep," he said, "for thinking of it, and often I feel so weighted down with sorrow that I have to get up in the night and go out and walk till I thoroughly weary myself before I can sleep." That was the only melancholy sentence I ever heard him utter, and the only time I ever saw that heartbroken look on his face.

> An account of Robert E. Lee during his visit to a student from Washington College (who had broken his leg) at his home in Lexington by the student's mother, quoted in Charles Flood, *Lee: The Last Years*, 1981.

I CAN'T understand it. I left a thousand men here.

> Lieutenant-General Lord Chelmsford, overheard upon discovering the massacre of his forces at Isandlwana in Zululand, 22 January 1879, quoted in Ian Knight, *Brave Men's Blood*, 1990.

WHEN I was a boy
the Sioux owned the world;
the sun rose and set on their land;
they sent ten thousand men to battle.
Where are the warriors today?
Who slew them? Where are their lands? Who
 owns them?

> Sitting Bull (c. 1831–1890).

ERRORS and defeats are more obviously illustrative of principles than successes are. . . . Defeat cries aloud for explanation; whereas success, like charity, covers a multitude of sins.

> Rear Admiral Alfred Thayer Mahan, *Naval Strategy*, 1911.

ANY ENGAGEMENT includes the abstract possibility of defeat and there is no other means for reducing the possibility than the organized preparation of the engagement.

> V.I. Lenin, quoted in *Voyenno istorichiskiy zhurnal*, 3/1986.

A BEATEN GENERAL is disgraced forever.

> Marshal of France Ferdinand Foch, *Precepts and Judgments*, 1919.

EVERYTHING seems quiet in Berlin for the time being. We are rather in a mess here unfortunately [German Army on the Eastern Front]. We shall not be able to hold Riga.

The troops will fight no more.

> General Max Hoffmann, 31 December 1918, *War Diaries and Other Papers*, II, 1929.

I HAVE SEEN much war in my lifetime and I hate it profoundly. But there are worse things than war; and all of them come with defeat.

> Ernest Hemingway, *Men at War*, 1942.

BATAAN is like a child in a family who dies. It lives in our hearts.

> General of the Army Douglas MacArthur, 9 April 1943, *New York Times*; on the first anniversary of the fall of Bataan.

POSITIONS are seldom lost because they have been destroyed, but almost invariably because the leader has decided in his own mind that the position cannot be held.

> General Alexander A. Vandegrift, 'Battle Doctrine for Front Line Leaders', Third Marine Division, 1944.

MAN IN WAR is not beaten, and cannot be beaten, until he owns himself beaten. Experience of all war proves this truth. So long as war persists as an instrument of policy, the objects of that policy can never be attained until the opponent admits his defeat. Total annihilation, even if it were possible, would recoil on the victor in the close-knit organization of the world's society. Moreover, it is not necessary to the military result. In all wars, and battles, decision is obtained at the moment when the survivors – normally the vast majority – realize that unless they yield their extinction has become inevitable.

The history of war shows that man tends to give way directly he recognizes a stronger – when it dawns upon his mind that he has no further hope of victory by continuing the fight. That is why in battle, contrary to popular impression, actual shock is the rarest episode. When an assault takes place, the weaker side – weaker in either numbers, morale, or momentum – have almost invariably surrendered or fled before the clash actually comes.

Captain Sir Basil Liddell Hart, *Thoughts on War*, 1944.

IN WAR there is no prize for the runner up.

General of the Army Omar N. Bradley, *Military Review*, 1950.

THE NUMBER ONE task is restoration of the wounded national honor. Since the Treaty of Versailles, the Germans know only too well where this wound can lead. The issue of Russia is the defeat of the Soviet Union in the cold war. Properly speaking, we are now fulfilling the conditions of a surrender declaration. We have burned up a few generations in order to build a "bright future." And today our heroes of yesterday must eke out a wretched existence and confess that their entire life was a mistake.

General Aleksander I. Lebed, *Nezavisimaya Gazeta* (Moscow), 29 August 1997.

DEFENCE

HERE were the best picked men detached in squads to stand the Trojan charge and shining Hector: a wall of them bulked together, spear-by-spear, shield-by-shield, the rims overlapping, buckler-to-buckler, helm-to-helm, man-to-man massed tight and the horsehair crests on glittering helmet horns brushed as they tossed their heads, the battalions bulked so dense, shoulder-to-shoulder close, and the spears they shook in daring hands packed into jagged lines of battle – single-minded fighters facing straight ahead, Achaeans primed for combat.

Homer, *The Iliad*, 13.152–162, c. 800 BC, tr. Robert Fagles, 1990; the Greeks drawing up a defensive formation to stop the Trojan onslaught on their ships pulled up on the beach.

LITTLE MINDS try to defend everything at once, but sensible people look at the main point only; they parry the worst blows and stand a little hurt if thereby they avoid a greater one. If you try to hold everything, you hold nothing.

Frederick the Great, quoted in Hermann Foertsch, *The Art of Modern Warfare*, 1940.

ONE OF the falsest notions in war is to remain on the defensive and let the enemy act offensively. In the long run it is inevitable that the party which stays on the defensive will lose.

Frederick the Great, letter 8 January 1779, *Politische Correspondenz Friedrichs des Grossen*, 1879–1939.

TO ME death is better than the defensive.

Field Marshal Prince Aleksandr V. Suvorov (1729–1800), quoted in W. Lyon Blease, *Suvorof*, 1920.

WHAT IS the concept of defense? The parrying of a blow. What is its characteristic feature? Awaiting the blow. It is this feature which turns any action into a defensive one; it is the only test by which defense can be distinguished from attack in war. Pure defense, however, would be completely contrary to the idea of war, since it would mean that only one side was waging it. . . . But if we are really waging war, we must return the enemy's blows; and these offensive acts in a defensive war come under the heading of "defense" – in other words, our offensive takes place within our own positions or theater of operations. Thus, a defensive campaign can be fought with offensive battles, and in a defensive battle, we can employ our divisions offensively. Even in a defensive position awaiting the enemy assault, our bullets take the offensive. So the defensive form of war is not a simple shield, but a shield made up of well-directed blows.

Major-General Carl von Clausewitz, *On War*, 6.1, 1832, tr. Michael Howard and Peter Paret, 1976.

WHAT IS the object of defense? Preservation. It is easier to hold ground than take it. It follows that defense is easier than attack, assuming both sides have equal means. Just what is it that makes preservation and protection so much easier? It is the fact that time which is allowed to pass unused accumulates to the credit of the defender. He reaps where he did not sow. Any omission of attack – whether from bad judgment, fear, or indolence – accrues to the defenders' benefit.

Major-General Carl von Clausewitz, *On War*, 6.1, 1832, tr. Michael Howard and Peter Paret, 1976.

HE WHO STAYS on the defensive does not make war, he endures it.

Field Marshal Colmar Baron von der Goltz, *The Nation in Arms*, 1883.

DEFENSIVE POSITIONS

ANY POSITION in which one accepts battle and makes use of terrain to protect oneself is a defensive position, and it makes no difference whether one's general attitude is mainly passive or mainly active.

Major-General Carl von Clausewitz, *On War*, 6.12, 1832, tr. Michael Howard and Peter Paret, 1976.

THE PERSON who is able to fully utilize all the equipment of military engineering and show a flexibility of mind and military inventiveness is always able to confront the enemy with unexpected events and unexpected dimensions of the defeat dealt it.

Marshal of the Soviet Union Mikhail N. Tukhachevskiy, April 1929, quoted in *Voyenno istorichiskiy zhurnal*, 2/1983.

ANYONE can realize that positions, however strong,

cannot repel an attack, when once they are deprived of a sufficient living garrison.

General Aleksei A. Brusilov, *A Soldier's Notebook*, 1930.

THE ITALIANS and Germans spent tremendous effort in time, labor, and money, building defensive positions. I am sure that just as in the case of the walls of Troy and the Roman walls across Europe, the fact that they trusted to defensive positions reduced their power to fight. Had they spent one-third as much effort fighting as they did in building, we never could have taken the positions.

General George S. Patton, Jr., July 1943, *The Patton Papers*, II, 1974.

LEAVE SOLDIERS in defensive positions too long and they begin to scare themselves to death. Every rustle of the wind sends shivers up their spine, and a single enemy sniper can paralyze an entire battalion. Instead of taking action to eliminate the threat, they hold back, convinced that any such attempt would only make matters worse and trigger a terrible retribution.

Colonel Harry Summers, 13 January 1989, *Washington Times*.

DEFIANCE

WHEN XERXES wrote again: "Deliver up your arms," he wrote back: "Come and take them."

King Leonidas of Sparta, 480 BC, at the Battle of Thermopylae, quoted in Plutarch, *The Lives*, c. AD 100 (*Plutarch on Sparta*, tr. Richard Talbert, 1988).

SOMETHING about six feet of English earth – a bit more as he is such a big man.

King Harold Godwinson of England, 25 September 1066, before the Battle of Stamford Bridge when the Norwegian Viking King Harald Hardrada, who was reputed to be seven feet tall, asked what the English king would pay him to leave England, quoted in David Howarth, *1066: The Year of the Conquest*, 1978.

KING OF ENGLAND, and you duke of Bedford . . . give up to the Maid sent here by the King of Heaven the key of all the noble cities of France you have taken and ravaged . . . I have come here . . . to drive you man for man from France . . . If you will not believe the Maid's message from God, wherever you happen to be we . . . shall make such a great hahaye as has not been made in France these thousand years.

Joan of Arc, 22 March 1429, letter to the English besieging Orléans.

TELL YOUR MASTER that this is the only territory that I will give him (pointing to the great ditch before the defenses of Malta). There lies the land which he may have for his own – provided only that he fills it with the bodies of his Janissaries.

Jean de la Valette, Grand Master of the Order of the Knights of St. John of Jerusalem, 30 June 1565, his reply to the emissary of Mustapha Pasha, commander of the Turkish Army besieging Malta, when offered terms of surrender, quoted in Ernle Bradford, *The Great Siege: Malta 1565*, 1961.

I HAVE SINGED the beard of the king of Spain.

Sir Francis Drake, after destroying a vast amount of shipping in the Harbour of Cadiz, 19 April 1587.

I KNOW I have the body of a weak and feeble woman, but I have the heart and stomach of a king, and of a king of England too.

Queen Elizabeth I, 29 July 1588, speech at Tilbury to her army as it awaited the Spanish Armada.

I WILL DIE in the last ditch.

William of Orange, later William III of England (1650–1702), quoted in Hume, *History of Great Britain*, II, 1757.

HEADS UP, for God's sake! Those are bullets – not turds!

General Lepic, 8 February 1807, to the Guard Horse-Grenadiers at Eylau as their losses to random fire lowered morale while they waited in reserve.

IF IT COST ME my throne, I will bury the world under its ruins!

Napoleon, 26 June 1813, reply to Prince Metternich's demands during the crisis of the 1813 campaign, quoted in R.M. Johnston, ed., *The Corsican*, 1910.

BY THE ETERNAL, they shall not sleep on our soil!

Major-General Andrew Jackson, 23 December 1814, upon learning that the British Army had landed near New Orleans.

MERDE! (Shit!)

'Le Mot de Cambronne', the actual reply of General Cambronne at Waterloo when called upon to surrender the Old Guard, not the more poetic, 'The Guard dies but does not surrender!'

I SHALL NEVER surrender nor retreat.

Lieutenant-Colonel William Barrett Travis, 24 February 1836, reply to General Santa Anna when called upon to surrender the Alamo.

TELL HIM to go to hell.

Major-General Zachary Taylor, 22 February 1847, reply to General Santa Anna's demand for his surrender at the Battle of Buena Vista.

GENERAL TAYLOR never surrenders.

General Thomas L. Crittenden, reply to General Santa Anna at the Battle of Buena Vista, 22 February 1847.

OUT OF the question!

The reply of Captain Jean Danjou, commanding the 3rd Company of the Foreign Legion Regiment at the battle of Camerone, 30 April 1863, in Mexico, in reply to the demand for surrender by Colonel Milan of the Mexican Army. The company's heroic last stand became the founding legend of the Foreign Legion. Afer Danjou was killed, the demand for surrender was made again and answered by the more earthy, 'Merde!', from the enlisted ranks.

THEY shall not pass. (*Ils ne passeront pas*.)
> Marshal Henri Phillipe Pétain, at Verdun, February 1916.

WE SHALL NOT flag or fail. We shall fight in France, we shall fight on the seas and oceans, we shall fight with growing confidence and growing strength in the air, we shall defend our island, whatever the cost may be, we shall fight on the beaches, we shall fight on the landing grounds, we shall fight in the fields and in the streets, we shall fight in the hills; we shall never surrender.
> Sir Winston S. Churchill, speech in the House of Commons after the evacuation of Dunkirk, 4 June 1940.

WE ARE WAITING for the long-promised invasion. So are the fishes. (*Nous attendons l'invasion promise de longue date. Les poissons aussi*.)
> Sir Winston S. Churchill, 21 October 1940, broadcast to the French people.

NUTS!
> Major-General Terry MacAullife, 22 December 1944, reply to the German demand that he surrender the 101st Airborne Division defending Bastogne.

DELAY

EVERY procrastinator is not a Fabius.
> King Gustavus II Adolphus, July 1630, to the colonel who could not make up his mind to surrender Stettin, quoted in Theodore Ayrault Dodge, *Gustavus Adolphus*, 1895.

WE MUST have the moral courage to make tough decisions in the face of uncertainty – and accept full responsibility for those decisions – when the natural inclination would be to postpone the decision pending more complete information. To delay action in an emergency because of incomplete information shows a lack of moral courage. We do not want to make rash decisions, but we must not squander opportunities while trying to gain more information.
> General Alfred M. Gray and Major John Schmitt, *Warfighting*, United States Marine Corps, 1989.

DELEGATION OF AUTHORITY

ACCORDING TO my custom . . . I was present at the attack near the monastery of Svyanty Kryzh, but held my tongue, not wishing in the least to detract from the praiseworthy, skilful and brave commands of my subordinates.
> Field Marshal Prince Aleksandr V. Suvorov (1729–1800).

THE BLOW wherever struck, must, to be successful, be sudden and heavy.
   The troops used, must be efficient and light. I cannot pretend at this distance to direct operations depending on circumstances unknown to me and requiring the exercise of discretion and judgment as to time and execution, but submit these suggestions for your consideration.
> General Robert E. Lee, letter to Major-General Thomas J. 'Stonewall' Jackson, during the Valley Campaign, 25 April 1862, quoted in *The Wartime Papers of R. E. Lee*, 1961.

I HAVE ALWAYS, whenever it was possible, avoided giving positive instructions to the commanding generals . . . leaving them the exercise of their own judgment, while giving them my opinion and advice.
> Major-General Henry W. Halleck, *The War of the Rebellion: A Compilation of the Official Records of the Union and Confederate Armies*, Vol. XX, Part 2, p. 670, U.S. Government Printing Office, 1880–1901.

I WILL DO no such thing. If we were personally present and knew the exact situation, we might assume such responsibility. If such orders are issued, you must issue them yourself. I hold that a General in command of an army in the field is the best judge of existing conditions.
> Major-General Henry W. Halleck, to Lincoln as he refused to change Burnside's plan of operation immediately before the Battle of Fredericksburg, December 1862, quoted in Haupt, *Reminiscences of General Herman Haupt*, 1901.

I AM CONFIDENT that at all times and in all places you will do all that can be done for the defence of the country and advancement of the service, and are ready to cooperate or act singly as circumstances dictate. I only wish you therefore to keep me advised of your movements that I may shape mine accordingly, and not to feel trammeled in your operations, other than is required by the general plan of operations, when an opportunity offers for you to advance the object of the campaign.
> General Robert E. Lee, letter to Lieutenant-General James A. Longstreet, 21 March 1863, quoted in *The Wartime Papers of R. E. Lee*, 1961.

BE CONTENT to do what you can for the well-being of what properly belongs to you; commit the rest to those who are responsible.
> General Robert E. Lee, quoted in William Jones, *Life and Letters of Robert Edward Lee*, 1906.

MY INTERFERENCE in battle would do more harm than good. . . . I have, then, to rely on my brigade and division commanders. I think and work with all my power to bring the troops to the right place at the right time; then I have done my duty. As soon as I order them forward into battle, I leave my army in the hands of God.

General Robert E. Lee, quoted in J.F.C. Fuller, *Grant and Lee*, 1933.

I DO NOT PROPOSE to lay down for you a plan of campaign . . . but simply lay down the work it is desirable to have done and leave you free to execute it in your own way. Submit to me, however, as early as you can, your plan of operation.

General of the Army Ulysses S. Grant, instructions to General Sherman, 4 April 1864, *Personal Memoirs*, II, 1885.

DO NOT HESITATE to give commands to officers in whom you have confidence, without regard to claims of others on account of rank. What we want is prompt and active movements after the enemy in accordance with the instructions you already have. I feel every confidence that you will do your best, and will leave you as far as possible to act on your own judgment, and not embarrass you with orders and instructions.

General of the Army Ulysses S. Grant, instructions to General Sheridan, early August 1864, quoted in Horace Porter, *Campaigning with Grant*, 1897.

WHEN a detachment is made, the commander thereof should be informed of the object to be accomplished, and left as free as possible to execute it in his own way. . . .

General of the Army William T. Sherman, *Memoirs*, II, 1875.

NO ARMY can be efficient unless it be a unit for action; and the power must come from above, not from below: The President delegates his power to the commander-in-chief, and he to the next, and so on down to the lowest actual commander of troops, however small the detachment. No matter how troops come together, when once united, the highest officer in rank is held responsible, and should be consequently armed with the fullest power of the Executive, subject only to law and existing orders. The more simple, the principle, the greater the likelihood of determined action; and the less a commanding officer is circumscribed by bounds or precedent, the greater is the probability that he will make the best use of his command and achieve the best results.

General of the Army William T. Sherman, *Memoirs*, II, 1875.

THE BATTALION OFFICER cannot be four company commanders.

General Mikhail I. Dragomirov (1830–1905), quoted in *Voyenno istorichiskiy zhurnal*, 9/1985.

YOU BRING OVER the papers that are going to win or lose a war – and you sign the others.

General of the Army Douglas MacArthur, c. 1919–1922, to Colonel Louis E. Hibbs, his adjutant while superintendent at West Point, when Hibbs asked MacArthur which papers he wanted to sign, quoted in Francis Miller, *General Douglas MacArthur*, 1942.

I ALSO SAID that he, as Supreme Comd., could not descend into the land battle and become a ground C-in-C; the Supreme Comd. has to sit on a very lofty perch and be able to take a detached view of the whole intricate problem – which involves land, sea, air, civil control, political problems, etc., etc. Someone must run the land battle for him; we had won a great victory in Normandy *because* of unified land control and *NOT in spite of it*.

Field Marshal Viscount Montgomery of Alamein, 1944, quoted in Ian Hamilton, *Master of the Battlefield*, 1983.

WHEN I SAY that the gift of persuading others to do what is wanted is more than half the art of command, I mean by others the "right men". For the art of selection is the secret of leadership. Without this power of devolution staleness seizes upon the harassed leader. In general men given great responsibility work too hard.

Baron Charles MacMoran Wilson Moran, *The Anatomy of Courage*, 1945.

A COMPANY COMMANDER can no more hope to supervise directly the acts of several hundred men in battle without reposing large faith in his lieutenants than the general can expect good results to come of by-passing his staff and his corps commanders and dealing directly with his divisions. But there are generals who have failed because they did not learn this lesson as captains.

Brigadier-General S.L.A. Marshal, *Men Against Fire*, 1947.

IF THE STATE of a command is such that the commander's hands are not free for the administration of his exterior tasks, it is an indication that the morale and leadership of the unit are based on incorrect principles and that insufficient authority has been delegated to subordinates. There can be no more miserable cause of failure though it is a weakness that is found in many conscientious officers. The man who cannot bring himself to trust the judgment and good faith of other men cannot command very long. He will soon break under the unnecessary strain he puts on himself. Sleeplessness, nervous irritation, and loss of self-control will be his lot until he is at last found totally unfit.

Brigadier-General S.L.A. Marshall, *The Armed Forces Officer*, 1950.

THEY (our company commanders) are now bound hand and foot by a whole new list of mandatory subjects. . . . You've delegated to the commander only the choice of what he is going to catch hell for.

General Creighton Abrams (1914–1974), quoted in *Military Review*, 4/1985.

EACH COMMANDER'S plan had to be clear so that every other commander would understand what his colleagues were doing – what their objectives were, and how they intended to accomplish them. By the time the order presentations and reviews were completed, they each knew the overall plan in detail, they knew how their own roles fit into the overall concept, they knew what their neighbors were trying to do and where they would be. They also knew that I trusted them to carry out their missions with an absolute minimum of interference. The field assignments were theirs, and my philosophy (as each commander understood) was that they would handle them best.

General Ariel Sharon, referring to the Battle of Agheila, 1967, *Warrior*, 1989.

ALL OF YOU heard me say earlier that "not one thing in Iraq is worth dying for," and that was true. Sometime in the next week, there is going to be a lot worth dying for in Iraq. We call them American soldiers and marines. When I said I want a minimum loss of life, we cannot draw distinctions between Americans who die. If a marine dies or a soldier dies, it's the same to me as one of you dying. For that reason, there will be no restriction placed on you by anyone. The individual fighter pilot or flight lead will decide what is necessary. That, individual courage and ability has always been and will continue to be our strength. God speed.

Lieutenant-General Buster Glosson, mid-February 1991, message to every fighter wing of the 14th Air Division just before the beginning of Desert Storm, 'The Price', Al Santoli, ed., *Leading the Way: How Vietnam Veterans Rebuilt the U.S. Military*, 1993.

COMMAND is lonely, I said, and that was not just a romantic cliché. Sharing a problem with the boss, in this corps, would not be seen as weakness or failure, but as a sign of mutual confidence. On the other hand, they did not have to buck every decision up to me. "I have a wide zone of indifference," I said. "I don't care if you hold reveille at five-thirty or five forty-five A.M. And don't ask me to decide."

General Colin Powell, *My American Journey*, 1995.

DEMOBILISATION

ALL THE Macedonians – about 10,000 all told – who were too old for service or in any way unfit, got their discharge at their own request. They were given their pay not only up to date, but also for the time they would take on the homeward journey. In addition to their pay they each received a gratuity of one talent. . . . he [Alexander] did . . . give the clearest proof of how warmly he felt for them, and of how much he would miss them when they had gone, by his decision to entrust them on their journey to the leadership and protection of Craterus, the most loyal of his officers and a man he loved as dearly as his own life. When he said good-bye to them, his eyes and the eyes of every man among them were wet with tears.

Arrian, of the release of Alexander's veterans in Babylon, 323 BC, *The Campaigns of Alexander*, 7.12, c. AD 150, tr. Aubrey de Sélincourt, 1987.

BY AGREEMENT between the officers appointed by Generals Lee and Grant to carry out the stipulations of the surrender of the Army of Northern Virginia, the evidence that an officer or enlisted man is a paroled prisoner of war is the fact of his possessing a printed certificate, certifying to the fact, dated at Appomattox C.H., April 10, 1865, and signed by his commanding officer or the staff officer of the same.

All guards, patrols, officers, and soldiers of the United States forces will respect such certificates, allow free passage to the holders thereof, and observe, in good faith, the provisions of the surrender that the holders shall remain unmolested in every respect.

General Order No. 43, Headquarters, 24th Corps, Army of the Potomac, a copy of which was given at General Grant's direction to every surrendered member of the Army of Northern Virginia (24th Corps had the printing press).

AFTER THE ARMIES had been reviewed in Washington, they were transported by the Government to fifty depots near their homes. They had been mustered out of service by officers appointed for that purpose, before they left the field. Their final muster-rolls were boxed up and transported with them, their final payment being made contingent upon their remaining in their ranks, and conducting themselves in an orderly manner until released. At the depots paymasters awaited them; and, having been transported and subsisted up to the last moment, they were paid in full, and discharged almost at their very homes. Thus it was that 800,963 men in arms were all released from military restraint and returned to the walks of civil life, within the space of two months, without a single act of lawlessness being reported.

Major-General E.D. Townsend, of the demobilisation of the volunteer regiments of the Union Army at the end of the Civil War, 1865, *Anecdotes of the Civil War*, 1884.

IT WAS NO demobilization, it was a rout.

General of the Army George C. Marshall, (1885–1959), on the rapid demobilisation of the U.S. Army after World War I.

THIS THING is exactly like a decomposing corpse and as Kipling says in his poem, "Gentlemen Rank [sic]": "We are dropping down the ladder rung by rung." I think you were very lucky not to come back and see our magnificent Army sloughing away.

> General George S. Patton, Jr., September 1945, letter to Colonel Charles Codman, on the rapid and feckless demobilisation of the U.S. Army in 1945, quoted in Carlo d'Este, *Patton: A Genius For War*, 1995.

DEMORALISATION

WHEN MEN are once checked in what they consider their special excellence, their whole opinion of themselves suffers more than if they had not at first believed in their superiority, the unexpected shock to their pride causing them to give way more than their real strength warrants. . . .

> Gylippus, Summer 413 BC, to the Syracusans before the last great naval battle with the Athenians in the harbour of Syracuse, quoted in Thucydides, *History of the Peloponnesian War*, 7.67, c. 404 BC, tr. Richard Crawley, 1910.

DEMORALIZE the enemy, then annihilate them.

> Lieutenant-General Johann von Ewald, *A Treatise Upon the Duties of Light Troops*, 1790.

THE MEN of both Lee's and Johnston's armies, like their brethren of the North, are as brave as men can be; but no man is so brave that he may not meet such defeats and disasters as to discourage and dampen his ardor for any cause, no matter how just he deems it.

> General of the Army Ulysses S. Grant, *Personal Memoirs of U.S. Grant*, II, 1885.

THE PRINCIPLE of Demoralization. As the principle of endurance has, as its primary object, the security of the minds of men by shielding their moral [morale] against the shock of battle, inversely the principle of demoralization has as its object the destruction of moral: first, in the moral attack against the spirit and nerves of the enemy's nation and government; secondly against this nation's policy; thirdly against the plan of its commander-in-chief, and fourthly against the moral of the soldiers commanded by him. Hitherto the fourth, the least important of these objectives, has been considered by the traditionally-minded soldier as the sole psychological objective of this great principle.

> Major-General J.F.C. Fuller, *The Reformation of War*, 1923.

DEPENDABILITY

EVEN WHEN in a battle that is beyond one's means to win, one should lift up his heart and be resolved that no one will surpass him in firmness. He should think to be another's strength and a man to be relied upon.

> Shiba Yoshimasa (1350–1410), *The Chikubasho*, 1383 (*Ideals of the Samurai*, tr. William Wilson, 1982).

DURING a critical phase of the Battle of the Bulge, when I commanded the 18th Airborne Corps, another corps commander just entering the fight next to me remarked: "I'm glad to have you on my flank. It's character that counts." I had long known him, and I knew what he meant. I replied: "That goes for me, too." There was no need for amplification. None was necessary. Each knew the other would stick however great the pressure; would extend help before it was asked, if he could; and would tell the truth, seek no self-glory, and everlastingly keep his word. Such feelings breed confidence and success.

> General Matthew B. Ridgway, 'Leadership', *Military Review*, 10/1966.

DESERTION/DESERTERS

THE POET'S SHIELD

A perfect shield bedecks some Thracian now;
I had no choice: I left it in a wood.
Ah, well, I saved my skin, so let it go!
A new one's just as good.

> Archilochus, c. 648 BC, tr. Sir William Morris, quoted in *The Oxford Book of Greek Verse in Translation*, 1930.

TO SEDUCE the enemy's soldiers from their allegiance and encourage them to surrender is of especial service, for an adversary is more hurt by desertion than by slaughter.

> Flavius Vegetius Renatus, *Military Institutions of the Romans*, c. AD 378, tr. Clark, 1776.

AN ENEMY SOLDIER who deserts to us, apart from some plot, is of the greatest advantage, for the enemy is hurt by deserters more than if the same men were killed in action.

> The Emperor Maurice, *The Strategikon*, c. AD 600 (*Maurice's Strategikon*, tr. George Dennis, 1984).

IF ANY of the enemy's troops desert him and come over to you, it is a great acquisition – provided they prove faithful; for their loss will be more than that of those killed in battle, although deserters will always be suspected by their new friends and odious to their old ones.

> Niccolo Machiavelli, *The Art of War*, 1521.

NO DANGERS can for me and mine be compared with the base desertion of such a noble cause – the honour of God, the peace of the provinces, the freedom of the Fatherland – and abandonment of the sacred and honourable side which I have up till now followed.

> Prince William I of Orange, 1584.

COME, come, let us fight another battle to-day: if I am beaten, we will desert together to-morrow.

> Frederick the Great (1712–1786), to a captured deserter, quoted in Campbell, *Frederick the Great*, 1843.

A SOLDIER who offers to quit his rank, or offers to flag, is to be instantly put to death by the officer who commands that platoon, or by the officer or sergeant in the rear of that platoon; a soldier does not deserve to live who won't fight for his king and country.
  Major-General Sir James Wolfe, 1755, order to the 20th Foot at Canterbury.

THOMAS CREEVY: "Do you calculate upon any desertion in Bonaparte's army?"
Wellington: "Not upon a man from the colonel to the private in a regiment – both inclusive. We may pick up a marshal or two; but not worth a damn."
  The Duke of Wellington, June 1815, before the Battle of Waterloo, quoted in Creevy, *The Creevy Papers*, 1934.

DESPERATION

I HAVE OFTEN myself witnessed occasions, and I have heard of many more from others where men who had been conquered by an enemy, having been driven quite to desperation, have renewed the fight, and retrieved their former disasters.
  Themistocles, quoted in Herodotus, *The Persian Wars*, 8.109, c. 430 BC, tr. George Rawlinson, 1942.

. . . AND THERE is nobody more terrible than the desperate.
  Field Marshal Prince Aleksandr V. Suvorov, 1799, account of his icy Swiss campaign.

I WAS CUT OFF and surrounded, night and day we attacked the enemy, in front and in the rear, captured his guns, which we were obliged to throw off the precipices owing to the shortage of pack animals, and inflicted on him losses four times heavier than ours. Everywhere we forced our way through as victors. . . .
  Field Marshal Prince Aleksandr V. Suvorov, 1799, account of his icy Swiss campaign.

DESTINY

IF THIS THING were going to cost me 80,000 men I wouldn't do it; but it won't take 12,000; it's mere child's play. I don't want to hurt anybody, but when my great political chariot is rolling, it's as well to stand from under the wheels.
  Napoleon, 1 May 1808, during the occupation of Spain, quoted in R.M. Johnston, ed., *The Corsican*, 1910.

AH, WHY DID the bullets spare my life if it was only to lose it in this wretched way?
  Napoleon, 5 April 1821, near death on St. Helena, quoted in R.M. Johnston, ed., *The Corsican*, 1910.

I FEEL that my destiny is in the hands of the Almighty. This belief, more than any other facts or reason, makes me brave and fearless as a I am.
  Major-General George Armstrong Custer, 1863, letter to his wife.

I DO NOT FEEL a person but an instrument of Destiny.
  General Charles de Gaulle, August 1944, upon entering Paris at its liberation.

ZHUKOV spun the wheel of history three times. First when he defended the Soviet Far East and smashed the Japanese forces. Then he conquered the Nazis in December 1941. His deeds were totally against military experience and doctrines, but he did them. And the third time was in the cold summer of 1953, when he executed Beriya.
  General Aleksandr I. Lebed, *Izvestiya* (Moscow), 20 November 1996.

DESTRUCTION OF THE ENEMY

AND FURTHERMORE it is my opinion that Carthage must be destroyed. (*Carthago delenda est*.)
  Marcus Porcius Cato, the Elder, c. 150 BC, quoted in Plutarch, *The Lives*, c. AD 100 (*The Makers of Rome*, tr. Ian Scott-Kilvert, 1965); the sentence with which he ended every speech in the Roman Senate based on his fear of a resurgent and vengeful Carthage.

THE OBJECTIVE is not the occupation of a geographical position but the destruction of the enemy force.
  General Piotr A. Rumyantsev (1725–1796), quoted in Parkinson, *Fox of the North*, 1976.

WHEN THE ENEMY is driven back, we have failed, and when he is cut off, encircled and dispersed, we have succeeded.
  Field Marshal Prince Aleksandr V. Suvorov (1729–1800), quoted in Reznichenko, *Tactica*, 1987.

THERE IS NO WAY of dealing with the Frenchman but to knock him down – to be civil to them is to be laughed at, why they are enemies.
  Admiral Viscount Nelson, 11 January 1798, of the capitulation of the French garrison at Capua to Captain T. Louis, quoted in Robert Southey, *Life of Nelson*, 1813.

HAD WE TAKEN ten sail and allowed the eleventh to escape, being able to get at her, I could never have called it well done.
  Admiral Viscount Nelson (1758–1805).

WE MAY DEPEND upon it that whenever we shall assemble an army, the French will consider its defeat and destruction their first object, particularly if

Buonoparte should be at the head of the French troops himself. . . .

> The Duke of Wellington, 1808, Portugal, advice to the British Cabinet on operations on the Iberian Peninsula, *The Dispatches of Field Marshal the Duke of Wellington, During His Various Campaigns in India, Denmark, Portugal, Spain, the Low Countries, and France*, IV, 1834–1838, p. 144.

STRIKE AN ENEMY once and for all. Let him cease to exist as a tribe or he will live to fly at your throat again.

> Shaka Zulu, c. 1811, advice to King Dingiswayo on the treatment of the defeated Ndwandwes, quoted in E.A. Ritter, *Shaka Zulu*, 1955.

THE MOST IMPORTANT goal of our actions is destruction of the enemy to the last limit of possibility.

> Field Marshal Prince Mikhail I. Kutuzov (1745–1813), quoted in Savkin, *Basic Principles of Operational Art and Tactics*, 1972.

A BATTLE gained is always a fine thing; but . . . [if we] simply force him to retreat without futher loss than that on the battle field . . . the enemy will soon be able to rally his forces and offer a new battle.

> Dennis Hart Mahan, *Advance-Guard, Out-Post, and Detachment Service of Troops with the Essential Principles of Strategy and Grand Tactics*, 1863.

THE BATTLES of Hannibal . . . have a particular character of stubbornness explained by the necessity for overcoming the Roman tenacity. It may be said that to Hannibal victory was not sufficient. He must destroy. Consequently he always tried to cut off all retreat for the enemy. He knew that with Rome, destruction was the only way of finishing the struggle.

He did not believe in the courage of despair in the masses; he believed in terror and he knew the value of surprise in inspiring it.

> Colonel Charles Ardant du Picq, *Battle Studies*, 1880, tr. Greely, 1957.

ONLY DESTRUCTION of the enemy can be called victory.

> Admiral Stepan O. Makarov, 1904, Port Arthur.

JOMINI'S DICTUM that the organized forces of the enemy are the chief objective, pierces like a two-edged sword to the joints and marrow of many specious propositions. . . .

> Rear Admiral Alfred Thayer Mahan, *From Sail to Steam*, 1907.

WHO WANTS a military leader incapable of understanding that the opponent is not going to surrender – that he must be crushed?

> Joseph Stalin to H.G. Wells, quoted in M. Berchin and E. Ben-Horin, *The Red Army*, 1942.

IN CASE opportunity for destruction of major portion

of the enemy fleet is offered or can be created, *such destruction becomes the primary task*.

> Admiral of the Fleet Chester W. Nimitz, operations order to Admiral Halsey in command of the Third Fleet in support of the invasion of the Philippines at Leyte Gulf, September 1944, quoted in Samuel Eliot Morison, *Leyte, June 1944–January 1945*, 1958.

WE SHALL LAND at Inchon and I shall crush them.

> General of the Army Douglas MacArthur, 23 August 1950, after being briefed on the difficulties of landing at Inchon, quoted in *The Congressional Record*, 15 January 1959, p. 669.

DID YOU EVER hear the story of the *Bismarck*? I forget the British Admiral's name. He told the story himself. He wirelessed Churchill. "The *Bismarck* is a wreck. The crew has left her but she won't sink. And I've got just enough oil in my ship to get home." The Prime Minister (Churchill) sent him a cable, "You stay there until the *Bismarck* is on the bottom; and we'll send out and tow you in."

> General of the Army Dwight D. Eisenhower, *The Military Churchill*, 1970.

WE ARE NOT going to attack into Kuwait. We are not going to go into the teeth of this. . . . We are going to hit him out here on the wing. Our objective will be to avoid the Iraqi main forces and go after his center of gravity. . . . we are going to destroy him. . . . We're going to push them back (against the Persian Gulf and the Euphrates River), and we're going to kill them in here.

> General H. Norman Schwarzkopf, mid-November 1990, briefing to his subordinate commanders on the coming Desert Storm campaign, quoted in Donnelly, 'The General's Plan', *Army Times*, 2 March 1992.

WE NEED to destroy not attack, not damage, not surround – I want you to destroy the Republican Guard.

> General H. Norman Schwarzkopf, *It Doesn't Take a Hero*, 1992.

DETAILS

APPRECIATE all those details; they are not without glory. It is the first step that leads to glory.

> Frederick the Great, *Art de la Guerre*, 1751.

I COULD as easily bail out the Potomac River with a teaspoon as attend to all the details of the army.

> President Abraham Lincoln, attributed by General James B. Fry; supposedly part of the reply given to a young soldier who had come to see Lincoln with a grievance, quoted in Allen Thorndyke Rice, *Reminiscences of Abraham Lincoln*, 1886.

IT IS ABSOLUTELY vital that a senior

commander should keep himself from becoming immersed in details, and I always did so. I would spend many hours in quiet thought and reflection in thinking out the major problems. In battle a commander has got to think how he will defeat the enemy. If he gets involved in details he cannot do this since he will lose sight of the essentials which really matter; he will then be led off on side issues which will have little influence on the battle, and he will fail to be that solid rock on which the staff can lean. Details are their province. No commander whose daily life is spent in the consideration of details, and who has not time for quiet thought and reflection, can make a sound plan of battle on a high level or conduct large-scale operations efficiently.

Field Marshal Viscount Montgomery of Alamein, *The Memoirs of Field Marshal Montgomery*, 1958.

DETERMINATION

WE WILL either find a way or make one.

Hannibal (247–183 BC).

THERE IS NOTHING impossible! . . . give your orders, support them with firmness, and you will see every obstacle vanish.

Lieutenant-General Johann von Ewald, *Treatise on the Duties of Light Troops*, 1790.

TRUE WISDOM for a general is in vigorous determination.

Napoleon, '*Précis des guerres de Frederic II*', *Correspondance de Napoléon Ier, publié par ordre de l'Empereur Napoléon III*, No. 209, Vol. XXXII, 1858–1870.

HE WHO understands the nature of a decision in practical affairs, especially in war where it must be made under the pressure of great responsibility and in the midst of a thousand uncertainties and contradictions, will appreciate that decisions cannot be made without many doubts; and what may seem a very simple problem often cannot be decided without the exercise of great determination. Conceiving plans for military operations is therefore the easiest part. . . .

Major–General Carl von Clausewitz, *Campaign of 1799 in Italy and Switzerland*, 1906.

DETERMINATION in a single instance is an expression of courage; if it becomes characteristic, a mental habit. But here we are referring not to physical courage but to the courage to accept responsibility, a courage in the face of moral danger. This has often been called *courage d'esprit*, because it is created by the intellect. That, however, does not make it an act of the intellect: it is an act of temperament. Intelligence alone is not courage; we often see that the most intelligent people are irresolute. Since in the rush of events a man is governed by feelings rather than by thought, the intellect needs to arouse the quality of courage, which then supports and sustains it in action.

Looked at in this way, the role of determination is to limit the agonies of doubt and the perils of hesitation when the motives for action are inadequate. . . .

Major-General Carl von Clausewitz, *On War*, 1.3, 1832, tr. Michael Howard and Peter Paret, 1976.

I STAND at the altar of murdered men and while I live I fight their cause.

Florence Nightingale, letter of August 1856, quoted in Cecil Woodham-Smith, *Florence Nightingale, 1820–1910*, 1951.

IF THE ENTIRE Union Army comes across here, I will kill them all.

Lieutenant-General James Longstreet, 13 December 1862, at Marye's Heights during the Battle of Fredericksburg.

MY TROOPS may fail to take a position, but are never driven from one.

Lieutenant-General Thomas J. 'Stonewall' Jackson (1824–1863).

I THINK it would be better to order up some artillery and defend the present location.

General of the Army Ulysses S. Grant, 1864, when members of his staff advised retreat at the Battle of the Wilderness.

SIMPLY TO EXALT the will as a force without limit tends only to create delusions about what may be accomplished by the exercise of it. These delusions in turn destroy the confidence of troops, then as confidence flags, they become unresponsive to the bidding of the commander. The quality of mind most worth seeking is not power of will but, as said by Marcus Aurelius, "Freedom of will and undeviating steadiness of purpose."

Brigadier-General S.L.A. Marshall, *Men Against Fire*, 1947.

IT IS TRUE that in war determination by itself may achieve results, while flexibility without determination in reserve, cannot, but it is only the blending of the two that brings final success. The hardest test of generalship is to hold this balance between determination and flexibility.

Field Marshal Viscount Slim of Burma, *Defeat Into Victory*, 1956.

THE DIRECT APPROACH

TO MOVE directly on an opponent consolidates his balance, physical and psychological, and by consolidating it increases his resisting power. For in the case of an army it rolls the enemy back towards his reserves, supplies, and reinforcements, so that as the original front is driven back and worn thin, new layers are added to the back. At most, it imposes a strain rather than producing a shock.

Captain Sir Basil Liddell Hart, *Strategy*, 1954.

MONTGOMERY was appalled at the inefficiency and lack of professional skill which led to failures and heavy casualties. It was not so much the casualties which horrified him as the waste, because nothing was achieved by them. He did not shrink from the direct approach, if it were efficiently done.

Field Marshal Lord Carver, *El Alamein*, 1962.

DISCIPLINE
General

BE MEN, my friends! Discipline fill your hearts!
Dread what comrades say of you here in bloody
  combat!
When men dread that, more men come through alive –
When soldiers break and run, good-bye glory,
good-bye all defenses!

Homer, *The Iliad*, 15.651–655, c. 800 BC, tr. Robert Fagles, 1990; Telamonian Ajax spurring on the Achaeans as their army lay at bay before the Trojan onslaught.

THE STRENGTH of an army lies in strict discipline and undeviating obedience to its officers.

Thucydides, *The Peloponnesian War*, Bk 2, c. 404 BC.

THE EXPENSE of keeping up good or bad troops is the same; but it depends wholly on you, most August Emperor, to restore the excellent discipline of the ancients and to correct the abuses of later times. This is a reformation the advantages of which will be equally felt by ourselves and our posterity.

Flavius Vegetius Renatus, *Military Institutions of the Romans*, c. AD 378, tr. Clark, 1776.

FEW MEN are brave by nature, but good order and experience make many so. Good order and discipline in any army are to be more depended upon than courage alone.

Niccolo Machiavelli, *The Art of War*, 1521.

ALL MILITARY history . . . records the triumphs of discipline and courage far more frequently than numbers and resources.

Robert E. Lee, 22 February 1865, Circular of the Army of Northern Virginia, quoted in William Jones, *Life and Letters of Robert Edward Lee*, 1906.

The Effects of Discipline

FOR WHERE there is no one in control nothing useful or distinguished can be done. This is roughly

true of all departments of life, and entirely true where soldiering is concerned. Here it is discipline that makes one feel safe, while lack of discipline has destroyed many people before now.

Xenophon, speech to the Greek officers after the defeat of Cyrus at Cunaxa, 401 BC, *Anabasis*, c. 360 BC (*The Persian Expedition*, 3.1, tr. Rex Warner).

DISCIPLINE is the soul of an army. It makes small numbers formidable; procures success to the weak, and esteem to all.

General George Washington, 29 July 1759, Letter of Instructions to the Captains of the Virginia Regiments.

TWO MAMELUKES held three Frenchmen; but one hundred French cavalry did not fear the same number of Mamelukes; three hundred vanquished the same number; one thousand French beat fifteen hundred Mamelukes.

Napoleon, quoted in Edward Earle, ed., *Makers of Strategy*, 1943.

AT NO TIME in the war has the necessity of close attention to this important subject been greater than at present, and at no time has its cultivation promised more valuable results. The proportion of experienced troops is larger in our army than in that of the enemy, while his numbers exceed our own. These are the circumstances most favorable for the display of the advantages of discipline, and in which the power it imparts will be most perfectly perceived.

Robert E. Lee, 22 February 1865, Circular of the Army of Northern Virginia, quoted in William Jones, *Life and Letters of Robert Edward Lee*, 1906.

THE IMPORTANCE and utility of thorough discipline should be impressed on officers and men on all occasions by illustrations taken from the experience of the instructor or from other sources of information. They should be made to understand that discipline contributes no less to their safety than to their efficiency. Disastrous surprises and those sudden panics which lead to defeat and the greatest loss of life are of rare occurrence among disciplined troops. It is well known that the greatest number of casualties occur when men become scattered, and especially when they retreat in confusion, as the fire of the enemy is then more deliberate and fatal. The experience of every officer shows that those troops suffer least who attack most vigorously, and that a few men retaining their organization and acting in concert accomplish far more with smaller loss than a larger number scattered and disorganized.

Robert E. Lee, 22 February 1865, Circular of the Army of Northern Virginia, quoted in William Jones, *Life and Letters of Robert Edward Lee*, 1906.

THE MORE MODERN war becomes, the more essential appear the basic qualities that from the beginning of history have distinguished armies from mobs. The first of these is discipline. We very soon learned in Burma that strict discipline in battle and in bivouac was vital, not only for success, but for survival. Nothing is easier in jungle or dispersed fighting than for a man to shirk. If he has no stomach for advancing, all he has to do is flop into the undergrowth; in retreat, he can slink out of the rear guard, join up later, and swear he was the last to leave. A patrol leader can take his men a mile into the jungle, hide there, and return with any report he fancies. Only discipline – not punishment – can stop that sort of thing; the real discipline that a man holds to because it is a refusal to betray his comrades. The discipline that makes a sentry, whose whole body is tortured for sleep, rest his chin on the point of his bayonet because he knows, if he nods, he risks the lives of the men sleeping behind him. It is only discipline, too, that can enforce the precautions against disease, irksome as they are, without which an army would shrivel away. At some stage in all wars armies have let their discipline sag, but they have never won victory until they made it taut again; nor will they. We found it a great mistake to belittle the importance of smartness in turn out, alertness of carriage, cleanliness of person, saluting, or precision of movement, and to dismiss them as naive, unintelligent parade-ground stuff. I do not believe that troops can have unshakable battle discipline without showing those outward and formal signs, which mark the pride men take in themselves and their units and the mutual confidence and respect that exist between them and their officers. It was our experience in a tough school that the best fighting units, in the long run, were not necessarily those with the most advertised reputations, but those who when they came out of battle at once resumed a more formal discipline and appearance.

Field Marshal Viscount Slim of Burma, *Courage and Other Broadcasts*, 1957.

Instilling Discipline

IF SOLDIERS are punished before they have grown attached to you, they will not prove submissive; and, unless submissive, they will be practically useless. If, when the soldiers have become attached to you, punishments are not enforced, they will still be useless.

Therefore soldiers must be treated in the first instance with humanity, but kept under control by means of iron discipline. This is a certain road to victory.

Sun Tzu, *The Art of War*, 9, c. 500 BC, tr. Giles, 1910.

YOU PICK OUT the big men! I'll make them brave.

Pyrrhus (319–272 BC) to his recruiters, quoted in Frontinus, *Stratagems*, 4.1, c. AD 84–96, tr. Charles E. Bennett, 1925.

AFTER the organization of troops, military discipline is the first matter that presents itself. It is the soul of armies. If it is not established with wisdom and maintained with unshakable resolution you will have

no soldiers. Regiments and armies will be only contemptible, armed mobs, more dangerous to their own country than to the enemy. Few orders are best, but they should be followed up with care; negligence should be punished without partiality and without distinction of rank or birth; otherwise, you will make yourself hated. One can be exact and just, and be loved at the same time as feared. Severity must be accompanied with kindness, but his should not have the appearance of pretense, but of goodness.

Field Marshal Maurice Comte de Saxe, *My Reveries*, 1732, tr. Phillips, 1940.

THE COMMANDER should practice kindness and severity, should appear friendly to the soldiers, speak to them on the march, visit them while they are cooking, ask them if they are well cared for, and alleviate their needs if they have any. Officers without experience in war should be treated kindly. Their good actions should be praised. Small requests should be granted and they should not be treated in an overbearing manner, but severity is maintained about everything regarding the service. The negligent officer is punished; the man who answers back is made to feel your severity by being reprimanded with the authoritative air that superiority gives; pillaging or argumentative soldiers, or those whose obedience is not immediate should be punished.

Frederick the Great, *Instructions to His Generals*, 1747, tr. Phillips, 1940.

BE STRICT in your discipline; that is, to require nothing unreasonable of your officers and men, but see that whatever is required be punctually complied with. Reward and punish every man according to his merit, without partiality or prejudice; hear his complaints; if well founded, redress them; if otherwise, discourage them, in order to prevent frivolous ones. Discourage vice in every shape, and impress upon the mind of every man, from the lowest to the highest, the importance of the cause, and what it is they are contending for.

General George Washington, letter of 10 November 1775, *The Writings of George Washington*, IV, John C. Fitzgerald, ed., 1931.

WITH SEVERITY, kindness is needed, or else severity is tyranny. I am strict in maintaining the health of the soldiers and a true sense of good conduct; kind soldierly strictness, and then general brotherhood. To me strictness by whim would be tyranny.

Field Marshal Prince Aleksandr V. Suvorov (1829–1800), *Dokumenty*, 1952.

MY SON, put a little order into your corps, it wants it badly. The Italians in particular commit atrocities, robbing and pillaging wherever they go. Shoot a few of them. Your affectionate father.

Napoleon, May 1813, letter to Prince Eugène who was to conduct a highly credible campaign against the Austrians.

IMPRESS upon your officers that discipline cannot be attained without constant watchfulness on their part. They must attend to the smallest particulars of detail. Men must be habituated to obey or they cannot be controlled in battle, and the neglect of the least important order impairs the proper influence of the officer.

In recommending officers or men for promotion you will always, where other qualifications are equal, give preference to those who show the highest appreciation of the importance of discipline and evince the greatest attention to its requirements.

> Robert E. Lee, 22 February 1865, Circular of the Army of Northern Virginia, quoted in William Jones, *Life and Letters of Robert Edward Lee*, 1906.

THE DISCIPLINE that makes the soldiers of a free country reliable in battle is not to be gained by harsh or tyrannical treatment. On the contrary, such treatment is far more likely to destroy than to make an army. It is possible to impart instruction and give commands in such a manner and in such a tone of voice as to inspire in the soldier no feeling but an intense desire to obey, while the opposite tone of voice cannot fail to excite strong resentment and a desire to disobey. The one mode or other of dealing with subordinates springs from a corresponding spirit in the breast of the commander. He who feels the respect which is due to others cannot fail to inspire in them regard for himself, while he who feels, and hence manifests, disrespect toward others, especially his inferiors, cannot fail to inspire hatred against himself.

> Lieutenant-General John M. Schofield, 11 August 1879, address to the Corps of Cadets at West Point, and now inscribed in the Sally Port.

IN CAMP, and especially in the presence of an active enemy, it is much easier to maintain discipline than in barracks in time of peace. Crime and breaches of discipline are much less frequent, and the necessity for courts-martial less. The captain can usually inflict all the punishment necessary, and the colonel should always.

> General of the Army William T. Sherman, *Memoirs*, II, 1875.

DISCIPLINE is not made to order, cannot be created off-hand; it is a matter of the institution of tradition. The Commander must have absolute confidence in his right to command, must have the habit of command, pride in commanding. It is this which gives a strong discipline to Armies commanded by an aristocracy, whenever such a thing exists.

> Colonel Charles Ardant du Picq, quoted in Ian Hamilton, *The Soul and Body of an Army*, 1921.

DISCIPLINE can only be obtained when all officers are so imbued with the sense of their awful obligation to their men and to their country that they cannot tolerate negligence. Officers who fail to

correct errors or to praise excellence are valueless in peace and dangerous misfits in war.

> General George S. Patton, Jr., *War As I Knew It*, 1947.

DISCIPLINE consists in obeying orders. If men do not obey orders in small things, they are incapable of being [led] in battle. I will have discipline – to do otherwise is to commit murder. . . . I cannot see what Fredendall did to justify his existence. Have never seen so little order or discipline.

> General George S. Patton, Jr., 13 March 1943, diary entry upon taking command of II Corps after the relief of Major-General Lloyd Fredendall, *Patton Papers*, II, 1974.

IT IS ABSURD to believe that soldiers who cannot be made to wear the proper uniform can be induced to move forward in battle. Officers who fail to perform their duty by correcting small violations and in enforcing proper conduct are incapable of leading.

> General George S. Patton, Jr., April 1943, *The Patton Papers*, II, 1974.

THAT'S THE CRUX of the matter. Discipline is something that is enforced, either by fear or by understanding. Even in an Army, it is not merely a question of giving orders; there is more to a soldier's discipline than blind obedience. To take men into your confidence is not a new technique invented in the last war. Good generals were doing that long before you and I got into khaki to save the world.

> Field Marshal Viscount Slim of Burma, *Courage and Other Broadcasts*, 1957.

The Lack of Discipline

POPULARITY, however desirable it may be to individuals, will not form, or feed, or pay an army; will not enable it to march, and fight; will not keep it in a state of efficiency for long and arduous service.

> The Duke of Wellington, letter from Portugal, 8 April 1811.

WITHOUT DISCIPLINE and good order, not only is an army unfit to be opposed to an enemy in the field, but it becomes a positive injury to the country by which it is maintained . . . The Commander in Chief assures the General and other Officers . . . that at the same time that he will be happy to draw the notice of Government, and to extol their good conduct, he will not be backward in noticing any inattention on the part of the officers of the army to the duties required from them . . . or any breach of discipline and orders by the soldiers.

> The Duke of Wellington, 1 January 1813, address to the Spanish Army, pleased at its improvement over the previous four years, but still cautious as to the stability of that improvement, quoted in Julian Rathbone, ed., *Wellington's War: His Peninsular Dispatches*, 1984.

OF LATE we have been doing everything in our

power, both by law and by publications, to relax the discipline by which alone such men can be kept in order. The officers of the lower ranks will not perform the duty required of them for the purpose of keeping their soldiers in order; and it is next to impossible to punish any officer for neglect of this description. As to the non-commissioned officers, as I have repeatedly stated, they are as bad as the men, and too near them, in point of pay and situation, by the regulations of late years, for us to expect them to do anything to keep the men in order. It is really a disgrace to have anything to say to such men as some of our soldiers are.

The Duke of Wellington, 2 July 1813, to Lord Bathurst, prompted by the breakdown in discipline and looting after the Battle of Vittoria, *The Dispatches of Field Marshal the Duke of Wellington, During His Various Campaigns in India, Denmark, Portugal, Spain, the Low Countries, and France*, X, 1834–1838, p. 496.

THE SPIRIT which animates our soldiers and the natural courage with which they are so liberally endowed have led to a reliance upon these good qualities to the neglect of those measures which would increase their efficiency and contribute to their safety. Many opportunities have been lost and hundreds of valuable lives uselessly sacrificed for want of a strict observance of discipline.

Robert E. Lee, 22 February 1865, Circular of the Army of Northern Virginia, quoted in William Jones, *Life and Letters of Robert Edward Lee*, 1906.

YOU CANNOT be disciplined in great things and undisciplined in small things . . . Brave, undisciplined men have no chance against the discipline and valor of other men. Have you ever seen a few policemen handle a crowd?

General George S. Patton, Jr., 17 May 1941, address to officers and men of the Second Armored Division, *The Patton Papers*, II, 1974.

THERE WAS no tactical organization other than tribal group, and few preparations were made for a campaign. There was a total lack of planning; battles were headlong assaults in rough phalangial order in which the warriors rapidly exhausted themselves and became disorganized; courage shattered itself upon the rocks of discipline.

Major-General J.F.C. Fuller, on the military organisation of the Gauls compared to the Romans, *Julius Caesar: Man, Soldier, Tyrant*, 1965.

The Nature of Discipline

IT IS the discipline which is the soul of armies, as indeed the soul of power in all intelligence. Other things – moral considerations, impulses of sentiment, and even natural excitement – may lead men to great deeds; but taken in the long run, and in all vicissitudes, an army is effective in proportion to its discipline.

Major-General Joshua L. Chamberlain, 1869, speech 'The Army of the Potomac'.

DISCIPLINE is a reciprocal question, that is, it is strong only where it exists not only from the bottom up but also from the top down, for the very law which imposes certain duties on the soldier also protects him from unjust violations and superiors who allow themselves such violations are the violators of both the law and discipline.

General Mikhail I. Dragomirov (1830–1905), quoted in *Voyenno istorichiskiy zhurnal*, 9/1985.

TO BE DISCIPLINED does not mean to keep silent, to do only what one thinks can be done without risk or being compromised, but it means acting in the spirit of the orders received, and to that end assuring by thought and planning the possibility of carrying out such orders, assuring by strength of character the energy to assume the risks necessary in their execution. The laziness of the mind results in lack of discipline as much as does insubordination. Lack of ability and ignorance are not either excuses, for knowledge is within reach of all who seek it.

Marshal of France Ferdinand Foch, *Principles of War*, 1913.

IT IS a mistaken idea that precision of movement and smartness of appearance, which for the popular mind are often the whole meaning of the word 'discipline', can only be obtained by a Prussian discipline, where the individuality of man is ground out until only a robot-like body is left. A century ago, Sir John Moore . . . introduced a new discipline based on intelligence and comradeship instead of on sullenness and fear. His work was justified by its fruits, and not only did the results show that this discipline of the thinking man instead of automata produces a more efficient soldier for war, but also that the former can rival the latter in order and smartness. Intelligent men whose minds are disciplined in the best sense can acquire these qualities as well, and more quickly, than the barrack-square product. But the reverse order of progress from the Frederican discipline to initiative is not possible. (Sept. 1925.)

Captain Sir Basil Liddell Hart, *Thoughts on War*, 1944.

WE HAD NO discipline in the sense in which it was restrictive, submergent of individuality, the Lowest Common Denominator of men. In peace-armies discipline meant the hunt, not of an average but of an absolute; the hundred per cent standard in which the ninety-nine were played down to the level of the weakest man on parade. The aim was to render the unit a unit, the man a type; in order that their effort might be calculable, and the collective output even in grain and bulk. The deeper the discipline, the lower was the individual excellence; also the more sure the performance.

By this substitution of a sure job for a possible masterpiece, military science made a deliberate sacrifice of capacity in order to reduce the uncertain element, the bionomic factor, in enlisted humanity.

Colonel T.E. Lawrence, *The Seven Pillars of Wisdom*, 1935.

FOR IT had seemed to me that discipline, or at least formal discipline, was a virtue of peace: a character or stamp by which to mark off soldiers from complete men, and obliterate the humanity of the individual. It resolved itself easiest into the restrictive, the making men not do this or that: and so could be fostered by a rule severe enough to make them despair of disobedience. It was a process of the mass, an element of the impersonal crowd, inapplicable to one man, since it involved obedience, a duality of will. It was not to impress upon men that their will must actively second the officer's, for then there would have been, as in the Arab Army and among irregulars, the momentary pause for thought transmission, or digestion; for the nerves to resolve the relaying of private will into active consequence. On the contrary, each regular Army sedulously rooted out this significant pause from its companies on parade. The drill-instructors tried to make obedience an instinct, a mental reflex, following as instantly on the command as though the motor power of the individual wills had been invested in the system.

This was well, so far as it increased quickness: but it made no provision for casualties, beyond the weak assumption that each subordinate had his will-motor not atrophied, but reserved in perfect order, ready at the instant to take over his late superior's office; the efficiency of direction passing smoothly down the great hierarchy till vested in the senior of the two surviving privates.

Colonel T.E. Lawrence, *The Seven Pillars of Wisdom*, 1935.

DISCIPLINE . . . is the basis of military efficiency. . . . the major factor of true military discipline consists in securing the voluntary cooperation of subordinates, thereby reducing the number of infractions of the laws and regulations to a minimum; by laying down the doctrine that the true test of the existence of a high state of discipline in a military organization is found in its cheerful and satisfactory performance of duty under all service conditions; and by reminding officers that a happy and contented detachment is usually a well disciplined detachment.

Major-General John A. Lejeune, *Reminiscences of a Marine*, 1929.

COMMANDING and obeying are the characteristics of the army, and the one is as hard as the other. Both are simplified in proportion as orders are given with prudence and intelligence and obedience is rendered with perception and confidence. Human nature demands compulsion when many are to be united for one purpose. Thus discipline becomes an inseparable feature of the army, and its nature and degree are the true measure of the army's efficiency. The more voluntary the nature of the discipline the better, but only a discipline that has become habit and matter of course can survive the test in the hour of danger.

Colonel-General Hans von Seekt, *Thoughts of a Soldier*, 1930.

IT IS the basic constituent of all armies. By virtue of discipline something resembling a contract comes into being between the leader and the subordinates. It is an understood thing that the latter owe obedience to the former, and that each single component of an organized body must, to the best of its ability, carry out the orders transmitted to him by a higher authority. In this way a fundamental attitude of good will is created which guarantees a minimum degree of cohesion. But it is not enough for a chief to bind his men into a whole through the medium of impersonal obedience. It is on the inner selves that he must leave the imprint of his personality. If he is to have a genuine and effective hold on his men, he must know how to make their wills part and parcel of his own, and so to inspire them as something of their own choosing. He must increase and multiply the effects of mere discipline and implant in those under him a sort of moral suggestion which goes far beyond reasoning, and crystallize round his own person all their potentialities of faith, hope, and devotion.

General Charles de Gaulle, *The Edge of the Sword*, 1932.

THE IDEA that real discipline is best instilled by fear of punishment is a delusion – especially in these days of open-order fighting. For such discipline kills the highest military qualities – initiative, and intelligent fulfillment of the superior's intentions. Moreover, the common notion that discipline is produced by drill is a case of putting the cart before the horse. A well-drilled battalion has often proved a bad one in the field. By contrast a *good* battalion is often good at drill – because if the spirit is right, it likes to do all things well. Here is the real sequence of causation. (June 1935.)

Captain Sir Basil Liddell Hart, *Thoughts on War*, 1944.

MILITARY DISCIPLINE, in the narrowest sense of the term, is the enforcement of instant obedience to orders through threat of punishment, supplemented by the control reflexes established through drill. In the wider sense it is bound up with the soldierly spirit. So far as this is susceptible to analysis, its components appear to be pride of manhood, the pride of arms (of being an initiate in the martial cult), the confidence that comes from skill at arms, the sense of comradeship, the sense of duty, and the sense of loyalty – to comrades, commanders, corps, and country. (Jan. 1936.)

Captain Sir Basil Liddell Hart, *Thoughts on War*, 1944.

IN ALL ARMIES, obedience of the subordinates to their superiors must be exacted . . . but the basis for soldier discipline must be the individual conscience. With soldiers, a discipline of coercion is ineffective, discipline must be self-imposed, because only when it is, is the soldier able to understand completely why he fights and how he must obey. This type of discipline becomes a tower of strength within the army, and it is the only type that can truly harmonize the relationship that exists between officers and soldiers.

Mao Tse-tung, *On Protracted War*, 1938.

WITHIN OUR SYSTEM, that discipline is nearest perfect which assures to the individual the greatest freedom of thought and action while at all times promoting his feeling of responsibility toward the group. *These twin ends are convergent and interdependent for the exact converse of the reason that it is impossible for any man to feel happy and successful if he is in the middle of a failing institution.*

Brigadier-General S.L.A. Marshall, *The Armed Forces Officer*, 1951.

HE (the soldier) recognizes a right and reasonable discipline as such, even though it causes him personal inconvenience, because he has acquired a sense of military values. But if it is either unduly harsh or unnecessarily lax, he likewise knows it and wears it as a hairshirt, to the undoing of his morale. Though the man, like the group, can be hurt by being pushed beyond sensible limits, his spirit will suffer even more sorely if no real test is put upon his abilities and moral powers. The greater his intelligence, the stronger will be his resentment. That is a law of nature. The enlightened mind has always the greatest measure of self-discipline but it also has a higher sense of what constitutes justice, fairplay and a reasonable requirement in the performance of duty. If denied these things, he will come to hold his chief, his job, and himself in contempt. The greater part of man's satisfactions comes of activity and only a very small remnant comes of passive enjoyment. Forgetting this rather obvious fact in human nature, social reformers aim at securing more leisure, rather than at making work itself more satisfactory. But it need not be forgotten in the military service.

Brigadier-General S.L.A. Marshall, *The Armed Forces Officer*, 1951.

WHEN WE SPEAK of conscious discipline, it means that it is built up on the basis of political consciousness of the officers and men, and the most important method of maintaining discipline is education and persuasion, thus making the army men of their own accord, respect and remind each other to observe discipline. When we speak of strict discipline, it means that everyone in the army, regardless of rank or office must observe discipline and no infringements are allowed.

General Vo Nguyen Giap, *People's War – People's Army*, 1961.

The Purpose of Discipline

REMEMBERING how great this city is which you are attacking, and what a fame you will bring on your ancestors and yourselves for good or evil according to the result, follow whithersoever you are led; maintain discipline and caution above all things, and be on the alert to obey the word of command. It is both the noblest and the safest thing for a great army to be visibly motivated by one spirit.

Archidamus II, King of Sparta, to the Spartan expeditionary force departing for Athens, 431 BC, quoted in Thucydides, *The Peloponnesian War*, 2.11, c. 404 BC, tr. Benjamin Jowett, 1881.

DO WE NOT SEE that every Nation under the Sun find their acct. therein; and without it no Order no regularity can be observed? Why then shou'd it be expected from us, (who are all young and inexperienced,) to govern, and keep up a proper spirit of Discipline with't Laws; when the best, and most Experienced, can scarcely do it with. Then if we consult our Interest, I am sure it is loudly called for.

General George Washington, 11 October 1775, to Robert Dinwiddie, *The Writings of George Washington*, I, p.202, John C. Fitzgerald, ed., 1931.

THE FIRMNESS requisite for the real business of fighting is only to be obtained by a constant course of discipline and service. I have never yet been witness to a single instance that would justify a different opinion; and it is most earnestly to be wished the liberties of America may no longer be trusted in any material degree to so precarious a dependence.

General George Washington, 15 September 1780, to the President of Congress, *The Writings of George Washington*, XX, p. 50, John C. Fitzgerald, ed., 1941.

IT IS NOT . . . by native gallantry, it is not by the exertion of bodily strength . . . that bodies . . . can contend effectually . . . bodies of men . . . must get into confusion unless regulated by discipline; unless accustomed to subordination, and obedient to command. I am afraid that panic is the usual attendance upon such confusion. It is then by the enforcement of rules of discipline, subordination, and good order, that such bodies can render efficient service to their King and Country; and can be otherwise than a terror to their friends, contemptible to their enemies, and burthen to the State.

The Duke of Wellington, 7 October 1834, speech upon the presentation of Colours to the 93rd Highlanders, *USJ*, 1834, III, quoted in Philip Haythornthwaite, *The Armies of Wellington*, 1994.

AS THE SEVERITY of military operations increases, so also must the sternness of the discipline. The zeal of the soldiers, their warlike instincts, and the interests and excitements of war may ensure obedience of orders and the cheerful endurance of perils and hardships during a short and prosperous campaign. But when fortune is dubious or adverse; when retreats as well as advances are necessary; when supplies fail, arrangements miscarry, and disasters impend, and when the struggle is protracted, men can only be persuaded to accept evil things by the lively realization of the fact that greater terrors await their refusal.

Sir Winston S. Churchill, *The River War*, 1899.

YOU MUST get it likewise: instant, cheerful, and automatic discipline, so that when we the quarterbacks give the signal of life or death in the near day of battle, you will not think and then act, but will act and if you will, think later – after the war. It is by discipline alone that all your efforts, all your patriotism, shall not have been in vain. Without it Heroism is futile. You will die for nothing. With DISCIPLINE you are IRRESISTIBLE.

General George S. Patton, Jr., summer 1918, lecture at the Army Staff College Course, Langres, France, quoted in Roger H. Nye, *The Patton Mind*, 1993.

DISCIPLINE, to which officer and private alike are subjected, was, in my opinion, the only basis on which an army could be effectively trained for war. Such a training could be acquired through long service. It is only what discipline makes second nature in a man that is lasting, and survives even the demoralizing impressions of the battle-field and the psychological changes wrought by a long campaign.

General Erich Ludendorff, *My War Memories, 1914–1918*, 1919.

[ALTHOUGH soldiers] carry within themselves a thousand and one seeds of diversity . . . men, in their hearts, can no more do without being controlled than they can live without food, drink or sleep. [Discipline is thus] the basic constituent of all armies [but must be] shaped by the conditions and moral climate of the times.

General Charles de Gaulle, *The Edge of the Sword*, 1932.

ALL HUMAN BEINGS have an innate resistence to obedience. Discipline removes this resistence and, by constant repetition, makes obedience habitual and subconscious. Where would an undisciplined football team get? The players react subconsciously to the signals. They must, because the split second required for thought would give the enemy the jump.

Battle is much more exigent than football. No sane man is unafraid in battle, but discipline produces in him a form of vicarious courage which, with his manhood, makes for victory. Self-respect grows directly from discipline. The Army saying, "Who ever saw a dirty soldier with a medal?" is largely true. Pride, in turn,

stems from self-respect and from the knowledge that the soldier is an American. The sense of duty and obligation to his comrades and superiors comes from a knowledge of reciprocal obligation, and from the sharing of the same way of life. Self-confidence, the greatest military virtue, results from the demonstrated ability derived from the acquisition of all preceding qualities and from exercise in the use of weapons.

General George S. Patton, Jr., *War As I Knew It*, 1947.

ONE of the primary purposes of discipline is to produce alertness. A man who is so lethargic that he fails to salute will fall an easy victim to the enemy.

General George S. Patton, Jr., *War As I Knew It*, 1947.

SOLDIERS can endure hardship. Most of their training is directed toward conditioning them for unusual privation and exertion. But no power on earth can reconcile them to what common sense says is unnecessary hardship which might have been avoided by greater intelligence in their superiors. The more intelligent the soldier, the more likely it is that he will see that as a sign of indiscipline up above and will answer it in the same way.

Brigadier-General S.L.A. Marshall, *Men Against Fire*, 1947.

BETWEEN these two things – discipline in itself and a personal faith in the military value of discipline – lies all the difference between military maturity and mediocrity. A salute from an unwilling soldier is as meaningless as the moving of a leaf on a tree; it is a sign only that the subject has been caught by a gust of wind. But a salute from the man who takes pride in the gesture because he feels privileged to wear the uniform, having found the service good, is an act of the highest military virtue.

Brigadier-General S.L.A. Marshall, *Men Against Fire*, 1947.

DISCIPLINE destroys the spirit and working loyalty of the general force when it is pitched to the minority of malcontented, undutiful men within the organization, whether to punish or appease them.

Brigadier-General S.L.A. Marshall, *The Armed Forces Officer*, 1951.

A MOST POTENT factor in spreading this belief in efficiency of an organization is a sense of discipline. In effect, discipline means that every man, when things pass beyond his own authority or initiative, knows to whom to turn for further direction. If it is the right kind of discipline he turns in the confidence that he will get sensible and effective direction. Every step must be taken to build up this confidence of the soldier in his leaders. For instance, it is not enough to be efficient; the organization must look efficient. If you enter the lines of a regiment where the quarter guard is smart and alert, and the men you meet are well turned out and salute briskly, you cannot fail to get an impression of efficiency. You are right; ten to one that unit is efficient. If you go into a headquarters and find the clerks scruffy, the floor unswept, and dirty tea mugs staining flyblown papers on the office tables, it may be efficient, but no visitor will think so.

Field Marshal Viscount Slim of Burma, *Defeat Into Victory*, 1956.

IT IS only discipline that enables men to live in a community and yet retain individual liberty. . . . You can have discipline without liberty but cannot have liberty without discipline. . . . The self-discipline of the strong is the safeguard of the weak.

Field Marshal Viscount Slim of Burma, *Courage and Other Broadcasts*, 1957.

DISLOCATION

EVERYTHING can collapse. Houses, bodies, and enemies collapse when their rhythm becomes deranged.

In large scale strategy, when the enemy starts to collapse you must pursue him without letting the chance go. If you fail to take advantage of your enemy's collapse, they may recover.

Miyamoto Musashi, *A Book of Five Rings*, 1645, tr. Victor Harris, 1984.

HOW IS the strategic dislocation produced? In the physical, or "logistical", sphere it is the result of a move which (a) upsets the enemy's dispositions and, by compelling a sudden 'change of front' dislocates the distribution and organization of his forces; (b) separates his forces; (c) endangers his supplies; (d) menaces the route or routes by which he could retreat in case of need and reestablish himself in his base or homeland.

Captain Sir Basil Liddell Hart, *Strategy*, 1954.

PSYCHOLOGICAL *dislocation fundamentally springs from this sense of being trapped.*

This is the reason why it has most frequently followed a physical move on to the enemy's rear. An army, like a man, cannot properly defend its back from a blow without turning round to use its arms in a new direction. "Turning" temporarily unbalances an army as it does a man, and with the former the period of instability is inevitably much longer. In consequence, the brain is much more sensitive to any menace to its back.

Captain Sir Basil Liddell Hart, *Strategy*, 1954.

DISUNITY

ONE SHOULD NOT carry maliciousness in his heart. In the *Chun Ch'an* it says, "If a malicious man is in a high position, his troops will fight among themselves to the last man."

Takeda Nobushige, *Opinions in 99 Articles*, 1588 (*Ideals of the Samurai*, tr. William Wilson, 1982).

I HAVE BEHELD no day since the commencement of hostilities that I have thought her liberties in such eminent danger as at present. Friends and foes seem now to combine to pull down the goodly fabric as we have hitherto been raising at the expense of so much time, blood, and treasure; and unless the bodies politick will exert themselves to bring things back to first principles, correct abuses, and punish our internal foes, inevitable ruin must follow.

General George Washington, letter to George Mason, 27 March 1779, *The Writings of George Washington*, XIV, John C. Fitzgerald, ed., 1936.

AT WHAT POINT then is the approach of danger to be expected? I answer, if it ever reach us, it must spring up amongst us. It cannot come from abroad. If destruction be our lot, we must ourselves be its author and finisher. As a nation of freemen, we must live through all time, or die by suicide.

President Abraham Lincoln, address before the Young Men's Lyceum, Springfield, Illinois, 27 January 1838, *The Collected Works of Abraham Lincoln*, I, 1953.

DIVINE FAVOUR

THERE SHALL NOT be any man be able to stand before thee all the days of thy life: as I was with Moses, so I will be with thee: I will not fail thee, nor forsake thee.

Joshua 1:1.

THEREFORE thus saith the LORD concerning the king of Assyria, He shall not come into this city, nor shoot an arrow there, nor come before it with shield, nor cast a bank against it.

By the way that he came, by the same shall he return, and shall not come into this city, saith the LORD.

For I will defend this city, to save it, for mine own sake, and for my servant David's sake.

And it came to pass that night, that the angel of the LORD sent out, and smote in the camp of the Assyrians an hundred fourscore and five thousand: and when they arose early in the morning, behold, they *were* all dead corpses.

So Sennacherib king of Assyria departed, and went and returned, and dwelt at Nineveh.

Samuel 19:32–35.

THE PROTECTRESS OF ATHENS

Our city, by the immortal gods' intent
and Zeus' decree, shall never come to harm:
for our bold champion, of proud descent,
Pallas of Athens shields us with her arm.

Solon, c. 594 BC, tr. Gilbert Highet, quoted in *The Oxford Book of Greek Verse in Translation*, 1930.

FREEDOM is a gift bestowed by nature even on the

dumb animals. Courage is the peculiar excellence of man, and the Gods help the braver side.

> Civilis, the German chieftain, inciting the Gauls to revolt against the Romans in the year of the Three Emperors, AD 69, quoted in Tacitus, *History*, 4.17, AD 98 (*The Complete Works of Tacitus*, tr. Alfred Church and William Brodribb, 1942).

I BRING YOU news from God, that our Lord will give you back your kingdom, bringing you to be crowned at Rheims, and driving out your enemies. In this I am God's messenger. Do you set me bravely to work, and I will raise the siege of Orléans.

> Joan of Arc, February–March 1429, to the Dauphin Charles, *Joan of Arc In Her Own Words*,1996.

COME HERE, Tepanecs. Are you ignorant of the fact that Huitzilopotchtli, god of the Actecs, fights for them and protects them with all his might? It seems to me folly to try to fight against the gods.

> Nezahualcoyotal, King of Texcoco, c. 1430, to a delegation from the city of Coyohuacan pleading war against the Aztecs, quoted in Diego Durán, *The History of the Indies of New Spain*, 1581, tr. Doris Heyden, 1994.

THEN you would have me disregard the protection of God?

> Gustavus II Adolphus (1594–1632), when his staff urged him to keep a bodyguard, quoted in Theodore Ayrault Dodge, *Gustavus Adolphus*, 1895.

GOD made them as stubble to our swords.

> Oliver Cromwell, 2 July 1644, of his victory at Marston Moor, quoted in Theodore Ayrault Dodge, *Gustavus Adolphus*, 1895.

. . . AS IT HAS BEEN a kind of destiny, that has thrown me upon this service, I shall hope that my undertaking it is designed to answer some good purpose. . . . I shall rely, therefore, confidently on that Providence, which has heretofore preserved and been bountiful to us.

> General George Washington, 8 June 1775, to Martha Washington, *The Writings of George Washington*, III, p. 294, John C. Fitzgerald, ed., 1931.

THE UNERRING HAND of providence shielded my men.

> Major-General Andrew Jackson, 26 January 1815, letter to Robert Hays of his victory at the Battle of New Orleans, *Correspondence*, II, p. 156.

THE FINGER of providence was upon me, and I escaped unhurt.

> The Duke of Wellington, 19 June 1815, of his victory at Waterloo, *Supplementary Despatches, Correspondence, and Memoranda of Field Marshal Arthur Duke of Wellington, K.G., 1794–1818*, X, 1863, p. 531.

FEAR NOT. God has pledged His word for the liberty of Greece, and He will not retract. We have been baptized once with holy ointment; we shall again be baptized in blood for the freedom of the Fatherland!

> Theodoros Kolokotrones, 1821, at the beginning of the Greek Revolution – Zeeto Ellas! *Theodoros Kolokotrones: Old Man of the Morea*, 1892.

DOCTRINE

A DOCTRINE of war consists first in a common way of objectively approaching the subject; second, in a common way of handling it, by adapting without reserve the means to the goal aimed at, to the object.

> Marshal of France Ferdinand Foch, *Precepts and Judgments*, 1919.

MILITARY DOCTRINE is military, and particularly, tactical philosophy; doctrine creates certainty, which is the soul of every action.

> General A.A. Svechin, 'The Foundations of Military Doctrine', 1920, quoted in Vitaly Rapoport and Yuri Alexeev, *High Treason*, 1985.

THE CENTRAL IDEA of an army is known as its doctrine, which to be sound must be based on the principles of war, and which to be effective must be elastic enough to admit of mutation in accordance with change in circumstances. In its ultimate relationship to the human understanding this central idea or doctrine is nothing else than common sense – that is, action adapted to circumstances.

> Major-General J.F.C. Fuller, *The Foundations of the Science of War*, 1926.

MILITARY DOCTRINE refers to the point of view from which military history is understood and its experience and lessons understood. Doctrine is the daughter of history. . . . Doctrine is needed so that in the realm of military thought an army not represent human dust, but a cohesive whole . . . should be predatory and stern, ruthless toward defeat and the defeated.

> General A.A. Svechin (1878–1938).

THE CRUMBLING of the whole system of doctrines and organization, to which our leaders had attached themselves, deprived them of their motive force. A sort of moral inhibition made them suddenly doubtful of everything, and especially of themselves. From then on the centrifugal forces were to show themselves rapidly.

> General Charles de Gaulle, *The Call to Honor*, 1955.

DOCTRINE provides a military organization with a common philosophy, a common language, a common purpose, and a unity of effort.

> General George H. Decker, 16 December 1960, speech given at the U.S. Army Command and General Staff College, Fort Leavenworth, Kansas.

AN INNER BATTLE took place in me. . . . At the beginning of the operation when we . . . had not yet felt to the end what destruction lengthy combat in this area might entail, I gave the order for encirclement.

[Then] the thought matured in me that we were obliged to seize the Silesian industrial area . . . whole, that is, that we had to leave the Hitlerites out of this trap. . . . On the other hand, it is precisely encirclement which is the highest form of operational art. . . . Then how could I . . . renounce it? It was not easy for me, a professional military person . . . to go against established doctrine . . . This was a difficult pyschological problem.

> Marshal of the Soviet Union Ivan S. Koniev, 1970, quoted in Leites, *The Soviet Style in War*, 1982.

AT THE VERY HEART of war lies doctrine. It represents the central beliefs for waging war in order to achieve victory. . . . It is the building material for strategy. It is fundamental to sound judgment.

> General Curtis LeMay, USAF, Air Force Manual 1-1, *Basic Doctrine* (Washington, DC: Department of the Air Force, 1984) frontispiece.

DOGMA

TO DOGMATIZE upon that which you have not practiced is the prerogative of ignorance; it is like thinking that you can solve, by an equation of the second degree, a problem of transcendental geometry which would have daunted Legrange or Laplace.

> Napoleon (1769–1821).

THE DOGMAS of the quiet past are inadequate to the stormy present. The occasion is piled high with difficulty, and we must rise with the occasion. As our case is new, so we must think anew, and act anew. We must disenthrall ourselves, and then we shall save our country.

> President Abraham Lincoln, 1 December 1862, 'Annual Message to Congress', *Collected Works of Abraham Lincoln*, V, 1953.

IT WILL BE BETTER to offer certain considerations for reflection than to make sweeping dogmatic assertions.

> Rear Admiral Alfred Thayer Mahan (1840–1914).

IN ITSELF, the danger of a doctrine is that it is apt to ossify into a dogma, and to be seized upon by mental emasculates who lack virility of judgment, and who are only too grateful to rest assured that their actions, however inept, find justification in a book, which, if they think at all, is, in their opinion, written in order to exonerate them from doing so. In the past many armies have been destroyed by internal discord, and some have been destroyed by the weapons of their antagonists, but the majority have perished through adhering to dogmas springing from their past successes – that is, self-destruction or suicide through inertia of mind.

> Major-General J.F.C. Fuller, *The Reformation of War*, 1923.

ADHERENCE to dogmas has destroyed more armies and lost more battles and lives than any other cause in war. No man of fixed opinions can make a good general; consequently, if this series of lectures, however hypothetical many of its contentions may seem, succeeds in unfixing dogmas, then certainly it will not have been written in vain.

> Major-General J.F.C. Fuller, *Lectures on F.S.R. III*, 1932.

PREJUDICE against novel methods is a phenomenon typical of an officer corps raised in a proven system. The Prussian Army was defeated for this reason by Napoleon. The same phenomenon showed up in this war, in German as well as British officer circles, where complicated theories obstructed the capability to see things in reality. A military dogma had been worked out in every last detail, and this was taken to represent the very peak of military wisdom. In their minds, the only military thought allowed acceptable was that which followed their own doctrine. Everything other than the rule was a game of chance; and it followed that success could only be the result of luck or accident. This attitude leads to fixed ideas, the consequences of which are incalculable.

> Field Marshal Erwin Rommel, letter of May/June 1942, quoted in John Pimlott, ed., *Rommel in His Own Words*, 1994.

DO OR DIE

FRIENDS! Fighting Danaans! Aides-in-arms of Ares! Fight like men, my comrades – call up your battle-fury! You think we have reserves in the rear to back us up? Some stronger wall to shield our men from disaster? No, there's no great citadel standing near with towers where we could defend ourselves and troops could turn the tide.
No – we're here on the plain of Troy – all Troy's in arms! Dug in, backs to the sea, land of our fathers far away! Fight – the light of safety lies in our fighting hands, not spines gone soft in battle.

> Homer, *The Iliad*, 15.851–859, c. 800 BC, tr. Robert Fagles, 1990; Telamonian Ajax's cry for support as he single-handedly held off the Trojan attack on the Greek ships.

TO FAIL to think fast when surrounded by the enemy is to have your back pressed to the wall;
And to fail to take the battle to the enemy when your back is to the wall is to perish.

> Sun Tzu, c. 500 B.C., a passage recovered from later encyclopaedic works and commentaries and not found in *The Art of War*, quoted in *Sun Tzu: The Art of Warfare*, 1993, tr. Roger Ames, 1993.

THROW YOUR TROOPS into positions whence there is no escape, and they will prefer death to flight. Officers and men alike will put forth their uttermost strength.

Soldiers when in desperate straits lose the sense of fear. If there is no place of refuge, they will stand firm. If they are in the heart of a hostile country, they will show a stubborn front. If there is no help for it, they will fight hard.

Sun Tzu, *The Art of War*, 11, c. 500 BC, tr. Giles, 1910.

AS TO THE FIELD of battle it is the abiding place of the dead. And he who decides to die will live, and he who wishes to live will die.

Wu C'hi (431–381 BC), *Art of War*, 3.4 (*Three Military Classics of China*, tr. A.L. Sadler, 1944).

WE HAVE nothing left in the world but what we can win with our swords. Timidity and cowardice are for men who can see safety at their backs – who can retreat without molestation along some easy road and find refuge in the familiar fields of their native land; but they are not for you: you must be brave; for you there is no middle way between victory or death – put all hope of it from you, and either conquer, or, should fortune hesitate to favour you, meet death in battle rather than in flight.

Hannibal, 218 BC, address to his troops after crossing the Alps into Italy as they faced their first Roman Army, quoted in Livy, *The History of Rome*, 21.44, c. AD 17 (*The War With Hannibal*, tr. Aubrey de Sélincourt, 1972).

GO, THEREFORE, to meet the foe with two objects before you, either victory or death. For men animated by such a spirit must always overcome their adversaries, since they go into battle ready to throw away their lives.

Scipio Africanus, 202 BC, address to the Roman Army before the Battle of Zama, quoted in Polybius, *Histories*, c. 125 BC, quoted in Liddell Hart, *A Greater Than Napoleon*, 1926.

WHEN MEN find they must inevitably perish, they willingly resolve to die with their comrades and with their arms in their hands.

Flavius Vegetius Renatus, *Military Institutions of the Romans*, c. AD 378, tr. Clark, 1776.

COURAGE shall be firmer, heart all the keener, spirit the greater, as our might grows less. Here lies our leader, fatally cut down, the good man in the dust. Forever shall that man mourn who now thinks to leave the battle! I am far advanced in years and I shall not leave. I intend to lie by the side of my dear lord.

Byrhtwold, one of Byrtnoth's huscarls, after the latter had been killed in battle against the Vikings and his household had gathered around to defend his body; from the fragmentary poem, *The Battle of Madon*, tr. C.B. Hieatt, 1967; one of the most famous passages in Anglo-Saxon literature.

IN THE COURSE of battle, as long as you are able to advance on foot, never take a step backward. Even when you are hemmed in amongst the enemy, never cease the struggle; you may with your bare fist knock the enemy out of the fight. And as long as they see activity, proving you to be in good fettle, they will stand in awe of you. At a time like this reconcile your heart with death. Under no conditions be afraid, but be bold; for a short blade grows longer in the hands of the brave.

Kai Ka'us Ibn Iskander, *A Mirror for Princes*, 1082, tr. Levy, 1951.

SIRS and fellows, as I am true knight and king, for me this day shall never England ransom pay.

King Henry V of England, 25 October 1415, address to his army before the Battle of Agincourt.

COURAGEOUS AZTECS, Tezcocans, Tepances, and all the men from the provinces: there is nothing we do here but conquer or die. For this we have come. Our enemy shows valor and a brave heart and has decided to defend the city. I beg of you to demonstrate bravery in this endeavor, for to die is to live forever in perpetual glory and honor.

Motecuhzoma II Xochoyotl, Aztec Emperor, 1506, exhorting his army before its assault on the city of Quetzaltepec, quoted in Durán, *The History of the Indies of New Spain*, 1581, tr. Doris Heyden, 1994.

AS FOR your statement, gentlemen, that we have lost fifty-five soldiers since we left the island of Cuba, from wounds, starvation, cold, sickness, and hardship, and that we are now few in number and all wounded and sick, God gives us the strength of many. It is clearly true that wars destroy men and horses and that we only sometimes eat well. We did not come here to take our ease, however, but to fight when the opportunity offered. Therefore I pray you, gentlemen, kindly to behave like gentlemen, I mean those whose habit is to encourage others whom they see displaying weakness. From now on, keep the island of Cuba and what you have left there out of your thoughts, and try to act, as you have done hitherto, like brave soldiers. For after God, who is our aid and support, we must rely on our own strong arms.

Hernan Cortes, 1519, exhorting his officers when many wanted to turn back on the road to the Valley of Mexico, quoted in Bernal Diaz, *The Conquest of New Spain*, c. 1565.

SOME COMMANDERS have forced their men to fight by depriving them of all means of saving themselves except victory; this is certainly the best method of making them fight desperately. This resolution is commonly heightened either by the confidence they put in themselves, their arms, armor, discipline, good order, and lately-won victories, or by the esteem they have for their general . . . or it is a result of the love for their country, which is natural to all men. There are various ways of forcing men to fight, but that is the strongest and most operative; it leaves men no other alternative but to conquer or die.

> Niccolo Machiavelli, *The Art of War*, 1521.

I SHALL surely prevent him [the Turk]. And even if this siege, contrary to my expectation, should end in a victory for the enemy, I declare to you all that I have resolved that no-one in Constantinople shall ever see a Grand Master of our Holy Order there in chains. If, indeed, the very worst should happen and all be lost, then I intend to put on the uniform of a common soldier and throw myself, sword in hand, into the thick of the enemy and perish there with my children and my brothers.

> Jean de la Valette, Grand Master of the Order of the Knights of St. John, 17 August 1565, his address to the council of the Order during the siege of Malta when informed that the Turks intended to drag him back to Constantinople in chains.

THERE IS one certain means by which I can be sure never to see my country's ruin: I will die in the last ditch.

> William III (William of Orange), King of England (1650–1702).

WE BEAT THEM tonight or Molly Stark's a widow.

> Brigadier-General John Stark, 16 August 1777, addressing his men before the Battle of Bennington.

IF WE HAD NOT driven them into hell . . . hell would have swallowed us.

> Field Marshal Prince Aleksandr V. Suvorov, 1787, of the Battle of Kinburn.

SIR ROBERT CALDER: There are eight sail of the line, Sir John.
Jervis: Very well, Sir.
Calder: There are 20 sail of the line, Sir John.
Jervis: Very well, Sir.
Calder: There are 25 sail of the line, Sir John.
Jervis: Very well, sir.
Calder: There are 27 sail of the line, Sir John, near double our own.
Jervis: Enough of that, Sir. If there are 50 sail of the line, I will go through them. The die is cast.

> Admiral Lord Vincent (Sir John Jervis), 14 February 1797, as the Spanish fleet came into sight before the Battle of Cape St. Vincent, quoted in David Walder, *Nelson*, 1978.

WESTMINSTER ABBEY or victory!

> Admiral Viscount Nelson, 14 February 1797, battle cry as he led a boarding party aboard a Spanish ship of the line during the Battle of Cape St. Vincent; Westminster Abbey was the sepulchre of the greatest of the English, quoted in Robert Southey, *Life of Nelson*, 1813.

THE TROOPS behaved admirably; if they had not done so, not a man of us would have quitted the field.

> The Duke of Wellington, 10 September 1800, on the conduct of his men after his victory at Hyderabad, quoted in Arthur Bryant, *The Great Duke*, 1972.

FAREWELL, my dear Lady Hester. If I can extricate myself and those with me from our present difficulties, and if I can beat the French I shall return to you with satisfaction; but if not, it will be better that I should never quit Spain.

> Lieutenant-General Sir John Moore, 24 November 1808, letter to Lady Hester Stanhope, quoted in Carola Oman, *Sir John Moore*, 1953.

TELL THE MEN to fire faster and not to give up the ship. Fight her til she sinks.

> Captain James Lawrence, 1813, order, as he lay dying, during the battle between his USS *Chesapeake* and HMS *Shannon*.

IF YOUR officer's dead and the sergeants look white,
Remember it's ruin to run from a fight;
So take open order, lie down, and sit tight,
An' wait for supports like a soldier.

> Rudyard Kipling, 'The Young British Soldier'.

IT SO OFTEN happens that, when men are convinced that they have to die, a desire to bear themselves well and to leave life's stage with dignity conquers all other sensations.

> Sir Winston S. Churchill, *Savonarola*, 1900.

WE ARE ABOUT to engage in a battle on which the fate of our country depends and it is important to remind all ranks that the moment has passed for looking to the rear; all our efforts must be directed to attacking and driving back the enemy. Troops that can advance no farther must, at any price, hold on to the ground they have conquered and die on the spot rather than give way. Under the circumstances which face us, no act of weakness can be tolerated.

> Marshal of France Joseph Joffre, early September 1914, message to the French Army as he began the counter-attack of the Battle of the Marne.

EVERY POSITION must be held to the last man: there must be no retirement. With our backs to the wall, and believing in the justice of our cause, each one of us must fight on to the end. The safety of our Homes and the Freedom of mankind alike depend on the conduct of each one of us at this critical moment.

> Field Marshal Earl Haig, Order of the Day, 12 April 1918, at the height of the German *Friedenstürm* offensive that nearly broke the British Army.

TODAY is Trinity Sunday. Centuries ago words were written to be a call and a spur to the faithful servants of truth and justice: "Arm yourselves, and be ye men of valor, and be in readiness for the conflict; for it is better for us to perish in battle than to look upon the outrage of our nation and our altar. As the Will of God is in Heaven, even so let it be."

Sir Winston S. Churchill, first address as Prime Minister, 19 May 1940, *Winston S. Churchill: His Complete Speeches 1987–1963*, VI, 1974, p. 6223.

OF THE 240 MEN on board this ship, 239 behaved as they ought to have and as I expected them to. . . . One did not. I had him brought before me a couple of hours ago, and he himself informed me that he knew the punishment for desertion of his post could be death. You will therefore be surprised to know that I propose to let him off with a caution, one caution to him and a second one to myself, for having failed in four months to impress my personality and doctrine on each and all of you to prevent such an incident from occurring. From now on I will try to make it clear that I expect every one of you to behave in the way that the 239 did, and to stick to their post in action to the last. I will under no circumstances whatever again tolerate the slightest suspicion of cowardice or indiscipline, and I know from now on that none of you will present me with any such problems.

I want to make it clear to all of you that I shall never give the order 'abandon ship', the only way you can leave the ship is if she sinks beneath your feet.

Earl Mountbatten of Burma, 1940 (as captain of HMS *Kelly*), quoted in Philip Ziegler, *Mountbatten*, 1985.

HERE we will stand and fight; there will be no further withdrawal. I have ordered that all plans and instructions dealing with further withdrawal are to be burnt at once. We will stand and fight here. If we can't stay here alive, then let us stay here dead. . . . Meanwhile, we ourselves will start to plan a great offensive; it will be the beginning of a campaign which will hit Rommel and his army for six, right out of Africa. . . . The great point to remember is that we are going to finish with this chap Rommel once and for all. It will be quite easy. There is no about it. He is definitely a nuisance. Therefore we will hit him a crack and finish with him.

Field Marshal Viscount Montgomery of Alamein, 13 August 1942, order to the Eighth Army upon his assumption of command.

IT IS ESSENTIAL to impress on all officers that determined leadership will be very vital in this battle, as in any battle. There have been far too many unwounded prisoners taken in this war. We must impress on our officers, N.C.O.'s and men that when they are cut off or surrounded, and there appears to be no hope of survival, they must organize themselves into a defensive locality and hold out where they are. By so doing they will add enormously to the enemy's difficulties; they will greatly assist the development of our own operations; and they will save themselves from spending the rest of the war in a prison camp.

Nothing is ever hopeless so long as troops have stout hearts, and have weapons and ammunition.

Field Marshal Viscount Montgomery of Alamein, 6 October 1942, instructions for Operation Lightfoot, the Battle of El Alamein, quoted in Francis de Guingand, *Operation Victory*, 1947.

BOB, I'm putting you in command at Buna. Relieve Harding. . . . [all] officers who won't fight . . . If necessary put sergeants in charge of battalions and corporals in charge of companies – anyone who will fight. Time is of the essence. . . . I want you to take Buna, or not come back alive.

General of the Army Douglas MacArthur, 29 November 1942, MacArthur's oral orders to General Robert L. Eichelberger, quoted in Jay Luvaas, ed., *Dear Miss Em: General Eichelberger's War in the Pacific*, 1972.

THERE WILL BE no Dunkirk, there will be no Bataan, a retreat to Pusan would be one of the greatest butcheries in history. We must fight until the end. Capture by these people is worse than death itself. We will fight as a team. If some of us must die, we will all die fighting together. Any man who gives ground may be personally responsible for the death of thousands of his comrades.

Major-General Walton Walker, 29 July 1950, his 'stand or die' order as the North Koreans were driving the U.S. Army back toward Pusan, quoted in Omar Bradley, *A General's Life*, p. 543.

WE HAVE always said that in our war with the Arabs we had a secret weapon – no alternative.

Prime Minister Golda Meir, *Life*, 3 October 1969.

DRILL AND CEREMONIES

DRILL is necessary to make the soldier steady and skilful, although it does not warrant exclusive attention.

Field Marshal Maurice Comte de Saxe, *My Reveries*, 1732, tr. Phillips, 1940.

I HAD NEVER LOOKED at a copy of tactics from the time of my graduation. My standing in that branch of studies had been near the foot of the class. In the Mexican war in the summer of 1846, I had been appointed regimental quartermaster and commissary and had not been at a battalion drill since.

General of the Army Ulysses S. Grant, *The Personal Memoirs of U.S. Grant*, I, 1885.

GIVE ME control of their *instinct* and you can have their *reason*.

An anonymous American drill sergeant, quoted in Richard Holmes, *Acts of War: The Behavior of Men in Battle*, 1985.

DRILL may be beautiful: but beauty is not perceptible when you are expecting a punishment every moment for not doing it well-enough. Dancing is beautiful: – because it's the same sort of thing, without the sergeant-major and the 'office'. Drill in the R.A.F. is always punitive: – it is always practice-drill, never exercise-drill or performance-drill. Airmen haven't the time to learn combined rhythm. If they did learn it, their (necessarily) individual work with screwdrivers & spanners would suffer. Rhythm takes months to acquire & years to lose.

> Colonel T.E. Lawrence, 6 November 1928, letter to Robert Graves; Lawrence's perspective at this time was that of an enlisted man, having resigned his wartime commission and enlisted in the RAF; quoted in Malcolm Brown, ed., *The Letters of T.E. Lawrence*, 1988.

ALL THROUGH your Army careers, you men have bitched about what you call "chicken shit drilling". That, like everything else in this Army, has a definite purpose. That purpose is alertness. Alertness must be bred into every soldier. I don't give a fuck for a man who's not always on his toes. You men are veterans or you wouldn't be here. You are ready for what's to come. A man must be alert at all times if he expects to stay alive. If you're not alert, sometime, a German son-of-an-asshole-bitch is going to sneak up behind you and beat you to death with a sockful of shit!

> General George S. Patton, Jr., 5 June 1944, 'Somewhere in England', speech to the men of the Third Army just before the Normandy Invasion, quoted in Charles M. Province, *The Unknown Patton*, 1983.

COMBAT EXPERIENCE has proven that ceremonies, such as formal guard mounts, formal retreat formations, and regular supervised reveille formations, are a great help, and, in some cases, essential, to prepare men and officers for battle, to give them that perfect discipline, that smartness of appearance, that alertness without which battles cannot be won.

> General George S. Patton, Jr., *War As I Knew It*, 1947.

THE MILITARY manifestations of discipline are many and various. At one end of the scale may be placed the outward display, such as saluting and smartness of drill, the meaning and value of which are often misunderstood and misused both inside the Army and outside. Saluting should be in spirit the recognition of a comrade in arms, the respect of a junior for a senior – a gesture of brotherhood on both sides. Good drill should either be a ceremony for the uplifting of the spirit or a time-saver for some necessary purpose – never mere formalism or pedantry. No one who has participated in it or seen it well done should doubt the inspiration of ceremonial drill.

> Field Marshal Viscount Wavell of Cyrenaica, *Soldiers and Soldiering*, 1953.

IF MEN are to give their best in war they must be united. Discipline seeks through drill to instill into all ranks this sense of unity, by requiring them to obey orders as one man. A Ceremonial parade, moreover, provides the occasion for men to express pride in their performance, pride in the Regiment or Corps and pride in the Profession of Arms.

> General Viscount Alexander of Tunis, November 1968.

DRINKING

AS PROOF that I will not, I may tell you that, just as I was starting to the Mexican War, a lady in Virginia prevailed on me to take a bottle of fine old whiskey, which she thought I could not get on without. I carried that bottle all through the war without having had the slightest occasion to use it, and on my return home I sent it back to my good friend, that she might be convinced that I could get on without liquor.

> General Robert E. Lee, upon being pressed to take two bottles of fine brandy by a friend, who assured him he would need it, spring 1861, as related by William Jones, *Personal Reminiscences, Anecdotes, and Letters of Gen. Robert E. Lee*, 1874.

UPON ONE OCCASION Jackson was suffering so much from fatigue, and severe exposure, that his surgeon prevailed upon him to take a little brandy. He made a very wry face as he swallowed it, and the doctor asked: "Why, General, is not the brandy good? It is some that we have recently captured, and I think it very fine." "Oh, yes!" was the reply, "it is very good brandy. I like liquor – its taste and its effect – *and that is just the reason I never drink it*." Upon another occasion, after along ride in a drenching rain, a brother officer insisted Jackson's taking a drink with him, but he firmly replied, "No, sir, I cannot do it. I tell you I *am more afraid of King Alcohol than of all the bullets of the enemy*."

> Lieutenant-General Thomas J. 'Stonewall' Jackson's opinion of drinking, as related by William Jones, *Personal Reminiscences, Anecdotes, and Letters of Gen. Robert E. Lee*, 1874.

I CANNOT CONSENT to place in the control of others one who cannot control himself.

> General Robert E. Lee, upon refusing to promote an officer who drank too freely, quoted in William Jones, *Personal Reminiscences, Anecdotes, and Letters of Gen. Robert E. Lee*, 1874.

DURING THE NIGHT of February 17th the greater portion of the city of Columbia was burned. The lurid flames could easily be seen from my camp, many miles distant. . . . I do not believe that General Sherman countenanced or was in any degree responsible for it. I believe the immediate cause of the disaster was a free use of whiskey (which was supplied to the soldiers by citizens with great liberality). A drunken soldier with a musket in one hand and a match in the other is not a pleasant visitor to have about the house on a dark, windy night, particularly when for a series of years you have urged him to come, so that you might have an opportunity of performing a surgical operation on him.

> Major-General Henry W. Slocum, of the burning of Columbia, South Carolina, 17 February 1865, 'Sherman's March from Savanah to Bentonville', in *Battles and Leaders of the Civil War, Being for the Most Part Contributions by Union and Confederate Officers*, IV, p. 686, Johnston and Buel, ed., 1887–1888.

GIVE 'EM beer and whiskey – that'll help some – and get rid of ice cream, candy and girls in training camps.

> Lieutenant-General Lewis B. 'Chesty' Puller, 1951, comment upon the decline in training evident in the other services during the first part of the Korean War, *United Press*.

AN OFFICER who won't drink whiskey may be some good, but he's got to prove it to me first!

> Lieutenant-General Lewis B. 'Chesty' Puller (1898–1971), quoting one of the old pre-1914 breed of marines, Lincoln Karmany, quoted in *Marine Corps League*, Summer 1992.

FOR MYSELF, I do not smoke and I drink no alcohol of any sort; this is purely because I dislike both tobacco and alcohol, and therein I am lucky because I believe one is in far better health without them. In general, I consider that excessive smoking and drinking tend to cloud the brain; when men's lives are at stake this must never be allowed to happen, and it does happen too often. You cannot win battles unless you are feeling well and full of energy.

> Field Marshal Viscount Montgomery of Alamein, *The Memoirs of Field Marshal Montgomery*, 1958.

IN 1993 I told myself I would no longer drink, that I would be the soberest man in the country. I made the decision and that was enough. But in Russia people drink from despair. We do not know where we are going, what we are building, or whether we are building at all. . . . I am sure that if you give people a goal they will still drink, but only in moderation, at celebrations, and no more.

> General Aleksandr I. Lebed, *Komsomolskaya Pravda* (Moscow), 7 February 1996.

DULCE ET DECORUM EST PRO PATRIA MORI
It is sweet and proper to die for country

SO FIGHT by the ships, all together. And that comrade who meets his death and destiny, speared or stabbed, Let him die! He dies fighting for fatherland – no dishonor there!
He'll leave behind wife and sons unscathed, His house and estates unharmed – once these Argives sail for home, the fatherland they love.

> Homer, *The Iliad*, 15.574–579, c. 800 BC, tr. Robert

Fagles, 1990; Hector, rallying the Trojans to storm the Greek camp.

AS FOR YOU, who now survive them, it is your business to pray for a better fate, but to think it your duty to preserve the same spirit and warmth of courage against your enemies; not judging of the expediency of this from a mere harangue – where any man indulging in a flow of words may tell you what you yourselves know as well as he, how many advantages there are in fighting valiantly against your enemies – but, rather making the daily-increasing grandeur of this community the object of your thoughts and growing quite enamored of it. And when it really appears great to your apprehensions, think again that this grandeur was acquired by brave and valiant men, by men who knew their duty, and in the moments of action were sensible of shame; who, whenever their attempts were unsuccessful, thought it no dishonor for their country to stand in need of anything their valor could do for it, and so made it the most glorious present. Bestowing thus their lives on the public, they have every one received a praise that will never decay, a sepulchre that will always be the most illustrious – not that in which their bones lie moldering, but that in which their fame is preserved, to be on every occasion, when honor is the employ of either word or act, eternally remembered. For the whole earth is the sepulchre of illustrious men. . . .

> Pericles, 431 BC, funeral oration for the Athenian war dead at the beginning of the Peloponnesian War, quoted in Thucydides, *The History of the Peloponnesian War*, 2.43, c. 404 BC, tr. Richard Crowley, 1910.

AND WHAT of those who have died in battle? Their death was noble, their burial illustrious; almost all are commemorated at home by statues of bronze; their parents are held in honour, with all dues of money or service remitted, for under my leadership not a man among you has ever fallen with his back to the enemy.

> Alexander the Great, 323 BC, speech to his troops at Opis in Babylonia, quoted in Arrian, *The Campaigns of Alexander*, 7.10, c. AD 150, tr. Aubrey de Sélincourt, 1987.

I REGRET the brave men you have lost, but they are dead on the field of honour.

> Napoleon, 16 October 1806, at Weimar, to Marshal Davout after his victory at Auerstadt, quoted in R.M. Johnston, ed., *The Corsican*, 1910.

EASY, but willing to die if God and my country think I have fulfilled my destiny and done my duty.

> Major-General J.E.B. Stuart, when asked how he felt as he lay dying of the wounds suffered at Yellow Tavern the day before, 12 May 1864, quoted by Major-General Fitzhugh Lee, in Early, *Southern Historical Society Papers*, I, January–June 1876.

THE WARMEST instincts of every man's soul declare the glory of the soldier's death. It is more appropriate to the Christian than to the Greek to sing:
Glorious his fate, and envied is his lot,
Who for his country fights and for it dies.
There is a true glory and a true honor; the glory of duty done – the honor of the integrity of principle.

> General Robert E. Lee, from his post-war writings, quoted in William Jones, *Life and Letters of Robert Edward Lee*, 1906.

IT IS FOOLISH and wrong to mourn the men who died. Rather we should thank God that such men lived.

> General George S. Patton, Jr., 7 June 1945, attributed, speech at the Copely Plaza Hotel, Boston, Massachusetts.

DUTY

YOU TELL ME to put my trust in birds,
flying off on their long wild wings? Never.
I would never give them a glance, a second thought,
whether they fly on the right toward the dawn and
    sunrise
or fly on the left toward the haze and coming dark!
No, no, put our trust in the will of mighty Zeus,
King of the deathless gods and men who die.
Bird signs!
Fight for your country – that is the best, the only omen!

> Homer, *The Iliad*, 12.274–82, c. 800 BC, tr. Robert Fagles, 1990; Hector, rebuking Polydamus for reliance on seers instead of on his sense of duty; a famous quotation from antiquity.

CEASE THEN – Our business in the field of fight
Is not to question, but to prove our might.

> Homer, *The Iliad*, 20.304–305, c. 800 BC, tr. Alexander Pope, 1743.

AND THEREFORE the general who in advancing does not seek personal fame, and in withdrawing is not concerned with avoiding punishment, but whose only purpose is to protect the people and promote the best interests of his sovereign, is the precious jewel of the state.

> Sun Tzu, *The Art of War*, c. 500 BC, tr. Samuel Griffith.

THE SENSE of duty makes the victor.

> Flavius Vegetius Renatus, *Military Institutions of the Romans*, c. AD 378, tr. Clark, 1776.

I THANK ALL for the advice which you have given me. I know that my going out of the city might be of some benefit to me, inasmuch as all that you foresee might really happen. But it is impossible for me to go away! How could I leave the churches of our Lord, and His servants the clergy, and the throne, and my people in such a plight? What would the world say about me? I pray you, my friends, in future do not say to me anything else but, "Nay, sire, do not leave us!" Never, never will I leave you! I am resolved to die here with you!

> The Emperor Constantine XI, in response to advice to flee Constantinople before the Turkish siege of 1453, quoted in Mijatovich, *Constantine: The Last Emperor of the Greeks*, 1892.

IF I GO away to sea,
    I shall return a corpse awash;
If duty calls me to the mountain,
    A verdant sward will be my pall;
Thus for the sake of the Emperor
    I will not die peaceful at home.

> Ancient Japanese war song, quoted in Inoguchi and Nakajimi, *The Divine Wind*, 1958.

LORD MALINCHE, I have assuredly done my duty in defense of my city and my vassals, and I can do no more. I am brought by force as a prisoner into your presence and beneath your power. Take the dagger that you have in your belt, and strike me dead immediately.

> The Aztec Emperor Cuauhtémoc (1521) brought before Cortes upon his capture, which ended the siege of Tenochtitlan, quoted in Bernal Diaz, *The Conquest of New Spain*, c. 1565.

THREE THINGS prompt men to a regular discharge of their Duty in time of Action: natural bravery, hope of reward, and fear of punishment. The first two are common to the untutor'd, and the Disciplin'd Soldiers; but the latter, most obviously distinguishes the one from the other. A Coward, when taught to believe, that if he breaks his Ranks, and abandons his Colours, he will be punished by Death by his own party, will take his chance against the Enemy.

> General George Washington, 9 February 1776, letter to the President of Congress, *The Writings of George Washington*, IV, John C. Fitzgerald, ed., 1931.

DUTY is the great business of a sea officer; all private considerations must give way to it, however painful it may be.

> Admiral Viscount Nelson, 1786, letter to Frances Nisbet.

FIRSTLY you must always implicitly obey orders, without attempting to form any opinion of your own respecting their propriety. Secondly, you must consider every man your enemy who speaks ill of your king; and thirdly you must hate a Frenchman as you hate the devil.

> Admiral Viscount Nelson, 1793, to a midshipman under his command in HMS *Agamemnon*.

ENGLAND expects every man will do his duty.

> Admiral Viscount Nelson, 21 October 1805, order to the fleet before the Battle of Trafalgar.

THANK GOD, I have done my duty.

> Admiral Viscount Nelson, 21 October 1805, dying of his wounds at Trafalgar on board HMS *Victory*.

I AM *NIMMUKWALLAH*, as we say in the east, that is, I have eaten of the King's salt and, therefore, conceive it to be my duty to serve with unhesitating zeal and cheerfulness where and whenever the King and his Government may think proper to employ me.

> The Duke of Wellington, 1805, upon accepting an obscure posting as brigade commander in a military backwater after his victories as an army commander in India, *The Dispatches of Field Marshal the Duke of Wellington, During His Various Campaigns in India, Denmark, Portugal, Spain, the Low Countries, and France*, IV, 1834–1838, p. 2.

THE BRAVE MAN inattentive to his duty, is worth little more to his country, than the coward who deserts her in the hour of danger.

> Major-General Andrew Jackson, 8 January 1815, to troops who had abandoned their lines during the Battle of New Orleans.

AND FOR MYSELF, I have done my duty. I have identified my fate with that of the heroic dead, & whatever lies these sordid exploiteurs of human misery spread about us these officials, there is a right & a God to fight for & our fight has been worth fighting. I do not despair – nor complain – It has been a great cause.

> Florence Nightingale, 8 March 1855, Scutari, The Barracks Hospital, letter to her sister, Parthenope, quoted in Goldie, ed., *'I have done my duty': Florence Nightingale in the Crimean War 1954–56*, 1987.

I HAVE MADE IT the rule of my life to ask no official favors, but to await orders and then obey them. Such is an officer's duty and his best policy.

> Admiral David Glasgow Farragut, 1857, reply to an inquiry from the Navy Department as to whether he wanted an extension of duty in San Francisco, quoted in Hugh Armstrong, 'Full Speed Ahead!', *Military History Magazine*, 2/1992.

NEITHER LET US be slandered from our duty by false accusations against us, nor frightened from it by menaces of destruction to the Government nor of dungeons to ourselves. LET US HAVE FAITH THAT RIGHT MAKES MIGHT, AND IN THAT FAITH, LET US TO THE END, DARE TO DO OUR DUTY AS WE UNDERSTAND IT.

> Abraham Lincoln, Cooper Institute Address, New York City, 27 February 1860, *Collected Works*, III, p. 547.

I HAVE NOW attained what I have been looking for all my life – a flag – and, having attained it, all that is necessary to complete the scene is a victory. If I die in the attempt, it will only be what every officer has to expect. He who dies in doing his duty to his country, and at peace with his God, has played out the drama of life to the best advantage.

> Admiral David G. Farragut, before running past the defences of New Orleans, 25 March 1862, quoted in Loyall Farragut, *The Life of David Glasgow Farragut*, 1879.

DON'T FLINCH from that fire, boys; there's a hotter fire than that for those who don't do their duty.

> Admiral David Glasgow Farragut, during the battle with the forts and flotilla guarding the city of New Orleans on 24 April 1862, quoted in Spears, *David G. Farragut*, 1905.

IT IS HARD TO SAY what would be the most wise policy to pursue toward this people, but for a soldier his duty is plain. He is to obey the orders of all those placed over him and whip the enemy wherever he meets him. "If he can" should only be thought of after an unavoidable defeat.

> General of the Army Ulysses S. Grant, letter to Congressman Elihu B. Washburne, 19 June 1862, after the Battle of Shiloh, quoted in Bruce Catton, *Grant Moves South*, 1960.

YES! All that is very sad, and might be a cause of self-reproach, *but that we are conscious that we have humbly tried to do our duty*. We may, therefore, with calm satisfaction, trust in God, and leave the results to him.

> General Robert E. Lee, in an 1866 conversation on the results of the war with William Jones, *Personal Reminiscences, Anecdotes, and Letters of Gen. Robert E. Lee*, 1874.

I DID ONLY what my duty demanded; I could have taken no other course without dishonor. And if all were to be done over again, I should act in precisely the same manner.

> General Robert E. Lee, June 1868, speaking to Wade Hampton of his decision to resign his commission in the U.S. Army and offer his services to Virginia in 1861, quoted in William Jones, *Personal Reminiscences, Anecdotes, and Letters of Gen. Robert E. Lee*, 1874.

SHALL I TELL YOU when he was on the Rappahannock, and they telegraphed him his child was dying – his darling little Flora – that he replied that "I shall have to leave my child in the hands of God; my duty to my country requires me here."

> Major-General J.E.B. Stuart, as recounted by Major-General Fitzhugh Lee, at a A.N.V. Banquet, 28 October 1875, quoted in Early, *Southern Historical Society Papers*, I, January–June 1876, p. 102.

DUTY is the sublimest word in our language. Do your duty in all things. You cannot do more. You should never do less.

> General Robert E. Lee, quoted in A.L. Long, *Memoirs of Robert E. Lee*, 1886.

THE ARMY are not satisfied with the change, and

consider the treatment of McClellan most ungracious and inopportune. Yet I do not sympathize in the movement going on to resist the order. "It is useless," I tell the gentlemen around me. "We are serving no one man: we are serving our country."

> Major-General Winfield Scott Hancock, 1862, on Lincoln's removal of McClellan for the second and last time, quoted in Almira R. Hancock, *Reminiscences of Winfield Scott Hancock*, 1887.

DUTY IS OURS; consequences are God's.

> Lieutenant-General Thomas J. 'Stonewall' Jackson, one of his favourite maxims, quoted in Mary Anne Jackson, *Life and Letters of General Thomas J. Jackson*, 1892.

SUCCESS is not in my hands; to do my duty is.

> Rear Admiral Samuel F. Du Pont, 10 March 1863, letter to his wife.

I MUST ABIDE the fortunes and share the fate of my people . . . I cannot leave my present position. I have a self-imposed task. I have led the young men of the South in battle. I must teach their sons to discharge their duty in life.

> General Robert E. Lee, post-war replies to lucrative offers to resettle outside the South, quoted in William Jones, *Life and Letters of Robert Edward Lee*, 1906.

DEFEAT is a common fate of a soldier and there is nothing to be ashamed of in it. The great point is whether we have performed our duty. I cannot but express admiration for the brave manner in which the officers and men of your vessels fought in the late battle for two days continuously. For you, especially, who fearlessly performed your great task until you were seriously wounded, I beg to express my sincerest respect and also my deepest regrets. I hope you will take great care of yourself and recover as soon as possible.

> Admiral Marquis Heihachiro Togo, 3 June 1905, to the wounded Russian Admiral Rodzhesvensky at his bedside after the Battle of Tsushima.

WE NEVER fail when we
   try to do our duty –
We always fail when we
   neglect to do it.

> Lieutenant-General Lord Baden-Powell, *Rovering to Success*, 1908.

YOU ARE ORDERED abroad as a soldier of the King to help our French comrades against an invasion of a common enemy. You have to perform a task which will need your courage, your energy, your patience. Remember that the honour of the British Army depends on your individual conduct. It will be your duty not only to set an example of discipline and perfect steadiness under fire but also to maintain the most friendly relations with those whom you are helping in this

struggle. In this new experience you may find temptations both in wine and women. You must entirely resist both temptations, and, while treating all women with perfect courtesy, you should avoid any intimacy. Do your duty bravely. Fear God. Honour the King.

> Field Marshal Earl Kitchener of Khartoum, a message to the soldiers of the British Expeditionary Force (BEF), 1914, to be kept by each soldier in his Active Service Pay Book, quoted in Sir G. Arthur, *Life of Kitchener*, III.

THE HIGHER the soldier rises on the military ladder, the graver becomes his duty; not in itself, for it only changes form – and no man can do more than his duty – but because to his own duty and his own honour is added the responsibility for the duty and the honour of his subordinates. Responsibility grows to immensity; at one time the lives and the honour of hundreds, of thousands, are at stake; at another, the security of the state itself.

> Colonel-General Hans von Seekt, *Thoughts of a Soldier*, 1930.

WHAT A STRANGE position I find myself in now having to make a decision diametrically opposed to my private opinion, with no choice but to push full speed in pursuance of that decision. Is that, too, fate? And what a bad start we've made.

> Admiral Isoroku Yamamoto, November 1941, letter to a friend as the Imperial Japanese Navy strike force departed for its attack on Pearl Harbor, quoted in John Toland, *The Rising Sun*, 1970.

THE DESTINY of mankind is not decided by material computation. When great causes are on the move in the world . . . we learn that we are spirits, not animals, and that something is going on in space and time and beyond space and time, which whether we like it or not, spells duty.

> Sir Winston S. Churchill, 1941, speech in Rochester, New York.

IF I DO my full duty, the rest will take care of itself.

> General George S. Patton, Jr., 8 November 1942, diary entry before the North African landings, *The Patton Papers*, II, 1974.

ANY COMMANDER who fails to attain his objective, and who is not dead or wounded, has not done his full duty.

> General George S. Patton, Jr., *War As I Knew It*, 1947.

FORWARD THEN. Forward! Let us go forward without fear into the future and let us dread naught when duty calls.

> Sir Winston S. Churchill (1874–1965).

WHILE WE HAVE strength we must discharge our duty. Neither taunts nor blandishments should move us from it.

> Sir Winston S. Churchill (1874–1965).

OUR HONOR lies in doing our duty toward our people and our fatherland as well as in the consciousness of our mutual obligation to keep faith with one another, so we can depend on each other. We must remember that, even in our technological age, it is a man's fighting spirit that ultimately decides between victory and defeat.

Major-General Hasso von Manteuffel, quoted in F.W. von Mellenthin, *German Generals of World War II*, 1977.

IF IT WERE ACCEPTED in principle that when a commander realized that the military situation was hopeless, it was his duty to advocate the conclusion of peace, even if that involved unconditional surrender, there would always be a danger that the struggle might be given up prematurely. As history shows, in war even a seemingly all but hopeless situation can sometimes be radically altered by unexpected political developments and similar occurrences.

Admiral Karl Dönitz, *Memoirs, Ten Years and Twenty Days*, 1959.

I HAD MISSED the boat in the war we had been told would end all wars. A soldier's place was where the fighting went on. I hadn't fully learned the basic lesson of the military – that the proper place for a soldier is where he is ordered by his superiors.

General of the Army Dwight D. Eisenhower, *At Ease: Stories I Tell My Friends*, 1967.

THE TOUGHEST VALUE has been duty. It demands more and gives less than any value I know. In the mind-numbing cold of a Grafenwohr, Germany, tank range in pitch blackness, in the lonely outpost of a border OP staring into a dark void across the Iron Curtain, in the daily battles in the jungle while far away, others decide their worth and where they will lead, in the loneliness of a decision to send your soldiers into an all-night tank battle, in the echo of taps in an otherwise still and silent landscape, in all of that, duty calls and you do it: you, and so many who have gone before you in those and sometimes even more demanding circumstances. You are aware of them. You know them from history, but you also know them because you and they are kindred spirits. You hear them talk to you across the centuries. You will not break the faith. You and your generation will do your duty as our country needs it done while you are there, then you will pass the torch to those who follow, those you have helped to prepare to take the torch.

General Fred Franks, Jr., quoted in Tom Clancy with General Fred Franks, Jr. (ret), *Into the Storm*, 1997.

MY FATHER [Admiral John McCain, commander in chief of the Pacific] gave the order to send B-52s – planes that did not have the precision guided munitions that so impress us all today – he gave the order to send them to bomb the city where the oldest son was held a prisoner of war. That is a pretty hard thing for father to do, but he did it because it was his duty, and he would not shrink from it. He did it because he didn't believe America should lose a war, or settle for a draw . . . He knew that leaders were expected to make hard choices in war. Would that the President [Clinton] had half the regard for the responsibilities of his office.

Senator John McCain, Jr., quoted in George Will, 'McCain's Honest Passion', *The Washington Post*, 1999.

E

ECONOMY OF FORCE
Principle of War

ONE MUST KNOW how to accept a loss when advisable, how to sacrifice a province (he who tries to defend everything saves nothing) and meanwhile march with *all* one's forces against the other forces of the enemy, compel them to battle, spare no effort for their destruction, and turn them against the others.

Frederick the Great (1712–1786), quoted in Foch, *The Principles of War*, 1913.

THE ART of war consists in having always more forces than the opponent, with an army weaker than his, at the point where one attacks, or where one is attacked.

Napoleon (1769–1821), quoted in Foch, *The Principles of War*, 1913.

I COULD LICK those fellows any day, but it would cost me 10,000 men, and, as this is the last army England has, we must take care of it.

The Duke of Wellington, 1810, during the Peninsular Campaign, quoted in Jac Weller, *On Wellington: The Duke and His Art of War*, 1998.

ONE OF THESE simplified features, or aids to analysis, is always to make sure that all forces are involved – always to ensure that no part of the whole force is idle. If a segment of one's force is located where it is not sufficiently busy with the enemy, or if troops are on the march – that is, idle – while the enemy is fighting, then these forces are being managed uneconomically. In this sense they are being wasted, which is even worse than using them inappropriately. When the time for action comes, the first requirement should be that all parts must act: even the least appropriate task will occupy some of the enemy's forces and reduce his overall strength, while completely inactive troops are neutralized for the time being.

Major-General Carl von Clausewitz, *On War*, 3.14, 1832, tr. Michael Howard and Peter Paret, 1976.

THE PRINCIPLE of economy of forces consists in throwing all one's forces at a given time on one point, in using there all one's troops, and, in order to render such a thing possible, having them always in communication among themselves instead of splitting them and of giving to each a fixed and unchangeable purpose.

Marshal of France Ferdinand Foch, *The Principles of War*, 1913.

TO ME, an unnecessary action, or shot, or casualty, was not only waste but sin.

Colonel T.E. Lawrence (1888–1935).

THE PRINCIPLE of Economy of Force. Economy of force may be defined as the efficient use of all means: physical, moral and material, towards winning a war. Of all the principles of war it is the most difficult to apply, because of its close interdependence on the ever changing conditions of war. In order to economize the moral energy of his men, a commander must not only be in spirit one of them, but must ever have fingers on the pulse of the fighters. What they feel he must feel, and what they think he must think; but while they feel fear, experience discomfort and think in terms of easy victory or disaster, though he must understand what all these mean to the men themselves, he must in no way be obsessed by them. To him economy of force first means planning a battle which his men *can* fight, and secondly, adjusting this plan according to the psychological changes which the enemy's resistence is producing on their endurance without forgoing his objective. This does not only entail his possessing judgment, but also foresight and imagination. His plan must never crystallize, for the energy of the battle front is always fluid. He must realize that a fog, or shower of rain, a cold night or unexpected resistance may force him to adjust his plan, and in order to enable him to do so, the grand tactical economy of force rests with his reserves, which form the staying power of the battle and the fuel of all tactical movement.

Major-General J.F.C. Fuller, *The Reformation of War*, 1923.

ECONOMY of force rightly means, not a mere husbanding of one's resources in man-power, but the employment of one's force, both weapons and men, in accordance with economic laws, so as to yield the highest possible dividend of success in proportion to the expenditure of strength. While husbanding the lives of the troops is a matter of common sense, full economy of force demands organized common sense – the habit of thinking scientifically, and weighing up tactical values and conditions. Economy of force is the supreme law of successful war.

Surprise is the psychological and Concentration the physical means to thoroughly *economic* "offensive action" – blows that will attain the maximum result at the minimum cost. Similarly, *information* and a correct *distribution* of our forces are the economic means to Security. *Flexibility* and *co-operation* increase Mobility – just as by choosing and steering the best course and by oiling and tuning-up the mechanism we get the best speed out of a motor-car. (Oct. 1924.)

> Captain Sir Basil Liddell Hart, *Thoughts on War*, 1944.

IN COLD TRUTH our small band, which at the most comprised some 300 Europeans and about 11,000 Askari, had occupied a very superior position for the whole war. According to what English officers told me, 137 Generals had been in the field, and in all about 300,000 men had been employed against us. The enemy's losses in dead would not be put too high at 60,000 for the English Press notice stated that about 20,000 Europeans and Indians alone had died or been killed, and to that must be added the large number of black soldiers who fell. The enemy had left 140,000 horse and mules behind in the battle area. Yet in spite of the enormously superior numbers at the disposal of the enemy, our small force, the rifle strength of which was only about 1,400 at the time of the armistice, had remained in the field always ready for action and possessed of the highest determination.

> Major-General Paul von Lettow-Vorbeck, *East African Campaigns*, 1957. Note: The defence of German East Africa (1914–1918) is undoubtedly the greatest demonstration of economy of force in modern military history.

ENDURANCE

NOW lead the way, wherever your fighting spirit
   bids you.
All of us right behind you, hearts intent on battle.
Nor do I think you'll find us short on courage,
long as our strength will last. Past his strength
no man can go, though he's set on mortal combat.

> Homer, *The Iliad*, 13.908–912, c. 800 BC, tr. Robert Fagles, 1990; Paris to his brother Hector during the battle for the Greek ships.

WHAT CAN a soldier do who charges when out of breath?

> Flavius Vegetius Renatus, *Military Institutions of the Romans*, c. AD 378, tr. Clark, 1776.

THE PRINCIPLE of Endurance. Springing directly from the principle of determination is the principle of endurance. The will of the commander-in-chief and the will of his men must endure, that is they must continue in the same state. It is the local conditions, mental and material, which continually weaken this state and in war often threaten to submerge it. To the commander endurance consists, therefore, in power of overcoming conditions – by foresight, judgment and skill. These qualities cannot be cultivated at a moment's notice, and the worst place to seek their cultivation is on the battlefield itself. The commander-in-chief must be, therefore, a mental athlete, his dumbbells, clubs, and bars being the elements of war and his exercises the application of the principles of war to the conditions of innumerable problems.

> Major-General J.F.C. Fuller, *The Reformation of War*, 1923.

COLLECTIVELY, in an army, endurance is intimately connected with numbers, and, paradoxical as it may seem, the greater the size of an army the less is its psychological endurance. The reason for this is a simple one: one man has one mind; two men have three minds – each his own and a crowd mind shared between them; a million men have millions and millions and millions of minds. If a task which normally requires a million men can be carried out by one man, this one man possesses pyschologically an all but infinitely higher endurance than any single man out of the million. Man, I will again repeat, is an encumbrance on the battlefield, psychologically as well as physically; consequently, endurance should not be sought in numbers, for one Achilles is worth a hundred hoplites.

> Major-General J.F.C. Fuller, *The Reformation of War*, 1923.

THE GREAT ADVANTAGE of the gain in moral force through all forms of physical training is that it is an unconscious gain. Will power, determination, mental poise, and muscle control all march hand-in-hand with the general health and well-being of the man. Fatigue will beat men down as quickly as any other condition, for fatigue brings fear with it. There is no quicker way to lose a battle than to lose it on the road for lack of adequate hardening of the troops. Such a condition cannot be redeemed by the resolve of a commander who insists on driving troops an extra mile beyond their general level of endurance. Extremes of this sort make men rebellious and hateful of command, and thus strike at tactical efficiency from two directions at once. For when men resent a commander, they will not fight as willingly for him, and when their bodies are spent, their nerves are gone. In this state the soldier's every act is mechanical. He is reduced to that automatism of mind which destroys his physical response. His courage is killed. His intellect falls asleep.

> Brigadier-General S.L.A. Marshall, *Men Against Fire*, 1947.

THE CIVIL COMPARISON to war must be that of a game, a very rough and dirty game, for which a robust mind and body are essential.

> Field Marshal Viscount Wavell of Cyrenaica, quoted in S.L.A. Marshall, *The Armed Forces Officer*, 1950.

IN WAR, it sometimes happens that the strain to which the commanders are subjected in critical situations becomes too severe and necessitates a change. This is not only the case with commanders at the front but also, and perhaps to an even greater degree, the higher command which has to make grave decisions alone and far from the theatre of war, from which conflicting and incomplete reports are received. This requires sure intuition, realistic imagination, and great strength of will, and entails a strain on the physical and mental forces which is sometimes overwhelming. If the troops at this time were exhausted, especially in the most exposed sectors, it is obvious that both the higher and lower commanders' endurance had also been severely tested.

Field Marshal Carl Baron von Mannerheim, *The Memoirs of Marshal Mannerheim*, 1953.

THE ENEMY
General

IN PRACTICE we always base our preparations against an enemy on the assumption that his plans are good; indeed, it is right to rest our hopes not on the belief in his blunders, but on the soundness of our provisions. Nor ought we to believe that there is much difference between man and man, but to think that the superiority lies with him who is reared in the severest school.

Archidamus II, (c. 469–427 BC), Eurypontid King of Sparta, quoted in *The History of the Peloponnesian War*, 1.84, c. 404 BC, tr. R. Crawley, 1910.

HE REMARKED that the Spartans do no ask how many the enemy are, but where they are.

Plutarch, paraphrasing Agis II (427–400 BC), son of Archidamus, Eurypontid King of Sparta, *The Lives*, c. AD 100 (*Plutarch on Sparta*, tr. Richard Talbert, 1988).

YOU NEED NOT imagine that victory will be as hard to win as the fame of our antagonists might suggest. Fortune is fickle: often a despised enemy has fought to the death, and a feather in the scale has brought defeat to famous nations and their kings. Take away the blinding brilliance of the name, and in what can the Romans be compared to you?

Hannibal, 218 BC, address to his army before the Battle of the Ticinus, quoted in Livy, *Universal History*, c. AD 17 (*The War With Hannibal*, tr. Aubrey de Sélincourt, 1972).

FOR EVERY ONE must confess that there is no greater proof of the abilities of a general than to investigate, with the utmost care, into the character and natural abilities of his opponent.

Polybius, *Histories*, 3.81, c. 125 BC (*Familiar Quotations from Greek Authors*, tr. Crauford Ramage, 1895).

IT IS BETTER to avoid a tricky opponent than one who never lets up. The latter makes no secret of what he is doing, whereas it is difficult to find out what the other is up to.

The Emperor Maurice, *The Strategikon*, c. AD 600 (*Maurice's Strategikon*, tr. George Dennis, 1984).

A GENERAL in all of his projects should not think so much about what he wishes to do as what his enemy will do; that he should never underestimate this enemy, but he should put himself in his place to appreciate difficulties and hindrances the enemy could not interpose; that his plans will be deranged at the slightest event if he has not foreseen everything and if he has not devised means with which to surmount the obstacles.

Frederick the Great, *Instructions to His Generals*, 3, 1747, tr. Phillips, 1940.

WHILE NEVER despising his enemy in his heart, he should never speak of him except with scorn and should compare carefully the advantages of our troops over the others.

Frederick the Great, *Instructions to His Generals*, 8, 1747, tr. Phillips, 1940.

WHAT DESIGN would I be forming if I were the enemy?

Frederick the Great, *General Principles of War*, 1748.

THE ONE who is to draw up a plan of operations must possess a minute knowledge of the power of his adversary and of the help the latter may expect from his allies. He must compare the forces of the enemy with his own numbers and those of his allies so that he can judge which kind of war to lead or undertake.

Frederick the Great, 1748, letter.

THE MAXIM in war, that your enemy is ever to be dreaded until at your feet, ought to be held inviolate.

Major-General Henry 'Light Horse Harry' Lee, *Memoirs of the War in the Southern Department*, 1869.

FIGHT the enemy with the weapons he lacks.

Field Marshal Prince Aleksandr V. Suvorov, quoted in Ossipov, *Suvorov*, 1945.

IN WAR one sees his own troubles and not those of the enemy.

Napoleon, 30 April 1809, to Eugene, *Correspondance de Napoléon Ier, publiée par ordre de l'Empereur Napoléon III*, No. 15144, Vol. XVIII, 1858–1870, p. 545.

NAPOLEON (watching Smolensk burn): An eruption of Vesuvius! Isn't that a fine sight, *Monsieur le Grand Ecuyer*?
Caulaincourt: Horrible, Sire.
Napoleon: Bah! Remember, gentlemen, remember the words of a Roman emperor: "A dead enemy always smells sweet."

Napoleon, the night of 17 August 1812, referring to the words of Vespasian, quoted in Armand de Caulaincourt, *With Napoleon in Russia*, 1935.

MAXIM 8. A general-in-chief should ask himself frequently in the day, What should I do if the enemy's army appeared now in my front, or on my right, or on my left? If he has any difficulty in answering these questions he is ill posted, and should seek to remedy it.

> Napoleon, *Military Maxims of Napoleon*, tr. George D'Aguilar, 1831 (David Chandler, ed., 1987).

MAXIM 16. It is an approved maxim in war, never to do what the enemy wishes you to do, for this reason alone, that he desires it. A field of battle, therefore, which he has previously studied and reconnoitered, should be avoided, and double care should be taken where he has had time to fortify or entrench. One consequence deducible from this principle is, never to attack a position in front which you can gain by turning.

> Napoleon, *Military Maxims of Napoleon*, tr. George D'Aguilar, 1831 (David Chandler, ed., 1987).

MEN are always more inclined to pitch their estimate of the enemy's strength too high than too low, such is human nature. Bearing this in mind, one must admit that partial ignorance of the situation is, generally speaking, a major factor in delaying the progress of military action. . . .

> Major-General Carl von Clausewitz, *On War*, 1.18, 1832, tr. Michael Howard and Peter Paret, 1976.

THE PRESIDENT once dropped a few kind words about the enemy. They were human beings – were they not? One could not be completely remorseless, even in war. The line must be drawn somewhere. An elderly woman in the reception room flashed a question; how could he speak kindly of his enemies when he should rather destroy them. "What, madam?" slowly as he gazed into her face, "do I not destroy them when I make them my friends?"

> Abraham Lincoln, recounted by Carl Sandburg, *Abraham Lincoln*, III, 1939.

IT IS ALWAYS proper to assume that the enemy will do what he should do.

> General Robert E. Lee, letter to Jefferson Davis, quoted in *Douglas Southall Freeman on Leadership*, 1993.

THOSE WHO OPPOSE our purposes are not always to be regarded as our enemies. We usually think and act from our local surroundings. The better rule is to judge our adversaries from their standpoint, not from our own.

> General Robert E. Lee, 1870, notes found in his desk at Washington College after his death, quoted in A.L. Long, *Memoirs of Robert E. Lee*, 1886.

DOCTOR, there is a good old book which I read and you preach from, which says, "Love your enemies, bless them that curse you, do good to them that hate you, and pray for them which despitefully use you and persecute you." Do you think your remarks this evening were quite in the spirit of that teaching? I have never cherished toward them bitter or vindictive feelings, and have never seen the day when I did not pray for them.

> General Robert E. Lee to a clergyman who after the

war had vehemently spoken against the possible indictment of Lee for treason, quoted in William Jones, *Personal Reminiscences*, 1874.

IN WAR a soldier must expect short commons, short sleep, and sore feet. Even an old soldier finds it difficult, and for a green one it is hard. But if it's hard for you it isn't easier for the enemy; maybe harder still. Only you see your own hardships, but don't see the enemy's.

> M.I. Dragomirov, *Notes for Soldiers*, c. 1890.

WHILE DISPOSITIONS taken in peace times can be weighted at length, and infallibly lead to the result desired, such is not the case with the use of forces in war, with operations. In war, once hostilities are begun, our will soon encounters the independent will of the enemy. Our dispositions strike against the freely-made dispositions of the enemy.

> Field Marshal Helmuth Graf von Moltke, quoted in Foch, *Principles of War*, 1913, p. 100.

I HOPE you have kept the enemy always in the picture. War-books so often leave them out.

> Colonel T.E. Lawrence, 9 February 1928, letter to Colonel A.P. Wavell.

IF WE TRY to give an exact answer to the question who deserves the most credit for the victory at Tannenberg, we must also briefly consider the conduct of the enemy, without whose blunders the success would not have been possible.

> General Max Hoffmann, *War Diaries and Other Papers*, II, 1929.

NEVER mistreat the enemy by halves.

> Sir Winston S. Churchill (1874–1965).

AN IMPORTANT difference between a military operation and a surgical operation is that the patient is not tied down. But it is a common fault of generalship to assume that he is. (May 1934.)

> Captain Sir Basil Liddell Hart, *Thoughts on War*, 1944.

HOWEVER ABSORBED a commander may be in the elaboration of his own thoughts, it is sometimes necessary to take the enemy into account.

> Sir Winston S. Churchill (1874–1965) – attributed.

I HAVE TODAY written General Bradley that if he can give me 2,000 tons of ammunition . . . and then guarantee a like amount daily, I can initiate an attack any time. I have learned from you to fight on a shoestring, and I realize further that the enemy is fighting on a shoestring which is even more frayed than ours.

> General George S. Patton, Jr., 19 October 1944, letter to General Eisenhower, *The Patton Papers*, II, 1974.

WHEN SPEAKING to a junior about the enemy confronting him, always understate their strength.

You do this because the person in contact with the enemy invariably overestimates their strength to himself, so, if you understate it, you probably hit the approximate fact, and also enhance your junior's self-confidence.

General George S. Patton, Jr., *War As I Knew It*, 1947.

I WANT to emphasize the importance of focusing on the enemy when planning and conducting combat operations. First, you must know your enemy. Second, you must develop your plan keeping the enemy foremost in mind. Third, you must wargame your plan to enhance your ability to develop or adjust the plan once enemy contact is made.

General H. Norman Schwarzkopf, 'Food for Thought', *How They Fight*, 1988.

A BATTLE PLAN is good only until enemy contact is made. From then on, your ability to execute the plan depends on what the enemy does. If your assessment of the enemy is good, then you probably have anticipated his actions or reactions and will be able to quickly develop or adjust your plan accordingly. If your assessment is bad, due to poor understanding of how the enemy fights or poor battlefield intelligence, then you will probably get surprised, react slowly, lose the initiative, and cause your unit to be defeated.

General H. Norman Schwarzkopf, 'Food for Thought', *How They Fight*, 1988.

Know Your Enemy

HENCE THE SAYING: If you know the enemy and know yourself, you need not fear the result of a hundred battles. If you know yourself but not the enemy, for every victory gained you will also suffer a defeat. If you know neither the enemy nor yourself, you will succumb in every battle.

Sun Tzu, *The Art of War*, 3, c. 500 BC, tr. Giles, 1910.

THEY ARE NO MATCH for us either in bodily strength or resolution, [and] will find their superiority in numbers of no avail. Our enemies are Medes and Persians, men who for centuries have lived soft and luxurious lives; we of Macedon for generations past have been trained in the hard school of danger and war. Above all, we are free men, and they are slaves. There are Greek troops, to be sure, in Persian service – but how different is their cause from ours! They will be fighting for pay – and not much of it at that; we, on the contrary, shall fight for Greece, and our hearts will be in it.

Alexander the Great, October 333 BC, exhortation to his men before the Battle of Issus, quoted in Arrian, *The Campaigns of Alexander*, 2.7, c. AD 150, tr. Aubrey de Sélincourt, 1987.

THAT GENERAL is wise who before entering into war carefully studies the enemy, and can guard against his strong points and take advantage of his weaknesses. For example, the enemy is superior in cavalry; he should destroy his forage. He is superior in number of troops; cut off their supplies. His army is composed of diverse peoples; corrupt them with gifts, favors, and promises. There is dissention among them; deal with their leaders. This people relies on the spear; lead them into difficult terrain. This people relies on the bow; line up in the open and force them into close, hand-to-hand fighting. Against Scythians or Huns launch your assault in February or March when their horses are in wretched condition after suffering through the winter. . . . If they march or make camp without proper precautions, make unexpected raids on them by night and by day. If they are reckless and undisciplined in combat and not inured to hardship, make believe you are going to attack, but delay and drag things out until their ardor cools, and when they begin to hesitate, then make your attack on them. The foe is superior in infantry; entice him into the open, not too close, but from a safe distance hit him with javelins.

The Emperor Maurice, *The Strategikon*, c. AD 600 (*Maurice's Strategikon*, tr. George Dennis, 1984).

"TO BECOME the enemy" means to think yourself into the enemy's position. In the world people tend to think of a robber trapped in a house as a fortified enemy. However, if we think of "becoming the enemy", we feel that the whole world is against us and that there is no escape. He who is shut inside is a pheasant. He who enters to arrest is a hawk. You must appreciate this.

Miyamoto Musashi, *A Book of Five Rings*, 1645, tr. Victor Harris, 1984.

IT IS VERY IMPORTANT to know the genius, character and talents of the enemy general; it is on this knowledge that one can develop plans . . .

Napoleon (1769–1821), quoted in David Chandler, *The Campaigns of Napoleon*, 1966.

MY DIE IS CAST . . . they may overwhelm me but I don't think they will outmanoeuvre me. First, because I am not afraid of them, as everyone else seems to be; and secondly, because if what I hear of their system of manoeuvres be true, I think it a false one, as against steady troops. I suspect all the continental armies are more than half beaten before the battle was begun. I, at least, will not be frightened beforehand.

The Duke of Wellington, 1808, giving his opinion of the French, upon embarking on the Peninsular Campaign, quoted in J. Crocker, *The Crocker Papers*, I, 1884.

THEY DO NOT know what they say. If it comes to a conflict of arms, the war will last at least four years. Northern politicians do not appreciate the determination and pluck of the South, and Southern politicians do not appreciate the numbers, resources, and patient perseverance of the North. Both sides forget that we are all Americans, and that it must be a terrible struggle if it comes to war. Tell General Scott that we must do all we can to avert war, and if it comes to the worst we must then do everything in our power to mitigate its evils.

> General Robert E. Lee, May 1861, interview with several Northern visitors after he had resigned his commission and moved to Richmond, quoted in William Jones, *Life and Letters of Robert Edward Lee, Soldier and Man*, 1906.

THE CONFEDERATES at Fort Morgan are making great preparations to receive us. That concerns me little. I know they will do all in their power to destroy us, and we will reciprocate the compliment. I hope to give them a fair fight if once I get inside. I expect nothing from them but that they will try to blow me up if they can.

> Admiral David G. Farragut (1801–1870), quoted in Alfred Thayer Mahan, *Admiral Farragut*, 1892.

THE NATURAL DISPOSITION of most people is to clothe a commander of a large army whom they did not know with almost superhuman abilities. A large part of the National army, for instance, and most of the press of the country, clothed General Lee with just such qualities, but I had known him personally, and knew that he was mortal; and it was just as well that I felt this.

> General Ulysses S. Grant, *Personal Memoirs*, II, 1885.

HE WHO RECKONS solely by the visible in war is reckoning falsely. The inherent worth of the soldier is everything. It was on that that I based my confidence. What I thought to myself was this:

The Russian may invade our Fatherland, and contact with the soil of Germany may lift up his heart, but that does not make him a German soldier, and those who lead him are not German officers. The Russian soldier had fought with the greatest obedience on the battlefields of Manchuria although he had no sympathy with the political ambitions of his rulers in the Pacific. It did not seem unlikely that in a war against the Central Powers the Russian Army would have greater enthusiasm for the war aims of the Tsar's Empire. On the other hand, I considered that, taking it all round, the Russian soldier and officer would not display higher military qualities in the European theatre than they had in the Asiatic, and believed that in comparing the two forces I was entitled to credit our side with a plus on the ground of intrinsic value instead of a minus for our numerical inferiority.

> Field Marshal Paul von Hindenburg, *Out of My Life*, 1920.

MOST PEOPLE think Americans love luxury and that their culture is shallow and meaningless. It is a mistake to regard the Americans as luxury-loving and weak. I can tell you Americans are full of the spirit of Justice, fight and adventure. Also their thinking is very advanced and scientific. Lindbergh's solo crossing of the Atlantic is the sort of valiant act which is normal for them. That is typically American adventure based on science.

> Admiral Isoroku Yamamoto, late 1940, an address to his old middle school in Nagaoaka, quoted in John Deane Potter, *Yamamoto*, 1965.

WHAT KIND of people do they [the Japanese] think we are?

> Sir Winston S. Churchill, speech to a joint session of the U.S. Congress, 26 December 1941.

FOR MORE than a dozen years I have been frustrated by my inability in formal briefings, lectures, and documents, either in the mud of gunnery ranges or in the comfort of theaters, to adequately transmit anything sufficiently meaningful about the men behind the Soviet guns. When asked what the Soviet military is "really like," I have often joked that it's a lot like sex: Much of what you've heard about it isn't true; when it's good, it can be amazing; but when it's bad, it's inexpressibly embarrassing.

> Lieutenant-Colonel Ralph Peters, *Red Army*, 1980.

Respect Your Enemy

COME,
let us give each other gifts, unforgettable gifts,
so any man may say, Trojan soldier or Argive,
"First they fought with heart-devouring hatred,
then they parted, bound by pacts of friendship."

> Homer, *The Iliad*, 7.345–349, c. 800 BC, tr. Robert Fagles, 1990; Hector calling a truce in his duel with Telemonian Ajax out of respect for his enemy's valour.

FRIENDS, until this time we have never fought a people who are our equal, as you are. It is just, then, that since we are equal in bravery, you should be honored in this same way.

> Tlacaelel, Aztec generalissimo, c. 1450, to the conquered Chalcas who then had their noses pierced to receive the ornaments of valor, quoted in Fray Diego Durán, *The History of the Indies of New Spain*, 1581, tr. Doris Heyden, 1994.

NEVER DESPISE your enemy, whoever he is. Try to find out about his weapons and means, how he uses them and fights. Research into his strengths and weaknesses.

> Field Marshal Prince Aleksandr V. Suvorov, 1789 or 1790, letter, quoted in Philip Longworth, *The Art of Victory*, 1966.

BUONOPARTE had never yet had to contend with an English officer, and he [Nelson] would endeavour to make him respect us.

> Admiral Viscount Nelson (writing in the second person), to the British authorities in Bombay notifying

them of his victory at the Battle of the Nile, 1 August 1798, quoted in Robert Southey, *Life of Nelson*, 1813.

I HOPE that you will be introduced to Buonoparte. You will hear him plentifully abused here – but I own tho' he has done many acts which are unpardonable, yet I cannot help having admiration and respect for him.
General Sir John Moore, early 1803, letter to Captain Gardiner, quoted in Carola Oman, *Sir John Moore*, 1953.

MOORE is the only General now worthy to contend with me. I shall move against him in person.
Napoleon, 19 December 1808, when he learned that Moore was audaciously moving on the French lines of communication in Spain, quoted in Carola Oman, *Sir John Moore*, 1953.

NOR BLAME THEM too much . . . nor us for not blaming them more. Although, as we believed, fatally wrong in striking at the old flag, misreading its deeper meaning and the innermost law of the people's life, blind to the signs of the times in the march of man, they fought as they were taught, true to such ideals as they saw, and put into their cause their best. For us they were fellow-soldiers as well, suffering the fate of arms. We could not look into those brave, bronze faces, and those battered flags we had met on so many fields where glorious manhood lent a glory to the earth that bore it, and think of personal hate and mean revenge. Whosoever had misled these men, we had not. We had led them back, home.
Major-General Joshua L. Chamberlain, *The Passing of the Armies*, 1915.

AS MY COMMAND, in worn-out shoes and ragged uniforms, but with proud mien, moved to the designated point to stack their arms and surrender their cherished battle-flags, they challenged the admiration of the brave victors. One of the knightliest soldiers of the Federal army, General Joshua L. Chamberlain of Maine, who afterward served with distinction as governor of his State, called his troops into line, and as my men marched in front of them, the veterans in blue gave a soldierly salute to those vanquished heroes – a token of respect from Americans to Americans, a final and fitting tribute from Northern to Southern chivalry.
General John B. Gordon, *Reminiscences of the Civil War*, 1903.

SO 'ERE'S TO YOU, Fuzzy-Wuzzy, at your 'ome in the Soudan;
You're a pore benighted 'eathen but a first-class fighting man;
An' ere's to you, Fuzzy-Wuzzy, with your 'ayrick 'ead of 'air –
You big black boundin' begger – for you broke a British Square!
Rudyard Kipling, 'Fuzzy-Wuzzy'.

NEWSPAPER libels on Fritz's courage and efficiency were resented by all trench-soldiers of experience.
Robert Graves, *Goodbye to All That*, 1929.

I HAVE ALWAYS said what I here expressly repeat in print, that the German people exhibited such astounding energy, doggedness, sturdy patriotism, courage, endurance, discipline, and readiness to die for their country, that, as a soldier, I cannot but salute them. They fought with lion-like bravery and an amazing tenacity against the whole world. The German soldier – and this means the German people – deserves unstinted respect.
General Aleksei A. Brusilov, *A Soldier's Notebook*, 1930.

EXCEPTIONS [to the panic among the Turkish troops] were the German detachments; and there, for the first time, I grew proud of the enemy who had killed my brothers. They were two thousand miles from home, without hope and without guides, in conditions mad enough to break the bravest nerves. Yet their sections held together, in firm rank, sheering through the wrack of Turk and Arab like armoured ships, high-faced and silent. When attacked they halted, took position, fired to order. There was no haste, no crying, no hesitation. They were glorious.
Colonel T.E. Lawrence, *The Seven Pillars of Wisdom*, 1935.

THE THING that worries me slightly is that, although the war's only been going for something over three months, a lot of people are feeling relieved, or saying they're "grateful to Admiral Yamamoto" because there hasn't been a single air raid. They're very wrong: the fact that the enemy hasn't come is no thanks to Admiral Yamamoto, but to the enemy himself. So if they want to express gratitude to somebody, I wish they'd express it to America. If the latter really made up its mind to wade in on us, there'd be no way of defending a city like Tokyo.
The "first stage of operations" has been a kind of children's hour, and will soon be over; now comes the adults' hour, so perhaps I'd better stop dozing and bestir myself.
Admiral Isoroku Yamamoto, 18 April 1942, to the geisha, Niwa Michi, just before the Doolittle raid on Tokyo, quoted in Agawa, *Reluctant Admiral*, 1979.

REMEMBER that these enemies, whom we shall have the honor to destroy, are good soldiers and stark fighters. To beat such men, you must not despise their ability, but you must be confident in your own superiority.
General George S. Patton, Jr., December 1941, *The Patton Papers*, II, 1974.

THE WILLINGNESS of the Allied pilots to engage us

in combat deserves special mention here, for, regardless of the odds, their fighters were always screaming in to attack. And it is important to point out that their fighter planes were clearly inferior in performance to our own Zeros. Furthermore, almost all of our pilots were skilled air veterans; coupled with the Zero's outstanding performance, this afforded us a distinct advantage. The men we fought then were among the bravest I have ever encountered, no less so than our own pilots who, three years later, went out willingly on missions from which there was no hope of return.

> Saburo Sakai, *Samurai!*, 1957; describing the air battles around Lae, 180 miles north of Port Moresby in 1942.

I NEVER UNDERESTIMATE the enemy. . . . I look at his capabilities and assume he has them until we find out differently.

> General H. Norman Schwarzkopf, 1991, quoted in Peter David, *Triumph in the Desert*, 1991.

ENERGY

NOW any weakling in the world will fight in a minute if he gets excited, but when it comes to actually taking up arms and seeking to do battle, this is being possessed by energy – when this energy wanes they will stop, get frightened, and feel regret. The reason that armies look upon strong enemies the way they look at virgin girls is that their aggressiveness is being taken advantage of, as they are stirred up over something.

> Ho Yen-hsi (Ho Yanxi), Sung dynasty (early 12th century) commentator, Sun Tzu, *The Art of War*, 7, c. 500 BC, tr. Thomas Cleary, 1988.

GENERALS wage war through the armed forces, the armed forces fight by energy. Energy prevails when it is drummed up. If you can energize your troops, don't do it too frequently, otherwise their energy will easily wane. Don't do it at too great a distance either, otherwise their energy will be easily exhausted. You should drum up the energy of your soldiers when enemies are within a calculated critical distance, having your troops fight at close range. When enemies wane and you prevail, victory over them is assured.

The rule is "Fight when full of energy, flee when drained of energy."

> Liu Ji (1310–1375), *Lessons of War* (*Mastering the Art of War*, tr. Thomas Cleary, 1989).

IF YOU wage war, do it energetically and with severity. This is the only way to make it shorter, and consequently less inhuman.

> Napoleon, 1799, letter to General Hedouville, quoted in Christopher Herold, ed, *The Mind of Napoleon*, 1955.

IF WE READ history with an open mind, we cannot fail to conclude that, among all the military virtues, *the energetic conduct of war* has always contributed most to glory and success.

> Major-General Carl von Clausewitz, *On War*, 4.3, 1832, tr. Michael Howard and Peter Paret, 1976.

THE TRUE SPEED of war is not headlong precipitancy, but the unremitting energy which wastes no time.

> Rear Admiral Alfred Thayer Mahan (1840–1914).

THE POWER to vivify an undertaking implies the energy sufficient to shoulder the burden of its consequence.

> General Charles de Gaulle, *The Edge of the Sword*, 1932.

THE CONSERVATION of men's powers, not the spending thereof, is the object of main concern to the truly qualified commander.

> Brigadier-General S.L.A. Marshall, *The Armed Forces Officer*, 1950.

THE ORGANIZATION of supplies, the command of men, anything in any way constructive requires more than intellect; it requires energy and drive and an unrelenting will to serve the cause, regardless of one's personal interests. Academic soldiers mostly look on war as a pure intellectual problem and demand energy and drive only from those whom they somewhat contemptuously refer to as "Troupier", but from themselves, never. They rest content with their professional qualifications, which are attested for them by others of the same ilk, and regard themselves as the source of all good and the "Troupier" as the source of all evil.

> Field Marshal Erwin Rommel, *The Rommel Papers*, 1953.

MENTAL CONCEPTION must be followed by immediate execution. This is a matter of energy and initiative. What the soldier needs is a combination of realist intellect and energy. Whatever is attempted must be carried through. The young officer must understand from the outset of his training that just as much energy is required of him as mental ability.

> Field Marshal Erwin Rommel, *The Rommel Papers*, 1953.

ENGINEERS/SAPPERS

GOOD ENGINEERS are so scarce, that one must bear with their humours and forgive them because we cannot be without them.

> Lord Galway, 1704, report from Spain to the Board of Ordnance, quoted in David Chandler, *The Art of War in the Age of Marlborough*, 1976.

THEIR SCIENCE demands a great deal of courage

and spirit, a solid genius, perpetual study and consumate experience in all the arts of war.

> Marshal of France Sebastien de Vauban, *A Manual of Siegecraft*, 1740.

THE SAPPERS raise permanent and field fortifications; they attack and defend fortresses. They accompany the army to war. On these three counts alone one can rest assured that no other military organization in the World possesses a higher degree of ability and patriotism than exists in our corps of engineers. Alexandria, Antwerp, Juliers – and five hundred more places constructed, restored or augmented – these achievements prove that the arts of Vauban have not fallen into decadence in the hands of the Marescots, the Chasseloups and the Haxos. All Europe has been covered by our redoubts and entrenchements.

> Napoleon (1769–1821), quoted in J. Ambert, *Equises d'l'Armée Française*, 1840.

MAXIM 85. A general of engineers who must conceive, propose and direct all the fortifications of an army, needs good judgment and a practical mind above all.

> Napoleon, *The Military Maxims of Napoleon*, tr. Burnod, 1827.

THE SIEGE of Badajoz was a most serious undertaking, and the weather did not favour us. The troops were up to their middles in mud in the trenches . . . The Assault was a terrible business, of which I saw the loss when I was ordering it. But we had brought matters to that state that we could do no more, and it was necessary to storm or raise the siege. I trust, however, that future armies will be equipped for sieges, with the people necessary to carry them on as they ought to be; and that our engineers will learn how to put their batteries on the crest of the glaçis, and to blow in the counterscarp, instead of placing them wherever the wall can be seen, leaving the poor officers and troops to get into and across the ditch as they can . . .

> The Duke of Wellington, 28 May 1812, to Major-General Murray on the absence of professional engineers, quoted in Julian Rathbone, *Wellington's War: His Peninsular Dispatches*, 1984.

CLEARLY, we would need great skill and even greater courage. But our first need was for men and equipment. It will be seen why the creation of engineer units was a top priority. In just over two years we succeeded in creating and training almost 40 engineer battalions, some of them highly specialized. It was our biggest coup and the foundation of our success. In his memoirs, the Israeli Chief of Staff, General David Elazaar, records that during a discussion in the Israeli High Command of the possibility of Egyptian forces attempting to cross the canal, General Dayan, the Israeli Defense Minister, said: "To cross the canal the Egyptians would need the support of both the American and the Soviet engineer corps." I do not hold Dayan's dismissive remark against him. I accept the tribute. I know how hard we worked.

> General Saad El Shazly, *The Crossing of the Suez*, 1980.

NO CORPS was more constantly in demand, so much master of so many tasks.

> General Sir David Fraser, of the Royal Engineers, *And We Shall Shock Them*, 1983.

UBIQUE (Everywhere); *Quo fas et gloria ducunt* (Wherever right and glory lead).

> Mottos of the Corps of Royal Engineers.

ESSAYONS! (Let's try!)

> The motto of the U.S. Army Corps of Engineers.

ENTHUSIASM/EXCITEMENT

I DO NOT like the enthusiastic man.

> Cornelius Scipio 'The Younger' Africanus Aemilianus (185–129 BC), quoted in Cicero, *De Oratore*, c. 50 BC.

IN ALL MEN there is an innate excitability and drive which is kindled by the heat of the fight, and it is the function of the general not to quench but to heighten the excitement. There is sound sense in the ancient practice of sounding trumpet blasts on all sides and raising a battle cry from all throats; these things, they thought, serve both to terrify the enemy and to heighten the ardor of one's own men.

> Julius Caesar, *The Gallic War*, c. 51 BC, tr. Moses Hadas, 1957.

MILITARY VIRTUES should not be confused with simple bravery, and still less with enthusiasm for a cause. Bravery is obviously a necessary component. But just as bravery, which is part of the natural make-up of a man's character, can be developed in a soldier – a member of an organization – it must develop differently in him than in other men. In the soldier the natural tendency for unbridled action and outbursts of violence must be subordinated to demands of a higher kind: obedience, order, rule, and method. An army's efficiency gains life and spirit from enthusiasm for the cause for which it fights, but such enthusiasm is not indispensable.

> Major-General Carl von Clausewitz, *On War*, 3.5, 1832, tr. Michael Howard and Peter Paret, 1976.

I ALREADY KNEW that even in the ordinary condition of mind enthusiasm is a potent element with soldiers, but what I saw that day convinced me that if it can be excited from a state of despondency its power is almost irresistible. I said nothing except to remark, as I rode among those on the road: "If I had been with you this morning this disaster would not have happened. We must face the other way; we will go back and recover our camp."

> General of the Army Phillip H. Sheridan, of how his army turned itself around in the midst of the rout at the Battle of Winchester (19 September 1864) at his appearance on the field, *Personal Memoirs of P.H. Sheridan*, II, 1888.

ENTRENCHMENTS

DOMITIUS CORBULO used to say that the pick was the weapon with which to beat the enemy.

> Frontinus, *Stratagems*, 4.7, c. AD 84–96, tr. Charles E. Bennett, 1925; speaking of the distinguished Roman general who successfully campaigned against the Parthians in the reign of Nero.

WHEN I HEAR talk of lines, I always think I am hearing talk of the walls of China. The good ones are those that nature has made and the good entrenchments are good dispositions and brave soldiers.

> Field Marshal Maurice Comte de Saxe, *My Reveries*, 1732, tr. Phillips, 1940.

MAXIM 17. In a war of march and manoeuvre, if you would avoid a battle with a superior army, it is necessary to entrench every night, and occupy a good defensive position. Those natural positions which are ordinarily met with, are not sufficient to protect an army against superior numbers without recourse to art.

> Napoleon, *The Military Maxims of Napoleon*, tr. George D'Aguilar, 1831 (David Chandler, ed., 1987).

INTRENCHMENTS, or continuous lines, of which great use was made in the old wars, are adapted to absolutely defensive operations. They are open to the great inconvenience of spreading the means of defence along a considerable extent, and consequently, of being weak upon all points which the enemy may attack.

They offer moreover the great disadvantage of forcing an army to abandon them the instant any part of them is carried.

> Marshal of France Michel Ney, Duc d'Elchingen, Prince de la Moskova, *The Memoirs of Marshal Ney*, 1834.

THE FEELING of the two armies now seems to be that the rebels can protect themselves only by strong intrenchments, whilst our army is not only confident of protecting itself without intrenchements, but that it can beat and drive the enemy wherever and whenever he can be found without its protection.

> General of the Army Ulysses S. Grant, letter to Major-General Halleck from Cold Harbor, 5 June 1864, *Personal Memoirs*, II, 1885.

I THINK the public, and probably a great many

officers, confound attacking field-works or intrenchments where there is a small body of men posted with attacking a whole army that has thrown up intrenchments. Now that is a different thing altogether. You may take fieldworks in which there are small garrisons by assault, but when you have to attack a whole army, well intrenched, you will suffer terribly in getting up to them.

> Major-General A.A. Humphreys, testimony to Congress on the conduct of the war, quoted in Pennypacker, *General Meade*, 1901.

IT WAS one of Professor Mahan's maxims that the spade was as useful in war as the musket, and to this I add the ax. The habit of intrenching certainly does have the effect of making new troops timid. When a line of battle is once covered by a good parapet, made by the engineers or by the labor of the men themselves, it does require an effort to make them leave it in the face of danger; but when the enemy is intrenched, it becomes absolutely necessary to permit each brigade and division of the troops immediately opposed to throw up a corresponding trench for its own protection in case of a sudden sally.

> General of the Army William T. Sherman, *Memoirs*, II, 1875.

THE TRICK EXPRESSION, "Dig or die," is much overused and much misunderstood. Wars are not won by defensive tactics. Digging is primarily defensive. The only time it is proper for a soldier to dig is when he has reached his final objective. . . . Personally, I am opposed to digging under such circumstances, as the chance of getting killed while sleeping normally on the ground is quite remote, and the fatigue from digging innumerable slit trenches is avoided. Also, the psychological effect on the soldier is bad, because if he thinks he has to dig he must think the enemy is dangerous, which he usually is not.

> General George S. Patton, Jr., *War As I Knew It*, 1947.

ENVELOPMENT

IT IS an invariable axiom of war to secure your own flanks and rear and endeavor to turn those of your enemy.

> Frederick the Great, *Instructions to His Generals*, 1747, tr. Phillips, 1940.

A GENERAL should show boldness, strike a decided blow, and maneuver upon the flank of his enemy. The victory is in his hands.

> Napoleon, *Maxims of War*, 1831.

THE GREATER CONDITIONS of warfare have remained unchanged. The battle of extermination may be fought today according to the same plan as elaborated by Hannibal in long forgotten times. The hostile front is not the aim of the principle attack. It is not against that point that the troops should be massed and the reserves disposed; the essential thing is to crush the flanks.

Field Marshal Alfred Graf von Schlieffen, *Cannae*, 1913.

IT MAY BE SEEN from all the battles, won or lost by Frederick the Great, that his aim was attack from the very beginning a flank or even the rear of the enemy, to push him, if possible against an insurmountable obstacle and then to annihilate him by enveloping one or both of his flanks.

Field Marshal Alfred Graf von Schlieffen, *Cannae*, 1913.

ENVELOPMENT. An enemy may be enveloped and so placed at a severe disadvantage. Envelopment, whether accomplished by converging or overlapping, presupposes a flank, a flank which may be tactically rolled up, or, if turned, will expose the command and lines of communication behind it. The attack by envelopment is a very common action in war, which more often than not has led to victory.

Major-General J.F.C. Fuller, *The Reformation of War*, 1923.

IF I HAD worried about flanks, I could never have fought the war.

General George S. Patton, Jr., *War As I Knew It*, 1947.

THE DEEP ENVELOPMENT based on surprise, which severs the enemy's supply lines, is and always has been the most decisive maneuver of war. A short envelopment which fails to envelop and leaves the enemy's supply system intact, merely divides your own forces and can lead to heavy loss and even jeopardy.

General of the Army Douglas MacArthur, 23 August 1950, conference before Inchon.

WE JUST WENT right around the enemy and were behind him in no time at all.

General H. Norman Schwarzkopf, 1991, of the great envelopment in the Gulf War, quoted in Peter David, *Triumph in the Desert*, 1991.

EPITAPHS AND MEMORIALS

O MAN, I am Cyrus son of Cambyses, who founded the empire of Persia and ruled over Asia. Do not grudge me my monument.

The inscription over the tomb of Cyrus the Great (c. 600–529 BC), quoted in Arrian, *The Campaigns of Alexander*, 6.29, c. AD 150, tr. Aubrey de Sélincourt.

GO, tell the Spartans, thou who passeth by, That here obedient to their will we lie.

Simonides of Keos, the inscription on the monument at the Pass of Thermopylae for the 300 Spartans who fell in 470 BC during the invasion of Greece

by the Persians, quoted in Mackail, ed., *Select Epigrams*.

INTO THE DARK death cloud they passed, to set Fame on their own dear land for fadeless wreath, and dying died not. Valour lifts them yet Into the splendour from the night beneath.

Simonides, on the Spartan monument at Platea, 479 BC, tr. H. Macnaghten, quoted in *The Oxford Book of Greek Verse in Translation*, 1930.

IF VALOUR'S BEST be gallantly to die, Fortune to us of all men grants it now. We to set Freedom's crown on Hellas' brow Laboured, and here in ageless honour lie.

Simonides, on the Athenian monument at Platea, 480 BC, tr. W.C. Lawton, quoted in *The Oxford Book of Greek Verse in Translation*, 1930.

NO ATHENIAN, through my means, ever wore mourning.

Pericles, 429 BC, his own epitaph on his deathbed, quoted in Plutarch, *Plutarch's Lives*, c. AD 100, tr. John Dryden.

FOR IF I HAVE accomplished any glorious feat, that will be my memorial. But if I have not, not even all the statues in the world – the products of vulgar, worthless men – would make any difference.

Agesilaus, Eurypontid King of Sparta (400–360 BC), to his servants as he lay dying, quoted in Plutarch, *The Lives*, c. AD 100 (*Plutarch on Sparta*, tr. Richard Talbert, 1988).

STRANGER, this man you behold was the guiding star of his country, Claudius Marcellus by name, born of a glorious line; Seven times consul, he led the armies of Rome into battle, Death and destruction he dealt to all who invaded his land.

Inscription on the statue of Claudius Marcellus, one of Hannibal's most dangerous foes, who fell in battle against the famed Carthaginian in 208 BC, quoted in Plutarch, *The Lives*, c. AD 100 (*Makers of Rome*, tr. Ian Scott-Kilvert, 1965).

HERE STOOD fewer than sixty men against an entire army. Its weight overwhelmed them. Life, sooner than courage, forsook these soldiers of France.

The inscription to the last stand of the Third Company of the Foreign Legion Regiment at Cambrone, Mexico, on 30 April 1863, a desperate action so heroic that it became the Legion's founding legend.

IN MEMORY of the brave warriors who fell here in 1879 in defence of the old Zulu order.

Inscription on the Ulundi battlefield monument, South Africa.

TO THE GLORY OF GOD

In Memory of the heroic Americans of the Seventh
  Army and of the
supporting units of the Navy and Air Force
who gave their lives for victory in the Sicilian
  campaign,
July 10–August 17, 1943
– From their General

> Inscription on a broken propeller placed in the
> British church in Palermo by General George S.
> Patton, Jr., quoted in Carlo d'Este, *Patton: A
> Genius For War*, 1995.

WHEN you go home
Tell them of us and say,
For their tomorrow
We gave our today.

> Inscription on the monument of the British Second
> Division on Garrison Hill at Kohima, India,
> commemorating the 17,587 British casualties at the
> Battle of Kohima, 5 April–30 May 1944.

THIS EMBATTLED shore, portal of freedom, is
forever hallowed by the ideals, the valor and the
sacrifices of our fellow countrymen.

> Inscription on the monument to the American dead on
> the Normandy battlefield, commemorating the
> Normandy Campaign, 6 June–1 August 1944.

"NOT IN VAIN" may be the pride of those who
survived and the epitaph of those who fell.

> Sir Winston S. Churchill, 28 September 1944, speech
> in the House of Commons in tribute to the British First
> Airborne Division's sacrifice at the Battle of Arnhem.

EQUILIBRIUM/BALANCE

MANY THINGS can cause a loss of balance. One
cause is danger, another is hardship, and another is
surprise. You must research this.
  In large-scale strategy it is important to cause loss
of balance. Attack without warning where the enemy
is not expecting it, and while his spirit is undecided
follow up your advantage and, having the lead,
defeat him.

> Miyamoto Musashi, *A Book of Five Rings*, 1645,
> tr. Victor Harris, 1984.

ALL IN ALL, loss of moral equilibrium must not be
underestimated merely because it has no absolute
value and does not always show up in the final
balance. It can attain such massive proportions that
it overpowers everything by its irresistible force. For
this reason it may in itself become a main objective
of the action. . . .

> Major-General Carl von Clausewitz, *On War*, 4.4,
> 1832, tr. Michael Howard and Peter Paret, 1976.

WAR is in itself only a matter of maintaining

harmonious proportion between the spiritual and
material elements. Fundamentally that is so. If no such
proportion is attained, however excellent an army may
be, it can do nothing against its adversaries.

> Marshal of France Ferdinand Foch, quoted in Liddell
> Hart, *Foch, the Man of Orleans*, 1931.

ESPRIT DE CORPS

ALL THAT can be done with the soldier is to give
him *esprit de corps* – i.e., a higher opinion of his
own regiment than all the other troops in the country.

> Frederick the Great, *Military Testament*, 1768.

PERSONAL BRAVERY of a single individual does
not decide on the day of battle, but the bravery of
the unit, and the latter rests on the good opinion
and the confidence that each individual places in
the unit to which he belongs. The exterior
splendour, the regularity of movements, the
adroitness, and at the same time the firmness of the
mass – all this gives the individual soldier the safe
and calming conviction that nothing can withstand
his particular regiment or battalion.

> Field Marshal Francois Comte de Guibert
> (1744–1790), quoted in Keegan, *Soldiers*, 1986.

. . . (ESPRIT DE CORPS) which does not forget
itself in the heat of action and which alone makes
true combatants. Then we have an army; and it is no
longer difficult to explain how men carried away by
passion, even men who know how to die without
flinching, without turning pale, really strong in the
presence of death, but without discipline, without
solid organization, are vanquished by others
individually less valiant, but firmly, jointly, and
severally knit into a fighting unit.

> Colonel Charles Ardant du Picq, *Battle Studies*, 1880,
> tr. Greely, 1957.

I HAVE ALLUDED before to the esprit de corps,
founded as it was upon the sentiment of saving life –
sentiment to which appeal has never failed. Other
factors went to strengthen it. It was braced by a high
standard of results demanded, by determination to
make good in spite of partial first success. But the
strongest element in it was the faith in our weapon –
the machine necessary to supplement the other
machines of war, in order to break the stalemate
produced by the great German weapon, the
machine-gun – our mobile offensive answer to the
immobile defensive man-killer.

> Major-General Hugh Elles, Commander of the British
> Tank Corps in WWI, quoted in the preface to William
> Ellis, *The Tank Corps*, 1919.

ESPRIT . . . is the product of a thriving mutual
confidence between the leader and the led, founded
on the faith that together they possess a superior
quality and capability. The failure of the spirit of any

military organization is less frequently due to what men have forgotten than to what they can't forget. No "imperishable record" of past greatness can make men serve with any greater vigor if they are being served badly. Nor can it sustain the fighting will of the organization so much as one mil beyond the radius within which living associations enable men to think great thoughts and act with nobility toward their fellows. Unless the organization's past conveys to its officers a sense of having been especially chosen, and unless they respond to this trust by developing a complete sense of duty toward their men, the old battle records might as well be poured down the drain, since they will not rally a single man in the hour of danger.

Brigadier-General S.L.A. Marshall, *The Armed Forces Officer*, 1950.

GIVEN SUCH OFFICERS, the organization comes to possess a sense of unity and of fraternity in its routine existence which express itself as the force of cohesion in the hour when all ranks are confronted by a common danger. It is not because of mutual enthusiasm for an honored name but because of mutual confidence in one another that the ranks of old regiments or the bluejackets serving a ship with a great tradition are able to convert their esprit into battle discipline. Under stress they move and act together because they have imbibed the great lesson, and experience has made its application almost instinctive, that only in unity is their safety. They believe that they can trust their comrades and commanders as they would trust their next of kin. They have learned the necessity of mutual support and a common danger serves but to bind the ranks closer.

Brigadier-General S.L.A. Marshall, *The Armed Forces Officer*, 1950.

WELL, the main thing – that I have remembered all my life – is the definition of **esprit de corps**. Now my definition – the definition I was taught, that I've always believed in – is that **esprit de corps** means love for one's military legion, in my case the United States Marine Corps. I also learned that this loyalty to one's Corps travels both ways, up and down.

Lieutenant-General Lewis B. 'Chesty' Puller, 13 August 1956, quoted in Burke Davis, *Marine!*, 1962.

I WANTED to imbue my crews with enthusiasm and a complete faith in their arm and to instill in them a spirit of selfless readiness to serve in it. Only those possessed of such a spirit could hope to succeed in the grim realities of submarine warfare. Professional skill alone would not survive.

Admiral Karl Dönitz, *Memoirs, Ten Years and Twenty Days*, 1959.

WITH THE 82d and the 101st living side by side, a new factor was added to the prejudice of good order and discipline: the growing rivalry between the members of the divisions which, as the war went on, became famous throughout the Army. Sometimes it was wholesome and constructive, sometimes it was partisan and acrimonious, but in whatever form it created many problems in unit and individual relationships. Actually it was the rivalry of twin brothers who were so much alike in temperament as to be indistinguishable to innocent bystanders who soon discovered to their sorrow how quickly they would put aside family quarrels to turn on outsiders. Having served in both divisions in the course of the war, I could never have chosen between them except for the inevitable bias which came from having commanded the 101st. One's own division is necessarily number one.

General Maxwell Taylor, *Swords and Ploughshares*, 1972.

EXAMPLE

QUIET!
They said in the presence of his majesty: "What is it like to go on this road which becomes so narrow? It is reported that the foe is there waiting on the outside, while they are becoming more numerous. Will not horse have to go after horse, and the army and the people similarly? Will the vanguard of us be fighting while the rear guard is waiting here in Aruna, unable to fight? Now two other roads are here. One of the roads – behold, it is to the east of us, so that it comes out at Taanach. The other – behold, it is to the north side of Djefti, and will come out to the north of Megiddo. Let our victorious lord proceed on the one of them which is satisfactory to his heart, but do not make us go on that difficult road!"

". . . I swear as Re loves me, as my father Amon favors me, as my nostrils are rejuvenated with life and satisfaction, my majesty shall proceed upon this Aruna road! Let him of you who wishes go upon these roads of which you speak, and let him of you who wishes come in the following of my majesty! "Behold," they will say, these enemies whom Re abominates, "has his majesty set out on another road because he has become afraid of us?" – so they will speak."

They said in the presence of his majesty: "May thy father Amon, Lord of the Thrones of the Two Lands, Presiding over Karnak, act according to thy desire! Behold, we are following thy majesty everywhere that thy majesty goes, for a servant will be after his lord."

Then his majesty laid a charge upon the entire army: "Ye shall hold fast to the stride of your victorious lord on that road which becomes so narrow. Behold, his majesty has taken an oath, saying: "I will not let my victorious army go forth ahead of my majesty in this place!" Now his majesty had laid it in his heart that he himself should go forth at the head of his army. Every man was made aware of his order of march, horse following horse, while his majesty was at the head of his army.

Thutmose III (c. 1469 BC), account of his first Asiatic Campaign leading to the Battle of Megiddo, quoted in Pritchard, ed., *The Ancient Near East*, I, 1958.

I CHARGED all countries, while I was alone, my infantry and my chariotry having forsaken me. Not one among them stood to turn about. I swear, as Re Loves me, as my father, Atum, favors me, that as for every matter which his majesty has stated, I did it in truth, in the presence of my infantry and my chariotry.

> Rameses II, 1284 BC, in his own words of the Battle of Kadesh when the Hittites surprised his camp and cut him off from even his escort; he rallied his men by charging single-handed into the mass of Hittite chariots to cut a way through, quoted in James Breasted, *Ancient Records of Egypt*, 1906.

THE GENERAL shares heat and cold, labor and suffering, hunger and satiety with the officers and men. Therefore when the masses of the Three Armies hear the sound of the drum they are happy, and when they hear the sound of the gong they are angry. When attacking a high wall or crossing a deep lake, under a hail of arrows and stones, the officers will compete to be first to scale the wall. When the naked blades clash, the officers will compete to be the first to go forward. It is not because they like death and take pleasure in being wounded, but because the general knows their feelings of heat and cold, hunger and satiety, and clearly displays his knowledge of their labor and suffering.

> The T'ai Kung, c. 1100 BC (*The Seven Military Classics of Ancient China*, tr. Ralph Sawyer, 1993).

BEFORE the army's watering hole has been reached, the commander does not speak of thirst; before the fires have food on them, the commander does not speak of hunger.

> Sun Tzu, c. 500 BC, a passage recovered from later encyclopaedic works and commentaries not found in *The Art of War*, quoted in *Sun Tzu: The Art of Warfare*, tr. Roger Ames, 1993.

ALL THESE SOLDIERS have their eyes on you. If they see you are discouraged they will all be cowards; but if you show that you are making preparations against the enemy, and if you call on them, you may be sure they will follow you and try to imitate you. Perhaps it is fair to expect you to be a bit better than they are. You are captain, you see, and you are in command of troops and companies, and while there was peace, you had more wealth and honour; then now when war has come, we must ask you to be better than the mob, and to plan and labour for their behalf, if necessary.

> Xenophon, rallying the few surviving officers of the Ten Thousand to action, after most of the officers were murdered under truce by the Persians in 401 BC, *The March Up Country*, c. 360 BC, tr. W.H.D. Rouse.

PERHAPS you will say, that in my position as your commander, I had none of the labours and distress which you had to endure to win for me what I have won. But does any man among you honestly feel that he has suffered more for me than I have suffered for him? Come now – if you are wounded, strip and show your wounds, and I will show mine. There is no part of my body but my back which has not a scar; not a weapon a man may grasp or fling the mark of which I do not carry upon me. I have sword-cuts from close fight; arrows have pierced me, missiles from catapults bruised my flesh; again and again I have been struck by stones or clubs – and all for your sakes: for your glory and your gain. Over every land and sea, across river, mountain, and plain I led you to the world's end, a victorious army.

> Alexander the Great, 323 BC, to his troops at Opis in Babylonia, quoted in Arrian, *The Campaigns of Alexander*, 7.10, c. AD 100, tr. Aubrey de Sélincourt, 1987.

IF THE GENERAL is in haste to finish some enterprise that he has on hand, he should not hesitate to be prominent in the work, for soldiers are not forced to activity so much by the threats of their immediate superiors as by the influence of men of higher rank. For a soldier seeing his officer the first to put his hand to the task not only realizes the need of haste too but also is ashamed not to work, and afraid to disobey orders; and the rank and file no longer feel that they are being treated as slaves under orders but are moved as though urged by one on the same footing as themselves.

> Onasander, *The General*, AD 58, (*Aeneas Tacticus, Aclepiodotus, Onasander*, tr. The Illinois Greek Club, 1923).

ACCORDING to the code of generalship, generals do not say they are thirsty before the soldiers have drawn from the well; generals do not say they are hungry before the soldiers' food is cooked; generals do not say they are cold before the soldiers' fires are kindled; generals do not say they are hot before the soldiers' canopies are drawn. Generals do not use fans in summer, do not wear leather in winter, do not use umbrellas in the rain. They do as everyone does.

> Zhuge Liang (AD 180–234), *The Way of the General* (*Mastering the Art of War*, tr. Thomas Cleary, 1989).

IN CARRYING OUT very critical operations the general ought not set himself apart as though such labor was beneath him, but he should begin the work and toil along with his troops as much as possible. Such behavior will lead the soldier to be more submissive to his officers, even if only out of shame, and he will accomplish more.

> The Emperor Maurice, *The Strategikon*, c. AD 600 (*Maurice's Strategikon*, tr. George Dennis, 1984).

THE GENERAL should set an example of how things ought to be done for his subordinates, training himself in the highest ideals, doing what is right and refraining from those things his soldiers should refrain from.

> The Emperor Maurice, *The Strategikon*, c. AD 600 (*Maurice's Strategikon*, tr. George Dennis, 1984).

ESSENTIAL to generalship is to share the pleasures and pains of the troops. If you encounter danger, do not abandon the troops to save yourself, do not seek personal escape from difficulties confronting you. Rather, make every effort to protect the troops, sharing their fate. If you do this, the soldiers will not forget you.

The rule is "When you see danger and difficulty, do not forget the troops" ("Sima's Art of War").

> Liu Ji (1310–1375), *Lessons of War* (*Mastering the Art of War*, tr. Thomas Cleary, 1989).

I USED TO SAY to them, "go boldly in among the English," and then I used to go boldly in myself.

> Joan of Arc, 3 March 1430, to her inquisitors who intimated that her success was due to luck, quoted in Edward Creasy, *Decisive Battles of the World*, 1899.

ONE SHOULD take care in his activities so that he will be without negligence. In the *Shih Chi* it says, "If the master acts correctly, his retainers will perform well, even if given no commands. But if the master acts incorrectly, even though he gives commands they will not be followed."

> Takeda Nobushige (1525–1561), *Opinions in 99 Articles*, 1558 (*Ideals of the Samurai*, tr. William Wilson, 1982).

I, YOUR KING and leader, will go ahead and show every one the path of honor.

> Gustavus II Adolphus, 14 November 1632, to his commanders on the day before the Battle of Lützen, where he met his death, quoted in Theodore Ayrault Dodge, *Gustavus Adolphus*, 1895.

I WILL NOT send troops to dangers which I will not myself encounter.

> The Duke of Marlborough (1650–1722), quoted in Sir Winston S. Churchill, *Marlborough*, 1933.

I AM NOW at an age when I find no heat in my blood that gives me temptation to expose myself out of vanity; but as I would deserve and keep the kindness of this army, I must let them see that when I expose them, I would not exempt myself.

> The Duke of Marlborough (1650–1722), quoted in Sir Winston S. Churchill, *Marlborough*, 1933.

DRILL your soldiers well, and give them a pattern yourself.

> Alexander V. Suvorov (1729–1800), quoted in W. Lyon Blease, *Suvorof*, 1920.

WELL, I will let you see that I was a grenadier before I was a marshal, and still am one!

> Marshal of France Jean Lannes, 23 April 1809, seizing a scaling ladder and advancing alone on the Austrian-held fortifications of Ratisbonne when his men hesitated, quoted in Baron Marbot, *The Memoirs of Baron Marbot*, I, 1892.

IS IT NOT the manner in which the leaders carry out the tasks of command, of impressing their resolution in the hearts of others, that makes them warriors, far more than all other aptitudes or facilities which theory may expect of them?

> General Gerhardt von Scharnhorst, quoted in George C. Marshall, ed., *Infantry in Battle*, 1939.

AS IF THE FORCES in one individual after another become prostrated, and can no longer be excited and supported by an effort of his own will, the whole inertia of the mass gradually rests its weight on the will of the commander: by the spark in his breast, by the light of his spirit, the spark of purpose, the light of hope, must be kindled afresh in others.

> Major-General Carl von Clausewitz, *On War*, 1832, tr. Michael Howard and Peter Paret, 1976.

I CAN'T BE absent, as my attention is necessary in preparing my troops for hard fighting, should it be required; and as my officers and soldiers are not permitted to visit their wives and families, I ought not to see mine. It might make the troops feel that they are badly treated, and that I consult my own comfort, regardless of theirs. . . .

> Lieutenant-General Thomas J. 'Stonewall' Jackson, quoted in Dabney, *Life of Jackson*, I, 1866.

I CANNOT CONSENT to be feasting while my poor soldiers are nearly starving.

> General Robert E. Lee, upon refusing all but the plainest fare when served an elegant dinner on a visit to a great house, quoted in William Jones, *Personal Reminiscences*, 1874.

JACKSON is with you . . . Rally, brave men, and press forward. Your general will lead you. Jackson will lead you. Follow me!

> Lieutenant-General Thomas J. 'Stonewall' Jackson, 9 August 1862, rallying his shattered troops during the Battle of Cedar Mountain, quoted in David Martin, *The Second Bull Run Campaign*, 1997.

AS TO MY exposing myself unnecessarily, you need not be concerned. I know better than C—— where danger lies and where I should be. Soldiers have a right to see and know that the man who guides them is near enough to see with his own eyes, and that he cannot see without being seen.

> General William T. Sherman, letter to his wife from a camp near Vicksburg, 28 January 1863, *Home Letters*, 1909.

THERE ARE TIMES when a corps commander's life does not count.

> Major-General Winfield Scott Hancock, 3 July 1863, remark to an officer who cautioned him not to expose himself as he rode along the stone wall at the High Water Mark at Gettysburg during the Confederate bombardment, as an example to the men of his glorious Second Corps awaiting Pickett's Charge.

REGULAR DISCIPLINE will bring men to any amount of endurance, but there is a natural fear of hidden dangers, particularly when so awfully destructive of human life as the torpedo, which requires more than discipline to overcome. . . . After I saw the Tecumseh, struck by a torpedo, disappear almost instantly, beneath the waves . . . I determined at once, as I had originally intended to take the lead; and . . . I dashed ahead with the Hartford and the ships followed on, their officers believing they were going to a noble death with their commander-in-chief.

> Admiral David G. Farragut, report of the Battle of Mobile Bay, 5 August 1864, quoted in John Spears, *David G. Farragut*, 1905. A 'torpedo' was what is now known as a 'mine'.

I HAVE NEVER, on the field of battle, sent you where I was unwilling to go myself; nor would I now advise you to a course which I felt myself unwilling to pursue. You *have been* good soldiers; you *can* be good citizens. Obey the laws, preserve your honor, and the Government to which you have surrendered can afford to be, and will be magnanimous.

> Lieutenant-General Nathan Bedford Forrest, 9 May 1865, farewell to Forrest's Cavalry Corps at Gainesville, Georgia, quoted in *As They Saw Forrest*, 1956.

OFFICERS should never seek for houses, but share the conditions of the men.

> General of the Army William T. Sherman, *Memoirs of General W.T. Sherman*, 1875.

I AM GETTING ON for sixty, and this old body of mine is no longer worth caring for. But you are all young men with futures before you, so take care of yourselves and continue living in order to serve your country.

> Admiral Marquis Heihachiro Togo, 1905, to his staff at the Battle of Tsushima, quoted in Dennis and Peggy Warner, *The Tide at Sunrise*, 1974.

YOU SHOULD NEVER forget the power of example. The young men serving as enlisted men take their cue from you. If you conduct yourselves at all times as officers and gentlemen should conduct themselves, the moral tone of the whole Corps will be raised, its reputation, which is most precious to all of us, will be enhanced, and the esteem and affection in which the Corps is held by the American people will be increased.

> Major-General John A. Lejeune, 19 September 1922, Letter No. 1. to the Officer of the Marine Corps from the Commandant.

THUS we see how surely the physical is the foundation of the moral, and how these physical defects, for defects they are in war, react upon a general's moral sense by subordinating it to intellectual achievements. More and more do strategical, administrative and tactical details occupy his mind and pinch out the moral side of his nature.

Should he be a man of ability, he becomes a thinker rather than a doer, a planner rather than a leader, until morally he is as far removed from his men as a chess player is from the chessmen on his board. The more he is thrown back upon the intellectual side of war, the more sedentary he becomes, until a kind of military scholasticism enwarps his whole life.

The repercussion of such generalship on subordinate command has always been lamentable, because whatever a general may be, he is always the example which the bulk of his subordinate commanders will follow. If he becomes an office soldier, they become office soldiers; not only because his work makes their work, but because his morale makes their morale: how can he order them into danger if he remains in safety? If the general-in-chief does not face discomfort and danger neither will they; if they do not, neither will their subordinates, until the repercussion exhausts itself in a devitalized firing line.

> Major-General J.F.C. Fuller, *Generalship: Its Diseases and Their Cure*, 1933.

BE AN EXAMPLE to your men, both in your duty and in private life. Never spare yourself, and let the troops see that you don't, in your endurance of fatigue and privation. Always be tactful and well mannered and teach your subordinates to be the same. Avoid excessive sharpness or harshness of voice, which usually indicates the man who has shortcomings of his own to hide.

> Field Marshal Erwin Rommel, 1938, remarks to graduating cadets of the Wiener Neustadt Military School.

BE A MODEL of valor by example and precept.

> Lieutenant-General Lewis B. 'Chesty' Puller, 1942, to his officers and NCOs before the landing of the First Marine Division on Guadalcanal, quoted in the Puller Collection, Marine Corps Historical Division.

GENTLEMEN, at least we've all been blooded now. I don't want you to be mooning over the losses and feeling sorry for yourselves or taking all the blame on your shoulders. We've all got to leave this world some day; we're all in the same pickle. And there are worse things than dying for your country. Some things about our action in the last four days I want you to remember forever. There are some we'd all like to forget – but they'll be in your mind's eye as long as you live. I hope we've all learned something. Now take care of your men, and make yourselves ready. We haven't seen anything yet.

One other thing. Back there on the hillside at Mount Austen, I had trouble getting company officers up. I hope you saw what that cost us in casualties. Never do I want to see that again in my command. I want to see my officers leading. I want you to know that you're leaders, and not simply commanders. You cannot operate a military force in the field under these conditions with commanders alone. Civilians wouldn't know what I was talking about, but you've found out now that it's true: There are many qualities in a man, but one that is absolutely necessary in an infantry leader is stark courage. Give that idea to your men in your own way.

Lieutenant-General Lewis B. 'Chesty' Puller, to his officers at Guadalcanal, 1943, quoted in Burke Davis, *Marine!*, 1962.

FEAR is always worse when man is isolated; it is least prominent when following an example. This consideration points to the true cellule of combat on which tactics should be built up. The little compact group formed of men who have long shared their training and recreation, following the leader they know and who has trained them, is the ideal formation for battle. Example is better, as an antidote to fear, than the companionship of equals.

Captain Sir Basil Liddell Hart, *Thoughts on War*, 1944.

IN COLD WEATHER, General Officers must be careful not to appear to dress more warmly than the men.

General George S. Patton, Jr., *War As I Knew It*, 1947.

TO THE YOUNG OFFICER who is conscious of his own reserve and is anxious to do something about it, I can suggest nothing better than to make a habit of full physical participation. That is, instead of watching the squad or platoon work out a problem and either directing or criticizing its action, let him pick up a weapon, relieve one man in the group, then let himself be one of the commanded until the conclusion of the operation. Is this course of conduct beneath the dignity of an American officer? Certainly not!

Brigadier-General S.L.A. Marshall, *Men Against Fire*, 1947.

THE SMALL UNIT commander who practices self-exposure to danger in the hope of having a good moral effect on men, instead, frays the nerves of troops and most frequently succeeds in getting himself killed under conditions which do no earthly good to the army. Troops expect to see their officers working and moving *with* them; morale is impaired when they see that their leaders are shirking danger. But they do not care to see them play the part of a mechanical rabbit, darting to the front so as to tease on the hounds. In extreme emergencies, when the stakes are high and the failure of others to act has made the need imperative, such acts are warranted. But their value lies largely in their novelty. A commander cannot rally his men by a spectacular intervention in the hour when they have lost their grip if they have grown accustomed to seeing him run unnecessary risks in the average circumstances of battle.

Brigadier-General S.L.A. Marshall, *Men Against Fire*, 1947.

OPTIMISM and pessimism are infectious and they spread more rapidly from the head downward than in any other direction. . . . I firmly determined that my

mannerisms and speech in public would always reflect the cheerful certainty of victory – that any pessimism and discouragement I might ever feel would be reserved for my pillow.

General of the Army Dwight D. Eisenhower (1890–1969), quoted in *Military Review*, 10/1990.

ONLY THOSE who have disciplined themselves can exact disciplined performance from others. When the chips are down, when privation mounts and the casualty rates rise, when the crisis is at hand, which commander, I ask, receives the better response? Is it the one who has failed to share the rough going with his troops, who is rarely seen in the zone of aimed fire, and who expects much and gives little? Or is it the one whose every thought is for the welfare of his men, consistent with the accomplishment of the mission; who does not ask them to do what he has not already done and stands ready to do again when necessary; who with his men has shared short rations, the physical discomforts and rigors of campaign, and will be found at the crisis of action where the issues are to be decided?

General Matthew B. Ridgway, 'Leadership', *Military Review*, 10/1966.

I HAD HAD the unpleasant duty of terminating the service of a young career officer who had ordered a soldier to proceed on a dangerous action while he himself sat in safety. A vehicle of ours was stuck close to the border of the Gaza Strip and was under heavy fire from the Egyptians. The officer in charge sent a driver to retrieve it, while he himself lay behind cover and issued directions from there. I told the cadets: "I would not have dismissed this officer if he had decided that the danger was too great and it was better to abandon the vehicle rather than endanger lives. But if he decided to take daring action and save the vehicle, he should have advanced with his troops and laid his own life on the line together with theirs. Officers of the Israeli army do not send their men into battle. They lead them into battle."

General Moshe Dayan, *The Story of My Life*, 1976.

THE POWER of example is very important to people under stress. For one thing it affords an outlet for hero worship, to which there seems to be an important and deep-rooted inclination in men. The person under stress is aware of inadequacies. He sees someone else apparently less burdened in this way. To some extent he identifies with that other person. This gives him some release. He is then likely to be grateful and become even more biddable. He will be even more open to the influence of suggestion and example than he was before.

General Sir John Hackett, *The Profession of Arms*, 1983.

OUR LEADERS will discover also that part of their duty involves teaching. Every great leader I have known has been a great teacher, able to give those around him a sense of perspective and to set the moral, social, and motivational climate among his followers. This takes wisdom and discipline and requires both the sensitivity to perceive philosophical disarray in one's charges and the knowledge of how to put things in order. A leader must aspire to a strength, a compassion, and a conviction several octaves above that held sufficient by the workaday world. He must be at home under pressure and can never settle for the lifestyle or the outlook of that sheltered man on the street whom Joseph Conrad characterized as ". . . skimming over the years of existence to sink gently into a placid grave, ignorant of life to the last, without ever being made to see all it may contain of perfidy, or violence, or terror."

Admiral James B. Stockdale, 'Educating Leaders', *Washington Quarterly*, Winter 1983.

HOW THE HELL are you going to lead troops if they're freezing their butts off beneath shelter halves and you're dozing in a warm tent? A warm man can't understand a cold man's problems.

Lieutenant-Colonel Jack Nix, quoted in *Newsweek*, 18 April 1988.

EXERCISES/MANOEUVRES

SO SENSIBLE were the Romans of the imperfections of valor without skill and practice that, in their language, the name of an Army, was borrowed from the word which signified exercise.

(*Exercitus* means Army in Latin)
Edward Gibbon, *Decline and Fall of the Roman Empire*, 1776.

[EXERCISES] cultivated self-reliance – the foundation of courage.

Field Marshal Prince Aleksandr V. Suvorov (1729–1800), quoted in K. Ossipov, *Suvorov*, 1945.

THE SPLENDID MOTTO of the Infantry School: "Follow Me" certainly refutes . . . training and maneuvers . . . [where] there are a good many backward glances for inspiration.

General George S. Patton, Jr., January 1928, *The Patton Papers*, I, 1972.

IF THE EXERCISE is subsequently discussed in the officers' mess, it is probably worth while; if there is argument over it in the sergeants' mess, it is a good excercise; while if it should be mentioned in the corporals' room, it is an undoubted success.

Field Marshal Viscount Wavell of Cyrenaica, *Journal of the Royal United Services Institution*, May 1933.

TACTICAL EXERCISES set to bring out . . . tactical lessons are not worth the setting. What an exercise

should bring out is the personality and common sense of the generals.

Major-General J.F.C. Fuller, *Generalship: Its Diseases and Their Cure*, 1933.

TO ME, as to Clausewitz, "war lies in the realm of chance"; then, surely, should peace exercises lie there also. Every problem, I held, is a new picture, yet set in an old frame – the principles of war. Peace exercises should, therefore, test out wits, and not merely knowledge of the regulations. The unexpected is, consequently, their essence; and to make certain of the unexpected, all that is necessary is to arrange a clash, and then leave it to Commanders to fight it out; not to win, but to prove which of the two is the livest man can apply the principles in the livest way.

Major-General J.F.C. Fuller, *Memoirs of an Unconventional Soldier*, 1936.

WAR makes extremely heavy demands on the soldier's strength and nerves. For this reason make heavy demands on your men in peacetime exercises.

Field Marshal Erwin Rommel, *Infantry Attacks*, 1944.

TO SUM UP, I think we are too ponderous and too infrequent in our maneuver efforts; that we are too limited as to terrain and play too much on the home grounds; that we do not obtain sufficient appropriations for this vitally important business; that a determined effort must be made to amend laws, change regulations, evolve systems which will enable us to offset the present theoretical training (due to too many desks and details, mostly unavoidable) in order that the Army may properly train for its real purpose, as a matter of annual routine. (1938)

General of the Army George C. Marshall, quoted in Pogue, *The Soldierly Spirit, December 1880–June 1939*, 1981.

THERE ARE NO bullets in maneuvers, and things sometimes get a little dull. But play the game; don't lie in the shade. . . . Try, above all things, to use your imagination. Think this is war. "What would I do if that man were really shooting at me?" That is the only chance, men, that you are going to have to practice. The next time, maybe, there will be no umpires, and the bullets will be very real, both yours and the enemy's.

General George S. Patton, Jr., 17 May 1941, address to the officers and men of the Second Armored Division, *The Patton Papers*, II, 1974.

EXHORTATIONS BEFORE THE BATTLE

BE MEN, my friends! Discipline fill your hearts, maintain your pride in the eyes of other men! Remember, each of you, sons, wives, wealth, parents –

are mother and father dead or alive? No matter,
I beg you for their sakes, loved ones far away –
now stand and fight, no turning back, no panic.

Homer, *The Iliad*, 15.769–774, tr. Robert Fagles, 1990;
King Nestor of Pylos exhorting the Achaean Army at
bay to stand and fight.

HE . . . said that there was no need for him to
inspire them to the fight; they had long ago been
inspired by their own bravery and by their many
splendid exploits in the past; but he required each
of them to encourage his own men; the infantry
captains their companies, the squadron
commanders their own squadrons, the battalion
commanders their battalions, and the infantry
commanders the phalanx of which each was placed
in charge. In this battle, he pointed out, they were
to fight, not as before, for Hollow Syria or Phoenicia
or Egypt: it was the sovereignty of all Asia that was
there and then to be decided. There was then no
need for them to employ long speeches to make
their men act with that sense of honour which was
born in them, but they were to urge each man in
the moment of danger to attend in his own place in
the line to the requirements of order, to keep
perfect silence when that was necessary in the
advance, and by contrast to give a ringing shout
when it was right to shout, and howl to inspire
greatest terror when the moment came to howl;
they themselves were to obey orders sharply and
to pass them on sharply to their regiments, and
every man should recall that neglect of his own
duty brought the whole cause into common danger,
while energetic attention to it contributed to their
common success.

Arrian, describing Alexander's instructions to his
officers before the Battle of Gaugamela (Arbela),
1 October 331 BC, *Anabasis of Alexander*, 3.9,
c. AD 150, tr. P.A. Brunt, 1976.

NOW IS gode tyme, for alle Engelond prayeth for us;
and therefore be of gode chere, and lette us go to
our iorney. . . . In the name of Almyghti God and
Saynt George, avant banerer! And Saynte George,
this day thyn help.

Henry V, 14 October 1415, at the Battle of Agincourt.

IN GOD'S NAME! Let us go bravely!

Joan of Arc, 6 May 1429, in the assault on the English
fortress of the Augustines, *Joan of Arc In Her Own
Words*, 1996.

OH, VALIANT WARRIORS, the entire land of
Xochimilco is against us and they outnumber
us, but let this not trouble you. Strength and
spirit are what matter! Be informed that our
enemy is very near us, in a place called Ocolco,
and the battle will take place there. Therefore,
O Aztecs, make your name ring out as you have
always done.

Tlacaelel, Generalissimo of the Aztecs (mid-1440s),

quoted in Fray Diego Durán, *The History of the Indies
of New Spain*, 1581, tr. Doris Heyden, 1994.

THE CITY and the buildings are mine; but I resign
to your valour the captives and the spoil, the
treasures of gold and beauty; be rich and be happy.
Many are the provinces of my empire: the intrepid
soldier who first ascends the walls of
Constantinople shall be rewarded with the
government of the fairest and most wealthy; and my
gratitude shall accumulate his honours and fortunes
above all measure of his own hopes.

Mehmet II the Conquerer, exhortation to his army at
the beginning of the siege of Constantinople (1453),
quoted in Edward Gibbon, *The Decline and Fall of the
Roman Empire*, III, 1776.

IT IS the great battle of the Cross and Koran, which
is now to be fought. A formidable army of infidels are
on the point of investing our island. We, for our part,
are the chosen soldiers of the Cross, and if Heaven
requires the sacrifice of our lives, there can be no
better occasion than this. Let us hasten then, my
brothers, to the sacred altar. There we will renew our
vows and obtain, by our Faith in the Sacred
Sacraments, that contempt for death which alone
can render us invincible.

Jean de la Valette, Grand Master of the Order of the
Knights of St. John of Jerusalem, mid-May 1565,
address to the Brethren of the Order just before the
epic siege of Malta by the fleet and army of Suleyman
the Magnificent, quoted in Ernle Bradford, *The Great
Siege, Malta 1565*, 1961.

MY LOVING PEOPLE! My loving people! We have
been persuaded by some that are careful of our
safety, to take heed how we commit ourselves to
armed multitudes from fear of treachery. But I do
assure you, I do not desire to live to distrust the
faithful and loving people.

Let tyrants fear! I have always so behaved
myself that, under God, I have placed my chiefest
strength and safeguard in the loyal hearts and
goodwill of my subjects. Therefore, I am come
amongst you as you see at this time, not for my
recreation and disport, but being resolved, in the
midst and heat of the battle, to live or die amongst
you all – to lay down for my God and for my
kingdoms, and for my people, my honor and my
blood even in the dust!

I know I have the body of a weak and feeble
woman, but I have the heart and stomach of a King,
and of a King of England too, and think foul scorn
that Parma or Spain, or any Prince of Europe should
dare to invade the borders of my realm, to which,
rather than any dishonour should grow by me, I
myself will take up arms.

Elizabeth I, 19 August 1588, the Tilbury Speech, to
the English Army assembled at Tilbury camp ready
to repel the invasion of the Spanish army aboard
the Armada.

HARK! I hear the drum.
Forward in God's name! Jesu! Jesu!
> Gustavus II Adolphus, 15 November 1632, to his army as he led it into the Battle of Lützen, where he met his death, quoted in Theodore Ayrault Dodge, *Gustavus Adolphus*, 1895.

WE HAVE BEATEN this same enemy, you and I. Today you fight not for Poland but for Christianity; not for your king, but for your God! I have but one order for you: Wherever you see your king, follow and fear not!
> Jan III Sobieski, 12 September 1683, as he led the Polish attack on the Ottoman Army besieging Vienna, quoted in Theodore Ayrault Dodge, *Gustavus Adolphus*, 1895.

BY PUSH of bayonets, no firing til you see the whites of their eyes.
> Frederick the Great, at Prague, 6 May 1757.

COMRADES, in front of you are 4,000 young men belonging to the richest families in Vienna; they have come with post-horses as far as Bassano; I recommend them to you.
> Marshal Masséna, 15 January 1797, at the Battle of Rivoli, to which his troops responded with a roar of laughter and advanced with a shout of *'En avant!'*, quoted in R.W. Phipps, *The Armies of the First French Republic*, IV, 1935–1939.

SOLDIERS! Forty centuries behold you!
> Napoleon, 21 July 1798, to his army before the Battle of the Pyramids, quoted in R.M. Johnston, ed., *The Corsican*, 1910.

ENGLAND expects every man will do his duty.
> Admiral Viscount Nelson, 21 October 1805, order to the fleet before the Battle of Trafalgar, quoted in Churchill, *A History of the English-Speaking Peoples: The Age of Revolution*, 1957. Robert Southey's *Life of Nelson* has 'England expects every may to do his duty'. Most other sources agree with the Churchill wording.

SOLDIERS, here at last is the battle that you have so long expected! Victory now depends on your efforts, and is essential. It will give us abundance, good winter quarters, and a speedy return to our country. Do what you did at Austerlitz, at Friedland, at Vitebsk, at Smolensk, and let posterity point with pride to your conduct on this day: let people say of you: "He was at that great battle fought under the walls of Moscow!"
> Napoleon, 7 September 1812, on the heights of Borodino, quoted in R.M. Johnston, ed., *The Corsican*, 1910.

AFTER the extraordinary successes we have daily achieved over the enemy, everywhere, we have now only to pursue him swiftly, and then, perhaps, the soil of Russia which he had dreamed of subjugating will be bestrewn with his bones. And so we shall pursue him tirelessly. Winter is coming with its blizzards and frost, but has it any terrors for you, children of the North? Our steel hearts fear neither the inclemency of the weather nor the wrath of our enemy: they form a reliable bulwark for our country against which everything is crushed. You will be able to stand temporary privation should this occur. Good soldiers are distinguished by their staunchness and patience; the veteran will set an example to the novice. Let every one of you remember Suvorov, who taught us to bear cold and hunger when victory and the glory of the Russian people were at stake.
> Field Marshal Mikhail Kutuzov (1812), exhortation to his army upon the pursuit of Napoleon after he abandoned Moscow, quoted in Bragin, *Field Marshal Kutuzov*, 1944.

SOLDIERS! This is the anniversary of Marengo and of Friedland, that twice decided the fate of Europe. Then, as at Wagram, as after Austerlitz, we were too generous; we believed in the protestations and the oaths of the princes whom we left on their thrones! And now, coalized against us, they are aiming at the independence and the most sacred rights of France. They have begun an unjust aggression. Forward! Let us march against them; are not they and we the same men?

Soldiers! You were one against three at Jena against these same arrogant Prussians; at Montmirail, you were one against six. Madmen! A moment's prosperity has blinded them. If they enter France they will find their graves. Soldiers, we have forced marches to make, battles to fight, dangers to encounter, but with constancy the victory will be ours; the rights, the honor, of our country will be reconquered. For every Frenchman who has courage the moment has come to conquer or to die!
> Napoleon, 14 June 1815, to the army before the Battles of Ligny and Waterloo, quoted in R.M. Johnston, ed., *The Corsican*, 1910.

UP! Children of Zulu, your day has come. Up! and destroy them all!
> Shaka Zulu, 1819, in the Second Ndwandwe War, quoted in E.A. Ritter, *Shaka Zulu*, 1955.

TO ARMS, then, all of you! All of you! And the oppressors and the mighty shall disappear like dust. You, too, women, cast away all the cowards from your embraces; they will give you only cowards for children, and you who are the daughters of the land of beauty must bear children who are noble and brave.
> Giuseppe Garibaldi, appeal to his soldiers, 1860, quoted in Lewis Copeland, *The World's Great Speeches*, 1952.

UP, MEN, and to your posts! Don't forget today that you are from Old Virginia.
> Major-General George Pickett, 3 July 1863, to his division just before the charge at Getttysburg.

COME ON, Lakotas! It's a good day to die!
> Crazy Horse, 25 June 1876, as he rallied the Lakota warriors to defend their women and children camped on the Little Big Horn River against Custer's attack.

COME, THEN, let us to the task, to the battle, to the toil – each to our part, each to our station. Fill the armies, rule the air, pour out the munitions, strangle the U-boats, sweep the mines, plough the land, build the ships, guard the streets, succour the wounded, uplift the downcast, and honour the brave. Let us go forward together in all parts of the Empire, in all parts of the Island. There is not a week, nor a day, nor an hour to lose.
> Sir Winston S. Churchill, 27 January 1940, speech as First Lord of the Admiralty at the Free Trade Hall in Manchester.

IT HAS BEEN my privilege to assume command at this time. The day is set and we are ready. Be alert, and when the enemy appears, shoot calmly, shoot fast, and shoot straight.
> General Alexander A. Vandergrift, 15 October 1943, Memorandum to All Hands of the First Marine Amphibious Corps before the assault on Tarawa.

NEXT STOP Kuwait. We're going to go fast and go violently!
> Lieutenant-General Walter E. Boomer, 15 February 1991, to his assembled staff shortly before Desert Storm, quoted in Charles J. Quilter II, *U.S. Marines in the Persian Gulf, 1990–1991*, 1993.

EXHORTATIONS IN BATTLE

COURAGE! Do not fall back: in a little the place will be yours. Watch! When the wind blows my banner against the bulwark, you shall take it!
> Joan of Arc, 7 May 1429, in the assault on the bridge at Orléans, *Joan of Arc In Her Own Words*, 1996.

RASCALS, would you live forever? (*Ihr Racker, wollt ihr ewig leben?*)
> Frederick the Great, 18 June 1757, when the Guards hesitated at the Battle of Kolin.

UP, GUARDS and at 'em!
> The Duke of Wellington, 18 June 1815, to the Brigade of Guards at Waterloo.

COME ON you sons of bitches! Do you want to live forever?
> Sergeant Dan Daly, 4 June 1918, leading marines at Belleau Wood.

TWO KINDS of people are staying on this beach, the dead and those who are going to die. Now let's get the hell out of here!
> Brigadier-General Norman D. Cotta, 6 June 1944, Omaha Beach, leading the men of the 29th Infantry

Division off the beach, quoted in Omar Bradley, *A General's Life*, 1983.

GET UP and get moving. Follow me!
> Major-General Aubrey S. Newman, 20 October 1944, during the landings of his regiment, of the 24th Infantry Division, in the Philippines.

EXPERIENCE
General

I HAVE NOT LIVED so long, Spartans, without having had the experience of many wars, and I see those among you of the same age as myself, who will not fall into the common misfortune of longing for war from inexperience or from the belief in its advantage and its safety.
> Archidamus II, King of Sparta, 432 BC, speech on the prospects of war with Athens, quoted in Thucydides, *History of the Peloponnesian War*, c. 404 BC, tr. Richard Crawley, 1910.

THE MORE your troops have been accustomed to camp duties on frontier stations and the more carefully they have been disciplined, the less danger they will be exposed to in the field.
Men must be sufficiently tried before they are led against the enemy.
> Flavius Vegetius Renatus, *Military Institutions of the Romans*, c. AD 378, tr. Clark, 1776.

NEVER LEAD soldiers into combat before having made sufficient trial of their courage.
> The Emperor Maurice, *The Strategikon*, c. AD 600 (*Maurice's Strategikon*, tr. George Dennis, 1989).

WE HAVE ACQUIRED this knowledge not simply from hearing about it but also from having been taught by a certain amount of experience. For one thing, the men who instructed and trained us in this method were the very ones . . . who invented it. Then, on our own, we have put it into practice and, as best we could, almost made it a part of us.
> The Emperor Nikephoros II Phokas, *Skirmishing*, c. AD 969 (*Three Byzantine Military Treatises*, tr. George Dennis, 1985).

WHEN A GENERAL makes no mistakes in war, it is because he has not been long at it.
> Marshal General Vicomte de Turenne (1611–1675).

WHAT IS the good of experience if you do not reflect?
> Frederick the Great, quoted in Fuller, *Decisive Battles of the U.S.A.*, 1953.

NO BATTLE can be won in the study, and theory without practice is dead.
> Field Marshal Prince Aleksandr V. Suvorov (1729–1800), quoted in K. Ossipov, *Suvorov*, 1945.

HABITS of practice give, to the soldier, such skill and management in the use of arms in the day of battle, as might be expected to be acquired by experience, in working, in unison, the separate parts of a machine of compound movement. The knowledge and ability, acquired by such experience, aided by a correct direction of powers in general movement, ensure the application of united impulse, at the proper time and in the proper circumstances of action, producing a powerful effect, and a calculable one, as depending upon a uniform rule. It is thus that experience of actual war imprints, upon the soldier, the character of a veteran – a courage; arising from knowledge of things, and a consciousness of superiority in the art of applying powers. Such courage is cool and tempered: that of unexperienced troops is impetuous, blind, and headlong – liable to mistake its purpose unless plain and prominent in all its aspects.

Robert Jackson, *A Systematic View of the Formation, Discipline, and Economy of Armies*, 1804.

[I] UNDERSTOOD as much of military matters as I have ever done since.

The Duke of Wellington, of his experience in India 1796–1805; quoted in Lord Stanhope, *Notes of Conversations with the Duke of Wellington*, 1888.

OUR BUSINESS, like any other, is to be learned by constant practice and experience; and our experience is to be had in war, not at reviews.

General Sir John Moore (1761–1809).

MAXIM 77. Generals-in-chief must be guided by their own experience or their genius. Tactics, evolutions, the duties and knowledge of an engineer or an artillery officer may be learned in treatises, but the science of strategy is only to be acquired by experience, and by studying the campaigns of all the great captains.

Napoleon, *Military Maxims of Napoleon*, tr. George D'Aguilar, 1831 (David Chandler, ed., 1987).

BATTLE EXPERIENCE overcomes friction, from troopers and riflemen up to the divisional commander.

Major-General Carl von Clausewitz, *On War*, 1832, tr. Michael Howard and Peter Paret, 1976.

IT IS a frequent contention of the "practical soldier" that length of experience in the field counts for more than depth of study as a means to a mastery of war. The inevitable corollary of this claim is that the man who has seen the most fighting must be the greatest authority on tactics.

In this connection one may recall the story of Marshal Saxe and the aged general who urged the acceptance of his opinion on the ground that he had seen more campaigns than anyone else, whereupon Saxe replied that he had a mule which had been through twenty campaigns "and was still a mule." (March 1923.)

Captain Sir Basil Liddell Hart, *Thoughts on War*, 1944.

UNLIKE MOST other professions, the military offers but rare opportunities for actual practice. Most of its operating experience is necessarily in the realm of make-believe. It is as if a surgeon was confined for his practice to the dissection of frogs and dead paupers. The rest of a soldier's training for command lies in the realm of theory.

Captain Sir Basil Liddell Hart, *The Ghost of Napoleon*, 1933.

THERE IS no better teacher of war than war.

Mao Tse-tung, *On the Study of War*, 1936.

A DIVISION represents not only the lives of 15,000 men and millions of dollars' worth of equipment, but it also represents a priceless investment in months and years of training. In the 1st Division that investment had been multiplied beyond measure by its long experience in battle. Thus in quality the 1st was worth the equal of several inexperienced divisions. It had become an almost irreplaceable weapon in the Normandy invasion.

General of the Army Omar Bradley, *A Soldier's Story*, 1951.

IN TUNISIA the Americans had to pay a stiff price for their experience, but it brought rich dividends. Even at that time, the American generals showed themselves to be very advanced in the tactical handling of their forces, although we had to wait until the Patton Army in France to see the most astonishing achievements in mobile warfare. The Americans, it is fair to say, profited far more than the British from their experience in Africa, thus confirming the axiom that education is easier than reeducation.

Field Marshal Erwin Rommel, *The Rommel Papers*, 1953.

DIRECT EXPERIENCE is inherently too limited to form an adequate foundation either for theory or for application. At best it produces an atmosphere that is of value in drying and hardening the structure of thought. The great value of indirect experience lies in its greater variety and extent.

Captain Sir Basil Liddell Hart, *Strategy: The Indirect Approach*, 1954.

ONE THING that some Pentagon people never understood is when you're a soldier – mainline or guerrilla – you get awfully good with what little you have. Our Marines got better and better when they were operating in the jungle every day, even if they didn't have the best equipment and logistic support. But what hurt us was the "one year rotation" policy. Just as a trooper was getting real smart, it was time for him to go home. Somebody brand new replaced him, disrupting unit cohesion and effectiveness. And in the last weeks before rotation, people made tragic mistakes by being overly careful.

General Alfred Gray, 'One Year Rotation', Al Santoli, ed., *Leading the Way: How Vietnam Veterans Rebuilt the U.S. Military*, 1993.

Lack of Experience

SOME DAY there is going to be a man sitting in my present chair who has not been raised in the military services and who will have little understanding of where slashes in their estimates can be made with little or no damage. If that should happen while we still have the state of tension that now exists in the world, I shudder to think of what could happen in this country . . .

President Dwight D. Eisenhower, letter to Everett E. 'Swede' Hazlett, 20 August 1956, quoted in William Bragg Ewald, Jr., *Eisenhower the President*, 1981.

NO THEORETICAL studies, no intellectual attainments on the part of the layman can be a substitute for the experience of having lived and delivered under the stress of war.

General Maxwell Taylor, graduation address at the U.S. Military Academy at West Point, June 1963.

Lessons Learned

I AM NOT sorry that I went, notwithstanding what has happened. One may pick up something useful from among the most fatal errors.

Major-General Sir James Wolfe, 1757, of the Rochefort Expedition.

OH, WELL. It's all the same. The students are a credit to their teachers. The French have taught you some terrible lessons, and you understand, at length, the art of making war as it should be.

A captured French veteran to his British captors, in Spain during the Peninsular War, Costello, *Adventures of a Soldier written by Himself*, 1852, quoted in Arthur Bryant, The Great Duke, 1972.

THESE BEASTS have learned something.

Napoleon, 1813, comment during the Battle of Lützen on the improved performance of the Prussian Army compared to the 1806 campaign.

I LEARNT what one ought not to do, and that is always something.

The Duke of Wellington, after the disastrous British campaign in Holland, 1794–1795, in which he served as the colonel of the 33rd Foot; quoted in Earl Stanhope, *Conversations with the Duke of Wellington*, 1888.

ON 12 November, 1918, twenty four hours after the Armistice, General Pershing visited the I Corps headquarters, and found the corps commander pouring over his maps. "Don't you know the war's over?" asked a bemused Pershing. Liggett replied, "I'm trying to see where we might have done better."

Major-General Hunter Liggett, 12 November 1918, quoted in Adolph Carlson, 'A Chapter Not Yet Written', in Robert Neilson, ed., *Sun Tzu and the Information Warfare*, 1997.

IT IS absolutely necessary to put the experience of the war in a broad light and collect this experience while the impressions won on the battlefield are still fresh and a major proportion of the experienced officers are still in leading positions. . . . [committees were to write] short, concise studies on the newly-gained experiences of the war and consider the following points: a). What new situations arose in the war that had not been considered before the war? b). How effective were our pre-war views in dealing with the above situations? c). What new guidelines have been developed from the use of new weaponry in the war? d). Which new problems put forward by the war have not yet found a solution?

Colonel-General Hans von Seekt, 1 December 1919, letter to the Truppenamt on the duties of the 57 committees he established to examine the lessons learned from WWI, quoted in James S. Corum, *Roots of Blitzkrieg*, 1992.

HE IMPRESSED ME with his absolute honesty by this unwillingness to cover up the shortcomings of his command, in the fear that it might lead to his relief. All he desired was an opportunity to profit by the lessons of the recent experience. As a matter of fact, I happened to hear the question of his relief discussed, and in my small way I most energetically protested. This particular General commanded his division in action most successfully a few weeks later.

General of the Army George C. Marshall, *Memoirs of My Service in the World War*, 1976.

I CLAIM we got a hell of beating. We got run out of Burma and it is as humiliating as hell. I think we ought to find what caused it, and go back and retake it.

General Joseph Stillwell after the Burma Campaign of 1942, *New York Times*, 26 May 1942.

LESSON NO. 1 from Fuller: "To anticipate strategy, imagine."
Lesson No. 2 from Martel: "Men, not weapons, will shape the future, so stick with fundamentals."

Brigadier-General S.L.A. Marshall, *Bringing Up the Rear*, 1979.

THOSE GUYS who were in my first platoon in Vietnam stay with me. The years have faded, and the memories have faded. But I still remember what they did.

The young sergeants took care of me when I was a green lieutenant. They taught me the right things about how to say alive in combat.

After the big Gulf War parade ended, I walked over to the Vietnam Veterans Memorial to talk to Sergeant Stanton. I told him and all my other soldiers who perished, "Closure complete. The lessons learned in Vietnam were good ones. We did the job in the Gulf." I didn't break faith with my guys.

The genesis of the victory in the Gulf was Vietnam. That's where it started. The commitment of the commanders in the Gulf were people who years ago said, "Never again. I will not let that happen to this army again."

What we learned in Vietnam we brought forward with us. If that saved the lives of thousands of Americans, and allied and Iraqi civilians, then the 58,000 who perished in Vietnam didn't die for nothing.

> Brigadier-General Joseph 'Keith' Kellog, 'The Circle', Al Santoli, ed., *Leading the Way: How Vietnam Veterans Rebuilt the U.S. Military*, 1993.

The Loss of Experience

THE SUCCESSIVE tactical regulations issued during the forty odd years of peace which separated the wars of 1870 and 1914 shed a curious light on the way the memory of pain fades – and still more of its cause. Thus it came about that the first regulations of 1875 [French Army] were nearest the reality of 1914, whereas the last of the series was framed for a battlefield on which there were no bullets.

> Captain Sir Basil Liddell Hart, *Reputations Ten Years After*, 1928.

EXPERIENCES can be lost. That is dangerous and is a fault. They may also harden into dogma, and become a dead letter – that is no less dangerous and is an offense, for it is not the office of experience to conjure up the past, but to build for the future. Experiences must always be checked, to see if their pre-suppositions have not changed. The basis of such test, however, must be founded on an understanding of present conditions, and of a study of the future.

> Colonel Hermann Foertsch, *The Art of Modern Warfare*, 1940.

OUR MINOR TACTICS [Korean War] were deplorable; it was as if junior leaders had thrown the book away. Outposting was being done at ten to fifteen yards; one might as well dispense with that type of outpost. On the march, the point was often at about the same interval – ten to fifteen yards – from the main body, which made it of no value. Company leaders had forgotten how to employ smoke, and when I talked to them, saying that we must come to the fullest possible employment of lights in night defense, they grimly protested. "That would be fatal. It would give the position away." Yet many of these officers had served in the line in World War II. I came to see in those days what I had not understood before – that one should never underrate the speed with which an officer body can put aside the most valid lessons out of personal experience in war.

> Brigadier-General S.L.A. Marshall, *Bringing Up the Rear*, 1979.

EXPLOITATION

THE GODS do not grant all their gifts to one man, Hannibal. You know how to conquer but not how to use your victory.

> Maharbal Barca, the commander of the Carthaginian cavalry after the battle of Cannae, when his brother, Hannibal, preferred to rest the army rather than pursue, 2 August 216 BC, quoted in Livy, *Annals of the Roman People*, 22, c. 25 BC–AD 17 (*Livy: A History of Rome*, tr. Moses Hadas and Joe Poe, 1962).

THOSE who know how to win are much more numerous than those who know how to make use of their victories.

> Polybius, *Histories*, c. 125 BC (*The Rise of the Roman Empire*, tr. Ian Scott-Kilvert, 1987).

TO-DAY the victory had been the enemy's had there been any one among them to gain it.

> Julius Caesar, 48 BC, of Pompey's success in the Battle of Dyrrhachium, which he failed to exploit, quoted in Plutarch, *The Lives*, c. AD 100, tr. John Dryden.

WHEN WE HAVE incurred the risk of a battle, we should know how to profit by the victory, and not merely content ourselves, according to custom, with possession of the field.

> Field Marshal Maurice Comte de Saxe, *My Reveries*, 1732, tr. Phillips, 1940.

BREAK THROUGH without stopping. . . . The head must not wait for the tail. . . . Commanders of units are not to wait to report, but are to act on their own initiative with speed and judgment. If the Turks ask for quarter, give it.

> Field Marshal Prince Aleksandr V. Suvorov, 1773, on the Danube, quoted in K. Ossipov, *Suvorov*, 1945.

A STRONG PURSUIT, give no time for the enemy to think, take advantage of victory, uproot him, cut off his escape route.

> Field Marshal Prince Aleksandr V. Suvorov (1729–1800), quoted in V.Ye. Savkin, *Basic Principles of Operational Art and Tactics*, 1972.

FIRST gain the victory, and then make the best use of it you can.

> Admiral Viscount Nelson, to his captains before the Battle of the Nile, 1 August 1797, quoted in Robert Southey, *Life of Nelson*, 1813.

IN WARFARE nothing is done, so long as anything remains to be done. No victory is complete so long as there is an enemy in the field. . . . In our present situation there is but one order to be issued – to inflict as great a loss as possible upon the enemy and to exploit our victory in every way.

> Marshal of France Louis-Alexandre Berthier, Prince de Neuchatel, Prince de Wagram, 3 December 1805,

order to General Soult on the pursuit of the defeated Russian and Austrian forces on the day after the Battle of Austerlitz. Derrécagaix, *Le Maréchal Berthier*, II, quoted in Watson, *By Command of the Emperor*, 1957.

MY BROTHER: I shall start at one in the morning so as to reach Burgos before dawn; there I will make my arrangements for the day, for a victory is nothing, it must be turned to account.

Napoleon, 10 November 1808, to his brother Joseph, quoted in R.M. Johnston, ed., *The Corsican*, 1910.

IT HAS afterwards been asserted that the battle of Spichern had been fought at the wrong place and that it had crossed the plans of the high-command. I admit, no provision had been made for it. In general, however, there will be very few cases where a tactical victory will not fit the strategical plan. Yet a victory will always be gratefully accepted and exploited.

Field Marshal Alfred Graf von Schlieffen, *Brief History of the Franco-Prussian War*, quoted in Freytag-Loringhoven, *Generalship in the Great War*, 1920.

FOR SUCCESS in the attack, two major problems must be solved – *dislocation* and *exploitation*. One precedes and one follows the actual blow, which in comparison is a simple act. You cannot hit the enemy with effect unless you have first created the opportunity; you cannot make that effect decisive unless you exploit the second opportunity that comes before he can recover. (May 1930.)

Captain Sir Basil Liddell Hart, *Thoughts on War*, 1944.

F

FAILURE

HE WHO in war fails to do what he undertakes, may always plead the accidents which invariably attend military affairs: but he who declares a thing to be impossible, which is subsequently accomplished, registers his own incapacity.

> The Duke of Wellington (1769–1852), quoted in William Fraser, *Words on Wellington*, 1889.

THE SERVICE cannot afford to keep a man who does not succeed.

> Lieutenant-General Thomas J. 'Stonewall' Jackson (1824–1863), quoted in G.F.R. Henderson, *Stonewall Jackson*, 1898.

ON THE HEELS of the South African War came the sleuth-hounds pursuing the criminals, I mean the customary Royal Commissions. Ten thousand words of mine stand embedded in their Blue Books, cold and dead as so many mammoths in glaciers. But my long spun-out intercourse with the Royal Commissioners did have living issue – my Manchurian and Gallipoli notes. Only constant witnesses could have shown me how fallible is the unaided military memory or have led me by three steps to a War Diary: –
(1) There is nothing certain about war except that one side won't win.
(2) The winner is asked no questions – the loser has to answer for everything.
(3) Soldiers think of nothing so little as failure and yet, to the extent of fixing intentions, orders, facts, dates firmly in their own minds, they ought to be prepared.
Conclusion: – in war, keep your own counsel, preferably in a note-book.

> General Sir Ian Hamilton, *Gallipoli Diary*, 1918.

IT IS HARD to fail, but it is worse never to have tried to succeed.

> Governor Theodore Roosevelt of New York, 10 April 1898, speech before the Hamilton Club, Chicago, Illinois, *Works of Theodore Roosevelt*, XIII, 1926.

A MAN'S LIFE is interesting primarily when he has failed – I well know. For it's a sign that he tried to surpass himself.

> Georges Clemenceau, conversation with Jean Martet, 1 June 1928, quoted in *Clemenceau, the Events of His Life as Told by Himself to His Former Secretary, Jean Martet*, tr. Milton Waldman, 1930.

ENCOURAGING INITIATIVE presupposes an understanding by seniors and juniors alike, that innovation is imprecise, that error and false starts must be expected, that to try and fail is much to be preferred to never trying at all.

> Lieutenant-General Victor H. 'The Brute' Krulak, 'A Soldier's Dilemma', *Marine Corps Gazette*, 11/1986.

FALLEN COMRADES

HOW ARE the mighty fallen in the midst of the battle! O Jonathan, thou wast slain in thine high places.
I am distressed for thee, my brother Johnathan: very pleasant has thou been unto me: thy love to me was wonderful, passing the love of women.
How are the mighty fallen, and the weapons of war perished.

> King David of Israel, lament for his friend, the warrior prince, Jonathan, son of King Saul, II Samuel, 1.25–27.

THE GAMES were over now. The gathered armies scattered,
each man to his fast ship, and fighters turned their minds
to thoughts of food and the sweet warm grip of sleep.
But Achilles kept on grieving for his friend,
the memory burning on . . .
and all-subduing sleep could not take him,
not now, he turned and twisted, side to side,
he longed for Patrocles' manhood, his gallant heart —
what rough campaigns they'd fought to an end together,
what hardships they had suffered, cleaving their way through wars of men and pounding waves at sea.
The memories flooded over him, live tears flowing,
and now he'd lie on his side, now flat on his back,
now face down again. At last he'd leap to his feet,
wander in anguish, aimless along the surf, and dawn on dawn
flaming over the sea and shore would find him pacing.
Then he'd yoke his racing team to the chariot-harness,
lash the corpse of Hector behind the car for dragging
and haul him three times round the dead Patroclus' tomb,
and then he'd rest again in his tents and leave the body
sprawled face down in the dust. . . .

> Homer, *The Iliad*, 24.1–25, c. 800 BC, tr. Robert Fagles, 1990; Achilles' inconsolable grief for his comrade Patroclus.

FAST FRIENDS, forest-companions,
we made one bed and slept one sleep
in foreign lands after the fray.
Scathach's pupils, two together
we'd set forth to comb the forest.
. . .

There is no man that ever ate,
no man that was ever born,
no joyous son of king or queen,
for whose sake I would do you harm.
. . .

When we were away with Scathach
learning victory overseas,
it seemed our friend would remain
unbroken till the day of doom.

I loved the noble way you blushed,
and loved your fine, perfect form.
I loved your blue clear eye,
your way of speech, your skillfulness [,]
. . .

your curled yellow hair
like a great lovely jewel,
the soft leaf-shaped belt
that you wore at your waist.

You have fallen to the Hound,
I cry for it, little calf.
The shield didn't save you
that brought you to the fray.
> The lament of the high hero Cuchulain for his fallen
> warrior foster brother, Ferdia, in the Irish epic, *Tain*,
> 1970, quoted in Cahill, *How the Irish Saved Civilization*
> tr. Thomas Kinsella, 1995.

ALAS! Zwide's son I have conquered, indeed, but he
has killed me in Mgobozi. . . . Let us go. My heart is
bitter. Every Ndwandwe not yet dead shall pay for this.
> Shaka Zulu, October 1826, upon the death of his
> dearest friend and chief general, Mogobozi, in battle
> with the Ndwandwe, whose survivors he would
> massacre, quoted in E.A. Ritter, *Shaka Zulu*, 1955.

IT IS ALL OVER now. Many of us are prisoners,
many are dead, many wounded, bleeding and dying.
Your soldier lives and mourns and but for you, my
darling, he would rather be back there with his dead,
to sleep for all time in an unknown grave.
> Major-General George Pickett, to his fiancée, 4 July
> 1863, quoted in *Gettysburg, The Confederate High
> Tide*, 1985.

NEXT MORNING we buried seven dead Rough
Riders in a grave on the summit of the trail, Chaplain
Brown reading the solemn burial service of the
Episcopalians, while the men stood around with
bared heads and joined in singing, "Rock of Ages."
Vast number of vultures were wheeling round and

round in great circles through the blue sky overhead.
There could be no more honorable burial than that of
these men in a common grave – Indian and cow-
boy, miner, packer, and college athlete – the man of
unknown ancestry from the lonely Western plains
and the man who carried on his watch the crest of
the Styvesants and the Fishes, one in the way they
met death, just as during life they had been one in
their daring and their loyalty.
> President Theodore Roosevelt, *The Rough Riders*,
> 1899; of the burial of men of his Rough Rider's
> Regiment in Cuba during the Spanish-American War.

THAT IS OUR WAR, and we will carry it with us as
we go on from one battleground to another until it is
all over, leaving some of us behind on every beach,
in every field. We are just beginning with the ones
who lie back of us here in Tunisia. I don't know
whether it was their good fortune or their misfortune
to get out of it so early in the game. I guess it
doesn't make any difference, once a man has gone.
Medals and speeches and victories are nothing to
them any more. They died and others lived and
nobody knows why it is so. They died and thereby
the rest of us can go on and on. When we leave
here for the next shore, there is nothing we can do
for the ones beneath the wooden crosses, except
perhaps to pause and murmur, "Thanks, pal."
> Ernie Pyle, *Here is Your War*, 1945.

FALLEN SONS

AND, BEHOLD, Cushi came; and Cushi said,
Tidings, my lord the king: for the LORD hath
avenged thee this day of all them that rose up
against thee.
   And the king said unto Cushi, Is the young man
Abasalom safe? And Cushi answered, The enemies
of my lord the king, and all that rise against thee to
do thee hurt, be as that young man is.
   And the king was much moved, and went up to the
chamber over the gate, and wept: and as he went,
thus he said, O my son Absalom, my son, my son
Absalom! Would God I had died for thee, O
Absalom, my son, my son!
> King David, II Samuel, 18.31–33, c. 1000 BC, of the
> death of his rebellious son Absalom at the hands of
> his general, Joab, after the King had expressly
> ordered him to spare the wayward prince so beloved
> of his father.

BUT I, dear god, my life so cursed by fate . . .
I fathered hero sons in the wide realm of Troy
and now not a single one is left, I tell you.
Fifty sons I had when the sons of Achaea came,
nineteen born to me from a single mother's womb
and the rest by other women in the palace. Many,
most them violent Ares cut the knees from under.
But one, one was left me, to guard my walls, my
   people –

the one you killed the other day, defending his
    fatherland,
my Hector! It's all for him I've come to the ships now,
to win him back from you – I bring a priceless ransom.
Revere the gods, Achilles! Pity me in my own right,
remember your own father! I deserve more pity . . .
I have endured what no one on earth has ever
    done before –
I put to my lips the hands of the man who killed
    my son.

> Homer, *The Iliad*, 24.577–591, c. 800 BC, tr. Robert
> Fagles, 1990; Priam begging Achilles for the body of
> his son, Hector, breaker of horses.

NO ONE is so foolish as to prefer peace to war, in
which, instead of sons burying their fathers, fathers
bury their sons.

> King Croesus of Lydia, to Cyrus the Great who had
> just rescued him from his own funeral pyre following
> his defeat at the hands of the founder of the Persian
> Empire in 546 BC, quoted in Herodotus, *The Persian
> Wars*, 1.87, c, 430 BC, tr. George Rawlinson, 1942.

BUT NEITHER should you to feel so much concern
about death, knowing that we must regard birth as
the beginning of man's course, and death as the end.
He had died, as he who was even ever so reluctant
would have died; but to die honourably is the part of
one who is willing to die, and who had been taught
what he ought to know. Happy therefore is Gryllus,
and whoever chooses, not the greatest prolongation
of life, but life distinguished by virtue; though the
gods granted him, indeed, but a short life.

> Xenophon, letter to Soteira of the death of his son,
> Gryllus, who 'fell with honour at the battle of
> Mantinea', 362 BC, *Xenophon's Minor Works*,
> c. 360 BC, tr. J.S. Watson, 1891.

IT GIVES ME great concern to undertake a task,
which is not only a bitter renewal of my own grief, but
must be a violent shock to an affectionate parent.

You have for your support, the assistance of
religion, good sense, and the experience of the
uncertainty of human happiness. You have for your
satisfaction, that your son fell nobly in the cause of
his country, honored and lamented by all his fellow-
soldiers; that he led a life of honor and virtue, which
must secure to him everlasting happiness.

When the keen sensibility of the passions begins
to subside, these considerations will give you real
comfort. That the Almighty may give you fortitude to
bear this severest of strokes, is the earnest wish of
your companion in affliction.

> General Marquis Cornwallis, letter to the father of
> Lieutenant-Colonel Webster of the 33rd Foot, killed at
> the Battle of Guilford Courthouse, 15 March 1781,
> quoted in Henry Lee, *Memoirs of the War in the
> Southern Department*, 1869.

MY DEAREST MARY,
I embrace the opportunity of addressing you,

afforded by the departure of the mail. My health is as
good as I could reasonably expect it to be under all
the circumstances which have surrounded me. An
impenetrable gloom hangs over my mind in
consequence of the death of my beloved Eddie. His
rapid development in every particular, his high
attainments and manly deportment, had filled to the
brim the cup of paternal pride, and perhaps he was
my idol; I feel now that I almost worshipped him, and
dwelt more upon the creature than upon the Creator.
My grief knows no bounds, but my sense of
propriety dictates, that He, who rules the universe
knows what is best for us all, that all is dictated by
Infinite Wisdom, and I am consequently constrained
to say, Our Father, "Thy will be done."

> Major-General John W. Geary, 6 November 1863,
> letter to his wife on the loss of their son Lieutenant
> Edward R. Geary, killed at the Battle of Wauhatchie,
> Tennessee, quoted in John Geary, *A Politician Goes to
> War*, 1995.

MARCH 13.–The bright, beautiful Sabbath. Another
day of solemn suspense. My son, my son! When I left
Washington it seemed as if dear Ully's death was the
greatest possible affliction. Now, I hardly know if I can
recover his body. How thoughts of him flit by me. The
last evening he was with me I gave him my last
memorandum in case I fell. Dear boy, he goes before
me! Here, too, I have a whole life to contemplate, from
the baby in the cradle to the distinguished Colonel
falling in battle; and yet I am in the vigor of life. My son!

> Rear Admiral John A. Dahlgren, 13 March 1864, diary
> entry while attempting to recover the body of his son,
> Colonel Ulric Dahlgren, from the Confederates, quoted
> in Madeleine Vinton Dahlgren, *Memoir of John A.
> Dahlgren*, 1891.

LITTLE FLORA is broken hearted, but very brave,
and Mother suffers as much and is even braver; for
Mother has the true heroism of heart. Well, it is very
dreadful; it is the old who ought to die, and not fine
and gallant youth with the golden morning of life still
ahead; but after all he died as the heroes of old died,
as brave and fearless men must die when a great
cause calls. If our country did not contain such men it
would not be our country. I bitterly mourn that he was
not married and does not leave his own children
behind him; but the children's children of his brothers
and of Ethel will speak of him with pride as long as
our blood flows in the veins of man or woman.

> President Theodore Roosevelt, 21 July 1918, letter to
> Archibald Roosevelt, of the death of his son Quentin a
> few days before in an aerial battle in France,
> Theodore Roosevelt Collection, quoted in Edward
> Reenan, Jr., *The Lion's Pride*, 1998.

FAME

THE GENERAL who advances without coveting fame
and retreats without fearing disgrace, whose only

thought is to protect his country and do good service for his sovereign, is the jewel of the kingdom.

Sun Tzu, *The Art of War*, 10, c. 500 BC, tr. Giles, 1910.

FAME is the perfume of heroic deeds.

Socrates (469–399 BC).

WHICH would you rather be – a victor at the Olympic games or the announcer of the victor?

Themistocles, upon being asked whether he would rather be Achilles or Homer, from Plutarch, *Apothegms, Themistocles*, c. AD 125.

O FORTUNATE YOUTH, to have found Homer as the herald of your glory!

Alexander the Great at the tomb of Achilles at Troy, from Cicero, *Pro Archia*, 62 BC (*Selected Works of Cicero*, tr. Harry Hubbell, 1948).

THERE WERE SOME who thought he was too eager for fame, and indeed the desire of glory is the last infirmity cast off even by the wise.

Cornelius Tacitus, *History*, 4.5, AD 98 (*The Complete Works of Tacitus*, tr. Alfred Church and William Brodribb, 1942); of Helvidius Priscus.

PUT A ROGUE in the limelight and he will act like an honest man.

Napoleon, *Maxims*, 1804–1815.

BUT WITH ME immortality is the recollection one leaves in the memory of man. That idea prompts to great actions. It would be better for a man never to have lived than to leave behind him no traces of his existence.

Napoleon, 1802, conversation with his private secretary, Louis de Bourrienne, *Memoirs of Napoleon Bonaparte*, II, 1855.

YOU HAVE miscalculated the heights to which misfortune, the injustice and persecution of your government, and your own conduct have raised the Emperor. His head wears more than an imperial crown – it wears a crown of thorns.

It is not in your power, or in that of the like of you, to obscure the radiance of that crown.

Napoleon, autograph letter to Sir Hudson Lowe, governor of St. Helena, 25 July 1817, *Correspondance de Napoléon Ier, publié par ordre de l'Empereur Napoléon III*, XXXII, quoted in Christopher Herold, ed., *The Mind of Napoleon*, 1955.

OF ALL the passions that inspire man in battle, none, we have to admit, is so powerful and so constant as the longing for honor and renown. The abuse of these noble ambitions has certainly inflicted the most disgusting outrages on the human race; nevertheless their origins entitle them to be ranked among the most elevated in human nature. In war they act as the essential breath of life that animates the inert mass. Other emotions may be more common and more venerated – patriotism, idealism, vengeance, enthusiasm of every kind – but there are no substitute for a thirst for fame and honor.

Major-General Carl von Clausewitz, *On War*, 1.3, 1832, tr. Michael Howard and Peter Paret, 1976.

THE ROAD to failure is the road to fame – such apparently must be the verdict on posterity's estimate of the world's greatest figures. The flash of the meteor impresses the human imagination more than the remoter splendour of the star, fixed immutably in the high heavens. Is it that final swoop earthwards, the unearthly radiance ending in the common dust, that, by its evidence of the tangible or the finite, gives to the meteor a more human appeal? So with luminaries of the human system, provided that the ultimate fall has a dramatic note, the memory of spectacular failure eclipses that of enduring success. Again, it may be that the completeness of his course lends individual emphasis to the great failure, throwing his work into clearer relief, whereas the man whose efforts are crowned with permanent success builds a stepping-stone by which others may advance still farther, and so merges his own fame in that of his successors.

Captain Sir Basil Liddell Hart, *A Greater Than Napoleon: Scipio Africanus*, 1926.

I'M APPARENTLY not famous in Baghdad.

General H. Norman Schwarzkopf, 1991, quoted in Peter David, *Triumph in the Desert*, 1991.

FAMILIARITY

THE LEADER, mingling with the vulgar host, Is in the common mass of matter lost.

Homer, *The Odyssey*, 4.397, c. 800 BC, tr. Alexander Pope, 1725–1726.

BE EASY and condescending in your deportment to your officers, but not too familiar, lest you subject yourself to a want of that respect, which is necessary to support a proper command.

General George Washington, *The Writings of George Washington*, IV, p. 81, John C. Fitzgerald, ed., 1931.

SOLDIERS must never be witnesses to the discussions of the commanders.

Napoleon, 31 March 1805, to Marshal de Moncey, *Correspondance de Napoléon Ier, publié par ordre de l'Empereur Napoléon III*, No. 8507, Vol. X, p. 279, 1858–1870.

EFFICIENCY in a general, his soldiers have a right to expect; geniality they are usually right to suspect.

Field Marshal Viscount Wavell of Cyrenaica, *Generals and Generalship*, 1941.

'FAMOUS LAST WORDS'

THE LORD GOD is my armour!
> Gustavus Adolphus, refusing the steel body armour offered by his aides, which would have saved his life from the bullets and swords of Wallenstein's Croatian cavalry at the Battle of Lützen, 16 September 1632.

I DID NOT mean to be killed today.
> Vicomte de Turenne, on a reconnaissance just before being struck by a cannonball at the Battle of Sasbach, 27 July 1675.

AN ALLIANCE with Russia would be very valuable. Only women and children are capable of supposing that (I) would lose myself in the deserts of Russia.
> Napoleon, 14 March 1807, quoted in R.M. Johnston, ed, *The Corsican*, 1910.

I TELL YOU Wellington is a bad general, the English are bad soldiers; we will settle the matter by lunch time.
> Napoleon, 18 June 1815, on the battlefield of Waterloo at 8:30 am; the battle began in the early afternoon, quoted in R.M. Johnston, ed., *The Corsican*, 1910.

THE REBEL ARMY is now the legitimate property of the Army of the Potomac. . . . The enemy is now in my power, and God Almighty cannot deprive me of them.
> Major-General Joseph Hooker, 1 May 1863, *The War of the Rebellion: A Compilation of the Official Records of the Union and Confederate Armies*, XXV, Part 2, p. 328, U.S. Government Printing Office, 1880–1901; just as his army was about to engage Lee at the Battle of Chancellorsville.

THEY COULDN'T hit an elephant at this dist . . .
> Major-General John Sedgwick, 9 May 1864, killed instantly by a sniper while carelessly peering over the parapet during the Battle of Spotsylvania.

HURRAH, boys, we've got them!
> General George Armstrong Custer, as the 7th Cavalry closed on the great Indian encampment along the Little Big Horn River, 25 June 1876, quoted by Giovanni Martini in Benteen, *The Custer Fight*, 1933.

MY ONLY FEAR is that the *Zulu* will not fight.
> Lieutenant-General Lord Chelmsford, commanding British forces, just before the invasion of Zululand, 1879.

JAPAN should never be so foolish as to make enemies of Great Britain and the United States.
> Admiral Isoroku Yamamoto, c. 1937, quoted in Masanori Ito, *The End of the Imperial Japanese Navy*, 1956.

THE RUHR will not be subjected to a single bomb. If an enemy bomber reaches the Ruhr, my name is not Hermann Goering: you can call me Meier!
> Reichsmarshal Hermann Goering, 9 August 1939, as Germany prepared for war, quoted in William L. Shirer, *The Rise and Fall of the Third Reich*, 1960.

IT IS SIGNIFICANT that despite the claims of air enthusiasts no battleship has yet been sunk by bombs.
> Caption to photograph of the USS *Arizona* in the Army-Navy football game programme, 29 November 1941.

THE ATOM BOMB will never go off, and I speak as an expert in explosives.
> Admiral William Leahy to President Harry Truman before the first atomic bomb was dropped on Hiroshima, 1945.

THE CHINESE have no Air Force. If they try to get down to P'yongnang there will be the greatest slaughter.
> General of the Army Douglas MacArthur, 15 October 1950, in reply to President Truman who asked if there was a chance of Chinese intervention in the Korean War.

IF YOU WANT to accept his proposal I will not prostrate myself on the road and I will not resign; but you might as well know that it is superfluous.
> Moshe Dayan, at 8.00 am, 6 October 1973, during an emergency meeting of the Israeli Cabinet, dismissing the proposal of the Chief of Staff of the Israeli Defence Force that mobilisation be ordered in the face of the Egyptian and Syrian preparations to attack Israel, quoted in Haim Herzog, *The War of Atonement*, 1975.

THE IRAQI PEOPLE are capable of fighting to the victorious end which God wants . . . the blood of our martyrs will burn you.
> Saddam Hussein, August 1990, quoted in Pimlott and Badsey, *The Gulf War Assessed*, 1992.

[GENERAL PAVEL] Grachev promised to the president to solve the Chechen crisis in two hours with an airborne regiment. The president believed him.
> Lieutenant-General Aleksander I. Lebed, of the Russian Defence Minister's rash promise in early December 1994 to easily suppress the Chechens in Groznyy, but which resulted in months of brutal and bloody city fighting, quoted in *Moshovshiya Novosti* (Moscow) No. 7, 29 January–5 February1995.

FATE

FATE is the same for the man who holds back, the same if he fights hard. We are all held in a single honour, the brave with the weaklings. A man dies still if he has done nothing, as one who has done much.
> Homer, *The Iliad*, 9.318–320, c. 800 BC, tr. Richard Lattimore, 1951; Achilles refusing Agamemnon's gifts to settle their dispute.

BUT THE WILL of Zeus will always overpower the will of men,
and tears away his triumph, all in a lightning flash,
and at other times he will spur a man to battle.

> Homer, *The Iliad*, 17.203–205, c. 800 BC, tr. Robert Fagles, 1990; Hector's reply to Glaucus for chiding him for not seeking out Ajax.

FATE often spares the undoomed man when his courage lasts.

> *Beowulf*, c. AD 1000 (*My Name is Beowulf*, tr. Frederick Rebsamen, 1971).

WHAT BETTER FATE could overtake me than to die doing my duty as king, in which place it has pleased heaven to set me?

> Gustavus II Adolphus (1594–1632), citing the example of Alexander the Great when taken to task by his senior general for unnecessarily risking his life, quoted in Theodore Ayrault Dodge, *Gustavus Adolphus*, 1895.

I COULD SEE clearly enough the fatal hour coming! My star was growing paler; I felt the reins slipping from my fingers; and I could do nothing. Only a thunderstroke could save us. I had, therefore, to fight it out; and day by day, by this or that fatality, our chances were becoming more slender!

> Napoleon, 19 October 1813, after the defeat at Leipzig, quoted in R.M. Johnston, *The Corsican*, 1910.

A COMET! It was the omen foretold the death of Caesar!

> Napoleon, 2 April 1821, on St. Helena, quoted in R.M. Johnston, *The Corsican*, 1910.

FATIGUE AND REST

AND GRANT ME to buckle upon my shoulders that armour of thine, in hope that the Trojans may take me for thee, and so desist from war, and the warlike sons of the Achaeans may take breath, wearied as they are; for scant is the breathing-space in battle. And lightly might we that are unwearied drive men that are wearied with the battle back to the city from the ships and the huts.

> Homer, *The Iliad*, 16, c. 800 BC, tr. A.T. Murray, 1928; Patrocles to Achilles as the Trojans stormed the Greek camp.

. . . AND THIS I know, that I wake earlier than you – and watch, that you may sleep.

> Alexander the Great, 323 BC, to his officers and men at Opis, quoted in Arrian, *The Campaigns of Alexander*, 7.9, c. AD 150, tr. Aubrey de Sélincourt, 1987.

I HAVE DECIDED to engage successively and without halt one body of troops after the other, until harassed and worn out the enemy will be unable to further resist.

> Mehmet II the Conquerer, 1453, Ottoman Sultan, at

the Siege of Constantinople, quoted in J.F.C. Fuller, A *Military History of the Western World*, 1967.

GENTLEMEN, the dispositions for tomorrow, or rather for today since midnight has gone, cannot be altered. You have heard them read out. We shall do our duty. But before a battle, there is nothing more important than to sleep well. Gentlemen, let us take some rest.

> Field Marshal Prince Mikhail I. Kutuzov, 1 December 1805, the evening before the Battle of Austerliz, quoted in Parkinson, *Fox of the North*, 1976.

IN MILITARY, public or administrative affairs there is a need for deep thought as well as deep analysis, and also for an ability to concentrate on subjects for a long time without sleep.

> Napoleon (1769–1821), *Correspondance de Napoléon Ier, publié par ordre de l'Empereur Napoléon III*, No. 337, Vol. I, 1858–1870.

YOU MUST NOT needlessly fatigue the troops.

> Napoleon, 29 July 1806, *Correspondance de Napoléon Ier, publié par ordre de l'Empereur Napoléon III*, No. 10563, Vol. XII, 1858–1870.

IT IS AT NIGHT when a commander must work: if he tires himself to no purpose during the day, fatigue overcomes him at night. . . . A commander is not expected to sleep.

> Napoleon, conversation with Gaspard Gourgaud, *Journal inédit de 1815 à 1818*, Vol. II, n.d.

OH GOD! Perhaps the rain of the 17th of June had more to do with the loss of Waterloo than we think! If I had not been so exhausted I would have spent the whole night on horseback. The apparently most trivial circumstances have often the greatest effect.

> Napoleon (1769–1821), quoted in F.M. Kircheisen, ed., *Memoirs of Napoleon I*, 1929.

I WAS OBLIGED to do so [sleep] when I fought battles that lasted three days; Nature was also to have her due: I took advantage of the smallest intervals, and slept where and when I could.

> Napoleon (1769–1821) quoted in Emmanuel de Las Casas, *Memorial de St. Hélène*, II, 1816.

IF NO ONE had the right to give his views on military operations except when he is frozen, or faint from heat and thirst, or depressed from privation and fatigue, objective and accurate views would be even rarer than they are.

> Major-General Carl von Clausewitz, *On War*, 1.5, 1832, tr. Michael Howard and Peter Paret, 1976.

FATIGUE, exertion, and privation constitute a separate destructive factor in war – a factor not essentially belonging to combat, but more or less intricately involved in it, and pertaining especially to the realm of strategy. This factor is also present in tactical situations, and possibly in its most intense form; but since tactical actions are of shorter duration, the effects . . . will be limited. On the strategic plane, however, where the dimensions of time and space are enlarged, the effects are always perceptible, and often decisive.

> Major-General Carl von Clausewitz, *On War*, 3.12, 1832, tr. Michael Howard and Peter Paret, 1976.

I HAVE just read your despatch about sore tongued and fatigued horses. Will you pardon me for asking what the horses of your army have done since the battle of Antietam that fatigues anything?

> President Abraham Lincoln, 24 October 1862, letter to Major-General George B. McClellan, about his slow pursuit of General Lee after the Battle of Antietam, *The Portable Lincoln*, 1992.

I OFTEN SENT small squads at night to attack and run in the pickets along a line of several miles. Of course, these alarms were very annoying, for no human being knows how sweet sleep is but a soldier. I wanted to use and consume the Northern cavalry in hard work. I have often thought that their fierce hostility to me was more on account of the sleep I made them lose than the number we killed or captured.

> Colonel John S. Mosby, *Mosby's War Reminiscences*, 1887.

NO HUMAN BEING knows how sweet sleep is but a soldier.

> Colonel John S. Mosby, *Mosby's War Reminiscences*, 1887.

BEFORE ELEVEN O'CLOCK the general-in-chief remarked to the staff: "We shall have a busy day to-morrow, and I think we had better get all the sleep we can to-night. I am a confirmed believer in the restorative qualities of sleep, and always like to get at least seven hours of it, though I have often been compelled to put up with much less." "It is said," remarked Washburne, "that Napoleon often indulged in only four hours of sleep, and still preserved all the vigor of his mental faculties." "Well, I, for one, never believed those stories," the general replied. "If the truth were known, I have no doubt it would be found that he made up for his short sleep at night by taking naps during the day."

> General of the Army Ulysses S. Grant, as recounted by Brigadier-General Horace Porter, *Campaigning With Grant*, 1897.

THAT MEN should be prepared to fight to the last is neither surprising nor unusual; it is counted upon, in fact in establishing any plan of operations; but that men who have been retreating continuously for ten days and are lying about half-dead with exhaustion can pick up their arms and go into the attack with bugles blowing is something that had never entered into our calculations, never been taught as even a remote possibility in our military schools.

> General Heinrich Von Kluck, 1920, on the Anglo-French counter-attack of the First Battle of the Marne, 1914, quoted in Georges Blond, *The Marne*, 1967.

THERE ARE two things I will not put up with in war; one of them is 'nerves', and the other a consequence of the first, the maintenance of units in a constant state of tension and readiness and alarm, since it is insupportable for men and horses. I have so often seen it during the war. I have always come to the conclusion that in cases of uncertainty the commanders had simply quite uselessly shifted the burden of preparedness on to the shoulders of their subordinates, instead of carrying it themselves with the help of their staff. Even in moments of gravity, I struggled with myself for a long time before dragging out an order for increased wariness and a state of alarm.

> Marshal Joseph Pilsudski, *The Memoirs of a Polish Revolutionary and Soldier*, 1931.

I SAW about twenty-seven of twenty-nine divisions in battle. There were more failures, more crushed careers of officers of considerable rank, which grew out of physical exhaustion more than any other one cause. One acquired judgement with the years, but lost the resiliency of tendons and muscles. Leadership in the field depends to an important extent on one's legs, stomach, nervous system, and on one's ability to withstand hardships and lack of sleep and still be disposed energetically and aggressively to command men and dominate men on the battlefield. In World War I, many men had to be relieved because their spirit – their tenacity of purpose, their power of leadership over tired men – was broke through physical fatigue. They became pessimistic.

> General of the Army George C. Marshall (1880–1959), quoted in Bernard Loeffke, *From Warrior to Healer*, 1998.

THE TANKS traveled, in a straight line, perhaps 570 kilometers. . . . But, Andreya Lavrentevich, their speedometers show more than 2,000. A man has no speedometer and nobody knows what wear and tear has taken place.

> General Mikhail Ye. Katukov, 1945, quoted in Cornelius Ryan, *The Last Battle*, 1966.

MEN OF GOODWILL saddled with the fate of others need great courage to be idle when only rest can clear their fuddled wits.

> Baron Charles MacMoran Wilson Moran, *The Anatomy of Courage*, 1945.

THERE ARE more tired corps and division commanders than there are tired corps and divisions.

> General George S. Patton, Jr., *War As I Knew It*, 1947.

FATIGUE makes cowards of us all.

> General George S. Patton, Jr., *War As I Knew It*, 1947.

IN BATTLE, whatever wears out the muscles reacts

on the mind and whatever impairs the mind drains physical strength.

Tired men take fright more easily.

Frightened men swiftly tire.

The arrest of fear is as essential to the recovery of physical vigor by men as is rest to the body which has been spent by hard marching or hard work.

We are therefore dealing with a chain reaction. Half of control during battle comes of the commander's avoiding useless expenditure of the physical resources of his men while taking action to break the hold of fear. The other half comes from sensible preparation beforehand.

> Brigadier-General S.L.A. Marshall, *The Soldier's Load*, 1980.

SEVERAL WEEKS at Lae taught me a new respect for the luxury of sleep. Life at the airdrome was reduced to its simplest terms. During the day we either flew fighter missions or waited on stand-by alert. At night we wished only to sleep. The enemy, however, had other ideas about the matter, and almost unfailingly his bombers punctured the darkness to string rows of bombs against the field and to send ribbons of tracers into the ground as they passed over at low height.

We could dispense with the foods we desired most, live in shacks, and fly from a primitive field, but we could not go without sleep. And the Americans and Australians exerted every effort to keep us awake at night.

> Saburo Sakai, *Samurai!*; of the air war around Lae, 180 miles north of Port Moresby in 1942.

IF THERE'S NO ESCAPE, you don't experience combat fatigue.

You may get the soul scared out of you – or pretty well shot out – but you won't be suffering from combat fatigue, so-called.

> General Curtis LeMay, *Mission With LeMay*, 1965.

FEAR and fatigue impacted on the body in the same way, draining it of energy. That being true, the overloaded soldier became more susceptible to fear; and the more heavily fear began to oppress him, the less strength he had to sustain his burdens. Overloading plus fear – result, mass panic under fire.

> Brigadier-General S.L.A. Marshall, *Bringing Up the Rear*, 1979.

YET HISTORIANS and tacticians do not get it. If they did, there would be less nonsense written on the subject of vigorous pursuit, such as the current criticism of General Meade for allowing the beaten Confederate Army to slip away after Gettysburg. The Union Army was spiritually and physically spent after three days of battle ending in victory. Getting away, the southerners were homeward bound with no need to be urged.

> Brigadier-General S.L.A. Marshall, *Bringing Up the Rear*, 1979.

FEAR

FEAR makes men forget, and skill which cannot fight is useless.

> Brasidas of Sparta, 429 BC, to the Peloponnesian Fleet before action in the Criseaen Gulf, quoted in Thucydides, *The Peloponnesian War*, c. 404 BC, tr. Jowett, 1881.

FEAR is apparently a formidable ally for a guard.

> Xenophon, *How To Be A Good Cavalry Commander*, c. 360 BC (*Hiero the Tyrant and Other Treatises*, tr. Robin Waterfield, 1997).

IN THAT CASE I should be an even greater coward than they say I am, if I were to abandon the plans I believe to be right because of a few sneers and words of abuse. There is nothing shameful in experiencing fear for your country's sake. But the man who allows himself to be frightened by the opinions of others or by their slanders or abuse, proves that he is unworthy of such a high office as this, since he makes himself the slave of the very men whom it is his duty to restrain and overrule when they go astray and their judgment deserts them.

> Fabius Maximus, 217 BC, Roman dictator during the Second Punic War, in response to attacks by subordinates that his delaying tactics were cowardly, quoted in Plutarch, *The Lives*, c. AD 100 (*Makers of Rome*, tr. Ian Scott-Kilvert, 1965).

DARIUS and his army remained during the night marshalled in their original order; for they had no proper camp surrounding them, and they also feared that the enemy would make a night attack. It did more harm than anything else to the Persian cause at this crisis, that they stood so long under arms and that the fear, which usually proceeds great dangers, was not produced suddenly by a crisis, but cultivated for a long period, til it mastered their minds.

> Arrian, *Anabasis of Alexander*, 3.11, c. AD 125, tr. P.A. Brunt, 1976; the night before the Battle of Gaugamela (Arbela), 331 BC.

FEAR is sharp-sighted, and can see things under ground, and much more in the skies.

> Miguel de Cervantes, *Don Quixote*, 1605–1615, tr. Peter Motteux and John Ozell.

HE WHO is afraid is half beaten.

> Field Marshal Prince Aleksandr V. Suvorov, *The Science of Victory*, 1799.

ON THE BATTLEFIELD the real enemy is fear and not the bayonet or bullet.

> Robert Jackson, *A Systematic View of the Formation, Discipline, and Economy of Armies*, 1804.

WAR is not at all such a difficult art as people think. . . . In reality it would seem that he is vanquished who is afraid of his adversary and that the whole secret of war is this.

Napoleon, 1807, comment to Alexander I at Tilsit.

ALL SOLDIERS run away, madam.

The Duke of Wellington (1769–1852), when asked whether British soldiers ever ran away.

FEAR is the beginning of wisdom.

General of the Army William T. Sherman (1820–1891).

FEAR

I am that dreadful, blighting thing,
Like ratholes to the flood,
Like rust that knaws the faultless blade,
Like microbes to the blood.

I know no mercy and no truth,
The young I blight, the old I slay.
Regret stalks darkly in my wake,
And ignominy dogs my way.

Sometimes, in virtuous garb I rove,
With facile talk of easier way;
Seducing where I dare not rape
Young Manhood, from its honor's sway.

Again, in awesome guise I rush,
Stupendous, through the ranks of war,
Turning to water, with my gaze,
Hearts that, before, no foe could awe.

The maiden, who has strayed from right,
To me must pay the mead of shame.
The patriot who betrays his trust,
To me must own his tarnished name.

I spare no class nor cult nor creed,
My course is endless through the year.
I bow all heads and break all hearts,
All owe me homage – I am FEAR.

General George S. Patton, Jr., 26 April 1920, *Cosmopolitan* magazine, March 1945.

THE EXCEPTIONAL MAN may not feel fear, but the great mass of men do – their nervous control alone stands between them and a complete yielding to fear.

This nervous control may be upset in two principal ways. It may be worn thin by a long-continued strain – it may be shattered in a single instant by sudden shock. Usually it gives under a combination of these influences. The control is worn away imperceptibly by the anxiety and suspense of waiting for the enemy's blow, by the noise and concussive effect of shellfire, and by loss of the sleep that renovates the tired will. Then without warning the shock of a sudden surprise danger snaps the fine drawn thread of the will to resist. Stubborn resistance changes in a moment to

panic-stricken flight. Fear becomes uncontrollable terror. (July 1921.)

Captain Sir Basil Liddell Hart, *Thoughts on War*, 1944.

FEW MEN are by nature devoid of physical fear. The blistering heat of battle withers many a building reputation when the poor shrinking flesh fails to sustain the soul midst the myriad forms of dissolution in which the reaper seems to stalk the field. To combat this it behooves us to develop an antitoxin to fear and with it to inoculate our men. The best virus is a mixture of race consciousness, a mind saturated with former deeds of heroism, an abundant sense of obligation and an insatiable desire for present distinction and posthumous celebrity, so that in the fateful hour he may subdue his weaker self with that might potion – fear of fear.

Like a cold bath the first plunge is the hardest. Later, if he live, custom, fatigue, fatalism and pride will make him master of his emotions, for devoid of fear no normal man can ever become. Once on the morning of battle an officer asked Turenne if his knees shook from the cold and the veteran replied: "No, my friend, they shake from fear but if they knew where I shall this day take them they would tremble more.". . .

We do not stress enough the necessity for personal exposure and rash boldness on the part of our officers. Man loves life and too often yields to the sophistry of the subtle demon Fear, when he whispers, oh, so temptingly: "Your men need you, you must save yourself for them," forgetting that the inspiration of an heroic act will carry men to victory . . . forgetful too that the blood of heroes like the dragons teeth will sprout new leaders to replace his loss.

General George S. Patton, Jr., from his 1925 lecture, 'On Leadership', The Patton Collection, Library of Congress.

FEAR unhinges the will, and by unhinging the will it paralyses the reason; thoughts are dispersed in all direction in place of being concentrated on one definite aim. Fear, again, protects the body; it is the barometer of danger; is danger falling or rising, is it potent or weak? Fear should answer these questions, especially physical fear, and, thus knowing that danger confronts us, we can secure ourselves against it. Whilst moral fear is largely overcome by courage based on reason, physical fear is overcome by courage based on physical means.

Major-General J.F.C. Fuller, *The Foundations of the Science of War*, 1926.

ONE of the greatest qualities which we have is the ability to produce in our enemy the fear of the unknown. Therefore, we must always keep moving, do not sit down, do not say "I have done enough," keep on, see what else you can do to raise the devil with the enemy. . . .

General George S. Patton, Jr., 17 May 1941, address

to the officers and men of the Second Armoured Division, *The Patton Papers*, II, 1974.

YOU ARE NOT all going to die. Only two percent of you here, in a major battle would die. Death must not be feared. Every man is frightened at first in battle. If he says he isn't he is a God damn liar. Some men are cowards, yes, but they fight just the same or get the hell scared out of them watching men who do fight and who are just as scared as they. The real hero is the man who fights even though he is scared. Some get over their fright in a few minutes under fire, some take hours, some take days. The real man never lets the fear of death over-power his honor, his duty to his country and his innate manhood.
    General George S. Patton, Jr., June 1944, speech to the Third Army.

TO MANY A MAN in the line today fear is not so much of death itself . . . [as] of the terror and anguish and utter horror that precedes death in battle.
    Ernie Pyle, his last column written in Okinawa before he was killed by a Japanese sniper in 1945, quoted in *The Washington Post*, 1 April 1995, p. C1.

BY COWARDICE I do not mean fear. Fear is the response of the instinct of self-preservation to danger. It is only morbid, as Aristotle taught, when it is out of proportion to the degree of danger. In invincible fear – "fear stronger than I am" – the soldier has to struggle with a flood of emotions; he is made that way. But fear even when morbid is not cowardice. That is a label we reserve for something that a man does. What passes through his mind is his own affair.
    Lord Moran, *The Anatomy of Courage*, 1945.

WHEN the infantryman's mind is gripped by fear, his body is captured by inertia, which is fear's Siamese twin. "In an attack half of the men on a firing line are in terror and the other half are unnerved." So wrote Major General J.F.C. Fuller when a young captain. The failure of the average soldier to fire is not in the main due to conscious recognition of the fact that the act of firing may entail increased exposure. It is a result of a paralysis which comes of varying fears. The man afraid wants to do nothing; indeed, he does not care even to think of taking action.
    Getting him on his way to the doing of one positive act – the digging of a foxhole or the administering of first-aid to a comrade – persuading him to make any constructive use of his muscle power, and especially putting him at a job which he can share with other men, may become the first step toward getting him to make appropriate use of his weapons under combat conditions. Action is the great steadying force. It helps clear the brain. The man who finds that he can still control his muscles will shortly begin to use them. But if he is to make a rapid and complete recovery, he requires help from others.
    Brigadier S.L.A. Marshall, *Men Against Fire*, 1947.

EVERYBODY gets frightened. This is basic. I do not believe that many soldiers are frightened of death. Most people are frightened of dying and everybody is frightened of being hurt. The pressures of noise, of weariness, of insecurity lower the threshold of a man's resistance to fear. All these sources of stress can be found in battle, and others too – hunger, thirst, pain, excess of heat or cold and so on. Fear in war finds victims fattened for the sacrifice.
    General Sir John Hackett, *The Profession of Arms*, 1983.

NEVER look a frightened man in the eye if you want to keep him going. Of course, it occurs to me now that this can operate the other way round too. One can also be found out oneself in this way.
    General Sir John Hackett, *The Profession of Arms*, 1983.

I'VE BEEN SCARED in every war I've ever been in.
    General H. Norman Schwarzkopf, 1991, quoted in Peter David, *Triumph in the Desert*, 1991.

FIGHTING
General

WAR – I know it well, and the butchery of men.
Well I know, shift to the left, shift to the right
my tough tanned shield. That's what the real drill,
defensive fighting means to me. I know it all,
how to charge in the rush of plunging horses –
I know how to stand and fight to the finish,
twist and lunge in the War-god's deadly dance.
On guard!
    Homer, *The Iliad*, 7.271–281, 800 BC, tr. Robert Fagles, 1990; Hector to Telemonian Ajax as they began their duel.

ITALIAN COMMANDER: "If you are a great general, come down and fight me."
Marius: "If you are a great general, come and make me fight you."
    Gaius Marius (c. 157–86 BC), in F.E. Adcock, *The Roman Art of War Under the Republic*, 1940.

YOU SEE my sword dripping with blood and my horse with sweat. It is thus that the Moors are beaten in the field of battle.
    El Cid (Rodrigo Diaz de Vivar), 1094, after routing the Almoravides before Valencia, quoted in *Cronica del Cid Ruy Diaz*, 1498.

THE OBJECT of a good general is not to fight, but to win. He has fought enough if he gains a victory.
    The Duke of Alva, c. 1560.

TO IMAGINE that it is possible to perform great military deeds without fighting is just empty dreams.
    Napoleon (1769–1821).

HARD POUNDING, this, gentlemen; try who can pound the longest.

> The Duke of Wellington, 18 June 1815, to his staff at the Battle of Waterloo, quoted in Elizabeth Longford, *Years of the Sword*, 1970.

ESSENTIALLY war is fighting, for fighting is the only effective principle in the manifold activities generally designated as war. Fighting, in turn, is a trial of moral and physical forces through the medium of the latter. Naturally moral strength must not be excluded, for psychological forces exert a decisive influence on the elements involved in war.

> Major-General Carl von Clausewitz, *On War*, 2.1, 1832, tr. Michael Howard and Peter Paret, 1976.

IT IS SAID that when the officer in command reported to Gen. Jackson, at Winchester, in the evening, and gave a rather sensational account of the recapture of Port Royal and repulse of his own regiment, Gen. Jackson looked up, and in his quick, nervous way, asked: "Colonel, how many men had you killed?" "None, I am glad to say, general." "How many wounded?" "Few or none, sir." "Do you call that fighting, sir?" said Jackson, and a few minutes afterwards the colonel was put under arrest.

> Lieutenant-General Thomas J. 'Stonewall' Jackson, quoted in Allan, *History of the Campaign of Gen. T.J. (Stonewall) Jackson in the Shenandoah Valley of Virginia*, 1880.

I HAVE NOT word of encouragement to give! . . . The fact is that people have not yet made up their minds that we are at war with the South. They have not buckled down to the determination to fight this war through; for they have got the idea into their heads that we are going to get out of this fix somehow by strategy! That's the word – *strategy*! General McClellan thinks he is going to whip the Rebels by strategy; and the army has got the same notion. . . . The people *have not* made up their minds that we are at war, I tell you! They think there is a royal road to peace, and that General McClellan is to find it. The army has not settled down into the conviction that we are in a terrible war that has got to be fought out – no; and the officers have not either . . .

> Abraham Lincoln, shortly after the Battle of Antietam, September 1862, quoted in Sandburg, *Abraham Lincoln*, II, pp. 194–195.

WAR means fighting . . . The business of the soldier is to fight . . . to find the enemy and strike him; to invade his country, and do him all possible damage in the shortest time.

> Lieutenant-General Thomas J. 'Stonewall' Jackson (1824–1863).

I AM TIRED of this playing war without risks. We must encounter risks if we fight, and we cannot carry on the war without fighting.

> Major-General George G. Meade, 2 January 1863, letter to his wife.

WAR means fighting, and fighting means killing.

> Lieutenant-General Nathan Bedford Forrest (1821–1877).

FIGHT EVERYTHING blue betwixt wind and water until yonder flag comes down.

> Lieutenant-General Nathan Bedford Forrest, command to halt the escape of the garrison of Fort Pillow by steamer, 12 August 1864, quoted in Wyeth, *The Life of Nathan Bedford Forrest*, 1899.

THE MORE you hurt the enemy, the less he will hurt you.

> Admiral David G. Farragut, quoted in Martin, *Damn the Torpedos!*, 1970.

WE STARTED with a few good officers of experience, but shall end with some of the best in the world. Our fellows are beginning to understand that war means fighting. It is the duty of an officer to save his men as much as possible, but in almost all cases there has to be a certain amount of sacrifice.

> Admiral David G. Farragut, just before the battle of Mobile Bay on 5 August 1864, quoted in John Spears, *David G. Farragut*, 1905.

I DO NOT advise rashness, but I do desire resolute and actual fighting, with necessary casualties.

> Major-General Philip H. Sheridan, 23 September 1864, message to Brigadier-General William W. Averall.

THIS IS a very suggestive age. Some people seem to think that an army can be whipped by waiting for rivers to freeze over, exploding powder at a distance, drowning out troops, or setting them to sneezing; but it will always be found in the end that the only way to whip an army is to go out and fight it.

> General of the Army Ulysses S. Grant, to Brigadier-General Horace Porter, *Campaigning With Grant*, 1897.

THE OBJECT of fighting is to kill without getting killed. Don't disperse your force; you can't punch with an open hand; clench your fist; keep your command together.

Fight when holding, advancing or retiring: always fight or be ready to fight.

Aim at surprise; see without being seen. If you meet a man in a dark room, you jump; you should always try to make your enemy jump, either by day or night. A jumping man can't hit.

Never remain halted without a look-out. Sentries must be posted, no matter what troops are supposed to be in front of you.

Guard your flanks and keep touch with neighboring units. Try to get at the enemy's flanks.

Send information back to your immediate Commander. Negative information is as important as positive. State time and place of your message. You cannot expect assistance from your superiors unless you tell them where you are and how you are situated.

Hold what you have got and what you gain. Never withdraw from a position until ordered to do so.

WHEN IN DOUBT, FIGHT IT OUT. (1918)

> Major-General J.F.C. Fuller, *Memoirs of an Unconventional Soldier*, 1936.

YOU CAN TELL the general and the admiral we're going to stick and fight it out.

> General David A. Shoup, 20 November 1943, as commander (colonel) of the Second Marine Regiment during the desperate first hours of the landing on Tarawa, message to the commander of the Second Marine Division, Major-General Julian Smith, and commander of the invasion task force, Admiral Harry Hill; quoted in *Shoup Journal*, Marine Corps Historical Center.

YOU'VE NEVER lived until you've almost died. For those who fight for it, life has a meaning the protected will never know.

> Popular saying in SOG (Studies and Operations Group – clandestine special operations) units in Vietnam, quoted in Leigh Wade, *The Protected Will Never Know*, 1998.

City Fighting

I AGAIN CAUTION all unit and formation commanders not to execute combat operations with entire units such as companies and battalions. The offensive should be organized mainly on a small-group basis, with automatic weapons, hand grenades, bottles of inflammable mixture and anti-tank rifles.

> Marshal of the Soviet Union Vasili I. Chuikov, while commanding the 62nd Army during the siege of Stalingrad, emphasising the fragmenting nature of city fighting, Army General Order No. 166, 23 September 1942, quoted in Geoffrey Jukes, *Stalingrad: The Turning Point*, 1968.

AS THE FIGHT began, Vietnamese and Marines made do without tank, artillery, and air support, in the hope of sparing the venerable city, so rich a part of Vietnamese heritage; but as the enemy held on tenaciously, that policy proved too costly in American and South Vietnamese lives. President Thieu subsequently authorized whatever was necessary to retake the city. . . . Destruction inevitably followed.

> General William C. Westmoreland, of the Battle for Hue, February 1968, *A Soldier Reports*, 1976.

WE DECLARE that only fools fight in cities and shut our eyes against the future. But in the next century, in an uncontrollably urbanizing world, we will not be able to avoid urban deployments short of war and even full-scale city combat. Cities have always been centers of gravity, but they are now more magnetic than ever before. Once the gatherers of wealth, then the processors of wealth, cities and their satellite communities have become the ultimate creators of wealth. They concentrate people and power, communications and control, knowledge and capability, rendering all else peripheral. They are also the postmodern equivalent of jungles and mountains – citadels of the dispossessed and irreconcilable. A military unprepared for urban operations across a broad spectrum is unprepared for tomorrow.

> Lieutenant-Colonel Ralph Peters, *Fighting For the Future*, 1999.

IN FULLY URBANIZED warfare . . . warfare becomes profoundly vertical, reaching up into towers of steel and cement and downward into sewers, subway lines, road tunnels, communications tunnels and the like. Even with the "emptying" of the modern battlefield, organizational behavior in the field strives for lateral contiguity and organizational integrity. But the broken spatial qualities of urban terrain fragments units and compartmentalizes encounters, engagements, and even battles. The leader's span of control can easily collapse, and it is very, very hard to gain and maintain an accurate picture of the multidimensional "battlefield."

> Lieutenant-Colonel Ralph Peters, *Fighting For the Future*, 1999.

Desert Fighting

DESERT OPERATIONS should be like . . . wars at sea, "in their mobility, their ubiquity, their independence of bases and communications, their lack of ground features, of strategic areas, of fixed directions, of fixed points."

> Colonel T.E. Lawrence, quoted in Liddell Hart, *Colonel Lawrence: The Man Behind the Legend*, 1934.

OF ALL THEATRES of operations, it was probably in North Africa that the war took on its most advanced form. The protagonists on both sides were fully motorized formations, for whose employment the flat and obstruction-free desert offered hitherto undreamed-of possibilities. It was the only theatre where the principles of motorized and tank warfare, as they had been taught theoretically before the war, could be applied in full – and further developed. It was the only theatre where pure tank battles between major formations were fought.

> Field Marshal Erwin Rommel, *The Rommel Papers*, 1953.

IMMOBILITY and a rigid adherence to pattern are bad enough in European warfare; in the desert they are disastrous. Here everything is in flux; there are no obstructions, no lines, water or woods for cover; everything is open and incalculable; the commander must adapt and reorientate himself daily, even hourly, and retain his freedom of action. Everything is in motion; he must be constantly on the alert, all the time on the edge of capture or destruction by a more cunning, wide-awake or versatile enemy. There can be no conservatism in thought or action, no relying on tradition or resting on the laurels of previous victory. Speed of judgment, and action to create changing situations and surprises for the enemy faster than he can react, never making dispositions in advance, these are the fundamentals of desert tactics.

General Fritz Bayerlein, quoted in Erwin Rommel, *The Rommel Papers*, 1953.

BEING BARREN, the desert cannot be conquered by armies. Of itself, as Winston Churchill once wrote, the desert yields nothing to them but hardship and suffocation. To occupy it is therefore purposeless and wasteful, unless occupation is an essential step toward ultimate security.

It is this very singleness of purpose about desert warfare that makes it unique. The arena is suitable for nothing except primordial combat, with death or survival as the issue. All movement is limited or regulated by the availability of water, and all maneuver seeks the destruction of the enemy force.

Brigadier-General S.L.A. Marshall, 'The Desert: It's Different', *Infantry*, 12/1970.

IN DESERT WARFARE you do not necessarily go after a terrain objective. What you do is seek to destroy the enemy's center of gravity. And there are a lot of ways you can do that without ever having to worry about house-to-house, dig-'em-out fighting.

General H. Norman Scwharzkopf, 13 September 1990, interview, quoted in Pyle, *Schwarzkopf, In His Own Words*, 1991.

Mountain Fighting

IN MY FIFTH CAMPAIGN the inhabitants of the cities . . . of Mount Nipur, a steep mountain, like the nest of the eagle, king of birds, – were not submissive to my yoke. I had my camp pitched at the foot of Mount Nipur and with my picked bodyguard and my relentless warriors, I, like a strong wild-ox, went before them. Gullies, mountain torrents and waterfalls, dangerous cliffs, I surmounted in my sedan chair. Where it was too steep for my chair, I advanced on foot. Like a young gazelle I mounted the highest peaks in pursuit of them. Whenever my knees gave out, I sat down on some mountain boulder and drank the cold water from the water skin to quench my thirst. To the summits of the mountains I pursued them and brought about their overthrow. Their cities I captured and I carried off their spoil; I destroyed, I devastated, I burned them with fire.

Sennacherib, King of Assyria (705–681 BC), quoted in Daniel Luckenbill, *Ancient Records of Assyria and Babylonia*, 1926.

DO NOT CLIMB heights in order to fight. So much for mountain warfare.

Sun Tzu, *The Art of War*, 9, c. 500 BC, tr. Giles, 1910.

IF THE NARROW PLACES through which our army had been intending to pass should be seized by the enemy, and they are well equipped and in strength . . . then we must not get close to that place and certainly not send the army recklessly and at great risk through another difficult road which is occupied by the enemy. We do not say this out of fear of the enemy, but as a warning to avoid rugged terrain which involves struggling and danger. Often enough one weak person who has the advantage of a strong position can successfully fight against many brave men. For wherever you are unable to use your hands, your horse, and your weapons, while the enemy is able to do so, then the danger is obvious.

General Nikephoros Ouranos (attributed), *Campaign Organization and Tactics*, c. AD 1000 (*Three Byzantine Military Treatises*, tr. George Dennis, 1985).

THOSE who wage war in mountains should never pass through defiles without first making themselves masters of the heights.

Field Marshal Maurice Comte de Saxe, *My Reveries*, 1732, tr. Phillips, 1940.

IN REGARD to mountain warfare in general, everything depends on the skill of our subordinate officers and still more on the morale of our soldiers. Here it is not a question of skillful maneuvering, but of warlike spirit and wholehearted devotion to the cause.

Major-General Carl von Clausewitz, *Principles of War*, 1812, tr. Gatzke, 1942.

MAXIM 14. Among mountains, a great number of positions are always to be found very strong in themselves, and which it is dangerous to attack. The character of this mode of warfare consists in occupying camps on the flanks or in the rear of the enemy, leaving him only the alternative of abandoning his position without fighting, to take another in the rear, or to descend from it in order to attack you. In mountain warfare the assailant has always the disadvantage. . . .

Napoleon, *The Military Maxims of Napoleon*, tr. George D'Aguilar, 1831 (David Chandler, ed., 1987).

THE CHIEF CHARACTERISTIC of mountain defense is its complete passivity; in this light, the tendency towards the defense of mountains was very natural before armies attained to their present capability of movement. . . . The offensive had thus again gained a preponderance through the greater mobility of troops; and it was only through the same means that the defense could seek for help. But mountainous ground by its nature is opposed to mobility.

Major-General Carl von Clausewitz, *On War*, 6.15, 1832, tr. Michael Howard and Peter Paret, 1976.

VERY FAR from seeing a refuge for the defensive, in a mountainous country, when a decisive battle is sought, we should rather advise a general in such a case to avoid such a field by every possible means. . . . mountains, both tactically and strategically, are in general unfavorable to the defensive. . . . The mountains limit the view and prevent movements in every direction; they force a state of passivity, and make it necessary to close up every avenue of approach, which always leads more or less to a war of cordons. We should therefore, if possible, avoid mountains with the principal mass of our force, and leave them on one side, or keep them before or behind us.

Major-General Carl von Clausewitz, *On War*, 6.16, 1832, tr. Michael Howard and Peter Paret, 1976.

MOUNTAIN OPERATIONS teach us . . . that in such a country a strong and heroic will is worth more than all the precepts in the world. . . . One of the principal rules of this kind of war is, not to risk one's self in the valleys without securing the heights. Shall I also say that in this kind of war, more than any other, operations should be directed upon the communications of the enemy?

Lieutenant-General Antoine-Henri Baron de Jomini, *Summary of the Art of War*, 1838, tr. Mendell and Craighill, 1862.

WITH BRAVE INFANTRY and bold commanders mountain ranges can usually be forced.

Lieutenant-General Antoine-Henri Baron de Jomini, *Summary of the Art of War*, 1838, tr. Mendell and Craighill, 1862.

Night Fighting

BY DAY certainly the combatants have a clearer notion, though even then by no means of all that takes place, no one knowing much of anything that does not go on in his own immediate neighborhood; but in a night engagement . . . how could anyone know anything for certain?

Thucydides, of the Athenian night attack on the defences of Syracuse at Epipolae, 413 BC, *History of the Peloponnesian War*, 7,43, c. 404 BC, tr. Richard Crawley, 1910.

SOME AUTHORITIES state that Parmenio went to Alexander's tent and advised a night attack, because the enemy would not be expecting it, and it would naturally cause alarm and confusion. Alexander and Parmenio were not alone in the tent; others were listening, and that, perhaps, was one reason for Alexander's reply: "I will not," he said, "demean myself by stealing victory like a thief. Alexander must defeat his enemies openly and honestly." However, these lofty words probably indicated confidence in danger rather than vanity, and in my own opinion they were based upon perfectly sound sense: night-fighting is a tricky business; unexpected things happen to both sides – to those who have carefully planned the attack as much as to those who are taken off their guard – and often enough the better men get the worst of it, while victory, contrary to everybody's expectation, goes to the weaker side. More often than not Alexander took risks in his battles; but on this occasion he felt the chances of a night attack to be too unpredictable. . . .

Arrian, of Alexander the Great before the Battle of Gaugamela (Arbela), 1 October 331 BC, *The Campaigns of Alexander*, 3.10, c. AD 150, tr. Aubrey de Sélincourt, 1987.

THE MORE DARKNESS in night attacks hinders and impedes the sight, the more must one supply the place of actual vision by skill and care.

Scipio Africanus (236–184 BC), quoted in Liddell Hart, *A Greater Than Napoleon: Scipio Africanus*, 1926.

THE AVERAGE PERSON thinks that fighting at night is a simple matter, not calling for any special concern or precision. But such is not the case. On the contrary, very careful organization is needed. Anyone planning on night operations must first find soldiers who expressly volunteer for this kind of warfare. Both commander and men should make an agreement under oath. We should swear that when the assignment has been completed, they shall receive their proper rewards. The men should profess their readiness to accept death rather than fail to carry out their night mission. We should also promise them under oath that, if any man is killed in action, his heirs shall receive the rewards he deserved.

Second, we should seek men who are familiar with the nocturnal security arrangements of the enemy.

Third, there should be no moon that night. Otherwise the enemy will observe us marching along and, while we are still a good distance off, make preparations to confront us.

Anonymous Byzantine general, *On Strategy* (*Peri Strategias*) c. AD 527–565 (*Three Byzantine Military Treatises*, tr. George Dennis, 1985).

IN GENERAL, I believe that night attacks are only good when you are so weak that you dare not attack the enemy in daylight.

Frederick the Great, *Instructions to His Generals*, 1747, tr. Phillips, 1940.

BASICALLY, a night attack is only an intensified raid. At first glance it looks highly effective: supposedly the defender is taken unawares, while the attacker, of course, is well prepared for what is about to happen. What an uneven contest! One imagines complete confusion on one side, and on the other an attacker concerned merely to profit by it. This image explains the many schemes for night attacks put forward by those who have neither to lead them or accept responsibility for them. In practice they are very rare.

Major-General Carl von Clausewitz, *On War*, 4.14, 1832, tr. Michael Howard and Peter Paret, 1976.

NIGHT OPERATIONS are not merely risky; they are also difficult to execute. This too limits their scale. Their essence being surprise, it must be a prime consideration to approach without being seen. This, too, is easier for small detachments than for large ones, and rarely feasible for the columns of an entire army.

> Major-General Carl von Clausewitz, *On War*, 4.14, 1832, tr. Michael Howard and Peter Paret, 1976.

NO OPERATION of war is more critical than a night march.

> Sir Winston Churchill, *The River War*, 1899.

ATTACKS under cover of darkness may provide both the elements of surprise and of reasonable security on the battle fields of the future.

> Major-General John A. Lejeune, *The Reminiscences of a Marine*, 1929.

I NEVER HEARD of troops who can withstand a night attack from the rear.

> Bernard Newman, *The Cavalry Came Through*, 1930.

DARKNESS is a friend to the skilled infantryman.

> Captain Sir Basil Liddell Hart, *Thoughts on War*, 1944.

SOLDIERS must be taught to move and fight at night. This is becoming more and more imperative, and it does not mean to make an approach march at night. It means to conduct lethal operations in the dark. To do this, previous and very accurate daylight reconnaissance is desirable and limited objective attacks are essential. In addition to the usual reserve following such an attack, a second reserve should be at hand to move up after daylight in case the enemy counterattacks.

> General George S. Patton, Jr., *War As I Knew It*, 1947.

NIGHT OPERATIONS are a boon to troops who know the terrain like the palm of their hand and a reckless risk for those who don't. . . . There is no easier way to scramble a force than to deploy it at night on jumbled, unfamiliar ground. Voice recognition is about five percent efficient in the dark. Too quickly, men drift away, units become mixed and all control is lost.

> Brigadier-General S.L.A. Marshall, 'The Desert: It's Different', *Infantry*, 12/1970.

FIREPOWER

BATTLES are won by superiority of fire.

> Frederick the Great, *Military Testament*, 1768.

BY CONCENTRATING our howitzers and cannon at a single point we will gain the local superiority, and perhaps be able to beat them. The real difficulty is to make the hole in the enemy line, but once we have done that we will overcome the remaining obstacles soon enough.

> Frederick the Great, 11 June 1778, letter to Prince Henry, *Politische Correspondenz Friedrichs des Grossen*, 1879–1939.

FIRE OPENS the gates of victory.

> Field Marshal Prince Aleksandr V. Suvorov, *The Science of Victory*, 1796, quoted in Bragin, *Field Marshal Kutuzov*, 1944.

MAXIM 92. In battle like in siege, skill consists in converging a mass of fire on a single point: once the combat is opened, the commander who is adroit will suddenly and unexpectedly open fire with a surprising mass of artillery on one of these points, and is sure to seize it.

> Napoleon, *The Military Maxims of Napoleon*, tr. Burnod, 1827.

THE BEST PROTECTION against the enemy's fire is a well directed fire from our own guns.

> Admiral David G. Farragut, 14 March 1863, General Order for the attack on Port Hudson.

FIRE kills.

> Marshal of France Henri-Phillipe Pétain (1856–1951).

A SUPERIORITY of fire, and therefore a superiority in directing and delivering fire and in making use of fire, will become the main factors upon which the efficiency of a force will depend.

> Marshal of France Ferdinand Foch, *Precepts and Judgments*, 1919.

THERE IS but one means to extenuate the effects of enemy fire: it is to develop a more violent fire oneself.

> Marshal of France Ferdinand Foch, *Precepts and Judgments*, 1919.

NO ENDURANCE, no physical force, no gregarious instinct and solidarity of the mass struggle could give preponderance in the era of high-speed small-caliber rifles, machine guns, intricate technical devices on vessels, and the loose formation in ground battles.

> V.I. Lenin, quoted in Savkin, *Basic Principles of Operational Art and Tactics*, 1972.

IT IS FIRE-POWER, and fire-power that arrives at the right time and place, that counts in modern war – not man-power. (March 1924.)

> Captain Sir Basil Liddell Hart, *Thoughts on War*, 1944.

ERRORS of conception were to cost more than any errors of execution. Lessons of the South African War that went wider than the selection of leaders had been overlooked. Read in the light of 1914–1918, the "Evidence taken before the Royal Commission on the War in South Africa" offers astonishing proof of how professional vision may miss the wood for the trees. There is little hint, among those who were to be the leaders in the next war, that they had recognized the root problem of the future – the dominating power of fire defence and the supreme difficulty of crossing the bullet-swept zone.

> Captain Sir Basil Liddell Hart, *A History of the World War 1914–1918*, 1935.

THE TENDENCY towards under-rating fire-power . . . has marked every peace interval in modern military history.

> Captain Sir Basil Liddell Hart, *Thoughts on War*, 1944.

THE GREATER the visible effect of fire on the attacking infantry, the firmer grows the defenders' morale, whilst a conviction of the impregnability of the defense rapidly intensifies in the mind of the attacking infantryman.

> Captain Sir Basil Liddell Hart, *Thoughts on War*, 1944.

I THINK if we should say that "Fire is the Queen of Battles," we should avoid arm arguments and come nearer telling the truth. Battles are won by fire and movement. The purpose of the movement is to get the fire in a more advantageous place to play on the enemy. This is from the flank or rear.

> General George S. Patton, Jr., *War As I Knew It*, 1947.

BATTLES are won by frightening the enemy. Fear is induced by inflicting death and wounds on him. Death and wounds are produced by fire. Fire from the rear is more deadly and three times more effective than fire from the front, but to get fire behind the enemy, you must hold him by frontal fire and move rapidly around his flank.

> General George S. Patton, Jr., *War As I Knew It*, 1947.

FIREPOWER KILLS, disrupts, suppresses, and causes dispersion.

It is doubtful if any of the people who are today writing on the effect of technology on warfare would consciously disagree with this statement. Yet, many of them tend to ignore the impact of firepower on dispersion, and as a consequence they have come to believe that the more lethal the firepower, the more deaths, disruption, and suppression it will cause. In fact, as weapons have become more lethal intrinsically, their casualty-causing capability has either declined or remained about the same because of greater dispersion of targets.

> Colonel T.N. Dupuy, *Understanding War*, 1987.

FIRST BATTLE

THEN FELL ON Polydore his vengeful rage, The youngest hope of Priam's stooping age: (Whose feet for swiftness in the race surpast) Of all his sons, the dearest, and the last.

To the forbidden field he takes his flight In the first folly of a youthful knight, To vaunt his swiftness, wheels around the plain, Vaunts not long, with all his swiftness slain. Struck where the crossing belts unite behind, And golden rings the double back-plate join'd: Forth thro' the navel burst the thrilling steel; And on his knees with piercing shrieks he fell; The rushing entrails pour'd upon the ground His hands collect; and darkness wraps him round.

> Homer, *The Iliad*, 20.471–484, c. 800 BC, tr. Alexander Pope, 1743; the death of Prince Polydorus, the youngest of the Trojan princes, who had disobeyed his father and gone into his first battle to die at the hands of Achilles.

IMPATIENT to flesh his virgin sword.

> Homer, *The Odyssey*, 20, c. 800 BC, tr. Alexander Pope, 1725–1726.

LET THE BOY win his spurs.

> King Edward III, 26 August 1346, of his son, the Black Prince, at the Battle of Crécy, when others urged the king to send help to his sorely pressed flank.

THAT shall be my music in the future!

> Charles XII, King of Sweden, 1700, at Copenhagen, the first time under fire as he listened to the bullets' whistle.

ONLY A FOOL will claim that he is as calm in his first battle as in his tenth. . . . I know that my heart was pounding when reveille sounded on the morning of that memorable day.

> Frederick the Great, referring to the Battle of Mollwitz, 10 April 1741, quoted in Duffy, *The Military Life of Frederick the Great*, 1985.

I HEARD the bullets whistle, and believe me, there is something charming in the sound.

> General George Washingtion, 3 May 1754, letter to his mother about his first action.

AS TO THE WAY in which some of our ensigns and lieutenants braved danger – the boys just come out from school – it exceeds all belief. They ran as at cricket.

> The Duke of Wellington (1769–1852), of the first action of new officers during the Peninsular War (1809–1813).

WAR LOSES a great deal of its romance after a soldier has seen his first battle. I have a more vivid recollection of the first than the last one I was in. It is a classical maxim that it is sweet and becoming to die for one's country; but whoever has seen the horrors of a battlefield feels that is far sweeter to live for it.

> Colonel John S. Mosby, *Mosby's War Reminiscences*, 1887.

IN COMPANY with this Lady [Mrs. Hoge] I made my first visit to a military hospital. We drove to the "Fifth

Street Hospital," and passed directly into a ward of the wounded from Fort Donelson. The sickening odor of blood and healing wounds almost overpowered me. In the nearest bed lay a young man whose entire lower jaw had been shot away, and his tongue cut off. A surgeon came to dress the poor fellow's wounds, and I was directed to render him what assistance he required. The process of healing had drawn down the upper part of the face, so that when the ghastly wound was concealed by plasters and bandages, the exposed portion of the face was sadly distorted. But when the bandages were removed by the surgeon for examination of the wound, its horrible nature became apparent. A deathly faintness came over me, and I was hurried from the ward to the outer air for recovery.

Three times I returned, and each time some new horror smote my vision, some more sickening odor nauseated me, and I was led out fainting. The horrors of that long ward, containing over eighty of the most fearfully wounded men, were worse than anything I had imagined; but not worse than scenes in which I afterwards spent weeks and weeks without a tremor of the nerves or a flutter of the pulse. This was my first experience.

Mary A. Livermore, *My Story of the War*, 1887.

WHEN FIRST under fire and you're wishful to duck,
Don't look or take heed at the man that is struck.
Be thankful you're living and trust to your luck,
And march to your front like a soldier.

Rudyard Kipling (1865–1936), 'The Young British Soldier'.

FOR THE Red Gods call us out and we must go!
Rudyard Kipling (1865–1936), 'The Feet of the Young Men'.

I MUST HAVE BEEN unconscious for sometime. When I came to, Sergeant Bentele was working over me. French shell and shrapnel were striking intermittently in the vicinity. . . . A quarter of an hour later, buglers sounded "regimental call" and "assembly." From all sides parts of the regiment worked their way toward the area west of Bleid. One after the other the different companies came in. There were many gaps in their ranks. In its first fight the regiment had lost twenty-five per cent of its officers and fifteen per cent of its men in dead, wounded, and missing. I was deeply grieved to learn that two of my best friends had been killed. . . .

Field Marshal Erwin Rommel, of the first battle of the 124th Infantry Regiment, August 1914, *Infantry Attacks*, 1944.

THE FIRST FIGHT, the first contact with war! I do not know what this held for others, but for me it had as much moving poetry as my first youthful love affair, my first kisses. (1918)

Marshal Jospeh Pilsudski, *The Memoirs of a Polish Revolutionary and Soldier*, 1931.

MANY OF YOU have not been fortunate enough to have engaged in combat, and owing to the foolish writings of sob-sisters and tear-jerkers, you may have erroneous ideas of what battle is like. You will read of men – imaginary men – who on the eve of battle sit around the camp fire and discuss their mothers, and their sisters, and their sweet-hearts, and talk regretfully of their past life and fear foolishly for their future. No one has a higher or more respectful devotion to women than I have; but the night before battle you do not sit around a fire. . . . You go to sleep and have to be kicked in the butt in the morning so as to start the war. You have not dreamed of dying or worried about your boyhood. You have slept the sleep of fighting males eager for the kill.

General George S. Patton, December 1941, *The Patton Papers*, II, 1974.

WE WERE ENTERING a new uncharted land, a field of military enterprise in which we were guided only by theory and peace-time maneuvers.

General Holland M. 'Howlin Mad' Smith, *Coral and Brass*, 1948, of the landing on Tarawa in November 1943; although not the first battle for the Marines in the Pacific (Guadalcanal was first), Tarawa was the first modern amphibious operation for which the Marine Corps had been preparing during the inter-war years.

FAR AS training went, our pilots were coming directly from basic trainers right into B-17's. They knew nothing about formation flying. We merely prayed to get 'em off the ground and get 'em down again.

You'd go to bed at night and think: *How could anybody every have the gall to bring a rabble like this into battle?*

And then you'd say to yourself: *You, too. How will you stand up? You've never been shot at, you don't know how you'll feel. Maybe you know more about the business of being a pilot; maybe you know more about navigation and bombardment, and even gunnery, than your men. But what do you know about how it feels to be in combat? Will you stand up? Will you have the nerve to ask them to stand up to it?*

Things like that you'd keep thinking. Then you'd be too exhausted to go to sleep.

General Curtis LeMay, *Mission With LeMay*, 1965.

FLEXIBILITY

ONE MUST NOT always use the same modes of operation against the enemy, even though they seem to be working out successfully. Often enough the enemy will become used to them, adapt to them, and inflict disaster on us.

The Emperor Maurice, *The Strategikon*, c. AD 600 (*Maurice's Strategikon*, tr. George Dennis, 1984).

STRATEGY is an art, and one who practices it must be supple and cunning and know how to make a timely alteration at every turn of it. For there is a time when it is not shameful to flee, if the occasion allows, and again to pursue relentlessly, each according to one's advantage; where success would seem more by cunning than by force, risking everything is to be deprecated. Since many and various matters lead toward one end, victory, it is a matter of indifference which one one uses to reach it.

General John Kinnamos, *Deeds of John and Manuel Comnenus*, 1976.

THE DUKE being asked how it was that he had succeeded in beating Napoleon's Marshals, one after another, said "I will tell you. They planned their campaigns just as you might make a splendid set of harness. It looks very well; and answers very well; until it gets broken; and then you are done for. Now I made my campaigns of ropes. If anything went wrong, I tied a knot; and went on."

The Duke of Wellington (1769–1852), quoted in William Fraser, *Words on Wellington*, 1889.

STRATEGIC DEPLOYMENT can, and must be, planned far ahead. Battles in a war of positions demand similar treatment, but in the war of movement and the actions incidental to it the situations which the commander has to visualize follow one another in motley succession. He has to decide in accordance with his instinct. Thus soldiering becomes an art, and the soldier a strategist.

General Erich Ludendorff, *My War Memories, 1914–1918*, 1919.

EVERY RED ARMY commander must firmly grasp the fact that slavery to routine and extreme enthusiasm for some specific plan or some specific method are the most dangerous thing of all for us . . . nothing can be absolute or solidly fixed; everything flows and changes, and any means, any methods might be used in a certain situation.

Mikhail V. Frunze (1885–1925), quoted in *Voyenno istorichiskiy zhurnal*, II/1984.

THE SUCCESS of a commander does not arise from following rules or models. It consists in absolutely new comprehension of the dominant facts of the situation at the time, and all the forces at work. Every great operation of war is unique. What is wanted is a profound appreciation of the actual event. There is no surer road to disaster than to imitate the plans of bygone heroes and fit them to novel situations.

Sir Winston S. Churchill, *Marlborough*, 1933–1938.

LET US NOW discuss flexibility. What is flexibility? It is the concrete realization of the initiative in military operations; it is the flexible employment of armed force. . . . the central task in directing a war, a task most difficult to perform well. In addition to organizing and educating the army and the people, the business of war consists in the employment of troops in combat, and all these things are done to win the fight. Of course it is difficult to organize an army, etc., but it is even more difficult to employ it, particularly when the weak are fighting the strong. To do so requires subjective ability of a very high order and requires the overcoming of the confusion, obscurity and uncertainty peculiar to war and the discovery of order, clarity and certainty in it; only thus can flexibility in command be realized.

Mao Tse-tung, *On Protracted War*, May 1938.

RENOUNCING this counterstrike . . . was insistently required by a change of the situation. And that decision, in my view, expresses one of the characteristic traits of the gift for military leadership of Nikolai Fedorovich Vatutin: the ability to precisely capture the smallest changes in the situation, to infer the further development of events from them . . . not even shrinking from basic changes in plans made earlier.

Marshal of the Soviet Union Kirill S. Moskalenko (1902–1985), speaking of the counterstrike of tank units on the Voronezh Front foreseen for 4 July 1943, quoted in Nathan Leites, *The Soviet Style in War*, 1982.

ENSURE that both plan and dispositions are flexible – adaptable to circumstances. Your plan should foresee and provide for a next step in case of success or failure, or partial success – which is the most common case in war. Your dispositions (or formation) should be such as to allow this exploitation or adaptation in the shortest possible time.

Captain Sir Basil Liddell Hart, *Strategy*, 1954.

IN BATTLE, the art of command lies in understanding that no two situations are ever the same; each must be tackled as a wholly new problem to which there will be a wholly new answer.

Field Marshal Viscount Montgomery of Alamein, *The Memoirs of Field Marshal Montgomery*, 1958.

I HAVE USED the word 'flexibility' for the last time. It seems that it is a large general purpose tent under which chaos, confusion, and incompetency are kept well hidden from the public.

General Creighton Abrams (1914–1974), quoted in *Military Review*, 4/1985.

THE MARK of a good military unit is versatility in a combat situation, not simply the ability to memorize and execute a set piece.

Lieutenant-General Arthur S. Collins, Jr., *Common Sense Training*, 1978.

THE FOG OF WAR

FREDERICK: That was a diabolical day. Did you understand what was going on?
Catt: Your Majesty, I had a good grasp of the preliminary march, and the first arrangements for the

---

battle. But all the rest escaped me. I could make no sense of the various movements.
Frederick: You were not the only one, my dear friend. Console yourself, you weren't the only one!

Frederick the Great, speaking of the Battle of Zorndorff, 1758, quoted in Catt, *Unterhaltungen mit Friedrich dem Grossen*, 1884.

THE GENERAL UNRELIABILITY of all information presents a special problem in war: all action takes place, so to speak, in a kind of twilight, which like fog or moonlight, often tends to make things seem grotesque and larger than they really are.

Whatever is hidden from full view in this feeble light has to be guessed at by talent, or simply left to chance. So once again for lack of objective knowledge one has to trust to luck.

Major-General Carl von Clausewitz, *On War*, 2.2, 1832, tr. Michael Howard and Peter Paret, 1976.

IN WAR obscurity and confusion are normal. Late, exaggerated or misleading information, surprise situations and counterorders are to be expected.

General of the Army George C. Marshall, *Infantry in Battle*, 1939.

ERRORS of judgment there must be in war, and few would cavil at them, especially those due to the fog of war. But it is different when the fog is self-created by confused thought and limited study.

Captain Sir Basil Liddell Hart, *Thoughts on War*, 1944.

THE VIETNAM WAR is the foggiest in my own personal experience. Moreover, it is the first war I know of wherein the fog of war is thicker away from the scene of conflict than on the battlefield.

General Earle G. Wheeler, 18 December 1967, address to the Economic Club of Detroit, quoted in *Joint Force Quarterly*, Autumn–Winter 1997–1998.

ALL ACTIONS in war take place in an atmosphere of uncertainty – the fog of war. Uncertainty pervades battle in the form of unknowns about the enemy, about the environment, and even about the friendly situation. While we try to reduce these unknowns by gathering information, we must realize we cannot eliminate them. The very nature of war makes absolute certainty impossible; all actions in war will be based on incomplete, inaccurate, and even contradictory information.

General Alfred M. Gray and Major John Schmitt, *Warfighting*, United States Marine Corps, 1989.

FOLLOW-UP

MANY GENERALS believe that they have done everything as soon as they have issued orders, and they order a great deal because they find many abuses. This is a false principle; proceeding in this fashion, they will never reestablish discipline in an army in which it has been lost or weakened. Few orders are best, but they should be followed up with care; negligence should be punished without partiality and without distinction of rank or birth; otherwise you will make yourself hated. One can be exact and just, and be loved at the same time as feared. Severity must be accompanied with kindness, but this should not have the appearance of pretense, but of goodness.

Field Marshal Maurice Comte de Saxe, *My Reveries*, 1732, tr. Phillips, 1940.

THE PRINCIPAL TASK of the general is mental, large projects and major arrangements. But since the best dispositions become useless if they are not executed, it is essential that the general should be industrious to see whether his orders are executed or not.

Frederick the Great, *Instructions to His Generals*, 1747, tr. Phillips, 1940.

IT IS NOT ENOUGH to give orders, they must be obeyed.

Napoleon, 11 June 1806, advice to his stepson, Prince Eugene, *Correspondance de Napoléon Ier, publié par ordre de l'Empereur Napoléon III*, No. 10350, XII, 1858–1870.

IF YOU WANT anything done well, do it yourself.

The Duke of Wellington, quoted in William Fraser, *Words on Wellington*, 1889.

THERE IS but one way; – to do as I did – to have A HAND OF IRON. The moment there was the slightest neglect in any department I was down on them.

The Duke of Wellington, cited in Elizabeth Longford, *Wellington: Years of the Sword*, 1970.

NO MAN of action, no commander, has finished when he has taken his decision and embodied it in an order. He remains to the last moment responsible for its execution in the way he intended and for the manifestation of his will in every stage of its accomplishment. . . . One evening before a battle I was taking steps to discover whether our order had reached all the quarters concerned, and I received the brief answer in an honest Berlin accent, *"Ich greife an,"** He had understood, and that was the essential thing.
**Ich greife an*, I attack.

Colonel-General Hans von Seekt, *Thoughts of a Soldier*, 1930.

COMMANDERS must remember that . . . the issuance of an order, or the devising of a plan, is only about 5 percent of responsibility of command. The other 95 percent is to insure, by personal observation, or through interposing of staff officers that the order is carried out.

General George S. Patton, Jr., quoted in *Military Review*, 9/1980.

IT IS A MISTAKE to think that once an order is given

there is nothing more to be done; you have got to see that it is carried out in the spirit which you intended. Once he has decided on his outline plan and how he will carry it out, the commander should himself draft the initial operational order or directive, and not allow his staff to do so. His staff and subordinates then begin their more detailed work, and this is based on the written word of the commander himself. Mistakes are thus reduced to a minimum. This was my method, beginning from the days when I commanded a battalion.

Field Marshal Viscount Montgomery of Alamein, *The Memoirs of Field Marshal Montgomery*, 1958.

YOU MAY HAVE HEARD this story about General Pershing in World War I. While inspecting a certain area, he found a project that was not going too well, even though the second lieutenant in charge seemed to have a pretty good plan. General Pershing asked the lieutenant how much pay he received, and when the lieutenant replied: "$141.67 per month, Sir," General Pershing said, "Just remember that you get $1.67 for making your plan and issuing the order, and $140.00 for seeing that it is carried out.

General of the Army Omar N. Bradley, 'Leadership', *Parameters*, Winter 1972.

I PAID a lot of surprise visits at night, mostly driving alone. I wanted to check whether units were in a constant state of readiness, ensure that there was always a responsible senior officer in every command headquarters, and talk to the soldiers returning from a night exercise or from guard duty at an outpost. Whenever there was an operational problem, I would see the head of the Operations Branch, the unit commander, and his junior platoon commanders. I wanted to learn what had happened, if it was after an action, or what special problems were envisaged, if it was before an operation. I wanted to hear things from them at first hand, without intermediaries, and I believed that the young officers should hear what I had to say directly from me, in my own words and in my own style.

General Moshe Dayan, *The Story of My Life*, 1976.

A UNIT does well only what the commander checks.

Old U.S. Army saying.

FOLLY

MANY CITIES of men he saw and learned their minds, many pains he suffered, heartsick upon the open sea, fighting to save his life and bring his comrades home. But he could not save them from disaster, hard as he strove –
the recklessness of their own ways destroyed them all, the blind fools. . . .

Homer, *The Odyssey*, 1.4–9, c. 800 BC, tr. Robert Fagles, 1996, of the folly of Odysseus' men that led to their destruction.

I WAS in a furious rage. The Turks should never, by the rules of sane generalship, have ventured back to Tafileh at all. It was simple greed, a dog-in-the-manger attitude unworthy of a serious enemy, just the sort of hopeless thing a Turk would do. How could they expect a proper war when they gave us no chance to honour them? Our morale was continually being ruined by their follies, for neither could our men respect their courage, nor our officers respect their brains. Also, it was an icy morning, and I had been up all night and was Teutonic enough to decide that they should pay for my changed mind and plan.

Colonel T.E. Lawrence, *The Seven Pillars of Wisdom*, 1935.

ANOTHER LESSON of history is that the most dangerous folly of all is man's failure to recognize his own aptitude for folly. That failure is a common affliction of authority.

Captain Sir Basil Liddell Hart, *Through the Fog of War*, 1938.

ONE NEVER attributes folly to his enemy – but then, of such stuff are surprises made.

Lieutenant-General Phillip B. Davidson, writing of the rashness of the 1968 Tet Offensive by the North Vietnamese, *Vietnam at War*, 1988.

FORCE

FORCE has no place, there is need of skill.

Herodotus, *The History*, c. 450 BC.

NOTHING is so weak and unstable as a reputation for power not based on force.

Cornelius Tacitus, *Annals*, AD 116.

IN EVERY COUNTRY, force yields to civic qualities. Bayonets are lowered before the priest who speaks in the name of Heaven and before the scholar who inspires respect for his science. I have predicted to certain military men, who had scruples, that military rule will never take root in France, unless the nation were stultified by fifty years of ignorance. All attempts will fail, and their authors will be the victims. I do not govern in the capacity of a general but by virtue of the civil qualities which in the eyes of the nation qualify me for the government. If the nation did not hold this opinion, the government would not last. I knew what I was doing when, as army commander, I styled myself "Member of the Institute"; I was sure of being understood by the last drummer boy.

Napoleon, 1802, meeting of the Council of State, quoted in Christopher Herold, ed., *The Mind of Napoleon*, 1955.

DO YOU KNOW what I admire most in this world? It's the total inability of force to organize anything. There are only two powers in the world – the sword and the spirit. By spirit I understand the civil and religious institutions. . . . In the long run, the sword is always beaten by the spirit.

Napoleon, 1808, conversation with Fontanes, quoted in Christopher Herold, ed., *The Mind of Napoleon*, 1955.

PEOPLE are very apt to believe that enthusiasm carried the French through their revolution, and was the parent of those exertions which nearly conquered the world; but if the subject is nicely examined, it will be found that enthusiasm was the name only, but that force was the instrument which brought forward those great resources . . . and that a perseverance in the same system of applying every individual and every description of property to the service of the army, by force, has since conquered Europe.

The Duke of Wellington, 22 August 1809 at Miajadas, letter to Lord Castlereagh, commenting on how the Spanish leadership attempted to govern with enthusiasm, but without regularity and order, quoted in Julian Rathbone, *Wellington's War: His Peninsular Dispatches*, 1984.

THE PEOPLE are always in the wrong when they are faced by the armed forces.

Napoleon, 2 October 1810, letter.

FORCE is only justifiable in extremes; when we have the upper hand, justice is preferable.

Napoleon, *Political Aphorisms*, 1848.

FORCE, to counter opposing force, equips itself with the inventions of art and science. Attached to force are certain self-imposed, imperceptible limitations hardly worth mentioning, known as international law and custom, but they scarcely weaken it. Force – that is, physical force, for moral force has no existence save as expressed in the state and the law – is thus the *means* of war; to impose our will on the enemy is its object. To secure that object we must render the enemy powerless; and that, in theory, is the true aim of warfare.

Major-General Carl von Clausewitz, *On War*, 1.1, 1832, tr. Michael Howard and Peter Paret, 1976.

NOT BY SPEECHES and decisions of majorities will the greatest problems of the time be decided – that was the mistake of 1848–49 – but by iron and blood.

Prince Otto von Bismarck, 29 September 1862, while ambassador to France, to a group of Prussian ministers.

AN EFFICIENT military body depends for its effect in war – and in peace – less upon its position than upon its concentrated force.

Rear Admiral Alfred Thayer Mahan, *Naval Administration and Warfare*, 1908.

ONE MUST KNOW the limitations of force; one must know when to blend force with a maneuver, a blow with an agreement.

Leon Trotsky, *What Next?*, 1923.

NOT BELIEVING in force is the same as not believing in gravitation.

Leon Trotsky (1879–1940).

BETWEEN two groups that want to make inconsistent kinds of worlds, I see no remedy but force.

Justice Oliver Wendell Holmes, Jr. (1841–1935).

THE ONE MEANS that wins the easiest victory over reason: terror and force.

Adolf Hitler, *Mein Kampf*, 1.2, 1924.

AGAINST NAKED FORCE the only possible defense is naked force. The aggressor makes the rules for such a war; the defenders have no alternative but matching destruction with more destruction, slaughter with greater slaughter.

President Franklin Roosevelt, 21 August 1941, message to young Democrats Convention, Louisville, Kentucky.

THE MORE I reflect on the experience of history the more I come to see the instability of solutions achieved by force, and to suspect even those instances where force has had the appearance of resolving difficulties.

Captain Sir Basil Liddell Hart, *Thoughts on War*, 1944.

ONCE YOU DECIDE to use force, you had better make sure you have plenty of it. If you need a battalion to do a job, it's much better to have the strength of a division. You probably won't suffer any casualties at all in that way.

General of the Army Dwight D. Eisenhower, *The New York Times*, 10 May 1965.

FORESIGHT/ANTICIPATION

AFTER AGREEING upon a treaty or a truce with the enemy, the commander should make sure that his camp is guarded more strongly and more closely. If the enemy chooses to break the agreement, they will only gain a reputation for faithlessness and the disfavor of God, while we shall remain in safety and be true to our word. A general should not have to say: "I did not expect it."

The Emperor Maurice, *The Stratigikon*, c. AD 600 (*Maurice's Strategikon*, tr. George Dennis, 1984).

AS IT TURNED OUT, they wished to do it all in safety and to fall upon us by night, when we were not watching. And as I was so much on my guard, they found me standing in front of their thoughts.

Hernan Cortes, 1519, on his entry into the Valley of Mexico, in Madariaga, *Hernan Cortes*, 1942.

MAXIM 8. A general-in-chief should ask himself frequently in the day, What should I do if the enemy's army appeared now in my front, or on my right, or on my left? If he has any difficulty in answering these questions he is ill posted, and should seek to remedy it.

> Napoleon, *Military Maxims of Napoleon*, tr. George D'Aguilar, 1831 (David Chandler, ed., 1987).

THINK to a finish!

> Field Marshal Viscount Allenby of Meggido, 1902, upon taking command of the Fifth Lancers.

THE VITAL POINT in actual warfare is to apply to the enemy what we do not wish to be applied to ourselves and at the same time not to let the enemy apply it to us. Therefore, it is most important that what we consider would embarrass the enemy we should apply to them before they can do the same to us; we must always forestall them.

> Admiral Marquis Heihachiro Togo, February 1905, to the officers of the Japanese Fleet, quoted in Ogasawara, Life of Admiral Togo, 1934.

DANGERS which are warded off by effective precaution and foresight are never even remembered.

> Sir Winston S. Churchill (1874–1965).

WANT OF FORESIGHT, unwillingness to act when action would be simple and effective, lack of clear thinking, confusion of counsel until emergency comes, until self-preservation strikes its jarring gong – these are the features which constitute the endless repetition of history.

> Sir Winston S. Churchill, speech in the House of Commons, 2 May 1935, *Winston S. Churchill: His Complete Speeches 1897–1963*, VI, 1974, p. 6499.

AGAIN for the small unit commander, there is need to seek the true meaning of the counsel insistently given by Major General Stuart Heintzelman, Major General Frank A. Ross, and others: "Anticipation is 60 per cent of the art of command."

But like ten years in the penitentiary, it is very easy to say "Anticipate!" and very hard to do it.

> Brigadier-General S.L.A. Marshall, *Men Against Fire*, 1947.

A COMMANDER must think two stages ahead.

> Field Marshal Viscount Montgomery of Alamein, *The Memoirs of Field Marshal Montgomery*, 1958.

WHILE ROMMEL was leading his troops in person against our strongly-held defensive positions on the Alam Halfa ridge, Montgomery was planning the battle of Alamein. That was the difference between the two.

> Lieutenant-General Sir Brian Horrocks, *Escape to Action*, 1961.

IT IS a cardinal responsibility of a commander to foresee insofar as possible where and when crises affecting his command are likely to occur. It starts with his initial estimate of the situation – a continuing mental process from the moment of entering the combat zone until his unit is pulled out of the line.

Ask yourself these questions. What are the enemy's capabilities? What shall I do, or what could I do, if he should exercise that one of his capabilities which would be most dangerous to me, or most likely to interfere with the accomplishment of my mission?

> General Matthew B. Ridgway, 'Leadership', *Military Review*, 10/1966.

THE JOB of a commander is to think ahead. A GHQ must be dealing with events foreseen two and preferably three or more days away. The imagination and foresight with which he manages that is one of the inescapable tests of a commander: because if there is one rule about a battle it is, "What is possible today may not be possible tomorrow."

> General Saad El Shazly, *The Crossing of the Suez*, 1980.

FORTIFICATIONS

WHEN SOMEBODY . . . asked why Sparta lacked fortification walls, he pointed to the citizens under arms and said: "These are the Spartans' walls."

> Plutarch, quoting Agesilaus, Eurypontid King of Sparta (400–360 BC), *The Lives*, c. AD 100 (*Plutarch on Sparta*, tr. Richard Talbert, 1988).

WHEN ANOTHER PERSON put the same question to him, his reply was: "Cities shouldn't be fortified with stones and timbers, but with the valour of their inhabitants."

> Plutarch, quoting Agesilaus, Eurypontid King of Sparta (400–360 BC), *The Lives*, c. AD 100 (*Plutarch on Sparta*, tr. Richard Talbert, 1988).

BY GOD'S THROAT, even if that castle were all built of butter and not of iron and stone, I have no doubt it would defend me against him [King of France] and all his forces.

> Richard I, 'The Lion Heart', King of England, 1198–1199, of his new castle, Gaillard.

THE ART of defending fortified places consists in putting off the moment of their reduction.

> Frederick the Great, *Instructions to His Generals*, 1747, tr. Phillips, 1940.

THE ONLY ADVANTAGE a fortified line may afford is to render the situation of the enemy so difficult as to induce him to operate incorrectly, which in turn may cause him to be defeated with numerically inferior forces. Or if one is confronted by a capable general, the fortifications may have the effect of compelling him methodically to negotiate the obstacles that one has created with due deliberation. In this manner time is gained.

> Napoleon, 1807, '*Notes sur la defence de l'Italie*', *Correspondance de Napoléon Ier, publié par ordre de l'Empereur Napoléon III*, No. 14704, Vol. XVIII, 1858–1870.

MAXIM 40. Fortresses are equally useful in offensive and defensive warfare. It is true they will not in themselves arrest an army, but they are an excellent means of retarding, embarrassing, weakening, and annoying a victorious enemy.

Napoleon, *The Military Maxims of Napoleon*, tr. George D'Aguilar, 1831 (David Chandler, ed., 1987).

MAXIM 103. When they are thoroughly understood, field fortifications are always useful and never injurious.

Napoleon, *The Military Maxims of Napoleon*, tr. Burnod, 1827.

FORTITUDE

WITHOUT ARROGANCE or the smallest deviation from the truth, it may be said that no history now extant, can furnish an instance of an Army's suffering such uncommon hardships as ours have done, and bearing them with the same patience and fortitude. To see men without clothes to clothe their nakedness, without blankets to lie on, without shoes, by which their marches might be traced by the blood from their feet, and almost as often without provisions as with; marching through frost and snow, and at Christmas taking up their winter quarters within a day's march of the enemy, without a house or hut to cover them till they could be built, and submitting to it without a murmur, is a mark of patience and obedience which in my opinion can scarce be paralleled.

General George Washington, 1777, at Valley Forge.

WAR is the realm of physical exertion and suffering. These will destroy us unless we can make ourselves indifferent to them, and for this birth our training must provide us with a certain strength of body and soul. If we do possess those qualities, then even if we have nothing but common sense to guide them we shall be well equipped for war: it is exactly these qualities that primitive and semicivilized peoples usually possess.

Major-General Carl von Clausewitz, *On War*, 1.3, 1832 tr. Michael Howard and Peter Paret, 1976.

FORTUNE

I WHO NEVER yet feared anything that was human, have amongst such as were divine, always had a dread of Fortune as faithless and inconstant. . . .

Lucius Aemilius Paulus, 216 BC, quoted in Plutarch, *Plutarch's Lives*, c. AD 100, tr. John Dryden.

IT IS DIFFICULT for a man to whom fortune has never proved false to reflect upon its uncertainties.

Hannibal, 202 BC, to Scipio Africanus on the day before the Battle of Zama, which ended the Second Punic War in the defeat of Carthage, quoted in Livy, *Annals of the Roman People*, c. 25 BC–AD 17 (*Livy: A History of Rome*, 30, tr. Moses Hadas and Joe Poe, 1962).

IN WAR we must always leave room for strokes of fortune and accidents that cannot be foreseen.

Polybius, *Universal History*, c. 125 BC (*The Rise of the Roman Empire*, tr. Ian Scott-Kilvert, 1987).

GO AHEAD, my friend. Be bold and fear nothing. You have got Caesar and Caesar's fortune with you in your boat.

Julius Caesar, 28 November 49 BC, during the Civil War, when the master of the boat in which he was travelling from Brindisium to Dyrrhaccium was so terrified of the rough sea that he was about to turn about, quoted in Plutarch, *The Lives*, c. AD 100 (*The Fall of the Roman Republic*, tr. Rex Warner, 1972).

FOR IT IS necessary to pray to Fortune to do its share, but not to consider that Fortune has entire control. Stupid are those who make disasters chargeable to Fortune alone, rather than to the negligence of commanders, as well as those who attribute successes to her, and to the skill of the generals.

Onasander, *The General*, AD 58 (*Aeneas Tacticus, Aclepiodotus, Onasander*, tr. The Illinois Greek Club, 1923).

FOR I KNOW WELL the terror and misfortune which have laid hold upon the enemy and compel them to become less brave, for the one fills them with fear because of what has already happened, and the other brushes aside their hope of success. For Fortune, once seen to be bad, straightway enslaves the spirit of those who have fallen in her way.

Count Belisarius, December AD 533, address to his army before the Battle of Tricamarum in North Africa, during which he destroyed the last hope of the Vandals, quoted in Procopius, *History of the Wars*, 4.1, c. AD 560, tr. H.B. Dewing, 1929.

IT IS BETTER to subdue an enemy by famine than by sword, for in battle, *fortuna* has often a much greater share than *virtu*.

Niccolo Machiavelli, *The Art of War*, 1521.

THERE IS NOTHING so subject to inconstancy of fortune as war.

Miguel de Cervantes, *Don Quixote*, 1615.

WHEN A GENERAL conducts himself with all prudence, he still can suffer ill fortune; for how many things do not cooperate at all with his labors! Weather, harvest, the officers, the health or sickness of his troops, blunders, the death of an officer on whom he counts, discouragement of the troops, exposure of your spies, negligence of the officers who should reconnoiter the enemy, and finally betrayal. These are the things that should be kept continually before your eyes so as to be prepared for them and so that good fortune will not blind us.

Frederick the Great, *Instructions to His Generals*, 1747, tr. Phillips, 1940.

INDEED the fate of states and the reputation of generals rest on the most trifling incidents. A few seconds are enough to determine their fortune.

Frederick the Great, *Oeuvres de Frederic le Grand*, (1846–1857).

RULE fortune.

Field Marshal Prince Aleksandr V. Suvorov (1729–1800), quoted in Blease, *Suvorof*, 1920.

IN WARFARE every opportunity must be seized; for fortune is a woman; if you miss her to-day, you need not expect to find her tomorrow.

Napoleon, 30 July 1800, quoted in R.M. Johnston, ed., *The Corsican*, 1910.

I PROPOSE to get into fortune's way. . . .

The Duke of Wellington, 10 December 1812, to Lord Beresford, *The Dispatches of Field Marshal the Duke of Wellington, During His Various Campaigns in India, Denmark, Portugal, Spain, the Low Countries, and France*, IX, 1834–1838, p. 609.

IS IT TRUE that the Poles want to leave me?

I went too far. I have made mistakes. Fortune has turned her back on me these last two years; but she's a woman, and will change. Who can tell? Perhaps it is your evil star has drawn mine on? In any case have you lost confidence in me?

Napoleon, 28 October 1813, to the Polish officers on the road near Schuluchterne after the disaster at Leipzig, quoted in R.M. Johnston, ed., *The Corsican*, 1910.

I SENSED that Fortune was abandoning me. I no longer had in me the feeling of final success. Not to venture is to do nothing when the moment is right, and one should never venture without being convinced of good luck.

Napoleon, on St. Helena, cited in Henry Lachouque, *Waterloo*, 1972.

. . . THE CONTINGENT element inseparable from the waging of war [which] gives to that activity both its difficulty and its grandeur.

General Charles de Gaulle, *The Edge of the Sword*, 1932.

I AM MORE than ever impressed with the part that good or bad fortune sometimes plays in tactical engagements. The authors give us credit, where no credit is due, for being able to choose the exact time for our attack on the Japanese carriers when they were at the great disadvantage – flight decks full of aircraft fueled, armed and ready to go. All I can claim credit for, myself, is a very keen sense of the urgent need for surprise and a strong desire to hit the enemy carriers with our full strength as early as we could reach them.

Admiral Raymond A. Spruance, foreword to *Midway: The Battle That Doomed Japan*, 1955; surely a description of how 'fortune favours the bold'.

FRICTION

. . . THE EFFECT of reality on ideas and intentions in war.

Major-General Carl von Clausewitz, to Marie von Brühl, 29 September 1806.

EVERYTHING in war is very simple, but the simplest thing is difficult. The difficulties accumulate and end by producing a kind of friction that is inconceivable unless one has experienced war. . . . Countless minor incidents – the kind you can never really foresee – combine to lower the general level of performance, so that one always falls far short of the intended goal. Iron will-power can overcome friction; it pulverizes every obstacle, but of course it wears down the machine as well.

Friction is the only concept that more or less corresponds to the factors that distinguish real war from war on paper. The military machine . . . is composed of individuals, every one of whom retains his potential for friction. . . . the least important of whom may chance to delay things or somehow make them go wrong.

Major-General Carl von Clausewitz, *On War*, 1.7, 1832, tr. Michael Howard and Peter Paret, 1976.

FRIENDLY RELATIONS contribute a lot to diminish the friction of war. Comradeship is the oil in the machine. If 'Bill' appeals to his friend 'Dick' he is more sure of good and prompt support than if an overtired O.C. 9th Battalion sends a formal message to an overburdened O.C. 999th Battery. It is thus important to lose no opportunity of creating a co-operative atmosphere by making touch. The military saying that "time spent in reconnaissance is rarely wasted" applies just as clearly to the more personal kind of reconnaissance within your own front. (July 1933.)

Captain Sir Basil Liddell Hart, *Thoughts on War*, 1944.

THE VERY ESSENCE of war as a clash between opposed wills creates friction. It is critical to keep in mind that the enemy is not an inanimate object but an independent and animate force. The enemy seeks to resist our will and impose his own will on us. It is the dynamic interplay between his will and ours that makes war difficult and complex. In this environment, friction abounds.

Friction may be mental, as in indecision over a course of action. Or it may be physical, as in effective enemy fire or a terrain obstacle that must be overcome. Friction may be external, imposed by enemy action, the terrain, weather, or mere chance. Or friction may be self-induced, caused by such factors as lack of a clearly defined goal, lack of coordination, unclear or complicated plans, complex task organizations or command relationships, or complicated communications systems. Whatever form it takes, because war is a human enterprise, friction will always have a psychological as well as a physical impact.

While we should attempt to minimize self-induced friction, the greater requirement is to fight effectively within the medium of friction. The means to overcome friction is the will; we prevail over friction through persistent strength of mind and spirit. While striving to overcome the effects of friction ourselves, we must attempt at the same time to raise our enemy's friction to a level that destroys his ability to fight.

General Alfred M. Gray and Major John Schmitt, *Warfighting*, United States Marine Corps, 1989.

FRIENDLY FIRE/FRATRICIDE

TRUE, but this is a necessary evil which we must endure, to arrest impending destruction.

General Marquis Cornwallis, 15 March 1781, to Brigadier-General O'Hara, of the necessity of firing on his own troops mixed with the advancing Americans at the Battle of Guilford Courthouse, quoted in Henry Lee, *Memoir of the War in the Southern Department*, 1869.

FRIENDLY fire, isn't.

U.S. Navy Seal list of quips published just before Operation Just Cause in Panama, December 1989.

I DETEST the term "friendly fire." Once a bullet leaves a muzzle or a rocket leaves an airplane, it is not friendly to anyone. Unfortunately, fratricide has been around since the beginning of war. The very chaotic nature of the battlefield, where quick decisions make the difference between life and death, has resulted in numerous incidents of troops being killed by their own fire.

General H. Norman Schwarzkopf, *It Doesn't Take a Hero*, 1992.

MUCH has been made of the casualties caused by friendly fire in DESERT STORM. One can deeply sympathize with families mourning their dead killed by accident rather than enemy action. I believe a large percentage of our casualties have been caused by errors or mistakes in all our wars. . . . And what if we did not employ the heavy firepower we use in battle to protect our troops and to offset numerically superior enemy forces? Would the casualties be less or greater? War is a brutal and dangerous endeavor in which men – and now women – are exposed to death and horrible wounds. Every leader worthy of the name keeps his casualties to the irreducible minimum, but the simple fact is that war is death and destruction. Lest I be judged too harshly for these observations, let me assure the reader that one of the high points of my life was during one of my World War II battalion's reunions, when several

wives thanked me for bringing their husbands safely home.

Lieutenant-General Louis Metzger, 'Some Thoughts on Combat', *Marine Corps Gazette*, 1/1993.

FUNERALS

THE GENERAL should take thought for the burial of the dead, offering as a pretext for delay neither occasion nor time nor place nor fear, whether he happens to be victorious or defeated. Now this is both a holy act of reverence toward the dead and also a necessary example for the living. For if the dead are not buried, each soldier believes that no care will be taken of his own body, should he chance to fall, observing what happens before his own eyes, and thereby judging of the future, feeling that he, likewise, if he should die, would fail of burial, waxes indignant at the contemptuous neglect of burial.

Onasander, *The General*, AD 58, quoted in *Aeneas Tacticus, Aclepiodotus, Onasander*, 1923.

THE FUNERAL PYRE was raised and gold was brought up from the hoard in payment of wergild for Hneaef. Upon the pyre were placed the dead warriors in bloodied corslets, gilded boar glittering above the helmets. Then Hildeburh in double grief ordered the body of her slain son to be placed by the side of her brother Hneaef, nephew at uncle's shoulder. She keened her sorrow as the bodies mounted to the pyre.

The fire swirled up to the heavens and roared above the mound. Heads melted and the wounded bodies burst with spring blood. Then the flames, greediest of spirits, swallowed up those taken away in battle, their glory gone with the smoke.

Beowulf, c. AD 1000 (*My Name is Beowulf*, tr. Frederick Rebsamen, 1971).

THERE SHOULD BE no real neglect of the dead, because it has a bad effect on the living; for each soldier values himself as highly as though he were living in a good house at home.

General of the Army William T. Sherman, *Memoirs of W.T. Sherman*, 1875.

THERE WAS a tenderness under the apple trees as powder-grimed officers and men brought in the dead; a tenderness for lost comrades, who had fought together so often and so well, that went beyond reverence and compassion . . . Funerals in the field, rough and ready though they be, seem less bleak than those performed with funeral rites, as though the soldier whose calling deals with sudden death can find a way to stand easy in its shadow.

Brigadier Lord Lovat, *March Past*, 1978.

G

GENERALS/GENERALSHIP

THERE ARE FIVE dangerous faults which may affect a general: (1) Recklessness, which leads to destruction; (2) cowardice, which leads to capture; (3) a hasty temper that can be provoked by insults; (4) delicacy of honor that is sensitive to shame; (5) over-solicitude for his men, which exposes him to worry and trouble. These are the five besetting sins of a general, ruinous to the conduct of war.

When an army is overthrown and its leader slain, the cause will surely be found among the five dangerous faults. Let them be a subject of meditation.
> Sun Tzu, *The Art of War*, 8, c. 500 BC, tr. Giles, 1910.

FOR A GENERAL must also be capable of furnishing military equipment and providing supplies for the men; he must be resourceful, active, careful, hardy, and quick-witted; he must be both gentle and brutal, at once straightforward and designing, capable of both caution and surprise, lavish and rapacious, generous and mean, skilful in defence and attack; and there are many other qualifications, some natural, some acquired, that are necessary to one who would succeed as a general. It is well to understand tactics too; for there is a wide difference between right and wrong disposition of the troops, just as stones, bricks, timber and tiles flung together anyhow are useless, whereas when the materials that neither rot nor decay, that is the stones and tiles, are placed at the bottom and the top, and the bricks and timber are put together in the middle, as in building, the result is something of great value, a house, in fact.
> Socrates (470–399 BC), quoted by Xenophon, *Memorabilia*, 3.6–7, c. 360 BC (tr. E.C. Marchant, 1923).

HE USED TO SAY that a general needs to show daring towards his opponents, goodwill towards his subordinates and a cool head in crisis.
> Plutarch, paraphrasing Agesilaus, Eurypontid King of Sparta (400–360 BC), *The Lives*, c. AD 100, (*Plutarch on Sparta*, tr. Richard Talbert, 1988).

WHEN PEOPLE said of Scipio Africanus that he lacked aggressiveness, he is reported to have answered: "My mother bore me a general, not a warrior."
> Scipio Africanus (236–184 BC), quoted in Frontinus, *Stratagems*, 4.7, c. AD 84–96, tr. Charles E. Bennett, 1925.

A GOOD GENERAL not only sees the way to victory; he also knows when victory is not possible.
> Polybius, *Histories*, 1, c. 125 BC.

IT WAS Caesar's hope that he could finish the business without fighting or casualties because he had cut his adversaries off from food supply. Why lose men, even for victory? Why expose soldiers who deserved so well of him to wounds? Why even tempt fortune. Victory through policy is as much a mark of the good general as victory by the sword.
> Julius Caesar, *The Civil War*, c. 45 BC, (*The Gallic Wars and other Writings by Julius Caesar*, tr. Moses Hadas, 1957).

THERE ARE five skills and four desires involved in generalship.

The five skills are: skill in knowing the disposition and power of enemies, skill in knowing the ways to advance and withdraw, skill in knowing how empty or how full countries are, skill in knowing nature's timing and human affairs, and skill in knowing the features of terrain.

The four desires are: desire for the extraordinary and unexpected in strategy, desire for thoroughness in security, desire for calm among the masses, and desire for unity of hearts and minds.
> Zhuge Liang (AD 180–234), *The Way of the General* (*Mastering the Art of War*, tr. Thomas Cleary, 1989).

A SHIP cannot cross the sea without a helmsman, nor can one defeat an enemy without tactics and strategy. With these and the aid of God it is possible to overcome not only an enemy force of equal strength but even one greatly superior in numbers. For it is not true, as some inexperienced people believe, that wars are decided by courage and numbers of troops, but, along with God's favor, by tactics and generalship, and our concern should be with these rather than wasting our time in mobilizing large numbers of men. The former provide security and advantage to men who know how to use them well, whereas the other brings trouble and financial ruin.
> The Emperor Maurice, *The Strategikon*, c. AD 600 (*Maurice's Strategikon*, tr. George Dennis, 1984).

It is safer and more advantageous to overcome the enemy by planning and generalship than by sheer force; in the one case the results are achieved without loss to oneself, while in the other some price has to be paid.

> The Emperor Maurice, *The Strategikon*, c. AD 600 (*Maurice's Strategikon*, tr. George Dennis, 1984).

THE COMMANDING GENERAL, as well as the general, the military governor, the ruling general: his office [is] warfare. [He is] the maneuverer of troops – a courageous warrior, one whose mission is to go to his death.

The good commanding general, [or] general, [is] able, prudent, a holder of vigil, a maneuverer of forces. He devises strategy; he declares, he assumes the responsibility of war. He distributes, he supervises the arms; he distributes, commands, supervises the provisioning. He lays out, he searches out the roads [to the foe]; he tracks [them]. He establishes the war huts, the prisons, the market places in enemy lands. He places the sentries, posts the chosen ones, stations the spies, the hidden ones, the concentrated ones. He interrogates them; he discovers the places where the enemy will approach.

The stupid commanding general, [or] general, causes trouble, causes death, leads one into danger.

> Aztec account of generalship, c. 1500, quoted in Fray Bernardino de Sahagún, *General History of the Things of New Spain, Book 10 – The People*, 1961.

PAY WELL, command well, hang well.

> General Sir Ralph Hopton (1596–1652), *Maxims for the Management of an Army*, 1643.

THE KNOWLEDGE of a real general must be varied. He must have an accurate idea of politics in order to be informed of the intention of princes and the forces of states and of their communications; to know the number of troops and the princes and their allies can put in the field; and to judge the condition of their finances. Knowledge of the country where he must wage war serves as the base for all strategy. He must be able to imagine himself in the enemy's shoes in order to anticipate all the obstacles that are likely to be placed in his way. Above all, he must train his mind to furnish him with a multitude of expedients, ways and means in case of need. All this requires study and exercise. For those who are destined for the military profession, peace must be a time of meditation, and war the period where one puts his ideas into practice.

> Frederick the Great, 'Reflexions sur la projets de campagne', *Oeuvres de Frederic le Grand*, 1846–1856, in Jay Luvaas, ed., *Frederick the Great on the Art of War*, 1966.

THOSE WHO are persuaded that valour alone

suffices for the general officer, deceive themselves greatly; it is an essential quality, no doubt, but it must be matched with much other knowledge . . . [The general] must use judgment in everything and how can he do this if he lacks knowledge?

> Frederick the Great, *Oeuvres de Frederic le Grand*, 29.4, 1846–1856, quoted in Azar Gat, *The Origins of Military Thought: from the Enlightenment to Clausewitz*, 1989.

A PERFECT GENERAL, like Plato's republic, is a figment. Either would be admirable, but it is not characteristic of human nature to produce beings exempt from human weaknesses and defects. The finest medallions have reverse sides. But in spite of this awareness of our imperfections it is not less necessary to consider all the different talents that are needed by an accomplished general. . . .

It is essential that a general should dissemble while appearing to be occupied, working with the mind and working with the body, ceaselessly suspicious while affecting tranquility, saving of his soldiers and not squandering them except for the most important interests, informed of everything, always on the lookout to deceive the enemy and careful not to be deceived himself. In a word he should be more than an industrious, active, and indefatigable man, but one who does not forget one thing to execute another, and above all who does not despise those little details which pertain to great projects.

> Frederick the Great, *Instructions to His Generals*, 1747, tr. Phillips, 1940.

MAXIM 81. It is exceptional and difficult to find all the qualities of a great general combined in one man. What is most desirable and distinguishes the exceptional man, is the balance of intelligence and ability with character or courage. If courage is predominant, the general will hazard far beyond his conceptions; and on the contrary, he will not dare to accomplish his conceptions if his character or his courage are below his intelligence.

> Napoleon, *The Military Maxims of Napoleon*, tr. Burnod, 1827.

THE MOST essential quality of a general is firmness of character and the resolution to conquer at any price.

> Napoleon, quoted in Gourgaud, *Journal inédit de 1815 à 1818*, Vol. II, 1816.

INTELLIGENT and fearless generals assure the success of affairs.

> Napoleon, to Marshal Mortier, 29 November 1806, *Correspondance de Napoléon Ier, publié par ordre de l'Empereur Napoléon III*, No. 113255, XIII, 1858–1870.

MAKE WAR seriously. You must be up at one in the morning. Your troops must be under arms at two, and you must be on the spot to receive reports from the reconnaissances sent out in all directions. You must not turn in again until eight, when you are sure there is nothing new.

Napoleon, 24 April 1807, to his brother Jérôme, quoted in R.M. Johnston, ed., *The Corsican*, 1910.

I HAVE SEEN the order of the day signed by you that makes you the laughing stock of Germany, Austria, and France. Have you no friend who will tell you the truth? You are King and brother of the Emperor, – ridiculous title in warfare! You must be a soldier, and again a soldier, and always a soldier! You must bivouac with your outposts, spend night and day in the saddle, march with your advance guard so as to get information, or else remain in your seraglio. You wage war like a satrap. By Heaven! Is it from me you have learned that! – from me, who with an army of 200,000 men live with my skirmishers?

Napoleon, 17 May 1809, to his brother Jérôme, quoted in R.M. Johnston, ed., *The Corsican*, 1910.

WAR is a singular art; I can assure you that fighting sixty battles taught me nothing I did not know at the first one. The essential quality of the general is firmness, and that is a gift from heaven.

Napoleon, 25 December 1817, St. Helena, quoted in R.M. Johnston, ed., *The Corsican*, 1910.

TO BE a good general a man must know mathematics; it is of daily help in straightening one's ideas. Perhaps I owe my success to my mathematical conceptions; a general must never imagine things, that is the most fatal of all. My great talent, the thing that marks me most, is that I see clearly; it is the same with my eloquence, for I can distinguish what is essential in a question from every angle. The great art in battle is to change the line of operations during the course of the engagement; that is an idea of my own, and quite new.

The art of war does not require complicated maneuvers; the simplest are the best, and common sense is fundamental. From which one might wonder how it is generals make blunders; it is because they try to be clever. The most difficult thing is to guess the enemy's plan, to sift the truth from all the reports that come in. The rest merely requires common sense; it is like a boxing match, the more you punch the better it is. It is also necessary to read the map well.

Napoleon, 29 January 1818, St. Helena, quoted in R.M. Johnston, ed., *The Corsican*, 1910.

A GENERAL'S principal talent consists in knowing the mentality of the soldier and in gaining his confidence.

Napoleon (1769–1821).

THE MOST ESSENTIAL qualities for a general will always be: *first*, a high moral courage, capable of great resolution; *second*, a physical courage which takes no account of danger. His scientific or military acquirements are secondary to these. It is not necessary that he should be a man of vast erudition; his knowledge may be limited but it should be thorough, and he should be perfectly grounded in the principles at the base of the art of war.

Next in importance come the qualities of his personal character. A man who is gallant, just, firm, upright, capable of esteeming merit in others instead of being jealous of it, and skillful in making his merit add to his own glory, will always be a good general and may even pass for a great man. . . . *finally*, the union of wise theory with great character will constitute the great general.

Lieutenant-General Antoine-Henri Baron de Jomini, *Summary of the Art of War*, 1838, tr. Mendell and Craighill, 1862.

A GENERAL has much to bear and needs strong nerves. The civilian is too inclined to think that war is only like the working out of an arithmetical problem with given numbers. It is anything but that. On both sides it is a case of wrestling with powerful, unknown physical and psychological forces, a struggle which inferiority in numbers makes all the more difficult. It means working with men of varying force of character and with their own views. The only quantity that is known and constant is the will of the leader.

General Erich Ludendorff, *My War Memories, 1914–1918*, 1919.

IF OUR western adversaries failed to obtain any decisive results in the battle from 1915 to 1917 it must mainly be ascribed to a certain unimaginativeness in their generalship. The necessary superiority in men, war material and ammunition was certainly not lacking, nor can it be suggested that the quality of the enemy troops would not have been high enough to satisfy the demands of a more vigorous and ingenious leadership. Moreover, in view of the highly-developed railway and road system, and the enormous amount of transport at their disposal, our enemies in the West had free scope for far greater strategic subtlety. However, the enemy commander did not make full use of these possibilities, and our long resistance was to be attributed, apart from other things, to a certain barrenness of the soil in which the enemy's plans took root.

Field Marshal Paul von Hindenburg, *Out of My Life*, 1920.

THESE, THEN, are the three pillars of generalship – courage, creative intelligence, and physical fitness; the attributes of youth rather than of middle age.

Major-General J.F.C. Fuller, *Generalship: Its Diseases and Their Cure*, 1933.

THE EVER-VICTORIOUS general is rare and there

have been very few of these in history, but what is necessary is that our generals should have studied the art of war and paid attention to its rules; it is then that, with this wisdom tempered by courage, our military leaders will have better chances of success.

  Mao Tse-tung, *On the Study of War*, 1936.

WHAT I HOLD to be the first essential of a general [is] the quality of robustness, the ability to stand the shocks of war.

  Field Marshal Viscount Wavell of Cyrenaica, 1939,
  'Lees Knowles Lectures', Trinity College, Cambridge.

I DON'T MIND being called tough, since I find in this racket it's the tough guys who lead the survivors.

  General Curtis LeMay, 1943.

HERE ARE six points which are important for successful generalship. A general must:
(a) Know his "stuff" thoroughly.
(b) Be known and recognized by the troops.
(c) Ensure the troops are given tasks that are within their powers. Success means mutual confidence – failure the reverse.
(d) See that subordinate commanders are disturbed as little as possible in carrying out their tasks.
(e) Command by personal contact.
(f) Be human and study the human factor.

  Major-General Sir Francis de Guingand, *Operation Victory*, 1947.

GENERALS are often prone, if they have the chance, to choose a set-piece battle, when all is ready, at their own selected moment, rather than to wear down the enemy by continued unspectacular fighting. They naturally prefer certainty to hazard. They forget that war never stops, but burns on from day to day with ever-changing results not only in one theatre but in all.

  Sir Winston S. Churchill (1874–1965).

I HAVE ALWAYS believed that a motto for generals must be "No Regrets," no crying over spilt milk.

  Field Marshal Viscount Slim of Burma, *Defeat Into Victory*, 1956.

TO EXERCISE high command successfully one has to have an infinite capacity for taking pains and for careful preparation; and one has also to have an inner conviction which at times will transcend reason. Having fought, possibly over a prolonged period, for the advantage and gained it, there then comes the moment for boldness. When that moment comes, will you throw your bonnet over the mill and soar from the known to seize the unknown? In the answer to this question lies the supreme test of generalship in high command.

  Field Marshal Viscount Montgomery of Alamein, *The Memoirs of Field Marshal Montgomery*, 1958.

LET ME GIVE you some advice, Lieutenant. Don't become a general. Don't ever become a general. If you become a general you just plain have too much to worry about.

  General of the Army Dwight D. Eisenhower, 9 May 1965.

I BELIEVE generals get to focus on and solve big problems in peace and war. They must know details and occasionally dip into those, but essentially they must figure out the few deciding issues or battles for their times and conditions and focus their energies on those. These are what I called points of main effort. They cannot be many. You have to decide what they are, and make them stick.

  Generals must have an imagination that lets them visualize what needs to be. They must synthesize to create a whole when others cannot see, and then communicate that whole with so much clarity and so much conviction that others will see it, too, and follow it. That is command. That is leadership at the senior levels.

  Generals decide where to be bold and where not to be bold.

  They must be strong and decisive, yet they must also keep their ego from clouding their judgments. Instead, they must use that ego to stick to doing what is right, even in the face of adversity.

  Generals decide where to intervene and where not to inervene.

  They decide where to tolerate imperfection and where not to tolerate imperfection.

  They must be intensely competitive. They must hate to lose.

  They need to demand a climate of dignity and respect, and to know that to lead is also to serve. They can do a lot of good for individuals every day.

  They must continue to grow. They must not be complacent.

  If they can, they should rest easy in the saddle and have a sense of humor. Smile once in a while.

  If generals can remember "Don't worry, General, we trust you," and do their best to fulfill that trust, they will have done their duty.

  General Fred Franks, Jr., quoted in Tom Clancy with General Fred Franks, Jr. (ret), *Into the Storm*, 1997.

GENERAL STAFF

NORMALLY it is not possible for an army simply to dismiss incompetent generals. The very authority which their office bestows upon generals is the first reason for this. Moreover, the generals form a clique, tenaciously supporting each other, all convinced that they are the best possible representatives of the army. But we can at least give them capable assistants. Thus the General Staff officers are those who support incompetent generals, providing the talents that might otherwise be wanting among leaders and commanders.

> General Gerhard von Scharnhorst (1755–1813), quoted in T.N. Dupuy, *A Genius for War*, 1977.

THE MOST highly trained general staff, with the best of ideas and principles cannot guarantee good leadership in an army by itself. It must be backed by a great general who serves as its leader and counterbalance, who from time to time prevents the staff from entangling itself in its own red tape. A good staff on the other hand is an indispensable aid for a general.

> Major-General Carl von Clausewitz (1780–1831), *The Campaign of 1799 in Italy and Switzerland*, 1906.

THE DIFFICULTY of always selecting a good general has led to the formation of a good general staff, which being near the general may advise him and thus exercise a beneficial influence over the operations. A well-instructed general staff is one of the most useful organizations, but care must be observed to prevent the introduction into it of false principles.

> Lieutenant-General Antoine-Henri Baron de Jomini, *Summary of the Art of War*, 1838, tr. Mendell and Craighill, 1862.

GREAT ACHIEVEMENTS, small display: more reality than appearance.

> Field Marshal Helmuth Graf von Moltke (1800–1891), motto of the German General Staff, quoted in Heinz Guderian, *Panzer Leader*, 1953.

A TRAINED general staff is even more necessary to a commander today than when Clausewitz wrote, because of the greater masses of men involved in operations today. There is little danger that such a staff will, as with the opponents of Napoleon, "entangle itself in its own red tape"; but there is another danger which has resulted from the highly technical character of general staff training. This is the tendency to overemphasize detail. We must take care that the mass of minutiae required in modern-day planning does not overshadow the spirit of the operation itself, and cause us to judge the operation by the excellence or insufficiency of its staff work, rather than by its scope and daring, as we should. To use Boyen's words, we must see that "industry without talent is not unduly rewarded." There is no better way to prevent this than to study the leadership of great generals of the past and endeavor to follow the workings of their minds. Only in this way can we gain for ourselves some part of the insight and determination they possessed.

> General der Infantrie Hugo Baron von Freytag-Loringhoven, *The Power of Personality in War*, 1911, tr. Spaulding, 1938.

THE GENERAL Staff officer was, so to speak, a man apart. As the war became more technical, his duties became more arduous. It was no longer sufficient for him to have a general knowledge of all arms and their employment. He had to be a good artilleryman and, in addition, to possess a sound knowledge of the use of aircraft, signalling, supply questions and a thousand other things, while he had to master many details which the divisional commander had no time to settle. In spite of every effort to keep them brief, the orders which had to draft grew ever longer and more complicated. The more technical the war became, the more did these orders grow into veritable works of art, involving infinite skill and knowledge. There was no other way, if things were to go smoothly. The variety of his functions often compelled the General Staff officer to keep many things in his own hands. Care had to be taken that the independence of other services did not suffer on this account, and that the commander, too, was not "shelved." I could never have allowed either of these developments.

> General Erich Ludendorff, *My War Memories, 1914–1918*, 1919.

THE GENERAL STAFF was certainly one of the most remarkable structures within the framework of our German Army. Side by side with the distinctly hierarchical form of the commands it constituted a special element which had its foundation in the great intellectual prestige of the Chief of Staff of the Army, Field Marshal Count von Moltke. The peace training of the General Staff officer offered a guarantee that in case of war all the commanders in the field should be controlled from a single source, and all their plans governed by a common aim. The influence of the General Staff on those commanders was not regulated by any binding order. It depended far more on the military and personal qualities of the individual officer. The first requirement of the General Staff officer was that he should keep his own personality and actions entirely in the background. He had to work out of sight, and therefore be more than he seemed.

> Field Marshal Paul von Hindenburg, *Out of My Life*, 1920.

GENERAL STAFF officers have no names.

> Colonel-General Hans von Seekt, quoted in Hermann Foertsch, *The Art of Modern Warfare*, 1940.

HISTORY has often shown that, where a particular aim has an instinctive appeal, a General Staff appreciation may have more resemblance to counsel's address to the jury on behalf of the client than to a judicial summing up. (May 1933.)

> Captain Sir Basil Liddell Hart, *Thoughts on War*, 1944.

NO SOLDIER can doubt the immense value of a general staff if it is the general's servant, and not the general's gaoler. I have said that the staff has no responsibilities; it has none, though it has duties; because it has no powers of decision or command. It can suggest, but it has no responsibility for actions resulting; the general alone is responsible, therefore the general alone should and must decide, and, more than this, he must elaborate his own decisions and not merely have them thrust upon him by his staff like a disc upon a gramophone.

> Major-General J.F.C. Fuller, *Generalship: Its Diseases and Their Cure*, 1933.

MY GENERAL STAFF training revolted against an operation of this sort. If old von Moltke thought I had planned this offensive he would turn in his grave.

> Field Marshal Gerd von Rundstedt, November 1944, referring to the plan for the Ardennes Offensive of December 1944.

PREREQUISITES for appointment to the General Staff were integrity of character and unimpeachable behavior and way of life both on and off duty. Next came military competence; a man had to have proved himself at the front, had to have an understanding for tactical and technical matters, a talent for organization and powers of endurance both physical and mental; he had also to be industrious, of sober temperament, and determined.

In selecting officers from this point of view it is possible that intellectual ability was sometimes overvalued in comparison to strength of character and particularly to warmth of personality; but these last two qualities are much less easily estimated, particularly since they do not by their very nature tend to be spectacular.

> Colonel-General Heinz Guderian, *Panzer Leader*, 1953.

THE GERMAN General Staff was a human institution, and it, too, had human frailties and weaknesses, which contributed, at least in part, to its two major defeats in this century. Yet the performance of that General Staff, and of the Army it designed and built in both of those disastrous wars, was comparable in terms of military excellence to Napoleon and Hannibal at their best. Perhaps, in this sense, it is not too much to say that in striving to institutionalize excellence in military affairs, the German General Staff can be said to have institutionalized military genius itself.

> Colonel T.N. Dupuy, *A Genius for War: The German General Staff and the German Army*, 1977.

IF ANY ONE aspect of military performance was emphasized more than any other in the General Staff and in all German military training, it was encouragement of initiative. American General Albert C. Wedemeyer, the last American officer who attended the War Academy before World War II, remembers this emphasis. It was summarized, he recalls, in the concept: "When in doubt, attack!"

> Colonel T.N. Dupuy, *A Genius For War: The German General Staff and the German Army*, 1977.

GENIUS

THEY [the Romans] failed to reckon with the talents of Archimedes or to foresee that in some cases the genius of one man is far more effective than superiority in numbers. This lesson they now learned by experience.

> Polybius, of the Roman attack on Syracuse in 214 BC, *Histories*, 8.3, c. 125 BC (*The Rise of the Roman Empire*, tr. Ian Scott-Kilvert, 1987).

THE PERSECUTION of genius fosters its influence.

> Cornelius Tacitus, *Annals*, 4.35, AD 116, (*The Complete Works of Tacitus*, tr. Alfred Church and William Brodribb, 1942).

GREAT GENIUSES have a sort of intuitive knowledge; they see at once the cause, and its effect, with the different combinations, which unite them: they do not proceed by common rules, successively from one idea to another, by slow languid steps, no: the *Whole*, with all its circumstances and various combinations, is like a picture, all together present to their mind; they want no geometry, but an age produces few of this kind of men: and in the common run of generals, geometry, and experience, will help them to avoid gross errors.

> Major-General Henry Lloyd, *History of the Late War in Germany*, 1766.

A GENIUS paramount in force and originality manifested in the character of a general, animates the operations of the army with one impulse. . . . It impresses an opinion of superiority on the mass: everyone views himself in the splendour of his commander, assimilates, in idea, with his excellence, and, being superior in opinion, soon becomes so in reality. Hence, it is not the dry mechanical wisdom of the plan of battle, so much as the animating spirit of the leader, which may be considered as the pledge of success in war. . . . It may be observed, in this place, that good officers abound among all nations who cultivate the art of war; the genuine military genius is of rare occurrence: no power of industry can produce it; and no one can define the path in which it moves. The genius which leads to conquest, like the genius of a poet, is original: it is a first impression, improved by study in the book of nature only. . . . the spirit which knows not to submit, which retires from no danger because it is formidable, is the soul of a soldier. The soldier fixes victory in his eye, as a passion rather than a reason. This forms what may be considered as genius – a paramount genius, which domineers and conquers and enslaves.

> Robert Jackson, *A Systematic View of the Formation, Discipline, and Economy of Armies*, 1804.

OF THE conquerors and eminent military characters who have at different times astonished the world, Alexander the Great and Charles the Twelfth of Sweden are two of the most singular; the latter of whom was the most heroic and the most extraordinary man of whom history has left any record. An army which had Alexander or Charles in its eye was different from itself in its simple nature, it imbibed a share of their spirit, became insensible of danger, and heroic in the extreme.

Robert Jackson, *A Systematic View on the Formation, Discipline, and Economy of Armies*, 1804.

ACHILLES was the son of a goddess and a mortal: he symbolizes the genius of war. Its divine half is composed of all those elements which depend on moral factors – on character, on talent, on the interests of your adversary, on public opinion, and on the morale of your troops, who are either strong and victorious or weak and beaten, depending on which they think they will be. Armaments, entrenchments, positions, order of battle, everything pertaining to the combinations of material factors – these make up the earthly half.

Napoleon, dictation at St. Helena (1815–1821), quoted in Christopher Herold, ed., *The Mind of Napoleon*, 1955.

GENIUS is sometimes only an instinct which is incapable of being perfected. In most cases the art of judging correctly is perfected only through observation and experience. A good thought is not always associated with good judgment, but good judgment always presupposes a good thought.

Napoleon (1769–1821) F.M. Kircheisen, ed., *The Memoirs of Napoleon*, 1929.

THERE IS NO genius who tells me suddenly and in secret what I must say or do in any circumstance unexpected by others, it is reflection, meditation.

Napoleon (1769–1821), quoted in Ferdinand Foch, *Principles of War*, 1913.

GENIUS is not extravagant; it is ardent, and it conceives great projects; but it knows beforehand how to attain the result, and it uses the simplest means, because its faculties are essentially calculating, industrious, and patient. It is creative, because its knowledge is vast; it is quick and preemptory, not because it is presumptuous, but because it is well-prepared.

General Sir William Napier (1782–1853), quoted in George F.R. Henderson, *Stonewall Jackson*, 1898.

EVERY SPECIAL calling in life . . . requires special qualities of intellect and temperament. When these are of a high order, and manifest themselves by extraordinary achievements, the mind to which they belong is termed genius . . . a superior mental capacity for certain activities. . . . The essence of military genius is to bring under consideration all of the tendencies of the mind and soul in combination towards the business of war. . . . We say "in combination," for military genius is not just one single quality bearing upon war – as, for instance courage . . . but it is a harmonious combination of powers, in which one or the other may predominate, but none must be in opposition.

Major-General Carl von Clausewitz, *On War*, 1.3, 1832, tr. Michael Howard and Peter Paret, 1976.

. . . THE REALM of genius, *which rises above all rules*.

Pity the soldier who is supposed to crawl among these scraps of rules, and not good enough for genius, which genius can ignore, or laugh at. No; what genius does is the best rule, and theory can do no better than show how and why this should be the case.

Major-General Carl von Clausewitz, *On War*, 2.2, 1832, tr. Michael Howard and Peter Paret, 1976.

TOWERING GENIUS disdains a beaten path. It seeks regions hitherto unexplored.

Abraham Lincoln, 27 January 1838, speech in Springfield, Illinois.

IN WAR there is a critical instant – a night – perhaps only a half hour, when everything culminates. He is the military genius who recognizes this instant and acts upon it, neither precipitating nor postponing the critical moment. There is thus good reason why great soldiers should be so rare that generations pass without producing a single one. A great soldier must have, in addition to all usual traits of intellect, a courage unmoved by the greatest danger, and cool under every emergency, and the quickness of lightning, not only in conceiving, but in enforcing an order.

Colonel Theodore Lyman (1833–1897), *Meade's Headquarters*, 1922.

GENIUS is, of course, an exception to all rules and is in a category by itself, as we see from the personality of Frederick, whose versatility is unequalled among military men. The Comte de Segur, as quoted by Pierron, says very pertinently: "Tremendous intellect, plus a vast amount of good sense, coupled with great strength of character add up to genius. The first two of these characteristics make it possible to see the critical point in any affair; the third enables one to employ all his force to reach it."

General-Lieutenant Hugo Baron von Freytag-Loringhoven, *The Power of Personality in War*, 1911, tr. Spaulding, 1938.

THE STROKE of genius that turns the fate of a battle? I don't believe it. A battle is a complicated operation, that you prepare laboriously. If the enemy does this, you say to yourself I shall do that. If such and such happens, these are the steps I shall take to meet it. You think out every possible development and decide on the way to deal with the situation created. One of these developments occurs; you put in operation your pre-arranged plan, and everyone says, "What genius to have thought of that at the critical moment!" Whereas the credit is really due to the labour of preparation done beforehand.

Marshal of France Ferdinand Foch, *Daily Mail* (London), 19 April 1919.

DESPITE every wish to give full weight to the genius of the Commander, we must fain recognize that there are immutable bounds set to what any individual can achieve. We know what a Lee can do against the good, ordinary General; yet – there are the appointed limits – as Gettysburg showed. A thrust is well-timed and deadly; the over-tasked blade breaks in the hand of the master. The stroke remains a master stroke; it did not penetrate, that was all!

General Sir Ian Hamilton, *The Soul and Body of an Army*, 1921.

OPPOSED to genius stand the men of logarithms, who, by their "if-he-does-this-I-shall-do-that," attempt to exhaust the cache of chances which God keeps stocked far away in starland. Genius is God's secret, that is all. Foch thinks he won the war because he "calculated," as the Yankees say. He forgets that the Germans equally pride themselves on calculations. He either forgets, or he is too modest to tell us, that he has in him like a burning fire a passion for sheer fighting, a fire of passion which burnt up all his sums and figures when the moment came. But if the great Marshal had only told us this, we should have known what weight to attach to his "if-he-does-this-I-shall-do-that."

General Sir Ian Hamilton, *Soul and Body of an Army*, 1921.

THE MILITARY GENIUS is he who can produce original combinations out of the forces of war; he is the man who can take all these forces and so attune them to the conditions which confront him that he can produce startling and, frequently, incomprehensible results. As an animal cannot explain the instincts which control it, neither can a man of genius explain the powers which control him. He acts on the spur of the moment, and he acts rightly, because this power is in his control. That some explanation exists cannot be doubted, but so far science has not revealed it, though the psychologist is working towards its fringe.

Major-General J.F.C. Fuller, *The Foundations of the Science of War*, 1926.

AS GENIUS is a personal gift, so is imitation a collective instinct. One man possessed of genius may alter the course of history, in fact, such a man has always altered the course of history, when alteration has been rapid. Three men of genius, working as a committee, could not do this, and still less so a crowd of normal men.

Major-General J.F.C. Fuller, *The Foundations of the Science of War*, 1926.

GENERALS have been legion; artists of war few. Many more evidences of military genius can be traced in the scantier records of irregular and guerrilla forces. The natural explanation is that the natural gifts of these leaders who have emerged straight from the womb of conflict, instead of a professional incubation chamber, have not been cramped or warped by convention. . . . it does cast a reflection upon the customary method of training leaders in organized armies. It is significant that in the American Civil War, which was the most fruitful field of generalship in modern times, most of the outstanding leaders were men who after an apprenticeship in the Regular Army had gone into some field of civil activity, which in varying degree freed their minds from the fetters of military convention and routine, while they retained a useful experience of the functioning of the military machine. (March 1937.)

Captain Sir Basil Liddell Hart, *Thoughts on War*, 1944.

"GENIUS" is a tiresome and misleading word to apply to the military art, if it suggests, as it does to many, one so gifted by nature as to obtain his successes by inspiration rather than through study. Nor does the definition of genius attributed to Carlyle as "an infinite capacity for taking pains" suit the great commander, as it suggests the pedant or martinet. Good generals, unlike poets, are made rather than born, and will never reach the first rank without much study of their profession; but they must have certain natural gifts – the power of quick decision, judgment, boldness and, I am afraid, a considerable degree of toughness, almost callousness, which is harder to find as civilization progresses.

Field Marshal Viscount Wavell of Cyrenaica, *Soldiers and Soldiering*, 1953.

THE GENTLEMAN

I FEEL every thing that hurts the Sensibility of a Gentleman.

General George Washington, to the Marquis de Lafayette, 1 September 1778, *The Writings of George Washington*, XII, p. 382, John C. Fitzgerald, ed., 1934.

RECOLLECT that you must be a seaman to be an officer; and also, that you cannot be a good officer without being a gentleman.

Admiral Viscount Nelson (1758–1805), to his midshipmen, quoted in Robert Southey, *Life of Nelson*, 1813.

YOU UNDERSTAND that with one arm lost in Mexico I might easily have kept out of the war, without anyone charging a want of zeal against me. But as a gentleman I felt called upon to act and not be idle. Besides, I firmly believe in the Union.

Major-General Philip Kearny, August 1861, letter to his wife.

WE HAVE only one rule here – to act like a gentleman at all times.

General Robert E. Lee, to a student who asked what the rules were at Washington College where Lee served as president after the Civil War (1865–1870).

THE FORBEARING use of power does not only form a touchstone, but the manner in which an individual enjoys certain advantages over others is a test of a true *gentleman*.

The power which the strong have over the weak, the magistrate over the citizen, the employer over the employed, the educated over the unlettered, the experienced over the confiding, even the clever over the silly – the forbearing or inoffensive use of all this power or authority, or a total abstinence from it when the case admits it, will show the gentleman in a plain light. The gentleman does not needlessly and unnecessarily remind an offender of a wrong he may have committed against him. He cannot only forgive, he can forget; and he strives for the nobleness of self and mildness of character which impart sufficient strength to let the past be but the past. *A true gentleman of honor feels humbled himself when he cannot help humbling others.*

> General Robert E. Lee, a note found in his satchel after his death, quoted in William Jones, *Personal Reminiscences, Anecdotes, and Letters of Gen. Robert E. Lee*, 1874.

WE WANT to make our nation entirely one of gentlemen, men who have a strong sense of honour, of chivalry towards others, of playing the game bravely and unselfishly for their side, and to play it with a sense of fair play and happiness in all.

> Lieutenant-General Baden-Powell, *Headquarters Gazette*, 1914.

THE IDENTITY of the officer with the gentleman should persist in his relations with men of all degree. In the routine of daily direction and disposition, and even in moments of exhortation, he had best bring courtesy to firmness. The finest officers that one has known are not occasional gentlemen, but in every circumstance: in commissioned company and, more importantly in contact with those who have no recourse against arrogance.

> Brigadier-General S.L.A. Marshall, *The Armed Forces Officer*, 1950.

GLORY

WHO IS the King of glory? The Lord of hosts, he is the King of glory.

> Psalms 24:10.

MOTHER tells me,
the immortal goddess Thetis with her glistening feet,
that two fates bear me on to the day of death.
If I hold out here and I lay siege to Troy,
my journey home is gone, but my glory never dies.
If I voyage back to the fatherland I love,
my pride, my glory dies . . .
true, but the life that's left me will be long,
the stroke of death will not come on me quickly.

> Homer, *The Iliad*, 9.497–505, c. 800 BC, tr. Robert Fagles, 1990; the 'choice of Achilles' between a long, dull life or a short one sweet with everlasting glory.

SO NOW I meet my doom. Well let me die –
but not without struggle, not without glory, no,
in some great clash of arms that even men to come
will hear of down the years!

> Homer, *The Iliad*, 22.359–362, c. 800 BC, tr. Robert Fagles, 1990; Hector aware that doom was rushing upon him in the shape of brilliant Achilles.

THE NEAREST WAY to glory – a short cut, as it were – is to strive to be what you wish to be thought to be.

> Socrates (469–399 BC), quoted in Cicero, *De Officiis*, 2.12.43, 44 BC, tr. Walter Miller.

MY OWN assessment of myself is based on the extent not of my life but of my glory. I could have been content with my father's inheritance, and within Macedonia's bounds have enjoyed a life of ease as I awaited an old age without renown or distinction (though even inactive men cannot control their destiny, and those who believe a long life is the only good are often overtaken by a premature death). But no – I count my victories, not my years and, if I accurately compute fortune's favours to me, my life has been long.

> Alexander the Great, quoted in Curtius, *The History of Alexander*, c. AD 41, tr. John Yardley, 1984.

IT IS MEN who endure toil and dare dangers that achieve glorious deeds, and it is a lovely thing to live with courage and to die leaving behind an everlasting renown.

> Alexander the Great (356–323 BC), quoted in Plutarch, *The Lives*, c. AD 100, tr. John Dryden.

STAND FIRM; for well you know that hardship and danger are the price of glory, and that sweet is the savour of a life of courage and of deathless renown beyond the grave.

> Alexander the Great, July 326 BC, in India when the Macedonians refused to go on, quoted in Arrian, *The Campaigns of Alexander*, 5.26, c. AD 150, tr. Aubrey de Sélincourt, 1971.

THE DESIRE for glory is the last infirmity cast off even by the wise.

> Cornelius Tacitus, *Histories*, 4.6, AD 104–109 (*The Complete Works of Tacitus*, tr. Alfred Church and William Brodribb, 1942).

WE ORDER that glory and honor and greatness not be inherited simply because one is born of nobles but must be acquired in war, by brave deeds. . . . And those courageous warriors will be awarded insignia of valor not once but many times and will be given gold and silver, precious stones, jewels, fine feathers. All of these can used by them always, and by no others. These things will remind them of us after we are dead; we will be remembered by our sons and grandsons and all our descendants.

Tlacaelel, generalissimo of the Aztecs, c. 1450, promulgation of the Aztec warrior code, quoted in Diego Durán, *History of the Indies of New Spain*, 1581, tr. Doris Heyden, 1994.

FROM WHERE the eagles are resting,
from where the tigers are exhalted,
the sun is invoked.

Like a shield that descends,
so does the Sun set,
In Mexico night is falling,
war rages on all sides,

Oh Giver of Life!
war comes near. . . .

Proud of itself
is the city of Mexico-Tenochtitlan.
Here no one fears to die in war.
This is our glory.
This is Your Command,
oh Giver of Life!
Have this in mind, oh princes,
do not forget it.
Who could conquer Tenochtitlan?
Who could shake the foundation of heaven?

With our arrows,
with our shields,
the city exists.
Mexico-Tenochtitlan remains.

Aztec poem, c. 1500, exhalting the glory of their great capital and its martial people, quoted in Miguel Leon-Portilla, *Pre-Columbian Literatures of Mexico*, 1969.

THERE MUST BE a beginning of any great matter, but the continuing unto the end until it be thoroughly finished yields the true glory.

Sir Francis Drake, 17 May 1587, to Lord Walsingham.

MY GREATEST happiness is to serve my gracious King and Country, and I am envious only of glory; for if it be a sin to covet glory, I am the most offending soul alive.

Admiral Viscount Nelson, 18 February 1800, letter to Lady Hamilton.

THE ART of war is the most difficult of all arts; therefore military glory is universally considered the highest, and the services of warriors are rewarded by a sensible government in a splendid manner and above all other services.

Napoleon (1769–1821).

WHERE IS the republic, ancient or modern, that has not granted honours? Call them trifles if you like, but it is by trifles that men are influenced. I would not utter such a sentiment as this in public, but here, among statesmen and thinkers, things should be spoken of as they are. In my opinion the French do not care for liberty and equality; they must be given distinctions. Do you suppose you can persuade men to fight by a process of analysis? Never; the process is valid only for the man of science in his study. The soldier demands glory, distinction, rewards.

Napoleon, 14 May 1802, in Paris, quoted in R.M. Johnston, ed., *The Corsican*, 1910.

DIE YOUNG, and I shall accept your death – but not if you have lived without glory, without being useful to your country, without leaving a trace of your existence: for that is not to have lived at all.

Napoleon, 1802, letter to Jérôme, quoted in Christopher Herold, ed., *The Mind of Napoleon*, 1955.

GLORY can only be won where there is danger.

Napoleon, 14 November 1806.

HOW GLORIOUS it is to be a Frenchman!

Marshal Ney, June 1807, after the Battle of Friedland, cited in Raymond Horricks, *Marshal Ney*, 1982.

A NEW Prometheus, I am nailed to a rock to be gnawed by a vulture. Yes, I have stolen the fire of Heaven and made a gift of it to France. The fire has returned to its source, and I am here!

The love of glory is like the bridge that Satan built across Chaos to pass from Hell to Paradise: glory links the past with the future across a bottomless abyss. Nothing to my son, except my name!

Napoleon, a note found written in his hand after his death on 5 May 1821, quoted in Christopher Herold, ed., *The Mind of Napoleon*, 1955.

THE EXCEEDING brightness of military glory – that attractive rainbow, that rises in showers of blood – that serpent's eye, that charms to destroy.

President Abraham Lincoln, 'Speech in the United States House of Representatives on the War with Mexico', 12 January 1848, *Collected Works of Abraham Lincoln*, I, 1953.

A SAILOR does not have a difficult or an easy path. There is just one, the glorious path.

Admiral P.S. Nakhimov, quoted in Ablamonov, *Admiral*, 1986.

THERE IS a true glory and a true honor, the glory of duty done, the honor of the integrity of principle.

General Robert E. Lee, in Early, *Southern Historical Society Papers*, XI.

IN THE HEARTS of most men there lurks a sentiment which they carefully try to hide from their fellow men. This foolish sentiment is that which causes man to aspire constantly to immortality. Not all men, however, succeed in inscribing their names on the walls of the temple of glory.

General Antonio Lopez de Santa Anna, *The Eagle: The Autobiography of Santa Anna*, c. 1870.

THE LOVE of glory, the ardent desire for honorable distinction by honorable deeds, is among the most potent and elevating of military motives.

Rear Admiral Alfred Thayer Mahan, *Life of Nelson*, 1897.

A NATION without glory is like a man without courage, a woman without virtue. It takes the first place in our human estimate of national fame. All States long for it, and certainly it is a big factor in the consciousness of national strength which commands the respect of both friends and enemies. It is a national heirloom of priceless value to the people to whom the world accord it and who are ready to fight rather than risk its loss. When the nation to whom it was once universally conceded begins to sneer at it as unimportant, and to ridicule its worth, the tide of that nation's greatness has surely turned. . . .

Glory to the nation is what sunlight is to all human beings. Without it the State dwindles in size and grows weak in strength, as the man in a dark dungeon becomes daily whiter, until at last his whiteness passes into the colourlessness of death.

Field Marshal Viscount Wolseley, *The Story of a Soldier's Life*, II, 1903.

COMMON MEN endure these horrors and overcome them, along with the insistent yearnings of the belly and reasonable promptings of fear; and in this, I think, is glory.

Colonel John W. Thomason, Jr. *Fix Bayonets*, 1926.

WHAT A GLORY shines on the brave and true.

Sir Winston S. Churchill (1874–1965).

HUMILITY must always be the portion of any man who receives acclaim earned in the blood of his followers and the sacrifices of his friends.

General of the Army Dwight D. Eisenhower, address, London, 12 June 1945.

THE GOLDEN BRIDGE

DO NOT THWART an enemy returning home.
To surround an enemy you must leave a way of escape
Do not press an enemy at bay.

Sun Tzu, *The Art of War*, c. 500 BC, tr. Samuel Griffith, 1969.

KING WEI asked, "How should one attack desperados?"
Master Sun answered, ". . . [Wait] until they find a way to leave."

Sun Bin, *The Lost Art of War*, c. 350 BC, tr. Thomas Cleary, 1996.

FOR NOTHING makes men so brave as the fear of what ills they will suffer if they surrender; indeed the expectation of the evils which will ensure from their subjection produces a terrible pertinacity in danger. Moreover, fighting is dangerous against desperate men, who expect from surrender no amelioration of the fate which will be theirs if they continue to fight, and therefore prefer, if they can inflict much harm, also to suffer much.

Onasander, *The General*, AD 58 (*Aeneas Tacticus, Aclepiodotus, Onasander*, tr. The Illinois Greek Club, 1923).

SCIPIO AFRICANUS used to say that a road not only ought to be afforded the enemy for flight, but that it ought even to be paved.

Frontinus, *Stratagems*, 4.7, c. AD 84–96, tr. Charles E. Bennett, 1925.

THE MAXIM of Scipio, that a golden bridge should be made for a flying enemy, has much been commended. For when they have free room to escape they think of nothing but how to save themselves by flight, and the confusion becoming general, great numbers are cut to pieces. The pursuers can be in no danger when the vanquished have thrown away their arms for greater haste. In this case the greater the numbers of the flying army, the greater the slaughter. Numbers are of no significance where troops once thrown into consternation are equally terrified at the sight of the enemy as at their weapons. But on the contrary, men when penned in, although weak and few, become a match for the enemy from the very fact that they have no resource but in despair. "The conquer'd's safety is to hope for none."

Flavius Vegetius Renatus, *Military Institutions of the Romans*, c. AD 378, tr. Clark, 1776.

WHEN the enemy is surrounded, it is well to leave a gap in our lines to give them the opportunity to flee, in case they judge that flight is better than remaining and taking their chances.

The Emperor Maurice, *The Strategikon*, c. AD 600 (*Maurice's Strategikon*, tr. George Dennis, 1984).

IN GOD'S NAME! they go. Let them depart. And go we to give thanks to God. We shall not follow them farther, for it is Sunday. Seek not to harm them. It suffices me that they go.

Joan of Arc, 8 May 1429, to her soldiers as the English raised the siege of Orléans, *Joan of Arc in Her Own Words*, 1996.

WHEN an enemy army is in flight, you must either build a golden bridge for it or stop it with a wall of steel.

Napoleon (1769–1821), quoted in Christopher Herold, ed., *The Mind of Napoleon*, 1955.

WHEN the two sides are too evenly matched to

offer a reasonable chance of early success to either, the statesman is wise who can learn something from the psychology of strategy. It is an elementary principle of strategy that, if you find your opponent in a strong position too costly to force, you should leave him a line of retreat – as the quickest way of loosening his resistance. It should, equally, be a principle of policy, especially in war, to provide your opponent with a ladder by which he can climb down.

> Captain Sir Basil Liddell Hart, *Strategy*, 1954.

WE DID NOT set ourselves the task of cutting the last path of retreat of the Hitlerites. If we had done this, it would then have been necessary to root them out there at length, and we would doubtlessly have destroyed the city [Cracow]. Tempting as it was to create a ring of encirclement, we did not do that, though it was possible for us to do so. Confronting the enemy with a real threat of envelopment, our troops pushed him out of the city through the straight strike of infantry and tanks.

> Marshal of the Soviet Union Ivan S. Koniev, 1970, quoted in Nathan Leites, *The Soviet Style in War*, 1982.

GREAT CAPTAINS/GREATNESS

IN A NARROW sphere great men are blunderers.

> Napoleon, *Maxims*, 1804–1815.

I AM a Shawnee. My forefathers were warriors. Their son is a warrior. From them I take only my existence. From my tribe I take nothing. I have made myself what I am.

> Tecumseh, 11 August 1810, meeting with General William Henry Harrison at Fort Knox, Kentucky.

A CONSECUTIVE series of great actions never is the result of chance and luck; it always is the product of planning and genius. Great men are rarely known to fail in their most perilous enterprises. . . . Is it because they are lucky that they became great? No, but being great, they have been able to master luck.

> Napoleon, 14 November 1816, conversation on St. Helena. Emmanuel Las Casas, *Mémorial de St. Hélène*, quoted in Christopher Herold, ed., *The Mind of Napoleon*, 1955.

MAXIM 18. A general of ordinary talent occupying a bad position, and surprised by a superior force, seeks his safety in retreat; but a great captain supplies all deficiencies by his courage, and marches boldly to meet the attack. By this means he disconcerts his adversary, and if this last shows any irresolution in his movements, a skilful leader profiting by his indecision may even hope for victory, or at least employ the day in manoeuvring – at night he entrenches himself, or falls back to a better position. By this determined conduct he maintains

the honour of his arms, the first essential to all military superiority.

> Napoleon, *The Military Maxims of Napoleon*, tr. George D'Aguilar, 1831 (David Chandler, ed., 1987).

THE RIGHT APPRECIATION of their opponents . . . the audacity to leave for a short space of time, a small force only before them, energy in forced marches, boldness in sudden attacks, the intensified activity which great souls acquire in the moment of danger, these are the ground of such victories.

> Major-General Carl von Clausewitz, *On War*, 1832, tr. Michael Howard and Peter Paret, 1976.

THE ACQUIREMENTS of the accomplished officer may enable him to see the right thing to be done under given conditions, and yet fail to lift him to the height of due performance. It is in the strength of purpose, in the power of rapid decision, of instant action, and if need be, of strenuous endurance through a period.

> Admiral David Glasgow Farragut, quoted in Christopher Marin, *Damn the Torpedos!*, 1970.

MANY A TIME has the soldier's calling exhausted strong characters, and that surprisingly quickly. The fine intellect and resolute will of one year give place to the sterile imaginings and faint heart of the next. That is perhaps the tragedy of military greatness.

> Field Marshal Paul von Hindenburg, *Out of My Life*, 1920.

IF I MAY hazard to set down the qualifications of the great captain, then I should say that they are:
(i) Imagination operating through reason.
(ii) Reason operating through audacity.
(iii) And audacity operating through rapidity of movement.

The first creates unsuspected forms of thought; the second establishes original forms of action; and the third impels the human means at the disposal of the commander to accomplish his purpose with the force and rapidity of a thunderbolt. From the mind, through the soul, we thus gain our ends by means of the body.

> Major-General J.F.C. Fuller, *The Foundations of the Science of War*, 1926.

IT MAY WELL BE that the greatest soldiers have possessed superior intellects, may have been thinkers; but this was not their dominant characteristic . . . [they] owed their successes to indomitable wills and tremendous energy in execution and achieved their initial hold upon the hearts of their troops by acts of demonstrated valor . . . the great leaders are not our responsibility, but God's.

> General George S. Patton, Jr., 27 October 1927, lecture, 'Why Men Fight', *The Patton Papers*, I, 1972.

HISTORY shows that rather than resign himself to a

direct approach, a Great Captain will take even the most hazardous indirect approach – if necessary, over mountains, deserts, or swamps, with only a fraction of his force, even cutting himself from his communications. Facing, in fact, every unfavourable condition rather than the risk of stalemate. (Oct. 1928.)

Captain Sir Basil Liddell Hart, *Thoughts on War*, 1944.

HE MUST ACCEPT the loneliness which according to Faguet, is the "wretchedness of superior beings." Contentment and tranquility and the simple joys which go by the name of happiness are denied to those who fill positions of great power. The choice must be made, and it is a hard one: whence that vague sense of melancholy which hangs about the skirts of majesty, in things no less than in people. One day somebody said to Napoleon, as they were looking at an old and noble monument: "How sad it is!" "Yes," came the reply, "as sad as greatness."

General Charles de Gaulle, *The Edge of the Sword*, 1932.

IT GOES without saying that the successes achieved by great men have always depended on their possessing many different faculties. Character alone, if unsupported by other qualities, results only in rashness and obstinacy. On the other hand, purely intellectual gifts, even of the highest order, are not sufficient. History is filled with examples of men who, though they were gifted beyond the ordinary, saw their labors brought to nothing because they were lacking in character. Whether serving, or betraying, their masters in the most expert fashion, they were entirely uncreative. Notable they may have been, but famous never.

General Charles de Gaulle, *The Edge of the Sword*, 1932.

"ENLIGHTENED Views and Supreme Wisdom" . . . are all a matter of intuition and character which no decree can compel, no instruction can impart. Only flair, intelligence and above all the latent eagerness to play a part which alone enables a man to develop ability and strength of character, can be of service. It all comes to this, that nothing great will ever be achieved without great men, and men are great only if they are determined to be so.

General Charles de Gaulle, *The Edge of the Sword*, 1932.

THE COMMANDER with the imagination – the genius, in fact – to use the new forces may have his name written among the 'great captains.' But he will not win that title lightly or easily; consider for a moment the qualifications he will require. On the ground he will have to handle forces moving at a speed and ranging at a distance far exceeding that of the most mobile cavalry of the past; a study of naval strategy and tactics as well as those of cavalry (tanks) will be essential to him. Some ideas on his position in battle and the speed at which he must make his decisions may be derived from the battle of Jutland; not much from Salisbury Plain or the Long Valley. Needless to say, he must be able to handle Air Forces with the same knowledge as forces on land.

Field Marshal Viscount Wavell of Cyrenaica, *Generals and Generalship*, 1941.

ONE MARK of a great man is the power of making lasting impressions upon the people he meets.

Sir Winston S. Churchill (1874–1965).

IT WAS because he really understood war that he became so good at securing peace. He was the least militaristic of soldiers, and free from the lust of glory. It was because he saw the value of peace that he became so unbeatable in war. For he kept the end in view, instead of falling in love with the means. Unlike Napoleon, he was not infected by the romance of war, which germinates illusions and self-deceptions. That was how Napoleon failed, and Wellington prevailed.

Captain Sir Basil Liddell Hart, 'Wellington', quoted in Barrett Parker, *Famous British Generals*, 1951.

H

HEALTH

WHEN YOU ARE at war, if your army has suffered a setback, it is imperative to examine the physical and mental health of the soldiers. If they are healthy, then inspire them to fight; if they are run down and low in spirits, then nurture their health for the time being, until they are again fit for service.
>Liu Ji (1310–1375), *Lessons of War* (*Mastering the Art of War*, tr. Thomas Cleary, 1984).

. . . FOR BAD INDEED is the condition of a general when he has a sickness among his men and an enemy to contend with at the same time. But nothing is more conducive to keeping an army in good health and spirits than exercise; the ancients used to exercise their troops every day. Proper exercise, then, is surely of great importance for it preserves your health in camp and secures you victory in the field.
>Niccolo Machiavelli, *The Art of War*, 1521.

THE SOLDIER'S HEALTH must come before economy or any other consideration.
>Napoleon, 17 June 1813, letter to Daru, *Correspondance de Napoléon Ier, publié par ordre de l'Empereur Napoléon III*, XXV, p. 396, 1858–1870.

IF THE FACILITIES for washing were as great as those for drink, our Indian Army would be the cleanest body of men in the world.
>Florence Nightingale, 1863, commenting as a member of the Royal Commission on the sanitary state of the Indian army.

GOOD HEALTH and a robust constitution are invaluable in a general. . . . In a sick body, the mind cannot possibly remain permanently fresh and clear. It is stunted by the selfish body from the great things to which it should be entirely devoted.
>Field Marshal Colmar Baron von der Goltz, *The Nation in Arms*, 1887.

HEALTH in a general is, of course, most important, but it is a relative quality only. We would all of us, I imagine, sooner have Napoleon sick on our side than many of his opponents whole. A great spirit can rule in a frail body, as Wolfe and others have showed us. Marlborough during his great campaigns would have been ploughed by most modern medical boards.
>Field Marshal Viscount Wavell of Cyrenaica, *Soldiers and Soldiering*, 1953.

HERO/HEROISM

THEY SAY: "Exhalted is the Sun of our land! We were lost in the land daily in the darkness, which King Rameses III has expelled. The lands and countries are stripped, and brought to Egypt as slaves; gifts gathered together for her gods' satiety, provisions, supplies, are a flood in the Two Lands. The multitude rejoices in this land, none is sad, for Amon has established his son upon his throne, all the circuit of the sun is united in his grasp; the vanquished Asiatics and the Tehenu. Taken are those who were spoiling the condition of Egypt. The land had been exposed in continual extremity, since the former kings. They were desolated, the gods as well as all people. There was no hero to seize them when they retreated. Lo, there was a youth like a gryphon, like a bull ready for battle upon the field. His horses were like hawks . . . roaring like a lion terrible in rage. . . . His name is a flame, the terror of him is in the countries."
>Rameses III, Egyptian Pharaoh, c. 1193 BC, description of his victory in the First Libyan War, quoted in James Breasted, *Ancient Records of Egypt*, 1906.

THE ACTION was one that rewarded itself.
>Scipio Africanus (236–184 BC), quoted in Polybius, *The Histories*.

[IN] THE VALIANT man [are] invincibility, robustness, unconquerability. [He is] powerful, rugged, strong.
  The good valiant man [is] one who excels others – a victor, a conqueror, a taker of captives. He is reckless; he destroys, he charges the foe; he takes captives; he besieges, he sweeps away [the foe]. He glorifies himself, he glorifies [his exploits].
  The bad valiant man [is] vainglorious, a boaster that he is an eagle warrior, an ocelot warrior, a brave warrior. He pretends to be a brave warrior; he brags of himself, he boasts that he is a brave warrior.
>An Aztec account of the valiant man, quoted in Fray Bernardino de Sahagún, *General History of the Things of New Spain, Book 10 – The People*, 1961.

THOUGH THE ACTIONS of our hero shine with great brilliancy, they must not be imitated, except with peculiar caution. The more resplendent they are, the more easily they seduce the youthful, headlong, and angry warrior, to whom we cannot often enough repeat that valor without wisdom is insufficient, and that the adversary with a cool head, who can combine and calculate, will finally be victorious over the rash individual.
>Frederick the Great, 'Reflections on Charles XII',

Posthumus Works of Frederick II, King of Prussia, tr. Holcroft, 1789; in Jay Luvaas, ed., *Frederick the Great on the Art of War*, 1966.

PERMIT ME, Your Highness, to report that heroes are to be found also in the lower ranks.
> Field Marshal Prince Aleksandr V. Suvorov, report to Prince Potemkin of the Battle of Kinburn during the 1787 Kherson campaign against the Turks, quoted in K. Ossipov, *Suvorov*, 1945.

HIGH AND DANGEROUS action teaches us to believe as right beyond dispute things for which our doubting minds are slow to find words of proof; out of heroism grows faith in the worth of heroism.
> Justice Oliver Wendell Holmes, Jr. (1841–1935).

AT THE GRAVE of the hero we end, not with sorrow at the inevitable loss, but with the contagion of his courage; and with a kind of desperate joy we return back to the fight.
> Justice Oliver Wendell Holmes, Jr. (1841–1935).

WAR IS, or anyhow should be, an heroic undertaking; for without heroism it can be no more than an animal conflict, which in place of raising man through an ideal, debases him through brutality.
> Major-General J.F.C. Fuller, *Generalship: Its Diseases and Their Cure*, 1933.

SOLDIERS, all men in fact, are natural hero worshippers. Officers with a flare for command realize this and emphasize in their conduct, dress and deportment the qualities they seek to produce in their men. . . . the influence one man can have on thousands is a never ending source of wonder to me.
> General George S. Patton, Jr., 6 June 1944, *The Patton Papers*, II, 1974.

IT IS an unfortunate and, to me tragic fact that, in our attempts to prevent war, we have taught our people to belittle the heroic qualities of the soldier. They do not realize that, as Shakespeare put it, the pursuit of "The bubble reputation even at the cannon's mouth" is not only a good military characteristic, but also very helpful to the young man when bullets and shells are whistling and cracking around him. Much more could be done if the women of America would praise their heroes.
> General George S. Patton, Jr., *War As I Knew It*, 1947.

ON A TRIP to the West Coast, President Kennedy was asked by a little boy, "Mr. President, how did you become a war hero?"
"It was involuntary. They sank my boat."
> President John F. Kennedy, quoted in Adler, *The Kennedy Wit*, 1964.

IT IS in disaster, not success, that the heroes and the bums really get sorted out.
> Admiral James B. Stockdale, 'In War, In Prison, In Antiquity', *Parameters*, 12/1987.

IT DOESN'T TAKE a hero to order men into battle. It takes a hero to be one of those men who goes into battle.
> General H. Norman Schwarzkopf, *It Doesn't Take a Hero*, 1992.

IT WAS during an assault . . . that Platoon Commander Lieutenant Aleksandr Aksenov caught two bullets in the stomach and died a day later. This was a robust, cheerful lad with the heart of lion who was born to be a winner and who believed, quite without justification and fatally, as, by the way, do all lieutenants, that death could find anyone you like, only not him. "Yes, they will wound and they will kill, but that is for the others; this is me. How could it be me? This cannot be. I am young, strong, powerful and superbly professionally trained, I am 23 years old, few can compete with me, I am destined to live. How can that be? Kill me? Joke if you like!" This psychology is inherent to youth and infects practically 100 percent of enlisted men and young officers. Heroism often is a very close neighbor with plain stupidity, sad as it is to write. And where common sense and elementary tactics suggest that one must go by bounds and crawling, a soldier or officer imbued with such psychology rolls up his sleeves, sticks a cigarette butt to his lower lip, takes his weapon at the ready and goes forward unhurriedly, with a sense of his own dignity, by his entire appearance demonstrating supreme contempt for everything and everyone: for his own life, for possible death, for the enemy.
> Lieutenant General Aleksandr I. Lebed, *I Hurt For This Great Country*, 1995.

LAST YEAR I was privileged to participate in the [Medal of Honor] ceremony in the White House. I sat there and observed the President of the United States, our Commander in Chief, issue to two widows the Medal of Honor, posthumously awarded to their husbands – two sergeants who were killed in a firefight in Mogadishu in 1993. Those noncomissioned officers of the United States Army, the United States of America, saw one of our helicopters go down and asked three times to go to the aid of their comrades.
They knew the risk; they did not hesitate. They did not hesitate. Courage! Courage!
They defended their wounded comrade. Loyalty!
They defended him with their last bullets. They defended him with their lives. Heroes! Three times.
> General Gordon R. Sullivan, 3 June 1995, Commencement Address to the graduating class at the United States Military Academy, West Point.

HIERARCHY/SENIORITY

THE MILITARY hierarchical system must come to the aid of subordination, even of ideas.
> Field Marshal Helmuth Graf von Moltke, 'The Italian Campaign of 1859', quoted in von Freytag-Loringhoven, *Generalship in the Great War*, 1920.

TO BE a really successful leader, a senior officer must avoid aloofness . . . He should not place himself on a pedestal and exercise command from a position far above the heads of his men, but he must come down to the ground where they are struggling and mingle with them as friend and as a father.

Major-General John A. Lejeune, *The Reminiscences of a Marine*, 1929.

IT FOLLOWS that the stuffed dummies of the hierarchy can never enjoy prestige, for they are parasites who take everything and give nothing in return, weak-kneed creatures forever trembling in their shoes, jumping jacks who will turn their coats without scruple at the first opportunity. They can often safeguard their official careers, their rank if they are soldiers, their portfolios if they are ministers. They even, on occasion, receive the deference which custom and convention accords to their office. . . . But such cold and shrewd intelligences can never command the confidence and enthusiasm of others.

General Charles de Gaulle, *The Edge of the Sword*, 1932.

IT IS a military convention that infallibility is the privilege of seniority. (May 1933.)

Captain Sir Basil Liddell Hart, *Thoughts on War*, 1944.

THE PRETENCE to infallibility is instinctive in a hierarchy. If military commanders are prone to it that is only because of the prominent part that authority plays in the military profession. But to understand the cause is not to underrate the harm that this pretence has produced – in every sphere. We learn from history that the critics of authority have always been rebuked in self-righteous tones – if no worse fate has befallen them – yet have often been justified by history. (Jan. 1934.)

Captain Sir Basil Liddell Hart, *Thoughts on War*, 1944.

HISTORY
General

MY PURPOSE is not to relate at length every motion, but only such as were conspicuous for excellence or notorious for infamy. This I regard as history's highest function, to let no worthy action be uncommemorated, and to hold out the reprobation of posterity as a terror to evil words and deeds.

Cornelius Tacitus, *Annals*, 4.65, AD 116, (*The Complete Works of Tacitus*, tr. Alfred Church and William Brodribb, 1942).

WHAT WILL history say – what will posterity think?

Napoleon, his favourite phrase according to de Bourriene, his confidant and secretary, 1797–1802, quoted in Louis de Bourriene, *Memoirs of Napoleon Bonaparte*, I, 1855, p. xxiv.

EVERYTHING on earth is soon forgotten, except the opinion we leave imprinted upon history.

Napoleon, 27 November 1802, to General Leclerc,

Correspondance de Napoléon Ier, publié par ordre de l'Empereur Napoléon III, VIII, p. 113, 1858–1870, quoted in Christopher Herold, ed., *The Mind of Napoleon*, 1955.

MY USUAL reading fare, when I go to bed, is the old chronicles of the third, fourth, and fifth centuries. I read them or have them translated for me. Nothing is more curious, or less known, than the change from the old way of life to the new, than the transition from the ancient political bodies to the new ones that were founded on their ruins.

Napoleon, 1806, at a meeting of the Council of State, quoted in Christopher Herold, ed., *The Mind of Napoleon*, 1955.

AS SOON AS histories are properly told there is no more need of romances.

Walt Whitman, preface to *Leaves of Grass*, 1855–1892.

FELLOW CITIZENS, we cannot escape history. . . . We will be remembered in spite of ourselves.

Abraham Lincoln, 1 December 1862, second annual message to Congress.

IT IS HISTORY that teaches us to hope.

General Robert E. Lee, c. 1866, letter to Colonel Charles Marshall.

PEOPLE get the history they deserve.

General Charles de Gaulle, 1920, lecture to cadets at St. Cyr.

FOR THE FIRST TIME in my life I have seen "History" at close quarters, and I know that its actual process is very different from what is presented to posterity.

General Max Hoffman, *War Diaries and Other Papers*, 1929.

THERE IS a modern, and too common, tendency to regard history as a specialist subject. On the contrary, it is the corrective to specialization. Viewed right, it is the broadest of studies, embracing every aspect of life. It lays the foundation of education by showing how mankind repeats its follies, and what those follies are. . . . It is universal experience – infinitely longer, wider, and more varied than any individual's experience. How often do we hear people claim a knowledge of the world and of life because they are sixty or seventy years old. Most of them might be described as a 'young sixty, or seventy'. There is no excuse for any literate person if he is less than three thousand years old in mind.

Captain Sir Basil Liddell Hart, *Through the Fog of War*, 1938.

THE HISTORY of free men is never really written by chance but by choice – their choice.

President Dwight D. Eisenhower, 9 October 1956, address in Pittsburgh, Pennsylvania.

HISTORY is the laboratory of the human race. All

other disciplines observe and record solely in the physical realm. History happens in the human mind as much as in the tangible world. And because man can act, choose, and to some degree control his environment, we look to history to instruct us. I look to history for insights and, yes, for strength.
> General Gordon R. Sullivan, 22 February 1992, West Point, speech at the U.S. Military Academy Department of History.

LITERATURE is history with the truth left in. I believe we can profit from the study of the classical texts as never before. The veneer of civilization, so recent and fragile, is being stripped from much of the world. The old problems are today's problems – and tomorrow's. If we want to know "Who is our enemy?" we must look within.
> Lieutenant-Colonel Ralph Peters, 'Our New Old Enemies', *Parameters*, Summer 1999.

Studying Military History

[HISTORY] hath triumphed over time, which besides it, nothing but Eternity hath triumphed over. . . .
In a word, we may gather out of history a policy no less wise than eternal; by the comparison and application of other men's forepassed miseries with our own like errors and ill deservings.
> Sir Walter Raleigh, *History of the World*, 1614.

IT IS NOT ONLY Experience and Practice which maketh a Soldier worthy of his Name: but the knowledge of the manifold Accidents which arise from the variety of humane actions, which is best, and most speedily learned by reading History: for upon the variety of Chances that are set forth, he may meditate on the Effects of other men's adventures, that their harms may be his warnings, and their happy proceedings his fortunate Directions in the Art Military.
> Anonymous Captain J.S. (probably John Smythe), *Military Discipline – Or the Art of War*, 1689.

IT IS NOT probable that any similar chain of causes should, in a short time, produce the same circumstances as those under which we were . . . generals are never placed in exactly similar situations. . . . past facts are good to store in the imagination and the memory; they furnish a repository of ideas whence a supply of materials may be obtained, but which ought to be purified by passing through the strainer of judgment.
> Frederick the Great, *The History of the Seven Years War, Posthumus Works*, II, pp. ix, xi, xii, quoted in Azer Gat, *The Origins of Military Thought: from the Enlightenment to Clausewitz*, 1989.

I HAD IT from Xenophon, but our friends here are astonished at what I have done because they have read nothing.
> Major-General Sir James Wolfe, of his use of light

infantry at the siege of Louisburg, 1758, quoted in Liddell Hart, *Great Captains Unveiled*, 1927.

HISTORY I conquered rather than studied: that is to say, I wanted from it and retained of it only what could add to my ideas, I spurned what was of no use, and I seized upon certain conclusions that pleased me.
> Napoleon, conversation with Mme de Rémusat, quoted in Christopher Herold, ed., *The Mind of Napoleon*, 1955.

MAXIM 78. Peruse again and again the campaigns of Alexander, Hannibal, Caesar, Gustavus Adolphus, Turenne, Eugene and Frederick. Model yourself upon them. This is the only means of becoming a great captain, and of acquiring the secret of the art of war. Your own genius will be enlightened and improved by this study, and you will learn to reject all maxims foreign to the principles of the great commanders.
> Napoleon, *The Military Maxims of Napoleon*, tr. George D'Aguilar, 1831 (David Chandler, ed., 1987).

THE KNOWLEDGE of higher leadership can only be acquired by the study of military history and actual experience. There are no hard and fast rules; everything depends on the plans of the general, the condition of his troops, the season of the year, and a thousand other circumstances, which have the effect that no one case will ever resemble another.
> Napoleon (1769–1821), quoted in von Freytag-Loringhoven, *Generalship in the Great War*, 1920.

ONLY THE STUDY of military history is capable of giving those who have no experience of their own a clear picture of what I have just called the friction of the whole machine.
> Major-General Carl von Clausewitz, *Principles of War*, 1812, tr. Gatzke, 1942.

IF WE READ history with an open mind, we cannot fail to conclude that, among all the military virtues, the energetic conduct of war has always contributed most to glory and success.
> Major-General Carl von Clausewitz, *On War*, 4.3, 1832, tr. Michael Howard and Peter Paret, 1976.

MILITARY HISTORY, accompanied by sound criticism, is indeed the true school of war.
> Lieutenant-General Antoine-Henri Baron de Jomini, *Summary of the Art of War*, 1838, tr. Mendell and Craighill, 1862.

IF A FEW prejudiced men, after reading this book and carefully studying the detailed and correct history of the campaigns of the great masters of the art of war, still contend that it has neither principles nor rules, I can only pity them and reply, in the famous words of Frederick, "a mule which had made twenty campaigns under Prince Eugene would not be a better tactician than at the beginning."
> Lieutenant-General Antoine-Henri Baron de Jomini,

Summary of the Art of War, 1838, tr. Mendell and Craighill, 1862.

IT IS in military history that we are to look for the source of all military science. In it we shall find those exemplifications of failure and success by which alone the truth and value of the rules of strategy can be tested.

Dennis Hart Mahan, *Advance-Guard, Out-Post, and Detachment Service of Troops, with the Essential Principles of Strategy and Grand Tactics*, 1863.

THE STUDY of military history thus becomes very instructive in a strategical point of view; whilst, on the other hand, in endeavoring to apply . . . the tactics of the ancients to our modern armies, errors of the gravest character might be committed. Every servile imitation in this latter case . . . from not having weighed the enormous difference . . . between . . . present day . . . firearms, and the weapons for like purpose used by the ancients . . . is greatly to be deprecated . . . Misapprehension of the value of a new agent renders all celerity, that secret of success, impossible.

Dennis Hart Mahan, *Advance-Guard, Out-Post, and Detachment Service of Troops, with the Essential Principles of Strategy and Grand Tactics*, 1863.

. . . THE MOST effective means of teaching war during peace.

Field Marshal Helmuth Graf von Moltke (1800–1891).

THE SMALLEST DETAIL, taken from the actual incident in war, is more instructive to me, a soldier, than all the Thiers and Jominis in the world. They speak, no doubt, for the heads of states and armies but they never show me what I wish to know – a battalion, a company, a squad in action.

Colonel Charles Ardant du Picq, *Battle Studies*, 1880, tr. Greely, 1957.

IT IS NOW accepted with naval and military men who study their profession, that history supplies the raw material from which they are to draw their lessons, and reach their working conclusions. Its teachings are not, indeed, pedantic precedents; but they are the illustrations of living principles.

Rear Admiral Alfred Thayer Mahan, *From Sail to Steam*, 1907.

TO EVERY ONE who desires to become a commander, there is available a book entitled 'military history' . . . This reading matter, I must admit, is not always highly flavored. One will have to work through a mass of ingredients anything but palatable. But behind it all one arrives just the same at the facts, often most gratifying facts; at the bottom lies the knowledge as to how everything happened, how it had to happen, and how it will happen again.

Field Marshal Alfred Graf von Schlieffen, 15 October 1910, speech at the centenary celebration of the

Kriegsakademie, quoted in von Freytag-Loringhoven, *Generalship in the Great War*, 1920.

HISTORY. – To keep the brain of an army going in time of peace, to direct it continually towards its task of war, there is no book more fruitful to the student than that of history. If war, in its just aspect, is but a struggle between two wills more or less powerful and more or less informed, then the accuracy of decisions arrived at in war will always depend upon the same considerations as those of the past. The same errors reappear, leading to the same checks. The art of war is always to be drawn from the same sources.

Marshal of France Ferdinand Foch, *Precepts and Judgments*, 1919.

THE ROAD to high command leads through a long path called the history of war. Like all long roads the scenery is not always interesting; there are desert stretches of prosaic facts. But now and again the traveler reaches eminences where he sees the most sublime panoramas ever vouchsafed to mortals – the deathless deeds of the great who have passed to Valhalla, which is death but not oblivion.

General George S. Patton, Jr., note card, c. 1920, entitled 'Training', from the Patton Collection, Library of Congress.

TO BE USEFUL in battle, military knowledge like discipline must be subconscious. The memorizing of concrete examples is futile for in battle the mind does not work well enough to make memory trustworthy. One must be so soaked in military lore that he does the military thing automatically. The study of history will produce this result. The study of algebra will not.

General George S. Patton, Jr., note card, c. 1920, entitled 'Training', from the Patton Collection, Library of Congress.

UNLESS HISTORY can teach us how to look at the future, the history of war is but a bloody romance.

Major-General J.F.C. Fuller, *British Light Infantry in the Eighteenth Century*, 1925.

DO MAKE IT clear that generalship, at least in my case, came of understanding, of hard study and brain-work and concentration. Had it come easy to me I should not have done it so well.

So please, if you see me that way and agree with me, do use me as a text to preach for more study of books and history, a greater seriousness in military art. With 2,000 years of examples behind us we have no excuse, when fighting, for not fighting well.

Colonel T.E. Lawrence, 26 April 1933, letter to Captain Sir Basil Liddell Hart, quoted in *The Liddell Hart Memoirs*, I, 1965.

WHAT A FINE mirror history is . . . In great events which pass to the bosom of history how clearly do the conduct and acts of those who take an active part in these events show their moral character.

General Kemal Mustapha Atatürk, quoted in Alan Moorehead, *Gallipoli*, 1956.

IF I AM doubted, then again must I ask the student to turn to military history, and not merely examine one or two incidents as I have done, but read and re-read the campaigns of the great captains and study operations of the great fools, for not only are these latter folk in the majority, but their art is immensely instructive. What will the student's verdict be? I imagine that it will agree with mine: namely, that we soldiers are mostly alchemists, and many of us little more than military sorcerers.

Major-General J.F.C. Fuller, *The Foundations of the Science of War*, 1926.

THE VALUE of the knowledge acquired by study must not be overestimated. The soldier faced with the necessity for independent decision must not mentally search the pages of his professional encyclopaedia nor seek to remember how the great generals of history, from Alexander to Zieten, would have acted in a similar case. Such knowledge as that derived from the study of the history of war is only of living practical value when it has been digested, when the permanent and the important has been extracted from the wealth of detail and has been incorporated with a man's own mental resources – and it is not every man who has the gift for this.

Colonel-General Hans von Seekt, *Thoughts of a Soldier*, 1930.

THE REAL WAY to get value out of the study of military history is to take particular situations, and as far as possible get inside the skin of the man who made a decision, realize the conditions in which the decision was made, and then see in what way you could have improved upon it.

Field Marshal Viscount Wavell of Cyrenaica, 1930, lecture to officers at Aldershot.

STUDY the human side of military history, which is not a matter of cold-blooded formulas or diagrams, or nursery-book principles, such as: Be good and you will be happy. Be mobile and you will be victorious. Interior lines at night are the general's delight. Exterior lines at morning are the general's warning. And so on.

Field Marshal Viscount Wavell of Cyrenaica, 1930, lecture to officers at Aldershot.

TO MAKE WAR without a thorough knowledge of the history of war is on a par with the casualness of a doctor who prescribes medicine without taking the trouble to study the history of the case he is treating. (Dec. 1933.)

Captain Sir Basil Liddell Hart, *Thoughts on War*, 1944.

MORE THAN MOST professions the military is forced to depend upon intelligent interpretation of the past for signpost charting the future. Devoid of opportunity, in peace, for self-instruction through actual practice of his profession, the soldier makes maximum use of historical record in assuring the readiness of himself and his command to function efficiently in emergency. The facts derived from historical analysis he applies to conditions of the present and the proximate future, thus developing a synthesis of appropriate method, organization, and doctrine.

General of the Army Douglas MacArthur, *Annual Report of the Chief of Staff, June 30, 1935*.

THE DISCOVERY of uncomfortable facts had never been encouraged in armies, who treated their history as a sentimental treasure rather than a field of scientific research. (June 1936.)

Captain Sir Basil Liddell Hart, *Thoughts on War*, 1944.

IT IS TRUE that full study of war will not seriously assist a subaltern on picket duty; but when it comes to understanding present war conditions and the probable origins of the next war, a deep and impartial knowledge of history is essential. Further still, as it is not subalterns or generals who make wars, but governments and nations, unless the people as a whole have some understanding of what war meant in past ages, their opinions on war . . . today will be purely alchemical.

Major-General J.F.C. Fuller, *Decisive Battles: Their Influence Upon History and Civilization*, 1939.

TO BE a successful soldier, you must know history. Read it objectively. . . . You must read biography and especially autobiography. . . .

General George S. Patton, Jr., 6 June 1944, letter to his son, *The Patton Papers*, II, 1974.

THE VALUE of military history is the creative perception of the experience and lessons of the past in the capability to disclose the regular laws of the development of methods for the conduct of war, in its boundless capabilities for the expansion of the military world outlook and military thinking of officers and generals.

Marshal of the Soviet Union Andrei Grechko, *Voyenno istorichiskiy zhurnal*, 2/1961.

IN MY VIEW, the single most important foundation for any leader is a solid academic background in history. That discipline gives perspective to the problems of the present and drives home the point that there is really very little new under the sun. Whenever a policymaker starts his explanation of how he intends to handle a problem with such phrases as "We are at the takeoff point of a new era . . . ," you know you are heading for trouble. Starting by ignoring the natural yardstick of 4,000 years of recorded history, busy people, particularly busy opportunists, have a tendency to see their dilemmas as so unique and unprecedented that they deserve to make exceptions to law, custom, or morality in their own favor to get around them. . . .

Admiral James B. Stockdale, 'Educating Leaders', *The Washington Quarterly*, Winter 1983.

MILITARY HISTORY is essential to the development of military science because – unlike most other sciences – military science is unable to test its theories and hypotheses in laboratory experiments. Military versions of experiments, such as field exercises, maneuvers, and tests, can never reproduce the essential ingredient of war, which is fear in a lethal environment. Such experiments are useful, but only to a limited degree.
> Colonel T.N. Dupuy, *Understanding War*, 1987.

I ALWAYS ENJOY reading military history. I tell people that history strengthens me – it helps me and, I hope, others realize that mortal man can overcome the obstacles in his path, transforming his situation through sound decisions and steadfast application of his will. The books I cite here have all helped me reach that conclusion, and I still refer to them even though I first encountered several of them many years ago.
> General Gordon R. Sullivan, 'From My Bookshelf', *Military Review*, 11/91.

Writing Military History

I SHALL BE content if those shall pronounce my History useful who desire to have a view of events as they did really happen, and as are very likely, in accordance with human nature, to repeat themselves at some future time – if not exactly the same, yet very similar.
> Thucydides, *The Peloponnesian War*, c. 404 BC, tr. Benjamin Jowett, 1881.

FEW PERSONS will understand me, but I write for the connoisseurs, trusting that they will not be offended by the confidence of my opinions.
> Field Marshal Maurice Comte de Saxe, *My Reveries*, 1732, tr. Phillips, 1940.

EXPERTS should not be offended by the assurance with which I deliver my opinions. They should correct them; that is the fruit I expect from my work.
> Field Marshal Maurice Comte de Saxe, *My Reveries*, 1732, tr. Phillips, 1940.

WRITE THE HISTORY of a battle? As well write the history of a ball.
> The Duke of Wellington, quoted in Richard Holmes, *Acts of War: Human Behavior in Battle*, 1985.

HE COULD NOT tell the whole truth without hurting the feelings of many worthy men, and without doing mischief. Expatiating on the subject, he related many anecdotes illustrating this observation, showing errors committed by generals and others – especially at Waterloo – errors so materially affecting his operations that he could not do justice to himself if he suppressed them, and yet by giving them publicity he would ungraciously affect the favour of many worthy men, whose only fault was dullness.
> General Sir William Napier, relating the Duke of Wellington's reluctance to write a history of his

campaigns, quoted in Charles Oman, *Wellington's Army 1809–1814*, 1913.

MY AMBITION was to write a book that would not be forgotten in two or three years, and which anyone interested in the subject would certainly take up more than once.
> Major-General Carl von Clausewitz, *On War*, 1832, p. 63, tr. Michael Howard and Peter Paret, 1976; notes on the genesis of his early manuscript, 1818.

I AM DESIROUS that the bravery and devotion of the Army of Northern Virginia be correctly transmitted to posterity. This is the only tribute that can now be paid to the worth of its noble officers and soldiers, and I am anxious to collect the necessary information for the history of the campaigns, including the operations in the Valley and in Western Virginia, from its organization to its final surrender. . . .
> General Robert E. Lee, from a circular letter sent to many of his general officers after the Civil War in an attempt to gather material for a history of the Army of Northern Virginia, quoted in Captain Robert E. Lee, *The Recollections and Letters of Robert E. Lee*, 1904.

ALTHOUGH the story of a campaign is made up of many details which cannot be omitted, since they are essential to the truth as well as the interest of the account, it is of paramount importance that the reader should preserve a general idea. . . . To appreciate the tale it is less necessary to contemplate the wild scenes and stirring incidents, than thoroughly to understand the logical sequence of incidents which all tend to ultimately culminate in a decisive trial of strength.
> Sir Winston S. Churchill, *The River War*, 1899.

I WANT to tell the story *professionally* & to comment freely on every professional feature as one w[oul]d comment on moves of chess.
> Brigadier-General Edward Porter Alexander, letter, 1901, referring to his writing of *Military Memoirs of a Confederate: A Critical Narrative*, 1907.

THE MILITARY HISTORIAN who is instructed in the principles of the art of war finds, as it were imposed upon him, the necessity of so constructing his narrative as to present a substantial unity in effect. Such familiar phrase as the "key of the situation," the decisive point for which he has been taught to look, upon the tenure of which depends more or less the fortune of war, sustains continually before his mind the idea, to which his treatment must correspond, of a central feature round which all else groups; not only subordinate but contributive. Here is no vague collocation of words, but the concrete, pithy expression of a trained habit of mind which dominates writing necessarily, even though unconsciously to the writer.
> Rear Admiral Alfred Thayer Mahan, *Naval Administration and Warfare*, 1908.

IT IS NOT the coloring, but in the grouping, that the true

excellence of the military historian is found; just as the battle is won, not by the picturesqueness of the scene, but by the disposition of the forces. Both the logical faculty and the imagination contribute to his success, but the former much exceeds the latter in effect. A campaign, or a battle, skillfully designed, is a work of art, and duly to describe it requires something of the appreciation and combinative faculty of an artist; but where there is no appeal over the imagination, to the intellect, impressions are apt to lack distinctness. While there is a certain exaltation in sharing, through vivid narrative, the emotions of those who have borne a part in some deed of conspicuous daring, the fascination does not equal that wrought upon the mind as it traces the sequence by which successive occurrences are seen to issue in their necessary results, or causes apparently remote converge upon a common end.
  Rear Admiral Alfred Thayer Mahan, *Naval Administration and Warfare*, 1908.

IN WAR TIME no soldier is free to say what he thinks; after a war no one cares what a soldier thinks.
  General Sir Ian Hamilton, *Ian Hamilton's Dispatches From the Dardenelles*, 1917.

TEN MILLION pities that G.B.S. [George Bernard Shaw] didn't raise the Arab Revolt and write the history of it. There is a book of books gone to waste, because nobody made him a Brigadier-General! It's easy to be wise afterwards, I suppose. If I'm Prime Minister for the next war, all independent commands shall be given to the finest writers of the generation. We may lose the war . . . but think of the glories to be published as the Peace rolls on!
  Colonel T.E. Lawrence, letter to Mrs. Charlotte Shaw, 15 October 1924, in *The Letters of T.E. Lawrence*, 1988.

THOSE ACCUSTOMED to the conventional military history and biography may complain that the account of battles is uncomfortably bare and scantily furnished in details. I shall welcome the complaint. This book is a study of life, not of still life. An exercise in human psychology, not in upholstery. To place the position and trace the action of battalions and batteries is only of value to the collector of antiques, and still more to the dealer in faked antiques. Those who believe that exactness is possible can never have known war, or must have forgotten it. And even if by supernatural means we could recreate the action in such detail, it would be historically valueless. For the issue of any operation of war is decided not by what the situation actually is, but by what the rival commanders think it is. Historically and practically, it is far more important to discover what information they had, and the times at which it reached them, than to know the actual situation of the "pieces." A battlefield is not a chessboard.
  Captain Sir Basil Liddell Hart, *Sherman: Soldier, Realist, American*, 1929.

IF TRUTH is many-sided, mendacity is many-tongued. History cannot proceed by silences. The chronicler of ill-recorded times has none the less to tell his tale. If facts are lacking, rumor must serve. Failing affidavits, he must build with gossip.
  Sir Winston S. Churchill, *Marlborough*, 1933.

A MILITARY PHILOSOPHER may recognize the inevitability of gradual evolution, but a military historian must point out how often it has proved fatal to nations. The money spent on armies that failed to adapt themselves to changing conditions has proved too literally a sinking fund – acting as a millstone around the investor's neck when he was plunged into the deep waters of war. (March 1934.)
  Captain Sir Basil Liddell Hart, *Thoughts on War*, 1944.

AFTER TWENTY YEARS of such work pure documentary history seems to me akin to mythology. For those who still put their faith in it, here is a short story with a moral. When the British front was broken in March, 1918, and French reinforcements came to help in filling the gap, an eminent French general arrived at a certain army corps headquarters, and there majestically dictated orders giving the line on which his troops would stand that night and start their counter-attack in the morning. After reading it, with some perplexity, the British corps commander exclaimed, "But that line is behind the German front; you lost it yesterday." To which he received the reply, made with a knowing smile: "C'est pour l'histoire."
  Captain Sir Basil Liddell Hart, *Through the Fog of War*, 1938.

DEEP is the gulf between history and historic truth, and perhaps never more so than in books dealing with military history. If one reason is that they are usually written by soldiers untrained as historians, and another that there is frequently some personal link, whether of acquaintance or tradition, between author and subject, a deeper reasons lies in a habit of mind. For the soldier, "My country," right or wrong, must be the watchword. And this essential loyalty, whether it be to a country, to a regiment, or to comrades, is so ingrained in him that when he passes from action to reflection it is difficult for him to acquire instead the historian's single-minded loyalty to truth.
  Captain Sir Basil Liddell Hart, *Through the Fog of War*, 1938.

NAVAL OFFICERS prefer to make history rather than write it – because of which preference they probably do a better job of the former.
  Admiral Ernest J. King, 1942, quoted in *Naval War College Review*.

IN THIS BOOK I have tried to achieve one purpose: to explain how war is waged on the field from the field command post. For it is there, midway between the conference table and the foxhole, that strategy is translated into battlefield tactics; there the field commander must calculate the cost of rivers, roads, and hills in terms of guns, tank tonnage – and most importantly in terms of the lives and limbs of his soldiers. How , then, did we reach our critical decisions? Why and how did we go where we did? These are the questions I have been asked most often. And these are the questions that give me justification for writing this book.

> General of the Army Omar N. Bradley, *A Soldier's Story*, 1951.

SOME READERS may think I have at times, whether as a subaltern or as a general, treated too lightly, even when in this minor key, the grim and tragic business of war. If they do, I can only plead guilty to a fault – or is it a virtue? – that has for centuries marked the British soldier. There would be fewer battle honours emblazoned on his colours had he lacked it.

> Field Marshal Viscount Slim of Burma, *Unofficial History*, 1959.

THE MILITARY HISTORY of a war written shortly after the end of that war is generally unsatisfactory because the silence demanded by considerations of security outweigh the benefit to be derived from publication – even if the scope is limited to recording the lessons learned. If military history is to have any real scholarly value from which something may be learned, it must be comprehensive, exhaustive, complete and objective. Writing that is distorted by bias or subjectivity, or is unable – for security reasons – to give all the facts, will not be of lasting value nor will it make a significant contribution to military science, though it may arouse ephemeral interest.

> General Yigal Allon, *The Making of Israel's Army*, 1970.

MOST BATTLES are more like a schoolyard in a rough neighborhood at recess time than a clash between football giants in the Rose Bowl. They are messy, inorganic, and uncoordinated. It is only much later, after the clerks have tidied up their reports and the generals have published their memoirs, that the historian with his orderly mind professes to discern an understandable pattern in what was essentially catch-as-catch-can, if not chaotic, at the time.

> Brigadier-General S.L.A. Marshall, *Ambush*, 1969.

MY OFFICIAL DUTIES required me to get a full and final accounting of what had happened on that field.

It was done by assembling the survivors of every unit that had fought, interviewing them as a group, and recording their experiences personal and in common from the beginning of movement till the end of fighting.

The method of reconstructing what develops in combat, relating cause to effect, and eliminating the fog, is my own. . . . It works because it is simple and because what one man remembers will stir recall in another. The one inviolable rule, if such group interviewing is to get valid results, is that the question-and-answer routine must be in sequence step-by-step from first to last.

> Brigadier-General S.L.A. Marshall, *The Fields of Bamboo*, 1971.

HONOUR

WHEN XERXES wrote to him [Leonidas]: "It is possible for you not to fight the gods but to side with me and be monarch of Greece," he wrote back: "If you understood what is honourable in life, you would avoid lusting after what belongs to others. For me, it is better to die for Greece than to be monarch of the people of my race."

> King Leonidas of Sparta, 480 BC, at Thermopylae, quoted in Plutarch, *The Lives*, c. AD 100 (*Plutarch on Sparta*, tr. Richard Talbert, 1988).

WHEN ASKED why the best men prefer an honourable death to a life without honour, he said: "Because they regard the latter as the gift of Nature, and the former as being in their own hands."

> King Leonidas of Sparta, 480 BC, quoted in Plutarch, *The Lives*, c. AD 100 (*Plutarch on Sparta*, tr. Richard Talbert, 1988).

THUS CHOOSING to die resisting, rather than to live submitting, they fled only from dishonour, but met danger face to face, and after one brief moment, while at the summit of their fortune, left behind them not their fear, but their glory.

> Pericles, 431/430 BC, funeral oration for the Athenian fallen, quoted in Thucydides, *History of the Peloponnesian War*, c. 404 BC, 2.42, tr. William Crawley, 1910, Robert Strassler, ed., *The Landmark Thucydides*, 1996.

FOR THE LOVE of honor alone is ever young; and not riches, as some say, but honor is the delight of men when they are old and useless.

> Pericles, 431/430 BC, funeral oration for the Athenian fallen, Thucydides, *The Peloponnesian War*, 2.44, tr. Benjamin Jowett, 1881.

ATHENIANS excel all others not so much in singing or in stature or in strength, as in love of honour, which is the strongest incentive to deeds of honour and renown.

> Socrates (470–399 BC), quoted by Xenophon, *Memorabilia*, 3.13, c. 360 BC (tr. E.C. Marchant, 1923).

LEARNING of his approach, Alexander rode and met him in advance of the line with a few Companions; halting his horse, he admired the stature of Porus, who was approximately over five cubits in height, his beauty, and the appearance he gave of spirit not enslaved, but of one man of honour meeting another after a fine struggle against another king for his own kingdom. Then Alexander spoke to him first and urged him to say what he desired to be done with him. Porus is said to have replied: "Treat me, Alexander, like a king," and Alexander, pleased with the reply, answered: 'that you shall have, Porus, for my own sake; now demand what you would wish for yours.' He replied that everything was comprised in this one request. Alexander was all the more pleased with this reply, and gave Porus the government of his Indians and added still further territory even greater in extent to his old realm. In this way he himself acted like a king in his treatment of a man of honour, while in Porus he found from this time entire fidelity.

> Arrian, *Anabasis of Alexander*, 5.19, c. AD 150, tr. P.A. Brunt; the meeting of Alexander the Great and Porus after the Battle of the Hydaspes, June 326 BC.

EVEN HONOR and virtue make enemies, condemning, as they do, their opposites by too close a contrast.

> Cornelius Tacitus, *Annals*, 4.33, AD 116, (*The Complete Works of Tacitus*, tr. Alfred Church and William Brodribb, 1942).

TO EVERY MAN posterity gives his true honour.

> Cornelius Tacitus, *Annals*, 15.59, AD 116, (*The Complete Works of Tacitus*, tr. Alfred Church and William Brodribb, 1942).

THE BEST MEMORIAL for a mighty man is to gain honour ere death.

> *Beowulf*, c. AD 1000.

YOUR MAJESTY may send me to attack the enemy batteries, and I will readily obey. But to act contrary to my honour, oath and duty is something which my will and conscience do not permit me to do.

> General F.C. von Saldern, 1761, response to Frederick the Great's order to commit the atrocity of destroying the royal palaces of Saxony, quoted in Christopher Duffy, *The Military Life of Frederick the Great*, 1985.

WAR must be carried on systematically, and to do it you must have men of character activated by principles of honor.

> General George Washington (1732–1799).

I WOULD LAY DOWN my life for America, but I cannot trifle with my honor.

> Admiral John Paul Jones, 4 September 1777, letter to A. Livingston.

THE NEAPOLITAN OFFICERS did not lose much honour, for, God knows, they had not much to lose; but they lost all they had.

> Admiral Viscount Nelson, writing of the rout of the Neapolitan Army by the French, 15 December 1798, quoted in Robert Southey, *Life of Nelson*, 1813.

WHEN A MAN chooses a calling, he must do everything that can be done in that calling, so that he can never suffer reproach for having done only half of his duty. On this account I keep among the mottos in my portfolio, the following from Boileau:
> Honor is like an island,
> Steep and without shore:
> They who once leave,
> Can never return.

> Lieutenant-General Johann von Ewald, entry on 17 May 1781, during his service as a young German *Jäger* captain, in the employ of the British, during the American Revolution, *Diary of the American War*, 1979.

THE BRAVEST MAN feels an anxiety '*circa praecordia*' as he enters the battle; but he dreads disgrace more.

> Admiral Viscount Nelson, quoted in Alfred Thayer Mahan, *The Life of Nelson*, 1897.

UNFIT as my ship was, I had nothing left for the honour of our country but to sail, which I did in two hours afterward.

> Admiral Viscount Nelson, 16 September 1793, letter from Naples.

WHAT I WANT you to preserve is honour, and not a few planks of wood.

> Napoleon, 15 September 1804, letter to the Minister of Marine, *Correspondance de Napoléon Ier, publié par ordre de l'Empereur Napoléon III*, IX, p. 527, 1858–1870.

ONE OBTAINS everything from men by appealing to their sense of honour.

> Napoleon, 1 March 1805, to Fouché, *Correspondance de Napoléon Ier, publié par ordre de l'Empereur Napoléon III*, VI, p. 178, 1858–1870.

IT IS NO DISHONOUR to be defeated by my army.

> Napoleon, 1805, to a captured Russian officer after the Battle of Austerlitz.

WHOEVER PREFERS death to ignominity will save his life and live in honour, but he who prefers life will die and cover himself with disgrace.

> Napoleon, 1 October 1809, letter to General Clarke, *Correspondance de Napoléon Ier, publié par ordre de l'Empereur Napoléon III*, XIX, p. 542, 1858–1870, quoted in Christopher Herold, ed., *The Mind of Napoleon*, 1955.

THE HONOUR of a general consists in obeying, in keeping subalterns under his orders on the honest path, in maintaining good discipline, devoting oneself solely to the interests of the State and the sovereign, and in scorning completely private interests.

> Napoleon, 8 June 1811, letter to Marshal Berthier, *Correspondance de Napoléon Ier, publié par ordre de l'Empereur Napoléon III*, No. 17782, Vol. XXII, 1858–1870.

THE BRITISH ARMY is what it is because it is officered by gentlemen; men who would . . . scorn to do a dishonourable thing and who have something more at stake than a reputation for military smartness.

> The Duke of Wellington (1769–1852), quoted in *The Autobiography of Sir Harry Smith*, I, 1901.

THE SOLDIER'S TRADE, if it is to mean anything at all, has to be anchored to an unshakeable code of honor. Otherwise, those of us who follow the drums become nothing more than a bunch of hired assassins walking around in gaudy clothes . . . a disgrace to God and mankind.

> Major-General Carl von Clausewitz, *On War*, 1832, tr. Michael Howard and Peter Paret, 1976.

HONOUR is manly decency. The shame of being found wanting in it means everything to us.

> Alfred Comte de Vigny, *Servitude and Grandeur of Arms*, 1835.

WHAT IS LIFE without honor? Degradation is worse than death. We must think of the living and of those who are come after us, and see that with God's blessing we transmit to them the freedom we have ourselves inherited.

> Lieutenant-General Thomas J. 'Stonewall' Jackson, August 1862, to an officer who requested leave to visit a dying member of his family.

A REALLY GREAT PEOPLE, proud and high-spirited, would face all the disasters of war rather than purchase that base prosperity which is bought at the price of national honor.

> President Theodore Roosevelt, 23 February 1907, speech at Harvard University.

BUT WHO OF US would endure a world . . . without the divine folly of honor? . . . In the midst of doubt, in the collapse of creeds, there is one thing I do not doubt, and that is that the faith is true and adorable which leads a soldier to throw away his life in obedience to a blindly accepted duty, in a cause which he little understands, in a plan of campaign of which he has no notion, under tactics of which he does not see the use.

> Justice Oliver Wendell Holmes, Jr., 'The Soldier's Faith', speech at Harvard University, *Speeches*, 1913.

THE MUSTER rolls on which the name and oath were written were pledges of honor redeemable at the gates of death. And they who went up to them, knowing this, are on the lists of heroes.

> Major-General Joshua L. Chamberlain, *The Passing of the Armies*, 1915.

AND AN OFFICER is so absorbed by the sense of responsibility for his men, for his cause, for the fight, that the thought of personal peril has no place whatever in governing his actions. The instinct to seek safety is overcome by the instinct of honor.

> Major-General Joshua L. Chamberlain, *The Passing of the Armies*, 1915.

NEVER GIVE IN, never give in, never, never, never – in nothing great or small, large or petty – never give in except in convictions of honour and good sense.

> Sir Winston S. Churchill, 29 October 1941, address at Harrow School.

AN OFFICER must teach his men to honor the country and the uniform and to respect the symbols of these things. But one way in which to do them

honor is to begin to understand the limits in which they operate as forces influencing the conduct and shaping the fortunes of combat troops. The rule for the soldier should be that given the Australian mounted infantryman when he asked the Sphinx for the wisdom of the ages: "Don't expect too much!"

> Brigadier-General S.L.A. Marshall, *Men Against Fire*, 1947.

A MAN has honor if he holds himself to a course of conduct because of a conviction that it is in the general interest, even though he is well aware that it may lead to inconvenience, personal loss, humiliation, or grave personal risk.

> Brigadier-General S.L.A. Marshall, *The Armed Forces Officer*, 1950.

WHEN MACARTHUR put out an order forbidding the confiscation of Japanese officers' swords, Halsey was indignant. The next time he saw the general he protested, saying he considered the order unwise for two reasons. First, the sword, a symbol of militarism would keep its spirit alive . . .

"That's true," said MacArthur, "but I was thinking of Appomattox, when Grant allowed Lee's troops to keep their side arms."

"That brings me to my second point," Halsey replied. "Grant was dealing with an honorable foe. We are not."

The general pondered a few moments, pacing his office. "You're right!" he exclaimed. "You're right! I'll revoke the order." He did.

> The exchange between Admiral Halsey and General of the Army MacArthur over an interpretation of honour, as related by E.B. Potter, *Bull Halsey*, 1985.

NO NATION can safely trust its martial honor to leaders who do not maintain the universal code which distinguishes between those things that are right and those things that are wrong.

> General of the Army Douglas MacArthur, February 1946, describing General Homma's conduct in The Philippines, 1942, in *Reminiscences*, 1962.

THE CHOICE of death or dishonour is one which has always faced the professional fighting man, and there must be no doubt in his mind what his answer must be. He chooses death for himself so that his country [or comrades] may survive, or on a grander scale so that the principles for which he is fighting may survive.

> Lieutenant-General Sir John Crowley, quoted in John D. Luck, *To Fight With Intrepidity*, 1998.

HOPE

WHEN HE HAD shared out or signed away almost all the property of the crown, Perdiccas asked him, "But your majesty, what are you leaving for yourself?" "My hopes!" replied Alexander.

> Alexander the Great, 334 BC, as he prepared to cross the Hellespont to conquer the Persian Empire on an

empty purse, quoted in Plutarch, *The Lives*, c. AD 100, (*The Age of Alexander*, tr. Ian Scott-Kilvert, 1972).

HOPE encourages men to endure and attempt everything; in depriving them of it, or in making it too distant, you deprive them of their very soul.
    Field Marshal Maurice Comte de Saxe, *My Reveries*, 1732, tr. Phillips, 1940.

THE FOE is conquered, not by destruction of his existence, but by the annihilation of his hopes of victory.
    Field Marshal Colmar Baron von der Goltz, *The Nation in Arms*, 1887.

LOSS OF HOPE, rather than loss of life, is the factor that really decides wars, battles, and even the smallest combats. The all-time experience of warfare shows that when men reach the point where they see, or feel, that further effort and sacrifice can do no more than delay the end they commonly lose the will to spin it out, and bow to the inevitable.
    Captain Sir Basil Liddell Hart, *Defence of the West*, 1950.

PURPOSEFUL leadership is to keep hope alive.
    Major-General Bernard Loeffke, quoted in the *Congressional Record*, 14 September 1992, p. E2605.

HORSES

HAST THOU given the horse strength? hast thou clothed his neck with thunder?
    Canst thou make him afraid as a grasshopper? the glory of his nostrils is terrible.
    He paweth in the valley, and rejoiceth in his strength; he goeth on to meet the armed men.
    He mocketh at fear, and is not afrighted; neither turneth he back from the sword.
    The quiver rattleth against him, the glittering spear and the shield.
    He swalloweth the ground with fierceness and rage: neither believeth he that *it is* the sound of the trumpet.
    He saith among the trumpets, Ha, Ha; and he smelleth the battle afar off, the thunder of the captains, and the shouting.
    Job 39:19–25.

OUT OF RANGE,
The horses of Achilleus, from the time
they sensed their charioteer downed in the dust
at the hands of deadly Hektor, had been weeping.
Automédôn, the son of Diorês,
laid often on their backs his flickering whip,
pled often in a low tone – or swore at them –
but neither toward the shipways and the beach
by Hellê's waters would they budge, nor follow
Akhaians into battle. No: stock-still
as a gravestone, fixed above the tomb
of a dead man or woman, they stood fast,

holding the beautiful war-car still: their heads
curved over to the ground, and warm tears flowed
from under eyelids earthward as they mourned
their longed-for driver. Manes along the yoke
were soiled as they hung forward under yokepads.
Seeing their tears flow, pitying them, Lord Zeus
bent his head and murmured in his heart:

"Poor things, why did I give you to King Pêleus,
a mortal, you who never age or die,
to let you ache with men in their hard lot?"
    Homer, *The Iliad*, 17, c. 800 BC, tr. Robert Fitzgerald; the sacred horses of Achilles mourning the death of Patrocles to whom Achilles had lent his armour and team to fight the Trojans.

THE FIRST THING to appreciate is that spirit in a horse is the equivalent of anger in a human being. So just as the best way to avoid infuriating some one is not to say or do anything that will irritate him, you are least likely to arouse a high-spirited horse if you avoid annoying it. . . . But the best piece of advice I can give, if you need a horse for war, is not to get one that is too high-spirited.
    Xenophon, *On Horsemanship*, c. 360 BC (*Hiero the Tyrant and Other Treatises*, tr. Robin Waterfield, 1997).

BUT GOOD HORSES with competent riders will manage to escape even from hopeless situations.
    Xenophon, *On Horsemanship*, c. 360 BC (*Hiero the Tyrant and Other Treatises*, tr. Robin Waterfield, 1997).

THE DISAPPEARANCE of the horse from war does not suggest the withdrawal of riding from an officer's education in peace. It suggests exactly the opposite.
    General Sir John Hackett, 1960, lecture to the Royal United Services Institute (RUSI).

IT WAS the horse, of course, that distinguished the cavalryman from the other branches, even the artillery, because of the manner in which they used them. It made the cavalry an elite branch of the service, and it was in horsemanship that most of the legends of the school originated. The horse doubled the work of training cavalrymen in comparison with that of training the dismounted branches, and it was the horse that increased the sense of responsibility of cavalrymen, they could not forget him for even one day.
    General Lucian C. Truscott, Jr., *The Twilight of the Cavalry*, 1989; speaking of the U.S. Army Cavalry School at Fort Riley, Kansas.

HUMANITY

KIND-HEARTED PEOPLE might of course think there was some ingenious way to disarm or defeat an enemy without too much bloodshed, and might imagine this is the true goal of the art of war. Pleasant as it sounds, it is a fallacy that must be exposed: war is such a dangerous business that the mistakes which come from kindness are the very worst.

> Major-General Carl von Clausewitz, *On War*, 1.1, 1832, tr. Michael Howard and Peter Paret, 1976.

MEN who take up arms against one another in public do not cease on this account to be moral beings, responsible to one another and to God.

> U.S. Army General Order No. 100, 1863.

THE GREATEST KINDNESS in war is to bring it to a speedy conclusion.

> Field Marshal Helmuth Graf von Moltke, 11 December 1880.

NO MAN is justified in doing evil on the ground of expediency.

> President Theodore Roosevelt, *The Strenuous Life*, 1900.

THE ART of leading, in operations large or small, is the art of dealing with humanity.

> Brigadier-General S.L.A. Marshall, *Men Against Fire*, 1947.

QUITE CONTRARY to trivial opinion, all professional military men do not walk blind and brutal. I have known some who demonstrated as much pity as they did courage, and they showed a lot of that.

When you are dealing firsthand with the quivering element of life and death – When you are trying to figure out the best manner in which to save certain lives as well as to take others, and in the same operation – You do not necessarily become calloused. Neither does a surgeon.

> General Curtis LeMay, *Mission With LeMay*, 1965.

YOU CAN only be compassionate on the battlefield if you are operating from a position of strength.

> General Walter E. Boomer, 17 June 1993, U.S. Naval War College, Newport, Rhode Island.

HUMOUR

WHAT IMPRESSED ME most at the time, and survives as an inspiring memory, was the steadiness and fortitude of the British private soldier combined with his queer ironic humour in days of deep privation and adversity.

> Herbert Asquith, *Moments of Memory*, 1937; referring to the crisis of the German *Friedensturm* of 1918 and the 'backs to the wall' resolve of the British Army.

DON'T BE CARELESS about yourselves – on the other hand not too careful. Live well but do not flaunt it. Laugh a little and teach your men to laugh – get good humour under fire – war is a game that's played with a smile. If you can't smile, grin. If you can't grin, keep out of the way until you can.

> Sir Winston S. Churchill (1874–1965).

THE THIRD FLEET'S sunken and damaged ships have been salvaged and are retiring at high speed toward the enemy.

> Admiral William 'Bull' Halsey, response to the repeated Japanese claim to have sunk his fleet during its raid on Taiwana and the Ryuku Islands in October 1944, in E.B. Potter, *Bull Halsey*, 1985.

TO SPEAK of the importance of a sense of humor would be futile, if it were not that what cramps so many men isn't that they are by nature humorless as that they are hesitant to exercise what humor they possess. Within the military profession, this is as unwise as to let the muscles go soft or to spare the mind the strain of original thinking. Great humor has always been in the military tradition.

> Brigadier-General S.L.A. Marshall, *The Armed Forces Officer*, 1950.

HUMOR is an effective but tricky technique in command and leadership, beneficial when used wisely and with skill, but it can backfire into a dangerous booby trap if overworked or crudely employed.

> Major-General Aubrey 'Red' Newman, *Follow Me*, 1981.

MIX EMPATHY with your humor; consider how the jest you have in mind will affect others before you utter it.

> Major-General Aubrey 'Red' Newman, *Follow Me*, 1981.

PEOPLE are afraid of a leader who has no sense of humor. They think that he is not capable of relaxing, and as a result of this there is a tendency for that leader to have a reputation for pomposity, which may not be the case at all. Humor has a tendency to relax people in times of stress.

> General Louis H. Wilson, quoted in Montor, *Naval Leadership: Voices of Experience*, 1987.

LEADERS Should Have a Sense of Humor. Most of the time, leaders should laugh at themselves rather than at others. They should generally be willing to tell jokes or even embarrassing stories about their own mistakes to let people know that they are human, that they err, and that they are willing to admit errors. They should let people know that life is not so important that you can't sit back and occasionally be amused by what's happening. Humor can be a great reliever of tension; a story or a joke at times of crisis or difficulty can be very therapeutic. Be relaxed, be humorous with people, but don't use humor against people. Humor, delivered with an acid tongue and aimed at subordinates, can be very counterproductive.

> Major-General Perry Smith, *Taking Charge: A Practical Guide for Leaders*, 1986.

HUNGER

ACHILLES, godlike and brave, send not the Achaeans thus against Ilium to fight the Trojans fasting, for the battle will be no brief one, when it is once begun, and heaven has filled both sides with fury; bid them first take food, both bread and wine, by the ships, for in this there is strength and stay. No man can do battle the livelong day to the going down of the sun if he is without food. However much he may want to fight his strength will fail him before he knows it; hunger and thirst will find him out, and his limbs will grow weary under him. But a man can fight all day if he is full fed with meat and wine; his heart beats high, and his strength will stay till he has routed all his foes.

>Homer, *The Iliad*, 19, c. 800 BC, tr. Samuel Butler; Odysseus urging Achilles, who was eager to avenge the death of Patrocles, to taste his revenge slightly cold.

HE [the general] should not hesitate to order the first meal at sunrise, lest the enemy, by a prior attack force his men to fight while still hungry. On the whole, this matter must not be considered of slight importance nor should a general neglect to pay attention to it; for soldiers who have eaten moderately, so as not to put too great a load into their stomachs, are more vigorous in battle; armies have often been overpowered for just this reason, their strength failing for lack of food – that is, whenever the decision rests, not on a moment's fighting, but when the battle lasts throughout the entire day.

>Onasander, *The General*, AD 58 (*Aeneas Tacticus, Aclepiodotus, Onasander*, tr. The Illinois Greek Club, 1923).

GAIUS CAESAR used to say that he followed the same policy towards the enemy as did many doctors when dealing with physical ailments, namely, that of conquering the foe by hunger rather than steel.

>Frontinus, *Stratagems*, 4.7, c. AD 84–96, tr. Charles E. Bennett, 1925.

FAMINE makes greater havoc in an army than the enemy, and is more terrible than the sword.

>Flavius Vegetius Renatus, *Military Institutions of the Romans*, c. AD 378, tr. Clark, 1776.

THE GENERAL achieves the most who tries to destroy the enemy's army more by hunger than by force of arms.

>The Emperor Maurice, *The Strategikon*, c. AD 600 (*Maurice's Strategikon*, tr. George Dennis, 1984).

FEW VICTORIES are won on an empty belly.

>Sir John Hawkwood (1320–1394).

THE GREATEST SECRET of war and the masterpiece of a skillful general is to starve his enemy. Hunger exhausts men more surely than courage, and you will succeed with less risk than by fighting.

>Frederick the Great, *Instructions to His Generals*, 1747, tr. Phillips, 1940.

THE FIRST ART of a military leader is to deprive the enemy of subsistence.

>Field Marshal Prince Aleksandr V. Suvorov (1729–1800).

A STARVING ARMY is actually worse than none. The soldiers lose their discipline and their spirit. They plunder even in the presence of their officers.

>The Duke of Wellington, August 1809, letter from Spain.

FOOD, FOOD, FOOD! Without it, there is no limit to the horrors this undisciplined mass of men may bring upon the town.

>Napoleon, 29 November 1812, letter to M. Maert, Minister for Foreign Affairs, of the approach of his starving army to Vilna on its retreat from Moscow, *Correspondance de Napoléon Ier, publié par ordre de l'Empereur Napoléon III*, XXIV, 19362, 1858–1870.

THERE IS an enemy I dread much more than the hostile Creek . . . that meagre-monster "Famine".

>Major-General Andrew Jackson, 23 October 1813, letter to Leroy Pope, *Correspondence*, I, p. 336.

THE PERSON selected to feed the army was a metaphysical dyspeptic, who it was said, lived on rice-water, and had a theory that soldiers could do the same. A man, to fill such a position well, should be in sympathy with hungry men, on the principle that he who drives fat oxen must himself be fat.

>Colonel John S. Mosby, *Mosby's War Reminiscences*, 1887.

THE WANING *MORAL* at home was intimately connected with the food situation. In the daily food the human body did not receive the necessary nourishment, especially albumen and fats, for the maintenance of physical and mental vigour. In wide quarters a certain decay of bodily and mental powers of resistance was noticeable, resulting in an unmanly and hysterical state of mind which under the spell of enemy progaganda encouraged the pacifist leanings of many Germans. In the summer of 1917 my first glimpse of this situation gave me a great shock. This state of mind was a tremendous element of weakness. It was all a question of human nature. It could be eliminated to some extent by strong patriotic feeling, but in the long run could only be finally overcome by better nourishment. More food was needed.

>General Erich Ludendorff, *My War Memories, 1914–1918*, 1919.

NOTHING undermines morale more decisively than hunger; quickest of all is the effect of any digestive upset. That was strikingly demonstrated in the late summer of 1918, when the moral slump of the German troops became most marked at a moment when stomach disorders, due to bad food, were rife among them. The old saying that "an army marches on its stomach" has a wider and deeper application than has yet been given to it. An army fights on its stomach, and falls if its stomach is upset. (May 1939.)

>Captain Sir Basil Liddell Hart, *Thoughts on War*, 1944.

IDEALISM/IDEALS

IT IS, indeed, an observable fact that all leaders of men, whether as political figures, prophets, or soldiers, all those who can get the best out of others, have always identified themselves with high ideals, and this has given added scope and strength to their influence. Followed in their lifetime because they stand for greatness of mind rather than self-interest, they are later remembered less for the usefulness of what they have achieved than for the sweep of their endeavors. Though sometimes reason may condemn them, feeling clothes them in an aura of glory.

General Charles de Gaulle, *The Edge of the Sword*, 1932.

MEN who are infused with a faith, even a false one, will beat men who have no faith; only a good one can withstand the impact. Those who complain of the younger generation's lack of patriotism should, rather, reproach themselves for their failure to define and teach patriotism in higher terms than the mere preservation of a geogpraphical area, its inhabitants, and their material interests. Such material appeal offers no adequate inspiration, nor cause for sacrifice to the young. Those who are concerned with practical questions of defence ought to realize the practical importance of ideals. (August 1936.)

Captain Sir Basil Liddell Hart, *Thoughts on War*, 1944.

MILITARY IDEALS are not different from the ideals that make any man sound in himself and in his relation to others. They are called military ideals only because the proving ground is a little more rugged in the Service than elsewhere. But they are all founded in hard military experience; they did not find expression because some admiral got in in his head one day to set an unattainable goal for his men, or because some general wished to turn pious face to the public, professing that his men were aspiring to greater virtue than anything the public knew.

Brigadier-General S.L.A. Marshall, *The Officer as Leader*, 1950.

IGNORANCE

ONE MUST OBEY these old fellows who, never having studied their profession, obsessed by an antiquated routine which they call experience, and taking advantage of a long existence which they consider a long life, set out to traduce, pull to pieces, and ridicule budding genius which they detest, because they are compelled to value it more than themselves.

Major-General Henry Lloyd, *Introduction of the History of the War in Germany*, 1766.

THERE IS an enemy greater than the hospital: the damned fellow who "doesn't know". The hint-dropper, the riddle-poser, the deceiver, the word-spinner, the prayer-skimper, the two-faced, the mannered, the incoherent. The fellow who "doesn't know" has caused a great deal of harm. . . . One is ashamed to talk about him. Arrest for the officer who "doesn't know" and house arrest for the field or general officer.

Field Marshal Prince Aleksandr V. Suvorov, *The Science of Victory*, 1796.

THE IGNORANT suspect no difficulties. They want to solve a problem of transcendental mathematics by means of a second-degree formula. All questions of grant tactics are indeterminate physico-mathematical equations that are incapable of solution by formulas of elementary mathematics.

Napoleon, dictation at St. Helena, *Correspondance de Napoléon Ier, publiée par ordre de l'Empereur Napoléon III*, XXXI, p. 338, 1858–1870, quoted in Christopher Herold, ed., *The Mind of Napoleon*, 1955.

AN IGNORANT OFFICER is a murderer. All brave men confide in the knowledge he is supposed to possess; and when the death-trial comes their generous blood flows in vain. Merciful God! How can an ignorant man charge himself with so much bloodshed? I have studied war long, earnestly and deeply, but yet I tremble at my own derelictions.

General Sir William Napier (1782–1853).

THE GREATEST DIFFICULTY I find is in causing orders and regulations to be obeyed. This arises not from a spirit of disobedience, but from ignorance.

General Robert E. Lee, quoted in Montross, *War Through the Ages*, 1960.

I HAVE KNOWN him for a long time. I am very fond of him, but he has not yet gone as far as Caesar's Commentaries in studying the history of war since he forgot the history he learned at West Point.

General of the Armies John J. Pershing, 1918, comments on a deficient officer, quoted in Frank Vandiver, *Black Jack*, 1977.

AN IGNORANT MAN cannot be a good soldier. He

may be brave and audacious, and, in the hand-to-hand struggles of the past, his ignorance may have appeared but a small defect, since he could rapidly clinch with danger. But to-day this defect has grown big; the stout arm of Cannae, of Crécy, or even of Inkerman, demands at least a cunning brain. Fighting intervals and distances have increased, and there is more room for ignorance to display its feathers, and the corridors of fear are long and broad.

Major-General J.F.C. Fuller, *The Foundations of the Science of War*, 1926.

WISDOM begins at the point of understanding that there is nothing shameful about ignorance; it is shameful only when a man would rather remain in that state than cultivate other men's knowledge.

Brigadier-General S.L.A. Marshall, *The Armed Forces Officer*, 1950.

IMAGINATION

WITHOUT that great gift [imagination] only a very inferior order of ambition in any walk of life can be satisfied, and certainly without it no one can ever become a renowned leader of armies. How largely it was possessed by Moses, Xenophon, Hannibal, Caesar, Turenne, Marlborough, Napoleon, and Wellington! It is said to rule the world. . . . And yet, whilst imagination may convert into a poet the man of poor physique, it would not of itself make an able general of him. He who aspires to lead soldiers in war should be not only a thorough master of the soldier's science, but he must possess a healthy strength of body, an iron nerve, calm determination, and that instinctive electric power which causes men to follow the leader who possesses it, as readily, as surely, as iron filings do the magnet. . . . It is the necessity for this rare, this exceptional combination of mental gifts with untiring physical power and stern resolution that accounts for the fact that the truly great commander is rare indeed among God's creations.

Field Marshal Viscount Wolseley, *The Story of a Soldier's Life*, 1869.

THE DEVELOPMENT of the power of imagination and its various ramifications is an essential part of general staff training, and an indispensable requisite for leaders of large forces distributed over a considerable area. The ability to form accurate mental pictures of a situation quickly is especially important today when the higher commander cannot hope to see his troops with his physical eyes.

General der Infantrie Hugo Baron von Freytag-Loringhoven, *The Power of Personality in War*, 1911, tr. Spaulding, 1938.

IMAGINATION forms one of the four parts of genius and has itself two clearly marked attributes: the one, fancy or the power of ornamenting facts as, for instance, making the wolf speak to Little Red Riding

Hood or describing the Battle of Le Cateau; the other, inventions; not fairy tales but machines. Inventions do not often make their first bow to armies on the battle-field. They have been in the air for some time; hawked about the ante-chambers of the men of the hour; spat upon by common sense; cold-shouldered by interests vested in what exists; held up by stale functionaries to whom the sin against the Holy Ghost is to 'make a precedent' – until, one day, arrives a genius who by his imagination sees; by his enthusiasm moves; by his energy keeps moving; by his courage cuts the painter of tradition.

General Sir Ian Hamilton, *The Body and Soul of an Army*, 1921.

THE MOST indispensable attribute of the great captain is imagination.

General of the Army Douglas MacArthur, 1959, letter to B.H. Liddell Hart.

IMPEDIMENTA

FIRST OF ALL, then, I propose that we burn the wagons we have, that the baggage-train may not be our captain, and we may go where is best for the army. Next, burn the tents too: for these are a nuisance to carry, they don't help us to fight or to find provisions. Further, let us get rid of superfluous baggage, keeping only what we need for battle or eating or drinking; so the greatest number of us will be under arms, and as few as possible carrying baggage. You know, of course, that if we are beaten, someone else owns all our goods; if we win, we may call the enemy our porters.

Xenophon, *Anabasis*, 3.2, c. 360 BC (*The March Up Country*, tr. W.H.D. Rouse, 1959); 401 BC, encouraging the stranded Greek Army to abandon its impedimenta to allow escape from the Persians.

FOR the purpose of limiting the number of pack animals, by which the march of the army was especially hampered, Gaius Marius had his soldiers fasten their utensils and food up in bundles and hang these on forked poles, to make the burden easy and to facilitate rest; whence the expression "Marius's Mules."

Frontinus, *Stratagems*, 4.6, c. AD 84–96, tr. Charles E. Bennett, 1925.

WHEN an army brings along a useless crowd, unnecessary baggage, luxury items, expensive equipment which services no purpose, then a journey of one day will not be completed in four. In crossing deep or swampy rivers, moreover, or passing over bridges the army will suffer no little delay because of the useless crowd. Then, too, there is the food supply which ought to be for the use of the fighting men along with a moderate number of necessary servants. But a useless crowd will devour that and swiftly reduce the army to want and force it to return home without having achieved anything. And so, often what even a strong force of the enemy has been unable to accomplish is brought about by want alone which stems from thoughtlessness. They are the very people who, growing weary of the work and fearful of the enemy, hasten to spread rumors and harmful stories, and they devise whatever tricks they can to overturn the plans which are in the interest of the emperor and to bring about a swift return.

> General Nikephoros Ouranos, *Campaign Organization and Tactics*, c. AD 994 (*Three Byzantine Military Treatises*, tr. George Dennis, 1985).

IT IS NECESSARY from time to time to inspect the baggage and force the men to throw away useless gear. I have frequently done this. One can hardly imagine all the trash they carry with them year after year. . . . It is no exaggeration to say that I have filled twenty wagons with rubbish which I have found in the review of a single regiment.

> Field Marshal Maurice Comte de Saxe, *My Reveries*, 1732, tr. Phillips, 1940.

WE CAN get along without anything but food and ammunition. The road to glory cannot be followed with much baggage.

> Lieutenant-General Richard S. Ewell, 1862, orders during the Valley campaign.

AN ARMY is efficient for action and motion exactly in the inverse ratio of its *impedimenta*.

> General of the Army William T. Sherman, *Memoirs of General W.T. Sherman*, II, 1875.

A SERIOUS HANDICAP on mobility lies in the tendency of armies to increase their requirement. The desire for stronger armament causes a demand for more transport; the desire for better communications leads to more complex communications; the desire for superior organization creates an additional organization to deal with the development. In building up its powers to overcome the enemy's resistance an army is apt to set up an internal resistance to its advance. Thus what has been gained by the advent of mechanized means of movement is largely offset by the growth of impedimenta. It is not a necessary growth, but military evolution has always tended to be a process of accretion, tacking new means on to the old body. The idea of remodelling design is foreign to tradition. And the result to-day is the paradoxical one that armies have become less mobile as their limbs have become more mobile. The hare dons the shell of the tortoise.

> Captain Sir Basil Liddell Hart, *Thoughts on War*, 1944.

INCOMPETENCE

MANY badly conceived enterprises have the luck to be successful because the enemy has shown an even smaller degree of intelligence.

> Thucydides, *The History of the Peloponnesian War*, c. 404 BC.

TO ME you will be worthless merely for a certain period; to yourself and the state for ever.

> Scipio the Younger, 133 BC, to the incompetent tribune Gaius Memmius, quoted in Frontinus, *Stratagems*, 4.1, c. AD 84–96, tr. Charles E. Bennett, 1925.

THOSE whose performance is consistently poor should not be entrusted even with just ordinary responsibilities.

> The Emperor Maurice, *The Strategikon*, c. AD 600 (*Maurice's Strategikon*, tr. George Dennis, 1984).

THE GENERAL has no plan, or even an idea of a plan nor do I believe he knows the meaning of the word Plan. I entered fully into a discussion upon the situation of the army the day before yesterday, in which I pointed out the inutility of augmenting his army here and the danger of the measure if he should not – and he could not – augment his means of supply, and I gave him papers to read upon the subject to his future operations. He had not uttered one word to me upon that subject from that time to this. And Moore told me last night that he had said to him, "You may either land your corps or not as you think proper," as if it was a matter of perfect indifference whether this army should have 10,000 men in addition or whether 15,000 additional mouths should be fed by means calculated for half the number. The people are really more stupid and incapable than any I have yet met with, and, if things go on in this disgraceful manner, I must quit them.

> The Duke of Wellington, 26 August 1808, after being superseded in command of the British forces in Portugal by incompetent general officers due to the iron rule of seniority, quoted in Arthur Bryant, *The Great Duke*, 1972.

WHEN I was at Tilsit with the Emperor Alexander and the King of Prussia, I was the most ignorant of the three in military affairs! These two sovereigns, especially the King of Prussia, were completely *au fait* as to the number of buttons there ought to be in front of a jacket, how many behind, and the manner in which the skirts ought to be cut. Not a tailor in the army knew better than Frederick how many measures of cloth it took to make a jacket. In fact, I was nobody in comparison with them. They continually tormented me with questions about matters belonging to tailors, of which I was entirely ignorant, though, in order not to affront them, I answered just as gravely as if the fate of an army depended upon the cut of a jacket. The King of Prussia changed his fashion every day. He was a tall, dry looking fellow, and would give a good idea of Don Quixote. At Jena, his army performed the finest and most showy manoeuvres possible, but I soon put a stop to their *coglionerie*, and taught them that to fight and to execute dazzling manoeuvres and wear splendid uniforms were very different affairs. If the French army had been commanded by a tailor, the King of Prussia would certainly have gained the day, from his superior knowledge and art!

> Napoleon, 16 May 1817, on St. Helena, cited in R.M. Johnston, ed., *The Corsican*, 1910.

THERE ARE field-marshals who would not have shone at the head of cavalry regiments and vice versa.

> Major-General Carl von Clausewitz, *On War*, 1832, tr. Michael Howard and Peter Paret, 1976.

THERE ARE plenty of small-minded men who, in time of peace, excel in detail, are inexorable in matters of equipment and drill, and perpetually interfere with the work of their subordinates.

They thus acquire an unmerited reputation, and render the service a burden, but they above all do mischief in preventing development of individuality, and in retarding the advancement of independent and capable spirits.

When war arises the small minds, worn out by attention to trifles, are incapable of effort, and fail miserably. So goes the world.

> The Archduke Albert (1817–1895), quoted in Fuller, *Generalship: Its Diseases and Their Cure*, 1933.

THE INCOMPETENCE of the authorities and of G.H.Q. is greater on the other side than with us; and that is saying a good deal.

> General Max Hoffmann, November 1915, *War Diaries and Other Papers*, I, 1929.

PRESUMABLY victory is our object. This war is a business proposition; it therefore requires ability. Nevertheless, our Army is crawling with "duds"; though habitual offenders, they are tolerated because of the camaraderie of the old Regular Army: an Army so small as to permit of all its higher members being personal friends. Good-fellowship ranks with us above efficiency; the result is a military trade union which does not declare a dividend.

> Major-General J.F.C. Fuller, 1918, *Memoirs of an Unconventional Soldier*, 1936.

MORE AND MORE does the "system" tend to promote to *control*, men who have shown themselves efficient *cogs* in the machine. It is especially so in the Army to-day. There are few commanders in our higher commands. And even these, since their chins usually outweigh their foreheads, are themselves outweighted by the majority of commanders who are essentially staff officers. These tend to be *desperately* conventional in organizing the Army and moulding its doctrines for war. And in war they would almost certainly prove *recklessly* cautious. (May 1936.)

> Captain Sir Basil Liddell Hart, *Thoughts on War*, 1944.

IT IS always a bad sign in an army when scapegoats are habitually sought out and brought to sacrifice for every conceivable mistake. It usually shows something very wrong in the highest command. It completely inhibits the willingness of junior commanders to take decisions, for they will always try to get chapter and verse for everything they do, finishing up more often than not with a miserable piece of casuistry instead of the decision which would spell release. The usual result is that the man who never does more than supinely pass on the opinion of his seniors is brought to the top, while the really valuable man, the man who accepts nothing ready-made but has an opinion of his own, gets put on the shelf.

> Field Marshal Erwin Rommel, *The Rommel Papers*, 1953.

IT TAKES a war to separate the men from the boys. To many serving officers, the army is simply a better 'ole. They do duty routinely in peace time and develop a keen eye for a secure spot where they will have minimum problems and maximum comfort.

Though some so-called line officers are in this category, their wearing of the crossed rifles or cannon is a masquerade; they are not interested in combat, and if they think of it at all, they are caught between chill and sweat. They have no intention of ever going into battle. Should the accident of assignment force them to do so, they invariably fall apart and are relieved for cause, provided they live long enough. This type of officer usually knows the regulations to the letter. To his mind, they are as inviolable as the tablets from Mount Sinai were intended to be. Being what he is, he cannot understand that regulations are nothing more than a general guidance to conduct, written to protect and advise the soldier, but never intended to fetter him and circumscribe his action when great daring and initiative are required in coping with some unprecedented problem.

> Brigadier-General S.L.A. Marshall, *Bringing Up the Rear*, 1979.

INDEPENDENCE OF COMMAND

THERE ARE . . . commands of the sovereign which must not be obeyed.

> Sun Tzu, *The Art of War*, 8, c. 500 BC, tr. Giles, 1910.

MAXIM 72. A general-in-chief has no right to shelter his mistakes in war under cover of his sovereign, or of a minister, when they are both distant from the scene of operation, and must consequently be either ill informed or wholly ignorant of the actual state of things.

Hence it follows that every general is culpable who undertakes the execution of a plan which he considers faulty. It is his duty to represent his reasons, to insist upon a change of plan; in short, to give in his resignation rather than allow himself to become the instrument of his army's ruin. Every general-in-chief who fights a battle in consequence of superior orders, with the uncertainly of losing, is equally blamable.

Napoleon, *The Military Maxims of Napoleon*, tr. George D'Aguilar, 1831 (David Chandler, ed., 1987).

TO FIELD MARSHAL ROMMEL:
In the situation in which you find yourself there can be no other thought but to stand fast and throw every gun and every man into the battle. The utmost efforts are being made to help you. Your enemy, despite his superiority, must also be at the end of his strength. It would not be the first time in history that a strong will has triumphed over the bigger battalions. As to your troops, you can show them no other road than that to victory or death.

ADOLF HITLER

This order demanded the impossible. Even the most devoted soldier can be killed by a bomb.

Erwin Rommel, Hitler's order from East Prussia to stand fast at El Alamein in North Africa and Rommel's comment, *The Rommel Papers*, 1953.

THE INDIRECT APPROACH

IN ALL FIGHTING, the direct method may be used for joining battle, but indirect methods will be needed in order to secure victory.

Indirect tactics, efficiently applied, are inexhaustible as Heaven and Earth, unending as the flow of rivers and streams; like the sun and moon, they end but to begin anew; like the four seasons, they pass but to return once more.

Sun Tzu, *The Art of War*, 5, c. 500 BC, tr. Giles, 1910.

WHEN ASKED how to cope with a great host of the enemy in orderly array and on the point of marching to the attack, I should say: "Begin by seizing something which your opponent holds dear; then he will be amenable to your will."

Sun Tzu, *The Art of War*, 11, c. 500 BC, tr. Giles, 1910.

IT IS WELL to hurt the enemy by deceit, by raids, or by hunger and never be enticed into a pitched battle, which is a demonstration more of luck than of bravery.

The Emperor Maurice, *The Strategikon*, c. AD 600 (*Maurice's Strategikon*, tr. George Dennis, 1984).

IF YOU WOULD shoot a general, first destroy his horse.

Japanese military proverb, quoted in Inoguchi and Nakajima, *The Divine Wind*, 1958.

THREE MEN behind the enemy are worth more than fifty in front of him.

Frederick the Great (1712–1786).

MAXIM 16. It is an approved maxim of war, never

do what the enemy wishes you to do, for this reason alone, that he desires it. A field of battle, therefore, which he has previously studied and reconnoitered, should be avoided, and double care should be taken where he has had time to fortify or entrench. One consequence deducible from this principle is, never to attack a position in front which you can gain by turning.

Napoleon, *The Military Maxims of Napoleon*, tr. George D'Aguilar, 1831 (David Chandler, ed., 1987).

TO SEE CORRECTLY a general must understand the nature of the changes which take place in war. The enemy does not attack him physically, but mentally; for the enemy attacks his ideas, his reason, his plan. The physical pressure directed against his men reacts on him through compelling him to change his plan, and changes in his plan react on his men by creating a mental confusion which weakens their morale. Psychologically, the battle is opened by a physical blow which unbalances the commander's mind, which in its turn throws out of adjustment the morale of his men, and leads to their fears impeding the flow of his will. If the blow is a totally unexpected one, the will of the commander may cease altogether to flow, and, the balance in the moral sphere being utterly upset, self-preservation fusing with self-assertion results in panic.

Major-General J.F.C. Fuller, *The Foundations of the Science of War*, 1926.

THROUGHOUT HISTORY the direct approach has been the normal form of strategy, and a purposeful indirect approach the rare exception. It is curious how often generals have adopted the latter, not as their intial strategy, but as a last resource. Yet it has brought them a decision where the direct approach had brought them failure – and thereby left them in a weakened condition to attempt the indirect. A decisive success obtained in such deteriorated conditions acquires all the greater signficance. (Oct. 1928.)

Captain Sir Basil Liddell Hart, *Thoughts on War*, 1944.

THE ART of the indirect approach can only be mastered, and its full scope appreciated, by study of and reflection upon the whole history of war. But we can at least crystallize the lessons into two simple maxims, one negative, and the other positive. The first is that in face of the overwhelming evidence of history no general is justified in launching his troops to a *direct* attack upon an enemy *firmly* in position. The second, that instead of seeking to upset the enemy's equilibrium by one's attack, it must be upset *before* a real attack is, or can be, successfully launched. . . . (Nov. 1928.)

Captain Sir Basil Liddell Hart, *Thoughts on War*, 1944.

BATTLE should no longer resemble a bludgeon fight, but should be a test of skill, a manoeuvre

combat, in which is fulfilled the great principle of surprise by striking "from an unexpected direction against an unguarded spot."
  Captain Sir Basil Liddell Hart, *Thoughts on War*, 1944.

YOU CAN TELL a man's character by the way he makes advances to a woman. Men like you, for example – when the fleet's in port and you go off to have a good time, you seem to have only two ways of going about things. First, you put it straight to the woman: "Hey, how about a lay?" Now, any woman, even the lowest whore, is going to put up at least a show of refusing if she's asked like that. So what do you do next? You either act insulted and get rough, or you give up immediately and go off to try the same thing on the next woman. That's all you're capable of. But take a look at Western men – they're quite different. Once they've set their sights on a woman, they invite her out for a drink, or to dinner, or to go dancing. In that way they gradually break down her defenses until, in the end, they get what they want, and in style at that. Where achieving a particular aim is concerned, that's surely a far wiser way of going about things. At any rate, they're the kind of men you'd be dealing with if there were a war, so you'd better give it some thought.
  Admiral Isoroku Yamamoto, 1939, to his junior officers, quoted in Agawa, *The Reluctant Admiral*, 1979.

USE steamroller strategy; that is, make up your mind on course and direction of action, and stick to it. But in tactics, do not steamroller. Attack weakness. Hold them by the nose and kick them in the pants.
  General George S. Patton, Jr., *War As I Knew It*, 1947.

NEVER ATTACK where the enemy expects you to come. It is much better to go over difficult ground where you are not expected than it is over good ground where you are expected.
  General George S. Patton, Jr., *War As I Knew It*, 1947.

THE ENEMY wanted to concentrate their forces. We compelled them to disperse. By successfully launching strong offensives on the points they had left relatively unprotected, we obliged them to scatter their troops all over the place in order to ward off our blows, and thus created favourable conditions for the attack at Dien Bien Phu, the most powerful entrenched camp in Indo-China, considered invulnerable by the Franco-American general staff. We decided to take the enemy by the throat at Dien Bien Phu.
  General Vo Nguyen Giap, *People's War, People's Army*, 1961.

ATTACKING the human body has been a sloppy and inefficient means of making war. Attacking the mind may prove the culmination of military history.
  Lieutenant-Colonel Ralph Peters, *Fighting for the Future*, 1999.

INFANTRY

THOSE who go on foot or on a war-horse, with the mettle to take on a hundred men, who are skilled in the use of close-range weapons, swords, and spears, are called infantry generals.
  Zhuge Liang (AD 180–234), *The Way of the General*.

THE INFANTRY must ever be valued as the very foundation and nerve of an army.
  Niccolo Machiavelli, *Discourses*, 1517.

THERE, it all depends upon that article whether we do the business or not. Give me enough of it, and I am sure.
  The Duke of Wellington, May 1815, pointing to a British infantryman on the eve of the Waterloo campaign, Creevy, *The Creevy Papers*, 1934.

IT WAS the most desperate business I ever was in. I never took so much trouble about any Battle [Waterloo], & never was so near being beat. Our loss is immense particularly in the best of All Instruments, British Infantry. I never saw the Infantry behave so well.
  The Duke of Wellington, 19 June 1815, the day after Waterloo, quoted in Brett-James, *The Hundred Days*, 1964.

MY OPINION is that the best troops we have, probably the best in the world, are the British infantry, particularly the old infantry that has served in Spain. This is what we ought to keep up; and what I wish above all others to retain.
  The Duke of Wellington, advice to British ministers intent on reducing the army after 1815, *The Dispatches of Field Marshal the Duke of Wellington During His Various Campaigns in India, Denmark, Portugal, Spain, the Low Countries, and France*, XII, 1834–1838, p. 668.

INFANTRY is the Queen of Battles.
  General Sir William Napier (1785–1860); later adopted as the motto of the U.S. Infantry.

MAXIM 93. The better the infantry is, the more it should be used carefully and supported with good batteries. Good infantry is, without doubt, the sinew of an army; but if it is forced to fight for a long time against a very superior artillery, it will become demoralized and will be destroyed.
  Napoleon, *The Military Maxims of Napoleon*, tr. Burnod, 1827.

IT IS ADMITTED by all military men that infantry is the great lever of war, and that the artillery and cavalry are only indispensable accessories. . . .
  Two essential conditions constitute the strength of infantry: –
  That the men be good walkers and inured to fatigue.
  That the firing be well-executed.

The physical constitution, and the national composition of the French armies, fulfill the former most advantageously; the vivacity and intelligence of the soldiers ensure the success of the latter.

Marshal of France Michel Ney, Duc d'Elchingen, Prince de la Moskova, *Memoirs of Marshal Ney*, 1834.

LET US remember the great part that is played by the infantry soldier in war. The artillery help us, the cavalry help us, and the engineers are there to confirm our success and overcome obstacles, but it is the infantry soldier, officer and man, who must bear the great stress of battle. He has no immovable gun to serve, and no horse to carry him forward; of his own initiative he advances against the enemy position with a fixed determination to drive him back and defeat him. It is not generally considered that he requires any very high training, and yet his training in the correct use of ground and of his rifle, in the dire stress of battle, is more complicated and more difficult than that of any other arm of the service. He is more influenced than any other soldier by those characteristics of the human mind which are adverse to success; ground is never the same and can never be treated in the same way, and therefore we can give no fixed rules to work by.

Captain R.C.B. Haking, *Company Training*, 1917.

IN THE END of ends, infantry is the deciding factor in every battle. I was in the infantry myself and was body and soul an infantry man. I told my sons to join the infantry. They did so, but, as happened to so many our our young men, the freedom of the air drew them from the trenches. But the fine saying of the old "Directions for Infantry Exercise," remain true in war: "The infantry bears the heaviest burden of a battle and requires the greatest sacrifice; so also it promises the greatest renown."

General Erich Ludendorff, *My War Memories, 1914–1918*, 1919.

INFANTRYMEN are they who in the frosts and storms of night watch over the sleep of camps, climb under fire the highest crests, fight and die, without their voluntary sacrifice receiving the reward of heroism.

General Francesco Franco, *Diario de Una Bandera*, 1922.

WHEN the smoke cleared away, it was the man with the sword, or the crossbow, or the rifle, who settled the final issue on the field.

General of the Army George C. Marshall, 3 February 1939, speech before the National Rifle Association.

I LOVE the infantryman because they are the underdogs. They are the mud-rain-and-wind boys. They have no comforts, and they learn to live without the necessities. And in the end they are the guys that wars can't be won without.

Ernie Pyle, *New York World Telegram*, 5 May 1943.

LOOK at an infantryman's eyes and you can tell how much war he has seen.

Sergeant William 'Bill' Mauldin, *Up Front*, 1944.

ANOTHER ELEMENT [of leadership] to be considered is the Man to be led, and with whose morale we are concerned. I am constantly reminded of this point by a cartoon which hangs over my desk at home which depicts an infantryman with his rifle across his knees as he sits behind a parapet. Above him is the list of the newest weapons science has devised and the soldier behind the parapet is saying: "But still they haven't found a substitute for ME."

General of the Army Omar N. Bradley, 'Leadership', *Parameters*, Winter 1972, p. 2.

. . . THE LEAST spectacular arm of the Army, yet without them you cannot win a battle. Indeed, without them, you can do nothing. Nothing at all, nothing.

Field Marshal Viscount Montgomery of Alamein, quoted in *Military Review*, 5/1981.

INITIATIVE
The Operational Dynamic

WHOEVER is first in the field and awaits the coming of the enemy, will be fresh for the fight; whoever is second in the field and has to hasten to the battle, will arrive exhausted.

Therefore the clever combatant imposes his will on the enemy, but does not allow the enemy's will to be imposed on him.

By holding out advantages to him, he can cause the enemy to approach of his own accord; or by inflicting damage, he can make it impossible for the enemy to draw near.

Sun Tzu, *The Art of War*, 6, c. 500 BC, tr. Giles, 1910.

THE ART of war is, in the last result, the art of keeping one's freedom of action.

Xenophon (431–352 BC).

HE WHO BRINGS danger upon another has more spirit than he who repels it. Add to this, that the terror excited by the unexpected is increased thereby. When you have entered the territory of an enemy you obtain a near view of his strong and weak points.

. . . you will hear at once that I have landed, and that Africa is blazing with war; that Hannibal is preparing to depart from this country. . . . Many things which are not now apparent at this distance will develop; and it is the part of a general not to be wanting when opportunity arises, and to bend its events to his designs. I shall, Quintus Fabius, have the opponent you assign me, Hannibal, but I shall rather draw him after me than be kept here by him.

Scipio Africanus, c. 203 BC, from Polybius, quoted in Liddell Hart, *A Greater Than Napoleon*, 1926.

A RULE that I practice myself and which I have

always found good is that in order to have rest oneself it is necessary to keep the enemy occupied. This throws them back on the defensive, and once they are placed that way they cannot rise up again during the entire campaign.

Frederick the Great, *Instructions to His Generals*, 1747, tr. Phillips, 1940.

IT IS an incontestable truth that it is better to forestall the enemy, than to find yourself anticipated by him.

Frederick the Great, 'Anti-Machiavelli', *Posthumous works of Frederick II, King of Prussia*, 1789, tr. Holcroft, quoted in Jay Luvaas, *Frederick the Great on the Art of War*, 1966.

IF YOU ARE frequently alarmed by the enemy, do not suffer it quietly, but alarm him still more frequently, in order to keep him in awe, and tire him out.

Lieutenant-General Johann von Ewald, *Treatise on the Duties of Light Troops*, 1790.

WE MUST get the upper hand, and if we once have that, we shall keep it with ease, and shall certainly succeed.

The Duke of Wellington, 17 August 1803, dispatch in India.

I BEGIN to fear that the enemy will not attack us. We shall therefore have to attack him.

General Robert E. Lee, 30 September 1861, letter to John B. Floyd.

THE PRESIDENT . . . directs me to suggest if the enemy had more occupation south of the river, his cavalry would not be so likely to make raids north of it.

Major-General Henry W. Halleck, to Major-General George McClellan, mid-October 1862, *The War of the Rebellion: A Compilation of the Official Records of the Union and Confederate Armies*, Vol. XIX, Part 2, p. 421, U.S. Government Printing Office, 1880–1901.

WHAT WE WANT is prompt and active movements after the enemy in accordance with the instructions you already have. I feel every confidence that you will do for the very best and will leave you as far as possible to act on your own judgement and not embarrass you with orders and instructions.

General of the Army Ulysses S. Grant, 7 August 1864, letter to Sheridan, *Papers of USG*, XI, 1982, p. 380.

INSTEAD of being on the defensive, I would be on the offensive; instead of guessing at what he [the enemy] means to do, he would have to guess at my plans. The difference in war is 25 per cent.

General of the Army William T. Sherman, 11 October 1864, letter to Grant urging his attack toward Atlanta and the sea, *The War of the Rebellion: A Compilation of the Official Records of the Union and Confederate Armies*, Series I, Vol. XXXIX, Part 3, p. 202, U.S. Government Printing Office, 1880–1901.

IN ANY FIGHT, it's the first blow that counts; and if you keep it up hot enough, you can whip 'em as fast as they come up.

Lieutenant-General Nathan Bedford Forrest (1821–1877).

THE VALUE of the "initiative" in war cannot be overstated. It surpasses in power mere accession of numbers, as it requires neither transport nor commissariat. Holding it, a commander lays his plans deliberately, and executes them at his own appointed time and in his own way. The "defensive" is weak, lowering the morale of the army reduced to it, enforcing constant watchfulness lest threatened attacks become real, and keeping commander and troops in a state of anxious tension.

Lieutenant-General Richard Taylor, *Destruction and Reconstruction*, 1879.

IT WAS to be considered that hostile troops would allow themselves to be held if we attacked, or at least threatened, the enemy at some really sensitive point. It was further to be remembered that, with the means available, protection of the Colony could not be ensured even by purely defensive tactics, since the total length of land frontier and coast-line was about equal to that of Germany. From these considerations it followed that it was necessary, not to split up our small available forces in local defence, but, on the contrary, to keep them together, to grip the enemy by the throat and force him to employ his forces for self-defence. . . .

Field Marshal Paul von Lettow-Vorbeck, *East African Campaigns*, 1957, describing the defence of German East Africa in WWI, during which German forces of fewer than 15,000 drew into the theatre a third of a million Allied troops.

EVERYONE of us knows from his personal experience how an opponent taking the initiative, though he be much weaker, confounds all calculations of his enemy, ruins his plans . . .

Mikhail Frunze, 1922.

THE INITIATIVE . . . means an army's freedom of action as distinguished from an enforced loss of freedom. Freedom of action is the very life of an army and, once it is lost, the army is close to defeat or destruction.

Mao Tse-tung, *On Protracted War*, 1938.

I DETERMINED to make no-man's land our land. We set out to besiege the besiegers.

Lieutenant-General Leslie Morshead, his principle of defence as Commander of the Tobruk garrison and the Ninth Australian Division, 1941, quoted in Horner, *The Commanders*, 1984.

THE PRIME characteristic of German tactical doctrine is maintenance of the initiative and avoidance of stabilization. The Germans believe absolutely that if a

trained commander prepares and executes aggressive moves, with even average ability and reasonable speed, the enemy will be kept too busy meeting them to carry out successful offensive measures.
> U.S. military observer of German Army training before WWII, quoted in U.S. War Department, *German Military Training*, 17 September 1942.

AS LONG AS you attack them, they cannot find the time to attack you.
> General George S. Patton, Jr., quoted in Robert H. Patton, *The Pattons*, 1994.

WHEN SO MUCH was uncertain, the need to recover the initiative glared forth.
> Winston S. Churchill, after Dunkirk, 1940, *Their Finest Hour*, 1949.

LEAVING ASIDE the failure of our allies, the Russians can credit their great victories to the fact that they have applied standard German command principles: Zhukov as military commander enjoys complete freedom within the framework of the task assigned to him; the Russians have adopted German tactics and German strategic doctrines. In the meantime, we have borrowed from the Russians their earlier system of rigidly laying down the law on virtually everything and going into the tiniest details, and therein lies the blame for our defeats. German military leaders who can think and act independently are discouraged – indeed both such qualities can lead to court-martial. Thus we have forfeited one of the fundamental requirements of a successful and versatile military command. We have become benumbed, and are incapable of strategic action (1942).
> General Reinhard Gehlen, *The Service*, 1942.

I HAVE NEVER given a damn what the enemy was going to do or where he was. What I have known is what I have intended to do and then have done it. By acting in this manner I have always gotten to the place he expected me to come about three days before he got there.
> General George S. Patton, Jr., August 1944, *The Patton Papers*, II, 1974.

DURING WAR the ball is always kicking around loose in the middle of the field and any man who has the will may pick it up and run with it.
> Brigadier-General S.L.A. Marshall, *The Armed Forces Officer*, 1950.

IN THE FAST MOVING dynamics of battle, soldiers shouldn't have to wait for orders. I don't want you to read my thoughts as commander. I want you to read the enemy's thoughts. Outmaneuver him. Whether you are on foot, in a tank or in an airplane, you must outthink that enemy.
> Colonel Michael Wyly, 'Revolution', Al Santoli, ed., *Leading the Way: How Vietnam Veterans Rebuilt the U.S. Military*, 1993.

HE WHO SHOOTS first laughs last.
> General Aleksandr I. Lebed's favourite Russian military maxim, *Sobesednik* (Moscow), March 1998.

HE WHO STRIKES first, strikes twice.
> Russian military proverb.

The Personal Quality

TRUE, when the man leaps in the breach that way no one can blame or disobey him, no Achaean, not when he spurs the troops and gives commands.
> Homer, *The Iliad*, 10.150–153, c. 800 BC, tr. Robert Fagles, 1990; King Nestor of Pylos speaking of Menalaus' initiative to organise resistance when the Trojans stormed the Greek camp.

TELL THE KING that after the battle my head is at his disposal, but meantime I hope he will permit me to exercise it in his service!
> General F.W. Seydlitz, to Frederick the Great who was continually ordering an ill-advised manoeuvre from the opposite end of the battlefield at Zorndorf, 25 August 1758, quoted in Christopher Duffy, *The Military Life of Frederick the Great*, 1986.

IT CERTAINLY WAS SO, and if ever you commit such a breach of your orders I will forgive you also.
> Admiral Lord St. Vincent, 14 February 1797, on the evening of the Battle of Cape St. Vincent when an officer complained that Nelson's action was a breach of orders, quoted in David Walder, *Nelson*, 1978.

WHEN the signal, No. 39, was made, the Signal Lieutenant reported to him. He continued his walk, and did not appear to take notice of it. The lieutenant meeting his Lordship at the next turn asked, "whether he should repeat it?" Lord Nelson answered, "No, acknowledge it." . . . his Lordship called after him, "Is No. 16 [for close action] still hoisted?" The lieutenant answering in the affirmative, Lord Nelson said, "Mind you keep it so." He now walked the deck considerably agitated, which was always known by his moving the stump of his right arm. After a turn or two, he said to me, in a quick manner, "Do you know what's shown on board the Commander-in-Chief, No. 39?" On asking him what that meant, he answered, "Why, to leave off action." "Leave off action!" he repeated, and then added, with a shrug, "Now damn me if I do." He also observed, I believe, to Captain Foley, "You know, Foley, I have only one eye – I have a right to be blind sometimes:" and with an archness peculiar to his character, putting the glass to his blind eye, he exclaimed, "I really do not see the signal."
> Admiral Viscount Nelson's refusal to abandon a successful action despite orders to do so during the Battle of Copenhagen, 2 April 1801, as described by Colonel William Parker, quoted in Alfred Thayer Mahan, *The Life of Nelson*, 1897.

WHEN I AM without orders, and unexpected occurrences arise, I shall always act as I think the honour and glory of my King and Country demand.

Admiral Viscount Nelson, November 1804, letter to Hugh Elliot.

BUT, IN CASE signals can neither be seen or perfectly understood, no captain can do very wrong if he places his ship alongside that of the enemy.

Admiral Viscount Nelson, 9 October 1805, memorandum to the fleet before Trafalgar.

THAT INDIVIDUALITY of action which so strongly characterizes the conduct of our troops in battle, if unguided or misdirected, can but produce confusion. But let the same idea control the mind of every man, let them apply these general principles to the incidents of battle as they arise, and success is certain.

Major-General James E.B. Stuart, General Order No. 26, Cavalry Tactics, 30 July 1863, *Letters of Major General James E.B. Stuart*, 1990.

I DO NOT propose to lay down for you a plan of Campaign but simply to lay down the work it is desirable to have done and leave you free to execute it in your own way. Submit to me however as early as you can your plan of operation.

General of the Army Ulysses S. Grant, 4 April 1864, letter to Sherman, prior to the 1864 campaign, quoted in *Papers of USG*, X, 1982, p. 252.

ALL IN ALL it seems . . . that an unusual spirit, of independence of those above and acceptance of responsibility, has grown up throughout the Prussian officer corps as it has in no other army. . . . Prussian officers will not stand for being hemmed in by rule and stereotypes as happens in Russia, Austria or Britain. . . . We follow the more natural course of giving scope to every individual's talent, of using a looser rein. We back up every success as a matter of course – even when it runs counter to the intentions of the commander-in-chief. . . . the subordinate commander exploits every advantage by taking initiatives off his own bat, without his superior's knowledge or permission.

Frederick III, 1860, essay, quoted in Richard Simpkin, *Race to the Swift*, 1985.

A FAVOURABLE SITUATION will never be exploited if commanders wait for orders. The highest commander and the youngest soldier must always be conscious of the fact that omission and inactivity are worse than resorting to the wrong expedient.

Field Marshal Helmuth Graf von Moltke (1800–1891).

THE [German Army] Field Service Regulations [of 1911] . . . require "every officer, under all conditions, to exercise initiative to the maximum extent, without fear of the consequences. Commanding officers must encourage and require this." This requirement is especially important during long periods of peace, when the necessity for maintaining discipline has a tendency to discourage independent action. All commanding officers, especially the higher ones, must, as their duty make every effort to develop initiative in their subordinates, and oppose indifference and routine service. They must also restrain their supervisory activities and avoid too frequent visits to troop instruction, which sometimes causes embarrassment.

General der Infantrie Hugo Baron Freytag-Loringhoven, *The Power of Personality in War*, 1911, tr. Spaulding, 1938.

YOU MUST frequently act without orders from higher authority. Time will not permit you to wait for them. Here again enters the importance of studying the work of officers above you. If you have a comprehensive grasp of the entire situation and can form an idea of the general plan of your superiors, that and your previous emergency training will enable you to determine that the responsibility is yours and to issue the necessary orders without delay.

Major A.C. Bach, 1917, farewell instructions to graduating student officers at Fort Sheridan, Wyoming.

MY AIM was to turn highly-disciplined troops into responsible men possessed of initiative. Discipline is not intended to kill character, but to develop it. The purpose of discipline is to bring about the uniformity in co-operating for the attainment of the common goal, and this uniformity can only be obtained when each one sets aside the thought of his own personal interests. This common goal is – Victory.

General Erich Ludendorff, *My War Memories, 1914–1918*, 1919.

THE MAGAZINE RIFLE with its low trajectory and smokeless powder, spoke volumes to the captain of 1899–1902. It told him he could still conduct his company into the zone of aimed fire, but that, having got them there, he must:
(1) Keep his direct command at the cost of double losses.
(2) Let each little group understand the common objective. Then leave them to the promptings of their own consciences of what was right rather than to the dread of what was wrong.

General Sir Ian Hamiliton, *The Soul and Body of an Army*, 1921.

IF, IN THE OPINION of the leader, the plan has, through change in conditions, become inoperative, then he ceases to be a leader and becomes, for the time being, an independent commander and must act as if he were a general-in-chief. That is to say, he must replace the inoperative plan by an operative one – that is, one which will permit of the economical expenditure of force. To carry on a plan which manifestly has failed is the act of a fool, whether he be the general-in-chief or a private soldier. Once again we come back to our starting-point, namely, intelligence.

Major-General J.F.C. Fuller, *The Foundations of the Science of War*, 1926.

THE CAPACITY for independent action of low-level infantry sub-units has long been our weakest point. The cry of "I'm waiting for orders," which really meant "I'm doing nothing," was the real scourge of our activities in the field.

Marshal of the Soviet Union Mikhail N. Tukhachevskiy, 1931–1932, quoted in Richard Simpkin, *Deep Battle*, 1987.

THERE ARE cases of . . . initiative exaggerated to the point of violating discipline and interfering with the concentration of the combined effort . . . In the last analysis, an exaggerated display of initiative is due in the first place to an absence or weakness of decision higher up. A spirit of enterprise in a commander is never a danger in itself.

. . . so it comes about that the authorities dread any officer who has the gift of making decisions and cares nothing for routine and soothing words. "Arrogant and undisciplined" is what the mediocrities say of him, treating the thoroughbred with a tender mouth as they would a donkey which refuses to move, not realizing that asperity is, more often than not, the reverse side of a strong character, that you can only lean on something that offers resistance, and that resolute and inconvenient men are to be preferred to easy-going natures without initiative.

General Charles de Gaulle, *The Edge of the Sword*, 1932.

UNFORESEEN circumstance and unexpected difficulties are bound to arise in the course of the battle. The overall commander must grasp all new information on the situation thoroughly, and take appropriate action forthwith.

The exercise of individual initiative by subordinates confronted with a sudden change in the situation is of enormous importance. The commander should encourage every sensible initiative taken by his subordinates in all possible ways, exploiting it in furtherance of the overall aim of the battle.

Marshal of the Soviet Union Mikhail N. Tukhachevskiy, 1937, quoted in Simpkin, *Deep Battle*, 1987.

EISENHOWER, the Department is filled with able men who analyze the problems well but feel compelled always to bring them to me for final solution. I must have assistants who will solve their own problems and tell me later what they have done.

General George C. Marshall, quoted in Stephen E. Ambrose, *Eisenhower: Soldier, General of the Army, President-Elect*, 1963.

I WISH to assure all officers and men that I shall never criticize them or go back on them for having done too much but that I shall certainly relieve them if they do nothing. You must keep moving. . . .

General George S. Patton, Jr., May 1941, *The Patton Papers*, II, 1974.

PEOPLE must try to use their imagination and when orders fail to come, must act on their own best judgment. A very safe rule to follow is that in case of doubt, push on just a little further and then keep on pushing. . . .

General George S. Patton, Jr., July 1941, *The Patton Papers*, II, 1974.

NEVER TELL PEOPLE *how* to do things. Tell them *what* to do and they will surprise you with their ingenuity.

General George S. Patton, Jr., *War As I Knew It*, 1947.

IMPROVISATION is the essence of initiative in all combat just as initiative is the outward showing of the power of decision.

Brigadier-General S.L.A. Marshall, *Men Against Fire*, 1947.

AS THE SITUATION demanded, Captain Müller was given the greatest freedom of action. If any promising objective presented itself during the march, he was to decide without hesitation what his best course was. I would bring up our main body and intervene unconditionally in his support, and, in any case, I would accept the situation he had created. The main thing was that he should not wait for special orders and instructions. I realized that in acting thus I was in a large measure placing the conduct of our operations in the hands of a subordinate officer. It was only possible because that subordinate officer possessed a very sound tactical judgment and great initiative.

Field Marshal Paul von Lettow-Vorbeck, *East African Campaigns*, 1957.

INITIATIVE I gave as the third of the qualities of an officer. Initiative simply means that you do not sit down and wait for something to happen. In war, if you do, it will all right, but it will be almighty unpleasant. Initiative for you means that you keep a couple of jumps ahead, not only of the enemy, but of your own men.

Field Marshal Viscount Slim of Burma, *Courage and Other Broadcasts*, 1957.

IT IS BETTER to struggle with a stallion when the problem is how to hold it back, than to urge on a bull which refuses to budge.

General Moshe Dayan (1915–1981).

COMMANDERS at all levels had to act more on their own; they were given greater latitude to work out their own plans to achieve what they knew was the Army Commander's intention. In time they developed to a marked degree the flexibility of mind and a firmness of decision that enabled them to act swiftly to take advantage of sudden information or changing circumstances without reference to superiors. . . . This acting without orders, in anticipation of orders, or without waiting for approval, yet always within the over-all intention, must become second nature in any form of warfare where formations do not fight closely *en cadre*, and must go down to the smallest units. It requires in the higher command a corresponding flexibility of mind, confidence in its subordinates, and the power to make its intentions clear right through the force.

Field Marshal Viscount Slim of Burma, *Defeat Into Victory*, 1956; of the command relationship within the British 14th Army in the Burma-India-China theatre during WWII.

TO MAKE perfectly clear that action contrary to orders was not considered as disobedience or lack of discipline, German commanders began to repeat one of Moltke's favorite stories, of an incident observed while visiting the headquarters of Prince Frederick Charles. A major, receiving a tongue-lashing from the Prince for a tactical blunder, offered the excuse that he had been obeying orders, and reminded the Prince that a Prussian officer was taught that an order from a superior was tantamount to an order from the King. Frederick Charles promptly responded: "His Majesty made you a major because he believed you would know when not to obey his orders." This simple story became guidance for all following generations of German officer.

Colonel T.N. Dupuy, *A Genius For War: The Army and the German General Staff, 1807–1945*, 1977.

SO HERE we have Rule 2 for superiors: Clear a path. Make sure that the road to the top is wide open for ideas, opinions, and criticism and that everyone knows that initiative is respected as a precious military jewel.

It is told that in 1862 Stonewall Jackson, leaning against a tree and staring down the Shenandoah Valley, was asked by one of his staff officers what he was doing. He is supposed to have replied, "I'm trying to figure out what the Yankees are up to. If anyone in this army thinks he knows tell them to come up here and see me." Jackson was clearing a path.

Lieutenant-General Victor H. 'The Brute' Krulak, 'A Soldier's Dilemma', *Marine Corps Gazette*, 11/1986.

INNOVATION

THE MIND is not interested by routine forms of duty; and, as it is important to success that the mind should be interested, it is useful . . . to endeavour to give a new cast, consequently a new force of impression, to military exercises and military forms of evolution, without changing the principles of such practices as are laid on a basis of truth. New modes

of military exercise interest the individual by their novelty; they even not infrequently communicate an animating energy to the arm of the actor, which goes beyond the limits of ordinary calculation: they seldom fail to intimidate the enemy as striking him by surprise. If this be so, it belongs to military genius to change the appearances of things, with a view to animate one part and to intimidate another. But, while this be done, especial care is to be taken that the fundamental principles of military tactic be not rashly violated.

Robert Jackson, *A Systematic View of the Formation, Discipline, and Economy of Armies*, 1804.

NO SOLDIER who has made himself conversant with the resources of his art, will allow himself to be trammelled by an exclusive system.

Dennis Hart Mahan, *Advance-Guard, Out-Post, and Detachment Service of Troops, with the Essential Principles of Strategy and Grand Tactics*, 1863.

THE UNRESTING progress of mankind causes continual change in the weapons; and with that must come a continual change in the manner of fighting – in the handling and disposition of troops or ships on the battlefield. . . . The battles of the past succeeded or failed according as they were fought in conformity with the principles of war; and the seaman who carefully studies the causes of success or failure will not only detect and gradually assimilate these principles, but will also acquire increased aptitude in applying them to the tactical use of the ships and weapons of his own day. He will observe that changes in tactics have not only taken place after changes in weapons which necessarily is the case, but the interval between such changes has been unduly long. An improvement of weapons is due to the energy of one or two men, while changes in tactics have to overcome the inertia of a conservative class; but it is a great evil. It can be remedied only by a candid recognition of each change, by careful study of the powers and limitations of the new ship or weapon, and by consequent adaptation of the method of using it to the qualities it possesses, which will constitute its tactics. History shows that it is vain to hope that military men generally will be at the pains to do this, but the one who does will go into battle with a great advantage, a lesson in itself of no mean value.

Rear Admiral Alfred Thayer Mahan, *The Influence of Sea Power Upon History, 1660–1783*, 1890.

IN WAR novelties of an atavistic nature are generally horrible; nevertheless, in the public mind, their novelty is their crime; consequently, when novelties of a progressive character are introduced on the battlefield, the public mind immediately anathematizes them, not necessarily because they are horrible but because they are new. Nothing insults a human being more than an idea his brains are incapable of creating. Such ideas detract from his dignity for they belittle his understanding. In April 1915, a few hundred British and French soldiers were gassed to death; gas being a novelty, Europe was transfixed with horror. In the winter of 1918–1919, the influenza scourge accounted for over 10,000,000 deaths, more than the total casualties killed throughout the Great War; yet the world scarcely twitched an eyelid, though a few people went so far as to sniff eucalyptus.

Major-General J.F.C. Fuller, *The Reformation of War*, 1923.

ACCUSING as I do without exception all the great Allied offensives of 1914, 1916 and 1917, as needless and wrongly conceived operations of infinite cost, I am bound to reply to the questions – what else could have been done? And I answer it, pointing to the Battle of Cambrai, "This could have been done". This in many variants, this in larger and better forms ought to have been done, and would have been done if only the generals had not been content to fight machine-gun bullets with the breasts of gallant men, and think this was waging war.

Sir Winston S. Churchill, on the first use of tanks on the battlefield, *The World Crisis*, 1923.

LOOKING BACK on the stages by which various fresh ideas gained acceptance, it can be seen that the process was eased when they could be presented, not as something radically new, but as the revival in modern terms of a time-honoured principle or practice that had been forgotten. This required not deception, but care to trace the connection – since "there is nothing new under the sun". A notable example was the way that the opposition to mechanization was diminished by showing the mobile armoured vehicle – the fast moving tank – was fundamentally the heir of the armoured horseman, and thus the natural means of reviving the decisive role which cavalry had played in past ages.

Captain Sir Basil Liddell Hart, *Sherman*, 1929.

PREJUDICE against innovation is a typical characteristic of an Officer Corps which has grown up in a well-tried and proven system.

Field Marshal Erwin Rommel, *The Rommel Papers*, 1953.

SCIENCE is in the saddle. Science is the dictator, whether we like it or not. Science runs ahead of both politics and military affairs. Science evolves new conditions to which institutions must be adapted. Let us keep our science dry.

General Carl M. Spaatz (1891–1974).

THE AFTER-ACTION report called the exercise a "fiasco." . . . Many of the Marines' critics said, "I told you so." Again the Marines saw it differently. In one observer's opinion, the fiasco at Culebra in 1924 identified enough errors to keep the Corps busy for

15 years. The experiment in 1924, and the subsequent experiments in the years leading up to World War II, allowed the Corps to forge ahead in the development of workable amphibious doctrine, tactics, and equipment that later proved decisive in not only the Pacific but the European and North African theaters as well.

General Charles C. Krulak, of the exercises on the island of Culebra in the Caribbean, which were the first tests of amphibious warfare concepts, *Marine Corps Gazette*, 12/1996.

INSPIRATION

THE FIRST CITY we shall see was built by Alexander. Our every step will evoke memories of the past worthy of emulation by Frenchmen.

Napoleon, 22 June 1798, proclamation to his troops at sea on the expedition to Egypt, quoted in R.M. Johnston, ed., *The Corsican*, 1910.

HENCE the difference between a mechanic and a man of genius entrusted with the command of an army. The one operates mechanically by the impulse of fear on the slavish passions of man; the other insensibly insinuates and incorporates himself with his soldiers, forming them into heroes . . . hence the same instruments, independent of the mechanical mode of application, move forward to victory or recoil to defeat, according to the mode in which they are animated.

Robert Jackson, *A Systematic View on the Formation, Discipline, and Economy of Armies*, 1804.

WHAT A THING is imagination! Here are men who don't know me, who have never seen me, but who only knew of me, and they are moved by my presence, they would do anything for me! And this same incident arises in all centuries and in all countries! Such is fanaticism! Yes, imagination rules the world. The defect of our modern institutions is that they do not speak to the imagination. By that alone can a man be governed; without it he is but a brute.

Napoleon, 17 June 1800, at Milan, after being cheered by German and Hungarian prisoners taken at the Battle of Marengo three days previously, men whom Napoleon had taken prisoner before in the campaigns of 1796 and 1797, quoted in R.M. Johnston, ed., *The Corsican*, 1910.

HE WHO SEEKS, finds, if he does not lose heart; and to me, continuously seeking, came from within the suggestion that control of the sea was an historic factor which had never been systematically appreciated and expounded. Once formulated consciously, this thought became the nucleus of all my writing for twenty years to come . . .

Rear Admiral Alfred Thayer Mahan, *From Sail to Steam*, 1907.

IT IS THIS animation which so largely constitutes the art of war, and of which it is so difficult to write. It is not one soul lighting another – this is mere fanaticism – but rather one mind illuminating many minds, by one heart causing thousands to beat in rhythm which, like a musical instrument, accompanies the mind in control. It is a union between intelligence and heart; between the will of the general and the willingness of his men; that fusion of the mental and moral spheres.

Major-General J.F.C. Fuller, *The Foundations of the Science of War*, 1926.

WHILE WAR is terribly destructive, monstrously cruel, and horrible beyond expressions, it nevertheless causes the divine spark in men to glow, to kindle, and to burst into a living flame, and enables them to attain heights of devotion to duty, sheer heroism, and sublime unselfishness that in all probability they would never have reached in the prosecution of peaceful pursuits.

Major-General John A. Lejeune, *The Reminiscences of a Marine*, 1929.

IT IS . . . an essential element in leadership. A commander has to work, not with a piece of clockwork which "goes" when it is wound up, but with "tool-using men". These men are afraid of death, and suffer from hunger, thirst, lack of sleep, and bad weather. Some are brave, some are not. Some are slow in the uptake, and others are mentally alert. Some are trusting and loyal, others jealous and insubordinate. In short, they carry within themselves a thousand and one seeds of diversity. To make them act as one it is not enough for a commander to decide in his own mind what should be done, nor even to limit himself to issuing orders for the carrying out of his intentions. He must be able to create a spirit of confidence in those under him. He must be able to exert his authority.

General Charles de Gaulle, *The Edge of the Sword*, 1932.

STUDY the human side of history . . . To learn that Napoleon in 1796 with 20,000 beat combined forces of 30,000 by something called economy of force or operating on interior lines is a mere waste of time. If you can understand how a young unknown man inspired a half-starved, ragged, rather Bolshie, crowd; how he filled their bellies; how he outmarched, outwitted, and outbluffed and defeated men who had studied war all their lives and waged it according to the text-books of their time, you will have learnt something worth knowing.

Field Marshal Viscount Wavell of Cyrenaica (1883–1950).

I HAVE NEVER accepted what many people have kindly said, namely that I inspired the nation. It was the nation and the race dwelling around the globe that had the lion heart. I had the luck to be called upon to give the roar.

Sir Winston S. Churchill, 30 November 1954, speech on his 80th birthday at Westminster Hall.

WHEN ALL the units had been briefed by their officers, I would stand out on the porch of the headquarters and watch the preparations. Soldiers would be going and coming, checking their weapons and equipment, loading trucks, talking to each other and their officers. The camp would be a beehive of activity, alive with purpose. Each one knew precisely what his job was, and how he was going to do it. Each had been readied by months of the hardest training. I could see the determination in their eyes, and invariably I would feel a surge of assurance. It was a reciprocal process, a flow of confidence from them to me and from me to them. A commander has to inspire his men, but it was always clear to me that they inspire him as well.

General Ariel Sharon, *Warrior*, 1989.

INSTINCT/INTUITION

CIRCUMSTANCES vary so enormously in war, and are so indefinable, that a vast array of factors has to be appreciated – mostly in the light of probabilities alone. The man responsible for evaluating the whole must bring to his task the quality of intuition that perceives the truth at every point. Otherwise a chaos of opinions and considerations would arise, and fatally entangle judgment. Bonaparte rightly said in this connection that many of the decisions faced by the commander in chief resemble mathematical problems worthy of the gifts of a Newton or Euler.

Major-General Carl von Clausewitz, *On War*, 1.3, 1832, tr. Michael Howard and Peter Paret, 1976.

AS WITH a man of the world, instinct becomes almost habit so that he always acts, speaks and moves appropriately, so only the experienced officer will make the right decision in major and minor matters – at every pulsebeat of war. Practice and experience dictate the answer. "This is possible, that is not."

Major-General Carl von Clausewitz, *On War*, 1, 1832, tr. Michael Howard and Peter Paret, 1976.

THE KNOWLEDGE needed by a senior commander is distinguished by the fact that it can only be attained by a special talent, through the medium of relfection, study and thought: an intellectual instinct which extracts the essence from the phenomenon of life, as a bee sucks honey from a flower. In addition to study and reflection, life itself serves as source.

Major-General Carl von Clausewitz, *On War*, 2, 1832, tr. Michael Howard and Peter Paret, 1976.

THE CONSECUTIVE achievements of a war are not premeditated but spontaneous and guided by military instinct.

Field Marshal Helmuth Graf von Moltke, *Instructions for the Commanders of Large Formations*, 1869.

THE GREATEST commander is he whose intuitions most nearly happen.
>Colonel T.E. Lawrence, 'The Science of Guerrilla Warfare', *Encyclopaedia Britannica*, 1929.

GREAT war leaders have always been aware of the importance of instinct. Was not what Alexander called his "hope," Caesar his "luck" and Napoleon his "star" simply the fact that they knew they had a particular gift of making contact with realities sufficiently closely to dominate them? For those who are greatly gifted, this facility often shines through their personalities. There may be nothing in itself exceptional about what they say or their way of saying it, but other men in their presence have the impression of a natural force destined to master events.
>General Charles de Gaulle, *The Edge of the Sword*, 1932.

THE FIGHTING INSTINCT is necessary to success on the battlefield – although even here the combatant who can keep a cool head has an advantage over the man who "sees red" – but should always be ridden on a tight rein. The statesman who gives that instinct its head loses his own; he is not fit to take charge of the fate of nations.
>Captain Sir Basil Liddell Hart, *Strategy*, 1954.

IF SOMETHING smells bad, sounds funny, or causes you to lose sleep at night, take another look. Your instincts combined with your experience can prevent you and your organization from walking off the cliff.
>Major-General Perry M. Smith, 'Learning to Lead', *Marine Corps Gazette*, January 1997.

INTEGRITY

I HATE the man like the very Gates of Death who says one thing but hides another in his heart.
>Homer, *The Iliad*, 9.378–380, c. 800 BC, tr. Robert Fagles, 1990; Achilles' opinion of Agamemnon, to Odysseus who encouraged his reconciliation with the King of Men.

FALSE WORDS are not only evil in themselves, but they infect the soul with evil.
>Socrates (c. 470–399 BC).

COMMANDERS must have integrity; without integrity, they have no power. If they have no power, they cannot bring out the best in their armies. Therefore, integrity is the hand of warriorship.
>Sun Bin, *The Lost Art of War*, c. 350 BC, tr. Thomas Cleary.

ACTING with integrity is a rich resource for warriors.
>Sun Bin, *The Lost Art of War*, c. 350 BC, tr. Thomas Cleary.

NO MATTER how lacking a man may be in

humanity, if he would be a warrior, he should first of all tell no lies. It is also basic that he be not the least bit suspicious, that he habitually stand on integrity, and that he know a sense of shame. The reason being that when a man who has formerly told lies and acted suspiciously participates in some great event, he will be pointed at behind his back and neither his allies nor his enemies will believe in him, regardless of how reasonable his words may be. One should be very prudent about this.
>Asakura Norikage, *Soteki Waki*, c. 1550 (*Ideals of the Samurai*, tr. William Wilson, 1982).

A MAN may cease to be lucky, for that is beyond his control; but he should not cease to be honest.
>Charles XII, 1714, to Axel Loewen.

I KNOW how to hold my tongue when it is necessary; but I do not know how to lie.
>Field Marshal Prince Eugene of Savoy, 1728, to the English diplomat, Lord Waldegrave.

A MAN ought not only to be virtuous in reality, but he must also always appear so.
>General George Washington (1732–1799), quoted by Major-General Henry Lee, *Memoirs of the War in the Southern Department*, 1869.

I HOLD the maxim no less applicable to public than to private affairs, that honesty is the best policy.
>General George Washington, 1796, farewell address as President.

NO MAN is justified in doing evil in the name of expediency.
>Theodore Roosevelt, *The Strenuous Life*, 1900.

I HAVE JUST been offered two hundred fifty thousand dollars and the most beautiful woman I have ever seen to betray my trust. I am depositing the money with the Treasury of the United States and request immediate relief from this command. They are getting close to my price.
>Major-General Arthur MacArthur (1845–1912), quoted by his son, Douglas MacArthur, *Reminiscences*, 1964.

THE PROPHETS must be stoned; that is their lot, and the test of their self-fulfillment. But a leader who is stoned may merely prove that he has failed in his function through a deficiency of wisdom, or through confusing his function with that of a prophet. Time alone can tell whether the effect of such a sacrifice redeems the apparent failure as a leader that does honour to him as a man. At the least, he avoids the more common fault of leaders – that of sacrificing the truth to expediency without ultimate advantage to the cause. For whoever habitually suppresses the truth in the interests of tact will produce a deformity from the womb of his thought.
>Captain Sir Basil Liddell Hart, *Sherman*, 1929.

IN ORDER to be a leader, a man must have followers. And to have followers, a man must have their confidence. Hence the supreme quality for a leader is unquestionably integrity. Without it, no real success is possible, no matter whether it is on a section gang, a football field, in an army, or in an office. The first great need, therefore, is integrity and high purpose.

> General of the Army Dwight D. Eisenhower, quoted in *Airpower*, Summer 1996.

FIDELITY . . . because it comes of personal decision, is the jewel within the reach of every officer who has the will to possess it. It is the epitome of character, and fortunately no other quality in the individual is more readily recognized and honored, by one's military associates.

> Brigadier-General S.L.A. Marshall, *The Armed Forces Officer*, 1950.

HE HAS INTEGRITY if his interest in the good of the Service is at all times greater than his peronal pride, and when he holds himself to the same line of duty when unobserved as he would follow if all of his superiors were present.

> Brigadier-General S.L.A. Marshall, *The Armed Forces Officer*, 1950.

INTEGRITY. And so to the greatest of the virtues on my list, one without which the leader is lost. Integrity, of course, embraces much more than just simple honesty. It means being true to your men, true to your outfit, and above all true to yourself. Integrity of purpose, loyalty upward and loyalty downward, humanity, unselfishness – these are its components. They come more easily to a man of conscience.

> Lieutenant-General Sir James Glover, 'A Soldier and His Conscience', *Parameters*, 9/1983.

INTEGRITY is one of those words that many people keep in that desk drawer labeled "too hard." It is not a topic for the dinner table or the cocktail party. When supported with education, one's integrity can give a person something to rely on when perspective seems to blur, when rules and principles seem to waver, and when faced with a hard choice of right and wrong. To urge people to develop it is not a statement of piety but of practical advice. Anyone who has lived in an intense extortion environment [POW] realizes that the most potent weapon an adversary can bring to bear is manipulation, the manipulation of a prey's shame. A clear conscience is one's only protection.

> Admiral James B. Stockdale, 'Educating Leaders', *Washington Quarterly*, Winter 1983.

THE INTEGRITY of society is approximately equal to the lowest common denominator of its people. If developing individuals observe that people with known moral defects, or people known to be crooked or liars, are accepted by society without

penalty, they may conclude that integrity is not worth their effort.

> Admiral Arleigh A. '31 Knot' Burke, 'Integrity', U.S. Naval Institute, *Proceedings*, 10/1985.

LEADERS Should Exude Integrity. Leaders should not only talk about integrity, they must also operate at a high level of integrity. They should emphasize both personal and institutional integrity. They should take corrective action when there are violations of integrity and upgrade the standards of institutional integrity over time. A leader should also ensure that everybody understands the leader's fundamental commitment to the values of their institutions. Soon after taking over a leadership position, a leader should look for ways to demonstrate this commitment to integrity. Institutional integrity cannot lie dormant until a crisis occurs; integrity must be ingrained and must be supported by the leader and the organizational community. Of all the qualities a leader must have, integrity is the most important.

> Major-General Perry M. Smith, *Taking Charge: A Practical Guide for Leaders*, 1986.

WE ALL HAD to weigh, in the balance, the difference between lives and lies.

> Lieutenant-Colonel Oliver North, 1989, during the Senate's Iran-Contra hearings.

SMOKE OUT those of low integrity. Leaders must sniff the air constantly to ensure high standards of ethics are maintained. In almost all large organizations, someone is walking out the back door with something. Expense accounts, personnel records, training reports, and contracts need regular scrutiny.

> Major-General Perry M. Smith, 'Learning to Lead', *Marine Corps Gazette*, 1/1997.

IT'S THE INNER VOICE, the source of self-control, the basis for the trust that is imperative in today's military. It's doing the right thing when nobody is looking.

> General Ronald R. Fogleman, quoted in *The Washington Times*, 10 July 1997, p. A23.

THE ELITE, too, produced its cowards and incompetents. But it also produced officers such as George Washington and George Patton, Robert E. Lee and George Marshall (the latter sprung from small-town gentry – even slight privilege once inspired obligation). Those officers had been imbued with social rules of integrity, both moral and financial, that set a tone for others to study and attain. Imagine but one of the men named above accepting a retirement job flogging metal for Lockheed Martin or Northrop Grumman. Such men knew when to take a stand, and would have turned in their stars before they acquiesced in looting the public.

> Lieutenant-Colonel Ralph Peters, 'Hucksters in Uniform', *The Washington Monthly*, 5/1999.

INTELLECT

TO THOSE who congratulated him on his victory in the battle against the Arcadians, he said: "It would be better if our intelligence were beating them rather than our strength."
> Archidamus III (d. 338 BC), Eurypontid King of Sparta, quoted in Plutarch, *The Lives*, c. AD 100 (*Plutarch on Sparta*, tr. Richard Talbert, 1988).

MEN with sharpness of mind are to be found only among those with a penchant for thought.
> Shiba Yoshimasa, *The Chikubasho*, 1380 (*Ideals of the Samurai*, tr. William Wilson, 1982).

WHAT DISTINGUISHED a man from a beast of burden is thought, and the faculty of bringing ideas together . . . a pack mule can go on the campaigns of Prince Eugene of Savoy, and still learn nothing of tactics.
> Frederick the Great (1712–1786).

THE DISCIPLINE of the mind is as requisite as that of the body to make a good soldier.
> General Sir John Moore, 1804, letter to Robert Brownrigg.

THE VITAL contribution of intelligence is clear throughout. No wonder then, that war, though it may appear to be uncomplicated, cannot be waged with distinction except by men of outstanding intellect.
> Major-General Carl von Clausewitz, *On War*, 1.3, 1832, tr. Michael Howard and Peter Paret, 1976.

WE ONLY WISH to represent things as they are, and to expose the error of believing that a mere bravo without intellect can make himself distinguished in war.
> Major-General Carl von Clausewitz, *On War*, 1.3, 1832, tr. Michael Howard and Peter Paret, 1976.

WHAT THIS TASK requires in the way of higher intellectual gifts is a sense of unity and a power of judgment raised to a marvelous pitch of vision, which easily grasps and dismisses a thousand remote possibilities that an ordinary mind would labor to identify and wear itself out in so doing.
> Major-General Carl von Clausewitz, *On War*, 1.3, 1832, tr. Michael Howard and Peter Paret, 1976.

MARKED intellectual capacity is the chief characteristic of the most famous soldiers. Alexander, Hannibal, Caesar, Marlborough, Washington, Frederick, Napoleon, Wellington, and Nelson were each and all of them something more than fighting men. Few of their age rivalled them in strength of intellect. It was this, combined with the best qualities of Ney and Blücher, that made them masters of strategy, and lifted them high above those who were tacticians and nothing more.
> Colonel George F.R. Henderson, *Stonewall Jackson and the American Civil War*, 1898.

IT IS TRUE that military men, exaggerating the relative powerlessness of the intelligence, will sometimes neglect to make use of it at all. Here the line of least resistance comes into its own. There have been examples of commanders avoiding all intellectual effort and even despising it on principle. Every great victory is usually followed by this kind of mental decline. The Prussian Army after the death of Frederick the Great, for instance of this. In other cases, the military men note the inadequacy of knowledge and therefore trust to inspiration alone or to the dictates of fate. That was the prevalent state of the French Army at the time of the Second Empire: "We shall muddle through, somehow."
> General Charles de Gaulle, *The Edge of the Sword*, 1932.

THERE IS one word in our language which I believe to be the most potent word in the dictionary. So that you do not forget it, I have written it on the blackboard – it is the word WHY. Whatever I say to you, whatever your instructors say to you, whatever you read, whatever you think, ask yourself the reason why. If you do not do so, however much you may strive to learn, you will be mentally standing at ease. Remember this: your brain is not a museum for the past, or a lumber room for the present; it is a laboratory for the future, even if the future is only five minutes ahead of you; a creative centre in which new discoveries are made and progress is fashioned.
> Major-General J.F.C. Fuller, lecture to students at the Camberley staff college, January 1933, *Memoirs of an Unconventional Soldier*, 1936.

THE INFLUENCE of thought on thought is the most influential factor in history.
> Captain Sir Basil Liddell Hart, *The Ghost of Napoleon*, 1934.

PHYSICAL EXUBERANCE does not go with mental fitness. A man who takes a lot of exercise rarely exercises his mind adequately – in developing his body he leaves his mind underdeveloped. Pain may intensify the feelings but can hardly clarify the thought.

The mind works best when the body is quiescent – when one is totally unaware of the body: as if one were detached from it altogether for the time. If the body is either unwell or too active it impinges on the mind.

We ought to take account of this factor when weighing the mental form of commanders. Allowance must be made for the physical effect of active service conditions, and also for the intense cultivation of physical fitness by excessive exercise. (May 1934.)
> Captain Sir Basil Liddell Hart, *Thoughts on War*, 1944.

WITH SOLDIERS, instinctive qualities play the chief part in action. The battlefield is not an intellectual sphere. But the organization and training of armies demand, above all, intellect based upon knowledge. Yet in the military system, these essentially different activities are treated as interchangeable. Here is the reason for so many failures. An army will produce a number of good fighting commanders, especially if their tactical sense is not atrophied by routine and discipline. But no army produces equally good strategists, because such can only be developed through a scientific approach to problems, and this is incompatible with the loyalty to other interests which the service demands. (November 1934.)

> Captain Sir Basil Liddell Hart, *Thoughts on War*, 1944.

THE ARMY for all its good points, is a cramping place for a *thinking man*. As I have seen too often, such a man chafes and goes – or else decays. And the root of the trouble is the Army's root fear of the truth. Romantic fiction is the soldierly taste. The heads of the Army talk much of developing character yet deaden it – frowning on younger men who show promise of the personality necessary for command, and the originality necessary for surprise. (October 1935.)

> Captain Sir Basil Liddell Hart, *Thoughts on War*, 1944.

FAITH MATTERS so much to a soldier in the stress of war that military training inculcates a habit of unquestioning obedience which in turn fosters an unquestioning acceptance of the prevailing doctrine. While fighting is a most practical test of theory, it is a small part of soldiering; and there is far more in soldiering that tends to make men the slaves of a theory. Moreover, the soldier must have faith in his power to defeat his enemy: that faith finds its fullest expression in the attack: hence to question, even on material grounds, the possibility of successful attack is a risk to faith. Doubt is unnerving save to philosophic minds: and armies are not composed of philosophers, either at the top or at the bottom. In no activity is optimism so necessary to success, for it deals so largely with the unknown – even unto death. The margin that separates optimism from blind folly is narrow. There is no cause for surprise that soldiers so often overstep it and become the victims of their faith.

> Captain Sir Basil Liddell Hart, *The War in Outline*, 1936.

THERE HAS BEEN no illustrious captain who did not possess taste and feeling for the heritage of the human mind. At the root of Alexander's victories one will always find Aristotle.

> General Charles de Gaulle, *The Army of the Future*, 1941.

EVERY MARINE has a basic responsiblity to study the profession of arms on his own. A leader without either interest in or knowledge of the history and theory of warfare – the intellectual content of his profession – is a leader in appearance only. Self-

study in the art and science of war is at least equal in importance – and should receive at least equal time – to maintaining physical condition. This is particularly true among officers; after all, an officer's principal weapon is his mind.

> General Alfred M. Gray and Major John Schmitt, *Warfighting*, United States Marine Corps, 1989.

SOME PEOPLE paint a picture of me as a rough tough tobacco chewin' guy. But I've always been a pretty good listener to the opposition, people with other views. Even with stars on my collar, my attitude isn't "You'd better learn this or else." My intention is to encourage people to use their minds to learn and grow.

Warfare, in many instances, is as much psychological as it is physical. The objective is to defeat the minds of your opponents.

> General Alfred M. Gray, 'Honest Criticism', Al Santoli, ed., *Leading the Way: How Vietnam Veterans Rebuilt the U.S. Military*, 1993.

WE CANNOT EXPECT today's military to think, because the thinking men have left the military. Neither rigorous reflection nor self-criticism are common virtues among senior officers.

> Lieutenant-Colonel Ralph Peters, 'Hucksters in Uniform', *The Washington Monthly*, 5/1999.

INTREPIDITY

O STRANGE! What will you do with this man, who can bear neither good nor bad fortune? He is the only man who neither suffers us to rest when he is victor, nor rests himself when he is overcome. We shall have, it seems, perpetually to fight with him; as in good success his confidence, and in ill success his shame, still urges him to some further enterprise.

> Hannibal, 209 BC, on the intrepidity of Marcus Claudius Marcellus, Roman proconsul, at the Battle of Asculum, quoted in Plutarch, *The Lives*, c. AD 100, tr. John Dryden.

TO FIGHT the enemy bravely with a prospect of victory is nothing; but to fight with intrepidity under the constant impression of defeat, and inspire irregular troops to do it, is a talent peculiar to yourself.

> Major-General Nathaniel Greene, letter to Colonel Francis 'Swamp Fox' Marion after his capture of Fort Watson, South Carolina, 23 April 1781.

FEW MEN can trust their judgment when in physical danger. On the other hand men's hearts go to the leader who is ready – as Marlborough and Wellington were – to risk his life. The intrepid General has gone more than half way to win the affections of his men.

> Baron Charles MacMoran Wilson Moran, *The Anatomy of Courage*, 1945.

INVENTION

ON SEEING an arrow shot from a catapult when it was first brought from Sicily, he exclaimed: "By Heracles, man's valour is done for."

Plutarch, quoting Archidamus III (d. 338 BC), Eurypontid King of Sparta, *The Lives*, c. AD 100 (*Plutarch on Sparta*, tr. Richard Talbert, 1988).

I WAS TOLD by Mr. Charles King, when President of Columbia College, that he had been present in company with [Admiral Stephen] Decatur at one of the early experiments in steam navigation. Crude as the appliances still were, demonstration was conclusive; and Decatur, whatever his prejudices, was open to conviction. "Yes," he said gloomily, to King, "it is the end of our business; hereafter any man who can boil a tea-kettle will be as good as the best of us."

Rear Admiral Alfred Thayer Mahan, *From Sail to Steam*, 1907.

THE PAST had its inventions and when they coincided with a man who staked his shirt on them the face of the world changed. Scythes fixed to the axles of war chariots; the moving towers which overthrew Babylon; Greek fire; the short bow, the cross-bow, the Welsh long bow and ballistra; plate armour, the Prussian needle gun; the Merrimac and Ericsson's marvellous coincidental reply. The future is pregnant with invention . . .

General Sir Ian Hamilton, *The Soul and Body of an Army*, 1921.

J

JUDGEMENT

THERE ARE roads which must not be followed, armies which must not be attacked, towns which must not be besieged, positions which must not be contested, commands of the sovereign which must not be obeyed.
  Sun Tzu, *The Art of War*, 8, c. 500 BC, tr. Giles, 1910.

REASON and judgment are the qualities of a leader.
  Cornelius Tacitus, *Annals*, 15.59, AD 116.

LOOK at the essence of a thing, whether it be a point of doctrine, of practice, or interpretation.
  The Emperor Marcus Aurelius (ruled AD 161–180), *Meditations*.

JUDGMENT, and not headlong courage, is the true arbiter of war.
  Count Belisarius (c. AD 505–565).

THE GENERAL should not be hasty in placing confidence in people who promise to do something; if he does, almost everyone will think he is light headed.
  The Emperor Maurice, *The Strategikon*, c. AD 600 (*Maurice's Strategikon*, tr. George Dennis, 1984).

IF I AM to be hanged for it, I cannot accuse a man who I believe has meant well, and whose error was one of judgment and not of intention.
  The Duke of Wellington, 31 July 1809. on the subject of General Crauford's handling of the Light Division.

THAT QUALITY which I wish to see the officers possess, who are at the head of the troops, is a cool, discriminating judgment when in action, which will enable them to decide with promptitude how far they can go and ought to go, with propriety; and to convey their orders, and act with such vigor and decision, that the soldier will look to them with confidence in the moment of action, and obey them with alacrity.
  The Duke of Wellington, General Order, 15 May 1811.

IN REVIEWING the whole array of factors a general must weigh before making his decision, we must remember that he can gauge the direction and value of the most important ones only by considering numerous other possibilities – some immediate, some remote. He must *guess*, so to speak: guess whether the first shock of battle will steel the enemy's resolve and stiffen his resistance, or whether, like a Bologna flask, it will shatter as soon as its surface is scratched; guess the extent of debilitation and paralysis that the drying up of particular sources of supply and the severing of certain lines of communication will cause in the enemy; guess whether the burning pain of an injury he has dealt will make the enemy collapse with exhaustion or, like a wounded bull, arouse his rage; guess whether the other powers will be frightened or indignant, and whether and which political alliances will be dissolved or formed. When we realize that he must hit upon all this and much more by means of his discreet judgment, as a marksman hits a target, we must admit that such an accomplishment of the human mind is no small achievement. Thousands of wrong turns running in all directions tempt his perception; and if the range, confusion and complexity of the issues are not enough to overwhelm him, the dangers and responsibilities may.
  Major-General Carl von Clausewitz, *On War*, 7.22, 1832, tr. Michael Howard and Peter Paret, 1976.

IF YOU TAKE a chance, it usually succeeds, presupposing good judgment.
  Lieutenant-General Sir Giffard Martel (1889–1958).

JUDGMENT comes from experience and experience comes from bad judgment.
  General Simon Bolivar Buckner, quoted by General of the Army Omar N. Bradley, 'Leadership', *Parameters*, Winter 1972.

THE CORE of leadership is the ability and willingness to exercise judgment. It is the judgment which sits at the center of the German Army's *Innere Fuehrung*, at the center of the Mongol Yassak, and the Roman Army's rules of the soldier, and it is judgment which sits at the center of leadership today. If judgment is vital to leadership, then it is clear that the code of values of the officer can never be the equivalent of bureaucratic rules.
  Lieutenant-Colonel Richard Gabriel, 'The Environment of Military Leadership', *Military Review*, 7/1980.

JUNIOR OFFICERS

A YOUNG OFFICER should never think he does too much; they are to attend to the looks of the men, and if any are thinner or paler than usual, the reason of their falling off may be enquired into.
  Major-General Sir James Wolfe (1727–1759), *Instructions for Young Officers*.

THERE ARE three things, young gentleman, which you are constantly to bear in mind. First, you must always implicitly obey orders, without attempting to form any opinion of your own respecting their propriety. Secondly, you must consider every man your enemy who speaks ill of your king; and thirdly, you must hate a Frenchman as you do the devil.

Admiral Viscount Nelson, 1792, to a midshipman aboard HMS *Agamemnon*, quoted in Robert Southey, *Life of Nelson*, 1813.

THE LIEUTENANT, in the absence of the captain, commands the company, and should therefore make himself acquainted with the duties of the station; he must also be perfectly acquainted with the duties of the non-commissioned officer and soldier, and see them performed with the greatest exactness. . . . he should endeavor to gain the love of his men, by his attention to every thing which may contribute to their health and convenience. He should often visit them at different hours; inspect into their manner of living; see that their provisions are good and well cooked, and as far as possible oblige them to take their meals at regulated hours. He should pay attention to their complaints, and when well founded, endeavour to get them redressed; but discourage them from complaining on every frivolous occasion. . . . He must not suffer the soldiers to be ill treated by the non-commissioned officers through malevolence, or from any pique or resentment; but must at the same time be careful that a proper degree of subordination is kept up between them.

Major-General Friedrich Baron von Steuben, *Revolutionary War Drill Manual*, 1794.

AS TO THE WAY in which some of our ensigns and lieutenants braved danger – the boys just come out from school – it exceeds all belief. They ran as at cricket.

The Duke of Wellington, quoted in Rodgers, *Recollections*, 1859.

BUT the *platoon commander* – that is a special item. This by no means a trifle; this the commander, the leader, the head of the basic military group – the platoon. It is impossible to build an edifice with loose sand. One must have good building material, one must have a good platoon, and this means – a good, reliable, class-conscious, confident platoon commander.

Leon Trotsky, 1 April 1922, 'Our Current Basic Military Tasks', *Military Writings*, 1969.

AS THE WAR dragged on into the autumn of 1916, the German Army, like our own, had need of underpinning. But the lynch-pins were missing. A German soldier writes:

The tragedy of the Somme battle was that the best soldiers, the stoutest-hearted men were lost; their numbers were replaceable, their spiritual worth never could be.

Our own forces were in no better plight. Most of those who were meant by nature to lead men had been struck down by two years of war.

That is the story of all wars. A national army is held together by young leaders. They are most needed when weariness has dulled the first purpose of such a force in the third or fourth year of war. But as time passes they have become scarce, for the best go first and have gone first since war began.

Dead like the rest, for this is true;
War never chooses an evil man but the good.
It is the theme of the *Iliad*. It runs through the humblest diary of the war.

Baron Charles MacMoran Wilson Moran, *The Anatomy of Courage*, 1945.

MODERN BATTLES are fought by platoon leaders. The carefully prepared plans of higher commanders can do no more than project you to the line of departure at the proper time and place, in proper formation, and start you off in the right direction.

General of the Army George C. Marshall, *Selected Speeches and Statements*, 1945.

NEVER in the history of warfare has individual leadership meant so much. Land fighting has almost inevitably broken down into mobile action by small units, and the ability of junior officers, non-commissioned officers and even privates to assume responsibility and initiative in a pinch has carried us through to victory. . . .

We have paid no small price. By their very leadership, men have multiplied their risks. An unusually heavy percentage of our outstanding young officers were killed in action on Iwo Jima – most of them shot down in front of their men. Such men will be sorely missed.

General Alexander A. Vandegrift, 1945.

THE CHARACTERISTICS which are required in the minor commander if he is to prove capable of preparing men for and leading them through the shock of combat with high credit may therefore be briefly described:
(1) Diligence in the care of men.
(2) Administration of all organizational affairs such as punishments and promotions according to a standard of resolute justice.
(3) Military bearing.
(4) A basic understanding of the simple fact that soldiers wish to think of themselves as soldiers and that all military information is nourishing to their spirits and their lives.
(5) Courage, creative intelligence, and physical fitness.
(6) Innate respect for the dignity of the position and the work of other men.

Brigadier-General S.L.A. Marshall, *The Armed Forces Officer*, 1950.

SAID a newly arrived lieutenant to an old sergeant of the 12th Cavalry: "You've been here a long time, haven't you?" "Yes sir," replied the sergeant. "The troop commanders, they come and go, but it don't hurt the troop."

Brigadier-General S.L.A. Marshall, *The Armed Forces Officer*, 1950.

THE PIOUS GREEK, when he had set up altars to all the great gods by name, added one more altar, "To the Unknown God". So whenever we speak and think of the great captains and set up our military altars to Hannibal and Napoleon and Marlborough and such-like, let us add one more altar, "To the Unknown Leader", that is, to the good company, platoon, or section leader who carries forward his men or holds his post, and often falls unknown. It is these who in the end do most to win wars.

Field Marshal Viscount Wavell of Cyrenaica, *Soldiers and Soldiering*, 1953.

THE MOST TERRIBLE warfare is to be a second lieutenant leading a platoon when you are on the battlefield.

General Dwight D. Eisenhower, 17 March 1954, remark.

JUSTICE

WHEN ASKED once which of the two virtues was finer, courage or justice, he declared: "Courage has no value if justice is not in evidence too; but if everyone were to be just, then no one would need courage."

Agesilaus, Eurypontid King of Sparta (400–360 BC),

quoted in Plutarch, *The Lives*, c. AD 100 (*Plutarch on Sparta*, tr. Richard Talbert, 1988).

COMMANDERS must be just; if they are not just, they will lack dignity. If they lack dignity, they will lack charisma; and if they lack charisma, their soldiers will not face death for them. Therefore justice is the head of warriorship.

Sun Bin, c. 350 BC, *The Lost Art of War*, tr. Thomas Cleary.

I SHALL NOT consider anyone of you a fellow-soldier of mine, no matter how terrible he is reputed to be to the foe, who is not able to use clean hands against the enemy. For bravery cannot be victorious unless it be arrayed along with justice.

Count Belisarius, AD 533, to his troops, at the beginning of the Vandalic War, who complained when he executed two soldiers who had murdered another, quoted in Procopius, *History of the Wars*, 3.12, c. AD 560, tr. H.B. Dewing.

THERE IS no authority without justice.

Napoleon, 12 March 1803, remark.

HE [a man] has justice if he acknowledges the interests of all concerned in any particular transaction rather than serving his own particular interests.

Brigadier-General S.L.A. Marshall, *The Armed Forces Officer*, 1950.

K

KILLING

AT THE WORD of Assur, the great lord, my lord, on flank and front I pressed upon the enemy like the onset of raging storm. With the weapons of Assur, my lord, and the terrible onset of my attack, I stopped their advance, I succeeded in surrounding them, I decimated the enemy host with arrow and spear. All of their bodies I bored through like a sieve. . . . Like the many waters of a storm I made the contents of their gullets and entrails run down upon the wide earth. My prancing steeds harnessed my riding, plunged into the streams of their blood as into a river. The wheels of my war chariot, which brings down the wicked and evil, were bespattered with blood and filth. With the bodies of their warriors I filled the plain, like grass. Their testicles I cut off, and tore out their privates like the seeds of cucumbers of June. Their hands I cut off. . . . The chariots and their horses, whose riders had been slain at the beginning of the terrible onslaught, and who had been left to themselves, kept running back and forth . . . I put an end to their riders' fighting. . . . They abandoned their tents and to save their lives they trampled the bodies of their fallen soldiers, they fled like young pigeons that are pursued. They were besides themselves; they held back their urine, but let their dung go into their chariots. In pursuit of them I dispatched my chariots and horses after them. Those among who had escaped, who had fled for their lives, wherever my charioteers met them, they cut them down with the sword.
> Sennacherib (705–681 BC), King of Assyria, quoted in Daniel Luckenbill, *Ancient Records of Assyria and Babylonia*, 1926.

DO NOT PUT a premium on killing.
> Li Ch'uan, Tang Dynasty commentator on Sun Tzu, *The Art of War*, 3, c. 500 BC, tr. Samuel Griffith, 1963.

WE MUST never forget our mission, as soldiers, is to kill, even though being killed ourselves. We must not shut our eyes to this fact. To make war – to kill without being killed is an illusion. To fight – to be killed without killing – that is clumsy, inept. One must know how to kill while being ready to be killed oneself. The man who is dedicated to death is terrible. Nothing can stop him if he is not shot down on the way.
> General Mikhail I. Dragomirov (1830–1905).

THE OVERFAITHFUL sword returns the user
His heart's desire at price of his heart's blood.
> Rudyard Kipling, 'The Proconsuls', 1905.

THE ETHICS of human destruction must necessarily be somewhat obscure. Neither rhetoric nor hysteria will help us to determine them.
> Winston S. Churchill, 24 October 1898, letter to the editor of the *Westminster Gazette*.

PUT YOUR HEART and soul into being expert killers with your weapons. The only good enemy is a dead enemy. Misses do not kill, but a bullet in the heart or a bayonet in the guts do. Let every bullet find its billet – in the body of your foes.
> General George S. Patton, Jr., 20 December 1941, *The Patton Papers*, II, 1974; speech to the members of the Second Armored Division after the Carolina manoeuvres.

CHILDREN of a free and sheltered people who have lived a generous life, we have not the pugnacious disposition of those oppressed beasts our enemies who must fight or starve. Our bravery is too negative. We talk too much of sacrifice, of the glory of dying that freedom may live. Of course we are willing to die but that is not enough. We must be eager to kill, to inflict on the enemy – the hated enemy – wounds, death, and destruction. If we die killing, well and good, but if we fight hard enough, viciously enough, we will kill and live. Live to return to our family and our girl as conquering heroes – men of Mars.
> General George S. Patton, Jr., March 1942.

CHRISTMAS [1944] dawned clear and cold; lovely weather for killing Germans, although the thought seemed somewhat at variance with the spirit of the day.
> General George S. Patton, Jr., *War As I Knew It*, 1947.

WAR is a savage business, a form of legalized murder, a business where killing one's fellow men without mercy is a duty and sometimes a form of sport. Nobody enjoys killing their fellow creatures, but in war one's likes and dislikes must take second place to defeat and survival. In this book there is much killing and I make no excuse for recording cases with satisfaction and often with relish, whilst on reflection one is shocked at depriving others, just as good as oneself, of their lives and for no better reason than that both of us are obeying orders and performing an unpleasant duty.
> Colonel Richard Meinertzhagen, *Army Diary 1899–1925*, 1960.

THE PURPOSE of the military is to kill, and if you cannot stomach that, you should not have a military.

Lieutenant-Colonel Ralph Peters, *Fighting for the Future*, 1999.

OF ALL the notions I have advanced over the years, the only one that has met with consistent rejection is the statement that men like to kill. I do not believe that all men like to kill. At the extreme, there are those saintly beings who would rather sacrifice their own lives before taking the life of another. The average man will kill if compelled to, in uniform in a war or in self-defense, but has no evident taste for it. Men react differently to the experience of killing. Some are traumatized. Others simply move on with their lives. But there is at least a minority of human beings – mostly male – who enjoy killing. That minority may be small, but it does not take many enthusiastic killers to trigger the destruction of a fragile society. Revolutions, pogroms, genocides, and civil wars are made not by majorities. The majority may gloat or loot, but the killing minority drives history.

Lieutenant-Colonel Ralph Peters, *Fighting for the Future*, 1999.

KNOW YOUR MEN

NOTHING is harder to see than into people's natures. Though good and bad are different, their conditions and appearances are not always uniform. There are some people who are nice enough but steal. Some people are outwardly respectful while inwardly making fools of everyone. Some people are brave on the outside yet cowardly on the inside. Some people do their best but are not loyal.

Hard though it be to know people, there are ways.

First is to question them concerning right and wrong, to observe their ideas.

Second is to exhaust all their arguments, to see how they change.

Third is to consult with them about strategy, to see how perceptive they are.

Fourth is to announce that there is trouble, to see how brave they are.

Fifth is to get them drunk, to observe their nature.

Sixth is to present them with the prospect of gain, to see how modest they are.

Seventh is to give them a task to do within a specific time, to see how trustworthy they are.

Zhuge Liang (AD 180–234), *The Way of the General* (*Mastering the Art of War*, tr. Thomas Cleary, 1989).

IF THE GENERAL knows the inclinations and tendencies of each officer and soldier, he will know better what duties should be assigned to each one.

The Emperor Maurice, *The Strategikon*, c. AD 600 (*Maurice's Strategikon*, tr. George Dennis, 1984).

A MAN with intelligence and a firm heart will be able to put others to use. People's ways are variant, and to use a man to whom one has taken a liking for all things – for example, to use a military man for literary matters, or a man untalented in speech as a messenger, or a slow-thinking man in a place where a quick wit is necessary – may bring about failure and even cause a man's life to be ruined. A man should be put to use in the line with which he seems most familiar.

When men are put to use in the same way that curved wood is used for the wheel and straight wood for the shaft, there will be no one without value.

Shiba Yoshimasa, *Chikubasho*, 1380 (*Ideals of the Samurai*, tr. William Wilson, 1982).

HE HAS great skill in fencing, no doubt, but he can't discriminate between those who need it and those who don't. A lord of the Empire, for instance, or a daimyo need not cut people down with his own hand, for if he is in a tight place in a fight he can call on his men to do it for him. What he needs first of all is the capacity to judge the capacity of the people he uses.

Tokugawa Ieyasu (1543–1616), commenting on the qualifications of a fencing master, quoted in A.L. Sadler, *The Maker of Modern Japan: The Life of Tokugawa Ieyasu*, 1937.

YOU MUST love soldiers in order to understand them, and understand them in order to lead them.

Marshal of France Vicomte de Turenne (1611–1675).

A GENERAL'S principal talent consists in knowing the mentality of the soldier and in winning his confidence. And, in these two respects, the French soldier is more difficult to lead than any other. He is not a machine to be put in motion but a reasonable being that must be directed.

Napoleon (1769–1821), quoted in Christopher Herold, ed., *The Mind of Napoleon*, 1955.

THE TRUTH IS, men are very hard to know, and yet, not to be deceived, we must judge them by their present actions, but for the present only.

Napoleon, *Maxims*, 1804–1815.

GENERALS should mess with the common soldiers. The Spartan system was a good one.

Napoleon, to Gaspard Gourgaud at St. Helena, 1815–1818.

IT IS NOT ENOUGH that we see the service in a different light, for it will acquire altogether different significance in service when we know how to act toward different people. We must not take uniformly identical steps against all and, under the guise of encouragement, beat everyone without distinction, with words and canes. Such uniformity in the actions of a commander shows that he has nothing in common with his subordinates and that he has no understanding at all of his countrymen. And this is very important.

Admiral P.S. Nakhimov (1802–1855), quoted in Danchenko and Vydrin, *Military Pedagogy*, 1973.

THE TRUE WAY to be popular with the troops is not to be free and familiar with them, but to make them believe you know more than they do.

General of the Army William T. Sherman, September 1864, remark to Bishop Henry C. Lay.

KNOW YOUR MEN, and be constantly on the alert for potential leaders – you never know how soon you may need them. During my two years in command of the 82nd Airborne Division in World War II, I was in close and daily touch with every regimental and most battalion commanders. Before acceding to command of the division, and while I was General Omar Bradley's assistant division commander, I had learned to call by name every infantry officer in the division.

Later, by frequent exchange of views with the infantry regimental commanders and the divisional artillery commander, I knew in advance whom they had earmarked for battalion command. I do not recall any instance where I thought the regimental commander had not picked the right man. The payoff came in Normandy. I went in with 12 battalion commanders – four regiments – and I had 14 new ones when we came out, for some battalions lost as many as three commanders during the 33 days we were in that fight.

General Matthew B. Ridgway, 'Leadership', *Military Review*, 10/1966.

I HAD always been one of those field commanders passionately concerned with minor tactics: the battlefield skills of the smallest section, platoon or company. The best plan in the world is useless if the young officer or his men do not have the training or will to carry it out. Every commander, however exalted, whatever armies he disposes, must keep in touch with his "poor bloody infantry" – know what they can do, sense what they can feel, imbue them in turn with what he feels and what he demands. Without that rapport he is no more than a "classroom commander," a master of maps maybe, but lost on the field.

General Saad el Shazly, *The Crossing of the Suez*, 1980.

L

LAST WORDS

REMEMBER my last saying: show kindness to your friends, and then shall you have it in your power to chastise your enemies.
> Cyrus the Great, c. 529 BC, quoted in Xenophon, *The Education of Cyrus*, tr. H.G. Dakyns, 1992.

TO the best (or strongest).
> Alexander the Great, 323 BC, on his deathbed in Babylon when asked to whom he bequeathed his empire, quoted in Curtius, *The history of Alexander*, c. AD 41, tr. John Yardley, 1984.

LET ME FREE the Roman people from their long anxiety, since they think it tedious to wait for an old man's death. . . . they have sent an ambassador to suggest to Prusias (king of Bithynia) the crime of murdering a guest.
> Hannibal, 183 BC, upon poisoning himself as the Romans pursued him even into exile.

UNGRATEFUL COUNTRY, you will not possess even my bones.
> Scipio Africanus, 183 BC, inscription to be engraved on his tomb in Campania, after he had been tried for bribery in Rome, quoted in Valerius Maximus, *De Dictis Factisque*, III.

THOU TOO, my son?
> Gaius Julius Caesar, 15 March 44 BC, to Marcus Junius Brutus, thought to be his son, as he stabbed Caesar in the Senate House in Rome, quoted in Suetonius, *The Lives of the Twelve Caesars*, AD 121, tr. Philemon Holland, 1606.

OH WRETCHED valour thou wert but a name, and yet I worshipped thee as real indeed. But now it seems thou wert but fortune's slave.
> Marcus Junius Brutus, 42 BC, as he fell upon his sword after the defeat of the assassins of Julius Caesar at the Battle of Philippi.

COME, give it to me, if we have anything to do.
> Emperor Septimius Severus, AD 211, still trying to accomplish imperial business as he expired, quoted in Dio Cassius, *Romaika*, 76.15.2, c. AD 230.

I DESIRE to leave to the men that come after me a remembrance of me in good works.
> King Alfred the Great, AD 901.

FORTH we go in our lines
Without our armour, against the blue blades.
The helmets glitter: I have no armour.
Our shrouds are down in those ships.
> Harald Hardraade, 25 September 1066, poem composed as the Battle of Stamford Bridge began, quoted in David Howarth, *The Year of the Conquest*, 1978; the shrouds referred to are the byrnies his men left in their ships.

GOD has promised me a great victory after my death.
> El Cid, 1094, after the rout of the Almoravides before Valencia, quoted in *Cronica Particular del Cid*, 1512.

NOW LET the rest go as it will, I care no more.
> Henry II, 6 July 1189, as he learned of the betrayal of his son, quoted in Marion Meade, *Eleanor of Aquitaine*, 1977.

YOUTH, I forgive thee. Take off his chains, give him 100 shillings, and let him go.
> Richard I, 1199, to the man who had caused his mortal wound with a crossbow bolt. Richard's wishes were not honoured: the archer was flayed alive after the King's death.

CARRY MY BONES before you on your march. For the rebels will not be able to endure the sight of me, dead or alive.
> Edward I, 1307.

REJOICE my departed soul with a beautiful series of victories.
> Osman I, 1326, quoted in Lord Kinross, *The Ottoman Centuries*, 1979.

MAKE MY SKIN into drumheads for the Bohemian cause.
> Jan Ziska, 1424.

I PRAY YOU, go to the nearest church, and bring me the cross, and hold it up level with my eyes until I am dead. I would have the cross on which God hung be ever before my eyes while life lasts in me.
Jesu, Jesus!
> Joan of Arc, 30 May 1431, at the stake, *Joan of Arc in Her Own Words*, 1996.

THE CITY is taken, and I am still alive!
> Emperor Constantine XI, 29 May 1453, before

plunging to his death in the midst of Turkish troops who were pouring through a breach in the walls of Constantinople, quoted in Lord Kinross, *The Ottoman Centuries*, 1979.

THE FLEETING pomp of the world is
like the green willow
. . . but at the end a sharp
axe destroys it, a north
wind fells it . . .
  King Nezahualcoyotl of Texcoco, 1472, quoted in Frances Gilmore, *Flute of the Smoking Mirror*, 1949.

PITY ME NOT: I die as a man of honour ought, in the discharge of my duty: they indeed are objects of pity who fight against their king, their country and their oath.
  God and my country!
  Pierre du Terrail, Chevalier de Bayard, 1524, to the Genoese rebel who offered him commiseration for his mortal wound; also 'Let me die facing the enemy'.

I KNEW what it was to trust to your false promises, Malinche; I knew that you had destined me to this fate, since I did not fall by my own hand when you entered my city of Tenochtitlan. Why do you slay me so unjustly? God will demand it of you!
  Emperor Cuahtémoc of the Aztecs, Lent 1525, just before Cortes had him hanged on trumped-up charges, quoted in William Prescott, *The History of the Conquest of Mexico*, 1843.

WHAT have I done, oh my children, that I should meet such a fate? And from your hands, too, you, who have met with friendship and kindness from my people, with whom I have shared my treasures, who have received nothing but benefits from my hands!
  Emperor Atahualpa of the Incas, 26 July 1533, just before Pizarro had him garrotted, quoted in William Prescott, *History of The Conquest of Peru*, 1847.

WHAT HO! traitors! have you come to kill me in my own house?
. . . Jesu!
  Francisco Pizarro, 26 June 1541, when the assassins broke into his house to murder him; he killed three before being overwhelmed, quoted in William Prescott, *History of the Conquest of Peru*, 1847.

IT HAS long been a question whether one can conscientiously hold property of Indian slaves. Since this point has not yet been determined, I enjoin it on my son Martin and his heirs that they spare no pains to come to an exact knowledge of the truth; as a matter which deeply concerns the conscience of each of them, no less than mine.
  Hernan Cortes, the final element of his will, which he executed shortly before his death on 2 December 1547 in Seville, quoted in William Prescott, *The History of the Conquest of Mexico*, 1843.

I HAVE enough, save thyself brother!
  Gustavus II Adolphus, 1632, to the Duke of Lauenberg as they were overtaken by Imperialist cavalry at the Battle of Lützen.

THEY DON'T want to listen to me when I'm alive, so why should they obey me when I'm dead.
  King John III of Poland (Jan Sobiewski), 1696.

I HAVE loved war too well.
  King Louis XIV of France, 1 September 1715.

THAT was once a man.
  The Duke of Marlborough, shortly before his death on 16 June 1722, 'One day he paced with failing steps the state rooms of his palace, and stood long and intently contemplating his portrait by Kneller. Then he turned away with the words above', quoted in Churchill, *Marlborough*, 1933.

NO, not quite naked; I shall have my uniform on. Herr Jesu, to Thee I live; Herr Jesu, to Thee I die: in life and death, Thou art my gain.
  King Frederick William I of Prussia, 1740, upon hearing the passage from the *Book of Job*, 'Naked I came into the world and naked shall I go.'

NOW GOD be praised, I will die in peace.
  Major-General James Wolfe, 13 September 1759, upon hearing that his forces had triumphed over the French at Quebec, quoted in Churchill, *A History of the English Speaking Peoples: The Age of Revolution*, 1957.

OH that I had served my Lord as faithfully as I have served my King.
  Major-General Louis-Joseph Marquis de Montcalm, 14 September 1759, the day after his defeat at the hands of Wolf on the Plains of Abraham outside Quebec, quoted in Parkman, *Montcalm and Wolfe*, 1884.

WE HAVE crossed the mountain; things will go better now.
  King Frederick the Great of Prussia, 17 August 1786, to the sun at his palace of Sans Souchi.

WAITING are they, waiting are they? Well, let 'em wait!
  Ethan Allen, 1789, upon being told that the angels were waiting for him.

GENOA . . . Battle . . . Forward!
  Field Marshal Aleksandr Suvorov, May 1800, quoted in Phillip Longworth, *The Art of Victory*, 1965.

I AM SATISFIED. Thank God, I have done my duty.
  Admiral Viscount Nelson, 21 October 1805, in the cockpit of HMS *Victory* as the Battle of Trafalgar waned and the British victory became apparent, quoted in Rober Southey, *The Life of Nelson*, 1813.

ARE the French beaten?
[When told yes] I hope the people of England

will be satisfied. I hope that my country will do me justice.
> Lieutenant-General Sir John Moore, 16 January 1809, to his surgeon after losing an arm to a cannon-ball at the Battle of Corunna in Portugal, quoted in Carola Oman, *Sir John Moore*, 1953.

NAPOLEON: "You will live, my friend:"
Lannes: "I trust I may, if I can still be of use to France and your Majesty."
> Marshal of France Jean Lannes, 21 May 1809, mortally wounded at Aspern-Essling.

GOOD GOD! To survive a hundred fields and die like this . . .
> Marshal of France Guillaume Marie Brunne, 1 August 1815, when about to be torn to pieces by a Royalist mob after Waterloo, quoted in R.F. Delderfield, *Napoleon's Marshals*, 1966.

SPARE the face, straight to the heart!
> Marshal of France Murat to his firing squad, 13 October 1815, quoted in R.F. Delderfield, *Napoleon's Marshals*, 1966.

SOLDIERS, when I give the command to fire, fire straight at my heart. Wait for the order. It will be my last to you. I protest against my condemnation. I have fought a hundred battles for France, and not one against her. . . . Soldiers, Fire!
> Marshal of France Michel Ney, after he had insisted on commanding his own firing squad, 7 December 1815, quoted in Raymond Horricks, *Marshal Ney: The Romance and the Real*, 1982.

NOSTITZ, you have learned many things from me. Now you are to learn how peacefully a man can die.
> Field Marshal Prince Gebhard von Blücher, 1819.

TÊTE d'Armée! (Head of the Army!)
> Napoleon, 5.30 pm, 5 May 1821, St. Helena.

HAU! You, too, Mbopa, son of Sitayi, you too, are killing me.
> Shaka Zulu, 1828, to one of his assassins, quoted in E.A. Ritter, *Shaka Zulu*, 1955.

LET US GO – let us go – this people don't want us in this land! Let's go, boys. Take my luggage on board the frigate.
> Simon Bolivar, 17 December 1830, after resigning in disillusionment as supreme chief of Columbia.

ORDER A.P. Hill to prepare for action! Pass the infantry to the front rapidly! Tell Major Hawks . . . (leaving the sentence unfinished he stopped, then a smile came over his face) Let us now cross over the river and rest under the shade of the trees.
> Lieutenant-General Thomas J. 'Stonewall' Jackson, 10 May 1863, quoted in John Selby, *Jackson As Military Commander*, 1968.

FORWARD MEN, forward for God's sake and drive those fellows out of those woods. . . .
> Major-General John Fulton Reynolds, 1 July 1863, while leading the Iron Brigade of his First Corps on the first day of the Battle of Gettysburg, quoted in Edward Coddington, *Gettysburg: A Study in Command*, 1968.

GIVE THEM the cold steel, men!
> Brigadier-General Lewis Armistead, 3 July 1863, as he climbed over the stone wall at Gettysburg, the 'high tide of the Confederacy'.

DOCTOR, I suppose I am going fast now. It will soon be over. But God's will be done. I hope I have fulfilled my destiny to my country and my duty to God. . . . I am resigned; God's will be done.
> Major-General James E.B. Stuart, 12 May 1864, as he lay dying from wounds suffered at Yellow Tavern, quoted in Douglas Southall Freeman, *Lee's Lieutenants*, 1944.

TELL A.P. Hill he must come up . . .
> General Robert E. Lee, 12 October 1870, quoted in Brigadier-General Fitzhugh Lee, *General Lee*, 1894.

NOW MARK THIS, if the Expeditionary Force, and I ask for no more than two hundred men, does not come in ten days, the town may fall; and I have done my best for the honour of our country. Goodbye.
> General Charles George Gordon, 14 December 1884, last diary entry while waiting for the relief of Khartoum.

I AM a great sufferer all the time . . . all that I can do is pray that the prayers of all these good people may be answered so far as to have us all meet in another and better world. I cannot speak even in a whisper.
> General Ulysses S. Grant, 23 July 1885, written as he lay dying of throat cancer.

LET ME GO! Let me go!
> Clara Barton, 12 April 1912, on her deathbed, quoted in Percy Epler, *The Life of Clara Barton*, 1915.

IT MUST COME to a fight. Only keep the right wing strong.
> Field Marshal Alfred Count von Schlieffen, 1913.

THIS I would say, standing as I do in view of God and Eternity: I realize that patriotism is not enough; I must have no hatred and bitterness towards anyone.
> Edith Cavell, 12 October 1915, to the chaplain attending her before her execution by German firing squad.

GENTLEMEN, the battle is done. The victory is ours!
> Admiral George Dewey, 1917.

DON'T you think I'll be back?
> Rittmeister Manfred Freiherr von Richthofen, the 'Red Baron', 21 April 1918, to his ground crew as he took off on his last mission.

HAVE YOU been dreaming about all this?
> Marshal of the Soviet Union N.T. Tukhachevskiy, early June 1937, to a fellow prisoner confessing to fantastic, trumpted-up charges during Stalin's Great Purges, quoted in Robert Conquest, *The Great Terror*, 1990.

LONG LIVE the Party! Long Live Stalin!
> General I.E. Yakir, as he was being led to the firing squad during Stalin's Great Purges, 11 June 1937, quoted in Robert Conquest, *The Great Terror*, 1990.

TO DIE by the hand of one's own people is hard.
> Field Marshal Erwin Rommel, 14 October 1944, to his son before he took the poison brought by Hitler's emissaries.

IT'S TOO DARK. . . . I mean too late.
> General George S. Patton, Jr., 21 December 1945, quoted in Carlo d'Este, *Patton: A Genius For War*, 1995.

I COULDN'T SLEEP last night – I had great difficulty. I can't have very long to go now. I've got to meet God – and explain all those men I killed at Alamein . . .
> Field Marshal Montgomery, among his last words, late February 1975, quoted in Nigel Hamilton, *Monty – the Last Years of the Field Marshal*, 1983.

THE LEADER

NOT WITHOUT fame, the men who rule in Lycia,
these kings of ours who eat fat cuts of lamb
and drink sweet wine, the finest stock we have.
But they owe it all to their own fighting strength –
our great men of war, they lead our way in battle.
> Homer, *The Iliad*, 12.369–373, c. 800 BC,
> tr. Robert Fagles, 1990.

THE LEADER must himself believe that willing obedience always beats forced obedience, and that he can get this only by really knowing what should be done. Thus he can secure obedience from his men because he can convince them that he knows best, precisely as a good doctor makes his patients obey him. Also he must be ready to suffer more hardships than he asks of his soldiers, more fatigue, greater extremes of heat and cold.
> Xenophon, *Cyropaedia*, c. 360 BC.

WHEN he was asked how someone might most surely earn people's esteem, he replied: "By the best words and the finest actions."
> Plutarch, quoting Agesilaus, Eurypontid King of Sparta (400–360 BC), *The Lives*, c. AD 100, (*Plutarch on Sparta*, tr. Richard Talbert, 1988).

AN ARMY of deer led by a lion is more to be feared than an army of lions led by a deer.
> Attributed to Chabrias (c. 420–357/6 BC) and to Philip of Macedon (382–336 BC).

A LEADER is a dealer in hope.
> Napoleon (1769–1821).

THE MORE the leader is in the habit of demanding from his men, the surer he will be that his demands will be answered.
> Major-General Carl von Clausewitz, *On War*, 1832, tr. Michael Howard and Peter Paret, 1976.

WHEN you join your organization you will find there a willing body of men who ask from you nothing more than the qualities that will command their respect, their loyalty, and their obedience.
> They are perfectly ready and eager to follow you so long as you can convince them that you have those qualities. When the time comes that they are satisfied you do not possess them you might as well kiss yourself goodbye. Your usefulness to that organization is at an end.
> Major C.A. Bach, 1917, farewell instructions to the graduating student officers, Fort Sheridan, Wyoming.

TO BE a highly successful leader in war four things are essential, assuming that you possess good common sense, have studied your profession and are physically strong.
> When conditions are difficult, the command depressed and everyone seems critical and pessimistic, you must be especially cheerful and optimistic.
> When evening comes and all are exhausted, hungry and possibly dispirited, particularly in unfavorable weather at the end of a march or in battle, you must put aside any thought of personal fatigue and display marked energy in looking after the comfort of your organization, inspecting your lines for tomorrow.
> Make a point of extreme loyalty, in thought and deed, to your chiefs personally; and in your efforts to carry out their plans or policies, the less you approve the more energy you must direct to their accomplishment.
> The more alarming and disquieting the reports received or the conditions viewed in battle, the more determined must be your attitude. Never ask for the relief of your unit and never hesitate to attack.
> I am certain in the belief that the average man who scrupulously follows this course of action is bound to win great success. Few seemed equal to it in this war, but I believe this was due to their failure to realize the importance of so governing their course.
> General of the Army George C. Marshall, 5 November 1920, letter to General John Mallory.

THE MORAL equilibrium of the man is tremendously affected by an outward calmness on the part of the leader. The soldier's nerves, taut from anxiety of what lies ahead, will be soothed and healed if the leader sets an example of coolness. Bewildered by the noise and confusion of battle, the man feels instinctively that

the situation cannot be so dangerous as it appears if he sees that his leader remains unaffected, that his orders are given clearly and deliberately, and that his tactics show decision and judgment. However "jumpy" the man feels, the inspiration of his leader's example shames him into swallowing his own fear. But if the leader reveals himself irresolute and confused, the more even than if he shows personal fear, the infection spreads instantly to his men. (July 1921.)
  Captain Sir Basil Liddell Hart, *Thoughts on War*, 1944.

TO BE a successful leader, a commander must not only gain contact with his men, but he must give them the impression of fearlessness.
  Major-General John A. Lejeune, *The Reminiscences of a Marine*, 1929.

WHAT, above all else, we look for in a leader is the power to dominate events, to leave his mark on them, and to assume responsibility for the consequences of his actions. The setting up of one man over his fellows can be justified only if he can bring to the common task the drive and certainty which comes of character. But why, for that matter, should a man be granted, free gratis and for nothing, the privilege of domination, the right to issue orders, the pride of seeing them obeyed, the thousand and one tokens of respect, unquestioning obedience, and loyalty which surround the seat of power? To him goes the greater part of the honor and glory. But that is fair enough, for he makes the best repayment that he can by shouldering risks. Obedience would be intolerable if he who demands it did not use it to produce effective results, and how can he do so if he does not possess the qualities of daring, decision, and intiative?
  General Charles de Gaulle, *The Edge of the Sword*, 1932.

THE REAL LEADER displays his quality in his triumphs over adversity, however great it may be.
  General of the Army George C. Marshall, 18 September 1941, address to the First Officer Candidate Class, Fort Benning, Georgia.

THE TRULY GREAT leader overcomes all difficulties, and campaigns and battles are nothing but a long series of difficulties to be overcome.
  General of the Army George C. Marshall, 18 September 1941, Fort Benning, Georgia.

NO MAN is a leader until his appointment is ratified in the minds and hearts of his men.
  Anonymous, *The Infantry Journal*, 1948.

A LEADER is a man who has the ability to get other people to do what they don't want to do, and like it.
  President Harry S. Truman, *Memoirs*, 1954.

THE GOOD military leader will dominate the events which surround him; once he lets events get the better of him he will lose the confidence of his men,

and when that happens he ceases to be of value as a leader.
  Field Marshal Viscount Montgomery of Alamein, *The Memoirs of Field Marshal Montgomery*, 1958.

WHEN ALL is said and done the leader must exercise an effective influence, and the degree to which he can do this will depend on the personality of the man – the "incandescence" of which he is capable, the flame which burns within him, the magnetism which will draw the hearts of other men toward him. What I personally would want to know about a leader is:
  Where is he going?
  Will he go all out?
  Has he the talents and equipment, including knowledge, experience and courage? Will he take decisions, accepting full responsibility for them, and take risks where necessary?
  Will he then delegate and decentralize, having first created an organization in which there are definite focal points of decision so that the master plan can be implemented smoothly and quickly?
  Field Marshal Viscount Montgomery of Alamein, *The Memoirs of Field Marshal Montgomery*, 1958.

A LEADER who doesn't hesitate before sending his nation into battle is not fit to be a leader.
  Golda Meir, *As Good as Golda*, 1970.

THE BEHAVIOR of a leader *in battle* is a distinct form of social behavior which has held a special place in the history of Western civilization and, indeed, in most other cultures as well. The role of Battle Leader possesses a special mystique and attendant value system. Combat officers are not viewed as merely another component of the larger societal technostructure that can be created cooky-cutter fashion from a training base little different from the Harvard Business School. The values, goals, and modes of action required of the combat officer are qualitively different from those associated with and expected from the commercial manager.
  Lieutenant-Colonel Richard Gabriel, *Crisis in Command*, 1978.

EVERY GREAT LEADER I have known has been a great teacher, able to give those around him a sense of perspective and to set the moral, social, and motivational climate among his followers.
  Admiral James B. Stockdale, 'Educating Leaders', *The Washington Quarterly*, 30 March 1983.

I'VE MADE the points that leaders under pressure must keep themselves absolutely clean morally (the relativism of the social sciences will never do). They must lead by example, must be able to implant high-mindedness in their followers, must have competence beyond status, and must have earned their followers' respect by demonstrating integrity.
  Admiral James B. Stockdale, 'Machiavelli, Management, and Moral Leadership', *Military Ethics*, 1987.

A LEADER establishes the ethical . . . environment in which the entire operation is going to be accomplished.

> General H. Norman Schwarzkopf, 1991, quoted in Peter David, *Triumph in the Desert*, 1991.

LET ME REPEAT – I have commanded everything it is possible to command, and I know that as a leader, it is simply impossible to please everybody.

> General Aleksandr I. Lebed, *Literaturnaya Gazeta* (Moscow), 17 May 1995.

I INVENTED the following formula: if a lion leads lions, victory is guaranteed; if a lion leads donkeys, the chances of success are fifty-fifty; but if a donkey leads lions, there is no hope.

> General Aleksandr I. Lebed, *El Pais* (Madrid), 15 March 1998.

THERE ARE three types of leaders: Those who make things happen; those that watch things happen; and those who wonder what happened!

> American military saying.

LEADERSHIP

THERE IS no command without leadership.

> Sun Bin, *The Lost Art of War*, c. 350 BC, tr. Thomas Cleary.

THE REAL SECRET of leadership in battle is the domination of the mass by a single personality. Influence over subordinates is a matter of suggestion. Discipline acquired during peace and the power of personal example are both used to exact great sacrifices.

> *General der Infantrie* Hugo Baron von Freytag-Loringhoven, *The Power of Personality in War*, 1911, tr. Spaulding, 1938.

THE QUALITY of leadership needs, above all, spirit, intelligence, and sympathy. Spirit is needed to fire men to self-sacrificing achievements; intelligence, because men will only respect and follow a leader whom they feel knows his profession thoroughly; sympathy, to understand the mentality of each individual in order to draw out the best that is in him. Given these qualities, men will conquer fear to follow a leader. (July 1921.)

> Captain Sir Basil Liddell Hart, *Thoughts on War*, 1944.

AT FIRST PUSH one would scarcely expect to find the behavior of a piece of cooked spaghetti an illustration of successful leadership in combat. . . . it scarcely takes demonstration to prove how vastly more easy it is to PULL a piece of cooked spaghetti in a given direction along a major axis than it is to PUSH it in the same direction. Further, the difficulty increases with the size of either the spaghetti or the command. . . .

> General George S. Patton, Jr., January 1928, *The Patton Papers*, I, 1972.

. . . WE WOULD HAVE responded more readily to the exercise of leadership than to a system based chiefly on compulsion.

> Major-General John A. Lejeune, on the U.S. Naval Academy of the 1880s, *Reminiscences of a Marine*, 1929.

FOR TEN YEARS I had burrowed into the essence of the work of leadership, the element – as Clausewitz says – of danger, the element of uncertainty, finally, as I put it, the element of eternal contradictions, which are not to be solved, but are cut like the Gordian knot by the sword of decision, the sword of command.

> Marshal Joseph Pilsudski, *The Memoirs of a Polish Revolutionary and Soldier*, 1931.

LEADERSHIP in war is an art, a free creative activity based on a foundation of knowledge. The greatest demands are made on the personality.

> Generals Werner von Fritsch and Ludwig Beck, *Troop Leadership*, 1933.

MUCH of what I have said has been by way of repetition of one thought which I wish you gentlemen to carry with you to your new duties. You will be responsible for a unit in the Army of the United States in this great emergency. Its quality, its discipline, its training will depend on your leadership. Whatever deficiencies there are must be charged to your failure or incapacity. Remember this: The truly great leader overcomes all difficulties, and campaigns and battles are nothing but a long series of difficulties to be overcome. The lack of equipment, the lack of food, the lack of this or that are only excuses; the real leader displays his quality in his triumphs over adversity, however great it may be.

> General of the Army George C. Marshall, 27 September 1941, address to the first graduates of the U.S. Army's Officer Candidate Schools, subsequently published in *The Army and Navy Register*, 4 October 1941.

LET US set up a standard around which the brave and loyal can rally.

> Sir Winston S. Churchill (1874–1965).

A FEW MEN had the stuff of leadership in them, they were like rafts to which all the rest of humanity clung for support and hope.

> Baron Charles MacMoran Wilson Moran, 12 May 1943, preface to *The Anatomy of Courage*, 1945.

LEADERSHIP in conference, even with subordinates, is as important as on the battlefield.

> General of the Army George C. Marshall, quoted in Forrest C. Pogue, *General George C. Marshall: Ordeal and Hope, 1939–1942*, 1965.

WAR is much too brutal a business to have room for brutal leading; in the end, its only effect can be to corrode the character of men, and when character is lost, all is lost. The bully and the sadist serve only to further encumber an army; their subordinates must waste precious time clearing away the wreckage that they make. The good company has no place for an officer who would rather be right than loved, for the time will quickly come when he walks alone, and in battle no man may succeed in solitude.

Brigadier-General S.L.A. Marshall, *Men Against Fire*, 1947.

IN THE British Army there are no good units and no bad units – only good and bad officers and NCOs. They make or break the unit. Today we cannot afford anything but the good ones. No man can be given a more honourable task than to lead his fellow countrymen in war. We, the officers and NCOs, owe it to the men we command and to our country that we make ourselves fit to lead the best soldiers in the world, that in peace the training we give them is practical, alive and purposeful, and that in war our leadership is wise, resolute and unselfish.

Leaders are made more often than they are born. You all have leadership in you. Develop it by thought, by training and by practice. . . .

Field Marshal Viscount Slim of Burma, 1949, Foreword to the first edition of the *British Army Journal*, later renamed *British Army Review*.

I HAVE BEEN very lucky in my service. In getting on for forty years I have commanded everything from a squad of six men to an Army Group of a million and a quarter, and, believe me, whether you command ten men or ten million, the essentials of leadership are the same. Leadership is that mixture of example, persuasion and compulsion which makes men do what you want them to do. If I were asked to define leadership, I should say it is the Projection of Personality. It is the most intensely personal thing in the world, because it is just plain you.

Field Marshal Viscount Slim of Burma, *Courage and Other Broadcasts*, 1957.

HERD-PSYCHOLOGY is a slightly different problem. Any schoolmaster can deal with an individual, few of them can manage a rebellious class. The test of statesmanship and leadership is ability to gauge and master mass- and mob-psychology. The hallmark of leadership is to comprehend the purpose of a crowd, its ingredients, its strength, its ability to achieve its object, its cohesive cement, its impetus and above all to search out its leadership.

Colonel Richard Meinertzhagen, *Army Diary 1899–1925*, 1960.

LEADERSHIP can be taught, but not character. The one arises from the other. A successful leader of men must have character, ability and be prepared to take unlimited responsibility. Responsibility can only be learned by taking responsibility; you cannot learn the piano without playing on one. Leadership is the practical application of character. it implies the ability to command and to make obedience proud and free.

One of the questions demanded by the War Office before 1914 of officers recommended for the Staff College was: Does this officer give commands in a manner likely to secure cheerful obedience? My Commanding Officer – Du Maurier, whose habits were slightly unorthodox – replied: "I do not know if this officer's orders would be cheerfully obeyed, but I can guarantee that they would be carried out."

The War Office were satisfied.

Colonel Richard Meinertzhagen, *Army Diary 1899–1925*, 1960.

LEADERSHIP and learning are indispensable to each other.

President John F. Kennedy, 22 November 1963, remark prepared for delivery at the Trade Mart in Dallas.

I HOLD that leadership is not a science, but an art. It conceives an ideal, states it as an objective, and then seeks actively and earnestly to attain it, everlastingly persevering, because the records of war are full of successes coming to those leaders who stuck it out just a little longer than their opponents.

General Matthew B. Ridgway, 'Leadership', *Military Review*, 9/1966.

ONE OF MY cardinal rules of battle leadership – or leadership in any field – is to be yourself, to strive to apply the basic principles of the art of war, and to seek to accomplish your assigned missions by your own methods and in your own way.

General Matthew B. Ridgway, *The Korean War*, 1967.

ONE FINAL ASPECT of leadership is the frequent necessity to be a philosopher, able to understand and to explain the lack of a moral economy in this universe, for many people have a great deal of difficulty with the fact that virtue is not always rewarded nor is evil always punished. To handle tragedy may indeed be the mark of an educated man, for one of the principal goals of education is to prepare us for failure. To say that is not to encourage resignation to the whims of fate, but to acknowledge the need for forethought about how to cope with undeserved reverses. It's important that our leadership steel themselves against the natural reaction of lashing out or withdrawing when it happens. The test of character is not "hanging in there" when the light at the end of the tunnel is expected but performance of duty and persistence of example when the situation rules out the possibility of the light ever coming.

Admiral James B. Stockdale, *Naval War College Review*, July–August 1979.

LEADERSHIP must be based on goodwill. Goodwill does not mean posturing and, least of all, pandering to the mob. It means obvious and wholehearted commitment to helping followers. We are tired of leaders we fear, tired of leaders we love, and most tired of leaders who let us take liberties with them. What we need for leaders are men of the heart who are so helpful that they, in effect, do away with the need of their jobs. But leaders like that are never out of a job, never out of followers. Strange as it sounds, great leaders gain authority by giving it away.

> Admiral James B. Stockdale, 'Machiavelli, Management, and Moral Leadership', *Military Ethics*, 1987.

WE NEVER lost sight of the reality that people, particularly gifted commanders, are what make units succeed. The way I like to put it, leadership is the art of accomplishing more than the science of management says is possible.

> General Colin Powell, *My American Journey*, 1995.

WHEN LEADERSHIP fails, sometimes a fundamental shift overtakes a unit, or a military service, or a nation, that is so profound that it can change an entire ethos. Most often it occurs gradually, not because of decisions taken by senior leaders so much as from their inaction, an acquiescence to insistent, incremental pressures generated from the outside. Usually, the leaders, reacting to and sometimes overwhelmed by these pressures, are the ones who comprehend the changes the least, and in some cases can not perceive what has happened until it is too late for them to protect even their own legacy.

> James H. Webb, Jr., 'The Silence of the Admirals', *Proceedings*, 1/1999.

LOGISTICS

MASTER SUN said: "A city might have walls of iron and be surrounded by moats of boiling water, but if it is inadequately provisioned, even a Chiang T'ai-kung or a Mo Ti would be unable to defend it."

> Sun Tzu, c. 500 BC, a passage recovered from later works not found in *The Art of War*, quoted in *Sun Tzu: The Art of Warfare*, tr. Roger Ames, 1993.

WITHOUT supplies neither a general nor a soldier is good for anything.

> Clearchus, 401 BC, speech to the Ten Thousand, quoted in Xenophon, *Anabasis*, 1.3, c. 360 BC (*The Persian Expedition*, tr. Rex Warner, 1949).

ON THE third day of his campaign Philip arrived at Onocarsis, a place in Thrace with a beautifully prepared grove; it was in every regard a pleasant place to spend time, especially in summer. He was going to camp in this beautiful area, but he learned that there was no feed for the animals.

"What kind of life are we leading," he said, "if we have to live at the pleasure of an ass?"

> King Philip II of Macedon, quoted in Alfred S. Bradford, *Philip II of Macedon: A Life from the Ancient Sources*, 1992.

AN ARMY cannot preserve good order unless its

soldiers have meat in their bellies, coats on their backs and shoes on their feet.

> The Duke of Marlborough, 1703, letter to Colonel Cadogan.

WITHOUT SUPPLIES no army is brave.

> Frederick the Great, *Instructions to his Generals*, 1747, tr. Phillips, 1940.

THE TROOPS will have observed the extreme difficulty of supplying them with bread in this part of the country, and the necessity that exists, that they should take care of that which is issued to them, and make it last for the time specified in General Orders; for want of attention to this object, and care of their bread, the best operations are necessarily relinquished.

> The Duke of Wellington, 17 May 1809, at Ruivaes in Portugal, *Selections from the General Orders of Field Marshal the Duke of Wellington During His Various Commands*, 1847.

THE MERE READINESS of the troops is nothing in comparison with the preparations required for the departments of the Service [logistics].

> The Duke of Wellington, quoted in Arthur Bryant, *The Great Duke*, 1972.

THERE IS no subordination with empty stomachs.

> Napoleon, quoted in Emmanuel Las Casas, *Mémorial de St. Hélène*, 1816.

AN ARMY marches on its stomach.

> Napoleon; source cited in *Oxford Dictionary of Quotations* as 'anonymous' and also attributed 'to Napoleon in *Windsor Magazine*, 1904, p. 268; probably condensed from a long passage in Las Casas . . .' (see quotation above).

THE WHOLE of military activity must relate directly or indirectly to the engagement. The end for which a soldier is recruited, clothed, armed, and trained, the whole object of his sleeping, eating, drinking, and marching is simply that he should fight at the right place and the right time.

> Major-General Carl von Clausewitz, *On War*, 1.2, 1832, tr. Michael Howard and Peter Paret, 1976.

THE "FEEDING" of an army is a matter of the most vital. One of the most effective ways of impeding the march of an army is by cutting off its supplies; and this is just as legitimate as to attack in line of battle.

> Colonel John S. Mosby, *Mosby's War Reminiscences*, 1887.

VICTORY is the beautiful, bright-colored flower. Transport is the stem without which it never could have blossomed.

> Sir Winston S. Churchill, *The River War*, 1899.

FUEL stands first in importance of the resources of the fleet. Without ammunition, a ship may run away,

hoping to fight another day but without fuel she can neither run, nor reach her station, nor remain on it, if remote, nor fight.
  Admiral Alfred Thayer Mahan (1840–1914).

CONTEMPORARY armies possess colossal vitality. Even the achievement of the utter defeat of the opponent at a definite moment does not assure the final victory so long as there is, behind the defeated units, a rear which is economically and morally strong. Given the presence of time and space which permit a new mobilization of human and material resources which are needed for the restoration of the fighting capacity of the army, such defeated units may reestablish the front and carry the struggle forward with hope of success.
  Mikhail V. Frunze (1885–1925).

MOBILITY is the true test of a supply system.
  Captain Sir Basil Liddell Hart, *Thoughts on War*, 1944.

THE HISTORY of war proves that nine out of ten times an army has been destroyed because its supply lines have been cut off. . . . We shall land at Inchon, and I shall crush them.
  General of the Army Douglas MacArthur, quoted in Roy Appleton, *South to the Naktong, North to the Yalu: The United States in the Korean War*, 1961.

GOOD LOGISTICS is combat power.
  Lieutenant-General William G. Pagonis, *Moving Mountains*, 1992.

LOGISITICS AND GENERALSHIP

THE COMMANDER who fails to provide his army with necessary food and other supplies is making arrangements for his own defeat, even with no enemy present.
  The Emperor Maurice, *The Strategikon*, c. AD 600 (*Maurice's Strategikon*, tr. George Dennis, 1984).

WHEN THE Duke of Cumberland has weakened his army sufficiently, I shall teach him that a general's first duty is to provide for its welfare.
  Field Marshal Maurice Comte de Saxe, 1747, before Laufeld.

UNDERSTAND that the foundation of an army is the belly. It is necessary to procure nourishment for the soldier wherever you assemble him and wherever you wish to conduct him. This is the primary duty of a general.
  Frederick the Great, *Instructions to His Generals*, 1747, tr. Phillips, 1940.

WHAT I WANT to avoid is that my supplies should command me.
  Field Marshal Francois Comte de Guibert, *Essai Général de la Tactique*, 1770.

IN ALL his letters General Marmont is always referring to the commissariat. I repeat that in a war of invasion and of rapid movements which the Emperor is waging there can be no depots, and the generals in command must themselves see to it that they procure the necessary supplies from the countries which they traverse.
  Marshal Berthier, 11 October 1805, letter to General Marmont during the Austrian campaign, quoted in S.J. Watson, *By Command of the Emperor*, 1957.

IT IS very necessary to attend to all this detail and to trace a biscuit from Lisbon into a man's mouth on the frontier and to provide for its removal from place to place by land or by water, or no military operations can be carried out.
  The Duke of Wellington, 1811, *The Dispatches of Field Marshal the Duke of Wellington During His Various Campaigns in India, Denmark, Portugal, Spain, the Low Countries, and France*, VII, 1834–1838, p. 406.

WHAT MAKES the general's task so difficult is the necessity of feeding so many men and animals. If he allows himself to be guided by the supply officers he will never move and his expedition will fail.
  Napoleon, *Maxims of War*, 1831.

THE "FEEDING" of an army is a matter of the most vital importance, and demands the earliest attention of the general intrusted with a campaign. To be strong, healthy, and capable of the largest measure of physical effort, the soldier needs about three pounds gross of food per day, and the horse or mule about twenty pounds. When a general first estimates the quantity of food and forage needed for any army of fifty to one hundred thousand men, he is apt to be dismayed, and here a good staff is indispensable, though the general cannot throw off on them the responsibility. He must give the subject his personal attention, for the army reposes in him alone, and should never doubt the fact that their existence overrides in importance all other considerations. Once satisfied of this, and that all has been done that can be, the soldiers are always willing to bear the largest measure of privation.
  General of the Army William T. Sherman, *Memoirs of General W.T. Sherman*, 1875,

I BELIEVE that the task of bringing the force to the fighting point, properly equipped and well-formed in all that it needs is at least as important as the capable leading of the force in the fight itself. . . . In fact it is indispensable and the combat between hostile forces is more in the preparation than the fight.
  General Sir John Monash (1865–1931), quoted in Horner, *The Commanders*, 1984.

THE MORE I SEE of war, the less I think that general principles of strategy count as compared with administrative problems and the gaining of intelligence. The main principles of strategy, e.g., to attack the other fellow in the flank or rear in preference to the front, to surprise him by any means in one's power and to attack his morale before you attack him physically are really things that every savage schoolboy knows. But it is often outside the power of the general to act as he would have liked owing to lack of adequate resources and I think that military history very seldom brings this out, in fact, it is almost impossible that it should do so without a detailed study which is often unavailable. For instance, if Hannibal had another twenty elephants, it might have altered his whole strategy against Italy.

> Field Marshal Viscount Wavell of Cyrenaica, 1942, letter to Liddell Hart.

[LOGISTICS] . . . the crux of generalship – superior even to tactical skill.

> Field Marshal Viscount Wavell of Cyrenaica (1883–1950).

MANY GENERALS have failed in war because they neglected to ensure that what they wanted to achieve operationally was commensurate with their administrative resources; and some have failed because they over-insured in this respect. The lesson is, there must always be a nice balance between the two requirements.

> Field Marshal Viscount Montgomery of Alamein, *The Memoirs of Field Marshal Montgomery*, 1958.

LOGISTICIANS

NOBODY ever heard of a quartermaster in history.

> Major-General Nathaniel Greene, 1778, letter to General George Washington upon receiving his appointment as Quartermaster General of the Continental Army.

I HAVE PREVAILED upon Lord Clive to appoint a Commissary of Stores . . . Matters can now be brought into some shape and we shall know what we are about, instead of trusting to the vague calculations of a parcel of blockheads who know nothing and have no data.

> The Duke of Wellington, 28 and 31 October 1798, in India to his brother, Sir Henry Wellesley, *Supplementary Despatches, Correspondence, and Memoranda of Field Marshal Arthur Duke of Wellington, K.G., 1794–1818*, I, 1858, pp. 124, 84, quoted in Elizabeth Longford, Wellington: The Years of the Sword, 1969.

EVERY MAN of you should be mentioned by name, soldiers of Verdun, soldiers in the line and soldiers in the rear. For if I give the place of honor, as is meet, to those who fell in the front of the battle, still I know that their courage would have availed nothing without the patient toil, continued day and night, to the last limit of their strength, on the part of the men to whose efforts were due the regular arrival of the reinforcements, of munitions, and of food, and the evacuation of wounded: the truck drivers along the Sacred Way, the railroad engineers, the ambulance force.

> Marshal of France Henri-Phillipe Pétain, 1927, at the dedication of the Ossuaire at Verdun, *Verdun*, 1930.

AN ADEQUATE supply system and stocks of weapons, petrol and ammunition are essential conditions for any army to be able to stand successfully the strain of battle. Before the fighting proper, the battle is fought and decided by the Quartermasters.

> Field Marshal Erwin Rommel, quoted in Archibald Wavell, *Soldiers and Soldiering*, 1953.

LOOTING/PILLAGE/PLUNDER/RAPINE

THEN HIS MAJESTY prevailed against them at the head of his army, and when they saw his majesty prevailing against them they fled headlong to Megiddo in fear, abandoning their horses and their chariots of gold and silver. . . . Now, if only the army of his majesty had not given their heart to plundering the things of the enemy, they would have captured Megiddo at this moment when the wretched foes of Kadesh and the wretched foe of this city were hauled up in haste to bring them into this city.

> Pharaoh Thutmose III, 1439 BC, at the Battle of Megiddo, quoted in James Breasted, *Ancient Records of Egypt*, 1906.

IT IS sometimes to your interest to give the enemy rein, and to allow him to lay waste as much of the land as he wishes, where, while plundering and laden with spoil, he will easily suffer punishment at your hands. For in this way all that has been taken would be recovered, and those who had done the damage would receive their just deserts.

> Aeneas Tacticus, *On the Defence of Fortified Positions*, 356 BC (*Aeneas Tacticus, Aclepiodotus, Onasander*, tr. The Illinois Greek Club, 1923).

OUR SOLDIERS must be restrained from plundering. Otherwise while they are scattered about doing this, the enemy army might reform and attack them.

> The Emperor Maurice, *The Strategikon*, c. AD 600 (*Maurice's Strategikon*, tr. George Dennis, 1984).

THE CITY and the buildings are mine; but I resign to your valour the captives and the spoil, the treasures of gold and beauty; be rich and be happy. Many are the provinces of my empire: the intrepid soldier who first ascends the walls of Constantinople shall be rewarded with the government of the fairest and most wealthy; and my gratitude shall accumulate his honours and fortunes above all measure of his own hopes.

> Mehmed II, exhortation to his army at the beginning of the siege of Constantinople (1453), quoted in Gibbon, *The Decline and Fall of the Roman Empire*, III, 1776–1788.

DO YOU THINK my men are nuns?

> General Count Johann Tilly, 1621, to the complaints of the rapine committed by his Imperialist troops, quoted in Theodore Ayrault Dodge, *Gustavus Adolphus*, 1895.

GOD be my witness, you are yourselves the destroyers, wasters and spoilers of your Fatherland. My heart is sickened when I look at you.

Gustavus II Adolphus, King of Sweden, September 1632, to the officers of his German Protestant allies who had stolen cattle during his invasion of Bavaria.

I FEAR the Turkish Army less than their camp.

Field Marshal Prince Eugene, quoted in Chandler, *Atlas of Military Strategy*, 1980; referring to the breakdown in discipline that would occur in the looting of the Turkish camp.

IT IS our business to give protection, and support, to the poor, distressed inhabitants; not to multiply and increase their calamities.

General George Washington, 21 January 1777, General Orders, *The Writings of George Washington*, VII, p. 47, John C. Fitzgerald, ed., 1932.

NO OFFICER of the army can appropriate any object unless authorized by the general-in-chief. The general-in-chief directs me to point out to you that it is an army on the march, not a horder of pillagers. Establish order and maintain discipline.

Marshal Berthier, 5 February 1797, order to General Victor whose corps was on the march to Rome through the Papal States, quoted in S.J. Watson, *By Command of the Emperor: A Life of Marshal Berthier*, 1957.

FIRE authorizes looting, which the soldier permits himself in order to save the rest from the remnants of the fire.

Napoleon, 20 September 1812, letter to Tsar Aleksandr I complaining of the burning of Moscow by incendiaries, *Correspondance de Napoléon Ier, publiée par ordre de l'Empereur Napoléon III*, XXIV, 19213, 1858–1870.

WE STARTED with the army in the highest order, and up to the day of battle nothing could get on better; but that event has, as usual, totally annihilated all order and discipline. The soldiers of the army have got among them about a million sterling in money . . . the night of the battle, instead of being passed in getting rest and food to prepare them for the pursuit of the following day, was passed by the soldiers in looking for plunder. The consequence was, that they were totally knocked up . . . This is the consequence of the state of discipline of the British army. We may gain the greatest victories; but we shall do no good until we shall so far alter our system, as to force all ranks to perform their duty. The new regiments are, as usual, the worst of all.

The Duke of Wellington, 29 June 1813, to Bathurst after the Battle of Vittoria, *The Dispatches of Field Marshal the Duke of Wellington During His Various Campaigns in India, Denmark, Portugal, Spain, the Low Countries, and France*, X, 1834–1838, p. 473.

I DO NOT CARE whether I command a large or a small army; but large or small, I will be obeyed and I will not suffer pillage.

The Duke of Wellington, early 1814, during the invasion of southern France when he suppressed looting by his army by frequent hangings in an effort to win the good will of the population, quoted in Arthur Bryant, *The Great Duke*, 1972.

. . . BUT AFTER three hours [having promised his soldiers the pillage of Pavia for 24 hours], I could bear it no longer, and I put an end to it. I had but 1200 men . . . the cries of the populace which reached my ears prevailed. If there had been 20,000 soldiers, their numbers would have drowned the complaints of the people, and I should have heard nothing of it. Happily, however, policy and morality are equally opposed to the system of pillage. I have meditated much on this subject: and have often been urged to gratify my soldiers in this manner. But nothing is so certain to disorganize and completely ruin an army. A soldier loses all discipline as soon as he gets an opportunity to pillage; and, if by pillage he enriches himself, he immediately becomes a bad soldier, and will not fight.

Napoleon, 1 July 1816, conversation with Count Emmanuel Las Casas on St. Helena, *The Life, Exile, and Conversations of the Emperor Napoleon*, II, 1890.

DISREPUTE having been brought upon our brave soldiers by the bad conduct of some of their numbers, showing on all occasions, when marching through territory occupied by sympathizers of the enemy, a total disregard of rights of citizens, and being guilty of wanton destruction of private property the Genl. commanding, desires and intends to enforce a change in this respect.

Interpreting Confiscation Acts by troops themselves, has a demoralizing effect, weakens them in exact proportion to the demoralization and makes open and armed enemies of many who, from opposite treatment would become friends or at worst non-combatants.

It is ordered, therefore, that the severest punishment, be inflicted upon every soldier, who is guilty of taking or destroying private property, and any commissioned officer guilty of like conduct, or of countenancing it shall be deprived of his sword and expelled from the camp, not to be permitted to return.

General Ulysses S. Grant, General Order No. 3, 13 January 1862, Head Quarters District of Cairo.

AH, GENERAL HOOD, when you Texans come about the chickens have to roost mighty high.

General Robert E. Lee, to General John B. Hood when he commanded the Texas Brigade, *Advance and Retreat*, 1880.

THE COMMANDING GENERAL considers that no greater disgrace could befall the army, and through it our whole people, than the perpetration of the barbarous outrages upon the unarmed, and defenceless and the wanton destruction of private property that have marked the course of the enemy in our own country.

Such proceedings not only degrade the perpetrators and all connected with them, but are subversive of the discipline and efficiency of the army, and destructive of the ends of our present movement.

It must be remembered that we make war only upon armed men, and that we cannot take vengeance for the wrongs our people have suffered without lowering ourselves in the eyes of all whose abhorrence has been excited by the atrocities of our enemies, and offending against Him to whom vengeance belongeth, without whose favor and support our efforts must all prove in vain.

The commanding general therefore earnestly exhorts the troops to abstain with most scrupulous care from unnecessary or wanton injury to private property, and he enjoins upon all officers to arrest and bring to summary punishment all who shall in any way offend against the orders on this subject.

> General Robert E. Lee, General Order No. 73, issued at Chambersburg, Pennsylvania, 27 June 1863, during the Gettysburg campaign, *The Wartime Papers of Robert E. Lee*, 1961.

INSULT to a soldier does not justify pillage, but it takes from the officer the disposition he would otherwise feel to follow up the inquiry and punish the wrong-doers.

> General of the Army William T. Sherman, letter to the editor of the *Bulletin*, 21 September 1862, *Memoirs*, I, 1875.

SHERMAN was right behind us with an army, an army that was no respecter of ducks, chickens, pigs, or turkeys, for they used to say of one particular regiment in Sherman's corps that it could catch, scrape, and skin a hog without a soldier leaving the ranks.

> Admiral David D. Porter, *Incidents and Anecdotes of the Civil War*, 1885.

THERE WAS only one serious feature. The success had not been as complete as it might have been, because a good division, instead of pressing on, stopped to go through an enemy supply depot.

> General Erich Ludendorff, of the breakdown in discipline among hungry German troops during the 1918 *Friedenstürm*, *My War Memories 1914–1918*, 1919.

WAR looses violence and disorder; it inflames passions and makes it relatively easy for the individual to get away with unlawful actions. But it does not lessen the gravity of the offense or make it less necessary that constituted authority put him down. The main safeguard against lawlessness and hooliganism in any armed body is the integrity of the officers. When men know that their commander is absolutely opposed to such excesses, and will take forceful action to repress any breach of discipline, they will conform. But when an officer winks at any

depradation by his men, it is no different than if he had committed the act.

> Brigadier-General S.L.A. Marshall, *The Armed Forces Officer*, 1950.

I WAS AFRAID that our wonderful captures of the last few weeks would tempt some of our Europeans to help themselves to things improperly, and I took advantage of the occasion to point out the evils of such behaviour. It must not be forgotten that war booty belongs to the State, and that the individual soldier has to notify superiors if he happens to want any particular object he has captured. An estimate is then made of the value of the object and he has to pay the amount. It was important for me to maintain the *morale* of our troops unconditionally if I was to be able to appeal to their sense of honour and make calls on their endurance.

> Major-General Paul von Lettow-Vorbeck, *East African Campaigns*, 1957.

THEFT is a crime no matter where or from whom. It is often from small beginnings that the rot sets in: a soldier "lifts" a few oranges from an orchard and gets away with it; an officer, held in the highest esteem, takes a revolver as booty from the enemy, carries off a few "finds" from an historic site, or in supposedly innocent mischief sends his wife a souvenir "from a house in occupied territory" or "found on an infiltrator". In this way the dam of army morals is burst asunder and the officer is powerless to prevent the spread of corruption to which he has himself succumbed. No distinction can be drawn here between the penny and the pound; petty or large-scale, crime can be called by no other name. No commander can demand discipline and honesty from his men if he himself does not serve as an example. And plainly the higher the rank the graver the crime – and the more rigorous punishment there must be.

> General Yigal Allon, *The Making of Israel's Army*, 1970.

LOYALTY

THOSE WHO WOULD be military leaders must have loyal hearts, eyes and ears, claws and fangs. Without people loyal to them, they are like someone walking at night, not knowing where to step. Without eyes and ears, they are as though in the dark, not knowing where to proceed. Without claws and fangs, they are like hungry men eating poisoned food, inevitably they die. . . . Therefore good generals always have intelligent and learned associates for their advisors, thoughtful and careful associates for their eyes and ears, brave and formidable associates for their claws and fangs.

> Zhuge Liang (AD 180–234), *The Way of the General*, (*Mastering the Art of War*, tr. Thomas Cleary, 1989).

IN ALL the military works it is written: To train samurai to be loyal separate them when young, or treat them according to their character. But it is no use to train them according to any fixed plan, they must be educated by benevolence. If the superior loves benevolence then the inferior will love his duty.

> Tokugawa Ieyasu (1543–1616), quoted in A.L. Sadler, *The Maker of Modern Japan: The Life of Tokugawa Ieyasu*, 1937.

THIS FAITH gave you victory at Shiloh and Vicksburg. Also, when you have completed your best preparations, you go into battle without hesitation as at Chattanooga – no doubts, no reserve; and, I tell you that it was this that made us act with confidence. I knew wherever I was that you thought of me and if I got into a tight place you would come, if alive.

> General of the Army William T. Sherman, 10 March 1864, near Memphis, letter to General Grant.

. . . A MONSTROUS THEORY, viz., that a regimental officer who is the only officer present with a party of soldiers actually and seriously engaged with the enemy can, under any pretext whatever, be justified in deserting them . . . The more helpless the position in which an officer finds his men, the more it is his bounden duty to stay and share their fortune, whether for good or ill.

> Field Marshal Sir Garnet Wolseley (1833–1913), quoted in Donald Morris, *The Washing of the Spears*, 1968.

LOYALTY is the marrow of honor.

> Field Marshal Paul von Hindenburg, *Out of My Life*, 1920.

A GOOD OFFICER ought to recognize that there is a higher loyalty than that to his immediate superiors – loyalty to the army and the nation. In action his first aim should be to prove a faithful subordinate, but in reflection he should maintain his critical sense. For that "criticism is the life-blood of science" is a greater truth than the idea, prevalent among weak-minded superiors, that it is a breach of discipline. (Dec. 1926.)

> Captain Sir Basil Liddell Hart, *Thoughts on War*, 1944.

MAN has two supreme loyalties – to country and to family. With most men the second, being more personal, is the stronger. So long as their families are safe they will defend their country, believing that by their sacrifice they are safeguarding their families also. But even the bonds of patriotism, discipline, and comradeship are loosened when the familiy is threatened. The soldier feels instinctively that if he was at home he could at least fight for the immediate protection of his family, work to gain food for it, and, at worst, die with it. But when the enemy is closer than he is, the danger and his fears are magnified by his remoteness. Every letter, every rumour is a strain on his nerves and on his sense of duty.

Hence the deadliest form of strategy in a war between nations is that which sets the two loyalties in opposition and so imposes a breaking strain on the will of the soldier. This "tug of war" in the soldier's mind can be created by giving a deeper sense and wider scope to the military idea of the "rear attack" – by developing it into an attack against the rear of a people, not merely of an army. (April 1929.)

> Captain Sir Basil Liddell Hart, *Thoughts on War*, 1944.

THOSE WHO ARE naturally loyal say little about it, and are ready to assume it in others. In contrast, the type of soldier who is always dwelling on the importance of "loyalty" usually means loyalty to his own interests. (Sept. 1932.)

> Captain Sir Basil Liddell Hart, *Thoughts on War*, 1944.

AN OFFICER . . . should make it a cardinal principle of life that by no act of commission or omission on his part will he permit his immediate superior to make a mistake.

> General Malin Craig, 12 June 1937, address to the graduating class of West Point.

WE LEARN from history that those who are disloyal to their own superiors are most prone to preach loyalty to their subordinates. Loyalty is a noble quality, so long as it is not blind and does not exclude the higher loyalty to truth and decency. But the word is much abused. For "loyalty," analyzed, is too often a polite word for what would be more accurately described as "a conspiracy for mutual inefficiency." In this sense it is essentially selfish. . . . "loyalty" is not a quality we can isolate – so far as it is real, and of intrinsic value, it is implicit in the possession of other virtues.

> Captain Sir Basil Liddell Hart, *Through the Fog of War*, 1938.

THERE IS a great deal of talk about loyalty from the bottom to the top. Loyalty from the top down is even more necessary and much less prevalent.

> General George S. Patton, Jr., *War As I Knew It*, 1947.

LOYALTY is the big thing, the greatest battle asset of all. But no man ever wins the loyalty of troops by preaching loyalty. It is given him by them as he proves his possession of the other virtues. The doctrine of a blind loyalty to leadership is a selfish and futile military dogma except in so far as it is ennobled by a higher loyalty in all ranks to truth and decency.

> Brigadier-General S.L.A. Marshall, *Men Against Fire*, 1947.

THE LOYALTY of men simply cannot be commanded when they become embittered by selfish action.

> Brigadier-General S.L.A. Marshall, *The Armed Forces Officer*, 1950.

LOYALTY is developed through the unifying of action. The more decisive the action becomes, the greater the bond.

> Brigadier-General S.L.A. Marshall, *The Armed Forces Officer*, 1950.

THE VERY TOUCHSTONE of loyalty is that just demands will be put upon it.
> Brigadier-General S.L.A. Marshall, *The Armed Forces Officer*, 1950.

I ALSO LEARNT that the discipline demanded from the soldier must become loyalty in the officer.
> Field Marshal Viscount Montgomery of Alamein, *The Memoirs of Field Marshal Montgomery*, 1958.

THE ESSENCE of Loyalty is the courage to propose the unpopular, coupled with a determination to obey, no matter how distasteful the ultimate decision. And the essence of leadership is the ability to inspire such behavior.
> Lieutenant-General Victor H. 'The Brute' Krulak, 'A Soldier's Dilemma', *Marine Corps Gazette*, 11/1986.

I EXPLAINED my idea of loyalty. "When we are debating an issue, loyalty means giving me your honest opinion, whether you think I'll like it or not. Disagreement, at this stage, stimulates me. But once a decision has been made, the debate ends. From that point on, loyalty means executing the decision as if it were your own."
> General Colin Powell, *My American Journey*, 1995.

LUCK

THE STATE benefits more from a lucky general than from a brave one. The first achieves his results with little effort, whereas the other does so at some risk.
> The Emperor Maurice, *The Strategikon*, c. AD 600 (*Maurice's Strategikon*, tr. George Dennis, 1984).

AS I RELY very much upon Providence, so I shall be ready of approving all occasions that may offer.
> The Duke of Marlborough, 4 May 1710, letter to the Earl of Godolphin.

ONE CAN SEE that a general should be skillful and lucky and that no one should believe so fully in his star that he abandons himself to it blindly. If you are lucky and trust in luck alone, even your success reduces you to the defensive; if you are unlucky you are already there.
> Frederick the Great, *Instructions to His Generals*, 1747, tr. Phillips, 1940.

I BASE my calculation on the expectation that luck will be against me.
> Napoleon (1769–1821).

THE AFFAIRS of war, like the destiny of battles, as well of empires, hang upon a spider's thread.
> Napoleon, *Political Aphorisms*, 1848.

LUCK in the long run is given only to the efficient.
> Field Marshal Helmuth Graf von Moltke (1800–1891).

LUCK is like a sum of gold, to be spent.
> Field Marshal Viscount Allenby of Meggido (1861–1936).

THOUGH IT IS no doubt true that luck in the long run pans out evenly, this is not true of a short campaign, still less of a battle. It can, in fact, play a disconcertingly prominent part in the issue.
> Colonel Alfred H. Burne, *The Art of War on Land*, 1947.

THERE IS such a thing as luck, and as soldiers you have to believe in it.
> Brigadier-General S.L.A. Marshall, quoted in Fitton, ed., *Leadership*, 1990.

THE HARDER I work, the luckier I get.
> Lieutenant-General Victor H. 'The Brute' Krulak, *Life Magazine*, 11/1965, a favourite motto.

THAT'S THE WAY it is in war. You win or lose, live or die – and the difference is just an eyelash.
> General of the Army Douglas MacArthur, *Reminiscences*, 1964.

THERE IS still another ingredient in this formula for a great leader . . . and that is LUCK. He must have opportunity. Then, of course, when opportunity knocks, he must be able to rise and open the door.
> General of the Army Omar N. Bradley, 'Leadership', *Parameters*, Winter 1972.

THE THEORY is debatable, of course; I am not imposing it on anyone. Nevertheless, I became accustomed long ago to dividing people, vehicles and subunits into lucky and unlucky. There are people who sense their death. They are still alive, they still walk, they chew something, they speak, but they already have a stamp across their forehead. At one time I did not stop two such people, which I regret, but later, after them, I began to scrutinize faces attentively, and if I noticed the very familiar signs, I did not take them on an operation under any far-fetched pretext, right down to out-and-out injustice. I do not know whether or not I was right, but I didn't take them.
> General Aleksandr I. Lebed, *I Cry For This Great Country*, 1995.

M

MAINTENANCE

IT HAS BEEN well said that Nelson took more care of his topgallant masts, in ordinary cruising, than he did of his whole fleet when the enemy was to be checked or beaten.
  Rear Admiral Alfred Thayer Mahan, *Lessons of the War with Spain*, 1899.

VEHICLES are maintained properly by tools, elbow grease, and dirty hands, not by pencils and forms.
  General Lesly J. McNair, in Kahn, *McNair, Educator of an Army*.

WE BUILD our equipment to military specs that are pretty tough. Sure, we have to change filters on engines. Sure, there will be a certain amount of corruption on helicopter blades. Yes, we will have to change engines on aircraft more often, but we know how to do all that. We know how to maintain our equipment. I absolutely do not expect to see huge breakdowns of equipment all over the kingdom.
  My aide-de-camp said it is like flossing your teeth. If you forget it once, your teeth are not going to fall out. If we are smart about it, we are not going to have that sort of problem.
  General H. Norman Schwarzkopf, 13 September 1990, interview with Richard Pyle, *Schwarzkopf: In His Own Words*, 1991.

MAN

THE MAN whose profession is arms should calm his mind and look into the depths of others. Doing so is likely the best of the martial arts.
  Shiba Yoshimasa, *Chikubasho*, 1380 (*Ideals of the Samurai*, tr. William Wilson, 1982).

MEN are your castles
Men are your walls
Sympathy is your ally
Enmity your foe
  Takeda Shingen (1521–1573), quoted in *Ideals of the Samurai*, tr. William Wilson, 1982.

IN ALL THINGS, think with one's starting point in man.
  Nabeshima Naoshige (1538–1618), quoted in *Ideals of the Samurai*, tr. William Wilson, 1982.

THE SAME TROOPS, who if attacking would have been victorious, may be invariably defeated in entrenchments. Few men have accounted for it in a reasonable manner, for it lies in human hearts and one should search for it there. No one has written of this matter which is the most important, the most learned, and the most profound of the profession of war. And without a knowledge of the human heart, one is dependent upon the favor of fortune, which sometimes is very inconstant.
  Field Marshal Maurice Comte de Saxe, *My Reveries*, 1732, tr. Phillips, 1940.

. . . THE HUMAN HEART – the groundwork of genius in the art of war.
  Major-General Henry 'Light Horse Harry' Lee, *Memoir of the War in the Southern Department*, 1869.

I START OUT by believing the worst [of men].
  Napoleon, repeated saying, quoted in Christopher Herold, ed., *The Mind of Napoleon*, 1955.

THE HUMAN HEART is an abyss that deceives all calculations. The most penetrating eyes cannot fathom it.
  Napoleon, 8 March 1804, letter to General Dessolle, *Correspondance de Napoléon Ier, publiée par ordre de l'Empereur Napoléon III*, IX, p. 274, 1858–1870.

THE HUMAN CHARACTER is the subject of the military officer's study; for it is upon man that his trials are made. He must, therefore, know, in the most precise manner, what man can do, and what he cannot do; he must also know the means by which his exertions are to be animated to the utmost extent of exertion. The general's duty is consequently an arduous duty; the capacity of learning it is the gift of Nature; the school is in the camp and the cottage rather than the city and the palace; for a man cannot know things in their foundations till he sees them without disguise; as he cannot judge of the hardships of service till he has felt them in experience. . . .
  Robert Jackson, *A Systematic View of the Formation, Discipline, and Economy of Armies*, 1804.

IT NEEDS a long experience of war to perceive its principles; one must have undertaken many offensive operations to realize how the slightest incident means encouragement or discouragement, brings about one result or another. In warfare men are nothing, a man is everything.
  Napoleon, 30 August 1808, a note on Spanish affairs, quoted in R.M. Johnston, ed., *The Corsican*, 1910.

MAN, not men, is the most important consideration.
Napoleon, *Maxims of War*, 1831.

SENTIMENT rules the world, and he who fails to take that into account can never hope to lead.
Napoleon (1769–1821).

YOU DO NOT know men. They are difficult to understand if you want to be just. Do they know themselves, can they explain themselves to themselves? Most of those who have deserted me perhaps would, had my luck held out, never have suspected their defection. There are vices and virtues born of circumstances.
Napoleon, 1815, conversation on St. Helena, quoted in Christopher Herold, ed., *The Mind of Napoleon*, 1955.

IF YOU WISH to study men, learn how far their patience can stretch.
Napoleon, 1816, conversation on St. Helena, quoted in Christopher Herold, ed., *The Mind of Napoleon*, 1955.

THE MORAL of this story doubtless is that men never change. This is not true; they change both for better and worse. A thousand other maxims which authors attempt to establish are all equally false. They affirm that men are ungrateful; but no, they are not so ungrateful as is supposed; and if ingratitude be frequently a subject of complaint, it is because the benefactor requires more than he gives.

It is also said that when you know a man's character, you have a key to his whole conduct. This is a mistaken notion. A man may commit a bad action, though he be fundamentally good; he may be led into an act of wickedness, without being himself wicked. This is because man is usually actuated not by the natural bent of his character, but by a secret momentary passion, which has lain dormant and concealed in the inmost recesses of his heart. Another error is to suppose that the face is the mirror of the mind. The truth is that it is very difficult to know a man's character. To avoid being deceived on this point, it is necessary to judge a person by his actions only; and it must be by his actions of the moment, and merely for that moment.

In truth, men have their virtues and their vices, their heroism and their perversity; men are neither generally good nor generally bad; but they possess and practice all that is good and bad in this world. This is the principle; natural disposition, education and accidental circumstances produce the application. I have always been guided by this opinion, and I have found it generally correct. However, I was deceived in 1814, when I believed France, at the sight of her dangers, would make common cause with me; but I was not deceived in 1815, on my return from Waterloo.
Napoleon, 20 May 1816, conversation on St. Helena, quoted in Emmanuel Las Casas, *Mémorial de Sainte Hélène*, II, 1840.

IN THE EYES of empire builders men are not men, but instruments.
Napoleon, *Maxims*, 1804–1815.

REMEMBER also that one of the requisite studies for an officer is *man*. Where your analytical geometry will serve you once, a knowledge of men will serve you daily. As a commander, to get the right man in the right place is one of the questions of success or defeat.
Admiral David G. Farragut, 13 October 1864, letter to his son.

THERE IS a soul to an army as well as to the individual man, and no general can accomplish the full work of his army unless he commands the souls of his men, as well as their bodies and legs.
General of the Army William T. Sherman, *Memoirs of General W.T. Sherman*, 1875.

THE MAN is the first weapon in battle. Let us study the soldier, for it is he who brings reality to it.
Colonel Charles Ardant du Picq, *Battle Studies*, 1880, tr. Greely, 1957.

ON FOOT, on horseback, on the bridge of a vessel, at the moment of danger, the same man is found. Anyone who knows him well, deduces from his action in the past what his future action will be.
Colonel Charles Ardant du Picq, *Battle Studies*, 1880, tr. Greely, 1957.

GIVE ME soldiers prepared to fight to the death, and I will look after the tactics. Men, men, and again men. Always men – they are the first and best instrument of battle.
General Mikhail I. Dragomirov (1830–1895).

IT IS the leader who reckons with the human nature of his troops, and of the enemy, rather than with their mere physical attributes, numbers, armament and the like, who can hope to follow in Napoleon's footsteps.
Colonel G.F.R. Henderson, quoted in Marshall, *The Armed Forces Officer*, 1950.

I WILL AGAIN sound the note of warning against that plausible cry of the day which finds all progress in material advance, disregarding that noblest sphere in which the mind and heart of man, in which all that is god-like in man, reign supreme; and against the temper which looks not to man, but to his armor.
Rear Admiral Alfred Thayer Mahan, *Naval Administration and Warfare*, 1908.

WE WILL have to say that in any case the decisive role does not belong to technology – behind technology there is always a living person without whom the technology is dead.
Mikhail Frunze (1885–1925), quoted in M. Gareyev, *Frunze, Military Theorist*, 1985.

WARS may be fought with weapons, but they are won by men. It is the spirit of the men who follow and the man who leads that gains the victory.
  General George S. Patton, Jr., in *The Cavalry Journal*, 9/1933.

IF I HAD TIME and anything like your ability to study war, I think I should concentrate entirely on the "actualities of war" – the effects of tiredness, hunger, fear, lack of sleep, weather . . . The principles of strategy and tactics, and the logistics of war are really absurdly simple: it is the actualities that make war so complicated and so difficult, and are usually so neglected by historians.
  Field Marshal Viscount Wavell of Cyrenaica to Liddell Hart, quoted in John Connell, 'Writing About Soldiers', *Journal of the Royal United Services Institute*, 8/1965.

A COMMANDER should have a profound understanding of human nature, the knack of smoothing out troubles, the power of winning affection while communicating energy, and the capacity for ruthless determination where required by circumstances. He needs to generate an electrifying current and to keep a cool head in applying it. (Oct. 1933.)
  Captain Sir Basil Liddell Hart, *Thoughts on War*, 1944.

THIS IS the so-called theory that "weapons decide everything", which constitutes a mechanical approach to the question of war and a subjective and one-sided view. Our view is opposed to this; we see not only weapons but also people. Weapons are an important factor in war, but not the decisive factor; it is people, not things, that are decisive. The contest of strength is not only a contest of military and economic power, but also a contest of human power and morale.
  Mao Tse-tung, *On Protracted War*, May 1938.

THE ART of leading, in operations large or small, is the art of dealing with humanity, of working diligently on behalf of men, of being sympathetic with them, but equally, of insisting they make a square facing toward their own problems.
  Brigadier-General S.L.A. Marshall, *Men Against Fire*, 1947.

AN ARMY must be as hard as steel in battle and can be made so; but, like steel, it reaches its finest quality only after much preparation and only provided the ingredients are properly constituted and handled. Unlike steel, an army is a most sensitive instrument and can easily become damaged; its basic ingredient is men and, to handle an army well, it is essential to understand human nature. Bottled up in men are great emotional forces which have got to be given an outlet in a way which is positive and constructive, and which warms the heart and excites the imagination. If the approach to the human factor is cold and impersonal, then you achieve nothing. But if you gain the confidence and trust of your men, and they feel their best interests are safe in your hands, then you have in your possession a priceless asset and the greatest achievements become possible.
  Field Marshal Viscount Montgomery of Alamein, *The Memoirs of Field Marshal Montgomery*, 1958.

IT IS ESSENTIAL to understand that battles are won primarily in the hearts of men.
  Field Marshal Viscount Montgomery of Alamein, *The Memoirs of Field Marshal Montgomery*, 1958.

I WAS BLAMED for excessive demands and exactness which I consider to be a necessary quality of any commander – bolshevik. Looking at this part, I realize that I was sometimes excessively demanding and I did not always control myself when offenses of my subordinates were involved. I used to lose control over myself because of carelessness in any work and in the behavior of the military men. Some of them did not understand that and I probably wasn't soft enough toward human weaknesses.
  Marshal of the Soviet Union Georgi K. Zhukov, quoted in Gareyev, *Frunze, Military Theorist*, 1985.

THE ESSENTIAL nature of war has not changed. Wars are fought by men, and there has been no discernable difference in the fundamental nature of man over the past five thousand years of recorded history. Because the nature of man has not changed, neither has his basic objective when he turns to war: the employment of lethal instruments to force his will upon other men with opposing points of view.
  Colonel N.T. Dupuy, *Understanding War*, 1987.

IT IS PEOPLE who win wars, not technology. If servicemen are not properly trained and motivated to use the equipment they have, they will achieve very little with it.
  General Sir Peter de la Billière, *Storm Command*, 1992.

ULTIMATELY, people, not machines define our success in war. Accordingly, we will equip our Marines, not man our equipment.
  General Charles C. Krulak, *Marine Corps Gazette*, 1996.

MAN, not space, is the last frontier. We must explore him.
  Lieutenant-Colonel Ralph Peters, 'Our New Old Enemies', *Parameters*, Summer 1999.

MANOEUVRE
Principle of War

SUN TZU said: In war, the general receives his commands from the sovereign.
  Having collected an army and concentrated his forces, he must blend and harmonize the different elements thereof before pitching his camp.
  After that, comes the tactical maneuvering, than which there is nothing more difficult. The difficulty of

tactical maneuvering consists in turning the devious into the direct, and misfortune into gain.

Sun Tzu, *The Art of War*, 7, c. 500 BC, tr. Giles, 1910.

MANEUVERING with an army is advantageous; with an undisciplined multitude, most dangerous.

Sun Tzu, *The Art of War*, 7, c. 500 BC, tr. Giles, 1910.

. . . FOR AS A SHIP, if you deprive it of its steersman, falls with all its crew into the hands of the enemy; so, with an army in war, if you outwit or out-maneuver its general, the whole will often fall into your hands.

Polybius, *Histories*, c. 125 BC.

THE ENEMY should see me marching when he believes me to be fettered by calculations of subsistence; this new kind of war must astonish him, must give him no chance to breathe anywhere, and make plain at his cost this constant truth – that there is scarcely any position tenable in face of a well-constituted, temperate, patient and manoeuvring army.

Field Marshal François Duc de Guibert, *Essai Général de Tactique*, 1770.

APTITUDE for maneuver is the supreme skill in a general; it is the most useful and rarest of gifts by which genius is estimated.

Napoleon (1769–1821), quoted in Commandant J. Colin, *The Transformation of War*, 1895.

[VICTORY/WINNING BATTLES] . . . more by the movement of troops than by fighting.

General of the Army William T. Sherman (1820–1891).

MANEUVERS are threats; he who appears most threatening wins.

Colonel Charles Ardant du Picq, *Battle Studies*, 1880, tr. Greely, 1957.

THE FUNDAMENTAL characterization of a strategy of maneuver is not the formal offensive but initiative and action.

Leon Trotsky, 1921.

NEARLY all the battles which are regarded as masterpieces of the military art, from which have been derived the foundation of states and the fame of commanders, have been battles of manoeuvre.

Sir Winston S. Churchill, *The World Crisis*, II, 1923.

BATTLES are won by slaughter and manoeuvre. The greater the general, the more he contributes in manoeuvre, the less he demands in slaughter.

Sir Winston S. Churchill, *The World Crisis*, II, 1923.

THE TRADITIONAL understanding of maneuver is a spatial one; that is, we must maneuver in space to gain a positional advantage. However, in order to maximize the usefulness of maneuver, we must consider maneuver in time as well; that is, we generate faster operational tempo than the enemy to gain a temporal advantage. It is through maneuver in both dimensions that an inferior force can achieve decisive superiority as the necessary time and place.

General Alfred M. Gray and Major John Schmitt, *Warfighting*, United States Marine Corps, 1989.

HE . . . saw that there was no point in fighting for a piece of sand. As he put it, it would be "rather like a sailor fighting for a wave or an airman for a cloud." A patch of sand, he decided, was an irrelevance. If some foolish Iraqi wished to dig a hole and sit in it, the best way of defeating him would be to go round behind him and deprive him of his water. As long as the Iraqis chose to defend sand, he reckoned "they had neutered themselves", and he set about training to fight a fast-moving battle in depth, as he put it, "fundamentally to alter the way we did business, to accommodate the reality of the circumstances."

General Sir Peter de la Billière, quoting Major-General Rupert Smith commanding the British First Armoured Division in its preparation for Desert Storm, December 1990, *Storm Command*, 1992.

MANHOOD/MANLINESS

BE MEN, my friends! Discipline fill your hearts, maintain your pride in the eyes of other men! Remember, each of you, sons, wives, wealth, parents – are mother and father dead or alive? No matter, I beg you for their sakes, loved ones far away – now stand and fight, no turning back, no panic.

Homer, *The Iliad*, 15.769–774, c. 800 BC, tr. Robert Fagles, 1990; Nestor, King of Pylos, appealing to the manhood of the panicking Greeks as the Trojans pressed them back upon their ships.

WHEN SOMEONE inquired of him what children should learn, he said: "What they will also use when they become men."

Plutarch, quoting Agesilaus, Eurypontid King of Sparta (400–360 BC), *The Lives*, c. AD 100 (*Plutarch on Sparta*, tr. Richard Talbert, 1988).

BEFORE a man can be manly the gift which makes him so must be there, collected by him slowly, unconsciously as his bones, his flesh, his blood.

Field Marshal Earl Roberts, *Diary*, 1876.

ARM and prepare to acquit yourselves like men, for the time of your ordeal is at hand.

Field Marshal Earl Roberts, *Message to the Nation*, 1912.

SEVERAL YEARS at a first-class military school or college would be of incalculable value to every

American boy in fitting him to engage in life's arduous struggle and in preparing him to perform the duties of American citizenship in time of peace.

> Major-General John A. Lejeune, *Reminiscences of a Marine*, 1929.

OUR CHILDREN don't need to be coddled, and they shouldn't be condemned. Above all, for heaven's sake, let your sons alone and let them grow up to be men.

> Lieutenant-General Lewis B. 'Chesty' Puller (1898–1971), comment at a meeting of the Parent-Teacher Association, Saluda, Virginia, after his retirement in 1955.

WAR makes everyone indecently naked. The essence of everyone is spread out on the palm of fate in three days for all to see: either you are a man and soldier or you have gotten male characteristics through a misunderstanding.

> Lieutenant-General Aleksandr I. Lebed, *I Hurt For This Great Country*, 1995.

MARCH TO THE SOUND OF THE GUNS

THE SAFEST WAY of achieving victory is to seek it among the enemy's battalions.

> Field Marshal Prince Aleksandr V. Suvorov (1729–1800), quoted in K. Ossipov, *Suvorov*, 1945.

MARCH to the sound of the guns.

> The Duke of York, 1793, to his commanders during the Dunkirk campaign.

MARSHAL GROUCHY had only left his camp at Gemlouz at ten in the morning, and was halfway to Wavres between noon and one o'clock. He heard the dreadful cannonade of Waterloo. No experienced man could have mistaken it: it was the sound of several hundred guns, and from that moment two armies were hurling death at each other. General Excelmans, commanding the cavalry, was profoundly moved by it. He went up to the Marshal and said to him: "The Emperor is at grips with the English army; there can be no doubt about it, such a furious fire can be no skirmish. Monsieur le Marechal, we must march towards the sound of the guns. I am an old soldier of the Army of Italy; I have heard General Bonaparte preach this principle a hundred times. If we turn to the left we shall be on the battlefield in two hours". . . .

> Napoleon (1769–1821), quoted in Somerset de Chair, ed., *The Waterloo Campaign*, 1957.

THE DRAWBACK to "marching to the sound of the guns", a type of subordinate initiative that was so much praised in and after the 1870 war, is that it may serve to nullify the higher commander's strategical plan. That particularly applies where a force is being used for manoeuvre. For it may be led

to swing in against the enemy's head, instead of continuing its circuit to strike the enemy's tail, and cut off his head. Thereby he may be given the chance to wiggle free. (Sept. 1928.)

> Captain Sir Basil Liddell Hart, *Thoughts on War*, 1944.

MARCHING

BUT ON the armies came
as if the whole earth were devoured by wildfire, yes,
and the ground thundered under them, deep as it does
for Zeus who loves the lightning, Zeus in all his rage
when he lashed the ground around Typhoeus in Arima,
there where they say the monster makes his bed of pain –
so the earth thundered under their feet, armies trampling,
sweeping through the plain at blazing speed.

> Homer, *The Iliad*, 2.887–895, c. 800 BC, tr. Robert Fagles, 1990.

AN ARMY is exposed to more danger on marches than in battles. In an engagement the men are properly armed, they see their enemies before them and are prepared to fight. But on a march the soldier is less on his guard, has not his arms always ready and is thrown into disorder by a sudden attack or ambuscade. A general, therefore, cannot be too careful and diligent in taking necessary precautions to prevent a surprise on the march.

> Flavius Vegetius Renatus, *Military Institutions of the Romans*, c. AD 378, tr Clark, 1776.

WE MARCH straight on; we march to victory.

> Harold Godwinson, King of England, 1066, refusing William of Normandy's offer of parly before the Battle of Hastings.

MARCHES are war.

> Napoleon, quoted in David Chandler, *The Campaigns of Napoleon*, 1966.

I HAVE accomplished my object; I have destroyed the Austrian army by simple marching. I have made 60,000 prisoners, taken 120 guns, more than 90 flags, and more than 30 generals.

> Napoleon, 19 October 1805, to Josephine, of the Ulm campaign, quoted in R.M. Johnston, ed., *The Corsican*, 1910.

SOLDIERS! The Russians boast that they are marching against us, we will move to meet them, we will spare them half the journey!

> Napoleon, 26 November 1806, at Potsdam, to his army upon the approach of the Russians, quoted in R.M. Johnston, ed., *The Corsican*, 1910.

MAXIM 9. The strength of an army, like power in mechanics, is reckoned by multiplying the mass by the rapidity. A rapid march increases the morale of an army, and increases its means of victory. Press on!

> Napoleon, *The Military Maxims of Napoleon*, tr. George D'Aguilar, 1831 (David Chandler, ed., 1987).

ONE OF the greatest difficulties in war is to have the men inured to marching. . . . The rapidity of a march, or rather skillful marches, almost always determines the success of a war. . . . It is this power of marching which constitutes the strength of infantry; and enterprises which seem to present the greatest difficulties, become comparatively easy by the advantages accruing from rapid marches.

> Marshal of France Michel Ney, Duc d'Elchingen, Prince de la Moskova, *Memoirs of Marshal Ney*, 1834.

THE HARDSHIPS of forced marches are more often painful than the dangers of battle. . . . I would rather lose one man marching than five in fighting. . . .

> Lieutenant-General Thomas J. 'Stonewall' Jackson, 1862, quoted in Henderson, *Stonewall Jackson*, 1898.

HIS [Jackson's] celerity of movement was a simple matter. He never broke down men by too-long-continued marching. He rested the whole column very often, but only for a few minutes at a time. I remember that he liked to see the men lie down flat on the ground to rest, and would say, "A man rests all over when he lies down."

> Brigadier-General John Imboden, in Underwood and Buel, ed., *Battles and Leaders of the Civil War, Being for the Most Part Contributions by Union and Confederate Officers*, II, 1887.

MARINES

NO PREVIOUS engagement had been so fierce and obstinate. Great was the eagerness with which the rowers on both sides rushed upon their enemies whenever the word of command was given; and keen was the contest between the pilots as they maneuvered against one another. The marines too were full of anxiety that, when ship struck ship, the service on deck should not fall short of the rest; everyone in the place assigned to him was eager to be foremost among his fellows . . . All the time that another vessel was bearing down, the men on deck poured showers of javelins and arrows and stones upon the enemy; and when the two closed, the marines fought hand to hand, and endeavored to board.

> Thucydides, of the great naval battle in the harbour of Syracuse, 413 BC, *The Peloponnesian War*, 7.70, c. 404 BC, tr. Benjamin Jowett, 1881.

THAT twelve hundred land Souldjers be forthwith raysed, to be in readinesse, to be distrubuted into his Mats Fleets prepared for sea Service . . .

> Charles II, 28 October 1664, Order in Council establishing the Royal Marines, the first permanent body of marines.

THAT TWO BATTALIONS of Marines be raised consisting of one Colonel, two lieutenant Colonels, two Majors & Officers as usual in other regiments, that they consist of an equal number of privates with other battalions; that particular care be taken that no person be appointed to office inlisted into said Battalions, but such are good seamen, or so acquainted with maritime affairs as to be able to serve to advantage by sea . . .

> Resolution of the Continental Congress, 10 November 1775, establishing the United States Marine Corps.

I NEVER KNEW an appeal made to them for honor, courage, or loyalty that they did not more than realize my highest expectations. If ever the hour of real danger should come to England they will be found the Country's Sheet Anchor.

> Admiral Lord St. Vincent, 1802, of the Royal Marines.

HOW MUCH might be done with a hundred thousand soldiers such as these.

> Napoleon, 15 July 1815, while inspecting the Royal Marine guard aboard HMS *Bellerophon*, following his surrender after Waterloo.

THE MARINES are properly the garrisons of His Majesty's ships, and upon no pretence ought they to be moved from a fair and safe communication with the ships to which they belong.

> The Duke of Wellington, 21 April 1837, to the House of Lords.

A SHIP without Marines is like a garment without buttons.

> Rear Admiral David Dixon Porter, 1863, letter to Colonel John Harris, USMC.

THE MARINES have landed and the situation is well in hand.

> Richard Harding Davis (1864–1916) – attributed.

"SOLDIER AN' SAILOR TOO"
(The Royal Regiment of Marines)

As I was spittin' into Ditch aboard o' the *Crocodile*,
I seed a man on a man-o'-war got up in the Reg'lars style
'E was scrapin' the paint from off of 'er plates, an' I sez to 'im, "'Oo are you?"
Sez 'e "I'm a Jolly – 'Er Majesty's Jolly – soldier an' sailor too!"
Now 'is work begins by Gawd knows when, and 'is work is never through;
'E isn't one o' the reg'lar Line, nor 'e isn't one of the crew.
'E's a kind of giddy harumfrodite – soldier an' sailor too!

An', after, I met 'im all over the world, a-doin' all kinds of things,
Like landin' 'isself with a Gatlin' gun to talk to them 'eathen kings;

'E sleeps in an 'ammick instead of a cot, an' 'e drills
    with the deck on a slew;
An' 'e sweats like a Jolly – 'Er Majesty's Jolly –
    soldier an' sailor too!
For there isn't a job on the top o' the earth the
    beggar don't know, nor do –
    Rudyard Kipling (1865–1936)

. . . "A GOOD MARINE." (The adjective had no
comparative or superlative. Nobody since 1775 had
ever been better than a good Marine.)
    Lawrence Stallings, *The Doughboys*, 1963; of the use
    of the term 'a good Marine' in 1918.

I WANT TO SEE it speedily recruited to full strength.
I want to see the very flower of American manhood
brought within the ranks. I want to see it a picked
body of loyal, America-loving young men not out for
a good time but for good service. We want only men
of ambition in this corps; young men who want to
better themselves.
    Major-General John A. Lejeune, quoted in interview,
    The Public Ledger (Philadelphia), 1 August 1920.

THE SPIRIT of comradeship and brotherhood in
arms which has traditionally existed throughout the
ranks of the Marine Corps is a vital characteristic of
the Corps. It must be fostered and kept alive and
made the moving force in all Marine Corps
organizations.
    Major-General John A. Lejeune, *Marine Corps
    Manual*, 1920.

WHEN the dominance of the seas passed from the
Phoenicians to the Greeks, the latter inherited the
sea-fighting organization of their predecessors
practically intact, with the same divisions remaining
between slaves, navigators, and fighting men. These
latter were given the special name "epibatae" to
distinguish them from the hoplites or heavy infantry
of the land, and this name is probably the first
distinctive designation for marines.
    Major-General John A. Lejeune, 'United States Marine
    Corps', U.S. Government Printing Office, 1925.

IN THE big war companies, 250 strong, you could
find every sort of man, from every sort of calling.
There were Northwesterners with straw-colored hair
that looked white against their tanned skins, and
delicately spoken chaps with the stamp of eastern
universities on them. There were large-boned fellows
from Pacific-coast lumber camps, and tall, lean
Southerners who swore amazingly in gentle,
drawling voices. There were husky farmers from the
corn-belt, and youngsters who had sprung, as it
were, to arms from the necktie counter. And there
were also a number of diverse people who ran
curiously to type, with drilled shoulders and a bone-
deep sunburn, and a tolerant scorn of everything on
earth. Their speech was flavored with navy words,
and the words culled from all the folk who live on the
seas and the ports where our war-ships go. In easy
hours their talk ran from the Tatar Wall beyond Pekin
to the Southern Islands, down under Manila; from
Portsmouth Navy Yard – New Hampshire and very
cold – to obscure bushwhackings in the West Indies,
where Cacao chiefs, whimsically sanguinary,
barefoot generals with names like Charlemagne and
Christophe, waged war according to the precepts of
the French Revolution and the Cult of the Snake.
They drank their *eau de vie* of Haute-Marne, and
reminisced on saki, and vino, and Bacardi Rum –
strange drinks in strange *cantinas* at the far ends of
the earth; and they spoke fondly of Milwaukee beer.
Rifles were high and holy things to them, and they
knew five-inch broadside guns. They talked
patronizingly of the war, and were concerned about
rations. They were the Leathernecks, the Old
Timers: collected from the ship's guard and shore
stations all over the earth to form the 4th Brigade of
Marines, the two rifle regiments, detached from the
navy by order of the President for service with the
American Expeditionary Forces. They were the old
breed of American regulars, regarding the service as
home and war as an occupation; and they
transmitted their temper and character and viewpoint to the high-hearted volunteer mass which filled
the ranks of the Marine Brigade.
    Colonel John W. Thomason, Jr., *Fix Bayonets!*, 1926.

THEY TELL the tale of an American lady of notable
good works, much esteemed by the French, who, at
the end of June, 1918, visited one of the field-
hospitals behind Degoutte's Sixth French Army.
Degoutte was fighting on the face of the Marne
salinet, and the 2d American Division, then in action
around the Bois de Belleau, northwest of Chateau
Thierry, was under his orders. It happened that
occasional casualties of the Marine Brigade of the
2d American Division, wounded toward the flank
where Degoutte's own horizon-blue infantry joined
on, were picked up by French stretcher-bearers and
evacuated to French hospitals. And this lady, looking
down a long, crowded ward, saw on a pillow a face
unlike the fiercely whiskered Gallic heads there
displayed in rows. She went to it.
    "Oh," she said, "Surely you are an American!"
    "No, ma'am," the casualty answered, "I'm a Marine."
    Colonel John W. Thomason, Jr., *Fix Bayonets!*, 1926.

GRADUALLY it has become recognized that while
Marines are not necessary as a police force on
board ship, yet their service afloat is necessary in
order to provide the Navy with an efficient
expeditionary force habituated to ship life,
accustomed to being governed by Navy laws and
regulations, and officered by a personnel whose
members have been closely associated with the
officers of the Navy officially and unofficially
throughout their entire naval careers.
    Major-General John A. Lejeune, *The Reminiscences of
    a Marine*, 1929.

THERE IS a wide and important field of usefulness for a military force with the characteristics of the Marine Corps. I refer to the field occupied by the expeditionary force, which accompanies the fleet in its overseas campaigns, for the conduct of such shore operations as are required for the expeditious and successful prosecution of the naval campaign.
> Major-General John A. Lejeune, *The Reminiscences of a Marine*, 1929.

THE OPERATIONS of . . . an expeditionary force are extraordinarily difficult and hazardous and require unusually skillful and resolute leadership, and troops which are especially trained for the accomplishment of their mission.
> Major-General John A. Lejeune, *The Reminiscences of a Marine*, 1929.

IN THE HANDS of its own officers . . . rests . . . [the Marine Corps'] future. If they allow the Corps to deteriorate, its mission as the Navy's expeditionary force in peace and war will pass into stronger and more capable hands and the Corps will be marked for extinction.
> Major-General John A. Lejeune, *The Reminiscences of a Marine*, 1929.

I ADOPTED as the guiding principle of my administration the rule that the good of the Corps, combined with the just treatment of all officers and men, was paramount and, therefore, took precedence over all other considerations.
> Major-General John A. Lejeune, on the guiding principle of his Commandancy of the U.S. Marine Corps, *The Reminiscences of a Marine*, 1929.

THE MARINE CORPS is part of the Naval Service, and its expeditionary duty with the Fleet in peace and in war is its chief mission.
> Major-General John A. Lejeune, *The Reminiscences of a Marine*, 1929.

NO ONE can ever say that the Marines have ever failed to do their work in handsome fashion.
> Major-General Johnson Hagood, *We Can Defend America*, 1937.

EVEN THOUGH you Navy officers do come in to about one thousand yards, I remind you that you have a little more armor. I want you to know that Marines are crossing the beach with bayonets, and the only armor they'll have is a khaki shirt.
> Major-General Julian C. Smith, November 1943, to the naval officers supporting the landing of his Second Marine Division at Tarawa, quoted in Bill D. Ross, *Iwo Jima*, 1985.

THE RAISING of that flag on Suribachi means a Marine Corps for the next 500 years.
> James Forrestal, 23 February 1945, to Lieutenant-General H.M. Smith.

IT IS a notable fact that few men ever leave the Marine Corps without a feeling of undying loyalty toward it.
> General Alexander A. Vandegrift, 6 May 1946, to the Senate Naval Affairs Committee, regarding the Army's proposals for abolition of the Marine Corps.

THE MARINES are ready, and if it came to a fight today I do not know who could replace them.
> General A.A. Vandegrift, 6 May 1946, to the Senate Naval Affairs Committee, regarding the Army's proposals for abolition of the Marine Corps.

THE MARINE CORPS, then, believes that it has earned this right – to have its future decided by the legislative body which created it – nothing more. Sentiment is not a valid consideration in determining questions of national security. We have pride in ourselves and in our past but we do not rest our case on any presumed gratitude owing us from the nation. The bended knee is not a tradition of our Corps. If the Marine as a fighting man has not made a case for himself after 170 years of service, he must go. But I think you will agree with me he has earned the right to depart with dignity and honor, not by subjugation to the status of uselessness and servility planned for him by the War Department.
> General A.A. Vandegrift, 6 May 1946, to the Senate Naval Affairs Committee, regarding the Army's proposals for abolition of the Marine Corps.

THE SITUATION is critical and Miryang may be lost. The enemy has driven a division-sized salient across the Naktong. More will cross the river tonight. If Miryang is lost . . . we will be faced with a withdrawal from Korea. I am heartened that the Marine Brigade will move against the Naktong Salient tomorrow. They are faced with impossible odds, and I have no valid reason to substantiate it, but I have the feeling they will halt the enemy.
. . . These Marines have the swagger, confidence, and hardness that must have been in Stonewall Jackson's Army of the Shenandoah. They remind me of the Coldstreams at Dunkirk. Upon this thin line of reasoning, I cling to the hope of victory.
> British military observer, 16 August 1950, wire dispatched from Miryang within the Pusan perimeter, quoted in T.R. Fehrenbach, *This Kind of War*, 1963.

THE MARINE CORPS is the Navy's police force . . . and as long as I am President that is what it will remain. They have a propaganda machine that is almost equal to Stalin's.
> President Harry S. Truman, 29 August 1950, letter to Congressman Gordon L. McDonough, *Time*, 18 September 1950.

I SINCERELY REGRET the unfortunate choice of language which I used in my letter of August 29 to

Congressman McDonough concerning the Marine Corps . . .

> President Harry S. Truman, 6 September 1950, to General C.B. Cates, Commandant of the United States Marine Corps.

I HAVE just returned from visiting the Marines at the front, and there is not a finer fighting organization in the world.

> General of the Army Douglas MacArthur, 21 September 1950, on the outskirts of Seoul.

WE'RE professional soldiers. We fight any enemy the President designates. We don't just keep talking Communism, Communism, Communism. You might build up hate against one enemy and find yourself fighting another.

> General David M. Shoup, *The New York Times*, 29 October 1961.

MEN, I'd rather be toting a rifle in the rear rank than going out now as a lieutenant general. If you're a Marine, you're all Marine. You'll put the Corps above your family, your country, even God and all else in some cases. You stick to your Corps. God bless you.

> Lieutenant-General Lewis B. 'Chesty' Puller, 1955, retirement comment to the 5,000 marines who crashed his retirement party at Camp Lejeune, North Carolina.

I DON'T FEEL our young Marine should be pampered. Solid training, deprivation and a few hard knocks are good for the soul.

> Lieutenant-General Lewis B. 'Chesty' Puller, 7 February 1962, comment to visiting Marine NCOs, Marine Corps press release.

THE BASIC SECRET of the Marine Corps is that every Marine is trained as a rifleman or a platoon leader.

> General Leonard F. Chapman, Jr., *The Washington Post*, 19 December 1971.

JUST REJOICE at the news and congratulate our forces and the marines. . . . Rejoice, rejoice.

> Prime Minister Margaret Thatcher, 26 April 1982, on the capture of the island of South Georgia during the Falklands War.

BE READY to go with whatever you have.

> Marine Corps dictum, quoted by Lieutenant-General Victor H. 'The Brute' Krulak, *First to Fight*, 1984.

. . . PROFESSIONAL independence, a conviction that the Marines' job, being different, is certain to have many different needs. It has long been understood that fulfilling those needs demands a willingness to acknowledge that nobody else is going to do it for us, coupled with a determination to find a way ourselves. Today's overbearing atmosphere of military standardization certainly makes resourceful improvisations . . . far more difficult. But, one way or another, the Marines are going to keep the pioneering spirit alive because it is very near to the heart of what the Corps is all about.

> Lieutenant-General Victor H. 'The Brute' Krulak, *First to Fight*, 1984.

IN 1935 I asked venerable Gunnery Sergeant Walter Holzworth just how the Marine Corps came by its reputation as one of the world's greatest fighting formations. "Well, lieutenant," the sergeant said, "they started right out telling everybody how great they were. Pretty soon they got to believing it themselves. And they have been busy ever since proving they were right."

> Lieutenant-General Victor H. 'The Brute' Krulak, *First to Fight*, 1984.

THE LAST DAY, as the country was collapsing, I listened to military radio and could still hear the South Vietnamese Marines fighting up near Danang. The North Vietnamese had overrun Danang weeks before we started the evacuation. The Marines went into the hills and were fighting back. Forty-three of their company commanders died while fighting in the hills. Great bravery.

> General Alfred Gray, 'Saigon Burning', Al Santoli, ed., *Leading the Way: How Vietnam Veterans Rebuilt the U.S. Military*, 1993.

BEING A MARINE is a rare experience. Savor it.

> Lieutenant-General Louis Metzger, 'It's Not All Bayonets and Bullets: A Memoir', *Marine Corps Gazette*, 4/1994.

TWO HUNDRED and twenty-three years ago, the Second Continental Congress created a Corps of Marines to defend the American colonies and to fight for the rich blessings of liberty and democracy. Since that day, Marines have protected the cherished ideals of our Founding Fathers and defended our Nation's interests around the globe. In their blood, they have authored our Corps' glorious history and punctuated it with legendary tales of honor, courage, and commitment – with our Touchstones of Valor.

> General Charles C. Krulak, 10 November 1998, birthday greetings to the United States Marine Corps from its Commandant, *Marine Corps Gazette*, 11/1998.

MARKSMANSHIP

IN ARCHERY we have three goals: to shoot accurately, to shoot powerfully, to shoot rapidly.

> Anonymous Byzantine general, *On Strategy (Peri Strategias)* c. AD 527–565 (*Three Byzantine Military Treatises*, tr. George Dennis, 1985.

EVERY English archer beareth under his girdle twenty-four Scots.

> English proverb, alluding to the 24 arrows each longbowman carried in his belt and the deadly accuracy of his marksmanship.

AIM for their shoelaces!

> Oliver Cromwell (1599–1658), during the English Civil War; an early recognition of the fact that most men shoot high.

TEACH the soldier how to load his musket properly, whether with cartridge or loose powder, with or without the bayonet fixed; how he should give fire under the different circumstances he will encounter; teach him never to fire without an order, and never to do so without aiming, thus avoiding waste of fire to no purpose.

> Marshal Jacques-Francois de Puységur, Art de la Guerre, 1748.

GREAT CARE should be observed in choosing active Marsksmen; the manifest Inferiority of inactive Persons, unused to Arms, in this kind of Service, although equal in Numbers, to lively Persons who have practised Hunting is inconceivable. The Chance against them is more than two to one.

> General George Washington, 16 April 1756, to Robert Dinwiddie, The Writings of George Washington, I, p. 313, John C. Fitzgerald, ed., 1931.

IT IS NOT sufficient that the soldier must shoot, he must shoot well.

> Napoleon (1769–1821).

GOOD MARKSMANSHIP is always the most important thing for the infantry.

> General Gerhard von Scharnhorst, 1812, memorandum.

YOU DON'T hurt 'em if you don't hit 'em.

> Lieutenant-General Lewis 'Chesty' Puller, quoted in Burke Davis, Marine, 1962.

MASS
Principle of War

THAT THE impact of your army may be like a grindstone dashed against an egg – that is effected by the science of weak points and strong.

> Sun Tzu, The Art of War, 5, c. 500 BC, tr. Giles, 1910.

USE the most solid to attack the most empty.

> The 'Martial' Emperor Ts'ao Ts'ao, AD 155–220, commentary to Sun Tzu, The Art of War, 5, c. 500 BC, tr. Samuel Griffith, 1963.

ONE SHOULD NOT be overly fond of famous swords and daggers. For even if one has a sword valued at 10,000 cash, he will not overcome 100 men carrying spears valued at 100 cash.

> Asakura Toshikage (1428–1481), The 17 Articles of Asakura Toshikage (Ideals of the Samurai, tr. William Wilson, 1982).

MOVE UPON the enemy in one mass on one line so that when brought to battle you shall outnumber him, and from such a direction that you compromise him.

> Napoleon (1769–1821).

NOT BY RAMBLING operations, or naval duels, are wars decided, but by force massed and handled in skillful combinations.

> Rear Admiral Alfred Thayer Mahan (1840–1914).

THE ART of making the weight of all one's forces successively bear on the resistances one may meet.

> Marshal of France Ferdinand Foch, Principles of War, 1913.

DO NOT LET my opponents castigate me with the blather that Waterloo was won on the playfields of Eton, for the fact remains geographically, historically and tactically, whether the great Duke uttered such nonsense or not, that it was won on fields in Belgium by carrying out a fundamental principle of war, the principle of mass; in other words by marching on to those fields three Englishmen, Germans or Belgiums to every two Frenchmen.

> Major-General J.F.C. Fuller, 'Principles of War with Reference to the Campaigns of 1914–1915', Royal United Services Institution Journal, LXI: 1, 1916.

THE FIFTH ACT of the great drama in Flanders opened on the 22nd October. Enormous masses of ammunition, such as the human mind had never imagined before the war, were hurled upon the bodies of men who passed a miserable existence scattered about in mud-filled shell holes. The horror of the shell-hole area of Verdun was surpassed. It was no longer life at all. It was more unspeakable suffering. And through this world of mud the attackers dragged themselves, slowly, but steadily, and in dense masses. Caught in the advanced zone by our hail of fire they often collapsed, and the lonely man in the shell-hole breathed again. Then the mass came on again. Rifle and machine-gun jammed in the mud. Man fought against man, and only too often the mass was successful.

> General Erich Ludendorff, My War Memories 1914–1918, 1919.

THE CONCENTRATION of all means on one . . . operation may yield a big economy of force. An enemy front capable of enduring dozens of small strikes may be broken by one big strike. In certain conditions, a certain mass of operation is necessary in order to obtain even minimal results.

> General A.A. Svechin, 1927.

WE MUST NOT replace crushing strikes against the

enemy with pinpricks. . . . It is necessary to prepare an operation which will be like an earthquake.

> Marshal of the Soviet Union Georgi K. Zhukov, 12 May 1944.

THE THEORY of human mass dominated the military mind from Waterloo to the World War. This monster was the child of the French Revolution by Napoleon. The midwife who brought it into the military world was the Prussian philosopher of war, Clausewitz, cloudily profound. He unfortunately died while his own thought was still fermenting – leaving his papers in sealed packets, with the significant note: "Should the work be interrupted by my death, then what is found can only be called a mass of formless conceptions . . . open to endless misconceptions." So they proved.

> Captain Sir Basil Liddell Hart, *Thoughts on War*, 1944.

MATÉRIEL

WHEN CONFIDENCE is placed in superiority of material means, valuable as they are against an enemy at a distance, it may be betrayed by the actions of the enemy. If he closes with you in spite of your superiority in means of destruction, the morale of the enemy mounts with your loss of confidence.

> Colonel Charles Ardant du Picq, *Battle Studies*, 1880, tr. Greely, 1957.

IN OUR DAY wars are not won by mere enthusiasm, but by technical superiority.

> V.I. Lenin, 1918, speech.

A FIGHTING revolutionary spirit and class self-awareness are the crucial factors in a revolutionary war, but revolutionary spirit alone without the necessary equipment cannot be victorious in modern war.

> Marshal of the Soviet Union Mikhail N. Tukhachevskiy, quoted in *Voyenno istorichiskiy zhurnal*, 2/1983.

TO-DAY, in the army we are faced with the problems of motorization and mechanization, just as the navy was seventy-odd years ago. Some think these changes good, and others bad; but their possible virtues and vices are insignificant problems if we lose sight of the greater problem which is this: The more mechanical become the weapons with which we fight, the less mechanical must be the spirit which controls them.

> Major-General J.F.C. Fuller, *Generalship: Its Diseases and Their Cure*, 1933.

MEDALS AND DECORATIONS

AT THE STORMING of a city the first man to scale the wall is awarded a crown of gold. In the same way those who have shielded and saved one of their fellow-citizens or their allies is honoured with gifts from the consul, and the men whose lives they have saved present them of their own free will with a crown; if not, they are compelled to do so by the tribunes who judge the case. Moreover, a man who has been saved in this way reveres his rescuer as a father for the rest of his life and must treat him as if he were a parent. And so by means of such incentives even those who stay at home feel the impulse to emulate such achievements in the field no less than those who are present and see and hear what takes place. For the men who receive these trophies not only enjoy great prestige in the army and soon afterwards in their homes, but they are also singled out for precedence in religious processions when they return. On these occasions nobody is allowed to wear decorations save those who have been honoured for their bravery by the consuls, and it is the custom to hang up the trophies they have won in the most conspicuous places in their houses, and to regard them as proofs and visible symbols of their valour. So when we consider this people's almost obsessive concern with military rewards and punishments, and the immense importance which they attach to both, it is not surprising that they emerge with brilliant success from every war in which they engage.

> Polybius, *Histories*, 6.39, c. 125 BC (*The Rise of the Roman Empire*, tr. Ian Scott-Kilvert, 1987).

HONOR THEM with titles, present them with goods, and soldiers willingly come join you. Treat them courteously, inspire them with speeches, and soldiers willingly die. Give them nourishment and rest so that they do not become weary, make the code of rules uniform, and soldiers willingly obey. Lead them into battle personally, and soldiers will be brave. Record even a little good, reward even a little merit, and the soldiers will be encouraged.

> Zhuge Liang (AD 180–234) commentary to Sun Tzu, *The Art of War* (*Mastering the Art of War*, tr. Thomas Cleary, 1989).

IT IS NOT titles that honor men, but men that honor titles.

> Niccolo Machiavelli, *Discourses*, 1517.

DRINKWATER: As for you, Commodore, they will make you a baronet.
Nelson: No, no. if they want to mark my services, it must not be in that manner.
Drinkwater: Oh, you wish to be made a Knight of the Bath?
Nelson: Yes, if my services have been of any value, let them be noticed in a way that the public may know me – or them.

> Admiral Viscount Nelson, 14 February 1797, after the victory at Cape St. Vincent, preferring the ribbon and star of a Knight of the Bath to display his valour, rather than the higher honour of being made a baronet.

SHOW ME a republic, ancient or modern, in which there have been no decorations. Some people call them baubles. Well, it is by such baubles that one leads men.

> Napoleon, 19 May 1802, on establishing the *Légion d'honneur* (Legion of Honour).

IN HONOUR I gained them, and in honour I will die with them.

> Admiral Viscount Nelson, 21 October 1805, at the Battle of Trafalgar, when urged not to wear his brilliant decorations, which ultimately attracted the aim of a French marksman who wounded him mortally, quoted in Robert Southey, *Life of Nelson*, 1813.

A SOLDIER will fight long and hard for a bit of colored ribbon.

> Napoleon, 15 July 1815, to the captain of HMS *Bellerophon*, upon entering exile.

I'D RATHER BE a second lieutenant with a DSC (Distinguished Service Cross) than a general without it.

> General George S. Patton, Jr., 1918, quoted in *The Washington Post*, 18 May 1996, p. C1.

A COWARD dressed as a brave man will change from his cowardice and, in nine cases out of ten, will on the next occasion demonstrate the qualities fortuitously emblazoned on his chest . . .

We must have more decorations and we must give them with no niggard hand . . .

War may be hell; but for John Doughboy there is a heaven of suggestion in anticipating what Annie Rooney will say when she sees him in his pink feather and his new medal.

> General George S. Patton, Jr., October 1927, *The Patton Papers*, I, 1972.

THE RESULT of decorations works two ways. It makes the men who get them proud and determined to get more, and it makes the men who have not received them jealous and determined to get some in order to even up. It is the greatest thing we have for building a fighting heart.

> General George S. Patton (1885–1945), quoted in Semmes, *Portrait of Patton*, 1955.

A MEDAL glitters, but it also casts a shadow.

> Sir Winston S. Churchill, 22 March 1944, speech in the House of Commons.

CIVILIANS may think it's a little juvenile to worry about ribbons, but a civilian has a house and a bankroll to show what he's done for the past four years.

> Bill Mauldin, quoted in *The Washington Post*, 18 May 1996, p. C1.

IT IS IMPOSSIBLE for the Nation to compensate for the services of a fighting man. There is no pay scale that is high enough to buy the services of a single soldier during even a few minutes of the agony of combat, the physical miseries of the campaign, or of the extreme personal inconvenience of leaving his home to go out to the most unpleasant and dangerous spots on earth to serve his Nation. But so that our troops might know that the Nation realizes this simple truth, the Army made it a determined policy to decorate men promptly for arduous service and for acts of gallantry while they were fighting.

> General of the Army George C. Marshall, *Biennial Reports of the Chief of Staff*, 1996.

THEY RECOMMENDED me for a Silver Star for that action, and back in Corps Headquarters at Noumea some jerk reduced it to a Bronze Star. What right have those people got to put their cotton-picking hands into things like that? They didn't see the action, and have no way on earth to judge. Wouldn't you think they could see what it does to morale? I can stand it. I've got enough damned medals. But what it does to the young kids is inexcusable.

> Lieutenant-General Lewis 'Chesty' Puller, quoted in Burke Davis, *Marine*, 1962.

NO ORDER taken by me while I was chief of staff gave me greater satisfaction than re-establishing the Order of the Purple Heart. It had not been in use for a century and a quarter.

This decoration is unique in several ways; first, it is the oldest in American history, and antedates practically all of the famous military medals in the world; second, it comes from the greatest of all Americans, George Washington, and thereby carries with it something of the reverence which haloes his great name; and third, it is the only decoration which is completely intrinsic in that it does not depend upon approval or favor by anyone. It goes only to those who are wounded in battle, and enemy action alone determines the award. It is a true badge of courage and every breast that wears it can beat with pride.

> General of the Army Douglas MacArthur, *Reminiscences*, 1964.

DURING THE WAR I found that men who won the Medal of Honor – and survived – were so conscious of the distinction that when they returned to combat they showed even greater courage, took greater risks and were far more likely to be killed than their comrades. This tendency was so pronounced that I instituted a policy of sending such men back to the states to train and inspire our untried troops. Usually they would protest bitterly, but I never let myself be swayed.

> General Mark Clark, 'Recapturing What Honor Really Means', *Rocky Mountain News*, 5 May 1984.

MEDICAL CORPS

WAR is the only proper school of the surgeon.

> Hippocrates, *Wounds of the Head*, c. 415 BC.

EIGHT OR TEN of the less-skilled soldiers in each tagma should be assigned as medical corpsmen to each bandon, especially in the first battle line. They should be alert, quick, lightly clothed, and without weapons. Their duty is to follow about a hundred feet to the rear of their own tagma, to pick up and give aid to anyone seriously wounded in the battle, or who has fallen off his horse, or is otherwise out of action, so they may not be trampled by the second line. For each person so rescued the corpsman should receive from the treasury one nomisma over above his pay. . . .

> The Emperor Maurice, *The Strategikon*, c. AD 600 (*Maurice's Strategikon*, tr. George Dennis, 1984).

YOU medical people will have more lives to answer for in the other world than even we do.

> Napoleon, quoted in Barry O'Meara, *Napoleon in Exile*, 1822.

YOU Gentlemen of England who sit at home in all the well-earned satisfaction of your successful cases, can have little idea from reading the newspapers of the Horror and Misery of operating upon these dying, exhausted men.

> Florence Nightingale, 1854, letter from the British hospital at Scutari to Dr. Brown during the Crimean War.

IT MAY SEEM a strange principle to enunciate as the very first requirement in a Hospital that it should do the sick no harm.

> Florence Nightingale, *Notes on Hospitals*, 1859.

A CORPS of Medical officers was not established soley for the purpose of attending the wounded and sick . . . the labors of Medical officers cover a more extended field. The leading idea, which should be constantly kept in view, is to strengthen the hands of the Commanding General by keeping his army in the most vigorous health, thus rendering it, in the highest degree, efficient for enduring fatigue and privation, and for fighting. In this view, the duties of such a corps are of vital importance to the success of an army, and commanders seldom appreciate the full effect of their proper fulfilment [sic].

> Major Jonathan Letterman (1824–1872), Medical Director of the Army of the Potomac.

IF I WERE to speak of war, it would not be to show you the glories of conquering armies but the mischief and misery they strew in their track; and how, while they march on with tread of iron and plumes proudly tossing in the breeze, some one must follow closely in their steps, crouching to the earth, toiling in the rain and darkness, shelterless like themselves, with no thought of pride or glory, fame or praise, or reward; hearts breaking with pity, faces bathed in tears and hands in blood. This is the side which history never shows.

> Clara Barton, quoted in Percy Epler, *The Life of Clara Barton*, 1915.

HYGIENE . . . has such bearing upon the efficiency of armed forces that its place in warfare cannot be denied. As to its usefulness to line officers, I will venture to quote words of my own: "The responsibility for the health of crews rests ultimately with the commanding officers; who, however they be guided ordinarily by the opinion of the surgeon, must be able on occasion to overrule intelligently the professional bias of the latter." A doctor's business is to save life; the admiral's or captain's to risk it, when necessary and possible to attain a given end.

> Rear Admiral Alfred Thayer Mahan, *Naval Administration and Warfare*, 1908.

FANNED by the fierce winds of war, medical science and surgical art have advanced unceasingly, hand in hand. There has certainly been no lack of subjects for the treatment. The Medical profession at least cannot complain of unemployment through lack of raw material.

> Sir Winston S. Churchill, 10 September 1947, speech to the International Congress of Physicians at the Guildhall, London.

MEETING ENGAGEMENT

AS THE THEBANS were retreating from Orchomenus towards Tegyrae, the Spartans, at the same time marching from Locris, met them. As soon as they came in view, advancing through the straits, one told Pelopidas, "We are fallen into our enemy's hands;" he replied, "And why not they into ours?"

> Pelopidas, at the Battle of Tegyrae, 375 BC, as told by Plutarch, *Plutarch's Lives*, c. AD 100, tr. John Dryden.

MEMOIRS/DIARIES

ANY MEMOIRS of my life, distinct and unconnected with the general history of the war, would rather hurt my feelings than tickle my pride whilst I lived. I had rather glide gently down the stream of life, leaving it to posterity to think and say what they please of me, than by any act of mine to have vanity or ostentation imputed to me. . . . I do not think vanity is a trait of my character.

> General George Washington, 25 March 1784, to Doctor James Craik, *The Writings of George Washington*, XXVII, p. 371, John C. Fitzgerald, ed., 1938.

WHAT the layman gets to know of the course of military events is usually nondescript. One action resembles another, and from a mere recital of events it would be impossible to guess what obstacles were faced and overcome. Only now and then, in the memoirs of generals or of their confidents, or as the result of close historical study, are some of the countless threads of the tapestry revealed. Most of the arguments and clashes of opinion that precede a major operation are deliberately concealed because they touch political interests, or they are simply forgotten, being considered as scaffolding to be demolished when the building is complete.

Major-General Carl von Clausewitz, *On War*, 1832, 1.3, tr. Michael Howard and Peter Paret, 1976.

I HAVE OFTEN needed a diary, an experience case record for reference. It is late to start at 38 1/2 years old, but I shall have some spare moments in the next ten days between here and Manila and I set my memory to work. Many things worthy of remembrance and reference have happened to me, especially in the last two years. To write them is to learn my lessons of experience anew. It will do me good. To live them over in memory will be like the review of a hard-studied study. It ought to polish the fixed and fix some floating principles in me, and help arrange knowledge and experience for convenient use.

Lieutenant-General Robert Lee Bullard, 26 November 1899, diary entry.

THIS BOOK should make a contribution towards perpetuating those experiences of the bitter war years; experiences often gained at the cost of great deprivations and bitter sacrifices.

Field Marshal Erwin Rommel, *Infantry Attacks*, 1937.

THE LAST WORD in the Foreword to this book is "truth." I have tried to write the truth. I suppose everyone claims that about his memoirs! Most official accounts of past wars are deceptively well written, and seem to omit many important matters – in particular, anything which might indicate that any of our commanders ever made the slightest mistake. They are therefore useless as a source of instruction. They remind me of the French general's reply to a British protest in 1918, when the former directed the British to take over a sector from the French which had already been overrun by the Germans forty-eight hours previously. The French general said: "Mais, mon ami, ca c'est pour l'histoire."

Field Marshal Viscount Montgomery of Alamein, *The Memoirs of Field Marshal Montgomery*, 1958.

I HEAR my generals are selling themselves dearly.

Sir Winston S. Churchill, of the flood of memoirs after WWII, quoted in Liddell Hart, *The Sword and the Pen*, 1976.

A GENERAL who has taken part in a campaign is by no means best fitted to write its history. That, if it is to be complete and unbiased, should be the work of someone less personally involved. Yet such a general might write something of value. He might, as honestly as he could, tell of the problems he faced, why he took the decisions he did, what helped, what hindered, the luck he had, and the mistakes he made. He might, by showing how one man attempted the art of command, be of use to those who later may themselves have to exercise it. He

might even give, to those who have not experienced it, some impression of what it feels like to shoulder a commander's responsibilities in war. These things I have tried to do in this book.

Field Marshal Viscount Slim of Burma, *Defeat Into Victory*, 1956.

I MEAN to record the course of events as I saw them. I shall be as objective as I feel possible to be, but I have no intention whatever of departing, for any reason, from my own honest opinion as to events and personalities. So often, people make great play about being completely unprejudiced. Frankly, I am completely prejudiced, and I accept as a guide and as warning, Goethe's saying:

"I can promise to be upright but not to be unprejudiced."

Air Marshal Lord Tedder, *With Prejudice: The War Memoirs of Marshal of the Royal Air Force Lord Tedder, G.C.B.*, 1966.

THE WORST THING that anybody can do . . . is to keep an exact diary, because then he will put down every little resentment he had against Bill Smith and Joe Doakes. He will note everything that annoys him. Finally, his editors get hold of this and they say, "Oh, this is a gold mine." They take the things that he said and even emphasize them – the frictional type of entry – instead of those things which show that he thought things were going pretty well. I despise daily biographies as showing real history. I don't believe they do.

General of the Army Dwight D. Eisenhower, *General Eisenhower on the Military Churchill*, 1970.

ONE OF the aims of a personal memoir is, perhaps, an impossible one: a hope of re-creating for a new generation the immediacy, the reality, the heart-thumping excitement of events which youngsters know only by legend or the printed page – or perhaps do not know about at all. I have talked to college freshmen whose information about World War II was so limited they did not know that the first effort of the American and British ground forces to assault Hitler's European empire proceeded through the back door – Africa. Most of them were familiar with the ultimate assault across the English Channel, but few of them had any understanding of the early days of the war when there were numerous pessimists to whom the task of defeating Germany seemed impossible. Not long ago an intelligent young woman put this question to me: "Why did we invade French North Africa? The French were our friends."

Major-General Ernest N. Harmon, *Combat Commander: Autobiography of a Soldier*, 1970.

HE WHO THINKS of the past also has the future in mind. He who speaks of the future has no right to forget the past. Having gone through the inferno of many battles I know at first hand what war means and I do not want mankind to face that again.

Each line in these memoirs is the fruit of my own observations, experiences and reflections which may sometimes be subjective but are always sincere. I have spoken and will continue to speak of the last war without holding anything back, laying bare my thoughts and all that has troubled my soul.

Marshal of the Soviet Union Vasili I. Chuikov, *The End of the Third Reich*, 1978.

A MAJOR DRAWBACK of certain memoirs which I have read is the limited viewpoint in describing the combat events by the army commanders and even the front commanders. . . . At times, the strange impression is created that seemingly an experienced and educated military man, in fighting in the war within his demarcation lines and having adjacent units to the right and left, forgets that not only his failures but also his successes are tied to their actions. He forgets that to the right and to the left of him units are fighting from the very same Soviet Army and to these proper due must be paid just as to his own units. He forgets that this is all the same army and not some other and that the Germans are fighting not specifically against his army or front but against the Soviet Army as a whole, against all the armies and all the fronts.

Marshal of the Soviet Union Georgi K. Zhukov, quoted in *Voyenno istorichiskiy zhurnal*, 12/1987.

IN RECENT YEARS, I have been reminded how "history strengthens" by reading the memoirs of Generals Ulysses S. Grant and William T. Sherman. Both of these remarkable men were outstanding warfighting generals, but their personalities were radically different. Those personalities shine through their writing, and I think everyone can learn about human diversity and strength in the face of adversity by reading their memoirs.

General Gordon R. Sullivan, 'From My Bookshelf', *Military Review*, 11/91.

MENTOR/PREFERMENT

TO ACT in concert with a great man is the first of blessings.

Marquis de Lafayette, 1778, letter to George Washington.

IT WOULD finish me, could I have taken a sprig of these brave men's laurels. They are, and I glory in them, my darling children; served in my school; and all of us caught our professional zeal and fire from the great and good Earl of St. Vincent.

Admiral Viscount Nelson, March 1800, letter to Lord Keith on the successful sea engagements fought by men he had trained, quoted in David Howarth, *Nelson: The Immortal Memory*, 1986.

I WOULD NEVER have believed this preference could have happened to me, that I could come out

before the others in intellectual qualities, but he [Gerhard von Scharnhorst] convinced me he had thought me the most able in the school, and when I believed myself capable of this, I went ahead with confidence.

Major-General Carl von Clausewitz, quoted in Roger Parkinson, *Clausewitz*, 1971.

THE NOTICE of others has been the start of many successful men.

General George S. Patton, Jr., 1915, quoted in Robert H. Patton, *The Pattons*, 1994.

ORIGINALITY never yet led to preferment.

Admiral Sir John Fisher, *Memories*, 1919.

NOTHING could be more stimulating to a man who has consecrated himself to the search for the essential truth of war than this task of instructing those who will be called upon to apply it on the battlefield, where the lives of their soldiers and the fate of their country are at stake. But if, when found, he expects to instil that truth into minds, open indeed, but which the influences of practical military life have rendered somewhat sceptical toward school studies, the search must never be relaxed until at last he has seized it and made it his very own.

Marshal of France Ferdinand Foch, *The Memoirs of Marshal Foch*, 1931.

BY THE WAY, I have a favor to ask. When you are handing out diplomas at West Point you will see a cadet named Clarence Gooding, about 120 in standing. I would greatly appreciate your making some personal comment to this young fellow when you hand him his diploma. He was my office orderly at Benning – for only a few months. Having just enlisted, I was greatly impressed with his efficiency, bearing and general intelligence. I found out that he had been trying for West Point and had had no success. Finally he enlisted for this purpose and was refused permission to join the candidates class of men being coached. Without his knowledge, I wrote to his congressman in Texas and got the promise of an appointment if a vacancy occurred. The first alternate dropped out at the eleventh hour and Gooding received his appointment. The principal failed and Gooding passed. He is a fine boy and would be electrified by a personal word from you.

General of the Army George C. Marshall, 2 June 1936, letter to General of the Armies John J. Pershing, *Papers of George C. Marshall: The Soldierly Spirit*, 1981.

THE BATTALION returned to England in 1913 and an officer of our 2nd Battalion was posted to it who had just completed the two-year course at the Staff College at Camberley. His name was Captain Lefroy. He was a bachelor and I used to have long talks with him about the Army and what was wrong with it, and especially how one could get to real grips with the military art. He was interested at once, and helped me tremendously with advice about what books to read and how to study. I think it was Lefroy who first showed me the path to tread and encouraged my youthful ambition. He was killed later in the 1914–18 war and was a great loss to me and to the Army. . . . All this goes to show how important it is for a young officer to come in contact with the best type of officer and the right influences early in his military career. . . . In my case, the ambition was there, and the urge to master my profession. But is required advice and encouragement from the right people to set me on the road, and once that was forthcoming it was plainer sailing.

Field Marshal Viscount Montgomery, *The Memoirs of Field Marshal Montgomery*, 1958.

NOW RELATIONS with Uborevich were good. I felt that he was working with me. He took a look at me, gave me various assignments, and forced me to report. Then he assigned me . . . a report on the actions of the French Cavalry during the battle on the Po River during World War I. . . . For me this report was an unusual and difficult undertaking. Particularly as I, the division commander, was to give this report in the presence of all the comanders of the district combat arms and corps commanders. But I prepared for the report and was lost only at first. I hung up all the maps and then stopped by them; I had to start but stood there in silence. But Uborevich was able to help me at that moment and by his question called me into the conversation. Subsequently, everything went normally and he judged my report as good. . . . I repeat, I felt him working patiently with me.

Marshal of the Soviet Union Georgi K. Zhukov, quoted in *Voyenno istorichiskiy zhurnal*, 12/1987.

ALL COMMANDERS should consider the professional development of their subordinates as a principal responsibility of command. Commanders should foster a teacher-student relationship with their subordinates. . . . Commanders should see the development of their subordinates as a direct reflection on themselves.

General Alfred M. Gray and Major John Schmitt, *Warfighting*, United States Marine Corps, 1989.

MERCENARIES

THE CARTHAGINIANS were in the habit of forming their armies of mercenaries drawn together from the different countries; if they did so for the purpose of preventing conspiracies, and of making the soldiers more completely under the control of their generals, they may seem perhaps, in this respect, not to have acted foolishly, for troops of this sort cannot easily unite together in factious counsels. But when we take another view of the question, the wisdom of the proceeding may be doubted, if we consider the difficulty there is to instruct, soften, and subdue the

minds of an army so brought together when rage has seized them, and when hatred and resentment have taken root among them, and sedition is actually begun. In such circumstances, they are no longer men, but beasts of prey. Their fury cannot be restricted within the ordinary bounds of human wickedness or violence, but breaks out into deeds the most terrible and monstrous that are to be found in nature.

Polybius, *Histories*, 1.67, c. 125 BC (*Familiar Quotations from Greek Authors*, tr. Crauford Taut Ramage, 1895).

IF ANY ONE supports his state by the arms of mercenaries, he will never stand firm or sure, as they are disunited, ambitious, without discipline, faithless, bold amongst friends, cowardly amongst enemies, they have no fear of God, and keep no faith with men. Ruin is only deferred as long as the assault is postponed; in peace you are despoiled by them, and in war by the enemy. The cause of this is that they have no love or other motive to keep them in the field beyond a trifling wage, which is not enough to make them ready to die for you. They are quite willing to be your soldiers so long as you do not make war.

Niccolo Machiavelli, *The Prince*, 1513.

I ROARED, loved and romped,
And what I lauded most was sin . . .
Seeking common whores,
Vagabonding, picking quarrels, cursing,
Drinking away money and blood,
Everything was splendidly good.

Georg Greflinger, a German mercenary and later scholar, quoted in Langer, *The Thirty Years War*, 1980.

LET US therefore animate and encourage each other, and show the whole world that a Freeman contending for *Liberty* on his own ground is superior to any slavish mercenary on earth.

General George Washington, 2 July 1776, General Order to the Continental Army.

THE GREEKS in the service of the Great King were not enthusiastic in his cause. The Swiss in French, Spanish, and Italian service were not enthusiastic in their causes. The troops of Frederick the great, mostly foreigners, were not enthusiastic in his cause. A good general, good training, and good discipline make good troops independently of the cause in which they fight. It is true, however, that fanaticism, love of fatherland, and national glory can inspire fresh troops to good advantage.

Napoleon (1769–1821), quoted in Christopher Herold, ed., *The Mind of Napoleon*, 1955.

BETTER to lose one's life for the Fatherland, than hang a foreign tassel to one's sword.

Konstantinos Rhigas' immortal war song, quoted in Kolokotrones, *Theodoros Kolokotrones*, 1892; referring to the fact that many Greeks had joined foreign armies while Greece suffered under the Turkocratia.

MILITARISM

THOSE who enjoy militarism, however, will perish; and those who are ambitious for victory will be disgraced. War is not something to enjoy, victory is not an object of ambition.
  Sun Bin, *The Lost Art of War*, c. 350 BC,
  tr. Thomas Cleary.

PRUSSIA was hatched from a cannon ball.
  Napoleon (1769–1821).

WHEN I COME in contact with a militarist, his stupidity depresses me and makes me realize the amount of human obtuseness that has to be overcome before we can make much progress towards peace.
  Captain Sir Basil Liddell Hart, *Thoughts on War*, 1944.

MILITARY EDUCATION

THE LACADAEMONIANS made war their chief study. They are affirmed to be the first who reasoned on the events of battles and committed their observations thereon to writing with such success as to reduce the military art, before considered totally dependent on courage or fortune, to certain rules and fixed principles.
  Flavius Vegetius Renatus, *Military Institutions of the Romans*, c. AD 378, tr Clark, 1776.

WAR is not an affair of chance. A great deal of knowledge, study, and meditation is necessary to conduct it well.
  Frederick the Great, *Instructions to His Generals*, 1747,
  tr. Phillips, 1940.

EVERY ART has its rules and maxims. One must study them: theory facilitates practice. The lifetime of one man is not long enough to enable him to acquire perfect knowledge and experience. Theory helps to supplement it, it provides a youth with premature experience and makes him skillful also through the mistakes of others. In the profession of war the rules of the art never are violated without drawing punishment from the enemy, who is delighted to find us at fault. An officer can spare himself many mistakes by improving himself. We even venture to say that he must do it, because the mistakes that he commits through ignorance cover him with shame, and even in praising his courage one cannot refrain from blaming his stupidity.
  What an incentive to work hard! What reasons to travel the thorny road to glory! And what loftier and nobler compensation is there than to have one's name immortalized for his pains, and by his work.
  Frederick the Great, 'Avant-propos', 1771, *Oeuvres*,
  Vol. XXIX, 1846–1856, in Jay Luvaas, ed., *Frederick the Great on the Art of War*, 1966.

NONE OTHER than a Gentleman, as well as seaman, both in Theory and practice is qualified to support the Character of a Commissioned Officer in the Navy, nor is any Man fit to Command a Ship of War, who is not also capable of communicating his Ideas on Paper in Language that becomes his Rank.
  Admiral John Paul Jones (1747–1792).

GNEISENAU, if I had only learned something, what might not have been made of me! . . . But I put off everything I should have learned. Instead of studying, I have given myself to gambling, drink, and women; I have hunted, and perpetrated all sorts of foolish pranks. That's why I know nothing now. Yes, the other way I would have become a different kind of fellow, believe me.
  Field Marshal Prince Gebhard von Blücher, to Gneisenau, his chief of staff, during the 1813 campaign.

CORRECT THEORIES, founded upon right principles, sustained by actual events of wars, and added to accurate military history, will form a true school of instruction for generals. If these means do not produce great men, they will at least produce generals of sufficient skill to take rank next after the natural masters of the art of war.
  Lieutenant-General Antoine-Henri Baron de Jomini,
  Summary of the Art of War, 1838, tr. Mendell and Craighill, 1862.

IT IS necessary that the study of the military sciences should be encouraged and rewarded as well as courage and zeal. The military corps should be esteemed and honored; this is the only way of securing for the army men of merit and genius.
  Lieutenant General Antoine-Henri Baron de Jomini,
  Summary of the Art of War, 1838, tr. Mendell and Craighill, 1862.

THE CLOSE of the siege of Vicksburg found us with an army unsurpassed, in proportion to its numbers, taken as a whole of officers and men. A military education was acquired which no other school could have given. Men who thought a company was quite enough for them to command properly at the beginning, would have made good regimental or brigade commanders; most of brigade commanders were equal to the command of a division, and one, Ransom, would have been equal to the command of a corps at least. Logan and Crocker ended the campaign fitted to command independent armies.
  General of the Army Ulysses S. Grant, *Personal Memoirs of U.S. Grant*, 1885.

IT IS EVIDENT that a theoretical knowledge is not sufficient to that end; there must be a free, practical, artistic development of the qualities of mind and character, resting of course on a previous military education and guided by experience, whether it be the experience of military history or actual experience in war.

Field Marshal Helmuth Graf von Moltke, quoted in Ferdinand Foch, *Principles of War*, 1913.

I HOPE the officers of her Majesty's army may never degenerate into bookworms. There is happily at present no tendency in that direction, for I am glad to say that this generation is as fond of danger, adventure, and all manly out-of-door sports as its forefathers were. At the same time, all now recognize that the officer who has not studied war as an applied science, and who is ignorant of modern military history, is of little use beyond the rank of captain.

Field Marshal Viscount Wolseley, Preface to the English edition of Colmar von der Goltz, *The Conduct of War*, 1897.

AS I PERCEIVED that for increasing the power of rapid judgment in questions of tactics, it would be useful to make the head alert by means of such a game as chess, I commenced recently to study the Englishman Jane's book on chess and although I have not yet been able to attain the results expected, still, if I can get new ideas and make some improvements, it cannot be said to have been a waste of time. If we exploit the idea of this game, we shall surely reach points which will be of use to the study of the art of war.

Admiral Marquis Heihachiro Togo, c. 1898.

NOT TO promote war but to preserve peace.

Elihu Root, 1902, motto of the U.S. Army War College, Carlisle Barracks, Pennsylvania.

BESIDES the care of the men and the education of the non-commissioned officers – an education which was also calculated to assist in their future callings – I attached the greatest importance to increasing the efficiency of the Officer Corps and the training of the younger officers. While the personnel of the Regular Officers' Corps is always the same, the officers of the Reserve, the N.C.O.'s and men change continually. So the Officers' Corps is the mainspring of the Army. The officers must therefore be thoroughly conversant with the Army's great deeds and possess a comprehensive knowledge of their country's history, as it is expected of all men who have to lead others.

General Erich Ludendorff, *My War Memories 1914–1918*, 1919.

THERE CAN BE no better school for a commander of a regiment, or a brigade, or a division than the work of educating the platoon commander. . . . the best training of all is received by a teacher in teaching his pupils.

Leon Trotksy, 1922, *Military Writings of Leon Trotsky*, 1969.

TO-DAY we meet together as students, and it is only through mutual loyalty to each other that we shall profit by the work which lies before us. . . . As the director of your studies, the ideal I intend to aim at is that we shall teach each other; first, because we all have a vast amount of war experience behind us, and secondly, because, in my opinion, it is only through free criticism of each other's ideas that truth can be thrashed out. Mere swallowing of either food or opinions does not of necessity carry with it digestion, and without digestion swallowing is but labour lost and food wasted. . . . During your course here no one is going to compel you to work, for the simple reason that a man who requires to be driven is not worth the driving. . . . thus you will become your own masters, and until you learn how to teach yourselves, you will never be taught by others.

Major-General J.F.C. Fuller, from his first lecture at Camberley staff college, 1923, quoted in *Memoirs of an Unconventional Soldier*, 1936.

THE FOURTEEN MONTHS at the War College constituted a very marked dividing line in my professional life . . . during the years that followed the completion of the course I have been conscious that I possessed greater mental power than I before realized, and have felt able to meet successfully any difficulty which might confront me, or to overcome any obstacle which I might find in my path.

Major-General John A. Lejeune, *Reminiscences of a Marine*, 1929.

THOUGH the military art is essentially a practical one, the opportunities of practicing it are rare. Even the largest-scale peace maneuvers are only a feeble shadow of the real thing. So that a soldier desirous of acquiring skill in handling troops is forced to theoretical study of Great Captains.

Field Marshal Viscount Wavell of Cyrenaica, c. 1930, lecture to officers at Aldershot.

FOR MY STRATEGY, I could find no teachers in the field: but behind me there were some little years of military reading, and even in the little that I have written about it, you may be able to trace the allusions and quotations, the conscious analogies.

Colonel T.E. Lawrence (1888–1935).

THIS IS just not another training pamphlet; it is a magazine and like all good magazines it will be interesting, stimulating and, I hope, at times amusing. In it you will find current military thought, tips on training, and the lessons of war illustrated by experience in battle.

You will be the authors of the articles; you will contribute the ideas and suggestions that will make alive your training and your leadership. We have all got a lot to learn and we have all got something which, out of our own experience and study, we can teach. This magazine is to enable us to share the results of that experience and that study. I want every officer and NCO to read the

British Army Journal and I want a lot of you to contribute to it.

> Field Marshal Viscount Slim of Burma, 1949, Foreword to the first edition of the *British Army Journal*, later renamed *British Army Review*.

HOWEVER COMPETENT an officer may be, and however thorough his earlier training, he is always a risky investment until he pays off in combat.

> General of the Army Omar N. Bradley, *A Soldier's Story*, 1951.

FUNDAMENTAL to the training of senior officers will be the most comprehensive instruction possible in technical and organizational matters. The object of this instruction will be to induce a certain independence of mind, so that particular value will need to be laid on teaching officers to think critically on questions of basic principle. Respect for the opinion of this or that great soldier must never be allowed to go so far that nobody dares to discuss it. A sure sense of reality must be aroused. Given a well-founded knowledge of basic principles, any man of reasonably cool and logical mind can work out most of the principles for himself, provided he is not inhibited in his thinking.

> Field Marshal Erwin Rommel, *The Rommel Papers*, 1953.

IT IS sometimes thought that when an officer is promoted to the next higher command, he needs no teaching in how to handle it. This is a great mistake. There is a tremendous difference between a brigade and a division, between a division and a corps; when an officer got promotion, he needed help and advice in his new job and it was up to me to see that he got it.

> Field Marshal Viscount Montgomery of Alamein, *The Memoirs of Field Marshal Montgomery*, 1958.

OFFICERS, particularly those in positions of command, must at all times be urged to expand the scope of their knowledge; nothing has a more damaging effect on the quality of the army than a hard core of commanders whose minds are narrow and inflexible. Educated, enlightened commanders will produce soldiers equally enlightened and thirsty for knowledge, soldiers who will understand why they were recruited and for what they must fight.

> General Yigal Allon, *The Making of Israel's Army*, 1970.

WHEN field grade officers complain of the weakness of company-grade officers and non-commissioned officers, and in the next breath say they do not have time for unit schools, then something is amiss in their own education.

> Lieutenant-General Arthur S. Collins, Jr., *Common Sense Training*, 1978.

I WAS always being asked by the Navy brass what a destroyer skipper needs to know about Immanuel Kant; a liberally educated person meets new ideas with curiosity and fascination. An illiberally educated person meets new ideas with fear.

> Admiral James B. Stockdale, *Newsweek*, 1 September 1980.

INSTRUCTION at West Point should be mind-developing: mathematics, English, history, natural and experimental philosophy, geography (since high schools seem to have abandoned the subject), and certain selected foreign languages. The mind is the thing, as it used to be in the old days. That, plus character and discipline.

> General Hamilton H. Howze, *A Cavalryman's Story*, 1996.

MILITARY ETHICS

SPECIAL EMPHASIS should be given to ethical training, for leadership through moral inspiration is indispensable to high commanders and important staff officers. Great attention, therefore, must be directed to inculcating, besides the necessary military knowledge and techniques, military morality and martial spirit.

> Generalissimo Chiang Kai-shek, 1930, description of the Army staff college.

ETHICS are enablers. Personal, social, or military, they allow us to interact without needless viciousness and without generalized violence to the soul, the body, or society. In the military sphere, ethics in war allows us to disguise psychologically the requirement to butcher other human beings, masking the blunt killing behind concepts such as just war, higher causes, and approved behaviors. Ethics in war on the part of a Western society do not so much protect the objects of our violence as they shield us from the verity of our actions. Military ethics are ceremonial in the religious sense: they codify the darkness, implying a comforting order in the chaos and void. So long as we believe that we have behaved ethically, we can, statistically, bear the knowledge of our deeds.

> Lieutenant-Colonel Ralph Peters, *Fighting for the Future*, 1999.

MILITARY INTELLIGENCE

THERE ARE five uses of intelligence:
There is Local Intelligence;
There is Inside Intelligence;
There is Counterintelligence;
There is Deadly Intelligence;
There is Secure Intelligence.

When the five Intelligences all occur together
And none know the method,
This is called the Divine Web.
It is the treasure of the Ruler.

Local Intelligence is Using natives to show the way.

Inside Intelligence is Using others' officials to show the way.

Counterintelligence is Using the opponent's Intelligence to show the way.

Deadly Intelligence is Working to deceive outwardly. We knowingly direct the Intelligence and pass it on to the opponent.

Secure Intelligence is falsifying reports.

Hence, in the Work of the Entire Force
Nothing should be as favorably regarded as Intelligence;
Nothing should be as generously rewarded as Intelligence;
Nothing should be as confidential as the Work of Intelligence;

Intelligence cannot be employed without enlightenment and intuition.
Intelligence cannot be used without humanity and generosity.
The Work of Intelligence cannot succeed without subtlety and ingeniousness.

Subtly, very subtly,
Nowhere neglect the Use of Intelligence.

But if the Work of Intelligence has not yet begun,
Those who discuss it beforehand, and those who listen,
Are both dangerous.
>   Sun Tzu, *The Art of War*, 13, c. 500 BC, tr. R.L. Wing, 1988.

IT IS ESSENTIAL to know the character of the enemy and of their principal officers – whether they be rash or cautious, enterprising or timid, whether they fight on principle or from chance.
>   Flavius Vegetius Renatus, *The Military Institutions of the Romans*, c. AD 378, tr Clark, 1776.

NOTHING is more worthy of the attention of a good general than the endeavour to penetrate the designs of the enemy.
>   Niccolo Machiavelli, *Discourses*, xviii, 1531.

. . . THAT NO WAR can be conducted successfully without early and good intelligence, and that such advices cannot be had but at very great expense.
>   The Duke of Marlborough (1650–1722), quoted in S.J. Watson, *By Command of the Emperor*, 1957.

GREAT ADVANTAGE is drawn from knowledge of your adversary, and when you know the measure of his intelligence and character you can use it to play on his weaknesses.
>   Frederick the Great, *Instructions to His Generals*, 1747, tr. Phillips, 1940.

HAVE GOOD SPIES; get to know everything that happens among your enemies; sow dissension in their midst. To crush tyranny every method is fair.
>   Lazare Carnot, 1793, message to General Pichegru.

THE MOST DIFFICULT thing is to discern the enemy's plans, and to detect the truth in all reports one receives: the remainder requires only common sense.
>   Napoleon (1769–1821), in S.J. Watson, *By Command of the Emperor*, 1957.

TO GET INFORMATION, it is necessary to seize the letters in the postal system, to question travelers. In one word, you have to look for it. Intelligence never comes by itself.
>   Napoleon (1769–1821), quoted in Chuqet, *Inédits Napoléoniens*, 1913.

TO GUESS at the intention of the enemy; to divine his opinion of yourself; to hide from him both your intentions and opinion; to mislead him by feigned manoeuvres; to invoke ruses, as well as digested schemes, so as to fight under the best conditions – this is and always was the art of war.
>   Napoleon, quoted in J.F.C. Fuller, *Memoirs of an Unconventional Soldier*, 1936.

THE WHOLE ART of war consists in getting at what lies on the other side of the hill, or, in other words, what we do not know from what we do know.
>   The Duke of Wellington (1769–1852).

BY "INTELLIGENCE" we mean every sort of information about the enemy and his country – the basis, in short, of our own plans and operations. If we consider the actual basis of this information, how unreliable and transient it is, we soon realize that war is a flimsy structure that can easily collapse and bury us in its ruins. The textbooks agree, of course, that we should only believe reliable intelligence, and should never cease to be suspicious, but what is the use of such feeble maxims? They belong to that wisdom which for want of anything better scribblers of systems and compendia resort to when they run out of ideas.
>   Major-General Carl von Clausewitz, *On War*, 1.6, 1832, tr. Michael Howard and Peter Paret, 1976.

MOST INTELLIGENCE is false, and the effect of fear is to multiply lies and inaccuracies. As a rule most men would rather believe bad news than good, and rather tend to exaggerate the bad news. The dangers that are reported may soon, like waves, subside; but like waves they keep recurring, without apparent reason.
>   Major-General Carl von Clausewitz, *On War*, 1.6, 1832, tr. Michael Howard and Peter Paret, 1976.

HOW CAN any man say what he should do himself if he is ignorant what his adversary is about?

> Lieutenant-General Antoine-Henri Baron de Jomini, *Summary of the Art of War*, 1838, tr. Mendell and Craighill, 1862.

NOTHING should be neglected in acquiring a knowledge of the geography and military statistics of other states, so as to know their material and moral capacity for attack and defense as well as the strategic advantages of the two parties. Distinguished officers should be employed in these scientific labors and should be rewarded when they demonstrate marked ability.

> Lieutenant-General Antoine-Henri Baron de Jomini, *Summary of the Art of War*, 1838, tr. Mendell and Craighill, 1862.

A GENERAL should neglect no means of gaining information of the enemy's movements. For this purpose he should make use of reconnaissance, spies, bodies of light troops commanded by capable officers, signals, and questioning of deserters and prisoners.

Ever multiply the means of obtaining information, for no matter how imperfect and contradictory they may be the truth may often be sifted from them.

Perfect reliance should be placed on none of these means.

> Lieutenant-General Antoine-Henri Baron de Jomini, *Summary of the Art of War*, 1838, tr. Mendell and Craighill, 1862.

WITHOUT Combat Intelligence a commander has no right to issue a combat order.

> Anonymous U.S. Army G2 (intelligence officer at division or higher echelon) in WWII, quoted in Stedman Chandler and Robert Robb, ed, *Front Line Intelligence*, 1946.

EXPECT only five per cent of an intelligence report to be accurate. The trick of a good commander is to isolate the five per cent.

> General of the Army Douglas MacArthur, quoted in Courtney Whitney, *MacArthur*, 1956.

WITHOUT an efficient Intelligence organization a commander is largely blind and deaf.

> Field Marshal Earl Alexander of Tunis, *Memoirs*, 1962.

NOTHING helps a fighting force more than correct information. Moreover, it should be in perfect order, and done well by capable personnel.

> Ernesto 'Che' Guevara, 1963, memorandum.

AMERICANS have always had an ambivalent attitude toward intelligence. When they feel threatened, they want a lot of it, and when they don't, they regard the whole thing as somewhat immoral.

> General Vernon A. Walters, *Silent Missions*, 1978.

THE SINGLE most important objective during the period immediately prior to DESERT STORM and before G-Day (24 February 1991) was to focus all intelligence endeavors downwardly, and from the ARCENT view, this was on the Corps, and through it to the Captains, Lieutenants, and Sergeants who fight the war. During peacetime, much intelligence tends to be academic. In Washington, it supports "the policy maker." In Army units in peacetime, it informs commanders and supports contingency plans. In exercises, it often supports training objectives which tends to make it less than realistic. In DESERT STORM, intelligence was real. It was a vital battlefield operating system, but the crucial link between what the XVIII Airborne Corps and VII U.S. Corps Commanders wanted and the intelligence provided did not come about automatically or easily. It took leadership and great team effort. The system to provide specific intelligence for specific purposes had to be established, and that was a very complex task, indeed.

> Major-General John F. Stewart, Jr., *Operation Desert Storm, The Military Intelligence Story: A view from the G-2, 3d U.S. Army*, April 1991.

ANALYSIS is the core discipline in intelligence. As we face a new century that promises to be brutal and dense with human conflict, the ability to understand and anticipate our enemies (and difficult allies) will be the intelligence skill most in demand.

It will never be enough to get the electronic intelligence signatures right, or to correlate the imagery in a timely manner.

Ultimately warfare is not about the characteristics of objects, but the subject of character. It is important to know how many tanks are out there, but is is vital to understand how an opponent is likely to employ them, what his goals are and how his will can be broken.

> Lieutenant-Colonel Ralph Peters, *Army Times*, 24 August 1998.

MILITARY JUSTICE

THE COMMANDER should be severe and thorough in investigating charges against his men, but merciful in punishing them. This will gain him their good will.

> The Emperor Maurice, *The Strategikon*, c. AD 600 (*Maurice's Strategikon*, tr. George Dennis, 1984).

WHEN certain offenses are common among soldiers, moderation is called for. Do not judge and punish all indiscriminately. Widespread resentment might draw them all together, and discipline would become even worse. It is wiser to punish just a few of the ring leaders.

> The Emperor Maurice, *The Strategikon*, c. AD 600 (*Maurice's Strategikon*, tr. George Dennis, 1984).

COME HERE, my son. Better that I punish thee, than that God, for thy sin, visit vengeance on me and the whole army.

> Gustavus II Adolphus (1594–1632), to a petty officer whom he had grasped by the hair and was handing over to the executioners, after discovering that the man had stolen a cow, quoted in Theodore Ayrault Dodge, *Gustavus Adolphus*, 1895.

FIRST, it is very well known to all men of experience and judgment in matters of arms that all such great captains as have been lieutenants general to emperors, kings, or formed commonwealths, or that with regiments of their own nation have served foreign princes as mercenaries, knowing that justice is the prince of all order and government both in war and peace, by which God is honored and served and magistrates and officers obeyed, have at the first forming of their armies or such regiments, by great advice of counsel, established sundry laws both politic and martial, with officers for the superintending and due execution of the same. These laws have been notified to all their men of war, as also, at every encamping or lodging, they have been set, written, or printed in certain tables in convenient places for all soldiers and men of war to behold, to the intent that none might transgress the same through ignorance.

> John Smythe (c. 1580–1631), *Certain Discourses Military*, 1966

HE [the general] should have a good disposition free from caprice and be a stranger to hatred. He should punish without mercy, especially those who are dearest to him, but never from anger. He should always be grieved when he is forced to execute the military rules and should have the example of Manlius constantly before his eyes. He should discard the idea that it is he who punishes and should persuade himself and others that he only administers the military laws. With these qualities, he will be loved, he will be feared, and, without doubt, obeyed.

> Field Marshal Maurice Comte de Saxe, *My Reveries*, 1732, tr. Phillips, 1940.

NO OFFENSE must go unpunished, for nothing can cause the men so much harm as lax discipline.

> Field Marshal Prince Aleksandr V. Suvorov (1729–1800), quoted in K. Ossipov, *Suvorov*, 1945.

MEASURED military punishment, together with a short and clear explanation of the offense, touches the ambitious soldier more than brutality which drives him to despair.

> Field Marshal Prince Aleksandr V. Suvorov (1729–1800), quoted in Philip Longworth, *The Art of Victory*, 1965.

ONE OF the great defects in our military establishment is the giving of weak sentences for military offenses. The purpose of military law is administrative rather than legal. As the French say,

sentences are for the purpose of encouraging the others. I am convinced that, in justice to other men, soldiers who go to sleep on post, who go absent for an unreasonable time during combat, who shirk in battle, should be executed; and that Army Commanders or Corps Commanders should have the authority to approve the death sentence. It is utterly stupid to say that General officers, as a result of whose orders thousands of gallant and brave men have been killed, are not capable of knowing how to remove the life of one miserable poltroon.

> General George S. Patton, Jr., *War As I Knew It*, 1947.

MILITARY LIFE

THAT VARIETY incident to a military life gives our profession some advantage over those of a more even and consistent nature. We have all our passions and affections roused and exercised, many of which must have wanted their proper employment, had not suitable occasions obliged us to exert them. Few men are acquainted with the degree of their own courage till danger prove them, and are seldom justly informed how far the love of honour and the dread of shame are superior to the love of life. . . . Constancy of temper, patience, and all the virtues necessary to make us suffer with a good grace are likewise parts of our character, and . . . frequently called in to carry us through unusual difficulties. . . .

> Major-General Sir James Wolfe (1727–1759), quoted in Liddell Hart, *Great Captains Unveiled*, 1927.

I HAVE MET many officers of the garrison who were with me in Mexico. You have often heard me say the cordiality and friendship in the army was the great attraction of the service. It is that, I believe, that has has kept me so long, and it is that which now makes me fear to leave it. I do not know where I should meet with so much friendship out of it.

> General Robert E. Lee, letter from Mobile, Alabama, 1849, quoted in Fitzhugh Lee, *General Lee*, 1894, pp. 43–85.

WELL, never leave the Corps until you are absolutely unable to continue. It's the greatest life there is. I miss it terribly.

> Lieutenant-General Lewis B. 'Chesty' Puller, 7 February 1962, comment after retirement to visiting Marine NCOs, Marine Corps press release.

MEN have joined armed forces at different times for different reasons. I do not see many young men joining for philosophical reasons. Almost always the desire for an active life has been prominent among reasons for taking up the profession of arms, but there have usually been contributory motives. These have often been ephemeral in value, and in kind accidental rather than essential.

> General Sir John Hackett, *The Profession of Arms*, 1963.

I AM WRITING my own obituary. . . .

I loved the Army: it reared me, it nurtured me, and it gave me the most satisfying years of my life. Thanks to it I have lived an entire lifetime in 26 years. It is only fitting that I should die in its service. . . .

And yet I deny that I died FOR anything – not my country, not my Army, not my fellow man. I LIVED for these things, and the manner in which I chose to do it involved the very real chance that I would die in the execution of my duties. . . .

. . . The Army is my life, it is such a part of what I was that what happened is the logical outcome of the life I loved. I never knew what it is to be too old or too tired to do anything. I lived a full life in the Army, and it has exacted the price. It is only just.

> Major John Alexander Hottell, written for the *West Point Alumni Quarterly* about a year before his death in a helicopter crash on 7 July 1970.

– "TAKE CHARGE of this post and all government property in view" – the Army's first general order.
– The mission is primary, followed by taking care of your soldiers.
– Don't stand there. Do something!
– Lead by example.
– "No excuse, sir."
– Officers always eat last.
– Never forget, you are an American infantryman, the best.
– And never be without a watch, a pencil, and a notepad.

> General Colin Powell, his maxims of military life, *My American Journey*, 1995.

I HAVE NEVER put pressure on him and do not intend to. A person must choose his own path in life. Romanticism always comes at first and then it turns into some more stable feeling. But this is not even romanticism but work which, in spite of all the numerous deprivations, gives you deep satisfaction. Constantly reaching beyond yourself. . . . This is not given to everyone, and not everyone likes it. You have to love it. . . .

> General Aleksandr I. Lebed, speaking of his son's career choice and his own choice of military life, *Sobesednik* (Moscow), 4/1995.

MILITARY MUSIC

NOBLE and manly music invigorates the spirit, strengthens the wavering man, and incites him to great and worthy deeds.

> Homer, *The Iliad*, c. 800 BC, tr. Fagles, 1990.

AFTER THIS they joined battle, the Argives and their allies advancing with haste and fury, the Spartans slowly and to the music of many flute players – a standing institution in their army, that has nothing to do with religion, but is meant to make them advance evenly, stepping in time, without breaking their order, as large armies are apt to do in the moment of engagement.

> Thucydides, *The History of the Peloponnesian War*, 5.70, c. 404 BC, tr. Richard Crowley, 1910; of the Spartans at the Battle of Mantinea, summer 418 BC.

WHEN SOMEONE asked why Spartiates go into battle to the music of pipes, he said: "So that, as they proceed in step to the music, both the cowards and the brave may be clearly distinguished."

> Plutarch, quoting Agesilaus, Eurypontid King of Sparta (400–360 BC), *The Lives*, c. AD 100 (*Plutarch on Sparta*, tr. Richard Talbert, 1988).

I DON'T BELIEVE we can have an army without music.

> General Robert E. Lee, quoted in Burke Davis, *Gray Fox*, 1956.

THEY WOULD MARCH away in the dark, singing to the beat of drums.

> Siegfried Sassoon, *Memoirs of a Fox-Hunting Man*, 1928.

A FEW DAYS later Colonel Sims came to see me at the command post. Accompanying him was the 7th Marines band leader, who reported his casualties in the following manner: "I lost my first trumpet, second trombone, one drum, and second chair in the clarinet," or words to that effect. Like all bandsmen he was a musician at all times and at all places.

> General Merrill B. Twining, *No Bended Knee*, 1994, referring to the losses suffered by the band of the Seventh Marines as it was pressed into battle on Guadalcanal in 1943.

TO MY SURPRISE I was promoted to full colonel and assigned to the command of the 13th Armored Regiment. This consisted of three tank battalions, each (at full strength) of fifty-four tanks, a reconnaissance company, a headquarters company, a maintenance company, and a band: altogether, about 3,000 officers and men and a whole flock of tanks and ancillary vehicles. I felt rewarded beyond my desserts.

You may wonder about the band. It was a damned fine band, and its playing contributed significantly to morale. And in combat it knocked itself out handling ammunition – 160-odd tanks use up a whale of a lot of shot. The whole regiment loved the band.

> General Hamilton H. Howze, *A Cavalryman's Story*, 1996.

MILITARY SCIENCE

WAR is a science replete with shadows in whose obscurity one cannot move with assured step. Routine and prejudice, the natural result of ignorance, are its foundation and support. All sciences have principles and rules. War has none.

The great captains who have written of it give us none. Extreme cleverness is required merely to understand them.

Field Marshal Maurice Comte de Saxe, *My Reveries*, 1732, tr. Phillips, 1940.

WAR is a science for those who are outstanding; an art for mediocrities; a trade for ignoramuses.

Frederick the Great (1712–1786).

. . . THE SCIENCE of winning . . .

Field Marshal Prince Aleksandr V. Suvorov (1729–1800).

MILITARY SCIENCE consists in first calculating all the possibilities accurately and then in making an almost mathematically exact allowance for accident. It is on this point that one must make no mistake; a decimal more or less may alter everything. Now, this apportioning of knowledge and accident can take place only in the head of a genius, for without it there can be no creation – and surely the greatest improvisation of the human mind is that which gives existence to the nonexistent. Accident thus always remains a mystery to mediocre minds and becomes reality for superior men.

Napoleon, conversation in the early 1800s, quoted in Christopher Herold, ed., *The Mind of Napoleon*, 1955.

NOTHING is better calculated to kill natural genius and to cause error to triumph, than those pedantic theories, based upon the false idea that war is a positive science, all the operations of which can be reduced to infallible calculations.

Lieutenant-General Antoine-Henri Baron de Jomini, *Summary of the Art of War*, 1838, tr. Mendell and Craighill, 1862.

IT [strategy] is more than science, it is the translation of science into practical life, the further development of the original governing idea, in accordance with the ever-changing circumstances; it is the art of taking action under the pressure of the most trying conditions.

Field Marshal Helmuth Graf von Moltke, *On Strategy*, 1871.

AT THE PRESENT TIME no one thinks to assert that there might be a military science; it is as unthinkable as is a science of poetry, of painting, of music.

General Mikhail I. Dragomirov (1830–1905).

AN AGGREGATE of "military principles" does not constitute a military science, for there is no more a science of war than there is a science of locksmithing. An army leader requires the knowledge of a whole number of sciences in order to feel himself fully equipped for his *art*. But military science does not exist; there does exist a military craft which can be raised to the level of military art.

Leon Trotsky, 8 May 1922, speech to the Military Scientific Society, *Military Writings*, 1969.

THE MARXIAN METHOD is a method of historical and social science. There is no "science" of war, and there never will be any. There are many sciences war is concerned with. But war itself is not a science; war is practical art and skill. How could it be possible to shape principles of military art with the help of Marxian method? It is as impossible as it is impossible to create a theory of architecture or to write a veterinary textbook with the help of Marxism.

Leon Trotsky, *How the Revolution Developed its Military Power* (Moscow, 1924).

A STUDY of military history brings ample confirmation of Rebecca West's *mot*: "Before a war military science seems a real science, like astronomy, but after a war it seems more like astrology."

Captain Sir Basil Liddell Hart, *Thoughts on War*, 1944.

MILITARY SERVICE

FOR THERE IS justice in the claim that steadfastness in his country's battles should be as a cloak to cover a man's other imperfections; since the good action has blotted out the bad, and his merit as a citizen more than outweighed his demerits as an individual.

Pericles, 431/430 BC, funeral speech for the Athenian dead, quoted in Thucydides, *The Peloponnesian War*, 2.42, c. 404 BC, tr. Richard Crawley, 1910.

HOWEVER LONG you live and whatever you accomplish, you will find that the time you spent in the Confederate army was the most profitably spent portion of your life. Never again speak of having lost time in the army!

General Robert E. Lee, quoted in Douglas Southall Freeman, *R.E. Lee*, IV, 1934.

THE ARMY taught me some great lessons – to be prepared for catastrophe – to endure being bored – and to know that however fine a fellow I thought myself in my usual routine there were other situations in which I was inferior to men that I might have looked down upon had not experience taught me to look up.

Justice Oliver Wendell Holmes, Jr. (1841–1935).

IF WE JUDGE the future from the past, we perceive that though there may be no war, we must not rest at ease. It appears to me that a warrior's life is continual war; there is no reason why his responsibility should grow lighter or heavier by being in time of peace or war. If war breaks out, we display our military power; and if we are at peace, we cultivate it. We must always discharge our duty.

Admiral Marquis Heihachiro Togo, 21 December 1905, farewell speech to the Japanese Fleet, quoted in Ogasawara, *Life of Admiral Togo*, 1934.

IT IS WELL, that not only the nation pay this great tribute of respect and gratitude once every year to those who fell in defence of its liberties, – but that those who struggled in the same noble cause, and survived, should meet, and in some manner, live over again the scenes which make, and forever must make up, to them the most important era of their lives.

For there is no true loyal soldier to-day, who served his term of enlistment in the war of the Rebellion, who, if asked for some portion of his past life to be taken out of his record and remembrance, but would say – "Take whatever three or four years of my existence you will, but leave the old army life untouched, – I did in those days what you never did, and I can never do again – leave that to me."

> Clara Barton, address on Memorial Day, 30 May 1869, quoted in Percy Epler, *The Life of Clara Barton*, 1915.

NATIONAL PREPAREDNESS means . . . first of all, the moral organization of the people, an organization which creates in the heart of every citizen a sense of his obligation for service to the nation in time of war.

> Major-General Leonard Wood, *Our Military History*, 1916.

IN THE FIRST PLACE it is more than usually difficult to attract men of outstanding ability into the army in prolonged periods of peace. What, fundamentally, tempts such men to adopt the profession of arms, is the prospect of power. There can be little doubt that no power is comparable to that of the war leader. So long, therefore, as the probability exists of some day being able to win distinction in the field, men of high quality and distinction will never be lacking worthily to fill the higher posts in the fighting services of countries with a strong military tradition. But a generation which is convinced that it will never again be called upon to fight, is unlikely to contain many individuals of first-class quality who will feel any inclination to become regular soldiers, the more so since in a pacifist period soldiers are considered of small use and have little to look forward to in terms either of reputation or money. The strong-minded, therefore, the enterprising, and those of marked personality, are not unnaturally inclined to embark on careers which will give them power and the consideration of their fellows.

> General Charles de Gaulle, *The Edge of the Sword*, 1932.

OUR SOLDIERS join the Army to serve the people, not the officers.

> Chu Teh (1886–1976), Commander of the People's Liberation Army (PLA).

IT IS my sole wish to serve the Emperor as his shield. I will not spare my honor or my life.

> Admiral Isoroku Yamamoto, 1941.

THE MAJORITY of men, so long as they are treated fairly and feel that good use is being made of their powers, will rejoice in a new sense of unity with new

companions even more than they will mind the increased separation from their old associations.

> Brigadier-General S.L.A. Marshall, *The Armed Forces Officer*, 1950.

A YOUNG MAN who does not have what it takes to perform military service is not likely to have what it takes to make a living. Today's military rejects include tomorrow's hard core unemployed.

> President John F. Kennedy, statement on the need for training or rehabilitation of Selective Service rejectees, 30 September 1963, *Public Papers of the Presidents of the United States: John F. Kennedy, 1963*, 1963.

WINNING our wars is the fundamental philosophical basis for anyone's military service to his country. I fought DESERT SHIELD based on this premise. I told my subordinate commanders and my staff, we are all serving a unified command.

> General H. Norman Schwarzkopf, Commander, U.S. CENTCOM, quoted in *Joint Pub 1, Joint Warfare of the US Armed Forces*, 1991.

THOSE who have sworn to serve their country in the Armed Forces are servants of the security and freedom of nations. If they carry out their duty honourably they truly contribute to the common good of the nation and to the maintenance of peace.

> Catechism of the Catholic Church, 1994.

I'M NOT SURE, but I rather think that the military service is a profession more personal and more emotionally charged than most of the others: a professional soldier, sailor, or airman, though he may on some occasions be disgusted with his current job – and his job changes constantly – is more inclined to be sentimentally inclined in respect to his career than would say, a lawyer or a shopkeeper. I don't think lawyers, for instance, have songs about regimental exploits – good, bad, and ridiculous – or about the virtues of dying on the field of honor, or, when they die, going to some special place "halfway down to hell" where there are a lot of good horses and whiskey. At least I hope they don't.

> General Hamilton H. Howze, *A Cavalryman's Story*, 1996.

FIRST, and most important to the formulation of military policy, are the elites. At the outset, I would offer you an important touchstone: The greatest lingering effect of the Vietnam era on our society is the notion that military service during time of war is not a prerequisite for moral authority or even respect. The idea has been accorded a quiet affirmation among our elites, usually whispered to one another, that some lives are worth more than others, that it is right and proper for the so-called best and brightest by virtue of an elite education to be excused from the dirty work of society.

> James H. Webb, Jr., 'The Silence of the Admirals', *Proceedings*, 1/1999.

AS I WRITE, we are waging a thoughtless demi-war in the Balkans. In a curious manner, it illustrates our loss of moral example. The shared drabness of service no longer informs president or senator, and ignorance of military matters rules. When the Kennedys no longer serve, the Clintons will not. Today's aspiring politicians regard military service as a blue-collar detour unworthy of their time. As a result, an administration unparalleled in its arrogance has blundered into a disaster that has swiftly cost a people its homeland, that threatens America's last shreds of strategic credibility, and that may gut the NATO alliance. While weeks lie between this electronic dash of ink and the printed page, even a miraculous turn-about in the Balkans will not erase the incompetence with which this adventure was begun. At the heart of our nation's government, not one person has worn a uniform.

> Lieutenant-Colonel Ralph Peters, 'Hucksters in Uniform', *The Washington Monthly*, 5/1999.

MILITARY SERVICES

BEING AN AMERICAN is more than paying taxes and obeying the speed limit. The sacrifices of the past inform the greatness of the present, and the sacrifices of the present provide security for the future, and it is above all the military services that connect us all in such a way.

> James H. Webb, Jr., 'The Silence of the Admirals', *Proceedings*, 1/1999.

MILITARY VIRTUE/SPIRIT

THE MILITARY virtues are: bravery in the soldier, courage in the officer, valour in the general, but guided by the principles of order and discipline, dominated by vigilance and foresight.

> Field Marshal Prince Aleksandr V. Suvorov (1729–1800).

THE CHIEF VIRTUES of a soldier are constancy and discipline. Valor comes only in second place.

> Napoleon, 25 December 1799, proclamation, *Correspondance de Napoléon Ier, publiée par ordre de l'Empereur Napoléon III*, VI, p. 39, 1858–1870, quoted in Christopher Herold, ed., *The Mind of Napoleon*, 1955.

IF VALOR is the soldier's first virtue, constancy is the second.

> Napoleon, 20 February 1801, *Correspondance de Napoléon Ier, publiée par ordre de l'Empereur Napoléon III*, VII, p. 40, 1858–1870, quoted in Christopher Herold, ed., *The Mind of Napoleon*, 1955.

WAR is a special kind of activity, different and separate from any other pursued by man. . . . An army's military qualities are based on the individual who is steeped in the spirit and essence of this activity; who trains the capacities it demands, rouses them, and makes them his own; who applies his intelligence to every detail; who gains ease and confidence through practice; and who completely immerses his personality in the appointed task.

> Major-General Carl von Clausewitz, *On War*, 2, 1832, tr. Michael Howard and Peter Paret, 1976.

AN ARMY that maintains its cohesion under the most murderous fire; that cannot be shaken by imaginary fears and resists well-founded ones with all its might; that, proud of its victories, will not lose the strength to obey orders and its respect and trust for its officers even in defeat; whose physical power, like the muscles of an athlete, has been steeled by training, privation and effort; a force that regards such efforts as a means to victory rather than a curse on its cause; that is mindful of all these duties and qualities by virtue of the single powerful idea of the honor of its arms – such an army is imbued with the true military spirit.

> Major-General Carl von Clausewitz, *On War*, 3.5, 1832, tr. Michael Howard and Peter Paret, 1976.

BY INURING armies to labor and fatigue, by keeping them from stagnation in garrison in times of peace, by inculcating their superiority over their enemies (without despising the latter too much), by inspiring a love for great exploits – in a word, by exciting their enthusiasm by every means in harmony with their tone of mind, by honoring courage, punishing weaknesss, and disgracing cowardice – we may expect to maintain a high military spirit.

> Lieutenant-General Antoine-Henri Baron de Jomini, *Summary of the Art of War*, 1838, tr. Mendell and Craighill, 1862.

THE OTHER distinct thing is that military virtues, as Arnold Toynbee calld them – fortitude, personal loyalty, consistency and compassion – make any group of men a better group to be in than one in which those qualities are absent.

The difference between the profession of arms and other professions then is that these qualities are not simply agreeable ones to have, but are functional necessities.

> General Sir John Hackett, quoted in 'Are Soldiers Civilized?', *Parameters*, Summer 1984.

MILITIA

THEY COME in you cannot tell how; go out you cannot see when; act you cannot tell where; consume your provisions; exhaust your stores; and leave you at last in a critical moment.

> George Washington (1732–1799), quoted in J.F.C. Fuller, *Decisive Battles of the U.S.A.*, 1953.

MEN just dragged from the tender Scenes of domestick life; unaccustomed to the din of Arms;

totally unacquainted with every kind of Military skill, which being followed by a want of confidence in themselves, when opposed to Troops regularly train'd, disciplined, and appointed, superior in knowledge, and superior in Arms, makes them timid, and ready to fly from their own shadows.

> George Washington, 24 September 1776, letter to the President of Congress, *The Writings of George Washington*, VI, p. 110, John C. Fitzgerald, ed., 1932.

NO MILITIA will ever acquire the habits necessary to resist a regular force. . . . The firmness requisite for the real business of fighting is only to be attained by a constant course of discipline and service. I have never yet been witness to a single instance that can justify a different opinion, and it is most ernestly to be wished that the liberties of America may no longer be trusted, in any material degree, to so precarious a dependence.

> George Washington, 15 September 1780, letter to the President of Congress, *The Writings of George Washington*, XX, p. 50, John C. Fitzgerald, ed., 1937.

I WOULD NOT have had a swamp in the view of the militia on any consideration; they would have made for it, and nothing could have detained them from it. And as to covering my wings, I knew my adversary, and was perfectly sure I should have nothing but downright fighting. As to retreat, it was the very thing I wished to cut off all hope of. I would have thanked Tarleton had he surrounded me with his cavalry. It would have been better than placing my own men in the rear to shoot down those who broke from the ranks. When men are forced to fight, they will sell their lives dearly. . . . Had I crossed the river, one half of the militia would immediately have abandoned me.

> Daniel Morgan, description of his use of militia at the Battle of Cowpens, 1781.

THE NORTH CAROLINA militia . . . abandoned us. . . . Many were missing, as is always the case with militia after battle; but they generally are to be found safe at their own firesides.

> Major-General Henry 'Light Horse Harry' Lee, of the militia at the Battle of Guilford Court House, 15 March 1781, *Memoirs of the War in the Southern Department*, 1869.

IN THIS peaceful service I imbibed the rudiments of the language and science of tactics, which opened a new field of observation and study. . . . The discipline and evolution of a modern battalion gave me a clearer notion of the Phalanx and the Legions, and the Captain of the Hampshire grenadiers (the reader may smile) has not been useless to the historian of the Roman Empire.

> Edward Gibbon (1737–1794), reminiscing on his militia service during the Seven Years War, *Autobiography*, 1962.

SUCH NOBLE REGIMENTS they have. Three field officers, four staff officers, ten captains, thirty lieutenants, and one private with a misery in his bowels.

> Lieutenant-General D.H. Hill, 24 April 1863, of the Confederate state militias.

MISTAKES

IN WAR there is never any chance for a second mistake.

> Lamarchus (465–414 BC), quoted in Plutarch, *Apothegms*.

I AM more afraid of our own blunders than of the enemy's devices.

> Pericles, 432 BC, speech to the Athenians encouraging a firm policy against the Spartans, quoted in Thucydides, *History of the Peloponnesian War*, 1.144, c. 404 BC, tr. Richard Crawley, 1910.

MISTAKES made in ordinary affairs can generally be remedied in a short while, but errors made in war cause lasting harm.

> The Emperor Maurice, *The Strategikon*, c. AD 600 (*Maurice's Strategikon*, tr. George Dennis, 1984).

WHEN a man has committed no faults in war, he can only have been engaged in it but a short time.

> Marshal of France Vicomte de Turenne, 1645, after the Battle of Marienthal.

GENTLEMEN, when the enemy is committed to a mistake, we must not interrupt him too soon.

> Admiral Viscount Nelson, quoted in Alfred Thayer Mahan, *The Life of Nelson*, 1897.

THE GREATEST general is he who makes the fewest mistakes.

> Napoleon (1769–1821).

IT SHOULD NOT be believed that a march of three or four days in the wrong direction can be corrected by a countermarch. As a rule, this is to make two mistakes instead of one.

> Napoleon, 2 July, 1808, note, *Correspondance de Napoléon Ier, publiée par ordre de l'Empereur Napoléon III*, XVII, p. 409, 1858–1870, cited in Christopher Herold, ed., *The Mind of Napoleon*, 1955.

IF I AM to be hanged for it, I cannot accuse a man who I believe has meant well . . . although my errors, and those of others also, are visited heavily upon me, that is not the way in which any, much less a British army, can be commanded.

> The Duke of Wellington, 1810, of General Craufurd, *Supplementary Despatches, Correspondence and Memoranda of Field Marshal Arthur Duke of Wellington, K.G., 1794–1818*, VI, 1860, p. 564.

AFTER it is all over, as stupid a fellow as I am can see the mistakes that were made. I notice, however, that my mistakes are never told me until it is too late, and you, and all my officers, know that I am always ready and anxious to have their suggestions.

> General Robert E. Lee, in remarks to Major-General Henry Heth, quoted in Early, ed., *Southern Historial Society Papers*, 153, 159–160, cited in Douglas Southall Freeman, *R.E. Lee, A Biography*, 1932.

I DRAW a distinction between mistakes. There is the mistake which comes through daring – what I call a mistake towards the enemy – in which you must sustain *your* commanders. . . . There are mistakes from the safety-first principle – mistakes of turning away from the enemy; and they require a far more acid consideration.

> Sir Winston S. Churchill (1874–1965).

MY GOD, Senator, that's the reason we do it. I want the mistake down in Louisiana, not over in Europe, and the only way to do this thing is try it out, and if it doesn't work, find out what we need to make it work.

> General of the Army George C. Marshall, to a senator who complained of the number of mistakes made in the Louisiana manoeuvres of 1940, quoted in Forrest Pogue, *George Marshall: Ordeal and Hope: 1939–1942*, 1965.

NOTHING is easy in war. Mistakes are always paid for in casualties and troops are quick to sense any blunder made by their commanders.

> General of the Army Dwight D. Eisenhower, *Crusade in Europe*, 1948.

VICTORY in battle – save where it is brought about by sheer weight of numbers, and omitting all question of the courage of the troops engaged – never comes solely as the result of the victor's planning. It is not only the merits of the victor that decide the issue, but also mistakes on the part of the vanquished.

> Field Marshal Erwin Rommel, *The Rommel Papers*, 1953.

THE TRAINING of armies is primarily devoted to developing efficiency in the detailed execution of the attack. This concentration on tactical technique tends to obscure the psychological element. It fosters a cult of soundness, rather than surprise. It breeds commanders who are so intent not to do anything wrong, according to "the book", that they forget the necessity of making the enemy do something wrong. The result is that their plans have no result. For, in war, it is by compelling mistakes that the scales are most often turned.

> Captain Sir Basil Liddell Hart, *Strategy*, 1954.

HAPPILY for the result of the battle – and for me – I was, like other generals before me, to be saved from the consequences of my mistakes by the resourcefulness of my subordinate commanders and the stubborn valour of my troops.

> Field Marshal Viscount Slim of Burma, *Defeat Into Victory*, 1956.

TO INQUIRE if and where we made mistakes is not to apologize. War is replete with mistakes because it is full of improvizations. In war we are always doing something for the first time. It would be a miracle if what we improvized under the stress of war should be perfect.

> Vice Admiral Hyman G. Rickover, April 1964, testimony before the House Military Appropriations Subcommittee.

YOU MUST BE able to underwrite the honest mistakes of your subordinates if you wish to develop their initiative and experience.

> Lieutenant-General Bruce C. Clarke (1901–1988).

INITIATIVE, the willingness to act on one's own judgment, is prerequisite for boldness. These traits carried to excess can lead to rashness, but we must realize that errors by junior leaders stemming from over-boldness are a necessary part of learning. We should deal with such errors leniently; there must be no "zero defects" mentality. Not only must we not stifle boldness and initiative, we must continue to encourage both traits *in spite of mistakes*. On the other hand, we must deal severely with errors of inaction or timidity. We will not accept lack of orders as justification for inaction; it is each Marine's duty to take initiative as the situation demands.

> General Alfred M. Gray and Major John Schmitt, *Warfighting*, United States Marine Corps, 1989.

MISTAKES are acts of commission. That is, you did something you thought was right, but it turns out that you made the wrong choice. It was a mistake. There are lessons to be learned from mistakes. Good leaders create an environment where subordinates are allowed to make mistakes, yet are not put into situations for which they are unprepared or in which the scope of the mistake could be dangerous. . . .

Frequently those who cannot tolerate mistakes are guilty of irresponsible behavior themselves. They have been given responsibility for the training and leadership development of their subordinate Marines. But how can they encourage imaginative training or promote safe risk taking, if their junior leaders retreat from new ideas for fear of making a mistake? If it is safer to repeat a proven course of action or to do nothing, why try something new? How do you develop a leader, a decision maker, if you never let them make decisions? These are the dilemmas to which a zero-defects mentality leads.

> General Charles C. Krulak, *Marine Corps Gazette*, 5/1997.

TO ERR is human; to forgive is divine, and neither is the policy of the U.S. Navy.

U.S. Navy saying, quoted in *Proceedings*, 2/1981.

MOBILITY/MOVEMENT

APTITUDE for war is aptitude for movement.

Napoleon, *Maxims of War*, 1831.

FORCE does not exist for mobility, but mobility for force.

Rear Admiral Alfred Thayer Mahan, *Lessons of the War with Spain*, 1899.

SUCCESS in war depends upon mobility and mobility upon time. Mobility leads to mass, to surprise and to security. Other things being equal, the most mobile side must win: this is a truism in war as in horse-racing. The tank first of all is a time-saving machine, secondly a shield – it is, in fact, a mechanical horse. If in a given time we can do three times as much as the enemy and lose a third less than he does, our possibilities of success are multiplied by nine.

Major-General J.F.C. Fuller, memorandum of 1917, *Memoirs of an Unconventional Soldier*, 1936.

MOVEMENT is the safety-valve of fear; unless we wish to risk a sudden collapse of the man's nerve control, we must open the valve. (July 1921.)

Captain Sir Basil Liddell Hart, *Thoughts on War*, 1944.

WE NEED bold and free flight, we need mobility.

Mikhail Frunze, 1921.

TWO THINGS stop the movement of armies: (a) bullets and fragments of shell which destroy the motive power of men, and (b) the confusion of the conflict.

Sir Winston S. Churchill, *The World Crisis*, 1923.

THE PRINCIPLE of Movement. If concentration of weapon-power be compared to a projectile and economy of force to its line of fire, then movement may be looked upon as the propellant and as a propellant is not always in a state of explosive energy, so neither is movement. Movement is the power of endowing mass with momentum; it depends, therefore, largely on security, which, when coupled with offensive power, results in liberty of action. Movement consequently, may be potential as well as dynamic, and, if an army be compared to a machine the power of which is supplied to it by a series of accumulators, should the object of its commander be to maintain movement, he can only accomplish this by refilling one set of accumulators while the other is in the process of being exhausted. The shorter the time available to do this the more difficult will the commander's task be; consequently, one of his most important duties, throughout war, is to increase the motive power of his troops, which depends on two main factors – moral and physical endurance.

Major-General J.F.C. Fuller, *The Reformation of War*, 1923.

AS IN individual combat, mobility is not only the link between security and surprise, but their mainstring. Mobility is economic movement, i.e. movement that fulfills the law of economy of force. The means to it are the direction given by the commander, the speed with which this is carried out, and the co-operation by which fulfilment is ensured without check or waste of energy – caused by friction, loss of touch, and misunderstanding of the plan or direction. (Jan. 1926.)

Captain Sir Basil Liddell Hart, *Thoughts on War*, 1944.

IT IS WORTH recalling that the Mongols, although their army was entirely composed of mobile troops, found neither the Himalayas nor the far-stretching Carpathians a barrier to progress. For mobile troops there is usually a way around. (Sept. 1927.)

Captain Sir Basil Liddell Hart, *Thoughts on War*, 1944.

BATTLE implies mobility, strategic and tactical. The army which seeks to fight another must be able to move quickly against it. On the battlefield the troops must be able to move forward in face of the enemy's fire. Once the issue is decided, the army must be able to follow up the beaten enemy, and complete the victory. Battle also implies the immobilization of the enemy – the paralysis of his powers of movement so that, in the first place, he may not be able to slip away, and second, that he may not be able to counter your strokes. (Jan. 1933.)

Captain Sir Basil Liddell Hart, *Thoughts on War*, 1944.

MOBILISATION

THE YOUNG MEN shall fight; the married men shall forge weapons and transport supplies; the women will make tents and serve in the hospitals; the children will make up old linen into lint; the old men will have themselves carried into the public squares to rouse the courage of the fighting men, and to preach hatred of kings and the unity of the Republic. The public buildings shall be turned into barracks, the public squares into munitions factories; the earthen floors of cellars shall be treated with lye to extract saltpetre. All suitable firearms shall be turned over to the troops; the interior shall be policed with fowling pieces and with cold steel. All saddle horses shall be seized for the cavalry; all draft horses not employed in cultivation will draw the artillery and supply wagons.

Decree of the Committee of Public Safety, France, 23 August 1793.

WHEN A NATION is without establishments and a military system, it is very difficult to organize an army.

Napoleon, *Maxims of War*, 1831.

IN MAKING an army, three elements are necessary – men, weapons and money. There must also be time.
 Sir Winston S. Churchill (1874–1965).

MOBILIZATION will inevitably mean war.
 German ultimatum to France, 1 August 1914, quoted in Captain Sir Basil Liddell Hart, *The Real War*, 1930.

THE ADVANCE of armies formed of millions of men . . . was the result of years of painstaking work. Once planned, it could not possibly be changed.
 General Count Helmuth von Moltke 'The Younger', 2 August 1914, to Kaiser Wilhelm's suggestion that the mobilisation to attack France be abandoned to concentrate instead on Russia, quoted in Captain Sir Basil Liddell Hart, *The Real War*, 1930.

EVERYONE will now be mobilized and all boys old enough to carry a spear will be sent to Addis Ababa. Married men will take their wives to carry food and cook. Those without wives will take any woman without a husband. Women with small babies need not go. The blind, those who cannot walk or for any reason cannot carry a spear are exempted. Anyone found at home after receipt of this order will be hanged.
 Emperor Haile Selassie's mobilisation order issued after the Italian invasion of Ethiopia in 1935.

WHAT DOES political mobilization mean? First, it means telling the army and the people about the political aim of the war. It is necessary for every soldier and civilian to see why the war must be fought and how it concerns him.
 Mao Tse-tung, *On Protracted War*, May 1938.

I WANT to make it clear that it is the purpose of the nation to build now with all possible speed every machine, every arsenal, every factory that we need to manufacture our defense material. We have the men – the skill – the wealth – and above all the will.
 President Franklin D. Roosevelt, 29 December 1940, 'Fireside Chat' on national security.

THE ARMY used to have all the time in the world and no money; now we've got all the money and no time.
 General of the Army George C. Marshall, January 1942, remark on the mobilisation for WWII.

MOMENTUM

IN BATTLE, momentum means riding on the force of the tide of events. If enemies are on the way to destruction, then you follow up and press them; their armies will surely collapse.
 The rule is "Use the force of momentum to defeat them . . ."
 Liu Ji (1310–1375), *Lessons of War* (*Mastering the Art of War*, tr. Thomas Cleary, 1989).

NEVER pull up during an attack.
 Field Marshal Prince Aleksandr V. Suvorov, *The Science of Victory*, 1796.

[THE BALANCE of rest and activity, the tricks to keep up the momentum] With this you get speed and the men don't get tired. The enemy reckons we're sixty miles away. . . . Suddenly we're on him like a cloudburst. His head whirls. Attack! That's why we came, that's why God sent us. Cavalry! Charge! Cut down, stab, chase, don't let them get away.
 Field Marshal Prince Aleksandr V. Suvorov, *The Science of Victory*, 1796.

MAXIM 9. The strength of an army, like the power in mechanics, is estimated by multiplying the mass by the rapidity; a rapid march augments the morale of an army, and increases all the chances of victory.
 Napoleon, *The Military Maxims of Napoleon*, tr. George D'Aguilar, 1831 (David Chandler, ed., 1987.

ABSTAINING from follow-on operations until the enemy army is completely destroyed deprives the victor of continued control of the situation. A pause faces him with the need to fight a new battle, in which the chances of success are more or less equal for both sides, just as they are in the initial operation. Above all a pause of this kind leads to indecisiveness of command, likewise to unpreparedness of service support – physical communications, signals and supplies.
 Marshal of the Soviet Union Mikhail N. Tukhachevskiy, 1924, quoted in Richard Simpkin, *Deep Battle*, 1987.

TWO fundamental lessons of war experience are – never to check momentum; never to resume mere pushing.
 Captain Sir Basil Liddell Hart, *Thoughts on War*, 1944.

MORAL ASCENDANCY/MORAL FORCE

MOVE FORWARD yourself with the cavalry and one battalion, and dash at the first enemy that comes into your neighborhood. You will either cut them up or drive them off . . . A long defensive war will ruin us . . . Dash at the first fellows that make their appearance and the campaign will be your own.
 The Duke of Wellington, 1800, in India, *The Dispatches of Field Marshal the Duke of Welllington, During His Various Campaigns in India, Denmark, Portugal, Spain, the Low Countries, and France*, II, 1834–1838, pp. 208, 210, 219.

WE MUST get the upper hand, and, if once we have that, we shall keep it with ease and shall certainly succeed.
 The Duke of Wellington, 17 August 1803, to Lieutenant-Colonel Close, quoted in Arthur Bryant, *The Great Duke*, 1972.

. . . THEY [the British soldiers] have obtained by their spirit and enterprise an ascendency over the French which nothing but great superiority of numbers on their part can get the better of.

> General Sir John Moore, 28 December 1808, to Castlereagh, from Benavente, quoted in Charles Oman, *History of the Peninsular War*, I, 1902.

MARCHING on Landshut I met Bessières retreating. I ordered him to march forward. He objected that the enemy were in force. – Go ahead, – said I, and he advanced. The enemy seeing him take the offensive thought he was stronger than they and retreated. In war that is the way everything goes. It is moral force more than numbers that wins victory.

> Napoleon, 14 June 1817, on St. Helena, quoted in R.M. Johnston, ed., *The Corsican*, 1910.

THE MORAL ELEMENTS are among the most important in war. They constitute the spirit that permeates war as a whole, and at an early stage they establish a close affinity with the will that moves and leads the whole mass of force, practically merging with it, since the will is itself a moral quantity. Unfortunately they will not yield to academic wisdom. They cannot be classified or counted. They have to be seen or felt.

> Major General Carl von Clausewitz, *On War*, 3.3, 1832, tr. Michael Howard and Peter Paret, 1976.

THEY [moral elements] are: *the skill of the commander, the experience and courage of the troops, and patriotic spirit*. The relative value of each cannot be universally established; it is hard enough to discuss their potential, and even more difficult to weight them against each other. The wisest course is not to underrate any of them – a temptation to which human judgment, being fickle, often succumbs. It is far preferable to muster historical evidence of the unmistakable effectiveness of all three.

> Major-General Carl von Clausewitz, *On War*, 3.4, 1832, tr. Michael Howard and Peter Paret, 1976.

LEE'S ARMY is really whipped. The prisoners we now take show it, and the action of his army shows it unmistakably. A battle with them outside of entrenchments cannot be had. Our men feel that they have gained the *morale* over the enemy, and attack him with confidence. I may be mistaken, but I feel that our success over Lee's army is already assured. The promptness and rapidity with which you have forwarded reinforcements has contributed largely to the feeling of confidence inspired in our men, and to break down that of the enemy.

> General of the Army Ulysses S. Grant, 26 May 1864, *Personal Memoirs of U.S. Grant*, II, 1885.

COMBAT TODAY requires . . . a moral cohesion, a unity more binding than at any other time. If one does not wish the bonds to break, he must make them more elastic to strengthen them.

> Colonel Charles Ardant du Picq, *Battle Studies*, 1880, tr. Greely, 1957.

IN BATTLE, two moral forces, even more than two material forces, are in conflict. The stronger conquers.

> Colonel Charles Ardant du Picq, *Battle Studies*, 1880, tr. Greely, 1957.

THE ARMY of the Tennessee had won five successive victories over the garrison of Vicksburg in the three preceding weeks. They had driven a portion of the army from Port Gibson with considerable loss, after having flanked them out of their stronghold at Grand Gulf. They had attacked another portion of the same army at Raymond, more than fifty miles farther in the interior of the State, and driven them back into Jackson with great loss in killed, wounded, captured and missing, besides loss of large and small arms; they had captured the capital of the State of Mississippi, with a large amount of materials of war and manufactures. Only a few days before, they had beaten the enemy then penned up in the town first at Champion's Hill, next at Big Black River Bridge, inflicting upon him a loss of fifteen thousand or more men . . . besides large losses in arms and ammunition. The Army of the Tennessee had come to believe that they could beat their antagonist under any circumstances.

> General of the Army Ulysses S. Grant, *Personal Memoirs*, 1885.

THE POWERFUL moral effect of our assuming the offensive, when nothing but surrender had been expected, seemed to bewilder them. Before they could recover from the shock of their surprise, Captain Flint, the leader, had fallen dead in their sight. Before the impetuous onset of my men they now broke and fled. No time was given them to re-form and rally.

> Colonel John S. Mosby, *Mosby's War Reminiscences*, 1887.

THEY CLAIM that to fire human grapeshot at the enemy without preparation, gives us moral ascendancy. But the thousands of dead Frenchmen, lying in front of the German trenches, are instead those who are giving moral ascendancy to the enemy. If this waste of human material keeps on, the day is not far off when the offensive capacity of our army, already seriously weakened, will be entirely destroyed.

> Lieutenant Abel Ferry, 1916, memorandum to the French Cabinet; Ferry was a Deputy in the French Assembly and a reserve officer in the field.

THE MOST solid moral qualities melt away under the effect of modern arms.

> Marshal of France Ferdinand Foch, *Precepts and Judgments*, 1919.

MORAL FORCES may take a back seat at Committees of Imperial Defense or in War Offices; at the front they are where Joab put Uriah.

General Sir Ian Hamilton, *The Soul and Body of an Army*, 1921.

MORAL FORCE is, unhappily, no substitute for armed force, but it is a very great reinforcement.

Sir Winston S. Churchill, 21 December 1937, speech in the House of Commons.

WHEN MEN become fearful in combat, the moral incentive can restore them and stimulate them to action. But when they become hopeless, it is because all moral incentive is gone. Soldiers who have ceased to hope are no longer receptive beings. They have become oblivious to all things, large and small.

Brigadier-General S.L.A. Marshall, *The Armed Forces Officer*, 1950.

SOLDIERS universally concede the general truth of Napoleon's much-quoted dictum that in war "the moral is to the physical as three to one". The actual arithmetical proportion may be worthless, for morale is apt to decline if the weapons are inadequate, and the strongest will is of little use if it is inside a dead body. But although the moral and physical factors are inseparable and indivisible, the saying gains its enduring value because it expresses the idea of the predominance of moral factors in all military decisions. On them constantly turns the issue of war and battle. In the history of war, they form the more constant factors, changing only in degree, whereas the physical factors are different in almost every war and every military situation.

Captain Sir Basil Liddell Hart, *Strategy*, 1954.

THERE IS no rule for the moral unifying of military forces under the pressures of the battlefield that is not equally good in the training that conditions troops to this eventuality. For the group to feel a great spiritual solidarity – for its members to be bound together by mutual confidence and the satisfactions of a rewarding comradeship – is the foundation of great enterprise. But it is more than that. Unaccompanied by a strengthening of the military virtues and a rise in the martial spirit, a friendly unity will not of itself point men directly toward the main object in training, or enable them to dispose themselves efficiently toward each other on entering battle.

Brigadier-General S.L.A. Marshall, *The Officer as a Leader*, 1966.

MORALE

Note: often spelled 'moral' in the 19th and early 20th centuries

A WHOLE ARMY may be robbed of its spirit; a commander-in-chief may be robbed of his presence of mind.

Now a soldier's spirit is keenest in the morning; by noonday it has begun to flag; and in the evening his mind is bent only on returning to camp.

A clever general, therefore, avoids an army when its spirit is keen, but attacks when it is sluggish and inclined to return. This is the art of studying moods.

Sun Tzu, *The Art of War*, 7, c. 500 BC, tr. Giles, 1910.

YOU ARE all aware that it is not numbers or strength that bring the victories in war. No, it is when one side goes against the enemy with the gods' gift of a stronger morale that their adversaries, as a rule, cannot withstand them.

Xenophon, *The Persian Expedition*, 3.1, c. 360 BC, tr. Rex Warner.

DEFEATED TROOPS should not be allowed to fall into despair, but they should be dealt with by stirring up hope and by various other means.

The Emperor Maurice, *The Strategikon*, c. AD 600 (*Maurice's Strategikon*, tr. George Dennis, 1984).

HE [Chevalier Folard] supposes all men to be brave at all times and does not realize that the courage of the troops must be reborn daily, that nothing is so variable, and that the true skill of the general consists of knowing how to guarantee it.

Field Marshal Maurice Comte de Saxe, *My Reveries*, 1732, tr. Phillips, 1940.

MY LORD, I never saw better horses, better clothes, finer belts and accoutrements; but money, which you don't want in England, will buy fine clothes and horses, but it can't buy the lively air, I see in everyone of these troopers.

Field Marshal Prince Eugene, June 1740, quoted in David Chandler, *The Art of War in the Age of Marlborough*, 1976.

A BATTLE is lost less through the loss of men than by discouragement.

Frederick the Great, *Instructions to His Generals*, 1747, tr. Phillips, 1940.

IN WAR, everything depends on morale; and morale and public opinion comprise the better part of reality.

Napoleon (1769–1821).

MORALE makes up three quarters of the game; the relative balance of man-power accounts only for the remaining quarter.

Napoleon, 27 August 1808, *Correspondance de Napoléon Ier, publiée par ordre de l'Empereur Napoléon III*, XVII, No. 14276, 1858–1870.

ONE FIGHTS well when the heart is light.

Napoleon, 17 February 1816, on St. Helena, to General Gaspard Gourgaud, *Sainte Hélène: Journal inédit de 1815 à 1818*, 1899.

MAXIM 6. At the commencement of a campaign, to

advance or not to advance is a matter for grave consideration, but when once the offensive has been assumed, it must be sustained to the last extremity. However skillful the manoeuvres, a retreat will always weaken the *moral* of an army, because in losing the chance of success, these last are transferred to the enemy. Besides, retreats cost always more men and *matériel* than the most bloody engagements, with the difference, that in a battle the enemy's loss is nearly equal to your own, whereas in a retreat the loss is on your side only.

    Napoleon, *The Military Maxims of Napoleon*, tr. George D'Aguilar, 1831 (David Chandler, ed., 1987).

PHYSICAL CASUALTIES are not the only losses incurred by both sides in the course of the engagement: their moral strength is also shaken, broken and ruined. In deciding whether or not to continue the engagement it is not enough to consider the loss of men, horses and guns; one also has to weigh the loss of order, courage, confidence, cohesion, and plan. The decision rests chiefly on the state of morale, which, in cases where the victor has lost as much as the vanquished, has been the single decisive factor.

    Major-General Carl von Clausewitz, *On War*, 4.4, 1832, tr, Michael Howard and Peter Paret, 1976.

THE MORALE of an army and its chief officers has an influence upon the fate of a war. This seems to be due to a certain physical effect produced by the moral cause. For example, the impetuous attack upon a hostile line by twenty thousand brave whose feelings are thoroughly enlisted in their cause will produce a much more powerful effect than the attack of forty thousand demoralized or apathetic men upon the same point.

    Lieutenant-General Antoine-Henri Baron de Jomini, *Summary of the Art of War*, 1838, tr. Mendell and Craighill, 1862.

NO SYSTEM of tactics can lead to victory when the *morale* of an army is bad, and even when it is excellent the victory may depend upon some occurrence like the rupture of the bridges over the Danube at Essling.

    Lieutenant-General Antoine-Henri Baron de Jomini, *Summary of the Art of War*, 1838, tr. Mendell and Craighill, 1862.

NOTE the army organizations and tactical formations on paper are always determined from the mechanical point of view, neglecting the essential coefficient, that of morale. They are almost always wrong.

    Colonel Charles Ardant du Picq, *Battle Studies*, 1880, tr. Greely, 1957.

THE ART of war is subject to many modifications by industrial and scientific progress. But one thing does not change, the heart of man. In the last analysis, success in battle is a matter of morale. In all matters which pertain to an army, organization, discipline and tactics, the human heart in the supreme moment of battle is the basic factor.

    Colonel Charles Ardant du Picq, *Battle Studies*, 1880, tr. Greely, 1957.

TO GENERAL SWINTON, too, is due the implanting into all ranks of the fundamental idea of the Tank as a weapon for saving the lives of infantry. This idea was indeed the foundation of the moral of the Tank Corps, for it spread from the fighting personnel to the depots and workshops, and even to the factories.

    More than anything else, it was this sentiment which kept men ploughing through the mud of 1917, in the dark days when often the chance of reaching an objective had fallen to ten per cent; which kept workshops in full swing all around the clock on ten and eleven hour shifts for weeks and, once, for months on end; which, finally, secured from the factories an intensive and remarkable output.

    Major-General Hugh Elles, Preface to Clough William-Ellis, *The Tank Corps*, 1919.

FIRST OF ALL you must build the morale of your own troops. Then you must look to the morale of your civilian population. Then, and only then, when these are in good repair should you concern yourself with the enemy's morale. And the best way to destroy the enemy's morale is to kill him in large numbers. There's nothing more demoralizing than that.

    Leon Trotsky (1879–1940), quoted in *RUSI*, 9/1984.

AS A RULE destroying the enemy by breaking his morale is an impossible task, since any such demoralization would turn largely on the social condition of his country. Demoralization of the remnants of an enemy army is a consequence of the destruction of his crucial main forces. It is thus a factor not just to be taken account of, but to be exploited.

    Marshal of the Soviet Union Mikhail N. Tukhachevskiy, 1924, quoted in Richard Simpkin, *Deep Battle*, 1987.

THE UNFAILING FORMULA for production of morale is patriotism, self-respect, discipline, and self-confidence within a military unit, joined with fair treatment and merited appreciation from without. It cannot be produced by pampering or coddling an army, and is not necessarily destroyed by hardship, danger, or even calamity. Though it can survive and develop in adversity that comes as an inescapable indicant of service, it will quickly wither of indifference or injustice on the part of their government or of ignorance, personal ambition, or ineptitude on the part of military leaders.

    General of the Army Douglas MacArthur, *Annual Report of the Chief of Staff, U.S. Army for the Fiscal Year Ending 30 June 1933*.

MORALE, only morale, individual morale as a

foundation under training and discipline, will bring victory.

> Field Marshal Viscount Slim of Burma, June 1941, to the officers of the Tenth Indian Infantry Division.

MORALE is a state of mind. It is steadfastness and courage and hope. It is confidence and zeal and loyalty. It is elan, esprit de corps and determination. It is staying power, the spirit which endures to the end – the will to win. With it all things are possible, without it everything else, planning, preparation, production, count for naught.

> General of the Army George C. Marshall, 15 June 1941, address at Trinity College, Hartford, Connecticut.

MACHINES are nothing without men. Men are nothing without morale.

> Admiral of the Fleet Ernest J. King, 19 June 1942, graduation address to the U.S. Naval Academy.

MORALE is when your hands and feet keep working when your head says it can't be done.

> Anonymous U.S. Navy seaman in WWII.

MORALE is the big thing in war. We must raise the morale of our soldiery to the highest pitch; they must be made enthusiastic, and must enter this battle with their tails high in the air and with the will to win.

> Field Marshal Viscount Montgomery of Alamein, 14 September 1942, instruction for Operation Lightfoot, the Battle of El Alamein, quoted in Francis de Guingand, *Operation Victory*, 1947.

TO WIN BATTLES you require good Commanders in the senior ranks, and good senior staff officers; all of these must know their stuff.

You also require an Army in which the morale of the troops is right on the top line. The troops must have confidence in their Commanders and must have the light of battle in their eyes; if this is not so you can achieve nothing.

> Field Marshal Viscount Montgomery of Alamein, 10 November 1942, quoted in Nigel Hamilton, *Master of the Battlefield*, 1983.

MORALE is the thinking of an army. It is the whole complex body of an army's thought: The way it feels about the soil and about the people from which it springs. The way that it feels about their cause and their politics as compared with other causes and politics. The way that it feels about its friends and allies, as well as its enemies. About its commanders and goldbricks. About food and shelter. Duty and leisure. Payday and sex. Militarism and civilianism. Freedom and slavery. Work and want. Weapons and comradeship. Bunk fatigue and drill. Discipline and disorder. Life and death. God and the devil.

> Brigadier-General S.L.A. Marshall, *Men Against Fire*, 1947.

TO THOSE who have known the firing line, it would scarcely be necessary to point out that morale in combat is never a steady current of force but a rapidly oscillating wave whose variations are both immeasurable and unpredictable.

It is this respect chiefly – the rapidity and capriciousness of its variations – that the morale problem in the zone of fire differs from rear area soldiering.

> Brigadier-General S.L.A. Marshall, *Men Against Fire*, 1947.

DO NOT place military cemeteries where they can be seen by replacements marching to the front. This has a very bad effect on morale, even if it adds to the pride of the Graves Registration Service.

> General George S. Patton, *War As I Knew It*, 1947.

VERY MANY FACTORS go into the building-up of sound morale in an army, but one of the greatest is that men be fully employed at useful and interesting work.

> Sir Winston S. Churchill, *The Gathering Storm*, 1948.

IT IS not enough to fight. It is the spirit which we bring to the fight that decides the issue. It is morale that wins the victory.

> General of the Army George C. Marshall, *Military Review*, 10/1948.

MORALE is the greatest single factor in successful war. . . . In any long and bitter campaign morale will suffer unless all ranks thoroughly believe that their commanders are concerned first and always with the welfare of the troops who do the fighting.

> General of the Army Dwight D. Eisenhower, *Crusade in Europe*, 1948.

TO GROW in knowledge of how to win a loyal and willing response from military forces, there must first be understanding of the springs of human action, what they are, and how they may be directed toward constructive ends. This done, the course which makes for the perfecting of forces during peacetime training need only be extended to harden them for the risk and stress of war.

> Brigadier-General S.L.A. Marshall, *The Armed Forces Officer*, 1950.

DILIGENCE in the care of men, administration of all organizational affairs according to a standard of resolute justice, military bearing in one's self, and finally, an understanding of the simple facts that men in a fighting establishment wish to think of themselves in that light and that all military information is nourishing to their spirits and their lives, are the four fundamentals by which the commander builds an all-sufficing morale in those in his charge.

> Brigadier-General S.L.A. Marshall, *The Armed Forces Officer*, 1950.

[SPIRITUAL FOUNDATION] Spiritual first, because

no other foundation of conduct will stand firm under real strain. I use the word "spiritual" not necessarily in the meaning of religious belief – though religion is and always has been one of the greatest foundations of morale – but in the sense of faith in a cause. A man must believe that what his organization is working for is worthy of all the labour and sacrifice he may be called upon to give – that it has a great and vitally necessary object – a noble object if you like. Next, he must feel intensely that he is part, even if only a small part, of that organization, and that what he is and what he does really counts.

[Mental Foundations] First, I think, the intelligent man must be convinced that the object of the organization is really attainable – difficult, perhaps, but not impossible. Second, he must feel that he belongs to an efficient show, one in which his efforts – perhaps his life – are not likely to be wasted. As the third mental foundation, he should, whenever possible, know why he is asked to do certain things.

[Material Foundations] . . . the material foundations of morale – where the man lives, the conditions under which he works, the tools he uses and what he gets for his labour. We are rightly increasingly concerned with these things, yet more dissatisfaction arises basically through neglect of the spiritual and intellectual foundations than in failure of the material. Often the material hardship is the irritant that inflames a deeper discontent. The specified grievance, although it may be justified, is not the real cause of the trouble. It is not that conditions are bad that upsets men so much as delay or failure to recognize that they are and to take steps to improve them. For example, few things are more discouraging than to ask men to work with obsolete or worn-out equipment – yet if it can be shown that there is a good reason why it cannot be replaced at the moment and that at the same time everyone above them is going all out to get the better tools, men will come to take a fierce pride in overcoming their difficulties.

Field Marshal Viscount Slim of Burma, *Courage and Other Broadcasts*, 1957.

THE MORALE of the soldier is the greatest single factor in war and the best way to achieve a high morale in war-time is by success in battle. The good general is the one who wins his battles with the fewest possible casualties; but morale will remain high even after considerable casualties, provided the battle has been won and the men know it was not wastefully conducted, and that every care has been taken of the wounded, and the killed have been collected and reverently buried.

Field Marshal Viscount Montgomery of Alamein, *The Memoirs of Field Marshal Montgomery*, 1958.

YOU MUST WATCH your own morale carefully. A battle is, in effect, a contest between two wills – your own and that of the enemy general. If your heart begins to fail you when the issue hangs in the balance, your opponent will probably win.

Field Marshal Viscount Montgomery of Alamein, *The Memoirs of Field Marshal Montgomery*, 1958.

MORALE is a state of mind. It is that intangible force which will move a whole group of men to give their last ounce to achieve something, without counting the cost to themselves; that makes them feel they are part of something greater than themselves.

Field Marshal Viscount Slim of Burma, *Serve to Lead*, 1959.

THE PENTAGON Whiz Kids are, I think, conscientious, patriotic people who are experts at calculating odds, figuring cost-effectiveness and squeezing the last cent out of contract negotiations. But they are heavy-handed butchers in dealing with that delicate, vital thing called "morale." This is the stuff that makes ships like the *Enterprise*, puts flags on top of Iwo Jima and wins wars. But I doubt if Mr. McNamara and his crew have any morale settings on their computers.

Admiral Daniel V. Gallery, *Eight Bells and All's Well*, 1965.

MORALE is born of loyalty, patriotism, discipline, and efficiency, all of which breed confidence in self and comrades. Most of all morale is promoted by unity – unity in service to the country and in the determination to attain the objective of national security. Morale is at one and the same time the strongest, and the most delicate of growths. It withstands schocks [sic], even disasters of the battlefield, but can be destroyed utterly by favoritism, neglect, or injustice. . . .

The Army should not be coddled or babied, for that does not produce morale, it merely condones and encourages inefficiency. But the Army should be taught to respect itself, and to render a quality of service that will command respect throughout the nation. Thus the population will come to look upon the uniform as the badge of loyalty, of duty, and of efficiency, and this feeling will be reflected, inescapably, in still higher performance in the Army.

General of the Army Dwight D. Eisenhower, *At Ease: Stories I Tell My Friends*, 1967.

GOOD MORALE is built when men have confidence in their leaders and their comrades, when they understand and value the tasks that are set before them. Good morale depends, primarily, upon the exercise of effective leadership. And the key to effective leadership is painstaking and persistent attention to communication: learning the concerns and needs of those who work with you and for you; clearly explaining what should be done and why; conveying to others your own confidence that the task at hand can be done and done well.

Major-General Ernest N. Harmon, *Combat Commander*, 1970.

MORALE does not develop suddenly or of its own accord. It is the result of example, of the actions and superior spirit of individuals among an elite coterie of people. Moral virtues are numbered among idealistic concepts. A man without ideas has no incentive. But those ideas can be developed only in association with known reality, with which the political and military leadership has to reckon.

> Major-General F.W. von Mellenthin, *German Generals of World War II*, 1977.

THE MORALE of soldiers comes from three things: a feeling that they have an important job to do, a feeling that they are trained to do it well, and a feeling that their good work is appreciated and recognized.

> Lieutenant-General Bruce C. Clarke, *Soldiers*, 3/1985.

I FOUGHT three different wars in Vietnam. . . . In all three tours, I never met an enemy with low morale. This means their indoctrination was good, their tactics simple, their discipline strong.

> Major-General Bernard O. Loeffke, letter, 1 October 1988, from Fort Clayton, Canal Zone, quoted in Michael Lanning and Dan Cragg, *Inside the VC and the NVA*, 1992.

MOTHERS

SO the voice of the king rang out in tears,
the citizens wailed in answer, and noble Hecuba
led the wives of Troy in a throbbing chant of sorrow:
"O my child – my desolation! How can I go on living?
What agonies must I suffer now, now you are dead
  and gone?
You were my pride throughout the city night and day –
a blessing to us all, the men and women of Troy:
Throughout the city they saluted you like a god.
You, you were their greatest glory while you lived –
now death and fate have seized you, dragged you
  down!"

> Homer, *The Iliad*, 22.504–512, c. 800 BC, tr. Robert Fagles, 1990; Hecuba, Queen of Troy, mourning her son, man-killing Hector.

WHEN ASKED by a woman from Attica: "Why are you Spartan women the only ones who can rule men?", she said: "Because we are also the only ones who give birth to men."

> Gorgo (born about 506 BC), wife of Leonidas, King of Sparta, quoted in Plutarch, *The Lives*, c. AD 100 (*Plutarch on Sparta*, tr. Richard Talbert, 1988).

ANOTHER WOMAN, as she handing her son his shield and giving him some encouragement, said: "Son, [return] either with this or on this."

> Anonymous Spartan mother, quoted in Plutarch, *The Lives*, c. AD 100 (*Plutarch on Sparta*, tr. Richard Talbert, 1988).

MAKE FRIENDS by being honest, keep them by being steadfast; be truthful, be sincere, be brave. . . . Andy, never tell a lie, nor take what is not your own, nor sue . . . for slander. . . . *Settle them cases yourself.*

> Elizabeth Jackson, 1781, to her son, Andrew Jackson, as she departed to nurse the sick American prisoners of war in British-held Charleston, where she would die of smallpox, quoted in Marquis James, *Andrew Jackson: Border Captain*, 1933.

ALL THAT I AM, or hope to be, I owe to my angel mother.

> President Abraham Lincoln, attributed in Josiah G. Holland, *The Life of Abraham Lincoln*, 1866, and George Alfred Townsend, *The Real Life of Abraham Lincoln*, 1867.

DEAR MADAM, I have been shown in the files of the War Department a statement of the Adjutant-General of Massachusetts that you are the mother of five sons who have died gloriously on the field of battle. I feel how weak and fruitless must be any words of mine which should attempt to beguile you from the grief of a loss so overwhelming. But I cannot refrain from tendering to you the consolation that may be found in the thanks of the Republic they died to save. I pray that our heavenly Father may assuage the anguish of your bereavement, and leave you only the cherished memory of the loved and lost, and the solemn pride that must be yours to have laid so costly a sacrifice on the altar of freedom.

> Abraham Lincoln, letter to Mrs Bixby, 21 November 1864 (Note: the records were in error; Mrs. Bixby had lost two sons for the Union despite being a Southern sympathiser).

MOTHERS – wives – and maidens, would there were some testimonials grand enough for you, – some tablet that could show to the world the sacrifice of American womanhood and American motherhood in that war! Sacrifices so nobly and so firmly – but so gently and beautifully made.

If like the Spartan mother she did not send her son defiantly to the field, – bidding him return only with his shield, or on it, – if like the Roman matron she did not take him by the hand and lead him proudly to the standard of the Republic; like the True Anglo-Saxon, – loyal and loving, tender and brave, – she hid her tears with one hand while with the other wrung her fond farewell, and passed him to the state.

> Clara Barton, quoted in Percy H. Epler, *The Life of Clara Barton*, 1905.

GLORY OF WOMEN
You love us when we're heroes, home on leave,
Or wounded in a mentionable place.
You worship decorations; you believe
That chivalry redeems the war's disgrace.
You make us shells. You listen with delight,
By tales of dirt and danger fondly thrilled.
You crown our distant ardours while we fight,
And mourn our laurelled memories when we're killed.

You can't believe that British troops "retire"
When hell's last horror breaks them, and they run,
Trampling the terrible corpses – blind with blood.
O German mother dreaming by the fire,
While you are knitting socks to send your son
His face is trodden deeper in the mud.

> Siegfried Sassoon (1886–1967).

SHAME ON YOU. Do not forget that you are the son of a Samurai, that tears are not for you.

> The mother of Saburo Sakai when, as a small boy, he would come home in tears after having been beaten up at school by the bigger boys, quoted in Saburo Sakai, *Samurai!*, 1957.

THE MOTTO Papa and I chose when he got his arms as a peer, will guide me as I know it will guide you; "In Honour Bound". . . . We who come from an old stock of a privileged family, that has not had to worry over material existence, has inherited that sense of duty towards our fellow men, those especially whose nation we belong to, and who look to us instinctively for example and guidance.

I know that you feel this too, more than ever in times like these. Let us live or die honourably. I am proud, with the old feelings of our ancestors, that you my son once more are called to such high service. My love for you and my pride in you are too deep for selfish worries or repining.

> Princess Victoria of Battenberg, 1 September 1939, in a letter to her son, later Earl Mountbatten of Burma, quoted in Philip Ziegler, *Mountbatten*, 1985.

AMONG WOMEN, too, it is the young of whom most is demanded. The lot of mothers who lose their sons is hard, but doubly hard is that of the young women who lose the chance of ever becoming wives and mothers. (Feb. 1939.)

> Captain Sir Basil Liddell Hart, *Thoughts on War*, 1944.

MOTIVATION

REGARD your soldiers as your children, and they will follow you into the deepest valleys; look on them as your own beloved sons, and they will stand by you even unto death.

> Sun Tzu, *The Art of War*, 10, c. 500 BC, tr. Giles, 1910.

MEN who think that their officer recognizes them are keener to be seen doing something honorable and more desirous of avoiding disgrace.

> Xenophon (381–c.352 BC).

TO GET PEOPLE to fly in the face of death without turning on their heels, in spite of poor management, is something even a legendary hero would find hard to do; so to put this responsibility on ordinary people is like trying to get a river to flow in reverse.

Therefore in battle formations, winners should be strengthened, losers should be replaced, the weary should be rested, the hungry should be fed. Then the people will only see the enemy, and won't see death; they will not turn on their heels even though they tread on naked blades. So when flowing water finds a course, it can even wash away boulders and snap boats in two; when people are employed in a manner consistent with their nature, then orders are carried out like a flowing current.

> Sun Bin, *The Lost Art of War*, c. 350 BC, tr. Thomas Cleary.

THE TWO ARMIES were now almost within striking distance. Alexander rode from one end of his line to the other with words of encouragement for all, addressing by name, with proper mention of rank and distinctions, not the officers of highest rank only but the captains of squadrons and companies; even the mercenaries were not forgotten, where any distinction or act of courage called for the mention of a name, and from every throat came the answering shout: "Wait no longer – forward to the assault!"

> Arrian, describing Alexander the Great at the Battle of Issus, October 333 BC, *The Campaigns of Alexander*, 2.10, c. AD 150, tr. Aubrey de Sélincourt. 1971.

WITH a joyous spirit and a willing and exultant heart they [soldiers] will choose to brave dangers on behalf of our holy emperors and all the Christian people. But what is more important than all else and more basic, what arouses their enthusiasm, increases their courage, and incites them to dare what nobody else would dare is the fact that their own households and those of the soldiers serving them and everyone about them possess complete freedom. This has provided them security and protection from the beginning and from antiquity. You will find that this has been legislated by the holy and blessed emperors of old and is written down in the tactical books. In addition to freedom, though, they should enjoy proper respect and not be despised and dishonored.

> Emperor Nikephorus II Phokas, *Skirmishing*, c. AD 969, (*Three Byzantine Military Treatises*, tr. George Dennis, 1985).

I HAD RATHER have a plain russet-coated captain that knows what he fights for, and loves what he knows, than that which you call a gentleman and is nothing more. I honor a gentleman that is so indeed.

> Oliver Cromwell, September 1643, letter to Sir William Springe.

THE CAVALRY REGIMENT that does not on this instant, on orders given, dash full plunge into the enemy, I will, directly after the battle, unhorse and make it a garrison regiment. The infantry battalion which, meet with what it may, shows the least sign of hesitancy, loses its colors and its sabers, and I cut the trimmings from its uniforms! Now, good night, gentlemen: shortly we have either beaten the enemy, or we never see one another again.

> Frederick the Great, to his officers before the Battle of Leuthen, 4 December 1757.

AS FOR the soldiers, all you can do is to imbue them with *esprit de corps*, in other words the conviction that their regiment is better than all the other regiments in the universe. It sometimes happens that the officers must lead them into considerable danger, and since ambition can exert no influence on the men, they must be made to fear their officers more than the perils to which they are exposed, otherwise nobody would be able to make them attack into a storm of missiles thundering from three hundred cannon. Good will can never motivate common men in dangers of this order – we must resort to force.

> Frederick the Great, *Testiment Politique*, 1768.

THREE THINGS prompt Men to a regular discharge of their Duty in time of Action: natural bravery, hope of reward, and fear of punishment. . . . The first two . . . are common to the untutor'd, and the Disciplin'd Soldiers: but the latter most obviously distinguishes the one from the other.

> General George Washington, 9 February 1776, letter to the President of Congress, *The Writings of George Washington*, IV, p. 316, John C. Fitzgerald, ed., 1931.

WITH what soldiers in the world could one do what was done by these men, who go about nearly naked and in the greatest privation? Deny the best-disciplined soldiers of Europe what is due them and they will run away in droves, and the general will soon be alone. But from this one can perceive what an enthusiasm – which the poor fellows call "Liberty" – can do!

> Lieutenant-General Johann von Ewald, *Diary of the American War*, 1979; his opinion of American soldiers written in 1791 after serving with the British as a captain of Hessian *Jägers* during the Revolution.

DIE for the Virgin, for your mother the Empress, for the royal family. The Church will pray to God for the dead. The survivor has honour and glory!

> Field Marshal Prince Aleksandr V. Suvorov, *The Science of Victory*, 1796.

INSTEAD of the lash, I would lead them by the stimulus of honor. I would instill a degree of emulation into their minds. I would promote every deserving soldier, as I did in France. . . . What might not be expected of the English army if every soldier hoped to be made a general provided he showed ability? [General] Bingham says, however, that most of your soldiers are brutes and must be driven by the stick. But surely the English soldiers must be possessed of sentiments sufficient to put them at least upon a level with the soldiers of other countries, where the degrading system of the lash is not used. Whatever debases man cannot be serviceable.

> Napoleon, 9 November 1816, on St. Helena, conversation on reform of the British Army, quoted in Christopher Herold, ed. *The Mind of Napoleon*, 1955.

A MAN does not have himself killed for a half-pence a day or for a petty distinction. You must speak to the soul in order to electrify him.

> Napoleon (1769–1821).

THE GREATEST GIFT a general can have is a bad temper [under control]. A bad temper gives you a sort of divine wrath, and it is only by the use of a divine wrath that you can drive men beyond their physical ability in order to save their lives.

> General George S. Patton, Jr., 4 March 1944, *The Patton Papers*, II, 1974.

I HOLD IT to be one of the simplest truths of war that the thing which enables an infantry soldier to keep going with his weapons is the near presence or the presumed presence of a comrade. The warmth which derives from human companionship is essential to the employment of the arms with which he fights as is the finger with which he pulls a trigger or the eye with which he aligns his sights.

> Brigadier-General S.L.A. Marshall, *Men Against Fire*, 1947.

ALSO remember that in any man's dark hour, a pat on the back and an earnest handclasp may work a small miracle.

> Brigadier-General S.L.A. Marshall, *The Armed Forces Officer*, 1950.

A FEW DAYS before the invasion of Sicily, Patton had all the general officers of the Seventh Army at his headquarters for a final briefing. He turned the conduct of the discussion of details over to members of his staff and took little personal part until the close of the day's work. Then he took the floor and gave us a moving address on the theme of the quality of the American soldiers whom we were leading into action, for most of us, our first action. He described their exploits in Tunisia, how well they had stood up against the German veterans of the Afrika Korps. He described with emotion the bravery of small units and there were tears rolling down his cheeks when he told of one company which had held its position until completely destroyed. It was pretty clear that with such men under our command, he considered that if anything went wrong it would be the fault of the generals. In a grand peroration he turned on us with a roar and, waving a menacing swaggerstick under our noses, he concluded: "Now we'll break up, and I never want to see you bastards again unless it's at your post on the shores of Sicily." We departed, convinced that it would be well to turn up on time and at the right place on the Sicilian beaches.

General Maxwell Taylor, *Swords and Plowshares*, 1972.

AWARDS that motivate only the top men are of little value in raising the ability of a unit. It takes awards to motivate the lower third to do that. A unit is measured by the ability of the lower third personnel in it to carry their part of the load.

Lieutenant-General Bruce C. Clarke (1901–1988).

A SOLDIER doesn't fight very hard for someone who is going to shoot him on a whim. That's not what leadership is all about.

General H. Norman Schwarzkopf, 27 February 1991, on the motivation of the Iraqi Army given during the 'Mother of All Briefings'.

MUTINY

HOW should base mutineers bound together by no rightful obligation, and united only by thirst for pillage and community of crime, display the intrepidity or obtain the success of honourable soldiers? Courage can never exist with the consciousness of guilt and speedily forsakes the man who has forsaken duty.

Count Belisarius, April AD 536, quoted in Mahon, *The Life of Belisarius*, 1829.

THAT LONG official neglect of intolerable grievance, and inexcusable supineness towards measures of progressive improvement had, as they sooner or later infallibly do, at last aroused illegal and exasperated enforcements of redress.

Jedediah Tucker, of the British naval mutinies of 1797, *Memoirs of Earl St. Vincent*, 1830.

I KNOW some generals are mutinous and preach revolt . . . let them take care. I am as high above a general as above a drummer boy and, if necessary, I will have the one shot as soon as the other.

Napoleon, October 1798, in Egypt, when generals began to complain about his leadership, quoted in S.J. Watson, *By Command of the Emperor*, 1957.

WHY does Colonel Grigsby refer to me to learn how to deal with mutineers? He should shoot them where they stand.

Lieutenant-General Thomas J. 'Stonewall' Jackson, May 1862, upon receiving a report of 12-month volunteers refusing duty.

WHERE SOLDIERS get into trouble of this nature, it is nearly always the fault of some officer who has failed in his duty.

Field Marshal Viscount Montgomery of Alamein, quoted in Ahrenfeldt, *Psychiatry in the British Army in the Second World War*, 1958.

N

NAVY

IN THE [Navy] there was a technology that blocked all my ideas. . . . No man capable of breaking away from its routine and doing creative work ever appeared. . . . I never could find an intermediary between me [and my sailors] who could get them moving.
> Napoleon, quoted in Charles de la Roncière and G. Clerc-Rampal, *Histoire de la Marine Française*, 1934.

THOSE far distant, storm-beaten ships, upon which [Napoleon's] Grand Army never looked, stood between it and the dominion of the world.
> Rear Admiral Alfred Thayer Mahan, referring to the Royal Navy in *The Influence of Sea Power Upon History*, II, 1892.

A THOROUGHLY GOOD navy takes a long time to build up. . . . Ships take years to build, crews take years before they become thoroughly expert, while the officers not only have to pass their early youth in a course of special training, but cannot possibly rise to supreme excellence in their profession unless they make it their life-work.
> President Theodore Roosevelt, 'Admiral Dewey', *McClure's Magazine*, 10/1899.

[THE GREAT WHITE FLEET] it afforded a convincing ocular demonstration of the power and might of America, and added immeasurably to the respect with which our nation was regarded.
> Major-General John A. Lejeune, *The Reminiscences of a Marine*, 1929.

FOR the Royal Navy, the watchword should be, "Carry on, and dread nought."
> Sir Winston S. Churchill, 6 December 1939, speech in the House of Commons.

DON'T TALK to me about naval tradition. It's nothing but rum, sodomy, and the lash.
> Sir Winston S. Churchill, during WWII when an admiral stated that a combined operation would be against naval tradition, quoted in Peter Gretton, *Former Naval Person*, 1968.

YOU SELDOM HEAR of the fleets except when there's trouble, and then you hear a lot.
> Admiral John S. McCain, 4 August 1964, *Norfolk Star Ledger*.

NECESSITY

IT MUST BE thoroughly understood that war is a necessity, and that the more readily we accept it, the less will be the ardor of our opponents, and that out of the greatest dangers communities and individuals acquire the greatest glory.
> Pericles, 432–431 BC, arguing for war with Sparta, Thucydides, *The Peloponnesian War*, 1.145, c. 404 BC, tr Richard Crawley, 1910.

IT IS the prime consideration of a general to secure victory – with its achievement unavoidable wrongs can later be remedied by kindness.
> Gonzalo de Corboba, 'El Gran Capitan', (1453–1515).

YOU MUST KNOW, then, that there are two methods of fighting, the one by law, the other by force: the first method is that of men, the second of beasts; but as the first method is often insufficient, one must have recourse to the second. It is therefore necessary for a prince to know how to use both the beast and the man.
> Niccolo Machiavelli, *The Prince*, 1513.

URGENT NECESSITY prompts many to do things, at the very thoughts of which they perhaps would start at other times.
> Miguel de Cervantes, *Don Quixote*, 1605–1615, tr. Peter Motteux and John Ozell.

NECESSITY hath no law.
> Oliver Cromwell, 1654, address to Parliament.

EXTORTIONS which are intolerable in their nature become excusable from the necessities of war.
> Cardinal Richelieu, 1633.

NECESSITY, dire necessity, will, nay must, justify my attack.
> General George Washington, 25 December 1776, attributed, before the daring attack on Trenton.

GREAT MEN are never cruel without necessity.
> Napoleon (1769–1821), quoted in Christopher Herold, ed., *The Mind of Napoleon*, 1955.

NECESSITY knows no law.
> President Abraham Lincoln, 27 August 1862, referring to the necessity of conscription, *Collected Works of Abraham Lincoln*, V, 1953.

EVERY OFFICER of the old army remembers how, in 1861, we were hampered with the old blue army-regulations, which tied our hands, and that to do any thing positive and necessary we had to tear it all to pieces – cut red-tape, as it was called – a dangerous thing for an army to do, for it was calculated to bring law and authority into contempt; but war was upon us, and overwhelming necessity overrides all law.

General of the Army William T. Sherman, *The Memoirs of General W.T. Sherman*, 1875.

NEGOTIATIONS

WHEN the Argives were disputing land boundaries with the Spartans and were maintaining that theirs was the fairer claim, he [Lysander] drew his sword and said: "The man who has this within his grasp argues best about land boundaries."

Plutarch, quoting Lysander (k. 395 BC), *The Lives*, c. AD 100, (*Plutarch on Sparta*, tr. Richard Talbert, 1988).

ONE CAN NEVER foresee the consequences of political negotiations under the influence of military eventualities.

Napoleon (1769–1821).

EVERY NEGOTIATION which does not have power behind it . . . [is] ridiculous and fruitless.

Adolf Hitler, 1924.

TO JAW-JAW is better than to war-war.

Sir Winston S. Churchill, 26 June 1954, speech.

ANY NEGOTIATIONS, even the most difficult, do mean no more corpses. A bad peace is better than a good quarrel.

General Aleksandr I. Lebed, *Nezavisimaya Gazeta* (Moscow), 29 August 1997.

NEUTRALITY

A PRINCE is further esteemed when he is a true friend or a true enemy, when, that is, he declares himself without reserve in favor of some one or against another. This policy is always more useful than remaining neutral. For if two neighboring powers come to blows, they are either such that if one wins, you will have to fear the victor, or else not. In either of these two cases it will be better for you to declare yourself openly and make war, because in the first case if you do not declare yourself, you will fall prey to the victor, to the pleasure and satisfaction of the one who has been defeated, and you will have no reason nor anything to defend you and nobody to receive you.

Niccolo Machiavelli, *The Prince*, 1513.

A NEUTRAL is bound to be hated by those who lose and despised by those who win.

Niccolo Machiavelli, 22 December 1514, letter to Francesco Vettor.

I SHALL TREAT neutrality as equivalent to a declaration of war against me.

Gustavus II Adolphus, King of Sweden, proclamation during the Thirty Years War, 1616–1648.

THE MOST sincere neutrality is not a sufficient guard against the depradations of nations at war.

General George Washington, 7 December 1796, Farewell Address.

NEVER break the neutrality of any port or place, but never consider as neutral any place from whence an attack is allowed to be made.

Admiral Viscount Nelson, 1804, letter of instruction.

WE NEED to educate our children on why we need a strong armed forces. Neutrality is a great thing but who is going to enforce neutrality?

General Lewis W. Walt, speaking in 1971, *New York Times*, 28 March 1989.

NON-COMBATANTS

DON'T HURT civilians, they give us food and drink; a soldier is not a footpad.

Field Marshal Prince Aleksandr V. Suvorov, *The Science of Victory*, 1796.

IT WILL REQUIRE the full exercise of the full powers of the Federal Government to restrain the fury of the noncombatants.

General Winfield Scott, April 1861, after the Confederate attack on Fort Sumter.

WHY, you craven fool, until this battle is decided, you do not know, neither do I, if you will have a government to apply to. . . . If I hear any more from you, I will give you a gun and send you to the front line to defend your rights.

Major-General George Gordon Meade, to a civilian who came to him during the artillery barrage that preceeded Pickett's charge, and complained that the Union forces were using his house as a hospital and littering his garden with graves and amputated limbs, 3 July 1863, quoted in John W. Storrs, *The 20th Connecticut Regiment*.

THOSE who live at home in peace and plenty want the duello part of this war to go on: but when they have to bear the burden by loss of property or comforts, they will cry for peace.

General of the Army Phillip H. Sheridan, 26 November 1864, telegram to Major-General Halleck from Kernstown, Virginia.

WHEN you've shouted "Rule Britannia", when you've sung "God Save the Queen",
When you've finished killing Kruger with your mouth.
> Rudyard Kipling (1865–1936), 'The Absent-Minded Beggar'.

ARRAS itself was fairly clear, as it was under shell fire; nevertheless, the Hotel de Commerce, where I pulled up for a drink, was doing good business. There was a dead soldier lying outside with a waterproof sheet over him; but inside, the place was crowded with soldiers drinking, chatting, and joking. The women serving them were now practically shell-proof, anyhow as regards nerves. You cannot terrorize a people for long, especially if there is money to be made.
> Major-General J.F.C. Fuller, note in 1917, *Memoirs of an Unconventional Soldier*, 1936.

THE MORALE of the civilians in a city which has not yet been touched by war is seldom as high as it is among the soldiers in the frontline.
> Alan Moorehead, *Gallipoli*, 1956.

NON-COMMISSIONED OFFICERS

THE CHOICE of non-commissioned officers is also an object of the greatest importance: the order and discipline of a regiment depends so much upon their behavior, that too much care cannot be taken in preferring none to that trust but those who by their merit and good conduct are entitled to it. Honesty, sobriety, and a remarkable attention to every point of duty, with a neatness in their dress, are indispensable requisites; a spirit to command respect and obedience from the men, an expertness in performing every part of the exercise, and an ability to teach it, are absolutely necessary; nor can a sergeant or corporal be said to be qualified who does not write and read in a tolerable manner.
> Major-General Friedrich Baron von Steuben, *Revolutionary Drill Manual*, 1794.

INSTRUCTIONS for the Sergeants and Corporals. It being on the non-commissioned officers that the discipline and order of a company in a great measure depend, they cannot be too circumspect in their behaviour towards the men, by treating them with mildness, and at the same time obliging every one to do his duty. By avoiding too great familiarity with the men, they will not only gain their love and confidence, but be treated with a proper respect whereas by contrary conduct they forfeit all regard, and their authority becomes despised.

Each sergeant and corporal will be in particular manner answerable for the squad committed to his care. He must pay particular attention to their conduct in every respect; that they keep themselves and their arms always clean; that they have their effects always ready, and put where they can get them immediately, even in the dark, without confusion; and on every fine day he must oblige them to air their effects.
> Major-General Friedrich Baron von Steuben, *Revolutionary Drill Manual*, 1794.

AS A RULE it is easy to find officers, but it is sometimes very hard to find noncommissioned officers.
> Napoleon, 28 January 1809, letter to General Clarke, quoted in Christopher Herold, ed., *The Mind of Napoleon*, 1955.

HIS EXCELLENCY also observes that the non-commissioned officers can do their duty, and can maintain the authority of their situation, only by having the support of the officers belonging to their company given to them upon all occasions, by constantly visiting the soldiers' quarters and by invariable attendance upon the parade, from the moment the soldiers are under arms.
> The Duke of Wellington, 4 April 1810, at Vizeu, *Selections from the General Orders of Field Marshal the Duke of Wellington During His Various Commands 1799–1818*, 1847.

WE HAVE in the service the scum of the earth as common soldier; and of late years we have been doing every thing in our power, both by law and by publications, to relax the discipline by which alone such men can be kept in order. . . . As to the non-commissioned officers, as I have repeatedly stated, they are as bad as the men. . . .
> The Duke of Wellington, 2 July 1813, to Lord Bathurst, *The Dispatches of Field Marshal the Duke of Wellington, During His Various Campaigns in India, Denmark, Portugal, Spain, the Low Countries, and France*, X, 1834–1838. p. 496.

ALL THE WORK is done by the non-commissioned officers of the Guards. It is true that they regularly get drunk once a day – by eight in the evening – and go to bed soon after, but then they always take care to do first what ever they were bid. . . . I am convinced that there would be nothing so intelligent, so valuable, as English soldiers of that rank, if you could get them sober, which is impossible.
> The Duke of Wellington, quoted in Maxwell, *The Life of Wellington*, II, 1899.

WE HAVE good corporals and sergeants and some good lieutenants and captains, and those are far more important than good generals.
> General of the Army William T. Sherman (1820–1891).

THE BACKBONE of the Army is the non-commissioned man!
> Rudyard Kipling, 'The 'Eathen', 1896.

PERHAPS of all the Marines I ever knew, [Sergeant Major John] Quick approached most nearly the perfect type of non-commissioned officer. A calm, forceful, intelligent, loyal and courageous man he was. I never knew him to raise his voice, lose his temper, or use profane language, and yet he exacted and obtained prompt and explicit obedience from all persons subject to his orders.

Major-General John A. Lejeune, *The Reminiscences of a Marine*, 1929.

EVEN to those who best understand the reasons for the regimenting of military forces, a discipline wrongfully applied is seen only as indiscipline. Invariably it will be countered in its own terms. No average rank-and-file will become insubordinate as quickly, or react as violently, as a group of senior non-commissioned officers, brought together in a body, and then mishandled by officers who are ignorant of the customs of the service and the limits of their own authority. Not only are they conscious of their rights, but they have greater respect for the state of decency and order which is the mark of a proper military establishment than for the insignia of rank. It is this firm feeling of the fitness of things, and his unbounded allegiance to an authority when it is based on character which makes the NCO and the petty officer the backbone of discipline within the United States fighting establishment.

Brigadier-General S.L.A. Marshall, *The Armed Forces Officer*, 1950.

MY MANY YEARS in the army have demonstrated that wherever confidence in NCOs is lacking and wherever they are continuously bossed by the officers, you have no real NCOs and no really combatworthy units.

Marshal of the Soviet Union Georgi K. Zhukov, *Reminiscences and Reflections*, 1974.

NUMBERS

IN WAR it is not numbers that give the advantage. If you do not advance recklessly, and are able to consolidate your own strength, get a clear picture of the enemy's situation, and secure the full support of your men, it is enough.

Sun Tzu, *The Art of War*, 9, c. 500 BC, tr. Roger Ames, 1993.

THE MEDES attacked at the charge, and many were killed; a second charge was made, and they were cut down in their hundreds – but they would not be driven back. All the same, it was clear to everyone, and especially to Xerxes, that his army contained plenty of men, but very few soldiers. The battle lasted throughout the day. The slaughter of the Medes was ghastly and they were at last replaced by the Persians. . . . These troops were called the King's Immortals, and were expected to finish off the Greeks easily. But when they came to grips they did

no better than the Medes – exactly the same, in fact – for they were fighting in a confined space, and using shorter spears than the Greeks. . . . The Spartans fought a masterly battle. They were battle-scarred men of long experience fighting raw recruits, and they showed it.

Herodutus (c. 484–420 BC), of the Battle of Thermopylae, 480 BC, *The Persian Wars*, 7.210.

WHEN SOMEONE said: "Leonidas, are you here like this, to run such a risk with a few men against many?", he replied: "If you think that I should rely on numbers, then not even the whole of Greece is enough, since it is a small fraction of their horde; but if I am to rely on courage, then even this number is quite adequate."

Leonidas, Agiad King of Sparta, 480 BC, at the Pass of Thermopylae, quoted in Plutarch, *The Lives*, c. AD 100 (*Plutarch on Sparta*, tr. Richard Talbert, 1988).

ONCE when he heard that the constant campaigning had made the allies discontented – there were large numbers of them following just a few Spartans – [Agesilaus] he was eager to demonstrate the unimportance of their mere numbers. He instructed the allies to sit down together at random, and the Spartans separately on their own. Next he announced that the potters should stand up first, and when they had done so, then the smiths second, then in turn carpenters, builders, and workers in every other craft. Thus virtually all the allies stood up, but not one of the Spartans, since there was a ban on their practising or learning a manual craft. So Agesilaus laughed and said: "Do you see, gentlemen, how many more soldiers we send out than you?"

Plutarch, quoting Agesilaus, Eurypontid King of Sparta (400–360 BC), *The Lives*, c. AD 100 (*Plutarch on Sparta*, tr. Richard Talbert, 1988).

VICTORY in war does not depend entirely upon numbers or mere courage; only skill and discipline will insure it. We find that the Romans owed the conquest of the world to no other cause than continual military training, exact observance of discipline in their camps and unwearied cultivation of the arts of war. . . . A handful of men, inured to war, proceeds to certain victory, while on the contrary numerous armies of raw and undisciplined troops are but masses of men dragged to slaughter.

Flavius Vegetius Renatus, *Military Institutions of the Romans*, c. AD 378, tr. Clark, 1776.

COURAGE and discipline are able to accomplish more than a large number of warriors. Often enough the lay of the land has been helpful in making the weaker force come out on top.

The Emperor Maurice, *The Strategikon*, c. AD 600 (*Maurice's Strategikon*, tr. George Dennis, 1984).

THAT'S ALL RIGHT. . . . The greater the enemy the more they will fall over one another, and the easier it will be for us to cut through. In any case, they're not numerous enough to darken the sun for us.

> Field Marshal Prince Aleksandr V. Suvorov
> (1729–1800), 1789, before the Battle of Rymnik.

I HEAR that General Hooker has more men than he can handle. I should like to have half as many more as I have today, and I would throw him into the river. . . . We have always had to put all our troops in the fighting line, and never had enough when we needed them most.

> Lieutenant-General Thomas J. 'Stonewall' Jackson,
> April 1863, before the Battle of Chancellorsville.

I JUST GOT THERE first with the most men.

> Lieutenant-General Nathan Bedford Forrest, to General
> John Hunt Morgan as the two compared notes on their
> operations, quoted in Henry, *Forrest*, 1944.

THE PRESIDENT has been powerfully reminded, by General Grant's present movements and plans, of his (President's) old suggestion so constantly made and as constantly neglected, to Buell & Halleck, et al., to move at once upon the enemy's whole line so as to bring into action to our advantage our great superiority in numbers. Otherwise by interior lines & control of the interior railroad system the enemy can shift their men rapidly from one point to another as they may be required. In this concerted movement, however, great superiority of numbers must tell: as the enemy, however successful where he concentrates, must necessarily weaken other portions of his line and lose important positions. This idea of his own, the Prest recognized with especial pleasure when Grant said it was his intention to make all the line useful – those not fighting could help the fighting. "Those not skinning can hold a leg," added this distinguished interlocutor.

> John Hay, diary entry for 30 April 1864, *Lincoln and
> the Civil War*, 1939.

THE DISPARITY of generalship often outweighs a difference of numbers, and . . . psychological incalculables are apt to make statistical calculations valueless – to the sore perplexity of military pedants, whose minds are fed on "balance sheet" history.

> Captain Sir Basil Liddell Hart, *Sherman*, 1929.

I HAVE never seen a company, platoon, or squad take a hill at 100 percent strength.

> Lieutenant-General Arthur S. Collins, Jr., *Common
> Sense Training*, 1978.

O

OBEDIENCE

A MAN submits though his heart breaks with fury. Better for him by far.
> Homer, *The Iliad*, 1.255–256, c. 800 BC,
> tr. Robert Fagles, 1990.

THE LEADER must himself believe that willing obedience always beats forced obedience, and that he can get this only by really knowing what should be done. Thus he can secure obedience from his men because he can convince them that he knows best, precisely as a good doctor makes his patients obey him. Also he must be ready to suffer more hardships than he asks of his soldiers, more fatigue, greater extremities of cold and heat.
> Xenophon, *Cyropaedia*, c. 360 BC.

HE who wishes to be obeyed must know how to command.
> Niccolo Machiavelli, *Discourses*, 1517.

THE LAWS of honour cannot necessarily be satisfied by throwing away one's life when it seems convenient. A soldier's duty is to obey.
> Jean de la Valette, Grand Master of the Order of the Knights of St. John, June 1565, forbidding his young knights to throw away their lives in a desperate sally against the Turks, who had invested the fort of St. Elmo during the siege of Malta.

I SPEAK HARSHLY to no one, but I will have your head off the instant you refuse to obey me.
> Marshal General Vicomte de Turenne (1611–1675), quoted in Maxime Weygand, *Turenne: Marshal of France*, 1930.

LET YOUR CHARACTER be above reproach, for that is the way to earn men's obedience.
> Field Marshal Johann von Schulenburg, 1709, letter to Field Marshal Maurice Comte de Saxe.

OBEDIENCE to the officers and subordination is so exact that no one ever questions an order, hours are observed exactly, and however little a general knows how to make himself obeyed, he is always sure to be. No one reasons about the possibility of an enterprise, and finally, its accomplishment is never despaired of.
> Frederick the Great, *Instructions to His Generals*, 1747, tr. Phillips, 1940.

WILLING OBEDIENCE always beats forced obedience.
> Major-General Frederich Baron von Steuben (1730–1794).

I WAS little satisfied . . . you received the order to proceed to Cairo and did not comply with it. *No event that may occur should prevent a soldier from obeying*, and talent in war consists in surmounting the difficulties liable to make an operation difficult.
> Napoleon, quoted in Ferdinand Foch, *Principles of War*, 1913.

THE EMPEROR, for the general direction of the operations, is in no need of advice, nor does he wish to have outlined to him any operation plans. No one knows his intentions, and it is our duty to obey him.
> Marshal of France Louis Berthier, Prince de Neuchatel, Prince de Wagram, 19 January 1807; Napoleon directed Berthier to send this letter to Marshal Ney, quoted in Foucart, *Campagne de Pologne*.

OFFICERS must recollect, that to perform their duty well in the field is but a small part of what is required of them; and that obedience to order, regularity, and accuracy in the performance of duties and discipline, are necessary to keep any military body together, and to enable them to perform any military operation with advantage to their country, or service to themselves.
> The Duke of Wellington, 17 August 1812, general order published in Madrid, quoted in Philip Haythornthwaite, *The Armies of Napoleon*, 1994.

I DO NOT BELIEVE in the proverb that in order to be able to command one must know how to obey. . . . Insubordination may only be the evidence of a strong mind.
> Napoleon, 1817, letter from St. Helena.

SOLDIERS must obey in all things. They may and do laugh at foolish orders, but they nevertheless obey, not because they are blindly obedient, but because they know that to disobey is to break the backbone of their profession.
> General Sir William Napier (1782–1853).

MEN must be habituated to obey or they cannot be controlled in battle and the neglect of the least important order impairs the proper influence of the officer.

> General Robert E. Lee, 1865, to the Army of Northern Virginia.

IT IS DIFFICULT for the non-military mind to realize how great is the moral effort of disobeying a superior, whose order on the one hand covers all responsibility and on the other entails the most serious personal and professional injury; if violated without due cause, the burden of proving rests with the junior. . . . He has to show, not that he meant to do right, but that he actually did right in disobeying in the particular instance. Under no less vigorous exactions can due military subordination be maintained.

> Rear Admiral Alfred Thayer Mahan, *The Life of Nelson*, 1897.

THE UGLY TRUTH is revealed that fear is the foundation of obedience.

> Sir Winston S. Churchill, *The River War*, 1899.

THE DUTY of obedience is not merely military but moral. It is not an arbitrary rule, but one essential and fundamental; the expression of a principle without which military organization would go to pieces and military success be impossible.

> Rear Admiral Alfred Thayer Mahan, *Retrospect and Prospect*, 1902.

THE SPIRIT of obedience, as distinguished from its letter, consists in faithfully forwarding the general object to which the officer's particular command is contributing.

> Rear Admiral Alfred Thayer Mahan, *Retrospect and Prospect*, 1902.

IN WAR, to obey is a difficult thing. For the obedience must be in the presence of the enemy, and in spite of the enemy, in the midst of danger, of varied and unforeseen circumstances, of a menacing unknown, in spite of fatigue of many causes.

> Marshal of France Ferdinand Foch, *Principles of War*, 1913.

THE MIND of the soldier, who commands and obeys without question, is apt to be fixed, drilled, and attached to definite rules.

> Field Marshal Viscount Wavell of Cyrenaica, *Generals and Generalship*, 1941.

ALL THROUGH your career of Army life, you men have bitched about what you call this chicken shit drilling. That is all for one reason, instant obedience to orders and it creates alertness. I don't give a damn for a man who is not always on his toes. You men are veterans or you wouldn't be here. You are ready. A man to continue breathing, must be alert at all times. If not, sometimes, some German son of a bitch will sneak up behind him and beat him to death with a sack full of shit.

> General George S. Patton, Jr., 6 June 1944, speech to the troops of the Third Army.

THE EFFICIENCY of a war administration depends mainly upon whether decisions emanating from the highest approved authority are in fact strictly, faithfully, and punctually obeyed.

> Sir Winston S. Churchill, *Their Finest Hour*, 1949.

ALL I WANT is compliance with my wishes, after reasonable discussion.

> Sir Winston S. Churchill, to the British Chiefs of Staff, quoted in Dwight D. Eisenhower, *General Eisenhower on the Military Churchill*, 1970.

TO KNOW how to command obedience is a very different thing from making men obey. Obedience is not the product of fear, but of understanding, and understanding is based on knowledge.

> Brigadier-General S.L.A. Marshall, *The Armed Forces Officer*, 1950.

THERE ARE admittedly cases where a senior commander cannot reconcile it with his responsibilities to carry out an order he has been given. Then, like Seydlitz at the Battle of Zorndorf, he has to say: "After the battle the King may dispose of my head as he will, but during the battle he will kindly allow me to make use of it." No general can vindicate his loss of a battle by claiming that he was compelled – against his better judgment – to execute an order that led to defeat. In this case the only course open to him is that of disobedience, for which he is answerable with his head. Success usually decides whether he was right or not.

> Field Marshal Erich von Manstein, *Lost Victories*, 1957.

THE OBJECTIVE
Principle of War

VICTORY in war is the main object in war. If this is long delayed, weapons are blunted and morale depressed. . . .

> Sun Tzu, *The Art of War*, 2, c. 500 BC, tr. Samuel Griffith, 1963.

WHITHER would you urge me? The most complete and most happy victory is to baffle the force of an enemy without impairing our own and in this favourable situation we are already placed. Is it not wiser to enjoy the advantages thus easily acquired, than to hazard them in the pursuit of more? Is it not enough to have altogether disappointed the arrogant hopes with which the Persians set out for this campaign and compelled them to a speedy and shameful retreat?

> Count Belisarius, AD 531, when his army demanded an attack of the retreating Persian Army, quoted in Mahon, *The Life of Belisarius*, 1829.

THE MAN who tries to hang onto everything ends up by holding nothing. Your essential objective must be the hostile army. . .

Frederick the Great, *General Principles of War*, 1748.

NEVER lose sight of your principle object; do not act contrary to your orders; do not be led astray by secondary issues; go straight for the main issue, and do not rest until you have conquered it. But do not be pedantic and small minded; if in carrying out an order you find that circumstances have changed since it was given you, disobey it resolutely, if your wits tell you you are doing right, but, if you do so, take care to acquaint the issuer of the order with what you have done. Fear nothing.

Lieutenant-General Johann von Ewald, *Treatise on the Duties of Light Troops*, 1790.

IF YOU START to take Vienna – take Vienna.

Napoleon (1769–1821).

MANY good generals exist in Europe, but they see too many things at once: I see but one thing, and that is the masses; I seek to destroy them, sure that the minor matters will fall of themselves.

Napoleon (1769–1821).

THE LOSS of Moscow is not the loss of Russia. My first obligation is to preserve the army, to get nearer to those troops approaching as reinforcements, and by the very act of leaving Moscow to prepare inescapable ruin for the enemy. . . . I will play for time, lull Napoleon as much as possible and not disturb him in Moscow. Every device which contributes to this object is preferable to the empty pursuit of glory.

Field Marshal Prince Mikhail I. Kutuzov, 1812, quoted in Parkinson, *Fox of the North*, 1976.

PURSUE one great decisive aim with force and determination – a maxim which should take first place among all causes of victory.

Major-General Carl von Clausewitz, *Principles of War*, 1812, tr Gatzke, 1942.

THE DESTRUCTION of the enemy forces is always the main object. . . .

Field Marshal August Wilhelm Graf von Gneisenau (1760–1831).

THE AIM of warfare is to disarm the enemy. . . . If the enemy is to be coerced you must put him in a situation that is even more unpleasant than the sacrifice you call on him to make. . . .

Major-General Carl von Clausewitz, *On War*, 1.1, 1832, tr. Michael Howard and Peter Paret, 1976.

SOMETIMES the political and military objective is the same – for example, the conquest of a province. In other cases the political object will not provide a suitable objective. In that event, another military objective must be adopted that will serve the political purpose and symbolize it in the peace negotiations.

Field Marshal Carl von Clausewitz, *On War*, 1.1, 1832, tr. Michael Howard and Peter Paret, 1976.

WHAT do we mean by the defeat of the enemy? Simply the destruction of his forces, whether by death, injury, or any other means – either completely or enough to make him stop fighting. Leaving aside all specific purposes of any particular engagement, the complete or partial destruction of the enemy must be regarded as the sole object of all engagements.

Field Marshal Carl von Clausewitz, *On War*, 4.3, 1832, tr. Michael Howard and Peter Paret, 1976.

NO ONE starts a war – or rather, no one in his senses ought to do so – without first being clear in his mind what he intends to achieve by that war and how he intends to conduct it. The former is its political purpose; the latter its operational objective. This is the governing principle which will set its course, prescribe the scale of means and effort which is required, and make its influence felt throughout down to the smallest operational detail.

Field Marshal Carl von Clausewitz, *On War*, 8.2, 1832, tr. Michael Howard and Peter Paret, 1976.

TO DO the greatest damage to our enemy with the least exposure to ourselves, is a military axiom lost sight of only by ignorance of the true ends of victory.

Dennis Hart Mahan, *Advance-Guard, Out-Post, and Detachment Service of Troops, with the Essential Principles of Strategy and Grand Tactics*, 1863.

SHERMAN will move at the same time you do, or two or three days in advance, Jo Johnston's Army being his objective point and the heart of Georgia his ultimate aim. . . . Lee's army will be your objective point. Wherever Lee goes, there you will go also.

General of the Army Ulysses S. Grant, 9 April 1864, orders to Major-General George Meade, *Papers of USG*, X, 1982, pp. 273–274.

I SHALL NOT give my attention so much to Richmond as to Lee's army, and I want all commanders to feel that hostile armies, and not cities, are to be their objectives.

General of the Army Ulysses S. Grant, 3 May 1864, comments to his staff at the beginning of the 1864 campaign, 3 May 1864, quoted in Porter, *Campaigning With Grant*, 1897.

OTHER great difficulties, experienced by every general, are to measure truly the thousand-and-one reports that come to him in the midst of conflict; to preserve a clear and well-defined purpose at every instant of time, and to cause all efforts to converge on that end.

General of the Army William T. Sherman, *Memoirs*, 1875.

WHY did you come to this war if you can't stand the gaff? War has always been this way. . . . The fat Old Man you talk about is going to win this campaign. When he does these things will be forgotten. It's the objective that counts, not the incidents.

General of the Armies John J. Pershing, as a first lieutenant, June 1898, to a fellow officer complaining of the supply problem and leadership of Brigadier-General William R. Shafter, during the campaign in Cuba, quoted in Donald Smyth, 'Pershing in the Spanish-American War', *Military Review*, Spring 1966.

. . . THAT EXCLUSIVENESS of purpose, which is the essence of strategy, and which subordinates, adjusts, all other factors and considerations to the one exclusive aim.

Rear Admiral Alfred Thayer Mahan, *Naval Strategy*, 1911.

IT MAY BE that the enemy's fleet is still at sea, in which case it is the great objective, now as always.

Rear Admiral Alfred Thayer Mahan, *Naval Strategy*, 1911.

IN WAR there is but one manner of considering every question, that is the *objective manner*. War is not an art of pleasure or sport, indulged in without other reason as one might go in for painting, music, hunting or tennis, which can be taken up or stopped at will. In war everything is co-related. Every move has some reason, seeks some object; once that object is determined it decides the nature and importance of the means to be employed.

Marshal of France Ferdinand Foch, *Principles of War*, 1913.

WAR means fighting for definite results. I am not waging war for the sake of waging war. If I obtain through the armistice the conditions we wish to impose upon Germany, I am satisifed. Once this object has been attained, nobody has the right to shed one drop of blood.

Marshal of France Ferdinand Foch, *Memoirs of Marshal Foch*, 1931.

THE STRATEGICAL OBJECTIVE: Irrespective of the arm employed, the principles of strategy remain immutable, changes in weapons affecting their application only. The first of all strategical principles is "the principle of the object," the object being "the destruction of the enemy's field armies – his fighting personnel."

Now, the potential fighting strength of a body of men lies in its organization; consequently, if we can destroy this organization, we shall destroy its fighting strength and so have gained our object.

There are two ways of destroying our object.
(i) By wearing it down (dissipating it).
(ii) By rendering it inoperative (unhinging it).

In war the first comprises the killing, wounding, capturing and disarming of the enemy's soldiers – body warfare. The second, the rendering inoperative of his power of command – brain warfare. Taking a single man as an example: the first method may be compared to a succession of slight wounds which will eventually cause him to bleed to death; the second – a shot through the brain.

Major-General J.F.C. Fuller, memorandum of 24 May 1918 for 'Plan 1919', *Memoirs of an Unconventional Soldier*, 1936.

WAR must entail some loss, but the less this loss is the greater will be the victory; consequently the military object of a nation is not to kill and destroy, but to enforce the policy of its government with the least possible loss of honour, life, and property. If the enemy can be compelled to accept the hostile policy without battle, so much the better. If he opposes it by military force, then it should never be forgotten that the strength of this force rests on the will of the government which employs it, and that, in its turn, this will rests on the will of the nation which this government represents. If the will of the nation cannot directly be attacked, then must the will of the army protecting it be broken.

Major-General J.F.C. Fuller, *The Reformation of War*, 1923.

THE TRUE military objective is a mental rather than a physical objective – the paralysis of the opposing command, not the bodies of the actual soldiers. For an army without orders, without co-ordination, without supplies, easily becomes a panic-stricken and famine-stricken mob, incapable of effective action. (March 1925.)

Captain Sir Basil Liddell Hart, *Thoughts on War*, 1944.

THE MILITARY OBJECT may be expressed in the one word "conquest," which presupposes victory in one form or another, and by conquest I understand that condition of success which will admit of a government imposing its will on the enemy's nation, and so attaining the execution of its policy. Conquest may also be considered as the grand strategical military idea, and victory the grand tactical means.

Major-General J.F.C. Fuller, *The Foundations of the Science of War*, 1926.

THE DANGER of carrying us away from the objective. . . . In an operation, there must be nothing superflous; it must be the incarnation of aim-directedness. The form of the operation . . . must recall . . . not the rococo . . . but a Greek temple.

General A.A. Svechin, 1927.

HISTORY shows that the unswerving pursuit of any one objective is almost certain to be barren of result.

"Variability" of objectives, like elasticity of dispositions, is necessary to fulfill an essential principle of war – *flexibility*. (Aug. 1929.)
  Captain Sir Basil Liddell Hart, *Thoughts on War*, 1944.

HERE WE ARE dealing with the elementary object of war, war as "politics with bloodshed", as mutual slaughter by opposing armies. The object of war is specifically "to preserve oneself and destroy the enemy" (to destroy the enemy means to disarm him or "deprive him of the power to resist", and does not mean to destroy every member of his forces physcially).
  Mao Tse-tung, *On Protracted War*, May 1938.

YOU ASK, What is our policy? I will say: It is to wage war by sea, land, and air, with all our might and with all the strength that God can give us; to wage war against a monstrous tyranny, never surpassed in the dark, lamentable catalog of human crime. That is our policy. You ask, What is our aim? I can answer in one word: Victory – victory at all costs, victory in spite of all terror; victory, however long and hard the road may be; for without victory there is no survival.
  Sir Winston S. Churchill, 13 May 1940, speech to the House of Commons.

REMEMBER that this is an invasion, not the creation of a fortified beach head.
  Sir Winston S. Churchill, 7 April 1944, at a meeting of senior Overlord commanders at St. Paul's School, Kensington, quoted in Patton, *The Patton Papers*, II, 1974.

THERE IS no purpose in capturing these manure-filled, water logged villages. The purpose of our operations is to kill or capture the German personnel and vehicles . . . so that they cannot retreat and repeat their opposition. Straight frontal attacks against villages are prohibited unless after careful study there is no other possible solution.
  General George S. Patton, Jr., 9 December 1944, letter of instruction for the Third Army, *The Patton Papers*, I, 1972.

UNITS must not be assigned impossible missions. That only contributes to heavy losses and a breakdown of morale. It is better to mount fewer offensive operations, and marshal forces for a decisive blow.
  Marshal of the Soviet Union Georgi Zhukov, 1945, quoted in Gareyev, *M.V. Frunze, Military Theorist*, 1985.

THE ALPHABET of war, Comrade General, says that victory is achieved not by taking towns but by destroying the enemy. In 1812, Napoleon forgot that. He lost Moscow – and Napoleon was no mean leader of men.
  General Andrei L. Getman, 1945, quoted in Cornelius Ryan, *The Last Battle*, 1966.

THE OBJECTIVE . . . is unquestionably the most important of all the principles of war. It is the connecting link which, alone, can impart coherence to war . . . Without the objective, all other principles are pointless. It gives the commander the "what." The other principles are guides in the "how."
  Admiral C.R. Brown, *The Principles of War*, June 1949.

IN TIME OF WAR the only value that can be affixed to any unit is the tactical value of that unit in winning the war. Even the lives of those men assigned to it become nothing more than tools to be used in the accomplishment of that mission. War has neither the time nor heart to concern itself with the individual and the dignity of man. Men must be subordinated to the effort that comes with fighting a war, and as a consequence men must die that objectives might be taken. For a commander the agony of war is not in its dangers, deprivations, or the fear of defeat but in the knowledge that with each new day men's lives must be spent to pay the costs of that day's objectives.
  General of the Army Omar N. Bradley, *A Soldier's Story*, 1951.

IN DISCUSSING the subject of the "objective" in war it is essential to be clear about, and keep clear in our minds, the distinction between the political and military objective. The two are different but not separate. For nations do not wage war for war's sake, but in pursuance of policy. The military objective is only the means to a political end. Hence the military objective should be governed by the political objective, subject to the basic condition that policy does not demand what is militarily – that, is practically – impossible.
  Captain Sir Basil Liddell Hart, *Strategy*, 1954.

KEEP your object always in mind, while adapting your plan to circumstances. Realize that there are more ways than one of gaining an object, but take heed that every objective should bear on the object. And in considering possible objectives weigh their possibility of attainment with their service to the object attained – to wander down a side-track is bad, but to reach a dead end is worse.
  Captain Sir Basil Liddell Hart, *Strategy*, 1954.

"YOU KNOW you never defeated us on the battlefield," said the American colonel. The North Vietnamese colonel pondered this remark a moment. "That may be so," he replied, "but it is also irrelevant."
  Colonel Harry G. Summers, Jr., when head of the Negotiations Division, U.S. Delegation, Four Party Joint Military Team, conversation with Colonel Tu, head of the North Vietnamese (DRV) Delegation, in Hanoi, 25 April 1975, *On Strategy*, 1981.

ONE of the most frustrating aspects of the Vietnam war from the Army's point of view is that as far as logistics and tactics were concerned we succeeded in everything we set out to do. At the height of the

war the Army was able to move almost a million soldiers a year in and out of Vietnam, feed them, clothe them, house them, supply them with arms and ammunition, and generally sustain them better than any Army had ever been sustained in the field. To project an Army of that size halfway around the world was a logistics and management task of enormous magnitude, and we had been more than equal to the task. On the battlefield itself, the Army was unbeatable. In engagement after engagement the forces of the Viet Cong and of the North Vietnamese Army were thrown back with terrible losses. Yet, in the end, it was North Vietnam, not the United States, that emerged victorious. How could we have succeeded so well, yet failed so miserably?
>Colonel Harry G. Summers, Jr., *On Strategy*, 1981.

THE FIRST PRINCIPLE of war is the principle of The Objective. It is the first principle because all else flows from it. It is the strategic equivalent of the mission statement in tactics and we must subject it to the same rigorous analysis as we do the tactical mission.
>Colonel Harry G. Summers, Jr., *On Strategy*, 1981.

OBJECTIVITY/REASON

BEFORE beginning operations you must, without any indulgence or self-deception, examine objectively every step that the enemy might undertake to thwart your plan, and consider in each conceivable case what means are open to you to fulfill your goal. The more you anticipate the difficulties in advance, the less surprised you will be should you encounter them during the campaign. Besides, you have already thought about these obstacles deliberately, and with composure you have perceived the means of avoiding them, so nothing can surprise you.
>Frederick the Great, 'Reflexions sur les projets de campagne', 1775, *Oeuvres de Frederic le Grand*, Vol. XXIX, 1846–1856, quoted in Jay Luvaas, ed., *Frederick the Great on the Art of War*, 1966.

THE PATH of nature and of truth is narrow but it is simple and direct; the devious paths are numerous and spacious; but they all lead to error and destruction.
>Robert Jackson, *A Systematic View of the Formation, Discipline and Economy of Armies*, 1804.

NOTHING should be concealed from the Emperor, either good or bad: to deceive him, even about things that are likely to be disagreeable to him is a crime.
>Marshal of France Louis Berthier, Prince de Neuchatel, Prince de Wagram, February 1807, letter to Marshal Lannes.

THIS IS the real way in which the matter must be viewed, and it is to no purpose, it is even against one's better interest, to turn away from the consideration of the real nature of affairs because of the horror of its elements excites repugnance.
>Major-General Carl von Clausewitz, *On War*, 1, 1832, tr. Michael Howard and Peter Paret, 1976.

PRECONCEIVED notions, especially in war, are dangerous, because they give their own particular colour to all information that comes in; and . . . stifle any real understanding of the actual situation. . . .
>General Aleksei A. Brusilov, March 1915, *A Soldier's Notebook*, 1930.

WE MUST have freedom of mind, no prejudices, no prepossession, no fixed ideas, no opinion accepted without discussion and merely because it has always been heard or practised. There should be only one test – reason.
>Marshal of France Ferdinand Foch, quoted in Liddell Hart, *Foch: The Man of Orleans*, 1931.

THE BUTTERFLY is the Fact – gleaming, fluttering, settling for an instant with wings fully spread to the sun, then vanishing in the shades of the forest. Whether you believe in Free Will or Predestination, all depends on the slanting glimpses you had of the colour of his wings.
>Sir Winston S. Churchill, *My Early Life*, 1930.

HAIG was an honourable man according to his lights – but his lights were dim. The consequences which have made "Passchendaele" a name of ill omen may be traced to the combined effect of his tendency to deceive himself; his tendency, therefore, to encourage his subordinates to deceive him; and their "loyal" tendency to tell a superior what was likely to coincide with his desires. Passchendaele is an object-lesson in this kind of well-meaning, if not disinterested truthfulness.
>Captain Sir Basil Liddell Hart, *Through the Fog of War*, 1938.

THE TRUTH is sought regardless of whether pleasant or unpleasant, or whether it supports or condemns our present organization of tactics.
>General Lesley J. McNair, round robin letter to his generals, quoted in E.J. Kahn, *McNair, Educator of an Army*, 1945.

WAR awakes a primitive strength in its servants, and primitive strength is only to be found in subjectivity, never in objectivity.
>Colonel Hans Ulrich Rudel, *Stuka Pilot*, 1958.

I THINK the difference in my attitude today compared with when I was composing those THOUGHTS ON WAR is that then I tended to assume that people could learn to think objectively about history and war; now, I just accept that few people can reason objectively about anything. I can still strive to pursue that aim, but I see the absurdities of life more than I did. I have come to see its nonsense, but one must try to live as if it could make sense.

Captain Sir Basil Liddell Hart, quoted in *Military Review*, 9/1966.

LEADERS Should Be Introspective. Leaders should be able to look at themselves objectively and analyze where they have made mistakes, where they've turned off people and where they've headed down the wrong path. They must be able to look in the mirror and determine what they did right today, and what they did wrong today, what decisions they need to go back to again, and how approachable they were. They should ask themselves if they have been too cooped up, too narrow, or too rigid. Introspection can be followed to a fault, however. Hamlets make poor leaders.

Major-General Perry Smith, *Taking Charge: A Practical Guide for Leaders*, 1986.

OBSTACLES

COUNTRY in which there are precipitous cliffs with torrents running between, deep natural hollows, confined places, tangled thickets, quagmires and crevasses, should be left with all possible speed and not approached.

While we keep away from such places, we should get the enemy to approach them; while we face them, we should let the enemy have them on his rear.

Sun Tzu, *The Art of War*, 9, c. 500 BC, tr. Giles, 1910.

THOSE EXPERT at preparing defences consider it fundamental to rely on the strength of such obstacles as mountains, rivers and foothills. They make it impossible for the enemy to know where to attack. They secretly conceal themselves as under the nine-layered ground.

Tu Yu (AD 735–812), commentator to Sun Tzu, *The Art of War*, 4, c. 500 BC, tr. Samuel Griffith, 1963.

MOUNTAINS can be crossed wherever goats cross, and winter freezes most rivers.

Frederick the Great, *Instructions to His Generals*, 1747, tr. Phillips, 1940.

NATURAL HAZARDS, however formidable, are inherently less dangerous and less uncertain than fighting hazards. All conditions are more calculable, all obstacles more surmountable, than those of human resistance. By reasoned calculation and preparation they can be overcome almost to timetable. While Napoleon was able to cross the Alps in 1800 "according to plan", the little fort of Bard could interfere so seriously with the movement of his army as to endanger his whole plan.

Captain Sir Basil Liddell Hart, *Strategy*, 1954.

AN OBSTACLE loses 50 per cent of its value if you stand back from it, allowing the enemy to

reconnoitre the approaches and subsequently to cross without interference.

Field Marshal Viscount Montgomery of Alamein, *A History of Warfare*, 1968.

OFFENCE AND DEFENCE
The Interrelationship

THE GENERAL who is skilled in defense hides in the most secret recesses of the earth; he who is skilled in attack flashes forth from the topmost heights of heaven. Thus on the one hand we have ability to protect ourselves; on the other, a victory is complete.

Sun Tzu, *The Art of War*, 4, c. 500 BC, tr. Giles, 1910.

PROJECTS of absolute defense are not practicable because while seeking to place yourself in strong camps the enemy will envelop you, deprive you of your supplies from the rear and oblige you to lose ground, thus disheartening your troops. Hence, I prefer to this conduct the temerity of the offensive with the hazard of losing the battle since this will not be more fatal than retreat and timid defensive. In the one case you lose ground by withdrawing and soldiers by desertion and you have no hope; in the other you do not risk more and, if you are fortunate, you can hope for the most brilliant success.

Frederick the Great, *Instructions to His Generals*, 1747, tr. Phillips, 1940.

MAXIM 19. The transition from the defensive to the offensive is one of the most delicate operations in war.

Napoleon, *The Military Maxims of Napoleon*, tr. George D'Aguilar, 1831 (David Chandler, ed., 1987).

IF THE DEFENSIVE is the stronger form of conducting war, but has a negative object, it follows of itself that we must only make use of it so long as our weakness compels us to do so, and that we must give up that form as soon as we feel strong enough to aim at the positive object. Now as the state of our circumstances is usually improved in the event of our gaining a victory through the assistance of the defensive, it is therefore, also, the natural course of war to begin with the defensive and end with the offensive.

Major-General Carl von Clausewitz, *On War*, 1832, tr. Michael Howard and Peter Paret, 1976.

A SUDDEN powerful transition to the offensive – the flashing sword of vengence – is the greatest moment for the defense. If it is not in the commander's mind from the start, or rather if it is not an integral part of his idea of defense, he will never be persuaded of the superiority of the defensive from; all he will see is how much of the enemy's resources he can destroy or capture. But these things do not depend on the way in which the knot is tied, but on the way in which it is untied. Moreover, it is a crude error to equate attack with the idea of assault alone, and therefore, to conceive of defense as merely misery and confusion.

> Major-General Carl von Clausewitz, *On War*, 6.5, 1832, tr. Michael Howard and Peter Paret, 1976.

THE BEST THING for an army on the defensive is to know how to take the offensive at a proper time, and *to take it*.

> Lieutenant-General Antoine-Henri Baron de Jomini, *Summary of the Art of War*, 1838, tr. Mendell and Craighill, 1862.

EVERY ARMY which maintains a strictly defensive attitude must, if attacked, be at last driven from its position; but if it takes advantage of the benefits of the defensive system and holds itself ready to take the offensive when occasion offers, it may hope for the greatest success.

> Lieutenant-General Antoine-Henri Baron de Jomini, *Summary of the Art of War*, 1838, tr. Mendell and Craighill, 1862.

THE OFFENSIVE knows what it wants. . . . the defensive is in a state of uncertainty.

> Field Marshal Helmuth Graf von Moltke, *Instructions for the Commanders of Large Formations*, 1869.

A CLEVER military leader will succeed in many cases in choosing defensive positions of such an offensive nature from the strategic point of view that the enemy is compelled to attack us in them.

> Field Marshal Helmuth Graf von Moltke (1800–1891).

IN WAR, the defensive exists mainly that the offensive may act more freely.

> Rear Admiral Alfred Thayer Mahan, *Naval Strategy*, 1911.

[CLAUSEWITZ, *On War*] "When we say that defense is a stronger form of war, that is, that it requires a smaller force, if soundly designed, we are speaking, of course, only of one certain line of operations. If we do not know the general line of operation on which the enemy intends to attack, and so cannot mass our force upon it, then defense is weak, because we are compelled to distribute our force so as to be strong enough to stop the enemy on any line of operations he may adopt."

Manifestly, however, a force capable of being strong enough on several lines of operation to stop an enemy possesses a superiority that should take the offensive.

> Rear Admiral Alfred Thayer Mahan, *Naval Strategy*, 1911.

A PURELY DEFENSIVE battle is a duel in which one of the fighters does nothing but *parry*. Nobody would admit that, by so doing, he could succeed in defeating his enemy. On the contrary, he would sooner or later expose himself, in spite of the greatest possible skill, to being touched, to being overcome by one of his enemy's thrusts, even if that enemy were the weaker party.

Hence the conclusion that the *offensive* form alone, be it resorted to at once or only after the *defensive*, can lead to results, and must therefore *always* be adopted – at least in the end.

> Marshal of France Ferdinand Foch, *Precepts and Judgments*, 1919.

AS THEY WERE depressed by defence their spirits rose in the offensive. The interests of the Army were best served by the offensive; in defence it was bound gradually to succumb to the ever increasing hostile superiority in men and material. This feeling was shared by everybody. In the West the Army pined for the offensive, and after Russia's collapse expected it with the most intense relief. Such was the feeling of the troops about attack and defence. It amounted to a definite conviction which obsessed them utterly that nothing but an offensive could win the war.

> General Erich Ludendorff, *My War Memories 1914–1918*, 1919.

WHERE THE PROBLEM of attack is difficult of solution it is worth considering the possibilities of an alternative form of action which throws the burden of that problem on the enemy, yet keeps the initiative. The alternative is what I would term the "baited offensive": the combination of offensive strategy with defensive tactics. Throughout history it has proved one of the most effective of moves, and its advantages have increased as modern weapons have handicapped other types of move. By rapidity of advance and mobility of manoeuvre, you may be able to seize points which the enemy, sensitive to the threat, will be constrained to attack. Thus you will invite him to a repulse which in turn may be exploited by a riposte. Such a counterstroke, against an exhausted attacker, is much less difficult than the attack on a defended position. The opportunity for it may also be created by a calculated withdrawal – what one may call the "luring defensive". Here is another gambit of future warfare. (Nov. 1935).

> Captain Sir Basil Liddell Hart, *Thoughts on War*, 1944.

THE INFLUENCE of growing firepower on tactical defense is evident. . . . The defensive is able more than before to carry out its original mission, which is to break the strength of the attacker, to parry his blows, to weaken him, to bleed him, so as to reverse the relation of forces and lead finally to the offensive, which is the only decisive form of warfare.

> Field Marshal Ritter Wilhelm von Leeb, *Defense*, 1938, tr. Possony, 1943.

THE *DEFENSE* has the advantage of being able to choose its own ground, and often, where there is plenty of room at its disposal, of even prescribing the time when its adversary must attack. The defensive waits upon the attacker. Its object is to conserve resources and to break down the attack of the opponent. If it wishes to avoid a decision, it moves away from the enemy, as far as time and space permit; it will drag the action out. As an attack proceeds, the attacker's resources diminish; he becomes weaker and wears himself out. He gets further and further from his base of operations, while for the defender this is not the case. The further the attacker advances, the more difficult his position becomes until he has gained the decision. Time in duration handicaps an attacker but is a gain for a defender.

> Colonels R. Ernest Dupuy and Trevor N. Dupuy, *The Military Heritage of America*, 1956.

THE HISTORY of wars convincingly testifies . . . to the constant contradiction between the means of attack and defense. The appearance of new means of attack has always (inevitably) led to the creation of corresponding means of counteraction, and this in the final analysis has led to the development of new methods for conducting engagements, battles, operations (and war in general).

> Marshal of the Soviet Union Nikolai V. Ogarkov, quoted in *Kommunist* (Moscow), 1978.

THE OFFENSIVE
Principle of War

I SHOULD SAY that in general the first of two army commanders who adopts an offensive attitude almost always reduces his rival to the defensive and makes him proceed in consonance with the movement of the former.

> Frederick the Great, *Instructions to his Generals*, 1747, tr. Phillips, 1940.

PUSHING OFF smartly is the road to success.

> Major-General Sir James Wolfe, 1758, letter to a friend.

AN OFFENSIVE, daring kind of war will awe the Indians and ruin the French. Blockhouses and a trembling defensive encourage the meanest scoundrel to attack us.

> Major-General Sir James Wolfe, 1758, letter to General Jeffery Lord Amherst regarding the imminent campaign in North America.

IN SHORT, I think like Frederick, one should always be the first to attack.

> Napoleon (1769–1821).

MAKE WAR offensively; it is the sole means to become a great captain and to fathom the secrets of the art.

> Napoleon, (1769–1821), *Correspondance de Napoléon Ier, publiée par ordre de l'Empereur Napoléon III*, XXXI, 1858–1870.

MAXIM 6. At the start of a campaign, to advance or not to advance is a matter for grave consideration, but when once the offensive has been assumed, it must be sustained to the last extremity.

> Napoleon, *The Military Maxims of Napoleon*, tr. George D'Aguilar, 1831 (David Chandler, ed., 1987).

IN ANY FIGHT, it's the first blow that counts; and if you keep it up hot enough, you can whip 'em as fast as they come up.

> Lieutenant-General Nathan Bedford Forrest (1821–1877).

WAR, once declared, must be waged offensively, aggressively. The enemy must not be fended off, but smitten down. You may then spare him every exaction, relinquish every gain; but till down he must be struck incessantly and remorselessly.

> Rear Admiral Alfred Thayer Mahan, *The Interest of America in Sea Power*, 1896.

IT IS this persistent widening and intensifying of the offensive – this pushing vigorously forward on carefully chosen objectives without excessive regard to alignment or close touch – that will give us the best results with the smallest losses. . . .

> Marshal of France Ferdinand Foch, 26 August 1918, letter to Field Marshal Haig, quoted in Liddell Hart, *Foch: Man of Orleans*, 1931.

HIT FIRST! Hit hard! Keep on hitting!

> Admiral Sir John 'Jackie' Fisher, *Memories*, 1919.

EVERY OFFENSIVE operation offers advantages in the first half of its duration . . . the offense gradually loses the advantages deriving from surprise and preparation. . . . one must not allow an offensive to drag on til its dying breath. . . .

> General A.A. Svechin, *Strategy*, 1927, quoted in Nathan Leites, *The Soviet Style in War*, 1982.

HAVING CROSSED the culmination point, the offensive very quickly acquires the nature of an adventure and any further development of it is only the enemy's most thorough preparation for a change from the pursuit of negative goals to the pursuit of positive goals which can receive the greatest scope. . . .

> General A.A. Svechin, *Strategy*, 1927, quoted in William F. Scott and Harriet Fast Scott, *The Soviet Art of War*, 1982.

IN WAR the only sure defense is offense, and the efficiency of the offense depends on the warlike souls of those conducting it.

> General George S. Patton, Jr., *War As I Knew It*, 1947.

SINCE I joined the Marines, I have advocated aggressiveness in the field and constant offensive action. Hit quickly, hit hard and keep right on hitting. Give the enemy no rest, no opportunity to consolidate his forces and hit back at you. This is the shortest road to victory.

General Holland M. 'Howlin' Mad' Smith, *Coral and Brass*, 1949.

THE *OFFENSIVE* alone embodies the positive qualities of combat which seek and promise decisive results. Attack seeks to strike the enemy, to destroy him on the field of battle. The attack has the advantage of the initiative. It forces action on the opponent and requires him to conform his activities to those of the attacker. It also has the factor of morale on its side.

R. Ernest Dupuy and Trevor N. Dupuy, *The Military Heritage of America*, 1956.

CARRYING THE WAR to the enemy and the destruction of his armed forces and his will to fight through the strategic offensive is the classic way wars are fought and won, hence the second principle of war is labeled *The Offensive*.

Colonel Harry G. Summers, Jr., *On Strategy*, 1981.

THE OFFENSIVE is the basic form of combat action. Only by a resolute offensive conducted at high tempo and to a great depth is total destruction of the enemy obtained.

Colonel-General V.G. Reznichenko, *Tactics*, 1984.

THE OFFICER

BUT IT IS NOT enough to cherish them at the moment when you have need of them and when their actions wring cheers from you. It is necessary that in time of peace they enjoy the reputation that they have so justly earned and that they be signally esteemed as men who have shed their blood solely for the honor and the well being of the state.

Frederick the Great, *Political Testament*, 1752.

WAR must be carried on systematically, and to do it, you must have good Officers, there are, in my Judgment, no other possible means to obtain them but by establishing your Army upon a permanent basis; and giving your officers good pay; this will induce Gentlemen, and Men of Character to engage; and till the bulk of your Officers are composed of such persons as are actuated by Principles of Honor, and spirit of Enterprize, you have little to expect from them.

General George Washington, 24 September 1776, letter to the President of Congress.

BE FRANK with your friends, temperate in your requirements and disinterested in conduct; bear an ardent zeal for the service of your Sovereign; love true fame, distinguish ambition from pride and vainglory; learn early to forgive the faults of others, and never forgive your own. . . .

Field Marshal Prince Aleksandr V. Suvorov (1729–1800), advice to a young officer cadet, quoted in W. Lyon Blease, *Suvorof*, 1920.

AS YOU from this day start the world as a man, I trust that your future conduct in life will prove you both an officer and a gentleman. Recollect that you must be a seaman to be an officer; and also that you cannot be a good officer without being a gentleman.

Admiral Lord Nelson (1758–1805) – attributed – advice to a young man upon his appointment as midshipman.

THE OFFICERS should feel the conviction that resignation, bravery, and faithful attention to duty are virtues without which no glory is possible and no army is respectable, and that firmness amid reverses is more honorable than enthusiasm in success – since courage alone is necessary to storm a position whereas it requires heroism to make a dificult retreat before a victorious and enterprising enemy, always opposing to him a firm and unbroken front.

Lieutenant-General Antoine-Henri Baron de Jomini, *Summary of the Art of War*, 1838, tr. Mendell and Craighill, 1862.

IN EVERY military system which has triumphed in modern war the officers have been recognized as the brain of the army, and to prepare them for their trust, governments have spared no pains to give them special education and training.

Colonel Emory Upton, *The Military Policy of the United States*, 1904.

OFFICERS used to serve, not for their starvation pay, but for love of their country and on the off-chance of being able to defend it with their lives. . . . They deliberately, indeed joyously, faced up to a life of adventure, roving action, exile, and poverty because it satisfied and reposed their souls.

General Sir Ian Hamilton, *The Soul and Body of an Army*, 1921.

THE OFFICER is a being apart, a kind of artist breathing the grand air in the brilliant profession of arms, in a uniform that is always seductive. . . . To me the officer is a separate race.

Mata Hari (1876–1917).

I DIVIDE my officers into four classes as follows: the clever, the industrious, the lazy, and the stupid. Each officer possesses at least two of these qualities. Those who are clever and industrious I appoint to the General Staff. Use can under certain circumstances be made of those who are stupid and lazy. The man who is clever and lazy qualifies for the highest leadership posts. He has the requisite nerves and the mental clarity of difficult decisions. But whoever is stupid and industrious must be got rid of, for he is too dangerous.

Attributed to General Kurt von Hammerstein Equord, c. 1933.

THE FOUNDATION of our National Defense system is the Regular Army, and the foundation of the

Regular Army is the officer. He is the soul of the system. If you have to cut everything out of the National Defense Act the last element should be the officer corps. If you had to discharge every soldier, if you had to do away with everything else, I would still professionally advise you to keep those 12,000 officers. They are the mainspring of the whole mechanism; each one of them would be worth a thousand men at the beginning of a war. They are the only ones who can take this heterogeneous mass and make it a homogeneous group.

> General of the Army Douglas MacArthur, 1933, statement before Congress defending the officer corps faced with proposed deep cuts, *Reminiscences*, 1964.

NEVER for an instant can you divest yourself of the fact that you are officers. On the athletic field, at the club, in civilian clothes, or even at home on leave, the fact that you are a commissioned officer in the Army imposes a constant obligation to higher standards than might ordinarily seem normal or necessary for your personal guidance. A small dereliction becomes conspicuous, at times notorious, purely by reason of the fact that the individual concerned is a commissioned officer.

But the evil result goes much further than a mere matter of unfortunate publicity. When you are commanding, leading men under conditions where physical exhaustion and privations must be ignored; where the lives of men may be sacrificed, then, the efficiency of your leadership will depend only to a minor degree on your tactical or technical ability. It will primarily be determined by your character, your reputation, not so much for courage – which will be accepted as matter of course – but by the previous reputation you have established for fairness, for that high-minded patriotic purpose, that quality of unswerving determination to carry through any military task assigned you.

The feeling which the men must hold for you is not to be compared to the popularity of a football coach or a leader of civic activities. Professional competence is essential to leadership, and your knowledge of arms, equipment, and tactical operations must be clearly superior to that possessed by your subordinates; at the same time, you must command their respect above and beyond those qualities.

> General of the Army George C. Marshall, 27 September 1941, address given to the first graduates of the U.S. Army's Officer Candidate Schools, published in *The Army and Navy Register*, 4 October 1941.

WE, as officers of the army, are not only members of the oldest of honorable professions, but are also the modern representatives of the demi-gods and heroes of antiquity. Back of us stretches a line of men whose acts of valor, of self-sacrifice and of service have been the theme of song and story since long before recorded history began. . . . In the days of chivalry . . . knights-officers were noted as well for courtesy and gentleness of behavior as for death-defying courage. . . . From their acts of courtesy and benevolence was derived the word, now pronounced as one, Gentle Man. . . . Let us be gentle. This is, courteous and considerate of the rights of others. Let us be Men. That is, fearless and untiring in doing our duty. . . . Our calling is most ancient and like all other old things it has amassed through the ages certain customs and traditions which decorate and ennoble it, which render beautiful the otherwise prosaic occupation of professional men-at-arms: killers.

> General George S. Patton, Jr. (1885–1945), quoted in Fitton, ed., *Leadership*, 1990.

THE MILITARY OFFICER is considered a gentleman, not because Congress wills it, nor because it has been the custom of the people at all times to afford him that courtesy, but specifically because nothing less than a gentleman is truly suited for his particular set of responsibilities.

> Brigadier-General S.L.A. Marshall, *The Armed Forces Officer*, 1950.

THE BADGE of rank which an officer wears on his coat is really a symbol of servitude – servitude to his men.

> General Maxwell Taylor, quoted in *Army Information Digest*, 1953.

IT IS precisely because life is so precious to me that I am prepared to die, and there is no paradox in this. The meaning I found in life is embodied in West Point; not just the place or the people, or even my four years there, but the total concept of the place. Its history reeks of nobility, its sons personify duty and honor, and that other great source of meaning, our country. It is the poetic words of MacArthur, gloom period, football weekends, "Ladies and Gentlemen, the United States Corps of Cadets." It is the pride in wearing your country's uniform and giving the troops something to believe in; it is the embodiment of the history of the American fighting man and, by damn, if I die taking part in that, I die happy and satisfied. Of the possible meanings of death, it is the best.

> Major Alexander Hottell, c. 1968, journal entry, quoted in John T. Murray, *Fallen Warriors*, 1996.

WITHOUT A SENSE of special calling, it is unlikely that an officer corps can develop leadership within itself. Leadership requires a special sense of sacrifice, a sense of risk and a devotion in courage that can never truly develop when the climate of the organization equates these demands with the values of the marketplace.

> Paul Savage and Lieutenant-Colonel Richard Gabriel, 'The Environment of Military Leadership', *Military Review*, 7/1980.

I TOOK the time to personally interview every new officer assigned to the division. For me, these interviews were quite revealing of the social corrosion caused by the protracted war of attrition in Vietnam and our bankrupt strategy. . . . I sensed that some of them had the makings of good professional officers and that, with a little encouragement, they might stay in the Army. An officer had to have two fundamentally important traits, I told them: integrity and courage, both physical and moral. If an officer lacked those qualities, no amount of careful planning or help from influential connections would bring them a successful career. Don't worry about your "career," I said. Solve the Army's problems and your career will take care of itself. If they felt at all inclined to become professional officers, they should "follow the sound of the cannon," go to Vietnam, lead men in battle, and, if they survived, then decide if they had a future in the Army.

> Major-General John K. Singlaub, as Assistant Division Commander of the Eighth Infantry Division, Germany, 1968, *Hazardous Duty: An American Soldier in the Twentieth Century*, 1991.

OFFICERS AND MEN

PAY HEED to nourishing the troops; do not unnecessarily fatigue them. Unite them in spirit; conserve their strength. Make unfathomable plans for the movement of the army.

Thus, such troops need no encouragement to be vigilant. Without extorting their support the general obtains it; without inviting their affection he gains it; without demanding their trust he wins it.

> Sun Tzu, *The Art of War*, c. 500 BC, tr. Samuel Griffith.

NOW as for me, my men, there is not one of you who has not with his own eyes seen me strike a blow in battle; I have watched and witnessed your valour in the field, and your acts of courage I know by heart, with every detail of when and where they took place: and this, surely, is not a thing of small importance. I was your pupil before I was your commander; I shall advance into the line with soldiers I have a thousand times praised and rewarded; and the enemy we shall meet are raw troops with a raw general, neither knowing anything of the other.

> Hannibal, 218 BC, address to his army before meeting the Roman Army under the Consul Cornelius Scipio on the River Ticinus, quoted in Livy, *The History of Rome*, 21.43, c. AD 17 (*The War With Hannibal*, tr. Aubrey de Sélincourt, 1965).

. . . FOR IF MEN have a spontaneous and natural love for their general, they are quick to obey his commands, they do not distrust him, and they cooperate with him in case of danger.

> Onasander, *The General*, AD 58, (*Aeneas Tacticus, Aclepiodotus, Onasander*, tr. The Illinois Greek Club, 1923).

NOTHING does so much honor to the abilities and application of the Tribune as the appearance and discipline of the soldiers, when their apparel is neat and clean, their arms bright and in good order and when they perform their exercises and evolutions with dexterity.

> Flavius Vegetius Renatus, *Military Institutions of the Romans*, c. AD 378, tr. Clark, 1776.

THE GENERAL who is overly harsh with his subordinates and the one who is too indulgent are both unfit for command. Fear leads to great hatred, and giving in too much results in being despised. It is safe to take the middle course.

> The Emperor Maurice, *The Strategikon*, c. AD 600 (*Maurice's Strategikon*, tr. George Dennis, 1984).

THE GENERAL'S WAY of life should be plain and simple like that of his soldiers; he should display a fatherly affection toward them; he should give orders in a mild manner; and he should always make sure to give advice and to discuss essential matters with them in person. His concerns ought to be with their safety, their food, and their regular pay. Without these it is impossible to maintain discipline in an army.

> The Emperor Maurice, *The Strategikon*, c. AD 600 (*Maurice's Strategikon*, tr. George Dennis, 1984).

WHAT MAKES soldiers in battle prefer to charge ahead rather than retreat even for survival is the benevolence of the military leadership. When soldiers know their leaders care for them as they care for their own children, then the soldiers love their leaders as they do their own fathers. This makes them willing to die in battle, to requite the benevolence of their leaders.

> Liu Ji (1310–1375), *Lessons of War* (*Mastering the Art of War*, tr. Thomas Cleary, 1989).

LOVE the soldier, and he will love you. That is the secret.

> Field Marshal Prince Aleksandr V. Suvorov (1729–1830).

UNDER such an officer [who understood them], they will conquer or die on the spot, while their action, their hardihood and abstinence enable them to bear up under a severity of fatigue under which larger and apparently stronger men would sink. But it is the principles of integrity and moral correctness that I admire most in Highland soldiers, and this was the trait that first caught my attention. It is this that makes them trustworthy, and makes their courage sure, and not that kind of flash in the pan which would scale a bastion to-day and tomorrow be alarmed at the fire of a picket. You Highland officers may sleep sound at night, and rise in the morning with the assurance that your men, your professional character and honour, are safe.

> Lieutenant-General Sir John Moore, 17 November 1804, letter to Colonel Alexander Napier, quoted in Carola Oman, *Sir John Moore*, 1953.

WHEN ASKED one day how, after so many years, he could recollect the names and numbers of the units engaged in one of his early combats, Napoleon responded, "Madam, this is a lover's recollection of his former mistresses."

> Napoleon, quoted in Count Emmanuel de Las Casas, *Memoirs of the Life, Exile and Conversations of the Emperor Napoleon*, 1836.

THE DUKE never claimed for one moment credit to himself where he did not feel that it was thoroughly deserved. Someone saying to him "How do you account, Duke, for your having so persistently beaten the French Marshals?" The Duke replied simply, "Well, the fact is their soldiers got them into scrapes: mine always got me out."

> The Duke of Wellington (1769–1852), quoted in William Fraser, *Words of Wellington*, 1889.

THE ONE MODE or the other of dealing with subordinates springs from a corresponding spirit in the breast of the commander. He who feels the respect which is due to others cannot fail to inspire in them regard for himself, while he who feels, and hence manifests, disrespect toward others, especially his inferiors, cannot fail to inspire hatred against himself.

> Major-General John M. Schofield (1831–1906), speech to the Corps of Cadets at West Point.

FOR AN OFFICER to be overbearing and insulting in the treatment of enlisted men is the act of a coward. He ties the man to a tree with ropes of discipline and then strikes him in the face, knowing full well that the man cannot strike back.

> Major C.A. Bach, 1917, farewell instructions to graduating student officers at Fort Sheridan, Wyoming.

THE RELATIONSHIP between officers and men should in no sense be that of superior and inferior nor that of master and servant, but rather that of teacher and scholar. In fact, it should partake of the nature of the relation between father and son, to the extent that officers, especially commanding officers, are responsible for the physical, mental, and moral welfare, as well as the discipline and military training of the young men under their command.

The recognition of this responsibility on the part of officers is vital to the well-being of the Marine Corps. It is especially so for the reason that so large a proportion of the men enlisting are under 21 years of age. These men are in the formative period of their lives and officers owe it to them, to their parents, and to the Nation, that when discharged from the service they should be far better men physically, mentally, and morally than they were when they enlisted.

> Major-General John A. Lejeune, *Marine Corps Manual*, 1920.

GOOD RELATIONS between commanders and the rank and file are like all other forms of friendship – if they are to be maintained and bear fruit they must be nourished. Soldiers are human beings – rather more human than other people – and they will never respond whole-heartedly to the commander who treats them as mere automata to be used for his own purpose according to order, and without any thought being given to them as ordinary men. On the other hand, they will always be ready to offer the last ounce of their strength in extricating from any difficulty into which he may have fallen the General in whom they have confidence as a personal friend. Our men are exceedingly accurate judges of an officer's worth and character, and whilst they intensely dislike the officer who does not enter into their feelings and treats them as if they had none, they have unbounded admiration for the one who treats them kindly as well as justly.

> Field Marshal Sir William Robertson, *From Private to Field-Marshal*, 1921.

BUT THERE the fundamental condition ensuring military might is lacking: there is no link between the upper and lower strata of society. The existence of a deep gulf dividing the command class from the exploited essentially reduces to nought all efforts to create a battleworthy military force.

> Mikhail Frunze (1885–1925), quoted in Gareyev, *Frunze, Military Theorist*, 1985.

WHEN the last bugle is sounded, I want to stand up with my soldiers.

> General of the Armies John J. Pershing, quoted in Hale and Turner, *The Yanks are Coming*, 1983.

SYMPATHY and understanding are vital faculties in a commander – because they evoke a similar response in subordinates, and thus create the basis of co-operation. Arbitrary control commonly breaks down unless it rests on the co-operation of minds attuned to the same key. Without this the first is but voice control. (May 1929.)

> Captain Sir Basil Liddell Hart, *Thoughts on War*, 1944.

MANY PEOPLE think that it is wrong methods that make for strained relations between officers and men and between the army and the people, but I always tell them that it is a question of basic attitude . . . of having respect for the soldiers and the people.

> Mao Tse-tung, *On Protracted War*, May 1938.

THE RELATIONSHIP between a general and his troops is very much like that between the rider and his horse. The horse must be controlled and disciplined, and yet encouraged: he should "be cared for in the stables as if he was worth 500 and ridden in the field as if he were worth half-a-crown".

> Field Marshal Viscount Wavell of Cyrenaica, *Generals and Generalship*, 1941.

ALL OFFICERS, and particularly General Officers, must be vitally interested in everything that interests the soldier. Usually you will gain a great deal of knowledge by being interested, but, even if you do not, the fact that you appear interested has a very high morale influence on the soldier.

General George S. Patton, Jr., *War As I Knew It*, 1947.

OFFICERS are responsible, not only for the conduct of their men in battle, but also for their health and contentment when not fighting. An officer must be the last man to take shelter from fire, and the first to move forward. Similarly, he must be the last man to look after his own comfort at the close of a march. He must see that his men are cared for. The officer must constantly interest himself in the rations of the men. He should know his men so well that any sign of sickness or nervous strain will be apparent to him, and he can take such action as may be necessary.

General George S. Patton, Jr., *War As I Knew It*, 1947.

THE EXAMPLE and personal conduct of officers and noncommissioned officers are of decisive influence on the troops. The officer who, in the face of the enemy, is cold-blooded, decisive, and courageous inspires his troops onward. The officer must, likewise, find the way to the hearts of his subordinates and gain their trust through an understanding of their feelings and thoughts, and through never-ceasing care of their needs.

Generals Werner von Fritsch and Ludwig Beck, *Troop Leadership*, 1933, quoted in U.S. War Department, *German Military Training*, 17 September 1942.

NOTHING more radical is suggested here than that the leader who would make certain of the fundamental soundness of his operation cannot do better than concentrate his attention on his men. There is no other worthwhile road. They dupe only themselves who believe that there is a brand of military efficiency which consists in moving smartly, expediting papers, and achieving perfection in formations, while at the same time slighting or ignoring the human nature of those whom they command. The art of leading, in operations large or small, is the art of dealing with humanity, of working diligently on behalf of men, of being sympathetic with them, but equally, of insisting that they make a square facing toward their own problems. These are the real bases of a commander's calculations. Yet how often do we hear an executive praised as an "efficient administrator" simply because he can keep a desk cleared, even though he is despised by everyone in the lower echelons and cannot command a fraction of their loyalty.

Brigadier-General S.L.A. Marshall, *The Armed Forces Officer*, 1950.

THE COMMANDER must have contact with his men. He must be capable of feeling and thinking with them. The soldier must have confidence in him. There is one cardinal principle which must always be remembered: one must never make a show of

false emotions to one's men. The ordinary soldier has a surprisingly good nose for what is true and what is false.

Field Marshal Erwin Rommel, *The Rommel Papers*, 1953.

HE [the soldier] will put up with this so long as he knows you are living in relatively much the same way; and he likes to see the C.-in-C. regularly in the forward area, and be spoken to and noticed. He must know that you really care for him and will look after his interests, and that you will give him all the pleasures you can in the midst of his discomforts.

Field Marshal Viscount Montgomery of Alamein, *The Memoirs of Field Marshal Montgomery*, 1958.

THE FIRST THING a young officer must do when he joins the Army is to fight a battle, and that battle is for the hearts of his men. If he wins that battle and subsequent similar ones, his men will follow him anywhere; if he loses it, he will never do any real good.

Field Marshal Viscount Montgomery of Alamein, *The Memoirs of Field Marshal Montgomery*, 1958.

THE MEN have a highly developed collective sense. They are almost never mistaken about their commander, and are the people best qualified to judge him. It is possible to mislead them by propaganda and publicity stunts. It is possible to create a cult of admiration for some military figure who rarely comes in contact with them. But it is quite impossible to deceive them as to the character and qualities of their direct commanders with whom they work day by day.

General Yigal Allon, *The Making of Israel's Army*, 1970.

SOLDIERS who know that their commander values them and has implicit faith in them, that he will spare no effort on their behalf and will evade no risk which they must take, that he has the ability to plan and conduct a battle well and that he at no time takes unfair advantage of his rank, will understand the limitations he imposes upon them and will reconcile themselves to the rigorous discipline he expects of them. They will go into battle knowing that it is unavoidable and that everything possible has been done to ensure its success. They will give of their best in executing their mission.

General Yigal Allon, *The Making of Israel's Army*, 1970.

THE BASIS of all good leadership is the relationship built up between a commander and his troops. Napoleon's greatest and, as it turned out, almost his only asset on his return from Elba was the devotion of his army. His physical condition might have deteriorated, his military genius might have waned, but so long as his soldiers were prepared to die for him the French Army was still a formidable fighting machine.

Lieutenant-General Sir Brian Horrocks, *Escape to Action*, 1961.

I DON'T LIKE being separated in comparative luxury from troops who are living hard.

> Field Marshal Sir Claude Auchinleck, 1976, interview with David Dimbleby.

SOLDIERS will go all out for an officer who does not waste their time through poor management when he has a tough job to do.

> General Bruce C. Clarke (1901–1988).

ENLISTED PEOPLE with a higher quality of intelligence need a different kind of leadership. You cannot run a unit just by giving orders and having the Uniform Code of Military Justice behind you.

> Admiral William Crowe, *Newsweek*, 18 April 1988.

I HAVE a strong belief in what young Marines can achieve if they are properly led. It never ceases to amaze me. In the desert, they built bases and moved vast distances that you wouldn't think anyone would be able to do. And all they ask in return is caring leadership. They are the first to know if you don't really care. And consequently, their performance will reflect that.

> General Walter Boomer, 'Up Front', Al Santoli, ed., *Leading the War: How Vietnam Veterans Rebuilt the U.S. Military*, 1993.

OFFICER SELECTION

IF YOU CHOOSE godly, honest men to be captains of horse, honest men will follow them.

> Oliver Cromwell, September 1643, letter to Sir William Springe.

WE WANT Men Capable of Command – who will fight and reduce their soldiers to strict obedience.

> Major-General Andrew Jackson, 15 September 1812, letter to Brigadier-General John Coffee, Library of Congress.

THERE IS another point to which I would invite your attention. The best troops are ineffective without good officers. Our volunteers, more than any others, require officers whom they can respect and trust. The best men for that position should be selected, and it is important to consider how it can be effected. It would be safe to trust men of the intelligence & character of our volunteers to elect their officers, could they at the time of election realize their dependent condition in the day of battle. But this they cannot do, & I have known them in the hour of danger repudiate & disown officers of their choice & beg for others. Is it right, then, for a State to throw upon its citizens a responsibility which they do not feel and cannot properly exercise? The colonel of a regiment has an important trust, & is a guardian of the honor of the State as well as of the lives of her citizens. I think it better for the field officers of the regiments in State service to be appointed by the governor, with the advice & consent of its legislature, & those in the Confederate service by the President & Congress.

> General Robert E. Lee, 24 December 1861, letter to Andrew G. Magrath on the pernicious effect of election of officers initially practised by the Confederates, *The Wartime Papers of Robert E. Lee*, 1961.

THE GREAT interests of the country are being sacrificed by appointing incompetent officers. I wish that if such appointments are continued, that the President would come in the field and command them, and not throw the responsibility upon me of defending the District when he throws such obstacles in my way.

> Lieutenant-General Thomas J. 'Stonewall' Jackson, 6 May 1862, letter to Alexander R. Boteler.

IF WE PERSUADE intelligent youth to hold aloof from the Army in peace, we ought not to complain if we are not properly led in war.

> Baron Charles MacMoran Wilson Moran, *The Anatomy of Courage*, 1945.

NO WRITTEN examination is a test of character, personality or leadership. Examinations are not a true test of ability and are not test at all of character or leadership. Some shine at examinations, others fail to disclose their knowledge of the subject. Brains of themselves are only of academic value. I have seen so many scholars fail in life through lack of application, character and personality. . . . Entrance examinations into the Army used to be particularly harmful. How can written examinations be a test of good officership? . . . Academic knowledge without character and personality is useless. The boy with average intelligence, with drive, character and practical ability – I knew so many of them who have had brilliant careers, leaving scholars behind. Scholars seldom enter the Army, preferring professions or politics. Successful soldiers have not been scholars, the one exception being Lord Wavell. I can think of no soldier who has reached the top of the ladder in recent years whose main assets have been scholarly ability. Our leading soldiers in both World Wars reached the top through character, personality, determination and leadership. All the very necessary and arduous brainwork is done by scholarly staff officers.

> Colonel Richard Meinertzhagen, *Army Diary 1899–1926*, 1960.

THE OLD SCHOOL

WE CANNOT DRAW our inspiration indifferently from Turenne, Conde, Prince Eugene, Villars, or Frederick the Great, even less from the tottering theories and degenerate forms of the last century.

The best of these doctrines answered a situation and needs which are no longer ours.

Marshal of France Ferdinand Foch, *The Principles of War*, 1913.

. . . FOR IF THERE IS anything more characteristic of the Navy than its fighting ability, it is the inertia to change, or conservatism, or the clinging to things that are old because they are old. It must be admitted that this characteristic has been in many things a safeguard; it is also true that in quite as many it has been a drag to progress.

Admiral of the Fleet Ernest J. King, 'Some Ideas About Organization on Board Ship', prize essay, 1909, *U.S. Naval Institute Proceedings* (written as a lieutenant).

HAVE WE the moral courage to accept the new idea and the energy to carry it out? We doubt it, for before us stands the serried phalanx of the "old school", who, like the ideal English bishop of Mrs. Browning –

". . . must not love truth too dangerously,
But prefer the interests of the Church."

Major-General J.F.C. Fuller, from his gold-medal-winning essay in R.U.S.I., 5/1920.

CAVALRY CIRCLES loathed the idea of giving up the horse, and thus instinctively decried the tank. They found much support both in the War Office and in Parliament. Wellington's reputed saying that the Battle of Waterloo was won on the playing-fields of Eton is merely a legend, but it is painfully true that the early battles of World War II were lost in the Cavalry Club.

Captain Sir Basil Liddell Hart, *The Memoirs of Captain Liddell Hart*, I, 1965.

OLD SOLDIERS

BUT now's the time
for the younger men to lock in rough encounters,
time for me to yield to the pains of old age.
But there was a day I shone among the
    champions.

Homer, *The Iliad*, 23.715–719, c. 800 BC, tr. Robert Fagles, 1990; King Nestor of Pylos' reminiscences at the games for Patrocles.

BUT there are still those moments when I can feel the strength and courage and wisdom move together in my head, and rich evening laughter of good men rises from the benches towards the dozing hawks in the beams above as the poet touches his harp and calls for me. Then I know that Beowulf is my name, and I in my youth with the strength of thirty men in my hand am proud and ready, and will sail again.

Beowulf, c. AD 600 (*Beowulf Is My Name*, tr. Frederick Rebsamen, 1971).

I DREAMED I was back in battle. I waded in blood up to my knees. I saw death as it is on the battle field. The poor boys with arms shot off and legs gone, were lying on the cold ground, with no nurses and no physicians to do anything for them. I saw the surgeons coming, too much needed by all to give special attention to any one. Once again I stood by them and witnessed those soldiers bearing their soldier pains, limbs being sawed off without opiates being taken, or even a bed to lie on. I crept around once more, trying to give them at least a drink of water to cool their parched lips, and I heard them at last speak of mother and wives and sweethearts, but never a murmur or complaint. Then I woke to hear myself groan because I have a stupid pain in my back, that's all. Here on a good bed, with every attention! I am ashamed that I murmur!

Clara Barton, 10 April 1912, two days before her death, quoted in Percy Epler, *The Life of Clara Barton*, 1915.

I 'EARD the feet on the gravel – the feet o' the men what drill –
An' I sez to my flutterin' 'eart-strings, I sez to 'em,
"Peace, be still!"

Rudyard Kipling, 'Back to the Army Again'.

THE SHADOWS are lengthening for me. The twilight is here. My days of old have vanished tone and tint; they have gone glimmering through the dreams of things that were. Their memory is one of wonderous beauty, watered by tears, and coaxed and caressed by the smiles of yesterday. I listen vainly, but with thirsty ear, for the witching melody of faint bugles blowing reveille, of far drums beating the long roll. In my dreams I hear again the crash of guns, the rattle of musketry, the strange mournful mutter of the battlefield. But in the evening of my memory, always I come back to West Point. Always there echoes and reechoes in my ears – Duty–Honor–Country.

Today marks my final call with you. But I want you to know that when I cross the river my last conscious thought will be of the Corps – and the Corps – and the Corps.

I bid you farewell.

General of the Army Douglas MacArthur, 12 May 1964, farewell address to the Corps of Cadets at Westpoint, *Reminiscences*, 1964.

OPERATIONAL ART

OPERATIONAL ART is the connecting link between strategy and tactics. It determines methods of preparing and conducting army and front operations, operations of groups of fronts, and also independent and joint operations of units of the different types of armed forces, in accordance with the requirements of strategy and for the achievement of strategic objectives. At the same time, operational art assigns missions to tactics, directing the tactical action of units and branches of arms in the interest of the operation .

> Chief Marshal of the Tank Forces Pavel A. Rotmistrov, 'On the Modern Soviet Military Art and Its Characteristics', *Voyennay Mysl'*, 2/1958, quoted in William Scott and Harriet Fast Scott, ed., *The Soviet Art of War*, 1982.

OPERATIONAL ART is the employment of military forces to attain strategic goals in a theater of war or theater of operations through the design, organization, and conduct of campaigns in a series of joint actions designed to attain a strategic objective in a theater of war. . . . Operational art thus involves fundamental decisions about when and where to fight and whether to accept or decline battle. Its essence is the identification of the enemy's center-of-gravity – his source of strength or balance – and the concentration of superior combat power against that point to achieve a decisive success. . . . Reduced to its essentials, operational art requires the commander to answer three questions:

(1) What military condition must be produced in the theater of war or operations to achieve the strategic goal?

(2) What sequence of actions is most likely to produce that condition?

(3) How should the resources of the force be applied to accomplish that sequence of actions?

> U.S. Army FM 100-5 *Operations*, 1986.

OPERATIONS

NO PLAN of operations can with any assurance look beyond the first meeting with the main enemy forces. Only a layman will think that he can see in the development of a campaign anything like a consistent pursuit of a previously conceived plan, one with all its details worked out beforehand and held to right to the end. The consecutive achievements of a war are not premeditated but spontaneous, and are guided by military instinct.

> Field Marshal Helmuth Graf von Moltke (1800–1891).

THIS APPROACH to an operation, this likening of it to the struggle of two wills, to the action of the "mass psyche" of one side on the other, amounts to pernicious military idealism. An operation consists in the organized struggle of each of the armies to achieve the complete destruction of the opponent's vital material strength. The operational aim cannot be the destruction of some imaginary, abstract nervous system of the army; it must be the destruction of the organism itself – of the force, and of an army's real nervous system, its communications.

> Marshal of the Soviet Union Mikhail N. Tukhachevskiy, 1924, quoted in Richard Simpkin, *Deep Battle*, 1987.

AN IMPORTANT difference between a military operation and a surgical operation is that the patient is not tied down. But it is a common fault of generalship to assume that he is. (May 1934.)

> Captain Sir Basil Liddell Hart, *Thoughts on War*, 1944.

OPINIONS

I NEVER SUFFER my mind to be so wedded to any opinions as to refuse to listen to better ones when they are suggested to me.

> Henry IV (Henry of Navarre), King of France (1553–1610).

I HAVE got you together to hear what I have written down. I do not wish your advice about the main matter – for that I have determined myself.

> President Abraham Lincoln, 22 September 1862, to his cabinet, quoted in Salman P. Chase, *Diary and Correspondence*, 1903.

AN OPINION can be argued with; a conviction is best shot.

> Colonel T.E. Lawrence (1888–1935).

YOU HAVE come here to acquire knowledge, to evolve it and to fit it to the men you will one day either command or administer. Knowledge is not only acquired in the lecture-room, but also in the mess and in your own private studies. Nothing clarifies knowledge like a free exchange of ideas; consequently, because I happen to be a Major, do not for a moment imagine that rank is a bar to free speech. If you disagree with me or the views of any of your instructors, openly state your disagreement; for we are all students, and the man who cannot change his opinions has mineralized his intellect – he is a walking stone.

> Major-General J.F.C. Fuller, *Memoirs of an Unconventional Soldier*, 1936.

I AM CONVINCED that the best service a retired general can perform is to turn in his tongue along with his suit and to mothball his opinions.

> General of the Army Omar N. Bradley, quoted in James Carlton, *The Military Quotation Book*, 1991.

WE ENJOY the comfort of opinions without the discomfort of thought.

> President John F. Kennedy, 11 June 1962, commencement address at Yale University, *Public Papers of Presidents of the United States: John F. Kennedy*, p. 234.

I CAN GIVE you my opinion, but remember this is just Al Gray talking: I'm too junior to make policy and too senior to make coffee.

> General Alfred M. Gray, *Soldier of Fortune*, 10/1981; while a major-general serving as the USMC's Development Director.

OPPORTUNITY

TO SECURE ourselves against defeat lies in our own hands, but the opportunity of defeating the enemy is provided by the enemy himself.
> Sun Tzu, *The Art of War*, 4, c. 500 BC, tr. Giles, 1910.

IF THE ENEMY leaves a door open, you must rush in.
> Sun Tzu, *The Art of War*, 11, c. 500 BC, tr. Giles, 1910.

. . . THE OPPORTUNITIES of war wait for no man.
> Pericles, reply to the Spartan ultimatum, 432/431 BC, quoted in Thucydides, *The History of the Peloponnesian War*, 1.142, c. 404 BC, tr. Richard Crowley, 1910.

TO OVERCOME the intelligent by folly is contrary to the natural order of things; to overcome the foolish by intelligence is in accord with the natural order. To overcome the intelligent by intelligence, however, is a matter of opportunity.
There are three avenues of opportunity: events, trends, and conditions. When opportunities occur through events but you are unable to respond, you are not smart. When opportunities become active through a trend and yet you cannot make plans, you are not wise. When opportunities emerge through conditions but you cannot act on them, you are not bold.
Those skilled in generalship always achieve their victories by taking advantage of opportunities.
> Zhuge Liang (AD 180–234), *The Way of the General* (*Mastering the Art of War*, tr. Thomas Cleary, 1989).

THE ART of certain victory, the mode of harmonizing with changes, is a matter of opportunity. Who but the perspicacious can deal with it? And of all avenues of seeing opportunity, none is greater than the unexpected.
> Zhuge Liang (AD 180–234), *The Way of the General* (*Mastering the Art of War*, tr. Thomas Cleary, 1989).

THOSE DESIGNS are best of which the enemy are entirely ignorant till the moment of execution. Opportunity in war is often more to be depended on than courage.
> Flavius Vegetius Renatus, *Military Institutions of the Romans*, c. AD 378, tr. Clark, 1776.

HE [the general] should often deliberate about his most serious problems and carry out what he has decided with as little delay and risk as possible. For opportunity is what cures problems.
> The Emperor Maurice, *The Strategikon*, c. AD 600 (*Maurice's Strategikon*, tr. George Dennis, 1984).

A GOOD GENERAL is one who utilizes his own skills to fit the opportunities he gets and the quality of the enemy.
> The Emperor Maurice, *The Strategikon*, c. AD 600 (*Maurice's Strategikon*, tr. George Dennis, 1984).

IN WAR opportunity is fleeting and cannot be put off at all.
> The Emperor Maurice, *The Strategikon*, c. AD 600 (*Maurice's Strategikon*, tr. George Dennis, 1984).

FOUR THINGS come back not:
The spoken word; the sped arrow;
Time past; the neglected opportunity.
> Omar I Ibn al-Khattab, Caliph (AD 581–644).

MY FEELING is that we should confront all the enemy's forces with all the forces of Islam; for events do not turn out according to man's will and we do not know how long a life is left to us, so it is foolish to dissipate this concentration of troops without striking a tremendous blow in the Holy War.
> Saladin, July 1187, his decision before the Battle of Hattin to make use of the opportunity presented by concentration, quoted by Ibn al-Athir in Gabrieli, *Arab Historians of the Crusades*, 1957.

I SHALL LAST a year, and but little longer: we must think to do good work in that year. Four things are laid upon me: to drive out the English; to bring you to be crowned and anointed at Rheims; to rescue the Duke of Orléans from the hands of the English; and to raise the siege of Orléans.
> Joan of Arc, March/April 1429, to Charles, Dauphin of France, *Joan of Arc in her Own Words*, 1996.

WHEN THERE IS a battle that can be won or a castle that can be taken, to concern oneself with the fortuitous day or direction and let time pass is extremely regrettable. There will be little value in sending a ship out in a storm, or having a single man face great numbers even if the day is propitious. For even though the day and place be "unlucky," if one will attain the minute details of the situation, prepare his attack in secret, adapt to the circumstances, and make strategy his foundation, the victory will surely be his.
> Asakura Toshikage (1428–1481), *The 17 Articles of Asakura Toshikage* (*Ideals of the Samurai*, tr. William Wilson, 1982).

NOTHING is of greater importance in time of war than knowing how to make the best use of a fair opportunity when it is offered.
> Niccolo Machiavelli, *The Art of War*, 1521.

NOT ONLY strike while the iron is hot, but make it hot by striking.
> Oliver Cromwell (1599–1658).

IT IS GOOD to exercise caution, but not to such an extent that all opportunities become lost. Hungry dogs bite best.
> Charles XII, King of Sweden (1682–1718).

THUS, on the day of battle, I should want the general to do nothing. His observations will be better for it, his judgment will be more sane, and he will be in better state to profit from the situations in which the enemy finds himself during the engagement. And when he sees an occasion, he should unleash his energies, hasten to the critical point at top speed, seize the first troops available, advance them rapidly, and lead them in person. These are the strokes that decide battles and gain victories. The important thing is to see the opportunity and to know how to use it.

> Field Marshal Maurice Comte de Saxe, *My Reveries*, 1732, tr. Phillips, 1940.

. . . LEARN to profit from local circumstances.

> Field Marshal Aleksandr V. Suvorov (1729–1800).

A SEA-OFFICER cannot, like a land-officer, form plans; his object is to embrace the happy moments which now and then offers, – it may be this day, not for a month, and perhaps never.

> Admiral Viscount Nelson, 1796, to the British Minister at Genoa.

ALL GREAT EVENTS hang by a single thread. The clever man takes advantage of everything, neglects nothing that may give him some added opportunity; the less clever man, by neglecting one thing, sometimes misses everything.

> Napoleon, 26 September 1797, letter to Tallyrand, *Correspondance de Napoléon Ier, publiée par ordre de l'Empereur Napoléon III*, III, p. 342, 1858–1870, quoted in Christopher Herold, ed., *The Mind of Napoleon*, 1955.

MAXIM 95. War is composed of nothing but accidents, and, although holding to general principles, a general should never lose sight of everything to enable him to profit from these accidents; that is the mark of genius.

In war there is but one favorable moment; the great art is to seize it.

> Napoleon, *The Military Maxims of Napoleon*, tr. Burnod, 1827.

WHEN this movement commences, I shall move out by my left, with all the force I can, holding present intrenched lines. I shall start with no distinct view, further than holding Lee's forces from following Sheridan. But I shall be along myself and will take advantage of anything that turns up.

> General of the Army Ulysses S. Grant, 1865, letter to Major-General Sherman from outside Petersburg, quoted in Liddell Hart, *Sherman*, 1930.

EVERYTHING comes to this: to be able to recognize the changed situation and order the foreseeable course and prepare it energetically.

> Field Marshal Helmuth Graf von Moltke, *Ausgewaehlte Werke*, I, 1925.

AN ADVANTAGE is an advantage, however offered or obtained; whether by an enemy's mistake, or by

the accidents of the ground that play so large a part in land war; and on either element a skillful defense looks warily for its opportunities to the enemy's mistakes, as well as to other conditions.

> Admiral Alfred Thayer Mahan, *Naval Strategy*, 1911.

ALL GREAT commanders have come with increasing experience of war to realize that opportunism is essential in war; that fixed purposes and objectives are contrary to its nature, and, if rigidly maintained, lead usually to a blank wall. But most of them have tended to develop a practice of pure opportunism – to take an obvious course and exploit any chance that occured. A few, like Sherman, have reached a more systematized practice of opportunism, seeking and finding a solution in variability, or elasticity in the choice of a line of operation leading to alternative objectives, combined with the development of formations that give them the power to vary their course and gain whichever the enemy leaves open. (April 1925.)

> Captain Sir Basil Liddell Hart, *Thoughts on War*, 1944.

THE BATTLE that turned the tide of the war in 1914 has given rise to an endless debate among generals and historians as to who was responsible for winning the Battle of the Marne. It is quite as apt to pose the question: "Was the Marne won by the Allies or lost by the Germans?" The reasonable answer is that most victories in history have been won by seizing opportunities offered by the loser. (June 1931.)

> Captain Sir Basil Liddell Hart, *Thoughts on War*, 1944.

FOR SUCCESS, two major problems must be solved – *dislocation* and *exploitation*. One precedes and one follows the actual blow – which in comparison is a simple act. You cannot hit the enemy with effect unless you have first created the opportunity; you cannot make that effect decisive unless you exploit the second opportunity that comes before he can recover.

> Captain Sir Basil Liddell Hart, *Strategy*, 1954.

THERE IS no security on this earth; there is only opportunity.

> General of the Army Douglas MacArthur, quoted in Courtney Whitney, *MacArthur: His Rendezvous with History*, 1955.

TO OUR MEN . . . the jungle was a strange, fearsome place; moving and fighting in it were a nightmare. We were too ready to classify it "impenetrable" . . . To us it appeared only as an obstacle to movement; to the Japanese it was a welcome means of concealed manoeuvre and surprise . . . The Japanese reaped the deserved reward . . . we paid the penalty.

> Field Marshal Viscount Slim of Burma, *Defeat into Victory*, 1956.

DECISIVE RESULTS in war are rarely the direct result of an initial, deliberate action. Rather, the initial action creates the conditions for subsequent actions which develop from it. As the opposing wills interact, they create various, fleeting opportunities for either foe. Such opportunities are often born of the disorder that is natural in war. They may be the result of our own actions, enemy mistakes, or even chance. By exploiting opportunities, we create in increasing numbers more opportunities for exploitation. It is often the ability and the willingness to ruthlessly exploit these opportunities that generate decisive results. The ability to take advantage of opportunity is a function of speed, flexibility, boldness, and initiative.

General Alfred M. Gray and Major John Schmitt, *Warfighting*, United States Marine Corps, 1989.

OPTIMISM

PERPETUAL optimism is a force multiplier.

General Colin Powell, *Reader's Digest*, 7/1995.

ORDER

THE ILLYRIANS, to those who have no experience of them, do indeed at first sight present a threatening aspect. The spectacle of their numbers is terrible, their cries are intolerable, and the brandishing of their spears in the air has menacing effect. But in action they are not the men they look, if their opponents will only stand their ground; for they have no regular order, and therefore are not ashamed of leaving any post in which they are hard pressed; to fly and to advance being alike honorable, no imputation can be thrown on their courage. When every man is his own master in battle, he will readily find a decent excuse for saving himself.

Brasidas of Sparta, to the Spartan Army, 423 BC, quoted in Thucydides, *The Peloponnesian War*, 4.126, c. 404 BC, tr. Benjamin Jowett, 1881.

IN MILITARY OPERATIONS, order leads to victory. If rewards and penalties are unclear, if rules and regulations are unreliable, and if signals are not followed, even if you have an army of a million strong it is of no practical benefit.

An orderly army is one that is mannerly and dignified, one that cannot be withstood when it advances and cannot be pursued when it withdraws. Its movements are regulated and directed; this gives it security and presents no danger. The troops can be massed but not scattered, can be deployed but not worn out.

Zhuge Liang (AD 180–234), *The Way of the General*, quoted in Thomas Cleary, *Mastering the Art of War*, 1989.

IF ALL is not in order, I will hang you despite my personal high regard.

Field Marshal Prince Aleksandr V. Suvorov, 1799, administrative order to his quartermaster-general during the Italian campaign.

ORDER marches with weighty and measured strides; disorder is always in a hurry.

Napoleon, *Maxims*, 1804–1815.

ENJOIN this upon the Officers, and let them inculcate, and press home to the Soldiery, the Necessity of Order and Harmony among them, who are embark'd in one common Cause, and mutually contending for all that Freeman [sic] hold dear. I am persuaded, if the Officers will but exert themselves, these Animosities, this Disorder, will in great Measure subside, and nothing being more essential to the Service than that it should, I am hopeful nothing on their Parts will be wanting to effect it.

General George Washington, letter to General Philip Schuyler, 17 July 1776, *The Writings of George Washington*, V, p. 290, John C. Fitzgerald, ed., 1932.

IT IS HARD to imagine why outrageous behavior was allowed to persist in the Army during that period [early 1970s]. In the institution, we had kind of lost our bearings in what was right and what was wrong. And what was appropriate discipline and what wasn't. We had misused some of the psychological stuff that management theorists were pushing on us. We started to think that we were running some kind of democratic day camp: Generals sitting around coffee houses talking to troops; troop councils reporting to battalion commanders about what they ought do. It was a breakdown of the command structure. Like inmates had taken over the asylum.

In the 2nd Division, we reinstalled discipline with the attitude: "Let me explain to you. I'm in charge and you ain't." That's what the troops needed to hear.

General Colin Powell, 'Fixing the System', Al Santoli, ed., *Leading the Way: How Vietnam Veterans Rebuilt the U.S. Military*, 1993.

WHAT THE HELL kind of democracy is it when one man has been given the right to send another man to his death? Well, what do we do here, conduct an assembly and count the votes? In a combat situation, the foremost sacred duty of a commander of any echelon is to immediately, without a court of investigation, shoot on the spot, like a mad dog, anyone, regardless of position or rank, who attempts to launch a similar type discussion. . . . no, there isn't and can't be a democratic army in the world. If that occurs, you can call that organization whatever you want to but not an army. An army without one-man command, without the force of order, without discipline – that is no more than a rabble. In any military clash, half of it will run away and half will be killed.

Aleksandr I. Lebed, *I Hurt For This Great Country*, 1995.

ORDERS

WHEN ASKED another time for what particular reason the Spartans enjoyed notably more success than others, he said: "Because more than others they train to give orders and to take them."

Plutarch, quoting Agesilaus, Eurypontid King of Sparta (400–360 BC), *The Lives*, c. AD 100 (*Plutarch on Sparta*, tr. Richard Talbert, 1988).

DURING any military affair, no matter how important the event may be, when something is communicated by word of mouth, the least bit of vagueness will invite grievous results.

Asakura Norikage, *Soteki Waki*, c. 1550 (*Ideals of the Samurai*, tr. William Wilson, 1982).

THE ORDERS I have given are strong, and I know not how my admiral will approve of them, for they are, in a great measure, contrary to those he gave me; but the Service requires strong and vigorous measures to bring the war to a conclusion.

Admiral Viscount Nelson, July 1795, letter to Admiral Collingwood.

TO SAY that an officer is never, for any object, to alter his orders, is what I cannot comprehend. The circumstances of this war so often vary, that an officer has almost every moment to consider, what would my superiors direct did they know what is passing under my nose? But, sir, I find few think as I do. To obey orders is all perfection. To serve my king and destroy the French, I consider as the great order of all, from which little ones spring; and if one of these militate against it (for who can tell exactly at a distance?), I go back, and obey the great order and object, to down – down with the damned French villains! My blood boils at the name of a Frenchman!

Admiral Viscount Nelson, March 1799, letter from Palermo to the Duke of Clarence, despairing at the army's lack of initiative in pressing the siege of Malta, quoted in Robert Southey, *Life of Nelson*, 1813.

I SHALL BE GLAD to know who commands this army – I or you? I establish one route, one line of communication – you establish another by ordering up supplies by it. As long as you live, sir, never do that again. Never do anything without my orders.

The Duke of Wellington, to Sir James McGrigor, who had moved some commissary supplies to Salamanca during the Peninsular campaign, cited in Charles Oman, *Wellington's Army*, 1913.

YOU MUST avoid countermanding orders: unless the soldier can see a good reason for benefit, he becomes discouraged and loses confidence.

Napoleon, 5 August 1806, advice to his stepson, Prince Eugene, *Correspondance de Napoléon Ier, publiée par ordre de l'Empereur Napoléon III*, No. 10699, XIII, 1858–1870.

YOUR DUTY is to obey me, not to act independently. Furthermore you have no right to

anticipate what may or may not be passing through my mind at any given time!

Napoleon, January 1807, to Marshal Ney after a reprimand for bringing on the manoeuvres that led to the Battle of Eylau without the Emperor's permission, cited in Raymond Horricks, *Marshal Ney*, 1982.

YOUR ORDERS of the day to the soldiers on the Burgos affair is wretched. Good God! Where should we be if I were given to writing four pages to the soldiers to tell them not to allow themselves to be disarmed, and to extol as a heroic deed the fact that a detachment of fifteen men fired on a mob? Frenchmen are too acute not to laugh at such proclamations, and mine is not the school at which you learned to write them. What will you do in a crisis if you lavish your proclamations now? Three orders of the day like yours would demoralize the army.

Napoleon, 26 April 1808, to Marshal Murat, quoted in R.M. Johnston, ed., *The Corsican*, 1910.

GIVE your orders so that they cannot be disobeyed.

Napoleon, 29 March 1811, to Marshal Berthier, *Correspondance de Napoléon Ier, publiée par ordre de l'Empereur Napoléon III*, No. 17529, XXI, 1858–1870.

I REGRET to hear from an officer that it is *impossible* to execute an order. If your cavalry will not obey your orders you must *make them* do it, and, if necessary, go out with them yourself. I desire you to go out and post your cavalry where you want them to stay, and arrest any man who leaves his post, and prefer charges and specifications against him, that he may be court-martialed. It will not do to say that men your men cannot be induced to perform their duty. *They must be made to do it.* . . .

Lieutenant-General Thomas J. 'Stonewall' Jackson, letter to Colonel Sincindiver, 11 February 1862, quoted in William Allan, *History of the Campaign of Gen. T.J. (Stonewall) Jackson in the Shenandoah Valley of Virginia*, 1880.

ON *Farragut's quarterdeck*: "Captain, you begin early in your life to disobey orders. Did you not see the signal flying for near an hour to withdraw from action? . . . I want none of this Nelson business in my squadron."

Later in Farragut's cabin: "I have censured you, sir, on my quarterdeck, for what appeared to be a disregard of my orders. I desire now to commend you and your officers and men for doing what you believe right under the circumstances. Do it again whenever in your judgment it is necessary to carry out your conception of duty."

Admiral David Glasgow Farragut, to Lieutenant Winfield Scott Schley, executive officer of the USS *Richmond*, during the action at Port Hudson, March 1863, quoted in Christopher Martin, *Damn the Torpedos!*, 1970.

I HAD WORDED my instructions so strongly, I thought they would wake up a dead man to his true condition.

> Major-General Joseph Hooker, April 1863, to his chief of cavalry, Brigadier-General Stoneman, prior to the Battle of Chancellorsville, 1–5 May 1863.

MEN bred as soldiers have no fancy for orders that carry want of faith on their face.

> Lieutenant-General James A. Longstreet, comments on Burnside's orders at the Battle of Fredericksburg, 13 December 1862, *From Manassas to Appomattox*, 1896.

IT IS the custom of military service to accept instructions of a commander as orders, but when they are coupled with conditions that transfer the responsibility of battle and defeat to the subordinate, they are not orders.

> Lieutenant-General James A. Longstreet, comments on Lee's vague orders to Ewell for the second day at Gettysburg, 2 July 1863, *From Manassas to Appomattox*, 1896.

IN ISSUING orders or giving verbal instruction, Jackson's words were few and simple; but they were so clear, so comprehensive and direct, that no officer could possibly misunderstand, and none dared disobey.

> Lieutenant-General John B. Gordon, quoted in Henderson, *Stonewall Jackson*, 1898.

REMEMBER, gentlemen, an order that can be misunderstood will be misunderstood.

> Field Marshal Helmuth Graf von Moltke (1800–1891).

ORDER, counter-order, disorder.

> Field Marshal Helmuth Graf von Moltke (1800–1891).

AN ORDER shall contain everything that a commander cannot do by himself, but nothing else.

> Field Marshal Helmuth Graf von Moltke (1800–1891).

THE HIGHER the commander, the shorter and simpler the orders must be.

> Field Marshal Helmuth Graf von Moltke (1800–1891), *Militaerische Werke*, II, 1892–1912.

IN WAR the first principle is to disobey orders. *Any fool can obey orders!*

> Admiral Sir John Fisher, after the Dogger Bank action, January 1915.

I JUST GAVE an order – quite a simple matter unless a man's afraid.

> General Sir Ian Hamilton, *Soul and Body of an Army*, 1921.

ALL ORDERS will have to be as brief as possible. They should be based on a profound appreciation of possibilities and probabilities which . . . will generally lead to a series of alternatives.

> Major-General J.F.C. Fuller (1878–1966).

PETAIN was once asked what part of an action called for the greatest effort. "Giving orders," he replied. There is, indeed, something irrevocable about the intervention of the human will in a sequence of events. Whether useful or not, opportune or misjudged, it is pregnant with unforeseeable consequences. The mere awareness of the audacity of such a proceeding is intimidating. Even in ordinary life there are many who do not find it easy to make decisions, and the number of those prepared to take the initiative is small in comparison with that of the obedient and submissive mass. How much more agonizing must be the call to decisive action in the case of a military commander who knows that so many poor lives depend upon his decision, and that on the highest as well as on the lowest levels it will be judged solely by its results. So heavy is the responsibility in such cases that few men are capable of shouldering the whole unaided. That is why the greatest intellectual qualities are not enough. No doubt they help; so, too, does instinct, but in the last resort, the decision is a moral one.

> General Charles de Gaulle, *The Edge of the Sword*, 1932.

IN WAR "thoughtless" orders often result in the useless sacrifice of men's lives. In peace, they often contribute to the sterilization of men's reason. And they inevitably make the man who transmits the order an accomplice in the crime, however unwilling. Unfortunately, few of the transmitters have the sensitiveness of perception to feel their responsibility. (July 1933.)

> Captain Sir Basil Liddell Hart, *Thoughts on War*, 1944.

THE ISSUANCE of an order is the simplest thing in the world. The important and difficult thing is to see: first, that the order is transmitted; and, second, that it is obeyed. . . .

> General George S. Patton, Jr., 8 July 1941, speech to the officers of the Second Armored Division, *The Patton Papers*, II, 1974.

I GIVE ORDERS only when they are necessary. I expect them to be executed at once and to the letter and that no unit under my command shall make changes, still less give orders to the contrary or delay execution through unnecessary red tape.

> Field Marshal Erwin Rommel, 22 April 1944, letter of instruction to subordinate commanders.

THE BEST WAY to issue orders is by word of mouth from one general to the next. Failing this, telephone conversation which should be recorded at each end. However, in order to have a confirmatory memorandum of all oral orders given, a short written order should always be made out, not necessarily at the time of issuing the order, but it should reach the junior prior to his carrying out the order; so that, if he has forgotten anything, he will be reminded of it, and, further, in order that he may be aware that his senior has taken definite responsibility for the operation ordered orally.

General George S. Patton, Jr., *War As I Knew It*, 1947.

AVOID as you would perdition issuing cover-up orders, orders for the record. This simply shows lack of intestinal fortitude on the part of the officer signing the orders, and everyone who reads them realizes it at once.

General George S. Patton, Jr., *War As I Knew It*, 1947.

AN OFFICER should not ask a man: "Would you like to do such-and-such a task?" when he has already made up his mind to assign him to a certain duty. Orders, hesitantly given, are doubtfully received. But the right way to do it is to instill the idea of collaboration. There is something irresistably appealing about such an approach as: "I need your help. Here's what we have to do."

Brigadier-General S.L.A. Marshall, *The Armed Forces Officer*, 1950.

OPERATIONS orders do not win battles without the valour and endurance of the soldiers who carry them out.

Field Marshal Viscount Wavell of Cyrenaica, *Soldiers and Soldiering*, 1953.

OPERATIONAL command in the battle must be direct and personal, by means of visits to subordinate H.Q. where orders are given verbally. A commander must train his subordinate commanders, and his own staff, to work and act on verbal orders. Those who cannot be trusted to act on clear and concise verbal orders, but want everything in writing are useless.

Field Marshal Viscount Montgomery of Alamein, *The Memoirs of Field Marshal Montgomery*, 1958.

IT IS highly desirable that a military man speak and write the English language clearly and forcibly. It is essential that he be articulate in the formation of orders and directives.

Admiral Thomas C. Kinkaid, *Proceedings*, 5/1959.

TO GRASP the spirit of order is not less important than to accept them cheerfully and keep faith with the contract. But the letter of an instruction does not relieve him who receives it from the obligation to exercise common sense.

Brigadier-General S.L.A. Marshall, *The Officer as Leader*, 1966.

ORDER a *naval rating* to "secure the house" and he'll enter it, close all the doors and windows, and probably throw a line over the roof and lash it down.

Order an *infantryman* to "secure the house" and he'll enter it, shoot anything that moves, and then probably dig trench about it.

Order an *airman* to "secure the house" and he'll

stroll down to the local estate agent and take out a 7-year lease on it.

British military adage, quoted in *JFQ Forum*, 95/96 Autumn/Winter

I AM NOT going to start World War III for you.

Lieutenant-General Michael Jackson, June 1999, refusing the order of NATO commander, General Wesley Clark, to stop by force the Russian *coup de main* aimed at seizing Pristina Airfield in Kosovo, quoted in *Newsweek*, 9 August 1999.

AN ORDER is a good basis for discussion.

Old military saying.

ORGANISATION

GENERALLY, management of the many is the same as management of the few. It is a matter of organization.

Sun Tzu, *The Art of War*, c. 500 BC, tr. Samuel Griffith, 1969.

A POLICY to quell disorder involves minimizing offices and combining duties, getting rid of embellishment in favor of substance.

First organize directives, then organize penalties. First organize the near at hand, then organize the far removed. First organize the inner, then organize the outer. First organize the basic, then organize the derivative. First organize the strong, then organize the weak. First organize the great, then organize the small. First organize yourself, then organize others.

Zhuge Liang (AD 180–234), *The Way of the General* (*Mastering the Art of War*, tr. Thomas Cleary, 1989).

THE PECULIAR strength of the Romans always consisted in the excellent organization of their legions. They were so denominated ab eligendo, from the care and exactness used in the choice of the soldiers.

Flavius Vegetius Renatus, *Military Institutions of the Romans*, c. AD 378, tr. Clark, 1776.

THE MASS needs, and we give it, leaders. . . . We add good arms. We add suitable methods of fighting. . . . We also add a rational decentralization . . . We animate with passion . . . An iron discipline . . . secures the greatest unit . . . But it depends also on supervision, the mutual supervision of groups of men who know each other well. A wise organization of comrades in peace who shall be comrades in war . . . And now confidence appears . . . Then we have an army.

Colonel Charles Ardant du Picq, *Battle Studies*, 1880, tr. Greely, 1957.

. . . BATTLES are rare events and that, meanwhile, the Army lives, marches, works, and has its being by organization and discipline. Further, after the first general action he will be surprised, if he thinks it over, to recollect how very great a part organization and discipline, or their absence, had to say to success or failure.

General Sir Ian Hamilton, *Soul and Body of an Army*, 1921.

THE PRIMARY OBJECT of organization is to shield people from unexpected calls upon their powers of adaptability, judgment and decision.

General Sir Ian Hamilton, *Soul and Body of an Army*, 1921.

ORGANIZATION is the vehicle of force; and force is threefold in nature; it is mental, moral, and physical. How will the idea affect these spheres of force? This is primarily a question of force and its expenditure. Thus, if the idea is complex, and does not permit of it being readily grasped by others, mistakes are likely to occur; and if its aim is beyond the moral and physical powers of the troops, should it be pushed beyond the limit of their endurance, though organization may for the time being be maintained, ultimately demoralization will set in, and a demoralized organization is one which has become so fragile that a slight blow, especially a surprise blow, will instantaneously shatter it to pieces.

Major-General J.F.C. Fuller, *The Foundation of the Science of War*, 1926.

ORIGINALITY AND THE CREATIVE MIND

. . . QUALIFICATIONS a general ought to possess . . . abilities to strike out something new of his own occasionally. For no man excelled in his profession who could not do that, and if a ready and quick invention is necessary and honourable in any profession, it must certainly be so in the art of war above all others.

Niccolo Machiavelli, *The Art of War*, 1521.

ONE OF the most important talents of a general we could call that of a "creative mind". . . Originality, not conventionality, is one of the main pillars of generalship. To do something that the enemy does not expect, is not prepared for, something which will surprise him and disarm him morally. To be always thinking ahead and to be always peeping around corners. To spy out the soul of one's adversary, and to act in a manner which will astonish and bewilder him, this is generalship. To render the enemy's general ridiculous in the eyes of his men, this is the foundation of success . . .

Field Marshal Colmar Baron von Der Goltz, quoted in J.F.C. Fuller, *Generalship: Its Diseases and Their Cure*, 1933.

ORIGINALITY is the most vital of all military virtues, as two thousand years of war attest. In peace it is at a discount, for it causes the disturbances of comfortable ways without producing dividends, as in civil life. But in war originality bears a higher premium than it can ever do in a civil profession. For its application can overthrow a nation and change the course of history in the proverbial twinkling of an eye. (August 1930.)

Captain Sir Basil Liddell Hart, *Thoughts on War*, 1944.

WE MUST hold our minds alert and receptive to the application of unglimpsed methods and weapons. The next war will be won in the future, not in the past. We must go on, or we will go under.

General of the Army Douglas MacArthur, 1931.

WHEN WE study the lives of the great captains, and not merely their victories and defeats, what do we discover? That the mainspring within them was originality, outwardly expressing itself in unexpected actions. It is in the mental past in which most battles are lost, and lost conventionally, and our system teaches us how to lose them, because in the schoolroom it will not transcend the conventional. The soldier who thinks ahead is considered, to put it bluntly, a damned nuisance.

Major-General J.F.C. Fuller, *Generalship: Its Diseases and Their Cure*, 1933.

THE BEST HOPE of tilting the scales and of overcoming the resistance inherent in conflict lies in originality – to produce something unexpected that will paralyze the opponent's freedom of action. . . . But in historical fact, such creative intelligence has been rare in the operations of war. And rarer still in preparation for war. Military history is filled with the record of military improvements that have been resisted by those who have profited richly from them. Between the development of new weapons or new tactics and their adoption there has always been a time-lag, often of generations. And that time-lag has often decided the fate of nations. (June 1936.)

Captain Sir Basil Liddell Hart, *Thoughts on War*, 1944.

WE SHOULD emphasize that not all creative ideas are good, however stubbornly they are held. But not all of them are bad either, and the superior who has the precious ability to discriminate between the two and the receptivity of mind to contemplate the new or the contrary idea is a man of great value. Conversely, the leader who does not possess those sovereign gifts is a continuing impediment to progress.

Once I heard two generals talking about Lt Col (later Gen) Merrill B. Twining. One said, "Well, the trouble with Twining is that he is always upsetting things with some new idea or other." What a wonderful tribute! What greater praise could one seek than to be identified as the man who is guilty of "upsetting things" with new ideas?

And the general who found Twining's creative behavior odious, how about him? It could be that he was not thinking, just rearranging his prejudices for the benefit of his audience. Or it could be that he had been misled by Ecclesiastes 1–18: "To increase knowledge only increases distress." But the sadder likelihood is that he was professionally long dead, frozen stiff under the icy hands of custom, convention, conformity, and timidity, a hazard to his Corps and best replaced.

Lieutenant-General Victor H. 'The Brute' Krulak, 'A Soldier's Dilemma', *Marine Corps Gazette*, 11/1986.

IN THE GREAT BATTLES at Cannae and Lepanto, at Tannenberg and Tsushima, at Cape St. Vincent and Chancellorsville and The Marne, we must acknowledge that a creative mind fashioned the setting for victory in each case. It was a mind that could think beyond the moment of crisis and see beyond the horizon of battle that set the scene for bravery and leadership to work their wonderful magic.

Lieutenant-General Victor H. 'The Brute' Krulak, 'A Soldier's Dilemma', *Marine Corps Gazette*, 11/1986.

FOR THREE YEARS I had a Medal of Honor recipient from Vietnam, Army Col Jack Jacobs, working for me. He is by far the most innovative person I have ever known. Well over 50 percent of his ideas were awful, but buried among these bad ideas was an occasional pearl of great wisdom. I learned that I had to protect Jack and my organization from his bad ideas while encouraging him to present all his ideas, so we could use his great ones.

Major-General Perry M. Smith, 'Learning to Lead', *Marine Corps Gazette*, 1/1997.

AMERICA thrives on eccentric talents, while its army rots as a last bastion of dumbed-down socialism.

Lieutenant-Colonel Ralph Peters, *Army Times*, 24 August 1998.

P

PACIFICATION

WHEN WE conquer our enemies by kind treatment, and by acts of justice, we are more likely to secure their obedience than by a victory in the field of battle. For in the one case they yield to necessity; in the other, it is their own free choice. Besides, how often is the victory dearly bought while the conquest of an enemy by affection may be brought about without expense or loss!

> Polybius, *Histories*, 5.12, c. 125 BC (*Familiar Quotations from Greek Authors*, tr. Crauford Ramage, 1895).

ROBBERS of the world, having by their universal plunder exhausted the land, they rifle the deep. If the enemy be rich, they are rapacious; if he be poor, they lust for dominion; neither the east nor the west has been able to satisfy them. Alone among men they covet with equal eagerness poverty and riches. To robbery, slaughter, plunder, they give the lying name of empire; they make a solitude and call it peace.

> Cornelius Tacitus, reporting the speech of the British rebel chieftain, Galgacus, during the reconquest of Britain, *Agricola*, 30, AD 98 (*The Complete Works of Tacitus*, tr. Alfred Church and William Brodribb, 1942).

SEVERITY is needed to govern the Turks; I order five or six heads to be sliced off every day in the streets of Cairo. Up till now we have had to behave mildly so as to counteract the reputation of terror that preceeded us; at present it is, on the contrary, better to assume the tone that commands obedience with these people, for with them obedience signifies fear.

> Napoleon, 31 July 1798, Cairo, quoted in R.M. Johnston, ed., *The Corsican*, 1910.

WE CAN still build a socialist Afghanistan if there are only one million Afghans.

> Soviet comment reported during the war in Afghanistan (c. 1984).

THE PACIFICATION program in its narrowest sense – the neutralization of the Viet Cong infrastructure in the countryside – was virtually complete by the end of 1970. It would hold firm, with minor shifts due to the combat situation, until the end of the GVN [Government of Vietnam] in 1975. Pacification in its broadest sense – to include reform of the GVN and RVNAF [Republic of Vietnam Armed Forces] – would never be won, but its narrow victory would constitute one of the resounding successes of Indochina War II.

> Lieutenant-General Phillip B. Davidson, *Vietnam at War*, 1988.

PACIFISM/ANTI-WAR ACTIVISM

ONCE INITIATED there were but few public men who would have the courage to oppose [war]. Experience proves that the man who obstructs a war in which his nation is engaged, no matter whether right or wrong, occupies no enviable place in life or history. Better for him, individually, to advocate "war, pestilence, and famine," than to act as obstructionist to a war already begun. The history of the defeated rebel will be honorable hereafter, compared with that of the Northern man who aided him by conspiring against his government while protected by it. The most favorable posthumous history the stay-at-home traitor can hope for is – oblivion.

> General of the Army Ulysses S. Grant, *Personal Memoirs of U.S. Grant*, 1885.

THE MAN who has formed a clear notion of the nature of war, of its necessities, requirements and consequences, to wit, the *soldier*, will take a far more serious view of the potentialities of war than the politician or the business man who coldly weighs its advantages and disadvantages. After all, it is not so difficult to sacrifice one's own life, but the professional duty of risking the lives of others weighs heavily on the conscience. The soldier, having experience of war, fears it far more than the doctrinaire who, being ignorant of war, talks only of peace; for the soldier has gazed into war's bloodshot eyes, he has observed from his point of vantage the battle-fields of a world war, he has had to witness the agonies of nations, his hair has turned grey over the ashes of countless burned homesteads and he has borne the responsibility for the life and death of thousands. The figure of the sabre-rattling, fire-eating general is an invention of poisoned and unscrupulous political strife, a figure welcome to stupid comic papers, a catchword personified. There is no reason why the soldier's attitude towards war should not be called "pacifism." It is a pacifism established on knowledge and born of a sense of responsibility, but it is not the pacifism engendered by national abasement or by a hazy internationalism. The soldier will be the first to welcome any effort to diminish the potentialities of war, but he does not march down the street to the slogan of "No more war!" because he knows that war and peace are decided by higher powers than princes, statesmen, parliaments, treaties and alliances – they are decided by the eternal laws which govern the growth and decay of nations. But the kind of pacifist who would deliberately make his own nation defenceless in such fateful encounters, who prefers to weaken it in alliance with a hostile neighbor rather than support his fellow-countrymen in preparation for legitimate resistance, deserves, as he always did, to be hanged to the nearest lamp-post, were it only a moral one.

> Colonel-General Hans von Seekt, *Thoughts of a Soldier*, 1930.

WE ARE for the abolition of war, we do not want war; but war can only be abolished through war, and to get rid of the gun, we must first grasp it in our hands.

> Mao Tse-tung, *Problems of War and Strategy*, 1938.

THE PACIFISTS are at it again. I met a visiting fireman of great eminence who told me this was the "LAST WAR." I told him that such statements since 2600 BC had signed the death warrant of millions of young men. He replied with the stock lie – "Oh yes but things are different now." My God! Will they never learn?

> General George S. Patton, Jr., 3 March 1944, letter to his wife, *The Patton Papers*, II, 1974.

RATIONAL pacifism must be based on a new maxim – "If you wish for peace, understand war."

> Captain Sir Basil Liddell Hart, *Thoughts on War*, 1944.

THE SUREST WAY to become a pacifist is to join the infantry.

> Bill Mauldin, *Up Front*, 1945.

WAR is never prevented by running away from it.

> Air Marshal Sir John Slessor, *Strategy for the West*, 1954.

PANIC

SO the Trojans held their watch that night but not
   the Achaeans –
Godsent Panic seized them, comrade of
   bloodcurdling Rout:
All their best were struck by grief too much to bear.
As crosswinds chop the sea where the fish swarm,
the North Wind and the West Wind blasting out
   of Thrace
in sudden, lightning attack, wave on blacker
   wave, cresting,

heaving a tangled mass of seaweed out along the
   surf –
so the Achaeans' hearts were torn inside their chests.

> Homer, *The Iliad*, 9.1–8, c. 800 BC, tr. Robert Fagles, 1990.

NOW for a little time it became a hand-to-hand fight, but when the cavalry with Alexander, and Alexander himself, pressed vigorously, shoving the Persians and striking their faces with their spears, and the Macedonian phalanx, solid and bristling with its pikes, had got to close quarters with them, and Darius, who had now long been in a panic, saw nothing but terrors all around, and he was himself the first to turn and flee.

> Arrian, *The Anabasis of Alexander*, 3.14, c. AD 125, tr. P.A. Brunt, 1976; the flight of Darius at the Battle of Gaugamela (or Arbela), 331 BC, which in turn panicked his army.

BOTH OFFICERS and troops must be warned against those sudden panics which often seize the bravest armies when they are not well-controlled by discipline, and when they do not recognize that the surest hope of safety lies in order. An army seized with panic is in a state of demoralization because when disorder is once introduced all concerted action on the part of individuals becomes impossible, the voice of the officers can no longer be heard. No maneuver for resuming the battle can be executed, and there is no course except in ignominious flight.

> Lieutenant-General Antoine-Henri Baron de Jomini, *Summary of the Art of War*, 1838, tr. Mendell and Craighill, 1862.

THE WORST enemy a Chief has to face in war is an alarmist.

> General Sir Ian Hamilton, *Gallipoli Diary*, 1920.

SINCE PANIC gathers volume like a snowball, I think we can take it that every large panic starts with some very minor event and that for the general purposes of control it is more important to have exact knowledge of the small cause than the large effect.
. . . the trouble began because somebody was thoughtless, somebody failed to tell other men what he was doing. . . . nothing is more likely to collapse a line of infantry in combat than the sight of a few of its number in full and unexplained flight. Precipitate motion in the wrong direction is an open invitation to disaster.

> Brigadier-General S.L.A. Marshall, *Men Against Fire*, 1947.

PATRIOTISM

THIS EMPIRE has been acquired by men who knew their duty and had the courage to do it, who in the hour of conflict had the fear of dishonor always present to them, and who, if ever they failed in an enterprise, would not allow their virtues to be lost to their country, but freely gave their lives to her as the fairest offering which they could present at her feast.

Pericles, 431 BC, funeral oration for the Athenian dead, quoted in Thucydides, *The Peloponnesian War*, c. 404 BC, tr. Benjamin Jowett, 1881.

THESE are the times that try men's souls. The summer soldier and the sunshine patriot will, in this crisis, shrink from the service of their country; but he that stands it now, deserves the love and thanks of man and woman. Tyranny, like hell, is not easily conquered; yet we have this consolation with us, that the harder the conflict, the more glorious the triumph. What we obtain too cheap, we esteem too lightly; 'tis dearness only that gives everything its value. Heaven knows how to put a price upon its goods, and it would be strange indeed if so celestial an article as freedom should not be highly rated.

Thomas Paine, *The American Crisis*, 23 December 1776.

MEN may speculate as they will; they may talk of patriotism; they draw a few examples from ancient story, of great achievements performed by its influence; but whoever builds upon it, as a sufficient Basis for conducting a long and bloody War, will find themselves deceived in the end. . . . We must take the passions of Men as Nature has given them, and those principles as a guide which are generally the rule of Action. I do not mean to exclude altogether the Idea of Patriotism. I know it exists, and I know it has done much in the present Contest. But I will venture to assert, that a great and lasting War can never be supported on this principle alone. It must be aided by a prospect of Interest or some reward. For a time, it may, of itself push Men to Action; to bear much, to encounter difficulties; but it will not endure unassisted by Interest.

General George Washington, 21 April 1778, letter to John Bannister, *The Writings of George Washington*, XI, p. 286, John C. Fitzgerald, ed., 1932.

IT IS but justice to assign great merit to the temper of those citizens whose estates were more immediately the scene of warfare. Their personal services were rendered without constraint, and the derangement of their affairs submitted to without dissatisfaction. It was the triumph of patriotism over personal considerations. And our present enjoyment of peace and freedom reward the sacrifice.

General George Washington, 1 December 1789, to the New Jersey Legislature, *The Writings of George Washington*, XXX, John C. Fitzgerald, ed., 1939.

OUR COUNTRY: in her intercourse with foreign nations may she always be in the right; but our country, right or wrong!

Admiral Stephen Decatur, April 1816, toast at a dinner in Norfolk, Virginia.

CERTAINLY no man has more that should make life dear to him than I have, in the affection of my home; but I do not want to survive the independence of my country.

Lieutenant-General Thomas J. 'Stonewall' Jackson, quoted in Henderson, *Stonewall Jackson*, II, 1898.

TRUE PATRIOTISM sometimes requires of men to act exactly contrary, at one period, to that which it does at another, and the motive which impels them – the desire to do right – is precisely the same.

General Robert E. Lee, 3 October 1865, letter to General P.G.T. Beauregard, quoted in Jones, *Life and Letters of Robert Edward Lee, Soldier and Man*, 1906.

MY COUNTRY, right or wrong; if right, to be kept right; and if wrong, to be set right.

Major-General Carl Schurz, 29 February 1872, speech.

OUR ORDERS home, and tidings of the attack on Fort Sumter, came by the same mail, and some time in June. The revulsion of feeling was immediate and universal, in that distant community and foreign land, as it had been two months before in the Northern States. The doughfaces were set at once, like flint. The grave and reverand seigniors, resident merchants, who had checked any belligerent utterance among us with reproachful regret that an American should be willing to fight Americans, reconverted or silenced. Every voice but one was hushed, and that voice said, "Fight."

Rear Admiral Alfred Thayer Mahan, recollections of the patriotic ardor felt by the U.S. Navy personnel and American residents in Montevideo upon news of the outbreak of the Civil War, *From Sail to Steam*, 1907.

PATRIOTISM is like a plant whose roots stretch down into race and place subconsciousness; a plant whose best nutrients are blood and tears; a plant which dies down in peace and flowers most brightly in war. Patriotism does not calculate, does not profiteer, does not stop to reason: in an atmosphere of danger the sap begins to stir; it lives; it takes possession of our soul.

General Sir Ian Hamilton, *The Soul and Body of an Army*, 1921.

THERE IS NOTHING more soulless than a religion without good works unless it be a patriotism which does not concern itself with the welfare and dignity of the individual. Only the officer who dedicates his thought and energy to his men can convert into coherent military force their inarticulate thoughts about their country; nor is any other in a position to stimulate their desire to be of service to it.

Brigadier-General S.L.A. Marshall, *Men Against Fire*, 1947.

THE MAN who is willing to fight for his country is finally the full custodian of its security. If there were no willing man, no power in government could ever rally the masses of the unwilling. But if the spirit and purpose which enable such men to find themselves and to act are to be safeguarded into the future, much more will have to be required of the country than that it point its young people toward the virtues of the production line. There is something almost fatally quixotic about a nation which professes lofty ideas in its international undertakings and yet disdains to talk patriotism to its citizens, as if this were beneath their dignity.

> Brigadier-General S.L.A. Marshall, *Men Against Fire*, 1947.

I ADMIRE men who stand up for their country in defeat, even though I am on the other side.

> Sir Winston S. Churchill, *The Gathering Storm*, 1948.

ASK NOT what your country can do for you – ask what you can do for your country.

> President John F. Kennedy, 20 January 1961, Inaugural Address.

PATRIOTISM is when love for your own people comes first; nationalism, when the hate for people other than your own comes first.

> General Charles de Gaulle, *Life*, 9 May 1969.

PAY

PAY the troops and fear no evil.

> Cornelius Tacitus (c. AD 56–120).

STABILITY between nations cannot be maintained without armies, nor armies without pay, nor pay without taxation.

> Cornelius Tacitus, *Histories*, 4.74, c. AD 98–117.

DO NOT disagree between yourselves. Give the soldiers money and despise everyone else.

> The Emperor Septimus Severus, AD 211, deathbed advice to his sons, quoted in Dio Cassius, *Romaika*, 76.15.2, c. AD 230.

TO RAISE any taxes is impracticable, since the provinces are in possession of the enemy, and the long arrear of pay which our soldiers vainly claim loosens every tie of discipline and duty. A debtor is but ill able to command.

> Count Belisarius (c. AD 505–565).

NOW the chief thing incumbent upon a general, in order to maintain his reputation, is to pay well and punish soundly for if he does not pay his men duly, he cannot punish them properly when they deserve it. Suppose, for instance, a soldier should be guilty of a robbery; how can you punish him for that when you give him no pay? And how can he help robbing when he has no other means of subsistence? But if you pay them well and do not punish them severely when they offend, they will soon grow insolent and licentious; then you will become despised and lose your authority; later, tumult and discord will naturally ensue in your army; and will probably end in ruin.

> Niccolo Machiavelli, *The Art of War*, 1521.

I THINK all men of experience and judgment in matters of war do know that the first and principal thing that is requisite to assemble and form an army or armies and to keep the same in obedience with good effect is treasure to maintain, pay, and reward, with severe execution of excellent military laws.

> John Smythe (c. 1580–1631), *Certain Discourses Military*, 1966

WITHOUT going into the different rates of pay, I shall say only that it should be ample. It is better to have a small number of well-kept and well-disciplined troops than to have a great number who are neglected in these matters. It is not the big armies that win battles; it is the good ones. Economy can be pushed only to a certain point. It has limits beyond which it degenerates into parsimony. If your pay and allowances for officers will not support them decently, then you will only have rich men who serve for debauchery or indigent wretches devoid of spirit.

> Field Marshal Maurice Comte de Saxe, *My Reveries*, 1732, tr. Phillips, 1940.

TRULY the only good officers are the impoverished gentlemen who have nothing but their sword and their cape; but it is essential that they should be able to live on their pay.

> Field Marshal Maurice Comte de Saxe, *My Reveries*, 1732, tr. Phillips, 1940.

THE SOLDIER should not have any ready money. If he has a few coins in his pocket, he thinks himself too much of a great lord to follow his profession, and he deserts at the opening of a campaign.

> Frederick the Great, *Instructions to His Generals*, 1747, tr. Phillips, 1940.

THERE IS nothing that gives a man consequence, and renders him fit for command, like a support that renders him independent of everybody but the State he serves.

> General George Washington, 24 September 1776, letter to the President of Congress from the Heights of Harlem.

MAXIM 40. Every means should be taken to attach the soldier to his colours. This is best accomplished by showing consideration and respect for the old soldier. His pay likewise should increase with his length of service. It is the height of injustice to give a veteran no greater advantages than a recruit.

> Napoleon, *The Military Maxims* of Napoleon, tr. George D'Aguilar, 1831 (David Chandler, ed., 1987).

WHILE BLAMING the illegal conduct of the troops and of certain officers, one cannot fail to recognize the right they have to complain when their pay is five months in arrears. . . . We have just surmounted one grave crisis; but I should not like to prophesy the outcome of another one if proper measures are not taken to give the soldier that to which he is legimately entitled.

> Marshal Berthier, Prince de Neuchatel, March 1798, letter to the Directory on the mutinies of French garrisons in occupied northern Italian cities, only suppressed when levies were made on the local populations to pay the troops, quoted in S.J. Watson, *By Command of the Emperor*, 1957.

WE THEN related to him a number of bon-mots made by our soldiers during his absence and on his return, with which he was much entertained. But what particularly excited his risability was the answer made by a grenadier at Lyons. A grand review was held there, just after the Emperor had landed on his return from Elba. The Commanding Officer remarked to his soldiers that they were well clothed and well fed, that their pay might be seen upon their persons: – "Yes, certainly," replied the grenadier to whom he addressed himself. – "Well!": continued the officer, with a confident air, "it was not so under Bonaparte. Your pay was in arrear, he was in your debt?" – "And what did that signify," said the grenadier smartly, "if we chose to give him credit?"

> A story told to Napoleon at St. Helena, 16 April 1816, quoted in Emmanuel Las Casas, *Memoirs of the Life, Exile, and Conversations of the Emperor Napoleon*, II, 1890.

MY present pay is not wholly for present work but is in great part for past services . . . What money will pay Meade for Gettysburg? What Sheridan for Winchester? What Thomas for Chickamauga?

> General of the Army William T. Sherman, 1870, letter on pending legislation to cut Army officers' pay.

THE FEELING of the soldier should be that, in every event, the sympathy and preference of his government is for him who fights, rather than for him who is on provost guard duty to the rear, and, like most men, he measures this by the amount of pay. Of course, the soldier must be trained to obedience, and should be "content with his wages;" but whoever has commanded an army in the field knows the difference between a willing, contented mass of men, and one that feels a cause of grievance.

> General of the Army William T. Sherman, *Memoirs of General W.T. Sherman*, 1875.

YOU CANNOT pay my Marines enough for what they do for this nation. But you sure can pay them too little.

> General Charles Krulak, testimony before the House Armed Services Committee, quoted in the *San Diego Union-Tribune*, 23 February 1999.

PEACE

IF ONE HAS a free choice and can live undisturbed, it is sheer folly to go to war.

> Pericles, at the beginning of the Peloponnesian War, quoted in Thucydides, *The Peloponnesian War*, c.404 BC.

PEACE is an armistice in a war that is continuously going on.

> Thucydides, *The Peloponnesian War*, c. 404 BC.

FOR PEACE, with justice and honour, is the fairest and most profitable of possessions, but with disgrace and shameful cowardice it is the most infamous and harmful of all.

> Polybius, *Histories*, 4, c. 125 BC (*The Rise of the Roman Empire*, tr. Ian Scott-Kilvert, 1987).

A BAD PEACE is even worse than war.

> Cornelius Tacitus, *Annals*, 3, AD 116.

THE FIRST blessing is peace, as is agreed upon by all men who have even a small share of reason. It follows that if any one should be a destroyer of it, he would be most responsible not only to those near him but also to his whole nation for the troubles which come. The best general, therefore, is that one who is able to bring about peace from war.

> Count Belisarius, AD 530, admonition to the Persian generals not to disrupt peace negotiations, quoted in Procopius, *History of the Wars*, I, c. AD 560.

I THINK it is evident to all men of wisdom and discretion that have read divers notable histories with consideration and judgment, as also that have well considered of this our age, that there are two things of all others that are the greatest enemies to the art and science military and have been the occasion of the great decay, and oftentimes the utter ruin, of many great empires, kingdoms, and commonswealths. . . . the first is long peace, which ensuing after great wars to divers nations that have had notable militias and exercises military in great perfection, they by enjoying long peace have so much given themselves to covetousness, effeminacies, and superfluities that they have either in great part or else utterly forgotten all orders and exercises military.

> John Smythe (c. 1580–1631), *Certain Discourses Military*, 1966.

THOUGH PEACE be made, yet it is interest that keeps peace.

> Oliver Cromwell, 4 September 1654, to Parliament.

WHAT my enemies call a general peace is my destruction. What I call peace is merely the disarmament of my enemies. Am I not more moderate than they?

> Napoleon, 1813, quoted in Christopher Herold, *The Mind of Napoleon*, 1955.

WARS are, of course, as a rule to be avoided; but they are far better than certain kinds of peace.

President Theodore Roosevelt, *Thomas Hart Benton*, 1897.

WE DESIRE a peace that will be honourable to both parties. And, as I understand this document, we are leaving honour behind us, for we are now not only surrendering our independence, but we are allowing every burgher to be fettered hand and foot. Where is the "honourable peace" for us? If we conclude peace, we have to do it as men who have to live and die here. We must not agree to a peace which leaves behind in the hearts of one party a wound that will never heal.

General Louis Botha, 19 May 1902, at the peace conference ending the Boer War, quoted in De Wet, *Three Years War*, 1902.

PEACE is generally good in itself, but it is never the highest good unless it comes as the handmaid of righteousness; and it becomes a very evil thing if it serves merely as a mask of cowardice and sloth, or as an instrument to further the ends of despotism or anarchy.

President Theodore Roosevelt, 1910, speech upon award of the Nobel Peace Prize.

I AM NOT worried about the war; it will be difficult but we shall win it; it is after the war that worries me. Mark you, it will take years and years of patience, courage and faith.

Field Marshal Jan Christian Smuts, quoted in Tedder, *With Prejudice*, 1948.

IF MAN does find the solution for world peace it will be the most revolutionary reversal of his record we have ever known.

General of the Army George C. Marshall, 1 September 1945, Biennial Report, Chief of Staff, U.S. Army.

THE OBJECT of war is a better state of peace – even if only from your own point of view. Hence it is essential to conduct war with constant regard to the peace you desire. That applies both to aggressor nations who seek expansion and to peaceful nations who only fight for self-preservation – although their views of what is meant by a better state of peace are very different.

Captain Sir Basil Liddell Hart, *Strategy*, 1954.

PEOPLE AND ARMY

AS COMMANDER of the Peloponnese, I led many thousands of men. I undertook expeditions and waged battles, but I confess in all honesty, that during the entire war I did not spend one single penny of my own, for I had none to spend. It was the people who fed me and who kept supplying all that my troops needed, and thanks to my sword I got horses and weapons from the Turks.

Theodoros Kolokotrones, August 1822, Nemea.

THE WELL-BEING of the people equally with the well-being of the Army requires a common sympathy and a common interest between them.

Major-General John Pope (1822–1892), to the veterans of the Army of the Tennessee.

AS TO the charge of want of loyalty, or zeal in the war, I assert, from as much opportunity for observation as any individual had, that no people ever displayed so much, under such circumstances, and with so little flagging, for so long a time continuously. This was proved by the long service of the troops without pay, and under exposure to such hardships, from the causes above mentioned, as modern troops have rarely endured; by the voluntary contributions of food and clothing sent to the armies from every district that furnished a regiment; by the general and continued submission of the people to the tyranny of the impressment system as practiced – such a tyranny, I believe, as no other high-spirited people ever endured – and by the sympathy and aid given by every house to all professing to belong to the army, or to be on the way to join it. And this spirit continued not only after all hope of success had died, but after the final confession of defeat by their military commanders.

General Joseph E. Johnston, *Narrative*, 1874.

THE NATION that will insist on drawing a broad line of demarkation between the fighting man and the thinking man is liable to find its fighting done by fools and its thinking done by cowards.

Lieutenant-General Sir William Butler (1838–1910).

IT HAS always been an article of my creed that Army and people have but one body and one soul, and that the Army cannot remain sound for ever if the nation is diseased.

General Erich Ludendorff, *My War Memories, 1914–1918*, 1919.

WHAT IS the true bastion of iron? It is the masses, the millions upon millions of people who genuinely and sincerely support our revolution. That is the bastion which it is impossible for any force on earth to smash.

Mao Tse-tung, 'Be Concerned with the Well-Being of the Masses', 27 January 1934, *Selected Works*, 1967.

CIVILIANS provide the manpower for our huge armies. Parents provide the sons who fight. They make sacrifices, enormous sacrifices for the cause. Wives lose their husbands, children lose their fathers, families lose their breadwinners. They go short of food, clothing and the comforts they are used to. They pay the heavy taxes required to finance our war effort . . . [hence] when they know that serious mistakes have been made they want to know why. After all they pay the cost of those mistakes.

> Lieutenant-General H. Gordon Bennett, *Why Singapore Fell*, 1944.

THE PEOPLE are like water and the army is like fish.

> Mao Tse-tung, 'Aspects of China's Anti-Japanese Struggle', 1948.

WHAT a society gets in its armed services is exactly what it asks for, no more and no less. What it asks for tends to be a reflection of what it is. When a country looks at its fighting forces it is looking in a mirror; the mirror is a true one and the face that it sees will be its own.

> General Sir John Hackett, *The Profession of Arms*, 1983.

WE EXIST today – we flourish today – not because of what we know we are, or what we know we can do, but because of what the grassroots of our country believes we are and believes we can do.

These thousands – millions – of people don't understand much about "comprehensive exercise of sea power" or "the security needs of a maritime nation," and they don't even absorb the full implication of "the balanced fleet." But that isn't too important, because what they do understand and believe about the Marine Corps is more powerful by far than these technical things.

Essentially, as a result of the unfailing conduct of our Corps over the years, they believe three things about the Marines. First, they believe that when trouble comes to our country there will be Marines – somewhere – who, through hard work, have made and kept themselves ready to do something useful about it, and do it at once. They picture these Marines as men – individual components of a lean, serious, professional outfit. . . .

Second, they believe that when the Marines go to war they invariably turn in a performance that is dramatically and decisively successful – not most of the time, but always. Their faith and their convictions in this regard are almost mystical. The mere association of the word Marines with a crisis is an automatic source of encouragement and confidence everywhere.

The third thing they believe about the Marines is that our Corps is downright good for the manhood of our country, that the Marines are master of a form of unfailing alchemy which converts unoriented youths into proud, self-reliant stable citizens – citizens into whose hands the nation's affairs may be safely entrusted. ·

> Lieutenant-General Victor H. 'The Brute' Krulak, *First to Fight*, 1984.

PERSEVERANCE

THE MERIT of the action lies in finishing it to the end.

> Genghis Khan (1162–1227).

THERE MUST be a beginning of any great matter, but the continuing unto the end until it be thoroughly finished yields the true glory.

> Sir Francis Drake, 17 May 1587, letter to Sir Francis Walsingham.

WE FIGHT, get beat, rise, and fight again.

> Major-General Nathaniel Greene, 22 June 1781, letter to Chevalier de la Luzerne on the campaign in the Carolinas.

A GENERAL in time of war is constantly bombarded by reports both true and false; by errors arising from fear or negligence or hastiness; by disobedience born of right or wrong interpretations, of ill will, of a proper mistaken sense of duty, of laziness, or of exhaustion; by accidents that nobody could have foreseen. In short, he is exposed to countless impressions, most of them disturbing, few of them encouraging. Long experience of war creates a knack of rapidly assessing these phenomena; courage and strength of character are as impervious to them as a rock to the rippling waves. If man were to yield to these pressure, he would never complete an operation. Perseverance in the chosen course is the essential counterweight, provided that no compelling reasons intervene to the contrary. Moreover, there is hardly a worthwhile enterprise in war whose execution does not call for infinite effort, trouble, and privation; and as man under pressure tends to give in to physical and intellectual weakness, only great strength of will can lead to the objective. It is steadfastness that will earn the admiration of the world and posterity.

> Major-General Carl von Clausewitz, *On War*, 3.11, 1832, tr. Michael Howard and Peter Paret, 1976.

I PROPOSE to fight it out on this line, if it takes all summer.

> General of the Army Ulysses S. Grant, 11 May 1864, dispatch from Spotsylvania Courthouse.

PERSONAL PRESENCE OF THE COMMANDER

IT IS NOT fitting for a good king and a brave captain to leave his own encampment.

> Ahuítzotl, 'The Lion of Anáhuac', Aztec Emperor, 1487, when a vassal lord offered the comfort of his palace while on campaign.

I SEE that it is only in my own hand, that my sword is invincible.

> Suleyman the Magnificent, late September 1565, upon the return of his defeated army and fleet from the epic

siege of Malta, the joint command of which he had delegated to his chief general, Mustapha Pasha, and his chief admiral, Piali, quoted in Ernle Bradford, *The Great Siege: Malta 1565*, 1961.

THE PRESENCE of a general is necessary: he is the head, he is the all in all of an army. It was not the Roman army conquered Gaul, but Caesar; it was not the Carthaginians made the armies of the Republic tremble at the very gates of Rome, but Hannibal; it was not the Macedonian army marched to the Indus, but Alexander; it was not the French army that carried war to the Weser and to the Inn, but Turenne; it was not the Prussian army that defended Prussia during the seven years against the three strongest Powers of Europe, but Frederick the Great.

> Napoleon, 30 July 1800, quoted in R.M. Johnston, ed., *The Corsican*, 1910.

FOR ALL the faith I have in French valor, I have equal faith in my lucky star, or perhaps in myself, and as a result I never count positively on victory unless I myself am in command.

> Napoleon, 1803, conversation, quoted in Christopher Herold, ed., *The Mind of Napoleon*, 1955.

I BELIEVE my arrival was most welcome, not only to the Commanders of the Fleet, but to almost every individual in it; and when I came to explain to them the Nelson touch it was like an electric shock. Some shed tears, all approved. "It was new – it was singular – it was simple!" and from admirals downwards it was repeated, – "It must succeed if ever they will allow us to get at them. You are, my Lord, surrounded by friends, whom you inspire with confidence."

> Admiral Viscount Nelson, October 1805, upon his return to the fleet before the Battle of Trafalgar when he had described his new tactics, quoted in David Walder, *Nelson*, 1978.

A GENERAL who sees with the eyes of others will never be able to command an army as it should be.

> Napoleon, 9 December 1817, to Barry E. O'Meara at St. Helena, *Napoleon in Exile*, 1822.

THE REAL REASON why I succeeded in my campaign [in India] is because I was always on the spot. I saw everything and did everything myself.

> The Duke of Wellington (1769–1852).

BY GOD! I don't think it would have been done if I had not been there.

> The Duke of Wellington (1769–1852), speaking of the Battle of Waterloo, 1815, quoted in *The Greevey Papers*, I, 1903.

OH YES – there was nothing like him. He suited a French army so exactly! Depend upon it, at the head of a French army there never was anything like him. In short, I used to say of him that his presence on the field made the difference of forty thousand men.

> The Duke of Wellington (1769–1852), quoted in Earl Stanhope, *Conversations With the Duke of Wellington*, 1888.

THE POSITION I am now placed in I feel will prove a trying one, but by having an eye to duty alone I shall hope to succeed. Placed in command of all the Armies as I have been it will be necessary for me to have an office and an A.A. Gen. in Washington, but I will not be there. I shall have Hd.Qrs. in the field and will move from one Army to another so as to be where my presence seems to be most required.

> General of the Army Ulysses S. Grant, letter to T. Lyle Dickey, 15 March 1864, *Papers of USG*, X, 1982, p. 208.

I HAVE SEEN your despatch in which you say, "I want Sheridan put in command of all the troops in the field, with instructions to put himself *south* of the enemy, and follow him to the *death*. Wherever the enemy goes, let our troops go also." This, I think, is exactly right, as to how our forces should move. But please look over the despatches you may have received from here, even since you made that order, and discover, if you can, that there is any idea in the head of any one here, of "putting our army south of the enemy," or of "following him to the death" in any direction. I repeat to you it will neither be done nor attempted unless you watch it every day, and hour, and force it.

> President Abraham Lincoln, 3 August 1864, to General Grant on the need for close supervision of the effort to send Sheridan to clean out the Shenandoah Valley (Grant left two hours after receipt of this message to effect that supervision), quoted in Grant, *Personal Memoirs and Selected Letters*, 1990.

HE [the general] must know perfectly the strength and quality of each part of his own army, as well as that of his opponent, and must be where he can personally see and observe with his own eyes, and judge with his own mind. No man can properly command an army from the rear, he must be "at its front;" and when a detachment is made, the commander thereof should be informed of the object to be accomplished, and left as free as possible to execute it in his own way; and when an Army is divided into several parts, the superior should always attend to that one which he regards as the most important.

> General of the Army William T. Sherman, *Memoirs of General W.T. Sherman*, II, 1875.

SOME MEN think that modern armies may be so regulated that a general can sit in an office and play on his several columns as on the keys of a piano; this is a fearful mistake. The directing mind must be at the very head of the army – must be seen there, and the effect of his mind and personal energy must be felt by every officer and man present with it, to secure the best results. Every attempt to make war easy and safe will result in humiliation and disaster.

General of the Army William T. Sherman, *The Memoirs of General W.T. Sherman*, II, 1875.

WHEN the battle becomes hot, they must see their commander, know him to be near. It does not matter even if he is without initiative, incapable of giving an order. His presence creates a belief that direction exists, and that is enough.

Colonel Charles Ardant du Picq, *Battle Studies*, 1880, tr. Greely, 1957.

GALLWITZ'S ARMY surged out against the Narew on both sides of Przasnysz. For this attack I went personally to the battlefield, not with any idea of interfering with the tactics of the Army Headquarters Staff, which I knew to be masterly, but only because I knew what outstanding importance Main Headquarters attached to the success of the break-through they had ordered at this point. I wanted to be on the spot so that in case of need I could intervene immediately if the Army Headquarters Staff needed any further help for the execution of its difficult task from the armies under my command.

Field Marshal Paul von Hindenburg, *Out of My Life*, 1920.

ON REACHING this camp on the 8th of February the Commander-in-Chief immediately proceeded to visit the troops, and by his cheery smile and friendly recognition did much to revive the spirits of those who were feeling disheartened owing to previous failures and disappointments. Lord Roberts possessed an attractive personality, took infinite pains to secure the confidence and esteem of his troops, and to show them that their interests were his – as they undoubtedly were. It is to be regretted that his example is not more frequently followed by other leaders, since the neglect of it greatly reduces the fighting value of the troops and cannot be made good by any other qualities of leadership, with the sole exception, perhaps, of an unbroken string of victories, and this rarely falls to the lot of the commander of whom regimental officers and men know and see little, and for whom they consequently care less.

Field Marshal Sir William Robertson, *From Private to Field-Marshal*, 1921.

PERHAPS the most damning comment on the plan which plunged the British Army in this bath of mud and blood [Third Battle of Ypres, 1917] is contained in an incidental revelation of the remorse of one who was largely responsible for it. This highly-placed officer from General Headquarters was on his first visit to the battle front – at the end of a four month's battle. Growing increasingly uneasy as the car approached the swamp-like edges of the battle area, he eventually burst into tears, crying "Good God, did

we really send men to fight in that?" To which his companion replied that the ground was far worse ahead. If the exclamation was a credit to his heart it revealed on what a foundation of delusion and inexcusable ignorance his indomitable "offensiveness" had been based.

Captain Sir Basil Liddell Hart, speaking of Lieutenant-General Sir Lancelot Kiggell, *The Real War, 1914–1918*, 1930.

THE MOST rapid way to shell-shock an army is to shell-proof its generals; for once the heart of an army is severed from its head the result is paralysis. The modern system of command has in fact guillotined generalship, hence modern battles have degenerated into saurian writhings between headless monsters.

Major-General J.F.C. Fuller, *Generalship: Its Diseases and Their Cure*, 1933.

WHAT troops and subordinate commanders appreciate is that a general should be constantly in personal contact with them, and should not see everything simply through the eyes of his staff. The less time a general spends in his office and the more with his troops the better.

Field Marshal Viscount Wavell of Cyrenaica, *Generals and Generalship*, 1941.

UPON going ashore at Sorrento, an officer approached a Ranger in uniform asking, "Do you know where I can find Colonel Darby?" A slow grin crossed the face of the husky soldier as he answered, "You'll never find him this far back."

As told by General William H. Baumer, of Colonel William O. Darby during the Allied landing in Italy on 9 September 1943, quoted in John D. Lock, *To Fight With Intrepidity*, 1998.

THE DAY of a commander in the field is one of constant vigilance. He must continually be getting about to see what is actually happening and be sure that his subordinates are in fact doing what is required of them in the best possible way. This getting about not only keeps the commander informed by first hand knowledge, but the confidence of the troops is raised when they constantly see him amongst themselves. No walk I ever did in New Guinea failed to pay a dividend, either by seeing or improving something or by maintaining the morale of the soldiers by having a chat with those I met.

Major-General George Vasey (1895–1945), quoted in Horner, *The Commanders*, 1984.

A STUDY of the map will indicate where critical situations exist or are apt to develop, and so indicate where the commander should be.

General George S. Patton, Jr., *War As I Knew It*, 1947.

FROM THE BATTALION down, the use of maps is of no value and is frequently fraught with great danger. I have never seen a good battalion commander

direct his units from a map. I have seen many bad battalion commanders indulge in this pusillanimous method of command.
General George S. Patton, Jr., *War As I Knew It*, 1947.

IN THE REAR AREAS the commander, high and low, wins the hearts of men primarily through a zealous interest in their general welfare. This is the true basis of his prestige and the qualifying test placed upon his soldierly abilities by those who serve under him. But at the front he commands their respect as it becomes proved to them that he understands their tactical problem and will do all possible to help them solve it.
Brigadier-General S.L.A. Marshall, *Men Against Fire*, 1947.

THE PLACE of all commanders of armour up to the divisional commander is on the battlefield, and within this wherever they have the best view of the terrain and good communications with the hard core of the tanks. I was always located where I could see and hear what was going on "in front", that is near the enemy and around myself – namely at the focal point! Nothing and nobody can replace a personal impression.
Major-General Hasso von Manteuffel, c. 1951, unpublished manuscript, quoted in Richard Simpkin, *Tank Warfare*, 1979.

EVERY experienced commander is familiar with this sort of panic which, in a critical situation, may seize an entire body of troops. Mass hysteria of this type can be overcome only by energetic actions and a display of perfect composure. The example set by a true leader can have miraculous effects. He must stay with his troops, remain cool, issue precise orders, and inspire confidence by his behavior. Good soldiers never desert such a leader. News of the presence of high ranking commanders up front travels like wildfire along the entire front line, bolstering everyone's morale. It means a sudden change from gloom to hope, from imminent defeat to victory.
Colonel-General Erhard Raus, *Defense Tactics Against Russian Breakthroughs*, D.A. Pam. No. 20-233, Department of the Army, 1951.

AS THE SITUATION was rather confused I spent the next day at the front again. It is of the utmost importance to the commander to have a good knowledge of the battlefield and of his own and his enemy's positions on the ground. It is often not a question of which of the opposing commanders is the higher qualified mentally, or which has the greater experience, but which of them has the better grasp of the battlefield. This is particularly the case when a situation develops, the outcome of which cannot be estimated. Then the commander must go up to see for himself; reports received second-hand rarely give the information he needs for his decisions.
Field Marshal Erwin Rommel, *The Rommel Papers*, 1953.

ACCURATE EXECUTION of the plans of the commander and his staff is of the highest importance. It is a mistake to assume that every unit officer will make all that there is to be made out of his situation; most of them soon succumb to a certain inertia. Then it is simply reported that for some reason or another this or that cannot be done – reasons are always easy enough to think up. People of this kind must be made to feel the authority of the commander and be shaken out of their apathy. The commander must be the prime mover of the battle and the troops must always have to reckon with his appearance in personal control.
Field Marshal Erwin Rommel, *The Rommel Papers*, 1953.

IN MOMENTS of panic, fatigue, or disorganization, or when something out of the ordinary has to be demanded . . . the personal example of the commander works wonders, especially if he has the wit to create some sort of legend 'round himself.
Field Marshal Erwin Rommel, *The Rommel Papers*, 1953.

I FELT utterly at sea. . . . My predecessor, von Rundstedt, rightly regarded himself as the heir to the tradition of the Supreme Command in World War One . . . With his finger on the pulse of things, he issued orders from his headquarters almost never visiting the front and rarely using the telephone. . . . Even if my ways were different I could still understand von Rundstedt's though I could not persuade myself to adopt them. . . . The laxity of discipline everywhere required personal contact with the commanders and troops. . . . One had to have a glimpse behind the scenes and into men's hearts.
Field Marshal Albert Kesselring, *The Memoirs of Field Marshal Kesselring*, 1953.

ONE of the most valuable qualities of a commander is a flair for putting himself in the right place at the vital time.
Field Marshal Viscount Slim of Burma, *Unofficial History*, 1957.

AS COMMANDER of a division or smaller unit, there will rarely be more than one crisis, one really critical situation facing you at any one time. The commander belongs right at the spot, not at some rear command post. He should be there before the crisis erupts, if possible. If it is not possible, then he should get there as soon as he can after it develops. Once there, then by personal observation of terrain, enemy fires, reactions, and attitudes of his own commanders on the spot – by his eyes, ears, brain, nose, and his sixth sense – he gets the best possible picture of what is happening and can best exercise his troop leadership and the full authority of his command. He can start help of every kind to his hard-pressed subordinates. He can urge commanders to provide additional fire support, artillery, air, and other infantry weapons. . . .

No other means will provide the commander with what his personal perceptions can provide, if he is present at the critical time and place. He can personally intervene, if he thinks that necessary, but only to the extent that such intervention will be helpful and not interfere with his subordinates. He is in a position to make instant decisions, to defend, withdraw, attack, exploit, or pursue.

If, at this time, he is at some rear command post, he will have to rely on reports from others, and time will be lost, perhaps just those precious moments which spell the difference between success and failure. Notwithstanding the console capabilities of future television in combat, I still believe what I have said is true. In any event, keep this time factor in mind. It is the one irretrievable, inextensible, priceless element in war.

General Matthew B. Ridgway, 'Leadership', *Military Review*, 9/1966.

FROM the practice of the first operations I concluded that those commanders failed most often who did not visit the terrain, where action was to take place, themselves only studied it on the map and issued written orders. The commanders who are to carry out combat missions must by all means know the terrain and enemy battle formations very well in order to take advantage of weak points in his dispositions and direct the main blow there.

Marshal of the Soviet Union Georgi K. Zhukov, *Reminiscences and Reflections*, 1974.

A COMMANDER should command from well forward. This allows him to see and sense firsthand the ebb and flow of combat, to gain an intuitive appreciation for the situation which he cannot obtain from reports. It allows him to exert his personal influence at decisive points during the action. It also allows him to locate closer to the events that will influence the situation so that he can observe them directly and circumvent the delays and inaccuracies that result from passing information up the chain of command. Finally, we recognize the importance of personal leadership. Only by his physical presence – by demonstrating the willingness to share danger and privation – can the commander fully gain the trust and confidence of his subordinates.

General Alfred M. Gray and Major John Schmitt, *Warfighting*, United States Marine Corps, 1989.

THE GULF WAR was fought with Marine leadership up front, which is the only place I believe that a leadership can fight from. I don't buy the argument that "because the battlefield had become more technical, the commander must stay back in his control room and manipulate from there."

Lieutenant-General Walter Boomer, 'Up Front', Al Santoli, ed., *Leading the Way: How Vietnam Veterans Rebuilt the U.S. Military*, 1993.

PART of maneuver warfare is reconnaissance-driven combat, where soldiers take action without orders. The commander isn't a Supreme Being sitting back at the command center. He needs to be up front leading. Because if he is fully informed, he can't do anything fast enough with the information. I don't care how much electronics or computer technology you give him.

Colonel Michael Wyly (USMC), 'Revolution', Al Santoli, ed., *Leading the Way: How Vietnam Veterans Rebuilt the U.S. Military*, 1993.

PERSONAL RISK OF THE COMMANDER

AFTER haranguing the Tenth Legion, Caesar started for the right wing where he saw his men under great pressure. The standards of the Twelfth were huddled in one place and the soldiers so cramped that their fighting was hampered. All the centurions of the fourth cohort were cut down, the standard bearer killed and standard lost, and almost all the centurions of the other cohorts were killed or wounded. . . . the enemy did not remit their pressure . . . and were pressing in from either flank. Caesar saw that the situation was critical, and there was no reserve to throw in. He snatched a shield from a soldier in the rear . . . and moved to the front line; he called upon the centurions by name, encouraged the men to advance, and directed them to open their lines out to give freer play with their swords. His coming inspired the men with hope and gave them new heart. Even in a desperate situation each man was anxious to do his utmost when his general was looking on, and the enemy's onset was somewhat slowed down.

Julius Caesar, 57 BC, when his camp was surprised by the Nervii on the Sambre River, *The Gallic War*, c. 51 BC, tr. Moses Hadas.

THE GENERAL should fight cautiously rather than boldly, or should keep away altogether from a hand-to-hand fight with the enemy. For even if in battle he shows that he is not to be outdone in valour, he can aid his army far less by fighting than he can harm it if he should be killed, since the knowledge of a general is far more important than his physical strength. Even a soldier can perform a great deed by bravery, but no one except the general can by his wisdom plan a greater one.

Onasander, *The General*, AD 58 (*Aeneas Tacticus, Aclepiodotus, Onasander*, tr. The Illinois Greek Club, 1923).

I WAS the first to set a ladder against the fortress on the bridge, and, as I raised it, I was wounded in the throat by a cross-bow bolt. But Saint Catherine comforted me greatly. And I did not cease to ride and do my work.

Joan of Arc, 7 May 1429, on the capture of the bridge at Orléans, *Joan of Arc in her Own Words*, 1996.

SOLDIERS! I will command your battalions in person, and I shall not expose myself if, with your usual courage, you throw the enemy's ranks into disorder and confusion. But should victory be for one moment uncertain, you would see your Emperor expose himself in the front rank, for there must be no question of victory on an occasion when the honour of the French infantry is at stake.

> Napoleon, 1 December 1805, bivouac near Austerlitz, quoted in R.M. Johnston, ed., *The Corsican*, 1910.

GET TO the front with your firing-line. It is no longer a case for acting as in recent years, but you must again put on your boots and your resolution of '93! When the French see your cocked hat with the skirmishers, and see you exposing yourself foremost to the enemy's fire, you can do what you like with them.

> Napoleon, 21 February 1814, letter to Marshal Augereau, quoted in R.M. Johnston, ed., *The Corsican*, 1910.

JACKSON is with you . . . Rally, brave men, and press forward. Your general will lead you. Jackson will lead you. Follow me!

> Lieutenant-General Thomas J. 'Stonewall' Jackson, 9 August 1862, rallying his shattered troops at the battle of Cedar Mountain, quoted in David Martin, *The Second Bull Run Campaign*, 1997.

I LONG AGO made up my mind that it was not a good plan to fight battles with paper orders – that is, for the commander to stand on a hill in the rear and send his aides-de-camp with written orders to the different commanders. My practice has always been to fight in the front rank.

> Major-General Phillip H. Sheridan, 24 October 1864, statement to Charles A. Dana.

IN ANY of these fights, a general officer who does his duty has got to expose himself. Otherwise, he cannot look himself in the face and order men to do things he is afraid to do himself. I am sure that whatever success I have had resulted from my adherence to this belief.

> General George S. Patton, Jr., 9 June 1943, letter to his nephew, Frederick Ayer, quoted in Roger H. Nye, *The Patton Mind*, 1993.

THE ADVANCE resumed on the following morning – D plus 2 and quickly developed a dramatic situation. Apparently unaware of our strength, a Red tank-infantry column drove directly into the lines of the advancing Marines and a pitched battle occurred at close quarters.

It was exciting for a while, but in a matter of 30 minutes, some 200 Red infantrymen were dead or captured and their tanks all smoking hulks.

Just about this time, General MacArthur chose to come ashore to inspect the front. Unaware of the hot battle in progress, the general's motorcade drove close up behind the action.

A young Marine officer ran up to him in a state of great agitation and said, "General, you can't come up here."

"Why?" MacArthur asked.

"We've just knocked out 5 Red tanks right over the top of this hill," the officer said.

MacArthur replied, "That was the proper thing to do," and walked up on the hill.

> Lieutenant-General Victor H. 'The Brute' Krulak, 1 December 1958, 'The Inchon Operation', address to the Cosmos Club, Washington, D.C., quoted in *The Congressional Record*, 15 January 1959, p. 671.

I'VE ALWAYS BELIEVED no officer's life, regardless of rank, is of such great value to his country that he should seek safety in the rear. . . . Officers should be forward with their men at the point of impact. That is where their character stands out and can do the most good. . . . Things work better that way. Men expect you to, and men look to officers and NCOs for example.

> Lieutenant-General Lewis 'Chesty' Puller (1898–1971), quoted in *Marine Corps Gazette*, 6/1998.

THE PETER PRINCIPLE

I HAVE SEEN very good colonels become very bad generals. I have known others who were great takers of villages, excellent for maneuvers within an army, but who, outside of that, were not even able to lead a thousand men in war, who lost their heads completely and were unable to take any decision.

If such a man arrives at the command of an army, he will seek to save himself by his dispositions, because he has no other resources. In attempting to make them understood better he will confuse the spirit of his whole army with multitudinous messages. Since the least circumstances changes everything in war, he will want to change his arrangements, will throw everything in horrible confusion, and infallibly will be defeated.

> Field Marshal Maurice Comte de Saxe, *My Reveries*, 1732, tr. Phillips, 1940.

AT MY SUGGESTION, he had been appointed to the command of the XII Army Corps, but in this post he already showed himself only a second-rate General lacking in determination. Apart from this, he attempted to do everything himself and would not trust any of his subordinates; and as he could not be everywhere at once on his vast front he left a great deal undone. In the smallish body of cavalry which he commanded for a long time, everyone knew him, loved him, and trusted him, and he was a success at his work. But with an increased number of troops and a large establishment of officers, his mistrustfulness, his air of gloom, and his silence prevented his men from loving him, trusting him, and understanding him any more than he understood them. Events proved clearly that his case was only another example of the familiar truth that every man has his limitations, which are fixed not only by his intelligence and his learning, but to a great extent by the particular bent of his personality.

General Aleksei A. Brusilov, *A Soldier's Notebook*, 1931.

EVERY OFFICER has his "ceiling" in rank, beyond which he should not be allowed to rise – particularly in war-time. An officer may do well when serving under a first class superior. But how will he shape when he finds himself the boss? It is one thing to be merely an advisor, with no real responsibility; it is quite another thing when you are the top man, responsible for the final decision. A good battalion commander does not necessarily make a good brigadier, nor a good divisional general a good corps commander. The judging of a man's ceiling in the higher ranks is one of the great problems which a commander must solve, and it occupied much of my time.

Field Marshal Viscount Montgomery of Alamein, *The Memoirs of Field Marshal Montgomery*, 1958.

PHYSICAL FITNESS

NO CITIZEN has any right to be an amateur in the matter of physical training. It is part of his profession as a citizen to keep himself in good condition, ready to serve his state at a moment's notice. The instinct of self-preservation demands it likewise: for how helpless is the state of the ill-trained youth in war or in danger! Finally, what a disgrace it is for a man to grow old without ever seeing the beauty and strength of which his body is capable.

Socrates (469–399 BC), according to Xenophon, quoted in Daniel Boorstein, *The Creators*, 1992.

DAILY PRACTICE of the military exercises is much more efficacious in preserving the health of an army than all the art of medicine.

Flavius Vegetius Renatus, *Military Institutions of the Romans*, c. AD 378, tr. Clark, 1776.

REMEMBER that victory depends on the legs; the hands are only the instruments of victory.

Field Marshal Prince Aleksandr V. Suvorov (1729–1800), quoted in W. Lyon Blease, *Suvorof*, 1920.

IN THIS SITUATION the real leaders of the Army stood forth in bold contrast to the ordinary clay. Men who had sustained a reputation for soldierly qualities, under less trying conditions, proved too weak for the ordeal and became pessimistic calamity howlers. Their organizations were quickly infected with the same spirit and grew ineffective unless a more suitable commander was given charge. It was apparent that the combination of tired muscles, physical discomforts, and heavy casualties weakened the backbone of many. Officers of high

rank who were not in perfect physical condition usually lost the will to conquer and took an exceedingly gloomy view of the situation.

General of the Army George C. Marshall, *Memoirs of My Service in the World War*, written 1923–1926, first published 1976.

I WANT THEM to be able to march 20 miles, the last five at double time, and then be ready to fight.

Lieutenant-General Lewis B. 'Chesty' Puller, 1951, upon his return from Korea to command a training brigade, quoted by Associated Press, 11 October 1971.

AT ITS BEST, the military is an environment in which we learn that we are more than we thought we were, can do more than we thought we could. Physical conditioning and courage are crucial ingredients, especially in combat. One of the greatest compliments that soldiers can bestow on an officer is their acknowledgment that "the old man can really hang in there."

Major-General Bernard Loeffke, *From Warrior to Healer*, 1998.

PLANNING/PLANS

FOR if many ill-conceived plans have succeeded through the still greater fatuity of an opponent, many more, apparently well laid, have on the contrary ended in disgrace. The confidence with which we form our schemes is never completely justified in their execution; speculation is carried on in safety, but, when it comes to action, fear causes failure.

Thucydides, *History of the Peloponnesian War*, 1.121, c. 404, tr. Richard Crawley, 1910.

PLAN what you have to do at night and carry out your decisions during the day. One cannot plan and act at the same time.

The Emperor Maurice, *The Strategikon*, c. AD 600 (*Maurice's Strategikon*, tr. George Dennis, 1984).

LONG and careful deliberation promises great safety in war, whereas hasty and impetuous generals usually commit serious blunders.

The Emperor Maurice, *The Strategikon*, c. AD 600 (*Maurice's Strategikon*, tr. George Dennis, 1984).

ONE SHOULD STUDY the possible courses in the light of the obstacles that have to be overcome, of the inconveniences or advantages that will result from the success of each branch, and, after taking account of the more likely objections, decide on the part which can lead to the greatest advantages, while employing diversions and all else that one can do to mislead the enemy and make him imagine that the main effort is coming at some other part. And in case all these diversions, countermarches or other ruses fail of their purpose – to hide the real aim – one must be ready to profit by a second or third branch of the plan without giving one's enemy time to consider it.

General Pierre de Bourcet, *Principes de la guerre de montagnes*, 1775.

IT IS BETTER to see and communicate the difficulties and dangers of an enterprise, and to endeavour to overcome them, than to be blind to everything but success till the moment of difficulty comes, and to despond.

The Duke of Wellington, 1798, *Supplementary Despatches, Correspondence and Memoranda of Field Marshal Arthur Duke of Wellington, K.G., 1794–1818*, I, 1858, pp. 195–196.

THERE IS no greater coward than I when I am drawing up a plan of campaign. I magnify every danger, every disadvantage that can be conceived. My nervousness is painful; but not that I show a cool face to those who are about me. I am like a woman in the throes of childbirth. When once my decision is made, however, I forget all, except what may carry it through to success.

Napoleon, 27 April 1800, quoted in R.M. Johnston, ed., *The Corsican*, 1910.

THE ENEMY is welcome to know my forces and positions, provided I know his, and he be ignorant of my plans.

Napoleon, May 1800, to his spy shortly before the Battle of Marengo, quoted in Louis de Bourrienne, *The Memoirs of Napoleon Bonaparte*, II, 1891.

IN WAR nothing is achieved except by calculation. Everything that is not soundly planned in its details yields no result.

Napoleon, 18 September 1806, to Joseph Bonaparte, *Correspondance de Napoléon Ier, publiée par ordre de l'Empereur Napoléon III*, No. 10809, Vol. XIII, p. 442, 1858–1870.

IF I TAKE so many precautions it is because it is my custom to leave nothing to chance.

Napoleon, 14 March 1808, to Marshal Murat, *Correspondance de Napoléon Ier, publiée par ordre de l'Empereur Napoléon III*, No. 13652, XVI, p. 418, 1858–1870.

WHO will attack tomorrow, I or Bonaparte? Bonaparte. Well, Bonaparte has not given me any idea of his projects; and, as my plans will depend upon his, how can you expect me to tell you what mine are? There is one thing certain, Uxbridge, that is, that whatever happens, you and I will do our duty.

The Duke of Wellington, June 1815, just before the Battle of Waterloo, to General Uxbridge, his nominal second-in-command, quoted in William Fraser, *Words on Wellington*, 1889.

I AM USED to thinking three or four months in advance about what I must do, and I calculate on the worst.

Napoleon (1769–1821).

IF I always appear prepared, it is because before entering on an undertaking, I have meditated for long and have foreseen what may occur. It is not genius which reveals to me suddenly and secretly what I should do in circumstances unexpected by others; it is thought and meditation.

Napoleon (1769–1821).

NOTHING succeeds in war except in consequence of a well prepared plan.

Napoleon (1769–1821).

BE AUDACIOUS and cunning in your plans, firm and persevering in their execution, determined to find a glorious end.

Major-General Carl von Clausewitz, *Principles of War*, 1812.

MAXIM 2. In forming the plan of a campaign, it is requisite to foresee everything the enemy may do, and to be prepared with the necessary means to counteract it.

Plans of campaign may be modified *ad infinitum* according to circumstances, the genius of the general, the character of the troops, and the features of the country.

Napoleon, *The Military Maxims of Napoleon*, tr. George D'Aguilar, 1831 (David Chandler, ed., 1987).

MAXIM 79. The first principle of a general-in-chief is to calculate what he must do, to see if he has all the means to surmount the obstacles with which the enemy can oppose him, and when he has made his decision, to do everything to overcome them.

Napoleon, *The Military Maxims of Napoleon*, tr. Burnod, 1827.

WAR PLANS cover every aspect of a war, and weave them all into a single operation that must have a single, ultimate objective in which all particular aims are reconciled.

Major-General Carl von Clausewitz, *On War*, 8.2, 1832, tr. Michael Howard and Peter Paret, 1976.

INDECISION is our bane. A bad plan, in my mind, followed out without wavering, is better than three or four good ones not so dealt with.

General Charles 'Chinese' Gordon, 1864, quoted in Paul Charrier, *Gordon of Khartoum*, 1965.

NO OPERATIONS PLAN will ever extend with any sort of certainty beyond the first encounter with the hostile main force. Only the layman believes to perceive in the development of any campaign a consistent execution of a preconceived original plan that has been thought out in all its details and adhered to to the very end.

Field Marshal Helmuth Graf von Moltke (1800–1891), quoted in von Freytag-Loringhoven, *Generalship in the World War*, 1920.

THE COMMANDER is compelled during the whole

campaign to reach decisions on the basis of situations which cannot be predicted. All consecutive acts of war are, therefore, not executions of a premeditated plan, but spontaneous actions, directed by military tact. The problem is to grasp in innumerable special cases the actual situation which is covered by the mist of uncertainty, to appraise the facts correctly and to guess the unknown elements, to reach a decision quickly and then to carry it out forcefully and relentlessly. . . . It is obvious that theoretical knowledge will not suffice, but that here the qualities of mind and character come to a free, practical and artistic expression, although schooled by military training and led by experiences from military history and from life itself.
  Field Marshal Helmut Graf von Moltke, quoted in Edward Earle, ed., *Makers of Modern Strategy*, 1943.

I NEVER PLAN beyond the first battle.
  Field Marshal Helmuth Graf von Moltke, *Ausgewaehlte Werke*, IV, 1925.

IT IS a delusion, when one believes that one can plan an entire campaign and carry out its planned end . . . The first battle will determine a new situation through which much of the original plan becomes inapplicable.
  Field Marshal Helmuth Graf von Moltke, *Militarische Werke*, IV, 1892-1212.

PLANNING is everything – Plans are nothing.
  Field Marshal Helmuth Graf von Moltke (1880–1891), sign above the entrance to the Joint Staff, Department of Defense, the Pentagon.

THE MAIN THING is always to have a plan; if it is not the best plan, it is at least better than no plan at all.
  General Sir John Monash, 1918, letter.

THE STROKE of genius that turns the fate of a battle? I don't believe in it. A battle is a complicated operation, that you prepare laboriously. If the enemy does this, you say to yourself I will do that. If such and such happens, these are the steps I shall take to meet it. You think out every possible development and decide on the way to deal with the situation created. One of these developments occurs; you put your plan in operation, and everyone says, "What genius . . ." whereas the credit is really due to the labor of preparation.
  Marshal of France Ferdinand Foch, April 1919, interview.

ONCE MORE I spent much time at the front and with the various Army Headquarters in active interchange of ideas on the tactics of offensive fighting, and on the attack itself. Many proposals and counter-proposals, many pros and cons were laid before me. . . . As was my duty, I had to give the ultimate decision. The tactical principles were considered to be correct and readily accepted by the troops. They left room for individual action in all directions.
  General Erich Ludendorff, *My War Memories 1914–1918*, 1919.

NOW, as every policy must be plastic enough to admit of fluctuations in national conditions, so must each plan be plastic enough to receive the impressions of war, that is power to change its shape without changing or cracking its substance. This plasticity is determined psychologically by the condition of mentality in the two opposing forces. There is the determination between the commanders-in-chief, and between them and their men, and ultimately, between the two forces themselves.
  Major-General J.F.C. Fuller, *The Reformation of War*, 1923.

WHEN MAKING a plan, try to put yourself in the enemy's mind, and think what course it is least probable he will foresee and forestall. The surest way to success in war is to choose the course of least expectation. (May 1930.)
  Captain Sir Basil Liddell Hart, *Thoughts on War*, 1944.

TO BE PRACTICAL, any plan must take account of the enemy's power to frustrate it; the best chance of overcoming such obstruction is to have a plan that can easily be varied to fit the circumstances met; to keep such adaptability, while still keeping the initiative, the best way is to operate along a line which offers alternative objectives. For thereby you put your opponent on the horns of a dilemma, which goes far to assure the gaining of at least one objective – whichever is least guarded – and may enable you to gain one after the other.
  Captain Sir Basil Liddell Hart, *How to Win Wars*.

THERE IS a close analogy between what takes place in the mind of a military commander when planning an action, and what happens to the artist at the moment of conception. The latter does not renounce the use of his intelligence. He draws from it lessons, methods, and knowledge. But his power of creation can operate only if he possesses, in addition, a certain instinctive faculty which we call inspiration, for that alone can give the direct contact with nature from which the vital spark must leap. We can say of the military art what Bacon said of the other arts: "They are the product of man added to nature."
  General Charles de Gaulle, *The Edge of the Sword*, 1932.

A PLAN, like a tree, must have branches – if it is to bear fruit. A plan with a single aim is apt to prove a barren pole. (Jan. 1933.)
  Captain Sir Basil Liddell Hart, *Thoughts on War*, 1944.

LET US NOW discuss the question of planning. Because of the uncertainty peculiar to war, it is much more difficult to prosecute war according to plan than is the case with other activities. Yet, since "preparedness ensures success and unpreparedness spells failure", there can be no victory in war without advance planning and preparations. There is no absolute certainty in war, and yet it is not without some degree of relative certainty. We are comparatively certain about our own situation. We are very uncertain about the enemy's, but here too there are signs for us to read, clues to follow and sequences of phenomena to ponder. These form what we call a degree of relative certainty, which provides an objective basis for planning in war.

Mao Tse-tung, *On Protracted War*, May 1938.

IT MAY BE of interest to future generals to realize that one makes plans to fit circumstances and does not try to create circumstances to fit plans. That way lies danger.

General George S. Patton, Jr., 26 February 1945, diary entry, *The Patton Papers*, II, 1974.

A GOOD PLAN violently executed Now is better than a perfect plan next week.

General George S. Patton, Jr., *War As I Knew It*, 1947.

THE PROBLEM that faces strategical planning (and also tactical planning, though in a more restricted sense) is twofold. We must, on the one hand, strive by all means to prevent the enemy from acting on sound principles; on the other hand, a supreme planning effort must be made to enable our forces to exploit those principles, in order to facilitate the achievement of our aims and objectives. For this purpose every principle which the enemy is likely to apply must serve as a target for the ingenuity of those who plan the operation of our forces.

General Yigael Yadin, article in *The Israeli Forces' Journal*, 9/1949.

ON the operational side a C.-in-C. must draw up a master plan for the campaign he envisages and he must always think and plan two battles ahead – the one he is preparing to fight and the next one – so that success gained in one battle can be used as a spring-board for the next. He has got to read the mind of his opponent, to anticipate enemy reactions to his moves, and to take quick steps to prevent enemy interference with his own plans. He has got to be a very clear thinker and able to sort out the essentials from the mass of factors which bear on every problem.

Field Marshal Viscount Montgomery of Alamein, *The Memoirs of Field Marshal Montgomery*, 1958.

THE PLAN of operations must always be made by the commander and must not be forced on him by his staff, or by circumstances, or by the enemy. He has got to relate what is strategically desirable with that which is tactically possible with the forces at his disposal; if this is not done he is unlikely to win. What is possible, given a bit of luck? And what is definitely impossible? That is always the problem. The plan having been made, there will be much detailed work to be done before the operation is launched; this detailed work must be done by the staff. The commander himself must stand back and have time to think: his attention must be directed to ensuring that the basic foundations and corner-stones of the master plan are not broken down by the mass of detail which will necessarily occupy the attention of the staff. If all these things are to be done successfully, a good Chief of Staff is essential.

Field Marshal Viscount Montgomery of Alamein, *The Memoirs of Field Marshal Montgomery*, 1958.

THE COMMANDER must decide how he will fight the battle *before it begins*. He must then decide how he will use the military effort at his disposal to force the battle to swing the way he wishes it to go; he must make the enemy dance to his tune from the beginning, and never vice versa. To be able to do this, his own dispositions must be so balanced that he can utilise but need not react to the enemy's move but can continue relentlessly with his own plan. The question of "balance" was a definite feature of my military creed.

Field Marshal Viscount Montgomery of Alamein, *The Memoirs of Field Marshal Montgomery*, 1958.

BUT IN TRUTH, the larger the command, the more time must go into planning; the longer it will take to move troops into position, to reconnoiter, to accumulate ammunition and other supplies, and to coordinate other participating elements on the ground and in the air. To a conscientious commander, time is the most vital factor in his planning. By proper foresight and correct preliminary action, he knows he can conserve the most precious elements he controls, the lives of his men. So he thinks ahead as far as he can. He keeps his tactical plan simple. He tries to eliminate as many variable factors as he is able. He has a firsthand look at as much of the ground as circumstances render accessible to him. He checks each task in the plan with the man to whom he intends to assign it. Then – having secured in almost every instance his subordinate's wholehearted acceptance of the contemplated mission and agreement on its feasibility – only then does he issue an order.

General Matthew B. Ridgway, *The Korean War*, 1967.

NATURALLY, in the course of a battle, one would like to fulfill the initial plan. . . . – but what does it mean to plan in war? We plan alone, but we fulfill our plans, if one may do so, together with the enemy, that is, taking account of his counteraction.

Marshal of the Soviet Union Ivan S. Koniev (1897–1973), 1972, quoted in Nathan Leites, *The Soviet Style in War*, 1982.

I GREW BIG with these plans. I had merely to cross a river, capture Brussels and then go on and take the port of Antwerp. And all this in the worst months of the year, December, January, February, through the countryside where snow was waist deep and there wasn't room to deploy four tanks abreast, let alone six armoured divisions; when it didn't get light until eight in the morning and was dark again at four in the afternoon; with divisions that had just been reformed and contained chiefly raw, untried recruits; and at Christmas time.

> General Josef 'Sepp' Dietrich (1892–1966), sarcastic comment on the German planning for the Battle of the Bulge, quoted in Charles Messenger, *Hitler's Gladiator*, 1987.

I EMPHASIZED meticulous planning not simply because I thought it was the most effective approach, which it is, but because by taking that approach you enforce on your subordinates the same necessity. They have to learn every detail of the topography, every position, every soldier they will be facing. And once they do that, they will be able to decide rationally – not intuitively – on the steps they have to take. They will make their decisions on the basis of knowledge. Experience had also taught me that if you lay your plans in detail before you are under the stress of fighting, the chances are much greater that you will be able to implement at least the outlines of the plans despite the contingencies of battle.

> General Ariel Sharon, *Warrior*, 1989.

ANY DAMNED FOOL can write a plan. It's the execution that gets you screwed up.

> General James F. Hollingsworth, quoted in John D. Lock, *To Fight With Intrepidity*, 1998.

THE PLAN was smooth on paper, only they forgot about the ravines.

> Russian military proverb.

POLITICS AND THE MILITARY

WHATEVER TALENTS I may possess (and they are but limited) are military talents. My education and training are military. I think the military and the civil talents are distinct, if not different, and full duty in either sphere is about as much as one man can qualify himself to perform. I shall not do the people the injustice to accept high civil office with whose questions it has not been my business to become familiar.

> General Robert E. Lee's conversation with Senator B.H. Hill, recounted in a post-war speech, quoted in William Jones, *Personal Reminiscences, Anecdotes, and Letters of Gen. Robert E. Lee*, 1874.

AVOID all political entanglements. I have always thought the most slavish life any man could lead was that of a politician. Besides I do not believe any man can be successful as a soldier whilst he has an anchor ahead for other advancement. I know of no circumstances likely to arise which could induce me to accept of any political office whatever. My only desire will be, as it has always

been, to whip out the rebellion in the shortest way possible and to retain as high a position in the Army afterwards as the Administration then in power may think me suitable for.

> General Ulysses S. Grant, 16 February 1864, letter to Commander Daniel Ammen, *Papers of USG*, X, 1982, pp. 132–133.

WAR cannot for a single minute be separated from politics.

> Mao Tse-tung, 1938, lecture.

MY LIFE is a mixture of politics and war. The latter is bad enough – but I've been trained for it! The former is straight and unadulterated venom! But I have to devote lots of my time, and much more of my good disposition, to it.

> General of the Army Dwight D. Eisenhower, 27 September 1943, letter to his wife.

THERE WAS a constant infiltration of enemy forces from the Laotian border, who were protected by the political restrictions from Washington that prevented us from knocking out their reinforcement bases or supply lines. We would constantly be pushing them back, but they had a damned sanctuary across the border guaranteed by American politicians. So we had to take back the same areas over and over again. I don't think there was a guy, from private to general, who didn't have a stench in his mouth from the politics of the war.

> Major-General James Day, 'Bushido Code', Al Santoli, ed., *Leading the Way: How Vietnam Veterans Rebuilt the U.S. Military*, 1993.

IN A NORMAL STATE, you cannot drive the army into politics with a stick. But our army [Russian] has been systematically politicized. Recall the slogans of 1993, not very long ago – the Army is outside politics. But who decided the outcome of the political confrontation in the fall of that very year at the White House? The Army. Who turned out to be the country's main political figure? The commander of a tank regiment. It was he who presented his 125-mm political arguments and decided the outcome of the campaign. One can only guess what would have happened had he presented his arguments on the other side.

> General Aleksandr I. Lebed, speaking of the participation of Russian Army elements in the suppression of the October 1993 coup in Moscow, *Literaturnaya Gazeta* (Moscow), 17 May 1995.

POWER

THE RIGHT USE of the sword is that it should subdue the barbarians while lying gleaming in its scabbard. If it leaves its sheath it cannot be said to be used rightly. Similarly the right use of military power is that it should conquer the enemy while concealed in the breast. To

take the field with an army is to be found wanting in the real knowledge of it. Those who hold the office of Shogun are to be particularly clear on this point.
Tokugawa Ieyasu (1543–1616), quoted in A.L. Sadler, *The Maker of Modern Japan: The Life of Tokugawa Ieyasu*, 1937.

POWER is my mistress. I have worked too hard in conquering her to allow anyone to take her from me or even to covet her.
Napoleon, in conversation with Pierre-Louis Roederer, 1804, *Journal du comte P.-L. Roederer*, 1909.

THERE ARE no manifestos like cannon and musketry.
The Duke of Wellington (1769–1852).

THE ONLY PRIZE much cared for by the powerful is power. The prize of the general is not a bigger tent, but command.
Justice Oliver Wendell Holmes, Jr., 15 February 1913, speech to Harvard Law School Association of New York.

POWER without responsibility: the prerogative of the harlot thoughout the ages.
Rudyard Kipling, *Kipling Journal*, December 1971.

ALL PEOPLES, whether they be orientals or occidentals, are far more impressed by an exhibition of power than by the perusal of diplomatic notes.
Major-General John A. Lejeune, *The Reminiscences of a Marine*, 1929.

POLITICAL POWER emanates from the barrel of a gun.
Mao Tse-tung, *On Guerrilla Warfare*, 1938.

WHOEVER has the army has power, and war decides everything.
Mao Tse-tung, *Selected Military Writings*, 1963.

LEADERS who share their power and their time can accomplish extraordinary things. The best leaders understand that leadership is the liberation of talent; hence they gain power not only by constantly giving it away, but also by not grabbing it back.
Major-General Perry M. Smith, 'Learning to Lead', *Marine Corps Gazette*, January 1997.

POWER is never handed over. It is taken.
General Aleksandr I. Lebed, *El Pais* (Madrid) 15 March 1998.

PRAISE

PRAISE from a friend, or censure from a foe,
Are lost on hearers that our merits know.
Homer, *The Iliad*, c. 800 BC, tr. Alexander Pope, 1743.

FOR MEN can endure to hear others praised only so long as they can severally persuade themselves of their ability to equal the actions recounted; when this point is passed, envy comes and with it incredulity.
Pericles, quoted in Thucydides, *History of the Peloponnesian War*, 2.120, c. 404 BC, tr. Richard Crowley, 1910.

THE MOST PLEASING of all sounds is that of your own praise.
Xenophon, *Hiero*, c. 360 BC, tr. Waterfield, 1997.

WHEN a general gives a public speech he ought also to say something in praise of the enemy. This will convince our men, even when you are praising others, that you will never deprive us of the praise we might receive from others and adorn them with our honors.
The Emperor Maurice, *The Strategikon*, c. AD 600 (*Maurice's Strategikon*, tr. George Dennis, 1984).

THE DESIRE to imitate brave actions will be aroused by praise. And these trifles will diffuse a spirit of emulation among troops which affects both officers and soldiers and in time will make them invincible.
Field Marshal Maurice Comte de Saxe, *My Reveries*, 1732, tr. Phillips, 1940.

THE GENERAL can even discuss the war with some of his corps commanders who are most intelligent, and permit them to express their sentiments freely in conversation. If you find some good among what they say, you should not remark about it then, but make use of it. When this has been done, you should speak about it in the presence of many others, it was so-and-so who had this idea; praise him for it. This modesty will gain the general the friendship of thinking men, and he will more easily find persons who will speak their sentiments sincerely to him.
Frederick the Great, *Instructions to His Generals*, 1747, tr. Phillips, 1940.

PRAISE from enemies is suspicious; it cannot flatter an honorable man unless it is given after the cessation of hostilities.
Napoleon, *The Military Maxims of Napoleon*, tr. Burnod, 1827.

PLEASE SAY a kind word to my army that I can repeat to them in general orders in regard to their conduct at Yorktown, Williamsburg, West Point, Hanover Court-House, and on the Chickahominy, as well as in regard to the Seven Days and the recent retreat.
No one has ever said anything to cheer them but myself. Say nothing about me. Merely give my men and officers credit for what they have done. It will do you much good, and will strengthen you much with

them, if you issue a handsome order to them in regard to what they have accomplished. They deserve it.

Major-General George B. McClellan, dispatch to Major-General Halleck, then General-in-Chief of the Union Armies, 18 August 1862, *McClellan's Own Story*, 1887.

AND DON'T FORGET a good word for the cooks.

Lieutenant-General Sir Leslie Morshead (1889–1959), at a commanders' conference after the Battle of El Alamein, quoted in Horner, *The Commanders*, 1984.

HUMILITY must always be the portion of any man who receives acclaim earned in the blood of his followers and the sacrifices of his friends.

General of the Army Dwight D. Eisenhower, 12 June 1945, address in London.

ALL a soldier desires to drive him forward is recognition and appreciation of his work.

General George S. Patton, Jr. (1885–1947).

YOU MUST get around and show interest in what your subordinates are doing even if you don't know much about the technique of their work. And when you are making these visits, try to pass out praise then due, as well as corrections and criticisms.

General of the Army Omar N. Bradley, 16 May 1967, speech to the U.S. Army Command and General Staff College.

A GENERAL must never be chary in alloting praise where it is due. People like to be praised when they have done well. In this connection Sir Winston Churchill once told me of the reply made by the Duke of Wellington, in his last years, when a friend asked him: "If you had your life over again, is there any way in which you could have done better?" The old Duke replied: "Yes, I should have given more praise."

Field Marshal Viscount Montgomery of Alamein, *A History of Warfare*, 1968.

IN COMMAND and leadership many qualities, attributes and techniques are required – including drive, force, judgment, perception and others. But nothing can replace the inspiration and lift that comes from commending a job well done.

Major-General Aubrey 'Red' Newman, *Follow Me*, 1981.

PRAYER

BEFORE doing anything else, you should offer up a sacrifice and ask the gods to ensure that the way in which you conduct your command – your thoughts, words and deeds – not only may afford them particular pleasure, but also may be particularly effective in bringing yourself, your friends and your state alliances, honour and general benefit.

Xenophon, *How To Be A Good Cavalry Commander*, c. 360 BC (*Hiero the Tyrant and Other Treatises*, tr. Robin Waterfield, 1997).

PRAYING HARD is fighting hard.

King Gustavus II Adolphus (1594–1632).

ON a lonely road just south of Pyongyang, a lonely commander was deeply troubled by the threat to the men he was charged with safeguarding. Could he do the job that was his to do and still give his men a fighting chance to survive? And out of the still of the night, as if from a great distance, came God's voice saying, "Be strong, have no fear, I am with you."

General Harold K. Johnson (1912–1983), of his experience as a battalion commander during the Korean War when asked to say a prayer at breakfasts and on similar occasions.

AS THE SOLDIER prays for peace he must be prepared to cope with the hardships of war and to bear its scars.

General William Westmoreland, *A Soldier Reports*, 1976.

PRAYERS AND HYMNS

IT IS GOD that girdeth me with strength, and maketh my way perfect.

He maketh my feet like hinds' feet, and setteth me upon my high places.

He teacheth my hands to war, so that a bow of steel is broken by my own arms.

Thou hast also given me the shield of thy salvation: and thy right hand hath holden me up, and thy gentleness hath made me great.

Thou hast enlarged my steps under me, that my feet did not slip.

I have pursued mine enemies, and over-taken: neither did I turn again till they were consumed.

I have wounded them that that they were not able to rise: they are fallen under my feet.

For thou hast girded me with strength unto the battle: thou hast subdued under me those that rose up against me.

Thou hast also given me the necks of mine enemies; that I might destroy them that hate me.

They cried, but *there was* none to save *them: even* unto the LORD, but he answered them not.

King David (d. 962 BC), Psalms 18:32–41.

EVEN THE GODS, I say, with incense, soothing vows, with full cups poured and the deep smoky savor men can bring them round, begging pardon when one oversteps the mark, does something wrong. We do have Prayers, you know, Prayers for forgiveness, daughters of mighty Zeus . . . and they limp and halt, they're all wrinkled, drawn, they squint to the side, can't look you in the eyes, and always bent on duty, trudging after Ruin, maddening, blinding Ruin. But Ruin is strong and swift – She outstrips them all by far, stealing a march,

leaping over the whole wide earth to bring mankind
to grief.
And the Prayers trail after, trying to heal the wounds.
And then, if a man reveres these daughters of Zeus
as they draw near him, they will help him greatly
and listen to his appeals. But if one denies them,
turns them away, stiff-necked and harsh – off they go
to the son of Cronus, Zeus, and pray that Ruin
will strike the man down, crazed and blinded
until he's paid the price.

Homer, *The Iliad*, 9.605–624, c. 800 BC,
tr. Robert Fagles, 1990; Thetis to her son, Achilles,
begging him to relent his vow not to fight for
the Achaeans until Agamemnon had assuaged
his honour.

MIGHTY ARES, golden-helmeted rider of chariots,
stout-hearted, shield-carrying and bronze-geared
savior of cities,
strong-handed and unwearing lord of the spear,
bulwark of Olympos,
father of fair Victory, and succorer of Themis.
You curb the unruly and lead truly just men,
O paragon of manly excellence, wheeling your
luminous orb
through the seven-pathed constellations of the sky,
where flaming
steeds ever carry you above the third heavenly arch.
Hearken, helper of mortals and giver of
flourishing youth,
and from above shine a gentle light on my life
and my martial prowess, that I may be able
to ward off bitter cowardice from my head,
to bend wisely my soul's beguiling impulse
and to restrain the sharp fury of my heart, whenever
it provokes me to enter chilling battle. But, O
blessed one,
give me courage to stay within the secure laws
of peace
and to escape the enemy's charge and violent death.

Homer, c. 800 BC, Hymn to Ares, the War
God, quoted in Athanassakis, *The Homeric
Hymns*, 1976.

I BEGIN to sing of Pallas Athena, defender of cities,
awesome goddess; she and Ares care for deeds
of war,
cities being sacked and cries of battle.
And she protects an army going to war and returning.
Hail, O goddess, and grant me good fortune and
happiness.

Homer, c. 800 BC, Hymn to Athena, quoted in
Athanassakis, *The Homeric Hymns*, 1976.

DEAR LORD, I pray Thee to suffer me not to see
Thy Holy City, since I cannot deliver it from the
hands of Thy enemies.

King Richard I, 'The Lion Heart', King of
England, 1192, on approaching Jerusalem,
the object of his Crusade, which he was never
to conquer.

O LORD GOD, when Thou givest to thy servants to
endeavor any great matter, grant us also to know
that it is not the beginning, but the continuing of the
same until it is thoroughly finished which yieldeth the
true glory.

Sir Francis Drake (c. 1540–1596).

OH LORD! Thou knowest how busy I must be this
day: if I forget Thee, do not Thou forget me. March
on, boys!

Sir Jacob Hill, 23 October 1642, before the Battle of
Edgehill during the English Civil War.

OH GOD, let me not be disgraced in my old days.
Or if Thou wilt not help me, do not help these
scoundrels; but leave us to try it ourselves.

Leopold I of Anhalt-Dessau, 'The Old Dessauer',
14 December 1745, before the Battle of Kesselsdorf.

DOWN, down with the French! . . . is my
constant prayer.

Admiral Viscount Nelson, December 1798, quoted in
Robert Southey, *Life of Nelson*, 1813.

MAY the Great God whom I worship grant to my
Country, and for the benefit of Europe in general,
a great and glorious victory; and may no
misconduct in any way tarnish it; and may
humanity after Victory be the predominant feature
in the British Fleet. For myself individually, I
commit my life to Him who made me, and may his
blessing light upon my endeavours for serving my
Country faithfully. To Him I resign myself and the
just cause which is entrusted to me to defend.
Amen. Amen. Amen.

Admiral Viscount Nelson, 21 October 1805, diary
prayer before the Battle of Trafalgar.

O LORD, if Thou wilt not be for us today, we ask that
Thou be not against us. Just leave it between the
French and ourselves.

Lieutenant-General Sir Alan Campbell of Erracht,
prayer before battle, c. 1809.

HYMM BEFORE ACTION
1896

The earth is full of anger
The seas are dark with wrath,
The nations in their harness
Go up against our path:
Ere yet we loose the legions
Ere yet we draw the blade,
Jehovah of the Thunders,
Lord God of Battles, aid!

Rudyard Kipling.

PLEASE GOD – let there be victory, before the
Americans arrive.

Field Marshal Douglas Earl Haig, 1917 diary entry
– attributed.

HIGH FLIGHT

Oh! I have slipped the surly bonds of Earth
And danced the skies on laughter-silvered wings;
Sunward I've climbed, and joined the tumbling mirth
of sun-split clouds, – and done a hundred things
You have not dreamed of – wheeled and soared
   and swung
High in the sunlit silence. Hov'ring there,
I've chased the shouting wind along, and flung
My eager craft through footless halls of air. . . .

Up, up the long delirious, burning blue
I've topped the wind-swept heights with easy grace
Where never lark nor ever eagle flew –
And, while with silent lifting mind I've trod
The high untrespassed sanctity of space,
Put out my hand, and touched the face of God.

Flying Officer John G. Magee, Royal Canadian Air
Force, 3 September 1941. An American volunteer in
the RCAF, Magee flew Spitfires in Britain and was
killed on a routine training mission on 11 December
1941. He had just sent the sonnet on the back of a
letter, saying, 'I am enclosing a verse I wrote the other
day. It started at 30,000 feet, and was finished soon
after I landed.'

FINALLY, knowing the vanities of man's effort and
the confusion of his purpose, let us pray that God
may accept our services and direct our endeavours,
so that when we shall have done all we shall see the
fruits of our labours and be satisfied.

Major-General Orde Wingate, February 1943, *Order of
the Day*, Imphal.

A PRAYER FOR THE FALLEN

With spirits righteous and perfected, repose the
soul of Thy servant, O Saviour; keeping it unto the
blessed life which is with Thee, O Thou Who
lovest mankind.

Amongst the Saints give rest, O Christ to the soul
of Thy servant: where no pain existeth, nor grief, nor
sighing, but life everlasting.

For Thou art the Resurrection of Thy departed
servants, O Christ our God, and unto Thee do we
bring hymns of glory, together with Thy Father, Who
is from everlasting, and Thine all-holy and righteous
and life-giving Spirit, now and ever, and unto the
ages of ages, Amen.

Be his memory eternal!

Orthodox Prayer Book, for the use of soldiers and
sailors of the United States of America, issued by the
Greek Orthodox Archdiocese of North and South
America, 1944.

ALMIGHTY GOD: Our sons, pride of our nation, this
day have set upon a mighty endeavor, a struggle to
preserve our republic, our religion, and our
civilization, and to set free a suffering humanity.
Lead them straight and true: Give strength to their
arms, stoutness to their hearts, steadfastness to
their faith.

President Franklin D. Roosevelt, 6 June 1944, D-Day
Prayer broadcast to the nation over the radio.

ALMIGHTY and most merciful Father, we humbly
beseech Thee, of Thy great goodness, to restrain
these immoderate rains with which we have had to
contend. Grant us fair weather for Battle. Graciously
harken to us as soldiers who call upon Thee that,
armed with Thy power, we may advance from victory
to victory, and crush the oppression and wickedness
of our enemies, and establish Thy justice among
men and nations. Amen.

Colonel James H. O'Neil, 24 December 1944, the
famous weather prayer that General George S.
Patton, Jr., ordered him to write as Chaplain of the
Third Army during the Battle of the Bulge, quoted in
Ladislas Farago, *Patton, Ordeal and Triumph*, 1964.

GOD of our Father, who by land and sea has ever
led us on to victory, please continue Your inspiring
guidance in this the greatest of our conflicts.

Strengthen my soul so that the weakening instinct of
self-preservation, which besets all of us in battle,
shall not blind me to my duty to my own manhood,
to the glory of my calling, and to my responsibility to
my fellow soldiers.

Grant to our armed forces that disciplined valor
and mutual confidence which ensures success
in war.

Let me not mourn for the men who have died
fighting, but rather let me be glad that such heroes
have lived.

If it be my lot to die, let me do so with courage and
honor in a manner which will bring the greatest harm
to the enemy, and please, oh, Lord, protect and
guide those I shall leave behind.

Give us victory, Lord.

General George S. Patton, Jr. (1885–1947).

PREPARATION

THE MAN who is prepared has his battle half fought.

Miguel de Cervantes, *Don Quixote*, 1615.

YOU HAVE NOT done anything in as much as you
still have something to do.

Napoleon (1769–1821).

VICTORY smiles in general upon those only who
know how to command it by good preparations. It is
seldom the effect of chance or of unexpected good
luck, but the fruit and recompense culled by the
experienced soldier, whose discernment is

supported by the resolution and boldness of his undertakings.

Marshal of France Michel Ney, Duc d'Elchingen, Prince de la Moskova, *Memoirs of Marshal Ney*, 1834.

NAPOLEON made sure that he might dare, and dared.

Napoleon, dictation c. 1817, St. Helena, on the capture of Malta, 1798, quoted in Christopher Herold, ed., *The Mind of Napoleon*, 1955.

THE ENEMY opened fire at 2:08 and our First Division bore it for a few minutes and replied at about 2:11. The number of enemy shells fired during these few minutes exceeded 300 and the *Mikasa* was damaged and had casualties before she had fired a shot. About a half hour later the enemy's battle formation was entirely out of order, so that the fate of our empire was really settled within this first half hour. The *Mikasa* and the eleven others of the main force had taken years of labor to design and build, and yet they were used for only half an hour of decisive battle. We, too, studied the art of war and trained ourselves in it, but it was put to use for only that short period. Though the decisive battle took such a short time, it required ten years of preparation.

Admiral Marquis Heihachiro Togo (1846–1934), speaking of the Battle of Tshushima, 1905, and his flagship, the *Mikasa*, quoted in Dennis and Peggy Warner, *The Tide at Sunrise*, 1974.

IT CANNOT BE too often repeated that in modern war, and especially in modern naval war, the chief factor in achieving triumph is what has been done in the way of thorough preparation and training before the beginning of war.

President Theodore Roosevelt, June 1902, graduation address at the U.S. Naval Academy.

THERE MUST BE no tendency to excuse incomplete readiness for war on the premise of future acquisition of trained personnel or modernized material . . . personnel shall be trained and rendered competent . . . existing material shall be maintained and utilized at its maximum effectiveness at all times.

Fleet Admiral Ernest J. King, *Fleet Admiral Ernest J. King, A Naval Record*, 1942.

PREPAREDNESS

NOW, it happened through this god, the lord of gods, that I was prepared and armed to trap them like wild fowl. He furnished my strength and caused my plans to prosper. I went forth, directing these marvelous things. I equipped my frontier in Zahi, prepared before them. The chiefs, the captains of infantry, the nobles, I caused to equip the harbor-mouths, like a strong wall, with warships, galleys and barges . . . They were manned completely from bow to stern with valiant warriors bearing their arms, soldiers of all the choicest of Egypt, being like lions roaring upon the mountain tops. The charioteers were warriors . . . and all good officers . . . ready of hand. Their horses were quivering in their every limb, ready to crush the countries under their feet. I was valiant Montu, stationed before them, that they might behold the hand-to-hand fighting of my own arms. I, King Rameses III, was made a far-striding hero, conscious of his might, valiant to lead his army in the day of battle.

Rameses III, Pharaoh of Egypt, c. 1190 BC, of the Northern War against Peoples of the Sea, quoted in James Breasted, *Ancient Records of Egypt*, 1906.

IF WE UNDERTAKE this war without preparation, we should by hastening its commencement only delay its conclusion.

Archidamus II, King of Sparta, 432 BC, speech on the prospects of war with Athens, quoted in Thucydides, *History of the Peloponnesian War*, 1.84, c. 404 BC, tr. Richard Crawley, 1910.

HE, therefore, who aspires to peace should prepare for war.

Flavius Vegetius Renatus, *Military Institutions of the Romans*, c. AD 378, tr. Clark, 1776.

SAGES are very careful not to forget about danger when secure, nor to forget about chaos in times of order. Even when there is peace in the land, it will not do to abandon the military altogether. If you lack foresight, you will be defenseless. It is necessary to develop cultured qualities internally while organizing military preparedness externally. Be considerate and gentle with foreigners, beware of the unexpected. Routine military exercises in each of the four seasons is the way to show that the nation is not oblivious to warfare. Not forgetting about warfare means teaching the people not to give up the practice of martial arts.

The rule is "Even if the land is at peace, to forget about warfare leads to collapse."

Liu Ji (1310–1375), *Lessons of War* (*Mastering the Art of War*, tr. Thomas Cleary, 1989).

HAPPY is that city which in time of peace thinks of war.

Inscription in the Armory of Venice.

THERE CANNOT BE good laws where there are not good arms.

Niccolo Machiavelli, *The Prince*, 1513.

A RICH MAN without arms must be prey to a poor soldier well armed.

Niccolo Machiavelli, *The Art of War*, 1521.

THE ARTS of peace and the arts of war are like two wheels of a cart which, lacking one, will have difficulty in standing. Naturally, the arts of peace are used during times of tranquility and those of war during times of confusion, but it is most essential to not forget the military during peaceful times nor to disregard scholastics during time of war. When the master of a province feels that the world is in peace and forgets the arts of war, first, military tactics will fall into disuse, the warriors of his clan will naturally become effeminate and lose interest in martial ways, the martial arts will be neglected, the variety of weapons will be insufficient, weapons handed down through the generations will become rusty and rot, and there will be nothing of any use during times of emergency. If the Way of the Warrior is thus neglected, ordinary military tactics will not be established; if a military situation were to suddenly arise there would be panic and confusion, consultation would be unprepared for, and the establishment of strategy would be difficult. When one has been born into the house of a military commander, he should not forget the arts of war even for a moment.

> Kuroda Nagamasa (1568–1623), *Notes on Regulations*, 1622 (*Ideals of the Samurai*, tr. William Wilson, 1982).

AFTER a fatal procrastination, not only of vigorous measures but of preparation for such, we took a step as decisive as the passage of the Rubicon, and now find ourselves plunged at once in a most serious war without a single requisition, gunpowder excepted, for carrying it on.

> General Sir John Burgoyne, letter from Boston, April 1775, after the Battles of Lexington and Concord.

THERE IS NOTHING so likely to produce peace as to be well prepared to meet an enemy.

> General George Washington, 29 January 1780, letter to Elbridge Gerry.

A FREE PEOPLE ought not only to be armed, but disciplined; to which end a uniform and well digested plan is requisite. . . .

> General George Washington, 8 January 1790, XXX, 1939, p. 491.

THAT PEOPLE will continue the longest in the enjoyment of peace who timely prepare to vindicate themselves and manifest a determination to protect themselves whenever they are wronged.

> Tecumseh, late 1811, to a great Indian council of the southern tribes, urging alliance against the expanding Americans.

DEFENSIVE POLICY of the U.S. – Does not alter PACIFIC POLICY of U.S. Be as pacific as you please but do not let the other fellow catch you unprepared.

> Lieutenant-General Robert L. Bullard, 1911, journal entry.

PREPAREDNESS does not mean militarism or an aggressive military spirit; it means simply the application to the military questions of the day of something of the experience and lessons of the past as well as those of the present. A man armed against thieves is not prone to become a thief unless he is one at heart. A nation can be strong without being immoral or a bully.

> Major-General Leonard Wood, *Our Military History: Its Facts and Fallacies*, 1916.

NATURALLY ENOUGH, military problems are anathema to the men in power. Nobody, whether a spendthrift or a miser likes getting bills. Though, in the last analysis, armaments are the consequences of policy, governments are afraid to impose them until immediate danger makes them obviously essential. On the contrary, when a long period of peace is promised, they are the first to put ships out of commission and disband regiments.

> General Charles de Gaulle, *The Edge of the Sword*, 1932.

TO MAINTAIN in peace a needlessly elaborate military establishment entails economic waste. But there can be no compromise with minimum requirements. In war there is no intermediate measure of success. Second best is to be defeated, and military defeat carries with it national disaster – political, economic, social, and spiritual disaster.

> General of the Army Douglas MacArthur, *Annual Report of the Chief of Staff, June 30, 1935*.

WANT OF FORESIGHT, unwillingness to act when action would be simple and effective, lack of clear thinking, confusion of counsel until the emergency comes, until self-preservation strikes its jarring gong – these are the features which constitute the endless repetition of history.

> Sir Winston S. Churchill, speech in the House of Commons, 2 May 1935, *Winston S. Churchill: His Complete Speeches, 1897–1963*, VI, 1974, p. 5592.

THE FIRST VICTORY we have to win is to avoid a battle; the second if we cannot avoid it, to win it.

> Sir Winston S. Churchill (1874–1965).

WE MUST be prepared. . . . [It] is good to be patient, it is good to be circumspect, it is good to be peace-loving – but it is not enough. We must be strong, we must be self-reliant.

> Sir Winston S. Churchill (1874–1965).

WITHOUT preparedness superiority is not real superiority and there can be no initiative either. Having grasped this point, a force which is inferior but prepared can often defeat a superior enemy by surprise attack.

> Mao Tse-tung, *On Protracted War*, May 1938.

VIRTUOUS MOTIVES, trammeled by inertia and timidity, are no match for armed and resolute wickedness. A sincere love of peace is not excuse for muddling hundreds of millions of humble folk into total war. The cheers of weak, well-meaning assemblies soon cease to echo, and their votes soon cease to count. Doom marches on.

Sir Winston S. Churchill, *The Gathering Storm*, 1948.

NO FOREIGN POLICY can have validity if there is no adequate force behind it and no national readiness to make the necessary sacrifices to produce that force.

Sir Winston S. Churchill, *The Gathering Storm*, 1948.

WE SLEEP safely in our beds because rough men stand ready in the night to visit violence on those who would harm us.

George Orwell (1903–1950), quoted in George Will, 'Rough and Ready', *The Washington Post*, 22 November 1998.

THE STRENGTH of the nation is dependent upon the integrity and wisdom of the government, upon the economic stability of the country, and upon the strength of the armed forces. . . . Not all the things that are desirable can be done. There must be balances between military requirements and requirements for the supporting (civilian) economy, between offensive and defensive measures, between military control and civilian control, between centralization and decentralization. There are balances within each of the services. . . . To win a war, or to keep the peace, the United States will require all hands, each with an appointed task, each doing that task well. . . .

Admiral Arleigh '31-Knot' Burke, *U.S. Naval Institute Proceedings*, 12/1948.

THE LACK of manpower became more and more desperate during the war, and the almost untrained troops who were brought up to fill the gaps in the ranks suffered disproportionately heavy losses. The economies achieved in time of peace had now to be paid for in blood. The officer cadres of peacetime were insufficient and largely used up after years of exhausting work. Both officers and non-commissioned officers of the reserve carried out their duties with the greatest devotion, but they could naturally not take the place of regular cadres. The war trained them, but the price was too high.

Field Marshal Carl Gustav Baron von Mannerheim, *The Memoirs of Marshal Mannerheim*, 1953.

GENERALS have often been reproached with preparing for the last war instead of for the next – an easy gibe when their fellow countrymen and their political leaders, too frequently, have prepared for no war at all. Preparation for war is an expensive, burdensome business, yet there is one important part of it that costs little – study. However changed and strange the new conditions of war may be, not only generals, but politicians and ordinary citizens, may find there is much to be learned from the past that can be applied to the future and, in their search for it, that some campaigns have more than others

foreshadowed the coming modern war. I believe that ours in Burma was one of these.

Field Marshal Viscount Slim of Burma, *Defeat Into Victory*, 1956.

IT IS customary in the democratic countries to deplore expenditures on armaments as conflicting with the requirements of social services. There is a tendency to forget that the most important social service a government can do for its people is to keep them alive and free.

Air Marshal Sir John Slessor (1897–1979).

THE MOST DIFFICULT military problem to resolve is that of establishing a security system, as inexpensively as possible in time of peace, capable of transforming itself very rapidly into a powerful force in case of the danger of aggression.

General André Beaufre, *Strategy for Tomorrow*, 1974.

IF the United States is ever defeated in a war, The Congress and the people will not be impressed by the services' education and social rehabilitation programs.

Lieutenant-General Arthur S. Collins, Jr., *Common Sense Training*, 1978.

PEACE is not preordained. It does not keep itself. If we really want to avoid war, if we want to prevent it and preserve peace, we must heed Secretary of War Elihu Root's admonition to General MacArthur's West Point class of 1903 and acknowledge that "according to all precedents in history, [there] will be another war and we must prepare for it." And the best way to do that, the surest prevention against war, is to have an army of substance with a genuine capacity to deter war and, if necessary, inflict real punishment in a timely manner. People really do pay attention to armies of substance.

General Gordon R. Sullivan, 3 June 1995, Commencement Address to the graduating class at the United States Military Academy at West Point.

THE PRESS

FOUR hostile newspapers were more to be feared than a thousand bayonets.

Napoleon, quoted in Liddell Hart, *The Sword and the Pen*, 1976.

YOU SEE ME master of France; well, I would not undertake to govern her for three months with liberty of the press.

Napoleon, to Prince Metternich, quoted in Louis de Bourrienne, *The Memoirs of Napoleon Bonaparte*, I, 1855.

POSSIBLE? Is anything possible? Read the newspapers.

The Duke of Wellington (1769–1821), quoted in William Fraser, *Words of Wellington*, 1889.

I WAS HONOURED by a good deal of abuse from some at home for telling the truth. But I could not tell lies or make things pleasant. . . . The only thing the partisans of misrule could allege was that I did not "make things pleasant" for the authorities and that, amid the filth and starvation, and deadly stagnation of the camp, I did not go about "babbling of green fields" of present abundances and of prospect of victory.

> William Howard Russell, the first of the great war correspondents, of his reporting during the Crimean War, *Crimea Despatches, 1854–1855*, 1966.

THEY DO NOT contribute to our self respect, or to a solution of the troubles of the country.

> General Robert E. Lee, referring to the nation's newspapers, letter to his wife, 2 July 1861, *The Wartime Papers of Robert E. Lee*, 1961.

SO you think the papers ought to say more about your husband! My brigade is not a brigade of newspaper correspondents.

> Lieutenant-General Thomas J. 'Stonewall' Jackson, 5 August 1861, letter to his wife after the First Battle of Manassas.

I AM SORRY, as you say, that the movements of the armies cannot keep pace with the expectations of the editors of papers. I know they can regulate matters satisfactorily to themselves on paper. I wish they could do so in the field. No one wishes them more success than I do & would be happy to see them have full swing. Genl Floyd has the benefit of three editors on his staff. I hope something will be done to please them.

> General Robert E. Lee, letter to his wife, 7 October 1861, quoted in *Wartime Papers of Robert E. Lee*, 1961.

SUPPRESS the entire press of Memphis for giving aid and comfort to the enemy by publishing in their columns every move made here by troops and every work commenced. Arrest the Editor of the Bulletin and send him here a prisoner, under guard, for his publication of present plans via New Carthage & Grand Gulf.

I am satisfied that much has found its way into the public press through that incorrigibly gassy man Col. Bissell of the Eng. Regt. I sent him to you thinking he could not do so much harm there as here. His tongue will have to be tied if there is anything going on where he is which you don't want made public. I feel a strong inclination to arrest him and trust to find evidence against him afterwards.

> General Ulysses S. Grant, letter to Major-General S.A. Hurlbut, commanding the 16th Corps, 9 April 1863, *Personal Memoirs of U.S.Grant, Selected Letters 1839–1865*, 1990.

THE PRESS caused the war, the press gives it point and bitterness, and as long as the press, both North and South, is allowed to fan the flames of discord and hostility, so long must the war last. The Southern press is just the same, and as long as people look to the press for truth and counsel so long will war and anarchy prevail. The liberty of the press, like that of individuals, must be restrained to just limits consistent with the good of the whole, and every fool must not be allowed to print and publish falsehood and slander as he pleases. . . .

> General William T. Sherman, 9 June 1864, letter to his wife from Acworth, Georgia, *Home Letters of General Sherman*, 1909.

WHY, SIR, in the beginning we appointed all our worst generals to command the armies, and all our best generals to edit the newspapers. As you know, I have planned some campaigns and quite a number of battles. I have given the work all the care and thought I could, and sometimes, when my plans were completed, as far as I could see, they seemed to be perfect. But when I have fought them through, I have discovered defects and occasionally wondered why I did not see some of the defects in advance. When it was all over, I found by reading a newspaper that these best editor generals saw all the defects plainly from the start. Unfortunately, they did not communicate their knowledge to me until it was too late. . . . I have no ambition but to serve the Confederacy, and do all I can to win our independence. I am willing to serve in any capacity to which the authorities assign me. I have done the best I could in the field, and have not succeeded as I could wish. I am willing to yield my place to these best generals, and I will do my best for the cause editing a newspaper.

> General Robert E. Lee's conversation with Senator B.H. Hill, as recounted in a post-war speech, quoted in J. William Jones, *Personal Reminiscences, Anecdotes, and Letters of Gen. Robert E. Lee*, 1874.

EVERY COUNTRY is finally answerable for the wanton mischief done by its newspapers, and the reckoning is liable to be presented some day in the shape of a final decision from some other country.

> Prince Otto von Bismarck, speech to the Reichstag, 6 February 1888, quoted in Lewis Copeland, ed., *The World's Great Speeches*, 1952.

THE PRINTING PRESS is the greatest weapon in the armory of the modern commander.

> Colonel T.E. Lawrence (1888–1935).

WHO can ascertain the truth about a cannon shot fired in the thick of night from a mutinous ship at a Czar's palace where the last government of the possessing classes is going out like an oil-less lamp? But just the same, the historian will make no mistake if he says that on October 25th not only was the electric current shut off in the government printing plant but an important page was turned in the history of mankind.

> Leon Trotsky, *History of the Russian Revolution*, 1932.

THE ESSENCE of successful warfare is secrecy. The essence of successful journalism is publicity.
British Regulations for War Correspondents, 1958.

IN GENERAL, journalism appears to nurture the pontifical judgment. I was on occasion reminded of General Eisenhower's remark to a publisher who had told him at length what was wrong with the conduct of World War II. "I thought it was only in the world's oldest profession," General Eisenhower said, "that amateurs think they can do better than professionals."
General William Westmoreland, *A Soldier Reports*, 1976.

IT MAY WELL BE that between press and officials there is an inherent, built-in conflict of interest. There is something to be said for both sides, but when the nation is at war and men's lives are at stake, there should be no ambiguity.
General William Westmoreland, *A Soldier Reports*, 1976.

WARS by definition require a hardness of heart that looks terrible on television. Ulysses Grant would have lost his job in a week if he had had to discuss his methods (industrial warfare: the grinder) with Deborah Norville.
Lance Morrow, 'A New Test of Resolve', *Time*, 3 September 1990.

I GUESS the one thing I would say to the press that I was delighted with is, in the very, very early stages of this operation, when we were over here building up and we didn't have very much on the ground, you all were giving us credit for a whole lot more over here. And as a result, that gave me quite a feeling of confidence that we might not be attacked quite as quickly as I thought we were going to be attacked.
General H. Norman Schwarzkopf, 27 February 1991, 'The Mother of All Briefings', in Riyadh as Operation Desert Storm was coming to a conclusion.

MILITARY LEADERS should plan adequately for dealing with the media. The objective is to ensure military operations are put in the proper context for the American public and audiences around the world. Commanders or senior military officials can no longer get away with a "no comment" answer regarding American troop use in trouble spots worldwide. Ignoring the media does not make them go away – it just forces them to contact alternative sources for their stories.
Refusing to talk to the media also guarantees the military's perspective will not be heard. Thus, it is to the military's benefit to cooperate with the media because "We don't win unless CNN says we win."
General H. Hugh Shelton, *Military Review*, November–December 1995.

THE MEDIA constantly needs news. They must file stories and will do it with or without the military's help. It is in the military's best interest to assist the media, because there are many good stories that can be told. . . . Credibility is too fragile an asset to waste on an unworthy or disingenuous news story.
. . . Soldiers invariably will do the right thing. Therefore, providing media access to them cements the bond between the society they come from and the military they support. Soldiers are ingenious and intelligent and their professionalism is obvious to everyone who comes in contact with them.
General H. Hugh Shelton, *Military Review*, November–December 1995.

THE PRINCIPLES OF WAR

I HAVE MADE my boundary beyond that of my fathers; I have increased that which was bequeathed me. I am a king who speaks and executes; that which my ear conceives is that which comes to pass by my hand; one who is eager to possess, and powerful . . . not allowing a matter to sleep in his heart . . . attacking him who attacks, silent in a matter, or answering a matter according to that which is in it; since if one is silent after an attack, it strengthens the heart of the enemy. Valiance is eagerness, cowardice is to slink back; he is truly a craven who is repelled on his own border.
Sesostris III, Pharaoh of Egypt (1887–1849 BC), c. 1871 BC; an early exposition of several of the principles of war: the objective, the offensive, security, quoted in James Breasted, *Ancient Records of Egypt*, 1906.

TO MAKE WAR with success the following principles should never be departed from:
To be superior to your enemy in numbers as well as in moral [morale]; to fight battles in order to spread terror in the country; to divide your army into as many corps as may be effected without risk, in order to undertake several objects at the same time; to treat well those who yield, to ill-treat those who resist; to secure your rear, and occupy and strengthen yourself at the outset in some post which shall serve as a central base point for the support of your future movements; to make yourself master of the great rivers and principal passes, and to establish your line of communications by getting possession of the fortresses by laying siege to them, and of the open country by giving battle; for it is vain to expect that conquests are to be achieved without combats, although when the victory is won they will be best maintained by uniting mildness with valour.
Field Marshal Prince Raimundo Montecuccoli (1609–1680), *Memoirs*, quoted in Chandler, *The Military Maxims of Napoleon*, 1988.

THE ART of war owns certain elements and fixed principles. We must acquire that theory, and lodge it in our heads – otherwise we will never get very far.
Frederick the Great, quoted in Duffy, *The Military Life of Frederick the Great*, 1985.

1. NOTHING but the offensive. 2. Speed in marches, swiftness. 3. Methodism is not needed. 4. Full authority to the commanding general. 5. Attack the enemy and hit him in the field. 6. Lose no time in sieges. . . . take fortresses chiefly by assaults or open force. . . . 7. Never divide forces for security of different points. If the enemy went around them, so much the better: he approaches in order to be defeated. . . . Never occupy yourself with vain maneuvers.

> Marshal Aleksandr V. Suvorov, his plan for the Italian Campaign (1799), quoted in *Voyennaya istoriya* (Moscow), 1971.

IT IS a principle of warfare, that when it is possible to make use of thunderbolts, they should be preferred to cannon.

> Napoleon, dictation on St. Helena, *Correspondance de Napoléon Ier, publiée par ordre de l'Empereur Napoléon III*, XXXI, p. 429, 1858–1870, quoted in Christopher Herold, ed., *The Mind of Napoleon*, 1955.

IT IS true that Jomini always argues for fixed principles. Genius works by inspiration. What is good in certain circumstances may be bad in others; but one ought to consider principles as an axis which holds certain relations to a curve. It may be good to recognize that on this or that occasion one has swerved from fixed principles of war.

> Napoleon, quoted in Gaspard Gourgaud, *Talks of Napoleon at St. Helena*, 1816.

TACTICS can be learned from treatises, somewhat like geometry, and so can the various military evolutions or the science of the engineers and the gunner; but knowledge of the grand principles of warfare can be acquired only through the study of military history and of the battles of the great captains and through experience. There are no precise, determinate rules: everything depends on the character that nature has bestowed on the general, on his qualities and defects, on the troops, on the range of the weapons, on the season of the year, and on a thousand circumstances which are never twice the same.

> Napoleon (1769–1821), dictation on St. Helena, *Correspondance de Napoléon Ier, publiée par ordre de l'Empereur Napoléon III*, XXXI, p. 365, 1858–1870, quoted in Christopher Herold, ed., *The Mind of Napoleon*, 1955.

PRINCIPLES of military art shine in history like the Sun on the horizon, so much the worse for blind men incapable of seeing them.

> Napoleon, quoted in *The Principles of Combined Arms Battle* (Moscow), 1992.

GET your principles straight; the rest is a matter of detail.

> Napoleon (1769–1821).

THESE three things you must always keep in mind: concentration of strength, activity, and a firm resolve to perish gloriously. They are the three principles of the military art which have disposed luck in my favor in all my operations.

> Napoleon, 1804, letter to General Lauriston, quoted in Christopher Herold, ed., *The Mind of Napoleon*, 1955.

THE PRINCIPLES of warfare are those which guided the great captains whose high deeds history has transmitted to us – Alexander, Hannibal, Caesar, Gustavus Adolphus, Turenne, Eugene of Savoy, Frederick the Great. . . . The history of their eighty-three campaigns would constitute a complete treatise on the art of war; the principles that must be followed in defensive and offensive warfare would flow from it as from a common source.

> Napoleon, on St. Helena, quoted in Christopher Herold, ed., *The Mind of Napoleon*, 1955.

MAXIM 112. All the great captains have done great things only by conforming to the rules and natural principles of the art; that is to say, by the wisdom of their combinations, the reasoned balance of means with consequences, and efforts with obstacles. They have succeeded only by thus conforming, whatever may have been the audacity of their enterprises and the extent of their success. They have never ceased to make war a veritable science. It is only under this title that they are our great models, and it is only in imitating them that one can hope to approach them.

> Napoleon, *The Military Maxims of Napoleon*, tr. Burnod, 1827.

KEEPING your forces united, being vulnerable at no point, moving rapidly on important points – these are the principles which assure victory, and, with fear, resulting from the reputation of your arms, maintain the faithfulness of allies and the obedience of conquered peoples.

> Napoleon, *Maxims of War*, 1831.

THE PRINCIPLES of war are the same as those of a siege. Fire must be concentrated at one point, and as soon as the breach is made, the equilibrium is broken and the rest is nothing.

> Napoleon, *Maxims of War*, 1831.

MAXIM 5. All wars should be governed by certain principles for every war should have a definite object, and be conducted according to the rules of art. War should only be undertaken with forces proportioned to the obstacles to be overcome.

> Napoleon, *The Military Maxims of Napoleon*, tr. George D'Aguilar, 1831 (David Chandler, ed., 1987)

ONLY THOSE general principles and attitudes that result from clear and deep understanding can provide a *comprehensive* guide to action. It is to these that opinions on specific problems should be anchored. The difficulty is to hold fast to these results of contemplation in the torrent of events and new opinions. Often there is a gap between principles and actual events that cannot always be bridged by a succession of logical deductions. Then a measure of self-confidence is needed, and a degree of skepticism is also salutary. Frequently nothing short of an imperative principle will suffice, which is not part of the immediate thought-process, but dominates it: that principle is in all doubtful cases *to stick to one's first impression and to refuse to change unless forced to do so by a clear conviction*. A strong faith in the overriding truth of tested principles is needed; the *vividness* of transient impressions must not make us forget that such truth as they contain is of a lesser stamp. By giving preference, in case of doubt, to our earlier convictions, by holding to them stubbornly, our actions acquire that quality of steadiness and consistency which is termed strength of character.

> Major-General Carl von Clausewitz, *On War*, 1.3, 1832, tr. Michael Howard and Peter Paret, 1976.

. . . A REAL AID or guiding star for those acting.

> Major-General Carl von Clausewitz, *On War*, 1832, quoted in *The Principles of Combined Arms Battle* (Moscow), 1992.

THERE EXISTS a small number of fundamental principles of war, which could not be deviated from without danger, and the application of which, on the contrary, has been in almost all time crowned with success.

> Lieutenant-General Antoine-Henri Baron de Jomini, *Summary of the Art of War*, 1838, tr. Mendell and Craighill, 1862.

ONE GREAT PRINCIPLE underlies all the operations of war – a principle which must be followed in all good combinations. It is embraced in the following maxims:

1. To throw by strategic movements the mass of an army, successively, upon the decisive points of a theater of war, and also upon the communications of the enemy as much as possible without compromising one's own.
2. To maneuver to engage fractions of the hostile army with the bulk of one's forces.
3. On the battlefield, to throw the mass of the forces upon the decisive point, or upon the portion of the hostile line which it is of the first importance to overthrow.
4. To so arrange that these masses shall not only be thrown upon the decisive point, but that they shall engage at the proper times and with ample energy.

> Lieutenant-General Antoine-Henri Baron de Jomini, *Summary of the Art of War*, 1838, tr. Mendell and Craighill, 1862.

IN WAR, as in every other art based upon settled principles, there are exceptions to all general rules. It is in discovering these cases that the talent of the general is shown.

> Dennis Hart Mahan, *Advance-Guard, Out-Post, and Detachment Service of Troops with the Essential Principles of Strategy and Grand Tactics*, 1863.

THE FIRST PRINCIPLE of war is to concentrate superior force at the decisive point, that is, upon the field of battle. But it is exceedingly seldom that by standing still, and leaving the initiative to the enemy, that this principle can be observed, for a numerically inferior force, if it once permits its enemy to concentrate, can hardly hope for success; to strike the enemy in detail and overthrow his columns in succession. And the highest art of all is to compel him to disperse his army, and then to concentrate superior force against each fraction in turn.

> Colonel George F. Henderson, *Stonewall Jackson*, 1898.

THE PRINCIPLES of the art of war are within reach of the most ordinary intelligence, but that does not mean that it is capable of applying them.

> General Mikhail I. Dragomirov (1830–1905), quoted in Foch, *Principles of War*, 1913.

WAR acknowledges principles, and even rules, but these are not so much fetters, or bars, which compel its movement aright, as guides which warn us when it is going wrong.

> Rear Admiral Alfred Thayer Mahan (1840–1914).

GENIUS is an immense capacity for taking pains.
Always do more than is required of you . . .
What then is death? Is not the taps of death but first call to the reveille of eternal life.
We live in deeds not years.
You can be what you will to be.

> General George S. Patton, Jr., August 1905, five personal principles that would guide his life, written after his first year at West Point, *1905 Notebook*, quoted in Carlo d'Este, *Patton: A Genius for War*, 1995.

(1) CUT line of communication; (2) cause enemy to form front to flank; (3) operate on internal lines; (4) separate bodies of enemy and fight in detail; and (5) direct attack.

> General George S. Patton, Jr., quoted in Carlo d'Este, *Patton: A Genius for War*, 1995.

THE FUNDAMENTAL principles of war are neither very numerous nor in themselves very abstruse, but the application of them is difficult and cannot be made subject to rules. The correct application of principles to circumstances is the outcome of sound military knowledge, built up by study and practice until it has become instinct.

> British Army *Field Service Regulations 1909*, quoted in Fuller, *The Foundations of the Science of War*, 1926.

TO CREATE a formula or a general rule . . . that would be appropriate in all situations is absurd. One must be able to think on one's feet to be able to make sense of each separate case.

> V.I. Lenin, quoted in Makhmut Gareyev, *Frunze, Military Theorist*, 1985.

THERE ARE eight principles of war, and they constitute the laws of every scientifically fought boxing match as of every battle. These principles are:

1st Principle. – The Principle of the objective
2nd Principle. – The Principle of the offensive
3rd Principle. – The Principle of security
4th Principle. – The Principle of concentration
5th Principle. – The Principle of economy of force
6th Principle. – The Principle of movement
7th Principle. – The Principle of surprise
8th Principle. – The Principle of co-operation.

No one of the above eight principles is of greater value than the other. No plan of action can be considered in harmony unless all are in harmony, and none can be considered in harmony unless weighed against the conditions which govern their application. Seldom can a perfect plan be arrived at because the fog of war seldom, if ever, rises. It is, however, an undoubted fact that the general who places his trust in the principles of war, and who trusts in them the more strongly the fog of war thickens, almost inevitably beats the general who does not.

> Major-General J.F.C. Fuller, *The Reformation of War*, 1923. Fuller was the first to define the principles of war as a coherent, interactive set of concepts; these principles, subsequently modified, are the basis of the Principles of War used by the U.S. and British Armies.

A GENERAL will seldom win without attacking, and he will seldom attack correctly unless he has chosen his objective with reference to the principles of war, and unless his attack is based on these principles. Imagination is a great detective, but imagination which is not based on the sound foundation of reason is at best a capricious leader. Even genius itself, unless it be stiffened by powerful weapons, a high morale, discipline and training, can only be likened to a marksman armed with a blunderbuss – ability wasted through insufficiency of means. Conversely, an efficient army led by an antiquated soldier may be compared to a machine gun in the hand of an arbalister.

> Major-General J.F.C. Fuller, *The Reformation of War*, 1923.

I WOULD GIVE you a word of warning on the so-called principles of war, as laid down in *Field Service Regulations*. For heaven's sake, don't treat those as holy writ, like the Ten Commandments, to be learned by heart, and as having by their repetition some magic, like the incantations of savage priests. They are merely a set of common-sense maxims, like "cut your coat according to your cloth," "a rolling stone gathers no moss," "honesty is the best policy," and so forth. . . . Clausewitz has a different set, so has Foch, so have other military writers. They are all simply common sense, and are instinctive to the properly trained soldier.

> Field Marshal Viscount Wavell of Cyrenaica, c. 1930, lecture to officers at Aldershot.

THE MILITARY STUDENT does not seek to learn from history the minutia of method and technique. In every age these are decisively influenced by the characteristics of weapons currently available and by means at hand for maneuvering, supplying and controlling combat forces. But research does bring to light those fundamental principles, and their combinations and applications, which, in the past, have been productive of success. These principles know no limitation of time. Consequently, the army extends its analytical interest to the dust-buried accounts of wars long past as well as to those still reeking with the scent of battle.

> General of the Army Douglas MacArthur, *Annual Report of the Chief of Staff for Fiscal Year Ending June 30, 1935*.

ADHERENCE to one principle frequently demands violation of another. Any leader who adheres inflexibly to one set of commmandments is inviting disastrous defeat from a resourceful opponent.

> Admiral C.R. Brown, *Principles of War*, June 1949.

RESPECT for the opinion of this or that great soldier must never be allowed to go so far that nobody dares to discuss it. A sure sense of reality must be aroused. Given a well-founded knowledge of basic principles, any man of reasonably cool and logical mind can work out most of the details for himself, provided he is not inhibited in his thinking.

> Field Marshal Erwin Rommel, *The Rommel Papers*, 1953.

AGAINST the principle of surprise – continuous activity by the various intelligence agencies. Against the principle of maintenance-of-aim – tactical diversionary attacks and strategical, psychological and political offensives. Against the principle of economy-of-force – attacks against lines of communications and stores in the rear, thereby pinning down the enemy's forces and dispersing them. Against the principle of coordination – strike against the channels of administration. Against the principle of concentration – diversionary attacks and air activity to split up the enemy's forces. Against the principles of security – sum total of the above activities and those that follow. Against the principle of offensive-spirit – offensive spirit. Against the principle of mobility – destruction of the lines of communication.

> General Yigael Yadin, *Israeli Forces Journal*, 9/1949.

THE PRINCIPLES of war, not merely one principle, can be condensed into a single word – "concentration". But for truth this needs to be amplified as the "concentration of strength against weakness". And for any real value it needs to be explained that the concentration of strength against weakness depends on the dispersion of your opponent's strength, which in turn is produced by a distribution of your own that gives the appearance, and partial effect of dispersion. Your dispersion, his dispersion, your concentration – such is the sequence, and each is a sequel. True concentration is the fruit of calculated dispersion.

Captain Sir Basil Liddell Hart, *Strategy*, 1954.

IN MOST military text books, more particularly *Field Service Regulations*, a list of the principles of war will be found. . . . There are several versions of these so-called principles, but they are no more than pegs on which to hang our tactical thoughts. There is nothing irrevocable about them; sometimes they may be discarded with impunity; but as a study of military history will show, they should only be discarded after deep consideration. They are very important guides rather than principles, and in the writer's opinion the simplest and most useful are derived from the seven tactical elements . . . aim or object, security, mobility, offensive power, economy of force, concentration of force, and surprise. Further, they are as applicable to strategy (operations in plan) as to tactics (operations in action), two terms which should never be separated by a bulkhead, because their components flow into each other and together constitute the art of war.

Major-General J.F.C. Fuller, *The Generalship of Alexander the Great*, 1958.

WAR remains an art and, like all arts, whatever its variation, will have its enduring principles. Many men, skilled either with sword or pen, and sometimes with both, have tried to expound those principles. I heard them once from a soldier of experience for whom I had a deep and well-founded respect. Many years ago, as a cadet hoping someday to be an officer, I was poring over the "Principles of War," listed in the old Field Service Regulations, when the sergeant-major came upon me. He surveyed me with kindly amusement. "Don't bother your head about all them things, me lad," he said. "There's only one principle of war, and that's this. Hit the other fellow as quick as you can and as hard as you can, where it hurts him the most, when he ain't lookin'!" As a recruit, I earned that great man's reproof often enough; now, as an old soldier, I would hope to receive his commendation. I think I might, for we of the Fourteenth Army held to his "Principle of War."

Field Marshal Viscount Slim of Burma, *Defeat Into Victory*, 1956.

I PERSONALLY was guided by them in preparing all operations. At the same time when these matters were treated formally, there was no success in battle, the engagement, or the operation.

Marshal of the Soviet Union G. V. Zhukov, quoted in *The Principles of Combined Arms Battle* (Moscow), 1992.

A *PRINCIPLE* indicates only the goal, which is why it is only a *regulator* of creativeness, the force directing

it onto the path of correct decisions, but it hardly is a substitute for it.

General G.A. Leyer, *Russkaya voyenno-teoreticheskaya mysl XIX i nachala XX veka*, 1960.

PRISONERS OF WAR (POWs)

NO PRISONER pleads well his case,
Framing it sorrowfully. But,
To comfort his distress, he can make a song.
My friends are many, though their gifts are few.
Shame upon them, if my ransom is not paid
These two winters in prison.

My friends and barons know well –
English, Norman, Poitevin and Gascon all –
That no friend of mine so low
Would I leave in prison for want of cash.
I mean no reproach
But still am I held captive.

Richard I *Coeur de Lion*, 1192, tr. Caitlin Matthews, song written while a prisoner of Leopold of Austria after having been captured on his return from Crusade.

I ENJOY too much pleasure in softening the Hardships of Captivity to with-hold any comfort from Prisoners; and beg you to do me the Justice to conclude, that no Requisition of this Nature, that should be made, will ever be denied.

General George Washington, 13 May 1777, to Leopold Phillip von Heister, *The Writings of George Washington*, VIII, p. 58, John C. Fitzgerald, ed., 1933.

WHEN the war is concluded, I am definitely of the opinion that all animosity should be forgotten, and that all prisoners should be released.

The Duke of Wellington, 1804, letter to E.S. Warring.

MAXIM 109. Prisoners of war do not belong to the power for which they have fought; they all are under the safeguard of honor and generosity of the nation that has disarmed them.

Napoleon, *The Military Maxims of Napoleon*, tr. Burnod, 1827.

LOSSES incurred during the battle consist mostly of dead and wounded; after the battle, they are usually greater in terms of captured guns and prisoners. While the former are shared more or less evenly by winner and loser, the latter are not. For that reason they are usually only found on one side, or at any rate in significant numbers on one side.

That is why guns and prisoners have always counted as the real trophies of victory: they are also its measure, for they are the tangible evidence of its scale. They are a better index to the degree of superior morale than any other factors, even when one relates them to the casualty figures. . . .

Major-General Carl von Clausewitz, *On War*, 4.4, 1832, tr. Michael Howard and Peter Paret, 1976.

AN OFFICER congratulating the General upon the great number of his prisoners, said jocularly, that they surrendered too easily, for the Confederacy would be embarrassed with their maintainence. He answered, smiling, "It's cheaper to feed them than to fight them."

> Lieutenant-General Thomas J. 'Stonewall' Jackson, during the Seven Days' Battles, 30 June 1862, quoted in R.L. Dabney, *Life of Lieut.-Gen. Thomas J. Jackson*, II, 1866.

I HOPE that few of the soldiers of this army will find it necessary at any time in the coming campaign to surrender themselves prisoners of war. WE cannot spare brave men to fill Federal prisons. Should, however, any be so unfortunate as to fall through unavoidable necessity into the hands of the enemy, it is important that they should preserve entire silence with regard to everything connected with the army, the positions, movements, organizations, or probable strength of any portion of it. I wish the commanding officers of regiments and companies to instruct their men, should they be captured, under any circumstances not to disclose the brigade, division, or corps to which they belong, but to give simply their names, company, and regiment, and not to speak of military matters even among their associates in misfortune. Proper prudence on the part of all will be of great assistance in preserving that secrecy so essential to success.

> General Robert E. Lee, circular to the Army of Northern Virginia, 7 April 1864, *The Wartime Papers of R. E. Lee*, 1961.

HE MADE very few comments upon the stirring events which were crowding so closely upon one another until the reports came in regarding the prisoners. When the large numbers captured were announced, he said, with the first trace of animation he had shown: "That's the kind of news I like to hear. I had hoped that a bold dash at daylight would secure a large number of prisoners. Hancock is doing well." This remark was eminently characteristic of the Union commander [U.S. Grant]. His extreme fondness for taking prisoners was manifested in every battle he fought. When word was brought to him of a success on any part of the line, his first and most eager question was always, "Have any prisoners been taken?" The love for capturing prisoners amounted to a passion with him. It did not seem to arise from the fact that they added so largely to the trophies of battle, and was no doubt chiefly due to his tenderness of heart, which prompted him to feel that it was always more humane to reduce the enemy's strength by captures than by slaughter. His desire in this respect was amply gratified, for during the war it fell to his lot to capture a larger number of prisoners than any general of modern times.

> Brigadier-General Horace Porter, *Campaigning With Grant*, 1897.

WE OUGHT NOT to make a single exchange nor release a prisoner on any pretext whatever until the war closes. We have got to fight until the Military power of the South is exhausted and if we release or exchange prisoners captured it simply becomes a war of extermination.

> General of the Army Ulysses S. Grant, 19 August 1864, letter to Secretary of State Seward, *Personal Memoirs and Selected Letters*, 1990.

PRISONER OF WAR guard companies, or an equivalent organization, should be as far forward as possible in action to take over prisoners of war, because troops heated with battle are not safe custodians. Any attempt to rob or loot prisoners of war by escorts must be strictly dealt with.

> General George S. Patton, Jr., *War As I Knew It*, 1947.

A PRISONER OF WAR is a man who tries to kill you and fails, and then asks you not to kill him.

> Sir Winston S. Churchill, 1952, quoted in *The Observer* (London).

IN the final choice a soldier's pack is not so heavy a burden as a prisoner's chains.

> General of the Army Dwight D. Eisenhower, Inaugural Address, 20 January 1953.

I SAW a group of soldiers clustered around a prisoner; as I drove up, one of them was hitting the Egyptian. I court-martialed the soldier on the spot, sentencing him to thirty-five days in the stockade. It was the kind of thing that brought my anger to the boiling point. In battle you fight and you have to kill. That's the nature of it. But once a man is your prisoner you never touch him.

> General Ariel Sharon, *Warrior*, 1989.

I MADE SURE that we treated prisoners humanely. Sadism is bad for morale, and, in the long run, humane treatment yields more information than brutality.

> Major-General John K. Singlaub, of his command of the Studies and Observations Group (unconventional warfare) during the opening stages of the U.S. deployment to Vietnam, *Hazardous Duty*, 1991.

THERE WAS only one moment at which Ahmad showed any emotion. He presented an accounting of coalition prisoners of war held by Iraq. "We have forty-one in all," he said. I made notes as he read them off:

17 Americans
2 Italians
12 British
1 Kuwaiti
9 Saudis

This left a number of people unaccounted for, and I quickly brought out our list of MIAs, but he stopped me. "And we would like to have the numbers of the POWs on our side as well."

"As of last night, sixty thousand," I replied. "Or sixty thousand plus, because it is difficult to count them completely." His face went completely pale: he had had no concept of the magnitude of their defeat.

> When the Iraqis treated for peace at Safwan,
> 31 March 1991, General H. Norman Scwharzkopf,
> *It Doesn't Take a Hero*, 1992.

THE PROFESSION OF ARMS

WAR is my homeland,
My armour is my house,
And fighting is my life.

> German soldiers' saying, 16th century, quoted in
> Langer, *The Thirty Years War*, 1980.

GENERALLY SPEAKING, the Way of the warrior is resolute acceptance of death. Although not only warriors but priests, women, peasants and lowlier folk have been known to die readily in the cause of duty or out of shame, this is a different thing. The warrior is different in that studying the Way of strategy is based on overcoming men.

> Miyamoto Musashi, *The Book of the Five Rings*, 1645,
> tr. Victor Harris, 1984.

THE PROFESSION of a Souldier is allowed to be lawful by the Word of God; and so Famous and Honourable amongst Men, that Emperours and Kings do account it a Great Honour to be of the Profession, and to have Experience in it.

> General George Monck, *Observations Upon Military
> and Political Matters*, 1671.

WAR is a trade for the ignorant and a science for the expert.

> Chevalier Jean Charles Folard (1669–1752).

THE MAN who devotes himself to war should regard it as a religious order into which he enters. He should have nothing, know no other home than his troop, and should hold himself honored in his profession.

> Field Marshal Maurice Comte de Saxe, *My Reveries*,
> 1732, tr. Phillips, 1940.

A SENSE of vocation is the greatest virtue of the military man.

> Field Marshal Prince Aleksandr V. Suvorov
> (1729–1800), quoted in *Morskoi Sbornik*, 5/1981.

FROM the nature of our profession we hold life by a more precarious tenure than many others, but when we fall, we trust it is to benefit our Country. So fell your Son by a cannon-ball under my immediate command at the Siege of Bastia. I had taken him on shore with me, from his abilities and attention to his duty.

> Admiral Viscount Nelson, 1794, letter to the father of
> Seaman Thomas Davies of the *Agamemnon*, who died
> at his side, quoted in David Walder, *Nelson*, 1978.

THERE ARE workers in buildings, in colours, in forms and in words – myself, I'm a worker in battles. It's my calling. – At thirty-five I've already made eighteen of them, called Victories. – I have to be paid for my work. And it's not expensive to pay with a throne. – Besides, I shall always go on working. You'll see plenty more. . . .

> Napoleon, 1804, conversation with Pope Pius VII at
> Fontainebleau, quoted by Alfred Comte de Vigny,
> *Servitude and Grandeur of Arms*, 1857.

THE MILITARY are a freemasonry . . . and I am the grand master of their lodges.

> Napoleon, 1809, conversation, quoted in Christopher
> Herold, ed., *The Mind of Napoleon*, 1955.

I LOVE a brave soldier who has undergone that baptism of fire, whatever nation he belongs to.

> Napoleon (1769–1821), on St. Helena, quoted in Barry
> O'Meara, *Napoleon in Exile*, 1822.

WHAT European soldier would not be inspired with respect at my approach!

> Napoleon, 28 May 1816, to Count Las Casas as
> British soldiers emptied their camp on St. Helena to
> watch the Emperor ride by, quoted in Emmanuel Las
> Casas, *Memoirs of the Life, Exile, and Conversations
> of the Emperor Napoleon*, II, 1890.

IN ANY CASE, who is asking anything of you? Who has asked you to feed me? If you stopped your provisions and I were hungry, these brave soldiers would take compassion on me. I could go to the mess of their grenadiers, and I am sure they would not deny the first, the oldest soldier of Europe.

> Napoleon, 18 August 1816, to Admiral Cockburn on
> St. Helena, referring to the men of the 58th Foot, the
> garrison of the island, cited in R.M. Johnston, ed., *The
> Corsican*, 1910.

I LIKE only those who make war.

> Napoleon, 1816, on St. Helena, quoted in Christopher
> Herold, ed., *The Mind of Napoleon*, 1955.

NO MATTER how clearly we see the citizen and the soldier in the same man, how strongly we conceive of war as the business of the entire nation, opposed diametrically to the pattern set by the *condottieri* of former times, the business of war will always remain individual and abstract. Consequently for as long as they practice this activity, soldiers will think of themselves as members of a kind of guild, in whose regulations, laws, and customs the spirt of war is given pride of place. And that does seem to be the case. No matter how much one may be inclined to take the most sophisticated view of war, it would be a serious mistake to underrate professional pride (*esprit de corps*) as something that may and must be present in an army to greater or lesser degree. Professional pride is the bond between the various natural forces that activate the military virtues; in the context of this professional pride they crystallize more readily.

> Major-General Carl von Clausewitz, *On War*, 3.5, tr. Michael Howard and Peter Paret, 1976.

WAR is a special profession, however general its relation may be and even if all the male population of a country capable of bearing arms were able to practice it, war would still continue to be different and separate from any other activity which occupies the life of man.

> Major-General Carl von Clausewitz (1780–1831).

ARMS is a profession that, if its principles are adhered to for success, requires an officer do what he fears may be wrong, and yet, according to military experience, must be done, if success is to be attained.

> Lieutenant-General Thomas J. 'Stonewall' Jackson, 11 April 1862, letter to his wife.

I WISH YOU to understand that the day is at hand when you will be called upon to meet the enemy in the worst form of our profession. . . . Hot and cold shot will, no doubt, be freely dealt to us, and there must be stout hearts and quick hands to extinguish the one and stop the holes in the other.

> Admiral David G. Farragut, general order before the attack past the forts guarding New Orleans on 24 April 1862, quoted in Loyall Farragut, *The Life of David Glasgow Farragut*, 1879.

IN NO EVENT will there be money in it; but there may always be honor and quietness of mind and worthy occupation – which are better guarantees of happiness.

> Rear Admiral Alfred Thayer Mahan, *The Navy as a Career*, 1895.

I DO NOT regard and have never regarded permanent soldiering as an attractive proposition for any man who has some other profession at his command. . . . if a man could command an income no larger in private practice than he could in military employment, I would recommend to him to stick to private practice every time. There is something about permanent military occupation which seems to confine a man's scope and limit his opportunities, and after he has had a few years under the circumscribed conditions of official routine, he generally finds himself wholly out of touch with civil occupation.

> General Sir John Monash, 6 January 1911, quoted in Horner, *The Commanders*, 1984.

THERE IS no more exacting profession or one that requires more painstaking attention to detail than the profession of arms in time of war.

> Major-General John A. Lejeune, *The Reminiscences of a Marine*, 1929.

THERE IS scope and occupation in the army for the highest mental as well as the highest physical efficiency. Whereas delight in the trade of arms, inherited and indulged from generation to generation, drives one man to the army, another may join from the desire to devote his ability and knowledge to the most immediate form of national service; one is attracted by a profession which gives pride of place to manly strength and personal value, and other by the prospect of activity in the open, another because he is interested in the machinery of war, and yet another because he loves horses.

'Αὐτὸς γὺρ ἐφέλκαι ἄνδρα σίδηρος'

Iron attracts man.

> Colonel-General Hans von Seekt, *Thoughts of a Soldier*, 1930.

MEN who adopt the profession of arms submit, of their own free will, to a law of perpetual constraint. Of their own accord they reject the right to live where they choose, to say what they think, to dress as they like. From the moment they become soldiers it needs but an order to settle them in this place, to move them to that, to separate them from their families and dislocate their normal lives. On the word of command they must rise, march, run, endure bad weather, go without sleep or food, be isolated in some distant post, work til they drop. They have ceased to be the masters of their fate. If they drop in their tracks, if their ashes are scattered to the four winds, that is all part and parcel of their job.

> General Charles de Gaulle, *The Edge of the Sword*, 1932.

OUR CALLING is most ancient, and like all other old things it has amassed through the ages certain customs and traditions which decorate it and ennoble it, which render beautiful the otherwise prosaic occupation of being professional men-at-arms: killers.

> General George S. Patton, Jr., quoted in Fitton, ed., *Leadership*, 1990.

THE POINT I wish to make here, and to repeat it for emphasis, is that the professional military man has three primary responsibilities:

First, to give his honest, fearless, objective, professional military opinion of what he needs to do the job the Nation gives him.

Second, if what he is given is less than the minimum he regards as essential, to give his superiors an honest, fearless, objective opinion of the consequences.

Third, and finally, he has the duty whatever the final decision, to do the utmost with whatever is furnished.

> General Matthew B. Ridgway, address to the Army Staff as Chief of Staff, 1954, quoted in Russel B. Reynolds, *The Officer's Guide, 1970–1971 Edition*, 1970.

WAR is the professional soldier's time of opportunity.
> Captain Sir Basil Liddell Hart, *Defence of the West*, 1956.

I FIND I have liked all of the soldiers of different races who have fought with me and most of those who have fought against me. This is not strange, for there is a freemasonry among fighting soldiers that helps them to understand one another even if they are enemies.
> Field Marshal Viscount Slim of Burma, *Unofficial History*, 1959.

WHEN there is visible enemy to fight in open combat . . . many serve, all applaud, and the tide of patriotism runs high. But when there is a long, slow struggle, with no immediate visible foe, your choice will seem hard indeed.
> President John F. Kennedy, address to a graduating class of the U.S. Naval Academy.

THE SOLDIER, be he friend or foe, is charged with the protection of the weak and unarmed. It is the very essence and reason of his being. When he violates this sacred trust, he not only profanes his entire cult but threatens the fabric of international society.
> General of the Army Douglas MacArthur, quoted in William Manchester, *American Caesar: Douglas MacArthur, 1880–1964*, 1978.

THE FUNCTION of the profession of arms is the ordered application of force in the resolution of a social problem. Harold Lasswell describes it as the management of violence, which is rather less precise. The bearing of arms among men for the purpose of fighting other men is found as far back as we can see. It has become at some times and in some places a calling resembling the priesthood in its dedication. It has never ceased to display a strong element of the vocational.

It has also become a profession, not only in the wider sense of what is professed, but in the narrower of an occupation with a distinguishable corpus of specific technical knowledge and doctrine, a more or less exclusive group coherence, a complex of institutions peculiar to itself, an educational pattern adapted to its own needs, a career structure of its own and a distinct place in the society which has brought it forth. In all these respects it has strong points of resemblance to medicine and law, as well as holy orders.
> General Sir John Hackett, *The Profession of Arms*, 1963.

IT IS WELL to remind those who quote the injunction in the Sermon on the Mount to "turn the other cheek also" to him who "shall smite thee on the right cheek", that, in the version in Saint Matthew's Gospel, this is preceded by the words, "I say unto you that ye resist not evil". The sad fact of life is that, if evil is not resisted, it will prevail. That is the justification for the use of force to deter, and if necessary, defeat those who turn to it to further their own ends, the justification for maintaining in the service of the community and the state, forces who are trained, skilled and well-equipped to meet that challenge when and wherever it arises. Their profession is an honourable one.
> Field Marshal Lord Carver, *Warfare Since 1945*, 1980.

THE MAN-AT-ARMS serves under an unlimited liability. . . . As John Ruskin said, the professional soldier has to offer himself to be slain.
> General Sir John Hackett, quoted in 'Are Soldiers Civilized', *Parameters*, Summer 1984.

THE MILITARY profession is a thinking profession. Officers particularly are expected to be students of the art and science of war at all levels – tactical, operational, and strategic – with a solid foundation in military theory and knowledge of military history and timeless lessons to be gained from it.
> General Alfred M. Gray and Major John Schmitt, *Warfighting*, United States Marine Corps, 1989.

MOST OF US were fascinated by the intellectual challenge [U.S. Army Command and General Staff College]. This certainly didn't mean we were eager for war. There aren't many professional soldiers who actually find combat pleasurable. Critics of the military – especially liberal academics and journalists – mistakenly believe that soldiers enjoy war. That's as logical as assuming surgeons enjoy cancer. We study the profession of arms not to wage war, but to defend the values of our civilization. This is an uncomplicated patriotic notion that is hard for sophisticated civilians to swallow. But our dedication to professional excellence does not mean career soldiers are especially cruel, or that we value human life less than our civilian counterparts. In fact, there is abundant proof to the contrary to be found in the thousands of citations for combat gallantry in actions to save lives.
> Major-General John K. Singlaub, *Hazardous Duty*, 1991.

SOMEONE asked me a few years ago why I wanted to be a soldier. I thought a few seconds before answering. Then I said, "If you like what our country stands for and are willing to fight to protect those ideals, you ought to be a soldier.

"If the sound of the national anthem and the sight of our flag stir something inside you, then you ought to be a soldier.

"If you want to be around a lot of other people who feel the same way about all that as you do, you ought to be a soldier.

"If you like a challenge, are not afraid of hard work, and think you are tough enough to meet the standards on the battlefield, you ought to be a soldier.

"If you and your family are strong enough to endure the many separations, often on a moment's notice, and can live that kind of life, then you ought to be a soldier.

"If the thought that at the end of your life you can say – or have said about you – that you served your country, if that appeals to you and you need no other reward than that, then you ought to be a soldier."

General Fred Franks, Jr., quoted in Tom Clancy with General Fred Franks, Jr. (ret), *Into the Storm*, 1997.

PROMOTION

I SAILED with King Amenhotep I triumphant, when he ascended the river to Kush in order extend the borders of Egypt. . . . I was at the head of our army; I fought incredibly; his majesty beheld my bravery. I brought off two hands, and took them to his majesty. . . . I brought his majesty in two days to Egypt from the upper well; he [the king] presented me with gold. Then I brought away two female slaves, in addition to those which I had taken to his majesty. One [the king] appointed me "Warrior of the Ruler."

Ahmose son of Abana, Egyptian naval officer during the reign of Pharaoh Amenhotep I (1557–1501 BC), quoted in James Breasted, *Ancient Records of Egypt*, 1906.

I REGRET to find every day proposals placed before me for the quick promotion of staff officers, lieutenants of not more than two, three, or four years' service. They think themselves veterans if they date back to 1799. And yet there is no regiment that does not average eight captains dating from 1792, wounded, and who have fought in every campaign. I count seven of them in the 1st regiment, eight in the 3d, fourteen in the 4th, fourteen in the 5th, fifteen in the 6th, and so on.

Napoleon, 21 January 1805, to Marshal Berthier, quoted in R.M. Johnston, ed., *The Corsican*, 1910.

I ASSEMBLED the officers and men; I asked them who had done well; and I promoted those who could read and write.

Napoleon, 23 November 1806, having reviewed the Fourth Corps following the Prussian campaign, quoted in R.M. Johnston, ed., *The Corsican*, 1910.

IF THE SKILL of a general is one of the surest elements of victory, it will readily be seen that the judicious selection of generals is one of the most delicate points in the science of government and one of the most essential parts of the military policy of a state. Unfortunately, this choice is influenced by so many petty passions that chance, rank, age, favor, party spirit, or jealousy will have as much to do with it as the public interest and justice.

Lieutenant-General Antoine-Henri Baron de Jomini, *Summary of the Art of War*, 1838, tr. Mendell and Craighill, 1862.

AS TO REWARDS and promotion, it is essential to respect long service and at the same time to open a way for merit. Three-fourths of the promotions in each grade should be according to the roster, with the remaining fourth reserved for those distinguished men of merit and zeal. In time of war, however, the regular order of promotion should be suspended, or at least reduced to a third of the promotions, leaving the majority for brilliant conduct and marked services.

Lieutenant-General Antoine-Henri Baron de Jomini, *Summary of the Art of War*, 1838, tr. Mendell and Craighill, 1862.

SUCH A DEGREE of public confidence and respect as puts it in one's power to serve his country, should be accepted and prized; but, apart from that, promotion among men is only a temptation and a trouble. Had this communication not come as an order, I should instantly have declined it, and continued in command of my brave old Brigade.

Lieutenant-General Thomas J. 'Stonewall' Jackson, comment on his appointment to an effectively independent command in the Valley, autumn 1861, quoted in R.L. Dabney, *The Life of Lieut.-Gen. Thomas J. Jackson*, I, 1864.

IN MY OPINION, an officer's pay, when he reaches the highest grade, is given him as a reward for long and faithful services. But the ignorant, as well as the wise and efficient, have risen to the command of squadrons and stations, according to their position on the Register; and when it was attempted to change the order of things, the law was ignored by the country and the President. . . . I have always been an advocate of promotion or distinction for professional services of a chivalrous character, and would never object to the promotion of any brother officer, who had the good fortune to be at the right place at the right time, and did an act by which he risked his life and reputation in the performance of his duty.

Admiral David G. Farragut, quoted in Loyall Farragut, *The Life of David Glasgow Farragut*, 1879.

DIFFERENCES of opinion must exist between the best of friends as to policies in war, and of judgment as to men's fitness. The officer who has the command, however, should be allowed to judge the fitness of the officers under him, unless he is very manifestly wrong.

General of the Army Ulysses S. Grant, *Personal Memoirs*, II, 1885.

WE ARE NOW at war, fighting for our lives, and we cannot afford to confine Army appointments to persons who have excited no hostile comment in their career.

Sir Winston S. Churchill, 19 October 1940, note to the Chief of the Imperial General Staff.

MORE AND MORE does the "System" tend to promote to *control*, men who have shown themselves efficient *cogs* in the machine. . . . There are few commanders in our higher commands. And even these, since their chins usually outweigh their foreheads are themselves outweighed by the majority – of commanders who are essentially staff officers.

Captain Sir Basil Liddell Hart, *Thoughts on War*, 1944.

THE FLAW in all these conscientious attempts to improve the system of promotion is that they tend inevitably to stress the formal record at the expense of the human element and that they aim at an improved flow of promotion when nothing less than an eruption will avail. In fact, the effort to make the Army "fairer" as a profession is contrary to the very nature of its object – war, which is essentially "unfair". The professional attitude was epitomized in a recent article by Admiral Harper, who scathingly criticized Mr. Churchill's selection of an officer for a certain command on the ground that Mr. Churchill had said that his choice was based on personal impressions and conversations rather than on official records. Yet outside the closely regulated professions what employer choosing a man for an important post would not weigh personality more than record? Admittedly, the value of a choice based on personal knowledge depends on the man who makes it, and even at the best it is highly unfair to those who fail through no fault of their own to catch the selector's eye. But it is the only system, or lack of a system, under which genius can be brought rapidly to the top. The lesson of military history is that genius and not mere competence decides the fate of warring nations. It was the shrewd dictum of one who, whatever his defects, was assuredly a genius – Lord Fisher – that "favouritism is the secret of efficiency". In our zeal for equalitarian fairness we have almost ruled out "favouritism", and the stalemate of 1914–1918 is a testimonial to our good intentions – which "paved the path to hell".

Captain Sir Basil Liddell Hart, *Thoughts on War*, 1944.

MY ONLY FEAR is that the extra stripe is going to interfere with my drinking arm.

Admiral William 'Bull' Halsey, upon the award of his fifth star and promotion to Fleet Admiral, quoted in E.B. Potter, *Bull Halsey*, 1985.

IF EVOLUTION were destined to favour the rise of those who, in the tragic hours when the storm sweeps away conventions and habits, are the only ones to remain on their feet and to be, therefore, necessary, would not that be all to the good?

General Charles de Gaulle, *War Memoirs: The Call to Honour 1940–1942*, 1955.

MY OWN FEELING now, after having been through two world wars, is that an extensive use of weedkiller is needed in the senior ranks after a war; this will enable the first class younger officers who have emerged during the war to be moved up.

Field Marshal Viscount Montgomery of Alamein, *Memoirs of Field Marshal Montgomery*, 1958.

BY GOOD FORTUNE in the game of military snakes and ladders, I found myself a general.

Field Marshal Viscount Slim of Burma, *Unofficial History*, 1959.

WE MAKE generals today on the basis of their ability to write a damned letter. Those kinds of men can't get us ready for war.

Lieutenant-General Lewis B. 'Chesty' Puller, quoted in Burke Davis, *Marine*, 1962.

IN THE EARLY DAYS of a tremendous undertaking, such as this war, appointments and selection of individuals are based upon a number of unimportant factors – among which, as we all know, are: personal propinquity, wild guesses, school records, past acquaintanceship, and a number of others, of which few really search down into the depths of character and ability. But the stark realities of distress, privation, and discouragement will bring character and ability into their own.

General of the Army Dwight D. Eisenhower, *At Ease: Stories I Tell My Friends*, 1967.

THIS is a long tough road we have to travel. The men that can do things are going to be sought out just as surely as the sun rises in the morning. Fake reputations, habits of glib and clever speech, and glittering surface performance are going to be discovered and kicked overboard. Solid, sound leadership, with inexhaustible nervous energy to spur on the efforts of lesser men, and ironclad determination to face discouragement, risk, and increasing work without flinching, will always characterize the man who has a sure-enough, bang-up fighting unit. Added to this he must have a darned strong tinge of imagination – I am continuously astonished by the utter lack of imaginative thinking among so many of our people that have reputations for being really good officers. Finally, the man has to be able to forget himself and his personal fortunes.

General of the Army Dwight D. Eisenhower, *At Ease: Stories I Tell My Friends*, 1967.

WE MUST CHOOSE the boldest. Only a man of complete bravery can take a plane off from a rolling deck and, without relying on any alternate airfields, head off into the blue, engage in combat, win and then, having located one's ship, bring one's aircraft back precisely on the dime of the runway . . .

Admiral of the Fleet of the Soviet Union Sergei G. Gorshkov, quoted in Ablamonov, *Admiral*, 1986.

PROMPTNESS

IT IS ESSENTIAL to be cautious and take your time in making plans, and once you come to a decision, carry it out right away without any hesitation or timidity. Timidity after all is not caution, but the invention of wickedness.

The Emperor Maurice, *The Strategikon*, c. AD 600 (*Maurice's Strategikon*, tr. George Dennis, 1984).

YOU WILL HAVE seen by what I have had occasion to delineate concerning war that promptness contributes a great deal to success in marches and even more in battles. That is why our army is drilled in such a fashion that it acts faster than others. Drill is the basis of these maneuvers which enable us to form in the twinkling of an eye.

Frederick the Great, *Instructions to His Generals*, 1747, tr. Phillips, 1940.

I HAVE ALWAYS been a quarter of an hour before my time, and it has made a man of me.

Admiral Viscount Nelson (1758–1805).

PROMPTNESS is the greatest of military virtues, evincing, as it does, zeal, energy and discipline. The success of arms depends more upon celerity than any one thing else.

Lieutenant-General D.H. Hill, 7 September 1863, circular to his troops in Chattanooga.

IN WAR, procrastination is a crime, and promptness is a handmaiden of victory.

Major-General John A. Lejeune, *The Reminiscences of a Marine*, 1929.

PROPAGANDA

HIS VICTORIES were published in all lands, to cause that every land together may see, to cause the glory of his conquests to appear; King Merneptah, the Bull, lord of strength, who slays his foes, beautiful upon the field of victory. . . . He has penetrated the land of Temeh in his lifetime, and put eternal fear in the heart of Meshwesh. He has turned back Libya, who invaded Egypt, and great fear of Egypt is in their hearts.

Merneptah, Pharaoh of Egypt, c. 1220 BC, celebrating his victory over the Libyans, quoted in James Breasted, *Records of Ancient Egypt*, 1906.

MY COUNTRYMEN, I know, from their form of government, and steady attachment to royalty, will come reluctantly to the idea of independence, but time and persecution bring many wonderful things to pass; and by private letters, which I have lately received from Virginia, I find [Paine's] "Common Sense" is working powerful change there in the minds of many men.

General George Washington, 1 April 1776, letter to Joseph Reed.

WE ARE HERE to guide public opinion, not to discuss it.

Napoleon, 1804, meeting of the *Conseil d'État*, quoted in Christopher Herold, ed., *The Mind of Napoleon*, 1955.

BARERE still believes that the masses must be stirred. On the contrary, they must be guided without noticing it.

Napoleon, 1804, letter to Fouché, quoted in Christopher Herold, ed., *The Mind of Napoleon*, 1955.

HAVE SOME well written articles published deriding the military movements of the Russians, the interview of the Emperor of Russia with the Emperor of Austria, and the absurd reports, phantoms born of the fogs and the spleen of England. Get active, and keep public opinion up. Tell the editors that although I am far away, I still read the papers, and that if they continue on the present tack I shall close their accounts.

Napoleon, 24 April 1805, to Fouché, quoted in R.M. Johnston, ed., *The Corsican*, 1910.

THIS WON'T DO; it will drive the people in England mad. Write me down a victory.

The Duke of Wellington, upon the news of the heavy British casualties suffered in the Battle of Albuera on 16 May 1811, which was described as a defeat, cited in Arthur Bryant, *The Great Duke*, 1972.

INSTEAD of all the stupidities with which the daily press is filled, why do you not send commissioners to visit the districts from which we have expelled the enemy and make them collect the details of the crimes that have been committed there? Nothing more powerful could be found to stir the minds than a recital of the details. What we need at this moment is real and serious things, not wit in prose and verse. My hair stands on end when I hear of the crimes committed by the enemy, and the police have not even thought of obtaining a single account of these happenings. . . . A picture drawn in large strokes will not convince the people. With ink and paper you can draw any pictures you like. Only by telling the facts simply and with details can we convince them.

Napoleon, 27 February 1814, letter to Savary, quoted in Christopher Herold, ed., *The Mind of Napoleon*, 1955.

WE WERE hypnotized by the enemy propaganda as a rabbit is by a snake. It was exceptionally clever and conceived on a great scale. It worked by strong mass-suggestion, kept in the closest touch with the military situation, and was unscrupulous as to the means it used. . . . The Army found no ally in a strong propaganda directed from home. While her Army was victorious on the field of battle, Germany failed in the fight against the *moral* of the enemy peoples.

General Erich Ludendorff, *My War Memories, 1914–1918*, 1919.

PROPAGANDA, as inverted patriotism, draws nourishment from the sins of the enemy. If there are no sins, invent them! The aim is to make the enemy appear so great a monster that he forfeits the rights of a human being. He cannot bring a libel action, so there is no need to stick at trifles.

> General Sir Ian Hamilton, *The Soul and Body of an Army*, 1921.

IT WAS more subtle than tactics, and better worth doing, because it dealt with uncontrollables, with subjects incapable of direct command. It considered the capacity for mood of our men, their complexities and mutability, and the cultivation of whatever in them promised to profit our intention. We had to arrange their minds in order of battle just as carefully and as formally as other officers would arrange their bodies. And not only our men's minds, though naturally they came first. We must also arrange the minds of the enemy, so far as we could reach them; then those other minds of the nation supporting us behind the firing line, since more than half the battle passed there in the back; then the minds of the enemy nation waiting the verdict; and of the neutrals looking on; circle beyond circle.

> Colonel T.E. Lawrence, *The Seven Pillars of Wisdom*, 1935.

DURING the great war a battle of propaganda was waged by all belligerents, though at its beginning few were prepared to wage it. Our object was to prove that the Germans were "dirty dogs," and that it was they who had started the war. I do not suggest that our contentions were wrong, but I cannot help feeling that when the Germans retaliated the means we employed to protect our national character were not of the best. In place of maintaining our reputation for fair play we hired a pack of journalists to defend us. These people, who had spent their lives in raking filth out of the law courts, went to mud with the alacrity of eels, and, though they undoubtedly succeeded in blackening the German nation, we ourselves became somewhat piebald in these gutter attacks.

> Major-General J.F.C. Fuller, *The Foundations of the Science of War*, 1926.

ALL THEY NEED do really is quietly let people know the truth. There is no need to bang the big drum. Official reports should stick to the absolute truth – once you start lying, the war's as good as lost. Information Division's outlook is all wrong. All this talk of guiding public opinion and maintaining the national morale is so much empty puff.

> Admiral Isoroku Yamamoto, 1942, quoted in Agawa, *The Reluctant Admiral*, 1979.

THE POLITICAL SKILL of the Communist government of North Vietnam in portraying their cause in terms that would elicit the support of liberal Americans must be judged one of the most successful in history. They oppressed the Catholic Church and somehow secured the support of a large number of American Roman Catholic clergy. They savagely suppressed any movement that seemed to diverge from the official party line and were supported by large numbers of academics, students, and clergy in the United States and around the world. They were good soldiers but they were world-class propagandists. They won in the media that which they could not win on the battlefield.

> Lieutenant-General William J. McCaffrey, 4 August 1988, letter, quoted in Lee and Cragg, *Inside the VC and the NVA*, 1992.

PSYCHOLOGICAL OPERATIONS

TO SEDUCE the enemy's soldiers from their allegiance and encourage them to surrender is of especial service, for an adversary is more hurt by desertion than by slaughter.

> Flavius Vegetius Renatus, *The Military Institutions of the Romans*, c. AD 378, tr. Clark, 1776.

LETTERS ought to be sent to deserters from our side who have joined the enemy in such a way that the letters will fall into the enemy's hands. These letters should remind the deserters of the prearranged time for their treachery, so that the enemy will become suspicious of them, and they will have to flee.

> The Emperor Maurice, *The Strategikon*, c. AD 600 (*Maurice's Strategikon*, tr. George Dennis, 1984).

AS FOR taking away the heart of their generals, the heart is the ruler of the general – order and disorder, courage and timidity, all are based on the mind. So those skilled in controlling opponents stir them into disorder, incite them to confusion, press them into fear – thus can the schemes in their hearts be taken away.

> Chang Yü (Zhang Yu), c. 1200, late Sung Dynasty commentator to Sun Tzu, *The Art of War*, 7, c. 500 BC, tr. Thomas Cleary.

IT IS your attitude, and the suspicion that you are maturing the boldest designs against him, that imposes on your enemy.

> Frederick the Great, *Instructions to His Generals*, 1747, tr. Phillips, 1940.

AS the excited passions of hostile people are of themselves a powerful enemy, both the general and his government should use their best efforts to ally them.

> Lieutenant-General Antoine-Henri Baron de Jomini, *Summary of the Art of War*, 1838, tr. Mendell and Craighill, 1862.

THE ENEMY bombards our front not only with a drumfire of artillery, but also with a drumfire of printed paper. Besides bombs which kill the body, his airmen also throw down leaflets which are intended to kill the soul.

> Field Marshal Paul von Hindenburg (1847–1934).

THE REAL TARGET in war is the mind of the enemy command, not the bodies of his troops. If we operate against his troops it is fundamentally for the effect that action will produce on the mind and will of the commander; indeed, the trend of warfare and the development of new weapons – aircraft and tanks – promise to give us increased and more direct opportunities of striking at this psychological target. (June 1926.)

Captain Sir Basil Liddell Hart, *Thoughts on War*, 1944.

FOR A STRONG adversary (corps) the opposition of twenty-four squadrons and twelve guns ought not to have appeared very serious, but in war the psychological factors are often decisive. An adversary who feels inferior is in reality so.

Field Marshal Carl Gustav Baron von Mannerheim, *The Memoirs of Field Marshal Mannerheim*, 1953.

LENIN had a vision of fundamental truth when he said that "the soundest strategy in war is to postpone operations until the moral disintegration of the enemy renders delivery of the mortal blow both possible and easy". This is not always practicable, nor his methods of propaganda always fruitful. But it will bear adaptation – "The soundest strategy in any campaign is to postpone battle and the soundest tactics to postpone attack, until the moral dislocation of the enemy renders the delivery of a decisive blow practicable".

Captain Sir Basil Liddell Hart, *Strategy*, 1954.

PUBLIC OPINION

NOTHING is more dangerous in wartime than to live in the temperamental atmosphere of a Gallup Poll, always feeling one's pulse and taking one's temperature. I see that a speaker at the week-end said that this was a time when leaders should keep their ears to the ground. All I can say is that the British nation will find it very hard to look up to leaders who are detected in that somewhat ungainly posture.

Sir Winston S. Churchill, speech in the House of Commons, 30 September 1941, *Winston S. Churchill: His Complete Speeches, 1897–1963*, VI, 1974, p. 6495.

WE ARE TOLD that we must not alarm the easygoing voter and public. How thin and paltry these arguments will sound if we are caught a year or two hence, fat, opulent and defenceless.

Sir Winston S. Churchill, quoted in James Hume, *The Wit & Wisdom of Winston S. Churchill*, 1995.

FINALLY, there is the matter of the U.S. public. The people, as a whole, find this war very hard to rationalize, so much so that many of them are unwilling to study or find out the facts. Without regard to what their personal viewpoint may be, I just wish that people were more curious. I think we could live

with informed hawks and informed doves. The thing we cannot live with are uninformed ostriches or, regrettably more often, uninformed mynah birds.

Lieutenant-General Victor H. 'The Brute' Krulak, 24 April 1968, address to the Navy League Convention, *Navy Magazine*, 6/1968.

PUNISHMENTS/REWARDS AND PUNISHMENTS

IN GENERAL, in employing rewards one values credibility; in employing punishments one values certainty. When rewards are trusted and punishments inevitable wherever the eye sees and the ear hears, then even where they do not see or hear there is no one who will not be transformed in their secrecy.

The T'ai Kung, c. 1100 BC (*The Seven Military Classics of Ancient China*, tr. Ralph Sawyer, 1993).

THE GENERAL creates awesomeness by executing the great and becomes enlightened by rewarding the small. Prohibitions are made effective and laws implemented by careful scrutiny in the use of punishments. Therefore if by executing one man the entire army will quake, kill him. If by rewarding one man the masses will be pleased, reward him. In executing, value the great; in rewarding, value the small. When you kill the powerful and the honored, this is punishment that reaches the pinnacle. When rewards extend down to the cowherds, grooms, and stablemen, these are rewards penetrating downward to the lowest. When punishments reach the pinnacle and rewards penetrate to the lowest, then your awesomeness has been effected.

The T'ai Kung, c. 1100 BC (*The Seven Military Classics of Ancient China*, tr. Ralph Sawyer, 1993).

BESTOW rewards without regard to rule, issue orders without regard to previous arrangements and you will be able to handle a whole army.

Sun Tzu, *The Art of War*, c. 500 BC, tr. Giles, 1910.

WHEN a Persian inquired what type of constitution met with his greatest approval, he said: "whichever gives brave men and cowards their due."

Plutarch, quoting Lysander (k. 395 BC), *The Lives*, c. AD 100, (*Plutarch on Sparta*, tr. Richard Talbert, 1988).

REWARDS and punishments must be reliable, otherwise troops will not halt at the sound of the gong or advance at the sound of the drum, so that even if there are a million of them, what use are they?

Wu Ch'i, d. 381 BC, quoted in Dennis and Ching Ping Bloodworth, *The Chinese Machiavelli*, 1976.

AND SO by means of such incentives even those who stay at home feel the impulse to emulate such achievements in the field no less than those who are present and see and hear what takes place. . . . When we consider this [the Roman] people's almost obsessive concern with military rewards and punishments, and the immense importance which they attach to both, it is not surprising that they emerge with brilliant success from every war in which they engage.

Polybius, *Histories*, 6.39, c. 125 BC (*The Rise of the Roman Empire*, tr. Ian Scott-Kilvert, 1987).

IN ONE DAY, then, six battles were fought, three at Durazzo and three at the earthworks. When an accounting was made we found that about 2,000 of the Pompeians had fallen, including many veterans and centurions . . . and that six of their military standards had been brought in. We lost not more than twenty men in all the battles; but in the redoubt every single man was wounded and four centurions of one cohort had lost their eyes. Wishing to produce evidence of their exertion and danger they counted out to Caesar some 30,000 arrows which had been shot into the redoubt, and when the shield of centurion Scaeva was brought forward 120 holes were found in it. In recognition of their services to himself and the state (it was clear that Scaeva was largely responsible for saving the redoubt) Caesar presented him with 200,000 sesterces, read a citation for him, and promoted him from the eighth rank to senior centurion. Later Caesar rewarded the cohort generously with double pay, grain, clothing, and military decorations.

Julius Caesar, *The Civil War*, c. 45 BC, tr. Moses Hadas.

REWARDS strengthen the self-esteem of those who have deserved well, and encourage others who desire similar rewards. . . . Whenever honour is paid to the brave and punishment of the cowardly is not neglected, then an army must have fair expectation; the latter are afraid to be found wanting, the former are ambitious to show prowess. It is not only necessary in victory to distribute rewards to the individual men but also make a recompense to the army as a whole.

Onasander, *The General*, AD 58 (*Aeneas Tacticus, Aclepiodotus, Onasander*, tr. The Illinois Greek Club, 1923).

THE PERSECUTION of genius fosters its influence; foreign tyrants, and all who have imitated their oppression, have merely procured infamy for themselves and glory for their victims.

Tacitus, *Annals*, 4.35, AD 116, (*The Complete Works of Tacitus*, tr. Alfred Church and William Brodribb, 1942).

A POLICY of rewards and penalties means rewarding the good and penalizing wrongdoers. Rewarding the good is to promote achievement; penalizing wrongdoers is to prevent treachery.

It is imperative that rewards and punishments be fair and impartial. When they know rewards are to be given, courageous warriors know what they are

dying for; when they know penalties are to be applied, villains know what to fear.

Therefore, reward should not be given without reason, and penalties should not be applied arbitrarily. If rewards are given for no reason, those who have worked hard in public service will be resentful; if penalties are applied arbitrarily, upright people will be bitter.

Zhuge Liang (AD 180–234), *The Way of the General* (*Mastering the Art of War*, tr. Thomas Cleary, 1989).

PUNISHMENT, and fear thereof, are necessary to keep soldiers in order in quarters; but in the field they are more influenced by hope and rewards.

Flavius Vegetius Renatus, *Military Institutions of the Romans*, c. AD 378, tr. Clark, 1776.

HE OUGHT NOT to be easy with those who have committed offenses out of cowardice or carelessness in the hope of being regarded as a good leader, for a good leader does not encourage cowardice or laziness. On the other hand, he ought not to punish hastily and without a full investigation just to show he can act firmly. The first leads to contempt and disobedience; the other to well-deserved hatred with all its consequences. Both of these are extremes. The better course is to join fear with justice, that is, impose a fitting punishment upon offenders after proof of guilt. This, for reasonable men, is not punishment, but correction, and aids in maintaining order and discipline.

The Emperor Maurice, *The Strategikon*, c. AD 600 (*Maurice's Strategikon*, tr. George Dennis, 1984).

PARADISE is under the shadow of our swords. Forward!

Omar I Ibn Al Khattab, Caliph, AD 637, at the Battle of Quadisiya.

FOR SOLDIERS to strive to scale high walls in spite of deep moats and showers of arrows and rocks, or for soldiers to plunge eagerly into the fray of battle, they must be induced by serious rewards; then they will prevail over any enemy.

The rule is "Where there are serious rewards, there will be valiant men."

Liu Ji (1310–1375), *Lessons of War* (*Mastering the Art of War*, tr. Thomas Cleary, 1989).

O SONS, brothers, and nephews who are here in the presence of the majesty of our ruler Motecuhzoma, I, Tlacaelel, wish to give more courage to those who are of a strong heart and embolden those who are weak so that the prize for their deeds will encourage them. I wish to compare the strong and the weak and mention their rewards or their retribution. When you go to the marketplace and see a precious ear ornament or nose pendant, or when you see splendid and beautiful feathers or a rich gilded shield, or weapons done in featherwork, do you not covet them, do you not pay the price that is asked? Know now that the king, who is here before you, has willed that labrets, golden garlands, many-colored feathers, ear ornaments, armbands, shields, weapons, insignia, rich mantles, and breechcloths are no longer to be purchased in the market by brave men. Now the sovereign will deliver them as payment and prize for heroic feats, for memorable deeds. Each one of you, when he goes into battle, to perform great feats, must keep in mind that, while he is carrying out these heroic acts in war, he has in reality gone to the marketplace where he will find all these priceless things, for upon returning from the war he will receive them according to his merits and so that he can display these as proof of his worth.

Tlacaelel, c. 1450, the promulgation of the Aztec code of the warrior, quoted in Diego Durán, *The History of the Indies of New Spain*, 1581, tr. Doris Heyden, 1994.

IF A MAN who serves indolently and a man who serves well are treated in the same way, the man who serves well may begin to wonder why he does so.

Asakura Toshikage (1428–1481), *The 17 Articles of Asakura Toshikage* (*Ideals of the Samurai*, tr. William Wilson, 1982).

THE CONSCIOUSNESS of having attempted faithfully to discharge my duty, and the approbation of my Country will be a sufficient recompense for my Services.

General George Washington, 18 March 1783, to the President of Congress, *The Writings of George Washington*, XXVI, p. 232, John C. Fitzgerald, ed., 1938.

I INTEND to make the generals and officers who have served me well so rich that there can be no excuse for their dishonouring the most noble of professions by their greed, while drawing upon themselves the contempt of the soldiers.

Napoleon, 15 November 1805, after the victory at Ulm, quoted in R.M. Johnston, ed., *The Corsican*, 1910.

. . . THEN there is this further observation (which I entreat the board to bear in mind), that the regularity, and order, and discipline of the corps, is not merely a public affair; it is not only that the regiment may be fit to do its service for the public, but I say that it is a positive breach of faith with the good man, if discipline should not be enforced. I will suppose that there are 100 men in a company, 80 of whom behave exceedingly well, and submit to all your regulations (and I apprehend that will be found to be pretty nearly the usual proportion); there will be 80 of them who will never commit a fault of any description; they lead a quiet life in the barracks, and do every thing that you require from them; but there are 20 that will not do so. What happens? These 20 are constantly disturbing the peace and the comfort of the 80, and there is perpetual riot and

disorder going on in the barracks besides. These men are perpetually in a state of punishment; they are either *billed-up*, or they are in confinement in the guard house, or they are in confinement in the gaol, or in some way or other. The consequence is, that these 80 are obliged to do their duty for them; so that, by not enforcing your own orders, and not punishing when those orders are not obeyed, you are doing the grossest injustice to those who do obey your orders.

The Duke of Wellington, evidence given before the Royal Commission for Inquiring into Military Punishments, n.d., *The Dispatches of Field Marshal the Duke of Wellington, During His Various Campaigns in India, Denmark, Portugal, Spain, the Low Countries, and France*, VIII, 1834–38, pp. 351–352.

ALL IS WELL with me. Every thing looks bright and favorable in this command. – I feel under many obligations to you for the interest you have taken in my welfare. But recollect that I have been highly honored already by the government and do not ask, or feel that I deserve, any thing more in the shape of honors or promotion. A success over the enemy is what I crave above every thing els (sic) and desire to hold such an influance (sic) over those under my command as to enable me to use them to the best advantage to secure this end.

General of the Army Ulysses S. Grant, 12 December 1863, letter to Senator Elihu B. Washburne, Chattanooga, quoted in *The Papers of USG*, IX, 1982, p. 522. At the time, Washburn had put forward a bill to revive the rank of lieutenant-general in the U.S. Army.

MEASURED military punishment, together with a short and clear explanation of the offense, touches the ambitious soldier more than brutality which drives him to despair.

General William T. Sherman, *Memoirs*, II, 1875.

THE GREAT MERIT in giving rewards is to give them promptly; it can not be considered generous when they are doled out too carefully.

Admiral David D. Porter, *Incidents and Anecdotes of the Civil War*, 1885.

DUE TO maudlin sentimentality it is not possible to cause the mass of a nation to view military punishments from their proper angle, namely as administrative rather than judicial acts, whose purpose in wartime is not to wreak vengence on the guilty but rather to restrain the innocent.

For example, the idea back of the death sentence for such acts as desertion, sleeping on post, skulking, etc., is not inherent in the offense itself. Desertion has perhaps no extenuation, but the other offenses usually have.

The poor tired boy who sleeps on his post is more to be pitied than blamed insofar as his individual case is concerned. But the act, harmless in itself, may have exposed scores or hundreds of his equally deserving comrades to capture, wounds and death. It is for their sake, not his fault, that the final penalty should be exacted of him.

A man may, under the influence of fatigue, so forget his obligation as to chance a term of imprisonment against a moment's oblivion, but he will think several times before he makes the same gamble with the certainty of death, his own death, not that of his comrades.

So with the skulker. . . . he cuts the very root of military virtue, which is based on mutual confidence.

The execution of a skulker is necessary, not for his sin but for his betrayal of his comrades. Judas is execrated for the betrayal of One, should he who betrays hundreds escape?

General George S. Patton, Jr. from his 1927 lecture, 'Why Men Fight', from the Patton Collection, United States Military Academy Library.

I MADE IT A RULE never to reprimand an enlisted man, or to censure an officer in the presence of his men. How could a Division Commander correct conditions among 28,000 men by shouting at an individual who might perhaps have his coat unbuttoned, or have on rubber boots under forbidden circumstances; or how could junior officers retain the respect of their men if scathingly rebuked in their presence?

Major-General John A. Lejeune, *The Reminiscences of a Marine*, 1929.

PURSUIT

AND HERE came Nestor
with orders ringing down the field: "My comrades –
Fighting Danaans, aides of Ares – no plunder now!
Don't lag behind, don't fling yourself at spoils
just to haul the biggest portion back to the ship.
Now's the time for killing! Later, at leisure,
strip the corpses up and down the plain!"
So he ordered, spuring each man's nerve –

Homer, *The Iliad*, 6.77–84, c. 800 BC, tr. Robert Fagles, 1990; Nestor urging the Achaeans not to be distracted from the pursuit of the fleeing Trojans.

A PURSUIT gives even cowards confidence.

Xenophon, 400 BC, speech to the Greek Army at Calpe on the Black Sea, *Anabasis*, c. 360 BC.

NO, you must realize what has been accomplished in this battle. In five days you will feast victoriously in the Capital. Follow me. I will go ahead with the cavalry and they will learn of your arrival before they know you are coming.

Maharbal Barca, the commander of the Carthaginian cavalry after the battle of Cannae, when his brother, Hannibal, preferred to rest the army rather than pursue, 2 August 216 BC, quoted in Livy, *Annals of the Roman People*, c. 25 BC–AD 17 (*Livy: A History of Rome*, 22, tr. Moses Hadas and Joe Poe, 1962).

IT IS a great feat to steer a policy to a successful conclusion or to overcome one's enemies in a campaign, but it requires a great deal more skill and caution to make good use of such triumphs. Thus we find that those who have won victories are far more numerous than those who have used them well . . .

Polybius, *Histories*, 10.36, c. 125 BC (*The Rise of the Roman Empire*, tr. Ian Scott-Kilvert, 1979).

HE WHO rashly pursues a flying enemy with troops in disorder, seems bent upon throwing away that victory which he had before obtained.

Flavius Vegetius Renatus, *Military Institutions of the Romans*, c. AD 378, tr. Clark, 1776.

AFTER gaining a victory the general who pursues the enemy with a scattered and disorganized army gives away his victory to the foe.

The Emperor Maurice, *The Strategikon*, c. AD 600 (*Maurice's Strategikon*, tr. George Dennis, 1984).

THE WORDS of the proverb: "A bridge of gold should be made for the enemy," is followed religiously. This is false. On the contrary, the pursuit should be pushed to the limit. And the retreat which had appeared such a satisfactory solution will be turned into a route [*sic*]. A detachment of ten thousand men can destroy an army of one hundred thousand in flight. Nothing inspires so much terror or occasions so much damage, for everything is lost. Substantial efforts are required to restore the defeated army, and in addition you are rid of the enemy for a good time. But many generals do not worry about finishing the war so soon.

Field Marshal Maurice Comte de Saxe, *My Reveries*, 1732, tr. Phillips, 1940.

ONCE the enemy has taken flight they can be pursued with no better weapons than air-filled bladders. But if the officer you have ordered in pursuit prides himself on the regularity of his formations and the precautions of his march . . . there is no use in having sent him. He must attack, push and pursue without cease.

Field Marshal Maurice Comte de Saxe, *My Reveries*, 1732, tr. Phillips, 1940.

THE ENEMY is pursued to the first defile; all the harm possible is to be done to him, but you should not allow yourself to become so drunk with success that you become imprudent. If the enemy is thoroughly defeated, make several marches after him and you will gain a prodigious amount of territory. But always camp in accordance with regulations!

Frederick the Great, *Instructions to His Generals*, 1747, tr. Phillips, 1940.

HE WHO never runs, can never be pursued.

Lieutenant-General Johann von Ewald, *A Treatise on the Duties of Light Troops*, 1790.

ONLY PURSUIT destroys a running enemy.
Field Marshal Prince Aleksandr V. Suvorov
(1729–1800).

DO NOT DELAY in the attack. When the foe has
been split off and cut down, pursue him
immediately and give him no time to assemble or
form up. . . . spare nothing. Without regard for
difficulties, pursue the enemy day and night until he
has been annihilated.
Field Marshal Prince Aleksandr V. Suvorov
(1729–1800).

PURSUE to the last man to the Adda and throw the
remains into the river.
Field Marshal Prince Aleksandr V. Suvorov, 1799,
during the Italian campaign.

A STRONG PURSUIT, give no time for the enemy to
think, take advantage of victory, uproot him, cut off
his escape.
Field Marshal Prince Aleksandr V. Suvorov
(1729–1800).

IN CASES of obstacles arising, don't be too
distracted by them. Time is more valuable than
anything else – one must know how to save it. Often
our previous victories remained without results
because of insufficient men. The falsest of rules is
the conviction that after an enemy defeat everything
is over, whereas the fact is that it is necessary to try
for even greater success.
Field Marshal Prince Aleksandr V. Suvorov
(1729–1800).

NOT DAYS nor hours, but even moments are
valuable in such a situation; want of provisions
cannot serve you as an excuse.
Field Marshal Prince Aleksandr V. Suvorov
(1729–1800).

FOLLOW a defeated enemy ruthlessly and put the
fear of Shaka into him.
Shaka Zulu (c. 1787–1828), military maxim, quoted in
E.A. Ritter, Shaka Zulu, 1955.

MAXIM 83. A general-in-chief should never allow
any rest either to the conqueror or to the
conquered.
Napoleon, The Military Maxims of Napoleon, tr.
Burnod, 1827.

NEXT to victory, the act of pursuit is the most
important in war.
Major-General Carl von Clausewitz, Principles of
War, 1812, tr. Gatzke, 1942.

PURSUIT of a beaten enemy begins the moment he
concedes the fight and abandons his position. At this
juncture victory, while assured, is usually still limited
and modest in its dimensions. Little positive

advantage would be gained in the normal course of
events unless victory were consummated by pursuit
on the first day. It is usually only then . . . that
trophies [prisoners, guns, etc.] tend to be taken
which will embody the victory . . .
Major-General Carl von Clausewitz, On War, 4.12,
1832, tr. Michael Howard and Peter Paret, 1976.

THE IMPORTANCE of the victory is chiefly
determined by the vigor with which the immediate
pursuit is carried out. In other words, pursuit makes
up the second act of victory and in many cases is
more important than the first. Strategy at this point
draws near to tactics in order to receive the
completed assignment from it; and its first exercise
of authority is to demand that the victory should
really be complete.
Major-General Carl von Clausewitz, On War, 4.12,
1832, tr. Michael Howard and Peter Paret, 1976.

. . . TO FOLLOW UP the success we gain with the
utmost energy. The pursuit of the enemy when
defeated is the only means of gathering up the fruits
of victory.
Major-General Carl von Clausewitz, On War, 1832, tr.
Michael Howard and Peter Paret, 1976.

A PURSUIT should generally be executed as boldly
and actively as possible, especially when it is
subsequent to a battle gained, because the
demoralized army may be wholly dispersed if
vigorously followed up.
Lieutenant-General Antoine-Henri Baron de Jomini,
Summary of the Art of War, 1838, tr. Mendell and
Craighill, 1862.

WHEN you strike the enemy and overcome him,
never give up the pursuit as long as your men have
strength to follow; for an enemy routed, if hotly
pursued, becomes panic-stricken, and can be
destroyed by half their number.
Lieutenant-General Thomas J. 'Stonewall' Jackson
(1824–1863).

DO NOT FAIL in that event to make the most of the
opportunity by the most vigorous attack possible, as
it may save us what we have most reason to
apprehend – a slow pursuit, in which he gains
strength as we lose it.
General of the Army William T. Sherman, 1864, quoted
in Liddell Hart, Sherman, 1930.

A PROMPT and vigorous pursuit is the only means
of ensuring complete success.
General of the Army Phillip H. Sheridan (1831–1888).

. . . NEVER on a battle-field to lose a moment's
time, but leaving the killed, wounded and spoils to
those whose special business it is to care for
them, to press on with every available man,
giving a panic-stricken and retreating foe no time

to rally, and reaping all the benefits of a success never complete until every enemy is killed, wounded or captured.

General Braxton Bragg, official report of the Battle of Shiloh, one of the most self-mocking statements ever made by a general, *The War of the Rebellion: A Compilation of the Official Records of the Union and Confederate Armies*, Serial No. I, Vol. X, p. 470, US Government Printing Office, 1880–1901.

THAT WHICH hitherto, on our part, had been a pursuit after a broken and routed army now resolved itself into an exciting chase after a panic-stricken, uncontrollable mob. It was no longer a question to be decided by force of arms, by skill, or by courage; it was simply a question of speed between pursuers and pursued; prisoners were taken by hundreds, entire companies threw down their arms and appeared glad when summoned to surrender.

Major-General George A. Custer, of the Battle of Cedar Creek, 19 October 1864, *The War of the Rebellion: A Compilation of the Official Records of the Union and Confederate Armies*, Series I, Vol. 43, Part 1, p. 535.

STRENUOUS, unrelaxing pursuit is therefore as imperative after a battle as is courage during it.

Rear Admiral Alfred Thayer Mahan, *Naval Strategy*, 1911.

IN PURSUIT you must always stretch possibilities to the limit. Troops having beaten the enemy will want to rest. They must be given as objectives, not those that you think they will reach, but the farthest they could possibly reach.

Field Marshal Viscount Allenby of Meggido, 1917, Order to XXI Corps, Philistia.

PURSUIT will hold the first place in your thoughts. It is at the moment when the victor is most exhausted that the greatest forfeit can be extracted from the vanquished.

Sir Winston S. Churchill, 13 December 1940, to Lord Wavell after his victory over the Italians in the Libyan desert.

WHILE COOLNESS in disaster is the supreme proof of a commander's courage, energy in pursuit is the surest test of his strength of will.

Field Marshal Viscount Wavell of Cyrenaica, unpublished *Recollections*, 1946.

Q

QUALITY

THE COMMANDER who has five or six thousand of our heavy cavalry and the help of God will need nothing more.
> The Emperor Nikephoros II Phokas (AD 912–969).

AT MY FIRST going out into this engagement I saw our men beaten at every hand. . . . "Your troops," said I, "are most of them old decayed serving-men, and tapsters, and such like fellows; and," said I, "their troops are gentlemen's sons, younger sons and persons of quality: do you think that the spirits of such base mean fellows will ever be able to encounter gentlemen, that have honor and courage and resolution in them? . . . You must get men of spirit: and take it not ill what I say, – I know you will not, – of a spirit that is likely to go on as far as gentlemen will go: or else you will be beaten still."
> Oliver Cromwell, October 1642, to John Hampden after the Battle of Edgehill.

IT IS NOT the big armies that win battles; it is the good ones.
> Field Marshal Maurice Comte de Saxe, *My Reveries*, 1732, tr. Phillips, 1940.

I HAVE a handsome army of about 1,700 "total" to wit: the 9th, 11th, 21st, and 25th regiments and two companies 2d artillery. . . . I am most partial to these regiments. The men are healthy, sober, cheerful, and docile. The field officers highly respectable, and many of the platoon officers are decent and emulous of improvement. If, of such materials, I do not make the best army now in service, by the 1st of June, I will agree to be dismissed from the service.
> Major-General Winfield Scott, 6 May 1814, letter to Brigadier William H. Winder at the end of the training programme that would take his brigade to victory at the Battle of Chippewa, 5 July 1814, *Ohio State Journal*, 26 October 1852.

NOT ALONE is the strength of the Fleet measured by the number of its fighting units, but by its efficiency, by its ability to proceed promptly where it is needed and to engage and overcome an enemy.
> Admiral Richard Wainwright, 1911.

IN DOWNSIZING military manpower, there is always a tendency to lose highly capable combat leaders who are ambitious and restless. They want to try other professions during peacetime. But at the same time, the military has always been able to keep a cadre of quality leaders who believe that their function in life is to rise to the top. They offset the numbers of quality people who leave the service. The farthest down the modern American military has been was right before World War II. The Army was gutted down to 136,000 people. Yet they were able to produce leaders like Eisenhower, MacArthur, and Patton.
> James Webb, 'Roles and Missions', Al Santoli, ed., *Leading the Way: How Vietnam Veterans Rebuilt the U.S. Military*, 1993.

MORE is not better, better is better.
> General Gordon R. Sullivan, quoted in *Military Review*, July–August 1996.

GOOD isn't enough. We need brilliant because the enemies we will face often will be the best their countries and cultures have to offer.
> Lieutenant-Colonel Ralph Peters, *Army Times*, 24 August 1998.

QUARTER

GLASDALE, Glasdale, yield to the King of Heaven. You have called me "whore": I pity your soul and the souls of your men.
> Joan of Arc, 7 May 1429, to the English commander in the assault on the bridge at Orléans, *Joan of Arc in her Own Words*, 1996.

WE MUST SPARE our enemies or it will be our loss, since they and all that belong to them must soon be ours.
> Anonymous Inca prince.

MAGDEBURG Quarter!
> For years after the massacre of the city of Magdeburg in May 1631, Imperialist soldiers attempting to surrender would be met with this Protestant response as they were shot down, quoted in C.V. Wedgwood, *The Thirty Years War*, 1938.

TARLETON Quarter!
> Battle cry of the American troops at the Battle of Cowpens, 17 January 1781, during the Revolution, referring to the merciless conduct of the British commander, Lieutenant-Colonel Banastre Tarleton, who had offered no quarter to the Americans in previous engagements.

QUOTATIONS AND MAXIMS

THE FACULTY of deciding at once and with certainty belongs only to him who, by his own experience, has tested the truth of the known maxims and possesses the manner of applying them; to him alone, in a word, who finds beforehand, in his positive acquirements, the conviction of the accuracy of his judgments.
The Archduke Charles of Austria (1771–1847).

I HATE quotations. Tell me what you know.
Ralph Waldo Emerson, *Journals*, 1849.

MAXIMS of war . . . are not so much positive rules as they are the development and applications of a few general principles. . . . the maxim rooting itself in a principle, formulates a rule generally correct under the conditions; but the teacher must admit each case has its own features – like the endless variety of the one human face – which modify the application of the rule, and may even make it at times wholly inapplicable. It is for the skill of the artist in war rightly to apply the principles and rules in each case.
Rear-Admiral Alfred Thayer Mahan, *Naval Strategy*, 1911.

IT IS a good thing for an uneducated man to read books of quotations.
Sir Winston S. Churchill, *My Early Life*, 1930.

CATCHWORDS and trite phrases are not the same thing as quotations, although not unrelated; for quotations also tend to have ridiculous and dangerous associations. At the same time it is undoubtedly convenient to find that someone else has already expressed the same thought in a happy and generally accepted form; not to mention the fact that literary people are agreeably surprised or impressed when they find a soldier occasionally quoting Goethe or even Greek, suggesting an intellectual capacity in excess of that required for reading the drill book. That is why I sometimes make quotations myself.
Colonel-General Hans von Seeckt, *Thoughts of a Soldier*, 1930.

THERE WAS a certain general, now dead but universally esteemed and respected in his day, who was a veritable fountain of information. Whenever he was asked to express an opinion on some military situation he would always begin by saying, "In such a situation Frederick the Great would say," etc., and then would follow some invariably apposite quotation. But the best quotation, the best parallel present to the mind will not relieve the soldier of the difficulty of decision.
Colonel-General Hans von Seekt, *Thoughts of a Soldier*, 1930.

PROFESSIONAL soldiers are sentimental men, for all the harsh realities of their calling. In their wallets they carry bits of philosophy, fragments of poetry, quotations from the Scriptures which in time of stress and danger speak to them with great meaning.
General Matthew B. Ridgway, *My Battles in War and Peace*, 1956.

NOTHING so comforts the military mind as the maxim of a great but dead general.
Barbara W. Tuchman, *The Guns of August*, 1962.

R

RANK

DO NOT look down on others because of your own elevated rank.
> Zhuge Liang (AD 189–234), *The Way of the General* (*Mastering the Art of War*, tr. Thomas Cleary, 1989).

THE RANK of Officers, which to me, Sir, is much dearer than the Pay.
> General George Washington, 29 May 1754, to Robert Dinwiddie, *Writings*, I, 1931, p. 83.

I WILL FIGHT under your command with the noblest abnegation. There are no rivalries as far as I am concerned when the independence of America is at stake. Be assured, General; come to Peru; count on my sincere cooperation. I shall be your lieutenant.
> General Jose de San Martin, c. 1822, letter to General Simon Bolivar, quoted in Ricardo Rojas, *San Martin*, 1957.

TRUTH TO SPEAK, I do not appreciate this matter of rank on paper, as you officers do. The world will not forget that you fought the battle of "Stone River" and it will never care a fig whether you rank General Grant on paper, or he ranks you.
> President Abraham Lincoln, 17 March 1862, letter to Major-General William S. Rosecrans, *Collected Works of Abraham Lincoln*, VI, 1953.

WHILE RANK should be *no patriot's motive*, it is nevertheless the acknowledged evidence of appreciation, and when withheld from one occupying a position corresponding to higher rank the inference is against the officer and prejudicial to him.
> Major-General J.E.B. Stuart, 6 February 1864, letter to Colonel A. Boteler, *Letters of Major General James E.B. Stuart*, 1990.

DO NOT hesitate to give commands to officers in whom you repose confidence without regard to claims of others on account of rank.
> General of the Army Ulysses S. Grant, August 1864, letter to Major-General Philip Sheridan, *Papers of USG*, XI, 1982, pp. 379–380.

I WILL ACCEPT no commission that would tend to create a rivalry with Grant. I want him to hold what he has earned and got. I have all the rank I want.
> General of the Army William T. Sherman, 22 January 1865, letter to his brother.

AT THE TIME [1862] he [Sherman] was my senior in rank and there was no authority of law to assign a junior to command a senior of the same grade. But every boat that came up with supplies or reinforcements brought a note of encouragement from Sherman, asking me to call upon him for any assistance he could render, saying that if he could be of service at the front I might send for him and he would waive rank.
> General of the Army Ulysses S. Grant, *Personal Memoirs*, I, 1885.

I THINK of rank but of trivial importance so that it is sufficient for the individual to exercise command.
> General Robert E. Lee (1807–1870).

FOR, apart from the fact that exposure is one of the penalties of rank in the navy, it will always be the aim of the enemy to destroy the flag-ship. . . .
> Admiral David G. Farragut, quoted in Alfred Thayer Mahan, *Admiral Farragut*, 1892.

AFTER the close of the war I was once conversing with Gen. Grant when he remarked playfully that in all the changes in rank which occurred to officers in our service he thought the one which was felt to be the most important was when one was promoted from Brevet 2nd Lieutenant to 2nd Lieutenant! (The General himself had served for more than two years a Brevet 2nd Lieutenant.) I admitted that that was certainly an important event in one's history, but according to my observation there was one change which beat it all to pieces. "What is that?" he asked. I replied "when one drops from a Major General to a Captain."
> Major-General John Gibbon, referring to the loss of wartime rank in the post-war army, *Personal Reminiscences of the Civil War*, 1928.

THE BARRIER of rank is the highest of all barriers in the way of access to the truth.
> Captain Sir Basil Liddell Hart, *Thoughts on War*, 1944.

THE BADGE of rank which an officer wears on his coat is really a symbol of servitude to his men.
> General Maxwell D. Taylor, *The Field Artillery Journal*, January/February 1947.

RANK should be used to serve one's subordinates. It should never be flaunted or used to get the upper hand of a subordinate in any situation save where he had already discredited himself in an unusually ugly or unseemly manner.

> Brigadier-General S.L.A. Marshall, *The Armed Forces Officer*, 1950.

RANK is only given you in the Army to enable you to better serve those below you and those above you. Rank is not given for you to exercise your idiosyncrasies.

> General Bruce C. Clarke (1901–1988), *Thoughts on Leadership*.

ONE of the problems inherent in possessing rank and owning the responsibility of command is that people don't think you're quite human. You can't get drunk even every now and then. (But there have never been too many teetotalers among the military, if we leave out Stonewall Jackson and – I suppose – Sir Galahad.)

> General Curtis LeMay, *Mission With LeMay*, 1965.

RASHNESS

REMEMBER, that even intrepidity must be restrained within certain moderate limits, and, when it becomes pernicious, ceases to be honourable.

> Count Belisarius, (c. AD 505–565), urging restraint upon his troops, quoted in Mahon, *Life of Belisarius*, 1829.

OUR COMMANDER ought to adapt his strategems to the disposition of the enemy general. If the latter is inclined to rashness, he may be enticed into premature and reckless action; if he is on the timid side, he may be struck down with continual surprise attacks.

> The Emperor Maurice, *The Strategikon*, c. AD 600 (*Maurice's Strategikon*, tr. George Dennis, 1984).

LONG and careful deliberation promises great safety in war, whereas hasty and impetuous generals usually commit serious blunders.

> The Emperor Maurice, *The Strategikon*, c. AD 600 (*Maurice's Strategikon*, tr. George Dennis, 1984).

I MAY BE accused of rashness but not of sluggishness.

> Napoleon, 6 May 1796, *Correspondance de Napoléon Ier, publiée par ordre de l'Empereur Napoléon III*, No. 337, Vol. I, 1858–1870.

RASHNESS succeeds often, still more often fails.

> Napoleon (1769–1821).

RASHNESS in war is prudence.

> Admiral Sir John Fisher, *Memories*, 1919.

READINESS

THE ART of war teaches us to rely not on the likelihood of the enemy's not coming, but on our own readiness to receive him; not on the chance of his not attacking but rather on the fact that we have made our positions unassailable.

> Sun Tzu, *The Art of War*, 8, c. 500 BC, tr. Giles, 1910.

A GENERAL who desires peace must be prepared for war, for the barbarians become very nervous when they face an adversary all set to fight.

> The Emperor Maurice, *The Strategikon*, c. AD 600 (*Maurice's Strategikon*, tr. George Dennis, 1984).

ORDERS should be given to the soldiers that they should be ready to march out on a holiday, in the rain, day or night. For this reason they should not be told the time or the day beforehand, so they may always be prepared.

> The Emperor Maurice, *The Strategikon*, c. AD 600 (*Maurice's Strategikon*, tr. George Dennis, 1984).

MAXIM 7. An army should be ready every day, every night, and at all times of the day and night, to oppose all the resistance of which it is capable. With this view, the soldier should be invariably complete in arms and ammunition; the infantry should never be without its artillery, its cavalry, and its generals.

> Napoleon, *The Military Maxims of Napoleon*, tr. George D'Aguilar, 1831 (David Chandler, 1987).

THE GODS who give the crown of victory to those who, by their training in peaceful times, are already victorious before they fight, refuse it to those who, satisfied with one victory, rest contentedly in peace. As the old saying goes, "After a victory, tighten the strings of your helmet."

> Admiral Marquis Heihachiro Togo, 21 December 1905, farewell to the Japanese Fleet after the Battle of Tsushima, quoted in Ogasawara, *Life of Admiral Togo*, 1934.

IT IS TOO LATE to learn the technique of warfare when military operations are already in progress, especially when the enemy is an expert in it.

> General Aleksei A. Brusilov, *A Soldier's Notebook*, 1931.

I AM NOT a bit anxious about my battles. If I am anxious I don't fight them. I wait until I am ready.

> Field Marshal Viscount Montgomery of Alamein (1887–1976) – attributed.

BEING READY is not what matters. What matters is winning after you get there.

> Lieutenant-General Victor H. 'The Brute' Krulak, *Life Magazine*, 30 April 1965.

A "READY" STATE of mind requires a positive, constructive approach to the Army's problems. The Army is not without problems now, nor will it ever be. Some of these problems have their roots outside the Army's gate, others are wholly our own, but we cannot allow ourselves to be overcome by them, nor can we stand idly by waiting for others to solve them. By facing these problems positively and fairly, without cant and without whitewash, we are improving our readiness and our ability to provide this country the land fighting force it needs. If we are to be ready, every member of the Army – our Army – must step forward to accept these challenges, bypass the trap of self-pity, and avoid becoming the unwitting captive of events. . . . We cannot (merely) look for readiness sometime in the future, but be ready in mind, in spirit and in attitude today. A better weapon on the drawing board, a new command and control system for the next decade, or a new concept for organizing the Army in the field may contribute to our readiness eventually, but as promises, they contribute little to our strength today. We cannot let tomorrow's promises deter us from meeting today's requirements.

General Creighton Abrams (1914–1974), quoted in *Military Review*, 4/1985.

THE REAR/REAR ATTACK/REAR GUARDS

MOST TERRIBLE, or rather most effective, of all manoeuvres, is sudden attack against the enemy's rear. . . . For no hope of safety would remain for them in flight, and they would be unable to turn backwards, since the opposing army would attack, or to go forward, because of the detachment assailing their rear.

Onasander, *The General*, AD 58, (*Aeneas Tacticus, Aclepiodotus, Onasander*, tr. The Illinois Greek Club, 1923).

REAR GUARDS are the safety of armies and often they carry victory with them.

Frederick the Great, *Instructions to His Generals*, 1747, tr. Phillips, 1940.

THE RISK of having to fight on two fronts, and the even greater risk of finding one's retreat cut off, tend to paralyze movement and the ability to resist, and so affect the balance between victory and defeat. What is more, in the case of defeat, they increase the losses and can raise them to their very limit – to annihilation. A threat to the rear can, therefore, make a defeat *more probable*, as well as *more decisive*.

Major-General Carl von Clausewitz, *On War*, 4.4, 1832, tr. Michael Howard and Peter Paret, 1976.

I NEVER SAW the rear of an army engaged in battle but I feared that some calamity had happened at the front – the apparent confusion, broken wagons, crippled horses, men lying about dead and maimed, parties hastening to and fro in seeming disorder, and a general apprehension of something dreadful about to ensue; all these signs, however, lessened as I neared the front, and there the contrast was complete – perfect order, men and horses full of confidence, and it was not unusual for general hilarity, laughing, and cheering. Although cannon might be firing, the musketry clattering, and the enemy's shot hitting close, there reigned a general feeling of strength and security that bore a marked contrast to the bloody signs that had drifted rapidly to the rear; therefore, for comfort and safety, I surely would rather be at the front than the rear line of battle. So also on the march, the head of a column moves on steadily, while the rear is alternately halting then rushing forward to close up the gap; and all sorts of rumors, especially the worst, float back to the rear.

General of the Army William T. Sherman, *The Memoirs of General W.T. Sherman*, 1875.

IT IS just as legitimate to fight an enemy in the rear as in the front. The only difference is the danger.

Colonel John S. Mosby, *Mosby's War Reminiscences*, 1887.

THE OBJECT of the rear attack is not itself to crush the enemy, but to unhinge his morale and dispositions so that his dislocation renders the subsequent delivery of a decisive blow both practicable and easy. (April 1929.)

Captain Sir Basil Liddell Hart, *Thoughts on War*, 1944.

GIVE THE ENEMY a spanking from behind. You can kill more soldiers by scaring them to death from behind with a lot of noise than by attacking them from the front.

General George S. Patton, Jr., 1940, *The Patton Papers*, II, 1974.

OUR MEN are taught that their own safety depends upon their getting to the enemy's rear and not in staying in front of him. This is fundamental to our training.

German officer, quoted in U.S. War Department, *German Military Training*, 17 September 1942.

A MOVE round the enemy's front against the rear has the aim not only of avoiding resistance on its way but in its issue. In the profoundest sense, it takes the line of least resistance. The equivalent in the psychological sphere is the line of least expectation. They are the two faces of the same coin, and to appreciate this is to widen our understanding of strategy.

Captain Sir Basil Liddell Hart, *Strategy*, 1954.

RECONCILIATION

LET US try in this way, if we can, to win back public opinion and gain a lasting victory. For all too many others have incurred hatred through their cruelty and failed to maintain their victory for long, with the exception of Sulla, and I do not wish to emulate him. Let this be a new way of gaining victory; let us secure ourselves through mercy and magnanimity!

Julius Caesar, early March 45 BC, letter after the Roman Civil War.

THE WAR will be eternal if nobody is forgiven. . . . I am decidedly of opinion that all animosity should be forgotten.

The Duke of Wellington, 12 March 1804 and 22 January 1804, in India, cited in Arthur Bryant, *The Great Duke*, 1972.

WITH MALICE toward none, with charity for all, with firmness in the right, as God gives us to see the right, let us strive on to finish the work we are in, to bind up the nation's wounds, to care for him who shall have borne the battle, and for his widow and orphans; to do all which may achieve and cherish a just and lasting peace among ourselves and with all nations.

Abraham Lincoln, 4 March 1865, Second Inaugural Address.

I WANT no one punished. Treat them liberally all around. We want those people to return to their allegience to the Union and submit to the laws.

President Abraham Lincoln, 28 March 1865, instructions to Generals Grant and Sherman and to Admiral Porter just before Lee's surrender.

ANY FEELING of personal resentment toward the late Confederates I would not counsel or cherish. Our countrymen – large numbers of them – combined and fought us hard for a cause. They failed and we succeeded; so that, in an honest desire for reconcilement, I would be the more careful, even in the use of terms, to convey no hatred or reproach for the past. Such are my real convictions, and certainly the intention of all my efforts is not to anger and separate, but to pacify and unite.

Major-General Oliver O. Howard, *Autobiography of Gen. O.O. Howard*, I, 1907.

IT MUST BE a peace without victory. . . . Victory would mean peace forced upon the loser, a victor's peace imposed upon the vanquished. It would be accepted in humiliation, under duress, at an intolerable sacrifice, and would leave a sting, a resentment, a bitter memory upon which terms of peace would rest, not permanently, but only as upon quicksand. Only a peace between equals can last.

President Woodrow Wilson, 22 January 1917, speech to the U.S. Senate.

RECONNAISSANCE

AGITATE the enemy and ascertain the pattern of his movement. Determine his dispositions and so ascertain the field of battle. Probe him and learn where his strength is abundant and where deficient.

Sun Tzu, *The Art of War*, 6, c. 500 BC, tr. Giles, 1910.

WE ARE NOT fit to lead an army on the march unless we are familiar with the face of the country – its mountains and forests, its pitfalls.

Sun Tzu, *The Art of War*, 7, c. 500 BC, tr. Giles, 1910.

SINCE it is good not to neglect any one of the factors which contribute to the common benefit of the army, it is necessary to have experienced and intelligent guides. We should treat them well, look out for them, and take good care of them, for without them nothing worthwhile will be accomplished. The men we call guides are not simply men who know the roads, for the lowliest peasant can do that, but men who, in addition to knowing roads, are able to conduct the army through the mountain passes, who can plan ahead, and who know the proper distances for the campsites, locations which are suitable and which have plenty of water, so the camp will not find itself in dire straits. They should know the topography of the enemy's country in detail, so they can lead the army into it to plunder and take captives.

General Nikephoros Ouranos, *Campaign Organization and Tactics*, c. AD 994 (*Three Byzantine Military Treatises*, tr. George Dennis, 1985).

WHEN IT IS desired to apply oneself to this essential part of war, the most detailed and exact maps of the country that can be found are taken and examined and reexamined frequently. If it is not in time of war, the places are visited, camps are chosen, roads are examined, the mayors of villages, the butchers, and the farmers are talked to. One becomes familiar with the footpaths, the depths of the woods, their nature, the depth of the rivers, the marshes that can be crossed and those which cannot . . . the road is chosen for such and such a march, the number of columns in which the march can be made estimated and all strong camping places on the route are examined.

Frederick the Great, *Instructions to His Generals*, 1747, tr. Phillips, 1940.

A PEASANT and a drover are not military men, and you will find that quite different descriptions of the same stretch of country will be given by an economist, a carter, a huntsman or a soldier.

Frederick the Great, 'Des Marches d'Armée', 1777, *Oeuvres*, XXIX, 1846–1857.

SINGLE MEN in the night will be more likely to ascertain facts than the best glasses in the day.

General George Washington, 10 July 1779, letter to General Anthony Wayne, *Writings*, XV, 1936, p. 397.

A RECONNAISSANCE? I don't need one. They're only necessary for the timid, and forewarn the enemy. If you really want to find the enemy, you'll find him without them. Bayonets, cold arms, attack, punch – these are my reconnaissances.

Field Marshal Prince Aleksandr V. Suvorov, 1799, during the Italian campaign, quoted in Phillip Longworth, *The Art of Victory*, 1966.

. . . SKILFULLY reconnoitering defiles and fords, providing himself with trusty guides, interrogating the village priest and the chief of relays, quickly establishing relations with the inhabitants, seeking out spies, seizing letters.

> Napoleon, on the duties of a chief of reconnaissance, *Maxims of War*, 1831.

BEAR IN MIND that your telegrams may make the whole Army strike tents, and night or day, rain or shine, take up the line of march. Endeavor, therefore, to secure accurate information. . . . Above all, vigilance! vigilance! vigilance!

> Major J.E.B. Stuart, 4 April 1864, letter to John R. Chambliss, quoted in Douglas Southall Freeman, *Lee's Lieutenants: Gettysburg to Appomattox*, 1944.

I HAVE no confidence in any scout.

> General Robert E. Lee (1807–1870).

WE WOULD seriously overestimate the value of our excellent modern maps, however, to imagine we can now dispense with personal reconnaissance. No matter how skillfully one may read today's maps of former battlefields, one cannot fully understand, without an examination of the ground, the reasons for events as they actually occurred. At Kolin, for example, the full difficulty of the attack could be appreciated only from the Austrian defensive position.

> *General der Infantrie* Hugo Baron von Freytag-Loringhoven, *The Power of Personality in War*, 1911, tr. Spaulding, 1938.

TIME spent on reconnaissance is seldom wasted.

> British Army *Field Service Regulations*, 1912.

IN ORDER to conquer that unknown which follows us until the very point of going into action, there is only one means, which consists in looking out until the last moment, even on the battlefield, for *information*.

> Marshal of France Ferdinand Foch, *Precepts and Judgments*, 1919.

YOU CAN never do too much reconnaissance.

> General George S. Patton, Jr., *War As I Knew It*, 1947.

JUNIOR OFFICERS of reconnaissance units must be very inquisitive. Their reports must be accurate and factual. Negative information is as important as positive information.

> General George S. Patton, Jr., *War As I Knew It*, 1947.

DO YOUR OWN reconnaissance. See for yourself and then get down to the job without delay.

> Field Marshal Erich von Manstein (1887–1973).

RECRUITS/RECRUITMENT

AN ARMY raised without proper regard to the choice of its recruits was never yet made good by the length of time.

> Flavius Vegetius Renatus, *Military Institutions of the Romans*, c. AD 378, tr. Clark, 1776.

NO ONE, I imagine, can doubt that the peasants are the most fit to carry arms for they from their infancy have been exposed to all kinds of weather and have been brought up to the hardest labor. They are able to endure the most intense heat of the sun, are unacquainted with use of baths and are strangers to the other luxuries of life. They are simple, content with little, inured to fatigue, and prepared in some measure for a military by their continual employment in their farm work, in handling the spade, digging trenches and carrying burdens.

> Flavius Vegetius Renatus, *Military Institutions of the Romans*, c. AD 378, tr. Clark, 1776.

MEN just dragged from the tender Scenes of domestick life; unaccustomed to the din of Arms; totally unacquainted with every kind of Military skill . . . when opposed to Troops regularly train'd, disciplined, and appointed, superior in knowledge, and superior in Arms, makes them timid and ready to fly from their own shadows.

> General George Washington, 24 September 1776, letter to the President of Congress, *Writings*, VI, 1932, p. 110.

I WILL RECEIVE 200 able-bodied men if they will present themselves at my headquarters by the first of June with a good horse and gun. I wish none but those who desire to be actively engaged. My headquarters for the present is at Corinth, Miss. Come on, boys, if you want a heap of fun and to kill some Yankees.
N.B. Forrest
Colonel, Commanding
Forrest's Regiment

> Lieutenant-General Nathan Bedford Forrest, April 1862, recruiting advertisement in the *Appeal*, run while he recuperated from wounds suffered at the Battle of Shiloh, quoted in Robert Henry, *First With the Most Forrest*, 1944.

THE COUNTRY LAD is generally the most humble, obedient, and easily governed; but the city-born recruit is, as a rule, the smartest, tidiest, and most easily trained.

> John Menzies, *Reminiscences of an Old Soldier*, 1883.

FOR THE Red Gods call us out and we must go!

> Rudyard Kipling, 'The Feet of the Young Men'.

THERE ARE those who say, "I am a farmer," or, "I am a student;" "I can discuss literature but not the military arts." This is incorrect. There is no profound difference between the farmer and the soldier. You must have courage. You simply leave your farms and become soldiers. . . . When you take your arms in hand, you become soldiers; when you are organized, you become military units.

> Mao Tse-tung, *On Guerrilla War*, 1937.

THE DIRECTOR of the CIA in my time was Army Gen. Beetle Smith, whom I had met on some

occasion during the war in Africa. One day as he entered the meeting, late, he announced that he had just left the Oval Office. He said the President (Truman) asked him why the Army was rejecting so many recruits for lack of physical fitness for military duty. "Why," said the President, "when I entered the Army one doctor would look up your rear while another looked down your throat. If they couldn't see each other, they'd sign you up."
> General Hamilton H. Howze, *A Cavalryman's Story*, 1996.

YOUR SOUL may belong to God, but your ass belongs to the Army.
> U.S. Army saying.

REFLECTION/MEDITATION

THE WISE must contemplate the intermixture of gain and loss. If they discern advantage [in difficult situations], their efforts can be trusted. If they discern harm [in prospective advantage], difficulties can be resolved.
> Sun Tzu, *The Art of War*, 8, c. 500 BC, tr. Ralph Sawyer, 1994.

NOWHERE can man find a quieter or more untroubled retreat than in his own soul.
> The Emperor Marcus Aurelius, *Meditations*, AD 161–180.

HE PONDERS the dangers inherent in the advantages, and the advantages inherent in the dangers.
> The 'Martial' Emperor Ts'ao Ts'ao (AD 155–220), commentary to *Sun Tzu*, 8, c. 500 BC, tr. Samuel Griffith, 1963.

THE GENERAL should not go to sleep before reflecting on what he should have done that he might have neglected and on what he has to do the next day.
> The Emperor Maurice, *The Strategikon*, c. AD 600 (*Maurice's Strategikon*, tr. George Dennis, 1984).

WHAT IS the good of experience if you do not reflect.
> Frederick the Great (1712–1786).

THE WINTERS wear away, so do our years, and so does life itself; and it matters little where a man passes his days and what station he fills, or whether he be great or considerable, but it imports him something to look to his manner of life. This day I am twenty-five years of age, and all that time is as nothing. . . . But it is worth a moment's consideration that one may be called away on a sudden, unguarded and unprepared; and the oftener these thoughts are entertained the less will be the dread or fear of death. You will judge by this sort of discourse that it is the dead of night, when all is quiet and at rest, and one of those intervals when men think of what they really are, and what they really should be;

how much is expected and how little performed. . . . The little time taken for meditation is the best employed in all our lives; for, if the uncertainty of our state and being is then brought before us, and that compared with our course of conduct, who is there that won't immediately discover the inconsistency of all his behaviour and the vanity of all his pursuits.
> Major-General Sir James Wolfe, quoted in Liddell Hart, *Great Captains Unveiled*, 1927.

IF I APPEAR to be always ready to reply to everything, it is because, before undertaking anything, I have meditated for a long time – I have foreseen what might happen. It is not a spirit which suddenly reveals to me what I have to say or do in a circumstance unexpected by others: it is reflexion, meditation.
> Napoleon, quoted in Barrett Parker, ed., *Famous British Generals*, 1951.

UNTIL TOMORROW; night brings counsel.
> Napoleon, his method of dealing with the matters of the greatest importance, compared to the quick dispatch of the great mass of his daily business, quoted in Chandler, *The Campaigns of Napoleon*, 1966.

GENERALSHIP, at least in my case, came not by instinct, unsought, but by understanding, hard study and brain concentration. Had it come easily to me, I should not have done it as well.
> Colonel T.E. Lawrence, 1932, letter to Liddell Hart.

AN ACQUAINTANCE with the "friction" of military movements and the actual conditions of the battlefield is invaluable. But the duration of experience matters less than the capacity for reflection. And the measure of this, in turn, counts for more than the extent of study. Given some acquaintance with actual war, and time for study, the mastery of strategy and tactics is likely to be in proportion to the capacity for reflection, analysis, and originality of thought.
> Captain Sir Basil Liddell Hart, *Thoughts on War*, 1944.

THE REGIMENT

THE REGIMENT is the family. The colonel, as the father, should have a personal acquaintance with every officer and man, and should instill a feeling of pride and affection for himself, so that his officers and men would naturally look to him for personal advice and instruction. In war the regiment should never be subdivided, but should always be maintained entire. In peace this is impossible.
> General of the Army William T. Sherman, *The Memoirs of General W.T. Sherman*, 1875.

AFTER THE TRAIN had been captured by 150 Boers, the last four men, though completely surrounded, and with no cover continued to fire until three were killed, the fourth wounded. On the Boers asking the survivor the reason why they had not surrendered, he replied, "Why, man, we are the Gordon Highlanders."

Field Marshal Viscount Kitchener, 10 August 1901, telegram from Pretoria to King Edward VII during the Boer War.

THE NOBLE COURAGE that has its origins in love of country and sense of duty is not confined to the well-born; it is to be equally found in the uneducated private soldier. What can be finer than his love of regiment, his devotion to its reputation, and his determination to protect its honour! To him "The Regiment" is mother, sister and mistress. That its fame may live and flourish he is prepared to risk all and to die without a murmur. What early cause calls forth greater enthusiasm? It is a high, an admirable phase of patriotism, for, to the soldier, his regiment is his country.

Field Marshal Viscount Wolseley, *The Story of a Soldier's Life*, 1903.

HEADS UP the Warwicks! Show the _____ yer cap-badges!

Field Marshal Viscount Slim of Burma, quoting the 'Incorrigible Rogue', a soldier in his company during the Mesopotamian campaign, 1916, *Unofficial History*, 1959 (see Preface).

NEVER FORGET: the Regiment is the foundation of everything.

Field Marshal Viscount Wavell of Cyrenaica (1883–1950), quoted in Fergusson, *The Trumpet in the Hall*, 1970.

THOUGH I shall maintain that good soldiers are not bred from bad stock, I do not doubt that many unpromising specimens were transformed by training; in particular by that part of training which consists in inculcating esprit de corps. I remember men recruited at the street corner by starvation who came to act on the principle that if the Regiment lived it did not matter if they died, though they did not put it that way. This was their source of strength, their abiding faith, it was the last of all the creeds that in historical times have steeled men against death.

Baron Charles MacMoran Wilson Moran, *The Anatomy of Courage*, 1945.

THE ART of command is the art of dealing with human nature. The soldier is governed through his heart and not through his head. The complete acceptance in the soldiers' training of that creed with all its implications is the particular contribution England has made to the business of making soldiers. It began, I think, with Moore – it was the foundation of the discipline of his camp at Shorncliffe. The men's response to kindness led them to accept the religion of the Regiment – that

only the Regiment matters; a faith which made our professional army before the last war [1914–1918], in German words, "a perfect thing apart".

Baron Charles MacMoran Wilson Moran, *The Anatomy of Courage*, 1945.

THEY WILL REMEMBER for a little while in England. The soldier does have his day. I want to remind you this afternoon that it is not enough to remember now. We've got to show what we think of their sacrifice in the way we conduct ourselves in the days ahead.

The Chaplain of the First Battalion, Gloucestershire Regiment (The Glosters), April 1951, memorial service in Korea for the battalion, which had been overrun after a heroic defence.

THERE IS a great source of strength in the regimental system itself. This sets up in the group a continuing focus of affection, trust and loyalty. It uses insignia, totems and a good deal of almost mystical paraphernalia to increase the binding grip of the whole upon its members. Some day I want to turn the ethnologists on to study of the regimental system as a means of strengthening group resistance to stress. Their advice may well be that instead of a quaint and decorative traditional survival, we have in the British regimental system a military instrument of deadly efficiency.

General Sir John Hackett, *The Profession of Arms*, 1983.

REGULARS AND VOLUNTEERS

REGULAR TROOPS alone are equal to the exigencies of modern war, as well as for defence as offence, and whenever a substitute is attempted it must prove illusory and ruinous.

General George Washington, 15 September 1780, to the President of Congress, *Writings*, XX, 1937, p. 49.

NO MILITIA will ever acquire the habits necessary to resist a regular force.

General George Washington, 15 September 1780, to the President of Congress, *Writings*, XX, 1937, p. 50.

THE FIRMNESS requisite for the real business of fighting is only to be attained by a constant course of discipline and service. I have never yet been witness to a single instance that can justify a different opinion; and it is most earnestly to be wished the liberties of America may no longer be trusted in any material degree to so precarious a dependence.

General George Washington, 15 September 1780, to the President of Congress, *Writings*, XX, 1937, p. 50.

WHEN the perfect order and discipline which are essential to regular troops are contemplated, and with what ease and precision they execute the difficult maneuvers indispensable to the success of offensive or defensive operations, the conviction cannot be resisted that such troops will always have a decided advantage over the more numerous forces composed of uninstructed militia or undisciplined recruits.

Major-General Alexander Hamilton (1755–1804).

WHEN defending itself against another country, a nation never lacks men, but too often, *soldiers*.

Napoleon, *Political Aphorisms*, 1848.

THE VICTORIES in Mexico were, in every instance, over vastly superior numbers. There were two reasons for this. Both General Scott and General Taylor had such armies as are not often got together. At the battles of Palo Alto and Resaca de la Palma, General Taylor had a small army, but it was composed exclusively of regular troops, under the best drill and discipline. Every officer, from the highest to the lowest, was educated in his profession, not at West Point necessarily, but in the camp, in garrison, and many of them in Indian wars. The rank and file were probably inferior, as material out of which to make an army, to the volunteers that participated in all the later battles of the war; but they were brave men, and then drill and discipline brought out all there was in them. A better army, man for man, probably never faced an enemy than the one commanded by General Taylor in the earliest two engagements of the Mexican war. The volunteers who followed were of better material, but without drill or discipline at the start. They were associated with so many disciplined men and professionally educated officers, that when they went into engagements it was with a confidence they would not have felt otherwise. They became soldiers themselves almost at once. . . .

General of the Army Ulysses S. Grant, *Personal Memoirs of U.S. Grant*, 1885.

IF A VOLUNTEER organization consists of good material, and is eager to learn, it can readily do so if it has one or two first-class regular officers to teach it. . . . and most important of all, officers and men alike were eager for fighting, and resolute to do well and behave properly, to encounter hardship and privation, and the irksome monotony of camp routine, without grumbling or complaining; they had counted the cost before they went in, and were delighted to pay the penalties inevitably attendant upon the career of a fighting regiment; and from the moment when the regiment began to gather, the higher officers kept instilling into those under them the spirit of eagerness for action and of stern determination to grasp at death rather than forfeit honor.

President Theodore Roosevelt, *The Rough Riders*, 1899; of his regiment of volunteers, The Rough Riders, during the Spanish-American War.

THAT WHEN a nation relies upon a system of regulars and volunteers, or regulars and militia, the men, in the absence of compulsion, or very strong inducements, will invariably enlist in the organizations most lax in discipline.

Colonel Emory Upton, *The Military Policy of the United States*, 1904.

DURING THE WAR young men of two or three years' service had to lead companies. Many succeeded, but others failed in many ways. The capacity for leadership is a gift, the result of education and tact. Zeal and courage cannot always take their place. Everything was done, at home and at the front, to secure the thorough training of company commanders, but there is no doubt that the complaints of the men as to their inexperience were, at bottom, justified. This was a very serious matter, involving the admirable relations that had hitherto existed between officers and men. . . . The excellent regular officer, so often the object of attacks, was no longer available. The green grass was growing on his grave. In the short period of the war, it was impossible to train a new generation of these men, with the same high professional qualities, the same thorough knowledge, and the same sense of responsibility towards their men as had been possessed by officers trained through a long course of years. Nothing could provide a more striking justification of our whole army system than the events of this war.

General Erich Ludendorff, *My War Memories, 1914–1918*, 1919.

AFTER hardly three months of war the greater part of our regular, professional officers and trained men had vanished, leaving only skeleton forces which had to be hastily filled with men wretchedly instructed who were sent to me from depots; while the strength of the officers was kept up by promoting subalterns, who likewise were inadequately trained. From this period onwards the professional character of our forces disappeared, and the Army became more and more like a sort of badly trained militia. The question of N.C.O.'s became a particularly acute one; we had to institute training squads so as to provide, hastily and anyhow, N.C.O.'s who assuredly could not take the place of their well-trained predecessors.

General Aleksei A. Brusilov, *A Soldier's Notebook*, 1931.

FROM THE BEGINNING I had to suppose that the attitude of the Austrian and German troops, standing armies with century-old traditions, would be one of profound scepticism as to the military value of our volunteer formation with the character of a militia. I was prepared for this, and knowing well the lofty ambition of the Strzelcy, I was very much afraid that I might not only wound this ambition of theirs at the first reverse, but even worse, destroy their faith in themselves as soldiers. And a reverse was very likely in the extremely poor state of our technical armament

and equipment. . . . Finally, as in every new foundation, our internal relations were so little consolidated that each individual commander had to devote much time to bringing order into everyday details, to founding some sort of internal *modus vivendi* between the men. I had constantly to settle a number of routine questions of a personal character resulting from the friction of the whole military machine. Questions of seniority amongst fellow officers, questions of the sphere of each man's competence, this was the hell in which I lived at the beginning of the War. I had to defend the soldiers not only from external humiliations, but also from the internal humiliation, to which a consciousness of being less efficient than those around them, and of being unable to execute the tasks they had taken upon themselves, could not but give rise.
> Marshal Joseph Pilsudski, of the founding of the Polish Army as volunteer allies of the Germans and Austrians during WWI, *Memoirs of a Polish Revolutionary and Soldier*, 1931.

I LONGED for more Regular troops with which to rebuild and expand the Army. Wars are not won by heroic militia.
> Sir Winston S. Churchill, *Their Finest Hour*, 1949.

REGULATIONS

NOT TO FOLLOW regulations is the same as a blind man not following a wall.
> Tsar Peter I, 'The Great', quoted in Savkin, *Basic Principles of Operational Art and Tactics*, 1972.

NOBODY in the British Army ever reads a regulation or an order as if it were to be a guide for his conduct, or in any other manner than as an amusing novel.
> The Duke of Wellington (1769–1852).

REGULATIONS are all very well for drill but in the hour of danger they are no more use. . . . You must learn to think.
> Marshal of France Ferdinand Foch (1851–1929).

METHOD, I explained, was laid down in the Training Manuals, which were written not for sages, but for normal men, many of whom are fools. Though they must be followed, "do not imagine for a moment," I said, "that they have been written to exonerate you from thinking."
> Major-General J.F.C. Fuller, *Memoirs of an Unconventional Soldier*, 1936.

YOU DO NOT rise by the regulations, but in spite of them. Therefore in all matters of active service the subaltern must never take "No" for an answer. He should get to the front at all costs.
> Sir Winston S. Churchill, *Ian Hamilton's March*.

ONE of the first regulations might be to think.
> Major-General Orlando Ward, under the pseudonym 'MacKenzie Hill', *The Field Artillery Journal*, c. 1938.

WELL, ultimately, the regulations are made by men. And not everything can be anticipated in the regulations. Of course, there are exceptional instances.
> Admiral of the Fleet of the Soviet Union Sergei G. Gorshkov, quoted in Ablamonov, *Admiral*, 1986.

REINFORCEMENTS

. . . OUR BEST CHANCE of establishing a panic among them, as a fresh assailant has always more terrors for an enemy than the one he is immediately engaged with.
> Brasidas, 422 BC, speech to his army before the Battle of Amphipolis, quoted by Thucydides, *History of the Peloponnesian War*, 5.9, c. 404 BC, tr. Richard Crawley, 1910.

IF A LITTLE HELP reaches you in the action itself, it determines the turn of fortune for you. The enemy is discouraged and his excited imagination sees the help as being at least twice as strong as it really is.
> Frederick the Great, *Instructions to His Generals*, 1747, tr. Phillips, 1940.

ONE always has enough troops when he knows how to use them.
> Napoleon, 26 June 1806, to Joseph Bonaparte, *Correspondance de Napoléon Ier, publiée par ordre de l'Empereur Napoléon III*, No. 10416, Vol. XII, 1858–1870.

GENERALS always make requests – it is in the nature of things. There is not a one who cannot be counted upon for that. It is quite natural that the man who is entrusted with only one task thinks only about it, and the more men he has the better guarantee he has for success.
> Napoleon, 4 March 1809, to Joseph Bonaparte, *Correspondance de Napoléon Ier, publiée par ordre de l'Empereur Napoléon III*, No. 14846, Vol. XVIII, 1858–1870.

A SEASONABLE reinforcement renders the success of a battle certain, because the enemy will always imagine it stronger than it really is, and lose courage accordingly.
> Napoleon, *Maxims of War*, 1831.

WE GET a large body of reinforcements together, and start them to the front; but after deducting the sick, the deserters, the stragglers, and the discharged, the numbers seriously diminish by the time they reach their destination. It's like trying to shovel fleas across a barnyard; you don't get 'em all there.

> President Abraham Lincoln, quoted in Horace Porter, *Campaigning With Grant*, 1897.

REINFORCE SUCCESS

THE MOMENT it becomes certain that an assault cannot succeed, suspend the offensive; but when one does succeed, push it vigorously, and if necessary pile in troops at the successful point from wherever they can be taken.

> General of the Army Ulysses S. Grant, 3 June 1864, at the Battle of Cold Harbor, quoted in Horace Porter, *Campaigning With Grant*, 1906.

A COMMANDER should never renew an attack along the same line (or in the same form) after it has once failed. A mere reinforcement of weight is not sufficient change, for it is probable that the enemy also will have strengthened himself in the interval. It is even more probable that his success in repulsing you will have strengthened him morally. (May 1930.)

> Captain Sir Basil Liddell Hart, *Thoughts on War*, 1944.

RELIEF

I MUST REMOVE this man, yes. Disgrace him I will not, lest in doing so I paralyze the initiative of another man.

> General Robert E. Lee, quoted in Douglas Southall Freeman, *Douglas Southall Freeman on Leadership*, 1993.

THE SERVICE cannot afford to keep a man who does not succeed.

> Lieutenant-General Thomas J. 'Stonewall' Jackson, quoted in Henderson, *Stonewall Jackson*, 1898.

JACKSON: Colonel, why do you not get your brigade together, keep it together, and move on? Colonel: It is impossible, General, I can't do it. Jackson: Do not say it is impossible! Turn your command over to the next officer. If he cannot do it, I will find someone who can, if I have to take him from the ranks!

> Lieutenant-General Thomas J. 'Stonewall' Jackson, 2 June 1862, quoted in Henry Kyd Douglas, *I Rode With Stonewall*, 1940.

TENDER consideration for worthless and incompetent officers is but another name for cruelty toward the brave men who fall sacrifices to these defects of their leaders.

> President Jefferson Davis, 8 October 1862, message to the Confederate Congress.

THE ORDER depriving me of the command created an immense deal of deep feeling in the army – so much so that many were in favor of my refusing to obey the order, and of marching upon Washington to take possession of the government. My chief purpose in remaining with the army as long as I did after being relieved was to calm this feeling, in which I succeeded.

> Major-General George B. McClellan, *McClellan's Own Story*, 1887.

LIEUTENANT-GENERAL J.B. Hood has been commissioned to the temporary rank of general, under the late law of Congress. I am directed by the Secretary of War to inform you that, as you have failed to arrest the advance of the enemy to the vicinity of Atlanta, far in the interior of Georgia, and express no confidence that you can defeat or repel him, you are hereby relieved from the command of the Army and Department of Tennessee, which you will immediately turn over to General Hood.

> General Samuel Cooper (Adjutant General), notification of President Davis' relief of General Joseph E. Johnston, quoted in Johnston, *Narrative*, 1874.

IF WARREN fails to attack promptly send Humphreys to command his corps and relieve him.

> General of the Army Ulysses S. Grant, 12 May 1864, Letter to Major-General Meade, *Papers of USG*, X, 1982.

HE [Grant] then proceeded to Washington, and on November 23 called upon the President and the Secretary of War, and had extended interviews with them. One object in his going to Washington was to make a determined effort to obtain promotion for his officers who had made themselves conspicuous for their gallantry and efficiency in the field. In order to create the necessary vacancies, he recommended that the inefficient general officers be mustered out of the service, and gave a list of eight major-generals and thirty-three brigadiers whose services the government could dispense with to advantage. In the matter of relieving these useless officers the general was entirely impartial, as the list contained a number of his warm personal friends. The President said to him: "Why, I find that lots of the officers on this list are very close friends of yours; do you want them all dropped?" The general replied: "That's very true, Mr. President; but my personal friends are not always good generals, and I think it but just to adhere to my recommendations."

> Brigadier-General Horace Porter, of Grant's willingness to relieve inefficient officers, meeting in November 1864, *Campaigning With Grant*, 1906.

WHAT am I going to do with him? He is not growing in his job, but where is a better man? Do you know one?

> General of the Armies John J. 'Black Jack' Pershing, 1918, discussing a deficient officer he was about to relieve, quoted in Frank Vandiver, *Black Jack*, 1977.

THERE WERE those who had been relieved from their commands who came in to tell me of the injustice which had been done them. It was hard to talk to men of this class, because in most instances I was convinced by what they told me that their relief was justified. To discuss with an old friend the smash-up of his career is tragic and depressing at best, and more practically when he feels that he has been treated unfairly and an honorable record forever besmirched.

General of the Army George C. Marshall, *Memoirs of My Service in the World War*, written between 1923 and 1926, published in 1976.

IN WAR you must either trust your general or sack him.

Field Marshal Sir John Dill, 1941, letter to Field Marshal Wavell.

THERE WERE INSTANCES in Europe where I relieved commanders for their failure to move fast enough. And it is possible that some were the victims of circumstance. For how can the blame for failure be laid fairly on a single man when there are in reality so many factors that can effect the outcome of any battle? Yet each commander must always assume total responsibility for every individual in his command. If his battalion or regimental commanders fail him in the attack, then he must relieve them or be relieved himself. Many a division commander has failed not because he lacked the capacity for command but only because he declined to be hard enough on his subordinates.

In the last analysis, however, the issue of relief resolves itself into one of mutual confidence.

General of the Army Omar N. Bradley, *A Soldier's Story*, 1951.

THE OCCASION for the relief of commanders may regrettably arise. If it does, there are three points to consider: Is your decision based on personal knowledge and observation, or on secondhand information? What will be the effect on the command concerned? Are you relieving a commander whose men think highly of him – even with affection – regardless of professional competence? And finally, have you a better man available?

Every man is entitled to go into battle with the best chance of survival your forethought as a leader can provide. What best helps you discharge this responsibility? Sharing things with your men; to be always in the toughest spots; always where the crisis is, or seems most likely to develop; always thinking of what help you can give your commanders who are executing your orders; doing your utmost to see that the best in rations, shelter, first aid, and evacuation facilities are available; being generous with praise, swift and fair with punishment when you have the facts, intolerant of demonstrated failure in leadership on which lives depend, yet making full allowances for human weaknesses and the stresses and strains of battle on individuals.

General Matthew B. Ridgway, 'Leadership', *Military Review*, 10/1966.

RELIGION

IF THOU wishest the gods to be propitious to thee, thou must honour the gods.

Xenophon, *Memorabilia*, c. 360 BC.

BEFORE getting into danger, the general should worship God. When he goes into danger, then, he can with confidence pray to God as a friend.

The Emperor Maurice, *The Strategikon*, c. AD 600 (*Maurice's Strategikon*, tr. George Dennis, 1984).

I THINK that when God grants me victory over the rest of Palestine I shall divide my territories, make a will stating my wishes, then set sail on this sea for their far-off lands and pursue the Franks there, so as to free the earth of anyone who does not believe in God, or die in the attempt.

Saladin (1138–1193), quoted by Baha Ad-Din in Gabarieli, *Arab Historians of the Crusades*, 1957.

HE WHO IS steadfast unto death shall be saved and they who suffer in a just cause theirs is the kingdom of heaven.

Edward, 'The Black Prince', 19 September 1356, address to his knights before the Battle of Poitiers, quoted in Froissart, *Chronicles*, 1523–1525.

IT WILL GIVE me great pleasure to fight for my God against your gods, who are a mere nothing.

Hernan Cortes, 1521, to the Aztec priesthood, quoted in *Five Letters*, 1522–1525.

YOU MAY WIN salvation under my command, but hardly riches.

King Gustavus II Adolphus (1594–1632).

I CAN SAY this of Naseby that when I saw the enemy drawn up and march in gallant order towards us, and we a company of poor ignorant men, to seek how to order our battle, the General having commanded me to order all the horse, I could not, riding alone about my business, but smile out to God in praises in assurance of victory, because He would, by things that are not, bring to naught things that are. Of which I had great assurance – and God did it.

The Lord Protector Oliver Cromwell, after the Battle of Naseby, 14 June 1644, quoted in Churchill, *A History of the English Speaking Peoples: The New World*, 1956.

TRULY I think he that prays and preaches best will fight best.

The Lord Protector Oliver Cromwell, 25 December 1650, letter to Colonel Francis Hacker, quoted in Ashely, ed., *Cromwell*, 1969.

PUT YOUR TRUST in God, but be sure to see that your powder is dry.

The Lord Protector Oliver Cromwell (1599–1658), to his troops when they were about to cross a river.

WHEN I lay me down to sleep, I recommend myself to the care of Almighty God; when I awake I give myself up to His direction. Amidst all the evils that threaten me, I will look up to Him for help, and question not but that He will either avert them or turn them to my advantage. Though I know neither the time nor the place of my death, I am not at all solicitous about it, because I am sure that He knows them both, and that He will not fail to support and comfort me.

Admiral Viscount Nelson, 1793, journal entry, quoted in David Howarth, *Nelson: The Immortal Memory*, 1988.

NOW I can do no more. We must trust to the Great Disposer of all events, and the justice of our cause. I thank God for this great opportunity of doing my duty.

Admiral Viscount Nelson, 21 October 1805, moments after his last signal to the fleet at Trafalgar, 'England expects every man to do his duty', quoted in Robert Southey, *Life of Nelson*, 1813.

THE SOLDIERS of the army have permission to go to mass, so far as this: they are forbidden to go into the churches during the performance of divine service, unless they go to assist in the performance of the service. I could not do more, for in point of fact soldiers cannot by law attend the celebration of mass excepting in Ireland. The thing now stands exactly as it ought; any man may go to mass who chooses, and nobody makes any inquiry about it. The consequence is, that nobody goes to mass, and although we have whole regiments of Irishmen, and of course Roman Catholics, I have not seen one soldier perform any one act of religious worship in these Catholic countries, excepting making the sign of the cross to induce the people of the country to give them wine.

The Duke of Wellington, 1809, *The Dispatches of Field Marshal the Duke of Wellington, During His Various Campaigns in India, Denmark, Portugal, Spain, the Low Countries, and France*, V, pp. 134–135, 1834–1838.

I NEVER HAD so grand and awful an idea of the resurrection as . . . [when] I saw . . . more than five hundred Britons emerging from the heaps of their dead comrades, all over the plain rising up, and . . . coming forward . . . as prisoners.

Major-General Andrew Jackson, of the survivors of the British attack on his defences during the Battle of New Orleans, 8 January 1815, quoted in James Parton, *A Life of Andrew Jackson*, II, 1859–1860.

EVERYTHING proclaims the existence of a God, that cannot be questioned; but all our religions are evidently the work of men. Why are there so many? – Why has ours not always existed? – Why does it consider itself exclusively the right one? – What becomes in this case of all the virtuous men who have gone before us? – Why do these religions revile, oppose, exterminate one another? – Why has this been the case ever and every where? – Because men are ever men; because priests have ever and every where introduced fraud and falsehood. However, as soon as I had power, I immediately re-established religion. I made it the ground-work and foundation upon which I built. I considered it as the support of sound principles and good morality, both in doctrine and in practice. Besides, such is the restlessness of man, that his mind requires that something undefined and marvellous which religion offers; and it is better for him to find it there, than to seek it of Cagliostro, of Mademoiselle Lenormand, or of the fortune-tellers and imposters.

Napoleon, 1 June 1816, conversation on St. Helena, quoted in Emmanuel Las Casas, *The Life, Exile, and Conversations of Napoleon Bonaparte*, II, 1890.

LOOK AT A MAN in his full vigor, look at those columns ready to throw themselves into the battlefield: the drum beats the charge; now they move; the grapeshot mows them down. There is no question of priests or confession.

Napoleon, 1819, conversation on St. Helena, quoted in F. Antommarchi, *Mémoires*, I, 1825, and in Christopher Herold, ed., *The Mind of Napoleon*, 1955.

THE PRESIDENT, Commander-in-Chief of the Army and Navy, desires and enjoins the orderly observance of the Sabbath by the officers and men in the military and naval service. The importance for man and beast of the prescribed weekly rest, the sacred rights of Christian soldiers and sailors, a becoming deference to the best sentiment of a Christian people, and a due regard for the Divine will, demand that Sunday labor in the Army and Navy be reduced to the measure of strict necessity.

The discipline and character of the national forces should not suffer, nor the cause they defend be imperiled, by the profanation of the day or name of the Most High. "At this time of public distress" – adopting the words of Washington in 1776 – "men may find enough to do in the service of God and their country without abandoning themselves to vice and immorality." The first General Order issued by the Father of his Country after the Declaration of Independence, indicates the spirit in which our institutions were founded and should ever be defended: "*The General hopes and trusts that every officer and man will endeavor to live and act as becomes a Christian soldier defending the dearest rights and liberties of his country.*"

President Abraham Lincoln, order for observance of the sabbath, Executive Mansion, Washington, 15 November 1862.

HELL, is that all? Detail forty men at once for baptism!

Major-General Daniel E. Sickles, 1862, when his brigade chaplain expressed concern that other brigades were converting more men than he was, quoted in *The Journals of Joseph Hopkins Twichell*, item dated 16 December 1905.

THE PRESIDENT of the Confederate States has, in the name of the people, appointed the 21st day of August as a day of fasting, humiliation and prayer. A strict observance of the day is enjoined upon the officers and soldiers of this army. All military duties, except such as are absolutely necessary, will be suspended. The commanding officers of brigades and regiments are requested to cause divine services, suitable to the occasion, to be performed in their respective commands.

Soldiers! we have sinned against Almighty God. We have forgotten his signal mercies, and have cultivated a revengeful, haughty and boastful spirit. We have not remembered that the defenders of a just cause should be pure in his eyes; that "our times are in his hands" – and we have relied too much on our own arms for the achievement of our independence. God is our only refuge and our strength. Let us humble ourselves before him. Let us confess our many sins, and beseech him to give us a higher courage, a purer patriotism and more determined will: that he will convert the hearts of our enemies: that he will hasten the time when war, with its sorrows and sufferings, shall cease, and that he will give us a name and place among the nations of the earth.

> General Robert E. Lee, 13 August 1863, *General Orders No. 83*, Army of Northern Virginia.

CAPTAIN, my religious belief teaches me to feel as safe in battle as in bed. God has fixed the time for my death. I do not concern myself about that, but to be always ready, no matter when it may overtake me. . . . That is the way all men should live, and then all would be equally brave.

> Lieutenant-General Thomas J. 'Stonewall' Jackson, to Brigadier-General John Imboden, quoted in *Battles and Leaders of the Civil War, Being for the Most Part Contributions by Union and Confederate Officers*, I, Johnston and Buel, ed., 1887.

DAILY in the great temple of nature, and at night by heaven's chandeliers, are audiences of from one to two thousand men anxious to hear the way of life. Many of them, neglected, as I must say they have been by Christians at home, are daily professing religion – men grown old in sin, and who never blanched in the presence of the foe, are made to tremble under a sense of guilt, and here in the forests and fields are being converted to God; young men, over whose departure from the paternal roof and from pious influences have been shed so many bitter tears, have been enabled, under the preaching of a few faithful ministers, to give parents and friends at home such assurances as to change those *bitter* tears into tears of rejoicing.

> Lieutenant-General John B. Gordon, quoted in Mary Anna Jackson, *Life of Jackson*, 1892.

PARSON! For God's sake, pray. Nothing but God Almighty can save that fort!

> Lieutenant-General Nathan Bedford Forrest,

14 February 1862, to David C. Kelley, a minister turned solder, at Fort Donelson.

SOME OF US must die. Cross yourselves and march forward.

> Major-General William Starke Rosecrans – attributed – 31 December 1862, to his men at the Battle of Stones River.

IT AMUSES ME to see the effect of religion. Everybody relies upon God until it comes to fighting; then they rely upon men. You can't make men fight unless they are so disposed. Remember the words, "Victory or success is with God." He must give Grant the power over his officers and men to fight, and himself the gift of foresight into results, and the daring to undertake. As I believe God is on our side, I believe He will sooner or later give us victory.

> Admiral David G. Farragut, 3 June 1864, on his flagship, USS *Hartford*, off Mobile Bay, quoted in Loyall Farragut, *The Life of David Glasgow Farragut*, 1879.

IN ONE THING we took "the touch of elbows." It was not uncommon incident that from close opposing bivouacs and across hushed breastworks at evening voices of prayer from over the way would stir our hearts, and floating songs of love and praise be caught up and broadened into a mighty and thrilling chorus by our men softening down in cadences like enfolding wings. Such moments were surely a "Truce of God."

> Major-General Joshua L. Chamberlain, *The Passing of the Armies*, 1915.

GOD disposes. This ought to satisfy us.

> General Robert E. Lee, a note found in his desk at Washington College after his death, quoted in A.L. Long, *Memoirs of Robert E. Lee*, 1886.

I PRAY DAILY to do my duty, retain my self-confidence, and accomplish my destiny. No one can live under the aweful responsibility I have without Divine help. Frequently I feel that I don't rate it.

> General George S. Patton, Jr., 19 June 1943, diary entry.

A CHAPLAIN visits our company. In a tired voice, he prays for the strength of our arms and for the souls of the men who are to die. We do not consider his denomination. Helmets come off. Catholics, Jews, and Protestants bow their heads and finger their weapons. It is the front-line religion: God and the Garand.

> Lieutenant Audie Murphy, *To Hell and Back*, 1949.

FINALLY, I do not believe that today a commander can inspire great armies, or single units, or even individual men, and lead them to achieve great victories, unless he has a proper sense of religious truth. He must always keep his finger on the spiritual pulse of his armies; he must be sure that the spiritual purpose which inspires them is right and true, and is

clearly expounded to one and all. Unless he does this, he can expect no lasting success. For all leadership, I believe, is based on the spiritual quality, the power to inspire others to follow; this spiritual quality may be for good, or evil. In many cases in the past this quality has been devoted towards personal ends, and was partly or wholly evil; whenever this was so, in the end it failed. Leadership which is evil, while it may temporarily succeed, always carries within itself the seeds of its own destruction.
Field Marshal Viscount Montgomery of Alamein, *The Memoirs of Field Marshal Montgomery*, 1958.

RELIGION and military life are wholly compatible in my mind. You can't go into this disciplined life, giving up so many things, without spiritual support.
Lieutenant-General Victor H. 'The Brute' Krulak, *Life Magazine*, 30 April 1965.

IN WAR, many of us become religious. We went to feel closer to God. The ever-present possibility of dying is a constant reminder to put our affairs in order.
Major-General Bernard Loeffke, *From Warrior to Healer*, 1998.

REMINISCENCES

CHIEF of the sailors, Ahmose, son of Ebana, triumphant; he says: "I will tell you, O all ye people; I will cause you to know the honors which came to me. I was presented with gold seven times in the presence of the whole land; male and female slaves likewise. I was endowed with many fields." The fame of one valiant in achievements shall not perish in this land forever.
Ahmose, son of Abana, Egyptian naval officer in the reign of Pharaohs Ahmose, Amenhotep I and Thutmose I (1580–1501 BC), quoted in James Breasted, *Ancient Records of Egypt*, 1906.

BUT NOW my heyday's gone –
I've had my share of blows. Yet look hard at the husk and you'll see, I think, the grain that gave it life.
By heaven, Ares gave me courage, Athena too,
  to break
the ranks of men wide open, once, in the olds days,
Whenever I picked my troops and formed an ambush,
plotting attacks to spring against our foes –
no hint of death could daunt my fighting spirit!
Far out of the front I'd charge and spear my man,
I'd cut down any enemy soldier backing off.
Such was I in battle, true, but I had no love
for working the land, the chores of households either,
the labor that raises crops of shining children. No,
it was always oarswept ships that thrilled my heart,
and wars, and the long polished spears and arrows,
dreadful gear that makes the next man cringe.
I loved them all – god planted that love inside me.
Each man delights in the work that suits him best.
Homer, *The Odyssey*, 14.244–260, c. 800 BC,

tr. Robert Fagles, 1996; the reminiscences of Odysseus in his wanderings.

I SHOULD HAVE given Suchet an army-corps under my command, I should have sent Davout a month earlier to organize my army, and appointed Clauzel Minister of War. Or I ought to have given Soult the command of the Guard. He did not wish me to employ Ney. I should have spent the night of the 15th in Fleurus, and given Grouchy's command to Suchet, and given the former the command of all the cavalry, as I had not got Murat. The soldiers did not know each other well enough to possess the proper *esprit de corps*. The cavalry were better than the infantry. It is a pity that I did not fall at Waterloo, for that would have been a fine ending. My situation is frightful! I am like a dead man, yet full of life!
Napoleon (1769–1821), of the Waterloo campaign, quoted in F.M. Kircheisen, *The Memoirs of Napoleon I*, 1929.

IN CONCLUSION, I must state that, as I have dedicated myself entirely to the mobile profession of defending my country, these last Memoirs may be lacking in literary style. In reading these pages, the reader will soon discover that the author is a soldier, not a writer. I leave it to my readers, in their infinite wisdom, to judge my character and deeds without prejudice. I will abide by their sentence.
General Antonio Lopez de Santa Anna, *The Eagle: The Autobiography of Santa Anna*, c. 1870.

TO BE at the head of a strong column of troops, in the execution of some task that requires brain, is the highest pleasure of war – a grim one and terrible, but which leaves on the mind and memory the strongest mark; to detect the weak point of an enemy's line; to break through with vehemence and thus lead to victory; or to discover some key-point and hold it with tenacity; or to do some other distinct act which is afterward recognized as the real cause of success. These all become matters that are never forgotten.
General of the Army William T. Sherman, *The Memoirs of General W.T. Sherman*, II, 1875.

IT WAS GIVEN to us to learn at the outset that life is a profound and passionate thing. And it is for us to bear the report to those who come after. . . . the one and only success it is man's to command is to bring to his work a mighty heart.
Justice Oliver Wendell Holmes (1841–1935).

TO CONCLUDE, I would again put on record the deep love and gratitude that I have always felt for all the troops who were in my charge. At a word from me, they faced wounds, agony, and death for Russia's sake. And all in vain! May I be pardoned, for the guilt is not mine; and I could not foresee the future.
General Aleksei A. Brusilov, *A Soldier's Notebook*, 1931.

I DECIDED to try sincerely and quietly to illustrate in

myself the truth of the essence of commanding weighed down as it is by the burden of dangers, uncertainties and contradictions. Evey soldier struggles with them because they are the essence of war. A commander bears in addition, the weight of responsibility for his subordinates and must feel on his cheek the stinging shame of humiliation when his work of commanding has failed and others have paid with their blood for his unsuccess.

Marshal Joseph Pilsudski, *The Memoirs of a Polish Revolutionary and Soldier*, 1931.

IT WAS seventeen years ago – those days of old have vanished, tone and tint; they have gone glimmering through the dreams of things that were. Their memory is a land where flowers of wondrous beauty and varied colors spring, watered by tears and coaxed and caressed into fuller bloom by the smiles of yesterday. Refrains no longer rise and fall from that land of used-to-be. We listen vainly, but with thirsty ear, for the witching melodies of days that are gone. Ghosts in olive drab and sky blue and German gray pass before our eyes; voices that have stolen away in the echoes from the battlefields no more ring out. The faint, far whisper of forgotten songs no longer floats through the air. Youth, strength, aspirations, struggles, triumphs, despairs, wide winds sweeping, beacons flashing across uncharted depths, movements, vividness, radiance, shadows, faint bugles sounding reveille, far drums beating the long roll, the crash of guns, the rattle of musketry – the still white crosses!
And tonight we are met to remember.

General of the Army Douglas MacArthur, 14 July 1935, address to the veterans of the 42nd 'Rainbow' Division, *A Soldier Speaks*, 1965.

THIS I have always felt; as a youth and now as a man well in middle age: That truth is courage intellectualized. Thus the idea of the great man is the human coping stone of my philosophy as it was of the philosophy of that great man – Thomas Carlyle. Therefore in my study of war I have always put the great man first. As my system was founded on the organization of the human body, of necessity it follows that to breathe life into it, those who can do so must be men who at least aspire towards greatness.

Major-General J.F.C. Fuller, *Memoirs of an Unconventional Soldier*, 1936.

AT A DIFFICULT TIME a prince of my royal family once sent me a small portrait of Frederick the Great on which he had inscribed these words that the great king addressed to his friend, the Marquis d'Argens, when his own defeat seemed imminent. "Nothing can alter my inner soul: I shall pursue my own straight course and shall do what I believe to be right and honorable." The little picture I have lost, but the king's words remain engraved on my memory and are for me a model. If, despite everything, I could not prevent the defeat of my country, I must

ask my readers to believe that this was not for lack of a will to do so.

Colonel-General Heinz Guderian, *Panzer Leader*, 1953.

WELL, I'd like to do it all over again. The whole thing.
And more than that – more than anything – I'd like to see once again the face of every Marine I've ever served with.

General Lewis 'Chesty' Puller, 26 June 1960, to his wife when she asked him what he would like to do after his retirement, quoted in Burke Davis, *Marine*, 1962.

WITH every passing year we draw further and further away from those years of war. A new generation of people has grown up. For them war only means our reminiscences of it. And the numbers of us who took part in those historic events are dwindling fast. But I am convinced that time cannot cause the greatness to fade. Those were extraordinarily difficult, but also truly glorious years. Once a person has undergone great trials and come through victorious, then throughout his life he draws strength from this victory.

Marshal of the Soviet Union Georgi K. Zhukov, *Reminiscences and Reflections*, 1974.

I WOULD LIKE to be rated not by what I wrote but by how I lived, for I wrote to live and not the other way around. Having tried in this accounting to bestride the various periods in my journeying as if they were so many stages along a road, largely with the hope of explaining fortune that I hardly understand myself, I find on looking back that there is little to lament and much to cheer. Good companions were always alongside to help me through trial; I needed them as they in turn needed me. My yesterdays were the best the country ever knew, or so I believe, for in living them to the hilt I helped make them.
I think I will leave it at that.

Brigadier-General S.L.A. Marshall, *Bringing Up the Rear*, 1979.

REORGANISATION

ANY military reorganization should conform to certain set principles: –
(1) Power must go with responsibility.
(2) The average human brain finds its effective scope in handling from three to six other brains.
If a man divides the whole of his work into two branches and delegates his responsibility, freely and properly, to two experienced heads of branches he will not have enough to do. The occasions when they would have to refer to him would be too few to keep him fully occupied. If he delegates to three heads he will be kept fairly busy whilst six heads of branches will give most bosses a ten hours' day. Those data are the results of centuries of the experiences of soldiers, which are greater, where

organization is in question, than those of politicians, business men or any other class of men by just so much as an Army in the field is a bigger concern than a general election, the Bank of England, the Standard Oil Company, the Steel Trusts, the Railway Combines of America, or any other part of politics or business. Of all the ways wasted there is none so vicious as that of your clever politician trying to run a business concern without having any notion of self-organization. One of them who took over Munitions for a time had so little idea of organizing his own energy that he nearly died of overwork through holding up the work of others; by delegating responsibility coupled with direct access to himself to seventeen sub-chiefs!

Now, it will be understood why a battalion has four companies (and not seventeen); why a brigade has three or four battalions (and not seventeen).
General Sir Ian Hamilton, *The Soul and Body of an Army*, 1921.

THE HYPOTHESIS of every reorganization of an army is, first of all, peace on the outer borders. That means several years of external peace and a state of political calm. . . . Before these conditions are achieved a successful military reorganization cannot be accomplished. Success cannot be attained while you are in a continual state of war.
Colonel-General Hans von Seekt, while a military advisor to Chiang Kai-shek during the 1930s, *Denkschrift für Marschall Chiang Kai-shek*, n.d.

REPLACEMENTS

I DON'T KNOW what effect these men will have on the enemy, but, by God, they frighten me.
The Duke of Wellington, 1809, impression of replacements sent to him in Spain.

THOSE PEOPLE think they are indispensable; they don't know I have a hundred division commanders who can take their place.
Napoleon, repeated remark about his marshals, quoted in Christopher Herold, ed., *The Mind of Napoleon*, 1955.

IT LOOKS HARD to put those brigades, now numbering less than 800 men, into battle. They feel discouraged, whereas if we could have a steady influx of recruits the living would soon forget the dead.
General William T. Sherman, letter to Major-General Halleck, 4 September 1864, *O.R.*, Series I, Vol. XXXVIII, Part 5, pp. 793–794.

THE FIGHTING TROOPS are not being replaced effectively, although masses of drafts are sent to the technical and administrative services, who were originally on the most lavish scale, and who have since hardly suffered at all by the fire of the enemy.

The first duty of the war office is to keep up the rifle infantry strength.
Sir Winston S. Churchill, 3 May 1943, note to the Chief of the Imperial General Staff.

REPLACEMENTS are like spare parts – supplies. They must be asked for in time by the front line, and the need for them must be anticipated in the rear.
General George S. Patton, Jr., *War As I Knew It*, 1947.

REPORTS

I NEVER suffer reports, unsupported by proofs, to have weight in my Mind.
General George Washington, 15 July 1781, to Richard Henry Lee, *Writings*, XXII, 1937, p. 382.

ALL REPORTS should be written clearly, precisely, as far as possible avoiding any inaccuracy, length or beauty of expression, in order not to cloud the thought.
Field Marshal Prince Aleksandr V. Suvorov, 1799, during his campaign in Northern Italy.

NOTHING should be concealed from the Emperor, either bad or good: to deceive him, even about things that are likely to be disagreeable to him is a crime.
Marshal Berthier, at the end of February 1807, after the Battle of Eylau, advice to General Savary temporary commander of Lannes' corps, on the matter of deserters, quoted in S.J. Watson, *By Command of the Emperor*, 1957.

I HAVE SHOWN the Emperor, Monsieur le général Pino, the report which you have sent me. It is essential that you write your reports more legibly, and especially show the date plainly; that which you have written is not clear; one cannot tell whether it is the 11th, the 21st, or the 22d. Besides the date, it is always necessary to show the hour at which you write, and the place.
Marshal Berthier, Prince de Neuchatel, quoted in Albert du Casse, *Mémoires de Prince Eugène*, VII, 1859.

REPORTS are not self executive.
Florence Nightingale, 1857, marginal comment on a document.

THE OFFICERS say I don't believe anything. I certainly believe very little that comes in the shape of reports. They keep everybody stirred up. I mean to be whipped or to whip my enemy, and not to be scared to death.
Admiral David G. Farragut, quoted in Alfred Thayer Mahan, *Admiral Farragut*, 1892.

AS IT WAS, nothing came of all the loss and effort, except a report which I sent over to the British headquarters in Palestine for the Staff's consumption. It was mainly written for effect, full of quaint smiles and mock simplicities; and made them

think me a modest amateur, doing his best after the great models; not a clown, leering after them where they with Foch, bandmaster, at their head went drumming down the old road of effusion of blood into the house of Clausewitz. Like the battle, it was a nearly-proof parody of regulation use.
Headquarters loved it, and innocently, to crown the jest, offered me a decoration on the strength of it. We should have more bright breasts in the Army if each man was able without witnesses, to write his own despatch.

> Colonel T.E. Lawrence, *The Seven Pillars of Wisdom*, 1926.

IN WAR nothing is ever as bad, or as good, as it is reported to Higher Headquarters. Any reports which emanate from a unit after dark – that is, where the knowledge has been obtained after dark – should be viewed with skepticism by the next higher unit. Reports by wounded men are always exaggerated and favor the enemy.

> General George S. Patton, Jr., *War As I Knew It*, 1947.

WHEN YOU RECEIVE reports of counter-attacks, find out who sent them – that is, the size of the unit which sent them. A squad occupying a position will report an enemy section approaching it as a counter-attack, but such a counter-attack has no material effect on a division or a corps.

> General George S. Patton, Jr., *War As I Knew It*, 1947.

IN A BATTLE nothing is ever as good or as bad as the first reports of excited men would have it.

> Field Marshal Viscount Slim of Burma, *Unofficial History*, 1959.

BAD NEWS is not like fine wine – it does not improve with age.

> General Creighton Abrams, quoted in *Parameters*, Summer 1987.

REPRISALS

THE OFFICERS and soldiers of the army must recollect that their nations are at war with France solely because the ruler of the French nation will not allow them to be at peace, and is desirous of forcing them to submit to his yoke; and they must not forget that the worst of the evils suffered by the enemy in his profligate invasion of Spain and Portugal have been occasioned by the irregularities of the soldiers, and their cruelties authorised and encouraged by their chiefs toward the unfortunate and peaceful inhabitants of the country.
    To revenge this conduct on the peaceable inhabitants of France would be unmanly and unworthy of the nations to whom the Commander of the Forces would now address himself, and at all events would be the occasion of similar and worse evils to the army at large than those which the enemy's armies have

suffered in the Peninsula, and would eventually prove highly injurious to the public interests.

> The Duke of Wellington, 23 June 1813, at Salvatierra, upon the invasion of France, *Selections from the General Orders of Field Marshal the Duke of Wellington During His Various Commands 1799–1818*, 1847.

WE MUST TAKE revenge for the many sorrows inflicted upon the nations, and for so much arrogance. If we do not, then we are miserable wretches indeed, and deserve to be shocked out of our lazy peace every two years and threatened with the scourge of slavery. . . . We must return the visits of the French to our cities, by visiting them in theirs. Until we do, our revenge and triumph will be incomplete. If the Silesian Army reaches Paris first, I shall at once have the bridges of Austerlitz and Jena blown up, as well as the Arc de Triomphe.

> Field Marshal August Graf von Gneisenau, at the beginning of the 1814 campaign, quoted in David Hamilton-Williams, *The Fall of Napoleon*, 1994.

THIS WAS a hard sight. Our men got very much exasperated & one day when I brought up the rear, I [had] some sad work in protecting helpless women and children from outrage, when the rebels had been firing from their houses on us, and the men were bent on revenge. I invariably gave them my protection which any man of honor will give any woman as long as she is a woman. But I have no doubt they were all "burnt out" before the whole army got by. It was a sad business. I am willing to fight men in arms but not *babes in arms*.

> Major-General Joshua L. Chamberlain, 14 December 1864, letter to his sister, describing the attitude of his troops after Union stragglers had had their throats cut by the Confederates.

WHEN WE ARRIVED there, 90 percent of Afghanistan's residents welcomed us but when we left, 100 percent of them hated us. It is not difficult to understand why. When Afghan fighters fired on a Russian convoy from a village, for example, a Soviet commander used to simply raze that village to the ground. At first it was just a village, then 10 villages, then 100 villages, until half of the country was destroyed, and then there was a nationwide war, when local men were deeply upset by the fact that their children and wives were being killed and their houses being destroyed and that they were deprived of means of survival. The same thing happened in Chechnya. When nine settlements were razed to the ground, the most uncontrollable and wild unit of fighters was formed from the residents of Bamut which had been destroyed. They had nothing to lose.

> General Aleksandr I. Lebed, *Argumenty I Fakty* (Moscow), 22 October 1996.

REVENGE is a dish that should be eaten cold.

> English proverb.

REPUTATION

ODYSSEUS probed his own great fighting heart:
"O dear god, what becomes of Odysseus now?
A disgraceful thing if I should break and run,
fearing their main force – but it's far worse
if I'm taken all alone. Look, Zeus just drove
the rest of my comrades off in panic flight.
But debate, my friend, why thrash things out?
Cowards, I know, would quit the fighting now
but the man who wants to make his mark in war
must stand his ground and brace for all he's worth –
suffer his wounds or wound his man to death.
> Homer, *The Iliad*, 11.483–487, c. 800 BC,
> tr. Robert Fagles, 1990.

AT LAST is *Hector* stretch'd upon the plain,
Who fear'd no vengeance for Patrocles slain:
Then Prince! you should have fear'd, what now
   you feel;
Achilles absent was *Achilles* still.
> Homer, *The Iliad*, 22.415–419, c. 800 BC, tr. Alexander
> Pope, 1743; Achilles taunting the dying Hector that he
> had forgotten there was deadly substance behind
> Achilles' reputation.

QUESTIONED as to how he had gained his great
reputation, he said: "By having despised death."
> Plutarch, quoting Agesilaus, Eurypontid King of Sparta
> (400–360 BC), *The Lives*, c. AD 100 (*Plutarch on
> Sparta*, tr. Richard Talbert, 1988).

WHEN . . . woman heard that her son was behaving
badly abroad, she wrote to him: "You've acquired a
bad reputation. Either shake this off or cease to exist."
> Plutarch, quoting an anonymous Spartan mother, *The
> Lives*, c. AD 100 (*Plutarch on Sparta*, tr. Richard
> Talbert, 1988).

WHAT OF the two men in command? You have
Alexander, they – Darius!
> Alexander the Great, 333 BC, address to his army
> before the Battle of Issus, quoted in Arrian, *The
> Campaigns of Alexander*, 2.7, c. AD 150, tr. Aubrey
> de Sélincourt.

BUT HOW MANY ships do you reckon my presence
is worth?
> King Antigonas II Gonatas (c. 319–239 BC).

NOR DID HE use his success for self-glorification, or
apply the name of campaigns and victories to the
repression of a conquered people. He did not even
describe his achievements in a laurelled letter. Yet
by this disguising his renown he really increased it,
for men inferred the grandeur of his aspirations from
his silence about services so great.
> Cornelius Tacitus, *Agricola*, AD 98 (*The Complete
> Works of Tacitus*, tr. Alfred Church and William
> Brodribb, 1942), of his father-in-law, Cnaeus Julius
> Agricola, governor of Britain.

BUT WHAT most commonly keeps an army
united, is the reputation of the general, that is,
of his courage and good conduct; without these,
neither high birth nor any sort of authority is
sufficient.
> Niccolo Machiavelli, *The Art of War*, 1521.

I HAVE TAMED men of iron in my day – shall I not
crush men of butter?
> Alvarez de Toledo, Duke of Alva (1507–1582), of his
> attempt to pacify the Netherlands.

IT IS MORE the nature of men to be less
interested in things which relate to others than
about those in which they themselves are
concerned. The reputation of an organization
becomes personal just as soon as it is an honor to
belong to it.
> Field Marshal Maurice Comte de Saxe, *My Reveries*,
> 1732, tr. Phillips, 1940.

SUBSTANTIAL SERVICE is what constitutes lasting
reputation; and your reports this campaign are the
best panegyric that can be given of your actions.
> Major-General Nathaniel Greene, 27 January
> 1782, to Major-General (then Lieutenant-Colonel)
> Henry 'Light Horse Harry' Lee, quoted in *Henry
> Lee, Memoirs of the War in the Southern
> Department*, 1869.

HE WHO FEARS to lose his reputation is sure to
lose it.
> Napoleon, 1797, letter, quoted in Christopher Herold,
> ed., *The Mind of Napoleon*, 1955.

A GREAT REPUTATION is a great noise; the more
there is made, the farther off it is heard. Laws,
institutions, monuments, nations, all fall; but the
noise continues and resounds in after ages.
> Napoleon, quoted in Louis de Bourrienne, *Memoirs of
> Napoleon Bonaparte*, I, 1855.

MY POWER proceeds from my reputation, and my
reputation from the victories I have won. My power
would fall if I were not to support it with more glory
and more victories. Conquest has made me what I
am; only conquest can maintain me.
> Napoleon, 30 December 1802, quoted in
> R.M. Johnston, ed., *The Corsican*, 1910.

HAD I SUCCEEDED, I should have died with the
reputation of the greatest man that ever lived.
> Napoleon (1769–1821), quoted in Barry O'Meara,
> *Napoleon in Exile*, 1822.

MANY FAULTS, no doubt, will be found in my
career; but Arcole, Rivoli, the Pyramids, Marengo,
Austerlitz, Jena, Friedland – these are granite: the
tooth of envy is powerless here.
> Napoleon, 1815, conversation, quoted in Christopher
> Herold, ed., *The Mind of Napoleon*, 1955.

I DESIRE that the terror of my name shall guard our frontiers more potently than chains or fortresses.
> General Mikhail Yermolov, during the pacification of the Caucasus in the 1830s, quoted in Blanch, *The Sabres of Paradise*, 1960.

GO BACK, give my compliments to them and tell the Stonewall Brigade to maintain her reputation!
> Lieutenant-General Thomas J. 'Stonewall' Jackson, 30 August 1862, on the second day of the Battle of Second Bull Run, when the Stonewall Brigade was hard-pressed and appealed to Jackson for reinforcements, quoted in James Robertson, *Stonewall Jackson*, 1997.

IN THE ARMY of the Shenandoah you were the *First Brigade*! In the army of the Potomac, you were the *First Brigade*! In the second corps of the army you are the *First Brigade*! You are the *First Brigade* in the affections of your general; and I hope by your future deeds and bearing you will be handed to posterity as the *First Brigade* in this our second war of independence. Farewell!
> Lieutenant-General Thomas J. 'Stonewall' Jackson, farewell to the Stonewall Brigade at Centerville, Virginia, 4 October 1862, quoted in Daniells, *The Life of Jackson*, 1863.

WHAT CAN I SAY to you as I go away?
When the heart is full it is not easy to speak. But I would say this to you:
"YOU have made this Army what it is. YOU have made its name a household word all over the world. Therefore, YOU must uphold its good name and its traditions."
> Field Marshal Viscount Montgomery of Alamein (then General), August 1943, to the Eighth Army, 'Personal Message from the Commander – to be read to all the troops'.

DON'T FORGET, you don't know I'm here at all. No word of that fact is to be mentioned in any letter. The world is not supposed to know what the hell they did with me. I'm not supposed to be commanding this army. I'm not even supposed to be in England. Let the first bastards to find out be the goddam Germans. Some day I want them to raise up their hind legs and howl: "Jesus Christ, it's that goddam Third Army and that sonofabitch Patton again!"
> General George S. Patton, Jr., part of his famous pre-battle speech to units of the Third Army before D-Day, 1944, quoted in Carlo d'Este, *Patton: A Genius For War*, 1995.

RESERVES

WARS are paid for by the possession of reserves.
> Thucydides, *Peloponnesian Wars*, c. 404 BC, tr. Rex Warner.

THE GENERAL should also have somewhere a picked corps, stationed apart from the phalanx as military reserves, that he may have them ready to give assistance to those detachments of his force that are exhausted. These fresh troops are of not a little advantage in attacking tired men; for, besides relieving those of their own men who are worn out, they attack in their full freshness a wearied enemy.
> Onasander, *The General*, AD 58 (*Aeneas Tacticus, Aclepiodotus, Onasander*, tr. The Illinois Greek Club, 1923).

IT IS BETTER to have several bodies of reserves than to extend your front too much.
> Flavius Vegetius Renatus, *Military Institutions of the Romans*, c. AD 378, tr. Clark, 1776.

A GENERAL should always have a body of chosen troops about him, whom he can send to the support of sections of the army which are hard pressed.
> The Emperor Maurice, *The Strategikon*, c. AD 600 (*Maurice's Strategikon*, tr. George Dennis, 1984).

WHEN ONE has a good reserve, one does not fear one's enemies.
> Richard I, 'The Lion Heart', King of England, 1194, after his victory at the Battle of Fréteval, quoted in *Histoire de Guillaume le Maréchal*, c. 1220.

PROVIDENCE is always on the side of the last reserve.
> Napoleon (1769–1821), *Sayings of Napoleon*.

FATIGUE the opponent, if possible, with few forces and conserve a decisive mass for the critical moment. Once this decisive mass has been thrown in, it must be used with the greatest audacity.
> Major-General Carl von Clausewitz, *Principles of War*, 1812.

THE GREAT SECRET of battle is to have reserve. I always had.
> The Duke of Wellington (1769–1852).

MAXIM 96. A general who retains fresh troops for the day after a battle is almost always beaten. He should, if helpful, throw in his last man, because on the day after a complete success there are no more obstacles in front of him; prestige alone will insure new triumphs to the conqueror.
> Napoleon, *The Military Maxims of Napoleon*, tr. Burnod, 1827.

A RESERVE has two distinct purposes. One is to prolong and renew action; the second, to counter unforeseen threats. The first purpose presupposes the value of the successive use of force. . . . The case of a unit being sent to a point that is about to be overrun is clearly an instance of the second category, since the amount of resistance necessary at that point had obviously not been foreseen. A unit that is intended merely to prolong the fighting in a particular engagement and for that purpose is kept in reserve, will be available and subordinate to the commanding officer, though posted out of the reach of fire.

> Major-General Carl von Clausewitz, *On War*, 3.13, 1832, tr. Michael Howard and Peter Paret, 1976.

THE SYSTEM of holding out a reserve as long as possible for independent action when the enemy has used his own, ought to be applied downwards. Each battalion should have its own, each regiment its own, firmly maintained.

> Colonel Charles Ardant du Picq, *Battle Studies*, 1880, tr. Greely, 1957.

IN THE BATTLE LINE, tactics merely consist in overcoming hostile resistance by a slow and progressive wear of the enemy's resources; for that purpose, the fight is kept up everywhere. It must be supported, and such is the use made of the reserves. They must become warehouses into which one dips to replace the wear and tear as it occurs. Art consists in still having a reserve when the opponent no longer has one, so as to have the last word in a struggle in which wearing-down is the only argument employed.

> Marshal of France Ferdinand Foch, *Principles of War*, 1913.

I HAVE NO MORE reserves. The only men I have left are the sentries at my gates. I will take them with me to where the line is broken, and the last of the English will die fighting.

> Field Marshal Sir John French, 1914, message to General Foch during the Battle of Ypres, quoted in Spears, Liaison 1914, *A Narration of the Great Retreat*.

THE RESERVE is a *club*, prepared, organized, reserved, carefully maintained with a view to carrying out the one act of battle from which a result is expected – the decisive attack.

> Marshal of France Ferdinand Foch, *Precepts and Judgments*, 1919.

THERE IS always the possibility of accident, of some flaw in materials, present in the general's mind: and the reserve is unconsciously held to meet it.

> Colonel T.E. Lawrence (1888–1935).

IT IS in the use and withholding of their reserves that the great Commanders have generally excelled. After all, when once the last reserve has been thrown in, the Commander's part is played. . . . The event must be left to pluck and to the fighting troops.

> Sir Winston S. Churchill, *Painting as a Pastime*, 1932.

TO FIGHT without a reserve is similar to playing cards without capital – sheer gambling. To trust to the cast of dice is not generalship.

> Major-General J.F.C. Fuller, *Memoirs of an Unconventional Soldier*, 1936.

A STUDY of Napoleon's tactics will show us that the first step he took in battle was not to break the enemy's front, and then when his forces were disorganized risk being hit by the enemy's reserves; but instead to draw the enemy's reserves into the fire fight, and directly they were drawn in to break through them or envelop them. Once this was done, security was gained; consequently, a pursuit could be carried out, a pursuit being more often than not initiated by troops disorganized by victory against troops disorganized by deafeat.

> Major-General J.F.C. Fuller, *Memoirs of an Unconventional Soldier*, 1936.

IN MECHANIZED WARFARE the value of a reserve cannot be exaggerated, for increased mobility carries with it the power of effecting innumerable surprises, and the more the unexpected becomes possible, the stronger must be the reserves.

> Major-General J.F.C. Fuller, *Armoured Warfare*, 1943.

RESIGNATION

MY REASONS for resigning were set forth in my letter of the 31st ult., and my views remain unchanged; and if the Secretary persists in this ruinous policy complained of, I feel that no officer can serve his country better than by making his strongest possible protest against it, which, in my opinion, is done by tendering his resignation, rather than be a willing instrument in prosecuting the war upon a ruinous principle. . . .

> Lieutenant-General Thomas J. 'Stonewall' Jackson, 6 February 1862, letter to Governor Letcher of Virginia, quoted in Allan, *History of the Campaign of Gen. T.J. (Stonewall) Jackson in the Shenandoah Valley of Virginia*, 1880.

IF IT EVER came to a choice between compromising my moral principles and the performance of my duties, I know I'd go with my moral principles. At the same time, however, I would also cease being an Army officer. I would have to resign my commission. But even at that I could be accomplishing my duty.

> General H. Norman Schwarzkopf, October 1991, interview with C.D.B. Bryan, quoted in Peter David, *Triumph in the Desert*, 1991.

RESISTANCE TO REFORM

I HAVE NOT written this book for military monks, but for civilians, who pay for their alchemy and mysteries. In war there is nothing mysterious, for it is the most common-sense of all the sciences. . . . If it possess a mystery, then that mystery is unprogressiveness, or it is a mystery that, in a profession which may, at any moment, demand the risk of danger and death, men are found willing to base their work on the campaigns of Waterloo and Sedan when the only possible war which confronts them is the next war.

Major-General J.F.C. Fuller, *The Reformation of War*, 1923.

IT [the Army] has been in the family for three hundred years, and he is naturally very loath to part with it and inhabit some horrible ferro-concrete house. He cannot afford to modernize it, and, to make both ends meet, he shuts up room after room, and so "economizes" his reduced income and hopes for better times. He cannot tear himself away from its memories and traditions and family ghosts, and so dry-rot creeps through its foundations and the rain percolates through its roof.

Major-General J.F.C. Fuller, *The Reformation of War*, 1923.

THERE ARE two kinds of treason. The first is constitutional and means betraying one's own country. The second means action whereby a party "betrays their trust." The Army and Navy are treasonable under that head for not giving proper improvements to the air service. Of course, I refer to the system and not to any individual.

Brigadier-General William 'Billy' Mitchell, 1925, at his court-martial.

THE PROBLEM which faces the reformer of armies in peace might be likened to that of an architect called on to alter and modernize an old-fashioned house without increasing its size, with the whole family still living in it (often grumbling at the architect's improvements, since an extra bathroom can only be added at the expense of someone's dressing room) and under the strictest financial limitations.

Field Marshal Viscount Wavell of Cyrenaica, 'The Army and the Prophets', *Royal United Services Institute (RUSI)*, May 1930.

THE REGULAR OFFICER has the traditions of forty generations of serving soldiers behind him, and to him the old weapons are the most honored.

Colonel T.E. Lawrence (1888–1935).

AN ARMY is an institution not merely conservative but retrogressive by nature. It has such natural resistance to progress that it is always insured against the danger of being pushed too fast. Far worse and more certain, as history abundantly testifies, is the danger of it slipping backward. Like a man pushing a barrow up a hill, if the soldier ceases to push, the military machine will run back and crush him. To be deemed a revolutionary in the army is merely an indication of vitality, the pulse-beat which shows that the mind is still alive. When a soldier ceases to be a revolutionary it is a sure sign he has become a mummy. (Jan. 1931.)

Captain Sir Basil Liddell Hart, *Thoughts on War*, 1944.

I FOUND that the technique and practices developed at Benning and Leavenworth would practically halt the development of an open warfare situation, apparently requiring an armistice or some understanding with a complacent enemy.

General of the Army George C. Marshall, 4 December 1933, quoted in Pogue, *George C. Marshall: Education of a General*, 1963.

CONVENTIONALISM takes a firm stand against innovations. But this inflexibility towards any immediate change is often followed in the long run by the most astounding reversals. When it ultimately changes, it often turns upside down and stands on its head. (April 1936.)

Captain Sir Basil Liddell Hart, *Thoughts on War*, 1944.

RESOLUTION/RESOLVE

I HAVE NOT the particular shining bauble or feather in my cap for crowds to gaze at or kneel to, but I have power and resolution for foes to tremble at.

Oliver Cromwell (1599–1658).

THE TRUE PRUDENCE of a general consists of energetic resolve.

Napoleon (1769–1821).

MAXIM 84. An irresolute general who acts without principles and without plan, even though he leads an army numerically superior to that of the enemy, almost always finds himself inferior to the latter on the field of battle. Fumblings, the *mezzo termine* [the middle course] lose all in War.

Napoleon, *The Military Maxims of Napoleon*, tr. Burnod, 1827.

IS IT NOT the manner in which the leaders carry out the task of command, of impressing their resolution in the hearts of others, that makes them warriors, far more than all other aptitudes or faculties which theory may expect of them?

General Gerhardt von Scharnhorst, at the time of Blücher's appointment to command the army of Silesia in 1813, quoted in Ferdinand Foch, *Principles of War*, 1913.

I WILL SMASH them, so help me god!

Major-General Andrew Jackson, 1815, at the Battle of New Orleans.

HARDSHIP, blood, and death create enthusiasts and martyrs and give birth to bold and desperate resolutions.

Napoleon (1769–1821), on St. Helena, quoted in Christopher Herold, ed., *The Mind of Napoleon*, 1955.

GREAT EXTREMITIES require extraordinary resolution. The more obstinate the resistance of an army, the greater the chances of success. How many seeming impossibilities have been accomplished by men whose only resolve was death!

Napoleon, *Maxims of War*, 1831.

THE PRESIDENT of the United States ordered me to break through the Japanese lines and proceed from Corregidor to Australia for the purpose, as I understand it, of organizing the American offensive against Japan, a primary object of which is the relief of the Philippines. I came through, and I shall return.

General of the Army Douglas MacArthur, 17 March 1942, upon his arrival in Australia, *Reminiscences*, 1964.

SINCE THE WAR began, tens of thousands of officers and men of matchless loyalty and courage have done battle at the risk of their lives, and have died to become guardian gods of our land.

Ah, how can I ever enter the imperial presence again? With what words can I possibly report to the parents and brothers of my dead comrades?

The body is frail, yet with a mind firm with unshakable resolve I will drive deep into the enemy's positions and let him see the blood of a Japanese man.

Wait but a while, young men! – one last battle, fought gallantly to the death, and I will be joining you!

Admiral Isoroku Yamamoto, late September 1942, a poem found in his desk before the fatal flight during which he was shot down by U.S. aircraft, quoted in Agawa, *Reluctant Admiral*, 1979.

I HAVE RETURNED. By the grace of God, our forces stand again on Philippine soil.

General of the Army Douglas MacArthur, 20 October 1944, landing on Leyte.

WHETHER WE ATTACK or whether we stay where we are is only death. But realizing that in death there is life, let us take this opportunity to exhalt Japanese manhood. I shall advance upon the Americans to deliver still another blow and leave my bones upon Saipan as a bulwark of the Pacific.

Vice-Admiral Chuichi Nagumo, 1944, quoted in *MHQ*, Spring 1955.

NEVER take "No" for an answer. Never submit to failure.

Sir Winston S. Churchill (1874–1965).

THIS is not time to go wobbly.

Prime Minister Margaret Thatcher, 26 August 1990, to President George Bush as she sought to strengthen his resolve to take military action against Saddam Hussein's invasion of Kuwait.

RESPONSIBILITY/ACCOUNTABILITY

INSPIRED with Nestor's voice and sent by Zeus, the dream cried out, "Still asleep, Agamemnon? The son of Atreus, the skilled breaker of horses?

How can you sleep all night, a man weighed down with duties?
Your armies turning over their lives to your command – responsibilities so heavy.

Homer, *The Iliad*, 2.25–29, c. 800 BC, tr. Robert Fagles, 1990.

RESPONSIBILITY is the test of a man's courage.

Admiral Lord St. Vincent (1735–1833).

OUR DISASTERS in Spain are as ridiculous as they are great, even the English think so. But the army has not lost its prestige. The army of Spain has no general, and was burdened with a King. I am bound to admit that the fundamental mistakes lie at my own door.

Napoleon, 20 July 1813, quoted in R.M. Johnston, ed., *The Corsican*, 1910.

THIS WAS all my fault, General Pickett. This has been my fight and blame is mine. Your men did all men could do. The fault is entirely my own.

General Robert E. Lee, 3 July 1863, at the Battle of Gettysburg, after Pickett's Charge when Lee rode out to meet the remnants of the attacking force, quoted in Stackpole, *They Met at Gettysburg*, 1956.

I HAVE NEVER had any cause of complaint either on account of deficiency in the Staff Deptmts or embarrassments trown (sic) in the way by the Authorities at Washington. The fact is I believe complaints are generally made to shift responsibility of inaction from commanders to Staff Departments or Washington Authorities.

General of the Army Ulysses S. Grant, 16 February 1864, letter to Brigadier-General Rufus Ingalls.

. . . RESPONSIBILITY, the best of educators.

Rear-Admiral Alfred Thayer Mahan, *The Life of Nelson*, 1897.

I DON'T KNOW who won the Battle of the Marne, but if it had been lost, I know who would have lost it.

Marshal of France J.C. Joffre, 1919, to the Briey Parliamentary Commission.

LEAVE THAT to me. I am the only one who must apologize to His Majesty.

Admiral Isoroku Yamamoto, 4 June 1942, when the question was raised as to how the Japanese Fleet could apologize to the Emperor for the defeat it had just suffered at Midway, quoted in John Deane Potter, *Yamamoto*, 1967.

BAD NEWS always comes first. There was no report of the enemy's losses. This is the hardest thing an area commander in the rear has to face. Your feeling is one of complete helplessness. You know you have put your men into a fight, and you hope you have done everything possible to make that fight successful, but you are always searching your mind for something you may have left undone. It is a great mental agony. You not only have your individual responsibility to your country and to the cause of the Allied Powers, but you have the responsibility of many lives on your shoulders, plus the material damage that may be inflicted on your forces.

Admiral of the Fleet William 'Bull' Halsey, observation while awaiting news of the outcome of the Battle of Guadalcanal, 12–13 November 1942, quoted in E.B. Potter, *Bull Halsey*, 1985.

IN FORTY HOURS I shall be in battle, with little information and on the spur of the moment will have to make most momentous decisions, but I believe that one's spirit enlarges with responsibility and that, with God's help, I shall make them and make them right. It seems that my whole life has been pointed to this moment. When this job is done, I presume I will be pointed to the next step in the ladder of destiny. If I do my full duty, the rest will take care of itself.

General George S. Patton, Jr., 6 November 1942, *War As I Knew It*, 1947.

A GENERAL OFFICER who will invariably assume the responsibility for failure, whether he deserves it or not, and invariably give the credit for success to others, whether they deserve it or not, will achieve outstanding success.

General George S. Patton, Jr., *War As I Knew It*, 1947.

TO MEN who have been long in battle and have thought about it deeply, there comes at last the awareness of this ultimate responsibility – that one man must go ahead so that a nation may live. No feeling of futility accompanies that thought. At the time one accepts it simply as the rule of life and of death, of struggle and of national survival. But in the long afterglow comes also the realization that a nation may perish because too few of its people have found this truth on the only field where it may be found and because too many of the others who have not found it, unconsciously resist it and rule it out because it has not been part of their experience.

Brigadier-General S.L.A. Marshall, *Men Against Fire*, 1947.

HINDENBURG once said that he was occasionally held responsible for victories, but always for defeats.

Field Marshal Albert Kesselring, *Memoirs of Field Marshal Kesselring*, 1953.

THE PRICE of greatness is responsibility.

Sir Winston S. Churchill (1874–1965).

ANY CLEVER PERSON can make plans for winning a war if he has no responsibility for carrying them out.

Sir Winston S. Churchill (1874–1965).

SOLDIERS of an army invariably reflect the attitude of their General. The leader is the essence. Isolated cases of rapine may well be exceptional, but

widespread and continuing abuse can only be a fixed responsibility of highest field authority. Resultant liability is commensurate with resulting crime. To hold otherwise would be to prevaricate the fundamental nature of the command function. This imposes no new hazard on a commander, no new limitation on his power. He has always, and properly, been subject to due process of law. Powerful as he may become in time of war, he still is not autocratic or absolute, he still remains responsible before the bar of universal justice. From time immemorial the record of high commanders, of whatever side, has been generally temperate and just.

General of the Army Douglas MacArthur, 21 March 1946, justifying the death penalty for General Masahara Homma, *A Soldier Speaks*, 1965.

I HAVE NEVER been a self-confident person. My lack of self-confidence has not prevented me from being decisive in my job. When one does a job, when one is responsible for it and makes decisions – here there is no place for doubts of oneself or a lack of confidence. You are completely engrossed in your job and in giving your all to this job and doing everything that you are capable of. But later, when the job is complete, when you reflect on what you have done, when you think not only of the past but also of the future, there is a heightened awareness that you lack something, something is missing, that you had to know a number of things which you did not know and this returning feeling causes you to rethink everything and decide: "Could you have not done better than what you did, if you had possessed all that you lacked?"

Marshal of the Soviet Union Georgi K. Zhukov (1896–1974), quoted in *Voyenno istorichiskiy zhurnal*, 12/1987.

EVERY GOOD SOLDIER in authority should be just as concerned with his responsibility to help those under him make the right turns.

Major-General Aubrey 'Red' Newman, *Follow Me*, 1981.

RESPONSIBILITY is a unique concept: It can only reside and inhere in a single individual. You may share it with others, but your portion is not diminished. You may delegate it, but it is still with you. You may disclaim it, but you can not divest yourself of it. Even if you do not recognize it or admit its presence, you cannot escape it. If the responsibility is rightfully yours, no evasion, or ignorance, or passing the blame can shift the burden to someone else.

Admiral Hyman G. Rickover (1900–1987), quoted in *The Washington Post*, 4 September 1998, p. A24.

AFTER multiple combat tours in Korea and Vietnam, there are friends who I lost that still stand out in my mind. I don't believe that is negative. Their memory doesn't disrupt me. In a way, they have helped me come to grips with my responsibility of Command.

General Alfred M. Gray, 'Gunfighters', Al Santoli, ed.,

Leading the Way: How Vietnam Veterans Rebuilt the U.S. Military, 1993.

ACCOUNTABILITY is critically important to good order and discipline of the force, and failure to ensure accountability will destroy the trust of the American public . . . who look to us, the members of their nation's Air Force, to embrace and live by the standards that are higher than those in the society we serve.

General Ronald R. Fogelman, 1995, USAF video, quoted by Colonel Harry Summers, *The Washington Times*, 10 July 1997.

WHEN you became a Marine, you were expected to take responsibility for yourself. In our Corps, however, it isn't long before you are expected to assume responsibility for others. You are now, or soon will be, expected to lead. At the same time you are entrusted to lead, you are also given the authority to get the job done. You are free to share authority within the ranks you have been entrusted to lead. This is called delegation. Sergeants delegate some of their authority to corporals and so on. And while the delegation of authority is a proven technique for mission success, attempts to delegate responsibility always end in failure. Responsibility can never be delegated. Responsibility, remember, is your decision to do what needs to be done, to do what is right.

So what of accountability? Accountability means that you must give account of your actions. It differs from responsibility in that it is not a decision or an action but a sum of what you have done. It is an end product. Is your rifle clean or not? You have been entrusted with the responsibility of the weapon, but on inspection day you will be held accountable for its condition. As you can see, accountability is the proof of whether you have been responsible. Accountability is what the Nation expects of the Corps. It is what I expect of you. Responsibility and accountability go hand in hand. The fusing of responsibility and accountability is what makes Marines effective leaders and followers.

General Charles C. Krulak, 'Responsibility, Accountability, and the Zero-Defects Mentality', *Marine Corps Gazette*, May 1997.

RETALIATION

I HEARD this afternoon from Stoneman that they (seesch) had murdered some of our men after they were taken prisoners. . . . I will pay them in their own coin, if they wish to carry on the war in that manner. I hope there is some mistake about the murders, for I do not wish to make reprisals. It is a sad business at best. . . .

Major-General George B. McClellan, 9 May 1862, letter, *McClellan's Own Story*, 1887.

THE GOVERNMENT of the United States will give the same protection to all its soldiers, and if the enemy shall sell or enslave anyone because of his color, the offense shall be punished by retaliation upon the enemy's prisoners in our possession.

It is therefore ordered that for every soldier of the United States killed in violation of the laws of war, a rebel soldier shall be executed; and for every one enslaved by the enemy or sold into slavery, a rebel soldier shall be placed at hard labor on the public works and continued at such labor until the other shall be released and receive treatment due to a prisoner of war.

President Abraham Lincoln, 30 July 1863, executive order, quoted in *The Portable Lincoln*, 1992.

I CANNOT recommend the execution of the prisoners who have fallen into our hands. . . . But I do not think that reason and reflection would justify such a course. I think it better to do right, even if we suffer in so doing, than to incur the reproach of our conscience and posterity. Nor do I think that under present circumstances policy dictates execution of these men. It would produce retaliation. How many and better men have we in the enemy's hands than they have in ours! But this consideration should have no weight, provided the course was in itself right. Yet history records instances where such considerations have prevented the execution of marauders and devastators of provinces.

General Robert E. Lee, letter to the Secretary of War, James A. Seddon, 6 March 1864, quoted in J. William Jones, *Life and Letters of Robert Edward Lee*, 1906.

SINCE the murder of my men, not less than seven hundred prisoners, including many officers of high rank, captured from your army by this command have been forwarded to Richmond; but the execution of my purpose of retaliation was deferred, in order, as far as possible, to confine its operation to the men of Custer and Powell. Accordingly, on the 6th instant, seven of your men were, by my order, executed on the Valley Pike – your highway of travel. Hereafter, any prisoners falling into my hands will be treated with the kindness due to their condition, unless some new act of barbarity shall compel me, reluctantly, to adopt a line of policy repugnant to humanity.

Colonel John S. Mosby, 11 November 1864, letter to Major-General Philip Sheridan, announcing his intention to execute Union prisoners in retaliation for the murder of seven of his own men, *Memoirs of Colonel John S. Mosby*, 1917.

RETIREMENT

HE SAYS, "I followed the Kings of Upper and Lower Egypt, the gods; I was with their majesties when they went to the South and North country, in every place where they went; from King Ahmose I, triumphant, King Amenhotep I, triumphant, King

Thutmose I, triumphant, King Thutmose II, triumphant, until this Good God, King Thutmose III who is given life forever.

I attained a good old age, having had a life of royal favor, having had honor under their majesties and the love of me having been in court.

Ahmose-Pen-Nekhbet, Egyptian general of the 18th Dynasty, c. 1580–1500 BC, quoted in James Breasted, *Ancient Records of Egypt*, 1906.

THE SCENE is at last closed.

General George Washington, 28 December 1783, on his return to Mount Vernon after the Revolutionary War, *Writings*, XXVII, 1938, p. 288.

I AM just beginning to experience that ease, and freedom from public cares which, however desirable, takes some time to realize; for strange as it may tell, it is nevertheless true, that it was not 'till lately I could get the better of my usual custom of ruminating as soon as I waked in the Morning, on the business of the ensuing day; and of my surprize, after having revolved many things in my mind, to find that I was no longer a public Man, or had any thing to do with public transactions.

General George Washington, 20 February 1784, *Writings*, XXVII, 1938, p. 340.

THE TIME FACTOR . . . rules the profession of arms. There is perhaps none where the dicta of the man in office are accepted with such an uncritical deference, or where the termination of an active career brings a quicker descent into careless disregard. Little wonder that many are so affected by the sudden transition as to cling pathetically to the trimmings of the past.

Captain Sir Basil Liddell Hart, *Thoughts on War*, 1944.

FOR an old soldier to say that it is a pleasure to take his last review is, in my mind at least, a stretch of the imagination and a far cry from the truth.

General Jonathan M. Wainwright, 31 August 1947, at his retirement ceremony, quoted in Duane Schultz, *Hero of Bataan*, 1981.

I JUST HOPE he never retires. He'll have to run the house then, and I'll have to get out.

Mrs. Victor H. Krulak, wife of 'The Brute', *Life Magazine*, 30 November 1965.

MARY AND I packed our possessions and turned Quarters One over to the Ridgways, not without a deep sense of loss. It had been our home for five and a half uninterrupted years, longer than we had ever lived in one place. As we walked away for the last time, it occurred to me that it had been forty-two years, almost to the day, since I checked in at the main gate at West Point. Now I was a mere sixty years old; an entirely new and quite different life lay ahead.

General of the Army Omar N. Bradley, *A General's Life*, 1983.

ON FRIDAY, August 30, I put on my battle fatigues and reported to the personnel office at Central Command. A young female soldier handed me my discharge form and said, "Sir, this is your DD-214. We recommend you put this form into your safe deposit box because this is the only real proof that you were ever in the service." I signed the papers, received my retiree ID card, and, after posing for a snapshot with all the young troops in my office, walked out to the car. Craig "Max" Maxum, the sergeant major who'd been in charge of my bodyguards since the beginning of Desert Storm and was still constantly at my side, asked, "Is that all?"

"Max, that's it."

"Sir, it's not right. Thirty-five years in the military and you just sign a piece of paper and it's over? Sir, it's not right. We ought to do something."

"We've had enough parades." But Max was disturbed.

The following night some friends gave Brenda and me a dinner party. We got home shortly before midnight. I'd just parked the car in the garage when Max said, "Only seventeen seconds more, sir."

At first I didn't understand. "What do you mean?" I asked. He looked at me funny and I realized he was talking about my retirement. "Shut up, Max. I don't want to talk about it." I laughed.

"Sir it just doesn't seem right. No rockets in the air, no big parade, no flyovers."

By then it was midnight. My Army career was over.

General H. Norman Schwarzkopf, *It Doesn't Take a Hero*, 1992.

IT'S ALMOST like jumping out of an airplane. You are weightless. There's no noise, or anything like that. The weight is off of you. You're not standing on your own feet. You're not bearing your own weight. You're just suspended in the air.

You don't know whether it's time to go home and die in a couple of years, or whether you're going to devote yourself to your grandchildren, or whatever you're going to do.

General Carl E. Mundy, *The Washington Post*, 5 June 1999, p. C2.

RETREAT

NO SHAME in running.
Fleeing disaster, even in pitch darkness.
Better to flee from death than feel its grip.

Homer, *The Iliad*, 14.96–98, c. 800 BC, tr. Robert Fagles, 1990; Agamemnon, having lost his nerve as the Trojans threatened the Greek camp and ships.

I DO NOT FLEE, but I give ground like the rams, in order that I might make my charge the mightier.

King Philip II of Macedon (382–336 BC), quoted in Alfred S. Bradford, *Philip II of Macedon: A Life from the Ancient Sources*, 1992.

FOR as it is a great and glorious achievement, if we

press on, to have accomplished so great a march, to have traversed forests and to have crossed estuaries, so, if we retire, our present most complete success will prove our greatest danger. We have not the same knowledge of the country or the same abundance of supplies, but we have arms in our hands, and in them we have everything. For myself I have long been convinced that neither for an army nor for a general is retreat safe. Better, too, is an honourable death than a life of shame, and safety and renown are for us to be found together. And it would be no inglorious end to perish on the extreme confines of earth and of nature.

> Cnaeus Julius Agricola, c. AD 83, address to his army before the last major battle of the reconquest of Britain, quoted in Tacitus, *Agricola*, AD 98, (*The Complete Works of Tacitus*, tr. Alfred Church and William Brodribb, 1942).

THERE IS no retreat, or, to put it more mildly, retirement, which does not bring an infinity of woes to those who make it, to wit: shame, hunger, loss of friends, goods and arms, and death, which is the worst of them, but not the last for infamy endures for ever.

> Hernan Cortes, 1520, address to his army, quoted in de Gomara, *Istoria de la Conquista de Mexico*, 1552, tr. Simpson.

TO WITHDRAW is not to run away, and to stay is no wise action, when there's more reason to fear than to hope.

> Miguel de Cervantes, *Don Quixote*, 1605–1615, tr. Peter Moteux and John Ozell.

IF YOU HAVE been obliged to withdraw repeatedly before the enemy, the troops get frightened. The same thing happens if you have suffered some check; even when a good opportunity presents itself to you, it must be allowed to escape as you see any wavering among the troops.

> Frederick the Great, *Instructions to His Generals*, 1747, tr. Phillips, 1940.

NEVER sound the retreat. Never. Warn the men that if they hear it, it is only a ruse on the part of the enemy.

> Field Marshal Prince Aleksandr V. Suvorov (1729–1800), quoted in Blanch, *The Sabres of Paradise*, 1960.

THERE ARE few generals that have run oftener, or more lustily than I have done. But I have taken care not to run too far, and commonly have run as fast forward as backward, to convince the Enemy that we were like a Crab, that could run either way.

> Major-General Nathaniel Greene, 18 July 1781, to Major-General Henry Knox.

IF we are defeated, we can think about retreating then, and in any case, I shall be dead, so why should I worry.

> Marshal of France Pierre Augereau, Duc de Castiglione, 1796, advice to Napoleon who considered

retreating before the Battle of Castiglione, quoted in Delderfield, *Napoleon's Marshals*, 1962.

COUNT PETER IVANOVITCH. The troops of Count Bellegarde from the Tyrol will come up to Alessandria uninstructed, strangers to the handling of the bayonet and sword. . . . visit me, and set off at once to Alessandria, and there reveal to the Bellegarde troops the secret of beating the enemy with cold steel, and carefully adapt them to this conquering attack; two or three lessons will be enough for the instruction of all the detachments, but if there is time, they can study more by themselves; but do you unlearn them how to retreat.

> Field Marshal Prince Aleksandr V. Suvorov, 1799, to Prince Bagration during the Italian campaign on how to deal with allied Austrian troops, quoted in W. Lyon Blease, *Suvorof*, 1920.

PEOPLE who think of retreating before a battle has been fought ought to have stayed home.

> Marshal of France Michel Ney, Duc d'Elchingen, Prince de La Moskova, 1805, to Baron Jomini, quoted in Raymond Horricks, *Marshal Ney, The Romance and the Real*, 1982.

HONORABLE RETREATS are no ways inferior to brave charges, as having less fortune, more of discipline, and as much valour.

> Lieutenant-General Sir William Napier, *A History of the War in the Peninsula*, 1828–1840

MAXIM 6. . . . However skilful the manoeuvres, a retreat will always weaken the *moral* [morale] of an army, because in losing the chances of success, these last are transferred to the enemy. Besides, retreats cost always more men and *matériel* than the most bloody engagements, with this difference, that in a battle the enemy's loss is nearly equal to your own, whereas in a retreat the loss is on your side only.

> Napoleon, *The Military Maxims of Napoleon*, tr. George D'Aguilar, 1831 (David Chandler, ed., 1987).

MAXIM 15. . . . In a retreat, besides the loss of the honour of the army, the loss is often equal to two battles. For this reason we should never despair while brave men are to be found with the colours. It is by this means we obtain victory, and deserve to obtain it.

> Napoleon, *The Military Maxims of Napoleon*, tr. George D'Aguilar, 1831 (David Chandler, ed., 1987).

TO KNOW when to retreat and to dare to do it.

> The Duke of Wellington, when asked for his opinion on the best test of greatness in a general, quoted in William Fraser, *Words on Wellington*, 1889.

WHEN a battle is lost, the strength of the army is broken – its moral even more than its physical strength. A second battle without the help of new and favorable factors would mean outright defeat, perhaps even absolute destruction. That is a military axiom. It is in the nature of things that a retreat should be continued until the balance of power is reestablished – whether by means of reinforcements or the cover of strong fortresses or major natural obstacles or the overextention of the enemy.

> Major-General Carl von Clausewitz, *On War*, 4.13, 1832, tr. Michael Howard and Peter Paret, 1976.

THE OFFICERS should feel . . . that firmness amid reverses is more honorable than enthusiasm in success, – since courage alone is necessary to storm a position, while it requires heroism to make a difficult retreat before a victorious and enterprising enemy always opposing to him a firm and unbroken front. A fine retreat should meet with a reward equal to that given for a great victory.

> Lieutenant-General Antoine-Henri Baron de Jomini, *Summary of the Art of War*, 1838, tr. Mendell and Craighill, 1862.

MY WOUNDED are behind me and I will never pass them alive.

> Major-General Zachary Taylor, 1847, upon receiving the order to retire at the Battle of Buena Vista.

RETREAT, hell! We just got over here.

> Major-General Wendell Neville, of the Marine Brigade, 3 May 1918, at the Second Battle of the Marne, when his Fifth Marines were moving up to the front and a French officer urged him to retreat, quoted in Lawrence Stallings, *The Doughboys*, 1963.

RETREAT is a concept which fully enters into that of the attack. I retreat over 100 to 200 kilometers so as to go over to the attack on a certain line at a certain moment decided by myself. . . . Retreat is one of the movements in the general course of offensive operations. . . . Retreat is not flight.

> Mikhail Frunze, 1922, quoted in Nathan Leites, *The Soviet Style in War*, 1982.

IT WILL BE readily understood that troops which have once begun to retreat lose heart, discipline slackens, and it is hard to say when or how they will stop and what their conditions will be when they do.

> General Aleksei A. Brusilov, *A Soldier's Notebook*, 1931.

THERE HAD BEEN last-minute reinforcements, a battalion of U.S. Army troops which fought its way through the enemy with heavy losses. Its colonel reported to Puller [USMC] for orders.

"Take your position along those hills and have your men dig in."

"Yes, sir. Now, where is my line of retreat?"

Puller's voice became low and hard: "I'm glad you asked me that. Now I know where you stand. Wait one minute." He took a field telephone and called his tank commander. The Army officer listened to the Marine order:

"I've got a new outfit," Puller said. He gave its position in detail. "If they start to pull back from that line,

even one foot, I want you to open fire on them." He hung up the telephone and turned to the Army officer: "Does that answer your question?"

> Lieutenant-General Lewis 'Chesty' Puller, 1950, at the Chosin Reservoir, quoted in Burke Davis, *Marine*, 1962.

THE SOLDIER who has been forced to retreat through no fault of his own loses confidence in the higher command; because he has withdrawn already from several positions in succession he tends to look upon retreat as an undesirable but natural outcome of a battle.

> Field Marshal Earl Alexander of Tunis, *The Alexander Memoirs 1940–1945*, 1961.

REVOLUTION

IN TIME of revolution, with perseverance and courage, a soldier should think nothing impossible.

> Napoleon, *Political Aphorisms*, 1848.

I ALWAYS HAD a horror of revolutionising any country for a political object. I always said, if they rise of themselves, well and good, but do not stir them up; it is a fearful responsibility.

> The Duke of Wellington, 1808, upon the suggestion of raising insurrections in the Spanish colonies in the Americas, quoted in The Earl of Stanhope, *Notes of Conversations with the Duke of Wellington*, 1888.

HE WHO SERVES a revolution ploughs the sea.

> General Simon Bolivar, December 1830, quoted in Salvador de Madariaga, *Bolivar*, 1852.

BE NOT deceived. Revolutions do not go backward.

> Abraham Lincoln, 19 May 1856, speech.

THE RIGHT of revolution is an inherent one. When people are oppressed by their government, it is a natural right they enjoy to relieve themselves of the oppression, if they are strong enough, either by withdrawal from it, or by overthrowing it and substituting a government more acceptable.

> General of the Army Ulysses S. Grant, *Personal Memoirs*, 1885.

EVERY great revolution brings ruin to the old army.

> Leon Trotsky, 1921, to Professor Milyukov.

WE ARE working for a revolution. If we do not start it by improving the life of the soldiers, all slogans of reforming and improving society are but empty words.

> Generalissimo Chiang Kai-shek, 1925, letter to Chou en Lai.

PEOPLE do not make revolution eagerly any more than they do war. There is a difference, however, that in war compulsion plays the decisive role, in revolution there is no compulsion except that of circumstances. A revolution takes place only when there is not other way out. And the insurrection, which rises above a revolution like a peak in the mountain chain of its events, can no more be evoked at will than the revolution as a whole. The masses advance and retreat several times before they make up their minds to the final assault.

Leon Troksky, *The History of the Russian Revolution*, III, 1932.

REVOLUTION is not a dinner party, not an essay, or a painting, nor a piece of embroidery; it cannot be advanced softly, gradually, carefully, considerately, respectfully, politely, plainly and modestly.

Mao Tse-tung, quoted in *Time*, 18 December 1950.

THE CENTRAL TASK and the highest form of a revolution is to seize political power by armed force, to settle problems by force.

Mao Tse-tung, *Problems of War and Strategy*, 1954.

ONE does not necessarily have to wait for revolutionary situation: it can be created.

Ernesto 'Che' Guevara, *Guerrilla Warfare*, 1961.

THE FUNDAMENTAL PRINCIPLE of revolutionary war: strike to win, strike only when success is certain; if not, then, don't strike.

General Vo Nguyen Giap, *People's War – People's Army*, 1961.

A REVOLUTIONARY WAR is never confined within the bounds of military action. Because its purpose is to destroy an existing society and its institutions and to replace them with a completely new state structure, any revolutionary war is a unity of which the constituent parts, in varying importance, are military, political, economic, social, and psychological.

Brigadier-General Samuel B. Griffith II, introduction to Mao Tse-tung, *On Guerrilla Warfare*, 1961.

THE ARMY is on the brink of exploding. All it would take is for blood to be shed somewhere in Russia and immediately all sorts of gang leaders and field commanders wanting to take on the Kremlin will appear. Two people with submachine guns will always persuade 100 wise men.

Lieutenant-General Aleksandr I. Lebed, *Argumentiy i Fakty* (Moscow), September 1998.

THE REVOLUTION IN MILITARY AFFAIRS (RMA)

GENTLEMEN: I hear many say, "What need so much ado and great charge in caliver, musket, pike, and corselet? Our ancestors won many battles with bows, black bills, and jacks." But what think you of that? *Captain*: Sir, then was then, and now is now. The wars are much altered since the fiery weapons first came up.

Robert Barret, *The Theory and Practice of Modern Wars*, 1598, quoted in John Smythe, *Certain Discourses Military*, 1966.

BUT SINCE the discovery of gunpowder has changed the art of war, the whole system has, in consequence, been changed. Strength of body, the first quality among the heros of antiquity, is at present of no significance. Stratagem vanquishes strength, and art overcomes courage. The understanding of the general has more influence on the fortunate or unfortunate consequences of the campaign than the prowess of the combatants. Prudence prepares and traces the route that valor must pursue; boldness directs the execution, and ability, not good fortune, wins the applause of the well informed.

Frederick the Great (1712–1786), 'Reflections on Charles XII', *Posthumus Works of Frederick the Great*, tr. Holcroft, 1789, quoted in Jay Luvaas, ed., *Frederick the Great on the Art of War*, 1966.

WHEREAS we had available for immediate purposes one hundred and forty-nine first class warships, we have now two, these being the *Warrior* and her sister *Ironside*. There is not now a ship in the English navy apart from these two that it would not be madness to trust to an engagement with that little [American] *Monitor*.

The Times (London), 1862, quoted in John Taylor Wood, 'The First Fight of Iron-Clads, *Battles and Leaders of the Civil War, Being for the Most Part Contributions by Union and Confederate Officers*, II, Johnston and Buel, ed., 1888.

I WAS TOLD by Mr. Charles King, when President of Columbia College, that he had been present in company with [Admiral Stephen] Decatur at one of the early experiments in steam navigation. Crude as the appliances still were, demonstration was conclusive; and Decatur, whatever his prejudices, was open to conviction. "Yes," he said gloomily, to King, "it is the end of our business; hereafter any man who can boil a tea-kettle will be as good as the best of us."

Rear-Admiral Alfred Thayer Mahan, *From Sail to Steam*, 1907.

THE DISTINGUISHING FEATURE of the development of the means of armed combat, under present-day conditions is the appearance of qualitatively new types of weapons and military equipment and their rapid mass introduction in the armed forces, which sharply increased in fighting capabilities of the latter and led to a fundamental break in the organization forms of the armed forces and the means for carrying out military operations in every scale. In military strategy, in military art, in military affairs as a whole, a revolution has taken place.

Marshal of the Soviet Union V.D. Sokolovskiy, quoted in Harriet Fast Scott, ed., *Soviet Military Strategy* (third edition), 1968.

THUS, the creation of new weapons and military equipment . . . also entails corresponding transformations in the methods of conducting military operations. But this does not take place immediately upon the appearance of new means of combat, but only when they begin to be used in a quantity which inevitably causes a new qualitative state of the phenomenon. As long as the new weapons and military equipment are used in limited numbers, they are most often merely adapted to the existing methods of armed conflict or, at best, introduce in them only a few partial adjustments.

> Marshal of the Soviet Union Nikolai V. Ogarkov, *History Teaches Vigilance*, 1985.

LIKE every other revolution, the American RMA involves big changes – changes that occur or can be recognized suddenly and that spread across institutions, doctrine, and the way we think about the use of force. What makes revolutions disturbing, of course, is not the scope, speed, and extent of innovation as much as what must be given up to consummate them. The problem with deep, fast, and rampant innovation is not getting people to accept the new but to surrender the old. Most will flirt with the future, but few want to embrace it at the expense of the comfortable past.

> Admiral William A. Owens, 'The American Revolution in Military Affairs', *Joint Force Quarterly*, Winter 1995/1996.

RISK

IT IS ALSO the mark of a sensible cavalry commander never to take risks, if he can help it, except when it is obvious that he will have the enemy at a disadvantage. Doing the enemy favours should be regarded as a betrayal of one's side rather than as courage.

> Xenophon, *How To Be A Good Cavalry Commander*, c. 360 BC (*Hiero the Tyrant and Other Treatises*, tr. Robin Waterfield, 1997).

LET US march on and go whither the tokens of the gods and the injurious dealings of our enemies call us. The die is cast (*Iacta alea est*).

> Julius Caesar, 11 January 49 BC, at the crossing of the Rubicon, quoted in Suetonius, 'Julius Caesar', 32, *Lives of the Twelve Caesars*, AD 121, tr. Philemon Holland, 1606.

RISKS should not be taken without necessity or real hope of gain. To do so is the same as fishing with gold as bait.

> The Emperor Maurice, *The Strategikon*, c. AD 600 (*Maurice's Strategikon*, tr. George Dennis, 1984).

WE MUST risk something for God!

> Hernan Cortes, 1519, when he smashed the idol of the God of the Smoking Mirror (Huitzilopochtli) in the Great Teocalli (Templo Mayor) in Tenochtitlan.

YOU SAY that I run too much risk. I don't do it because I want to but because I am obliged to. If I don't go into danger, nobody else will. They are all volunteers; I can't force them.

> King Henry IV (Henry of Navarre) of France (1553–1610).

WE SHOULD on all occasions avoid a general Action, or put anything to Risque, unless compelled by a necessity, into which we ought never to be drawn.

> General George Washington, September 1776, letter to the President of Congress.

IT IS TRUE that I must run great risk; no gallant action was ever accomplished without danger.

> Admiral John Paul Jones, 1778, letter to the American Commissioners in Paris.

THE RULES of conduct, the maxims of action, and the tactical instincts that serve to gain small victories may always be expanded into the winning of great ones with suitable opportunity; because in human affairs the sources of success are ever to be found in the fountains of quick resolve and swift stroke; and it seems to be a law inflexible and inexorable that he who will not risk cannot win.

> Admiral John Paul Jones, 1791, letter to Vice-Admiral Kersaint.

IF THE ART of war consisted merely in not taking risks glory would be at the mercy of very mediocre talent.

> Napoleon (1769–1821).

IN ALL great action there is risk.

> The Duke of Wellington, September 1803, in India to his brother, shortly before the Battle of Assaye, quoted in Arthur Bryant, The Great Duke, 1972.

EVERY naval expedition we have attempted since I have been at the head of the government has failed, because the admirals see double and have picked up the idea, I don't know where, that you can make war without running risks.

> Napoleon, 12 September 1804, to his naval minister, Decrès, quoted in R.M. Johnston, ed., *The Corsican*, 1910.

I WAS AWARE that I was risking infinitely too much, but something must be risked for the honor of the Service.

> General Sir John Moore, December 1808, letter from Spain.

THE TORMENT of precautions often exceeds the dangers to be avoided. It is sometimes better to abandon one's self to destiny.

> Napoleon, *Maxims*, 1804–1815.

FIRST reckon, then risk.

> Field Marshal Helmuth Graf von Moltke (1800–1891).

WE MUST encounter risks if we fight, and we cannot carry on war without fighting. . . . McClellan's vice . . . was always waiting to have everything just as he wanted before he would attack, and before he could get things arranged as he wanted them, the enemy pounced on him and thwarted all his plans. There is now no doubt that he allowed three distinct occasions to take Richmond slip through his hands for want of nerve to run what he considered risks. Such a general will never command success, though he may avoid disaster.

> Major-General George G. Meade, 2 January 1863, letter to his wife, *The Life and Letters of George Gordon Meade*, 1913.

I AM WELL AWARE that extreme outposts are always exposed, and for that reason they should be sleeplessly vigilant. If we do not run risks we never shall know anything of the enemy.

> Major-General George H. Thomas, 24 April 1864, message to Absalom Baird.

CALCULATED RISK guided by skill is the right way to interpret the motto, "l'audace, toujours l'audace". (Sept. 1925.)

> Captain Sir Basil Liddell Hart, *Thoughts on War*, 1944.

WHEN I considered the state of our armament, and thought of this test – and for soldiers the test is always battle – I repeated to myself: "Careful, careful, and once more careful with fire. Don't be a child, and don't give rein to your fancy." But all the character, will, pride and ambition within me rebelled against these cunctatorial "prudent" reflections. Besides, in my opinion there was no escape. I do not deny that the test of battle was an extraordinarily dangerous undertaking, but we could only win what we needed above all to win, self-confidence and the military respect of those around us, by taking risks, and big risks.

> Marshal Joseph Pilsudski, *Memoirs of a Polish Revolutionary and Soldier*, 1931.

MEN have bad luck and their luck may change. But anyhow you will not get generals to run risks unless they feel they have behind them a strong government.

> Sir Winston S. Churchill (1874–1965).

DEAREST LU,
We've been attacking since the 31st with dazzling success. There'll be consternation amongst our masters in Tripoli and Rome, perhaps in Berlin too. I took the risk against all orders and instructions because the opportunity seemed favourable. No doubt it will all be pronounced good later and they'll all say they'd have done exactly the same in my place. We've already reached our first objective, which we weren't supposed to get to until the end of May. The British are falling over each other to get away. Our casualties small. Booty can't yet be estimated. You will understand that I can't sleep for happiness.

> Field Marshal Erwin Rommel, 3 April 1941, letter to his wife, *The Rommel Papers*, 1953.

THE HABIT of gambling contrary to reasonable calculations is a military vice which, as the pages of history reveal, has ruined more armies than any other cause.

> Captain Sir Basil Liddell Hart, *Thoughts on War*, 1944.

TAKE calculated risks. That is quite different from being rash.

> General George S. Patton, Jr., 6 June 1944, letter to his son, *The Patton Papers*, II, 1974.

IN MAKING WAR there must be three parts risk and seven parts security, in addition to one's own subjective effort.

> General Lin Piao, 1946, quoted in Dennis and Ching Ping Bloodworth, *The Chinese Machiavelli*, 1976.

WAR IS RISK. Either its ends permit of honest differences of opinion about what should best be done, or operations long since would have become an exact science and general staff work would be as routine as logarithms.

> Brigadier-General S.L.A. Marshall, *Men Against Fire*, 1947.

IN ENTERPRISES in which one risks everything, there usually comes a moment when the person responsible feels that fate is being determined. By a strange convergence the thousand trials in the midst of which he is struggling seem suddenly to blossom into a decisive episode. If it turns out well, fortune will be in his hands.

> General Charles de Gaulle, *War Memoirs: The Call to Honor 1940–1942*, 1955.

WHEN you stop a dictator there are always risks. But there are greater risks in not stopping a dictator.

> Prime Minister Margaret Thatcher, 5 April 1982, interview.

BY ITS NATURE, uncertainty invariably involves the estimation and acceptance of risk. Risk is inherent in war and is involved in every mission. Risk is also related to gain; normally, greater potential gain requires greater risk. Further, risk is equally common to action and inaction.

> General Alfred M. Gray and Major John Schmitt, *Warfighting*, United States Marine Corps, 1989.

RIVERS

WHEN an invading force crosses a river in its onward march, do not advance to meet it in midstream. It will be best to let the army get across and then deliver your attack.

Sun Tzu, *The Art of War*, 8, c. 500 BC, tr. Giles, 1910; presumably, the object is to trap the enemy against the river.

I SHOULD BE ashamed of myself if a little trickle of water like this were too much for us to cross without further preparation, when I had no difficulty whatever in crossing the Hellespont. Such hesitancy would be unworthy of the fighting fame of our people and of my own promptitude in the face of danger. Without doubt it would give the Persians added confidence; nothing has yet happened to them to cause them alarm, and they would begin to think they were as good soldiers as we are.

Alexander the Great, May 334 BC, quoted in Arrian, *The Campaigns of Alexander*, 1.13, c. AD 150, tr. Aubrey de Sélincourt; reply to his second-in-command, Parmenio, who urged Alexander to use stratagem to cross the Granicus the following morning instead of making a direct assault.

THE DEFENSE of a river crossing is the worst of all assignments especially if the front that you are to defend is long; in this case defense is impracticable.

Frederick the Great, *Instructions to His Generals*, 1747, tr. Phillips, 1940.

NEVER base your defense on rivers unless they cut between rocks and have steep banks. You can defend a river that lies behind the army, but it has yet to be shown how a river in front of the armies can successfully be held. As many times as you take up a position behind a river to keep the enemy from crossing it, that often you will be duped, because sooner or later the enemy, forced to display cunning, finds a suitable moment for stealing his crossing.

Therefore this is what I propose: the only way to defend a river is to keep it behind you.

Frederick the Great, 'Reflexions sur les projets de campagn', and 'Éléments de castramertire et de tactique', *Oeuvres de Frederic le Grand*, 1846–1857, quoted in Jay Luvaas, ed., *Frederick the Great on the Art of War*, 1966.

THE NEAREST VILLAGES are Aspern, Essling, and Enzersdorf. To cross a river like the Danube in the presence of an enemy knowing the ground thoroughly, and having the sympathies of the inhabitants, is one of the most difficult military operations conceivable.

Napoleon, 22 May 1809, at his bivouac on the island of Lobau during the Austrian campaign, quoted in R.M. Johnston, ed., *The Corsican*, 1910.

A RIVER must always be regarded as an obstacle which is unable to hold up the enemy more than a few days. One can prevent him from crossing only by holding in readiness strong forces in bridgeheads on the hostile shore, with a view to attacking as soon

as the enemy begins to cross. . . . Nothing is more dangerous than the attempt at defending seriously a river line by keeping his side of the river occupied; for if the enemy were to cross suddenly with surprise effect – and that he will always be able to do somehow or other – he would find the defender in extensive positions from which the latter will be unable to assemble in time.

Napoleon, 15 March 1813, letter to Jérôme, *Correspondance de Napoléon Ier, publiée par ordre de l'Empereur Napoléon III*, No. 19, Vol. XXV, 1858–1870.

I WOULD NOT TAKE any risk of being entangled upon the river, like an ox jumped half over a fence, and liable to be torn by dogs, front and rear, without a fair chance to gore one way or kick the other.

Abraham Lincoln, 5 June 1863, letter to Major-General Joseph Hooker, *Collected Works of Abraham Lincoln*, VI, 1953.

A RIVER will in any case enable the defender to gain time, require the attacker to make special technical preparations, and warn the latter to be cautious. As a prerequisite for success in effecting a river crossing, the deceit of the defender as to the real intentions has always been considered essential.

General der Infantrie Hugo Baron von Freytag-Loringhoven, *Generalship in the Great War*, I, 1920.

THE TROOPS which forced the Dnieper exhibited outstanding staunchness and courage. . . . they pushed onward as soon as they reached the river; without waiting for pontoons or other heavy bridge-building equipment, they used anything that came to hand – timber rafts, ferries, fishermen's row-boats and motor-boats. Everything that happened to be there was used. On the opposite bank there was fierce fighting for bridgeheads. Having no time to dig in, our troops immediately engaged the enemy, who did everything they could to force them back into the river . . .

Marshal of the Soviet Union Georgi K. Zhukov, *Reminiscences and Reflections*, 1974, of the assault crossing of the mighty Dnieper River in Ukraine during September 1943.

QUESTION: What is more important, a bridge across the Rhine or the fighting down here?
Patton: A bridge over the Rhine.

General George S. Patton, Jr., 17 March 1945, at a press conference; on 22–23 March, his Fifth Infantry Division made a surprise crossing, *The Patton Papers*, II, 1974.

ROUT

SURELY if there is one military maxim of universal value, it is to press hard on a rout.

Colonel T.E. Lawrence, quoted in Liddell Hart, *Colonel Lawrence: The Man Behind the Legend*, 1935.

MARSHAL TIMOSHENKO told me that the army had been so utterly routed by the enemy that the only way to rally the troops was to set up mobile field kitchens and hope that the soldiers would return when they got hungry.
  Nikita Khrushchev, of the Soviet disaster at Kiev in 1941, quoted in Charles Messenger, *The Blitzkrieg Story*, 1976.

RUSE

UTTERANCE of his majesty to the king's-children, the princes, the king's butlers, and the charioteers: "Behold ye, the great might of my father, Amon-Re. The countries which came from their isles in the midst of the sea, they advanced on Egypt, their hearts relying upon their arms. The net was made ready for them, to ensnare them. Entering stealthily into the harbor-mouth, they fell into it. Caught in their place, they were dispatched, and their bodies stripped. I showed you my might which was in that which my majesty wrought while I was alone. My arrow struck, and none escaped my arms nor my hand. I flourished like a hawk among fowl; my talons descended upon their heads. Amon-Re was upon my right and upon my left, his might and power were in my limbs, a tumult for you; commanding for me that my counsels and my designs should come to pass. . . .
  Rameses III, Pharaoh of Egypt, c. 1190 BC, the defeat of the Sea Peoples in their descent upon Egypt, quoted in James Breasted, *Ancient Records of Egypt*, 1906.

RUSES are of great usefulness. They are detours which often lead more surely to the objective than the wide road which goes straight ahead. Animals have only one method of acting, but intelligent men have inexhaustable resources.
  You outwit the enemy to force him to fight, or to prevent him from it.
  Frederick the Great, *Instructions to His Generals*, 1747, tr. Phillips, 1940.

YOU FEAR a retreat through Moscow, but I regard it as far-sighted. It will save the army. Napoleon is like a stormy torrent which we are as yet unable to stop. Moscow will be the sponge that sucks him in.
  Field Marshal Prince Mikhail I. Kutuzov, 1812, quoted in Parkinson, *Fox of the North*, 1976.

WE ARE BRED UP to feel it a disgrace even to succeed by falsehood; the word spy conveys something as repulsive as slave; we will keep hammering along with the conviction that honesty is the best policy, and that truth always wins in the long run. These pretty little sentiments do well for a child's copy book, but a man who acts on them had better sheathe his sword forever.
  Field Marshal Viscount Wolseley, *A Soldier's Pocket-Book*, 1869.

THE CONDUCT of operations is too much influenced by the experience of peacetime exercises. In the conditions of real war, the feeling of uncertainty is magnified, and this makes the opponent much more sensitive to crafty deceptions – so that even the most threadbare ruse has succeeded time after time. (Aug. 1928.)
  Captain Sir Basil Liddell Hart, *Thoughts on War*, 1944.

S

SACRIFICE

SO FIGHT by the ships, all together. And that comrade
who meets his death and destiny, speared or stabbed,
Let him die! He dies fighting for fatherland –
no dishonor there!
He'll leave behind him wife and sons unscathed,
His house and estates unharmed – once these
Argives sail for home,
the fatherland they love.
> Homer, *The Iliad*, 15.574–580, c. 800 BC, tr. Robert
> Fagles, 1990; Hector, rallying the Trojans and urging
> them to storm the Greek camp.

WHEN the ephors said: "Haven't you decided to take
any action beyond blocking the passes against the
Persians?", "In theory, no," he said, "but in fact I plan
to die for the Greeks."
> Leonidas, King of Sparta, 480 BC, quoted in Plutarch,
> *The Lives*, c. AD 100 (*Plutarch on Sparta*, tr. Richard
> Talbert, 1988).

WHEN another woman heard that her son had fallen
in the battleline, she said:
Let there be weeping for cowards; but you, child,
  without a tear
Do I bury: you are my son, and Sparta's too.
> Plutarch, quoting an anonymous Spartan mother, *The
> Lives*, c. AD 100 (*Plutarch on Sparta*, tr. Richard
> Talbert, 1988).

GOD FORBID that I should live an Emperor without an
Empire! As my city falls, I will fall with it! Whosoever
wishes to escape, let him save himself if he can; and
whoever is ready to face death, let him follow me!
> Emperor Constantine XI, May 1453, at the fall of
> Constantinople, quoted in Mijatovich, *Constantine: The
> Last Emperor of the Greeks*, 1892.

WE SWORE obedience when we joined the Order.
We swore on the vows of chivalry that our lives
would be sacrificed for the faith whenever, and
wherever, the call might come. Our brethren in St.
Elmo must now make that sacrifice.
> Jean de la Valette, Grand Master of the Order of the
> Knights of St. John, 20 June 1565, letter to the Viceroy
> of Sicily, on the fate of the Order's defenders of the fort
> of St. Elmo during the Turkish siege of Malta in 1565.

WHO LIVES for honour must know how to die for
the universal good.
> Gustavus II Adolphus, 30 April 1632, to his

commanders, who commented on how close he had
come to death in the day's fighting along the River
Lech, quoted in Theodore Ayrault Dodge, *Gustavus
Adolphus*, 1895.

PERISH yourself but rescue your comrade!
> Field Marshal Prince Aleksandr V. Suvorov
> (1729–1800).

IN DECISIVE CASES there are moments when
victory demands sacrifices and when it becomes
necessary to burn your own warships. If military art
consisted of always taking a safe position, then glory
would become the property of mediocre people.
> Napoleon (1769–1821).

I HAVE NEVER had much value for the public spirit
of any man who does not sacrifice his private views
and convenience when it is necessary.
> The Duke of Wellington, 25 March 1801, to his brother
> Henry Wellesley, cited in Arthur Bryant, *The Great
> Duke*, 1972.

NEVER, I believe, have soldiers shown such great
self-sacrifice as mine have for me! In spite of of all
my defeats, no soldier has ever cursed me, not even
when dying. Never have troops served a man more
faithfully than they have served me! To the last drop
of blood that flowed from their veins, they called:
"Long live the Emperor!"
> Napoleon, quoted in F.M. Kircheisen, *Memoirs of
> Napoleon I*, 1929.

LET US STOP being selfish. . . . To the idea of the
common good and of our existence, everything must
be sacrificed. . . . The lack of funds does not even
allow us to take care of the most elementary
things. . . . As from today our salaries are cut in half.
. . . I shall measure patriotism by generosity. . . .
From this moment on, luxury and comforts must
make us ashamed.
> General Jose de San Martin, 1815, quoted in Ricardo
> Rojas, *San Martin*, 1967.

IF THE ENEMY is to be coerced you must put him in
a situation that is even more unpleasant than the
sacrifice you call on him to make. The hardships of
the situation must not of course be merely transient –
at least not in appearance. Otherwise the enemy
would not give in but would wait for things to improve.
> Major-General Carl von Clausewitz, *On War*, 1.1,
> 1832, tr. Michael Howard and Peter Paret, 1976.

THERE IS no more gallant deed recorded in history. I ordered these men in there because I saw I must gain five minutes in time. Reinforcements were coming on the run, but I knew that before they could reach the threatened point, the Confederates would seize the position. I would have ordered that regiment in if I had known every man would have been killed. It had to be done. I was glad to find such a gallant body of men at hand willing to make the terrible sacrifice that the occasion demanded.

> Major-General Winfield Scott Hancock, of his order throwing the First Minnesota into the path of two oncoming Confederate brigades at the crisis of the battle at Gettysburg on 2 July 1863.

I AM much obliged to you, gentlemen . . . for the kind things you have said. I haven't done much, no more than I ought; neither have you. I am glad you are going to give twelve hundred dollars a month for the poor fellows in the hospitals; for it's no more than you ought to do, and it isn't half as much as the soldiers in the hospitals have given for you. Suppose, gentlemen, you had got to give to-night one thousand dollars or your right arm; five thousand dollars or both your eyes; all that you are worth for your life?

But I have got eighteen hundred boys in my hospital at Chattanooga who have given one arm and one leg, and some have given both; and yet they don't seem to think they have done a great deal for their country. And the graveyard behind the hospital, and the battle-field a little farther off, contain the bodies of thousands who have freely given their lives to save you and your homes and your country from ruin. Oh, gentlemen of Milwaukee, don't let us be telling of what we have given, and what we have done! *We* have done nothing, and given nothing, in comparison to *them*! And it's our duty to keep on giving and doing just as long as there's a soldier down South fighting or suffering for us.

> Mary A. 'Mother' Bickerdyke, late winter 1863, to a gathering of the Milwaukee Chamber of Commerce, quoted in Livermore, *My Story of the War*, 1887.

THEIR BLOOD and their toil, their endurance and patriotism, have made us and all who come after us forever their debtors. . . . our homage must not only find expression on our lips; it must also show itself forth in our deeds.

> President Theodore Roosevelt, 15 October 1903, referring to the 'great dead' of the Civil War in his speech at the dedication of the monument to General William Tecumseh Sherman in Washington.

I, NOGI MARESUKE, commander-in-chief of the Third Imperial Army before Port Arthur, celebrate with sake and many offerings a fete in honor of you. . . . I wish to tell you that your noble sacrifice has not been in vain, for the enemy's fleet has been destroyed, and Port Arthur has at last surrendered. I,

Nogi Maresuke, took oath with you to conquer or seek oblivion in death. I have survived to receive the Imperial thanks, but I will not monopolize the glory. With you, Spirits of the Dead, who achieved this great result, I desire to share my triumph.

> General Maresuke Nogi, 1905, quoted in Dennis and Peggy Warner, *The Tide at Sunrise*, 1974.

BUT WAR is a ruthless taskmaster, demanding success regardless of confusion, shortness of time, and paucity of tools. Exact justice for the individual and a careful consideration of his rights is quite impossible. One man sacrifices his life on the battlefield and another sacrifices his reputation elsewhere, both in the same cause. The hurly-burly of the conflict does not permit commanders to draw fine distinctions; to succeed, they must demand results, close their ears to excuses, and drive subordinates beyond what would ordinarily be considered the limit of human capacity. Wars are won by the side that accomplishes the impossible.

> General of the Army George C. Marshall, *Memoirs of My Services in the World War* (written between 1923 and 1926), 1976

A NATION which makes the final sacrifice for life and freedom does not get beaten.

> Kemal Atatürk, quoted in M.M. Mousharrafa, *Atatürk*, 1944.

THE SOLEMN characteristic feature of the soldier's profession is the readiness to die in discharge of duty. Other professions, too, may require the risk of life in discharge of duty, every man may be faced, outside his profession, with the necessity for the last great sacrifice, as an ethical duty; but in no other profession do killing and its corollary, readiness to die, form the essence of professional duty. If the true art of war lies in destroying the enemy, then its exponent must also be prepared to be destroyed himself. This conception of the soldier's function justifies us in speaking of soldiering as something unique. It is the responsibility for life and death which gives the soldier his special character, his gravity, and self-consciousness – not only the responsibility for his own life, which may be sacrificed, not light-heartedly but from a feeling of duty, but the simultaneous responsibility for the lives of comrades and, in the end, for the life of the enemy, whose death is not an act of independent free will on the part of the killer, but an acknowledgement of professional duty. The feeling of responsibility for oneself and others is one of the most vital characteristics of the soldier's life. Responsibility towards oneself demands the most exacting inward and outward training for the military profession, so that the final sacrifice may not be made in vain.

> Colonel-General Hans von Seekt, *Thoughts of a Soldier*, 1930.

THE SOLDIER, above all other men, is required to perform the highest act of religious teaching – sacrifice. In battle and in the face of danger and death he discloses those divine attributes which his Maker gave when He created man in his own image. No physical courage and no brute instincts can take the place of the divine annunciation and spiritual uplift which will alone sustain him. However horrible the incidents of war may be, the soldier who is called upon to offer and to give his life for his country is the noblest development of mankind.

General of the Army Douglas MacArthur, 14 July 1935, address to the veterans of the Rainbow (42nd) Division, *A Soldier Speaks*, 1965.

I WOULD SAY to the House, as I said to those who have joined this Government: "I have nothing to offer but blood, toil, tears, and sweat."

We have before us an ordeal of the most grievous kind. We have before us many, many long months of struggle and of suffering. You ask, What is our policy? I will say: "It is to wage war, by sea, land, and air, with all our might and with all the strength that God can give us: to wage war against a monstrous tyranny, never surpassed in the dark, lamentable catalogue of human crime. That is our policy." You ask, What is our aim? I can answer in one word: Victory – victory at all costs, victory in spite of all terror, victory however long and hard the road may be; for without victory there is no survival. Let that be realized; no survival for the British Empire; no survival for all the British Empire has stood for; no survival for the urge and impulse of the ages, that mankind will move forward towards its goal. But I take up my task with buoyancy and hope. I feel sure that our cause will not be suffered to fail among men. At this time I feel entitled to claim the aid of all, and I say, "Come, then, let us go forward together with our united strength."

Sir Winston S. Churchill, 13 May 1940, first speech to the House of Commons as Prime Minister, *Blood, Sweat, and Tears*, 1941.

OUT of the depths of sorrow and sacrifice will be born again the glory of mankind.

Sir Winston S. Churchill (1874–1965).

I CONSIDER IT no sacrifice to die for my country. In my mind we came here to thank God that men like these have lived rather than to regret that they died.

General George S. Patton, Jr., 11 November 1943, speech at an Allied cemetery in Italy, quoted in Semmes, *Portrait of Patton*, 1955.

THE GLORY of taking the fort is not worth the sacrifices in men which it would demand.

General George S. Patton, Jr., October 1944, remark to General Bradley about Fort Driant at Verdun, *The Patton Papers*, II, 1974.

I WANT YOU to remember that no bastard ever won a war by dying for his country. He won it by making the other poor dumb bastard die for his country.

General George S. Patton, Jr., 1944, speech to his troops.

REFRESHINGLY
After the violent storm
The moon rose radiant.

Vice-Admiral Takijiro Ohnishi, Commander, Kamikaze Special Attack Force – his final *haiku* before committing suicide, 15 August 1945, quoted in Inoguchi and Nakajima, *The Divine Wind*, 1955.

ARCHIBALD RUTLEDGE once wrote that there can be no real love without a willingness to sacrifice. Tuck this away in your inner minds. It may pay off in some crisis coming to you in the years now hidden beyond the horizon. Do you love your country and its flag? Do you love the branch in which you are serving, the men with whom you will be privileged to share service and to command? If you do, then you will be prepared to sacrifice for them, if your responsibilities or the situation demands.

General Matthew B. Ridgway, 'Leadership', *Military Review*, 10/1966.

SAFETY

FOR THEY HAD learned that true safety was to be found in long previous training, and not in eloquent exhortations uttered when they were going into action.

Thucydides, *The History of the Peloponnesian War*, c. 404 BC.

THE DESIRE for safety stands against every great and noble enterprise.

Cornelius Tacitus, *Annals*, c. AD 116.

EVERY ATTEMPT to make war easy and safe will result in humiliation and disaster.

General of the Army William T. Sherman, *The Memoirs of General W.T. Sherman*, II, 1875.

SELF-PRESERVATION is the keystone in the arch of war, because it is the keystone in that greater arch called life. No normal man wishes to be killed in battle, though he may long to die in battle rather than to die in his bed. He does not wish to do so, because there is not virtue in merely dying, for virtue is to be sought in living and living rightly.

Major-General J.F.C. Fuller, *Generalship: Its Diseases and Their Cure*, 1933.

DISCIPLINE APART, the soldier's chief cares are, first, his personal comfort, i.e., regular rations, proper clothing, good billets, and proper hospital arrangements (square meals and a square deal in fact); and secondly, his personal safety, i.e., that he shall be put into a fight with as good a chance for victory and survival.

Field Marshal Viscount Wavell of Cyrenaica (1883–1950).

"SAFETY FIRST" is the road to ruin in war.

Sir Winston S. Churchill, 3 November 1940, telegram to Anthony Eden.

SUCCESS cannot be guaranteed. There are no safe battles.

Sir Winston S. Churchill (1874–1965).

VICTORY will never be found by taking the line of least resistance.

Sir Winston S. Churchill (1874–1965).

SAILORS/SEAMEN

IT MUST be kept in mind that seamanship, just like anything else, is a matter requiring skill, and will not admit of being taken up occasionally as an occupation for times of leisure; on the contrary, it is so exacting as to leave leisure for nothing else.

Pericles, 432 BC, arguing for war with Sparta, quoted in Thucydides, *History of the Peloponnesian War*, 1.142, c. 404 BC, tr. Richard Crawley, 1910.

MY SEAMEN are now what British seamen ought to be . . . almost invincible; they really mind shot no more than peas.

Admiral Viscount Nelson, February 1794, off Bastia in Corsica, quoted in David Howarth, *Nelson: The Immortal Memory*, 1988.

THE SAILOR in a squadron fights only once in every campaign; the soldier fights every day. The sailor, whatever may be the fatigues and dangers on the sea, undergoes fewer of these than the soldier. He never suffers from hunger or thirst; he has always with him his quarters, his kitchen, his hospital and his pharmacy.

Napoleon, *Maxims of War*, 1831.

THE SEAMAN is the main engine on a military ship, and we are only the springs which act on it. . . . The seaman controls the sails, it is he too who aims the weapon at the enemy; the seaman carries out boarding operations if need be; the seaman does everything.

Admiral P.S. Nakhimov (1802–1855).

THEY [the Confederates] forgot the ingenuity of the American seaman.

Admiral David D. Porter, of his ironclads' escape from the narrow Yazoo bayous, March 1863, *Incidents and Anecdotes of the Civil War*, 1885.

SALUTE

A COMPLIANCE with the minutiae of military courtesy is a mark of well disciplined troops. The exchange of military salutes between officers and men should not be overlooked. Its omission indicates a poor state of discipline.

Major-General John A. Lejeune, 19 September 1922, *Letter No. 1 to the Officers of the Marine Corps from the Commandant*.

THE SALUTE is the mutual greeting of respect and loyalty between members of a fighting organization.

General George S. Patton, Jr., May 1941, address to the officers of the Second Armored Division, *The Patton Papers*, II, 1974.

ONE MORNING long ago, as a brand new second lieutenant, I was walking on to parade. A private soldier passed me and saluted; I acknowledged his salute with an airy wave of the hand. Suddenly, behind me, a voice rasped out my name. I spun round. There was my Colonel, for whom I had a most wholesome respect, and with him the Regimental Sergeant Major, of whom, if truth must be told, I stood in some awe. "I see," said the Colonel, "you don't know how to return a salute. Sergent Major, plant your staff in the ground and let Mr. Slim practise saluting it until he does know how to return a salute!" So to and fro I marched in sight of the whole battalion, saluting the Sergeant Major's cane. I could cheerfully have murdered the Colonel, the Sergeant Major and, more than cheerfully, my fellow subalterns grinning at me. At the end of ten minutes the Colonel called me up to him. All he said was, "Now remember, discipline begins with the officers!"

Field Marshal Viscount Slim of Burma, *Courage and Other Broadcasts*, 1957.

A SALUTE from an unwilling man is as meaningless as the moving of a leaf on a tree; it is a sign only that the subject has been caught by a gust of wind. But a salute from the man who takes pride in the gesture because he feels privileged to wear the uniform of the United States, having found military service good, is the epitome of military virtue.

Brigadier-General S.L.A. Marshall, *The Officer As Leader*, 1950.

THE SCHOOL SOLUTION

IN THIS ART as in poetry and eloquence, there are many who can trace the rules by which a poem or an oration should be composed, and even compose, according to the exactest rule; but for want of that enthusiastic and divine fire, their productions are languid and insipid; so in our profession, many are to be found who know every precept of it by heart;

but alas! when called upon to apply them, are immediately at a stand. They then recall their rules and want to make everything, the rivers, the woods, ravines, mountains, etc. subservient to them; whereas their precepts should, on the contrary, be subject to these, who are the only rules, the only guide we ought to follow; whatever manoeuvre is not formed on them is absurd and ridiculous.

These form the great book of war; and he who cannot read it, must be forever content with the title of a brave soldier and never aspire to that of great general.

> Major-General Henry Lloyd, *History of the Late War in Germany*, 1766–1782.

ONE need only be on one's guard against the bottomless pit of systematic rules.

> Field Marshal Prince Aleksandr V. Suvorov (1729–1800), quoted in Blease, *Suvorof*, 1920.

THERE ARE no precise or determined rules; everything depends on the character that nature has given to the general, on his qualities, his shortcomings, on the nature of the troops, on the range of the firearms, on the season and on a thousand other circumstances which are never the same.

> Napoleon (1769–1821), 'Notes sur l'art de la guerre', *Correspondance de Napoléon Ier, publiée par ordre de l'Empereur Napoléon III*, Vol. XXXI, 1858–1870.

MAXIM 42. There is no authority in war without exception. . . .

> Napoleon, *The Military Maxims of Napoleon*, tr. George D'Aguilar, 1831 (David Chandler, ed., 1987).

UNHAPPY the general that comes upon the field of battle with a system.

> Napoleon, *Maxims*, 1804–1815.

PITY the warrior who is contended to crawl about in the beggardom of rules! . . . What genius does must be the best of rules, and theory cannot do better than show how and why it is so.

> Major-General Carl von Clausewitz, *On War*, 2.2, 1832, tr. J.J. Graham, 1908.

I HAVE HEARD in the old army an anecdote very characteristic of [Braxton] Bragg. On one occasion, when stationed at a post of several companies commanded by a field officer, he was himself commanding one of the companies and at the same time acting as post quartermaster and commissary. . . . As commander of the company he made a requisition upon the quartermaster – himself – for something he wanted. As quartermaster he declined to fill the requisition, and endorsed on the back of it his reasons for so doing. As company commander he responded to this, urging that his requisition called for nothing but what he was entitled to, and that it was the duty of the quartermaster to fill it. As quartermaster he still persisted that he was right. In this condition of affairs

Bragg referred the whole matter to the commanding officer. The latter, when he saw the nature of the matter referred, exclaimed: "My God, Mr. Bragg, you have quarrelled with every officer in the army, and now you are quarrelling with yourself!"

> General of the Army Ulysses S. Grant, *Personal Memoirs*, 1885.

IF MEN make war in slavish obedience to rules, they will fail.

> General of the Army Ulysses S. Grant, *Personal Memoirs*, I, 1885.

WHENEVER I met one of them fellers that fit by note, I generally whipped h–ll out him before he got his tune pitched.

> Lieutenant-General Nathan Bedford Forrest, quoted in *As They Saw Forrest*, 1956.

NO SERVITUDE is more hopeless than that of unintelligent submission to an idea formally correct, yet incomplete. It has all the vicious misleading of a half-truth unqualified by appreciation of modifying conditions; and so seamen who disdained theories, and hugged the belief in themselves as "practical" became *doctrinaires* in the worst sense.

> Rear-Admiral Alfred Thayer Mahan, *Types of Naval Officers*, 1901.

WE MUST first understand truths, and therefore have an open mind, without prejudice, ready-made ideas, or theories blindly accepted merely because they rest on tradition. One standard alone, that of reason. Then we must apply these truths to specific cases, on the map at first, on the ground later, the battlefield ultimately. Let us not look for similarities, let us not appeal to our memory, it would desert us at the first cannon shot, and let us avoid all charts or formulae. We wish to reach the field with a trained power of judgment; it only need to have us train it, to have us begin training it today. Let us for that purpose seek the reason of things; that will show us how to use them.

> Marshal of France Ferdinand Foch, *Principles of War*, 1913.

WHEN confronted with a situation, do not try to recall examples given in any particular book on the subject; do not try to remember what your instructor said . . . do not try to carry in your minds patterns of particular exercises or battles, thinking they will fit new cases, because no two sets of circumstances are alike.

> General of the Armies John J. Pershing, 1918, address to the First Infantry Division, quoted in Vandiver, *Black Jack*, 1977.

THE PRINCIPLES which regulate the use of all available means in war – the economic employment by a commander of the forces at his disposal, the building up of a concentration (and, consequently, advances by phases or forward bounds), surprise for the enemy, security for oneself – are of value only (how often has this been said before!) insofar as they are adapted to the circumstances of the given situation. There is nothing specifically military about this generalization; it is as true for politics and industry as it is for armies in the field.

> General Charles de Gaulle, *The Edge of the Sword*, 1932.

OFFICIAL MANUALS, by the nature of their compilation, are merely registers of prevailing practice, not the log-books of a scientific study of war.

> Captain Sir Basil Liddell Hart, *Thoughts on War*, 1944.

THERE IS no approved solution to any tactical situation.

> General George S. Patton, Jr., *War As I Knew It*, 1947.

NORMALLY, there is no ideal solution to military problems; every course has its advantages and disadvantages. One must select that which seems best from the most varied aspects and then pursue it resolutely and accept the consequences. Any compromise is bad.

> Field Marshal Erwin Rommel, *The Rommel Papers*, 1953.

SCORCHED EARTH

IN CASE OF a forced retreat of Red Army units, all rolling stock must be evacuated; to the enemy must not be left a single engine, a single railway car, not a single pound of grain or gallon of fuel . . . In occupied regions conditions must be made unbearable for the enemy and all his accomplices. They must be hounded and annihilated at every step and all their measures frustrated.

> Joseph V. Stalin, 3 July 1941, address to the Soviet people.

SEA POWER

NOT WHOLLY can Pallas win the heart of
  Olympian Zeus,
Though she prays him with many prayers and all
  her subtlety;
Yet will I speak to you this other word, as firm as
  adamant:
Though all else shall be taken within the bound of
  Cecrops
and the fold of the holy mountain of Cithaeron,
Yet Zeus the all-seeing grants to Athene's prayer
That the wooden wall only shall not fall, but help
  you and your children.
But await not the host of horse and foot coming
  from Asia,
Nor be still, but turn your back and withdraw from
  the foe.
Truly a day will come when you will meet him face
  to face.

Divine Salamis, you will bring death to women's sons
When the corn is scattered, or the harvest
  gathered in.

> Delphic Oracle, June 480 BC, the famous oracle who predicted that the Athenian Navy would be the decisive factor in the defence of Greece against the Persian invasion, quoted in Peter Green, *The Greco-Persian Wars*, 1996.

HE who commands the sea has command of everything.

> Themistocles (c. 528–462 BC) quoted in Cicero, *Epistolae ad Atticum*.

MINOS is the first to whom tradition ascribes the possession of a navy. He made himself master of a great part of what is now termed the Hellenic Sea; he conquered the Cyclades, and was the first colonizer of most of them, expelling the Carians and appointing his own sons to govern them. Lastly, it was he who, from a natural desire to protect his growing revenues, sought, as far as he was able, to clear the sea of pirates.

> Thucydides, *The Peloponnesian War*, I.24, c. 404 BC, tr. Benajmin Jowett, 1881.

FOR OUR NAVAL SKILL is of more use to us for service on land, than their military skill for service at sea. Familiarity with the sea they will not find an easy acquisition. If you who have been practising at it ever since the Median invasion have not yet brought it to perfection, is there any chance of anything considerable being effected by an agricultural, unseafaring population, who will besides be prevented from practicing by the constant presence of strong squadrons of observation from Athens? With a small squadron they might hazard an engagement, encouraging their ignorance by numbers; but the restraint of a strong force will prevent their moving, and through want of practice they will grow more clumsy, and consequently more timid. It must be kept in mind that seamanship, just like everything else, is a matter of art, and will not admit of being taken up occasionally as an occupation for times of leisure; on the contrary, it is so exacting as to leave leisure for nothing else.

> Pericles, 432/431 BC, address to the Athenians on the virtues of sea power, quoted in Thucydides, *The History of the Peloponnesian War*, 1.142, c. 404 BC, tr. Richard Crawley, 1910.

THE RULE of the sea is indeed a great matter.

> Pericles, 432/431 BC, address to the Athenians on the virtues of sea power, quoted in Thucydides, *The History of the Peloponnesian War*, 1.144, c. 404 BC, tr. Richard Crawley, 1910.

HE WHO RULES on the sea will very shortly rule on the land also.

> Khayer ad-Din, 'Barbarossa', (d. 1546).

THIS MUCH is certain; that he that commands the

sea is at great liberty, and may take as much and as little of the war as he will. Whereas these, that be strongest by land, are many times nevertheless in great straits.

> Francis Bacon, *On the True Greatness of Kingdoms and Estates*, 1597.

WHOSOEVER commands the sea commands the trade; whosoever commands the trade of the world commands the riches of the world, and consequently the world itself.

> Sir Walter Raleigh, *Historie of the Worlde*, 1616.

A FLEET could easily without putting itself out of breath outrun the soldiers that coast it.

> Sir Walter Raleigh, *Historie of the Worlde*, 1616.

A MAN OF WAR is the best ambassador.

> Oliver Cromwell (1599–1658).

WITHOUT a respectable Navy – alas, America!

> Admiral John Paul Jones, 17 October 1776, letter to Robert Morris.

UNDER all circumstances, a decisive naval superiority is to be considered a fundamental principle, and the basis upon which all hope of success must ultimately depend.

> General George Washington, 1780, letter.

WITHOUT a decisive naval force we can do nothing definitive, and with it everything honorable and glorious.

> General George Washington, 20 December 1780, letter to Benjamin Franklin.

IT IS in our own experience, that the most sincere Neutrality is not a sufficient guard against the depredations of Nations at War. To secure respect to a neutral Flag, requires a naval force, organized, and ready to vindicate it, from insult or aggression. This may even prevent the necessity of going to War, by discouraging the belligerent Powers from committing such violations of the rights of the neutral party, as may first or last, leave no other option.

> General George Washington, 7 December 1796, Eighth Annual Address to Congress, *The Writings of George Washington*, XXXV, p. 314, John C. Fitzgerald, ed., 1940.

I DO NOT SAY the Frenchman will not come; I only say he will not come by sea.

> Admiral Lord St. Vincent, 1803, as First Lord of the Admiralty to the British Cabinet on the possibility of a French invasion, quoted in G.J. Marcus, *The Age of Nelson*, 1971.

WHEREVER wood can swim, there I am sure to find this flag of England.

> Napoleon, July 1815, at Rochefort upon his surrender to the Royal Navy.

HAD I BEEN master of the sea, I should have been lord of the Orient.

> Napoleon (1769–1821).

NOR MUST Uncle Sam's Web-feet be forgotten. At all the watery margins they have been present. Not only on the deep sea, the broad bay, and the rapid river, but also up the narrow muddy bayou, and wherever the ground was a little damp, they have been, and made their track.

> President Abraham Lincoln, 26 August 1863, letter to James C. Conkling.

IT IS NOT the taking of individual ships or convoys, be they few or many, that strikes down the money power of a nation; it is the possession of that overbearing power on the sea which drives the enemy's flag from it, or allows it to appear only as the fugitive; and by controlling the great common, closes the highway by which commerce moves to and from the enemy's shores. This overbearing power can only be exercised by great navies.

> Rear-Admiral Alfred Thayer Mahan, *The Influence of Sea Power Upon History*, 1890.

SEA POWER in the broad sense . . . includes not only the military strength afloat that rules the sea or any part of it by force of arms, but also the peaceful commerce and shipping from which alone a military fleet naturally and healthfully springs, and on which it securely rests.

> Rear-Admiral Alfred Thayer Mahan, *The Influence of Sea Power Upon History*, 1890.

THE WORLD has never seen a more impressive demonstration of the influence of sea power upon history. Those far distant, storm-beaten ships, upon which the Grand Army never looked, stood between it and the dominion of the world.

> Rear-Admiral Alfred Thayer Mahan, referring to the Royal Navy, *The Influence of Sea Power Upon the French Revolution and Empire*, II, 1892.

THE NAVY is the 1st, 2nd, 3rd, 4th . . . ad infinitum Line of Defence! If the Navy is not supreme, no Army however large is of the slightest use.

> Admiral Sir John Fisher, speaking before WWI, quoted in Arthur Marder, *The Anatomy of British Sea Power*, 1940.

THE WHOLE PRINCIPLE of naval fighting is to be free to go anywhere with every damned thing the Navy possesses.

> Admiral Sir John Fisher, 1914.

WHEN we speak of command of the seas, it does not mean command of every part of the sea at the same moment, or at every moment. It only means that we can make our will prevail ultimately in any part of the seas which may be selected for operations, and thus indirectly make our will prevail in every part of the seas.

Sir Winston S. Churchill, 11 October 1940, to the House of Commons.

THE NET RESULT is that naval forces are able, without resorting to diplomatic channels, to establish offshore, anywhere in the world, airfields completely equipped with machine shops, ammunition dumps, tank farms, warehouses, together with quarters and all types of accomodations for personnel. Such task forces are virtually as complete as any air base ever established. They constitute the only air base that can be made available near enemy territory without assault and conquest, and furthermore, they are mobile offensive bases that can be employed with the unique attribute of secrecy and surprise, which contributes equally to their defensive as well as offensive effectiveness.

Admiral of the Fleet Chester A. Nimitz (1885–1966), quoted in Potter, *Nimitz*, 1976.

HISTORY shows that those states which do not have naval forces at their disposal have not been able to hold the status of a great power for very long.

Admiral of the Fleet of the Soviet Union Sergei G. Gorshkov, *Red Sea Rising*, 1974.

SECRECY

O DIVINE ART of subtlety and secrecy! Through you we learn to be invisible, through you inaudible; and hence hold the enemy's fate in our hands.

Sun Tzu, *The Art of War*, 6, c. 500 BC, tr. Giles, 1910.

NOW of all the precautions that have been mentioned, the first that the general of an army ought to attend to is secrecy. He ought to take care that his designs be not disclosed by his countenance betraying the joyful expectation of success, or the sadness of defeat, nor yet by feelings of friendship or affection for those around him. He should communicate his intention to none except to those without whose assistance his plans cannot be carried into execution, and not even to them till the time when their services are required make it necessary that they should be made acquainted with them. Nor should the tongue only be silent, but still more must the mind itself be on its guard; for it has often happened that many, who have a strict watch over their tongue, have betrayed their intentions by some external signs, and sometimes by their actions.

Polybius, *Histories*, 9.13, c. 125 BC (*Familiar Quotations from Greek Authors*, tr. Crauford Ramage, 1895).

CONSULT with many on proper measures to be taken, but communicate the plans you intend to put in execution to few, and those only of the most assured fidelity. Or better, trust no one but yourself.

Flavius Vegetius Renatus, *Military Institutions of the Romans*, c. AD 378, tr. Clark, 1776.

FOR WHAT should be done seek the advice of many; for what you will actually do take council with only a few trustworthy people; then off by yourself alone decide on the best and most helpful plan to follow, and stick to it.

The Emperor Maurice, *The Strategikon*, c. AD 600 (*Maurice's Strategikon*, tr. George Dennis, 1984).

THE GENERAL who wants to keep his plans concealed from the enemy should never take the rank and file of his own troops into his confidence.

The Emperor Maurice, *The Strategikon*, c. AD 600 (*Maurice's Strategikon*, tr. George Dennis, 1984).

ONLY THOSE battle plans are successful which the enemy does not suspect before we put them into action.

The Emperor Maurice, *The Strategikon*, c. AD 600 (*Maurice's Strategikon*, tr. George Dennis, 1984).

TO KEEP your actions and your plans secret always has been a very good thing. For that reason Metellus, when he was with armies in Spain, replied to one who asked him what he was going to do the next day, that if his shirt knew it he would burn it. Marcus Crassus said to one who asked him when he was going to move the army: "Do you believe that you will be the only one not to hear the trumpet?"

Niccolo Machiavelli, *The Art of War*, 1521.

KALCKSTEIN: Your Majesty, am I right in thinking there is going to be a war?
Frederick: Who can tell!
Kalckstein: The movement seems to be directed on Silesia.
Frederick: Can you keep a secret? (Taking him by the hand.)
Kalckstein: Oh yes, Your Majesty.
Frederick: Well, so can I!

Frederick the Great, 1740, during his preparation for the seizure of Silesia, quoted in Christopher Duffy, *The Military Life of Frederick the Great*, 1985.

SECRECY is so necessary to a general that the ancients have even said that there was not a human being able to hold his tongue. But there is a reason for that: If you form the finest plans in the world but divulge them, your enemy will learn about them, and then it will be easy for him to parry them.

Frederick the Great, *Instructions to His Generals*, 1747, tr. Phillips, 1940.

THE NECESSITY of procuring good Intelligence is apparent and need not be further urged – All that remains for me to add, is that you keep the whole matter as secret as possible. For upon Secrecy, Success depends in most Enterprizes of the kind, and for want of it, they are generally defeated, however well planned + promising a favourable issue.

General George Washington, 26 July 1777, letter to Colonel Elias Dayton.

TAKE NOBODY into your confidence, not even your chief of staff.

Napoleon, 26 May 1812, to his brother Jérôme, *Correspondance de Napoléon Ier, publiée par ordre de l'Empereur Napoléon III*, No. 18727, XXIII, 1858–1870.

FREDERICK the Great was right when he said that if his night-cap knew what was in his head he would throw it into the fire.

Lieutenant-General Antoine-Henri Baron de Jomini, *Summary of the Art of War*, 1838, tr. Mendell and Craighill, 1862.

LINCOLN adopted a set form to meet one question and, according to the Chicago *Journal*, the dialogue ran:
VISITOR: When will the army move?
LINCOLN: Ask General Grant.
VISITOR: General Grant will not tell me.
LINCOLN: Neither will he tell me.

President Abraham Lincoln, quoted in Carl Sandburg, *Abraham Lincoln*, II, 1964.

NO SERVING SOLDIER can tell his fellow-countryman anything about an Army which is not (1) quite commonplace; (2) an expression of the views of the Authorities at the moment.

General Sir Ian Hamilton, *The Soul and Body of an Army*, 1921.

WAR and truth have a fundamental incompatibility. The devotion to secrecy in the interests of the military machine largely explains why, throughout history, its operations commonly appear in retrospect the most uncertain and least efficient of human activities.

Captain Sir Basil Liddell Hart, *Thoughts on War*, 1944.

SECURITY
Principle of War

IN MAKING tactical dispositions, the highest pitch you can attain is to conceal them; conceal your dispositions and you will be safe from the prying of the subtlest of spies, from the machinations of the wisest brains. How victory may be produced for them out of the enemy's own tactics – that is what the multitude cannot comprehend.

All men can see these tactics whereby I conquer, but what none can see is the strategy out of which victory is evolved.

Sun Tzu, *The Art of War*, c. 500 BC, tr. Giles, 1910.

THE COURSE of war cannot be foreseen, and its

attacks are generally dictated by the impulse of the moment; and where overweening self-confidence has despised preparations, a wise apprehension has often been able to make head against superior numbers. Not that confidence is out of place in an army of invasion, but in an enemy's country it should also be accompanied by the precautions of apprehension: troops will by this combination be best inspired for dealing a blow, and best secured against receiving one.

Archidamus II, King of Sparta, 431 BC, speech to the Peloponnesian allied army upon its invasion of Attica, quoted in Thucydides, *The History of the Peloponnesian War*, c. 404 BC, tr. Richard Crawley, 1910.

A GENERAL who has been defeated in a pitched battle, although skill and conduct have the greatest share in beating him, may in his defense throw the blame to fortune. But if he has suffered himself to be surprised or drawn into the snares of his enemy, he has no excuse for his fault, because he might have avoided such a misfortune by taking proper precautions and employing spies on whose intelligence he could depend.

Flavius Vegetius Renatus, *Military Institutions of the Romans*, c. AD 378, tr. Clark, 1776.

THE PERSON who wants to wage war against an enemy must first make sure that his own lands are secure. By secure I mean not only the security of the army but of the cities and the entire country, so that the people who live there may suffer no harm at all from the enemy.

Anonymous Byzantine general, *On Strategy*, c. AD 527–565, quoted in George Dennis, *Three Byzantine Military Treatises*, 1985.

IT WAS NOT my wish to disclose to all what I am thinking. For talk carried about through a camp cannot keep secrets, for it advances little by little until it is carried out even to the enemy.

Count Belisarius, AD 541, to his officers when they questioned his judgement during the Persian Wars, quoted in Procopius, *History of the Wars*, 2.18, c. AD 560, tr. H.B. Dewing.

EVEN in friendly territory a fortified camp should be set up; a general should never have to say: "I did not expect it."

The Emperor Maurice, *The Strategikon*, c. AD 600 (*Maurice's Strategikon*, tr. George Dennis, 1984).

AFTER A VICTORY we must not become careless, but be on our guard all the more against surprise attacks by the vanquished.

The Emperor Maurice, *The Strategikon*, c. AD 600 (*Maurice's Strategikon*, tr. George Dennis, 1984).

A GENERAL who takes nothing for granted is secure in war.

The Emperor Maurice, *The Strategikon*, c. AD 600 (*Maurice's Strategikon*, tr. George Dennis, 1984).

NO ENTERPRISE is more likely to succeed than one concealed from the enemy until it is ripe for execution.
Niccolo Machiavelli, *The Art of War*, 1521.

SKEPTICISM is the mother of security. Even though fools trust their enemies, prudent persons never do. The general is the principal sentinel of the army. He should always be careful of its preservation and see that it is never exposed to misfortune. One falls into a feeling of security after battles, when one is drunk with success and when one believes the enemy completely disheartened. Also when a skillful enemy amuses you with pretended peace proposals. One does this through mental laziness and lack of calculation concerning the intentions of the enemy.
Frederick the Great, *Instructions to His Generals*, 1747, tr. Phillips, 1940.

DO NOT NEGLECT the principles of foresight and know that often, puffed up with success, armies have lost the fruit of their heroism through a feeling of false security.
Frederick the Great, *Instructions to His Generals*, 1747, tr. Phillips, 1940.

THE PRINCIPLE OF SECURITY. The objective in battle being to destroy or paralyse the enemy's fighting strength, consequently the side which can best secure itself against the action of its antagonist will stand the best chance of winning, for by saving its men and weapons, its organization and moral [morale], it will augment its offensive power. Security is, therefore, a shield and not a lethal weapon, consequently the defensive is not the strongest form of war, but merely a prelude to the accomplishment of the objective – the defeat of the enemy by means of the offensive invigorated by defensive measures. The offensive being essential to success, it stands to reason that security without reference to the offensive is no security at all, but merely delayed suicide.
Major-General J.F.C. Fuller, *The Reformation of War*, 1923.

AS DANGER and the fear of danger are the chief moral obstacles of the battlefield, it follows that the imbuing of troops with a sense of security is one of the chief duties of a commander; for, if weapons be of equal power, battles are won by a superiority of nerve rather than by a superiority of numbers. This sense of security, though it may be supplemented by earth works or mechanical contrivances, is chiefly based on the feeling of moral ascendence due to fighting efficiency and confidence in command. Thus, a man who is a skilled marksman will experience a greater sense of security when lying in the open than an indifferent rifleman in a trench.

Given the skilled soldier, the moral ascendency resulting from his efficiency will rapidly evaporate unless it be skilfully directed and employed. As in all undertakings – civil or military, ultimately we come back to the impulse of the moment, to the brains which control impulse and to each individual nerve which runs through the military body. To give skilled troops to an unskilled leader is tantamount to throwing snow on hot bricks. Skill in command is, therefore, the foundation of security, for a clumsy craftsman will soon take the edge off his tools.
Major-General J.F.C. Fuller, *The Foundations of the Science of War*, 1926.

SELF-CONFIDENCE

OFTEN there is a gap between principles and actual events that cannot always be bridged by a succession of logical deductions. Then a measure of self-confidence is needed.
Major-General Carl von Clausewitz, *On War*, 1, tr. Michael Howard and Peter Paret, 1976.

NEVER take counsel of your fears.
Lieutenant-General Thomas J. 'Stonewall' Jackson, 18 June 1862, to Major Hotchkiss.

WILSON, I am a damned sight smarter than Grant. I know a great deal more about war, military history, strategy, and grand tactics than he does; I know more about organization, supply, and administration, and about everything else than he does. But I tell you where he beats me, and where he beats the world. He don't care a damn for what the enemy does out of his sight, but it scares me like hell. . . . I am more nervous than he is. I am more likely to change my orders, or to countermarch my command than he is. He uses such information as he has, according to his best judgment. He issues his orders and does his level best to carry them out without much reference to what is going on about him.
General of the Army William T. Sherman, quoted in Harry T. Williams, *McClellan, Sherman and Grant*, 1962.

I KNOW the greatest anxiety is now felt in the North for the success of this move, and that the anxiety will increase when it is once known that the Army is in motion. I feel well myself. Do not know that this is any criterion to judge results because I have never felt otherwise. I believe it has never been my misfortune to be placed where I lost my presence of mind, unless indeed it has been when thrown in strange company, particularly of ladies. Under such circumstances I know I must appear like a fool.
General Ulysses S. Grant, letter to Julia Dent Grant, 2 May 1864, shortly before the beginning of the great campaign of 1864, *Papers of USG*, X, 1982.

OFTEN . . . a decision is made which cannot be justified by any accepted principle, and the urge to modify such a decision, no matter how well-thought-out it may have been, becomes particularly hard to resist. Remaining steadfast here calls for a vast amount of confidence in oneself, as well as a certain degree of skepticism. One's main help . . . is faith in the time-tested principles used to frame the decision, backed up by this maxim: In case of doubt, hold to your first decision, and make no change until positive conviction forces it.

> General der Infantrie Hugo Baron von Freytag-Loringhoven, *The Power of Personality in War*, 1911, tr. Spaulding, 1938.

THE MOST VITAL quality a soldier can possess is self-confidence, utter, complete and bumptious.

> General George S. Patton, Jr., 6 June 1944, letter to his son, *The Patton Papers*, II, 1974.

YOU CAN have doubts about your good looks, about your intelligence, or about your self-control, but to win in a war, you must have no doubt about your ability as a soldier.

> General George S. Patton, Jr., quoted in Robert H. Patton, *The Pattons*, 1994.

WHEN I THINK of the greatness of my job and realize that I am what I am, I am amazed, but on reflection, who is as good as I am? I know of no one.

> General George S. Patton, Jr., *The Patton Papers*, II, 1974.

ONE of the most interesting points to my mind about all this business of making war is the way that people try and shake your confidence in what you are doing, and suggest that your plan is not good, and that you ought to do this, or that. If I had done all that was suggested I would still be back in the Alamein area.

> Field Marshal Viscount Montgomery of Alamein, quoted in Nigel Hamilton, *Master of the Battlefield*, 1983.

SELF-CONTROL

SELF-CONTROL is the chief element in self-respect, and self-respect is the chief element in courage.

> Thucydides, *The History of the Peloponnesian War*, c. 404 BC.

LET THE ARMY see that you are not unduly elated over successes nor utterly cast down by failures.

> The Emperor Maurice, *The Strategikon*, c. AD 600 (*Maurice's Strategikon*, tr. George Dennis, 1984).

IT IS WELL for the general to exercise self-control at all times, but especially in war.

> The Emperor Maurice, *The Strategikon*, c. AD 600 (*Maurice's Strategikon*, tr. George Dennis, 1984).

THE GENERAL should be calm in emergencies, prudent in counsel, courteous to his associates. He will be most successful in battle if he charges against the enemy, not like a wild beast, but in a calculated manner.

> The Emperor Maurice, *The Strategikon*, c. AD 600 (*Maurice's Strategikon*, tr. George Dennis, 1984).

THERE IS nothing more base than for a man to lose his temper too often. No matter how angry one becomes, his first thought should be to pacify his mind and come to a clear understanding of the situation at hand. Then, if he is in the right, to become angry is correct.

> Shiba Yoshimasa (1350–1410), *The Chikubasho*, 1380, (*The Ideals of the Samurai*, tr. William Wilson, 1982).

BUT it might be closer to the truth to assume that the faculty known as *self-control* – the gift of keeping calm even under the greatest stress – is rooted in temperament. It is itself an emotion which serves to balance the passionate feelings in strong characters without destroying them, and it is this balance alone that assures the dominance of the intellect. . . .

> Major-General Carl von Clausewitz, *On War*, 1.3, 1832, tr. Michael Howard and Peter Paret, 1976.

GENERAL MEADE was an officer of great merit with drawbacks to his usefulness which were beyond his control. . . . He made it unpleasant at times, even in battle, for those around him to approach him with information.

> General of the Army Ulysses S. Grant, *Personal Memoirs*, II, 1885.

IF THERE ARE persons with steel nerves on a patrol boat, then their night attacks will be completely successful. Persons with great self-control can achieve miracles, while weak will of the executors and a lack of tenacity to a significant degree diminish the result.

> Admiral Stepan O. Makarov (1849–1904), quoted in Ablamonov, *Admiral*.

BUT the priceless advantage which may be instilled in the military crowd by a proper training is that it also possesses the means of recovery. That possibility – the resolution of order out of chaos – reposes within every file who has gained within the service a confidence that he has some measure of influence among his fellows. The welfare of the unit machinery depends upon having the greatest possible number of human shock absorbers – men who in the worst hour are capable of stepping forward and saying: "This calls for something extra and that means me." The restoration of control upon the battlefield, and the process of checking fright and paralysis and turning men back to essential tactical duties, does not come simply of constituted authority again finding its voice and articulating its strength to the extremities of the unit boundary. Control is a man-to-man force under fire. No matter how lowly his rank, any man who controls himself contributes to the control of others. A private can steady a general as surely as a cat can look at a king. There is no better ramrod for the back of a senior, who is beginning to buckle, than the sight of a junior who has kept his nerve. Land battles, as to the fighting part, are won by the intrepidity of men in grade from private to captains mainly. Fear is contagious but courage is not less so. The courage of any one man reflects in some degree the courage of all those who are within vision. To the man who is in terror and bordering on panic, no influence can be more steadying than that of seeing some other man near him who is retaining self-control and doing his duty.

> Brigadier-General S.L.A. Marshall, *The Armed Forces Officer*, 1950.

AN OFFICER should never speak ironically or sarcastically to an enlisted man, since the latter doesn't have a fair chance to answer back. The use of profanity and epithets comes under the same heading. The best argument for a man keeping his temper is that nobody else wants it; and when he voluntarily throws it away, he loses a main prop to his own position.

> Brigadier-General S.L.A. Marshall, *The Armed Forces Officer*, 1950.

EXPLOSIONS of temper do not necessarily ruin a general's reputation or influence with his troops; it is almost expected of them ("the privileged irascibility of senior officers", someone has written), and it is not always resented, sometimes even admired, except by those immediately concerned. But sarcasm is always resented and seldom forgiven. In the Peninsula the bitter sarcastic tongue of Craufurd, the brilliant but erratic leader of the Light Division, was much more wounding and feared than the more violent outbursts of Picton, a rough, hot-tempered man.

> Field Marshal Viscount Wavell of Cyrenaica, *Soldiers and Soldiering*, 1953.

SELF-INTEREST

WHEN tremendous dangers are involved, no one can be blamed for looking to his own interest.

> Thucydides, *The Peloponnesian War*, 1.6, c. 404 BC, tr. Rex Warner.

HOW TRUE it is that we feel public misfortune only in so far as it affects our private interests! And it takes a money loss to make us feel the pinch. So when the spoils of war were being stripped from vanquished Carthage, and you saw her left naked and unarmed amidst all the many armed tribes of Africa, no one raised a moan; but today, when contributions have to be made from private property, you behave like mourners at your country's funeral.

> Hannibal, 201 BC, to the Senate of Carthage when the first instalment of the peace indemnity levied by Rome at the end of the Second Punic War became due, quoted in Livy, *History of Rome*, c. 29 BC–AD 17 (*The War With Hannibal*, tr. Aubrey de Sélincourt, 1972).

THIS WAR is not being conducted for the benefit of officers or to enrich them by the capture of prizes, and every commander is deficient in the high moral character which has always been inherent in the Navy who for a moment consults his private interests in preference to the public good, hesitates to destroy what is the property of the enemy, or attempts to benefit himself at the expense of others.

> Admiral David Dixon Porter, 9 November 1864, General Order No. 41.

THE LOSS of property weighs more heavily with the most of mankind; heavier often, than the sacrifices made on the field of battle. Death is popularly considered the maximum punishment of war, but it is not; reduction to poverty brings prayers of peace more surely and more quickly than does the destruction of human life, as the selfishness of man has demonstrated in more than one conflict.

> General of the Army Phillip H. Sheridan, *Personal Memoirs of P.H. Sheridan*, 1888.

SIC TRANSIT GLORIA MUNDI

THE EAGLE has ceased to scream, but the parrots will now begin to chatter. The war of the giants is over and the pigmies will now start to squabble.

> Sir Winston S. Churchill, 7 May 1945, comment upon the announcement of VE Day, quoted in Kay Halle, *Irrepressible Churchill*, 1966.

THUS, then, on the night of the tenth of May, at the outset of this mighty battle, I acquired the chief power in the State, which henceforth I wielded in ever-growing measure for five years and three months of world war, at the end of which time, all our enemies having surrendered unconditionally or being about to do so, I was immediately dismissed by the British electorate from all further conduct of their affairs.

> Sir Winston S. Churchill, *The Gathering Storm*, 1948.

WHEN a soldier's tour of duty is over, it's over.

> General Wesley Clark, July 1999, upon the news that, despite his victory over Serbia, he would be dismissed early from his position as NATO Commander.

SIMPLICITY
Principle of War

THE ART of war is a simple art; everything is in the performance. There is nothing vague in it; everything in it is common sense; ideology does not enter in.

> Napoleon, dictation on St. Helena, quoted in Christopher Herold, ed., *The Mind of Napoleon*, 1955.

THE ART of war is like everything else that is beautiful and simple. The simplest moves are the best. If MacDonald, instead of doing whatever he did, had asked a peasant for the way to Genoa, the peasant would have answered, "Through Bobbio" – and that would have been a superb move.

Napoleon, 1818, conversation, quoted in Christopher Herold, ed., *The Mind of Napoleon*, 1955.

IF ONE has never personally experienced war, one cannot understand in what the difficulties constantly mentioned really consist, nor why a commander should need any brilliance and exceptional ability. Everything looks simple; the knowledge required does not look remarkable, the strategic options are so obvious that by comparison the simplest problem of higher mathematics has an impressive scientific dignity. Once war has actually been seen the difficulties become clear; but it is still extremely hard to describe the unseen, all-pervading element that brings about this change of perspective.

Major-General Carl von Clausewitz, *On War*, 1.7, 1832, tr. Michael Howard and Peter Paret, 1976.

IN WAR only what is simple can succeed.

Field Marshal Paul von Hindenburg (1847–1934).

SPARTAN simplicity must be observed. Nothing will be done merely because it contributes to beauty, convenience, comfort, or prestige.

Circular from the Office of the Chief Signal Officer, U.S. Army, 29 May 1945.

SIMPLICITY contributes to successful operations. Direct, simple plans and clear, concise orders minimize misunderstanding and confusion. If other factors are equal, the simplest plan is preferred.

U.S. Army Field Manual 100-5, 19 February 1962.

THE KISS principle: KEEP IT SIMPLE, STUPID!

Anglo-American military maxim.

SITUATION

MILITARY TACTICS are like unto water; for water in its natural course runs away from high places and hastens downwards. So in war, the way to avoid what is strong is to strike what is weak.

Water shapes its course according to the ground over which it flows; the soldier works out his victory in relation to the foe he is facing.

Therefore, just as water retains no constant shape, so in warfare there are no constant conditions.

He who can modify his tactics in relation to his opponent and thereby succeed in winning, may be called a heaven-born captain.

Sun Tzu, *The Art of War*, 6, c. 500 BC, tr. Giles, 1910.

THE GENERAL should be ignorant of none of the situations likely to occur in war. Who can attempt to accomplish what he does not understand? Who is able to furnish assistance in situations whose dangers he does not understand?

The Emperor Maurice, *The Strategikon*, c. AD 600 (*Maurice's Strategikon*, tr. George Dennis, 1984).

RULES and norms arise any time it is necessary to apply an unconditional principle to a conditional situation. . . . Rules and norms . . . are conditional, i.e., they are true only under certain conditions of the situation.

General G.A. Leyer, *Methods of Military Science*, 1894, quoted in V.Ye. Savkin, *Soviet Operational Art*, 1972.

[BASE ONE'S ACTIONS]. . . on the one hand, on a deep respect for fundamental principles, and on the other, on just as deep a respect for the situation.

General G.A. Leyer, *Key Questions*, 1898, quoted in V.Ye. Savkin, *Soviet Operational Art*, 1972.

SITUATIONS in war are of unlimited variety. They change often and suddenly and are rarely discernable at an early point. Incalculable elements are often of great influence. The independent will of the enemy is pitted against ours. Frictions and mistakes are an every day occurrence.

Generals Werner von Fritsch and Ludwig Beck, *Troop Leadership*, 1933.

OBSCURITY of the situation is the rule. Seldom will one have exact information of the enemy. Clarification of the hostile situation is a self-evident demand. However, to wait in tense situations for information is seldom a token of strong leadership, but often one of weakness. . . . The teaching of the conduct of war cannot be concentrated exhaustively in regulations. The principles so enunciated must be employed dependent upon the situation. . . .

The emptiness of the battlefield demands independently thinking and acting fighters, who, considering each situation, are dominated by the determination to act boldly and decisively, and to arrive at success.

Generals Werner von Fritsch and Ludwig Beck, *Troop Leadership*, 1933.

SKILL

FORCE has no place where there is need of skill

Herodotus (c. 484–420 BC), *The Histories of Herodotus*.

CERTES the Frenchmen and Rutters, deriding our new archery . . . will not let in open skirmish, if any leisure serve, to turn up their tails and cry, "Shoot, English!" and all because our strong shooting is decayed and laid in bed. But if some of our Englishmen now lived that served Edward the Third in his wars with France, the breech of such a varlet should have been nailed to his bum with an arrow and another feathered in his bowels before he should have turned about to see who shot the first.

> William Harrison, quoted in Holinshed, *Chronicles*, 1807.

MR. AMERY, author of *The Times* history of the War, probed a weak spot in the prevailing European theory by arguing that superior skill now counted more than superior numbers, and that its proportionate value would increase with material progress. The same note was struck by General Baden-Powell, who urged that the way to develop it was to give officers responsibility when young – he was left to find his channel for proving this in the Boy Scout movement, and not in the Army.

> Captain Sir Basil Liddell Hart, *A History of the World War 1914–1918*, 1935.

VERY FEW PEOPLE will use skill if brute force will do the trick. The worst thing for a good general is to have superior numbers.

> Colonel T.E. Lawrence, 31 March 1929, letter to B.H. Liddell Hart, *T.E. Lawrence to his Biographers*, 1963.

SOLDIERS

JUST THINK of how the soldier is treated. While still a child he is shut up in the barracks. During his training he is always being knocked about. If he makes the least mistake he is beaten, a burning blow on his body, another on his eye, perhaps his head is laid open with a wound. He is battered and bruised with flogging. On the march he has to carry bread and water like the load of an ass; the joints of his back are bowed; they hang heavy loads round his neck like that of an ass. . . .

> An onymous Egyptian scribe expressing the usual distaste of the pen for the sword, quoted in Cotrell, *The Warrior Pharaohs*.

YOU are the disaster.
Would to god you commanded another army,
a ragtag crew of cowards, instead of ruling us,
the men whom Zeus decrees, form youth to old age,
must wind down our brutal wars to the bitter end
until we drop and die, down to the last man.

> Homer, *The Iliad*, 14.103–107, c. 800 BC, tr. Robert Fagles, 1990; Odysseus to Agamemnon, who panicked and urged the Greeks to flee from the danger of the Trojan assault on their camp.

IF, HOWEVER, you are indulgent, but unable to make your authority felt; kind-hearted but unable to enforce your commands; and incapable, moreover, of quelling disorder, then your soldiers must be likened to spoiled children; they are useless for any practical purpose.

> Sun Tzu, *The Art of War*, 10, c. 500 BC, tr. Giles, 1910.

ROUGH and unpolished, but great on great occasions.

> Euripides (c. 484–406 BC), his description of Herakles, which Plutarch said also applied to the Roman people,

quoted in Plutarch, *The Lives*, c. AD 100 (*The Age of Alexander*, tr. Ian Scott-Kilvert, 1965).

REMEMBER that zeal, honor, and obedience mark the good soldier.

> Brasidas, 422 BC, speech to the Spartans and their allies before the Battle of Amphipolis, quoted in Thucydides, *History of the Peloponnesian War*, 5.9, c. 404 BC, tr. Richard Crawley, 1910.

MANY think the genius of the soldier wants subtlety, because military law, which is summary and blunt, and apt to appeal to the sword, finds no exercise for the refinements of the forum.

> Cornelius Tacitus, *Agricola*, AD 98 (*The Complete Works of Tacitus*, tr. Alfred Church and William Brodribb, 1942); to this preface, he contrasted the character of his father-in-law, Cnaeus Julius Agricola, later governor of Britain.

FOR WHO OUGHT to be more faithful than a man that is entrusted with the safety of his country, and has sworn to defend it to the last drop of his blood? Who ought to be fonder of peace than those that suffer by nothing but war? Who are under greater obligations to worship God than Soldiers, who are daily exposed to innumerable dangers, and have most occasion for his protection?

> Niccolo Machiavelli, *The Art of War*, 1521.

THE DISTINCTIVE MARK of the soldier is that all his desires are despotic; that of the civilian is that he submits everything to discussion, to truth, to reason.

> Napoleon, 4 May 1802, quoted in R.M. Johnston, ed., *The Corsican*, 1910.

SOLDIERS generally win battles; generals generally get the credit for them.

> Napoleon, 1815, to General Gaspard Gourgaud on St. Helena.

I HATE that cheering. If once you allow soldiers to express an opinion, they may on some other occasion hiss instead of cheer.

> The Duke of Wellington, 1815, to Lady Shelley in Paris, *The Diary of Frances Lady Shelley*, II, 1912.

SIR, when soldiers have been christened by the fire of the battle-field, they have all one rank in my eyes.

> Napoleon, 16 May 1816, to Major-General Sir Hudson Lowe, the Governor of St. Helena and his jailer, who had suggested that officers of his staff rather than the officer established at Napoleon's residence, accompany him on his rides; quoted in Emmanuel Las Casas, *The Life, Exile, and Conversations of Emperor Napoleon Bonaparte*, II, 1891.

MME. DE MONTHOLON: Which were the best troops? Napoleon: Those that win battles, madam. And they are fickle, they must be taken on their day, like you ladies. The best troops have been, the

Carthaginians under Hannibal, the Romans under the Scipios, the Macedonians under Alexander, the Prussians under Frederick. Some day my army of Italy and that of Austerlitz may be equalled, but, surely never surpassed.

Napoleon, 28 August 1816, quoted in R.M. Johnston, ed., *The Corsican*, 1910.

TROOPS are made to let themselves be killed.

Napoleon, 1817, conversation on St. Helena, cited in Christopher Herold, ed., *The Mind of Napoleon*, 1955.

MAXIM 58. The first qualification of a soldier is fortitude under fatigue and privation. Courage is only the second; hardship, poverty, and want are the best school of the soldier.

Napoleon, *The Military Maxims of Napoleon*, tr. George D'Aguilar, 1831 (David Chandler, ed., 1987).

I HAVE NEVER been able to join in the popular cry about the recklessness, sensuality, helplessness of the soldier. On the contrary I should say (& no woman perhaps has ever seen more of the manufacturing & agricultural classes of England than I have – before I came out here) that I have never seen so teachable & helpful a class as the army generally.

Give them an opportunity promptly & securely to send money home – & they will use it.

Give them a School & lecture & they will come to it.

Give them a book & a game & a Magic Lanthorn & they will leave off drinking.

Give them suffering & they will bear it.

Give them work & they will do it.

I had rather have to do with the Army generally than with any other class I have ever attempted to serve.

And I speak with *intimate* experience of 18 months which I have had since I "joined the Army" – no woman (or man either) having seen them under such conditions.

And when I compare them with the Medical Staff Corps, the Land Transport Corps, the Army Works Corps, I am struck with the soldier's superiority as a moral & even as an intellectual being.

If Officers would but think thus of their men, how much might not be done for them.

Florence Nightingale, 6 March 1856, Scutari, The Barracks Hospital, letter to Lieutenant-Colonel Lefroy, quoted in Goldie, ed., *'I have done my duty': Florence Nightingale in the Crimean War 1854–1856*, 1987.

THIS extraordinary war in which we are engaged falls heavily upon all classes of people, but the most heavily upon the soldier. For it has been said, all that a man hath will he give for his life; and while all contribute of their substance the soldier puts his life at stake, and often yields it up in his countries cause. The highest merit, then, is due to the soldier.

President Abraham Lincoln, 18 March 1864, remarks at the closing of a sanitary fair, Washington D.C., quoted in Roy P. Baslar, ed., *The Collected Works of Abraham Lincoln*, VII, 1953.

THE ONLY CHANGE that breech-loading arms will probably make in the art and practice of war will be to increase the amount of ammunition to be expended, and necessarily to be carried along; to still further "thin out" the lines of attack, and to reduce battles to short, quick decisive conflicts. It does not in the least affect the grand strategy, or the necessity for perfect organization, drill,and discipline. The companies and battalions will be more dispersed, and the men will be less under the immediate eye of their officers, and therefore a higher order of intelligence and courage on the part of the individual soldier will be an element of strength.

General of the Army William T. Sherman, *The Memoirs of General W.T. Sherman*, II, 1875.

BOYS are soldiers in their hearts already – and where the harm? Soldiers are not pugnacious. Paul bade Timothy to be a good soldier. Christ commended the centurion. Milton urged teachers to fit their pupils for all the offices of war. The very thought of danger and self-sacrifice are inspirations.

General Sir Ian Hamilton, *The Soul and Body of an Army*, 1921.

AS IN THE SHADES of a November evening I, for the first time, led a platoon of Grenadiers across the sopping fields . . . the conviction came into my mind with absolute assurance that the simple soldiers and their regimental officers, armed with their cause, would by their virtues in the end retrieve the mistakes and ignorance of Staffs and Cabinets, or Admirals, Generals, and politicians – including, no doubt, many of my own. But, alas, at what a needless cost!

Sir Winston S. Churchill, *The World Crisis*, 1923.

WHAT are the qualities of a good soldier, by the development of which we make the man war-worthy – fit for any war? . . . The following four – in whatever order you place them – pretty well cover the field: discipline, physical fitness, technical skill in the use of weapons, battle-craft.

Field Marshal Viscount Wavell of Cyrenaica, 15 February 1933, lecture at the Royal United Service Institution (RUSI).

THEY WISH to hell they were someplace else, and they wish to hell they would get relief. They wish to hell the mud was dry and they wish to hell their coffee was hot. They want to go home. But they stay in their wet holes and fight, and then they climb out and crawl though minefields and fight some more.

Bill Mauldin, *Willie and Joe*.

THE FIGHTING SOLDIER . . . was fighting for his life, and killing then for him was as much a profession as writing was for me.

He wanted to kill individually or in vast numbers. He wanted to see the Germans overrun, mangled, butchered in the Tunisian trap. He spoke excitedly of seeing great heaps of dead, of our bombers sinking whole shiploads of fleeing men, of Germans by the thousands dying miserably in the final Tunisian holocaust of our own creation.

In that one respect the front-line soldier differed from all the rest of us. All the rest of us – you and me and even the thousands of soldiers behind the lines in Africa – we wanted terribly yet only academically for the war to be over. The front-line soldier wanted it to be terminated by the physical process of his destroying enough Germans to end it. He was truly at war. The rest of us, no matter how hard we worked, were not. Say what you will, nothing can make a complete soldier except battle experience.
  Ernie Pyle, *Here is Your War*, 1945.

THE SOLDIER is the Army. No army is better than its soldiers. The soldier is also a citizen. In fact, the highest obligation and privilege of citizenship is that of bearing arms for one's country. Hence it is a proud privilege to be a soldier – a good soldier. Anyone, in any walk of life, who is content with mediocrity is untrue to himself and to American tradition. To be a good soldier a man must have discipline, self-respect, pride in his unit and in his country, a high sense of duty and obligation to his comrades and to his superiors, and self-confidence born of demonstrated ability.
  General George S. Patton, Jr., *War As I Knew It*, 1947.

THE SOLDIER is a man; he expects to be treated as an adult, not a schoolboy. He has rights; they must be made known to him and thereafter respected. He has ambition; it must be stirred. He has a belief in fair play; it must be honored. He has a need of comradeship; it must be supplied. He has imagination; it must be stimulated. He has a sense of personal dignity; it must be sustained. He has pride; it can be satisfied and made the bedrock of character once he has been assured that he is playing a useful and respected role. To give a man this is the acme of inspired leadership. He has become loyal because loyalty has been given to him.
  General of the Army George C. Marshall (1880–1959).

I RELAPSE into silence and go into the tent. For a long time afterwards the man Steen is the subject of my thoughts. Now I understand him better than I did. I realize how much virile strength and strength-giving understanding can be passed from one man to another in a quiet talk at the front. It is not the soldier's way to be communicative. He expresses himself very differently from a civilian. His talk is every bit as uncivilian and tongue-tied as it is popularly represented. And because war jerks a man out of all pretence and hypocrisy, the things a warrior says, even if they only take the form of an oath or a primitive sentimentality, are integrally sincere and genuine, and therefore finer stuff than all the glib rhetoric of the civilian world.
  Colonel Hans Ulrich Rudel, *Stuka Pilot*, 1958.

I HAVE WRITTEN much of generals and staff officers . . . the war in Burma was a soldier's war. There comes a moment in every battle against a stubborn enemy when the result hangs in the balance. Then the general, however skilful and farsighted he may have been, must hand over to his soldiers, to the men in the ranks and to their regimental officers and leave them to complete what he has begun.
  Field Marshal Viscount Slim of Burma, *Defeat Into Victory*, 1956.

BY PEOPLE I do not mean "personnel." I do not mean "end Strength." I mean living, breathing, serving, human beings. They have needs and interests and desires. They have spirit and will, and strengths and abilities. They have weaknesses and faults; and they have names. They are the heart of our preparedness . . . and this preparedness – as a nation and as an Army – depends upon the spirit of our soldiers. It is the spirit that gives the Army . . . life. Without it we cannot succeed.
  General Creighton Abrams (1914–1974), quoted in *Parameters*, 6/1981.

THERE IS no mystery to what we do as soldiers and as an Army. When called to do so, we fight and win our nation's wars as part of a joint team. We spend a lifetime getting ready to do that. I was no different.
  General Fred Franks, Jr., quoted in Tom Clancy with General Fred Franks, Jr. (ret), *Into the Storm*, 1997.

SOLDIERS AND POLITICIANS

IT IS easy enough to say to a general, go to Italy, win battles, and sign peace at Vienna. But the doing of it is not so easy. I have never paid the least attention to the plans sent to me by the Directoire. Only fools could take stock in such rubbish.
  Napoleon, 21 March 1797, in R.M. Johnston, ed., *The Corsican*, 1910.

I UNDERSTAND why Bonaparte is accused; it's for concluding peace. But I warn you, I speak in the name of 80,000 men; the time when cowardly lawyers and low chatterers could send soldiers to the guillotine has passed, and if you drive them to it, the soldiers of Italy will march to the Clichy gate with their general: but, if they do, look out for yourselves!
  Napoleon, 30 June 1797, to the Directoire, quoted in R.M. Johnston, *The Corsican*, 1910.

IF EVER I have the luck to set foot in France again, the reign of chatter is over.
  Napoleon, 11 August 1799, in Cairo, quoted in R.M. Johnston, ed., *The Corsican*, 1910.

I HAD RATHER talk to soldiers than to lawyers. Those . . . made me nervous. I am not accustomed to assemblies; it may come in time.
  Napoleon, 10 November 1799, after a stormy session with the Council of Ancients, Paris, quoted in R.M. Johnston, ed., *The Corsican*, 1910.

I DO NOT desire to place myself in the most perilous of all positions: – *a fire upon my rear, from Washington, and the fire, in front, from the Mexicans*.
Lieutenant-General Winfield Scott, 21 May 1846, letter to the Secretary of War.

I START early in the morning. . . . Those hounds in Washington are after me again.
Major-General George B. McClellan, *McClellan's Own Story*, 1887.

THE GOVERNMENT seems determined to apply the guillotine to all unsuccessful generals. It seems rather hard to do this where a general is not in fault, but perhaps with us now, as in the French Revolution, some harsh measures are required.
Major-General Henry W. Halleck, *The War of the Rebellion: A Compilation of the Official Records of the Union and Confederate Armies*, Vol. XVI, Part 2, p. 421.

IF THEY [politicians] would only follow the example of their ancestors, enter a herd of swine, run down some steep bank and drown themselves in the sea, there would be some hope of saving the country.
Major-General Henry W. Halleck, *The War of the Rebellion: A Compilation of the Official Records of the Union and Confederate Armies*, Vol. XXII, Part 1, p. 793.

I AM A SOLDIER. It is my duty to obey orders. It is enough to turn one's hair grey to spend one day in the Congress. The members are patriotic and earnest, but they will neither take the responsibility of action nor will they clothe me with the authority to act for them.
General Robert E. Lee, quoted in John B. Gordon, *Reminiscences*, 1903.

SO LONG as we can gain success, the interference of politicians in military matters can be resisted; but on the first disaster they press upon us like a pack of hungry wolves.
Major-General Henry W. Halleck, letter to Schofield, 7 July 1863, *John M. Schofield Manuscripts* (LOC).

KEEP YOUR HANDS off the regiment, ye iconoclastic civilian officials who meddle and muddle in Army matters. Clever politicians you may be, but you are not soldiers and you do not understand them; they are not pawns on a chessboard. Leave the management of our fighting men to soldiers of experience in our British Army of old renown, and do not parody us by appearing in public decked for the nonce in a soldier's khaki coat. You might as well put your arm in a sling, or tie your head up in the bandage of some poor maimed soldier, to whom, when wounded and unable to earn a livelihood, your regulations allow a pension of sixpence a day!
Field Marshal Viscount Wolseley, *The Story of a Soldier's Life*, 1903.

A MILITARY MAN in the political world is a complete innocent. A military man turned politician never achieves anything worthwhile. The more confidence he has, the less he can do.
Admiral Isoroku Yamamato, 1938, quoted in Agawa, *The Reluctant Admiral*, 1979.

ALL the reproaches that have been levelled against the leaders of the armed forces by their countrymen and by the international courts have failed to take into consideration one very simple fact: that policy is not laid down by soldiers, but by politicians. This has always been the case and is so today. When war starts, the soldiers can only act according to the political and military situation as it then exists. Unfortunately it is not the habit of politicians to appear in the conspicuous places when the bullets begin to fly. They prefer to remain in some safe retreat and to let the soldiers carry out "the continuation of politics by other means."
Colonel-General Heinz Guderian, *Panzer Leader*, 1953.

THE SOLDIER always knows that everything he does . . . will be scrutinized by two classes of critics – by the government that employs him and by the enemies of that Government.
Field Marshal Viscount Slim of Burma, *Unofficial History*, 1959.

SPEECHES AND THE SPOKEN WORD

STUDENT: Do you mean that in addition to his other duties a cavalry leader must take care to be a good speaker?
Socrates: Did you suppose that commander of cavalry should be mum? Did you never reflect that all the best we learned according to custom – the learning, I mean, that teaches us how to live – we learned by means of words, and that every other good lesson to be learned is learned by means of words; that the best teachers rely most on the spoken word and those with the deepest knowledge of the greatest subjects are the best talkers?
Socrates (470–399 BC), quoted by Xenophon, *Memorabilia*, 3.11–12, c. 360 BC, tr. E.C. Marchant, 1923.

GREAT ELOQUENCE, like fire, grows with its material; it becomes fiercer with movement, and brighter as it burns.
Cornelius Tacitus, *Oratory*, 36, c. AD 75 (*The Complete Works of Tacitus*, tr. Alfred Church and William Brodribb, 1942).

THE GENERAL who possesses some skill in public speaking is able, as in the past, to rouse the weak-hearted to battle and restore courage to a defeated army.
The Emperor Maurice, *The Strategikon*, c. AD 600 (*Maurice's Strategikon*, tr. George Dennis, 1984).

YOU KNOW what words can do to soldiers.
> Napoleon, 12 March 1800, to General Brunne, *Correspondance de Napoléon Ier, publiée par ordre de l'Empereur Napoléon III*, VI, p. 178, quoted in Christopher Herold, ed., *The Mind of Napoleon*, 1955.

MAXIM 61. It is not speeches at the moment of battle that render soldiers brave. The veteran scarcely listens to them, and the recruit forgets them at the first discharge. If discourses and harangues are useful, it is during the campaign; to do away unfavourable impressions, to correct false reports, to keep alive proper spirit in the camp, and to furnish materials and amusement for the bivouac. All printed orders should keep in view these objects.
> Napoleon, *The Military Maxims of Napoleon*, tr. George D'Aguilar, 1831 (David Chandler, ed., 1987).

ACTION employs men's fervour, but words arouse it.
> General Charles de Gaulle, quoted in F.M. Richardson, *Fighting Spirit*, 1978.

OLD MAN, when you have something to say to officers or men, make it snappy. The fewer words, the better. They won't believe you if you shoot bull. When you face ranks of men and try that, you can hear 'em sigh in despair when you open your mouth, if they sense you're a phoney. They can usually look at you and tell. Maybe it doesn't sound like it, but that's an important thing in a Marine's career.
> Lieutenant-General Lewis 'Chesty' Puller, quoted in Burke Davis, *Marine*, 1962.

MEN who can command words to serve their thoughts and feelings are well on their way to commanding men to serve their purposes.
> Brigadier-General S.L.A. Marshall, *The Armed Forces Officer*, 1950.

THE COMMANDER must have contact with his men. He must be capable of feeling and thinking with them. The soldier must have confidence in him. There is one cardinal principle which must always be remembered: one must never make a show of false emotions to one's men. The ordinary soldier has a surprisingly good nose for what is true and what is false.
> Field Marshal Erwin Rommel, *The Rommel Papers*, 1953.

THE TROOPS must be brought to a state of wild enthusiasm before the operation begins. They must have that offensive eagerness and that infectious optimism which comes from physical well-being. They must enter the fight with the light of battle in their eyes and definitely wanting to kill the enemy. In achieving this end, it is the spoken word which counts, from the commander to his troops; plain speech is far more effective than any written word.
> Field Marshal Viscount Montgomery of Alamein, *The Memoirs of Field Marshal Montgomery*, 1958.

SPEED

RAPIDITY is the essence of war. Take advantage of the enemy's unreadiness, make your way by unexpected routes, and attack unguarded spots.
> Sun Tzu, *The Art of War*, 11, c. 500 BC, tr. Giles, 1910.

IT IS ESSENTIAL to be cautious and take your time in making plans, and once you come to a decision carry it out right away without any hesitation or timidity. Timidity after all is not caution but the invention of wickedness.
> The Emperor Maurice, *The Strategikon*, c. AD 600 (*Maurice's Strategikon*, tr. George Dennis, 1984).

IF YOU MOVE rapidly, above all if the work of your scouts, your intelligence and your couriers is reliable, you can be certain of defeating a battalion with a detachment, an army with a battalion.
> Anonymous Byzantine general, 10th-century treatise on tactics, quoted in Guerdan, *Byzantium, Its Triumphs and Tragedy*.

IN MILITARY PRACTICE one must plan quickly and carry on without delay, so as to give the enemy no time to collect himself.
> Field Marshal Prince Aleksandr V. Suvorov (1729–1800), quoted in W. Lyon Blease, *Suvorof*, 1920.

I WORK in minutes, not in hours.
> Field Marshal Prince Aleksandr V. Suvorov (1729–1800), quoted in W. Lyon Blease, *Suvorof*, 1920.

IT IS the moment which gives victory, master it by the swiftness of Caesar, who knew so well how to surprise his enemies, even in broad daylight, to turn them and attack them where and when he wished, without ever being compelled to cut off their supplies of food and fodder.
> Field Marshal Prince Aleksandr V. Suvorov (1729–1800), quoted in W. Lyon Blease, *Suvorof*, 1920.

TO DO GOOD one must make haste.
> Field Marshal Prince Aleksandr V. Suvorov (1729–1800), quoted in W. Lyon Blease, *Suvorof*, 1920.

SWIFTNESS and impact are the soul of genuine warfare.
> Field Marshal Prince Aleksandr V. Suvorov (1729–1800), quoted in V.Ye.. Savkin, *Basic Principles*, 1972.

JUST AS LIGHTNING has already struck when the flash is seen, so when the enemy discovers the head of the army, the whole should be there, and leave him no time to counteract its dispositions.
> Field Marshal Francois Comte de Guibert (1744–1790).

IT IS very advantageous to rush unexpectedly on an enemy who has erred, to attack him suddenly and come down on him with thunder before he sees the lightning.

   Napoleon (1769–1821).

IN ORDER to smash, it is necessary to act suddenly.

   Napoleon (1769–1821).

THE THIRD RULE is never to waste time. Unless important advantages are to be gained from hesitation, it is necessary to set to work at once. By this speed a hundred enemy measures are nipped in the bud, and public opinion is won most rapidly.

   Major-General Carl von Clausewitz, *Principles of War*, 1812, tr. Gatzke, 1942.

SPEED shall be the motto of this campaign. We shall not allow Morillo any time to threaten our rear, for when he can do something against us, we shall be coming back on him with twice or thrice as much force as we are taking away.

   General Simon Bolivar, May 1819, quoted in Salvador de Madariaga, *Bolivar*, 1952.

SPEED is one of the chief characteristics of strategical marches, as it is of ordinary movements on the battle field. In this one quality reside all the advantages that a fortunate initiative may have procured; and by it we gain in the pursuit all the results that a victory on the battle field has placed in our hands.

   Dennis Hart Mahan, *Advance-Guard, Out-Post, and Detachment Service of Troops with the Essential Principles of Strategy and Grand Tactics*, 1863.

NO GREAT SUCCESS can be hoped for in war in which rapid movements do not enter as an element. Even the very elements of Nature seem to array themselves against the slow and over-prudent general.

   Dennis Hart Mahan, *Advance-Guard, Out-Post, and Detachment Service of Troops with the Essential Principles of Strategy and Grand Tactics*, 1863.

SPEED is the essential requisite for a first-class ship of war – but essential only to go into action, not out of it.

   Rear-Admiral John A. Dahlgren (1809–1870).

THE TRUE SPEED of war is not headlong precipitancy, but the unremitting energy which wastes no time.

   Rear-Admiral Alfred Thayer Mahan, *Lessons of the War With Spain*, 1899.

SPEED of mind to seize an opening and exploit an unforeseen advantage is the product not only of the commander's training and natural ability, but also of the promptness of his information – through personal touch with the progress of the battle, and the instant rendering of reports. (Oct. 1925.)

   Captain Sir Basil Liddell Hart, *Thoughts on War*, 1944.

NOTHING is more important to the future efficiency of the Army than to multiply its rate of movement. A law of physics that applies with equal force to warfare is that while striking force increases directly with the mass applied, it increases according to the square of the speed of the application. Through proper organization in all echelons, through the development and perfection of reliable combat machines capable of speedy maneuver, and through the improvement of transportation, maintenance, and communication, and supply arrangements, the objective of greater and still greater speed must be pursued.

   General of the Army Douglas MacArthur, *Annual Report of the Chief of Staff June 30, 1935.*

SPEED of action in conjunction with organization, expert maneuver and dextrous application to the terrain, with an account of the enemy's air, is a basic guarantee of success in battle. Troops having quickly executed a disposition, quickly regrouped with a changing situation, quickly arising from rest, quickly perfecting a campaign movement, quickly falling out in combat order and opening fire, having quickly attacked and pursued the opponent, can always count on success.

   Red Army *Field Service Regulations* (1936), attributed to Marshal of the Soviet Union Mikhail N. Tukhachevskiy, quoted in R.L. Garthoff, *Soviet Military Doctrine*, 1953.

SPEED is acquired by making the necessary reconnaissance, providing the proper artillery and other tactical support . . . bringing up every man, and then launching the attack with a predetermined plan so that the time under fire will be reduced to the minimum.

   General George S. Patton, Jr., *War As I Knew It*, 1947.

DON'T DELAY: The best is the enemy of the good. By this I mean that a good plan violently executed *now* is better than a perfect plan next week. War is a very simple thing, and the determining characteristics are self-confidence, speed, and audacity. None of these things can be perfect, but they can be good.

   General George S. Patton, Jr., *War As I Knew It*, 1947.

IN SMALL OPERATIONS, as in large, speed is the essential element of success. If the difference between two possible flanks is so small that it requires thought, the time wasted in thought is not well used.

   General George S. Patton, Jr., *War As I Knew It*, 1947.

ONE of the first lessons I had drawn from my experience of motorized warfare was that speed of manoeuvre in operations and quick reaction in command are decisive. Troops must be able to carry out operations at top speed and in complete coordination. To be satisfied with norms is fatal. One

must constantly demand and strive for maximum performance, for the side which makes the greater effort is the faster – and the faster wins the battle.
  Field Marshal Erwin Rommel, *The Rommel Papers*, 1953.

EXCEPT for Napoleon, probably no other general appreciated as fully as Alexander the value of mobility in war. From the opening of his career until its close, speed dominated all his movements, and the result was that, by increasing the time at his disposal, in any given period he could proportionately accomplish more than his opponent.
  Major-General J.F.C. Fuller, *The Generalship of Alexander the Great*, 1960.

THERE IS only one sound way to conduct war as I read history: Deploy to the war zone as quickly as possible sufficient forces to end it at the earliest moment. Anything less is a gift to the other side.
  Brigadier-General S.L.A. Marshall, 'Thoughts of Vietnam', in Thompson, *The Lessons of Vietnam*, 1977.

LIGHTNING SPEED, more lightning speed; boldness, more boldness.
  Motto of the North Vietnamese General Staff, quoted in Colonel Harry Summers, *On Strategy*, 1981.

SPEED is life.
  United States Marine Corps maxim.

SPIRIT

NOW as for the host of the Vandals, let no one of you consider them. For not by numbers of men nor by measure of body, but by valour of soul, is war want to be decided.
  Count Belisarius, December AD 533, address to his army before the Battle of Tricamarum in North Africa, in which he destroyed the last hope of the Vandals, quoted in Procopius, *History of the Wars*, 4.1, c. AD 560, tr. H.B. Dewing.

THE SPIRIT of the commander is naturally communicated to the troops, and there is an ancient saying that that it is better to have an army of deer commanded by a lion than an army of lions commanded by a deer.
  The Emperor Maurice, *The Strategikon*, c. AD 600 (*Maurice's Strategikon*, tr. George Dennis, 1984).

PERSEVERANCE and spirit have done Wonders in all ages.
  General George Washington, 20 August 1775, letter to Philip Schuyler, *The Writings of George Washington*, III, p. 437, John C. Fitzgerald, ed., 1931.

DO NOT compare your physical forces with those of the enemy's, for the spirit should not be compared with matter. You are men, they are beasts; you are free, they are slaves. Fight and you shall conquer. God grants victory to constancy.
  General Simon Bolivar, 1814, quoted in Salvador de Madariaga, *Bolivar*, 1952.

A WARLIKE SPIRIT, which alone can create and civilize a state, is absolutely essential to national defense and to national perpetuity. . . . The more warlike the spirit of the people, the less need for a large standing army. . . . Every male brought into existence should be taught from infancy that the military service of the Republic carries with it honor and distinction, and his very life should be permeated with the ideal that even death itself may become a boon when a man dies that a nation may live and fulfill its destiny.
  General of the Army Douglas MacArthur, *Infantry Journal*, 3/1927.

THERE IS no substitute for the spiritual, in war. Miracles must be wrought if victories are to be won, and to work miracles men's hearts must needs be afire with self-sacrificing love for each other, for their units, for their division, and for their country.
  Major-General John A. Lejeune, *The Reminiscences of a Marine*, 1929.

AS LONG AS you are generous and true, and also fierce, you cannot hurt the world or even seriously distress her. She was made to be wooed and won by youth. She has lived and thrived only by repeated subjugations.
  Sir Winston S. Churchill, *My Early Life*, 1930.

IT IS the cold glitter in the attacker's eye not the point of the questing bayonet that breaks the line. It is the fierce determination of the drive to close with the enemy not the mechanical perfection of the tank that conquers the trench. It is the cataclysmic ecstasy of conflict in the flier not the perfection of his machine gun that drops the enemy in flaming ruin.
  General George S. Patton, Jr. (1885–1947).

IT IS not enough to fight. It is the spirit which we bring to the fight that decides the issue. It is morale that wins the victory.
  General of the Army George C. Marshall, *Military Review*, 10/1948.

I HAVE ALWAYS held the view that an army is not merely a collection of individuals, with so many tanks, guns, machine-guns, etc., and that the strength of the army is not just the total of all these things added together. The real strength of an army is, and must be, far greater than the sum total of its parts; that extra strength is provided by morale, fighting spirit, mutual confidence between the leaders and the led and especially with the high command, the quality of comradeship, and many other intangible spiritual qualities.
  Field Marshal Viscount Montgomery of Alamein, *The Memoirs of Field Marshal Montgomery*, 1958.

TO BE AMONG them made every day good. Theirs was a beaten, battered division, almost drained of flesh and blood, its rifle companies cut to fifteen or twenty men per unit. They understood the enormity of their misfortune, yet the few who survived glorified it by their spirit.

Brigadier-General S.L.A. Marshall, of the men of the Second Infantry Division in 1951, *Bringing Up the Rear*, 1979.

SPIT AND POLISH

BAD LUCK to this marching,
Pipe-claying and starching;
How neat one must be to be killed by the French!

Soldiers' song from the Peninsular War, 1811, *Mickey Free's* lyrical complaint to the 14th Light Dragoons, quoted in C. Lever, *Charles O'Malley*, 1905.

THE EASIEST and quickest path into the esteem of traditional military authorities is by the appeal to the eye rather than to the mind. The "polish and pipeclay" school is not yet extinct, and it is easier for the mediocre intelligence to become an authority on buttons than on tactics. (March 1925.)

Captain Sir Basil Liddell Hart, *Thoughts on War*, 1944.

THE WAY of endurance lay primarily in deadening reflection with action; but where action was restricted, trivialities came to the rescue. Here rests the defence not only for gossip and "camp rumours" but for much seemingly futile "spit and polish". In the training camp its abuse was a hindrance to the development of military intelligence, and thus a handicap on war efficiency, yet in the rest camp it had a healing virtue that has often been misunderstood, not least by its advocates.

Captain Sir Basil Liddell Hart, *The Memoirs of Captain Liddell Hart*, 1965.

WHEN spit-and-polish are laid on so heavily that they become onerous, and the ranks cannot see any legitimate connection between the requirements and the development of an attitude which will serve as clear fighting purpose, it is to be questioned that the exactions serve any good object whatever.

Brigadier-General S.L.A. Marshall, *The Armed Forces Officer*, 1950.

SPORT

AGGRESSIVE fighting for the right is the noblest sport the world affords.

President Theodore Roosevelt (1858–1919), *The Works of Theodore Roosevelt*, XV, 1926, p. xxxiii.

UPON the fields of friendly strife
Are sown the seeds

That, upon other fields, on other days
Will bear the fruits of victory.

General of the Army Douglas MacArthur, *Reminiscences*, 1964, p. 82; lines written by MacArthur while Superintendent at West Point (1919–1922), which he ordered to be carved over the entrance to the gymnasium.

NOTHING more quickly than competitive athletics brings out the qualities of leadership, quickness of decision, promptness of action, mental and muscular co-ordination, aggressiveness, and courage. And nothing so firmly establishes that indefinable spirit of group interest and pride which we know as morale.

General of the Army Douglas MacArthur, c. 1919–1922, while Superintent at West Point, quoted in Francis Miller, *General Douglas MacArthur*, 1942.

LORD WELLINGTON is supposed to have said that the battle of Waterloo was won on the cricket fields of England . . . I believe it to be almost universally accepted as sound policy that the cultivation of athletics in a military organization is extremely beneficial to the personnel from the standpoint of improved physique and improved morale. For these reasons, a comprehensive athletic policy for the Marine Corps was put into effect, and athletic activity, especially in connection with football and baseball, everywhere prevailed.

Major-General John A. Lejeune, *The Reminiscences of a Marine*, 1929.

IN SPORT, in courage, and in the sight of Heaven, all men must meet on equal terms.

Sir Winston S. Churchill (1874–1965).

AT WEST POINT I learned how important it is to provide opportunities for "friendly strife" to warriors. Through fiercely competitive athletics, the warrior spirit is strengthened. Sports build a soldier's confidence, stamina and physical strength – qualities that are much needed in combat. Team sports are especially effective at revealing the importance of a well thought out, flexible strategy, knowledge of the opponent's (and one's own) strengths and weaknesses, clear goals and objectives and clearly defined roles for each member of the team. They also reveal the importance of esprit de corps, belief in the wisdom of the team's leaders, and belief in the capabilities of oneself and the other team members.

Major-General Bernard Loeffke, *From Warrior to Healer*, 1998.

THE STAFF

BUT ABOVE ALL, a general should take care to have men of proven fidelity, wisdom, and long experience in military affairs near his person as a sort of council. From such men a general may learn not only the state of his own army, but also that of the enemy's.

Niccolo Machiavelli, *The Art of War*, 1521.

IN ALL AGES and times, all emperors, kings, and formed commonwealths . . . have established a council of men of great sufficiency both in war and peace to assist their generals. . . . to the intent that their generals in all important matters should consult with them, the conclusion and resolution of such consultations notwithstanding to remain in the wisdom, judgment, and valor of the generals.

John Smythe (c. 1580–1631), *Certain Discourses Military*, 1966.

LARGE STAFFS – small victories.

Field Marshal Prince Aleksandr V. Suvorov (1729–1800).

THIS OFFICER [liaison officer] must set down nothing by hearsay. He must see everything with his own eyes, report nothing but what he has seen; and, when he is obliged to report something that he has not seen, say that he has not seen it.

Napoleon, August 1803, instructions to his aide-de-camp, Philippe de Ségur, quoted in S.J. Watson, *By Command of the Emperor*, 1957.

EVERY STAFF OFFICER must be considered as acting under the direct orders and superintendence of the superior officer for whose assistance he is employed, and who is responsible for his acts. To consider the relative situation of the general officer and the staff officer in any other light, would tend to alter the nature of the Service, and, in fact, might give the command of the troops to a subaltern staff officer instead of to their general officer.

The Duke of Wellington, cited in Sir Charles Oman, *Wellington's Army*, 1913.

A GOOD STAFF has the advantage of being more lasting than the genius of a single man.

Lieutenant-General Antoine-Henri Baron de Jomini, *Summary of the Art of War*, 1838, tr. Mendell and Craighill, 1862.

I DO NOT WANT to make an appointment on my staff except of such as are early risers.

Lieutenant-General Thomas J. 'Stonewall' Jackson, 1862, letter to his wife.

A BULKY STAFF implies a division of responsibility, slowness of action, and indecision, whereas a small staff implies activity and concentration of purpose. The smallness of Grant's staff throughout the civil war forms the best model for future generations.

General of the Army William T. Sherman, *The Memoirs of General W.T. Sherman*, 1875.

THE MORE intimately it [the staff] comes into contact

with the troops, the more useful and valuable it becomes. The almost entire separation of the staff from the line, as now practiced by us, and hitherto by the French, has proved mischievous, and the great retinues of staff-officers with which some of our earlier generals began the war were simply ridiculous.

General of the Army William T. Sherman, *The Memoirs of General W.T. Sherman*, 1875.

GREAT CAPTAINS have no need for counsel. They study the questions which arise, and decide them, and their entourage has only to execute their decisions. But such generals are stars of the first magnitude who scarcely appear once in a century. In the great majority of cases, the leader of the army cannot do without advice. This advice may be the outcome of the deliberations of a small number of qualified men. But within this small number, one and only one opinion must prevail. The organization of the military hierarchy must ensure subordination even in thought and give the right and duty of presenting a single opinion for the examination of the general-in-chief to one man and only one.

Field Marshal Helmuth Graf von Moltke, 1862, letter.

THAT IS just one illustration of how time may be lost in handling troops, and of the need of an abundance of competent staff officers by the generals in command. Scarcely any of our generals had half of what they needed to keep a *constant & close supervision on the execution of important orders*. And that always to be done. An army is like a great machine, and in putting it into battle it is not enough for a commander to merely issue the necessary orders. He should have a staff ample to supervise the execution of each step, & to promptly report any difficulty or misunderstanding.

Brigadier-General Edward Porter Alexander, of the delays in positioning troops at Gettysburg on 2 July 1863, *Fighting for the Confederacy* (written between 1900 and 1907, but not published until 1989).

THE TYPICAL staff officer is the man past middle life, spare, unwrinkled, intelligent, cold, passive, noncommittal; with eyes like a codfish, polite in contact but at the same time unresponsive, cool, calm and as damnably composed as a concrete post or a plaster-of-paris cast; a human petrification with a heart of feldspar and without charm or the friendly germ; minus bowels, passion or a sense of humor. Happily they never reproduce and all of them finally go to hell.

General Freiherr Kurt von Hammerstein Equord (1878–1943).

NO MILITARY or naval force, in war, can accomplish anything worthwhile unless there is back of it the work of an efficient, loyal, and devoted staff.

Lieutenant-General Hunter Liggett (1857–1935).

WITHOUT a staff, an army could not peel a potato.

Lieutenant-General Hunter Liggett (1857–1935).

THERE IS a type of staff officer who seems to think that it is more important to draft immaculate orders than to get out a reasonably well-worded order in time for action to be taken before the situation changes or the opportunity passes. (June 1933.)

Captain Sir Basil Liddell Hart, *Thoughts on War*, 1944.

THE STAFF becomes an all-controlling bureaucracy, a paper octopus squirting ink and wriggling its tentacles into every corner. Unless pruned with an axe it will grow like a fakir's mango tree, and the more it grows the more it overshadows the general. It creates work, it creates offices, and, above all, it creates rear-spirit. No sooner is a war declared than the general-in-chief (and many a subordinate general also) finds himself a Gulliver in Lilliput, tied down to his office stool by innumerable threads woven out of the brains of his staff and superior staffs.

Major-General J.F.C. Fuller, *Generalship: Its Diseases and Their Cure*, 1933.

A YES MAN on a staff is a menace to a commander. One with the courage of his convictions is an asset.

Major-General Orlando Ward, c. 1934.

THE MILITARY STAFF must be adequately composed: it must contain the best brains in the fields of land, air, and sea warfare, propaganda war, technology, economics, politics and also those who know the people's life.

General Erich Ludendorff, *Total War*, 1935.

A PERFECT COMMANDER is a man who does things by himself and of his own will [in furtherance of the objectives set down by his government's policy makers]. He will have about him aides to advise, and to put into execution what he demands and without whom the greatest genius cannot prevail. [These assistants comprise the commander's staff]. They are indeed his instruments, who as men understand the machinery of transmitting orders, as the soldier understands his weapons. But they must retire behind the personality of their chief.

Colonel Hermann Foertsch, *The Art of Modern War*, 1940.

THEM potted palms up at division, they get promoted because they can write a good letter.

General Lewis 'Chesty' Puller, 1942, when a battalion commander on Guadalcanal, quoted in Merrill B. Twining, *No Bended Knee*, 1994.

ONE of the inevitable problems with the Marine Corps or any other military service is that staff officers take over the minute a war is ended. The combat people run things when the chips are down and the country's life is at stake but when the guns stop, nobody's got a use for a combat man.

The staff officers are like rats; they stream out of hiding and take over. It's true. Just watch what happens to paperwork. God, in peacetime they put

out enough to sink a small-size nation into the sea – and when war breaks, most of it just naturally stops. That's the way they do everything. There must always be staff people, of course, or we'd never get anything done – but if we don't stop this empire building of the staff, somebody's going to come along and lick us one of these days. We'll be so knotted in red tape that we can't move.

Lieutenant-General Lewis 'Chesty' Puller, June 1946, letter to his wife, quoted in Burke Davis, *Marine*, 1962.

THERE IS certainly no black magic about becoming a successful Army staff officer in the field. Youth and brains are the important things. With a comparatively small amount of training and experience most staff appointments can be filled by non-regulars. In 21st Army Group a number of important posts were held by young ex-civilians. One could not have wished for better men.

Montgomery backed youth and the "clever chap," and this policy paid him enormously.

Major-General Sir Francis de Guingand, *Operation Victory*, 1947.

STAFF WORK . . . has its own particular rewards. Chief among them are the broadening of perspective, a more intimate contact with the views, working methods, and personality characteristics of higher commanders and chance to become acquainted with administrative responsibility from the viewpoint of policy. Although it sounds mysterious and even forbidding until one has done it, the procedures are not more complex or less instructive than in any other type of assignment.

Brigadier-General S.L.A. Marshall, *The Armed Forces Officer*, 1950.

WHEN you carry a paper in here, I want you to give me every reason you can think of why I should not approve it. If, in spite of your objections, my decision is still to go ahead, then I'll know I'm right.

General of the Army George C. Marshall, instructions to his staff, quoted in Bradley, *A Soldier's Story*, 1951.

I NOW WANT you to consider the general in relation to his troops. I will begin with a few words about his staff, who are the means by which he controls and directs his army. I will give you two simple rules which every general should observe: first, never to try to do his own staff work; and, secondly, never to let his staff get between him and his troops. What a staff appreciates is that it should receive clear and definite instructions, and then be left to work out the details without interference. What troops and subordinate commanders appreciate is that a general should be constantly in personal contact with them, and should not see everything simply through the eyes of his staff. The less time a general spends in his office and the more with his troops the better.

Field Marshal Viscount Wavell of Cyrenaica, *Soldiers and Soldiering*, 1953.

I WAS EVACUATED to hospital in England and for some months I took no further part in the war. I had time for reflection in hospital and came to the conclusion that the old adage was probably correct: the pen was mightier than the sword. I joined the staff.

> Field Marshal Viscount Montgomery of Alamein, after being wounded in 1914, *The Memoirs of Field Marshal Montgomery*, 1958.

MY WAR experience led me to believe that the staff must be the servants of the troops, and that a good staff officer must serve his commander and the troops but himself be anonymous.

> Field Marshal Viscount Montgomery of Alamein, *The Memoirs of Field Marshal Montgomery*, 1958.

THE QUALITIES of a leader are not limited to commanders. The requirements for leadership are just as essential in the staff officer, and in some respects more exacting, since he does not have that ultimate authority which can be used when necessary and must rely even more than his commander on his own strength of character, his tact and persuasion in carrying out his duties.

> General Matthew B. Ridgway, 'Leadership', *Military Review*, 10/1966.

IT'S LIKE dropping a pound of mercury on the floor. It scatters all over but pretty soon you find it all together over in the corner of the room.

> General Creighton Abrams (1914–1974), speaking of the difficulty in reducing the Army Staff, quoted in *Military Review*, 4/1985.

THE STAFF is there because it serves a vital purpose. Recognition is rare, medals are few, but the successful staff officer can at least take pride in having served as midwife at the birth of great events.

> General Merrill B. Twining, *No Bended Knee*, 1994.

IT'S MY "porcupine" theory of command. No commander can know everything. He must rely on deputies, competent in the narrow areas assigned them. His responsibility is to make sure none of them tugs the blanket to one side of the bed. A deputy who answers "Yes, sir" to every stupid thing his commander says can get his boss into serious trouble. He must have the courage to take a stand and be able to defend it.

> Lieutenant-General Aleksandr Lebed, *Time Magazine*, 27 February 1995.

STRATEGY

ATTACK BY STRATEGEM. Sun Tzu said: In the practical art of war, the best thing of all is to take the enemy's country whole and intact; to shatter and destroy it is not so good. So, too, it is better to capture an army entire than to destroy it, to capture a regiment, detachment or a company entire than to destroy them.

Hence to fight and conquer in all your battles is not supreme excellence; supreme excellence consists of breaking the enemy's resistance without fighting.

> Sun Tzu, *The Art of War*, 3, c., 500 BC, tr. Giles, 1910.

IN PLANNING, never a useless move; in strategy, no step taken in vain.

> Ch'ên Hao, early commentator on Sun Tzu, *The Art of War*, 4., tr. Samuel Griffith, 1963.

I KNOW WELL that war is a great evil and the worst of all evils. But since our enemies clearly look upon the shedding of blood as one of their basic duties and the height of virtue, and since each one must stand up for his country and his own people with word, pen, and deed, we have decided to write about strategy. But putting it into practice we shall be able not only to resist our enemies but even to conquer them. . . . Strategy is the means by which a commander may defend his own lands and defeat his enemies. The general is the one who practices strategy.

> Anonymous Byzantine general, *On Strategy*, c. AD 527–565, quoted in George Dennis, *Three Byzantine Military Treatises*, 1985.

THE MOST COMPLETE and happy victory is this: to compel one's enemy to give up his purpose, while suffering no harm oneself.

> Count Belisarius (c. AD 505–565).

STRATEGY is the craft of the warrior.

> Miyamoto Musashi, *A Book of Five Rings*, 1645, tr. Victor Harris, 1984.

STRATEGY is based on the forces you have, on the strength of the enemy, on the situation of the country where you want to carry the war, and on the actual political condition of Europe.

> Frederick the Great (1712–1786), 'Pensées et règles générales pour la guerre', *Oeuvres de Frederic le Grand*, XXVIII, 1846–1856.

STRATEGY means the combination of individual engagements to attain the goal of the campaign.

> Major-General Carl von Clausewitz, *Principles of War*, 1812, tr. Gatzke, 1942.

STRATEGY is the science of making use of space and time. I am more jealous of the latter than of the former. We can always recover lost ground, but never lost time.

> Field Marshal August Graf von Gneisenau (1761–1831), quoted in Hermann Foertsch, *The Art of Modern War*, 1940.

. . . THE ART of employment of battles as a means to gain the object of the war.

> Major-General Carl von Clausewitz, *On War*, 1832, tr. Michael Howard and Peter Paret, 1976.

STRATEGY is a system of *ad hoc* expedients; it is more than knowledge, it is the application of knowledge to practical life, the development of an original idea in accordance with continually changing circumstances. It is the art of action under the pressure of the most difficult conditions.

Field Marshal Helmut Graf von Moltke, quoted in Edward Earle, ed., *Makers of Modern Strategy*, 1943.

STRATEGY is a system of makeshifts. It is more than a science, it is the application of science to practical affairs; it is carrying through an originally conceived plan under a constantly shifting set of circumstances. It is the art of acting under the pressure of the most difficult kind of conditions. Strategy is the application of common sense in the work of leading an army; its teachings hardly go beyond the first requirement of common sense; its value lies entirely in its concrete application. It is a matter of understanding correctly at every moment a constantly changing situation, and then doing the simplest and most natural thing with energy and determination. This is what makes war an art, an art that is served by many sciences. Like every art, war cannot be learned rationally, but only by experience. In war, as in art, there can be no set standards nor can code of rules take the place of brains.

Field Marshal Helmuth Graf von Moltke, *On Strategy*, 1871.

A CLEVER military leader will succeed in many cases in choosing defensive positions of such an offensive nature from the strategic point of view that the enemy is compelled to attack us in them.

Field Marshal Helmuth Graf von Moltke (1800–1891).

THE MAIN THING in true strategy is simply this: first deal as hard blows at the enemy's soldiers as possible, and then cause so much suffering to the inhabitants of a country that they will long for peace and press their Government to make it. Nothing should be left to the people but eyes to lament the war.

General of the Army Phillip H. Sheridan, quoted in Forbes, *Memories and Studies in War and Peace*, 1895.

BUT even if history had not shown that principles of strategy have held good under circumstances so many and various that they may be justly assured of universal value, to sea as well as to land, there would still remain the same mental training afforded by the examination of successive modifications that have been introduced into the art of war by the great generals.

Rear-Admiral Alfred Thayer Mahan, 6 August 1888, address at the U.S. Naval War College.

AS IN A BUILDING, which, however fair and beautiful the superstructure, is radically marred and imperfect if the foundation be insecure – so, if the strategy be wrong, the skill of the general on the battlefield, the valor of the soldier, the brilliancy

of the victory, however otherwise decisive, fail of their effect.

Rear-Admiral Alfred Thayer Mahan, *Naval Administration and Warfare*, 1908.

PRINCIPLES of strategy never transcend common sense.

Motto of the highest school of the German Army before 1914, quoted in Leon Trotsky, *Military Writings*, 1967.

WHERE the strategist is empowered to seek a military decision, his responsibility is to seek it under the most advantageous circumstances in order to produce the most profitable results. Hence *his true aim is not so much to seek battle, as to seek a strategic situation so advantageous that if it does not of itself produce the decision, its continuation by a battle is sure to achieve this*. In other words, dislocation is the aim of strategy; its sequel may be either the enemy's dissolution or his disruption in battle. Dissolution may involve some partial measure of fighting, but this has not the character of a battle. (Oct. 1928.)

Captain Sir Basil Liddell Hart, *Thoughts on War*, 1944.

IT IS the art of strategy to bring about a battle under the most favorable conditions possible, both as to the ground and the timing, and to force it on the opponent under conditions that are most unpropitious to him.

Colonel Hermann Foertsch, *The Art of Modern War*, 1940.

KILL JAPS, kill Japs, and keep on killing Japs.

Admiral of the Fleet William 'Bull' Halsey, strategy for winning the war, November 1942, quoted in E.B. Potter, *Bull Halsey*, 1985.

STRATEGY is the determination of the direction of the main blow – The plan of strategy is the plan of the organization of the decisive blow in the direction in which the blow can most quickly give the maximum results.

In other words, *to define the direction of the main blow means to predetermine the nature of operations in the whole period of war, to determine nine-tenths of the fate of the entire war*. In this is the main task of strategy.

Joseph Stalin, quoted in R.L. Garthoff, *Soviet Military Doctrine*, 1953.

THE AIM of strategy is to clinch a political argument by means of force instead of words. Normally this is accomplished by battle, the true object of which is not physical destruction, but mental submission on the part of the enemy.

Major-General J.F.C. Fuller, *Armoured Warfare*, 1943.

THE HISTORY of strategy is, fundamentally, a record of the application and evolution of the indirect approach.

Captain Sir Basil Liddell Hart, *Strategy*, 1954.

. . . THE ART of distributing and applying the military means to fulfill the ends of policy.
> Captain Sir Basil Liddell Hart, *Strategy*, 1954.

THE ESSENCE of strategy is the abstract interplay which, to use Foch's phrase, springs from the clash between two opposing wills. It is the art which enables a man, no matter what the techniques employed, to master the problems set by any clash of wills and as a result to employ the techniques available with maximum efficiency. It is therefore the art of the dialectic of force or, more precisely, *the art of the dialectic of two opposing wills using force to resolve their dispute*.
> General Andre Beaufre, *An Introduction to Strategy*, 1965.

THE LAWS of strategy are objective and apply impartially to both hostile sides.
> Marshal of the Soviet Union V.D. Sokolovksiy, *Soviet Military Strategy* (Third edition), 1968.

LESSON NO. 1 from Fuller: "To anticipate strategy, imagine."
Lesson No. 2 from Martel: "Men, not weapons, will shape the future, so stick with fundamentals."
> Brigadier-General S.L.A. Marshall, referring to Generals J.F.C. Fuller and Giffard Martel, *Bringing Up the Rear*, 1979.

THERE ARE probably more kinds of strategy, and more definitions of it, than there are varieties and definitions of economics or politics. It is a loose sort of a word.
> Rear-Admiral Joseph C. Wylie, *Military Strategy: A General Theory of Power Control* 1967.

OUR STRATEGY to go after this army is very, very simple. First we're going to cut it off, and then we're going to kill it.
> General Colin Powell, *The Washington Post*, 23 January 1991, speaking of the Iraqi Army just before the beginning of Operation Desert Storm.

STRATEGY is theology with the hope left out.
> Lieutenant-Colonel Ralph Peters, *Fighting for the Future*, 1999.

STRENGTH

NOW lead the way, wherever your fighting spirit bids you.
All of us right behind you, hearts intent on battle.
Nor do I think you'll find us short on courage,
long as our strength will last. Past his strength
no man can go,though he's set on mortal combat.
> Homer, *The Iliad*, 13.908–912, c. 800 BC, tr. Robert Fagles, 1990; Prince Paris to his brother, Hector.

LIKE STRENGTH is felt from hope, and from despair, and each contends, as his were all the war.
> Homer, *The Iliad*, 15.852, c. 800 BC, tr. Alexander Pope, 1743, 1715–1720; describing the climactic struggle at the ships.

A GREAT PRINCIPLE only carries weight when it is associated with the movement of great forces.
> Sir Winston S. Churchill (1874–1965).

PEACE is our aim and strength the only way of getting it.
> Sir Winston S. Churchill (1874–1965).

IF WE ARE STRONG, our character will speak for itself. If we are weak, words will be of no help.
> President John F. Kennedy, undelivered address, Dallas, 22 November 1963.

STRESS

IN THIS SITUATION the real leaders of the Army stood forth in bold contrast to those of ordinary clay. Men who had sustained a reputation for soldierly qualities, under less trying conditions, proved too weak for the ordeal and became pessimistic calamity howlers. Their organizations were quickly infected with the spirit and grew ineffective unless a more suitable commander was given charge. It was apparent that the combination of tired muscles, physical discomforts, and heavy casualties weakened the backbone of many. Officers who were not in perfect physical condition usually lost the will to conquer and took an exceedingly gloomy view of the situation.
> General of the Army George C. Marshall, *Memoirs of My Services in the World War* (written between 1923 and 1926, but not published until 1976).

THE GENERAL is dealing with men's lives, and must have a certain mental robustness to stand the strain of this responsibility.
> Field Marshal Viscount Wavell of Cyrenaica, *Generals and Generalship*, 1941.

[I] REALIZED how inexorably and inescapably strain and tension wear away at the leader's endurance, his judgment and his confidence. The pressure becomes more acute because of the duty of a staff constantly to present the commander the worst side of an eventuality. In this situation, the commander has to preserve optimism in himself and in his command. Without confidence, enthusiasm and optimism in the command, victory is impossible.
> General of the Army Dwight D. Eisenhower, quoted in *Military Review*, 10/1990.

THE MILITARY is a long, hard road, and it makes extraordinary requirements of every individual. In war, particularly, it puts stresses upon men such as

they have not known elsewhere, and the temptation to "get our from under" would be irresistable if their spirits had not been tempered to the ordeal.
Brigadier-General S.L.A. Marshall, *The Armed Forces Officer*, 1950.

ONE of the common ways that seniors induce self-defeating stress in their juniors is to over-supervise them. Another is to summon them repeatedly to report in person about inconsequential administrative details.
Major-General Aubrey 'Red' Newman, *Follow Me*, 1981.

STRESS is essential to leadership. Living with stress, knowing how to handle pressure, is necessary for survival. It is related to a man's ability to wrest control over his own destiny from the circumstances that surround him. Or, if you like, to prevail over technology. Tied up with this ability is something I can express in one word, "improvisation." I mean man's ability to prepare a response to a situation while under pressure.
Admiral James Stockdale, 'Education for Leadership and Survival', *Military Ethics*, 1987.

STRIKE WEAKNESS

YOU MAY ADVANCE and be absolutely irresistible, if you make for the enemy's weak points; you may retire and be safe from pursuit if your movements are more rapid than those of the enemy.
Sun Tzu, *The Art of War*, 6, c. 500 BC, tr. Giles, 1910.

MILITARY TACTICS are like unto water; for water in its natural course runs away from high places and hastens downwards. So in war, the way to avoid what is strong is to strike what is weak.
Sun Tzu, *The Art of War*, 6, c. 500 BC, tr. Giles, 1910.

ANOTHER sound principle is always to aim for the weak point of the enemy's position, even if it is a long way off. After all, pushing yourself to make a great effort is less risky than engaging a superior force.
Xenophon, *How To Be A Good Cavalry Commander*, c. 360 BC (*Hiero the Tyrant and Other Treatises*, tr. Robin Waterfield, 1997).

TO MAKE SURE you attack where there is no defense is what is crucial to warriorship. . . .
Sun Bin, *The Lost Art of War*, c. 350 BC, tr. Thomas Cleary.

GO INTO emptiness, strike voids, bypass what he defends, hit him where he does not expect you.
The 'Martial' Emperor Ts'ao Ts'ao (AD 155–220), commentary to Sun Tzu, *The Art of War*, 6, c. 500 BC, tr. Samuel Griffith, 1963.

PRESIDENT of the Directoire: "You often defeated a stronger foe with fewer forces."
Bonaparte: "But in this case, too, the lesser forces

still suffered defeat at the hands of the larger forces. With an enemy army superior in numbers against me, I dashed like lightning to its flank, smashed it, took advantage of the enemy's disarray, and again rushed with all my forces to other points. Thus, I inflicted defeat piecemeal, and the victory which I won was, as you see, nothing more than the victory of the stronger over the weaker."
Napoleon, quoted in Colonel V.Ye. Savkin, *Operational Art and Tactics*, 1972.

EVERYBODY has a weak spot, and the first thing I try to do is to find out where it is, and pitch into it with the biggest shell or shot that I have, and repeat that dose until it operates.
Admiral David G. Farragut, quoted in Alfred Thayer Mahan, *Admiral Farragut*.

WE WON the victory where it was easy to win and not over something that was hard to conquer. . . . each division of the combined squadrons did its work well and not more. There was nothing remarkable in our bravery. We regard ourselves as a fit example of good fight. . . .
Admiral Marquis Heihachiro Togo, remarking on the Battle of Tsushima (27–28 May 1905), quoted in Dennis and Peggy Warner, *The Tide at Sunrise*, 1974.

UNLESS very urgent reasons to the contrary exist, strike at one end rather than at the middle, because both ends can come up to help the middle against you quicker than one can can get to help the other; and, as between the two ends, strike at the one upon which the enemy most depends for reinforcements and supplies to maintain his strength.
Rear-Admiral Alfred Thayer Mahan, *Sea Power in its Relations with the War of 1812*, 1905.

HAVE BEEN giving everyone a simplified directive of war. Use steamroller strategy; that is, make up your mind on course and direction of action, and stick to it. But in tactics, do not steamroller. Attack weakness. Hold them by the nose and kick them in the pants.
General George S. Patton, Jr., 6 November 1942, *War As I Knew It*, 1947.

STYLE

IN the profession of war, like that of letters, each man has his style.
Napoleon, 6 June 1806, letter to Joseph, *Correspondance de Napoléon Ier, publiée par ordre de l'Empereur Napoléon III*, No. 10325, Vol. XII, 1858–1870.

AT THE HEAD of an army, nothing is more becoming than simplicity.
Napoleon, *Political Aphorisms*, 1848.

STYLE . . . is first and above all the expression of a man's personality, as characteristic as any other trait; or, as some one has said – was it Buffon? – style is the man himself. From this point of view it is susceptible of training, of development, or of pruning; but to attempt to pattern it on that of another person is a mistake. For one chance of success there are a dozen of failure; for you are trying to raise a special product from a soil probably uncongenial, or a fruit from an alien stem – figs from vines.
  Rear-Admiral Alfred Thayer Mahan, *From Sail to Steam*, 1907.

THERE ARE apparently two types of successful soldiers. Those who get on by being unobtrusive and those who get on by being obtrusive. I am of the latter type and seem to be rare and unpopular; but it is my method. One has to choose a system and stick to it. People who are not themselves are nobody.
  General George S. Patton, Jr., 6 June 1944, *The Patton Papers*, II, 1974.

ONE of my cardinal rules of battle leadership – or leadership in any profession – is to be yourself, to strive to apply the basic principles of the art of war, and to seek to accomplish your assigned missions by your own methods in your own way.
  General Matthew B. Ridgway, *The Korean War*, 1967.

SUBORDINATES

ENCOURAGE and listen well to the words of your subordinates. It is well known that gold lies hidden underground.
  Nabeshima Naoshige (1538–1618), quoted in William Wilson, *Ideals of the Samurai*, 1982.

A MAJOR GULF exists between a commander-in-chief – a general who leads the army as a whole or commands in a theater of operations – and the senior generals immediately subordinate to him. The reason is simple: the second level is subjected to much closer control and supervision, and thus gives far less scope for independent thought. People therefore often think outstanding intellectual ability is called for only at the top, and that for all other duties common intelligence will suffice. A general of lesser responsibility, an officer grown gray in the service, his mind well-blinkered by long years of routine, may often be considered to have developed a certain stodginess; his gallantry is respected, but his simplemindedness makes us smile. We do not intend to champion and promote these good men; it would contribute nothing to their efficiency, and little to their happiness.
  Major-General Carl von Clausewitz, *On War*, 1.3, 1832, tr. Michael Howard and Peter Paret, 1976.

WHILST I have been eminently successful in this War, in at least gaining the confidence of the public, no one feels more than me how much of this success is due to the energy and skill, of those who it has been my good fortune to have occupying a subordinate position under me. There are many officers to whom these remarks are applicable to a greater or less degree, proportionate to their ability as soldiers, but what I want is to express my thanks to you and McPherson as the men to whom, above all others, I feel indebted for whatever I have had of success. How far your advice and suggestions have been of assistance, you know. How far your execution of whatever has been given you to do entitles you to the reward I am receiving you cannot know as well as me. I feel all the gratitude this letter would express, giving it the most flattering construction.
  General of the Army Ulysses S. Grant, 4 March 1864, letter to General Sherman, *Personal Memoirs and Selected Letters*, 1990.

TODAY I decided to stay in . . . There is nothing that I can do at the front except bother people, as they are all doing a swell job, and I believe advancing very rapidly. One of the hardest things that I have to do to – and I presume any General has to do – is not to interfere with the next echelon of command when the show is going all right.
  General George S. Patton, Jr., 18 November 1944, letter to his sister Nita, *The Patton Papers*, II, 1974.

COMMANDERS and staffs should visit units two echelons below their own, and their maps should be so kept. In other words, Corps Commanders or their staffs should visit Division and Regimental Command Posts; the Division Commander should visit Regimental and Battalion Command Posts; the visits above referred to are for command purposes. What might be called inspirational visits should go farther up. The more senior the officer who appears with a very small unit at the front, the better the effect on the troops. If some danger is involved in the visit, its value is enhanced.
  General George S. Patton, Jr., *Was As I Knew It*, 1947.

THE MORE SENIOR the officer, the more time he has. Therefore, the senior should go forward to visit the junior rather than call the junior back to see him. The exception to this is when it is necessary to collect several commanders for the formulation of a coordinated plan.
  General George S. Patton, Jr., *War As I Knew It*, 1947.

THERE HAVE BEEN great and distinguished leaders in our military Services at all levels who had no particular gifts for administration and little for organizing the detail of decisive action either within battle or without. They excelled because of a superior ability to make use of the brains and command the loyalty of well-chosen subordinates. Their particular function was to judge the goal according to their resources and audacity, and then to hold the team steady until the goal was gained. So doing, they complemented the power of the faithful lieutenants who might have put them in the shade in any IQ test.

Brigadier-General S.L.A. Marshall, *The Armed Forces Officer*, 1950.

OF COURSE a commander must know in what way to give verbal orders to his subordinates. No two will be the same; each will require different treatment. Some will react differently from the others; some will be happy with a general directive whilst others will like more detail. Eventually a mutual confidence on the subject will grow up between the commander and his subordinates; once this has been achieved there will never be any more difficulties or misunderstandings.

Field Marshal Viscount Montgomery of Alamein, *The Memoirs of Field Marshal Montgomery*, 1958.

CLOSELY AKIN to the relationship with staff officers is keeping in close personal touch with your principal subordinate commanders – in the division, with your brigade and separate battalion commanders; in the corps with your division commanders, their chiefs of staff, and as many of the commanders of attached corps units as you can; and in the army, with corps and division commanders and their chiefs of staff. There is always time for these visits; administrative work can be done at night. By day you belong with your troops.

General Matthew B. Ridgway, 'Leadership', *Military Review*, 10/1966.

I HAD TO WALK that tightrope familiar to all top commanders in any profession, civilian as well as military: To maintain the proper balance between according sufficient latitude to the subordinate commander in carrying out broadly stated directives, and in exercising adequate supervision, as befitted the man who would bear the ultimate responsibility for the success or failure of the entire effort.

General Matthew B. Ridgway, *The Korean War*, 1967.

SUBORDINATION

ONE CIRCUMSTANCE, in this important Business, ought to be cautiously guarded against, and that is, the Soldier and Officer being too nearly on a level. Discipline and Subordination add life and Vigour to Military movements. The person Commanded yields but a reluctant obedience to those, he conceives, are undeservedly made his Superiors. The degrees of Rank are frequently transferred from Civil Life into the Departments of the Army. The true criterion to judge by (when past Services do not enter into the Competition) is, to consider whether the Candidate for Office has a just pretention to the Character of a Gentleman, a proper sense of Honor, and some reputation to loose.

General George Washington, 5 October 1776, letter to Governor Patrick Henry of Virginia, *The Writings of George Washington*, VI, p. 167, John C. Fitzgerald, ed., 1932.

TO BRING MEN to a proper degree of subordination is not the work of a day, a month, or a year.

General George Washington, quoted in S.L.A. Marshall, *The Armed Forces Officer*, 1950.

SUBORDINATION is the mother of discipline, or the art of war.

Field Marshal Prince Aleksandr V. Suvorov, field training order issued after the Battle of Kinburn in 1787, quoted in K. Ossipov, *Suvorov*, 1945.

SUCCESS

'TIS MAN'S to fight, but Heaven's to give success.

Homer, *The Iliad*, 6.427, c. 800 BC, tr. Alexander Pope, 1743.

SUCCESS is a matter of planning and it is only careless people who find that Heaven will not help their mortal designs.

Themistocles, 480 BC, the year of the Battle of Salamis, quoted in Herodotus (c. 484–420 BC), *The Struggle for Greece*, tr. Cavandar.

AND LET the strongest motive, which actuates men come to your minds, namely, pride in past achievement. For it is a shame, for those at least who have reason, to fall short of one's own self and to be found inferior to one's own standard of valour.

Count Belisarius, December AD 533, address to his army before the Battle of Tricamarum in North Africa, in which he destroyed the last hope of the Vandals, quoted in Procopius, *History of the Wars*, 4.1, c. AD 560, tr. H.B. Dewing.

WHOSOEVER desires constant success must change his conduct with the times.

Niccolo Machiavelli, *Discourses*, 1517.

IT WILL BE a consolation to you to reflect that the thinking part of Mankind do not form their judgment from events; and that their equity will ever attach equal glory to those actions which deserve success, as to those which have been crowned with it.

General George Washington, 11 September 1778, to General Comte d'Estaing, *The Writings of George Washington*, XII, John C. Fitzgerald, ed., 1934.

ALTHOUGH I cannot insure success, I will endeavour to deserve it.

Admiral John Paul Jones, 1780, letter.

I AM SURE you will deserve success. To mortals is not given the power of commanding it.

Admiral Lord St. Vincent, 14 July 1797, letter to Nelson before sailing against Tenerife.

THEY WON'T draw me from my cautious system. I'll fight them only where I am pretty sure of success.

The Duke of Wellington, autumn 1810, while watching

Marshal Masséna's army starving outside his lines at Torres Vedres, *Supplementary Despatches, Correspondence, and Memoranda of Field Marshal Arthur Duke of Wellington, K.G., 1794–1818*, VI, 1858–1872, p. 612.

SUCCESS is only to be obtained by simultaneous efforts, directed upon a given point, sustained with constancy, and executed with decision.

Archduke Charles of Austria (1771–1841).

. . . IN WAR many roads lead to success, and that they do not all involve the opponent's defeat. They range from *the destruction of the enemy's forces, the conquest of his territory, to a temporary occupation or invasion, to projects with an immediate purpose, and finally passively awaiting the enemy's attacks*. Any one of these may be used to overcome the enemy's will: the choice depends on the circumstances.

Major-General Carl von Clausewitz, *On War*, 1.2, 1832, tr. Michael Howard and Peter Paret, 1976.

SUCCESS in war, like charity in religion, covers a multitude of sins.

General Sir William Napier (1785–1860).

TO HAVE FOUGHT my own command daily, on equal terms and in open combats against the thousands that could have brought against it by the North, would soon have resulted in its entire annihilation. I endeavored to compensate for my limited resources by stratagems, surprises, and night attacks, in which the advantage was generally on my side, notwithstanding the superior numbers we assailed. For this reason, the complaint has often been made against me that I would not fight fair . . . in one sense the charge that I did not fight fair is true. I fought for success and not for display. There was no man in the Confederate army who had less of the spirit of knight-errantry in him, or took a more practical view of war than I did.

Colonel John S. Mosby, *Mosby's War Reminiscences*, 1887.

MY SUCCESS had been so uninterrupted that the men thought that victory was chained to my standard. Men who go into a fight under the influence of such feelings are next to invincible, and generally are the victors before it begins.

Colonel John S. Mosby, *Mosby's War Reminiscences*, 1887.

TOO MUCH SUCCESS is not wholly desirable; an occasional beating is good for men – and nations.

Rear-Admiral Alfred Thayer Mahan, *The Life of Nelson*, 1897.

A MAN who says that his success is due to himself is a fool. Success is one-third ability and two-thirds good fortune – or perhaps more exactly, one-third ability, one third luck (or providence), and one-third

the power to "stick it", to keep on pegging away until fortune turns, as it usually does sooner or later. (Oct. 1932.)

Captain Sir Basil Liddell Hart, *Thoughts on War*, 1944.

SUCCESS is how high you bounce when you hit bottom.

General George S. Patton (1889–1945), quoted in *Reader's Digest*, April 1995, p. 177.

NO ONE can guarantee success in war, but only deserve it.

Sir Winston S. Churchill, *Their Finest Hour*, 1948.

SUCCESS is disarming. Tension is the normal state of mind and body in combat. When the tension suddenly relaxes through the winning of a first objective, troops are apt to be pervaded by a sense of extreme well-being and there is apt to ensue laxness in all of its forms and with all of its dangers.

Brigadier-General S.L.A. Marshall, *Men Against Fire*, 1947.

POSSIBLY the big difference between the basic discipline of the front and rear areas could be best summed this way: when the chips are down, the main question is not how you go about your mission but whether it succeeds.

Brigadier-General S.L.A. Marshall, *Men Against Fire*, 1947.

WHAT IS SUCCESS? I think it is a mixture of having a flair for the thing that you are doing; knowing that it is not enough, that you have got to have hard work and a certain sense of purpose.

Prime Minister Margaret Thatcher, *Parade*, 13 July 1986.

THERE ARE no secrets to success; don't waste time looking for them . . . Success is the result of perfection, hard work, learning from failure, loyalty to those for whom you work and persistence. You must be ready for opportunity when it comes.

General Colin Powell, quoted in *The Washington Post*, 15 January 1989.

SUICIDE

AND THE BATTLE went sore against Saul, and the archers hit him; and he was sore wounded of the archers.
Then said Saul unto his armourbearer Draw thy sword, and thrust me through therewith; lest these uncircumcised come and thrust me through, and abuse me. But his armourbearer would not; for he was sore afraid. Therefore Saul took a sword, and fell upon it.

Samuel I, 31.3–4; of the death of King Saul fighting the Philistines at the Battle of Mount Gilboa c. 1006 BC.

S

YES, we must escape, but this time with our hands, not our feet.

> Marcus Brutus, shortly after his defeat at the Second Battle of Philippi, 26 November 42 BC, just before he fell upon his sword, quoted in Plutarch, *The Lives*, c. AD 100 (Makers of Rome, tr. Ian Scott-Kilvert, 1965).

YOU MUST NOT pity me in this last turn of fate. You should rather be happy in the remembrance of our love and in the recollection that of all men I was once the most powerful and now at the end have fallen not dishonourably, a Roman by a Roman vanquished.

> Mark Antony, 30 BC, to Cleopatra as he lay dying after falling upon his own sword following his flight from the destruction of the fleet at the Battle of Actium.

I FEEL that I am reserved for one end or other.

> Robert Lord Clive (1725–1774), comment when his pistol failed to go off twice when attempting to commit suicide.

THERE IS as much courage in supporting with firmness the afflictions of the soul as there is in standing steady under the grape of a battery of guns. To give one's self up to grief without resistance, to kill one's self to escape it, is to abandon the battlefield defeated.

> Napoleon, 14 May 1802, at St. Cloud, quoted in R.M. Johnston, ed., *The Corsican*, 1910.

DURING THE FIGHT at Aracis-sur-Aube I did all I could to meet with a glorious end defending the soil of our country inch by inch. I exposed myself continuously. Bullets rained all around me; my clothes were full of them; but not one touched me. I am condemned to live.

> Napoleon, 20 March 1814, quoted in R.M. Johnston, ed., *The Corsican*, 1910.

TO KILL MYSELF would be a gambler's death. I am condemned to live. Besides, only the dead do not return.

> Napoleon, 11 April 1814, after his abdication, *Correspondance de Napoléon Ier, publiée par ordre de l'Empereur Napoléon III*, Vol. XXXI, pp. 485–486, 1858–1870.

WHEN the nerves break down, there is nothing left but to admit that one can't handle the situation and to shoot oneself.

> Adolf Hitler, February 1943, upon hearing of the surrender of Field Marshal Paulus at Stalingrad, quoted in Clark, *Barbarossa*, 1965.

SUPERIORITY

BY DISCOVERING the enemy's dispositions and remaining invisible ourselves, we can keep our forces concentrated while the enemy must be divided.

We can form a single united body, while the enemy must split up into fractions. Hence there will be a whole pitted against separate parts of a whole, which means that we shall be many to the enemy's few.

And if we are thus able to attack an inferior force with a superior one, our opponents will be in dire straits.

> Sun Tzu, *The Art of War*, 6, c. 500 BC, tr. Giles, 1910.

ONE who has few must prepare against the enemy; one who has many makes the enemy prepare against him.

> Sun Tzu, *The Art of War*, 6, c. 500 BC, tr. Samuel Griffith, 1963.

RELATIVE SUPERIORITY, that is, the skillful concentration of superior strength at the decisive point, is much more frequently based on the correct appraisal of this decisive point, on suitable planning from the start; which leads to appropriate disposition of forces, and on the resolution needed to sacrifice nonessentials for the sake of essentials – that is, the courage to retain the major part of one's forces united. This is particularly characteristic of Frederick the Great and Bonaparte.

> Major-General Carl von Clausewitz, *On War*, 3.8, 1832, tr. Michael Howard and Peter Paret, 1976.

THE FUNDAMENTAL OBJECT in all military combinations is to gain local superiority by concentration.

> Rear-Admiral Alfred Thayer Mahan, *Naval Strategy*, 1911.

ONE is always liable to be smashed by superior force, but one should never be caught unprepared to do one's best.

> Field Marshal Viscount Allenby of Megiddo, 1900, letter to his wife during the Boer War.

ARMIES and nations are mainly composed of normal men, not of abnormal heroes, and once these realize the *permanent* superiority of the enemy they will surrender to *force majeure*.

> Captain Sir Basil Liddell Hart, *Thoughts on War*, 1944.

SUPPORT

THE HARDEST TASK in war is to lie in support of some position or battery, under fire without the privilege of returning it; or to guard some train left in the rear, within hearing but out of danger; or to provide for the wounded and dead of some corps which is too busy ahead to care for its own.

> General of the Army William T. Sherman, *The Memoirs of General W.T. Sherman*, 1875

CLOSELY ALLIED to the confidence which is due to good leadership is that which is caused by the

feeling of being supported. Troops, led well, will forget self, will risk the sacrifice of their own lives by advancing to close with the enemy, but only so long as they feel that other troops are coming on to back them up. Men who are assigned to fill the van of an attack will only sacrifice themselves readily if they feel that their efforts will not be in vain. It is, again, the idea of isolation which undermines morale.

Captain Sir Basil Liddell Hart, *Thoughts on War*, 1944.

NOTHING will throw an infantry attack off stride as quickly as to promise it support which is not precisely delivered both in time and volume.

On the other hand, an artillery fire which is promptly delivered or an armor which advances steadily and confidently is like a shot in the arm. It moves the men mentally and sometimes bodily, thereby breaking the concentration of fear. But it is wiser to promise nothing than to default on anything. The memory of a default lingers and men consider it proof that the higher command is letting them down.

Brigadier-General S.L.A. Marshall, *Men Against Fire*, 1947.

GOOD senior commanders once must be trusted and "backed" to the limit. Any commander is entitled to help and support from his immediate superior; sometimes he does not get it, a factor to be taken into account if the man fails. If, having received the help he might normally expect, a man fails – then he must go.

Field Marshal Viscount Montgomery of Alamein, *The Memoirs of Field Marshal Montgomery*, 1958.

SURPRISE
Principle of War

BEHOLD, the wretched, vanquished chief of Kheta [Hittite king] together with numerous allied countries, were stationed in battle array, concealed on the northwest of the city of Kadesh, while his majesty [Ramses II] with his bodyguard, and the division of Amon was marching behind him. The division of Re crossed over the river-bed on the south side of the town of Shabtuna, at the distance of [app. 1.4 miles] from the division of Amon; the division of Ptah was on the south of the city of Aranami; and the division of Sutekh was marching on upon the road. His majesty had formed the first rank of all the leaders of his army . . .

They [Hittites] came forth from the southern side of Kadesh, and they cut through the division of Re in its middle, while they were marching without knowing and without being drawn up for battle. The infantry and the chariotry of his majesty retreated before them. Now, his majesty had halted on the north of the city of Kadesh, on the western side of the Orontes. Then came one to tell his majesty.

His majesty shone like his father Montu, when he took the adornments of war; as he seized his coat of mail, he was like Baal in his hour. The great span [chariot] which bore his majesty called: "Victory in Thebes," from the great stables of Ramses II, was in the midst of the leaders. His majesty halted the rout; by himself and none other with him. When his majesty went to look behind him, he found 2,500 chariotry surrounding him. . . .

The Poem of Pentaur, Rameses II suffering the first great reported surprise attack in history at the Battle of Kadesh, 1294 BC (Rameses would have also suffered the first recorded great defeat had he not by personal example fought his way out and rallied his army to pull off at least a draw), quoted in James Breasted, *Ancient Records of Egypt*, 1906.

THE SPOT where we intend to fight must not be made known; for then the enemy will have to prepare against a possible attack at several different points; and his forces being thus distributed in many directions, the numbers we shall have to face at any given point will be proportionately few.

For should the enemy strengthen his van, he will weaken his rear; should he strengthen his rear, he will weaken his van; should he strengthen his left, he will weaken his right. Should he strengthen his right, he will weaken his left. If he sends reinforcements everywhere, he will be everywhere weak.

Sun Tzu, *The Art of War*, 6, c. 500 BC, tr. Giles, 1910.

THE EXECUTION of a military surprise is always dangerous, and the general who is never taken off his guard himself, and never loses an opportunity of striking at an unguarded foe, will be most likely to succeed in war.

Thucydides, *History of the Peloponnesian War*, c. 404 BC.

WHATEVER a thing may be, be it pleasant or terrible, the less it has been foreseen the more it pleases or frightens. This is seen nowhere better than in war, where *surprise* strikes with terror even those who are much the stronger party.

Xenophon (c. 431–352 BC).

AMONG the enemy, when they saw him advancing so unexpectedly, there was a total lack of steadiness. Some were running to take up their positions, others forming into line, others bridling their horses, others putting on their breastplates. The general impression was one of people expecting to suffer rather than cause damage.

Xenophon, of the onset of the Theban Army led by Epaminondas at the Battle of Mantinea in 362 BC, *Hellinca*, c. 360 BC (*A History of My Times*, tr. Rex Warner, 1966).

SAMENESS is inadequate to attain victory; therefore difference is used, for surprise. Therefore stillness is surprise to the mobile, relaxation is surprise to the weary, fullness is surprise to the hungry, orderliness is surprise to the unruly, many are a surprise to the

few. When the initiative is direct, holding back is surprise; when a surprise attack is launched without retaliation, that is victory. Those who have an abundance of surprises excel in gaining victories.
> Sun Bin, *The Lost Art of War*, c. 350 BC, tr. Thomas Cleary, 1966

EVEN brave men are dismayed by sudden perils.
> Cornelius Tacitus, *Annals*, 15.59, c. AD 115–117 (*The Complete Works of Tacitus*, tr. Alfred Church and William Brodribb, 1942).

NOVELTY and surprise throw an enemy into consternation but common incidents have no effect.
> Flavius Vegetius Renatus, *Military Institutions of the Romans*, c. AD 378, tr. Clark, 1776.

THE GENERAL must make it one of his highest priorities and concerns to launch secret and unexpected attacks upon the enemy whenever possible. If he is successful in this sort of operation, with only a small group of men, he will put large numbers of the enemy to flight.
> Emperor Nikephoros II Phokas, *Skirmishing*, c. AD 969 (*Three Byzantine Military Treatises*, tr. George Dennis, 1985).

EVERYTHING which the enemy least expects will succeed the best. If he relies for security on a chain of mountains that he believes impracticable and you pass these by roads unknown to him, he is confused to start with, and if you press him he will not have time to recover from his consternation. In the same way, if he places himself behind a river to defend the crossing and you find some ford above or below by which to cross, this surprise will derange and confuse him.
> Frederick the Great, *Instructions to His Generals*, 1747, tr. Phillips, 1940.

ANY OFFICER or non-commissioned officer who shall suffer himself to be surprised . . . must not expect to be forgiven.
> Major-General Sir James Wolfe, 1759, General Orders during the Quebec Expedition.

JUST AS lightning has already struck when the flash is seen, so when the enemy discovers the head of the army, the whole should be there, and leave them no time to counteract its dispositions.
> Field Marshal Francois Comte de Guibert, *Essai général de tactique*, 1770, quoted in Liddell Hart, *The Ghost of Napoleon*, 1933.

WHO can surprise well must conquer.
> Admiral John Paul Jones, 10 February 1778, letter to Benjamin Franklin, quoted in Lorenz, *John Paul Jones*, 1943.

WHATEVER is unexpected strikes the mind with fear, and when you hazard most, most is to be

gained. . . . The word surprisal, properly speaking, should not be known in war. . . . For to say an officer has been surprised, is the same as saying he has lost by his own negligence, ignorance, or obstinacy, the honour, liberty or lives of himself and many men who are entrusted to his care.
> Lieutenant-General Johann von Ewald, *Treatise on the Duties of Light Troops*, 1790.

TO ASTONISH is to vanquish.
> Field Marshal Prince Aleksandr V. Suvorov (1729–1800), quoted by Chuikov, in Leites, *The Soviet Style in War*, 1982.

THE ENEMY reckons we're sixty miles away. . . . Suddenly we're on him like a cloudburst. His head whirls. Attack! Cut down, stab, chase, don't let him get away.
> Field Marshal Aleksandr V. Suvorov (1729–1800), 1799, quoted in Philip Longworth, *The Art of Victory*, 1966.

. . . NOTHING so pregnant with dangerous consequences, or so disgraceful to an Officer in arms, as a surprise.
> Admiral Lord St. Vincent, 1798, memorandum to the Fleet off Cadiz.

SOLDIERS! On the 5th of June the Russian army attacked us in our cantonments. The enemy had mistaken the reason for our inactivity. They discovered too late that our slumber was that of the lion.
> Napoleon, 22 June 1807, to the army, quoted in R.M. Johnston, ed., *The Corsican*, 1910.

IT IS a principle of warfare, that when it is possible to make use of thunderbolts, they should be preferred to cannon.
> Napoleon (1769–1821), dictation on St. Helena, quoted in Christopher Herold, ed., *The Mind of Napoleon*, 1955.

MAXIM 95. War is composed of nothing but surprises. While a general should adhere to general principles, he should never lose the opportunity to profit by these surprises. It is the essence of genius. In war there is only one favorable moment. Genius seizes it.
> Napoleon, *The Military Maxims of Napoleon*, tr. Burnod, 1827.

TO BE DEFEATED is pardonable; to be surprised – never!
> Napoleon, *Maxims of War*, 1831.

THE UNIVERSAL DESIRE for relative numerical superiority – leads to another desire, which is consequently no less universal: that is *to take the enemy by surprise*. This desire is more or less basic to all operations, for without it superiority at the decisive point is hardly conceivable.

We suggest that surprise lies at the root of all operations without exception, though in widely varying degrees depending on the nature and circumstances of the operation.

> Major-General Carl von Clausewitz, *On War*, 3.9, 1832, tr. Michael Howard and Peter Paret, 1976.

THE TWO FACTORS that produce surprise are secrecy and speed. Both presuppose a high degree of energy on the part of the government and the commander; on the part of the army, they require great efficiency. Surprise will never be achieved under lax conditions and conduct.

> Major-General Carl von Clausewitz, *On War*, 3.9, 1832, tr. Michael Howard and Peter Paret, 1976.

FOR THE SIDE that can benefit from the psychological effects of surprise, the worse the situation is, the better it may turn out, while the enemy finds himself incapable of making coherent decisions. This holds true not only for senior commanders, but for everyone involved; for one peculiar feature of surprise is that it loosens the bonds of cohesion, and individual action can easily become significant.

> Major-General Carl von Clausewitz, *On War*, 3.9, 1832, tr. Michael Howard and Peter Paret, 1976.

THE OFFICERS and men who permit themselves to be surprised deserve to die, and the commanding general will spare no efforts to secure them their deserts.

> Lieutenant-General D.H. Hill, February 1863, address to his troops upon assumption of command.

THE WAY to destroy the enemy's morale, to show him that his cause is lost, is therefore surprise in every sense of the word, bringing into the struggle something "unexpected and terrible," which therefore has a great effect. It deprives the enemy of the power to reflect, and consequently to discuss.

Under various forms we always find the same principle of *surprise*, seeking to produce on the enemy the same moral result, *terror*; creating in him, by the sudden appearance of something unexpected and overwhelming, the feeling of impotence, the assurance that he cannot win; that is, that he is beaten.

> Marshal of France Ferdinand Foch, *Principles of War*, 1913.

INACTION leads to surprise, and surprise to defeat, which is after all only a form of surprise.

> Marshal of France Ferdinand Foch, *Precepts and Judgments*, 1919.

SURPRISE consists in the hard fact that the enemy suddenly appears in considerable numbers, without his *presence* having been known to be so *near*, for want of *information*, and without it being possible to *assemble*, for want of *protection*; for want, in one word, of a security service.

> Marshal of France Ferdinand Foch, *Precepts and Judgments*, 1919.

SURPRISE – the pith and marrow of war!

> Admiral Sir John Fisher, *Memories*, 1919.

LACK OF SECURITY, or a false interpretation of the principle of security, leads directly to being surprised. The principle of surprise, like a double-edged tool, is an exceedingly dangerous one in unskilled hands; for, being mainly controlled by psychological factors, its nature is less stable and the conditions affecting it are more difficult to gauge.

> Major-General J.F.C. Fuller, *The Reformation of War*, 1923.

AN ENEMY may be surprised, which implies that he is thrown off balance. This is the best method of defeating him, for it is so economical, one man taking on to himself the strength of many. Surprise may be considered under two main headings: surprise effected by doing something that the enemy does not expect, and surprise effected by doing something that the enemy cannot counter. The first may be denoted as moral surprise, the second as material.

> Major-General J.F.C. Fuller, *The Reformation of War*, 1923.

THE SUBJECT of surprise is an immense one, and one which influences all forms and modes of war. It is one which is nearly always lost sight of during peace-time, because danger and fear are more often than not abstract quantities; but in wartime they manifest, and with them manifests surprise – the demoralizing principle.

> Major-General J.F.C. Fuller, *The Foundations of the Science of War*, 1926.

OF ALL KEYS to success in war "unexpectedness" is the most important. By it a commander, whether of an army or a platoon, can often unlock gates which are impregnable to sheer force. (July 1929.)

> Captain Sir Basil Liddell Hart, *Thoughts on War*, 1944.

MOVEMENT generates surprise, and surprise gives impetus to movement.

> Captain Sir Basil Liddell Hart, 'Strategy', *Encyclopaedia Britannica* (1929 edition).

SURPRISE has a stunning effect. Therefore all troop action must be accomplished with the greatest secrecy and speed. Swiftness of action in combination with organization, skilful maneuver, and the ability to adapt to the terrain . . . are the basic guarantees of success in battle.

> Red Army *Field Service Regulations* (1936), attributed to Marshal of the Soviet Union, Mikhail N. Tukhachevskiy (1893–1937).

TACTICS must change if surprise is to be obtained,

for surprise does not merely mean hitting the enemy at some unexpected point, but also hitting him in an unexpected way.

> Major-General J.F.C. Fuller, *Memoirs of an Unconventional Soldier*, 1936.

ABSOLUTE SUPERIORITY *everywhere* is unattainable, hence it must frequently be replaced by relative superiority *somewhere*. To achieve relative superiority somewhere is the main objective of almost all military movements and the essential purpose of generalship. Since relative superiority will hardly be accomplished if the enemy knows the plan of concentration before the hour of attack, the principle of surprise is of importance equal to that of the principle of concentration.

> General Waldemar Erfurth, *Surprise*, 1938, tr. Possony, 1943.

FREQUENTLY, surprise reduces the unity of the enemy forces and induces the commanders of the enemy army to issue conflicting orders. . . . Modern wars offer many examples of panic which led to the frantic flight of whole armies.

> General Waldemar Erfurth, *Surprise*, 1938, tr. Possony, 1943.

A MILITARY MAN can scarcely pride himself on having "smitten a sleeping enemy"; it is more a matter of shame, simply, for the one smitten.

> Admiral Isoroku Yamamoto, 9 January 1942, quoted in Agawa, *The Reluctant Admiral*, 1979.

WE HAVE INFLICTED a complete surprise on the enemy. All our columns are inserted in the enemy's guts.

> Major-General Orde Wingate, 11 March 1944, Order of the Day to the Third Indian Division.

. . . TO DO something which the enemy cannot prevent, and to do something which he does not suspect. The first action may be compared to surprising a man with his eyes open, in the other, the man has his eyes shut.

> Major-General J.F.C. Fuller, *The Generalship of Alexander the Great*, 1958.

SINCE TIME immemorial there have been lively, self-confident commanders who have exploited the principle of surprise – the means whereby inferior forces may snatch victory, and turn downright impossible conditions to their own advantage. The effects on the morale of both parties are immense – but his every element of incalculability proves a deterrent to the ponderous spirits, and this is probably why they are so reluctant to embrace new weapons, even when the inadequacy of the old ones is all too clear.

> General Heinz Guderian, *Achtung – Panzer!*, 1992 (first published in German in 1937).

SURPRISES are a commonplace in war – and reconsidered opinions too.

> General Robert L. Eichelberger (1886–1961).

MOST OPPONENTS are at their best if they are allowed to dictate the battle; they are not so good when they are thrown off balance by manoeuvre and are forced to react to your own movements and thrusts. Surprise is essential. Strategical surprise may often be difficult, if not impossible, to obtain; but tactical surprise is always possible and must be given an essential place in training.

> Field Marshal Viscount Montgomery of Alamein, *A History of Warfare*, 1968.

A FORCE within striking distance of an enemy must be suitably disposed with regard to its battle positions, being ready *at all times* to fight quickly if surprised.

> Field Marshal Viscount Montgomery of Alamein, *A History of Warfare*, 1968.

SURPRISE makes it possible to take the enemy unawares, to cause panic in his ranks, to paralyze his will to resist, to drastically reduce his fighting efficiency, to contain his actions, to disrupt his troops' control, and to deny him the opportunity to take effective countermeasures quickly. As a result, this makes it possible to successfully rout even superior enemy forces with the least possible losses to friendly forces.

> Colonel-General V.G. Reznichenko, *Taktika*, 1984.

SURPRISE must form the basis of all troop combat activities. Surprise achieved at the beginning of an engagement may become exhausted after a while. Its effect is limited to the time that the enemy needs to eliminate the unequal conditions caused by the unanticipated actions on the part of the opposing side. This is why it is necessary during an engagement to strive both to make maximum use of surprise already achieved and to achieve a new surprise in the actions of all troop elements.

> Colonel-General V.G. Reznichenko, *Taktika*, 1984.

SURPRISE substantially enhances combat power. Achieving surprise in combat has always been important. It is perhaps more important today than ever. Quantitative analysis of historical combat shows that surprise has increased the combat power of military forces in those engagements in which it was achieved. Surprise has proven to be the greatest of all combat multipliers. It may be the most important of the Principles of War; it is at least as important as Mass and Maneuver.

> Colonel T.N. Dupuy, *Understanding War*, 1987.

SURPRISE is paralysis, if only partial and temporary, of the enemy's ability to resist. The advantage gained by surprise depends on the degree of surprise and the enemy's ability to adjust and recover. Surprise is based on speed, secrecy, and deception. It means doing the unexpected thing, which in turn normally means doing the more difficult thing in hopes that the enemy will not expect it. In fact, this is the genesis of maneuver – to circumvent the enemy's strength to strike him where he is not prepared.

General Alfred M. Gray and Major John Schmitt, *Warfighting*, United States Marine Corps, 1989.

WHILE the element of surprise is often of decisive importance, we must realize that it is difficult to achieve and easy to lose. Its advantages are only temporary and must be quickly exploited. Friction, the dominant attribute of war, is the constant enemy of surprise. We must also recognize that while surprise is always desirable, the ability to achieve it does not depend solely on our own efforts. It depends at least as much on our enemy's susceptibility to surprise – his expectations and preparedness. Our ability to achieve surprise rests on our ability to appreciate and then dislocate the enemy's expectations. Therefore, while surprise can be decisive, it is a mistake to depend on it alone for the margin of victory.

General Alfred M. Gray and Major John Schmitt, *Warfighting*, United States Marine Corps, 1989.

SURRENDER

SIR, –
I have the mortification to inform your excellency, that I have been forced to give up the posts of York and Gloucester, and to surrender the troops under my command, by capitulation, on the 19th instant, as prisoners of war, to the combined forces of America and France.

General Charles Marquis Cornwallis, 17 October 1781, to General Sir Henry Clinton, announcing the surrender of his army at Yorktown, quoted in Henry Lee, *War in the Southern Department*, 1869.

MAXIM 67. To authorize generals or other officers to lay down their arms in virtue of a particular capitulation, under any other circumstances than when they are composing the garrison of a fortress, affords a dangerous latitude. It is destructive of all military character in a nation to open such a door to the cowardly, the weak, or even to the misdirected brave. Great extremities require extraordinary resolution. The more obstinate the resistance of an army, the greater the chances of assistance or of success.

How many seeming impossibilities have been accomplished by men whose only resource was death!

Napoleon, *The Military Maxims of Napoleon*, tr. George D'Aguilar, 1831 (David Chandler, ed., 1987).

MAXIM 68. There is no security for any sovereign, for any nation, or for any general, if officers are permitted to capitulate in the open field, and to lay down their arms in virtue of conditions, favourable to the contracting party, but contrary to the interests of the army at large. To withdraw from danger, and thereby to involve their comrades in greater perils, is the height of cowardice. Such conduct should be proscribed, declared infamous, and made punishable with death. All generals, officers, and soldiers who capitulate in battle to save their own lives, should be decimated.

He who gives the order, and those who obey are alike traitors, and deserve capital punishment.

Napoleon, *The Military Maxims of Napoleon*, tr. George D'Aguilar, 1831 (David Chandler, ed., 1987).

MAXIM 69. There is but one honourable mode of becoming prisoner of war. That is, by being taken separately; by which is meant, being cut off entirely, and when we can no longer make use of our arms. In this case there can be no conditions, for honour can impose none. We yield to an irresistable necessity.

Napoleon, *The Military Maxims of Napoleon*, tr. George D'Aguilar, 1831 (David Chandler, ed., 1987).

YOUR ROYAL HIGHNESS: victimized by the factions which divide my country, and by the hostility of the European powers, I have ended my political career; and I come, as Themistocles did, to claim a seat by the hearth of the British people. I put myself under the protection of British law – a protection which I claim from your Royal Highness, as the strongest, the stubbornest, and most generous of my foes.

Napoleon, 14 July 1815, letter to the Prince Regent of England from Ile d'Aix after his defeat at Waterloo, *Correspondance de Napoléon Ier, publiée par ordre de l'Empereur Napoléon III*, XXVIII, 22066, 1858–1870.

SIR: yours of this date proposing armistice and appointment of commissioners to settle terms of capitulation, is just received. No terms except an unconditional and immediate surrender can be accepted. I propose to move immediately upon your works.

General of the Army Ulysses S. Grant, 16 November 1862, to the Confederate commander of Fort Donelson, *Personal Memoirs*, I, 1885.

THEN there is nothing left for me but to go and see General Grant, and I would rather die a thousand deaths.

General Robert E. Lee, 9 April 1865.

I KNOW they will say hard things of us. They will not understand how we were overwhelmed by numbers. But that is not the question, Colonel: The question is, is it right to surrender this army. If it is right, then I will take all the responsibility. . . . How easily I could be rid of this [life] and be at rest! I have only to ride along the line and all will be over. But it is our duty to live. What will become of the women and children of the South if we are not here to protect them?

General Robert E. Lee, quoted in A.L. Long, *Memoirs of Robert E. Lee*, 1886.

AFTER FOUR YEARS of arduous service, marked by unsurpassed, courage and fortitude, the Army of Northern Virginia has been compelled to yield to overwhelming numbers and resources. I need not tell the survivors of so many hard-fought battles, who have remained steadfast to the last, that I have consented to this result from no distrust of them; but, feeling that valor and devotion could accomplish nothing that could compensate for the loss that would have attended the continuation of the contest, I have determined to avoid the useless sacrifice of those whose past services have endeared them to their countrymen.

With an increasing admiration of your constancy and devotion to your country, and a grateful remembrance of your kind and generous consideration of myself, I bid you an affectionate farewell.

> General Robert E. Lee, farewell message to the Army of Northern Virginia, 10 April 1865, after the surrender at Appomattox.

TELL GENERAL HOWARD I know his heart. What he told me before I have in my heart. I am tired of fighting. Our chiefs are killed. Looking Glass is dead. Too-hul-hule-sute is dead. The old men are all dead. It is the young men who say yes or no. He who once led them is dead. It is cold and we have no blankets.

The little children are freezing to death. My people, some of them, have run away to the hills, and have no blankets, no food; no one knows where they are – perhaps freezing to death. I want to have time to look for my children and see how many of them I can find. Maybe I shall find them among the dead. Hear me, my chiefs. I am tired; my heart is sick and sad. From where the sun now stands I will fight no more forever.

> Chief Joseph of the Nez Perce, upon his surrender to a representative of General O.O. Howard, 5 October 1877, quoted in Mathieson, *The Nez Perce Indian War*, 1964.

I WOULD FIGHT without a break. I would fight in front of Amiens. I would fight in Amiens. I would fight behind Amiens. I would never surrender.

> Marshal of France Ferdinand Foch, 26 March 1918, to Sir Douglas Haig during the German *Friedensturm* offensive.

NATIONS which went down fighting rose again, but those which tamely surrendered were finished.

> Sir Winston S. Churchill (1874–1965).

HELPLESSNESS induces hopelessness, and history attests that loss of hope and not loss of life is what decides the issue of war.

> Captain Sir Basil Liddell Hart, *The Real War 1914–1918*, 1930.

IT IS with a broken heart and head bowed in sadness but not in shame, that I report to Your Excellency that I must go today to arrange terms for the surrender of the fortified islands of Manila Bay.

There is a limit of human endurance, and that limit has long since been past. Without prospect of relief I feel it is my duty to my country and to my gallant troops to end this useless effusion of blood and human sacrifice. If you agree, Mr. President, please say to the nation that my troops and I have accomplished all that is humanly possible and that we have upheld the best tradition of the United States and its Army. May God bless and preserve you and guide you and the nation in the effort to ultimate victory.

With profound regret and with continued pride in my gallant troops, I go to meet the Japanese commander. Goodbye, Mr. President.

> General Jonathan M. Wainwright's message to President Roosevelt, 6 May 1942, as he was about to surrender Corregidor to the Japanese under General Homma, quoted in Duane Schultz, *Hero of Bataan*, 1981.

LET NO MAN surrender so long as he is unwounded and can fight.

> Field Marshal Viscount Montgomery of Alamein, 30 October 1942, message to the Eighth Army on the eve of the Battle of Alamein.

SURRENDER is forbidden. Sixth Army will hold their positions to the last man and the last round, and by their heroic endurance will make an unforgettable contribution to the establishment of a defensive front and the salvation of the western world.

> Adolf Hitler, 23 February 1943, to Field Marshal Paulus, commander of the German Sixth Army surrounded in Stalingrad.

THEY [the German delegation sent by Admiral Doenitz to open negotiations for surrender] were brought to my caravan site and were drawn up under the Union Jack, which was flying proudly in the breeze. I kept them waiting for a few minutes and then came out of my caravan and walked towards them. They all saluted, under the Union Jack. It was a great moment; I knew the Germans had come to surrender and that the war was over.

> Field Marshal Viscount Montgomery of Alamein, 5 May 1945, taking the surrender of the Germans in northern Germany, *The Memoirs of Field Marshal Montgomery*, 1958.

TO RECEIVE the unconditional surrender of half a million enemy soldiers, sailors and airmen must be an event which happens to few people in the world. I was very conscious that this was the greatest day of my life.

> Admiral Earl Mountbatten, 12 September 1945, upon the Japanese surrender in Singapore, *Personal Diary of Admiral the Lord Louis Mountbatten*, 1988.

THERE IS almost always a way out, even of an apparently hopeless position, if the leader makes up his mind to face the risks.

> General Paul von Lettow-Vorbeck, *East African Campaigns*, 1957.

I WAS CONVINCED that an effective way really to impress on the Japanese that they had been beaten in the field was to insist on this ceremonial surrender of swords. No Japanese soldier, who had seen his general march up and hand over his sword, would ever doubt that the Invincible Army was invincible no longer. We did not want a repetition of the German First War legend of an unconquered army. With this in mind, I was dismayed to be told that General MacArthur in his over-all instruction for the surrender had decided that the "archaic" ceremony of the surrender of swords was not to be enforced. I am afraid I disregarded his wishes. In Southwest Asia all Japanese officers surrendered their swords to British officers of similar or higher rank; the enemy divisional and army commanders handed theirs in before large parades of their already disarmed troops. Field-Marshal Terauchi's sword is in Admiral Mountbatten's hands; General Kimura's is on my mantelpiece, where I always intended that one day it should be.

> Field Marshal Viscount Slim of Burma, *Defeat Into Victory*, 1956.

SWEARING/PROFANITY/ INVECTIVE/BLASPHEMY

I WILL TELL YOU never to employ with your soldiers heartless words, dishonorable oaths, and never use profanity or degrading language in their presence. The colonel who uses these expression with his soldiers degrades himself, and if he is speaking to his officers, he commits an extremely evident blunder. Never forget the officers of your regiment are men, French, your equals, and that you must, consequently, employ a tone and language when giving them orders which is suitable to those persons in whom honor is the motivating factor.

> Marshal of France Charles-Louis de Belle Isle, Duc de Gisors (1684–1761), letter to his son upon the latter's assumption of command of a French regiment, in Fitton, *Leadership*, 1990.

NOTHING justifies profanity.

> Lieutenant-General Thomas J. 'Stonewall' Jackson, to Brigadier-General John Imboden, quoted in *Battles and Leaders of the Civil War, Being for the Most Part Contributions by Union and Confederate Officers*, I, Johnston and Buel, ed., 1887–1888.

THE DAY before the fight, Hooker said to a general officer, "God Almighty could not prevent me from winning a victory tomorrow." Pray, could we expect a victory after that? . . . Success cannot come to us through such profanity.

> Major-General Winfield Scott Hancock, of Major General Joseph Hooker's boast to defeat Robert E. Lee immediately prior to the Battle of Chancellorsville (1–5 May 1863), quoted in Almira Hancock, *Reminiscences of Winfield Scott Hancock*, 1887.

WHILE SITTING with him around the camp fire one night, after every one else had gone to bed, I said to him: "General, it seems singular that you have gone through all the rough and tumble of army service and frontier life, and have never been provoked into swearing. I have never heard you utter an oath or use an imprecation." "Well, somehow or other, I never learned to swear," he replied. "When a boy I seemed to have an aversion to it, and when I became a man I saw the folly of it. I have always noticed, too, that swearing helps to rouse a man's anger; and when a man flies into a passion his adversary who keeps cool always gets the better of him. In fact, I could never see the use of swearing. I think it is the case with many people who swear excessively that it is a mere habit, and that they do not mean to be profane; but, to say the least, it is a great waste of time." His example in this respect was once quoted in my hearing by a member of the Christian Commission to a teamster in the Army of the Potomac, in the hope of lessening the volume of rare oaths with which he was italicizing his language, and upon which he seemed to be placing his main reliance in moving his mule-team out of a mud-hole. The only reply evoked from him was: "Then thar's one thing sart'in: the old man never druv mules."

> Brigadier-General Horace Porter, *Campaigning With Grant*, 1897.

IN THE CLEARING north of the woods, his face blackened by gunsmoke, Sheridan ran into his commanding general. "Here we are," he told Rosecrans, "all that are left of us." He spoke the truth; in four hours of furious combat, culminating in one of the bravest fighting retreats of the war, he had lost more than 1,600 men, including three brigade commanders. Sill, Roberts, and Harrington were dead; soon Schaefer would join that terrible list. Sheridan was cursing, not so much from despair as from frustration. "Watch your language," Rosecrans ordered. "Remember, the first bullet may send you to eternity." With a third of his division heaped among the rocks and cedars behind him, Sheridan scarcely needed a lecture on the destructive capabilities of bullets. He shrugged. "Unless I swear like hell the men won't take me seriously," he said.

> General of the Army Phillip H. Sheridan, in an account of the Battle of Stones River, 31 December 1863, by Roy Morris, *Sheridan*, 1992.

WHEN I want my men to remember something important, to really make it stick, I give it to them double dirty. It may not sound nice to some bunch of little old ladies at an afternoon tea party, but it helps my soldiers remember. You can't run an army without profanity; and it has to be eloquent profanity. An army without profanity couldn't fight its way out of a piss-soaked paper bag. As for the types of comments I make, sometimes I just, by God, get carried away with my own eloquence.

> General George S. Patton, Jr. (1885–1945), to his nephew, quoted in Charles M. Province, *The Unknown Patton*.

UNLIKE MYSELF, strong emotion did not make him [MacArthur] profane. He did not need to be; profanity would have merely discolored his eloquence.

> Admiral William 'Bull' Halsey (1882–1959), quoted in E.B. Potter, *Bull Halsey*, 1985.

IT IS STRANGE for me to read in the regulation the command: "Charge, Forward!" I make bold to assert that one hears it in that regulation wording only during practice assaults. Not once in my life have I myself heard it, and I have inquired particularly about this matter among veterans, and they confirmed that, yes, this dry phrase will not raise people up for a real assault. Invective is the foundation of command and control in a combined-arms battle.

> Colonel-General Aleksandr I. Lebed, *I Hurt For This Great Country*, 1995.

THE SWORD AND THE PEN

IT IS SAID that the warrior's is the twofold Way of pen and sword, and he should have a taste for both Ways.

> Miyamoto Musashi, *A Book of Five Rings*, 1645, tr. Victor Harris, 1984.

I WOULD rather have written that poem, gentlemen, than take Quebec tomorrow.

> Major-General Sir James Wolfe, 12 September 1759, referring to Grey's *Elegy* on the day before his death in victory at the Battle of Quebec.

IT IS NOT the business of naval officers to write books.

> Rear-Admiral F.M. Ramsay, 1893, endorsement on the unfavourable fitness report made on Alfred Thayer Mahan.

IT IS OFTEN SAID that a man who writes well cannot be a good soldier; most of the great commanders, from King David, Xenophon, and Caesar to Wellington, not only wrote well, but extremely well.

> Field Marshal Viscount Wolseley, *The Story of a Soldier's Life*, II, 1903.

OUR REGULATIONS governing the publication by soldiers of their views on military matters are veritable Lettres de Cachet, consigning the intellects of our Service to the Bastille of ignorance.

> General Sir Ian Hamilton, *The Soul and Body of an Army*, 1921.

THE WRITTEN ESSAY or appreciation is a good test of character and grasp of the principles of war. It is apt to explode the legend of the "strong, silent man" – who is usually silent because his mind is so hazy that he fears to commit himself to the risk of logical argument. The man who writes gives proof that at any rate he possesses some knowledge, whereas it is quite a possibility that the mind of the inarticulate one may be a military vacuum. Further, arguments that would pass muster in verbal conferences are easily seen to be lacking in logic when written, for cold print is a merciless exposer of mental fog. (March 1923.)

> Captain Sir Basil Liddell Hart, *Thoughts on War*, 1944.

BATTLES are won through the ability of men to express themselves in clear and unmistakable language.

> Brigadier-General S.L.A. Marshall, *The Armed Forces Officer*, 1950.

THERE IS one quality above all which seems to me essential for a good commander, the ability to express himself clearly, confidently, and concisely, in speech and on paper; to have the power to translate his intentions into orders and instructions which are not merely intelligible but unmistakable, and yet brief enough to waste no time. My experience of getting on for fifty years' service has shown me that it is a rare quality amongst Army Officers, to which not nearly attention is paid in their education. It is one which can be acquired, but seldom is, because it is seldom taught.

> Field Marshal Viscount Wavell of Cyrenaica, *Soldiers and Soldiering*, 1953.

THE NOTION that the pen is mightier than the sword is a fantasy. Try waving a book at the man who comes after you with a machete or a gun. Yet the pen can inform the sword.

> Lieutenant-Colonel Ralph Peters, *Fighting for the Future*, 1999.

T

TACTICS

TO ENSURE that your whole host may withstand the brunt of the enemy's attack and remain unshaken – this is effected by maneuvers direct and indirect.

That the impact of your army may be like a grindstone dashed against an egg – that is effected by science of weak and strong points.

In all fighting, the direct methods may be used for joining battle, but indirect methods will be needed in order to secure victory.

Indirect tactics, efficiently applied, are inexhaustable as Heaven and Earth, unending as the flow of rivers and streams; like the sun and moon, they end but to begin anew; like the four seasons, they pass but to return once more.

There are not more than five musical notes, yet the combinations of these five give rise to more melodies than can ever be heard. There are not more than five primary colors, yet in combination they produce more hues than can ever be seen. There are not more than five cardinal tastes, yet combinations of them yield more flavours than can ever be tasted.

In battle, there are not more than two methods of attack – the direct and indirect; yet these two in combination give rise to an endless series of maneuvers. The direct and indirect lead on to each other in turn. It is like moving in a circle – you never come to an end. Who can exhaust the possibilities of their combinations?

Sun Tzu, *The Art of War*, 5, c. 500 BC, tr. Giles, 1910.

TACTICS is a science which enables one to organize and maneuver a body of armed men in an orderly manner. Tactics may be divided into four parts: proper organization of men for combat; distribution of weapons according to the needs of each man; movement of an armed body of troops in a manner appropriate to the occasion; the management of war, of personnel and materials, including an examination of ways and causes as well as of what is advantageous.

Anonymous Byzantine general (anonymous Vari), *Strategy*, c. AD 527–565, quoted in George Dennis, *Three Byzantine Military Treatises*, 1983.

IN TACTICS every engagement, great or small, is a defensive one if we leave the initiative to the enemy.

Major-General Carl von Clausewitz, *On War*, 1832, tr. Michael Howard and Peter Paret, 1976.

HOW DIFFERENT is almost every military problem,

except in the bare mechanism of tactics. In almost every case the data on which a solution depends is lacking. . . . Too often the general has only conjectures to go on, and these based on false premises. . . . What is true now, at the next moment may have no existence, or exist in a contrary sense. . . . These considerations explain why history produces so few captains.

Dennis Hart Mahan, *Advance-Guard, Out-Post, and Detachment Service of Troops with the Essential Principles of Strategy and Grand Tactics*, 1863.

TACTICS is an art based on the knowledge of how to make men fight with maximum energy against fear, a maximum which organization alone can give.

Colonel Charles Ardant du Picq, *Battle Studies*, 1880, tr. Greely, 1957.

I PERCEIVED at once, however, that Hardee's tactics – a mere translation from the French with Hardee's name attached – was nothing more than common sense . . . I found no trouble in giving commands that would take my regiment where I wanted it to go. . . . I do not believe that the officers of the regiment ever discovered that I had never studied the tactics that I used.

General of the Army Ulysses S. Grant, *Personal Memoirs*, 1885.

IN WAR we resemble a man endeavoring to seek an enemy in the dark, and the principles which govern our action will be similar to those which he would naturally adopt. The man stretches out one arm in order to grope for his enemy (Discover). On touching his adversary he feels his way to the latter's throat (Reconnoiter). As soon as he has reached it, he seizes him by the collar or throat so that his antagonist cannot wriggle away or strike back at him effectively (Fix). Then with his other fist he strikes his enemy, who is unable to avoid the blow, a decisive knock-out blow (Decisive Attack). Before the enemy can recover, he follows up his advantage by taking steps to render him finally powerless (Exploit).

Captain Sir Basil Liddell Hart, 'The Essential Principles of War . . .', *United Services Magazine*, 4/1920.

NINE-TENTHS of tactics are certain, and taught in books; but the irrational tenth is like the kingfisher flashing across the pool and that is the test of generals. It can only be ensured by instinct, sharpened by thought practising the stroke so often that at the crisis it is as natural as a reflex.

Colonel T.E. Lawrence, 'The Science of Guerrilla Warfare', *Encyclopaedia Britannica*, 1929.

TACTICS are the cutting edge of strategy, the edge which chisels out the plan into an action; consequently the sharper this edge is the clearer will be the result.

Major-General J.F.C. Fuller, *Grant and Lee, A Study in Personality and Generalship*, 1933.

THERE IS only one tactical principle which is not subject to change. It is: to use the means at hand to inflict the maximum amount of wounds, death and destruction on the enemy in the minimum of time.

General George S. Patton, Jr., *War As I Knew It*, 1947.

IT SEEMS ALSO that he who devises or develops a new system of tactics deserves special advancement on the military honor role of fame. All tactics since the earliest days have been based on evaluating an equation in which x=mobility, y=armour, and z=hitting power. Once a satisfactory solution has been found and a formula evolved, it tends to remain static until some thinking soldier (or possibly civilian) recognizes that the values of x,y,z have been changed by the progress of inventions since the last formula was accepted and that a new formula and new systems of tactics are required.

Field Marshal Viscount Wavell of Cyrenaica, *Soldiers and Soldiering*, 1953.

ON THE OPENING PAGE of his great work *On War*, Clausewitz makes a very simple yet profound remark. It is, that "War is nothing but a duel on an extensive scale", and he likens it to a struggle between two wrestlers; between two pugilists would be a more apt comparison. If so, then the primary elements of tactics are to be seen in their simplest form in a fight between two unarmed men. They are: to think, to guard, to move and to hit.

Before a bout opens, each man must consider how best to knock out his adversary, and though as the fight proceeds he may be compelled to modify his means, he must never abandon his aim. At the start he must assume a defensive attitude until he has measured up his opponent. Next, he must move under cover of his defence towards him, and lastly by foot-play, and still under cover of his defence, he must assume the offensive and attempt to knock him out. In military terms, the four primary tactical elements are: the aim or object, security, mobility and offensive power.

If two pugilists are skilled in their art, they will recognize the value of three accentuating elements. They will economize their physical force, so as not to exhaust themselves prematurely; they will concentrate their blows against the decisive point selected, the left or right of their opponents jaw, or his solar plexus, and throughout will attempt to surprise him – that is, take him off-guard, or do something which he does not expect, or cannot guard against. In military terms these accentuating elements are: economy of force, concentration of force, and surprise.

Major-General J.F.C. Fuller, *The Generalship of Alexander the Great*, 1958.

TACTICS AND STRATEGY

ALL MEN can see these tactics whereby I conquer, but what none can see is the strategy out of which victory evolved.

Sun Tzu, *The Art of War*, c. 500 BC.

SIR, my strategy is one against ten, my tactics are ten against one.

The Duke of Wellington (1769–1852).

THE CONDUCT of war . . . consists in the planning and conduct of fighting. . . . It consists of a greater or lesser number of single *acts each complete in itself*, which . . . are called "engagements" and which form new entities. This gives rise to the completely different activity of *planning and executing these engagements themselves*, and of *coordinating* each of them with the others in order to further the object of the war. One has been called *tactics*, and the other *strategy*.

According to our classification, then, tactics teaches *the use of armed forces in the engagement*; strategy, *the use of engagements for the object of the war*.

Major-General Carl von Clausewitz, *On War*, 2.1, 1832, tr. Michael Howard and Peter Paret, 1976.

THE ORIGINAL MEANS of strategy is victory – that is, tactical success; its ends, in the final analysis, are those objects which will lead directly to peace. The application of these means for these ends will also be attended by factors that will influence it to a greater or lesser degree.

These factors are the geographical surroundings and the nature of the terrain . . . the time of day . . . and the weather.

Strategy, in connecting these factors with the outcome of an engagement, confers a special significance on that outcome and thereby on the engagement: *it assigns a particular aim to it*. Yet, insofar as that aim is not the one that will lead directly to peace, it remains subsidiary and is also to be thought of as a means. Successful engagements or victories in all stages of importance may therefore be considered as strategic means.

Major-General Carl von Clausewitz, *On War*, 2.2, 1832, tr. Michael Howard and Peter Paret, 1976.

TACTICAL SUCCESSES, those attained *in the course* of the engagement, *usually occur during the phase of disarray and weakness*. On the other hand, the strategic success, the overall effect of the engagement, the completed victory, whether great or insignificant, *already lies beyond that phase*. The strategic outcome takes shape only when the fragmented results have combined into a single independent whole. . . .

Major-General Carl von Clausewitz, *On War*, 3.12, 1832, tr. Michael Howard and Peter Paret, 1976.

STRATEGY is the art of making war upon the map, and comprehends the whole theater of operations. Grand tactics is the art of posting troops upon the battlefield according to the characteristics of the ground, of bringing them into action, and of fighting upon the ground, in contradiction to planning upon a map. Logistics comprises the means and arrangements which work out the plans of strategy and tactics. Strategy decides where to act; logistics brings the troops to this point; grand tactics decides the manner of execution and the employment of the troops.

Lieutenant-General Antoine-Henri Baron de Jomini, *Summary of the Art of War*, 1838, tr. Mendell and Craighill, 1862.

STRATEGY furnishes tactics with the opportunity to strike and with the prospect of success, through its conduct of the armies and of their concentration on the field of battle. On the other hand, however, it accepts the results of every single engagement, and builds upon them. Strategy retires when a tactical victory is in the making, in order to exploit the newly created situation.

Field Marshal Helmuth Graf von Moltke, quoted in Hermann Foertsch, *The Art of Modern War*, 1940.

A TACTICAL SUCCESS is only really decisive, if it is gained at the strategically correct spot.

Field Marshal Helmuth Graf von Moltke, quoted in Hermann Foertsch, *The Art of Modern War*, 1940.

. . . CONTACT (a word which perhaps better than any other indicates the dividing line between strategy and tactics). . . .

Rear-Admiral Alfred Thayer Mahan, *The Influence of Sea Power Upon History*, 1890.

AS A RULE, strategy concerns itself with those large-scale measures which serve to bring the forces into play at the decisive point under the most favorable conditions possible, while tactics relates to what is done in the engagement itself. Strategy might be called the science of generalship, while tactics is that of handling troops.

Field Marshal Colmar Baron von der Goltz (1843–1916).

IT SEEMS TO ME personally that attempts to define and separate these two fields are mistaken. I don't believe that strategy and tactics can be isolated in any event. Strategy and tactics are attributes of a single phenomenon; the difference is only one of degree.

Mikhail V. Frunze (1885–1925), quoted in M. Gareyev, *M.V. Frunze, Military Theorist*, 1985.

THE GREATER the certainty with which the success of the main force attack can be predicted in advance, the easier the task set that main force will be. One must not count on the heroism of the troops. *The strategy must ensure that the tactical task is a readily feasible one.*

Marshal of the Soviet Union Mikhail N. Tukhachevskiy, 1924, quoted in Richard Simpkin, *Deep Battle*, 1987.

AS REGARDS the relation of strategy to tactics, while in execution the borderline is often shadowy, and it is difficult to decide exactly where a strategical movement ends and a tactical movement begins, yet in conception the two are distinct. Tactics lies in, and fills the province of, fighting. Strategy not only stops on the frontier, but has for its purpose the reduction of fighting to the slenderest proportions. (Oct. 1928.)

Captain Sir Basil Liddell Hart, *Thoughts on War*, 1944.

IN PEACE we concentrate so much on tactics that we are apt to forget that it is merely the handmaiden of strategy. (Sept. 1930.)

Captain Sir Basil Liddell Hart, *Thoughts on War*, 1944.

SO FAR AS I can see strategy is eternal, and the same and true: but tactics are the ever-changing languages through which it speaks. A general can learn as much from Belisarius as from Haig – but not a soldier. Soldiers have to know their means.

Colonel T.E. Lawrence, Whit Monday 1933, quoted in *T.E. Lawrence to His Biographers*, 1963.

TACTICS is the art of handling troops on the battlefield, strategy is the art of bringing forces to the battlefield in a favourable position.

Field Marshal Viscount Wavell of Cyrenaica, quoted in David Chandler, *The Atlas of Military Strategy*, 1980.

I RATE the skilful tactician above the skilful strategist, especially him who plays the bad cards well.

Field Marshal Viscount Wavell of Cyrenaica, *Soldiers and Soldiering*, 1953.

THE GENERAL PRINCIPLES of strategy apply to tactics too, only that their application is different. A glance back at history will show that while tactics, like strategy, is based on certain truths and laws of permanent worth, the application of these laws will show that tactical forms have changed and developed along with the times, and in accordance with the means which the times provide.

Colonel Hermann Foertsch, *The Art of Modern War*, 1940.

. . . DEFINITION of strategy as – "the art of distributing and applying military means to fulfill the ends of policy". For strategy is concerned not merely with the movement of forces – as its role is often defined – but with the effect. When the application of the military instrument merges into actual fighting, the dispositions for and control of such direct action are termed "tactics". The two categories, although convenient for discussion, can never be truly divided into separate compartments because each not only influences but merges into the other.

Captain Sir Basil Liddell Hart, *Strategy*, 1954.

IN STRATEGY . . . calculation is simpler and a closer approximation to truth possible than in tactics. For in war the chief incalculable is the human will, which manifests itself in resistence, which in turn lies in the province of tactics. Strategy has not to overcome resistence, except from nature. Its purpose is to diminish the possibility of resistence, and it seeks to fulfill this purpose by exploiting the elements of movement and surprise.

Captain Sir Basil Liddell Hart, *Strategy*, 1954.

TALENT FOR WAR

THE BEST GENERAL is not the man of noble family, but the man who can take pride in his own deeds.

The Emperor Maurice, *The Strategikon*, c. AD 600 (*Maurice's Strategikon*, tr. George Dennis, 1984).

UNLESS a man is born with a talent for war, he will never be other than a mediocre general. It is the same with all talents; in painting, or in music, or in poetry, talent must be inherent for excellence. All sublime arts are alike in this respect. That is why we see so few outstanding men in science. Centuries pass without producing one. Application rectifies ideas but does not furnish a soul for that is the work of nature.

Field Marshal Maurice Comte de Saxe, *My Reveries*, 1732, tr. Phillips, 1940.

IT IS BAD to lack good fortune, but it is a misfortune to lack talent. . . . The fortune of war is on the side of the soldier of talent.

Field Marshal Aleksandr V. Suvorov (1729–1800), quoted in K. Ossipov, *Suvorov*, 1945.

WAR is a serious sport, in which one can endanger his reputation and his country: a rational man must feel and know whether or not he is cut out for this profession.

Napoleon, to Prince Eugene, 30 April 1809, *Correspondance de Napoléon Ier, publiée par ordre de l'Empereur Napoléon III*, No. 15144, Vol. XVIII, 1858–1870, p. 525.

HEADLONG, dogged, or innate courage, overmastering ambition, or long familiarity with danger – all must be present to a considerable degree if action in this debilitating environment is not to fall short of achievements that in the study would appear as nothing out of the ordinary.

Major-General Carl von Clausewitz, *On War*, 1.4, 1832, tr. Michael Howard and Peter Paret, 1976.

THE CAPITAL ROLE played by instinct in this matter of conception is recognized in our common parlance.

We say of a statesman, a soldier, or a man of business who conceives rightly, that is to say in accordance with what is, that he has a "sense of reality," that he has "a gift," or that he is possessed of "vision" or "flair." Where action is concerned, nothing can take the place of this effort supplied by nature itself. To it alone is due the fact that men whose intelligence does not call attention to itself, who do not excel at speculation, who do not shine in "paper work" or in theoretical argument, are transformed into masters of the battlefield.

General Charles de Gaulle, *The Edge of the Sword*, 1932.

EVERYONE is born for something, whether it is to be a soldier or a journalist. I was born to be a soldier. Even in my horoscope, which I do not believe in. I am an Aries born in the year of the Tiger – therefore, a warrior twice over. I spent 26 years in the Army and it felt as if it was a day. It was not heavy work. I was never afraid. I did not mind the mud, or the cold, or the blood.

Lieutenant-General Aleksandr I. Lebed, *El Pais* (Madrid), 15 March 1998.

TANKS

I MANAGED to get astride one of the German trenches . . . and opened fire with Hotchkiss machine-guns. There were some Germans in the dug-outs and I shall never forget the look on their faces when they emerged. . . .

Captain H.W. Mortimore, 15 September 1916, commander of the first tank in action, quoted in Trevor Wilson, *The Myriad Faces of War*, 1986.

EMPLOYMENT of tanks in mass is our greatest enemy.

General Erich Ludendorff, quoted in Richard Simpkin, *Race to the Swift*, 1985.

THAT THE application of petrol to land warfare will prove as great a step in tactics as that of steam in naval warfare.

That the characteristics of security, offensive power and mobility, which the tank combines in a higher degree than any single other weapon, are those which are fundamental to success in war.

That the tank enables the main advantages of sea warfare, unrestricted movment, to be to a great extent superimposed on that of land warfare. . . .

That the application of machinery to land warfare is as great a saver of man-power as its application to manufacture. That is: the tank does not create another man-power problem, but is a solution to existing problems.

Major-General J.F.C. Fuller, memorandum of 1918, *Memoirs of an Unconventional Soldier*, 1936.

BUT it is not, of course, enough that the Tank offers protection to those who fight in it. A trench or a hole in the ground will do the same. But the Tank is essentially a mobile weapon of *offense*. It is the weapon for the nation which does not fight willingly, but when it fights, fights to win, and to win quickly with as little bloodshed as possible. It is the weapon for men who, if they must fight, like to fight like intelligent beings still subjecting the material world to their will, and who are most unwillingly reduced to the roles of mere marching automata, bearers of burdens and diggers of the soil, roles from which the patient German did not seem adverse.

Major Clough Williams-Ellis, *The Tank Corps*, 1919.

THE TANK marks as great a revolution in land warfare as an armored steamship would have marked had it appeared amongst the toilsome triremes of Actium.

General Sir Ian Hamilton, *The Soul and Body of an Army*, 1921.

THERE never was a moment when it was possible to say that a tank had been "invented". There never was a person about whom it could be said "this man invented the tank". But there was a moment when the actual manufacture of the first tanks was definitely ordered, and there was a moment when an effective machine was designed as the direct outcome of this authorization.

Sir Winston S. Churchill, *The World Crisis*, 1923.

"IT WAS Mr. Churchill who, as First Lord of the Admiralty, gave the first order for eighteen tanks, or "landships" as they were then called, on March 26, 1915. He did not inform either the War Office or the Treasury – an almost unprecedented and certainly unconstitutional reticence, dictated by fear that conventional minds might stifle a great idea."

Sir Winston S. Churchill, quoted in Colin Coote, ed., *Maxims and Reflections*, 1949.

ONCE appreciate that tanks are not an extra arm or mere aid to infantry but the modern form of heavy cavalry and their true military use is obvious – to be concentrated and used in as large masses as possible for a decisive blow against the Achilles' heel of the enemy army, the communications and command centres which form its nerve system.

Captain Sir Basil Liddell Hart, writing in the *Westminster Gazette*, 1925.

THE READER will find in Fuller many interesting ideas about tank actions. He should pay particular attention to the actions of tanks in the enemy's rear, which, together with a simultaneous frontal assault, must undoubtedly result in more intensive manoeuvre and more decisive tactical action in modern battles. To the turning movement and the flank and rear attack (the sphere of classical, conventional manoeuvre) are added the seizure of rear boundaries, complete penetrations and sudden machine-gun attacks in depth . . . by tanks.

Marshal of the Soviet Union Mikhail N. Tukhachevskiy,

preface to Russian-language edition of J.F.C. Fuller's *The Reformation of War*, 1931.

THE SETTING UP of a deep battle – that is the simultaneous disruption of the enemy's tactical layout over its entire depth – requires two things of tanks. On the one hand they must help the infantry forward and accompany it; on the other they must penetrate into the enemy's rear, both to disorganize him and to isolate his main forces from the reserves at his disposal. This deep penetration by tanks must create in the enemy's rear an obstcle for him, onto which he must be forced back and on which his main forces must be destroyed.

Marshal of the Soviet Union Mikhail N. Tukhachevskiy, 'New Questions of War', written 1931/1932, but published finally in *Voyenno istoritchiskiy zhurnal*, 2/1962, quoted in Richard Simpkin, *Deep Battle*, 1987.

. . . THE INTERNAL-COMBUSTION engine which is ready to carry whatever one wants, wherever it is needed, at all speeds and distances . . . the internal-combustion engine which, if it is armoured, possesses such a fire power and shock power that the rhythm of the battle corresponds to that of its movements.

General Charles de Gaulle, *The Army of the Future*, 1934.

ON THE other side of the coin, a group of comrades looked not a little askance at the introduction into the army of tanks in mass. They were scared of rain, snow, autumn, spring and the like. Some comrades said that, because of our roads and climatic conditions, tanks would only be able to operate "for something like six weeks in the year." However the tank's talent for lively action soon stood the misgivings of these timid theorists on their heads. Tanks perform perfectly well in summer, winter, spring, and autumn.

Marshal of the Soviet Union Mikhail N. Tukhachevskiy, Red Army *Field Service Regulations* (1936), quoted in Richard Simpkin, *Deep Battle*, 1987.

UNTIL our critics can produce some new and better method of making a successful land attack other than self-massacre, we shall continue to maintain our belief that tanks – properly employed, needless to say – are today the best means available for a land attack.

Colonel-General Heinz Guderian, *Achtung! Panzer!*, 1937.

(THE TANK) is therefore the weapon of potentially decisive attack. Mobility and firepower will only be exploited to the full if the attack achieves deep penetration and the armoured force, having broken out, can go over to the pursuit. . . . The higher the concentration of tanks, the faster, greater and more sweeping will be the success – and the smaller our own losses. . . . Tanks must attack with surprise, and as far as possible where the enemy is known or presumed to be weak. . . . The tank needs supporting arms which complement it and can go everywhere with it. . . . Even in defence, the tank must be employed offensively. Concentration is even more important here, so that the enemy's superiority can be offset at least in one spot.

> Colonel-General Heinz Guderian, *Panzer Marsch!*, 1937, quoted in Richard Simpkin, *The Race to the Swift*, 1985.

THE SHORTER the battle, the fewer men will be killed and hence the greater their self-confidence and enthusiasm. To produce a short battle, tanks must advance rapidly but not hastily. . . . Mobile forces should be used in large groups and [be] vigorously led. They must attempt the impossible and dare the unknown.

> General George S. Patton, Jr., 1939, after reading an article by Heinz Guderian on tanks, *The Patton Papers*, II, 1974.

I WANT to bring to the attention of every officer here the professional significance which will attach to the success or failure of the 2d Armored Division in the Tennessee maneuvers. There are a large number of officers, some of them in high places in our country, who through lack of knowledge as to the capability of an armored division are opposed to them and who would prefer to see us organize a large number of old fashioned divisions about whose ability the officers in question have more information. It is my considered opinion that the creation of too many old type divisions will be distinctly detrimental and that the future of our country may well depend on the organization of a considerably larger number of armored divisions than are at present visualized. Therefore it behooves everyone of us to do his uttermost to see that in these forthcoming maneuvers we are not only a success but such an outstanding success that there could be no possible doubt in the minds of anyone as to the effectiveness of the armored divisions. Bear this in mind every moment.

> General George S. Patton, Jr., address to the officers of the Second Armored Division, May 1941, *The Patton Papers*, II, 1974.

ALTHOUGH the tactical consequences of motorisation and armour had been pre-eminently demonstrated by British military critics, the responsible British leaders had not taken the risk either of using this hitherto untried system as a foundation for peacetime training, or of applying it in war.

> Field Marshal Erwin Rommel, *The Rommel Papers*, 1953.

THE OFFICERS of a panzer division must learn to think and act independently within the framework of the general plan and not wait until they receive orders.

> Field Marshal Erwin Rommel, *The Rommel Papers*, 1953.

IT WAS principally the books and articles of the Englishmen, Fuller, Liddell Hart, and Martel, that excited my interest and gave me food for thought. These far-sighted soldiers were even then trying to make of the tank something more than just an infantry support weapon. They envisaged it in relationship to the growing motorization of our age, and thus they became the pioneers of a new type of warfare on the largest scale.

I learned from them the concentration of armor, as employed in the battle of Cambrai. Further, it was Liddell Hart who emphasized the use of armored forces for long-range strokes, operations against the opposing army's communications, and also proposed a type of armored division combining panzer and panzer-infantry units. Deeply impressed by these ideas I tried to develop them in a sense practicable for our own army. So I owe many suggestions of our further development to Captain Liddell Hart.

> Colonel-General Heinz Guderian, *Panzer Leader*, 1953.

I WAS BROUGHT UP in the Israeli Army which no doubt, was very much influenced by your unorthodoxic [sic] school of thought, and of course I am strongly in favor of your ideas.

> General Ariel Sharon, letter to Liddell Hart.

ARMOR – The Combat Arm of Decision.

> Motto of the U.S. Army Armor Branch.

FEAR naught.

> Motto of the British Royal Tank Corps.

TEAM/TEAMWORK

NESTOR, the mission stirs my fighting blood.
I'll slip right into enemy lines at once –
these Trojans, camped at our flank.
If another comrade would escort me, though,
there'd be more comfort in it, confidence too.
When two work side-by-side, one or the other spots
    the opening first if a kill's at hand.
When one looks out for himself, alert but alone,
his reach is shorter – his sly moves miss the mark.

> Homer, *The Iliad*, 10.258–266, c. 800 BC, tr. Robert Fagles, 1990; King Diomedes of Argos, asking for a companion when he volunteered to reconnoitre the Trojan camp.

FOUR BRAVE MEN who do not know each other will not dare to attack a lion. Four less brave, but knowing each other well, sure of their reliability and consequently of their mutual aid, will attack resolutely.

> Colonel Charles Ardant du Picq, *Battle Studies*, 1880, tr. Greely, 1957.

BUT AFTER ALL, no leadership or expert naval direction could be successful unless it were supported by the whole body of officers and men of the Navy. It is upon these faithful, trusty servants in the great ships and cruisers that the burden falls directly day after day.

Sir Winston S. Churchill, speech in the House of Commons, 18 December 1939, *Blood, Sweat, and Tears*, 1941.

AN ARMY is a team. It eats, sleeps, lives and fights as a team. All this stuff you've been hearing about individuality is a bunch of crap. The billious bastard who wrote that kind of stuff for the Saturday Evening Post didn't know anymore about real battle than he did about fucking. . . .

. . . Every man, every department, every unit, is important to the vast scheme of things. The ordnance men are needed to supply the guns, the QM to bring up the food and the clothes for us, for where we are going, there isn't a hell of a lot for us to steal. Every man in the mess hall, even the one who heats the water to keep us from getting diarrhea, has a job to do. Even the chaplain is important, for if we get killed and he isn't there to bury us, we would all go to hell.

General George S. Patton, Jr., speech to the Third Army, June 1944, 'A General Talks to His Army', 1944.

OUR MILITARY FORCES are one team – in the game to win regardless of who carries the ball. This is no time for "fancydans" who won't hit the line with all they have on every play, unless they can call the signals. Each player on the team – whether he shines in the spotlight of the backfield or eats dirt in the line – must be All-American.

General of the Army Omar N. Bradley, 19 October 1949, testimony to Congress.

THE CHINESE were now on the position and firing at whatever was coming or going on the slope below them. At that point I issued the shortest "five paragraph field combat order" of my career, "F? it, LET'S GO!" As if by magic the squads and fire teams dropped their heavy packs, spread out and assaulted, the BARs [Browning automatic rifles] gaining fire superiority as we went. It was just like the endless assault drills we practiced at Camp Tripoli while in reserve. Like the working of the human hand, each finger is different and moves independently, but all work in harmony to do what the hand needs to do. A well trained unit, with perfect trust in one another, operates the same way. . . .

Lieutenant-General Bernard E. Trainor, observations of combat in Korea, March 1952, 'On Fighting in a Forgotten War', *Marine Corps Gazette*, August 1998.

TEMPO

DEFEAT the enemy with cold steel, bayonets, swords, and pikes. . . . Don't slow down during an attack. When the enemy is broken, shattered, then pursue him at once, and don't give him time either to collect or re-form. If he surrenders, spare him; only order him to throw down his arms. During the attack call on the enemy to surrender. . . . Spare nothing, don't think of your labours; pursue the enemy night and day, so long as anything is left to be destroyed.

Field Marshal Prince Aleksandr V. Suvorov, *The Science of Victory*, 1796.

KEEP GOING all the time and always forward.

Major-General John A. Lejeune, personal motto, *The Public Ledger* (Philadelphia), 1 August 1920.

A CERTAIN DEGREE of disorganization attends every stage of an advance. Immobilization is ever the child of disorganization. Troops start an attack in a certain formation; movement and enemy fire gradually destroy its integrity; unit of action becomes dissipated at the same rate. The result is that unless the commander is thinking always beyond the immediate objective and planning the means by which he can restore impetus after the object is won, the attack will bog down even though the unit hasn't suffered critical losses in man strength.

Brigadier-General S.L.A. Marshall, *Men Against Fire*, 1947.

A COMMANDER must accustom his staff to a high tempo from the outset, and continuously keep them up to it. If he once allows himself to be satisfied with norms, or anything less than an all-out effort, he gives up the race from the starting post, and will sooner or later be taught a bitter lesson.

Field Marshal Erwin Rommel, *The Rommel Papers*, 1953.

IT IS physically impossible to sustain a high tempo of activity indefinitely, although clearly there will be times when it is advantageous to push men and equipment to the limit. Thus, the tempo of war will fluctuate – from periods of intense activity to periods in which activity is limited to information gathering, replenishment, or redeployment. Darkness and weather can influence the tempo of war but need not halt it. A competitive rhythm will develop between the opposing wills, with each belligerent trying to influence and exploit tempo and the continuous flow of events to suit his purposes.

General Alfred M. Gray and Major John Schmitt, *Warfighting*, United States Marine Corps, 1989.

TENACITY

IF the military leader is filled with high ambition and if he pursues his aims with audacity and strength of will, he will reach them in spite of all obstacles.

Major-General Carl von Clausewitz, *Principles of War*, 1812, tr. Gatzke, 1942.

THE ENEMY hold our front in very strong force, and evince a strong determination to interpose between us and Richmond to the last. I shall take no backward steps. . . .

> General of the Army Ulysses S. Grant, letter to Major-General Halleck during the Battle of Spottsylvania, 10 May 1864, quoted in Horace Porter, *Campaigning With Grant*, 1897.

I HAVE SEEN your despatch expressing your unwillingess to break your hold where you are. Neither am I willing. Hold on with a bulldog grip, and chew and choke as much as possible.

> President Abraham Lincoln, 17 August 1864, dispatch to General Grant on the James River, supporting Grant's refusal of General Halleck's suggestion that he detach troops to help quell expected disturbances over another draft call, quoted in Horace Porter, *Campaigning With Grant*, 1897.

WHEN GRANT gets possession of a place, he holds on to it as if he had inherited it.

> President Abraham Lincoln to Major-General Butler, 22 June 1864, quoted in Horace Porter, *Campaigning With Grant*, 1897.

I HAVE to take this place. The chances are that I shall lose some of my vessels by torpedoes or the guns of the enemy, but with some of my fleet afloat I shall eventually be successful. I can not lose all. I will attack, regardless of consequences, and never turn back.

> Admiral David G. Farragut, quoted in Loyall Farragut, *The Life of David Glasgow Farragut*, 1879.

TENACITY of purpose and untiring energy in execution can repair a first mistake and baffle deeply laid plans.

> Rear-Admiral Alfred Thayer Mahan (1840–1914).

VICTORY will come to the side that outlasts the other.

> Marshal of France Ferdinand Foch, 7 September 1914, order during the First Battle of the Marne.

I KNEW my ground, my material and my allies. If I met fifty checks I could yet see a fifty-first way to my object.

> Colonel T.E. Lawrence (1888–1935).

ONCE an action is begun, it should be carried through regardless of difficulties. If the going is hard, one should think of the enemy's losses and his fear, and so carry on to victory. A commander should not ignore the possibility of help coming to the enemy, nor should he be overly worried about it. An action begun and broken off when tenaciousness might have secured victory only breaks down morale. To persist and win through reveals a commander's strong will to win. On the other hand, when an action has been ordered, or even initiated, and circumstances so change the situation as to make it hopeless, a reversal of the order reveals a commander's versatility.

> General Lin Piao, 1946, quoted in Ebon, *Lin Piao*, 1970.

POSITIONS are seldom lost because they have been destroyed, but almost invariably because the leader has decided in his own mind that the position cannot be held.

> General Alexander A. Vandegrift (1887–1973), quoted in *Warfighting*, Fleet Marine Force Manual (FMFM) 1, 1990.

TERRAIN

THE NATURAL FORMATION of the country is the soldier's best ally.

> Sun Tzu, *The Art of War*, 10, c. 500 BC, tr. Giles, 1910.

THE NATURE of the ground is often of more consequence than courage.

> Flavius Vegetius Renatus, *The Military Institutions of the Romans*, c. AD 378, tr. Clark, 1776.

WE SHOULD CHOOSE the terrain not only to suit our armament, but also with a view to the various peoples. Parthians and Gauls handle themselves well on the Plains. The Spanish and Ligurians fight better in the mountains and hills, and the Britons in the woods, while the Germans are more at home in the swamps.

Whatever terrain the general chooses, he should make his troops familiar with it. They will then be able to avoid the rough spots and because of their knowledge of the area will fight the enemy with confidence.

> The Emperor Maurice, *The Strategikon*, c. AD 600 (*Maurice's Strategikon*, tr. George Dennis, 1984).

A GENERAL should possess a perfect knowledge of the localities where he is carrying on a war.

> Niccolo Machiavelli, *Discourses*, 1517.

KNOWLEDGE of the country is to a general what a rifle is to an infantryman and what the rules of arithmetic are to a geometrician. If he does not know the country he will do nothing but make gross mistakes. Without this knowledge his projects, be they otherwise admirable, become ridiculous and often impracticable. Therefore study the country where you are going to act!

> Frederick the Great, *Instructions to His Generals*, 1747, tr. Phillips, 1940.

TERRAIN for the military man is the same as the chess board for the player who wants to deploy and move his pawns, knights and elephants in the most effective way.

> Frederick the Great, *Testament Politique*, 1768.

IN EVERY OCCASION where it is a question of attacking the enemy, the way in which you must fight depends upon the terrain and the advantages that the enemy is skillful enough to procure for himself. . . . Terrain is the foremost oracle that one must consult, after which he can fathom the enemy dispositions by his own knowledge of the rules of war.

> Frederick the Great, '*Pensées et règles générales pour*

la guerre', 1755, *Oeuvres de Frederic le Grand*, Vol. XXVII, 1846–1856, quoted in Jay Luvaas, ed., *Frederick the Great on the Art of War*, 1966.

AS MANY different terrains as there are in existence, just so many different battles will there be.
> Frederick the Great (1712–1786), quoted in Hugo von Freytag-Loringhoven, *Generalship in the Great War*, 1920.

WHERE a deer can cross, a soldier can cross.
> Field Marshal Prince Aleksandr V. Suvorov (1729–1800), quoted in K. Ossipov, *Suvorov*, 1945.

MAXIM 104. An army can march anywhere and at any time of the year, wherever two men can place their feet.

MAXIM 105. Conditions on the ground should not alone decide the organization for combat, which should be determined from consideration of all circumstances.

MAXIM 111. The geographical conditions of a country, life in plains or mountains, education or discipline, have more influence than climate on the character of the troops.
> Napoleon, *The Military Maxims of Napoleon*, tr. Burnod, 1827.

NOW we must address ourselves to a special feature of military activity – possibly the most striking even though it is not the most important – which is not related to temperament, and involves merely the intellect. I mean the relationship between warfare and terrain.
> This relationship . . . is *a permanent factor* – so much so that one cannot conceive of a regular army operating except in a definite space. Second, its importance is *decisive in the highest degree*, for it affects the operations of all forces, and at times entirely alters them. Third, its influence may be felt in the *very smallest feature of the ground*, but it can also dominate *enormous areas*.
> Major-General Carl von Clausewitz, *On War*, 1.3, 1832, tr. Michael Howard and Peter Paret, 1976.

TERRAIN difficulties can be overcome only by a special faculty we sometimes call "a sense of locality [*ortsinn*]." It is an ability to form an accurate mental picture of the country, and readily orient one's self with it. This sense of locality is largely imagination, coming in part from actual visual impressions, and part from a mental process which uses knowledge gained from study and experience to fill in missing points and make a complete whole of the fragments determined by physical sight. The power of imagination then brings this whole picture before the minds eye, makes it into a picture, or a mental map, and maintains it permanently present and unbroken.
> Major-General Carl von Clausewitz, *On War*, 1.3, 1832, tr. Michael Howard and Peter Paret, 1976.

COULD a dog pass? Then that's enough. Where a dog can go, so can a Russian soldier.
> General Veliaminov, 1828, describing warfare in the Caucasus, quoted in Blanch, *The Sabres of Paradise*, 1960.

EVERY DAY I feel more and more in need of an atlas, as the knowledge of the geography in its minutest details is essential to a true military education.
> General of the Army William T. Sherman, quoted in Chandler, ed., *Atlas of Military Strategy*, 1980.

DETAILED map studies can easily divert us from close examination of the ground. . . . Taine calls our attention to the clarity of Napoleon's insight – a faculty we seem to have been losing for the past three hundred years by reason of our indoor education and studies in the fields of science. He says "Instead of things themselves we study the conventional signs for them; instead of the ground we study the map."
> General Baron Hugo von Freytag-Loringhoven, *The Power of Personality in War*, 1911, tr. Spaulding, 1938.

NATURAL HAZARDS, however formidable are inherently less dangerous and uncertain than fighting hazards.
> Captain Sir Basil Liddell Hart, *Strategy*, 1954.

THEORY AND PRACTICE

EVERY ART has its rules and maxims; they must be studied. Theory facilitates practice. The lifetime of one man is not sufficiently long to enable him to acquire perfect knowledge and experience; theory helps to supplement it; it provides youth with early experience and makes him skilful also through the mistakes of others. In the profession of war the rules of the art are never transgressed without punishment from the enemy.
> Frederick the Great, *Oeuvres*, 29. 58–59, quoted in Azer Gat, *The Origins of Military Thought*, 1989.

PITY the theory that conflicts with reason! No amount of humility can gloss over the contradiction; indeed, the greater the humility, the sooner it will be driven off the field of real life by ridicule and contempt.
> Major-General Carl von Clausewitz, *On War*, 2.2, 1832, tr. Michael Howard and Peter Paret, 1976.

THEORY becomes infinitely more difficult as soon as it touches the realm of moral values.
> Major-General Carl von Clausewitz, *On War*, 2.2, 1832, tr. Michael Howard and Peter Paret, 1976.

IT IS simply not possible to construct a model for the art of war that can serve as scaffolding on which the commander can rely for support at any time. Whenever he has to fall back on his innate talent, he will find himself outside the model and in conflict with it; no matter how versatile the code, the situation will

always lead to the consequences we have already alluded to: *talent and genius operate outside the rules, and theory conflicts with practice.*
> Major-General Carl von Clausewitz, *On War*, 2.2, 1832, tr. Michael Howard and Peter Paret, 1976.

THEORY will have fulfilled its main task when it is used to analyze the constituent elements of war, to distinguish precisely what at first sight seems fused, to explain in full the properties of the means employed and to show their probable effects, to define clearly the nature of the ends in view, and to illuminate all phases of warfare in a thorough critical inquiry. Theory then becomes a guide to anyone who wants to learn about war from books; it will light his way, ease his progress, train his judgment, and help him to avoid pitfalls.
> Major-General Carl von Clausewitz, *On War*, 2.2, 1832, tr. Michael Howard and Peter Paret, 1976.

THEORY exists so that one need not start afresh each time sorting out the material and plowing through it, but will find it ready to hand and in good order. It is meant to educate the mind of the future commander or, more accurately, to guide him in his self-education, not to accompany him to the battlefield.
> Major-General Carl von Clausewitz, *On War*, 2.2, 1832, tr. Michael Howard and Peter Paret, 1976.

THEORY cannot equip the mind with formulas for solving problems, nor can it mark the narrow path on which the sole solution is supposed to lie by planting a hedge of principles on either side. But it can give the mind insight into the great mass of phenomena and of their relationships, then leave it free to rise into the higher realms of action.
> Major-General Carl von Clausewitz, *On War*, 8.1, 1832, tr. Michael Howard and Peter Paret, 1976.

ONE of the surest ways of forming good combinations in war would be to order movements only after obtaining perfect information of the enemy's proceedings. In fact, how can any man say what he should do himself, if he is ignorant of what his adversary is about? Even as it is unquestionably of the highest importance to gain this information, so it is a thing of the utmost difficulty, not to say impossibility. This is one of the chief causes of the great difference between the theory and the practice of war.
> Lieutenant-General Antoine-Henri Baron de Jomini, *Summary of the Art of War*, 1838, tr. Mendell and Craighill, 1862.

WHEN the application of a rule and the consequent maneuver have procured victory a hundred times for skillful generals, shall their occasional failure be a sufficient reason for entirely denying their value and for distrusting the effect of the study of the art? Shall a theory be pronounced absurd because it has only three-fourths of the whole number of chances in its favor?
> Lieutenant-General Antoine-Henri Baron de Jomini,

Summary of the Art of War, 1838, tr. Mendell and Craighill, 1862.

IF THEORY went wrong, it is due to the fact that very few theorists had seen war. . . .
> General Mikhail I. Dragomirov (1830–1905), quoted in Ferdinand Foch, *Principles of War*, 1913.

FOR US theory is the basis of confidence in the actions being taken. . . .
> V.I. Lenin (1870–1924).

TO THOSE COMRADES who wish to build in military affairs by means of the Marxist method I recommend that they review our field statutes in this light and indicate just what changes – from the standpoint of Marxism – should be introduced into the rules for gathering intelligence, for securing one's lines, for artillery preparation, or for attack. I should very much like to hear at least a single new word in this sphere arrived at through the Marxist method – not just "an opinion or so" but something new and practical.
> Leon Trotksy, 8 May 1922, opening remarks to the Military Scientific Society, *Military Writings*, 1969.

DUE TO the facility with which men, material, and even situations may be created on paper, many writers produce theses on war as admirable as they are impractical. Due also to our school experiences where such intangible factors as morale, training, discipline, fatigue, equipment, and supply cannot be considered, we adopt the simple course of first omitting reference to these factors, and later of assuming them all satisfactory . . .
Duped by the historians who explain defeat and enhance victory by assuring us that both result from the use of PERFECT armies, the fruit of super-thinking, we never stop to consider the inaptness of the word perfect as a definition for armies.
> General George S. Patton, Jr., January 1928, *The Patton Papers*, I, 1972.

I HAVE NOTHING to say against theoretical training, and certainly nothing against practical training. Whoever would become master of his craft must have served as apprentice and journeyman; only a genius can bridge gaps in this sequence of instruction. Every man of action is an artist, and he must know the material with which, in which, and against which he works before he begins his task.
> Colonel-General Hans von Seekt, *Thoughts of a Soldier*, 1930.

THE OBJECTIVE value of a broad survey of war is not limited to the research for new and true doctrine. If a broad survey is an essential foundation for any theory of war, it is equally necessary for the ordinary military student who seeks to develop his own outlook and judgment. Otherwise his knowledge of

war will be like an inverted pyramid balanced
precariously on a slender apex.

Captain Sir Basil Liddell Hart, *Strategy*, 1954.

THOSE LEFT BEHIND

SO his whole head was dragged down in the dust.
And now his mother began to tear her hair . . .
she flung her shining veil to the ground and raised
a high, shattering scream, looking down at her son.
Pitifully his loving father groaned and round the king
his people cried with grief and wailing seized the city –
for all the world as if all Troy were torched and
    smoldering
down from the looming brows of the citadel to
    her roots.
Priam's people could hardly hold the old man back,
frantic, mad to go rushing out the Dardan Gates.
He begged them all, groveling in the filth,
crying out to them, calling each man by name,
"Let go, my friends! Much as you care for me,
let me hurry out of the city, make my way,
all on my own, to Achaea's waiting ships!
I must implore that terrible, violent man . . .
Perhaps – who knows? – he may respect my age,
may pity an old man. He has a father too,
as old as I am – Peleus sired him once,
Peleus reared him to be the scourge of Troy
but most of all to me – he made my life a hell.
So many sons he slaughtered, just coming into
    bloom . . .
and stabbing grief for him will take me down to Death –
my Hector – would to god he had perished in
    my arms!
Then his mother who bore him – oh so doomed,
she and I could glut ourselves with grief."

Homer, *The Iliad*, 22.477–503, c. 800 BC, tr. Robert
Fagles, 1990; the grief of King Priam of Troy, having
just witnessed the death of his son Hector at the
hands of Achilles beneath the walls of the city.

THOSE who are not here are eating earth that we
might live. Are we to forget the sorrowing mothers
who bore them, and let their younger brothers and
sisters go in want, because they gave their lives for
our Zululand? Have we not a saying that a grieving
mother's heart is soothed by a stomach full of meat?
Well then, let us give to the bereaved the reward
which the departed warriors would have received
had they lived, and let us give a double measure,
with both hands, to take the taste of bitter aloes from
the mouths of the sorrowing ones.

Shaka Zulu, 1819, after the Second Ndwandwe War,
quoted in E.A. Ritter, *Shaka Zulu*, 1955.

JULY 14, 1861
Camp Clark, Washington

My very dear Sarah:
    The indications are very strong that we shall move

in a few days – perhaps tomorrow, and lest I should
not be able to write again, I feel impelled to write a
few lines that may fall under your eye when I shall
be no more. . . .
    I have no misgivings about, or lack of confidence
in the cause in which I am engaged, and my
courage does not halt or falter. I know how American
Civilization now leans on the triumph of the
Government, and how great a debt we owe to those
who went before us through the blood and suffering
of the Revolution. And I am willing – perfectly willing
– to lay down all my joys in this life, to help maintain
this Government, and to pay the debt. . . .
    Sarah my love for you is deathless, it seems to bind
me with mighty cables that nothing but Omnipotence
could break; and yet my love of Country comes over
me like a strong wind and bears me unresistably with
all these chains to the battle field.
    The memories of the blissful moments I have
enjoyed with you come crowding over me, and I feel
most deeply grateful to God and to you that I have
enjoyed them so long. And how hard it is for me to
give them up and burn to ashes the hopes of future
years, when, God willing, we might still have lived
and loved together, and see our boys grown up to
honourable manhood, around us. If I do not return,
my dear Sarah, never forget how much I loved you,
nor when my last breath escapes me on the battle
field, it will whisper your name. Forgive me my
faults, and the many pains I have caused you. How
thoughtless, how foolish I have often times been!
    But, O Sarah! if the dead can come back to this
earth and flit unseen around those they love, I shall
always be with you; in the brightest day and the
darkest night . . . always, always; and when the soft
breeze fans your cheek, it shall be my breath, or the
cool air your throbbing temple, it shall be my spirit
passing by. Sarah do not mourn me dead; think I am
gone and wait for me, for we shall meet again. . . .

Major Sullivan Ballou, Second Rhode Island
Volunteers, letter to his wife in Smithfield, written a
week before his death at the Battle of First Bull Run,
quoted in Ken Burns, *The Civil War*, 1990.

WAIT FOR ME

Wait for me, and I'll return.
Only wait very hard . . .
Wait, when you are filled with sorrow
As you watch the yellow rain,
Wait, when the wind sweeps the snowdrifts,
Wait, in the sweltering heat,
Wait, when others have stopped waiting,
Forgetting their yesterdays.
Wait, even when from afar no letters come to you,
Wait, even when others are tired of waiting,
Wait, even when my mother and son think I am no
    more,
And when friends sit around the fire drinking to my
    memory,
Wait, and do not hurry to drink to my memory too;

Wait for I'll return,
Defying every death,
And let those who do not wait
Say I was lucky.
They will never understand
That in the midst of death,
You with your waiting saved me.
Only you and I will know how I survived, –
It's because you waited,
As no one else did.
    Konstantin Simonov, c. 1943, the most famous
    Russian poem of WWII.

I DON'T THINK there's ever been . . . even in the history of warfare, been a successful count of the dead . . . The people who will know [the count] best, unfortunately, are the families that won't see their loved ones come home.
    General H. Norman Schwarzkopf, 27 February 1991,
    briefing to the press corps, Saudi Arabia.

THEY ARE the gold star children, war's innocent victims, and their pain shimmers across the years pure and undimmed. They pass through life with an empty room in their hearts where a father was supposed to live and laugh and love.
    All their lives they listen for the footstep that will never fall, and long to know what might have been.
    Lieutenant-General Harold G. Moore, *We Were
    Soldiers Once . . . and Young*, 1992.

TIME/TIMING

KNOWING the place and time of a coming battle, we may concentrate from great distances in order to fight.
    But if neither time nor place be known, then the left wing will be impotent to succor the right, the right equally impotent to succor the left, the van unable to relieve the rear, or the rear to support the van. How much more so if the furthest portions of the army are anything under a hundred li apart and even the nearest are separated by several li.
    Sun Tzu, *The Art of War*, 6, c. 500 BC, tr. Giles, 1910.

IT IS BETTER to be at the right place with ten men than absent with ten thousand.
    Tamerlane (AD 1336–1405), quoted in Harold Lamb,
    Tamerlane, The Earth Shaker, 1928.

DISINTEGRATION happens to everything. When a house crumbles, a person crumbles, or an adversary crumbles, they fall apart by getting out of rhythm with the times.
    In the art of war on a large scale, it is also essential to find the rhythm of opponents as they come apart, and pursue them so as not to let openings slip by. If you miss the timing of vulnerable moments, there is the likelihood of counterattack.
    In the individual art of war it also happens that an adversary will get out of rhythm in combat and start to

fall apart. If you let such a chance get by you, the adversary will recover and thwart you. It is essential to follow up firmly on any loss of poise on the part of an adversary, to prevent the opponent from recovering.
    Miyamoto Musashi, *Book of the Five Spheres* (*The
    Japanese Art of War*, tr. Thomas Cleary, 1991).

THE MOMENT provides the victory. One moment decides the outcome of a battle and one – the success of a campaign. I do not operate in hours, but rather in minutes.
    Field Marshal Prince Aleksandr V. Suvorov
    (1729–1800), quoted in *Voyenny Vestnik*, 11/1986.

ADMIRAL, we have no time to lose. Fortune gave me three days only.
    Napoleon, 1 July 1798, to Admiral Brueys at
    Alexandria when the admiral protested at Napoleon's
    command to land his army immediately; Nelson's fleet
    had only departed three days before; quoted in
    S.J. Watson, *By Command of the Emperor*, 1957.

IN MILITARY OPERATIONS, hours determine success and campaigns.
    Napoleon, 20 March 1800, to Admiral Mazarredo,
    *Correspondance de Napoléon Ier, publiée par ordre
    de l'Empereur Napoléon III*, No. 4689, Vol. VI,
    1858–1870.

WHAT A PITY it is that I cannot move on for want of grain! My troops are in high health, order and spirits, but the unfortunate defect of arrangement . . . previous to my arrival has ruined everything. . . . If I had been able to reach the river one day sooner I should have been across before it filled. . . . How true it is that in military operations, time is everthing.
    The Duke of Wellington, 30 June 1800, to Lieutenant-
    Colonel Close, after failing by one day to ford a river
    before the monsoon broke, quoted in Arthur Bryant,
    The Great Duke, 1972.

GO, SIR, gallop, and don't forget that the world was made in six days. You can ask me for anything you like, except time.
    Napoleon, 11 March 1803, to a courier to the Tsar,
    quoted in R.M. Johnston, ed., *The Corsican*, 1910.

TIME is everything in military operations.
    The Duke of Wellington, *The Dispatches of Field
    Marshal the Duke of Wellington, During His Various
    Campaigns in India, Denmark, Portugal, Spain, the
    Low Countries, and France*, Vol. II, 1834–1838.

TIME is everything; five minutes make the difference between victory and defeat.
    Admiral Viscount Nelson (1758–1805).

THE LOSS of time is irretrievable in war; the excuses that are advanced are always bad ones, for operations go wrong only through delays.
    Napoleon, 20 March 1806, to Joseph Bonaparte,

Correspondance de Napoléon Ier, publiée par ordre de l'Empereur Napoléon III, No. 9997, Vol. XII, 1858–1870.

IT MAY BE that in the future I may lose a battle, but I shall never lose a minute.
Napoleon, quoted in Liddell Hart, *Strategy*, 1954.

STRATEGY is the art of making use of time and space. I am less chary of the latter than of the former; space we can recover, time never.
Napoleon, *Correspondance de Napoléon Ier, publiée par ordre de l'Empereur Napoléon III*, Vol. XVIII, No. 140707, 1858–1870, p. 218.

RAPIDITY! Activity! Activity! All lies with you!
Napoleon, 18 April 1809, to Marshal Masséna during the Austrian campaign, quoted in R.M. Johnston, ed., *The Corsican*, 1910.

COME. Every moment is precious, your presence is useless here; join the advance guard . . . I need a man who understands me; today's battle will be decisive.
Napoleon to Marshal Masséna, 22 April 1809, before the Battle of Eckmühl, quoted in General Koch, *Mémoires de Masséna*, VI, 1850.

FORCE AND TIME in this kind of operation amount to almost the same thing, and each can to a very large extent be expressed in terms of each other.
A week lost was about the same as a division. Three divisions in February could have occupied the Gallipoli Peninsula with little fighting. Five could have captured it after March 18. Seven were insignificant at the end of April, but nine just might have done it. Eleven might have sufficed at the beginning of July. Fourteen were to prove insufficient on Aug. 7.
Sir Winston S. Churchill, of the Gallipoli campaign in 1915.

THE WAR of 1914–1918 changed all ideas of time, in a military sense, and especially in the duration of its battles. For several thousand years of warfare a battle, however great its scale, had been a matter of hours. With the World War this standard became months – because the battles became sieges, without being recognized or scientifically treated as such. The change, it is to be hoped, is a transitory one, for quantity does not imply quality, whereas duration does not imply immobility and indecisiveness – which are the negation of generalship. Whether from the standpoint of military science or from that of the drain of human life, long battles are bad battles. (March 1926.)
Captain Sir Basil Liddell Hart, *Thoughts on War*, 1944.

MOBILITY of troops economizes time in battle. *Time in war is all*.
Marshal of the Soviet Union Aleksandr I. Yegorov (1883–1939), quoted in R.L. Garthoff, *Soviet Military Doctrine*, 1953.

OUR CARDS were speed and time, not hitting power, and these gave us strategical rather than tactical strength. Range is more to strategy than force.
Colonel T.E. Lawrence, 'The Science of Guerrilla Warfare', *Encyclopaedia Britannica*, 1929.

ONE of the deeper truths of war has been aptly expressed by Lawrence – "timing in war depends on the enemy as much as upon yourself." Timetables too often enable the enemy to turn the tables on you. (Aug. 1933.)
Captain Sir Basil Liddell Hart, *Thoughts on War*, 1944.

THE HISTORY of failure in war can almost be summed up in two words: too late. Too late in comprehending the deadly purpose of a potential enemy; too late in realizing the mortal danger; too late in preparedness; too late in uniting all possible forces for resistance; too late in standing with one's friends. Victory in war results from no mysterious alchemy of wizardry but entirely upon the concentration of superior force at the critical points of combat. To face an adversary in detail has been the prayer of every conquerer in history.
General of the Army Douglas MacArthur, 16 September 1940, statement for the Committee to Defend America by Aiding the Allies, *A Soldier Speaks*, 1965.

DEATH in battle is a function of time. The longer the troops remain under fire, the more men get killed. Therefore, everything must be done to speed up movement.
General George S. Patton, Jr., April 1943, *The Patton Papers*, II, 1974.

TIME is neutral; but it can be made the ally of those who will seize it and use it to the full.
Sir Winston S. Churchill (1874–1965).

A GOOD SOLUTION applied with vigor now is better than a perfect solution ten minutes later.
General George S. Patton, Jr., *War As I Knew It*, 1947.

TIME is the essence in war, and while a defeat may be balanced by a battle won, days and hours – even minutes – frittered away, can never be regained.
Brigadier-General Samuel B. Griffith II, *The Battle for Guadalcanal*, 1963.

A BATTALION this week can often be more effective than a division next month.
British Army motto.

TIMIDITY

A GENERAL good at commanding troops is like one sitting in a leaking boat or lying under a burning roof. For there is not time for the wise to offer counsel nor the brave to be angry. All must come to grips with the enemy. And therefore it is said that of all the dangers in employing troops, timidity is the greatest and that the calamities which overtake an army arise from hesitation.

> Wu Ch'i (430–381 BC), *Art of War*, 3.2, in Appendix I, Sun Tzu, *The Art of War*, c. 500 BC, tr. Samuel Griffith, 1963.

IT IS essential to be cautious and take your time in making plans, and once you come to a decision to carry it out right away without any hesitation or timidity. Timidity, after all is not caution, but the invention of wickedness.

> The Emperor Maurice, *The Strategikon*, c. AD 600 (*Maurice's Strategikon*, tr. George Dennis, 1984).

HE either fears his fate too much,
or his deserts are small,
That puts it not unto the touch,
to win or lose it all.

> James Graham, Marquis of Montrose (1612–1650).

"HELP, danger," and other figments of the imagination are all right for old women, who are afraid to get off the stove because they may break their legs, and for lazy, luxurious people, and blockheads – for miserable self-protection, which in the end, whether good or bad, in fact, always passes for bravery with the story tellers.

> Field Marshal Prince Aleksandr V. Suvorov (1729–1800), quoted in W. Lyon Blease, *Suvorof*, 1920.

THE TORMENT of precautions often exceeds the dangers to be avoided. It is sometimes better to abandon one's self to destiny.

> Napoleon (1769–1821).

WHEN one wants to open a campaign there is nothing can stand as an obstacle, and a river has never been a real obstacle. If Moreau wants to cross the Rhine, he will cross; if he had already crossed it, we could dictate our conditions of peace imperiously; but the man who fears for his reputation is certain to lose it. I have crossed the Julian Alps over three feet of ice; I have carried my artillery through places where never a cart has passed. Had I thought only of the repose of my army and my private interests, I should have stopped on the banks of the Isonzo; I threw myself into Germany to disengage the army of the Rhine. I am at the gates of Vienna, and its haughty court has sent its plenipotentiaries to my headquarters.

> Napoleon, 16 April 1797, to the *Directoire*, at Leoben, quoted in R.M. Johnston, ed., *The Corsican*, 1910.

GIVEN the same amount of intelligence, timidity will do a thousand times more damage in war than audacity.

> Major-General Carl von Clausewitz, *On War*, 3.6, 1832, tr. Michael Howard and Peter Paret, 1976.

WHEN told by Hamilton of [Douglas] Haig's appointment to take charge of a column, he remarked, "Haig will do nothing! He's quite all right, but he's too_____cautious: he will be so fixed on not giving the Boers a chance he'll never give himself one. If I were to go to him one evening and offer to land him at daybreak next morning within galloping distance of 1,000 sleeping Boers, I know exactly what he'd do: he'd insist on sending out someone else to make sure the Boers were really there – to make sure no reinforcements were coming up to them, and to make so dead sure in fact, then when he did get there not a single d_____d Boer would be within ten miles of him.

> Colonel Aubrey Woolls-Sampson, comment during the Boer War (1899–1902) on Douglas Haig, who was later to command the British Expeditionary Force (BEF) in WWI, quoted in Liddell Hart, *Through the Fog of War*, 1938.

TOMMY ATKINS

OUR *GOD* and *Souldiers* we alike adore;
Ev'n at the Brink of danger; not before:
After deliverance, both alike required;
Our *God's* forgotten, and our *Souldiers* slighted.

> Francis Quarles, 'Of Common Devotion', *The Complete Works in Prose and Verse of Francis Quarles*, II, 2, Alexander B. Grosart, ed., 1880.

HONOR to the Soldier, and Sailor everywhere, who bravely bears his country's cause. Honor also to the citizen who cares for his brother in the field, and serves, as he best can, the same cause – honor to him, only less than to him, who braves, for the common good, the storms of heaven and the storms of battle.

> President Abraham Lincoln, letter to George Opdyke and others, 2 December 1863, *The Collected Works of Abraham Lincoln*, VII, 1953.

FOR IT'S Tommy this, an' Tommy that, an' "Chuck him out, the brute!"
But it's "Saviour of 'is country" when the guns begin to shoot;
An' it's Tommy this, an' tommy that, an' anything you please;
An' Tommy ain't a bloomin' fool – you bet that Tommy sees!

> Rudyard Kipling, 'Tommy Atkins'.

ONE SUNDAY before the regiment disbanded I supplemented Chaplain Brown's address to the men by a short sermon of a rather horatory character. I told them how proud I was of them, but warned them not to think that they could now go back and rest on their laurels, bidding them remember that though for ten days or so the world would be willing to treat them as heroes, yet after that time they would find they had to get down to hard work just like everyone else, unless they were willing to be regarded as worthless do-nothings.

> President Theodore Roosevelt, *The Rough Riders*, 1899; of his volunteer regiment, the Rough Riders, at the end of the Spanish-American War.

I HAD FINISHED riding up the New York streets on the back seat of a Cadillac convertible like many before, waving, nodding, and watching torn pieces of paper come down like snow. The police were busy holding back a mob of well-wishers. A middle-aged man with a thin face and graying at the temples broke through the line and grabbed me by the arm. A policeman grabbed him and started to put him behind the line, but I said: "Wait a minute. I think he wants to tell me something."

He did: "Enjoy it today, my boy, because they won't give you a job cleaning up the streets tomorrow."

Colonel Gregory 'Pappy' Boyington, *Baa Baa Black Sheep*, 1958.

SEVEN MONTHS ago, I could give a single command and 541,000 people would immediately obey. Today, I can't get a plumber to come to my house.

General H. Norman Schwarzkopf, c. April 1992.

TRADITION

. . . NONE have inherited a past more crowded with great deeds; and many are heartened by such a heritage and encouraged to care for virtue and prove their gallantry.

Socrates (470–399 BC), of the Athenians, quoted by Xenophon, *Memorabilia*, 5.3, c. 360 BC, tr. E.C. Marchant, 1923.

THE EXPOSITION that I have been giving is based on the teachings of experience, but what you must do is to make your dispositions in accordance with the requirements of the situation with which you are confronted by the urgency of the actual moment. Tradition does not give the answer. The degree of the strength of God's help [i.e., of the commander's capacity for intuitive improvization – Arnold Toynbee] is the determining factor in deciding the outcome of war.

Anonymous Byzantine general, *Peri Parathromis Polemon*, 10th century.

TO GIVE reputation to the army of any state, it is necessary to revive the discipline of the ancients, cherish and honor it, and give it life, so that in return it may give reputation to the state.

Niccolo Machiavelli, *Discourses*, 1517.

NOTHING is so disgraceful as slavishness to custom; this is both a result of ignorance and a proof of it.

Field Marshal Maurice Comte de Saxe, *My Reveries*, 1732, 1732, tr. Phillips, 1940.

EVERY TRIFLE, every tag or ribbon that tradition may have associated with the former glories of a regiment should be retained, so long as its retention does not interfere with efficiency.

Colonel Clifford Walton, *History of the British Standing Army, 1660–1700*, 1894.

THE VALUE of tradition to the social body is immense. The veneration for practices, or for authority, consecrated by long acceptance, has a reserve of strength which cannot be obtained by any novel device.

Rear-Admiral Alfred Thayer Mahan, 'The Military Rule of Obedience', *National Review*, 3/1902.

AS DESCENDENTS of the men who gained such splendid victories in so many battles from 1702 onwards we are simply unable to be cowardly. We've got to win our battles, whatever the cost, so that people will say "They were worthy descendents of the 32nd" and that's saying a hell of a lot.

Unidentified British colonel of the regiment, quoted in F.M. Richardson, *Fighting Spirit*, 1978.

YOU WILL hardly fade away until the sun fades out of the sky and the earth sinks into the universal blackness. For already you form part of that great tradition of the Dardenelles which began with Hector and Achilles. In another few thousand years the two stories will have blended into one, and whether when "the iron roaring went up to the vault of heaven through the unharvested sky," as Homer tells us, it was the spear of Achilles or whether it was a 100-lb shell from Asiatic Annie won't make much odds to the Almighty.

General Sir Ian Hamilton, in a preface addressed to his Gallipoli soldiers, quoted in Alan Moorehead, *Gallipoli*, 1956.

IT TAKES the Navy three years to build a ship. It would take three hundred to rebuild a tradition.

Admiral Sir Andrew Browne Cunningham, May 1941, rejecting his staff's recommendation to abandon British ground forces on Crete in order to protect the Royal Navy's ships.

THE SPIRIT of discipline, as distinct from its outward and visible guises, is the result of association with martial traditions and their living embodiment.

Captain Sir Basil Liddell Hart, *Thoughts on War*, 1944.

FORTUNE is rightly malignant to those who break with the traditions and customs of the past.

Sir Winston S. Churchill, 23 April 1943, note to the Foreign Secretary.

HOWEVER GOOD and well trained a man may be as an individual, he is not a good soldier till he has become absorbed into the corporate life of his unit and has been entirely imbued with its traditions.

Field Marshal Viscount Wavell of Cyrenaica, *Soldiers and Soldiering*, 1953.

HOWEVER PRAISEWORTHY it may be to uphold tradition in the field of soldierly ethics, it is to be resisted in the field of military command.

Field Marshal Erwin Rommel, *The Rommel Papers*, 1953.

EVERY EUROPEAN nation has a strong tendency to

be tied by tradition even in matters of science. It was not, therefore, surprising that after World War I, in which the respective commands had exploited the then existing means of war to their uttermost limit, many of the European General Staffs became rigidly doctrinaire in their outlook. While unquestioningly accepting the views of great men in matters of principle, they themselves became lost in the detail, tangled it all up into a dreadful complexity, turned warfare into an exchange of memoranda and stuck to their ideas through thick and thin. Soon they were unable to see even the simplest possibilities of a situation, and they never failed to find in their followers and fellow-thinkers a sounding-board for their theories.

> Field Marshal Erwin Rommel, *The Rommel Papers*, 1953.

THERE CAN BE no doubt that old traditions are in theory of great value to any army. The characters of the more eminent General Staff officers of the past should have provided a younger generation with good models without, at the same time, hindering or perhaps even preventing contemporary development. But in practice tradition is not always regarded as simply supplying ideals of behavior, but rather as a source of practical example, as though an imitation of what was done before could reproduce identical results despite the fact that meanwhile circumstances and methods have completely altered. Hardly any mature institution can avoid this fallacious aspect of tradition.

> Colonel-General Heinz Guderian, *Panzer Leader*, 1953.

SOME PEOPLE scoff at tradition. They are right if tradition is taken to mean that you must never do something for the first time; but how wrong they are if you regard tradition as a standard of conduct, handed down to you, below which you must never fall. Then tradition, instead of being a pair of handcuffs to fetter you, will be a handrail to steady and guide you in steep places. One of those traditions, perhaps the greatest of them, is leadership, for the be-all and the end-all of an officer is to be a leader.

> Field Marshal Viscount Slim of Burma, *Courage and Other Broadcasts*, 1957.

THE TRADITIONS of the Foreign Legion – four main principles:
the will to serve well
a sense of discipline and honour
pride in a task well done
the cult of remembrance

> Quoted in John Robert Young, *The French Foreign Legion*, 1984.

THE END of the short-lived Cold War means that the Royal Navy can now get back to its proper business – fighting the French!

> Rear-Admiral Guy F. Liardet, after-dinner speech, 'Trend and Change', quoted in James Goldrick and John B. Hattendorf, ed., *Mahan is Not Enough*, 1993.

TRAINING
General

THE LACEDAEMONIANS, both in their warsongs and in the words which a man spoke to his comrade, did but remind one another of what their brave spirits knew already. For they had learned that true safety was to be found in long previous training, and not in eloquent exhortations uttered when they were going into action.

> Thucydides, of the Spartans at the Battle of Mantinea, summer 418 BC, *The Peloponnesian War*, V, c. 404 BC, tr. Benjamin Jowett, 1881.

MARCHING WELL and keeping ranks are skills which can only be acquired through long drill. The most valiant men in the world would fight very badly if they were not trained, and it is clear that men of the most moderate courage can become warlike by working hard at this profession. . . . In truth, you will be able to make brave through practice those who are not so by nature and to show that with care one can make good soldiers out of all sorts of men.

> Louis XIV, King of France, *Mémoires de Louis XIV*, 1860, quoted in Ralston, *Soldiers and States*, 1966.

TRAINING is light, and lack of training is darkness. The problem fears the expert. If a peasant doesn't know how to plough, he can't grow bread. A trained man is worth three untrained: that's too little – say six – six is too little – say ten to one. We will beat them all, roll them up, take them prisoner! In the last campaign the enemy lost 75,000 counted, but more like 100,000 in fact. He fought with skill and desperation, but we didn't lose 500. You see, lads! Military training! Gentlemen, what a marvellous thing it is!

> Field Marshal Prince Aleksandr V. Suvorov, *The Science of Victory*, 1796.

DO I WANT to see you eaten by vultures and hyaenas after the next battle, merely because you were too stupid or lazy to understand that what I am trying to teach you today will save you tomorrow?

> Mgobozi, c. 1818, to his Zulu recruits, quoted in E.A. Ritter, *Shaka Zulu*, 1955.

EVERY OFFICER and soldier who is able to do duty ought to be busily engaged in military preparation, by hard drilling, etc., in order that, through the blessing of God, we may be victorious in the battles which, in His all-wise providence, may await us. If the war is carried on with vigour, I think, under the blessing of God, it will not last long.

> Lieutenant-General Thomas J. 'Stonewall' Jackson, quoted in R.L. Dabney, *Life of Jackson*, I, 1864.

THAT TROOPS become reliable only in proportion as they are disciplined; that discipline is the fruit of long training, and cannot be attained without the existence of good corps of officers.

> Colonel Emory Upton, *The Military Policy of the United States*, 1904.

MILITARY SWAY lies not merely in warships and arms, but also in the immaterial power that wields them. If we consider that a gun whose every shot tells can hold its own against a hundred guns which can hit only one shot in a hundred, we seamen must seek military power spiritually. The cause of the recent victory of our navy [Tsushima], though it was in a great degree due to the Imperial virtue, must also be attributed to our training in peaceful times which produced its fruit in war.

> Admiral Marquis Heihachiro Togo, 21 December 1905, his farewell to the Japanese Fleet, quoted in Ogasawara, *Life of Admiral Togo*, 1934.

MORE IMPORTANT even than military education is practical military training.

> Major-General John A. Lejeune, *The Reminiscences of a Marine*, 1929.

IN WAR the issues are decided not by isolated acts of heroism but by the general training and spirit of an army.

> Field Marshal Albert Kesselring, *Memoirs of Field Marshal Kesselring*, 1953.

THE DEFINITION of military training is success in battle. In my opinion that is the only objective of military training. It wouldn't make any sense to have a military organization on the backs of the American taxpayers with any other definition. I've believed that ever since I've been a Marine.

> Lieutenant-General Lewis 'Chesty' Puller, 2 August 1956, quoted in Burke Davis, *Marine*, 1962.

THE ESSENTIAL characteristics of a good army are that it be well trained and well disciplined. These two characteristics are apparent in every unit achievement, whether in peace or in war. Discipline derives and flows from training and serves to emphasize a fundamental point essential to a philosophy of training: that training is all-encompassing. Training permeates everything a military organization does.

> Lieutenant-General Arthur S. Collins, Jr., *Common Sense Training*, 1978.

IT IS astounding what well-trained and dedicated soldiers can accomplish in the face of death, fear, physical privation, and an enemy determined to kill them.

> Lieutenant-General Arthur S. Collins, Jr., *Common Sense Training*, 1978.

PERHAPS somewhere in the primal reaches of our Army's memory, left over from the days ten thousand years ago when armies first began, there's a simple and fundamental formula: SKILL + WILL = KILL.

> Colonel Dandridge M. Malone, *Army Magazine*, 9/1979.

The Conduct of Training

PEOPLE DIE because they are incapable and are defeated because they are unsuitable. Therefore the most important thing in handling troops is to train them. If one man is trained for war he can teach ten, if ten are trained they can instruct a hundred, a hundred can train a thousand, a thousand ten thousand and ten thousand an army corps (37,500).

> Wu Ch'i (430–381 BC), *Art of War*, 3.5 (*Three Military Classics of China*, tr. A.L. Sadler, 1944).

WE ARE INFORMED by the writings of the ancients that, among their other exercises was that of the post. They gave their recruits round bucklers woven with willows, twice as heavy as those used on real service, and wooden swords double the weight of the common ones. They exercised them with these at the post both morning and afternoon. . . .

Every soldier, therefore, fixed a post firmly in the ground, about the height of six feet. Against this, as against a real enemy, the recruit was exercised with the above mentioned arms, as with the common shield and sword, sometimes aiming at the head or face, sometimes at the sides, at others endeavoring to strike at the thighs or legs. He was instructed in what manner to advance and retire, and in short how to take every advantage of his adversary; but was thus above all particularly cautioned not to lay himself open to his antagonist while aiming his stroke at him.

. . . This was the method of fighting principally used by the Romans, and their reason for exercising recruits with arms of such a weight at first was, that when they came to carry the common ones, which were so much lighter, the difference might enable them to act with greater security and alacrity in time of action.

> Flavius Vegetius Renatus, *Military Institutions of the Romans*, c. AD 378, tr. Clark, 1776.

THE MAN who spends more sleepless nights with his army and who works harder in drilling his troops runs the fewest risks in fighting the foe.

> The Emperor Maurice, *The Strategikon*, c. AD 600 (*Maurice's Strategikon*, tr. George Dennis, 1984).

THERE IS no other possible way, as far as strategy and experience are concerned, for you to prepare for warfare except by first exercising and training the army under your command. You must accustom them to and train them in the handling of weapons and get them to endure bitter and wearisome tasks and labors. They should not be allowed to become slack or lazy or to give themselves completely to drunkenness, luxury, or other kinds of debauchery. They certainly ought to receive their salaries and money for provisions regularly, as well as gifts and bonuses, more than are customary or stipulated.

> The Emperor Nikephoros II Phokas, *Skirmishing*, c. AD 969 (*Three Byzantine Military Treatises*, tr. George Dennis, 1985).

WHEN emperor Manuel took over the imperial office, he became concerned as to how the Romans might improve their armament for the future. It had previously been customary for them to be armed with round shields and for the most part to carry quivers and decide battles by bows, but he taught them to hold ones [shields] reaching to their feet, and trained them to wield long lances and skillfully practice horsemanship. Desiring to make respites from war preparation for war, he was frequently accustomed to practice riding; making a pretence of battle, he placed formations opposite one another. Thus charging with blunted lances, they practiced maneuvering in arms. So in brief time the Roman [Byzantine] excelled the French and Italians.

General John Kinnamos, *Deeds of John and Manuel Comnenus*, 1176.

AGAIN, all wise and sufficient generals and colonels have always had special regard, when the enemy hath not been near at hand, that their sergeants major, captains, and other officers should oftentimes in the field reduce their bands and regiments into divers forms, and to teach their soldiers all orders military, with the use of their weapons in every degree, time, and place; as also how to lodge in their quarters orderly, and therewithal to understand the orders of watches, bodies of watches, sentinels, rounds, and counterrounds, with many other matters military whereby they might be made prompt and ready to encounter the enemy.

John Smythe (c. 1580–1631), *Certain Discourses Military*, 1966.

THE TROOPS should be exercised frequently, cavalry as well as infantry, and the general should often be present to praise some, to criticize others, and to see with his own eyes that the orders . . . are observed exactly.

Frederick the Great, *Instructions to His Generals*, 1747, tr. Phillips, 1940.

THE SOLDIERS like training provided it is carried out sensibly.

Field Marshal Prince Aleksandr V. Suvorov (1729–1800), *The Suzdal Manual*, 1768, quoted in K. Ossipov, *Strategy*, 1945.

TRAINING is hard work, but it does not have to be dull. Much military training is presented in boring fashion. The troops lose interest and do not absorb the instruction, the training program fails, and the morale of the troops drops. Good training requires a lot of mental effort; the commander must devise ways to make training intellectually and physically challenging to the troops. The unfortunate thing is that so many commanders don't recognize dull training. But their troops do.

Lieutenant-General Arthur S. Collins, Jr., *Common Sense Training*, 1978.

Individual Training

WE MUST REMEMBER that one man is much the same as another, and that he is best who is trained in the severest school.

Thucydides, *The History of the Peloponnesian War*, 1, c. 404 BC.

FEW MEN are born brave; many become so through training and force of discipline.

Flavius Vegetius Renatus, *Military Institutions of the Romans*, c. AD 378, tr. Clark, 1776.

THE ANCIENTS have passed on to us the necessity of training and organizing the army, which is obviously useful and quite fundamental. They would train not only the army as a unit, but they would also teach each individual soldier and have him practice how to use his weapons skillfully. In actual combat, then, bravery, assisted experience and skill in handling weapons, should make him invincible. There is, assuredly, a need for exercises and for careful attention to weapons. For many of the Romans and Greeks of old with small armies of trained and experienced men put flight armies of tens of thousands of troops.

General Nikephoros Ouranos, *Campaign Organization and Tactics*, c. AD 994 (*Three Byzantine Military Treatises*, tr. George Dennis, 1985).

EVERY SOLDIER must be brought to the state where it can be said of him: "You have learned all there is to be learned, take care not to forget it."

Field Marshal Aleksandr V. Suvorov (1729–1800), favourite maxim on training, quoted in K. Ossipov, *Suvorov*, 1945.

BODY and spirit I surrendered whole
To harsh insructors – and received a soul.

Rudyard Kipling, 'The Wonder', *Epitaphs*, 1919.

THE FIRST DAY I was at camp I was afraid I was going to die. The next two weeks my sole fear was that I wasn't going to die. And after that I knew I'd never die because I'd become so hard nothing could kill me.

Anonymous American soldier, quoted in Cowing, *Dear Folks at Home*, 1919.

PARTICIPATION in sport may help turn a mild bookkeeper into a warrior if it has conditioned his mind so that he relishes the contest. The act of teaching one man to participate with other men in any training endeavor is frequently the first step in the development of new traits of receptiveness and outward giving in his character. It is from the acquiring of the habit of working with the group and of feeling responsible to the group that his thoughts are apt to turn ultimately to the welfare of the group when tactical disintegration occurs in battle; the more deeply this is impressed into his consciousness, the quicker will he revert under pressure to thinking and acting on behalf of the group.

Brigadier-General S.L.A. Marshall, *Men Against Fire*, 1947.

EVERY NORMAL MAN needs to have some sense of a contest, some feeling of resistence overcome, before he can make the best use of his facilities. Whatever experience serves to give him confidence that he can compete with other men helps to increase his solidarity with other men.

Brigadier-General S.L.A. Marshall, *The Armed Forces Officer*, 1950.

ONE GREAT DIFFICULTY of training the individual soldier in peace is to instil discipline and yet to preserve the initiative and independence needed in war. The best soldier in peace (officer or man) is not necessarily the best soldier in war – though he is so more often than not – and it is not always easy in peace conditions to recognize the man who will make good in war. The soldier who is a thorough nuisance in barracks is occasionally a treasure in the field, though not nearly as often as Hollywood and the sentimental novelists would have us believe.

Field Marshal Viscount Wavell of Cyrenaica, *Soldiers and Soldiering*, 1953.

THE WHOLE TRAINING of an officer seeks to accomplish one purpose – to instill in him the ability to take over in battle in a time of crisis.

General Matthew B. Ridgway, *Soldier*, 1956.

DURING TRAINING, the [Israeli] soldier is thrown more on his own than under the United States system. All instruction is pointed toward sharpening the power of decision in the average individual. Physical exercise and lecture courses are aimed to test and increase personal initiative. Israeli trainees believe that teaching the man to think clearly, observe keenly and report accurately is the main object of the school of the soldier.

Brigadier-General S.L.A. Marshall, *Sinai Victory*, 1958.

NOTHING comes off – except what you have practiced.

German dive-bomber pilots' maxim, quoted by Colonel Hans Ulrich Rudel, *Stuka Pilot*, 1958.

INDIVIDUAL TRAINING is the foundation on which unit effectiveness is built. It is the source of a soldier's confidence and trust in the Army.

Lieutenant-General Arthur S. Collins, Jr., *Common Sense Training*, 1978.

Lack of Training

NO SPEECH of admonition can be so fine that it will at once make those who hear it good men if they are not good already; it would surely not make archers good if they had not had previous practice in shooting; neither could it make lancers good, nor horsemen; it cannot even make men able to endure bodily labor, unless they have been trained to it before.

Cyrus the Younger (d. 401 BC).

. . . FOR IDLENESS makes the body soft and weak, while relaxation makes the soul cowardly and worthless; since pleasures capturing the passions by enticement of daily habit, corrupt even the most courageous man. For this reason the soldiers must never be without occupation. When after some time spent in idleness they are compelled to go against the enemy, they do not go willingly nor do they stand their ground, but because they have departed from their formal habits, they quickly become dismayed, even before making trial of danger, and even if they do not make trial, they quickly retreat, being incapable either of feeling hope or of sustaining the stress of battle.

Onasander, *The General*, AD 58 (*Aeneas Tacticus, Aclepiodotus, Onasander*, tr. The Illinois Greek Club, 1923).

THAT GOVERNMENT is a murderer of its citizens which sends them to the field uninformed and untaught, where they are to meet men of the same age and strength mechanized by education and discipline for battle.

Major-General Henry 'Light Horse Harry' Lee (1756–1818).

WITH A RAW ARMY it is possible to carry a formidable position, but not to carry out a plan or design.

Napoleon, quoted in Liddell Hart, *Reputations Ten Years After*, 1928.

MY FLEET looked well at Toulon, but when the storm came on, things changed at once. The sailors were not used to storms; they were lost among the mass of soldiers; these from seasickness lay in heaps about the decks; it was impossible to work the ships; hence yardarms were broken and sails were carried away. Our losses resulted as much from clumsiness and inexperience as from defects in the materials supplied by the dockyard.

Admiral Pierre Villeneuve, early 1805, to Admiral Decrés on the effects of the short voyage between Toulon and Corsica on his poorly trained crews, quoted in David Howarth, *Nelson: The Immortal Memory*, 1988.

A COLLECTION of untrained men is neither more nor less than a mob, in which individual courage goes for nothing. In movement each person finds his liberty of action merged in a crowd, ignorant and incapable of direction. Every obstacle creates confusion, speedily converted into panic by opposition.

Lieutenant-General Richard Taylor, *Destruction and Reconstruction*, 1879.

UNTUTORED COURAGE is useless in the face of educated bullets.

General George S. Patton, Jr., in the *Cavalry Journal*, 4/1922.

IN NO OTHER profession are the penalties for employing untrained personnel so appalling or so irrevocable as in the military.
> General of the Army Douglas MacArthur, *Annual Report of the Chief of Staff, U.S. Army, 1933*.

WE HAVE verified the inevitable – that inadequately trained officers cannot train troops effectively.
> General Lesley J. McNair, 1943, quoted in Kahn, *McNair, Educator of an Army*, 1945.

PROBABLY our most fundamental and important advantage over the enemy in North Africa was that when my army arrived in Africa in 1941, it was in a better position to benefit from further training on modern lines than were the British. My officers, particularly the younger commanders and General Staff Officers, were up to date in their thinking and not hampered by the conservatism of the British officer.
> Field Marshal Erwin Rommel, *The Rommel Papers*, 1953.

ONE of the biggest reasons for failure in the field of battle is not knowing what to do next and, in most cases, this is the result of not having been trained thoroughly in what to expect on the battlefield.
> General Orlando Ward, quoted in Gubler, *Combat Actions in Korea*, 1954.

THE ARMY is an instrument of war: its sole purpose is to fight the country's enemies, and tactical preparedness is an essential element of success in this struggle. An army lacking in tactical training is forced to learn in the course of fighting at the cost of unnecessary losses.
> Marshal of the Soviet Union Georgi K. Zhukov, *Reminiscences and Reflections*, 1974.

Physical Training

THE YOUNG RECRUITS in particular must be exercised in running, in order to charge the enemy with vigor, to occupy on occasion an advantageous post with greater expedition, and balk the enemy in their designs upon the same; and that they may, when sent to reconnoiter, advance with speed, and return with celerity and more easily overtake the enemy in pursuit.
> Flavius Vegetius Renatus, *Military Institutions of the Romans*, c. AD 378, tr. Clark, 1776.

THE FOUNDATION of training depends on the legs and not the arms. All the mystery of maneuvers and combats is in the legs, and it is to the legs that we should apply ourselves. Whoever claims otherwise is but a fool and not only in the elements of what is called the profession of arms.
> Field Marshal Maurice Comte de Saxe, *My Reveries*, 1732, 1732, tr. Phillips, 1940.

IS IT really true that a seven-mile cross-country run is enforced upon all in this division, from generals to privates? . . . It looks to me rather excessive. A colonel or a general ought not to exhaust himself in trying to compete with young boys running across country seven miles at a time. The duty of officers is no doubt to keep themselves fit, but still more to think of their men, and to take decisions affecting their safety or comfort. Who is the general of this division, and does he run the seven miles himself? If so, he may be more useful for football than for war. Could Napoleon have run seven miles across country at Austerlitz? Perhaps it was the other fellow he made run. In my experience, based on many years' observation, officers with high athletic qualifications are not usually successful in the higher ranks.
> Sir Winston S. Churchill, 4 February 1941, note to the Secretary of State for War.

A PINT of sweat will save a gallon of blood.
> General George S. Patton, Jr., 8 November 1942, message to his forces before the landing at Casablanca.

A MAN who takes a lot of exercise rarely exercises his mind adequately.
> Captain Sir Basil Liddell Hart, *Thoughts on War*, 1944.

MORE EMPHASIS will be placed on the hardening of men and officers. All soldiers and officers should be able to run a mile with combat pack in ten minutes and march eight miles in two hours. When soldiers are in actual contact with the enemy, it is almost impossible to maintain physical condition, but if the physical condition is high before they gain contact, it will not fall off sufficiently during contact to be detrimental.
> General George S. Patton, Jr., *War As I Knew It*, 1947.

TRULY THEN, it is killing men with kindness not to insist upon physical standards during training which will give them a maximum fitness for the extraordinary stresses of campaigning in war.
> Brigadier-General S.L.A. Marshall, *Men Against Fire*, 1947.

WHEN TROOPS lack the coordinated response which comes of long, varied and rigorous exercises, their combat losses will be excessive, and they will lack cohesion in their action against the enemy, and they will uselessly expend much of their initial velocity.
> Brigadier-General S.L.A. Marshall, *The Armed Forces Officer*, 1950.

THE HIGHEST FORM of physical training that an officer can undergo is the physical conditioning of his own men.
> Brigadier-General S.L.A. Marshall, *The Armed Forces Officer*, 1950.

ALL MILITARY FORCES remain relatively

undisciplined until physically toughened and mentally conditioned to unusual exertion.

> Brigadier-General S.L.A. Marshall, *The Armed Forces Officer*, 1950.

AN INTRAMURAL company athletic program constitutes training, which is everybody's business. The development of greater endurance, improved agility, and coordination results in a better state of health and a better mental attitude. Commanders' reluctance to take the time to improve both physical conditioning and mental attitude through this program must be overcome. Too many of them wear blinders, particularly at battalion and brigade level.

> Lieutenant-General Arthur S. Collins, Jr., *Common Sense Training*, 1978.

Small Unit Training

THE TRAINING of an infantry company for war, considered by the uninitiated as one of the simplest things in the world, is in reality the most complex; it is one constant struggle against human nature, and incessant variations of the tactical situation and of the ground, to say nothing of the frequent changes in the company as regards junior officers and noncommissioned officers.

> Captain R.C.B. Haking, *Company Training*, 1917.

BATTLES are fought by platoons and squads. Place emphasis on small unit combat instruction so that it is conducted with the same precision as close-order drill.

> General George S. Patton, Jr., *War As I Knew It*, 1947.

IN THE MATTER of training, all higher headquarters must seek to cut to a proper minimum the required hours for specified subjects, in an endeavor to leave the company or battery commander a reasonable latitude in the training of his unit in subjects which he selects as requiring greater emphasis. . . . In training it is also necessary to avoid over-supervision. By this I do not mean that battalion, regimental, or higher commanders should spend any less time in the field and in inspection of training, but the company commander must have the feeling that he is being trusted with the training of his company and that each move he makes is not being supervised by a hovering senior. . . . We have made the routine tactical problem a pretty dull affair. Troops spend long periods doing nothing, thinking nothing, learning nothing. . . . At all costs we must avoid a false front.

> General Anthony McAuliffe, 1954, quoted in Arthur S. Collins, *Common Sense Training*, 1978.

DEFEATS, collapses, and panics start with small units, and victories are determined by their measure of success. Skillful senior commanders can bring their armies into battle under favorable conditions, but the small-unit leaders at the company level are the ones who win the battle. Given anything like equal terms, the best-trained army will win. Even if the odds are markedly against an army which has well-trained small units and small-unit commanders, that army will often defeat a force superior in numbers and equipment. At a minimum, it will not be routed and will survive to fight on.

> Lieutenant-General Arthur S. Collins, Jr., *Common Sense Training*, 1978.

Train as You Fight

IF ANY ONE does but attend to the other parts of their [Roman] military discipline, he will be forced to confess that their obtaining so large a dominion, hath been the acquisition of their valor, and not the bare gift of fortune; for they do not begin to use their weapons first in time of war, nor do they the then put their hands first into motion, while they avoided so to do in times of peace; but as if their weapons did always cling to them, they have never any truce from warlike exercises; nor do they stay till times of war admonish them to use them; for their military exercises differ not at all from the real use of their arms, but every soldier is every day exercised, and that with great dilligence, as if it were in time of war which is the reason why they bear the fatigue of battles so easily; for neither can any disorder remove them from their usual regularity, nor can fear affright them out of it, nor can labor tire them; which firmness of conduct makes them always to overcome those that have not the same firmness; nor would he be mistaken that should call those their exercises unbloody battles, and their battles bloody exercises.

> Flavius Josephus (AD 37–c.100), *The Wars of the Jews*, tr. William Whiston, 1736.

MAKE PEACE a time of training for war, and battle an exhibition of bravery.

> The Emperor Maurice, *The Strategikon*, c. AD 600 (*Maurice's Strategikon*, tr. George Dennis, 1984).

MY TROOPS are good and well-disciplined, and the most important thing of all is that I have thoroughly habituated them to perform everything that they are required to execute. You will do something more easily, to a higher standard, and more bravely when you know that you will do it well.

> Frederick the Great, *Principes Généraux*, 1748.

BUONAPARTE has often made his boast that our fleet would be worn out by keeping the sea, and that his was kept in order and increasing by staying in port; but now he finds, I fancy, if Emperors hear the truth, that his fleet suffers more in a night than ours in a one year.

> Admiral Viscount Nelson, 1805, letter to Captain Collingwood, quoted in David Howarth, *Nelson: The Immortal Memory*, 1988.

THE TROOPS should learn in peacetime only what must done in wartime.

General Mikhail I. Dragomirov, quoted in *Voyenno istorichiskiy zhurnal*, 9/1985.

THERE IS no studying the battlefield. It is then simply a case of doing what is possible, to make use of what one knows and, in order to make a little possible, one must know much.

Marshal of France Ferdinand Foch, quoted in Marshall, *Infantry in Battle*, 1939.

ALL INSTRUCTIONS must contemplate the assumption of vigorous offensive. This purpose will be emphasized in every phase of training until it becomes settled habit in thought.

General of the Armies John J. Pershing, *Final Report of Gen. John J. Pershing*, quoted in J.F.C. Fuller, *Decisive Battles of the U.S.A.*, 1953.

THE TRAINING of troops when intelligently directed is the greatest of morale builders, as they are quick to sense that they are being prepared to meet effectively any emergency that may arise . . .

Major-General John A. Lejeune, *Reminiscences of a Marine*, 1929.

TROOPS must be toughened mentally so that adverse conditions will not divert them from their mission. Fatigue, loss of sleep, limited rations, adverse weather conditions, and other hardships must not weaken the determination to find and destroy the enemy.

General Lesley J. McNair, quoted in Kahn, *McNair, Educator of an Army*, 1945.

THE COMMANDER must be at constant pains to keep his troops abreast of all the latest tactical experience and developments, and must insist on their practical application. He must see to it that his subordinates are trained in accordance with the latest requirements. The best form of welfare for the troops is first-class training, for this saves unnecessary casualties.

Field Marshal Erwin Rommel, *The Rommel Papers*, 1953.

TRAINING is all-encompassing and should be related to everything a unit does or can have happen to it.

Lieutenant-General Arthur S. Collins, Jr., *Common Sense Training*, 1978.

TREACHERY/TREASON

ONCE when the ephors said to him: "Take the young man and march against this man's country: he will personally conduct you to the acropolis," Agis son of Archidamus replied, "And how is it proper, ephors, for so many young men to trust this one man who is betraying his own country?"

Agis II, Eurypontid King of Sparta (427–400 BC), quoted in Plutarch, *The Lives*, c. AD 100 (*Plutarch on Sparta*, tr. Richard Talbert, 1988).

SUCH was the crop of traitors then sprouting everywhere in Greece that, when Phillip wished to take a certain city protected by its inaccessibility, he asked if gold could not climb over the wall.

Plutarch, *Moralia*, of King Phillip II of Macedon, quoted in Alfred A. Bradford, *Phillip II of Macedon: A Life from the Ancient Sources*, 1992.

IT IS NOT the fat, sleek-headed men I am afraid of, but the pale, lean ones.

Julius Caesar, c. 44 BC; an appraisal of the type of men he feared most, having Cassius and Brutus in mind, quoted in Plutarch, *The Lives*, c. AD 100 (*Makers of Rome*, tr. Ian Scott-Kilvert, 1965).

THE TREASON pleases, but the traitors are odious.

Miguel de Cervantes, *Don Quixote*, 1605–1615, tr. Peter Motteux and John Ozell.

THIS [Major-General Benedict Arnold's treason] is an event that occasions me equal regret and mortification; but traitors are an outgrowth of every country and in a revolution of the present nature, it is more to be wondered at, that the catalogue is so small than there have been found a few.

General George Washington, to the Comte de Rochambeau, 27 September 1780, *The Writings of George Washington*, XX, p. 97, John C. Fitzgerald, ed., 1937.

TREATIES/DIPLOMACY

IF YOU SIN against this treaty which [your] lord Esarhaddon, king of Assyria, has established with you on behalf of the crown prince designate Ashurbanipal, his brothers by the mother of the crown prince designate Ashurbanipal, and the rest of the sons begotten by Esarhaddon, king of Assyria, may Ashur, father of the gods, strike you down with his fierce weapons. . . .

May they [the gods] break your bow and make you crouch at the feet of your enemies, may they make the bow refuse to bend in your hands, may they turn backwards your chariots. . . .

Just as the chariot is spattered with blood up to its running board, so may they spatter your chariots in the midst of your enemy with your own blood. . . .

If you abandon Esarhaddon, king of Assyria, or the crown prince designate Ashurbanipal, and disperse right and left, may swords consume the one who goes to the right, may swords consume the one too who goes to the left. . . .

May Nabu, who holds the tablets of fate of the gods, erase your name, and make your descendants disappear from the land.

Esarhaddon (d. 669 BC), King of Assyria, his vassal treaty with Ramataya, city ruler of Urakazabanu, quoted in James Pritchard, *The Ancient Near East*, 1975.

IN NO WAY should a sworn agreement made with the enemy be broken.

> The Emperor Maurice, *The Strategikon*, c. AD 600 (*Maurice's Strategikon*, tr. George Dennis, 1984).

ALL TREATIES are broken from considerations of interest; and in this respect republics are much more careful in the observance of treaties than princes. . . . I speak of the breaking of treaties from some extraordinary cause; and here I believe, from what has been said, that the people are less frequently guilty of this than princes, and are therefore more to be trusted.

> Niccolo Machiavelli, *Discourses*, 1517.

DIPLOMACY without arms is music without instruments.

> Frederick the Great (1712–1786).

TREATIES are observed as long as they are in harmony with interests.

> Napoleon, *The Military Maxims of Napoleon*, tr. Burnod, 1827.

MAY THE diplomatists not again spoil with their pens, that which the armies have at so much cost won with their swords!

> Field Marshal Gebhard von Blücher, 1815, at a dinner given by the Duke of Wellington in Paris, following the Allied victory over Napoleon at Waterloo.

I ONLY WISH I had you, gentlemen of the pen, exposed for once to a pretty smart skirmishing fire, that you might learn what it is when the soldier is obliged to repair with his life's blood the errors you so thoughtlessly commit on paper.

> Field Marshal Gebhard von Blücher, 1815, to the Prussian Foreign Minister, Prince Hardenberg, in Paris after the Allied victory over Napoleon at Waterloo.

DOES THE cessation of diplomatic notes stop the political relations between different nations and governments: Is not war merely another kind of writing and language for their thought: It has, to be sure, its own grammar, but not its own logic.

> Major-General Carl von Clausewitz, *On War*, 1832, tr. Michael Howard and Peter Paret, 1976.

DIPLOMACY has rarely been able to gain at the conference table what cannot be gained or held on the battlefield.

> General Walter Bedell Smith, 1954, after a conference on Indochina.

TREATIES are like flowers and young girls – they last while they last.

> General Charles de Gaulle, on a Franco-German treaty, *Time Magazine*, 12 July 1963.

THE TROOPS
Take Care of the Troops

PHILLIP, when he heard that Pythias, a certain first rate soldier, was estranged from him, because he had three daughters whom in his poverty he could hardly feed and he received no help from the king – and some of Phillip's Companions warned him that he should beware of Pythias – Phillip said, "What? If part of my body were sick, would I cut it off and not try to cure it?"

And, as though Pythias were a member of his family, he called in to himself, learned the truth, and arranged for some money. And he had a more devoted and faithful man than he had had before he offended him.

> King Phillip II of Macedon (382–336 BC), from Frontinus, *Strategematicon*, IV, vii, 37, quoted in Alfred S. Bradford, *Phillip II of Macedon*, 1992.

NEXT DAY, despite a sword wound in his thigh, Alexander went round to see the wounded; he gathered together the dead and gave them a splendid military funeral, the whole army marshalled in their finest battle array. His speech contained citations of all whom he knew, from his own eyes or from the agreed report of others, to have distinguished themselves in the battle; he honoured each of them by a donation suitable to their worth.

> Arrian, of Alexander the Great at the Battle of Issus, October 333 BC, *The anabasis of alexander*, 2.12, c. AD 150, tr. P.A. Brunt, 1976.

YOU CAN BE of no service to me, go to the soldiers, to whom you can be useful.

> Lieutenant-General Sir John Moore, 16 January 1809, to two surgeons who rushed to him as he lay mortally wounded on the field of Corunna, quoted in Carola Oman, *Sir John Moore*, 1953.

THE OFFICERS of the army are much mistaken if they suppose that their duty is done when they have attended to the drill of their men, and to the parade duties of the regiment: the order and regularity of the troops in camp and quarters, the subsistence and comfort of the soldiers, the general subordination and obedience of the corps, afford constant subjects for the attention of the field officers in particular, in which, by their conduct in the assistance they will give the Commanding officer, they can manifest their zeal for the service, their ability and their fitness for promotion to the higher ranks, at least equally as by an attention to the drill and parade discipline of the corps.

> The Duke of Wellington, 16 September 1809, at Badajoz, *Selections from the General Orders of Field Marshal the Duke of Wellington During His Various Commands 1799–1818*, 1847.

THE ATTENTION of commanding officers has been

frequently called to the expediency of supplying the soldier with breakfast.

> The Duke of Wellington (1769–1852), during the Peninsular War, quoted in Arthur Bryant, *The Great Duke*, 1972.

I GAINED the hearts of my soldiers (who would do anything for me) not by my justice, etc., but by looking after them when sick and continually visiting the Hospitals.

> General Charles 'Chinese' Gordon, letter to Florence Nightingale, 22 April 1888, quoted in Cecil Woodham-Smith, *Florence Nightingale, 1820–1910*, 1951.

THEY HURRIED FORWARD, often at a double-quick, waded the Shenandoah River, which was waist-deep to the men, ascended the Blue Ridge at Ashby's Gap, and, two hours after midnight, paused for a few hours' rest at the little village of Paris, upon the eastern slope of the mountain. Here General Jackson turned his brigade into an enclosure occupied by a beautiful grove, and the wearied men fell prostrate upon the earth, without food. In a little time an officer came to Jackson, reminded him that there were no sentries posted around his bivouac, while the men were all wrapped in sleep, and asked if some should be aroused, and a guard set. "No," replied Jackson, "let the poor fellows sleep; I will guard the camp myself." All the remainder of the night he paced around it, or sat upon the fence watching the slumbers of his men. . . .

> An account of Lieutenant-General Thomas J. 'Stonewall' Jackson's solicitude towards his men after a gruelling march on 21 July 1861, in Dabney, *Life of Jackson*, I, 1866.

BE KINDLY and just in your dealing with your men. Never play favorites. Make them feel that justice tempered with mercy may always be counted on. This does not mean a slackening of discipline. Obedience to orders and regulations must always be insisted upon, and good conduct on the part of the men exacted. Especially should this be done with reference to civilian inhabitants of foreign countries in which Marines are serving.

> Major-General John A. Lejeune, 19 September 1922, *Letter No. 1 to the Officers of the Marine Corps from the Commandant*.

LEADERS should get up in the morning thanking people; at noontime they should thank more people; before going home at night, they should thank still more. Thanking people is an important part of taking care of them because it's taking care of their psychological health. Leaders should sponsor outstanding subordinates while avoiding the pitfalls of cronyism. They should follow Pierce Chapron's advice when he helps people: "He who receives a benefit should never forget it; he who bestows should never remember it."

> Major-General Perry Smith, *Taking Charge: A Practical Guide for Leaders*, 1986.

Talk and Listen to the Troops

THE GREAT IMPEDIMENT to action, is in our opinion, not discussion, but the want of that knowledge which is gained by discussion preparatory to action. For we have a peculiar power of thinking before we act and of acting too, whereas other men are courageous from ignorance but hesitate upon reflection. And they are surely to be esteemed the bravest spirits who, having the clearest sense of both the pains and pleasures of life, do not on that account shrink from danger.

> Pericles, 431 BC, funeral oration for the first Athenians to fall in the Peloponnesian War, quoted in Thucydides, *The Peloponnesian War*, 2.40, c. 404 BC, tr. Benjamin Jowett, 1881.

IT IS IMPOSSIBLE for the General to explain to his army the motive for the movement he directs. The Commander of the Forces can, however, assure the army that he has made none since he left Salamanca which he did not foresee, and was not prepared for, and as far as he is a judge, they have answered the purposes for which they were intended. When it is proper to fight a battle, he will do it; and he will choose the time and place he thinks most fit: in the meantime he begs the Officers and Soldiers of the army to attend diligently to discharge their parts, and to leave to him and to the General Officers, the decision of measures which belong to them alone.

The army may rest assured that there is nothing he has more at heart than their honour – and that of their country.

> Lieutenant-General Sir John Moore, General Order of 27 December 1808, on the retreat from Spain, quoted in Carola Oman, *Sir John Moore*, 1953.

YOU ENGLISH are aristocrats. You keep a great distance between yourselves and the *popolo*. Nature formed all men equal. It was always my custom to go amongst the soldiers and rabble, to converse with them, hear their little histories, and speak kindly to them. This I found to be the greatest benefit to me.

> Napoleon, 3 April 1817, on St. Helena, quoted in R.M. Johnston, ed., *The Corsican*, 1910.

WHEN HE reviewed the troops he asked the officers, and often the soldiers, in what battles they had been engaged, and to those who had received serious wounds he gave the cross. Here, I think, I may appropriately mention a singular piece of charlatanism to which the Emperor had recourse, and which powerfully contributed to augment the enthusiasm of his troops. He would say to one of his *aides de camp*, "Ascertain from the colonel of such a regiment whether he has in his corps a man who has served in the campaigns of Italy or the campaigns of Egypt. Ascertain his name, where he was born, the particulars of his family, and what he has done. Learn his number in the ranks, and to what company he belongs, and furnish me with the information."

On the day of the review Bonaparte, at a single glance, could perceive the man who had been described to him. He would go up to him as if he recognised him, address him by his name, and say, "Oh! so you are here! You are a brave fellow – I saw you at Aboukir – how is your old father? What! Have you not got the cross? Stay, I will give it you." Then the delighted soldiers would say to each other, "You see the Emperor knows us all; he knows our families; he knows where we have served." What a stimulus was this to soldiers, whom he succeeded in persuading that they would all some time or other become Marshals of the Empire!

Louis Antoine Fauvelet de Bourrienne, Napoleon's private secretary (1797–1802), *The Memoirs of Napoleon Bonaparte*, II, 1855.

I HAVE many a time crept forward to the skirmish-line to avail myself of the cover of the pickets' "little fort", to observe more closely some expected result; and always talked familiarly with the men, and was astonished to see how well they comprehended the general object, and how accurately they were informed of the state of facts existing miles away from their particular corps. Soldiers are very quick to catch the general drift and purpose of a campaign, and are always sensible when they are well commanded or well cared for. Once impressed with this fact, and that they are making progress, they bear cheerfully any amount of labor and privation.

General of the Army William T. Sherman, *Memoirs*, II, 1875.

THE POWER to command has never meant the power to remain mysterious, but rather to communicate, at least to those who immediately execute our orders, the idea which animates our plans. If any one ever had the chance of playing the mysterious role in war it was Napoleon. For his authority was beyond question, and he had taken upon himself to think out everything and decide everything for his army. Yet in his correspondence he always put his views and his programme for several days to come before the Commanders of his army corps. And if we call to mind a number of his proclamations we shall see that his very troops were made aware of the manoeuvre he intended. Souvarov said exactly the same thing. Every soldier should understand the manoeuvre in which he is engaged. He was convinced that one can get anything out of a force to which one speaks frankly, because such a force will understand what is asked of it and will then itself ask no better than to do what is required of it.

Marshal of France Ferdinand Foch, *Precepts and Judgments*, 1919.

. . . THE LED put the worst construction on the silence of the leaders, that they assume no news to be bad news, despite all the proverbs.

Captain Sir Basil Liddell Hart, *A Greater Than Napoleon: Scipio Africanus*, 1926.

RUMORS spread like wildfires, and at each repetition are grossly exaggerated, especially in war or insurrection, and by the same token surmises are repeated as facts and dreams as realities.

Major-General John A. Lejeune, *The Reminiscences of a Marine*, 1929.

IN THE CORPS, we ask our young combat officers to share our faith in the superior intelligence of American fighting men by taking every man of their command, down to the newest Private, into their confidence during battle. The men must have the feeling of team effort, and the confidence that their officer is treating them all with fairness.

This can be created by letting them know the immediate plan of action, and why it has been chosen. A man fights much better when he has a sense of the common objective, rather than merely a knowledge of how things look from his own foxhole.

Time after time, I have seen men carry on when all their leaders have been knocked out, using the knowledge given them in talks, and conferences, in advance of the action.

This individual ability gives us an important margin over our enemies. It is generally acknowledged that we have better equipment, better weapons, and greater productive powers, than our enemies, but these advantages would lose their significance if our forces, man for man, were not superior in skill and initiative.

General Alexander A. Vandegrift, 28 January 1944, address at the Pennsylvania Military College, Navy Department press release.

THERE IS among the mass of individuals who carry rifles in a war an amount of ingenuity and efficiency. If men can talk naturally to their officers, the product of their resourcefulness becomes available to all.

General of the Army Dwight D. Eisenhower (1890–1969), quoted in S.L.A. Marshall, *The Armed Forces Officer*, 1950.

IT IS never a waste of time for the commander to talk to his people about their problems; more times than not, the problem will seem small to him, but so long as it looms large to the man, it cannot be dismissed with a wave of the hand. He will grow in esteem of his men as he treats their affairs with respect.

Brigadier-General S.L.A. Marshall, *The Armed Forces Officer*, 1950.

THE HABIT of talking down to troops is one of the worst vices that can afflict an officer.

Brigadier-General S.L.A. Marshall, *The Armed Forces Officer*, 1950.

TO LIE to American troops to cover up a blunder in combat rarely serves any valid purpose. They have a good sense of combat and an uncanny instinct for ferreting out the truth when anything goes wrong

tactically. They will excuse mistakes but they will not forgive being treated like children.
Brigadier-General S.L.A. Marshall, *The Armed Forces Officer*, 1950.

BUT IT IS not enough to have a worthy object; you have got to convince everyone in the party that it *is* a worthy object. What might have seemed obvious to me, sitting in Army HQs surrounded by maps, reports and returns, might not be so self-evident to the orderly at my door who hadn't seen his wife for four years, or to the wet, hungry soldier up there in the jungle who was being shot at. It may not be so plain to a lot of people now.
Field Marshal Viscount Slim of Burma, *Courage and Other Broadcasts*, 1957.

WE FOUND that the best way to convince men that what they were doing was worthwhile was to tell them yourself. The spoken word, delivered in person – not over the wireless – is the greatest instrument. An occasional talk by the man who holds the responsibility for the show counts a lot. It doesn't need an orator. Any man who holds control over others should be able to talk to them, provided he has two qualifications. First, that he is clear in his own mind about what he wants to put over, and secondly that he believes it himself. That last is important.
Field Marshal Viscount Slim of Burma, *Courage and Other Broadcasts*, 1957.

I HAVE always remembered Cromwell's saying that a soldier fights better when he knows what he is fighting for. Ever since I commanded twenty men in the first Desert Patrol in 1931, I have constantly collected all those under my command and explained to them every detail of the situation in which we have found ourselves. I have then invited questions and discussion.
Lieutenant-General Sir John Glubb, *A Soldier With the Arabs*, 1957.

THE NEED for truth is not always realized. A leader must speak the truth to those under him; if he does *not* they will find it out and then their confidence in him will decline. I did not always tell *all* the truth to the soldiers in the war; it would have compromised secrecy and it was not necessary.
I told them all they must know for the efficient carrying out of their tasks. But what I did tell them was always true and they knew it; that produced a mutual confidence between us.
Field Marshal Viscount Montgomery of Alamein, *The Memoirs of Field Marshal Montgomery*, 1958.

I CAN ANSWER questions and hold a detailed dialogue with a group of soldiers or even with a lone guard in a lookout post where there is a mutual interest in the subjects: What is happening on the enemy side: What are our defects? How can they be rectified: I am also interested in the personal lives of the men. Where do they come from? How do their families live? Do they rest or work when they are on leave? Do they support their parents?
I always found that the troops answered freely and were never afraid to criticize or complain. But these were more in the nature of question and answer than true dialogue. In this respect, I suppose there was no basic difference between my talk with an anonymous private in a Golan Heights outpost and my discussions with the top officials of the Ministry of Defense.
General Moshe Dayan, *The Story of My Life*, 1976.

ALL COMMANDERS use directives to a degree, but I tried a novel approach. Mine were, for a start, irregular, each one inspired by a specific incident, a particular mistake. But I tried to go beyond mere correction of error, important as that was. I tried to instill new ideas and new concepts. Every word was chosen with care. I put everything I had into their composition. The papers had differing grades of secrecy. Some were distributed only at brigade level, others to battalion; but most were directed to company commanders with instructions that they should pass on their messages to their men. Whenever I visited the forces, I made a point of questioning all levels to see if they knew the applicable directives. I was astonished by the results. One of the happiest moments of my career came at the Suez front on October 8 [1973], two days after our crossing. Wherever I went, the troops cheered and shouted: "Directive 41, we did it!" In Directive 41, I had laid down how our infantry divisions would cross the canal.
General Saad el Shazly, *The Crossing of the Suez*, 1980.

SQUINT with your ears. The most important skill for leaders is listening. Introverts have great edge, since they tend to listen quietly and usually don't suffer from being an "interruptaholic." Leaders should "squint with their ears." Too many bosses are thinking about what they will say next, rather than hearing what is being said now.
Major-General Perry M. Smith, 'Learning to Lead', *Marine Corps Gazette*, January 1997.

TRUCE

WE BROKE our sworn truce. We fight as outlaws. True, and what profit for us in the long run? Nothing –
Homer, *The Iliad*, 7.404–406, c. 800 BC, tr. Robert Fagles, 1990; Antenor speaking to the Trojan assembly after one of the gods had tricked a Trojan into breaking the truce with the Achaeans.

WHEN without a previous understanding the enemy asks for a truce, he is plotting.
Sun Tzu, *The Art of War*, 9, c. 500 BC, tr. Samuel Griffith, 1963.

IF without reason one begs for a truce it is assuredly because affairs in his country are in a dangerous state and he is worried and wishes to make a plan to gain a respite. Or otherwise he knows that our situation is susceptible to his plots and he wants to forestall our suspicions by asking for a truce. Then he will take advantage of our unpreparedness.

> Ch'ên Hao, commentory to Sun Tzu, *The Art of War*, 9, c. 500 BC, tr. Samuel Griffith, 1963.

I HAVE ISSUED the strictest orders that on no account is intercourse to be allowed between the opposing troops. To finish this war quickly we must keep up the fighting spirit. . . . I am calling for particulars as to names of officers and units who took part in this Christmas gathering with a view to disciplinary action. . . . War to the knife is the only way to carry out a campaign of this sort.

> General Sir Horace Smith-Dorrien, 26 December 1914, general order forbidding further instances of informal truces, as occurred on Christmas Day 1914 when British and German troops stopped fighting to celebrate the holiday together.

TRUST

KING WEI asked, "How can I get my people to follow orders as an ordinary matter of course?" Master Sun said, "Be trustworthy as a matter of course.

> Sun Bin, *The Lost Art of War*, c. 350 BC, tr. Thomas Cleary.

TRUST is a distinguished reward for warriors.

> Sun Bin, *The Lost Art of War*, c. 350 BC, tr. Thomas Cleary.

FOR IF MEN have a spontaneous and natural love for their general, they are quick to obey his commands, they do not distrust him, and they cooperate with him in case of danger.

> Onasander, *The General*, AD 58 (*Aeneas Tacticus, Aclepiodotus, Onasander*, tr. The Illinois Greek Club, 1923).

I COMMAND a great army. It is founded on trust. The minds of those who have been given permission to depart are already set on home like arrows. Their wives and children are counting the hours that they must wait for them. Although the battle before us may be fraught with danger, that trust cannot be broken.

> Zhuge Liang (AD 180–234), *The Way of the General*, when urged by his officers, at the approach of an enemy army, to revoke the leave promised to a number of his troops. He personally urged the troops to go, but they refused, and the enemy suffered a decisive defeat, quoted in Bloodworth, *The Chinese Machiavelli*, 1976.

WHAT makes soldiers in battle prefer to charge ahead rather than retreat even for survival is the benevolence of the military leadership. When soldiers know their leaders care for them as they care for their own children, then the soldiers love their leaders as they do their own fathers. This makes them willing to die in battle, to requite the benevolence of their leaders.

> Liu Ji (1310–1375), *Lessons of War* (*Mastering the Art of War*, tr. Thomas Cleary, 1989).

THE SPECIAL TRUST and confidence which is expressly reposed in each officer by his commission is the distinguishing privilege of the officer corps. It is the policy of the Marine Corps that this privilege be tangible and real; it is the corresponding obligation of the officer corps that it be wholly deserved.

Commanders will ensure that local policies, directives, and procedures reflect the special trust and confidence reposed in each member of the officer corps. Full credit will be given to his statements and certificates, he will be allowed maximum discretion in the exercise of authority vested in him, and he and his dependents will be accorded all prerogatives and perquisites which are traditional and otherwise appropriate. Except where the security of classified material and installations impose more stringent demands, an officer's uniform will amply attest his status as an officer, and his . . . statement will serve to identify him and his dependents.

As a concomitant, commanders will impress upon all subordinant officers the fact that the presumption of integrity, good manners, sound judgment, and discretion, which is the basis for the special trust and confidence reposed in each officer, is jeopardized by the slightest transgression on the part of any member of the officer corps. Any offense, however minor, will be dealt with promptly, and with sufficient severity to impress on the officer at fault, and on his fellow officers, the effects of the offense on the stature and reputation of the officer corps. It is an obligation to the officer corps as a whole, and transcends the bonds of personal friendship.

> Major-General John A. Lejeune, *The Marine Corps Manual*, 1920.

MUTUAL TRUST is the surest basis of discipline in necessity and danger.

> Generals Werner von Fritsch and Ludwig Beck, German Army, *Troop Leadership*, 1933, quoted in U.S. War Department, *German Military Training*, 17 September 1942.

THE COMMANDER stakes his reputation, his career, all that he is and may be in his profession, on the issue of a fight in which his instinct must derive so much that is unknown and his science weigh all that is imponderable: above all, he stakes the coin he values most – the trust that his officers and men have in him.

> Lieutenant-General Sir Francis Tuker, quoted in D.M. Horner, *The Commanders*, 1984.

TRUST is a many-splendored thing which pervades human relations at all levels in the military service.

> Major-General Aubrey 'Red' Newman, *Follow Me*, 1981.

TRUST is Vital. If you lead a large organization, it is essential to be able to trust your subordinate leaders. Such trust is difficult for some leaders who want to direct every aspect of their organization. These leaders cannot find their way clear to trust people and, as a result, they do not nurture subleaders or give them the opportunity to exercise their full creative talents. To be a truly effective leader, particularly of a large organization, requires a great deal of trust in one's subordinates. This trust needs to be balanced with a willingness to remove people who cannot be trusted, and to make some tough decisions. Without trust and mutual respect among leaders and subordinate leaders, a large organization will often suffer a combination of low performance and poor morale. In the words of Frank Crane, "You may be deceived if you trust too much, but you will live in torment if you do not trust enough."

> Major-General Perry M. Smith, *Taking Charge: A Practical Guide for Leaders*, 1986.

TRUST is an essential trait among leaders – trust by seniors in the abilities of their subordinates and by juniors in the competence and support of their seniors. Trust must be earned, and actions which undermine trust must meet with strict censure. Trust is a product of confidence and familiarity. Confidence among comrades results from demonstrated professional skill. Familiarity results from shared experience and a common professional philosophy.

> General Alfred M. Gray and Major John Schmitt, *Warfighting*, United States Marine Corps, 1989.

I BUILT trust among my components because I trusted them. . . .

> General H. Norman Schwarzkopf, quoted in *Joint Pub 1, Joint Warfare of the U.S. Armed Forces*, 1991.

THE NOTION of trust may convey even more than teamwork. It's critically important that you have trust, especially at the commander level. Issues are raised from time to time, but you can ask the questions that will defuse matters, because you're certain your fellow component commander wouldn't do or say that.

> Lieutenant-General Walter E. Boomer, quoted in *Joint Pub 1, Joint Warfare of the U.S. Armed Forces*, 1991.

TRUTH

TRUTH gains strength by notoriety and time, falsehood by precipitancy and vagueness.

> Cornelius Tacitus, *Annals*, 4.35, c. AD 116 (*The Complete Works of Tacitus*, tr. Alfred Church and William Brodribb, 1942).

THE PATH of nature and of truth is narrow but it is simple and direct; the devious paths are numerous and spacious; but they all lead to error and destruction.

> Robert Jackson, *A Systematic View of the Formation, Discipline and Economy of Armies*, 1804.

NOTHING should be concealed from the Emperor, either good or bad: to deceive him, even about things that are likely to be disagreeable to him is a crime.

> Marshal of France Louis Berthier, Prince de Neuchatel, Prince de Wagram, February 1807, letter to Marshal Lannes.

HAIG was an honourable man according to his lights – but his lights were dim. The consequences which have made "Passchendaele" a name of ill omen may be traced to the combined effect of his tendency to deceive himself; his tendency, therefore, to encourage his subordinates to deceive him; and their "loyal" tendency to tell a superior what was likely to conclude with his desires. Passchendaele is an object-lesson in this kind of well-meaning, if not disinterested truthfulness.

> Captain Sir Basil Liddell Hart, *Through the Fog of War*, 1938, referring to Field Marshal Douglas Haig, the commander of the British Expeditionary Force (BEF) during WWI.

THE TRUTH is uncontrovertible. Panic may resent it; ignorance may deride it; malice may destroy it, but there it is.

> Sir Winston S. Churchill (1874–1965).

THE TRUTH is sought regardless of whether pleasant or unpleasant, or whether it supports or condemns our present organization of tactics.

> General Lesley J. McNair, round-robin letter to his generals, quoted in Kahn, *McNair, Educator of an Army*, 1945.

OF COURSE it's the same old story. Truth usually is the same old story.

> Prime Minister Margaret Thatcher, *Time Magazine*, 1981.

U

UNCERTAINTY/THE UNEXPECTED/ THE UNKNOWN

WAR involves in its progress such a train of unforeseen and unsupposed circumstances that no human wisdom can calculate the end. It has but one thing certain, and that is to raise taxes.

  Thomas Paine (1737–1809), *Prospects on the Rubicon*, 1787.

ALTHOUGH our intellect always longs for clarity and certainty, our nature often finds uncertainty fascinating. It prefers to day-dream in the realms of chance and luck rather than accompany the intellect on its narrow and tortuous path of philosophical inquiry and logical deduction only to arrive – hardly knowing how – in unfamiliar surroundings where all the usual landmarks seems to have disappeared. Unconfirmed by narrow necessity, it can revel in a wealth of possibilities; which inspire courage to take wing and dive into the element of daring and danger like a fearless swimmer into the current.

  Major-General Carl von Clausewitz, *On War*, 1.1, 1832, tr. Michael Howard and Peter Paret, 1976.

THE COMMANDER in war must work in a medium which his eyes cannot see; which his best deductive powers cannot always fathom; and with which because of constant changes he can rarely become familiar.

  Major-General Carl von Clausewitz, *On War*, 1.3, 1832, tr. Michael Howard and Peter Paret, 1976.

WAR is the realm of uncertainty; three quarters of the factors on which action in war is based are wrapped in a fog of greater or lesser uncertainty. A sensitive and discriminating judgment is called for; a skilled intelligence to scent out the truth.

  Major-General Carl von Clausewitz, *On War*, 1.3, 1832, tr. Michael Howard and Peter Paret, 1976.

HE who wars walks in a mist through which the keenest eye cannot always discern the right path.

  General Sir William Napier, *History of the War in the Peninsula*, 1828–1840.

YOU WILL usually find that the enemy has three courses of action open to him, and of these he will adopt the fourth.

  Field Marshal Helmuth Graf von Moltke (1800–1891).

THE *UNKNOWN* is the governing condition of war. Everybody is familiar with the principle (so you might think), and being familiar with it will distrust the unknown and master it; the unknown will no longer exist.

This is not true in the least. All armies have lived and marched amidst the unknown.

  Marshal of France Ferdinand Foch, *Precepts and Judgments*, 1919.

UNIFORMS

AND NOW, bursting with rage against the men
  of Troy,
he donned Hephaestus' gifts – magnificent armor
the god of fire forged with all his labor.
First he wrapped his legs with well-made greaves,
fastened behind his heels with silver ankle-clasps,
next he strapped the breastplate around his chest,
then over his shoulder Achilles slung his sword,
the fine bronze blade with its silver-studded hilt,
then hoisted the massive shield flashing far and wide
like a full round moon – gleaming bright as the light
that reaches the sailors out at sea, the flare of a
  watch fire
burning strong in a lonely sheepfold up some
  mountain slope
when the gale winds hurl the crew that fights
  against them
far over the fish-swarming sea, far from loved ones –
so the gleam from Achilles' well-blazoned shield
shot up and hit the skies. Then lifting his
  rugged helmet
he set it down on his brows, and the horsehair crest
shone like a star and the waving golden plumes shook
that Hephaestus drove in bristling thick along its ridge.
And brilliant Achilles tested himself in all his gear,
Achilles spun on his heels to see if it fit tightly,
see if his shining limbs ran free within it, yes,
and it felt like buoyant wings lifting the great captain.

  Homer, *The Iliad*, 19.434–456, c. 800 BC, tr Fagles, 1990; Achilles donning his new divinely-wrought armour.

ON MAY 31, 1740, Frederick William I died, and when those around him sang the hymn, "Naked came I into the world and naked I shall go," he had just sufficient strength to mutter, "No, not quite naked; I shall have my uniform on."

  Frederick William I of Prussia, quoted by Major-General J.F.C. Fuller, *A Military History of the Western World*, II, 1955.

I HAVE an insuperable bias in favor of an elegant

uniform and a soldierly appearance, so much so that I would rather risk my life and reputation at the head of the same men in an attack, clothed and appointed as I could wish, merely with bayonets and a single charge of ammunition, than to take them as they appear in common with sixty rounds of cartridges.

Major-General 'Mad' Anthony Wayne to George Washington, 1776.

A WELL-DRESSED SOLDIER has more respect for himself. He also appears more redoubtable to the enemy and dominates him; for a good appearance is itself a force.

Joseph Joubert (1754–1824).

I THINK IT indifferent how a soldier is clothed, provided it is in a uniform manner; and that he is forced to keep himself clean and smart, as a soldier ought to be.

The Duke of Wellington, letter to the War Office, 1811.

I HEAR that measures are in contemplation to alter clothing, caps &c. of the army.

There is no subject of which I understand so little; and, abstractly speaking, I think it indifferent how a soldier is clothed, provided it is in a uniform manner; and that he is forced to keep himself clean and smart, as a soldier ought to be. But there is one thing I deprecate, and that is any imitation of the French in any manner.

It is impossible to form an idea of the inconveniences and injury which result from having anything like them. . . . I only beg that we may be as different from the French in everything.

The Duke of Wellington, 1811, letter to the Horse Guards, The Dispatches of Field Marshal the Duke of Wellington, During His Various Campaigns in India, Denmark, Portugal, Spain, the Low Countries, and France, VIII, 1834–1838, pp. 378–379.

DRESS THEM in red, blue, or green – they'll run away just the same.

Fernando I, King of the Two Sicilies, c. 1800, on the futility of trying to make good soldiers of his subjects by appealing to martial dress.

A SOLDIER must learn to love his profession, must look to it to satisfy all his tastes and his sense of honor. That is why handsome uniforms are useful.

Napoleon (1769–1821) to General Gaspard Gourgaud, 1815, on St. Helena.

I AM ASHAMED for strangers to see my barefoot, ragged boys in camp, but I would be glad for all the world to see them on the field of battle.

General Robert E. Lee, to an English visitor to the Army of Northern Virginia as his ragged army passed on parade, quoted in Lieutenant-General D.H. Hill, 'Address before the Mecklenburg (N.C.) Historical Society', Southern Historical Society Papers, I, January–June 1876, p. 397.

THE BETTER you dress a soldier, the more highly will he be thought of by women.

Field Marshal Lord Wolseley, The Soldier's Pocketbook, 1869.

AT THE SIGHT of the first few regiments of the enemy we were thrilled with interest. After three hours they had passed in one unbroken steel gray column [and] we were bored. But when hour after hour passed and there was not halt, no breathing time, no open spaces in the ranks, the thing became uncanny, inhuman. You returned to watch it, fascinated. It held the mystery and menace of fog rolling toward you across the sea.

The gray of the uniforms worn by both officers and men helped this air of mystery. Only the sharpest eye could detect among the thousands that passed the slightest difference. All moved under a cloak of invisibility. Only after the most numerous and severe tests at all distances, with all materials and combinations of colors that give forth no color could this gray have been discovered. That it was selected to clothe and disguise the German when he fights is typical of the German staff striving for efficiency to leave nothing to chance, to neglect no detail.

After you have seen this service uniform under conditions entirely opposite you are convinced that for the German soldier it is his strongest weapon. Even the most expert marksman cannot hit a target he cannot see. It is a gray green, not the blue gray of our Confederates. It is the gray of the hour just before daybreak, the gray of unpolished steel, of mist among green trees.

Richard Harding Davis, observing the German Army marching through Brussels, Tribune (New York), 23 August 1914.

THE SECRET of uniform was to make a crowd solid, dignified, impersonal: to give it the singleness and tautness of an upstanding man.

Colonel T.E. Lawrence, Revolt in the Desert, 1927.

IT IS PROVERBIAL that well dressed soldiers are usually well behaved soldiers. This thought led to the restoration to the Marine Corps of the blue uniform, to the successful endeavor to induce American manufacturers to produce a khaki cloth of high grade both as to texture and dye, and to improvements in the design and cut of all articles of uniform.

Major-General John A. Lejeune, The Reminiscences of a Marine, 1930.

SELF-RESPECT and esprit de corps demand some form of outward expression. Hence the justification of the uniform as the mark of a special class. The uniform indicates the soldier's responsibility; it is the outward sign of inward comradeship; it supports and confirms discipline.

Colonel-General Hans von Seekt, Thoughts of a Soldier, 1930.

UNITY OF COMMAND
Principle of War

RAGE – Goddess, sing the rage of Peleus' son
Achilles,
murderous, doomed, that cost the Achaeans
countless losses,
hurling down to the house of Death so many
sturdy souls,
great fighters' souls, but made their bodies carrion,
feasts for dogs and birds,
and the will of Zeus was moving toward its end.
Begin, Muse, when the two first broke and clashed,
Agamemnon lord of men and brilliant Achilles.

> Homer, *The Iliad*, 1.1–8, c. 800 BC, tr. Robert Fagles,
> 1990; the invocation of the Muse, the opening lines
> that announce an underlying theme of *The Iliad*, the
> breakdown in Greek leadership.

TOO MANY kings can ruin an army – mob rule!
Let there be one commander, one master only,
endowed by the son of crooked-minded Cronus
with kingly scepter and royal rights of custom:
whatever one man needs to lead his people well.

> Homer, *The Iliad*, 2.225–229, c. 800 BC, tr. Robert
> Fagles, 1990; Odysseus restoring order to the Achaean
> ranks.

FOR WHAT should be done seek the advice of
many, for what you will actually do take council with
only a few trustworthy people; then off by yourself
alone decide on the best and most helpful plan to
follow, and stick to it.

> The Emperor Maurice, *The Strategikon*, c. AD 600
> (*Maurice's Strategikon*, tr. George Dennis, 1984).

NOW in war there may be one hundred changes in
each step. When one sees he can, he advances;
when he sees that things are difficult, he retires. To
say that a general must await commands of the
sovereign in such circumstances is like informing a
superior that you wish to put out a fire. Before the
order to do so arrives the ashes are cold. And it is
said one must consult the Army Supervisor in these
matters! This is as if in building a house beside the
road one took advice from those who pass by. Of
course the work would never be completed!

To put a rein on an able general while at the
same time asking him to suppress a cunning
enemy is like tying up the Black Hound of Han and
then ordering him to catch elusive hares. What is
the difference?

> Ho Yen-hsi, Chinese military theorist of the Sung
> Dynasty, c. AD 1000, commentary on Sun Tzu, *The
> Art of War*, 3, c. 500 BC, tr Samuel Griffith, 1963.

AN ARMY should have but one chief; a greater
number is detrimental.

> Niccolo Machiavelli, *Discourses*, 1517.

NEVER will I accept a divided command – no, not
even were God Himself to be my colleague in office.
I must command alone, or not at all.

> Albert von Wallenstein, quoted in B.H. Liddell Hart,
> *Great Captains Unveiled*, 1927.

THE FIRST security for success is to confer the
command on one individual. When the authority is
divided, opinions are divided likewise, and the
operations are deprived of that *ensemble* which is
the first essential of victory. Besides, when an
enterprise is common to many, and not confined to a
single person, it is conducted without vigour, and
less interest is attached to the result.

> Field Marshal Count Raimond Montecuccoli
> (1609–1680), quoted in David Chandler, ed., *The
> Military Maxims of Napoleon*, 1987.

IT IS generally agreed that of all situations in which
the uncontested authority of one man may be
necessary to the public good, it is most evidently so
in war. Here everyone knows that resolutions must
be prompt, discipline exact, orders unquestioned,
and obedience absolute, that the least instant that is
lost in discussion may cause a golden opportunity to
escape forever and that the slightest mistakes that
one commits are often paid for in blood. . . .

Indeed what may one expect but tumult and
confusion in a body where those who must obey
cannot be sure who has the right to give them
commands, where those who aspire to authority
think more of settling their own private disputes than
of looking out for the welfare and the security of the
troops that have been entrusted to them.

> Louis XIV, King of France, *Mémoires de Louis XIV*,
> 1860, in David Ralston, *Soldiers and States*, 1966.

THAT NEEDS only a single general, but also that
nothing shall interfere with his movements and
operations. I have carried on this campaign without
consulting anyone; I should have done no good had
I had to come to terms with the viewpoint of another.
Lacking everything, I have got the better of far
superior forces because, in the belief that I had your
confidence, my movements have been as rapid as
my thought.

> Napoleon, 14 May 1796, letter to the Executive
> Directory after the Battle of Lodi on 10 May,
> complaining of the Directory's intention to appoint
> General Kellermann to share his command.

KELLERMANN would command the army quite as
well as I do; for I am certain that our victories are
due to the bravery and daring of the men. But I am
convinced that to combine Kellermann and myself in
Italy would be to court disaster. I cannot willingly
serve alongside a man who considers himself to be
the best general in Europe. In any case, I am certain
that one bad general is better than two good ones.
Fighting is like governing; it needs tact.

> Napoleon, 14 May 1796, letter to Citizen Carnot, after
> the Battle of Lodi on 10 May, complaining of the

Directory's intention to appoint General Kellermann to share his command, *Correspondance de Napoléon Ier, publiée par ordre de l'Empereur Napoléon III*, I, 421, 1858–1870.

IN WAR the commander alone understands the importance of certain things. He alone by his will and superior insight can conquer and overcome all difficulties.
Napoleon (1769–1821).

MAXIM 64. NOTHING is so important in war as an undivided command: for this reason, when war is carried on against a single power, there should be only one army, acting upon one base, and conducted by one chief.
Napoleon, *The Military Maxims of Napoleon*, tr. George D'Aguilar, 1831 (David Chandler, ed., 1987).

THE INEVITABLE END of multiple chiefs is that they fade and disappear for lack of unity.
Napoleon (1769–1821).

DO THE FINGERS know what the head intends the feet to do?
Shaka Zulu, c. 1818, quoted in E.A. Ritter, *Shaka Zulu*, 1955.

IT HAS BEEN SAID that one bad general is better than two good ones; and the saying is true, if taken to mean no more than that an army is better directed by a single mind, though inferior, than by two superior ones, at variance, and cross-purposes with each other.
And the same is true, in all joint operations wherein those engaged, can have none but a common end in view, and can differ only as to the choice of means. In a storm at sea, no one on board can wish the ship to sink; and yet, not unfrequently, all go down together, because too many will direct, and no single mind can be allowed to control.
President Abraham Lincoln, Annual Message to Congress, 31 December 1861, quoted in *Lincoln: Speeches, etc.*, 1989, p. 295.

AN ARMY is a collection of armed men obliged to obey one man. Every change in the rules which impairs the principle weakens the army.
General of the Army William T. Sherman (1820–1891).

NO; I will not direct any one to do what I would not do myself under similar circumstances. I never held what might be called formal councils of war, and I do not believe in them. They create a divided responsibility, and at times prevent that unity of action so necessary in the field. Some officers will in all likelihood oppose any plan that may be adopted; and when it is put into execution, such officers may, by their arguments in opposition, have so far

convinced themselves that the movement will fail that they cannot enter upon it with enthusiasm, and might possibly be influenced in their actions by the feeling that a victory would be a reflection upon their judgment. I believe it is better for a commander charged with the responsibility of all the operations of his army to consult his generals freely but informally, get their views and opinions, and then make up his mind what action to take, and act accordingly. There is too much truth in the old adage, "Councils of war do not fight."
General Ulysses S. Grant, comments on the suggestion that Sherman hold a council of war to determine whether he should march to the sea from Atlanta, early October 1864, quoted in Horace Porter, *Campaigning With Grant*, 1897.

SUBORDINATES can advise, urge, help and pray, but only one man, in his own mind and heart, can decide "Do we or do we not." The stakes are the highest and the penalties are expressed in terms of loss of life. . . . So the struggle is to do one's best; to keep the brain and the conscience clear; never be swayed by unworthy motives or inconsequential reasons but to strive to unearth the basic factors involved and then do one's duty.
General of the Army Dwight D. Eisenhower, 15 February 1943, letter to his wife.

YOU CAN'T RUN a military operation with a committee of staff officers in command. It will be nonsense.
Field Marshal Viscount Montgomery of Alamein, quoted in Francis de Guingand, *Operation Victory*, 1947.

NOW with the United States, it's a very simple thing. The War Department and the government decide that they have to do a certain thing with military forces. They look at the problem and say, "This is the mission for our forces." They pick a man. They confer with him about how much he'll need: How many divisions, how much air and navy, and all the rest of it. They say, all right, it's your job.
General of the Army Dwight D. Eisenhower, *General Eisenhower on the The Military Churchill*, 1970.

WHEN our front line infantry man or young sailor looked to his officer or NCO in the South Atlantic he was looking for guidance on how to improve his contribution. And this can be and was projected upwards. The ability to operate central joint command of our national force was war winning. Much was left unsaid because we knew our people and could rely on their flexibility, commonsense and sense of purpose. We were thus able to be truly joint. We won because we were unified, the enemy were not.
Major-General Sir Jeremy Moore, 'The Falklands Experience', *RUSI*, 1 March 1983.

V

VACILLATION/HESITATION/IRRESOLUTION

OF THE many harms that can beset an army, vacillation is the greatest. Of disasters that can befall an army, none surpasses doubt.
> The T'ai Kung, c. 1100 BC (*The Seven Military Classics of Ancient China*, tr. Ralph Sawyer, 1993).

VACILLATION is nothing less than disaster for an army.
> Takeda Nobushige, *Opinions in 99 Articles*, 1558 (*Ideals of the Samurai*, tr. William Wilson, 1982).

POSTPONEMENT breeds difficulties.
> Field Marshal Prince Aleksandr V. Suvorov (1829–1800), quoted in Philip Longworth, *The Art of Victory*, 1966.

HESITATION and half measures lose all in war.
> Napoleon, *Maxims of War*, 1831.

IRRESOLUTION in war is the most dangerous defect in a commander, more especially when the enemy is approaching. He must make his mind up without long deliberation, and above all things prevent French soldiers from giving way to their propensity for criticism. The most distinguished men in the career of arms have never ceased repeating this axiom: "Make your preparation for attack or defence instantly on the enemy's approach; should you even be obliged to execute them with disadvantage, do not hesitate." The enemy, who is a good observer, would take advantage of your indecision. It is often better to come to a bad decision immediately, than to hesitate between several good ones; for the bad one has always some favourable side by which success may be obtained. Moreover a vigilant mind is never embarrassed by the presence of the enemy, which on the contrary will tend to facilitate the boldness of its conceptions.
> Marshal of France Michel Ney, Duc d'Elchingen, Prince de la Moskova, *The Memoirs of Marshal Ney*, 1834.

PROCRASTINATION is like death.
> V.I. Lenin (1870–1924).

HE who will delay and shilly-shally in his place awaiting a clarified situation will himself inform the enemy and lose the initiative.
> Red Army, *Cavalry Combat Regulations*, 1936.

VALOUR

NOW those who discuss generals always think of their valour. But valour is only one of the many qualities of a general, and the valorous type of general is apt to join battle lightly and carelessly, without knowing how to profit by it, so that he cannot win.
> Wu C'hi (c. 430–381 BC), *The Art of War*, 1.4 (*Three Military Classics of China*, tr. A.L. Sadler, 1944).

IN VALOR there is hope.
> Cornelius Tacitus, *Annals*, c. AD 116.

VALOR is superior to numbers.
> Flavius Vegetius Renatus, *Military Institutions of the Romans*, c. AD 378, tr. Clark, 1776.

VALOR lies halfway between rashness and cowheartedness.
> Miguel de Cervantes, *Don Quixote*, 1615.

IF VALOUR can make amends for the want of numbers, we shall probably succeed.
> Major-General Sir James Wolfe, 1759, letter from Halifax to the Elder Pitt before the attack on Quebec.

AMONG the men who fought on Iwo Jima, uncommon valor was a common virtue.
> Admiral Chester W. Nimitz, March 1945.

HIDDEN VALOR is as bad as cowardice.
> Roman proverb.

VETERANS

AS FOR the cavalry, it should never be touched; old troopers and old horses are good, and recruits of either are absolutely useless. It is a burden, it is an expense, but it is indispensible.
  In regard to the infantry, as long as there are a few old heads you can do what you want with the tails; they are the greatest number, and the return of these men in peace is a noticeable benefit to the nation, without a serious diminution of the military forces.
> Field Marshal Maurice Comte de Saxe, *My Reveries*, 1732, tr. Phillips, 1940.

CALL A MEETING of the War Committee, and draft a measure to provide for discharged and wounded soldiers, by giving them preference in appointments to such administrative posts in the Forestry, Post

Office, Tobacco, Taxation, and in fact all departments, as can profitably be held by discharged officers and men. It is unfair, and contrary to my intention, to give such posts to people who have done nothing.

Napoleon, 27 January 1811, to General Count Andréossy, President of the War Committee of the State Council, *Correspondance de Napoléon Ier, publiée par ordre de l'Empereur Napoléon III*, XXI, 17301, 1858–1870.

THUS terminated the war, and with it all remembrance of the veteran's services.

General Sir William Napier, *History of the War in the Peninsula*, 1828–1840.

WHEN we got here the army was ragged and hard up, but already our new clothing is issued, and I will challenge the world to exhibit a finer looking set of men, brawny, strong, swarthy, a contrast to the weak and sickly fellows that came to me in Kentucky three years ago. It is a general truth that men exposed to the elements don't "catch cold," and I have not heard a man cough or sneeze for three months, but were these same men to go into houses in a month the doctor would have half of them. Now the doctors have no employment.

General of the Army William T. Sherman, 5 April 1865, letter to his wife from the vicinity of Goldsboro, North Carolina, *Home Letters*, 1909.

I BELIEVE that five hundred new men added to an old and experienced regiment were more valuable than a thousand men in the form of a new regiment, for the former by association with good, experienced captains, lieutenants, and non-commissioned officers, soon became veterans, whereas the latter were generally unavailable for a year.

General of the Army William T. Sherman, *Memoirs of General W.T. Sherman*, II, 1875.

IT WAS a sight never before witnessed in this country, and perhaps to be never again. Reviews of large numbers of troops, up to as high as one hundred thousand at a time, had been held as part of the preparatory discipline for battle. But here were the war-worn and generally shabbily-clad veterans, whose battles were finished. Before, on their way to the field, their new and fresh-looking banners were borne with the air of men determined to stand by them to the last. Now, they were brought back torn in shreds by bullets, and dingy with the smoke of war, vastly more prized than ever, and sending to the hearts of spectators a strange thrill of admiration for those men who had fulfilled their silent pledge, and brought back what was left of their colors, enveloped in glorious histories.

Brigadier-General E.D. Townsend, of the armies at the Grand Reviews of 23/24 May 1864, *Anecdotes of the Civil War*, 1884.

THE CITIZEN SOLDIERS were associated with so many disciplined men and professionally educated officers, that when they went into engagements it was with a confidence they would not have felt otherwise. They became soldiers themselves almost at once.

General of the Army Ulysses S. Grant, *Personal Memoirs of U.S. Grant*, I, 1885.

A MAN who is good enough to shed his blood for his country is good enough to be given a square deal afterwards. More than that no man is entitled to, and less than that no man shall have.

President Theodore Roosevelt, 7 December 1903.

THERE IS no sight in all the pageant of war like young, trained men going up to battle. The columns look solid and business-like. . . . They go on like a river that flows very deep and strong. Uniforms are drab these days, but there are points of light on the helmets and bayonets, and light in the quick steady eyes and the brown young faces, greatly daring. There is no singing – veterans know, and they do not sing much – and there is no excitement at all; they are schooled craftsmen, going up to impose their will, with the tools of their trade, on another lot of fellows; and there is nothing to make a fuss about.

Colonel John W. Thomason, Jr., *Fix Bayonets!*, 1926.

IT TAKES very little yeast to leaven a lump of dough. . . . It takes a very few veterans to leaven a division of doughboys.

General George S. Patton, Jr., *War As I Knew It*, 1947.

VICTORY
General

GREAT JOY has come in Egypt, rejoicing comes forth from the towns of Tomeri. They converse of the victories which Merneptah has achieved among the Tehenu: "How amiable is he, the victorious ruler! How magnified is the king among the gods! How fortunate is he, the commanding lord! Sit happily down and talk, or walk far out upon the way, for there is no fear in the heart of the people. The strongholds are left to themselves, the wells are opened again. The messengers skirt the battlements of the walls, shaded from the sun, until their watchmen wake. The soldiers lie sleeping, and the border scouts are in the field at their own desire. The herds of the field are left as cattle sent forth, without herdsmen, crossing at will the fullness of the stream. There is no uplifting of a shout in the night: "Stop! Behold, one comes, one comes with the speech of strangers!" One comes and goes with singing, and there is no lamentation of mourning people. The towns are settled again anew; as for the one that ploweth his harvest, he shall eat it. Re has turned himself to Egypt; he was born, destined to be her protector, the King Merneptah."

Merneptah, Pharaoh of Egypt (1225–1215 BC), celebration of victory over the Libyans, quoted in James Breasted, *Ancient Records of Egypt*, 1906.

VICTORY shifts, you know, now one man, now another.
> Homer, *The Iliad*, 6.401, c. 800 BC, tr. Robert Fagles, 1990.

THUS it is that in war the victorious strategist only seeks battle after the victory has been won, whereas he who is destined to defeat first fights and afterwards looks for victory.
> Sun Tzu, *The Art of War*, c. 500 BC, tr. Giles, 1910.

IT IS when you are proceeding against an enemy you expect to defeat that you should draw on all available resources. After all, an easy victory never gave anyone cause for regret.
> Xenophon, *How To Be A Good Cavalry Commander*, c. 360 BC (*Hiero the Tyrant and Other Treatises*, tr. Robin Waterfield, 1997).

ALEXANDER and Victory!
> The battle cry of Alexander the Great (356–323 BC), quoted in Plutarch, *The Lives*, c. AD 100.

TODAY the enemy would have won, if they had a commander who was a winner.
> Julius Caesar, 20 May 44 BC, after the Battle of Dyrrhacium, in which he had been defeated by Pompey who failed to press his advantage, quoted in Plutarch, *The Lives*, c. AD 100 (*The Fall of the Roman Republic*, tr. Rex Warner, 1972).

THE GREATEST happiness is to vanquish your enemies, to chase them before you, to rob them of their wealth, to see those dear to them bathed in tears, to clasp to your bosom their wives and daughters.
> Genghis Khan (1162–1227).

MAN does not enter battle to fight, but for victory. He does everything he can to avoid the first and obtain the second.
> Colonel Charles Ardant du Picq, *Battle Studies*, 1880, tr. Greely, 1957.

THE LAURELS of victory are at the point of the enemy bayonets. They must be plucked *there*; they must be carried by a hand-to-hand fight if one really means to conquer.
> Marshal of France Ferdinand Foch, *Precepts and Judgments*, 1919.

FAITH in victory determines victory.
> Marshal of France Louis-Hubert Lyautey, 8 July 1920.

THERE IS nothing certain about war except that one side won't win.
> General Sir Ian Hamilton, *Gallipoli Diary*, 1920.

I'M violently opposed to losing wars.
> Lieutenant-General Lewis B. 'Chesty' Puller (1898–1971), comment after his retirement in 1955, quoted in Burke Davis, *Marine*, 1964.

The Consequences of Victory

WAR will of itself discover and lay open the hidden and rankling wounds of the victorious party.
> Cornelius Tacitus, *Histories*, AD 104–109, 2.77, tr. Alfred Church and William Brodribb, 1942.

THE PROBLEMS of victory are more agreeable than those of defeat, but they are no less difficult.
> Sir Winston S. Churchill, 11 November 1942, in the House of Commons.

THE SHADOW of victory is disillusion: the reaction from extreme effort and prostrations.
> Sir Winston S. Churchill (1874–1965).

THE VENGEFUL passions are uppermost in the hour of victory.
> Captain Sir Basil Liddell Hart, *Defence of the West*, 1950.

IT IS very important that if we commit again to any kind of battle that we are sure to understand the ramifications of what happens if we do accomplish our objectives.
> General H. Norman Schwarzkopf, 1991, interview with C.D.B. Bryan, quoted in Peter David, *Triumph in the Desert*, 1991.

WHEN the Soviet Union collapsed, I think we all expected something different than what we actually got. We expected peace. We hoped for it. After all, we sacrificed a lot of blood and wealth to defeat communism. If the world was fair, we would have gotten peace.

Instead, we got a lot of trouble.

We hoped for a peace dividend. We ended up with a mailbox full of unexpected, unwanted bills – Somalia, Bosnia, more trouble with Iraq. Secretary of Defense Aspin said it best: "The new world order seems to be long on new and short on order." He is exactly right.
> General Gordon R. Sullivan, 6 August 1993, speech to the American Veterans Convention, New Orleans, Louisiana.

The Cost of Victory

I AM TIRED of the sickening sight of the battlefield, with its mangled corpses & poor suffering wounded! Victory has no charms for me when purchased at such cost.
> Major-General George Brinton McClellan, 2 June 1862, letter to his wife.

IT WAS a lovely day for strolling along the seashore. Men were sleepiing on the sand, some of them sleeping forever. Men were floating in the water, but they didn't know they were in the water, for they were dead. . . .

On the beach lay, expended, sufficient men and mechanism for a small war. They were gone forever now. And yet we could afford it.

We could afford it because we were one, we had our toehold, and behind us there were such enormous replacements for this wreckage on the beach that you could hardly conceive of their sum total. Men and equipment were flowing from England in such a gigantic stream that it made the waste on the beachead seem like nothing at all, really nothing at all.

> Ernie Pyle, of the Normandy beaches, 'This Is The Way It Really Was', *Washington Daily News*, 16 June 1944.

VICTORY was never in doubt. Its cost was. What was in doubt, in all our minds, was whether there would be any of us left to dedicate our cemetery at the end, or whether the last Marine would die knocking out the last Japanese gun and gunner.

> Major-General Graves B. Erskine, 14 March 1945, at the dedication of the Third Marine Division cemetery on Iwo Jima, quoted in Bill D. Ross, *Iwo Jima*, 1985.

The Elements of Victory

THUS we may know that there are five essentials for victory: (1) He will win who knows when to fight and when not to fight. (2) He will win who knows how to handle both superior and inferior forces. (3) He will win whose army is animated by the same spirit throughout all the ranks. (4) He will win who, prepared himself, waits to take the enemy unprepared. (5) He will win who has military capacity and is not interfered with by his sovereign. Victory lies in the knowledge of these five points.

Hence the saying: If you know the enemy and know yourself, you need not fear the result of a hundred battles. If you know yourself but not the enemy, for every victory gained you will also suffer a defeat. If you know neither the enemy nor yourself, you will succumb in every battle.

> Sun Tzu, *The Art of War*, 3, c. 500 BC, tr. Giles, 1910.

VICTORY in war does not depend entirely upon numbers or mere courage; only skill and discipline will insure it.

> Flavius Vegetius Renatus, *The Military Institutions of the Romans*, AD 378, tr. Clark, 1776.

VICTORY is achieved only through the combination of courage and military art.

> Field Marshal Prince Aleksandr V. Suvorov (1729–1800), quoted in M. Gareyev, *Frunze, Military Theorist*, 1985.

IF IN CONCLUSION we consider the total concept of a victory, we find that it consists of three elements:
1. The enemy's greater loss of material strength
2. His loss of morale
3. His open admission of the above by giving up his intentions.

> Major-General Carl von Clausewitz, *On War*, 4.4, 1832, tr. Michael Howard and Peter Paret, 1976.

THE DECISION can never be reached too soon to suit the winner or delayed long enough to suit the loser. A victory is greater for having been gained quickly; defeat is compensated for by having been long postponed.

> Major-General Carl von Clausewitz, *On War*, 5.6, 1832, tr. Michael Howard and Peter Paret, 1976.

IN VIEW of all of these intrinsic characteristics of war, we say there is only one result that counts: *final victory*. Until then, nothing is decided, nothing won, and nothing lost. In this form of work we must always keep in mind that it is the end that crowns the work.

> Major-General Carl von Clausewitz, *On War*, 8.3, 1832, tr. Michael Howard and Peter Paret, 1976.

THE WILL to conquer is victory's first condition, and therefore every soldier's first duty.

> Marshal of France Ferdinand Foch, *Principles of War*, 1913

WHAT we call victory is never won save by bits and scraps. The two trays of the scales counterbalance for a long time, and the slightest additional touch suffices to weigh one of them down.

> Marshal of France Ferdinand Foch, *Precepts and Judgments*, 1919.

VICTORY is an inclined plain. On condition that you do not check your movement the moving mass perpetually increases its speed.

> Marshal of France Ferdinand Foch, *Precepts and Judgments*, 1919.

THE SPACE separating defeat and victory is often very small, and the more powerful assailant does not always prevail. "The battle, sir," said Patrick Henry, "is not to the strong alone; it is to the vigilant, the active, the brave." Most often, the ingredients of victory are initiative, resourcefulness, adroitness, and improvisation.

> Lieutenant-General Victor H. 'The Brute' Krulak, *First to Fight*, 1984.

THE ARMY had a policy that you don't just beat him [the enemy] a little bit.

> Lieutenant-General John Yeosock, quoted in Donnelly, 'The Generals Plan', *Army Times*, 2 March 1992.

Generalship and Victory

THE EXPERT at battle seeks his victory from strategic advantage (*shih*) and does not demand it from his men. He is thus able to select the right men and exploit the strategic advantage (*shih*). He who exploits the strategic advantage (*shih*) sends his men into battle like rolling logs and boulders. It is the nature of logs and boulders that on flat ground, they are stationary, but on steep ground, they roll; the square in shape tends to stop but the round tends to roll. Thus, that the strategic advantage (*shih*) of the expert commander in exploiting his men in battle can be likened to rolling round boulders down a steep ravine thousands of feet high says something about his strategic advantage (*shih*).

Sun Tzu, *The Art of Warfare*, 5, c. 500 BC, tr. Roger Ames, 1993.

A GOOD GENERAL not only sees the way to victory; he also knows when victory is impossible.

Polybius, *Histories*, 1, c. 125 BC.

BEWARE of rashness, but with energy, and sleepless vigilance, go forward and give us victories.

President Abraham Lincoln, 26 January 1863, to Major-General Joseph Hooker.

I HAVE never in my life taken a command into battle, and had the slightest desire to come out alive unless I won.

General Philip H. Sheridan, when told by Brigadier-General Porter that he had exposed himself too much at the Battle of Five Forks, 1 April 1865, quoted in Horace Porter, *Campaigning With Grant*, 1897.

FINAL VICTORY has never been held the acid test of generalship, even where two professional armies have met. Ultimate defeat does not blind us to the skill of Hannibal, Napoleon, and Lee. (Jan. 1924.)

Captain Sir Basil Liddell Hart, *Thoughts on War*, 1944.

The Necessity of Victory

IF VICTORIOUS, we have everything to live for. If defeated, there will be nothing left to live for.

General Robert E. Lee, 3 May 1864, comment before the Battle of the Wilderness.

WE REGRET our companions in arms and shed a tear over their remains, but if these rebels should succeed we would have nothing left us and our lives would be spent in terror and sorrow.

Rear-Admiral David Dixon Porter, 17 January 1865, report to Gideon Welles, Secretary of the Navy.

VICTORY at all costs, victory in spite of terror, victory however long and hard the road may be; for without victory there is no survival.

Sir Winston S. Churchill, 13 May 1940, to the House of Commons.

IF WE WIN, nobody will care. If we lose, there will be nobody to care.

Sir Winston S. Churchill, secret session of the House of Commons, 25 June 1941, *Winston S. Churchill: His Complete Speeches, 1897–1963*, VI, 1974, p. 6438.

A CONVERSATION between this Commander and his political commissar, the latter saying: "I was with the troops today, spoke with people. They have only one thought: we shall stay to the death, we shall not let the Fascists go through."

– To stay is little. The Germans . . . can go through on our corpses. It is necessary to beat them. . . .

General P.A. Belov, autumn 1941, on the approaches to Moscow, quoted in Nathan Leites, *The Soviet Style in War*, 1982.

IN WAR there is no second prize for the runner-up.

General of the Army Omar N. Bradley, *Military Review*, 2/1950.

BUT once war is forced upon us, there is no other alternative than to apply every available means to bring it to a swift end. War's very object is victory, not prolonged indecision.

In war, there is no substitute for victory.

General of the Army Douglas MacArthur, 19 April 1951, address to Congress.

Pyrrhic Victory

THE ARMIES separated; and, it is said, Pyrrhus replied to one that gave him joy of his victory that one other such would utterly undo him. For he had lost a great part of the forces he brought with him, and almost all his particular friends and principal commanders; there were no others there to make recruits, and he found the confederates in Italy backward. On the other hand, as from a fountain continually flowing out of the city, the Roman camp was quickly and plentifully filled up with fresh men, not all abating in courage from the loss they sustained, but even from their very anger gaining new force and resolution to go on with the war.

Plutarch, *The Lives*, c. AD 100, tr. John Dryden, of the coining of the term 'Pyrrhic Victory' from the heavy, self-defeating losses taken in battle with the Romans, at Asculum in 279 BC, by Pyrrhus, King of Epirus.

THE PURSUIT of victory without slaughter is likely to lead to slaughter without victory.

The Duke of Marlborough (1650–1722).

IF GOD give us another defeat like this, your Majesty's enemies will be destroyed.

Marshal Claude-Louis-Hector de Villars, 11 September 1711, of the devastating losses he inflicted on Marlborough's infantry at Malplaquet, despite having to withdraw in good order from the field, a technical defeat.

MORE THAN ONCE have most promising opportunities been lost for want of men to take advantage of them, and victory itself has been made to put on the appearance of defeat, because our diminished and exhausted troops have been unable to renew a successful struggle against fresh numbers of the enemy. The lives of our soldiers are too precious to be sacrificed in the attainment of successes that inflict no loss upon the enemy beyond the actual loss in battle.

General Robert E. Lee, 10 January 1863, letter to James A. Seddon, *Confederate Secretary of War*.

AN ASSEGAI was thrust into the belly of the nation. There are not enough tears to mourn for the dead.

King Cetshwayo of Zululand, upon hearing of the fearful Zulu losses in wiping out the British column at Isandhlwana on 22 January 1879.

IF we have learned anything from our Vietnam experience, we should understand that the application of military power unsupported by adequate political consensus and resolve is insufficient to insure victory. Our military forces cannot operate in a political vacuum, for we are a consensus-oriented society, served rather than dominated by its defense establishment. The violation of this principle can only lead to the worst form of pyrrhic victory – when an army wins virtually every battle only to lose the highly political act that we call war. Thus, when reminded that his army had not defeated the U.S. Army on the battlefield, a North Vietnamese officer aptly replied, "That may be so, but it is also irrelevant."

Colonel Stuart A. Herrington, *Peace With Honor*, 1983; quoting Colonel Harry G. Summers, Jr. *On Strategy: A Critical Analysis of the Vietnam War*, 1982.

Reports of Victory

I CAME, I saw, I conquered.

Julius Caesar, 47 BC, the slogan carried in his Pontic Triumph, signifying how quickly he had dispatched this war, quoted in Suetonius, *Lives of the Twelve Caesars*, AD 121, tr. Philemon Holland, 1606.

THE ENEMY came to us. They are beaten. God be praised! I have been a little tired all day. I bid you good-night and am going to bed.

General Marshal Vicomte de Turenne, 14 June 1658, report of his victory that day in the Battle of the Dunes, quoted in Maxime Weygand, *Turenne, Marshal of France*, 1930.

I HAVE NOT time to say more, but to beg you will give my duty to the queen, and let her know her army has had a glorious victory, Mons. Tallard and two other generals are in my coach and I am following the rest. The bearer, my aide-de-camp, Colonel Parke, will give her an account of what has pass'd. I shall doe it in a day or two by another more at large.

The Duke of Marlborough, 13 August 1704, report of his victory that day at the Battle of Blenheim, quoted in Sir John Fortescue, *History of the British Army*, I, 1899.

WE HAVE MET the enemy, and they are ours: Two ships, two brigs, one schooner and one sloop.

Captain Oliver Hazard Perry, 10 September 1813, report to General William Henry Harrison of victory over the British at the Battle of Lake Eire on that date.

I YESTERDAY, after a most severe and bloody contest, gained a complete victory, and pursued the French till dark. They are in complete confusion; and I have I believe, 150 pieces of cannon; and Blücher, who continued the pursuit all night, my soldiers being tired to death, sent me word this morning that he had got 60 more . . . The finger of providence was upon me, and I escaped unhurt.

The Duke of Wellington, 19 June 1815, letter about Waterloo to Lady Frances Webster, *Supplementary Despatches, Correspondence, and Memoranda of Field Marshal Arthur Duke of Wellington, K.G., 1794–1818*, X, 1863, p. 531.

IT WAS a grand battle, and is in my judgment a most decided victory, though I did not annihilate or bag the Confederate Army. This morning they retired in great haste into the mountains, leaving their dead unburied and their wounded on the field. They awaited one day, expecting that flushed with success, I would attack them when they would play their old game of shooting us from behind breastworks – a game we played this time to their entire satisfaction. The men behaved splendidly; I really think they are becoming soldiers. They endured long marches, short rations, and stood one of the most terrific cannonadings I ever witnessed. . . . The army are in the highest spirits, and of course I am a great man. The most difficult part of my work is acting without correct information on which to predict action.

Major-General George G. Meade, 5 July 1863, letter to his wife on the day after Lee began his retreat from Gettysburg.

THE CAPTURE of Vicksburg has proved a bigger thing than I supposed it would. There was over thirty one thousand rebel troops still left when we entered the city. The number of small arms will reach 50,000 stands I think, and the amount of Ordnance and Ordnance stores is enormous. Since crossing the Miss. River an army of (60,000) sixty thousand men has, in the various battles been killed wounded, captured, and scattered so as to be lost to the Confederacy, and an armament for an army of (100,000) one hundred thousand men has departed from there forever.

General of the Army Ulysses S. Grant, 11 July 1863, to Brigadier-General L. Thomas, Adjutant General of the Army, in Johnston and Buel, ed., *Battles and Leaders of the Civil War, Being for the Most Part Contributions by Union and Confederate Officers*, III, 1888.

CASUALTIES many; percentage dead unknown; combat efficiency: We are winning.

General David Shoup, 21 November 1943, situation report from Betio Island in Tarawa Atoll, quoted in James R.Stockman, *The Battle for Tarawa*, 1947.

Soldiers and Victory

WHOEVER wants to keep alive must aim at victory. It is the winners who do the killing and the losers who get killed.

> Xenophon, *Anabasis*, 2.3, 401 BC (*The Persian Expedition*, tr. Rex Warner, 1949); speech to the Greek Army stranded in the midst of the Persian Army after the defeat of their employer, Cyrus, at the Battle of Cunaxa.

MEN, if you will do as I say I will always lead you to victory.

> Lieutenant-General Nathan Bedford Forrest, 12 April 1862, speech to his men after their escape from Fort Pillow.

HIS [Bragg] many retreats, too, had alienated the rank and file from him, or at least had taken away that enthusiasm which soldiers feel for the successful general, and which makes them obey his orders without question, and thus wins for him other successes. The one thing that a soldier never fails to understand is victory, and the commander who leads him to victory will be adored by him whether that victory has been won by great skill or by blundering, by the masterly handling of a few troops against great odds, or by the awkward use of overwhelming numbers. Long before Stonewall Jackson had risen to the height of his great fame, he had won the implicit confidence of his troops in all his movements. "Where are you going?" one inquired of the "foot cavalry" as they were making the usual stealthy march to the enemy's rear. "We don't know, but old Jack does," was the laughing answer. The trust was the fruit of past victories, and it led to other and greater achievements.

> Lieutenant-General D.H. Hill, 'Chickamauga – The Great Battle of the West', in Johnston and Buel, ed., *Battles and Leaders of the Civil War, Being for the Most Part Contributions by Union and Confederate Officers*, III, p. 639, 1887–1888.

THE MEN of the Eighth Army were brown-skinned and white-eye-browed from the desert sun. Most of them were in shorts, and they were a healthy-looking lot. Their spirit was like a tonic. The spirit of our own troops was good, but those boys from the burning sands were throbbing with the vitality of conquerors.

They were friendly, cocky, confident. They had been three years in the desert, and they wore the expression of victory on their faces. We envied them, and we were proud of them.

> Ernie Pyle, meeting of the U.S. First and British Eighth Armies in Tunisia in 1942, *Here is Your War*, 1945.

The Uses of Victory

FOR as we have often observed, it is no doubt a great thing to be successful in our undertakings, and to defeat our enemy in the field of battle; but it is a proof of greater wisdom, and requires more skill, to make a good use of victory. For many know how to conquer; few are able to use their conquest aright.

> Polybius, *Histories*, 10.36, c. 125 BC (*Familiar Quotations from Greek Authors*, tr. Crauford Ramage, 1895).

A VICTORY on the battlefield is of little account if it has not resulted either in breakthrough or encirclement. Though pushed back, the enemy will appear again on different ground to renew the resistance he momentarily gave up. The campaign will go on.

> Field Marshal Alfred Graf von Schlieffen (1833–1913).

THE TRUE national object in war, as in peace, is a more perfect peace. The experience of history enables us to deduce that gaining military victory is not in itself equivalent to gaining the object of war. (Oct. 1925.)

> Captain Sir Basil Liddell Hart, *Thoughts on War*, 1944.

VICTORY, in the true sense, implies that a nation's prospects after the war are better than if it had not made war. Victory, in this sense, is only possible if the result is quickly gained – for which only an aggressor can hope – or the effort is economically proportioned to the national resources. Favoured by geography, it has been Britain's distinction to excel in this wise economy of force. In a far-sighted fulfillment of the principle, looking beyond war to peace, lay the secret of her unbroken prosperity during three centuries. (Jan. 1931.)

> Captain Sir Basil Liddell Hart, *Thoughts on War*, 1944.

IF YOU concentrate exclusively on victory, with no thought for the after effect, you may be too exhausted to profit by the peace, while it is almost certain that the peace will be a bad one, containing the germs of another war. (April 1939.)

> Captain Sir Basil Liddell Hart, *Thoughts on War*, 1944

VICTORY in the true sense implies that the state of peace, and of one's people, is better after the war than before. Victory in this sense is only possible if a quick result can be gained or if a long effort can be economically proportioned to the national resources. The end must be adjusted to the means. Failing a fair prospect of such a victory, wise statesmanship will miss no opportunity for negotiating peace. Peace through stalemate, based on a coincident recognition by each side of the opponent's strength, is at least preferable to peace through common exhaustion – and has often provided a better foundation for lasting peace.

> Captain Sir Basil Liddell Hart, *Strategy*, 1954.

VIOLENCE

THOSE who despise violence are warriors fit to work for kings.

> Sun Bin, *The Lost Art of War*, c. 350 BC, tr. Thomas Cleary, 1996.

WAR therefore is an act of violence intended to compel our opponent to fulfill our will.

Violence arms itself with inventions of art and science in order to contend against violence. Self-imposed restrictions, almost imperceptible and hardly worth mentioning, termed usages of international law, accompany it without essentially impairing its power. Violence, that is to say, physical force (for there is no moral force without the conception of states and law), is therefore the *means*; the compulsory submission of the enemy to our will is the ultimate *object*.

Major-General Carl von Clausewitz, *On War*, 1.1.2, 1832, tr. J.J. Graham, 1908.

WAR is among the greatest horrors known to mankind; it should never be romanticized. The means of war is force, applied in the form of violence. It is through the use of violence – or the credible threat of violence – that we compel our enemy to do our will. In either event, violence is an essential element of war, and its immediate result is bloodshed, destruction, and suffering. While the magnitude of violence may vary with the object and means of war, the violent essence of war will never change. Any study of war that neglects this characteristic is misleading and incomplete.

General Alfred M. Gray and Major John Schmitt, *Warfighting*, United States Marine Corps, 1989.

RELIGIONS and civilizations may be seen as attempts to discipline mankind, to trim our worst excesses. Traditionally, religions and civilizations acknowledged mankind's propensity for violence and imposed appropriate strictures. Certainly, no religion or civilization has believed that it could ignore violent behavior as peripheral. Yet our contemporary American approach is to treat violence as an aberration, the product of a terrible misunderstanding. It is the mentality of the born victim, of the spouse who believes every weeping apology, of the social worker who believes in the mass murderer's rehabilitation. Our willful denial of the full spectrum of man's nature, from the sublime to the beastly, is a privilege of our wealth. It is a privilege that will be extended to our soldiers.

Lieutenant-Colonel Ralph Peters, *Fighting For the Future*, 1999.

MORALLY, the best among us may be those who argue for disarmament. But they are mistaken. The heart of the problem is not the weapon, but the man who builds and wields it. Were we to eliminate all weapons of mass destruction, as well as every last handgun and pocketknife, the killers among us would take up wooden clubs and rocks. The will to violence is within us – it is not merely a function of the availability of tools.

Lieutenant-Colonel Ralph Peters, 'Our New Old Enemies', *Parameters*, Summer 1999.

I'VE GOT to get the maximum violence out of this campaign – now!

General Wesley Clark, on escalating the bombing campaign against Serbia, quoted in 'The Commander's War', *The Washington Post*, 21 September 1999, A16.

SOME MEN thrive on violence and killing. Some few enjoy it ecstatically. It takes but a small band of such men, armed and determined, to destroy a fragile society. If the worst thugs are not removed – or killed – the victimized society has no chance of reconstruction. Mass murderers do not reform, they just rearm. We love the idea of redemption, but the rest of the world wants revenge . . . those who thrive by the gun generally only understand a larger gun pointed at them. Violence cannot be halted without the will to respond in kind. Those who shake the hands of tyrants become their accomplices.

Lieutenant-Colonel Ralph Peters, 'Sierra Leone's Blood Is On America's Hands', *Wall Street Journal*, 11 May 2000.

VOLUNTEERS

I AM NOT influenced by the expectation of promotion or pecuniary reward. I wish to be useful, and every kind of service necessary for the public good, becomes honorable by being necessary.

Captain Nathan Hale, September 1776, to Captain William Hull, who was trying to dissuade him from volunteering to be a spy, quoted in Isaac William Stuart, *Life of Nathan Hale*, 1856.

THE PATRIOT volunteer, fighting for his country and his rights, makes the most reliable soldier on earth.

Lieutenant-General Thomas J. 'Stonewall' Jackson, quoted in Henderson, *Stonewall Jackson and the American Civil War*, 1898.

THIS CONFLICT is one thing I've been waiting for. I'm well and strong and young – young enough to go to the front. If I can't be a soldier I'll help soldiers. . . . when there is no longer a soldier's arm to raise the Stars and Stripes above our Capitol, may God give strength to mine.

Clara Barton, 1861, quoted in National Park Service, *Clara Barton* (Handbook 110), 1981.

IT IS a striking feature, so far as my observation goes, of the present volunteer army of the United States, that there is nothing which men are called upon to do, mechanical or professional, that accomplished adepts cannot be found for the duty required in almost every regiment.

General of the Army Ulysses S. Grant, 6 July 1863, report on the Vicksburg campaign.

IF YOU ARE only ready to go when you are

fetched, where is the merit of that? Are you only going to do your duty when the law says you must? Does the call to duty find no response in you until reinforced, let us rather say, superseded, by the call of compulsion.

Field Marshal Earl Kitchener, 1915, speech at the Guildhall, London.

OUR voluntary service regulars are the last descendents of those rulers of the ancient world, the Roman legionnaires.

Major-General Sir Ian Hamilton, *Gallipoli Diary*, 1920.

THE VOLUNTEER principle is all very well, and those who volunteer deserve honour; but it skims the cream off units.

Brigadier Sir Bernard Fergusson, *The Trumpet in the Hall*, 1970.

WE CAN BUILD a strong, capable, effective Army with volunteers as long as we have that foundation of pride. We cannot buy pride; we cannot legislate it, we cannot do without it.

General Creighton W. Abrams, address to the National Aviation Club, Washington, 1974.

W

WAR
The Causes of War

. . . SO they waited,
the old chiefs of Troy, as they sat aloft the tower.
And catching sight of Helen moving along the
   ramparts,
they murmured one to another, gentle, winged words:
"who on earth could blame them? Ah, no wonder,
the men of Troy and Argives under arms have suffered
years of agony all for her, for such a woman.
Beauty, terrible beauty!"
A deathless goddess – so she strikes our eyes!
But still,
ravishing as she is, let her go home in the long ships
and not be left behind . . . for us and our children
down the years an irresistible sorrow."
> Homer, *The Iliad*, 3.183–194, c. 800 BC, tr. Robert
> Fagles, 1990; Helen, the cause of the Trojan War,
> summoned to the walls of Troy to witness the duel
> between Menelaus and Paris.

WARS spring from unseen and generally
insignificant causes.
> Thucydides, *The Peloponnesian War*, c. 404 BC.

THE REAL though unavowed cause [of the
Peloponnesian War] I believe to have been the
growth of the Athenian power, which terrified the
Lacedaemonians and forced them into war.
> Thucydides, *The Peloponnesian War*, 1.24, c. 404 BC,
> tr. Benjamin Jowett, 1881.

AND THEREFORE let none hesitate to accept war
in exchange for peace. Wise men refuse to move
until wronged, but brave men as soon as they are
wronged go to war, and when there is a good
opportunity make peace again. They are not
intoxicated by military success; but neither will they
tolerate injustice from a love of peace and ease. For
he whom pleasure makes a coward will quickly lose,
if he continues inactive, the delights of ease which
he is so unwilling to renounce.
> Thucydides, *The Peloponnesian War*, 1.120,
> c. 404 BC, tr. Benjamin Jowett, 1881; the Corinthian
> delegate to the assembly of the Spartan allies urging
> war with Athens.

ONE must never allow disorder to continue so as to
escape a war. One does not escape: The war is
merely postponed to one's disadvantage.
> Niccolo Machiavelli, *The Prince*, 1513.

THE POSSESSION of battle-ready troops, a well-
filled state treasury and a lively disposition, these
were the real things which moved me to war.
> Frederick the Great, on the invasion of Silesia, *a
> History of My Times*, 1741.

TWO different motives make men fight one another:
hostile feelings and *hostile intentions*. Our definition
is based on the latter, since it is the universal
element. Even the most savage, almost instinctive,
passion of hatred cannot be conceived as existing
without hostile intent; but hostile intentions are often
unaccompanied by any sort of hostile feelings – at
least by none that predominate. Savage peoples are
ruled by passion, civilized peoples by the mind. The
difference, however, lies not in the respective nature
of savagery and civilization, but in their attendant
circumstances, institutions, and so forth. The
difference, therefore, does not operate in every
case, but it does in most of them. Even the most
civilized of peoples, in short, can be fired with
passionate hatred of each other.
> Major-General Carl von Clausewitz, *On War*, 1.1.3,
> 1832, tr. Michael Howard and Peter Paret, 1976.

I HAD NO FEELING of self-reproach, for I fully
believed the contest was inevitable and was not of
our seeking. The United States was called upon not
only to defend its sovereignty, but its right to exist as
a nation. . . . To me it was simply a contest,
politically speaking, as to whether virtue or vice
should rule.
> Major-General Abner Doubleday, who commanded
> Fort Sumter in 1861 when the Confederates attacked
> it, firing the first shots of the Civil War, *Reminiscences
> of Forts Sumter and Moultrie, 1860–'61*, 1876.

STATES which are weak from a military standpoint,
and which are surrounded by stronger neighbors
invite war, and if they neglect their military
organizations from false motives, they court dangers
by their own supineness.
> Field Marshal Colmar Baron von der Goltz, *Nation in
> Arms*, 1883.

IF EVER there is another war in Europe, it will come
out of some damned silly thing in the Balkans.
> Chancellor Otto von Bismarck (1815–1898).

BLOOD, race, tradition, trade and a host of other
influences, capped by ambition to go on, to lead, to
expand, will always produce strife.

War, whether it be for good or evil, is among men.
Major-General Leonard Wood, *Our Military History: Its Facts and Fallacies*, 1916.

WHERE EVIL is mighty and defiant, the obligation to use force – that is war – arises.
Rear-Admiral Alfred Thayer Mahan, *Naval Strategy*, 1911.

I ASK the House from the point of view of British interests to consider what may be at stake. If France is beaten to her knees . . . if Belgium fell under the same dominating influence and then Holland and then Denmark . . . if, in a crisis like this, we run away from these obligations of honor and interest as regards the Belgian Treaty . . . I do not believe for a moment that, at the end of this war, even if we stood aside, we should be able to undo what had happened, in the course of the war, to prevent the whole of the West of Europe opposite us from falling under the domination of a single power . . . and we should, I believe, sacrifice our respect and good name and reputation before the world and should not escape the most serious and grave economic consequences.
Sir Edward Grey, British Foreign Secretary, 3 August 1914, speech to the House of Commons on the grounds for war with Germany, quoted in Barbara Tuchman, *The Guns of August*, 1962.

ONCE in a generation a mysterious wish for war passes through the people. Their instinct tells them that *there is no other way* of progress and of escape from habits that no longer fit them. Whole generations of statesmen will fumble over reforms for a lifetime which are put into full-blooded execution within a week of a declaration of war. There is *no other way*. Only by intense sufferings can the nations grow, just as a snake once a year must with anguish slough off the once beautiful coat which has now become a strait jacket.
General Sir Ian Hamilton, *Gallipoli Diary*, 1918.

NATIONAL INSECURITY is one of the fundamental causes of war, especially if the nation concerned is militarily powerful. All nations are impelled by the instinct of national preservation to seek secure frontiers, and, if secure frontiers cannot be gained by peaceful methods, powerful nations will seek to secure them by war. A strong frontier is nothing else than a natural fortress, which, when garrisoned, secures the nation against attack. The object is the security of the nation, consequently . . . the breaking down of the national will is the surest means of forcing the fortress to collapse.
Major-General J.F.C. Fuller, *The Foundation of the Science of War*, 1926.

THE MORE I study war, the more I come to feel that the cause of war is fundamentally psychological rather than political or economic. When I come in contact with a militarist, his stupidity depresses me and makes me realize the amount of human obtuseness that has to be overcome before we can make progress towards peace. But contact with pacifists too often has the effect of making me almost despair of the elimination of war, because in their very pacifism the element of pugnacity is so perceptible. Moreover, with this active dislike, which in itself hinders understanding, there is mingled an attitude toward it rather like the Arabs' attitude to disease – that it is an affliction of Providence, against which "charms" may avail, but not scientific study. Until we understand war in the fullest sense, which involves an understanding of men in war, among other elements, it seems to me that we can have no more prospect of preventing war than the savage has of preventing plague. (May 1934.)
Captain Sir Basil Liddell Hart, *Thoughts on War*, 1944.

THERE IS no merit in putting off a war for a year, if when it comes, it is a far worse war or one much harder to win.
Sir Winston S. Churchill, *The Gathering Storm*, 1948.

WAR for an aggressor nation is actually a nearly complete collapse of policy. Once war comes, then nearly all prewar policy is utterly invalid because the setting in which it was designed to function no longer corresponds with the facts of reality. When war comes, we at once move into a radically different world.
Rear-Admiral Joseph C. Wylie (1911–1993).

FROM the beginning of man's recorded history physical force, or the threat of it, has been freely and incessantly applied to the resolution of social problems. It persists as an essential element in the social pattern. History suggests that as a society of men grows more orderly the application of forces tends to become better ordered. The requirement for it has shown no sign of disappearing.
General Sir John Hackett, *The Profession of Arms*, 1963.

ONE clear picture emerges: that the wars . . . none of them were inevitable. They were not the product of forces beyond human control, nor were they the inescapable result of the development of the armed forces themselves and the trade in arms which supplied them, although both influence the policies which governments pursued in support of what they believe to be the interests of their nations. It was those policies which were themselves the causes of war.
Field Marshal Lord Carver, *Twentieth Century Warriors*, 1987.

MOREOVER, the internal tension in the country, the protests and these notorious scandals again. All of this requires a small, victorious war which allows everything to be written off. War writes everything off.
Lieutenant-General Aleksandr I. Lebed, speaking of a possible U.S. strike against Iraq for the purpose of diffusing the Lewinsky scandal, quoted in *El Pais* (Madrid), 15 March 1998.

Civil War

LOST to the clan,
lost to the hearth, lost to the old ways, that one
who lusts for all the horrors of war with his
  own people.
  Homer, *The Iliad*, 9.73–76, c. 800 BC, tr. Robert
  Fagles, 1990; speech by King Nestor of Pylos to
  reconcile Agamemnon and Achilles.

ALAS for Greece, how many brave men have you
killed with your own hands! If these men were still
alive, they could have conquered all the barbarians
in the world.
  Agesilaus (444–360 BC), Eurypontid King of Sparta,
  his distress at the large number of Greeks killed in
  battle against other Greeks, quoted in Plutarch, *The
  Lives*, c. AD 100 (*The Age of Alexander*, tr. Ian Scott-
  Kilvert, 1973).

NOW they [the Romans] were thoroughly
convinced that civil dissentions were much more to
be dreaded than a war carried out in a foreign
country against a foreign enemy.
  Polybius, *Histories*, 1.71, c. 125 BC (*Familiar Quotations
  from Greek Authors*, tr. Crauford Ramage, 1895).

IN CIVIL STRIFE, where action is more needed than
deliberation, nothing is safer than haste.
  Cornelius Tacitus, *History*, 1.62, AD 98 (*The Complete
  Works of Tacitus*, tr. Alfred Church and William
  Brodribb, 1942).

UNHAPPY it is though to reflect, that a Brother's
Sword has been sheathed in a Brother's breast, and
that, the once happy and peaceful plains of America
are either to be drenched with Blood, or Inhabited by
Slaves. Sad alternative! But can a virtuous Man
hesitate in his choice?
  General George Washington, 31 May 1775, to George
  William Fairfax, *The Writings of George Washington*,
  III, p. 292, John C. Fitzgerald, ed., 1931.

I AM ONE of those who have probably passed a
longer period of my life engaged in war than most
men, and principally in civil war; and I must say
this, that if I could avoid, by any sacrifice whatever,
even one month of civil war in the country to which
I was attached, I would sacrifice my own life in
order to do it.
  The Duke of Wellington, March 1829, to the House
  of Lords.

THIS WAR was never really contemplated in
earnest. I believe if either the North or the South had
expected that their differences would result in this
obstinate struggle, the cold-blooded Puritan and the
cock-hatted Huguenot and Cavalier would have
made a compromise.
  Major-General George Pickett, 27 June 1862, letter to
  his fiancée during the American Civil War.

The Conduct of War

IN WAR events of importance are the results of
trivial causes.
  Julius Caesar, *The Gallic War*, c. AD 51.

WAR is waged not with numbers but with wits.
  Field Marshal Prince Aleksandr V. Suvorov
  (1729–1800), quoted in M. Gareyev, *Frunze, Military
  Theorist*, 1985.

WAR justifies everything.
  Napoleon, 1808, quoted in Christopher Herold, ed.,
  The Mind of Napoleon, 1955.

THE CONDUCT of war resembles the workings of
an intricate machine with tremendous friction, so that
combinations which are easily planned on paper can
be executed only with effort.
  Major-General Carl von Clausewitz, *Principles of
  War*, 1812, Gatzke, 1942.

THE CONDUCT of war branches out in almost all
directions and has no definite limits; while any
system, any model, has the finite nature of a
synthesis. An irreconcilable conflict exists between
this type of theory and actual practice.
  Major-General Carl von Clausewitz, *On War*, 2.2,
  1832, tr. Michael Howard and Peter Paret, 1976.

AND SO it is that intelligence, instinct, and the
leader's authority combine to make the conduct of
war what it is. But what are these faculties if not the
expression of a powerful and resourceful
personality? Other things being equal, it is safe to
say that the value of the fighting man is in exact
proportion to the value, in terms of personality, of
those under whose command he serves. Training for
war is, first and foremost, training in leadership, and
it is literally true, for armies as well as for nations,
that where the leadership is good, the rest shall be
added to them.
  General Charles de Gaulle, *The Edge of the
  Sword*, 1932.

1. THE CONDUCT of war is an art, depending upon
free, creative activity, scientifically grounded. It
makes the highest demands upon individuals.
2. The conduct of war is based on continuous
development. New means of warfare call forth ever
changing employment.
  Generals Werner von Fritsch and Ludwig Beck, *Troop
  Leadership*, 1933.

THERE IS only one way to conduct war as I read
history: Deploy to the war zone as quickly as
possible sufficient forces to end it at the earliest
moment. Anything else is a gift to the enemy.
  Brigadier-General S.L.A. Marshall, 'Some Thoughts
  on Vietnam', quoted in Thompson, ed., *The Lessons
  of Vietnam*.

. . . ABOUT the general conduct of war. There are, in the end, no humanitarian wars. War is serious and it is deadly. Casualties, including civilian casualties, are to be expected. Trying to fight a war with one hand tied behind your back is the way to lose it. We always regret the loss of lives. But we should have no doubt that it is the men of evil, not our troops or pilots, who bear the guilt.

Margaret Thatcher, 20 April 1999, speech.

The Economy of War

A STATE is impoverished by its armies when it has to fight at a distance. . . . On the other hand, in the vicinity of the armies, the price of goods goes up. . . . All your strength is spent on the battlefield, and the families on the home front are left destitute. The toll to the people will have been some 70 percent of their property; the toll to the public coffers in terms of broken-down chariots and worn-out horses, body armor and helmets, crowsbows and bolts, halberds and bucklers, lances and shields, draft oxen and heavy supply wagons will be some 60 percent of its reserves.

Sun Tzu, *The Art of Warfare*, 5, c. 500 BC, tr. Roger Ames, 1993.

WAR is a matter not so much of arms as of money, which makes arms of use.

Archidamus II, King of Sparta, 432 BC, speech on the prospect of war with Athens, quoted in Thucydides, *History of the Peloponnesian War*, 1.83, c. 404 BC, tr. Richard Crawley, 1910.

FIGHT thou with shafts of silver and thou shalt conquer in all things.

Response of the Delphic Oracle to Philip of Macedon asking how he might be victorious in war, quoted from Plutarch, *Apothegms*.

WHEN the allies were inquiring how much money would suffice and were demanding that he fix their contributions, he said: "War does not call for set amounts."

Plutarch, quoting Archidamus III, Eurypontid King of Sparta (ruled 360–338 BC), *Plutarch on Sparta*, tr. Richard Talbert, 1988.

A KING'S RAW MATERIALS and instruments of rule are a well-peopled land, and he must have men of prayer, men of war, and men of work.

Alfred the Great, King of England (AD 849–901).

MONEY, more money, always money.

Marshal Gian Giacomo de Trivulce (1441–1518), when François I, King of France, asked him what he needed to make war.

EVERY ONE may begin a war at his pleasure, but cannot so finish it. . . And money alone, so far from being a means of defense, will only render a prince the more liable to being plundered. There cannot, therefore, be a more erroneous opinion than money is the sinews of war.

I maintain, then, contrary to the general opinion, that the sinews of war are not gold, but good soldiers; for gold alone will not procure good soldiers, but good soldiers will always procure gold. By making their wars with iron, they never suffered for the want of gold.

Niccolo Machiavelli, *Discourses*, 1517.

MEN, arms, money, and provisions are the sinews of war, but of these four, the first two are the most necessary; for men and arms will always find money and provisions, but money and provisions cannot always raise men and arms.

Niccolo Machiavelli, *The Art of War*, 1521.

THE ARMY is a school in which the miser becomes generous, and the generous prodigal; miserly soldiers are like monsters, very rarely seen.

Miguel de Cervantes, *Don Quixote*, 1615.

WE ARE without money, and have been so for a long time; without provision and forage, except what is taken by impress; without clothing, and shortly shall be (in a manner) without men. In a word, we have lived upon expedients till we can live no longer; and it may truly be said, that the history of this war is a history of false hopes and temporary devices, instead of system – and economy, which results from it.

General George Washington, 22 October 1780, letter to George Mason, quoted in Henry Lee, *War in the Southern Department*, 1869.

THE ARMY is a sack with no bottom.

General Simon Bolivar (1783–1830), quoted in *Military History*, 8/1988.

HE who has his thumb on the purse has the power.

Chancellor Otto von Bismarck, 21 May 1869, speech.

THE MEANS of waging war are the means of waging peace. Practically everything which in peace time possesses energy, can in war time be turned into war energy – newspapers, sewing machines, motor cars, dye works, watch factories, royal academicians; in fact all industries, trades, and professions; all the moral physical, economic, intellectual, and even spiritual, forces of the nation. At the apex of these we have the navy, army and air force which can attack the enemy physically, economically and morally, that is by fighting, starvation, and terror.

Major-General J.F.C. Fuller, *Lectures on F.S.R. II*, 1931.

FOR WEEKS and weeks now I have been trying to make bricks without straw, which in itself is bad enough, but which is made much worse when others believe you have the straw.

Major-General George Alan Vasey (1895–1945), quoted in Horner, *The Commanders*, 1984.

CLAUSEWITZ had observed (and Vietnam was to prove) the economic approach to military strategy "stood in about the same relationship to combat as the craft of the swordsmith to the art of fencing."
   Colonel Harry Summers, *Parameters*, Summer 1987.

Guerrilla/Partisan War

IT IS not to be expected that the rebel Americans will risk a general combat or a pitched battle, or even stand at all, except behind intrenchments as at Boston. Accustomed to felling of timber and to grubbing up trees, they are very ready at earthworks and palisading, and will cover and intrench themselves wherever they are for a short time left unmolested with surprising alacrity. . . . Composed as the American Army is, together with the strength of the country, full of woods, swamps, stone walls, and other inclosures and hiding places, it may be said of it that every private man will in action be his own general, who will turn every tree and bush into a kind of temporary fortress, and from whence, when he hath fired his shot with all deliberation, coolness, and uncertainty which hidden safety inspires, he will skip as it were to the next, and so on for a long time till dislodged either by cannon or by a resolute attack of light infantry.
   Lieutenant-General John 'Gentleman Johnny' Burgoyne (1722–1792), quoted in Lloyd, *A Review of the History of Infantry*, 1908.

THE MORE the enemy extends himself, the greater is the effect of an armed populace. Like a slow, gradual fire it destroys the bases of the enemy force.
   Major-General Carl von Clausewitz, *On War*, 1832, tr. J.J. Graham, 1908.

THE MILITARY VALUE of a partisan's work is not measured by the amount of property destroyed or the number of men killed or captured, but by the number he keeps watching.
   Colonel John S. Mosby, *Mosby's War Reminiscences*, 1887.

TO OPPOSE successfully such bodies of men as our burghers had to meet during this war demanded *rapidity of action* more than anything else. We had to be quick at fighting, quick at reconnoitring, quick (if it became necessary) at flying!
   Christiaan R. de Wet, *Three Years War*, 1902.

GOVERNMENTS saw men only in mass; but our men, being irregulars, were not formations, but individuals. An individual death, like a pebble dropped in water, might make but a brief hole; yet rings of sorrow widened out therefrom. We could not afford casualties.
   Materials were easier to replace. It was our obvious policy to be superior in some one tangible branch; gun-cotton or machine-guns or whatever could be made decisive. Orthodoxy had laid down

the maxim, applied to men, of being superior at the critical point and moment of attack. We might be superior in equipment in one dominant moment or respect; and for both things and men we might give the doctrine a twisted negative side, for cheapness' sake, and be weaker than the enemy everywhere except in that one point or matter. The decision of what was critical would always be ours. Most wars were wars of contact, both forces striving into touch to avoid tactical surprise. Ours should be a war of detachment. We were to contain the enemy by the silent threat of a vast unknown desert, not disclosing ourselves till we attacked. The attack might be nominal, directed not against him, but against his stuff. . . .
   Colonel T.E. Lawrence, *The Seven Pillars of Wisdom*, 1926.

GUERRILLA WAR is far more intelligent than a bayonet charge.
   Colonel T.E. Lawrence, 'The Science of Guerrilla Warfare', *Encyclopaedia Britannica*, 1929.

[GUERRILLA WAR] must have a friendly population, not actively friendly, but sympathetic to the point of not betraying rebel movements to the enemy. Rebellions can be made by two percent active in a striking force, and 98 passively sympathetic.
   Colonel T.E. Lawrence, 'The Science of Guerrilla Warfare', *Encyclopaedia Britannica*, 1929.

THE ADVANTAGES are nearly all on the side of the guerrilla in that he is bound by no rules, tied by no transport, hampered by no drill-books, while the soldier is bound by many things, not the least by his expectation of a full meal every so many hours. The soldier usually wins in the long run, but very expensively.
   Field Marshal Viscount Wavell of Cyrenaica, 30 August 1932, critique on a counter-guerrilla exercise, Blackdown.

THE ABILITY to run away is precisely one of the characteristics of guerillas. Running away is the chief means of getting out of passivity and regaining the initiative.
   Mao Tse-tung (1893–1976), quoted in Simpkin, *The Race to the Swift*, 1985.

FLEXIBLE employment of forces is more indispensible in guerrilla warfare than in regular warfare . . . and the chief ways of employing forces consist in dispersing, concentrating and shifting them. . . . In general the shifting of forces should be done secretly and swiftly.
   Mao Tse-tung (1893–1976), quoted in Simpkin, *The Race to the Swift*, 1985.

WHEN the enemy advances, we retreat.
When he escapes we harass.
When he retreats we pursue.

When he is tired we attack.
When he burns we put out the fire.
When he loots we attack.
When he pursues we hide.
When he retreats we return.
Mao Tse-tung (1893–1976).

GUERRILLA WAR, too, inverts one of the main
principles of orthodox war, the principle of
"concentration" – and on both sides. Dispersion is an
essential condition of survival and success on the
guerrilla side, which must never present a target and
thus can operate only in minute particles, though
these may momentarily coagulate like globules of
quicksilver to overwhelm some weakly guarded
objective. For guerrillas as the principle of
"concentration" has to be replaced by that of "fluidity
of force" . . .
Captain Sir Basil Liddell Hart, *Strategy*, 1954.

IN MANY WAYS this war [against Sinn Fein] was far
worse than the Great War which had ended in 1918.
It developed into a murder campaign in which, in the
end, the soldiers became very skilful and more than
held their own. But such a war is thoroughly bad for
officers and men; it tends to lower their standards of
decency and chivalry, and I was glad it was over.
Field Marshal Viscount Montgomery of Alamein, *The
Memoirs of Field Marshal Montgomery*, 1958.

CONCENTRATION of troops to realize an
overwhelming superiority over the enemy where he is
sufficiently exposed in order to destroy his
manpower; initiative, suppleness, rapidity, surprise,
suddenness in attack and retreat. As long as the
strategic balance of forces remains disadvantageous,
resolutely to muster troops to obtain absolute
superiority in combat in a given place, and at a given
time. To exhaust little by little by small victories the
enemy forces and at the same time to maintain and
increase ours. In these concrete conditions it proves
absolutely necessary not to lose sight of the main
objective of the fighting that is the destruction of the
enemy manpower. Therefore losses must be avoided
even at the cost of losing ground.
General Vo Nguyen Giap, *People's War, People's
Army*, 1961.

THERE IS a malevolent definition that says: "The
guerrilla fighter is the Jesuit of warfare." By this is
indicated a quality of secretiveness, of treachery, of
surprise that is obviously an essential element of
guerrilla warfare. It is a special kind of Jesuitism,
naturally prompted by circumstances, which
necessitates acting at certain moments in ways
different from the romantic and sporting conceptions
with which we are taught to believe war is fought.
Che Guevara, *Guerrilla Warfare*, 1961.

ADVANCE like foxes, fight like lions, and fly like birds.
Northeastern American Indian tactical maxim.

Information War

NOW, we enter the information age. To be
successful, battlefield commanders must attack the
enemy commander's ability to make decisions and
disseminate them. We must get inside the enemy's
decision cycle, and at the right time, we must be
able to disrupt it.
Major-General John F. Stewart, 'Intelligence Strategy
for the 21st Century', *Military Review*,
September–October 1995.

IF YOU ARE looking for an easy war, fight an
information-controlling state. If you are looking for a
difficult investment, invest in an information-controlling
state. If you are hunting a difficult conflict, enter the civil
strife that arises after the collapse of an information-
controlling state. If you are looking for a good
investment, find an emerging or "redeemed" state
unafraid of science, hard numbers, and education.
Lieutenant-Colonel Ralph Peters, 'Spotting the
Losers', *Parameters*, Spring 1998.

WE HAVE entered an age of constant conflict.
Information is at once our core commodity and the most
destabilizing factor of our time. Until now, history has
been a quest to acquire information; today, the
challenge lies in managing information. Those of us who
can sort, digest, synthesize, and apply relevant
knowledge soar – professionally, financially, politically,
militarily, and socially. We, the winners, are in a minority.
Lieutenant-Colonel Ralph Peters, *Fighting For the
Future*, 1999.

Just War

YOU YOURSELF acknowledge that you were the
aggressors and of this the gods are witnesses. They
granted to us a righteous victory in that war, and
shall grant us victory now.
Scipio Africanus, 202 BC, his reply to Hannibal the
day before the Battle of Zama, which ended the
Second Punic War with the defeat of Carthage, quoted
in Livy, *Annals of the Roman People*, c. 25 BC–AD 17
(*Livy: A History of Rome*, 30, tr. Moses Hadas and Joe
Poe, 1962).

FOR IT IS my opinion that war is no doubt much to be
dreaded, but still not to such a degree that we should be
willing to submit to every kind of insult rather than
engage in it. For why should we value so highly equality
of government, liberty of speech, and the glorious name
of freedom, if nothing is to be preferred to peace?
Polybius, *The Histories*, 4.34, c. 125 BC (*Familiar
Quotations from Greek Authors*, tr. Crauford
Ramage, 1895).

THE CAUSE of war must be just.
The Emperor Maurice, *The Strategikon*, c. AD 600
(*Maurice's Strategikon*, tr. George Dennis, 1984).

THE WAR is just which is necessary.
Niccolo Machiavelli, *The Prince*, 22, 1513.

IT IS most necessary for a general in the first place to approve his cause, and settle an opinion of right in the minds of his officers and soldiers.
General George Monck (1608–1670).

THE MOST just war is one which is founded upon undoubted rights and which, in addition, promises to the state advantages commensurate with the sacrifices required and the hazards incurred.
Lieutenant-General Antoine-Henri Baron de Jomini, *Summary of the Art of War*, 1838, tr. Mendell and Craighill, 1862.

WAR is a dreadful thing, and unjust war is a crime against humanity. But it is such a crime because it is unjust, not because it is war.
President Theodore Roosevelt, 23 April 1910, speech at the Sorbonne.

The Love of War

ONE can achieve his fill of good things,
even of sleep, even of making love . . .
rapturous song and the beat and sway of dancing
A man will yearn for his fill of all these joys
before his fill of war.
Homer, *The Iliad*, 13.743–746, c. 800 BC, tr. Robert Fagles, 1990; Menelaus appealing to Zeus to slake the Trojan blood lust.

. . . A MAN whose passion was war. When he could have kept at peace without shame or damage, he chose war; when he could have been idle, he wished for hard work that he might have war; when he could have kept wealth without danger, he chose to make it less by making war; there was a man who spent upon war as if it were a darling lover or some other pleasure.
Xenophon, *Anabasis*, c. 360 BC (*The March Up Country*, tr. W.H.D. Rouse, 1959), describing the Spartan mercenary general Clearchus.

A SHOT through the mainmast knocked a few splinters about us. He observed to me, with a smile, "It is warm work, and this day may be the last to any of us at a moment;" and then, stopping short at the gangway, he used an expression never to be erased from my memory, and said with emotion, "but mark you, I would not be elsewhere for thousands."
Admiral Viscount Nelson, 2 April 1801, during the Battle of Copenhagen, as related by Colonel William Parker, quoted in Alfred Thayer Mahan, *The Life of Nelson*, II, 1897.

HEAR THEM shoot; see them charge! It's in their blood! It's in their blood!
Marshal of France Michel Ney, Duc d'Elchingen, Prince de la Moskova, 6 July 1809, of his men at the Battle of

Wagram, quoted in John Lejuene, 'It's in Their Blood!', *Marine Corps Gazette*, 6 December 1921.

WE DO NOT, generally speaking, like the thoughts of peace. I expect I shall remain abroad for three or four years, which, individually, I would sooner spend in war than in peace. There is something indescribably exciting in the former.
General Charles 'Chinese' Gordon, 1856, quoted in Paul Charrier, *Gordon of Khartoum*, 1965.

IT IS WELL that war is so terrible – we would grow too fond of it.
General Robert E. Lee to Lieutenant-General James Longstreet, *Battle of Fredericksburg*, 13 December 1862.

THE YOUNG BLOODS of the South: sons of planters, lawyers about towns, good billiard-players and sportsmen, men who never did work and never will. War suits them, and the rascals are brave, fine riders, bold to rashness, and dangerous subjects in every sense. . . . The men must all be killed or employed by us before we can hope for peace.
General of the Army William T. Sherman, 17 September 1863, letter to Major-General Henry Halleck.

TO RIDE BOLDLY at what is in front of you, be it fence or enemy; to pray, not for comfort, but for combat; to remember that duty is not to be proved in the evil day, but then to be obeyed unquestioning; to love glory more than the temptations of wallowing at ease.
Justice Oliver Wendell Holmes, Jr., (1841–1935).

THERE ARE poets and writers who see naught in war but carrion, filth, savagery, and horror . . . They refuse war the credit of being the only exercise in devotion on the large scale existing in this world. The superb moral victory over death leaves them cold. Each one to his taste. To me this is no valley of death – it is a valley brim full of life at its highest power.
General Sir Ian Hamilton, 30 May 1915, diary entry at Gallipoli.

I'M AFRAID the war will end very soon now, but I suppose all good things come to an end sooner or later, so we mustn't grumble.
Field Marshal Earl Alexander of Tunis, 1917, letter to his mother while a subaltern during WWI.

THROUGH A GLASS, DARKLY

Through all the travail of ages,
Midst the pomp and toil of war
Have I fought and strove and perished
Countless times upon this star.

In the forms of many peoples
In all panoplies of time
Have I seen the luring vision
Of the victory Maid, sublime.
> General George S. Patton, Jr., 27 May 1922, quoted in
> Roger N. Nye, *The Patton Mind*, 1993.

WAR is conflict, fighting an elemental exposition of the age-old effort to survive. It is the cold glitter of the attacker's eye, not the point of the questing bayonet, that breaks the line. It is the fierce determination of the driver to close with the enemy, not the mechanical perfection of a Mark VIII tank that conquers the trench. It is the cataclysmic ecstasy of conflict in the flier not the perfection of his machine gun which drops the enemy in flaming ruin. . . .

In war tomorrow we shall be dealing with men subject to the same emotions as were the soldiers of Alexander; with men but little changed . . . from the starving shoeless Frenchmen of 1796. With men similar save in their arms to those who the inspiring powers of a Greek or a Corsican changed at a breath to bands of heroes all enduring all capable. . . .
> General George S. Patton, Jr., from his 1926 lecture,
> 'The Secret of Victory', from the Patton Collection,
> United States Military Academy Library.

I LOVE WAR and responsibility and excitement. Peace is going to be hell on me.
> General George S. Patton, Jr. (1885–1945).

WAR is the only place where a man really lives.
> General George S. Patton, Jr., letter to General of the
> Armies John J. Pershing, quoted in Carlo D'Este,
> *Patton: A Genius For War*, 1995.

IT IS respectfully requested that my present assignment to a combat unit be extended until the downfall of the Japanese Government.
> Lieutenant-General Lewis B. 'Chesty' Puller, early
> in WWII, request to the Commandant of the
> Marine Corps, quoted in the *Richmond Times
> Dispatch*, 6 August 1946.

I WAS SATISFIED by my years with a battalion in France that there is a breed of men who do not seem to fit into the structure of society; these men are vaguely discontented with the vast inhuman life of cities, its prudent, punctual existence, with its money saving, its daily stress on the need of security; they find in the army at least an alternative to the prison life of great towns. "All warlike people are a little idle, and love danger better than travail."
> Baron Charles MacMoran Wilson Moran (quoting
> Bacon), *The Anatomy of Courage*, 1945.

IF THE GERMANS are a warrior race, they are certainly militarist also. I think they love the military pageant and the panoply of war; and the feeling of strength and power that a well-organized and disciplined unit gives to each and every individual member of that unit. I am quite willing to admit that I myself share this curious attraction for the strength and elegence of beautifully trained and equipped formations, with all the art and subtlety of their movements in action against an enemy. I can well understand the enthusiasm which the soldiers – from marshals to the private soldier – showed for Napoleon; and why they followed their leader without doubt or question in his victorious campaigns. Feeling thus, they shared the glory of his conquests.
> Field Marshal Earl Alexander of Tunis, *The Alexander
> Memoirs*, 1961.

WAR is the most exciting and dramatic thing in life. In fighting to the death you feel terribly relaxed when you manage to come through.
> General Moshe Dayan, *The Observer* (London),
> 13 February 1972.

The Nature of War

THE LORD is a man of war: The LORD is his name.
> Exodus, 15:3.

THE ART of war is of vital importance to the state. It is a matter of life and death, a road either to safety or to ruin. Hence it is a subject of inquiry which can on no account be neglected.
> Sun Tzu, *The Art of War*, 1, c. 500 BC, tr. Giles, 1910.

IT IS only one who is thoroughly acquainted with the evils of war that can thoroughly understand the profitable way of carrying it on.
> Sun Tzu, *The Art of War*, 2, c. 500 BC, tr. Giles, 1910.

WAR is the last of all things to go according to programme.
> Thucydides, *The Peloponnesian War*, c. 404 BC.

IT IS not the object of war to annihilate those who have given provocation for it, but to cause them to mend their ways; not to ruin the innocent and guilty alike, but to save both.
> Polybius, *Histories*, 5, c. 125 BC.

EVEN WAR is a good exchange for a miserable peace.
> Cornelius Tacitus, *Annals*, 3.44, c. AD 115–117 (*The
> Complete Works of Tacitus*, tr. Alfred Church and
> William Brodribb, 1942).

. . . NOT A RIVER, nor a lake, but a whole ocean of all sorts of evil.
> Gustavus II Adolphus (1594–1632), quoted in Nils
> Ahnlund, *Gustavus Adolphus the Great*, 1940.

WAR is nothing but a duel on a larger scale. Countless duels go to make up war, but a picture of it as a whole can be formed by imagining a pair of wrestlers. Each tries through physical force to compel the other to do his will; his *immediate* aim is to *throw* his opponent in order to make him incapable of further resistence.

War is thus an act of force to compel our enemy to do our will.

Major-General Carl von Clausewitz, *On War*, 1.1, 1832, tr. Michael Howard and Peter Paret, 1976.

IF WE NOW consider briefly, the *subjective nature* of war – the means by which war has to be fought – it will look more than ever like a gamble. The element in which war exists is danger. The highest of all moral qualities in time of danger is certainly *courage*. Now courage is perfectly compatible with prudent calculation but the two differ nonetheless, and pertain to different psychological forces. Daring, on the other hand, boldness, rashness, trusting in luck are only variants of courage, and all these traits of character seek their proper element – chance.

Major-General Carl von Clausewitz, *On War*, 1.1.2, 1832, tr. Michael Howard and Peter Paret, 1976.

WAR is an act of force, and there is no logical limit to the application of that force. Each side, therefore, compels its opponent to follow suit; a reciprocal action is started which must lead, in theory, to extremes.

Major-General Carl von Clausewitz, *On War*, 1.1.3, 1832, tr. Michael Howard and Peter Paret, 1976.

WAR is not a pastime; it is no mere joy in daring and winning, no place for irresponsible enthusiasts. It is a serious means to a serious end, and all its colorful resemblance to a game of chance, all the vicissitudes of passion, courage, imagination, and enthusiasm it includes are merely its special characteristics.

Major-General Carl von Clausewitz, *On War*, 1.1.23, 1832, tr. Michael Howard and Peter Paret, 1976.

WAR is a pulsation of violence, variable in strength and therefore variable in the speed with which it explodes and discharges its energy. War moves on its goal with varying speeds; but it always lasts long enough for influence to be exerted on the goal and for its own course to be changed in one way or another – long enough, in other words, to remain subject to the action of a superior intelligence.

Major-General Carl von Clausewitz, *On War*, 1.1.23, 1832, tr. Michael Howard and Peter Paret, 1976.

WAR is more than a true chameleon that slightly adapts its characteristics to the given case. As a total phenomenon its dominant tendencies always make war a remarkable trinity – composed of primordial violence, hatred, and enmity, which are to be regarded as a blind force; of the play of chance and probability within which the creative spirit is free to roam; and of its element of subordination, as an instrument of policy, which makes it subject to reason alone.

Major-General Carl von Clausewitz, *On War*, 1.1.28, 1832, tr. Michael Howard and Peter Paret, 1976.

WAR is not an exercise of the will directed at inanimate matter, as is the case with the mechanical arts, or at matter which is animate but passive and yielding, as is the case with the human mind and emotions in the fine arts. In war, the will is directed at an animate object that *reacts*.

Major-General Carl von Clausewitz, *On War*, 2.3, 1832, tr. Michael Howard and Peter Paret, 1976.

ALL WAR presupposes human weakness, and seeks to exploit it.

Major-General Carl von Clausewitz, *On War*, 4.10, 1832, tr. Michael Howard and Peter Paret, 1976.

EVERY AGE has its own kind of war, its own limiting conditions and its own peculiar preconceptions.

Major-General Carl von Clausewitz, *On War*, 8.6, 1832, tr. Michael Howard and Peter Paret, 1976.

YOU SPEAK so lightly of war. You don't know what you are talking about. War is a terrible thing. I know you are a brave fighting people but for every day of actual fighting, there are months of marching, exposure, and suffering. More men die in war from sickness than are killed in battle. At best war is a frightful loss of life and property, and worse still is the demoralization of the people.

General of the Army William T. Sherman, January 1861, to his friend David French Boyd at the Louisiana military academy, to which Sherman had been appointed head, upon news of the secession of South Carolina, quoted in 'Sherman: In search of a meaning to his life', *The Washington Times*, 12 March 1994, p. B3.

IT IS painful enough to discover with what unconcern they speak of war and threaten it. I have seen enough of it to make me look upon it as the sum of all evils.

Lieutenant-General Thomas J. 'Stonewall' Jackson, April 1861, letter.

WAR is simply power unrestrained by constitution or compact.

General of the Army William T. Sherman, 31 January 1864, letter to Roswell M. Sawyer.

WAR, like the thunderbolt, follows its laws and turns not aside even if the beautiful, the virtuous and charitable stand in its path.

General of the Army William T. Sherman, 21 April 1864, letter to Charles A. Dana.

YOU MIGHT as well appeal against the thunderstorm as against the terrible hardships of war.

General of the Army William T. Sherman, 12 September 1864, letter to James C. Calhoun, the Mayor of Atlanta.

YOU CANNOT qualify war in harsher terms than I will. War is cruelty, and you cannot refine it, and those who brought war into our country deserve all the curse and maledictions a people can pour out.

General of the Army William T. Sherman, 12 September 1864, letter to James C. Calhoun, the Mayor of Atlanta.

WAR is at best barbarism . . . Its glory is all moonshine. It is only those who have neither fired a shot nor heard the shrieks and groans of the wounded who cry aloud for blood, more vengeance, more desolation. War is hell.

General of the Army William T. Sherman, 1879, speech during a graduation ceremony at the Michigan Military Academy, also speech in Columbus, Ohio, on 11 August 1880.

NO TRIUMPH of peace is quite so great as the supreme triumphs of war. The courage of the soldier, the courage of the statesman who has to meet storms which can be quelled only by soldierly virtues – this stands higher than any quality called out merely in time of peace.

President Theodore Roosevelt, 2 June 1897, speech at the U.S. Naval War College.

I SHALL NOT essay to enlighten you upon the subject of war. Were I to attempt it, I should doubtless miserably fail, for it has long been said, as to amount to an adage, that "women don't know anything about war."

I wish men didn't either. They have always known a great deal too much about it for the good of their kind. They have worshipped at Valkyria's shrine, and followed her siren lead, till it has cost a million times more than the whole world is worth, poured out the best blood and crushed the fairest forms the good God has ever created.

Clara Barton, quoted in Percy Epler, *The Life of Clara Barton*, 1915.

THE REAL WAR will never get in the books. Of the many-threaded drama with its sudden and strange surprises, its confounding prophesies, its moments of despair, the dread of foreign intervention, the interminable campaigns, the bloody battles, the mighty cumbrous and green armies, the drafts, the bounties – the immense money expenditure like a heavy-pouring constant rain – with, over the whole land the last three years of the struggle, an unending, universal mourning wail of women, parents, orphans – the marrow of tragedy concentrated in those army hospitals (it seemed some times as if the whole interest of the land, North and South, was one vast central hospital, and all the rest of the affair but flanges – those forming the untold and unwritten history of the war) – infinitely greater (like life) than the few scraps and distortions that are ever told or written or painted.

Walt Whitman, quoted in *The Washington Times*, 2 September 1995, p. B3.

WAR is an integral part of God's ordering of the universe. In war, man's noblest virtues come into play. Courage and renunciation, fidelity to duty and a readiness for sacrifice that does not stop short of offering up life itself. Without war the world would become swamped in materialism.

Field Marshal Helmuth Graf von Moltke (1800–1891), quoted in Toynbee, *War and Civilization*, 1950.

WAR is a perpetual struggle with embarrassments.

Field Marshal Colmar Baron von der Goltz, *The Nation in Arms*, 1883.

WAR is a game to be played with a smiling face.

O, horrible war! Amazing medley of the glorious and the squalid, the pitiful and the sublime! If modern men of light and leading saw your face closer, simple folk would see it hardly ever.

Sir Winston S. Churchill, *London to Ladysmith*, 1900.

FROM JOMINI also I imbibed a fixed disbelief in the thoughtlessly accepted maxim that the statesman and general occupy unrelated fields. For this misconception I substituted a tenet of my own, that war is simply a violent political movement; and from an expression of his, "The sterile glory of fighting battles merely to win them," I deduced, what military men are prone to overlook, that "War is not fighting, but business."

Rear-Admiral Alfred Thayer Mahan, *From Sail to Steam*, 1907.

LET US learn our lessons. Never, never, never believe any war will be smooth and easy, or that anyone who embarks on the strange voyage can measure the tides and hurricanes he will encounter . . . Antiquated War Offices, weak, incompetent or arrogant Commanders, untrustworthy allies, hostile neutrals, malignant Fortune, ugly surprises, awful miscalculations – all take their seats at the Council Board on the morrow of a declaration of war. Always remember, however, sure you are that you can easily win, that there would not be a war if the other man did not think he also had a chance.

Sir Winston S. Churchill, *A Roving Commission*.

FOUR THINGS greater than all things are, –
Women and Horses and Power and War.

Rudyard Kipling, 'The Ballad of the King's Jest', stanza 5, *The Collected Works of Rudyard Kipling*, XXV, 1941, p. 234.

IN WAR there are nothing but particular cases; everything has there an individual character; nothing ever repeats itself.

Marshal of France Ferdinand Foch, *Principles of War*, 1913.

VICTORY smiles upon those who anticipate the

changes in the character of war, not those who wait to adapt themselves after they occur.

General Giulio Douhet, *Command of the Air*, 1921.

WAR will not suffer any set form. Measures which on one section of the front and on a certain occasion – be it in attack or defense – resulted in a complete success, proved in a different place and under different circumstances failures. The reason for this is found in the fact that war has been carried on, from time immemorial, by men against men, and this holds true even to-day, in spite of the progress made in technical means. *Therefore, in the last analysis, it is the moral qualifications which, as in the past, will also decide the issue to-day.*

General der Infantrie Hugo Baron von Freytag-Loringhoven, *Generalship in the Great War*, 1921.

WAR is a specific form of relations between men. In consequence, war methods and war usages depend upon the anatomical and psychical qualities of individuals, upon the form of organization of the collective man, upon his technology, his physical and cultural-historical environment, and so on. The usages and methods of warfare are thus determined by changing circumstances and, therefore, they themselves can in no wise be eternal.

Leon Trotsky, 1922, *Military Writings*, 1969.

WAR, which used to be cruel and magnificent, has now become cruel and squalid. It is all the fault of democracy and science. From the moment that either of these meddlers and muddlers was allowed to take part in actual fighting, the doom of War was sealed. Instead of a small number of well-trained professionals championing their country's cause with ancient weapons and a beautiful intricacy of archaic movement, we now have entire populations, including even women and children, pitted against each other in brutish mutual extermination, and only a set of blear-eyed clerks left to add up the butcher's bill. From the moment when Democracy was admitted to, or rather forced itself upon, the battlefield, War ceased to be a gentleman's pursuit.

Sir Winston S. Churchill, *My Early Life*, 1930.

THE STORY of the human race is war.

Sir Winston S. Churchill, *Marlborough*, 1933.

IT IS not the horrors of war that will deter any virile young man from welcoming it, but the plain truth that, instead of a gallant adventure, he is setting out on a farcical futility. The best antidote to war is a widening sense of humour and a keener sense of the ridiculous. (Nov. 1934.)

Captain Sir Basil Liddell Hart, *Thoughts on War*, 1944.

THE SWORD is the axis of the world and its power is absolute.

General Charles de Gaulle, *Army of the Future*, 1934.

I HAVE SEEN WAR.
I have seen war on land and sea.
I have seen blood running from the wounded . . .
I have seen the dead in the mud.
I have seen cities destroyed . . .
I have seen children starving.
I have seen the agony of mothers and wives.
I hate war.

President Franklin D. Roosevelt, 14 August 1936, speech at Chautauqua, New York.

WAR is a series of local emergency measures.

Major-General J.F.C. Fuller, *Memoirs of an Unconventional Soldier*, 1936.

WAR is a contest of strength, but the original pattern of strength changes in the course of the war. Here the decisive factor is subjective effort – winning more victories and committing fewer errors. The objective factors provide the possibility for such change, but in order to turn this possibility into actuality both correct policy and subjective effort are essential. It is then that the subjective plays the decisive role.

Mao Tse-tung, *On Protracted War*, 1938.

WAR and truth have a fundamental incompatibility. The devotion to secrecy in the interests of the military machine largely explains why, throughout history, its operations commonly appear in retrospect the most uncertain and least efficient of human activities.

Captain Sir Basil Liddell Hart, *Through the Fog of War*, 1938.

WARFARE today is a thing of swift movement – of rapid concentrations. It requires the building up of enormous fire power against successive objectives with breathtaking speed. It is not a game for the unimaginative plodder.

General of the Army George C. Marshall, 18 September 1941, Fort Benning, Georgia.

THIS WAR . . . is one of those elemental conflicts which usher in a new millenium and which shake the world.

Adolf Hitler, 1942, speech in the Reichstag.

THERE IS no working middle course in wartime.

Sir Winston S. Churchill, 2 July 1942, speech in the House of Commons.

WAR creates such a strain that all the pettiness, jealousy, ambition and greed, and selfishness begin to leak out of the seams of the average character. On top of this are the problems created by the enemy.

General of the Army Dwight D. Eisenhower, 16 December 1942, *Letters to Mamie*, 1978.

WAR is very simple, direct, and ruthless. It takes a simple, direct, and ruthless man to wage war.

General George S. Patton, Jr., 15 April 1943, diary entry.

WAR, like politics, is a series of compromises.
  Captain Sir Basil Liddell Hart, *Thoughts on War*, 1944.

THE MAIN ethical objection to war for intelligent people is that it is so deplorably dull and usually so inefficiently run. . . . Most people seeing the muddle of war forget the muddles of peace and the general inefficiency of the human race in ordering its affairs.
  Field Marshal Viscount Wavell of Cyrenaica, unpublished 'Recollections', 1947.

WAR in its technical aspect is always a movement of societies. The passions that animate it and the pretexts it invokes unfailingly cloak a dispute over the material or spiritual destiny of men. Alexander's victories were those of a civilization. It was the barbarian's passionate hunger which caused the fall of the Roman Empire. There would have been no Arab invasion without the Koran. No crusades without the Gospels. The *ancien régime* in Europe rose against France when the Assembly proclaimed, "Men are born free and equal by law."
  General Charles de Gaulle, *Salvation 1944–1946*, 1960.

WAR is a very simple thing, and the determining characteristics are self confidence, speed, and audacity. None of these things can ever be perfect, but they can be good.
  General George S. Patton, Jr., *War As I Knew It*, 1947.

WAR is always a matter of doing evil in the hope that some good may come of it.
  Captain Sir Basil Liddell Hart, *Defense of the West*, 1950.

WAR has changed little *in principle* from the beginning of recorded history. The mechanized warfare of today is only an evolution from the time when men fought with clubs and stones, and its machines are as nothing without the men who invent them, man them and give them life. War is force – force to the utmost – force to make the enemy yield to our own will – to yield because they see their comrades killed and wounded – to yield because their own will to fight is broken. War is men against men. Mechanized war is still men against men, for machines are masses of inert metal without the men who control – or destroy them.
  Admiral of the Fleet Ernest J. King, *Fleet Admiral King: A Naval Record*, 1952.

WAR is not to be likened to a task which can be completed by installments, bit by bit, part of which when done is done forever. War is rather a race of an extraordinary character which, once started, has to be run through to the end.
  Sir Winston S. Churchill (1874–1965).

WAR is very cruel. It goes for so long.
  Sir Winston S. Churchill (1874–1965).

WAR is a crime. Ask the infantry and ask the dead.
  Ernest Hemingway (1899–1961).

AS EVERY combat veteran knows, war is primarily sheer boredom punctuated by moments of stark terror.
  Colonel Harry G. Summers, Jr., *On Strategy*, 1981.

WAR is fear cloaked in courage.
  General William C. Westmoreland, quoted in Moore, *We Were Soldiers Once . . . And Young*, 1992.

IT'S NOT NEAT; it's not tidy; and once you resort to it, it's uncertain and it's a mess.
  Admiral William Crowe, 28 November 1991, testifying to Congress before the Gulf War, quoted in *Armed Forces Journal*, February 1991.

SOME PEOPLE asked me when we attacked retreating Iraqi forces near Basrah, wasn't that "extreme violence." They missed the point. War is extreme violence. And the way to halt the suffering is to get the war over as quickly and decisively as you possibly can.
  General Charles Horner, 'Extreme Violence', Al Santoli, ed., *Leading the Way: How Vietnam Veterans Rebuilt the U.S. Military*, 1993.

WAR affects and maims the psyche for everyone without exception to a different degree. It forces and obligates us to look closely at the world around us in some kind of new, hitherto unfamiliar light. It makes nerve endings painfully sensitive. Everything falls into place, without admixture or embellishment: baseness as baseness, cowardice as cowardice. No high, beautiful, green fences can shield you from this sudden illumination.
  Lieutenant-General Aleksandr I. Lebed, *I Hurt For This Great Country*, 1995.

The Next War

THE LAWS of successful war in one generation would insure defeat in another.
  General of the Army Ulysses S. Grant (1822–1885).

THE IDEA that every war has been different from the last is the delusion of those who know no history. The next war has normally begun where the last left off, with, perhaps, a slight modification, governed not by the actual development of weapons in the interval but by such fractions of that development as have been recognized and incorporated by the peacetime armies. The generals, however, have usually begun more nearly where the last war began. In consequence, they are discomfited. And public opinion complains that they have stood still while warfare has changed. It fails to realize that the generals have moved – backwards. (April 1930.)
  Captain Sir Basil Liddell Hart, *Thoughts on War*, 1944.

MY PART in the next war will be to be destroyed by it . . .

Air Marshal Sir Arthur Harris, referring to the expected use of nuclear weapons, *Bomber Offensive*, 1947.

ORGANIZATIONS created to fight the last war better are not going to win the next.

General James M. Gavin (1907–1990).

HISTORY knows many examples when the armed forces of individual countries prepared for a future war, taking into account only the clearly manifested relationships of the past war, without examining the dialectical relationships and their dependence on changes which are taking place in the world. Such an approach usually leads to major errors.

Marshal of the Soviet Union Nikolai V. Ogarkov, *History Teaches Vigilance*, 1985.

IN 1981 I began formulating this theory and teaching the ideas of maneuver warfare in my classes. There was an immediate division among students. Some were electrified by new ideas that encouraged them to think and have their own ideas. Others asked questions, "Why am I studying this if it's not going to get me promoted?"

My answer was, "You are studying this so that we can win the next war."

Colonel Michael Wyly, 'Revolution', Al Santoli, ed., *Leading the Way: How Vietnam Veterans Rebuilt the U.S. Military*, 1993.

The Objectives of War

IT IS the object only of war that makes it honorable.

Thomas Paine, *The American Crisis*, V, 21 March 1778.

MODERN WARS are not internecine wars in which the killing of the enemy is the object. The destruction of the enemy in modern war, and, indeed modern war itself are means to obtain that object of the belligerent which lies beyond the war.

General Order 100, War Department, 24 April 1863.

THE legitimate object of war is a more perfect peace.

General of the Army William T. Sherman, 20 July 1865, speech in St. Louis.

WE HAVE no selfish ends to serve. We desire no conquest, no dominion. We seek no indemnities for ourselves, no material compensation for the sacrifice we shall freely make. We are but one of the champions of mankind

President Woodrow Wilson, 6 April 1917, Declaration of War against Germany.

THE OBJECT of war is to attain a better peace – even if only from your own point of view. Hence it is essential to conduct war with constant regard to the peace you desire. This is the truth underlying Clausewitz's definition of war as a "continuation of policy by other means" – the prolongation of that policy through the war into the subsequent peace must always be borne in mind. A State which expends its strength to the point of exhaustion bankrupts is own policy, and future.

Captain Sir Basil Liddell Hart (1895–1970)..

IF there should be a war between Japan and America, then our aim, of course, ought not to be Guam or the Philippines, nor Hawaii or Hong Kong, but a capitulation at the White House, in Washington itself. I wonder whether the politicians of the day really have the willingness to make sacrifices, and the confidence, that this would entail?

Admiral Isoroku Yamamoto, January 1941, letter to Sasakawa Ryoichi, quoted in Agawa, *The Reluctant Admiral*, 1979. Note: Misrepresented during WWII as a boastful reference to complete victory, in fact this statement was a cold-blooded, cautionary appraisal of the only possible objective of a war against an aroused America.

Politics/Policy and War

A GREAT COUNTRY can have no such thing as a little war.

The Duke of Wellington, 1815.

IT IS CLEAR . . . that war is not a mere act of policy but a true political instrument, a continuation of political activity by other means. What remains peculiar to war is simply the peculiar nature of its means. War in general, and the commander in any specific instance, is entitled to require that the trend and designs of policy shall not be inconsistent with these means. That, of course, is no small demand; but however much it may affect political aims in a given case, it will never do more than modify them. The political object is the goal, war is the means of reaching it, and means can never be considered in isolation from their purpose.

Major-General Carl von Clausewitz, *On War*, 1.1.24, 1832, tr. Michael Howard and Peter Paret, 1976.

THE FIRST, the supreme, the most far-reaching act of judgement that the statesman and commander have to make is to establish . . . the kind of war on which they are embarking; neither mistaking it for, nor trying to turn it into, something that is alien to its nature. This is the first of all strategic questions and the most comprehensive.

Major-General Carl von Clausewitz, *On War*, 1.1, 1832, tr. Michael Howard and Peter Paret, 1976.

WE ARGUE that a commander-in-chief must also be a statesman, but he must not cease to be a general. On the one hand, he is aware of the entire political situation; on the other, he knows exactly how much he can achieve with the means at his disposal.

Major-General Carl von Clausewitz, *On War*, 1.3, 1832, tr. Michael Howard and Peter Paret, 1976.

THE DEGREE of force that must be used against the enemy depends on the scale of political demands on either side. These demands, so far as they are known, would show what efforts each must make; but they seldom are fully known – which may be one reason why both sides do not exert themselves to the same degree.

> Major-General Carl von Clausewitz, *On War*, 8.3, 1832, tr. Michael Howard and Peter Paret, 1976.

THE PROBABLE CHARACTER and general shape of any war should mainly be assessed in the light of political factors and conditions.

> Major-General Carl von Clausewitz, *On War*, 8.3, 1832, tr. Michael Howard and Peter Paret, 1976.

THE ONLY QUESTION . . . is whether . . . the political point of view should give way to the purely military (if a purely military point of view is conceivable at all) . . . Subordinating the political point of view to the military would be absurd, for it is policy that creates war. Policy is the guiding intelligence and war only the instrument, not vice versa. No other policy exists, then, than to subordinate the military point of view to the political.

> Major-General Carl von Clausewitz, *On War*, 8.6, 1832, tr. Michael Howard and Peter Paret, 1976.

POLITICS uses war for the attainment of its ends; it operates decisively at the beginning and at the end, of course in such manner that it refrains from increasing its demand during the war's duration or from being satisfied with an inadequate success. . . . Strategy can only direct its efforts toward the highest goal which the means available make attainable. In this way, it aids politics best, working only for its objectives, but in its operations independent of it. . . . There is uncertainty in war, but the aims of policy remain. Policy must go hand in hand with strategy.

> Field Marshal Helmuth Graf von Moltke, *Ueber Strategie*, 1871.

PLACE in the hands of the King of Prussia the strongest possible military power, then he will be able to carry out the policy you wish; this policy cannot succeed through speeches, and shooting matches and songs; it can only be carried through blood and iron.

> Chancellor Prince Otto von Bismarck, 28 January 1886, speech in the Reichstag.

THAT THE SOLDIER is but the servant of the statesman, as war is but the instrument of diplomacy, no educated soldier will deny. Politics must always exercise an extreme influence on strategy; but it cannot be gainsaid that interference with the commanders in the field is fraught with the gravest danger.

> Colonel George F.R. Henderson, *Stonewall Jackson*, 1898.

. . . POLITICS is the reason, and war is only the

tool, not the other way around. Consequently, it remains only to subordinate the military point of view to the political.

> V.I. Lenin (1870–1924), *On War*.

HISTORY causes the military problem to become the essence of the political problem.

> V.I. Lenin, 1921, speech.

POLICY is a thought process, while war is merely a tool, and not the reverse.

> V.I. Lenin (1870–1924), quoted in Gorshkov, *Sea Power of the State*, 1979.

THE STATE must determine the nature of overall, and particularly military, policy in advance, outline accordingly the possible objectives of its military goals, work out and establish a definite plan of statewide action which allows for future conflicts and makes timely provision for their success with appropriate utilization of national energy.

> Mikhail V. Frunze (1885–1925).

WAR is not only a means of politics and is not limited only to combat operations. The Actions of the armed forces are accompanied by the organized and combined pressure and strikes on all fronts of the struggle (economic, political, etc.).

> Marshal of the Soviet Union Mikhail N. Tukachesvskiy (1893–1937), quoted in Gareyev, *Frunze, Military Theorist*, 1985.

WAR is not the continuation of policy. It is the breakdown of policy.

> Colonel-General Hans von Seekt, *Thoughts of a Soldier*, 1930.

IN THE THEATER of peacetime, it is the statesman who plays the chief role. Whether the masses greet him with applause or boos, it is for him first of all that they have eyes and ears. Then suddenly war calls another actor from the wings, pushes him to the middle of the stage, and trains the limelight on him: the military chief appears. A drama is about to begin which will be played by statesman and soldier in concert. No matter how great the crowd of extras, how noisy the audience, it is on these two performers that attention will be centered. So closely interwoven is their dialogue that nothing said by either has any relevance, point, or effect except with reference to the other. If one of them misses his cue, then disaster overwhelms them both. However widely in fact the work of the civil government differs from that of the High Command, no one would seriously question the interdependence of the two authorities. What policy can hope to succeed if the country's arms are brought low? Of what use is strategical planning if the means of carrying it out are not forthcoming?

> General Charles de Gaulle, *The Edge of the Sword*, 1932.

THE NATIONAL STRATEGY of any war, that is, the selection of national objectives and the determination of the general means and methods to be applied in obtaining them, as well as development of the broad policies applicable to the prosecution of the war, are decisions that must be made by the head of state, acting in conformity with the expressed will of the Government.

> General of the Army Douglas MacArthur, *Military Situation in the Far East*, presented to the 82nd Congress, 1932.

THERE ARE some militarists who say: "We are not interested in politics but only in the profession of arms." It is vital that these simple-minded militarists be made to realize the relationship that exists between politics and military affairs. Military action is a method used to attain a political goal. While military affairs and political affairs are not identical, it is impossible to isolate one from the other.

> Mao Tse-tung, *On Guerrilla Warfare*, 1937.

WAR has its own particular characteristics and in this sense it cannot be equated with politics in general. . . . When politics develops to a certain stage beyond which it cannot proceed by the usual means, war breaks out to sweep the obstacles from the way . . . When the obstacle is removed and our political aim attained, the war will stop. But if the obstacle is not completely swept away, we will have to continue till the aim is fully accomplished . . . It can therefore be said that politics is war without bloodshed while war is politics with bloodshed.

> Mao Tse-tung, *On Protracted War*, 1938.

WHEN policy is too stiff, and its war-aims too absolute, strategy forfeits the power to keep its plans flexible, to adopt a new line when one is blocked, and to retrieve advantage from the mishaps inevitable in war. An uncompromising attitude hinders the essential adaptability of strategy to events as well as to conditions. (July 1939.)

> Captain Sir Basil Liddell Hart, *Thoughts on War*, 1944.

HISTORY shows that gaining military victory is not in itself equivalent to gaining the object of policy. But as most of the thinking about war has been done by men of the military profession there has been a very natural tendency to lose sight of the basic national object, and identify it with the military aim. In consequence, whenever war has broken out, policy has too often been governed by the military aim – and this has been regarded as an end in itself, instead of as merely a means to the end.

> Captain Sir Basil Liddell Hart, *Strategy*, 1954.

POLITICS, from an elevation of military and political factors, selects the most propitious moment to start a war, taking into account all the strategic considerations.

> Marshal of the Soviet Union V.D. Sokolovskiy, *Soviet Military Strategy*, 1961.

Protracted War

AREN'T YOU SICK of being caged inside those walls? Time was when the world would talk of Priam's Troy as the city rich in gold and rich in bronze – but now our houses are stripped of all their sumptuous treasures,
troves sold off and shipped to Phrygia, lovely Maeonia, once great Zeus grew angry . . .

> Homer, *The Iliad*, 18.332–338, c. 800 BC, tr. Fagles, 1990; Hector's account of the cost to Troy of the Trojan War, then in its tenth year.

WHEN you engage in actual fighting, if victory is long in coming, the men's weapons will grow dull and their ardour will be damped. If you lay siege to a town, you will exhaust your strength. Again, if the campaign is protracted, the resources of the State will not be equal to the strain.

Now, when your weapons are dulled, your ardour damped, your strength exhausted and your treasure spent, other chieftains will spring up to take advantage of your extremity. Then no man, however wise, will be able to avert the consequences that must ensue.

Thus, though we have heard of stupid haste in war, cleverness has never been associated with long delays. There is no instance of a country having been benefited by a prolonged war.

> Sun Tzu, *The Art of War*, 2, c. 500 BC, tr. Giles, 1910.

A FRIEND came to see me on one of the evenings of the last week – he thinks it was on Monday August 3. We were standing at a window of my room in the Foreign office. It was getting dusk, and the lamps were being lit in the space below on which we were looking. My friend recalls that I remarked on this with the words: "The lamps are going out all over Europe; we shall not see them lit again in our lifetime."

> Sir Edward Grey, British Foreign Secretary, 3 August 1914, the day Germany declared war on France.

THE LONGER the war drags on and the more acute it becomes, the more the government themselves foster – and must foster – the activity of the masses, whom they call upon to make extraordinary effort and self-sacrifice. The experience of war, like the experience of any crisis in history, of any great calamity and any sudden turn in human life, stuns and breaks some people, but *enlightens and tempers others*. . . .

> V.I. Lenin, June 1915, *Collected Works*, XXI, 1960–1970, pp. 215–216.

THE GERMAN PEOPLE, both at home and at the front, have suffered and endured inconceivable hardships in the four long years of war. The war has undermined and disintegrated patriotic feeling and the whole national *moral* [morale].

Poisonous weeds grew in this soil. All German

sentiment, all patriotism, died in many breasts. Self came first. War profiteers of every kind, not excluding the political variety, who took advantage of the country's danger and the Government's weakness to snatch political and personal advantages, became more and more numerous. Our resolution suffered untold harm. We lost confidence in ourselves.

General Erich Ludendorff, *My War Memories, 1914–1918*, 1919.

THERE ARE still a lot of Japs left to kill.

Lieutenant-General Victor H. 'The Brute' Krulak, *Washington Star*, 21 November 1943; as a battalion commander (lieutenant-colonel) after the landing of his battalion as a diversion on Choiseul Island before the attack on Bougainville.

BUT ONCE war is forced upon us, there is no other alternative than to apply every available means to bring it to a swift end. War's very object is victory, not prolonged indecision.

General of the Army Douglas MacArthur, 19 April 1951, address to Congress.

THE EXPERIENCE of history brings ample evidence that the downfall of civilized states tends to come not from the direct assaults of foes but from internal decay, combined with the consequences of exhaustion in war. A State of suspense is trying – it has often led nations as well as individuals to commit suicide because they were unable to bear it. But suspense is better than to reach exhaustion in pursuit of the mirage of victory. Moreover, a truce to actual hostilities enables a recovery and development of strength, while the need for vigilance helps keep a nation on "its toes".

Captain Sir Basil Liddell Hart, *Strategy*, 1954.

The Results of War

THE END and perfection of our victories is to avoid the vices and infirmities of those whom we subdue.

Alexander the Great (356–323 BC), quoted in Plutarch, *The Lives*, c. AD 100, tr. John Dryden.

SURELY it would have been best if the gods had granted our fathers forebearance – if yours had been content to be masters of Italy, ours, to rule over Africa. Even for you Sicily and Sardinia are not sufficient return for the loss of so many fleets, so many armies, so many great generals. But the past is more readily lamented than corrected. We coveted the wealth of others and we have had to fight to keep our own. It has meant war for us in Africa, for you in Italy: You have seen the standards of an enemy almost within your gates and on your walls; in Carthage we can hear the armies of the Roman camp.

Hannibal, 202 BC, his unsuccessful plea to Scipio Africanus for a negotiated peace on the day before the Battle of Zama, which ended the Second Punic War with the defeat of Carthage, quoted in Livy, *Annals of the Roman People*, c. 25 BC–AD 17 (*Livy: A History of Rome*, 30, tr. Moses Hadas and Joe Poe, 1962).

WAR will of itself discover and lay open the hidden and rankling wounds of the victorious party.

Cornelius Tacitus, *Histories*, AD 104–109 (*The Complete Works of Tacitus*, tr. Alfred Church and William Brodribb, 1942).

WEAPONS are instruments of ill omen, war is immoral.

Really they are only to be resorted to when there is no other choice. It is not right to pursue aggressive warfare because one's country is large and prosperous, for this ultimately ends in defeat and destruction. Then it is too late to have regrets. Military action is like a fire – if not stopped it will burn itself out. Military expansion and adventurism soon lead to disaster.

The rule is "Even if a country is large, if it is militaristic it will eventually perish."

Liu Ji (1310–1375), *Lessons of War* (*Mastering the Art of War*, tr. Thomas Cleary, 1989).

I HOPE to God that I have fought my last battle. It is a bad thing to be always fighting. While in the thick of it I am too much occupied to feel anything; but it is wretched just after. It is quite impossible to think of glory. Both mind and feelings are exhausted. I am wretched even at the moment of victory, and I always say that, next to a battle lost, the greatest misery is a battle gained. Not only do you lose those dear friends with whom you have been living, but you are forced to leave the wounded behind you. To be sure, one tries to do the best for them, but how little that is! At such moments every feeling in your breast is deadened. I am now just beginning to regain my natural spirits, but I never wish for any more fighting.

The Duke of Wellington, 1815, to Lady Shelley after Waterloo.

IT IS not enough that our armies are victorious, that our enemies vanish from our territory, nor that the whole world recognizes our independence; we need something more: to be free under the auspices of liberal laws, emanating from the most sacred spring, which is the will of the people.

General Simon Bolivar, 1818.

WHAT a cruel thing is war: to separate and destroy families and friends, and mar the purest joys and happiness God has granted us in this world; to fill our hearts with hatred instead of love for our neighbors, and to devastate the fair face of this beautiful world.

General Robert E. Lee, 25 December 1862, letter to his wife.

I BEGIN to regard the death and mangling of a couple thousand men as a small affair, a kind of morning dash – and it may well be that we become so hardened.

General of the Army William T. Sherman, July 1864, letter to his wife.

ETERNAL PEACE is a dream, and not even a good dream, for war is part of God's world ordinance. In war, the noblest virtues flourish that otherwise would slumber and decay – courage and renunciation, the sense of duty and sacrifice, even to the giving of one's life. The experience of war stays with a man, and steels him all his life.

Field Marshal Helmuth Graf von Moltke (1800–1891).

A WAR, even the most victorious, is a national misfortune.

Field Marshal Helmuth Graf von Moltke, 1880, letter.

WAR, with its many acknowledged sufferings, is above all harmful when it cuts a nation off from others and throws it back upon itself.

Rear-Admiral Alfred Thayer Mahan, *The Influence of Sea Power Upon History*, 1890.

I AM NOT WORRIED about the war; it will be difficult but we shall win it; it is after the war that worries me. Mark you, it will take years and years of patience, courage, and faith.

Field Marshal Jan Christian Smuts (1870–1950).

WAR stirs in men's hearts the mud of their worst instincts. It puts a premium on violence, nourishes hatred, and gives free rein to cupidity. It crushes the weak, exalts the unworthy, and bolsters tyranny. Because of its blind fury many of the noblest schemes have come to nothing and the most generous instincts have more than once been checked. Time and time again it has destroyed all ordered living, devastated hope, and put the prophets to death. But, though Lucifer has used it for his purposes so, sometimes, has the Archangel. With what virtues has it not enriched the moral capital of mankind! Because of it, courage, devotion, and nobility have scaled the peaks. It has conferred greatness of spirit on the poor, brought pardon to the guilty, revealed the possibilities of self-sacrifice to the commonplace, restored honor to the rogue, and given dignity to the slave. It has carried ideas in the baggage wagons of its armies, and reforms in the knapsacks of its soldiers. It has blazed a trail for religion and spread across the world influences which have brought renewal to mankind, consoled it, and made it better. Had not innumerable soldiers shed their blood there would have been no Hellenism, no Roman civilization, no Christianity, no Rights of Man, and no modern developments.

General Charles de Gaulle, *The Edge of the Sword*, 1932.

TO SOME the game of war brings prizes, honor, advancement or experience; to some the consciousness of duty well discharged. . . . But here were those who had drawn the evil numbers – who had lost their all, to gain only a soldier's grave. Looking at those shapeless forms confined in a regulation blanket, the pride of race, the pomp of Empire, the glory of war appeared but the faint unsubstantial fabric of a dream.

Sir Winston S. Churchill (1874–1965).

THE COST of war is constantly spread before me, written neatly in many ledgers whose columns are gravestones.

General of the Army George C. Marshall, quoted in *MHQ*, Spring 1995.

MUSSOLINI said in the early 1930s: "War alone brings all human energies to their highest tension, and sets a seal of nobility on the people who have the virtue to face it." This is rubbish, and dangerous rubbish at that. War does not ennoble. Kant's view that war has made more bad people than it has destroyed is probably nearer the mark. But the interesting thing is that although war almost certainly does not ennoble, the preparation of men to fight in it almost certainly can and very often does.

General Sir John Hackett, *The Profession of Arms*, 1963.

A PROFESSIONAL soldier understands that war means killing people, war means maiming people, war means families left without fathers. All you have to do is hold your first dying soldier in your arms, and have that terribly futile feeling that his life is flowing out and you can't do anything about it. Then you understand the horror of war. Any soldier worth his salt should be antiwar. And still there are things worth fighting for.

General H. Norman Schwarzkopf, *Reader's Digest*, 8/1995.

WE HAVE LOST far too many people in this century – to war, revolution, persecution. A total of 75 million Russians have died in this way. We have enough space, enough resources, to ensure a life with human dignity in our territory. We have simply never been allowed to do so, because we have had to go to war all the time and kill.

Colonel-General Aleksandr I. Lebed, *Det fri Aktuelt* (Copenhagen), 2 July 1997.

PERHAPS, at some opportune moment, one of our military leaders should summon the courage to explain to Mr. Clinton that deaths do tend to occur in military operations and that, before threatening to use force, the president might want to consider that unpleasant reality. Warfare kills people and destroys objects. The dream of "bloodless war" remains just that. Contrary to the nonsense droned out of Washington think tanks – perhaps the most inappropriately termed institutions in history – the application of military power remains an equation of flesh and blood and destruction.

Lieutenant-Colonel Ralph Peters, *Wall Street Journal*, 17 November 1998.

A GREAT WAR leaves the country with three armies: an army of cripples, an army of mourners, and an army of thieves.

American proverb.

Revolutionary/People's War

ACCORDING to our idea of a People's War, it should, like a kind of nebulous vapoury essence, never condense into a solid body. . . . Still, however, it is necessary that this mist should collect at some points into denser masses, and form threatening clouds from which now and again a formidable flash of lightning may burst forth.

Major-General Carl von Clausewitz, *On War*, 6.26, 1832, tr. J.J. Graham, 1908.

IF WE WANTED to win swiftly, success could not be ensured. For that reason, in the process of making preparations, we continued to follow the enemy's situation and checked and rechecked our potentialities again. And we came to the conclusion that we could not secure success if we struck swiftly. In consequence, *we resolutely chose the other tactic: to strike surely and advance surely*. In taking this correct decision, we strictly followed this fundamental principle of the conduct of revolutionary war: strike to win, strike only when success is certain; if it is not, then don't strike.

General Vo Nguyen Giap, *People's War, People's Army*, 1961.

THEY CAN'T get it into their heads that the Vietnam War has to be understood in terms of the strategy of People's War, that it's not a question of men and material, that these things are irrelevant to the problem.

General Vo Nguyen Giap, *The Military Art of People's War*, 1970.

FIRST, revolutionary war is a political war. Its aim is to achieve political dominance within a state, and military power is a tool by which to gain this political end. . . . The second characteristic of revolutionary war is its totality. Its aim is victory, and not some vague middle ground. It is waged by all the people and all agencies under the control of the revolutionaries.

Lieutenant-General Phillip B. Davidson, *Vietnam at War*, 1988.

Total/Absolute War

SINCE BONAPARTE, then, war, first among the French and subsequently among their enemies, again became the concern of the people as a whole,

took on an entirely different character, or rather closely approached its true character, its absolute perfection. There seemed no end to the resources mobilized; all limits disappeared in the vigor and enthusiasm shown by governments and their subjects. Various factors powerfully increased that vigor: the vastness of available resources, the ample field of opportunity, and the depth of feeling generally aroused. The sole aim of war was to overthrow the opponent. Not until he was prostrate was it considered possible to pause and try to reconcile the opposing interests.

Major-General Carl von Clausewitz, *On War*, 8.3, 1832, tr. Michael Howard and Peter Paret, 1976.

WAR . . . should be "pure and simple" as applied to the belligerents. I would keep it so, till all traces of the war are effaced; till those who appealed to it are sick and tired of it, and come to the emblem of our nation, and sue for peace. I would not coax them, or even meet them half-way, but make them so sick of war that generations would pass before they would again appeal to it.

General of the Army William T. Sherman, 17 September 1863, letter to Major-General Halleck.

I WOULD MAKE this war as severe as possible, and show no symptoms of tiring till the South begs for mercy; indeed, I know, and you know, that the end would be reached quicker by such a course than by any seeming yielding on our part.

General of the Army William T. Sherman, 17 September 1863, letter to John A. Rawlins.

IF THE TERM "absolute war" has any meaning it is that of a fight until the capacity of one side for further resistance is exhausted. In practice, this may well mean that its conqueror is on the verge of exhaustion, too weak to reap the harvest of his victory. In other words, absolute war is war in which the conductor allows the fighting instinct to usurp the control of reason.

Captain Sir Basil Liddell Hart, *Thoughts on War*, 1944.

War of Revenge

I STOOD upon the ashes of my own home where my own wigwam had sent up its fire to the Great Spirit, and there I summoned the spirits of the braves who had fallen in their vain attempt to protect their homes from the grasping invader, and as I sniffed up the smell of their blood from the ground I swore once more eternal hatred – the hatred of an avenger.

Tecumseh, early March 1812, upon his return to the ruins of Prophet's Town, destroyed by U.S. forces on 6 November 1811.

THE WHOLE ARMY is burning with an insatiable desire to wreak vengeance upon South Carolina. I almost tremble at her fate, but feel that she deserves all that seems in store for her.

> General of the Army William T. Sherman, 24 December 1864, letter to Major-General Halleck on the feeling within the Union Army that it was South Carolina's obsession with secession that caused the Civil War.

THE WAR will go on forever [the Chechen War]. The lesson we learned in Afghanistan was the following: The man who came home in the evening and found his house ruined and his family killed was transformed into a wolf. This wolf will fight to the last with every means at his disposal. That we are sending 18-year olds into battle with wolves like this is absurd and laughable.

> Lieutenant-General Aleksandr I. Lebed, *Aftenposten* (Oslo), 15 May 1995; negating his own prediction, Lebed – as Yeltsin's envoy, but on his own initiative – hammered out a peace with the Chechens in 1996.

Termination of War

WARS begin when you will, but they do not end when you please.

> Niccolo Machiavelli, *History of Florence*, 1521–1524.

IT WAS EASY to begin the war, but no man knew where it would end.

> The Earl of Manchester, 1644, after the Battle of Marston Moor during the English Civil War.

TO END a war while it's going favourably for one's own side requires a special, different kind of effort. Even the Russo-Japanese War was only brought to a favourable conclusion with great difficulty.

> Admiral Isoruko Yamamoto, January, 1942, quoted in Agawa, *The Reluctant Admiral*, 1979.

SIXTEEN HOURS ago an American plane dropped a bomb on Hiroshima. . . . It is an atomic bomb. It is a harnessing of the basic power of the universe. The force from which the sun draws its power has been loosed against those who brought war to the Far East.

> President Harry S. Truman, 6 August 1945, message to the nation.

WAR CORRESPONDENTS

I HAVE MADE arrangements for the correspondents to take the field . . . and I have suggested to them that they wear a white uniform to indicate the purity of their profession.

> Major-General Irvin McDowell, quoted in William Russell, *My Diary North and South*, 1861.

THE NEWSPAPERS are after me again; I published an order they must not come along on pain of being treated as spies. I am now determined to test the question. Do they rule or the commanding general? If they rule I quit. I have ordered the arrest of one, shall try him, and if possible execute him a spy. They publish all the data for our enemy and it was only by absolute secrecy that we could get to the Post of Arkansas without their getting ahead. They did reveal our attempts to attack Haine's Bluff. I will never gain command an army in America if we must carry along paid spies. I will banish myself to some foreign country first. I shall notify Mr. Lincoln of this if he attempts to interfere with the sentence of any court ordered by me. If he wants an army he must conform to the well established rules of military nations and not attempt to keep up the open rules of peace. The South at the start did these things, and the result has been, they move their forces from Virginia to Mississippi and back without a breath spoken or written. . . .

> General of the Army William T. Sherman, 28 January 1863, letter to his wife from a camp near Vicksburg, *The Home Letters of General Sherman*, 1909.

I REGRET exceedingly the jealousies, heart-burnings, and other evil consequences resulting from the crude misstatements of newspaper correspondents, who have necessarily a very limited acquaintance with the facts about which they write, and who magnify the deeds of troops from their own States at the expense of others. But I can see no remedy for this. Men seem to prefer sowing discord to inculcating harmony. . . .

I believe it would be better to have no correspondents of the press with the army. . . .

> General Robert E. Lee, 9 September 1863, letter to Secretary of War James A. Seddon, quoted in J. William Jones, *Life and Letters of Robert Edward Lee, Soldier and Man*, 1906.

NEWSPAPER correspondents with an army, as a rule, are mischievous. They are the world's gossips, pick up and retail the camp scandal, and gradually drift to the headquarters of some general, who finds it easier to make reputation at home than with his own corps or division. They are also tempted to prophesy events and state facts which, to an enemy, reveal a purpose in time to guard against it. Moreover, they are always bound to see facts coloured by the partisan or politcal character of their own patrons, and thus bring army officers into the political controversies of the day, which are always mischievous and wrong. Yet, so greedy are the people at large for war news, that it is doubtful whether an army commander can exclude all reporters, without bringing down on himself a clamor that may imperil his own safety. Time and moderation must bring a just solution to this modern difficulty.

> General William T. Sherman, *Memoirs of General W.T. Sherman*, II, 1875.

THOSE newly invented curse to armies . . . that race of drones who are an encumbrance to an army; they eat the rations of the fighting man and do not work at all.

Field Marshal Viscount Wolseley, *The Soldier's Pocket-book*, 1869.

THE BRITISH PUBLIC likes to read sensational news, and the best war correspondent is he who can tell the most thrilling lies.

Field Marshal Earl Haig, 1898, of the Sudan campaign, letter to his sister.

SO the presence of a correspondent on the firing-line, or his absence from it, does not prove that he is not doing his full duty to his paper. The best correspondent is probably the man who by his energy and resource sees more of the war, both afloat and ashore, than do his rivals, and who is able to make the public see what he saw.

Richard Harding Davis, 'Our War Correspondents in Cuba and Puerto Rico', *Harper's Monthly*, May 1899.

"ALL THE DANGER of war and one-half per cent of the glory": such is our motto, and that is the reason why we [the press] expect large salaries.

Sir Winston S. Churchill, *Ian Hamilton's March*, 1900.

THERE IS no parallel . . . between the work of a war correspondent and the obligation of the serving soldier. The latter has to stick it and has no choice about the risks he will run. With very few notable exceptions, our war correspondents will not stay with combat danger long enough to begin to understand the ordeal of troops. They are another variety of sightseer. They flit in and out of the scene, hear a few shells explode, take a quick look at frontal living conditions, ask a few trivial questions of the hometown boys, and then beat it back to secure billets to pound out tear-jerking pieces about the horrors of war. With few exceptions, they will not stay on the job.

Brigadier-General S.L.A. Marshall, *Bringing Up the Rear*, 1979.

TO ATTACK journalists is as pointless as fighting against women. If you lose to them, you just stand there foolishly. If you win, you just stand there twice as foolishly.

General Aleksandr I. Lebed, *Nezavisimaya Gazeta* (Moscow), 29 August 1997.

WAR GAMES

THE ENEMY of our games was always Japan – and the courses were so thorough that after the start of WWII – nothing that happened in the Pacific was strange or unexpected. Each student was required to plan logisitic support for an advance across the Pacific – and we were well-prepared for the fantastic logistics efforts required to support operations during the war.

Admiral of the Fleet Chester W. Nimitz, 1965, quoted in 'Admiral Raymond A. Spruance and the Naval War College', *Naval War College Review*, 3/1971.

I COULD NOT shake a lingering doubt that many human factors of decisive importance are not reflected in war games and the mathematical answers that are derived by them. I think it very possible that the French did indeed lose the battle at Waterloo because Napoleon had piles. How do you put hemorrhoids into a war game?

General Hamilton H. Howze, *A Cavalryman's Story*, 1996.

WARMONGER

HE who is the author of a war lets loose the whole contagion of hell and opens a vein that bleeds a nation to death.

Thomas Paine, *The American Crisis*, V, 21 March 1778.

WOE to him who sets Europe on fire.

Field Marshal Helmuth Graf von Moltke, 1890, his prophetic farewell speech in the Reichstag, quoted by Holger H. Herwig, 'The Prussian Model and Military Planning Today', *Joint Forces Quarterly*, Spring 1998.

HE who preaches up a war is a fit chaplain for the devil.

American proverb.

WAR OFFICE/PENTAGON

IT IS a good thing to see the inside of the War Ofice for a short time, as it prevents one from having any respect for an official letter, but it is a mistake to remain there too long.

Field Marshal Earl Haig, 1909, upon leaving the War Office, quoted in Marhall-Cornwall, *Haig as Military Commander*, 1973.

TRAINING was, in fact, largely a case of trying to make bricks without straw, and there was much truth in what a distinguished General once said to me: "Never forget, Robertson, that we have two armies – the War Office army and the Aldershot army. The first is always up to strength, and is organized, reorganized, and disorganized almost daily. The second is never up to strength, knows nothing whatever about the first, and remains unaffected by any of these organizing activities. It just cleans its rifle and falls in on parade."

Field Marshal Sir William Robertson, *From Private to Field-Marshal*, 1921.

SIR HENRY WILSON was right, for though it is true that, whatever the circumstances might have been, he could not have reorganised the Army, with such an instrument as the War Office headed by the Army Council it was impossible for any man, even had he possessed the wisdom of Athena and the driving force of Mars, to organize anything. He was in the position of a painter of miniatures equipped with a boot brush. Seeing how foolish it all was, he daubed out caricatures to make people laugh, and in this he was eminently successful.

Before we can blame him or any soldier in his position, it is necessary to understand what a Government Department is like; yet in all probability, in 1919, the War Office was more alive than most others. I began to realise this soon after the war ended, when a naval officer came over from the Admiralty to see me about persuading us to introduce intelligence tests in our recruiting. I said to him: "'Intelligence,' that is not exactly the word for us, surely?" To which he replied: "Oh! You are far more alive on this side of Whitehall. Do you realise that on our side, there are old, old men lost in the cellars of the Admiralty still counting the round shot we fired at Sebastopol?"

Major-General J.F.C. Fuller, *Memoirs of an Unconventional Soldier*, 1936.

IT WAS a dull January morning when an elderly Major-General strolled into the War Office to pass the time of day. Finding his friend engaged, he waited in one of the passages on the second floor. A young Staff Captain with a large bundle of branch memoranda approached him, and the Major-General, no longer able to contain himself, turned to him and said:

"Isn't it ridiculous? Winston has been made Secretary for War."

The Staff Captain looked at him wearily and answered:

"It is ridiculous. The only man who could put this business straight is Trotsky!"

Major-General J.F.C. Fuller, *Memoirs of an Unconventional Soldier*, 1936.

A DIFFERENT illustration of the dangers of taking things too seriously was provided by an episode which casts a startling light on how "official machinery" can go wrong, and served to show that no staff system should be regarded as infallible. One day we received an order for the immediate demobilization of an officer whom we in the General Staff branch had specially asked to retain. Feeling that it must be a mistake I asked the Adjutant-General's branch to check the order with the War Office, but was told that it would be improper to question such a clear and precise order. Not willing to be put off, I set out in person to trace back the course of the order through the various channels, and eventually tracked it down to a typist's mistake in extending a bracket one line too far when making a combined list of officers who were to be respectively retained or demobilised.

Captain Sir Basil Liddell Hart, 1920, *The Memoirs of Captain Liddell Hart*, I, 1965.

THE PENTAGON was a sorry place to light after having commanded a theater of war.

General Dwight D. Eisenhower, 15 December 1945, letter to his son, John, quoted in Stephen Ambrose, *Eisenhower*, I, 1983.

THE FORTUNES and affairs of the denizens of the Pentagon are closer and more understandable to the civilian leadership than are the more remote problems and responsibilities of those who man the operating forces.

Admiral Robert B. Carney, 31 May 1963, address to the Naval War College, Newport, Rhode Island.

WARRIORS

THEY ARE WARRIORS. They are heirs to warriors. They should be used precisely to build up the airborne and border guard units. They are people who have war in their blood. They are winners by nature. Well, we have to forget the misleading opinion that anyone can serve in the Army. Not everyone can serve in the Army. Not everyone can be a designer, pilot, or doctor. Those who are capable should serve in the Army. Winners and warriors should come to the army.

General Aleksandr I. Lebed, 7 July 1996, speaking on television of the rebirth of the Cossack Hosts in Russia after the fall of Soviet power.

WE in the West are conditioned to protect the weak. The warrior butchers them. We fight to preserve the rule of law. The warrior thrives on lawlessness and havoc. He does not respect treaties, no matter the flourish with which they are signed, and he doesn't obey orders when he's not in the mood.

The warrior has been around since Cain killed Abel. It is the soldier, with his codes of conduct, who is new – developed in Europe and America over the past three centuries and imitated elsewhere. It seemed the warrior was in retreat. But now, as empires have disintegrated, and multiple revolutions – from a deluge of information to the emancipation of women – threaten the prejudices of traditional societies and failing states, the warrior is back. He is brutal as ever, and far better armed.

Lieutenant-Colonel Ralph Peters, 'Soldier vs. Warrior', *The Washington Post*, 7 March 1999, p. B1.

WEAPONS

AFTER GOD, we should place our hopes of safety in our weapons, not in our fortifications alone.

The Emperor Maurice, *The Strategikon*, c. AD 600 (*Maurice's Strategikon*, tr. George Dennis, 1984).

THE SWORD is the soul of the warrior. If any forget or lose it he will not be excused.

Tokugawa Ieyasu (1543–1616), quoted in A.L. Sadler, *The Maker of Modern Japan: The Life of Tokugawa Ieyasu*.

MAXIM 59. There are five things the soldier should never be without: his firelock, his ammunition, his knapsack, his provisions (for at least four days), and his entrenching tool. The knapsack may be reduced to the smallest size possible, but the soldier should always have it with him.

> Napoleon, *The Military Maxims of Napoleon*, tr. George D'Aguilar, 1831 (David Chandler, ed., 1987).

THE MEANS of destruction are approaching perfection with frightful rapidity.

> Lieutenant-General Antoine-Henri Baron de Jomini, *Summary of the Art of War*, 1838, tr. Mendell and Craighill, 1862.

NEW WEAPONS would seem to be regarded merely as an additional tap through which the bath of blood can be filled all the sooner.

> Captain Sir Basil Liddell Hart, *Paris, Or the Future of War*, 1925.

THE MORAL and material are interdependent. Weapons without courage are ineffective, but so are the bravest troops without sufficient weapons to protect them and their morale. Courage soon oozes when soldiers lose confidence in their weapons. (Dec. 1929.)

> Captain Sir Basil Liddell Hart, *Thoughts on War*, 1944.

AS LONG AGO as January 1919 I pointed out in *Weekly Tank Notes* that "Tools or weapons, if only the right ones can be discovered, form 99 per cent. of victory," and that all other things are no more than the "1 per cent. which makes the whole possible. Indeed, 'Savage animalism is nothing, inventive spiritualism is all.' . . ." I pointed out that though Napoleon was an infinitely greater General than Lord Raglan, the Minié rifle of 1854 would have enabled Lord Raglan to have annihilated him in 1815, and that had Napoleon, in 1805, "placed down as a challenge to the mechanical intellect of France 25,000,000 francs to produce a weapon 100 per cent. more efficient than the 'Brown Bess,' it is almost a certainty that, in 1815, he would have got it; that he would have won Waterloo, and that the whole course of history would have been changed. . . ."

> Major-General J.F.C. Fuller, *Memoirs of an Unconventional Soldier*, 1936.

NO NEW weapons can be introduced without changing conditions, and every change in condition will demand a modification in the application of the principles of war.

> Major-General J.F.C. Fuller, *Armoured Warfare*, 1943.

THERE ARE two universal and important weapons of the soldier which are often overlooked – the boot and the spade. Speed and length of marching has won many victories; the spade saved many defeats and gained time for victory.

> Field Marshal Earl Wavell of Cyrenaica, *The Good Soldier*, 1948.

A CAREFUL STUDY of past military history and particularly of the "little picture" of our own infantry operations in the past war leads to the conclusion that weapons when correctly handled in battle seldom fail to gain success. There is no other touchstone to tactical success, and it is a highly proper doctrine which seeks to ingrain in the infantry soldier a confidence that superior use of superior weapons is the surest protection.

> Brigadier-General S.L.A. Marshall, *Men Against Fire*, 1947.

I SPY my service pistol. Automatically I pick it up, remove the clip, and check the mechanism. It works with buttered smoothness. I weigh the weapon in my hand and admire the cold, blue glint of its steel. It is more beautiful than a flower; more faithful than most friends.

> First-Lieutenant Audie Murphy, *To Hell and Back*, 1949. Murphy was referring to the U.S. Army's Colt .45-calibre semi-automatic pistol, but using the older term 'service pistol'.

ENGLAND were but a fling, save for the crooked stick and the greygoose wing.

> English proverb, referring to the longbow, the clothyard arrow and the deadly skill of the English archer.

WEATHER

CLIMATE is what you expect but weather is what you get.

> American military saying.

IT IS always necessary to shape operation plans . . . on estimates of the weather, and as this is always changing, one cannot imitate in one season what has turned out well in another.

> Frederick the Great, *Instructions to His Generals*, 1747, tr. Phillips, 1940.

COMPLAINTS have been brought to my attention that the infantry have got their feet wet. That is the fault of the weather. The march was made in the service of the most mighty monarch. Only women, dandies, and lazy-bones need good weather.

> Field Marshal Prince Aleksandr V. Suvorov, 1799, to the commander of the Austrian allied force, who complained of having to march in bad weather, quoted in Philip Longworth, *The Science of Victory*, 1966.

I CANNOT command winds and weather.

> Admiral Viscount Nelson, April 1796.

THE RUSSIAN LAND which he dreamed of enslaving will be strewn with his bones. We will pursue tirelessly. Let winter, blizzards, and the cold come. Will you fear them, children of the north? Your iron breast fears neither the severity of weather nor the malice of enemies. It is the reliable wall of the homeland, against which all collapses.

Field Marshal Prince Mikhail I. Kutuzov, 1812, exhorting his troops during Napoleon's invasion of Russia, *Sbornik dokumentov* (*A Collection of Documents*), 1955.

RUSSIA has two generals in whom she can confide – Generals Janvier and Février.

Emperor Nicholas I, *Punch*, 10 March 1853.

WEATHER is not only to a great extent a controller of the condition of ground, but also of movement. It is scarcely necessary to point out the influence of heat and cold on the human body, or the effect of rain, fog, and frost on tactical and administrative mobility; but it is necessary to appreciate the moral effect of weather and climate, for in the past stupendous mistakes have resulted through deficiency in this appreciation.

Unless the headquarters staff have intimate experience of the conditions surrounding the fighters, two types of battle are likely to be waged – the first between the brains of the army and the enemy, in which case this action will be rendered impotent on account of the muscles being unable to execute the commands of the brains; and the second between the muscles and the enemy, which battle will be disorganized, not so much through the enemy's opposition as through the receipt of orders which are impossible to carry out.

Major-General J.F.C. Fuller, *The Foundation of the Science of War*, 1926.

WE MUST BEGIN our next offensive early, in order to make the most of the fine weather. It is no good waiting until August and then gambling with the Almighty. "*Gott mit uns*" is all very well; but the Deity expects man to consult the almanac before He obliges him by tampering with the seasons.

Major-General J.F.C. Fuller, *Memoirs of an Unconventional Soldier*, 1936.

THE ADMIRAL cannot take up a position that only in ideal conditions of tide and moon can the operation be begun. It has got to be begun as soon as possible, as long as conditions are practicable, even though they are not the best. People have to fight in war on all sorts of days, and under all sorts of conditions.

Sir Winston S. Churchill, note to General Ismay regarding the Dakar operation, 19 August 1940.

THIS IS sheer torture for the troops, and for our cause it is a tragedy, for the enemy is gaining time, and in spite of all our plans we are being carried deeper into winter. It really makes me sad. The best of intentions are wrecked by the weather. The

unique opportunity to launch a really great offensive recedes further and further, and I doubt if it will ever recur. God alone knows how things will turn out. One must just hope and keep one's spirits up, but at the moment it is a great test.

Colonel-General Heinz Guderian, November 1941, quoted in von Mellenthin, *German Generals of World War II*, 1977.

WHEN AND WHERE TO FIGHT

NOW a soldier's spirit is keenest in the morning; by noonday it has begun to flag; and in the evening his mind is bent only on returning to camp.

A clever general, therefore, avoids an army when its spirit is keen, but attacks it when it is sluggish and inclined to return. This is the art of studying moods.

Disciplined and calm, to await the appearance of disorder and hubbub amongst the enemy – this is the art of retaining self-possession.

To be near the goal while the enemy is still far from it, to wait at ease while the enemy is toiling and struggling, to be well fed while the enemy is famished – this is the art of husbanding one's strength.

To refrain from intercepting an enemy whose banners are in perfect order, to refrain from attacking an army drawn up in calm and confident array – this is the art of studying circumstances.

It is a military axiom not to advance up hill against the enemy, nor to oppose him when he comes downhill.

Do not pursue an enemy who simulates flight; do not attack soldiers whose temper is keen.

Do not swallow a bait offered by the enemy. Do not interfere with an army that is returning home.

When you surround an army leave an outlet free. Do not press a desperate foe too hard.

Such is the art of warfare.

Sun Tzu, *The Art of War*, 7, c. 500 BC, tr. Giles, 1910.

TO KNOW our troops can attack and yet be unaware that the enemy is not open to attack, reduces our chances of victory to half; to know the enemy is open to attack and yet be unaware that our own troops cannot attack, reduces our chances of victory again to half; to know the enemy is open to attack and our troops can attack, and yet be unaware that the terrain does not favor us in battle, reduces the chances of victory once again to half.

Thus when one who understands war moves, he does not go the wrong way, and when he takes action, he does not reach a dead end.

Hence it is said:

Know the other, know yourself,
And the victory will not be at risk;
Know the ground, know the natural conditions,
And the victory will be total.

Sun Tzu, *The Art of Warfare*, 8, c. 500 BC, tr. Roger Ames, 1993.

WARFARE is like hunting. Wild animals are taken by scouting, by nets, by lying in wait, by stalking, by circling around, and by other such stratagems rather than by sheer force. In waging war we should proceed in the same way, whether the enemy be many or few. To try simply to overpower the enemy in the open, hand to hand and face to face, even though you might appear to win, is an enterprise which is very risky and can result in serious harm. Apart from extreme emergency, it is ridiculous to try to gain victory which is so costly and brings only empty glory.

> The Emperor Maurice, *The Strategikon*, c. AD 600 (*Maurice's Strategikon*, tr. George Dennis, 1984).

GOOD OFFICERS never engage in general actions unless induced by opportunity or obliged by necessity.

> The Emperor Maurice, *The Strategikon*, c. AD 600 (*Maurice's Strategikon*, tr. George Dennis, 1984).

I THINK I also have something left to say relating to the precautions a general should take before he leads his army to battle; in the first place, it is my opinion that he should never engage unless he has an advantage over the enemy, or he is compelled to act. Now the advantage may arise from the terrain or from the order, superiority, or bravery of his army, he may be compelled to engage by a conviction that if he does not, he must inevitably be ruined.

> Niccolo Machiavelli, *The Art of War*, 1521.

THE DIFFERENT circumstances under which a battle should be avoided or declined are, when there is greater danger to be apprehended from defeat than advantage to be derived from victory; when you are very inferior to your enemy in numbers, and are expecting reinforcements; above all, when the enemy is advantageously posted, or when he is contributing to his own ruin by some inherent defect in positions or by the errors and divisions of his generals.

> Field Marshal Count Raimond Montecuccoli (1609–1680).

DECLINE the attack altogether unless you make it with advantage.

> Field Marshal Maurice Comte de Saxe, *My Reveries*, 1732, tr. Phillips, 1940.

IF . . . you are inferior in numbers do not despair of winning, but do not expect any other success than that gained by your skill. It is necessary to seek mountainous country and use artifices, so that if you were to be forced to battle, the enemy would not be able to face you with a front superior to your own, and so that you may be able definitely to protect your flanks.

> Frederick the Great, *Instructions to His Generals*, 1747, tr. Phillips, 1940.

MAXIM 31. When you determine to risk a battle, reserve to yourself every possible chance of

success, more particularly if you have to deal with an adversary of superior talent, for if you are beaten, even in the midst of your magazines and your communications, woe to the vanquished!

> Napoleon, *The Military Maxims of Napoleon*, tr. George D'Aguilar, 1831 (David Chandler, ed., 1987).

IF A SOLUTION cannot be reached without battle, this imposes on you the strategic aim to force battle at the time, and under the conditions, most favourable tactically to yourself.

> Rear-Admiral Alfred Thayer Mahan (1840–1914).

BUT THE SAFETY of the State, the lives and freedom of our own fellow countrymen, to whom they owe their position, make it right and imperative in the last resort, or when a final and definitive conviction has been reached, that the use of force should not be excluded. If the circumstances are such as to warrant it, force may be used. And if this be so, it should be used under the conditions which are most favourable. There is no merit in putting off a war for a year if, when it comes, it is a far worse war or one much harder to win. These are tormenting dilemmas upon which mankind has throughout its history been so frequently impaled. Final judgment upon them can only be recorded by history in relation to the facts of the case as known to the parties at the time, and also as subsequently.

> Sir Winston S. Churchill, *The Gathering Storm*, 1948.

STILL, if you will not fight for the right when you can easily win without bloodshed; if you will not fight when your victory will be sure and not too costly; you may come to the moment when you will have to fight with all the odds against you and only a precarious chance of survival. There may even be a worse case. You have to fight when there is no hope of victory, because it is better to perish than live as slaves.

> Sir Winston S. Churchill, *The Gathering Storm*, 1948.

WILL

AS EACH man's strength gives out, as it no longer responds to his will, the inertia of the whole gradually comes to rest on the commander's will alone. The ardor of his spirit must rekindle the flame of purpose in all others; his inward fire must revive their hope. Only to the extent that he can do this will he retain his hold on his men and keep control.

> Major-General Carl von Clausewitz, *On War*, 1832, 1, tr. Michael Howard and Peter Paret, 1976.

WILL springs from the two elements of moral sense and self-interest.

> Abraham Lincoln, 26 June 1857, speech in Springfield, Illinois.

IN BATTLE, two moral forces, even more than two material forces, are in conflict. The stronger conquers. The victor has often lost . . . more men than the vanquished . . . With equal or even inferior power of destruction, he will win who is determined to advance.

Colonel Charles Ardant du Picq, *Battle Studies*, 1880, tr. Greely, 1957.

THE WILL to conquer: such is the first condition of victory, consequently the first duty of every soldier; and it is also the supreme resolution with which the commander must fill the soul of his subordinates.

Marshal of France Ferdinand Foch, *Principles of War*, 1913.

A BATTLE WON is a battle in which one will not confess himself beaten.

Marshal of France Ferdinand Foch, *Precepts and Judgments*, 1919.

IN ANY WAR victory is determined in the final analysis by the state of mind of the masses which shed their blood on the field of battle.

Mikhail V. Frunze (1885–1925).

I HAVE BEEN awarded the Iron Cross for my modest share in the battle of Tannenberg. I had never thought that this finest of all military decorations would be won by sitting at the end of a telephone line. However, I realize now that there must be someone there who keeps his nerve, and by brute determination and will to victory overcomes difficulties, panics and suchlike nonsense.

General Max Hoffmann, 9 September 1914, *War Diaries and Other Papers*, I, 1929.

IN WAR the chief incalculable is the human will.

Captain Sir Basil Liddell Hart, *Encyclopaedia Britannica*, 1929.

BUT IN WAR it often happens that the impossible is in the end made possible by the might of one's utmost efforts and a steadfast will.

General Aleksei A. Brusilov, September 1914, *A Soldier's Notebook, 1914–1918*, 1931.

HINDENBURG was right when he said that the man who wins a war is the one whose nerves are the strongest. Our nerves proved particularly feeble, because we had so long been forced by the inadequacy of our technical equipment to make up the deficit by an excessive wastage of life. One cannot fight successfully with bare hands against an enemy provided with all the resources of modern warfare and inspired by patriotism.

General Aleksei A. Brusilov, *A Soldier's Notebook*, 1931.

IT IS not simply the weapons one has in one's arsenal that give one flexibility, but the willingness and ability to use them.

Mao Tse-tung (1893–1976).

IF WE CLEAR the air of the fog of catchwords which surround the conduct of war, and grasp that in the human will lies the source and mainspring of all conflict, as of all other activities of man's life, it becomes clear that our object in war can only be attained by the subjugation of the opposing will. All acts, such as defeat in the field, propaganda, blockade, diplomacy, or attack on the centres of government and population, are seen to be but means to that end.

Captain Sir Basil Liddell Hart, *Thoughts on War*, 1944.

THE WILL does not operate in a vacuum. It cannot be imposed successfully if it runs counter to reason. Things are not done in war primarily because a man wills it; they are done because they are do-able. The limits for the commander in battle are defined by the general circumstances. What he asks of his men must be consistent with the possibilities of the situation.

Brigadier-General S.L.A. Marshall, *Men Against Fire*, 1947.

WHAT can be sucessfully willed must first be clearly seen and understood. If amid the confusions of battle the commander sees what is required by the situation, if amid the miscarriage of arrangements and the assailing doubts of other men he measures the means of doing it, and if he then gives his order and holds his men to their duty, this is the ultimate triumph of the will on the field of battle. To reflect on this thought is to note that he exercises his will far less upon his men than upon himself.

Brigadier-General S.L.A. Marshall, *Men Against Fire*, 1947.

FOR POWER of will comes from the exercise of it. In the military commander strength of will does not automatically flourish apace with the growth of knowledge in the material things of war. But unless it does so, experience is had to no broad purpose and knowledge does not become wisdom. Equally, if the will power of the commander is in excess of his knowledge, it cannot be exercised for the good of the commanded. Thus, true strength of will in the commander develops from his study of human nature, for it is in the measure that he acquires knowledge of how other men think that he perfects himself in the control of their thoughts and acts.

Brigadier-General S.L.A. Marshall, *Men Against Fire*, 1947.

IT IS FATAL to enter any war without the will to win it.

General of the Army Douglas MacArthur, 7 July 1952, address to the Republican National Convention.

YOUR JOB as an officer is to make decisions and to see them carried out; to force them through against the opposition not only of the enemy, that is fair enough, but against that of your own men. Against colleagues who want it done another way, of allies – there is only one thing worse than having allies and that is not to have them – and of all opposition of man and nature that will bar your way. You cannot be a leader at all without this strength of will, this determination.

Field Marshal Viscount Slim of Burma, *Courage and Other Broadcasts*, 1957.

THE ULTIMATE TEST of willpower surely is the ability to dominate events rather than be dominated by them. I refer to the leader who can stand his ground cooly and imperturbably, when chaos surrounds him. A strong will is the function of a sound conscience. And judging from my own limited experience, the prime flaw in those commanders who have cracked under pressure has usually been a lack of willpower to stand up to the pressures of people and events – or possibly an inability to relax.

Lieutenant-General Sir James Glover, 'A Soldier and His Conscience', *Parameters*, 9/1983.

WITHDRAWAL

IF WE HAPPEN to be too weak for attack, then we strive to detach ourselves from the embraces of the enemy in order later to gather ourselves into a fist and to strike at the enemy's most vulnerable spot.

Leon Trotsky, 1921, *Military Writings of Leon Trotsky*, 1969.

THE WITHDRAWAL should be thought of as an offensive instrument, and exercises be framed to teach how the enemy can be lured into a trap, closed by counterstroke or devastating circle of fire.

Sir Basil Liddell Hart, *Thoughts on War*, 1944.

OF ALL operations of war, a withdrawal under heavy enemy pressure is probably the most difficult and perilous. Indeed it is recorded of the great Moltke, that when he was praised for his generalship in the Franco-Prussian War, and was told by an admirer that his reputation would rank with such great captains as Napoleon, Frederick, and Turenne, he answered, "No, for I have never conducted a retreat."

Major-General F.W. von Mellenthin, *Panzer Battles*, 1971.

WIVES

THAT CRY – that was Hector's honored mother
    I heard!
My heart's pounding, leaping up in my throat,
the knees beneath me paralyzed – Oh I know it . . .
something terrible's coming down on Priam's children.
Pray god the news will never reach my ears!
Yes but I dread it so – what if great Achilles
has cut my Hector off from the city, daring Hector,
and driven him out across the plain, and all alone? –

He may have put an end to that fatal headstrong pride
that always seized my Hector – never hanging back
with the main force of men, always charging ahead,
giving ground to no man in his fury!"

So she cried,
dashing out of the royal halls like a madwoman,
her heart racing hard, her women close behind her.
But once she reached the tower where soldiers
    massed
she stopped on the rampart, looked down and saw it
    all –
saw him dragged before the city, stallions galloping,
dragging Hector back to Achaea's beaked warships –
ruthless work. The world went black as night
before her eyes, she fainted, falling backward,
gasping away her life breath . . .
she flung to the winds her glittering headdress,
the cap and the coronet, braided band and veil,
all the regalia golden Aphrodite gave her once,
the day that Hector, helmet aflash in sunlight,
led her home to Troy from her father's house
with countless wedding gifts to win her heart.

Homer, *The Iliad*, 22.530–555, c. 800 BC, tr. Robert Fagles, 1990; of Andromache, Hector's wife, on his death at the hands of brilliant Achilles.

WHEN LEAVING for Thermopylae to fight the Persians, his wife Gorgo inquired if he had any instructions for her, and he said: "To marry good men and bear good children."

Leonidas, Agiad King of Sparta, 480 BC, quoted in Plutarch, *The Lives*, c. AD 100 (*Plutarch on Sparta*, tr. Richard Talbert,1988).

IF I must say anything on the subject of female excellence to those of you who will now be in widowhood, it will be all comprised in this brief exhortation. Great will be your glory in not falling short of your natural character, and greatest will be hers who is least talked of among the men whether for good or for bad.

Pericles, 431/430 BC, funeral oration for the Athenian dead, quoted in Thucydides, *The History of the Peloponnesian War*, c. 404 BC, tr. Richard Crawley, 1910.

O GREAT LORD of All Things, remember your servant
Who has gone to exalt your honour and the
    greatness of your name.
He will offer blood in that sacrifice which is war.
Behold, Lord, that he did not go out to work for me
Or for his children! He did not abandon us to
    obtain things
to support his home, with his tump line on his head,
Or with his digging stick in his hand. He went for
    your sake.
In your name, to obtain glory for you. Therefore,
    O Lord,
Let your pious heart have pity on him, who with
    great labor

And affliction now goes through the mountains
  and valleys,
Hills and precipices, offering you the moisture from
  his brow,
His sweat. Give him victory in this war so that he
  may return
To rest in his home and so that my children and I
  may see
His countenance again and feel his presence.

> The prayer of Aztec womanhood, recited every day at
> dawn until their husbands, sons, brothers and other
> relatives returned from the wars (15th/early 16th
> centuries), quoted in Durán, *The Aztecs: The History of
> the Indies of New Spain*, 1581, tr. Doris Heyden, 1994.

MARRIAGE is good for nothing in the
military profession.

> Napoleon, *Political Aphorisms*, 1848.

MARRIAGE for young warriors is a folly. Their first
and last duty is to protect the nation from its
enemies. This they cannot do efficiently if they have
family ties. . . . I tell you all, in future a man will have
to prove his worth to be a father, before he receives
permission to marry.

> Shaka Zulu, c. 1818, quoted in E.A. Ritter, *Shaka
> Zulu*, 1955.

I DOUBT if history affords a parallel to the deep
and bitter enmity of the women of the South. No
one who sees them and hears them but must feel
the intensity of their hate. Not a man is seen;
nothing but women with houses plundered, fields
open to the cattle and horses, pickets lounging on
every porch, and desolation sown broadcast,
servants all gone and women and children bred in
luxury, beautiful and accomplished, begging with
one breath for the soldiers' rations and in another
praying that the Almighty or Joe Johnston will come
and kill us, the despoilers of their homes and all
that is sacred.

> General of the Army William T. Sherman, 27 June
> 1863, letter to his wife, *The Home Letters of General
> Sherman*, 1909.

A WOMAN who hampers a man at the beginning of
his career is a hateful abomination, and he always
thinks so sooner or later. So you had best not
consider me at all in making your decision [to stay in
the Service]. The family might not thank me for
telling you this but I think it. . . . A girl might just ruin
a man's life by upsetting it at the beginning. You can
decide better if you consider your self as one instead
of as two. You must decide alone and then I will go
with you any where.

> Beatrice Ayer, the future wife of George S. Patton
> 17 January 1909, *The Patton Papers*, I, 1972.

A SOLDIER has no business to be married.

> General Sir Ian Hamilton, *Soul and Body of an
> Army*, 1921.

SCOTT was the last man to paint an unduly dark
picture. I knew his men were almost at the end of
their strength and in a desperate position. I could not
help wishing that he had not been so close a friend.
I thought of his wife and of his boys. There were lots
of other wives, too, in England, India, and Burma
whose hearts would be under that black cloud a
couple of miles away. Stupid to remember that now!
Better get it out of my head.

> Field Marshal Viscount Slim of Burma, *Defeat Into
> Victory*, 1956.

MAYBE the first lesson in leadership that this book
can offer is, "Marry well." Marry someone who has
the ability to give you unique perspectives on your
people, and who wants to be part of your career. I
did, and I'm forever glad of it.

> Lieutenant-General William G. Pagonis, of his wife,
> Cheri, *Moving Mountains*, 1992.

I CAN'T tell you how I've valued your letters. It's
them, and the close touch with you, that have kept
my spirits up when I was under most pressure.

> General Sir Peter de la Billière, to his wife, Bridget, at
> the end of the Gulf War, *Storm Command*, 1992.

I HOPE that in the final moments of your father's life,
his last thoughts were not of us. As he lay dying, I
wanted him to think only of his mission to which he
pledged himself. . . . He chose the military, and "I
shall not fail those with whom I serve" became his
simple religion.

> Mrs. Carmen Gordon, a letter to her two children on
> responsibility, following the death of their father,
> Army Ranger Master Sergeant Gary I. Gordon, who
> died trying to save downed helicopter pilots in
> Mogadishu, Somalia, 3 October 1993, reprinted in
> *Newsweek*, 1 August 1994.

WOMEN IN WAR

SHE may not have the strength for the exploits that
are expected of a man, but she has the spirit to fight
as nobly for her country as any of us.

> Marcus Brutus, 43 BC, of his wife Portia's devotion, as
> he prepared to flee from the Second Triumvirate,
> quoted in Plutarch, *The Lives*, c. AD 100 (*Makers of
> Rome*, tr. Ian Scott-Kilvert, 1965).

LORD RAGLAN, in his last visit to me, asked me
"if my father liked my coming out." I said with pride
my father is not as other men are, he thinks that
daughters should serve their country as well as
sons – he brought me up to think so – he has no
sons – & therefore he has sacrificed me to my
country – & told me to come home with my shield
on [*sic* "or"] upon it. He does not think, (as I once
heard a father & a very good & clever father say,)
"The girls are all I could wish – very happy, very
attentive to me, & very amusing." He thinks that

God sent women, as well as men, into the world to be something more than "happy", "attentive" & "amusing". Happy & "*dull*", *religion* is said to make us – "happy & *amusing*" *social life* is supposed to make us – but my father's religious & social ethics make us strive to be the pioneers of the human race & let "happiness" & amusement" take care of themselves.

Florence Nightingale, 14 November 1855, Balaklava, letter to her father, quoted in Sue M. Goldie, ed., '*I have done my duty' Florence Nightingale in the Crimean War 1854–56*, 1987.

MISS NIGHTINGALE was in an adventurous mood, and proposed to go still farther into the trenches up to the Three-Mortar Battery. Her Friends Mr. Bracebridge, Dr. Anderson, and M. Soyer were favourable to her wish, but the sentry was in a great state of consternation.
"Madam," said he, "if anything happens I call on these gentlemen to witness that I did not fail to warn you of the danger."
"My good young man," replied Miss Nightingale, "more dead and wounded have passed through my hands than I hope you will ever see in the battlefield during the whole of your military career; believe me, I have no fear of death."

Florence Nightingale, c. 1855, quoted in Sarah A. Tooley, *The Life of Florence Nightingale*, 1905.

THEN, perhaps, to relax, Ewell directed the placement of a battery to cover the ford. At that moment a woman rode up to him to report what she had seen of the Federal advance. Ewell was no romantic like Beauregard or Rosser. He had little use for such heroines, and abruptly told her there would be firing here soon. "You'll get killed," he said. "You'll be a *dead damsel* in less than a minute. *Get away from here! Get away!*" When Madam declined to leave, Ewell was astonished at her bravery. "Women," he said to Gordon, jerking his thumb in the lady's direction. "I tell you, sir, women would make a grand brigade – if it was not for snakes and spiders! They don't mind bullets – women are not afraid of bullets; but one big black-snake would put a whole army to flight."

Lieutenant-General Richard S. Ewell, 21 July 1861, before the Battle of First Bull Run, quoted in Davis, *Battle at Bull Run*, 1977.

WE WERE in a slight hollow and all shell which did not break our guns in front, came directly among or over us, bursting above our heads or burying themselves in the hills beyond.
A man lying upon the ground asked for a drink, I stopped to give it, and having raised him with my right hand, was holding him.
Just at this moment a bullet sped its free and easy way between us, tearing a hole in my sleeve and found its way into his body. He fell back dead. There was no more to be done for him and I left him to his rest. I have never mended that hole in my sleeve. I wonder if a soldier ever does mend a bullet hole in his coat?

Clara Barton, diary notes at Antietam 1862, quoted in Percy Epler, *The Life of Clara Barton*, 1915.

YOU HAVE just made the change from peacetime pursuits to wartime tasks – from the individualism of civilian life to the anonymity of mass military life. You have given up comfortable homes, highly paid positions, leisure. You have taken off silk and put on khaki. And all for essentially the same reason – you have a debt and a date. A debt to democracy, a date with destiny.

Colonel Oveta Culp Hobby to the first Officer Candidate Class of the Women's Army Auxiliary Corps (WAAC), 23 July 1942, quoted in Mattie Treadwell, *The Women's Army Corps*, 1954.

TO ME, one of the most stimulating aspects of our war effort has been the amazing development of the WAAC organization in quality, discipline, capacity for performing a wide variety of jobs, and the fine attitude of the women themselves. Commanders to whom the Waacs have been assigned have spoken in the highest terms of their efficiency and value. The best evidence in the matter are the demands now being made on the War Department for increased allotments of WAAC organizations. . . .
I wish you would reassure your subordinates of the confidence and high respect in which they are held in the Army.

General of the Army George C. Marshall, Chief of Staff of the Army, personal letter to Colonel Oveta Culp Hobby, Director of the Women's Army Auxiliary Corps, 15 January 1943.

I MOVED my WACs forward early after occupation of occupied territory because they were needed and they were soldiers in the same manner that my men were soldiers. Furthermore, if I had not moved my WACs when I did, I would have had mutiny . . . as they were eager to carry on where needed.

General of the Army Douglas MacArthur, statement to Colonel Boyce in Tokyo, 14 October 1945, quoted in Mattie Treadwell, *The Women's Army Corps*, 1954.

I REMEMBER we received our first consignment of Women's Army Corps personnel, then known as Women's Auxiliary Army Corps. Until my experience in London I had been opposed to the use of women in uniform. But in Great Britain I had seen them perform so magnificently in various positions, including serving in active anti-aircraft batteries, that I had been converted. In Africa many officers were still doubtful of women's usefulness in uniform – the older commanders in particular were filled with misgivings and open skepticism. What these men had failed to note was the changing requirements of war. The simple headquarters of a Grant or Lee were gone forever. An army of filing clerks, stenographers, office managers, telephone operators, and chauffeurs had become essential, and it was scarcely less than criminal to recruit these from needed manpower when great numbers of highly qualified women were available. From the day they first reached us their reputation as an efficient, effective corps continued to grow. Toward the end of the war the most stubborn die-hards had become convinced – and demanded them in increasing numbers. At first the women were kept carefully back at GHQ and secure bases, but as helpfulness grew, so did the scope of their duties in positions progressively nearer the front. Nurses had, of course, long been accepted as a necessary contingent of a fighting force. From the outset of this war our nurses lived up to traditions tracing back to Florence Nightingale; consequently it was difficult to understand the initial resistance to the employment of women in other activities. They became hospital assistants, dieticians, personal assistants, and even junior staff officers in many headquarters. George Patton, later in the war, was to insist that one of his most valuable assistants was his WAC office manager.

> General of the Army Dwight D. Eisenhower, *Crusade in Europe*, 1948.

HOW WISE you were to bring your women into your military and into your labor force. Had we done that initially, as you did, it could well have affected the whole course of the war. We would have found out, as you did, that women were equally effective, and for some skills, superior to males.

> Albert Speer (1905–1981), master of the German war industries, conversation with Lieutenant-General Ira C. Eaker, quoted in *Air Force Magazine*, 6 December 1976.

WORK

AND CALL each man by his name and father's line, show them all respect. Not too proud now.
We are the ones who ought to do the work.
On our backs, from the day that we were born, it seems that Zeus has piled his pack of hardships.

> Homer, *The Iliad*, 10.78–82, c. 800 BC, tr. Robert Fagles, 1990; Agamemnon urging the Greek leaders to set an example by doing their utmost to resist Hector's assault on their camp.

FOR A MAN who is a man, work, in my belief, if it is directed to noble ends, has no object beyond itself.

> Alexander the Great, July 326 BC, in India, to his men when they refused to go on, quoted in Arrian, *The Campaigns of Alexander*, 5.26, c. AD 150, tr. Aubrey de Sélincourt, 1971.

NOTHING more than effort and work.

> Frederick William I (1688–1740), motto of the father of Frederick the Great.

FAR AND AWAY the best prize that life offers is the chance to work hard at work worth doing.

> President Theodore Roosevelt, 1903, Labor Day address in Syracuse, New York.

I DO NOT KNOW anyone who has got to the top without hard work. That is the recipe. It will not always get you to the top, but it should get you pretty near.

> Prime Minister Margaret Thatcher, *Daily Telegraph*, 21 March 1986.

THE WOUNDED

AFTER THE BATTLE the general should give prompt attention to the wounded and see to burying the dead. Not only is this a religious duty, but it greatly helps the morale of the living.

> The Emperor Maurice, *The Strategikon*, c. AD 600 (*Maurice's Strategikon*, tr. George Dennis, 1984).

IT IS RIGHT to be very concerned about the wounded. If we neglect them, we will find that the rest of the troops will deliberately not fight well, and our remissness will cause us to lose some who could have been saved.

> The Emperor Maurice, *The Strategikon*, c. AD 600 (*Maurice's Strategikon*, tr. George Dennis, 1984).

ON THIS DAY the Turks made four assaults . . . They made all these assaults hoping to wear out our small force . . . During these engagements, many convalescents, although not yet fully recovered, used to come to the works and helped as best they could, because, like men of spirit, they preferred to die fighting rather than be cruelly butchered in their quarters if it were our misfortune that the Turks should win.

> Francesco Balbi de Correggio, 1565, at the siege of Malta.

THINK ALSO of the poor wounded of both armies. Especially have paternal care for your own and do not be inhuman to those of the enemy.

> Frederick the Great, *Instructions to His Generals*, 1747, tr. Phillips, 1940.

THERE IS nothing which gains an officer the love of his soldiers more than his care of them under the distress of sickness; it is then he has the power of exerting his humanity in providing them every comfortable necessary, and making their situation as agreeable as possible.

> Major-General Friedrich Baron von Steuben, *Revolutionary War Drill Manual*, 1794.

PAY every attention to the sick and wounded. Sacrifice your baggage, everything for them. Let the wagons be devoted to their use, and if necessary your own saddles. . . .

Napoleon (1769–1821), quoted in David Chandler, *The Campaigns of Napoleon*, 1966.

THERE ARE no greater patriots than those good men who have been maimed in the service of their country.

Napoleon, *Political Aphorisms*, 1848.

MY WOUNDED are behind me, and I will never pass them alive.

Major-General Zachary Taylor, 22 February 1847, when advised to retreat at Buena Vista.

THE WOUNDED had been taken off the battle-field by their general, who ordered his medical director, Dr McGuire, to send them to the rear. As the army was retreating, the surgeon said: "But that requires time. Can you stay to protect us?" "Make yourself easy about that," replied he; "this army stays here until the last wounded man is removed." And then with deep feeling he said: "Before I will leave them to the enemy I will lose many more men."

Mary Anne Jackson, of General Jackson's care for the wounded at the Battle of Kernstown, 22 March 1862, *The Life and Letters of General Thomas A. Jackson*, 1892.

PASSING through Douclon woods, we heard the moans of wounded men all around us. It was a gruesome sound. A low voice from a nearby bush called "*Kamerad, Kamerad!*" A youngster from the 127th lay with a breast wound on the cold stony ground. The poor lad sobbed as we stooped over him – he did not want to die. We wrapped him in his coat and shelter half, gave him some water, and made him as comfortable as possible. We heard the voices of wounded men on all sides now. One called in a heart-breaking way for his mother. Another prayed. Others were crying with pain and mingled with the voices we heard the sound of French: "*Des blessés, camarade!*" It was terrible to listen to suffering and dying men. We helped friend and foe without distinction.

Field Marshal Erwin Rommel, of his experiences during 1914, *Infantry Attacks*, 1937.

IT IS more fruitful to wound than to kill. While the dead man lies still, counting only one man less, the wounded man is a progressive drain upon his side. Comrades are often called upon to bandage him, sometimes even to accompany him back; stretcher-bearers and ambulance drivers to carry him back; doctors and orderlies to tend him in hospital. And on his passage thither the sight of him tends to spread depression among the beholders, acting on morale like the drops of cold water which imperceptibly wear away the stone. (April 1930.)

Captain Sir Basil Liddell Hart, *Thoughts on War*, 1944.

EVACUATE me, hell! Take that tag and label a bottle with it. I will remain in command.

Lieutenant-General Lewis B. 'Chesty' Puller, 8 November 1942, on Guadalcanal, to a doctor who had just pinned an evacuation tag on him after he had received seven wounds that day, Puller Collection, Marine Corps Historical Division.

MEN, all I can say is, if I had been a better general, most of you would not be here.

General George S. Patton, Jr., 1945, to wounded soldiers at Walter Reed Army Hospital in Washington, DC.

I FEEL like a fugitive from th' law of averages.

William 'Bill' Mauldin, comment from one of his G.I. veterans in a cartoon, *Up Front*, 1944.

DURING BATTLE, it is very important to visit frequently hospitals containing newly wounded men. Before starting such an inspection, the officer in charge of the hospital should inform the inspecting general which wards contain men whose conduct does not merit compliments.

General George S. Patton, Jr., *War As I Knew It*, 1947.

I REALIZED vividly now that the real horrors of war were to be seen in hospitals, not on the battlefield.

Lieutenant-General Sir John Glubb, *Into Battle: A Soldier's Diary of the Great War*, 1978.

WOUNDS

BUT DOES any man among you honestly feel that he has suffered more for me than I have suffered for him? Come now – if you are wounded, strip and show your wounds, and I will show mine. There is no part of my body but my back which has not a scar; not a weapon a man may grasp or fling the mark of which I do not carry upon me. I have sword-cuts from close fight; arrows have pierced me, missiles from catapults bruised my flesh; again and again I have been struck by stones or clubs – and all for your sakes: for your glory and gain.

Alexander the Great, July 323 BC, quelling the mutiny of the Macedonians at Opis, quoted in Arrian, *The Campaigns of Alexander*, 7.10, c. AD 150, tr. Aubrey de Sélincourt, 1971.

IN the naval battle of Lepanto he lost his left hand as a result of a harquebus shot, a wound which, however unsightly it may appear, he looks upon as beautiful, for the reason that it was received on the most memorable and sublime occasion that past ages have known or those to come may hope to know; for he was fighting beneath the victorious banner of the sons of that thunderbolt of war, Charles V of blessed memory.

Miguel de Cervantes, of himself, quoted in Daniel Boorstin, *The Creators*, 1992.

LET ME ALONE: I have yet my legs left, and one arm. Tell the surgeon to make haste, and get his instruments. I know I must lose my right arm; so the sooner it is off the better.

Admiral Viscount Nelson, 24 July 1797, after the assault on Santa Cruz de Tenerife, as he refused help in climbing up the side of his ship with his right arm almost shot away, quoted in Robert Southey, *Life of Nelson*, 1813.

WHEN he [Tsar Alexander I] reviewed the French Army and at Napoleon's side watched the Old Guard march past he was struck by the scars and wounds which many of these veterans bore. "And where are the soldiers who have given these wounds?" he exclaimed to Ney. "Sire, they are dead."

Sir Winston S. Churchill, *The Age of Revolution*, 1957, of the meeting of Napoleon and Alexander I of Russia at Tilsit, 7–9 July 1807.

I CONSIDER these wounds a blessing; they were given me for some good and wise purpose, and I would not part with them if I could.

Lieutenant-General Thomas J. 'Stonewall' Jackson, as he lay on his deathbed after the Battle of Chancellorsville, quoted in J.M. Daniells, *The Life of Stonewall Jackson*, 1863.

Y

YOUTH

AH for a young man
all looks fine and noble if he goes down in war,
hacked to pieces under a slashing bronze blade –
he lies there dead . . . but whatever death lays bare,
all wounds are marks of glory. When an old
 man's killed
and the dogs go at the gray head and the gray beard
and mutilate the genitals – that is the cruelest sight
in all our wretched lives.
> Homer, *The Iliad*, 22.84–88, c. 800 BC, tr. Robert
> Fagles, 1990; King Priam mourning his dead heroic
> son, Hector, and contemplating his own fate.

THOU dost know
The faults to which the young are ever prone;
The will is quick to act, the judgment weak;
> Homer, *The Iliad*, Vol. 4, tr. William Cullen Bryant,
> 1905, p. 139.

NEITHER TOO YOUNG nor too old; since the
young man does not inspire confidence, the old
man is feeble, and neither is free from danger, the
young man lest he err through reckless daring, the
older lest he neglect something through physical
weakness. The ideal lies between the two, for
physical vigour is found in the man who has not
yet grown old, and discretion in the man who is
not too young. Those who value physical strength
without discretion, or discretion without physical
strength, have failed to accomplish anything. For
a weak mind can contribute no valuable ideas,
nor can strength unsupported bring to completion
any activity.
> Onasander, *The General*, AD 58 (*Aeneas Tacticus,
> Aclepiodulus, Onasander*, tr. The Illinois Greek
> Club, 1923).

I WILL NOT withdraw so long as those banners still
wave in the wind. I am seventy one. How is it
possible for a man of my age to die more gloriously
than in the midst of my friends and brothers, in the
service of God?
> Jean de la Valette, Grand Master of the Order of the
> Knights of St. John, August 1565, as he prepared to
> die in a breach in the defences made by the Turks
> during the siege of Malta.

MY OLD SOLDIERS were the first who perceived
our situation, and I was foresaken by many of them,
but the young lads stood by me in the innocence of
their hearts, and to them I owed the preservation of
myself and my party.
> Lieutenant-General Johann von Ewald, *A Treatise
> Upon the Duties of Light Troops*, 1790; recounting an
> experience during the American Revolution on 26
> October 1776.

I NEVER should if I had not been very young.
> The Duke of Wellington, 3 July 1803, to Lieutenant-
> General Stuart, describing how he was able to cope
> with the responsibilities of command in India, quoted
> in George Chad, *The Conversations of the First Duke
> of Wellington with George William Chad*, 1956.

ONE has only a certain time for war. I will be good
for six years more; after that even I must cry halt.
> Napoleon, after 1805, comment to his valet, Baron W.
> Constant, *Mémoires*, V, 1896, quoted in David
> Chandler, *The Campaigns of Napoleon*, 1966.

WHAT a number of great Generals arose suddenly
during the revolution; Pichergru, Kléber, Masséna,
Marceau, Desaix, Hoche, &c., *and almost all were
originally private soldiers*. But here the efforts of
nature seem to have been exhausted; for she has
produced nothing since, or at least nothing so great.
At that period every thing was submitted to
competition among thirty millions of men, and nature
necessarily asserted her rights; whereas
subsequently, we were again confined within the
narrower limits of order and the forms of society. . . .
 Another circumstance, not less remarkable, was
the extreme youth of some of these Generals, who
seemed to have started ready made from the hands
of nature. Their characters were perfectly suited to
the circumstances in which they were placed, with
the exception of Hochc whose morals were by no
means pure. The others had no object in view save
glory and patriotism, which formed their whole circle.
They were men after the antique model.
> Napoleon, 10 May 1816, conversation on St. Helena,
> quoted in Emmanuel Las Casas, *Mémoir de St.
> Hélène*, 1816.

I HAVE to perform the labours of Hercules at an age
when strength forsakes me, debility increases, in
one word when hope, the comforter of the
distressed, begins to fail me.
> Napoleon, 1817. Major-General J.F.C. Fuller,
> *Generalship: its Diseases and Their Cure*, 1933.

I CONSIDER IT a great advantage to obtain

command young, having observed as a general thing that persons who come into authority late in life shrink from responsibility, and often break down under its weight.

Admiral David G. Farragut, 1819, journal entry.

BOLDNESS grows less common in the higher ranks. . . . Nearly every general known to us from history as mediocre, even vacillating, was noted for dash and determination as a junior officer.

Major-General Carl von Clausewitz, *On War*, 3.6, 1832, tr. Michael Howard and Peter Paret, 1976.

THROUGH great good fortune, in our youth our hearts were touched with fire. It was given to us to learn at the outset that life is a profound and passionate thing.

Oliver Wendell Holmes, associate justice, Supreme Court of Massachusetts, address to the John Sedgwick Post No. 4, Grand Army of the Republic, Keene, New Hampshire, 30 May 1884, *Speeches of Oliver Wendell Holmes*, 1934.

I TOLD HIM that our real difficulty was not man-power, but brain-power, and that so long as our Generals would think in terms of 1870, there could be no progress.

"1870?" he queried after a long pause, "1870?" – they must be very old men."

"Very old," I answered; "from their knowledge of warfare, most of them might have fought at the battle of Hastings."

Major-General J.F.C. Fuller, 1918, to Sir Henry Wilson.

AS REGARDS MYSELF, you wonder how it is that I have served for over twenty years without getting blunted. I think the answer is, that it is in no way necessary for a doctor whose work compels him to look after lunatics to go mad himself. I quite agree that one's position is frequently very trying, and for long I have been convinced that the two secrets of continuing mentally young are: (a) never get obsessed by detail, and (b) never be contented with anything.

Major-General J.F.C. Fuller, April 1922, letter to a friend, quoted in *Memoirs of an Unconventional Soldier*, 1936.

I AM DOUBTFUL whether the fact that a man has gained the Victoria Cross for bravery as a young officer fits him to command an army twenty or thirty years later. I have noticed more than one serious misfortune which arose from such assumptions. . . .

Sir Winston S. Churchill, on Sir Redvers Buller, *My Early Life*, 1930.

FEW YOUTHS of spirit are content at eighteen with comforts or even caresses. They seek physical fitness, movement, and the comradeship of their equals under hard conditions. They seek distinction, not favour, and exult in their manly independence.

Sir Winston S. Churchill, *Marlborough*, 1933.

IN WAR it is almost impossible to exaggerate the evil effects of age upon generalship, and through generalship on the spirit of the army. In peace time it may be otherwise, but in war time the physical, intellectual and moral stresses and strains which are at once set up immediately discover the weak links in a general's harness. First, war is obviously a young man's occupation; secondly, the older a man grows the more cautious he becomes, and thirdly, the more fixed become his ideas. Age may endow a man with experience, but in peace time there can be no moral experience of war, and little physical experience. Nothing is more dangerous in war than to rely upon peace training; for in modern times when war is declared, training has always been proved out of date. Consequently, the more elastic a man's mind is, that is the more it is able to receive and digest new impressions and experiences, the more common sense will be the actions resulting. Youth, in every way, is not only more elastic than old age, but less cautious and far more energetic. In a moment youth will vault into the saddle of a situation, whilst old age is always looking around for someone to give it a leg up.

Physically an old man is unable to share with his men the rough and tumble of war; instinctively he shuns discomfort, he fears sleeping under dripping hedges, dining of a biscuit, or partaking of a star-lit breakfast, not because he is a coward, but because for so many years he has slept between well-aired sheets, dined off a well-laid table and breakfasted at 9 o'clock, that he instinctively feels that if these things are changed he will not be himself, and he is right for he will be an uncomfortable old man.

Major-General J.F.C. Fuller, *Generalship: Its Diseases and Their Cure*, 1933.

LONG TRAINING tends to make a man ever more expert in execution, but that skill may be gained at the expense of fertility of ideas, originality of conception, and elasticity of views. It is too hopeful to expect generals whose minds have become set to make effective use of new weapons or tactics. Youth is surprise and surprise is war. (March 1923.)

Captain Sir Basil Liddell Hart, *Thoughts on War*, 1944.

. . . THE QUESTION of age v. youth. The advocates of the claims of age and experience cannot pretend that intellect is any more the prerogative of age than of youth. They may, however, urge that age has had greater opportunity for study. But rare is the senior officer who could honestly claim to have devoted his lifetime to intensive study. More often the hours spent in study steadily decline with the gradual extention of responsibilities. Few, indeed, have been able to devote even a year or two during their career to intensive study. In the case of the majority, study has been desultory. Thus where, as so often happens with genius, the intellect ripens early, the young student may have spent more hours in reading and reflection by the time he is twenty-five or thirty than most men spend in their whole lifetimes. (March 1923.)

Captain Sir Basil Liddell Hart, *Thoughts on War*, 1944.

THE PRESENT general officers of the line are for the most part too old to command troops in battle under the terrific pressures of modern war. . . . I do not propose to send our young citizen-soldier into action, if they must go into action, under commanders whose minds are no longer adaptable to the making of split-second decisions in the fast-moving war of today. . . . They'll have their chance to prove what they can do, but I doubt that many of them will come through satisfactorily. Those that don't will be eliminated.

General of the Army George C. Marshall (1880–1959), quoted in Eric Larrabee, *Commander in Chief: Franklin Delano Roosevelt, His Lieutenants and Their War*, 1987.

A LEADER must have the physical resources for the part. A man is as old as his arteries – the old tag is most true in war – and he who makes these calls upon his will power is spendthrift of his days. I have the impression that many senior soldiers and sailors who held high command in the first German war died before their time; they were worn out.

Baron Charles MacMoran Wilson Moran, *The Anatomy of Courage*, 1945.

IT IS SAD to remember that, when anyone has fairly mastered the art of command, the necessity for that art usually expires – either through the termination of the war or through the advanced age of the commander.

General George S. Patton, Jr., *War As I Knew It*, 1947.

NEXT comes the vexed question of age. One of the ancient Roman poets has pointed out the scandal of old men at war and old men in love. But at exactly what age a general ceases to be dangerous to the enemy and a Don Juan to the other sex is not easy to determine. It is impossible really to give exact values to the fire and boldness of youth as against the judgment and experience of riper years; if the mature mind still has the capacity to conceive and to absorb new ideas, to withstand unexpected shocks, and to put into execution bold and unorthodox designs, its superior knowledge and judgment will give the advantage over youth. At the same time there is no doubt that a good young general will usually beat a good old one.

Field Marshal Viscount Wavell of Cyrenaica, *Soldiers and Soldiering*, 1953.

Select Bibliography

Agawa, Hiroyuki, *The Reluctant Admiral: Yamamoto and the Imperial Navy*, tr. John Bester, Tokyo and New York, Kondansha International, 1979.

Alexander, Edward Porter, *Fighting for the Confederacy: The Personal Recollections of General Edward Porter*, Gary W. Gallegher ed., Chapel Hill, University of North Carolina Press, 1989.
Military Memoirs of a Confederate: A Critical Narrative, New York, Scribner's, 1907.

Alexander, Harold, *The Alexander Memoirs 1940–1945*, London, Cassell, and New York, McGraw-Hill, 1962.

Alexander, Joseph H., *Utmost Savagery: The Three Days of Tarawa*, New York, Ivy Books, 1995.

Allon, Yigal, *The Making of Israel's Army*, London, Vallentine, Mitchell, 1970, and New York, Universe Press, 1971.

Ardant du Picq, Charles, *Battle Studies*, 1880, tr. John L. Greely and Robert C. Cotton, Harrisburg, Stackpole Books, 1957.

Arrian, *The Campaigns of Alexander the Great*, tr. Aubrey de Sélincourt, London, Penguin, 1958, 1971.
anabasis of alexander, Books I–IV, tr. P.A. Brunt, Cambridge, MA, and London, Harvard University Press, 1976.
Anabasis of Alexander, Books V–VII, and *Indica*, tr. P.A. Brunt, Cambridge, MA, and London, Harvard University Press, 1976.

Barker, Thomas M., *The Military Intellectual and Battle: Raimondo Montecuccoli and the Thirty Years War*, Albany, State University of New York Press, 1975.

Beaufre, André, *an Introduction to Strategy*, New York, Praeger, 1965.

Bernhardi, Friedrich von, *On War of Today*, tr. Karl von Donat, London, Hugh Rees, 1913.
The War of the Future, tr. F.A. Holt, New York, Appleton, 1921.

Billière, Peter de la, *Storm Command: A Personal Account of the Gulf War*, London, HarperCollins, 1992.

Boatner, Mark M. III, *Biographical Dictionary of World War II*, Novato, CA, Presidio, 1996.

Borritt, Gabor S., ed., *Of the People, By the People, For the People and other Quotations from Abraham Lincoln*, New York, Columbia University Press, 1996.

Bourcet, Jean de, *The Defence of the Piedmont*, London, Oxford University Press, 1927.

Bourrienne, Louis Antoine Fauvelet de, *Memoirs of Napoleon Bonaparte*, London, Butler, 1855.

Bowder, Diana, ed., *Who Was Who in the Greek World: 776 BC–30 BC*, London, Phaidon Press, 1982, and New York, Washington Square Books, 1984.

Bradley, Omar N., *a Soldier's Story*, New York, Henry Holt, 1951, and London, Eyre & Spottiswoode, 1952.

Breasted, James H., *ancient Records of Egypt*, Vol. 1–4, Chicago, University of Chicago Press, and London, Luzac, 1906.

Brusilov, Aleksei A., *a Soldier's Notebook 1914–1918*, London, Macmillan, 1931.

Bryant, Arthur, *The Great Duke or the Invincible General*, London, Collins, 1971, and New York, Morrow, 1972.

Cadwallader, Sylvanus, *Three Years With Grant*, Lincoln, University of Nebraska Press, 1996.

Caesar, Julius, *The Gallic War and Other Writings of Julius Caesar*, tr. Moses Hadas, New York, Random House, 1957.

Carver, Michael, *War Since 1945*, London, Weidenfeld & Nicolson, 1980.

Chamberlain, Joshua Lawrence, *The Passing of the Armies: An Account of the Final Campaign of the Army of the Potomac*, New York, Putnam's, 1915.

Chandler, David, *The Campaigns of Napoleon: The Mind and Method of History's Greatest Soldier*, New York, Macmillan, and London, Weidenfeld, 1966.
ed., *The Dictionary of Battles: The World's Key Battles from 405 BC to Today*, New York, Henry Holt, 1987.
A Guide to the Battlefields of Europe: From the Siege of Troy to the Second World War, 2nd edition, London, Patrick Stephens, 1989.

Churchill, Sir Winston S., *Blood, Sweat, and Tears*, New York, Putnam's, 1941.
Great Contemporaries, New York, Putnam's, 1937.
Marlborough: His Life and Times, London, Harrap, 1933–1938.
Maxims and Reflections, Colin Coote, ed., Boston, Houghton Mifflin, 1949.
My Early Life, London, Butterworth, and New York, Scribner's, 1930.
The River War: An Historical Account of the Reconquest of the Soudan, London, Longmans, Green, 1899.
The Second World War, London, Cassell, and Boston, Houghton Mifflin, 1948–1954.
The World Crisis, London, Butterworth, and New York, Scribner's, 1923–1931.

Clancy, Tom with Franks, Fred, Jr., *Into the Storm: On the Ground in Iraq*, New York, J. Putnam, 1997.

Clausewitz, Carl von, *The Campaign of 1812 in Russia*, London, Greenhill, 1992.
On War, 1832, tr./ed. Michael Howard and Peter Paret, Princeton, Princeton University Press, 1976.
Principles of War, 1812, tr./ed. Hans W. Gatzke, Harrisburg, Stackpole Books, 1942.

Collins, Arthur S., *Common Sense Training*, San Rafael, Presidio, 1978.

Cox, Jacob D., *Atlanta*, New York, Scribner's, 1882.

Cromwell, Oliver, *Writings and Speeches of Oliver Cromwell*, Cambridge, Harvard University Press, 1947.

Dabney, R.I., *Life of Lieut.-Gen. Thomas J. Jackson (Stonewall Jackson)*, New York, Blalock, 1864–1866.

Dahlgren, Madeleine Vinton, *Memoir of John A. Dahlgren, Rear-Admiral, United States Navy*, New York, Charles W. Webster, 1891.

Davis, Burke, *Marine! The Life of Lt. Gen. Lewis (Chesty) Puller, USMC*, Boston, Little, Brown, 1962.

Dayan, Moshe, *Moshe Dayan: The Story of My Life*, London, Weidenfeld & Nicolson, and New York, Morrow, 1976.

Dodge, Theodore Ayrault, *Gustavus Adolphus*, Boston, Houghton Mifflin, 1895, and London, Greenhill, 1996.

Dönitz, Karl, *Memoirs: Ten Years and Twenty Days*, tr. R.H. Stevens, London, Weidenfeld, and Cleveland, World, 1959; London, Greenhill, 1990.

Duffy, Christopher, *The Military Life of Frederick the Great*, London, Routledge and Kegan Paul, 1985, and New York, Atheneum, 1986.

Dupuy, R. Ernest and Dupuy, Trevor N., *The Encyclopedia of Military History from 3500 B.C. to the Present*, New York and Evanston, Harper & Row, 1970.
The Military Heritage of America, New York, McGraw Hill, 1984.

Dupuy, Trevor N., *A Genius for War: The German Army and the General Staff*, Englewood Cliffs, Prentice Hall, 1977.
The Harper Encyclopedia of Military Biography, New York, HarperCollins, 1992.
Understanding War: History and Theory of Combat, New York, Paragon House, and London, Leo Cooper, 1987.

Durán, Fray Diego, *The History of the Indies of New Spain*, 1581, tr./ed. Doris Heyden, Norman, University of Oklahoma Press, 1994.

Earle, Edward Mead, ed., *Makers of Modern Strategy: Military Leaders from Machiavelli to Hitler*, Princeton, Princeton University Press, 1943.

Early, Jubal A., Jones, William, Brock, Robert A., Smith, James P., Eckenrode, Hamilton J., Freeman, Douglas Southall, and Vandiever, Frank E., ed., *Southern Historical Society Papers*, 52 vol., Richmond, VA, Southern Historical Society, 1876–1959.

Eicher, David J., *The Civil War in Books: An Analytical Bibliography*, Urbana and Chicago, University of Illinois Press, 1997.

Eisenhower, Dwight D., *At Ease: Stories I Tell My Friends*, New York, Doubleday, and London, Heinemann, 1967.
Crusade in Europe, Garden City, Doubleday, and London, Heinemann, 1948.
The Papers of Dwight David Eisenhower: The War Years, Alfred D. Chandler, Jr. and Stephen E. Ambrose, ed., Baltimore, Johns Hopkins, 1970.

Epler, Percy H., *The Life of Clara Barton: Angel of the Battlefield*, New York, Macmillan, 1915.

Era of the Civil War – 1820–1876, Special Bibliographic Series Number 11, Carlisle Barracks, PA, US Army Military History Institute, 1982.

Erfurth, Waldemar, *Surprise*, tr. Dr. Stefan T. Possony and Daniel Vilfroy, 1943, Harrisburg, Military Services Publishing Co., 1957; also published in Phillips, ed., *Roots of Strategy*, Book 3, Harrisburg, Stackpole, 1991.

Farragut, Loyall, *The Life of Admiral David Glasgow Farragut: First Admiral of the United States*, New York, Appleton, 1879.

Fisher, John A., *Memories and Records*, London, Hodder & Stoughton, 1919–1920, and New York, George H. Doran, 1920.

Fitton, Robert A., *Leadership: Quotations from the Military Tradition*, Boulder, Westview Press, 1990.

Flavius Vegetius Renatus, *see* Vegetius.

Foch, Ferdinand, *The Memoirs of Marshal Foch*, tr. T. Bentley Mott, London, Heinemann, 1931.
Precepts and Judgments, tr. Hillaire Belloc, London, Chapman and Hall, 1919.
The Principles of War, tr. J. de Morinini, New York, H.K. Fly, 1918; originally published in France, 1913.

Foertsch, Hermann, *The Art of Modern Warfare*, tr. Theodore W. Knauth. New York, Veritas Press, 1940.

Fraser, David, *And We Shall Shock Them: The British Army in World War II*, London, Hodder & Stoughton, 1983.

Fraser, William, *Words on Wellington*, London, Routledge, 1889.

Frederick II, *Frederick the Great on the Art of War*, Jay Luvaas, ed., New York, The Free Press, 1966.
Instructions to His Generals , 1747; published in Phillips, ed., *Roots of Strategy*, Book 1, Harrisburg, Stackpole, 1960.

Freeman, Douglas Southall, *R.E. Lee: A Biography*, New York and London, Scribner's, 1932–1934.
Douglas Southall Freeman on Leadership, 1920, Annapolis, Naval Institute Press, 1990.

Freytag-Loringhoven, Hugo von, *Generalship in the Great War*, manuscript, U.S. Army Command and General Staff College, Fort Leavenworth, Kansas; tr. U.S. Army War College, 1934.
The Power of Personality in War, 1911, tr. Spaulding, 1938; also published in Phillips, ed., *Roots of Strategy*, Book 3, Harrisburg, Stackpole, 1991.

Frontinus, *Stratagems, Aqueducts*, tr. Charles E. Bennett, Cambridge, MA, and London, Harvard University Press, 1925.

Fuller, J.F.C., *The Conduct of War 1789–1961*, London, Eyre & Spottiswoode, 1961.
The Foundations of the Science of War, London, Hutchinson, 1926.
The Generalship of Alexander the Great, London, Eyre & Spottiswoode, 1958.
Generalship: Its Diseases and Their Cure, London, Faber & Faber, 1933.
Grant and Lee: A Study in Personality and Generalship, London, Eyre and Spottiswoode, 1933.
Lectures on F.S.R. II, London, Sifton Praed, 1931.
Lectures on F.S.R. III, London, Sifton Praed, 1932.
Memoirs of an Unconventional Soldier, London, Nicholson and Watson, 1936.
A Military History of the Western World, New York, Minerva Press, 1967.
The Reformation of War, London, Hutchinson, 1923.

Gabriel, Richard A. and Savage, Paul L., *Crisis in Command: Mismanagement in the Army*, New York, Hill and Wang, 1978.

Gabrieli, Francesco, *Arab Historians of the Crusades*, 1957, Berkeley, University of California Press, 1984.

Gareyev, Makhmut, *M.V. Frunze: Military Theorist*, Moscow, Voyenizdat, 1985.

Gaulle, Charles de, *The Army of the Future*, London, Hutchinson, 1940, and New York, Lippincott, 1941; originally published as *Vers l'armée de métier*, Paris, Plon, 1934.
The Edge of the Sword, tr. Gerard Hopkins, London, Faber & Faber, and New York, Criterion, 1960; originally published as *Le fil de l'épée*, Paris, Berger-Levraul, 1932.
War Memoirs, tr. Richard Howard, London, Weidenfeld, 1955–1960, and New York, Simon and Schuster, 1955–1961; originally published as *Mémoires de Guerre*, Paris, 1954.

Gavin, James M., *On to Berlin*, New York, Viking, 1978.

Geary, John White, *A Politician Goes to War: The Civil War Letters of John White Geary*, ed., William Alan Blair, University Park, PA, Pennsylvania State University Press, 1995.

Giap, Vo Nguyen, *People's War – People's Army*, Hanoi, Foreign Languages Publishing House, 1961.

Gibbon, John, *Personal Recollections of the Civil War*, New York, Putnam, 1928.

Glubb, John Bagot, *A Soldier With the Arabs*, London, Hodder & Stoughton, and New York, Harper, 1957.

Goldie, Sue M., ed., *'I Have Done My Duty'*, *see* Nightingale, Florence.

Goltz, Colmar von der, *The Conduct of War*, 1897, tr. F.G. Leverson, London, Kegan Paul, Trench, Trübner, 1908.
The Nation in Arms, 1883, tr. Philip A. Ashworth, London, W.H. Allen, 1887.

Gordon, John B., *Reminiscences of the Civil War*, New York, Scribner's, 1903.

Grant, Ulysses S., *Personal Memoirs*, New York, Charles L. Webster, 1885.
Personal Memoirs of U.S. Grant, Selected Letters 1839–1865, New York, Literary Classics of the United States, 1990.

Graves, Robert, *Poems About War*, William Graves, ed., Mount Kisco, NY, and London, Moyer Bell, 1988.

Graves, Robert, and Liddell Hart, Basil H., *T.E. Lawrence to his Biographers*, London, Cassell, and Garden City, Doubleday, 1963.

Griffith, Samuel B. II, *The Battle for Guadalcanal*, Philadelphia, Lippincott, 1963.

Guderian, Heinz, *Panzer Leader*, tr. Constantine Fitzgibbon, London, Michael Joseph, 1953.
Achtung – Panzer!, tr. Christopher Duffy, London, Arms and Armour Press, 1992.

Guedalla, Philip, *The Duke of Wellington*, London, Hodder, and New York, Harper, 1931.

Guevera, Che, *Guerrilla Warfare*, Lincoln, University of Nebraska Press, 1985.

Guingand, Francis de, *Operation Victory*, London, Hodder & Stoughton, and New York, Scribner's, 1947.

Hackett, John Winthrop, *The Profession of Arms*, London, Sidgwick & Jackson, 1983.

Hamilton, Ian, *Gallipoli Diary*, London, Allen and Unwin, 1918–1920.
The Soul and Body of an Army, London, Edward Arnold, 1921.

Hancock, *Almira, Reminiscences of General Hancock*, New York, Charles L. Webster, 1887.

Harbage, Alfred, gen. ed., *William Shakespeare: The Complete Works*, London and Baltimore, Penguin, 1970.

Harbord, James G., *The American Army in France*, Boston and New York, Houghton Mifflin, 1936.

Harris, Arthur, *Bomber Offensive*, London, Collins, 1947, and Greenhill, 1990.

Haskell, Frank A., *The Battle of Gettysburg*, Boston, MOLLUS, Massachusetts Commandery, 1908; also published in Frank L. Byrne and Andrew T. Weaver, ed., *Haskell of Gettysburg: His Life and Civil War Papers*, Kent, OH, Kent State University Press, 1989.

Hayden, Lieutenant-Colonel H.J., *see* US Marine Corps.

Henderson, George F.R., *Stonewall Jackson and the American Civil War*, London and New York, Longmans, Green, 1898, 1906.

Herodotus, *The Persian Wars*, tr. George Rawlinson, New York, The Modern Library, 1942.

Herold, J. Christopher, *see* Napoleon.

Higham, T.F. and Bowra, C.M., *The Oxford Book of Greek Verse in Translation*, Oxford, Oxford University Press, 1938.

Hindenburg, Paul von, *Out of My Life*, tr. F.A. Hoyt, London, Cassell, 1920.

Hoffmann, Max, *War Diaries and Other Papers*, tr. Eric Sutton, London, Martin Secker, 1929.

Holmes, Oliver Wendell, *Touched With Fire*, Cambridge, Harvard University Press, 1948.

Homer, *The Iliad*, c. 800 BC, tr. Robert Fagles, New York, Viking Penguin, and London, Penguin, 1990.
The Iliad, tr. Richard Lattimore, Chicago and London, University of Chicago Press, 1951.
The Iliad of Homer, tr. Alexander Pope (1743), London and New York, Penguin, 1996.
The Odyssey, c. 800 BC, tr. Robert Fagles, New York, Viking Penguin, and London, Penguin, 1996.
The Odyssey of Homer, tr. T.E. Lawrence, Oxford, Oxford University Press, 1932.

Hornblower, Simon, and Spawforth, Antony, *the Oxford Classical Dictionary*, Oxford and New York, Oxford University Press, 1996.

Horner, D.M., *The Commanders: Australian Military Leadership in the twentieth Century*, Sydney, London and Boston, Allen & Unwin, 1984.

Horricks, Raymond, *Marshal Ney: The Romance and the Real*, London, Archway, 1982.

Horrocks, Brian, *Corps Commander*, London, Sidgwick & Jackson, and New York, Scribner's, 1977.
A Full Life, London, Collins, 1960, and Leo Cooper, 1974; also published as *Escape to Action*, New York, St. Martin's Press, 1961.

Howarth, David and Stephen, *Nelson: The Immortal Memory*, London, Dent, and New York, Viking, 1986.

Howze, Hamilton H., *a Cavalryman's Story*, Washington, Smithsonian Institution Press, 1996.

Jackson, Mary Anne, *Life and Letters of General Thomas J. Jackson (Stonewall Jackson)*, New York, Harper, 1892.

Jackson, Robert, *a Systematic View of the Formation, Discipline, and Economy of armies*, London, Cadell, 1804, and Parker, Furnivall and Parker, 1845.

Jang Chu, *the Precepts of Ssu Ma Jang Chu*, tr. A.L. Sadler in *three Military Classics of China*, Sydney, Australian Medical Publishing, 1944.

Joan of Arc, *Joan of Arc In Her Own Words*, tr. Willard Trask, New York, B.O.O.K.S, 1996.

Johnston, Joseph E., *Narrative of Military Operations Directed During the Late War Between the States*, New York, Appleton, 1874.

Johnston, R.M., *The Corsican: A Diary of Napoleon's Life in His Own Words*, New York, Houghton Mifflin, 1910.

Johnston, Robert Underwood and Buel, Clarence Clough, ed., *Battles and Leaders of the Civil War, Being for the Most Part Contributions by Union and Confederate Officers*, New York, Century, 1887–1888.

Jomini, Antoine-Henri de, *The Art of War*, Philadelphia, Lippincott, 1862, and London, Greenhill, 1992.
Summary of the Art of War, 1838, tr. Mendell and Craighill, Harrisburg, Stackpole Books, 1862, 1965.

Jones, J. William, *Life and Letters of Robert Edward Lee, Soldier and Man*, New York and Washington, Neale Publishing, 1906.
Personal Reminiscences, Anecdotes, and Letters of Gen. Robert E. Lee, New York, Appleton, 1874.

Josephus, *The Works of Josephus: Complete and Unabridged*, tr. William Whiston, Peabody, MA, Hendrickson, 1987.

Kai Ka'us Ibn Iskander, *A Mirror for Princes*, 1082, tr. Levy, New York, E.P. Dutton, 1951.

Kesselring, Albert, *The Memoirs of Field Marshal Kesselring*, London, William Kimber, 1953, and Greenhill, 1988.

King, Ernest J. and Whitehill, Walter Muir, *Fleet Admiral King: A Naval Record*, New York, Norton, 1952.

Kinnamos, John, *Deeds of John and Manuel Comnenus*, New York, Columbia University Press, 1976.

Kipling, Rudyard, *A Choice of Kipling's Verse*, T.S. Eliot, ed., London and Boston, Faber & Faber, 1941.

Kircheisen, F.M., *Memoirs of Napoleon I compiled from his Writings*, tr. Frederick Collins, London, Hutchinson, and New York, Duffield, 1929.

Kolokotrones, Theodoros, *Theodoros Kolokotrones: The Old Man of the Morea*, tr. Elizabeth Edmonds, London, T. Fisher Unwin, 1892, and Brookline, NY, Hellenic College Press, 1983.

Konev, I., *Year of Victory*, tr. David Mishne, Moscow, Progress Publishers, 1969.

Krulak, Victor H., *First to Fight: An Inside View of the U.S. Marine Corps*, Anapolis, Naval Institute Press, 1984, 1991.

Laffin, John, *Brassey's Dictionary of Battles*, London, Brassey's, 1986, and New York, Barnes and Noble, 1995.

Lande, Nathaniel, ed., *Dispatches From the Front: A History of the American War Correspondent*, New York and Oxford, Oxford University Press, 1995.

Lanning, Michael Lee and Cragg, Dan, *Inside the VC and the NVA: The Real Story of North Vietnam's Armed Forces*, New York, Ivy Books, 1992.

Lawrence, T.E., *The Seven Pillars of Wisdom*, privately published, 1926; London, Cape, and New York, Doubleday, 1935.

Lee, Henry, *Memoirs of the War in the Southern Department of the United States*, Robert E. Lee, ed., New York, 1869.

Lee, Robert E., *The Wartime Papers of Robert E. Lee*, Clifford Dowdey, ed., Boston, Little, Brown, 1961.

Lee, Robert E., Jr., *The Recollections and Letters of Robert E. Lee*, New York, Doubleday Page, 1904.

Leeb, Ritter Wilhelm von, *Defense*, 1938, tr. Dr Stefan T. Possony and Daniel Vilfroy, 1943; also published in Phillips, ed., *Roots of Strategy*, Book 3, Harrisburg, Stackpole, 1991.

Leites, Nathan, *The Soviet Style in War*, New York, Crane Russak, 1982.

LeMay, Curtis E., *Mission With LeMay*, Garden City, Doubleday, 1965.

Lettow-Vorbeck, Paul von, *East African Campaigns*, New York, Robert Speller, 1957.
My Reminiscences of East Africa, London, Hurst and Blackett, 1920.

Liddell Hart, Basil H., *Colonel Lawrence: The Man Behind the Legend*, London, Cape, and New York, Dodd, Mead, 1934.
Foch: The Man of Orleans, London, Eyre & Spottiswoode, 1931, and Boston, New York, 1932.
The Ghost of Napoleon, London, Faber & Faber, and New Haven, Yale, 1933.
Great Captains Unveiled, London, Blackwood, 1927, and Greenhill, 1989.
A Greater Than Napoleon: Scipio Africanus, London, Blackwood, 1926, and New York, Biblo and Tannen, 1971; also published as *Scipio Africanus: Greater than Napoleon*, London, Greenhill Books, 1992.
The Memoirs of Captain Liddell Hart, London, Cassell, 1965, and New York, Putnam, 1965–1966.
The Other Side of the Hill, London, Cassell, 1948; also published as *The German Generals Talk*, New York, Morrow, 1948.
The Real War 1914–1918, London, Faber & Faber, and Boston, Little, Brown, 1930.
Reputations: Ten Years After, London, John Murray, and Boston, Little, Brown, 1928.
Strategy: The Indirect Approach, London, Faber & Faber, and New York, Frederick A. Praeger, 1954.
The Sword and the Pen, New York, Thomas Y. Crowell, 1976, and London, Cassell, 1978.
thoughts on War, London, Faber & Faber, 1944.
Through the Fog of War, London, Faber & Faber, and New York, Random House, 1938.

Livermore, Mary A., *My Story of the War*, Hartford, CT, published by the author, 1887.

Livy, *Livy: A History of Rome*, tr. Moses Hadas and Joe P. Poe, New York, The Modern Library, 1962.
Rome and the Mediterranean, tr. Henry Bettenson, London, Penguin, 1976.
The War With Hannibal, tr. Aubrey de Sélincourt, London, Penguin, 1972.

Long, A.L. and Wright, Marcus J., *Memoirs of Robert E. Lee: His Military and Personal History, Embracing a Large Amount of Information Hitherto Unpublished*, New York, J.M. Stoddart, 1886.

Longford, Elizabeth, *Wellington: The Years of the Sword*, London, Weidenfeld, and New York and Evanston, Harper & Row, 1969.

Longstreet, James, *From Manassas to Appomattox*, Philadelphia, Lippincott, 1896.

Longworth, Phillip, *The Art of Victory: The Life and Achievements of Field Marshal Suvorov 1729–1800*, London, Constable, 1965, and New York, Holt, Rinehart and Winston, 1966.

Luckenbill, Daniel D, *Ancient Records of Assyria and Babylonia*, Chicago, University of Chicago Press, 1926.

Ludendorff, Erich von, *My War Memories 1914–1918*, London, Hutchinson, 1919.

Luvaas, Jay, tr./ed., *Frederick the Great on the Art of War*, New York, The Free Press, and London, Collier-Macmillan, 1966.
Napoleon on the Art of War, New York, The Free Press, 1999.

MacArthur, Douglas, *A Soldier Speaks: Public Papers and Speeches of General of the Army Douglas MacArthur*, New York and London, Praeger, 1965.
Reminiscences, New York, McGraw-Hill, 1964, and London, Heinemann, 1975.

McClellan, George B., *McClellan's Own Story: The War for the Union, the Soldiers Who Fought It, the Civilians Who Directed It, His Relations to It and to Them*, New York, Charles L. Webster, 1887.

Machiavelli, Niccolo, *The Art of War*, 1521, tr. Ellis Farneworth, Indianapolis, Bobbs-Merrill, 1965.

Madariaga, Salvador de, *Hernan Cortes: Conqueror of Mexico*, Coral Gables, University of Miami Press, 1942.

Mahan, Alfred Thayer, *Admiral Farragut*, New York, Appleton, 1892.
From Sail to Steam: Recollections of a Naval Life, New York, Harper, 1907.
The Influence of Sea Power Upon History 1660–1783, Boston, Little, Brown, 1890–1892.
Life of Nelson: The Embodiment of the Sea Power of Great Britain, Boston, Little, Brown, 1897.
Naval Administration and Warfare, Boston, Little, Brown, 1908.
Naval Strategy, Compared and Contrasted with the Principles of Military Operations on Land, Boston, Little, Brown, 1911.

Mahan, Dennis Hart, *Advance-Guard, Out-Post, and Detachment Service of Troops, with the Essential Principles of Strategy and Grand Tactics*, New York, John Wiley, 1863.

Mahon, Philip Henry, *The Life of Belisarius*, London, John Murray, 1829.

Mannerheim, Carl, *The Memoirs of Marshal Mannerheim*, tr. Eric Lewenhaupt, New York, E.P. Dutton, 1953, and London, Cassell, 1954.

Manstein, Erich von, *Lost Victories*, tr./ed. Anthony G. Powell, London, Methuen, and Chicago, Henry Regnery, 1958; Novato, Presidio, 1984, London, Greenhill, 1987.

Mao Tse-tung, *Selected Military Writings of Mao Tse-tung*, Peking, Foreign Languages Press, 1963, 1967.

Marius, Richard, ed., *The Columbia Book of Civil War Poetry*, New York, Columbia University Press, 1994.

Marshall, George C., *Biennial Reports of the Chief of Staff of the United States Army to the Secretary of War, 1 July 1939–30 June 1945*, Washington, Center of Military History, United States Army, 1996.

Memoirs of My Service in the World War 1917–1918, Boston, Houghton Mifflin, 1976.

Selected Speeches and Statements of General of the Army George C. Marshall, Chief of Staff, United States Army, Washington, The Infantry Journal, 1945.

Marshall, S.L.A., *The Armed Forces Officer*, Washington, U.S. Government Printing Office, 1950.

Bringing Up the Rear, San Rafael, Presidio, 1979.

Men Against Fire, New York, Morrow, 1947.

The Officer as Leader, Harrisburg, Stackpole, 1950.

The Soldier's Load and the Mobility of a Nation, 1950, Quantico, The Marine Corps Association, 1980.

Martin, Christopher, *Damn the Torpedos*, New York, Abelard, Schuman, 1970.

Mauldin, William, *Up Front*, New York, World, 1945.

Maurice, *The Strategikon*, tr. George T. Dennis, Philadelphia, University of Pennsylvania Press, 1984.

Meinertzhagen, Richard, *Army Diary 1899–1926*, Edinburgh, Oliver & Boyd, 1960.

Mellenthin, F.W. von, *Panzer Battles*, tr. H. Betzler, L.C.F. Turner, ed., Norman, Oklahoma University Press, 1971.

Mijatovich, Chedomil, *Constantine: The Last Emperor of the Greeks*, London, Sampson Low, Marston, 1892.

Miyamoto Musashi, *a Book of Five Rings*, 1645, tr. Victor Harris, London, Flamingo (HarperCollins), 1984, and Woodstock, Overlook, 1983.

Moltke, Helmuth von, *Strategy: Its Theory and Application: The Wars for German Unification 1866–1871*, Westport, Greenwood, 1971.

Monash, John, *The Australian Victories in France in 1918*, London, Hutchinson, 1920, and New York, E.P. Dutton, 1925.

Montgomery, Bernard Law, *The Memoirs of Field Marshal Montgomery*, London, Collins, and Cleveland, World, 1958.

Moore, Harold G. and Galloway, Joseph L., *We Were Soldiers Once . . . and Young: Ia Drang – The Battle That Changed the War in Vietnam*, New York, Random House, 1992.

Moore, John, *The Diary of Sir John Moore*, J.F. Maurice, ed., London, Edward Arnold, 1904.

Moran, Charles MacMoran Wilson, *The Anatomy of Courage*, London, Constable, 1945, and Garden City Park, NY, Avery, 1987.

Morison, Samuel Eliot, *John Paul Jones: A Sailor's Biography*, Boston, Little, Brown, 1959.

Mosby, John S., *The Memoirs of Colonel John S. Mosby*, Boston, Little, Brown, 1917.

Mosby's War Reminiscences and Stuart's Cavalry Campaigns, New York, Dodd, Mead, 1887.

Murray, John F., *Fallen Warriors: The West Point Class of 1964*, Fuquay-Varina, NC, Research Triangle Publishing, 1996.

Napier, William F., *History of the War in the Peninsula and the South of France From the Year 1807 to the Year 1814*, London, John Murray, 1828–1840.

Napoleon, *Correspondance de Napoléon Ier, publiée par ordre de l'Empereur Napoléon III*, 32 vol., Paris, Plon, Dumaine, 1858–1870.

The Military Maxims of Napoleon, tr. George C. D'Aguilar, 1831; David Chandler, ed., London, Greenhill, 1987.

The Military Maxims of Napoleon, tr. General Burnod, 1827; published in Phillips, ed., *Roots of Strategy*, Book 1, Harrisburg, Stackpole, 1985.

The Mind of Napoleon: A Selection from his Written and Spoken Words, J. Christopher Herold, ed., New York, Columbia University Press, 1955.

Napoleon's Memoirs, Somerset de Chair, ed., London, Golden Cockerel Press, 1945.

Newman, Aubrey S., *Follow Me: The Human Element in Leadership*, Novato, Presidio, 1981.

Ney, Michel, *The Memoirs of Marshal Ney*, London, Bull & Churton, 1834.

Nightingale, Florence, *'I Have Done My Duty': Florence Nightingale in the Crimean War 1854–56*, Sue M. Goldie, ed., Iowa City, University of Iowa Press, 1987.

Official Records of the Union and Confederate Navies in the War of the Rebellion, 31 vol., Washington, U.S. Government Printing Office, 1894–1927.

Ogasawara, Nagayo, *Life of Admiral Togo*, Tokyo, Seit Shorin Press, 1934.

Oman, Carola, *Sir John Moore*, London, Hodder & Stoughton, 1953.

Onasander, *The General*, tr. The Illinois Greek Club, Loeb Classical Library, 1923; Cambridge, Harvard University Press, 1937.

Ouranos, Nikephoros, *Campaign Organization and Tactics*, tr./ed. George T. Dennis in *Three Byzantine Military Treatises*, Washington, Dumbarton Oaks, 1985.

Pagonis, William G., *Moving Moutains: Lessons in Leadership and Logistics from the Gulf War*, Boston, Harvard Business School Press, 1992.

Parkinson, Roger, *The Fox of the North: The Life of Kutuzov, General of War and Peace*, London, Davies, and New York, David McKay, 1976.

Parry, Melanie, ed., *Chambers Biographical Dictionary*, 6th edition, Edinburgh, Chambers, 1997.

Patton, George S., Jr., *The Patton Papers*, Martin Blumenson, ed., Boston, Houghton Mifflin, 1972–1974.

War As I Knew It, Boston, Houghton Mifflin, 1947.

Perrett, Bryan, *The Battle Book: Crucial Conflicts in History from 1469 BC to the Present*, London, Arms and Armour Press, 1992.

Pershing, John J., *My Experiences in the World War*, New York, Stokes, 1931.

Peters, Ralph, *Fighting for the Future*, Mechanicsburg, Stackpole, 1999.

Pfiffer, Robert H., *State Letters of Assyria*, New Haven, American Oriental Society, 1935.

Phillips, Thomas R., ed., *Roots of Strategy*, Harrisburg, Stackpole, 1985–1991.

Phokas, Nikephoros, *Skirmishing*, tr./ed. George T. Dennis in *Three Byzantine Military Treatises*, Washington, Dumbarton Oaks, 1985.

Pickett, LaSalle Corbell, *Picket and His Men*, Atlanta, Foote and Davis, 1900.

Pilsudski, Joseph, *The Memoirs of a Polish Revolutionary and Soldier*, tr. D.R. Gillie, London, Faber & Faber, 1931.

Plutarch, *The Age of Alexander: Nine Greek Lives by Plutarch*, tr. Ian Scott-Kilvert, London, Penguin, 1973.

Fall of the Roman Republic: Six Lives by Plutarch, tr. Rex Warner, London, Penguin, 1972.

Makers of Rome: Nine Lives by Plutarch, tr. Ian Scott-Kilvert, London, Penguin, 1965.

Plutarch on Sparta, tr. Richard J.A. Talbert, London, Penguin, 1988.

Plutarch: The Lives of the Noble Grecians and Romans, tr. John Dryden, New York, The Modern Library.

The Rise and Fall of Athens: Nine Greek Lives, tr. Ian Scott-Kilvert, London, Penguin, 1960.

Selected Lives and Essays, Roslyn, NY, Walter J. Black, 1951.

Polybius, *The Rise of the Roman Empire*, tr. Ian Scott-Kilvert, London, Penguin, 1979.

Porter, David Dixon, *Incidents and Anecdotes of the Civil War*, New York, Appleton, 1885.

Porter, Horace, *Campaigning With Grant*, New York, Century, 1897.

Potter, John Deane, *Yamamoto: The Man Who Menaced America*, New York, Viking, 1965; also published as *Admiral of the Pacific: The Life of Yamamoto*, London, Heinemann, 1965.

Powell, Colin with Persico, Joseph E., *My American Journey*, New York, Random House, 1995.

Pritchard, Richard, ed., *The Ancient Near East: An Anthology in Texts and Pictures*, Cambridge, Princeton University Press, 1958.

Procopius, *A History of the Wars*, tr. H.B. Dewing, Loeb Classical Library, Cambridge, Harvard University Press, 1929.

Pyle, Ernie, *Brave Men*, New York, Holt, 1944.
Here Is Your War, Cleveland and New York, World, 1945.

Ralston, David B., *Soldiers and States: Civil-Military Relations in Modern Europe*, Boston, D.C. Heath, 1966.

Rathbone, Julian, *Wellington's War: His Peninsular Dispatches*, London, Michael Joseph, 1984.

Ridgway, Matthew B., *The Korean War*, Garden City, NY, Doubleday, 1967.
Soldier: The Memoirs of Matthew B. Ridgway, New York, Harper, 1956.

Ritter, E.A., *Shaka Zulu*, London, Longmans, 1955, and Greenhill, 1990.

Robertson, William, *From Private to Field-Marshal*, Boston, Houghton Mifflin, 1921.

Rojas, Ricardo, *San Martin: Knight of the Andes*, tr. Herschel Brickell and Carlos Videla, New York, Cooper Square, 1967.

Rommel, Erwin, *Infantry Attacks*, 1937, tr. G.E. Kiddé, Washington, The Infantry Journal, 1944, and London, Greenhill, 1990.
The Rommel Papers, tr. Paul Finlay, B.H. Liddell Hart, ed., London, Collins, and New York, Harcourt Brace, 1953.

Royal, Trevor, *Dictionary of Military Quotations*, London, Routledge, 1990.

Sadler, A.L., *The Maker of Modern Japan: The Life of Tokugawa Ieyasu*, London, George Allen & Unwin, 1937.

St. Exupéry, Antoine de, *Flight to Arras*, tr. Lewis Galantiere, New York, Reynal & Hitchcock, and London, Heinemann, 1942.

Santoli, Al, ed., *Leading the Way: How Vietnam Veterans Rebuilt the U.S. Military*, New York, Ballantine Books, 1993.

Savkin, Ye. V., *Basic Principles of Operational Art and Tactics*, Moscow, Voenizdat, 1972.

Sawyer, Ralph D., tr./ed., *The Seven Military Classics of Ancient China*, Boulder, Westview Press, 1993.

Saxe, Maurice de, *My Reveries Upon the Art of War*, 1732, tr. Thomas Phillips, 1940, in Phillips, ed., *Roots of Strategy*, Book 1, Harrisburg, Stackpole, 1985.

Schlieffen, Alfred von, *Cannae*, Fort Leavenworth, U.S. Army Command and General Staff College Press, 1931.

Schwarzkopf, H. Norman, with Petre, Peter, *It Doesn't Take a Hero*, New York, Bantam Books, 1992.

Scott, William F. and Harriet Fast, *The Soviet Art of War: Doctrine, Strategy, and Tactics*, Boulder, Westview Press, 1982.

Seekt, Hans von, *Thoughts of a Soldier*, tr. Gilbert Waterhouse, London, Ernest Benn, 1930.

Senger und Etterlin, Frido von, *Neither Fear Nor Hope: The Wartime Memoirs of the German Defender of Cassino*, tr. George Malcolm, London, Macdonald, 1963, and Novato, Presidio, 1989.

Sharon, Ariel, *Warrior: An Autobiography*, New York, Simon and Schuster, and London, Macdonald, 1989.

Shazly, Saad el, *The Crossing of the Suez*, San Francisco, American Mideast Research, 1980.

Sheridan, Phillip H., *Personal Memoirs of Phillip Henry Sheridan*, Charles L. Webster, 1888.

Sherman, William T., *Memoirs of General W.T. Sherman: Written by Himself*, New York, Appleton, 1875.

Simpkin, Richard, *Deep Battle: The Brainchild of Marshal Tukhachevskii*, London, Brassey's, 1987.

Singlaub, John K., *Hazardous Duty: An American Soldier in the Twentieth Century*, New York, Summit Books, 1991.

Slim, William, *Courage and Other Broadcasts*, London, Cassell, 1957.
Defeat Into Victory, London, Cassell, 1956, and New York, David McKay, 1963.
Unofficial History, London, Cassell, 1959.

Smith, Perry M., *Taking Charge: A Practical Guide for Leaders*, Washington, National Defense University, 1986.

Smythe, John, *Certain Discourses Military*, Ithaca, Cornell University Press, 1966.

Sokolovskiy, V.D., *Soviet Military Strategy*, tr./ed. Harriet Fast Scott, New York, Crane, Russak, 1975.

Southey, Robert, *Life of Nelson*, London, John Murray, 1813, and J.M. Dent (Everyman Library), 1942.

Stallings, Lawrence, *The Doughboys: The Story of the AEF*, New York, Harper & Row, 1963.

Steuben, Frederick William von, *Revolutionary Drill Manual*, 1794, New York, Dover, 1985.

Stockdale, James B., *A Vietnam Experience: Ten Years of Reflections*, Stanford, Hoover Institute Press, 1984.

Suetonius, *The Lives of the Twelve Caesars*, AD 121, tr. Philemon Holland, 1606, New York, Heritage Press, 1965.

Sullivan, Gordon R., *The Collected Works of the Thirty-Second Chief of Staff United States Army Gordon R. Sullivan, General, U.S. Army, Chief of Staff, 1991–1995*, Washington, Department of the Army.

Summers, Harry G., Jr., *On Strategy: The Vietnam War in Context*, Carlisle Barracks, U.S. Army War College, 1981.

[Sun Bin] Sun Tzu II, *The Lost Art of War*, tr./ed. Thomas Cleary, New York, Harper Collins, 1996.

Sun Tzu, *The Art of Strategy*, tr./ed. R.L. Wing, New York and London, Doubleday, 1988.
The Art of War, c. 500 BC, tr./ed. Thomas Cleary, Boston, Shambhala Press, 1988.
The Art of War, tr./ed. Lionel Giles, 1910; also published in Philips, ed., *Roots of Strategy*, Book 1, Harrisburg, Stackpole, 1985.
The Art of War, tr./ed. Samuel Griffith, Oxford and New York, Oxford University Press, 1963.
The Art of War, tr./ed. Ralph D. Sawyer, Boulder, Westview Press, 1985.
The Art of Warfare, tr./ed. Roger Ames, New York, Ballantine, 1993.

Tacitus, *The Complete Works of Tacitus*, tr. Alfred J. Church and William J. Brodribb, New York, The Modern Library, 1942.

Taylor, Richard, *Destruction and Reconstruction*, New York, Appleton, 1879.

Tedder, Arthur W., *With Prejudice: The War Memoirs of Marshal of the Royal Air Force Lord Tedder, G.C.B.*, London, Cassell, and Boston, Little, Brown, 1966.

Thomason, John W., *Fix Bayonets!*, New York, Scribner's, 1926, and London, Greenhill, 1989.

Thucydides, *History of the Peloponnesian War*, tr. Richard Crawley, London, J.M. Dent, 1910.
The Peloponnesian War, tr. Benjamin Jowett, 1881, New York, Bantam, 1960.

Treadwell, Mattie E., *The Women's Army Corps* (United States Army in World War II: Special Studies), Washington, Office of the Chief of Military History, 1954.

Trotsky, Leon, *History of the Russian Revolution*, New York, Simon & Schuster, 1932.
Military Writings, 1922, New York, Merit, 1969.

Truscott, Lucian K., Jr., *The Twilight of the Cavalry: Life in the Old Army, 1917–1942*, Lucian K. Truscott III, ed., Lawrence, University of Kansas Press, 1989.

Twining, Merrill B., *No Bended Knee: The Battle for Guadalcanal*, Novato, Presidio, 1997.

Upton, Emory, *The Military Policy of the United States Since 1775*, Washington, Government Printing Office, 1904.

US Marine Corps. *Warfighting*, FMFM1, General Alfred M. Gray and Major John Schmitt, ed., Washington, Department of the Navy, 1989, also published with *Campaigning*, FMFM1-1, and *Tactics*, FMFM1-3, as *Warfighting: Manoeuvre Warfare in the US Marine Corps*, Lieutenant-Colonel H.J. Hayden, ed., London, Greenhill, 1995.

Vegetius, *The Military Institutions of the Romans*, AD 378, tr. John Clark, 1776, published in Phillips, ed., *Roots of Strategy*, Book 1, Harrisburg, Stackpole, 1940, 1965.

Vigny, Alfred Victor de, *Servitude and Grandeur of Arms*, 1857, tr. Roger Gard, London, Penguin, 1996.

Walder, David, *Nelson*, London, Hamish Hamilton, and New York, The Dial Press/James Wade, 1978.

The War of the Rebellion: A Compilation of the Official Records of the Union and Confederate Armies, 70 vol., Washington, U.S. Government Printing Office, 1880–1901.

Washington, George, *Maxims of George Washington*, Mount Vernon, The Mount Vernon Ladies Association, 1989.
The Writings of George Washington, 39 vol., John C. Fitzgerald, ed., Washington, U.S. Government Printing Office, 1931–1944.

Watson, S.J., *By Command of the Emperor: A Life of Marshal Berthier*, London, Bodley Head, 1957.

Wavell, Archibald P., *Allenby: A Study in Greatness*, London, Harrap, 1940–1943, and New York, Oxford University Press, 1941–1943.
Generals and Generalship, London, Penguin, and New York, Macmillan, 1941.
The Good Soldier, London, Macmillan, 1948.
Other Men's Flowers, London, Cape, 1944.
Soldiers and Soldiering, London, Cape, 1953.

Webb, Henry J., *Elizabethan Military Science: The Books and Practice*, Madison, University of Wisconsin Press, 1965.

Webster's American Military Biographies, Springfield, MA, G. & C. Merriam, 1978.

Webster's New Biographical Dictionary, Springfield, MA, Merriam-Webster, 1988.

Wellington, Duke of, *The Dispatches of Field Marshal the Duke of Wellington, During His Various Campaigns in India, Denmark, Portugal, Spain, the Low Countries, and France*, compiled by Lieutenant-Colonel Gurwood, 12 vol., London, John Murray, 1834–1838.
Selections from the General Orders of Field Marshal the Duke of Wellington During His Various Commands 1799–1818, Colonel Gurwood, ed., London, Parker, Furnivall and Parker, 1847.
Supplementary Despatches, Correspondence, and Memoranda of Field Marshal Arthur Duke of Wellington, K.G., 1794–1818, 15 vol., the Duke of Wellington (son), ed., London, John Murray, 1858–1872.

Westmoreland, William C., *A Soldier Reports*, Garden City, NY, Doubleday, 1976.

Wet, Christiaan R. de, *A Three Years War*, London, Archibald Constable, 1902.

Weygand, Max, *Turenne: Marshal of France*, Boston, Houghton Mifflin, 1930.

Williams-Ellis, Clough and A., *The Tank Corps*, London, Country Life, 1919.

Wilson, William Scott., ed./tr., *Ideals of the Samurai: Writings of Japanese Warriors*, Burbank, Ohara Publications, 1982.

Wolseley, Garnet J., *The Soldier's Pocket-book for Field Service*, London, 1869.
The Story of a Soldier's Life, London, Archibald Constable, 1903.

Wood, Leonard, *The Military Obligation of Citizenship*, Princeton, Princeton University Press, 1915.

Wu Chi, *Wu Chi on the Art of War*, tr./ed. A.L. Sadler in *Three Military Classics of China*, Sydney, Australian Medical Publishing, 1944.

Xenophon, *Hiero the Tyrant and Other Treatises*, tr. Robin Waterfield, London, Penguin, 1997.
A History of My Times, tr. Rex Warner, London, Penguin, 1966.
The March Up Country, tr. W.H.D. Rouse, London, Thomas Nelson, 1947.
Memorabilia, Oeconomicus, Symposium, Apology, tr. E.C. Marchant and O.J. Todd, Cambridge, MA, and London, Loeb Classical Library, Harvard University Press, 1923.
The Persian Expedition, tr. Rex Warner, London and Baltimore, Penguin, 1949.

Young, Desmond, *The Desert Fox*, London, Collins, and New York, Harper & Row, 1950.

Zhuge, Liang and Liu Ji, *Mastering the Art of War: Zhuge Liang & Liu Ji*, tr./ed. Thomas Cleary, Boston, Shambhala Press, 1989.

Zhukov, Georgi K., *Reminiscences and Reflections*, tr. Vic Schneierson, Moscow, Progress Publishers, 1974.

Index of Well-Known Quotations

These are the times that try men's souls. (Paine) PATRIOTISM 352

These beasts have learned something. (Napoleon) EXPERIENCE 187

They couldn't hit an elephant at this dist . . . (Sedgwick) 'FAMOUS LAST WORDS' 194

They fled only from dishonour. (Thucydides) HONOUR 236

They make a solitude and call it peace. (Tacitus) PACIFICATION 350

The Third Fleet's sunken and damaged ships have been salvaged and are retiring at high speed toward the enemy. (Halsey) HUMOUR 240

This was all my fault, General Pickett. (Lee) RESPONSIBILITY AND ACCOUNTABILITY 417

. . . this is the last army England has, we must take care of it. (Wellington) ECONOMY OF FORCE 165

This is not the time to go wobbly. (Thatcher) RESOLUTION/RESOLVE 417

This order demanded the impossible. Even the most devoted soldier can be killed by a bomb. (Rommel) INDEPENDENCE OF COMMAND 246

Those far distant, storm-beaten ships, upon which the Grand Army never looked, stood between them and dominion of the world. (Mahan) NAVY 320

Time spent on reconnaissance is seldom wasted. (British Field Service Regulations) RECONNAISSANCE 400

To be a successful soldier, you must know history. (Patton) HISTORY – Studying Military History 233

To be defeated is pardonable; to be surprised – never! (Napoleon) SURPRISE 460

Treaties are like flowers and young girls – they last while they last. (de Gaulle) TREATIES/DIPLOMACY 488

Troops are made to let themselves be killed. (Napoleon) SOLDIERS 442

Truth usually is the same old story. (Thatcher) TRUTH 494

Untutored courage is useless in the face of educated bullets. (Patton) TRAINING – Lack of Training 485

Upon the fields of friendly strife are sown the seeds that upon other fields on other days will bear the fruits of victory. (MacArthur) SPORT 448

Valor is superior to numbers. (Vegetius) VALOUR 499

Victory at all costs, victory in spite of terror, victory however long and hard the road may be. (Churchill) VICTORY – The Necessity of Victory 503

Victory will come to the side that outlasts the other. (Foch) TENACITY 474

War involves in its progress such a train of unforeseen and unsupposed circumstances. (Paine) UNCERTAINTY/THE UNEXPECTED/THE UNKNOWN 495

War . . . is . . . continuation of political activity by other means. (Clausewitz) WAR – Politics/Policy and War 520

War is a pulsation of violence . . . (Clausewitz) WAR – The Nature of War 516

War is cruelty, and you cannot refine it. (Sherman) WAR – The Nature of War 517

War is hell. (Sherman) WAR – The Nature of War 517

The war is just which is necessary. (Machiavelli) WAR – Just War 514

War is not simply the continuation of policy; it is the breakdown of policy. (Seekt) WAR – Politics/Policy and War 521

War is simply power unrestrained by constitution or compact. (Sherman) WAR – The Nature of War 517

War is the last of things to go according to programme. (Thucydides) WAR – The Nature of War 516

War is the only place where a man really lives. (Patton) WAR – Love of War 515

War is the realm of uncertainty. (Clausewitz) UNCERTAINTY/THE UNEXPECTED/THE UNKNOWN 495

War means fighting, and fighting means killing. (Forrest) FIGHTING – General 200

Wars may be fought with weapons, but they are won by men. (Patton) MAN 283

Wars spring from unseen and generally insignificant causes. (Thucydides) WAR – Causes of War 508

We all had to weigh . . . the difference between lives and lies. (North) INTEGRITY 257

. . . we cannot escape history. (Lincoln) HISTORY – General 230

We fight, get beat, rise, and fight again. (Greene) PERSEVERANCE 356

We have met the enemy, and they are ours. . . . (Perry) VICTORY – Reports of Victory 504

. . . we humbly beseech Thee, of Thy great goodness, to restrain these immoderate rains. (O'Neil) PRAYERS AND HYMNS 370

We sleep soundly in our beds because rough men stand ready in the night to visit violence on those who would harm us. (Orwell) PREPARATION/PREPAREDNESS 373

Westminster Abbey or victory! (Nelson) DO OR DIE 157

. . . we will give them the bayonet. (Jackson) THE BAYONET 56

What can a soldier do who charges when out of breath? (Vegetius) ENDURANCE/PHYSICAL FITNESS/HEALTH 166

What counts is not necessarily the size of the dog in the fight – it's the size of the fight in the dog. (Eisenhower) AGGRESSIVENESS 31

What is life without honor? Degradation is worse than death. (Jackson) HONOUR 238

. . . when an enemy is committed to a mistake, we must not interrupt him too soon. (Nelson) MISTAKES 307

When Grant gets possession of a place, he holds on to it as if he had inherited it. (Lincoln) TENACITY 473

When I am without orders . . . I shall always act as I think the honour and glory of my King and Country demand. (Nelson) JUDGEMENT 261

When we assumed the soldier, we did not lay aside the citizen. (Washington) CITIZEN SOLDIER 84

Wherever the enemy goes, let our troops go also. (Grant) CONTACT 113

Wherever wood can swim, there I am sure to find this flag of England. (Napoleon) SEA POWER 433

Who dares wins. (SAS motto) DARING 129

The winds and waves are on the side of the ablest navigators. (Gibbon) ABILITY 25

Without supplies, no army is brave. (Frederick) LOGISTICS 274

The worst cowards, banded together, have their courage. (Homer) COHESION 90

Write the history of a battle? As well write the history of a ball. (Wellington) HISTORY – Writing Military History 234

You can ask me for anything you like, except time. (Napoleon) TIME/TIMING 478

You don't hurt 'em if you don't hit 'em. (Puller) MARKSMANSHIP 290

You know how to conquer but not how to use your victory. (Maharbal) EXPLOITATION 180

You may be whatever you resolve to be. (Jackson) CHARACTER 78

Biographical Index

Index of Battles and Campaigns

Index of Generals, Soldiers and War Leaders